MICROPROCESSORS AND INTERFACING

68000 VERSION

MICROPROCESSORS AND INTERFACING

PROGRAMMING AND HARDWARE

68000 VERSION

DOUGLAS V. HALL
ANDREW L. ROOD

GLENCOE

Macmillan/McGraw-Hill

Lake Forest, Illinois   Columbus, Ohio   Mission Hills, California   Peoria, Illinois

IBM PC, IBM PC/XT, IBM PC/AT, IBM PS/2, and MicroChannel Architecture are registered trademarks of IBM Corporation. The following are registered trademarks of Intel Corporation: 386, i486, i860, ICE, iRMX. Borland, Sidekick, Turbo Assembler, TASM, Turbo Debugger, and Turbo C++ are registered trademarks of Borland International, Inc. Microsoft, MS, MS DOS, Windows 3.0, Codeview, and MASM are registered trademarks of Microsoft Corporation. Apple and Macintosh are registered trademarks of Apple Computer Inc. UNIX is a registered trademark of AT&T Inc. The URDA P68000 MLab is a registered trademark of University Research and Development Associates. Consulair is a registered trademark of Consulair Inc. Think C is a registered trademark of Semantec. MC68000, 68008, 68010, 68020, 68030, and 68030 are registered trademarks of Motorola Inc. Other product names are registered trademarks of the companies associated with the product name referred to in the text or figure.

Hall, Douglas V.
    Microprocessors and interfacing : programming and hardware : 68000 version / Douglas V. Hall, Andrew L. Rood.
        p. cm.
    Includes bibliographical references and index.
    ISBN 0-07-025691-8 (text). — ISBN 0-07-025692-6 (experiments manual). — ISBN 0-07-025693-4 (instructor's manual)
    1. Microprocessors—Programming.   2. Microprocessors.   3. Computer interfaces.   I. Rood, Andrew L.   II. Title.
QA76.6.H2994 1992   91-48370
004.165—dc20   CIP

Send all inquiries to:
GLENCOE DIVISION
Macmillan/McGraw-Hill
936 Eastwind Drive
Westerville, OH 43081

ISBN 0-07-025691-8

Printed in the United States of America

1 2 3 4 5 6 7 8 9 A–KP 99 98 97 96 95 94 93 92

TO OUR STUDENTS

Let us go forward together into the future.

CONTENTS

PREFACE

This book is written for a wide variety of introductory microprocessor courses. The only prerequisite for this book is some knowledge of diodes, transistors, and simple digital devices.

My experience as an engineer and as a teacher indicates that it is much more productive to first learn one microprocessor family very thoroughly and from that strong base learn others as needed. For this edition of the book we chose the Motorola 68000/68008/68010/68020/68030/68040 family of microprocessors. Devices in this family are used in millions and millions of personal computers, including the Apple Macintosh and many "clones." The 68000 was the first member of this family, and although it has been superseded by newer processors, the 68000 is still an excellent entry point for learning about microprocessors. You don't need to know about the advanced features of the newer processors until you learn about multiuser/multitasking systems. Therefore, the 68000 is used for most of the hardware and programming examples until Chapter 15, which discusses the features of the newer processors and how these features are used in multiuser/multitasking systems.

CONTENT AND ORGANIZATION

All chapters begin with fundamental objectives and conclude with a review of important terms and concepts. Each chapter concludes with a generous supply of questions and problems that reinforce both the theory and applications presented in the chapters.

To help refresh your memory, Chapter 1 contains a brief review of the digital concepts needed for the rest of the book. It also includes an overview of basic computer mathematics and arithmetic operations on binary, HEX, and BCD numbers.

Chapters 2–10

Chapters 2–10 provide you with a comprehensive introduction to microprocessors, including interrupt applications, digital and analog interfacing, and industrial controls. These chapters include an overview of the 68000 microprocessor family and its architecture, programming language, and systems connections and troubleshooting.

Because I came into the world of electronics through the route of vacuum tubes, my first tendency in teaching microprocessors was to approach them from a hardware direction. However, the more I designed with microprocessors and taught microprocessor classes, the more I became aware that the real essence of a microprocessor is what you can program it to do. Therefore, Chapters 2–5 introduce you to writing structured assembly language programs for the 68000 microprocessor. The approach taken in this programming section is to solve the problem, write an algorithm for the solution, and then simply translate the algorithm to assembly language. Experience has shown that this approach is much more likely to produce a working program than just writing down assembly language instructions. The 68000 instruction set is introduced in Chapters 2–5 as needed to solve simple programming problems, but for reference Chapter 6 contains a dictionary of all 68000 instructions with examples for each.

Chapter 7 discusses the signals, timing, and system connections for a simple 68000-based microcomputer. Also discussed in Chapter 7 is a systematic method for troubleshooting a malfunctioning 68000-based microcomputer system and the use of a logic analyzer to observe microcomputer bus signals.

Chapter 8 discusses how the 68000 responds to interrupts, how interrupt-service procedures are written, and the operation of a peripheral device called a priority-interrupt controller.

Chapters 9 and 10 show how a microprocessor is interfaced with a wide variety of low-level input and output devices. Chapter 9 shows how a microprocessor is interfaced with digital devices such as keyboards, displays, and relays. Chapter 10 shows how a microprocessor is interfaced with analog input/output devices such as A/Ds, D/As, and a variety of sensors. Chapter 10 also shows how all the "pieces" are put together to produce a microprocessor-based scale and a simple microprocessor-based process control system. Chapter 10 concludes with a discussion of how microprocessors can be used to implement digital filters.

Chapters 11–15

Chapters 11–14 are devoted to the hardware, software, and peripheral interfacing for a microcomputer such as those in the Apple Macintosh Family. Chapter 11 discusses motherboard circuitry, including DRAM systems, caches, math coprocessors, and peripheral interface buses. Chapter 11 also shows how to use a schematic capture program to draw the schematic, a simulator program to verify the logic and timing of the design, and a layout program to design a printed-circuit board for the system. Knowledge of these electronic design automation tools is essential for anyone developing high-speed microprocessor systems.

At the request of many advisors from industry, Chapter 12 introduces you to the C programming language, which is used to write a large number of system-level programs. This chapter takes advantage of the fact that it is very easy to learn C if you are already familiar with 68000-type assembly language. A section in this chapter also shows you how to write simple programs that contain both C and assembly language modules.

Chapter 13 describes the operation and interfacing of common peripherals such as CRT displays, magnetic disks, and printers. Chapter 14 shows how a microcomputer is interfaced with communication systems such as modems and networks.

Finally, Chapter 15 starts with a discussion of the needs that must be met by multiuser/multitasking operating system and then describes how the features of the 68020, 68030, and 68040 processors meet these needs. This section of the chapter also includes discussions of how to develop programs for the 68020 in a variety of environments. The chapter and the book conclude with an introduction to parallel processors, and I think you will find these developing areas as fascinating as I have.

SUGGESTIONS FOR ASSIGNMENTS

Flexible Organization

The text is comprehensive, yet flexible in its organization. Chapter 1 could be easily omitted if students have a solid background in basic binary mathematics and digital fundamentals.

Chapters 2–10

I suggest following Chapters 2–10 as an instructional block, as each chapter builds on the preceding chapter. These nine chapters represent ideal coverage for a "short course" in microprocessors. The remaining chapters represent an opportunity for the instructor to tailor assignments for the students' needs or perhaps to give an individual student added study in recent developments in the architecture in microprocessors.

Chapter 11

Individual topics from Chapter 11 could be selected for study as students gain knowledge of the "tools" available for designing computer-based systems. The DRAM section is very important.

Chapter 12

Instructors may wish to assign or leave for outside reading Chapter 12 on programming in C, a new chapter. At the very least you should take a careful look at the simple programming examples and the development of tools for C. If class time does not permit assigning this chapter, you may wish to use selected examples and programs in your lecture presentations. This chapter can be included in any course sequence that does not have a separate class in C programming.

Chapter 13

Portions of the peripherals chapter may be assigned as required, depending upon the course syllabus. The CRT, disk, and printer sections are highly recommended.

Chapter 14

This is an important chapter, given the ever-expanding use of data communications. It should be assigned, if at all possible, unless the curriculum includes a separate course in data communications. Of primary importance are the sections on modems and LANs.

Chapter 15

The final chapter is on the cutting edge of the development of new microprocessors. It is our hope that all students will have the opportunity to read this chapter. At the very least students should read the section on the 68030. This is a final chapter, yet it is only the beginning of their study of microprocessors.

SPECIAL FEATURES

In response to feedback from industry and from a variety of electronics instructors of the INTEL version of *Microprocessors and Interfacing: Programming and Hardware*, this book contains these new or enhanced features.

1. The order of the topics in Chapters 4 and 5 has been improved, based on instructor feedback.
2. A greatly expanded section on digital signal processing hardware and software has been added to Chapter 10.
3. A section in Chapter 11 describes and shows an example of how electronic design automation tools such as schematic capture programs, simulator programs, and PC board layout programs are used to develop the hardware for a microcomputer system.
4. At the request of industry advisors, Chapter 12 is a completely new chapter that contains a solid introduction to the C programming language, including examples of programs with C and assembly language modules.
5. Chapters 13 and 14, the systems peripherals chapters, have been updated to reflect advances in technology such as VGA graphics, optical-disk storage, laser printers, and digital video interactive. The chapters now include both assembly language and C interface program examples.
6. The network section of Chapter 14 has been expanded to reflect the current importance of networks.
7. Chapter 15 now contains an extensive description of the features of the

68030 and 68040 processors and a discussion of how these features are used in multitasking environments such as UNIX.

IMPORTANT SUPPLEMENTS

This book and the Experiments Manual written to accompany it contain many hardware and software exercises students can do to solidify their knowledge of microprocessors. An IBM PC or IBM PC-compatible computer, or an Apple Macintosh can be used to edit, assemble, link/locate, run, and debug many of the 68000 assembly language programs.

The Experiments Manual contains 40 laboratory exercises that are directly coordinated to the text. Each experiment includes chapter references, required equipment, objectives, and experimental procedures.

The Instructor's Manual contains answers to the review questions. It also includes experimental notes and answers to selected questions for the Experiments Manual.

The Instructor's Manual includes disk directories. There are two disks available. This set of disks contains the source code for all the programs in the text and Experiments Manual. The disks are available for instructors and may be obtained directly from the publisher. The Instructor's Manual contains instructions for obtaining the disks.

ADDITIONAL GOALS

One of the main goals of this book is to teach you how to decipher manufacturer's data sheets for microprocessor and peripheral devices, so the book contains relevant parts of many data sheets. Because of the large number of devices discussed, however, it was not possible to include complete data sheets. If you are doing an in-depth study, it is suggested that you acquire or gain access to the latest editions of Motorola *Microprocessors* and *Peripherals* handbooks. The bibliography at the end of the book contains a list of other books and periodicals you can refer to for further details on the topics discussed in the book.

ACKNOWLEDGMENTS

I wish to express my profound thanks to the people around me who helped make this book a reality. Thanks to Pat Hunter, whose cheerful encouragement helped me through seemingly endless details. She proofread the original manuscript, worked out the answers to the end-of-chapter problems to verify that they are solvable, and made suggestions and contributions too numerous to mention. Thanks to Richard Cihkey of New England Technical Institute in New Britain, Connecticut, who meticulously worked his way through the original manuscript and made many valuable suggestions. Thanks to Mike Olisewski of Instant Information, Inc., who helped me "C the light" in Chapter 12 and contributed his industry perspective on the topics that should be included in the book. Thanks to Dr. Michael A. Driscoll of Portland State University, who helped me fine-tune Chapter 15. Thanks to Intel Corporation for letting me use many drawings from their data books so that this book could lead readers into the real world of data books. Finally, thanks to my wife Rosemary, my children Linda, Brad, Mark, Lee, and Kathryn, and to the rest of my family for their patience and support during the long effort of rewriting this book.

Douglas V. Hall

The 68000 version of this text was produced from Douglas Hall's original Intel version and his updated notes for the second edition of the Intel version. Thanks to Motorola Incorporated, to University Research and Development Associates, to Consulair Incorporated, to Semantec, and to Apple Computer Incorporated for their excellent products, which are used in many real-world applications as well as many instructional environments. Thanks to Douglas Hall for asking me to participate. Thanks to John Beck and to the entire team at Glencoe (Macmillan/McGraw-Hill) for their help, inspiration, and guidance in helping me complete work on the 68000 version. Thanks also to my parents: to my mother for always encouraging my writing interests and to my father for his own explorations into the writing of textbooks. Finally, sincere thanks to my wife, Terry, for her constant support and encouragement during the years it has taken to complete this version of the text.

If you have suggestions for improving the book or ideas that might clarify a point for someone else, please communicate with us through the publisher.

Andrew L. Rood

MICROPROCESSORS AND INTERFACING

68000 VERSION

CHAPTER

Computer Number Systems, Codes, and Digital Devices

Before starting our discussion of microprocessors and microcomputers, we need to make sure that some key concepts of the number systems, codes, and digital devices used in microcomputers are fresh in your mind. If the short summaries of these concepts in this chapter are not enough to refresh your memory, then it is a good idea to review the concepts in a current digital text before going on in this book.

OBJECTIVES

At the conclusion of this chapter, you should be able to

1. Convert numbers between the following codes: binary, octal, hexadecimal, and BCD.

2. Define the terms *bit, nibble, byte, word, most significant bit,* and *least significant bit.*

3. Use a table to find the ASCII or EBCDIC code for a given alphanumeric character.

4. Perform addition and subtraction of binary, octal, hexadecimal, and BCD numbers.

5. Describe the operation of gates, flip-flops, latches, registers, ROMs, dynamic RAMs, static RAMs, and buses.

6. Describe how an arithmetic logic unit can be instructed to perform arithmetic or logical operations on binary words.

COMPUTER NUMBER SYSTEMS AND CODES

Review of Decimal

To understand the structure of the binary number system, the first step is to review the familiar decimal, or base-10, number system. Figure 1-1a shows a decimal number with the value of each placeholder, or digit, expressed as a power of 10. The digits in the decimal number 5346.72 then tell you that you have 5 thousands, 3 hundreds, 4 tens, 6 ones, 7 tenths, and 2 hundredths. The number of symbols needed in a number system of any base is equal to the base number. In

the decimal number system, then, there are 10 symbols, 0 through 9. When the count in any digit position passes that of the highest-value symbol, a carry of 1 is added to the next digit position and the other digit rolls back to zero. A car odometer is a good example of this.

A number system can be built using powers of any number as place holders or digits, but some bases are more useful than others. It is difficult to build electronic circuits that can store and manipulate 10 different voltage levels, but it is relatively easy to build circuits that can handle 2 levels. Therefore, a *binary,* or *base*-2, number system is used.

The Binary Number System

Figure 1-1b shows the value of each digit in a binary number. Each binary digit represents a power of 2. A binary digit is often called a *bit.* Note that digits to the right of the *binary point* represent fractions used for numbers less than 1. The binary system uses only two symbols, zero (0) and one (1). Therefore, in binary you count as follows: 0, 1, 10, 11, 100, 101, 110, 111, etc.

Binary numbers are often called *binary words,* or just *words.* Binary words of certain numbers of bits have also acquired special names. A 4-bit binary word is called a *nibble,* and an 8-bit binary word is called a *byte.* A 16-bit binary word is often referred to just as a *word,* and a 32-bit binary word is referred to as a *doubleword.* The rightmost, or *least significant, bit* of a binary word is usually referred to as the LSB. The

$$5 \quad 3 \quad 4 \quad 6 \quad . \quad 7 \quad 2$$
$$10^3 \ 10^2 \ 10^1 \ 10^0 \quad 10^{-1} \ 10^{-2}$$

(a)

$$1 \quad 0 \quad 1 \quad 1 \quad 0 \quad . \quad 1 \quad 1$$
$$2^7 \ 2^6 \ 2^5 \ 2^4 \ 2^3 \ 2^2 \ 2^1 \ 2^0 \quad 2^{-1} \ 2^{-2}$$
$$128 \ 64 \ 32 \ 16 \ 8 \ 4 \ 2 \ 1 \quad \frac{1}{2} \quad \frac{1}{4}$$

(b)

FIGURE 1-1 Digit values in decimal and binary. (a) Decimal. (b) Binary.

leftmost, or *most significant, bit* of a binary word is usually called the MSB.

To convert a binary number to its equivalent decimal number, multiply each digit times the decimal value of the digit and find the sum of these products. The binary number 101, for example, represents

$$(1 \times 2^2) + (0 \times 2^1) + (1 \times 2^0), \quad \text{or} \quad 4 + 0 + 1 = \text{decimal } 5$$

The binary number 10110.11 represents

$$(1 \times 2^4) + (0 \times 2^3) + (1 \times 2^2) + (1 \times 2^1) + (0 \times 2^0) + (1 \times 2^{-1}) + (1 \times 2^{-2}) = 16 + 0 + 4 + 2 + 0 + 0.5 + 0.25$$
$$= \text{decimal } 22.75$$

To convert a decimal number to binary, there are two common methods. The first (Figure 1-2a) is simply a reverse of the binary-to-decimal method just given. For example, to convert the decimal number 21 (sometimes written as 21_{10}) to binary, first subtract the greatest power of 2 that is less than the number. The greatest power of 2 less than 21_{10} is 16, or 2^4. Subtracting 16 from 21 gives a remainder of 5. Put a 1 in the 2^4 digit position and see if the next-lower power of 2 is less than the remainder. Since 2^3 is 8 and 8 is not less than the remainder of 5, put a zero in the 2^3 digit position. Then try the next-lower power of 2, which is 2^2, or 4. This is less than the remainder of 5. Therefore, a 1 is put in the 2^2 digit position. When 2^2, or 4, is subtracted from the old remainder of 5, a new remainder of 1 is left. Since 2^1, or 2, is not less than this remainder, a zero is put in that position. A 1 is put in the 2^0 position because 2^0 is equal to 1; this is exactly equal to the remainder of 1. The result shows that 21_{10} is equal to 10101 in binary. The conversion process is somewhat messy to describe but easy to do. Try converting 46_{10} to binary. You should get 101110.

Another method of converting a decimal number to binary is shown in Figure 1-2b. Divide the decimal number by 2 and write the quotient and remainder as shown. Divide this quotient and following quotients by 2 until the quotient reaches zero. The column of remainders will be the binary equivalent of the given decimal number. Note that the MSD, or most significant digit, is on the bottom of the column and the LSD, or least significant digit, is on the top of the column if you perform the divisions in order from the top to the bottom of the page. You can demonstrate that the binary number is correct by converting from binary to decimal, as shown in the right-hand side of Figure 1-2b.

You can convert decimal numbers less than 1 to binary by multiplying successively by 2 and recording carries until the quantity to the right of the decimal point becomes zero, as shown in Figure 1-2c. The carries represent the binary equivalent of the decimal number, with the *MSB* at the top of the column. Decimal 0.625 equals 0.101 in binary. For decimal values that do not convert exactly the way this one did (that is, the quantity to the right of the decimal never becomes zero), you can continue the conversion process until you get the number of binary digits desired.

At this point it is interesting to compare the number of digits required to express numbers in decimal with the number required to express them in binary. In decimal, one digit can represent 10 numbers, 0–9; two digits can represent 10^2, or 100, numbers, 0–99; and three digits can represent 10^3, or 1000, numbers, 0–999. In binary, a similar pattern exists. One binary digit can represent two numbers, 0–1; two binary

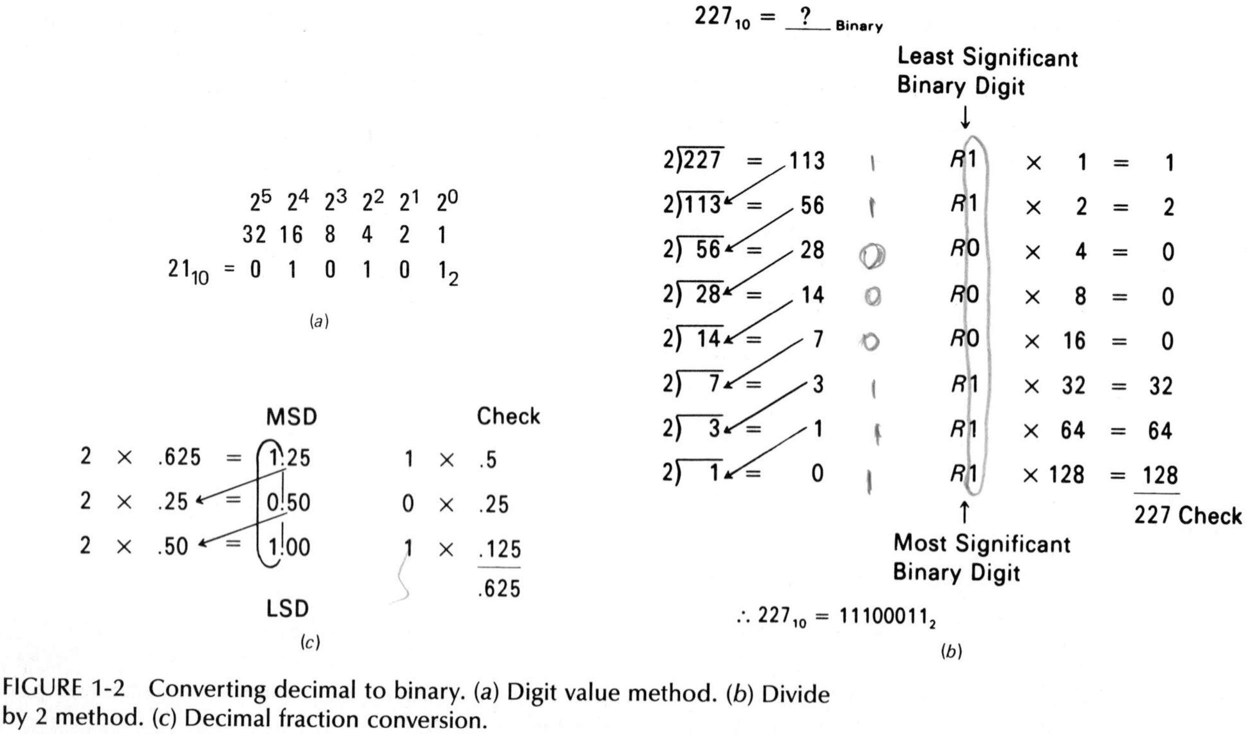

FIGURE 1-2 Converting decimal to binary. (a) Digit value method. (b) Divide by 2 method. (c) Decimal fraction conversion.

digits can represent 2^2, or 4, numbers, 0–11; and three binary digits can represent 2^3, or 8, numbers. Thus N decimal digits can represent 10^N numbers and N binary digits can represent 2^N numbers. Eight binary digits can represent 2^8, or 256, numbers, 0–255.

Octal

Binary is not a very compact code. This means that it requires many more digits to express a number than does, for example, decimal. Twelve binary digits can describe a number only up to 4095_{10}. Computers require binary data, but people working with computers have trouble remembering the long binary words produced by the verbose code. One solution to the problem is to use the *octal*, or *base-8* code. As you can see in Figure 1-3a, the digits in this code represent powers of 8. The symbols then are 0–7. You can convert a decimal number to the octal equivalent number with the same trick you used to convert decimal to binary. Figure 1-3b shows the technique for decimal-to-octal conversion. Decimal 327 is equal to 507_8. Verification of this is shown by converting the octal to decimal in the second half of Figure 1-3b.

Because 8 is an integral power of 2, conversions from binary to octal and from octal to binary are quite simple. If you have a binary number such as 1 0101 1111, starting from the binary point and moving to the left, mark off the binary digits in groups of three, as shown in Figure 1-3c. Each group of three binary digits is equal to one octal digit. For this example, 111 is a 7, 011 is a 3, and 101 is a 5. Therefore, 101011111_2 is equal to 537_8.

$$4096\ 512\ 64\ 8\ 1 \quad \tfrac{1}{8}\quad \tfrac{1}{64}\quad \tfrac{1}{512}$$
$$8^4 \quad 8^3 \quad 8^2\ 8^1 8^0 . \ 8^{-1}\ 8^{-2}\ 8^{-3}$$

(a)

$$327_{Decimal} = \underline{\ ?\ }_{Octal} \qquad 327_D = 507_8$$

LSD

8)327	=	40	R	7	× 1 =	7
8) 40	=	5	R	0	× 8 =	0
8) 5	=	0	R	5	× 64 =	320

MSD   327

(b)

Binary 101 011 111 .
Octal   5   3   7 └ Binary Point

(c)

FIGURE 1-3   Octal numbers. (a) Value of placeholders. (b) Conversion of decimal to octal. (c) Conversion of binary to octal.

You convert from octal to binary by replacing each octal digit with its 3-bit binary equivalent.

Hexadecimal

Some once-popular minicomputers, such as the PDP-8, have 12 parallel data lines. Four octal digits provide an easy way to represent the binary data word on these 12 parallel lines. For example, 100001010111 binary is easily written as 4127 octal. Most microprocessors have 4-bit, 8-bit, 16-bit, or 32-bit data words. For these microprocessors, it is more logical to use a code that groups the binary digits in groups of four rather than three. *Hexadecimal*, or base 16, code does this. Figure 1-4a shows the digit values for hexadecimal, which is often just called *hex*. Since hex is base 16, you need 16 possible symbols for each digit. The table in Figure 1-4b show the symbols for hex code. Following the decimal symbols 0 through 9, the letters A through F are used for values 10 through 15.

As mentioned before, each hex digit is equal to four binary digits. To convert the binary number 11010110 to hex, mark off groups of four, moving to the left from the binary point, as shown in Figure 1-4c. Then write the hex symbol for the value of each group of four. The 0110 group is equal to 6 and the 1101 group is equal to 13. Since 13 is D in hex, 11010110 binary is equal to D6 in hex. Thus, 8 bits are represented by 2 hex digits. In order to make it easier to read binary numbers, we will follow the convention of adding a space between every four digits. Thus 11010110 will be written 1101 0110.

In Motorola's manuals, a dollar sign ($) is used before a number to indicate that it is a hexadecimal number. For example, D6 hex is usually written $D6. Intel's manuals for the 8086 family use an H after a number to indicate hexadecimal. For example, D6 hex is written D6H in Intel manuals. The Motorola syntax is used in this text.

If you want to convert from decimal to hexadecimal, Figure 1-4d shows a familiar trick to use. The result shows that 227_{10} is equal to $E3. As you can see, hex is an even more compact code than decimal. Two hexadecimal digits can indicate a number up to 255. Only 4 hex digits are needed to represent a 16-bit binary number.

To illustrate how hexadecimal numbers are used in digital logic, a service manual tells you that the 8-bit wide data bus of a 68008 microprocessor should contain $3F during a certain operation. Converting $3F to binary gives the pattern of 1s and 0s (0011 1111) you would expect to find with your oscilloscope or logic analyzer on the parallel lines. The $3F is simply a shorthand that is easier to remember and less prone to errors.

To convert from octal code to hex code, the easiest way is to write the binary equivalent of the octal and then convert the binary digits, four at a time, into the appropriate hex digits. Reverse the procedure to get from hex to octal.

$$16^3 \quad 16^2 \quad 16^1 \quad 16^0 . \quad 16^{-1} \quad 16^{-2} \quad 16^{-3}$$

$$4096 \quad 256 \quad 16 \quad 1 \qquad \tfrac{1}{16} \quad \tfrac{1}{256} \quad \tfrac{1}{4096}$$

(a)

Dec		Hex
0	=	0
1	=	1
2	=	2
3	=	3
4	=	4
5	=	5
6	=	6
7	=	7
8	=	8
9	=	9
10	=	A
11	=	B
12	=	C
13	=	D
14	=	E
15	=	F

(b)

$$\underbrace{1101}_{D} \quad \underbrace{0110}_{6}{}_2 \qquad \text{HEX}$$

(c)

$$227_{10} = \underline{\quad ? \quad}_{\text{Hex}}$$

$$16\overline{)227} = 14 \qquad R3 \quad \times \ 1 \ = \ 3$$
$$16\overline{)\ 14} = 0 \qquad RE \quad \times 16 = 224$$
$$\overline{\qquad\qquad 227}$$

$$227_{10} = E3_{16}$$

(d)

FIGURE 1-4 Hexadecimal numbers. (a) Value of placeholders. (b) Symbols. (c) Binary-to-hexadecimal conversion. (d) Decimal-to-hexadecimal conversion.

BCD Codes

STANDARD BCD

In applications such as frequency counters, digital voltmeters, or calculators, where the output is a decimal display, a binary-coded decimal, or BCD, code is often used. The advantage of BCD for these applications is that information for each decimal digit is contained in a separate 4-bit binary word. As you can

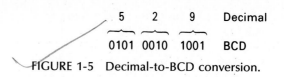

5	2	9	Decimal
0101	0010	1001	BCD

FIGURE 1-5 Decimal-to-BCD conversion.

see in Table 1-1, the simplest BCD code uses the first 10 numbers of standard binary code for the BCD numbers 0 through 9. The hex codes A through F are invalid BCD codes. Each decimal digit then is individually represented by its 4-bit binary equivalent, as illustrated in Fig. 1-5.

GRAY CODE

Gray code is another important binary code, which is often used for encoding shaft-position data from machines such as computer-controlled lathes. This code has the same possible combinations as standard binary, but as you can see in the 4-bit example in Table 1-1, they are arranged in a different order. Notice that only one binary digit changes at a time as you count up in this code.

If you need to construct a Gray-code table larger than that in Table 1-1, a handy way to do so is to observe the pattern of 1s and 0s and just extend it. The LSD column starts with one 0 and then has alternating groups of two 1s and two 0s as you go down the column. The second LSD column starts with two 0s and then has alternating groups of four 1s and four 0s. The third column starts with four 0s and then has alternating groups of eight 1s and eight 0s. By now you should see the pattern. Try to figure out the Gray code for the decimal number 16. You should get 1 1000.

Seven-Segment Display Code

Since seven-segment displays such as the one shown in Fig. 1-6 are now so common in everything from

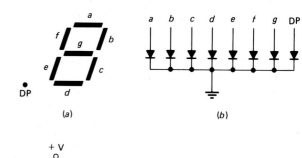

(a)

(b)

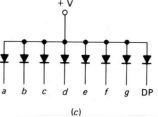

(c)

FIGURE 1-6 Seven-segment LED display. (a) Segment labels. (b) Schematic of common-cathode type. (c) Schematic of common-anode type.

TABLE 1-1
COMMON NUMBER CODES

DECIMAL SYSTEM	BINARY	OCTAL	HEXA-DECIMAL	8421 BCD	2421	5421	EXCESS-3	REFLECTED GRAY CODE	A	B	C	D	E	F	G	DISPLAY
				DECIMAL CODES					SEVEN-SEGMENT DISPLAY (1 = ON)							
0	0000	0	0	0000	0000	0000	0011 0011	0000	1	1	1	1	1	1	0	0
1	0001	1	1	0001	0001	0001	0011 0100	0001	0	1	1	0	0	0	0	1
2	0010	2	2	0010	0010	0010	0011 0101	0011	1	1	0	1	1	0	1	2
3	0011	3	3	0011	0011	0011	0011 0110	0010	1	1	1	1	0	0	1	3
4	0100	4	4	0100	0100	0100	0011 0111	0110	0	1	1	0	0	1	1	4
5	0101	5	5	0101	1011	1000	0011 1000	0111	1	0	1	1	0	1	1	5
6	0110	6	6	0110	1100	1001	0011 1001	0101	1	0	1	1	1	1	1	6
7	0111	7	7	0111	1101	1010	0011 1010	0100	1	1	1	0	0	0	0	7
8	1000	10	8	1000	1110	1011	0011 1011	1100	1	1	1	1	1	1	1	8
9	1001	11	9	1001	1111	1100	0011 1100	1101	1	1	1	1	0	1	1	9
10	1010	12	A	0001 0000	0001 0000	0001 0000	0100 0011	1111	1	1	1	0	1	1	1	A
11	1011	13	B	0001 0001	0001 0001	0001 0001	0100 0100	1110	0	0	1	1	1	1	1	B
12	1100	14	C	0001 0010	0001 0010	0001 0010	0100 0101	1010	1	0	0	1	1	1	0	C
13	1101	15	D	0001 0011	0001 0011	0001 0011	0100 0110	1011	0	1	1	1	1	0	1	D
14	1110	16	E	0001 0100	0001 0100	0001 0100	0100 0111	1001	1	0	0	1	1	1	1	E
15	1111	17	F	0001 0101	0001 1011	0001 1000	0100 1000	1000	1	0	0	0	1	1	1	F

calculators to gasoline pumps, the segment code for such displays has been included in Table 1-1. Some single seven-segment displays will display the last six numbers (10–15) of this code as the hexadecimal digits A–F. In Table 1-1, a 1 indicates that the segment is lighted, which is true for displays such as the common-cathode LED display in Figure 1-6b. For some displays, such as the common-anode LED display shown in Figure 1-6c, a low actually lights the segment, so you have to invert all the values.

Alphanumeric Codes

When communicating with or between computers, you need a binary-based code that can represent letters of the alphabet as well as numbers. Common codes used for this have from 5 to 12 bits per word and are referred to as *alphanumeric codes.* To detect possible errors in these codes, an additional bit, called a *parity bit,* is often added as the most significant bit.

Parity is a term used to identify whether a data word has an odd or even number of 1s. If a data word contains an odd number of 1s, the word is said to have *odd parity.* The binary word 011 0111 with five 1s has odd parity. The binary word 011 0000 has an even number of 1s (two), so it has *even parity.*

In practice the parity bit may function as follows. The system that is sending a data word checks the parity of the word. If the parity of the data word is odd, the system will set the parity bit to a 1. This makes the parity of the data word plus parity bit even. If the parity of the data word is even, the sending system will reset the parity bit to a 0. This again makes the parity of the data word plus parity even. The receiving system checks the parity of the data word plus parity bit that it receives. If the receiving system detects odd parity in the received data word plus parity, it can assume an error occurred and tells the sending system to send the data again. The system is then said to be using even parity. The system could have been set up to use (maintain) odd parity in a similar manner.

The difficulty with this method of detecting errors introduced during transmission is that two errors introduced into a data word may keep the correct parity; therefore, the parity checker won't indicate an error. Other, more complex methods, such as CRC and Hamming codes, can be used to detect multiple errors in transmitted data and even to correct errors. Some of these are described in a later chapter on data communication and formats for data memory storage.

ASCII

Table 1-2 shows several alphanumeric codes. The first of these is *ASCII,* or American Standard Code for Information Interchange. This is shown in the table as a 7-bit code. With 7 bits you can code up to 128 characters, which is enough for full upper- and lowercase alphabets, numbers, punctuation marks, and control characters. The code is arranged so that if only uppercase letters, numbers, and a few control characters are needed, only the lower 6 bits are required. If a

parity check is wanted, a parity bit is added to the basic 7-bit code in the MSB position. The binary word 1100 0100, for example, is the ASCII code for uppercase D with odd parity. Table 1-3 gives the meanings of the control character symbols used in the ASCII code table.

BCDIC

BCDIC code is the Binary-Coded Decimal Interchange Code used with some computers. It uses 7 bits plus a parity bit. The lower 4 bits are referred to as the *numeric bits.* The upper 4 bits contain a parity bit and 3 zone bits. The arrangement of these bits is shown at the bottom of Table 1-2. To save space in Table 1-2, the hex equivalent of the binary digits is used for the BCDIC code expressed with even parity.

EBCDIC

Another alphanumeric code commonly encountered in IBM equipment is the Extended Binary-Coded Decimal Interchange Code, or *EBCDIC.* This is an 8-bit code without parity. A ninth bit can be added for parity. To save space in Table 1-2, the 8 binary digits of EBCDIC are represented with their 2-digit hex equivalent.

SELECTRIC

Selectric is a 7-bit code used in the familiar IBM spinning-ball typewriters and printers. Table 1-2 also shows this code, for reference. Each bit position in the code controls an operation of the spinning ball.

From most significant to least significant bit, the meaning of the seven bits are ROTATE 5, TILT 1, TILT 2, SHIFT, ROTATE 2A, ROTATE 2, and ROTATE 1. In addition to this 7-bit code, Selectrics have separate machine commands for space, return, backspace, tabs, bell, and index.

HOLLERITH

Hollerith is a 12-bit code used to encode data from those computer cards that threaten you with a fate worse than death if you "fold, spindle, or mutilate" them. Figure 1-7 shows a standard 12-row by 80-column card. The 12 data rows are labeled, starting from the top, as 12, 11, 0, 1, 2, 3, 4, 5, 6, 7, 8, 9. The top 3 rows are called *zone punches* and the bottom 10 rows are called *digit punches.* Note that the zero row is included in both categories. A punched hole represents a 1 and a data word is described by the 12 bits in a vertical column. The card in Figure 1-7 shows the Hollerith code for the numbers and letters printed across the top of the card. Table 1-3 shows the entire code and the punched-hole equivalent for each character. Since Hollerith code uses very few of the possible combinations for 12 bits, it is not very efficient. Therefore, it is usually converted to ASCII or EBCDIC for use.

ADDING AND SUBTRACTING BINARY, OCTAL, HEX, AND BCD NUMBERS

The previous section of this chapter reviewed common number systems and codes used with computers. This

ASCII SYMBOL	HEX CODE FOR 7-BIT ASCII	BCDIC SYMBOL	HEX CODE FOR EP BCDIC	EBCDIC SYMBOL	HEX CODE FOR EBCDIC	SELECTRIC SYMBOL	HEX CODE FOR SELECTRIC	HOLLERITH SYMBOL	HOLES PUNCHED CODE FOR HOLLERITH
N U L	0 0			N U L	0 0			N U L	12 0 9 8 1
S O H	0 1			S O H	0 1			S C H	12 9 1
S T X	0 2			S T X	0 2			S T X	12 9 2
E T X	0 3			E T X	0 3			E T X	12 9 3
E O T	0 4			E O T	3 7			E C T	9 7
E N Q	0 5			E N Q	2 D			E N Q	0 9 8 5
A C K	0 6			A C K	2 E			A C K	0 9 8 6
B E L	0 7			B E L	2 F			B E L	0 9 8 7
B S	0 8			B S	1 6			B S	11 9 6
H T	0 9			H T	0 5			H T	12 9 5
L F	0 A			L F	2 5			L F	0 9 5
V T	0 B	‡	9 A	V T	0 B			V T	12 9 8 3
F F	0 C			F F	0 C			F F	12 9 8 4
C R	0 D	‡	F F	C R	0 D			C R	12 9 8 5
S O	0 E			S O	0 E			S O	12 9 8 6
S I	0 F			S I	0 F			S I	12 9 8 7
D L E	1 0			D L E	1 0			D L E	12 11 9 8 1
D C 1	1 1			D C 1	1 1			D C 1	11 9 1
D C 2	1 2			D C 2	1 2			D C 2	11 9 2
D C 3	1 3			D C 3	1 3			D C 3	11 9 3
D C 4	1 4			D C 4	3 5			D C 4	9 8 4
N A K	1 5			N A K	3 D			N A K	9 8 5
S Y N	1 6			S Y N	3 2			S Y N	9 2
E T B	1 7			E O B	2 6			E T B	0 9 6
C A N	1 8			C A N	1 8			C A N	11 9 8
E M	1 9			E M	1 9			E M	11 9 8 1
S U B	1 A			S U B	3 F			S U B	9 8 7
E S C	1 B			B Y P	2 4			E S C	0 9 7
F S	1 C			F L S	1 C			F S	11 9 8 4
G S	1 D			G S	1 D			G S	11 9 8 5
R S	1 E			R D S	1 E			R S	11 9 8 6
U S	1 F			U S	1 F			U S	11 9 8 7
S P	2 0	S P	0 0	S P	4 0			S P	NO PNCH
!	2 1	!	6 A	!	5 A	½!	2 7	!	12 8 7
"	2 2	⧻	5 F	"	7 F	"	2 D	"	8 7
#	2 3	#	4 B	#	7 B	#	7 E	#	8 3
$	2 4	$	2 B	$	5 B	$	7 9	$	11 8 3
%	2 5	%	5 C	%	6 C	%	3 D	%	0 8 4
&	2 6	&	3 0	&	5 0	&	7 D		12
'	2 7	V	1 D	'	7 D	'	2 5		8 5
(	2 8	Blank	5 0	(	4 D	(	3 8	(	12 8 5
)	2 9	△	6 F	)	5 D	)	3 9	)	11 8 5
*	2 A	*	6 C	*	5 C	*	7 C	*	11 8 4

(continued)

TABLE 1-2 Common alphanumeric codes.

ASCII SYMBOL	HEX CODE FOR 7-BIT ASCII	BCDIC SYMBOL	HEX CODE FOR EP BCDIC	EBCDIC SYMBOL	HEX CODE FOR EBCDIC	SELEC-TRIC SYMBOL	HEX CODE FOR SELEC-TRIC	HOL-LERITH SYMBOL	HOLES PUNCHED CODE FOR HOLLERITH
+	2 B			+	4 E	+	0 E	+	12 8 6
,	2 C	,	1 B	,	6 B	,	4 4	,	0 8 3
−	2 D			−	6 0	−	0 0	−	11
.	2 E	.	7 B	.	4 B	.	2 6	.	12 8 3
/	2 F	/	1 1	/	6 1	/	4 1	/	0 1
0	3 0	0	0 A	0	F 0	0	3 1	0	0
1	3 1	1	4 1	1	F 1	1	7 7	1	1
2	3 2	2	4 2	2	F 2	2	3 6	2	2
3	3 3	3	0 3	3	F 3	3	7 6	3	3
4	3 4	4	4 4	4	F 4	4	7 1	4	4
5	3 5	5	0 5	5	F 5	5	3 5	5	5
6	3 6	6	0 6	6	F 6	6	3 4	6	6
7	3 7	7	4 7	7	F 7	7	7 5	7	7
8	3 8	8	4 8	8	F 8	8	7 4	8	8
9	3 9	9	0 9	9	F 9	9	3 0	9	9
:	3 A	:	4 D	:	7 A	:	4 D	:	8 2
;	3 B	;	2 E	;	5 E	;	4 5	;	11 8 6
<	3 C	<	7 E	<	4 C			<	12 8 4
=	3 D	√	0 F	=	7 E	=	0 6	=	8 6
>	3 E	>	4 E	>	6 E			>	0 8 6
?	3 F	?	3 A	?	6 F	?	4 9	?	0 8 7
@	4 0	@	0 C	@	7 C	@	3 E	@	8 4
A	4 1	A	7 1	A	C 1	A	6 C	A	12 1
B	4 2	B	7 2	B	C 2	B	1 8	B	12 2
C	4 3	C	3 3	C	C 3	C	5 C	C	12 3
D	4 4	D	7 4	D	C 4	D	5 D	D	12 4
E	4 5	E	3 5	E	C 5	E	1 D	E	12 5
F	4 6	F	3 6	F	C 6	F	4 E	F	12 6
G	4 7	G	7 7	G	C 7	G	4 F	G	12 7
H	4 8	H	7 8	H	C 8	H	1 9	H	12 8
I	4 9	I	3 9	I	C 9	I	2 C	I	12 9
J	4 A	J	2 1	J	D 1	J	0 7	J	11 1
K	4 B	K	2 2	K	D 2	K	1 C	K	11 2
L	4 C	L	6 3	L	D 3	L	5 9	L	11 3
M	4 D	M	2 4	M	D 4	M	6 F	M	11 4
N	4 E	N	6 5	N	D 5	N	1 E	N	11 5
O	4 F	O	6 6	O	D 6	O	6 9	O	11 6
P	5 0	P	2 7	P	D 7	P	0 D	P	11 7
Q	5 1	Q	2 8	Q	D 8	Q	0 C	Q	11 8
R	5 2	R	6 9	R	D 9	R	6 D	R	11 9
S	5 3	S	1 2	S	E 2	S	2 9	S	0 2
T	5 4	T	5 3	T	E 3	T	1 F	T	0 3

(continued)

TABLE 1-2 Common alphanumeric codes (continued).

ASCII SYMBOL	HEX CODE FOR 7-BIT ASCII	BCDIC SYMBOL	HEX CODE FOR EP BCDIC	EBCDIC SYMBOL	HEX CODE FOR EBCDIC	SELECTRIC SYMBOL	HEX CODE FOR SELECTRIC	HOLLERITH SYMBOL	HOLES PUNCHED CODE FOR HOLLERITH
U	5 5	U	1 4	U	E 4	U	5 E	U	0 4
V	5 6	V	5 5	V	E 5	V	6 E	V	0 5
W	5 7	W	5 6	W	E 6	W	2 8	W	0 6
X	5 8	X	1 7	X	E 7	X	5 F	X	0 7
Y	5 9	Y	1 8	Y	E 8	Y	0 9	Y	0 8
Z	5 A	Z	5 9	Z	E 9	Z	3 F	Z	0 9
[	5 B	[	7 D	[	A D	[	7 F	[	12 8 2
\	5 C	\	1 E	N L	1 5			\	0 8 2
]	5 D	]	2 D	]	D D			]	11 8 2
^	5 E	□	3 C	¬	5 F			^	11 8 7
—	5 F	—	6 0	—	6 D	—	0 8	—	0 8 5
`	6 0			R E S	1 4			`	8 1
a	6 1			a	8 1	a	6 4	a	12 0 1
b	6 2			b	8 2	b	1 0	b	12 0 2
c	6 3			c	8 3	c	5 4	c	12 0 3
d	6 4			d	8 4	d	5 5	d	12 0 4
e	6 5			e	8 5	e	1 5	e	12 0 5
f	6 6			f	8 6	f	4 6	f	12 0 6
g	6 7			g	8 7	g	4 7	g	12 0 7
h	6 8			h	8 8	h	1 1	h	12 0 8
i	6 9			i	8 9	i	2 4	i	12 0 9
j	6 A			j	9 1	j	0 7	j	12 11 1
k	6 B			k	9 2	k	1 4	k	12 11 2
l	6 C			l	9 3	l	5 1	l	12 11 3
m	6 D			m	9 4	m	6 7	m	12 11 4
n	6 E			n	9 5	n	1 6	n	12 11 5
o	6 F			o	9 6	o	6 1	o	12 11 6
p	7 0			p	9 7	p	0 5	p	12 11 7
q	7 1			q	9 8	q	0 4	q	12 11 8
r	7 2			r	9 9	r	6 5	r	12 11 9
s	7 3			s	A 2	s	2 1	s	11 0 2
t	7 4			t	A 3	t	1 7	t	11 0 3
u	7 5			u	A 4	u	5 6	u	11 0 4
v	7 6			v	A 5	v	6 6	v	11 0 5
w	7 7			w	A 6	w	2 0	w	11 0 6
x	7 8			x	A 7	x	5 7	x	11 0 7
y	7 9			y	A 8	y	0 1	y	11 0 8
z	7 A			z	A 9	z	3 7	z	11 0 9
{	7 B			{	8 B			{	12 0
|	7 C			|	4 F			|	12 11
}	7 D			}	9 B			}	11 0
~	7 E			¢	4 A			~	11 0 1
D E L	7 F			D E L	0 7			D E L	12 9 7

BCDIC

$$\underbrace{\text{HEX DIGIT}}_{\text{PCBA}} \quad \underbrace{\text{HEX DIGIT}}_{2^3 2^2 2^1 2^0}$$

SELECTRIC

$$\underbrace{R_5 T_1 T_2}_{\text{HEX DIGIT}} \quad \underbrace{SR_{2_A} R_2 R_1}_{\text{HEX DIGIT}}$$

TABLE 1-2 Common alphanumeric codes (*continued*).

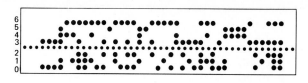

(a)

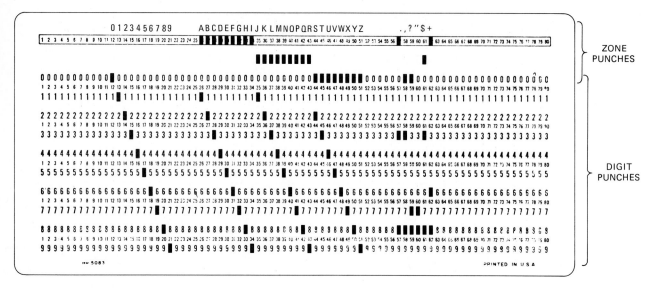

(b)

FIGURE 1-7   Hollerith punched card.

section reviews how to do computations in the previously described number systems.

Binary

ADDITION

Figure 1-8a shows the truth table for addition of two binary digits and carry in (C_{IN}) from addition of previous digits. Figure 1-8b shows the result of adding two 8-bit binary numbers using these rules. Note that since the result can be only a 0 or 1, $1 + 0 + C_{IN} = 0$ plus a carry into the next digit, and $1 + 1 + C_{IN} = 1$ plus a carry into the next digit.

2's COMPLEMENT BINARY

One way of representing negative numbers in binary is by using 2's complement binary. When you handwrite a number which represents some physical quantity such as temperature, you can simply put a + sign in front of the number when you wish to indicate that the number is positive. You can write a − sign when you wish to indicate that the number is negative. However, if you want to store values such as temperatures, which can be positive or negative, in a computer memory, there is a problem. Since the computer memory can only store 1s or 0s, some way must be established to represent the sign of the number with a 1 or a 0.

The way to do this is to reserve the MSB of the data word as a *sign bit* and to use the rest of the bits of the data word to represent the size (magnitude) of the quantity. A computer that works with 8-bit words will represent signed numbers with the MSB (bit 7) as the sign bit and the lower 7 bits as a representation of the

NUL	NULL	DC2	DIRECT CONTROL 2
SOH	START OF HEADING	DC3	DIRECT CONTROL 3
STX	START TEXT	DC4	DIRECT CONTROL 4
ETX	END TEXT	NAK	NEGATIVE
EOT	END OF TRANSMIS-		ACKNOWLEDGE
	SION	SYN	SYNCHRONOUS
ENQ	ENQUIRY		IDLE
ACK	ACKNOWLEDGE	ETB	END TRANSMIS-
BEL	BELL		SION BLOCK
BS	BACKSPACE	CAN	CANCEL
HT	HORIZONTAL TAB	EM	END OF MEDIUM
LF	LINE FEED	SUB	SUBSTITUTE
VT	VERTICAL TAB	ESC	ESCAPE
FF	FORM FEED	FS	FORM SEPARATOR
CR	CARRIAGE RETURN	GS	GROUP SEPARATOR
SO	SHIFT OUT	RS	RECORD
SI	SHIFT IN		SEPARATOR
DLE	DATA LINK ESCAPE	US	UNIT SEPARATOR
DC1	DIRECT CONTROL 1		

TABLE 1-3   Definitions of control characters.

INPUTS			OUTPUTS	
A	B	C_{IN}	S	C_{OUT}
0	0	0	0	0
0	0	1	1	0
0	1	0	1	0
0	1	1	0	1
1	0	0	1	0
1	0	1	0	1
1	1	0	0	1
1	1	1	1	1

$$S = A \oplus B \oplus C_{IN}$$

$$C_{OUT} = A \cdot B + C_{IN}(A \oplus B)$$

(a)

```
     10011010
  +  11011100
  [1] 01110110
        └── Carry
```

(b)

FIGURE 1-8   Binary addition. (a) Truth table for 2 bits plus carry. (b) Addition of two 8-bit words.

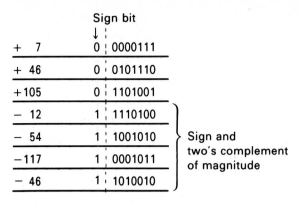

FIGURE 1-9   Positive and negative numbers represented with a sign bit and 2's complement.

magnitude of the numbers. The usual convention is to represent a positive number with a 0 sign bit and a negative number with a 1 sign bit.

To make computations with signed numbers easier, the magnitude of negative numbers is represented in a special form called 2's complement. The 2's complement of a binary number is formed by inverting each bit of the data word and adding 1 to the result. Some examples should help clarify this.

The number $+7_{10}$ is represented in 8-bit sign-and-magnitude form as 0000 0111. The sign bit is zero, which indicates a positive number. The magnitude of positive numbers is represented in straight binary, so the least significant bits of 0000 0111 represent 7_{10}.

To represent -7_{10} in 8-bit 2's complement sign-and-magnitude form, start with the 8-bit code for +7, 0000 0111. Invert each bit to get 1111 1000. Then add 1 to get 1111 1001. This result is the correct representation of -7_{10}. Figure 1-9 shows other examples of positive and negative numbers expressed in 8-bit sign-and-magnitude form. For practice, try generating each of these yourself to see if you get the same result as shown.

To reverse this procedure and find the magnitude of a number expressed in sign-and-magnitude form, proceed as follows. If the number is positive, as indicated by a sign bit of 0, then the least significant 7 bits represent the magnitude directly in binary. If the

number is negative, as indicated by a sign bit of 1, then the magnitude is expressed in 2's complement. To get the magnitude of this negative number expressed in standard binary, invert each bit of the data word, including the sign bit, and add 1 to the result. For example, given the word 1110 1011, invert each bit to get 0001 0100. Then add 1, resulting in 0001 0101. This equals 21_{10}, so you know that the original numbers represent -21_{10}. Again, try converting a few of the numbers in Figure 1-9 for practice.

Figure 1-10 shows some examples of addition of signed binary numbers of this type. Sign bits are added together, just as the other bits are. Figure 1-10a shows the results of adding two positive numbers. The sign bit of the result is zero, so the result is positive. The second example, in Figure 1-10b, adds -9 to +13, or, in effect, subtracts 9 from 13. As indicated by the zero sign bit, the result of this, 4, is positive and is in true binary form.

Figure 1-10c shows the result of adding -13 to a smaller positive number, +9. The sign bit of the result is a 1. This indicates that the result is negative and the magnitude is in 2's complement form. Remember, to convert a 2's complement result to a signed number in true binary form,

1.   Invert each bit, to produce 1's complement.

2.   Add 1.

3.   Place a minus sign in front of the number to indicate that the result is negative.

The final example in Figure 1-10d shows the results of adding two negative numbers. The sign bit of the result is a 1, and the result is negative and in 2's complement form. Again, inverting each bit, adding 1, and prefixing a minus sign will put the result in a more recognizable form.

Now let's consider the range of numbers that can be represented with 8 bits in sign-and-magnitude form. Eight bits can represent a maximum of 2^8, or 256, numbers. Since we are representing both positive and

```
  +13      00001101
  + 9      00001001
  +22      00010110
              └─ Sign bit is 0
                 so result is positive
                    (a)

+13      00001101
- 9      11110111 2's complement for -9 with sign bit
+ 4    1│00000100
            ↑└─ Sign bit is 0
                 so result is positive
          └─ Ignore carry
                    (b)

+ 9      00001001
-13      11110011 2's complement for -13 with sign bit
- 4      11111100 Sign bit is 1
         00000011 So invert each bit
       +        1 Add 1
       -00000100 Prefix with minus sign
                    (c)

- 9      11110111⎫ 2's complement,
-13      11110011⎭ sign-and-magnitude form
-22      11101010 Sign bit is 1
         00010101 So invert each bit
       +        1 Add 1
       -00010110 Prefix with minus sign
                    (d)
```

FIGURE 1-10 Addition of signed binary numbers.
(a) +9 and +13. (b) -9 and +13. (c) +9 and -13.
(d) -9 and -13.

negative numbers, half of this range will be positive and half negative. Therefore, the range is 0 to +127 and -1 to -128. Figure 1-11 shows the sign-and-magnitude binary representations for these values. If you like number patterns, you might notice that this scheme shifts the normal codes for 128 to 255 downward to represent -128 to -1.

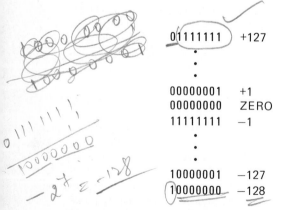

```
01111111    +127
   .
   .
   .
00000001    +1
00000000    ZERO
11111111    -1
   .
   .
   .
10000001    -127
10000000    -128
```

FIGURE 1-11 Range of signed numbers that can be represented with 8 binary bits.

If a computer is storing signed numbers as 16-bit words, then a much larger range of numbers can be represented. Since 16 bits gives 2^{16}, or 65,536, possible values, the range for 16-bit sign-and-magnitude numbers is -32,768 to +32,767. Operations with 16-bit sign-and-magnitude numbers are done the same as was demonstrated above for 8-bit sign-and-magnitude numbers.

BINARY SUBTRACTION

There are two common methods for doing binary subtraction, the "pencil" method and the 2's complement add method. Figure 1-12a shows the truth table for binary subtraction of two binary digits A and B. Also included in the truth table is the effect of a borrow in, B_{IN}, from subtracting previous digits. Figure 1-12b shows an example of the pencil method of subtracting two 8-bit numbers. Using a truth table, this method is the same as decimal subtraction.

A second method of performing binary subtraction is by adding the 2's complement representation of the bottom number (subtrahend) to the top number (minuend). Figure 1-12c shows how this is done. First represent the top number in sign-and-magnitude representation form. Then form the 2's complement sign-and-magnitude representation for the negative of the bottom number. Finally, add the two parts formed. For the example in Figure 1-12c, the sign of the result is a zero, which indicates the result is positive and in true form. The final carry produced by the addition can be ignored. Figure 1-12d shows another example of this method of subtraction. In this case the bottom number is larger than the top number. Again, represent the top number in sign-and-magnitude form, produce the 2's complement sign-and-magnitude form for the negative of the bottom number, and add the two together. The sign bit of the result is a 1 for this example. This indicates that the result is negative, and so its magnitude is represented in 2's complement form. To get the result into a form that is more recognizable to you, invert each bit of the result, add 1 to it, and put a minus sign in front of it, as shown in Figure 1-12d.

The examples shown use 8 bits, but the process works for any number of bits. This method may seem awkward, but it is easy for a computer or microprocessor to do because it requires only the simple operations of inverting and adding.

BINARY MULTIPLICATION

There are several methods of doing binary multiplication. Figure 1-13 shows what might be called the pencil method because it is the same as the way you learned to multiply decimal numbers. The top number, or multiplicand, is multiplied by the LSD of the bottom number, or multiplier. The partial product is recorded. The top number is multiplied by the next digit of the multiplier. The resultant partial product is written under the last product but shifted one place to the left. Adding all the partial products gives the total product. This method works well when doing multiplication by hand, but it is not practical for a computer because the

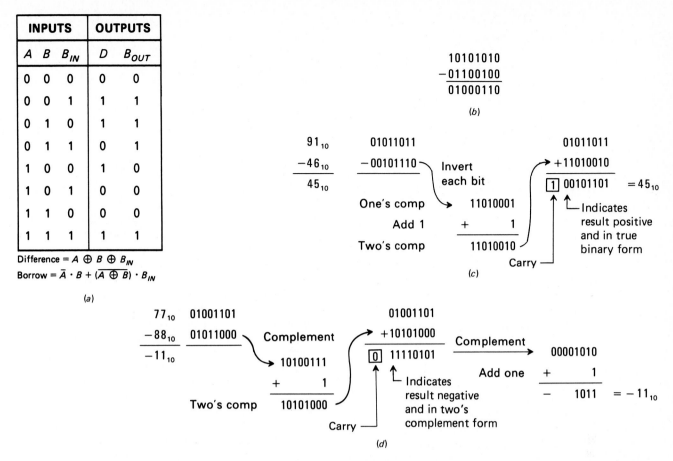

INPUTS			OUTPUTS	
A	B	B_{IN}	D	B_{OUT}
0	0	0	0	0
0	0	1	1	1
0	1	0	1	1
0	1	1	0	1
1	0	0	1	0
1	0	1	0	0
1	1	0	0	0
1	1	1	1	1

Difference $= A \oplus B \oplus B_{IN}$

Borrow $= \bar{A} \cdot B + (\overline{A \oplus B}) \cdot B_{IN}$

(a)

```
   10101010
 −01100100
   01000110
```

(b)

```
  91₁₀      01011011                        01011011
 −46₁₀     −00101110 ─ Invert            ┌→+11010010
  ─────                  each bit         │ ┌─────────
   45₁₀                                   │ │1│00101101  = 45₁₀
              One's comp    11010001      │  ↑↑
                                          │  └─Indicates
              Add 1        +        1     │     result positive
                          ──────────      │     and in true
              Two's comp    11010010 ─────┘     binary form
                                       Carry ─
```

(c)

```
  77₁₀   01001101                        01001101
 −88₁₀   01011000 ─ Complement        ┌→+10101000       Complement
 ─────                                 │ ┌─────────    ──────────→    00001010
 −11₁₀              10100111           │ │0│11110101                  Add one   +    1
                                       │   ↑                                    ──────
                  +        1           │   └─Indicates                          −  1011   = −11₁₀
                 ──────────            │      result negative
      Two's comp   10101000 ──────────┘      and in two's
                                Carry ─       complement form
```

(d)

FIGURE 1-12 Binary subtraction. (a) Truth table for two bits and borrow. (b) Pencil method. (c) 2's complement positive result. (d) 2's complement negative result.

type of shifts required make it awkward to implement.

One of the multiplication methods used by computers is repeated addition. To multiply 7 × 55, for example, the computer can just add seven 55s. For large numbers, however, this method is slow. To multiply 786 × 253, for example, requires 252 add operations.

Most computers use an add-and-shift-right method. This method takes advantage of the fact that, for binary multiplication, the partial product can only be either the top number if the multiplier digit is a 1 or a 0 if the multiplier digit is a 0. The method does the same thing as the pencil method except that the partial products are added as they are produced and the sum

of the partial products is shifted right rather than each partial product being shifted left.

A point to note about multiplying numbers is the number of bits the product requires. For example, multiplying two 4-bit numbers can give a product with as many as 8 bits, and two 8-bit numbers can give a 16-bit product.

BINARY DIVISION

Binary division can also be performed in several ways. Figure 1-14 shows two examples of the pencil method. This is the same process as decimal long division. However, it is much simpler than decimal long division because the digits of the result (quotient) can be only 0 or 1. A division is attempted on part of the dividend. If this is not possible because the divisor is larger than that part of the dividend, a 0 is entered into the quotient. Another attempt is then made to divide using one more digit of the dividend. When a division is possible, a 1 is entered in the quotient. The divisor is then subtracted from the portion of the dividend used. The process is continued as with standard long division until all the dividend is used. As shown in Figure 1-14b, 0s can be added to the right of the binary point and division continued to convert a remainder to a binary equivalent.

```
    11           1011        Multiplicand
  × 9         ×  1001        Multiplier
  ────         ───────
   99            1011 ⎫
                 0000 ⎪
                 0000 ⎬  Partial products
                 1011 ⎭
              ─────────
              1100011        Product
```

FIGURE 1-13 Binary multiplication.

```
        01100   Quotient
Divisor 110) 1001000   Dividend        12
        −110                          6)72
        ─────
         110
        −110
        ─────
           0
```

(a)

```
        110.01                6.25
100) 11001.00              4)25.00
    −100
    ────
     100
    −100
    ────
      01 00
```

(b)

FIGURE 1-14   Binary division.

Another method of division that is easier for computers and microprocessors to perform uses successive subtractions. The divisor is subtracted from the dividend and from each successive remainder until a borrow is produced. The desired quotient is 1 less than the number of subtractions needed to produce a borrow. This method is simple, but for large numbers it is slow.

For faster division of large numbers, computers use a subtract-and-shift-left method that is essentially the same process you go through with a pencil long division.

Octal and Hexadecimal Addition and Subtraction

People working with computers or microprocessors often use octal or hexadecimal as a shorthand way of representing long binary numbers such as memory addresses. It is therefore useful to be able to add and subtract octal and hexadecimal numbers.

OCTAL ADDITION

Figure 1-15 shows two ways of adding the octal numbers 47 and 36. The first way is to convert both numbers to their binary equivalents. Remember, each octal digit represents three binary digits. These binary numbers are then added using the rules for binary addition from Figure 1-8a. The resultant binary sum is then converted back to octal.

The second method works directly with the octal form: 7 added to 6 gives 13, which is a carry to the next digit and a remainder of 5. The 5 is recorded and the carry is added to the next digit column. Then 4 plus 3 plus a carry gives 8, which is a carry with no remainder. The 0 is written and the carry is added to the next digit column. This is the same process you use for

```
                                        Carry
                                          ↓
   47₈          100 111              ¹47₈
  +36₈        +  011 110            +  36₈
  ────        ─────────           ──────────
              1 000 101           8₁₀ 13₁₀
                1  0   5₈           1  0  5₈
```

(a)   *(b)*

FIGURE 1-15   Octal addition. (a) Adding binary equivalents. (b) Direct octal addition.

decimal addition, but a carry is produced any time the sum is 8 or greater, rather than 10 or greater.

HEXADECIMAL ADDITION

As shown in Figure 1-16 the same approaches can be used to add two hexadecimal numbers. For converting to binary, remember that each hex digit represents four binary digits. The binary numbers are added, and the result is converted back to hexadecimal.

The second method works directly with the hex numbers. With hex addition, a carry is produced whenever the sum is 16 or greater. An A in hex is a 10 in decimal, and an F is 15 in decimal. These add to give 25, which is a carry with a remainder of 9. The 9 is written and the carry is added to the next digit column. Then 7 plus 3 plus the carry gives decimal 11, or B in hex.

You may use whichever method seems easier to you and gives you consistently correct answers. If you are doing a great deal of octal or hexadecimal arithmetic you might buy an electronic calculator specifically designed to do decimal, octal, and hexadecimal arithmetic.

OCTAL SUBTRACTION

Octal subtraction is shown in Figure 1-17. Since the least significant digit of the top number is smaller than the least significant digit of the bottom number, a borrow must be done. In octal subtraction, 8 is borrowed from the next digit position and added to the top number. The bottom number is then subtracted and the remainder is recorded. The process is continued until all digits are subtracted. If you are uncomfortable borrowing 8s, you can just convert the number to decimal, subtract, and convert the result back to octal.

```
                                        Carry
                                          ↓
   7A       0111  1010            7  ¹  A₁₆
  +3F      +0011  1111           +  3     F₁₆
  ────     ──────────           ──────────────
   B9       1011  1001          11₁₀   25₁₀
                                  B₁₆    9₁₆
```

(a)   *(b)*

FIGURE 1-16   Hexadecimal addition.

$$\begin{array}{r} 34_8 \\ -17_8 \\ \hline 15_8 \end{array} \qquad \begin{array}{r} 28_{10} \\ -15_{10} \\ \hline 13_{10} \end{array}$$

FIGURE 1-17 Octal subtraction.

HEXADECIMAL SUBTRACTION

Hexadecimal subtraction is similar to octal subtraction except that when a borrow is needed, 16 is borrowed from the next MSD. Figure 1-18 shows this. It may help you to follow the example if you do partial conversions to decimal in your head. For example, 7 plus a borrowed 16 is 23. Subtracting B, or 11, leaves 12, or C in hexadecimal. Then 3 from the 6 left after a borrow leaves 3, so the result is $3C.

BCD Addition and Subtraction

In systems where the final result of a calculation is to be displayed, such as a calculator, it may be easier to work with numbers in a BCD format. These codes, as shown in Table 1-1, represent each decimal digit, 0 through 9, with a 4-bit binary word. The BCD words are the same as the binary equivalents for 0 through 9.

BCD ADDITION

BCD can have no digit-word with a value greater than 9. Therefore, a carry must be generated if the result of a BCD addition is greater than 1001, or 9. Figure 1-19 shows three examples of BCD addition. The first, in Figure 1-19a, is very straightforward because the sum is less than 9. The result is the same as it would be for standard binary.

For the second example, in Figure 1-19b, adding BCD 7 to BCD 5 produces 1100. This is a correct binary result of 12, but it is an illegal BCD code. To convert the result to BCD format, a correction factor of 6 is added. The result of adding 6 is 0001 0010, which is the legal BCD code for 12.

Figure 1-19c shows another case where a correction factor must be added. The initial addition of 9 and 8 produces 0001 0001. Even though the lower four digits are less than 9, this is an incorrect BCD result because a carryout of bit 3 of the BCD digit-word was produced. This carryout of bit 3 is often called an *auxiliary carry*. Adding the correction factor of 6 gives the correct BCD result of 0001 0111, or 17.

To summarize, a correction factor of 6 must be added to the result if the result in the lower 4 bits is greater than 9 or if the initial addition produces a carryout of bit 3 of any BCD digit-word. This correction is sometimes called a *decimal-adjust operation*.

$$\begin{array}{rcr} 77_{16} & = & 119_{10} \\ -3B_{16} & = & -59_{10} \\ \hline 3C_{16} & & 60_{10} \end{array}$$

FIGURE 1-18 Hexadecimal subtraction.

$$\begin{array}{rc}
 & \text{BCD} \\
35 & 0011\ \ 0101 \\
+23 & +0010\ \ 0011 \\
\hline
58 & 0101\ \ 1000
\end{array}$$

(a)

$$\begin{array}{rcl}
 & \text{BCD} & \\
7 & 0111 & \\
+\ 5 & +\ 0101 & \\
\hline
12 & 1100 & \text{Incorrect BCD} \\
 & +\ \ \ 110 & \text{Add 6} \\
\hline
 & 00010010 & \text{Correct BCD 12}
\end{array}$$

(b)

$$\begin{array}{rcl}
 & \text{BCD} & \\
9 & 1001 & \\
+\ 8 & +\ 1000 & \\
\hline
17 & 00010001 & \text{Incorrect BCD} \\
 & 110 & \text{Add 6} \\
\hline
 & 00010111 & \text{Correct BCD 17}
\end{array}$$

(c)

FIGURE 1-19 BCD addition. (a) No correction needed. (b) Correction needed due to illegal BCD result. (c) Correction needed due to carry out of BCD digit.

The reason for the correction factor of 6 is that in BCD we want a carry into the next digit after 1001, or 9, but in binary a carryout of the lower 4 bits does not occur until after 1111, or 15, which is 6 more than 9.

BCD SUBTRACTION

Figure 1-20 shows a subtraction of BCD 17 (0001 0111) minus BCD 9 (0000 1001). The initial result, 0000 1110, is not a legal BCD number. Whenever this occurs in BCD subtraction, 6 must be *subtracted* from the initial result to produce the correct BCD result. For the example shown in Figure 1-20, subtracting 6 gives a correct BCD result of 0000 1000, or 8.

The correction factor of 6 must be subtracted from any BCD digit-word if that digit-word is greater than 1001 or if a borrow from the next-higher digit occurred during the subtraction.

$$\begin{array}{rcl}
17 & 1\ \ 0111 & \\
-\ 9 & 0\ \ 1001 & \\
\hline
8 & 0\ \ 1110 & \text{Illegal BCD} \\
 & -\ \ \ 110 & \text{Subtract 6} \\
\hline
 & 1000 & = 8_{10}
\end{array}$$

FIGURE 1-20 BCD subtraction.

BASIC LOGIC GATES

Microcomputers such as those we discuss throughout this book often contain basic logic gates as "glue" between LSI (large-scale-integration) devices. For troubleshooting these systems, it is important to be able to predict logic levels at any point directly from the schematic rather than having to work your way through a truth table for each gate. This section should help refresh your memory of basic logic functions and help you remember how to analyze logic gate circuits quickly.

Inverting and Noninverting Buffers

Figure 1-21 shows the schematic symbols and truth tables for simple buffers and logic gates. The first thing to remember about these symbols is that the shape of the symbol indicates the logic function performed by the device. The second thing to remember about these symbols is that a bubble or lack of bubble indicates the *assertion* level for an input or output signal. Let's review how modern logic designers use these symbols.

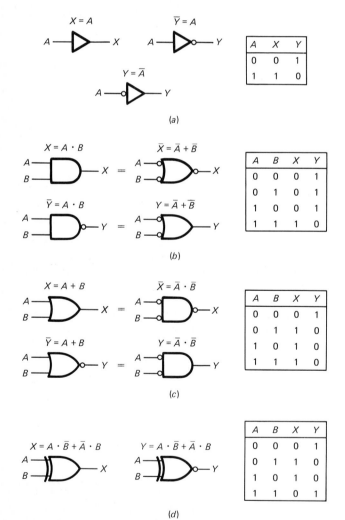

FIGURE 1-21   Buffers and logic gates. (a) Buffers. (b) AND-NAND. (c) OR-NOR. (d) Exclusive OR.

The first symbol for a *buffer* in Figure 1-21a has no bubbles on the input or output. Therefore, the input is active high and the output is active high. We read this symbol as follows. If the input, A, is asserted high, then the output, Y, will be asserted high. The rest of the truth table is covered by the assumption that if the A input is not asserted high, then the Y output will not be asserted high.

The next two symbols for a buffer each contain a bubble. The bubble on the output of the first of these indicates that the output is active low. The input has no bubble, so it is active high. You can read the function of the device directly from the schematic symbol as follows. If the A input is asserted high, then the Y output will be asserted low. This device then simply changes the assertion level of a signal. The output, Y, will always have a logic state that is the complement, or inverse, of that on the input, so the device is usually referred to as an *inverter*.

The second schematic symbol for an inverter in Figure 1-21a has the bubble on the input. We draw the symbol this way when we want to indicate that we are using the device to change an asserted-low signal to an asserted-high signal. For example, if we pass the signal CS through this device, it becomes $\overline{CS}$. The symbol tells you directly that if the input is asserted low, then the output will be asserted high. Now let's review how you express the functions of logic gates using this approach.

Logic Gates

Figure 1-21b shows the symbols and truth tables for simple logic gates. A symbol with a flat back and a round front indicates that the device performs the logical *AND* function. This means that the output will be asserted if the A input is asserted AND the B input is asserted. Again, a bubble or lack of bubble is used to indicate the assertion level of each input and output. The first AND symbol in Figure 1-21b has no bubbles, so the inputs and the output are active high. The output then will be asserted high if the A input is asserted high AND the B input is asserted high. The bubble on the output of the second AND symbol in Figure 1-21b indicates that this device, commonly called a *NAND* gate, has an active low output. If the A input is asserted high and the B input is asserted high, then the Y output will be asserted low. Look at the truth table in Figure 1-21b to see if you agree with this.

Figure 1-21c shows the other two possible cases for the AND symbol. The first of these has bubbles on the inputs and on the outputs. If you see this symbol in a schematic, you should immediately see that the output will be asserted low if the A input is asserted low AND the B input is asserted low. The second AND symbol in Figure 1-21c has no bubble on the output, so the output will be asserted high if the A AND B inputs are both asserted low.

A logic symbol with a curved back indicates that the output of the device will be asserted if the A input is asserted OR the B input of the device is asserted. Again a bubble or lack of bubble is used to indicate the assertion level for an input or output. Note in Figure 1-21b and 1-21c that each of the AND symbol forms has an equivalent OR symbol form. An AND symbol with active high inputs and an active high output, for example, represents the same device (a 74LS08, perhaps) as an OR symbol with active low inputs and an active low output. Use the truth table in Figure 1-21b to convince yourself of this. The bubbled-OR representation tells you that if one input is asserted low, the output will be low, regardless of the state on the other input. As we will show later in this chapter, this is often a useful way to think of the operation of an AND gate.

Figure 1-21d shows the symbol and truth table for an *exclusive*-OR gate. The output of this device will be asserted if the *A* input is asserted OR if the *B* input is asserted, but the output will not be asserted if both *A* AND *B* are asserted.

You need to be able to read any of these symbols because most logic designers will use the symbol that best describes the function they want a device to perform in a particular circuit.

Latches, Flip-flops, Registers, and Counters

THE D LATCH

A *latch* is a digital device that stores a 1 or a 0 on its output. Figure 1-22a shows the schematic symbol and truth table for a D latch. The device functions as follows. If the *enable* input, E, is low, any data present on the D input will have no effect on the Q or $\bar{Q}$ outputs. This is indicated in the truth table by an X in the D column. If the enable input is high, a high or a low on the D input will be passed to the Q output. In other words, the Q output will follow the D input as long as the enable input is high. The $\bar{Q}$ output will contain the complement of the logic state on Q. When the enable input is made low again, the state on Q at that time will be latched there. Any changes on D will have no effect on Q until the enable input is made high again. When the enable input goes low, then, the state present on D just before the enable goes low will be stored on the Q output. Keep this operation in mind as you read about the D flip-flop in the next section.

THE D FLIP-FLOP

The first type of *flip-flop* to review is the D type. Figure 1-22b shows the schematic symbol and the truth table for a typical D flip-flop. Note that this device has a *clock* input, CK, in place of the enable input on the D latch. Also note the up arrows in the clock column of the truth table. These arrows are used to indicate that a 1 or 0 on the D input will be copied to the Q output at the instant the clock input goes from low to high. In other words, the D flip-flop takes a snapshot of whatever state is on the D input when the clock goes high and displays the photo on the Q output. If the clock input is low, a change on D will have no effect on the output. Likewise, if the clock input is high, a change on D will have no effect on the Q output. Contrast this operation

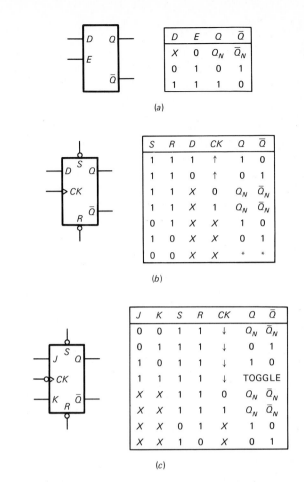

D	E	Q	$\bar{Q}$
X	0	Q_N	$\bar{Q}_N$
0	1	0	1
1	1	1	0

(a)

S	R	D	CK	Q	$\bar{Q}$
1	1	1	↑	1	0
1	1	0	↑	0	1
1	1	X	0	Q_N	$\bar{Q}_N$
1	1	X	1	Q_N	$\bar{Q}_N$
0	1	X	X	1	0
1	0	X	X	0	1
0	0	X	X	*	*

(b)

J	K	S	R	CK	Q	$\bar{Q}$
0	0	1	1	↓	Q_N	$\bar{Q}_N$
0	1	1	1	↓	0	1
1	0	1	1	↓	1	0
1	1	1	1	↓	TOGGLE	
X	X	1	1	0	Q_N	$\bar{Q}_N$
X	X	1	1	1	Q_N	$\bar{Q}_N$
X	X	0	1	X	1	0
X	X	1	0	X	0	1

(c)

FIGURE 1-22 Latches and flip-flops. (a) D latch. (b) D flip-flop. (c) JK flip-flop.

with that of the D latch to make sure you understand the difference between the two devices.

The D flip-flop in Figure 1-22b also has *direct set* (S) and *reset* (R) inputs. A flip-flop is considered *set* if its Q output is a 1. It is *reset* if its Q output is a 0. The bubbles on the set and reset inputs tell you that these inputs are active low. The truth table for the D flip-flop in Figure 1-22b indicates that the set and reset inputs are *asynchronous*. This means that if the set input is asserted low, the output will be set, regardless of the state on the D and the clock inputs. Likewise, if the reset input is asserted low, the Q output will be reset, regardless of the state of the D and clock inputs. The Xs in the D and CK columns of the truth table remind you that these inputs are "don't cares" if set or reset is asserted. The condition indicated by the asterisks (*) is a nonstable condition; that is, it will not persist when reset or clear inputs return to their inactive (high) level.

THE JK FLIP-FLOP

Figure 1-22c shows the schematic symbol and the truth table for a common *JK flip-flop* such as the 74LS76. The two data inputs, J and K, make this device more versatile than a D flip-flop. The bubble on the clock input of the symbol and the downward arrows in the truth table indicate that the Q and $\bar{Q}$

outputs will change only when the clock input goes from a high to a low. Changes on J or K will have no effect on the output if the clock input is low or if the clock input is high.

If J and K are both low when the CK input goes low, the outputs will remain the same as they were before the clock edge. This is indicated by Q_N and $\overline{Q}_N$ in the truth table. If J is low and K is high at the time of the clock edge, Q will become a zero. If J is high and K is low at the time of the clock edge, Q will become a 1. If J and K are both high at the time of the clock edge, the Q output will *toggle*. This means that it will change to the opposite state of what it was before the clock edge. The JK flip-flop also has asynchronous set and reset inputs, which function the same as those of the D flip-flop described previously.

REGISTERS

Flip-flops can be used individually or in groups to store binary data. A *register* is a group of D flip-flops connected in parallel, as shown in Figure 1-23a. A binary word applied to the data inputs of this register will be transferred to the Q outputs when the clock input is made high. The binary word will remain stored on the Q outputs until a new binary word is applied to the D inputs and a low-to-high signal is applied to the clock input. Other circuitry can read the stored binary word from the Q outputs at any time without changing its value.

If the Q output of each flip-flop in the register is connected to the D input of the next, as shown in Figure 1-23b, then the register will function as a *shift register*. A 1 applied to the first D input will be shifted to the first Q output by a clock pulse. The next clock pulse will shift this one to the output of the second flip-flop. Each additional clock pulse will shift the one to the next flip-flop in the register. Some shift registers allow you to load a binary word into the register and shift the loaded word left or right when the register is clocked. As we will show later in this chapter, the ability to shift binary numbers is very useful.

COUNTERS

Flip-flops can also be connected in parallel to make *counters*. Figure 1-24 shows a schematic symbol and count sequence for a presettable 4-bit binary counter. The main point we want to review here is how a presettable counter functions, so there is no need to go into the internal circuitry of the device. If the reset input is asserted, the Q outputs will all be made zeros. After the reset signal is unasserted, each clock pulse will cause the binary count on the outputs to be incremented by 1. As shown in Figure 1-24b, the count sequence will go from 0000 to 1111. If the outputs are at 1111, then the next clock pulse will cause the outputs to "roll over" to 0000 and a carry pulse to be sent out the carry output. This carry pulse can be used as the clock input for another counter.

Now, suppose that we want the counter to start counting from some number other than 0000. We can do this by applying the desired number to the four data inputs and asserting the load input. For example, if we apply a binary 6, 0110, to the data inputs and assert the load input, this value will be transferred to the Q outputs. After the load signal is unasserted, the next clock signal will increment the Q outputs to 0111, or 7. Counters such as this can be connected in series (cascaded) to produce counters of any desired number of bits.

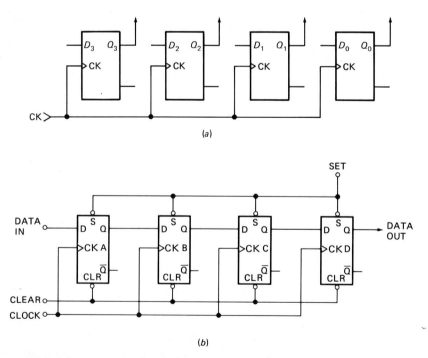

(a)

(b)

FIGURE 1-23   Registers. (a) Simple data storage. (b) Shift register.

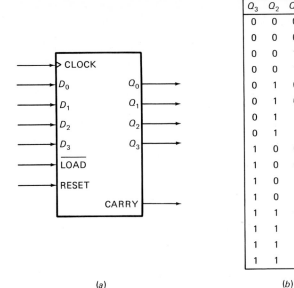

Q_3	Q_2	Q_1	Q_0
0	0	0	0
0	0	0	1
0	0	1	0
0	0	1	1
0	1	0	0
0	1	0	1
0	1	1	0
0	1	1	1
1	0	0	0
1	0	0	1
1	0	1	0
1	0	1	1
1	1	0	0
1	1	0	1
1	1	1	0
1	1	1	1

(a)   (b)

FIGURE 1-24 Four-bit, presettable binary counter. (a) Schematic symbol. (b) Count sequence.

ROMs, RAMs, and Buses

The next topics we need to review are the devices which store large numbers of binary words and how combinations of these devices can be connected together.

ROMs

The term ROM stands for *read-only memory*. There are several types of ROM that can be written to, read, erased, and written to with new data, but the main feature of ROMs is that they are *nonvolatile*. This means that the information stored in them is not lost when the power is removed from them.

Figure 1-25a shows the schematic symbol of a common ROM. As indicated by the eight *data* outputs, D0–D7, this ROM stores 8-bit data words. The data outputs are *three-state* outputs. This means that each output can be at a logic low state, a logic high state, or in a high-impedance, floating state. In the high-impedance state an output is essentially disconnected from anything connected to it. If the *CE* input of the ROM is not asserted, then all the outputs will be in the high-impedance state. Also, most ROMs switch to a lower power consumption condition if *CE* is not asserted. If the *CE* input is asserted, the device will be powered up, and the output buffers will be enabled. Therefore, the outputs will be at a normal logic low or logic high state. You will soon see why this is important if you don't happen to remember.

You can think of the binary words stored in the ROM as being in a long, numbered list. The number that corresponds to each stored word is called its *address*. In order to get a particular word onto the outputs of the ROM, you have to do two things: You have to apply the address of that word to the address inputs, A_0–A_{14}, and you have to assert the *CE* input to turn on the outputs. Incidentally, you can tell the number of binary words stored in the ROM by the number of address inputs; the number of words is equal to 2^N, where N is the number of address lines. The device in Figure 1-25a has 15 address lines, A_0–A_{14}, so the number of words is 2^{15}, or 32,768. In a data sheet this device would be referred to as a 32K × 8 ROM. This means 32K addresses by 8 bits per address.

Now, let's see why we want three-state outputs on this ROM. Suppose that we want to store more than 32K data words. We can do this by connecting two or

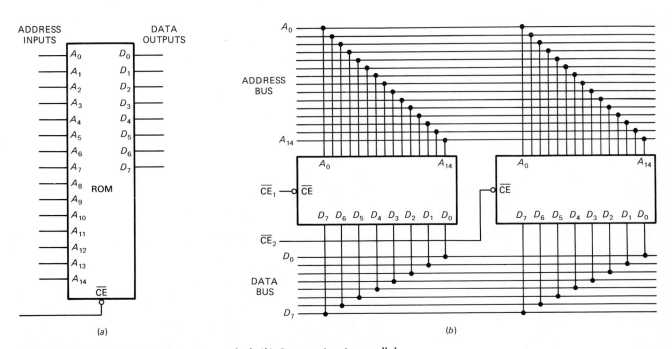

FIGURE 1-25 ROMs. (a) Schematic symbol. (b) Connection in parallel.

more ROMS in parallel, as shown in Figure 1-25b. The address lines connect to each device to allow us to address one of the 32,768 words in each. A set of parallel lines used to send addresses or data to several devices in this way is called a *bus*. The data outputs of the ROMs are likewise connected in parallel, so that any one of the ROMs can output data on the common data bus. If these ROMs had standard two-state outputs, a serious problem would occur, because each device would be trying to output an addressed word onto the data bus. The resulting argument between data outputs would probably destroy some of the outputs and give meaningless information on the data bus. Since the ROMs have three-state outputs, however, we can use external circuitry to make sure that only one ROM at a time has its outputs enabled. The very important principle here is that whenever several outputs are connected on a bus, the outputs should all be three-state, and only one set of outputs should be enabled at a time.

At the beginning of this section we mentioned that some ROMS can be erased and rewritten or reprogrammed with new data. Here is a summary of the different types of ROM:

Mask-programmed ROM—Programmed during manufacture; cannot be altered.

PROM—User-programmed by blowing fuses; cannot be altered except by blowing additional fuses.

EPROM—Electrically programmed by user; erased by ultraviolet light shone on quartz window in package.

EEPROM—Electrically programmed by user; erased with electrical signals instead of ultraviolet light.

STATIC AND DYNAMIC RAMs

The name RAM stands for *random-access memory*, but since ROMs are also random-access memories, a better name would probably be read-write memories. RAMs are also used to store binary words. A *static* RAM is essentially a matrix of flip-flops. Therefore, we can write a new data word in a RAM location at any time by applying the word to the flip-flop data inputs and clocking the flip-flop. The stored data word will remain on the flip-flop outputs as long as the power is left on. This type of memory is *volatile* because data is lost when the power is turned off.

Figure 1-26 shows the schematic symbol for a common RAM. This RAM has 12 address lines, A_0-A_{11}, so it stores 2^{12} (4096) binary words. The eight data lines tell you that the RAM stores 8-bit words. When we are reading a word from the RAM, these lines function as outputs. When we are writing a word to the RAM, these lines function as inputs. The *chip enable* input, $\overline{CE}$, is used to enable the device for a read or for a write. The read/write (R/$\overline{W}$) input will be asserted high if we want to read from the RAM, and it will be asserted low if we want to write a word to the RAM. Here's how all these lines work for reading from and writing to the device.

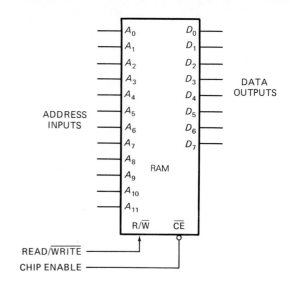

FIGURE 1-26   RAM schematic symbol.

To write to the RAM, we apply the desired address to the address inputs, assert the $\overline{CE}$ input low to turn on the device, and assert the R/$\overline{W}$ input low to tell the RAM we want to write to it. We then apply the data word we want to store to the data lines of the RAM for a specified time. To read a word from the RAM, we address the desired word, assert $\overline{CE}$ low to turn on the device, and assert R/$\overline{W}$ high to tell the RAM we want to read from it. For a read operation, the output buffers on the data lines will be enabled and the addressed data word will be present on the outputs.

The static RAMs we have just reviewed store binary words in a matrix of flip-flops. In *dynamic* RAMs (DRAMs), binary 1s and 0s are stored as electrical charges or no charges on a tiny capacitor. Since these tiny capacitors take up less space on a chip than a flip-flop would, a dynamic RAM chip can store many more bits than a static RAM chip of the same size. The disadvantage of dynamic RAMs is that the charge leaks off the capacitors. The logic state stored in each capacitor must be *refreshed* every 2 ms or so. A device called a *dynamic RAM refresh controller* can be used to refresh a large number of dynamic RAMs in a system. Some newer dynamic RAM devices contain built-in refresh circuitry, so they appear static to external circuitry.

Arithmetic Logic Units

Previous sections of this chapter reviewed ANDing, ORing, exclusive-ORing, adding, and subtracting of binary numbers. A device that can perform any of these functions and others on binary words is an *arithmetic logic* unit, or ALU. Figure 1-27a shows a block diagram for the 74LS181, which is a 4-bit ALU. This device can perform any one of 16 logic functions or any one of 16 arithmetic functions on two 4-bit binary words. The function performed on the two words is determined by the logic level applied to the

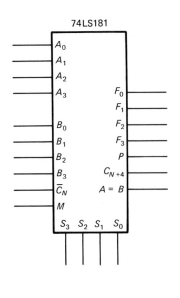

74LS181

SELECTION				ACTIVE-HIGH DATA		
				$M = H$ LOGIC FUNCTIONS	$M - L$; ARITHMETIC OPERATIONS	
S3	S2	S1	S0		$\overline{C}_N = H$ (no carry)	$\overline{C}_N = L$ (with carry)
L	L	L	L	$F = \overline{A}$	$F = A$	$F = A$ PLUS 1
L	L	L	H	$F = \overline{A + B}$	$F = A + B$	$F = (A + B)$ PLUS 1
L	L	H	L	$F = \overline{A}B$	$F = A + \overline{B}$	$F = (A + \overline{B})$ PLUS 1
L	L	H	H	$F = 0$	$F = $ MINUS 1 (2's COMPL)	$F = $ ZERO
L	H	L	L	$F = \overline{AB}$	$F = A$ PLUS $A\overline{B}$	$F = A$ PLUS $A\overline{B}$ PLUS 1
L	H	L	H	$F = \overline{B}$	$F = (A + B)$ PLUS $A\overline{B}$	$F = (A + B)$ PLUS $A\overline{B}$ PLUS 1
L	H	H	L	$F = A \oplus B$	$F = A$ MINUS B MINUS 1	$F = A$ MINUS B
L	H	H	H	$F = A\overline{B}$	$F = A\overline{B}$ MINUS 1	$F = A\overline{B}$
H	L	L	L	$F = \overline{A} + B$	$F = A$ PLUS AB	$F = A$ PLUS AB PLUS 1
H	L	L	H	$F = \overline{A \oplus B}$	$F = A$ PLUS B	$F = A$ PLUS B PLUS 1
H	L	H	L	$F = B$	$F = (A + \overline{B})$ PLUS AB	$F = (A + \overline{B})$ PLUS AB PLUS 1
H	L	H	H	$F = AB$	$F = AB$ MINUS 1	$F = AB$
H	H	L	L	$F = 1$	$F = A$ PLUS A	$F = A$ PLUS A PLUS 1
H	H	L	H	$F = A + \overline{B}$	$F = (A + B)$ PLUS A	$F = (A + B)$ PLUS A PLUS 1
H	H	H	L	$F = A + B$	$F = (A + \overline{B})$ PLUS A	$F = (A + \overline{B})$ PLUS A PLUS 1
H	H	H	H	$F = A$	$F = A$ MINUS 1	$F = A$

(a)

(b)

	A_3	A_2	A_1	A_0
A	1	0	1	0
	B_3	B_2	B_1	B_0
B	0	1	1	0
	F_3	F_2	F_1	F_0
$A \cdot B$	0	0	1	0
	F_3	F_2	F_1	F_0
$A + B$	1	1	1	0
	F_3	F_2	F_1	F_0
$A \oplus B$	1	1	0	0

(c)

FIGURE 1-27   Arithmetic logic unit (ALU). (a) Schematic symbol. (b) Truth table.
(c) Sample AND, OR, XOR operations.

mode input, M, and by the 4-bit binary code applied to the select inputs, $S_0 – S_3$.

Figure 1-27b shows the truth table for the 74LS181. In this truth table A represents the 4-bit binary word applied to the $A_0 – A_3$ inputs and B represents the 4-bit binary word applied to the $B_0 – B_3$ inputs. F represents the 4-bit binary word produced on the $F_0 – F_3$ outputs. If the mode input, M, is high, the device will perform one of 16 logic functions on the two words applied to the A and B inputs. For example, if M is high and we make S_3 high, S_2 low, S_1 high, and S_0 high, the 4-bit word on the A inputs will be ANDed with the 4-bit word on the B inputs. The result of this ANDing will appear on the F outputs. Each bit of the A word is ANDed with the corresponding bit of the B word to produce the result on F. Figure 1-27c shows an example of ANDing two words with this device. As you can see in this example, an output bit is high only if the corresponding bit is high in both the A word AND in the B word.

For another example of the operation of the 74LS181, suppose that the M input is high, S_3 is high, S_2 is high, S_2 is high, and S_0 is low. According to the truth table, the device will now OR each bit in the A word with the corresponding bit in the B word and give the result on the corresponding F output. Figure 1-27c shows the result that will be produced by ORing two 4-bit words. Figure 1-27c also shows, for your reference, the result that would be produced by exclusive-ORing these two 4-bit words together.

If the M input of the 74LS181 is low, then the device will perform one of 16 arithmetic functions on the A and B words. Again, the result of the operation will be put on the F outputs. Several 74LS181s can be cascaded to operate on words longer than 4 bits. The ripple-carry input, $\overline{C}_N$, allows a carry from an operation on previous words to be included in the current operation. If the $\overline{C}_N$ input is asserted low, then a carry will be added to the results of the operation on A and B. For example, if the M input is low, S_3 is high, S_2 is low, S_1 is low, S_0 is high, and C_n is low, the F outputs will have the sum of A plus B plus a carry.

The real importance of an ALU such as the 74LS181 is that it can be programmed with a binary instruction applied to its mode and select inputs to perform many different functions on two binary words applied to its data inputs. In other words, instead of having to build a different circuit to perform each of these functions, we have one programmable device. We can perform any of the operations that we want in a computer with a sequence of simple operations, such as those of the 74LS181. Therefore, an ALU is a very important part of the microprocessors and microcomputers that we discuss in the next chapter.

CHECKLIST OF IMPORTANT TERMS AND CONCEPTS IN THIS CHAPTER

If there are terms or concepts in this list you do not remember, use the index to find them in the chapter.

Binary, bit, nibble, byte, word, double word

LSB, MSB, LSD, MSD

Octal, hexadecimal, standard BCD, Gray code

Seven-segment display code

Alphanumeric codes: ASCII, BCDIC, EBCDIC, Selectric, Hollerith

Parity bit, odd parity, even parity

Converting between binary, octal, hexadecimal, BCD

Arithmetic with binary, octal, hexadecimal, BCD

BCD decimal-adjust operation

Signed numbers, sign bit

2's complement—sign-and-magnitude form

Signal assertion level

Inverting and noninverting buffers

Symbols and truth tables for AND, NAND, OR, NOR, and XOR logic gates

D latch, D flip-flop, JK flip-flop

Register, shift register, binary counter

ROM
    Address lines, data lines, bus lines
    Nonvolatile
    Three-state
    Cascaded outputs
    Enable input

PROM, EPROM, EEPROM

RAM
    Static, dynamic
    Volatile
    READ/WRITE input

ALU

REVIEW QUESTIONS AND PROBLEMS

1. Convert the following decimal numbers to binary.
   a. 22
   b. 76
   c. 500

2. Convert the following binary numbers to decimal.
   a. 1011
   b. 1101 0001
   c. 1110 1110 0101 1001

3. Convert the following numbers to octal.
   a. 110 101 001 binary
   b. 11 decimal
   c. 111 011 101 100 binary

4. Convert the following octal numbers to decimal.
   a. 314
   b. 74
   c. 43

5. Convert the following numbers to hexadecimal.
   a. 53 decimal
   b. 756 decimal
   c. 011 0110 0010 binary
   d. 110 0001 0111 binary

6. Convert the following numbers to decimal.
   a. \$D3
   b. \$3FE
   c. \$44

7. Convert the following decimal numbers to BCD.
   a. 86
   b. 62
   c. 33

8. The L key is depressed on an ASCII-encoded keyboard. What pattern of 1s and 0s would you expect to find on the seven parallel data lines coming from the keyboard? What pattern would a carriage return, CR, give?

9. Define parity and describe how it is used to detect an error in transmitted data.

10. Show each addition.
    a. $1\ 0011_2$ and 1011_2 in binary
    b. 37_{10} and 25_{10} in BCD
    c. 37_8 and 25_8 in octal
    d. \$4A and \$77

11. Express the following decimal numbers in 8-bit sign-and-magnitude form.
    a. +26
    b. −7
    c. −26
    d. −125

12. Show the subtraction, in binary, of the following decimal numbers using both the pencil method and the 2's complement addition method.
    a. 7 − 4
    b. 37 − 26
    c. 125 − 93

13. Show the multiplication of 1001 and 011 by the pencil method. Do the same for 1 1010 and 101.

14. Show the division of 110 0100 by 1010 using the pencil method.

15. Perform the indicated operations on the following numbers.
    a. Add octal numbers 27 and 16.
    b. Subtract octal number 45 from octal number 132.
    c. $3A + $94
    d. $17A − $4C
    e.   0101 1001 BCD
       + 0100 0010 BCD

    f.   0111 1001 BCD
       + 0100 1001 BCD

    g.   0101 1001 BCD
       − 0010 0110 BCD

    h.   0110 0111 BCD
       − 0011 1001 BCD

16. Use the circuit in Figure 1-28.
    a. Is the Y output active high or active low?
    b. Is the C signal active high or active low?
    c. What input conditions on A, B, and C will cause the Y output to be asserted?

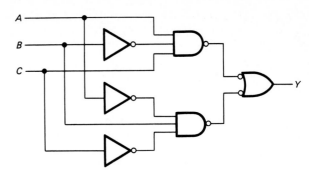

FIGURE 1-28   Circuit for problem 1-16.

17. What is the main difference between a D latch and a D flip-flop?

18. The National Semiconductor INS8298 is a 65,536-bit ROM organized as 8192 words or bytes of 8 bits. How many address lines are required to address one of the 8192 bytes?

19. Why do most ROMs and RAMs have three-state outputs?

20. Using Figure 1-27, show the programming of the select and mode inputs the 74181 requires to perform the following arithmetic functions.
    a. $A + B$
    b. $A - B - 1$
    c. $A \cdot B + A$

21. Show the output word produced when the following binary words are ANDed with each other and when they are ORed with each other.
    a. 1010 and 0111
    b. 1011 and 1100
    c. 1101 0111 and 11 1000

22. ANDing an 8-bit binary number with 1111 0000 is sometimes referred to as "masking" the lower 4 bits. Why?

CHAPTER 2

Computers, Microcomputers, and Microprocessors—An Introduction

We live in a computer-oriented society, and we are constantly bombarded with a multitude of terms relating to computers. Before getting started with the main topics in the book, we will try to clarify some of these terms and give an overview of computers and computer systems.

OBJECTIVES

At the conclusion of this chapter, you should be able to

1. Define the terms *microcomputer, microprocessor, hardware, software, firmware, timeshare, multitasking, distributed processing,* and *multiprocessing.*

2. Describe how a microcomputer fetches and executes an instruction.

3. List the registers and other parts in the 68000 family of CPUs.

4. Describe the function of the 68000 prefetch queue.

5. Demonstrate the way in which the 68000 addresses memory.

COMPUTERS

What Is a Computer?

Figure 2-1 shows a block diagram for a simple computer. The major parts are the *central processing unit* (CPU), *memory,* and the *input and output* (I/O) circuitry. Connecting these parts are three sets of parallel lines called *buses.* The three buses are the *address bus,* the *data bus,* and the *control bus.*

MEMORY

The *memory* section usually consists of a mixture of RAM (random-access memory) and ROM (read-only memory). It may also have magnetic floppy disks, magnetic hard disks, or laser optical disks. Memory has two purposes. The first purpose is to store the

binary codes for the sequence of instructions you want the computer to carry out. When you write a computer program, what you are really doing is just writing a sequential list of instructions for the computer. The second purpose of the memory is to store the binary-coded data with which the computer is going to be working. This data might be the inventory records of a supermarket, for example.

INPUT/OUTPUT

The *input/output,* or I/O, section allows the computer to take in data from the outside world or send data to the outside world. Peripherals such as keyboards, video display terminals, printers, and modems are connected to the I/O section. These allow the user and the computer to communicate with each other. The actual physical devices used to interface the computer buses to external systems are often called *ports.* Ports function in a computer just as shipping ports do in a country. An *input port* allows data from a keyboard, an A/D (analog-to-digital) converter, or some other source to be read into the computer under control of the CPU. An *output port* is used to send data from the computer to some peripheral such as a video display terminal, a printer, or a D/A (digital-to-analog) converter. Physically, an input or output port is often just a set of parallel D flip-flops that let data pass through when they are enabled or clocked by a control signal from the CPU.

CENTRAL PROCESSING UNIT

The *central processing unit,* or CPU, controls the operation of the computer. It fetches binary-coded instructions from memory, decodes the instructions into a series of simple actions, and carries out these actions. The CPU contains an *arithmetic logic unit,* or ALU, which can perform add, subtract, OR, AND, invert, or exclusive-OR operations on binary words when instructed to do so. The CPU also contains an *address counter,* which is used to hold the address of the next instruction or data to be fetched from memory; general-purpose registers, which are used for temporary storage of binary data; and circuitry that generates the control bus signals.

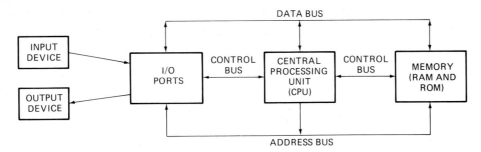

FIGURE 2-1 Block diagrams of a simple computer or microcomputer.

ADDRESS BUS

The *address bus* consists of 16, 20, 24, or more parallel signal lines. On these lines the CPU sends out the address of the memory location that is to be written to or read from. The number of memory locations that the CPU can address is determined by the number of address lines. If the CPU has N address lines, then it can directly address 2^N memory locations. For example, a CPU with 16 address lines can address 2^{16}, or 65,536, memory locations, a CPU with 20 address lines can address 2^{20}, or 1,048,576, locations, and a CPU with 24 address lines can address 2^{24}, or 16,777,216, locations. When the CPU reads data from or writes data to a port, the port address is also sent out on the address bus.

DATA BUS

The *data bus* consists of 8, 16, 32, or more parallel signal lines. As indicated by the double-ended arrows on the data bus line in Figure 2-1, the data bus lines are *bidirectional*. This means that the CPU can read data in on these lines from memory or from a port as well as send data out on these lines to a memory location or to a port. The outputs of many devices in a system are connected to the data bus, but the outputs of only one device at a time are enabled. Any device outputs connected on the data bus must be three-state outputs so that they can be floated when the device is not in use.

CONTROL BUS

The *control bus* consists of 4 to 10 parallel signal lines. The CPU sends out signals on the control bus to enable the outputs of addressed memory devices or port devices. Typical control bus signals are *memory read, memory write, I/O read,* and *I/O write.* To read a byte of data from a memory location, for example, the CPU sends out the address of the desired byte on the address bus and then sends out a memory-read signal on the control bus. The memory-read signal enables the addressed memory device to output the byte of data onto the data bus, where it is read by the CPU.

HARDWARE, SOFTWARE, AND FIRMWARE

When working around computers you almost constantly hear the terms hardware, software, and firm-

ware. *Hardware* is the name given to the physical devices and circuitry of the computer. *Software* refers to the programs written for the computer. *Firmware* is the term given to programs stored in ROMs or in other devices that keep their stored information when the power is turned off.

Execution of a Three-Instruction Program

EXECUTION SEQUENCE

To give you a better idea of how the parts of a computer function together, we will now describe the actions a simple computer might go through to carry out (*execute*) a simple program. The three instructions of the program are

1. Input a value from a keyboard connected to the port at address $C015.

2. Add 7 to the value read in.

3. Output the result to a display connected to the port at address $C010.

Figure 2-2a shows in diagram form the actions that the computer will perform to execute these three instructions.

For this example assume that the CPU fetches instructions and data from memory one word at a time. Also assume that the binary codes for the instructions are in sequential memory locations starting at address $4000. Figure 2-2b shows the binary codes that would be required in successive memory locations to execute this program on a 68008-based microcomputer.

The first action a computer will do is to fetch the first instruction byte from memory. To do this the CPU sends out the address of the first instruction byte, in this case $4000, to memory. This action is represented by line 1A in Figure 2-2a. The CPU then sends out a memory-read signal on the control bus (line 1B in the figure). This causes the memory to output the first instruction byte ($10) on the data bus, as represented by line 1C. This three-step procedure is repeated in lines 2A, 2B, and 2C, sending the address $4001 and receiving from memory the second instruction byte ($38). 68000-family CPUs use 2-byte instructions; that

FIGURE 2-2   (a) Execution of a three-step computer program. (b) Memory addresses and memory contents for three step program. (c) Assembler listing for three-step program.

PROGRAM

1. Input a value from a port at address $C015.
2. Add 7 to the value.
3. Output the result to a port at address $C010.

SEQUENCE

1A CPU sends out address of first byte of instruction to memory
1B CPU sends out MEMORY READ control signal to enable memory
1C memory sends out instruction byte from address
       specified to CPU on data bus
2A CPU addresses next memory location to get second instruction byte
2B Send MEMORY READ control signal to enable memory
2C memory sends instruction byte back to the CPU
2D CPU begins processing instruction, determines it needs an address
3A CPU send out next address to request first port address byte
3B CPU sends out MEMORY READ control signal to enable memory
3C memory sends next byte from addressed memory location to CPU on data bus
4A CPU sends out next memory address to request second byte of port address
4B CPU sends out MEMORY READ control signal to enable memory
4C memory places second address byte on data bus
4D CPU combines address bytes and places port address on address bus
4E CPU sends out READ control signal to enable I/O port
4F I/O port (Keyboard) places byte data on data bus from I/O device
4G CPU receives data byte and places it in low byte of the accumulator
5A CPU sends out memory address of next instruction's first byte
5B CPU sends out MEMORY READ control signal to enable memory
5C memory sends instruction byte on data bus
6A CPU sends out address of next instruction byte on address bus
6B CPU sends out MEMORY READ signal on control bus to enable memory
6C memory places next byte on data bus and CPU reads it
6D CPU decodes instuction and adds 7 to the low byte of the accumulator
7A CPU sends out address of next instruction byte
7B CPU sends out MEMORY READ control signal on control bus to enable memory
7C memory sends out byte from location addressed onto data bus, CPU reads it
8A CPU sends out address of next instruction byte
8B CPU sends out MEMORY READ control signal on control bus to enable memory
8C memory sends out byte from location addressed onto data bus, CPU reads it
8D CPU begins decoding instruction and determines that an address is requred
9A CPU sends address of first byte of I/O port address
9B CPU sends out MEMORY READ control signal to enable memory
9C memory sends out first byte of I/O port
       address as data on data bus and CPU reads it
10A CPU sends address of second byte of I/O port address
10B CPU sends out MEMORY READ control signal to enable memory
10C memory sends out second byte of I/O port
       address on data bus and CPU reads it
10D CPU combines I/O port address bytes and sends
       out I/O port address on address bus
10E CPU places low byte of the accumulator on the
       data bus; this is the value to write
10F CPU sends out a WRITE enable control signal
       on control bus to enable I/O port
10G I/O port (display) moves data byte from data bus to computer display

(a)

MEMORY ADDRESS	CONTENTS (Binary)	CONTENTS (Hex bytes)	OPERATION
$4000	00010000	10	Input from
$4001	00111000	38	Port at address
$4002	11000000	C0	$C015
$4003	00010101	15	
$4004	01011110	5E	Add 7
$4005	00000000	00	
$4006	00010001	11	Output to
$4007	11000000	C0	Port at address
$4008	11000000	C0	$C010
$4009	00010000	10	

(b)

MEMORY ADDRESS	CONTENTS (Binary)	CONTENTS (Hex words)	OPERATION
$4000	00010000	1038	Input from port at
$4002	11000000	C015	Address $C015
$4004	01011110	5E00	Add 7
$4006	00010001	11C0	Output to port at
$4008	11000000	C010	Address $C010

(b)

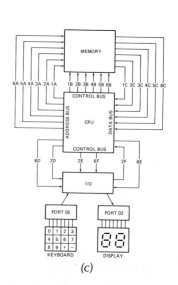

(c)

is, every instruction is exactly 2 bytes (1 word) long. A 68008 uses an 8-bit-wide data path so it can access 1 byte of data per memory access. Two accesses are required to read an entire instruction word.

The CPU reads the bytes from the data bus and composes them into one instruction word. The CPU then *decodes* the instruction, by which we mean that the CPU determines from the binary code read in what actions it is supposed to take. In this case the CPU determines that the code read in represents an input (read) instruction. Also, from decoding this instruction word the CPU determines that it needs more information before it can carry out the instruction. The CPU must fetch from memory the input port address. To do this the CPU sends out the next sequential address ($4002) to memory, as indicated by line 3A in the figure. The CPU also sends out another memory-read signal on the control bus (line 3B in Figure 2-2a). This enables the memory to put the addressed byte on the data bus (line 3C). This byte ($C0) is the first byte of the port address. On lines 4A and 4B the CPU requests the second byte of the I/O port address by sending the address $4003 and enabling memory. The memory responds (line 4C) by placing the byte on the data bus. When the CPU reads in this fourth byte, $15, it has all the information it needs to execute the instruction.

To execute the input instruction, the CPU sends out the port address ($C015) on the address bus (line 4D) and sends out an I/O read signal on the control bus (line 4E). The addressed port device then puts a byte of data on the data bus (line 4F). The CPU reads in the byte of data and stores it in an internal register called the *accumulator*. This completes the first instruction.

Having completed the first instruction, the CPU must now fetch its next instruction from memory. To do this it sends out the next sequential address ($4004) on the address bus (line 5A). The CPU then sends out a memory-read signal on the control bus (line 5B). This allows the memory to put the addressed byte ($5E) on the data bus (line 5C). The CPU reads in the instruction byte from the data bus. On lines 6A, 6B, and 6C the CPU reads the second byte of the instruction word and decodes the instruction. From the instruction word the CPU determines that it is supposed to add 7 to the number stored in the accumulator. Assume the result of the addition is left in the accumulator. This completes the second instruction.

The CPU must now fetch its next instruction. To do this it sends out the next sequential address ($4006) on the address bus (line 7A), sends out a memory-read signal on the control bus (line 7B), and reads in the addressed byte ($11) from the data bus (line 7C). On lines 8A, 8B, and 8C the CPU reads the second instruction byte. From these bytes the CPU determines that it is now supposed to do an output (write) operation to a port. The CPU also determines that it must go to memory again to get the address of the port to which it is supposed to output. To do this it sends out the next sequential address ($4008) on the address bus (line 9A), sends out a memory-read signal on the control bus (line 9B), and reads in the byte ($C0) put on the data bus by the memory (line 9C). The CPU reads the second

byte of the I/O port address ($10) on lines 10A, 10B, and 10C. The CPU now has all the information that it needs to execute the instruction. To output a data byte to a port, the CPU first sends out the address of the desired port on the address bus (line 10D). Next, it puts the data byte from the accumulator onto the data bus (line 10E). The CPU then sends out an I/O write signal on the control bus (line 10F). This signal enables the addressed output port device so the data from the data bus lines can pass through it (line 10G). When the CPU removes the I/O write signal to proceed with the next instruction, the data output remains latched on the output pins of the port device. Therefore, the computer does not have to keep outputting a value in order for it to remain there.

All the steps just described may seem like a great deal of work just to input a value from a keyboard, add 7 to it, and output the result to a display. Even a simple computer, however, can run through all these steps in a few microseconds.

Summary of Simple Computer Operation

1. A simple computer CPU fetches instructions or reads data from memory (reads memory) by sending out an address on the address bus and a memory-read signal on the control bus. The addressed instruction or data is sent from memory to the CPU on the data bus.

2. The CPU can write data in RAM memory by sending out an address on the address bus, sending out the data to be written on the data bus, and sending out a memory-write signal on the control bus.

3. To read data from a port, the CPU sends the port address out on the address bus and sends an I/O read signal on the control bus. Data from the port comes into the CPU on the data bus.

4. To write data to a port, the CPU sends out the port address on the address bus, sends the data to be written to the port out on the data bus, and sends an I/O write signal out on the control bus.

5. A microcomputer fetches each program instruction in sequence, decodes the instruction, and executes it.

Types of Computers

MAINFRAMES

Computers come in a wide variety of sizes and capabilities. The largest and most powerful are often called *mainframes*. Mainframe computers may fill an entire room. They are designed to work at very high speeds using large data words, typically 64 bits or greater, and they have massive amounts of memory. Computers of this type are used for military defense control, business data processing (an insurance company, for example), and for creating computer graphics displays for science fiction movies. Examples of this type of computer are the IBM 4831, the Honeywell DPS8, and the CRAY X-MP/48. Figure 2-3*a* shows a photograph of an IBM 4381 mainframe.

MINICOMPUTERS

Scaled-down versions of mainframe computers are often called *minicomputers*. The main unit of a minicomputer usually fits in a single rack or box. A minicomputer runs more slowly, works directly with smaller data words (often 32-bit words), and does not have as much memory as a mainframe. Computers of this type are used for business data processing, industrial

(a)

(b)

FIGURE 2-3   (a) Photograph of IBM mainframe computer. (*IBM Corp.*) (b) Photograph of DEC minicomputer. (*Digital Equipment Corp.*)

control (an oil refinery, for example), and scientific research. Examples of this type of computer are the Digital Equipment Corp. VAX 11/730, the Hewlett Packard 9000/350, and the Data General MV/8000II. Figure 2-3*b* shows a photograph of a Digital Equipment Corp. VAX 11/730 minicomputer.

MICROCOMPUTERS

As the name implies, *microcomputers* are small computers. They range from small controllers that work directly with 4-bit words and can address a few thousand bytes of memory to larger units that work directly with 32-bit words and can address millions or billions of bytes of memory. Some of the more powerful microcomputers have all or most features of earlier minicomputers. Therefore, it has become very hard to draw a sharp line between these two types. One distinguishing feature of a microcomputer has been that the CPU in a microcomputer is usually a single integrated circuit called a *microprocessor*. Older books often used the terms microprocessor and microcomputer interchangeably, but actually the microprocessor is the CPU, to which you add ROM, RAM, and ports to make a microcomputer. A later section in this chapter discusses the evolution of different types of microprocessors. Microcomputers are used in everything from smart sewing machines to computer-aided design systems. Examples of microcomputers are the URDA® P68000 Microlab™ (a single-board microprocessor development system, or MDS), the IBM Personal Computer (PC), and the Apple Macintosh® Personal Computer. Figure 2-4*a* shows a block diagram of the URDA MDS, Figure 2-4*b* is a photograph of the URDA MDS board, Figure 2-4*c* shows the IBM PC microcomputer, and Figure 2-4*d* shows the Apple Macintosh II microcomputer. The purpose of this book is to teach you how microprocessors are connected with other components to build microcomputers, how the microcomputers are interfaced with peripheral components to build microcomputer systems, and how these systems are programmed. We use the IBM PC and the URDA MDS as example systems throughout this book. An available laboratory manual, written to accompany this book, shows you how to get started using the URDA MDS and the IBM PC or the Apple Macintosh for assembly language programming.

Summary of Important Points

1. A computer or microcomputer consists of memory, a CPU, and some input/output circuitry.

2. These three parts are connected together by the address bus, the data bus, and the control bus.

3. The sequence of instructions, or program, for a computer is stored as binary numbers in successive memory locations.

4. The CPU fetches an instruction from memory, decodes the instruction to determine what actions must be done for the instruction, and carries out these actions.

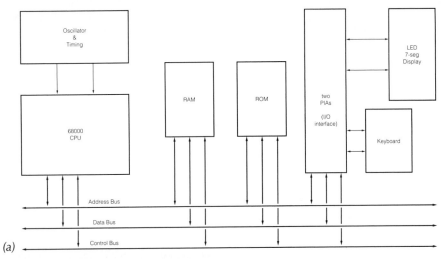

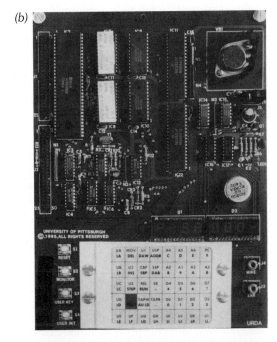

FIGURE 2-4 (a) Block diagram of URDA 68000 MDS.
(b) Photograph of URDA 68000 MDS. (c) Photograph
of IBM PC. (*IBM Corp.*) (d) Photograph of Apple
Macintosh II.

5. Three types of computer are mainframes, minicomputers, and microcomputers.

6. The CPU in a microcomputer is called a microprocessor.

How Computers and Microcomputers are Used: An Example

The following sections are intended to give you an
overview of how computers are interfaced with users to
do useful work. These sections should help you under-

stand many of the features designed into current microprocessors and where this book is heading.

COMPUTERIZING AN ELECTRONICS FACTORY—PROBLEM

Now, suppose that we want to *computerize* an electronics company. By this we mean that we want to make computer use available to as many people in the company as possible as cheaply as possible. We want the engineers to have access to a computer that can help them design circuits. People in the drafting department should have access to a computer that can be used for computer-aided drafting. The accounting department should have access to a computer for doing all the financial bookkeeping. The warehouse should have access to a computer to help with inventory control. The manufacturing department should have access to a computer for controlling machines and testing finished products. The president, vice presidents, and supervisors should have access to a computer to help them with long-range planning. Secretaries should have access to a computer for word processing. Salespeople should have access to a computer to help them keep track of current pricing, product availability, and commissions. There are several ways to provide all the needed computer power. The next sections discuss some of the ways that are used to give people access to a computer.

BATCH PROCESSING

In the 1960s the available computers were very large and were kept in separate air-conditioned rooms. When a programmer wanted to run a program, he or she brought the program to the computer room. Usually the program was in the form of a batch of punched cards. A computer operator would then run the program. A new programming job could not be started until the last one finished. Therefore, if a large job was being run, there might be a considerable wait before a programmer could get his or her job run. Also, if an error was found when the program ran, the programmer had to punch new cards and either bribe the computer operator or put the corrected program cards on the bottom of the jobs-to-be-done pile. Needless to say, a system of this sort is not acceptable for computerizing our electronics company because it serves only one user at a time and does not allow easy back-and-forth interaction between the computer and the user.

MULTIPROGRAMMING

An improvement over the basic batch system is a *multiprogramming* system. In this type of system several programs are put in the computer's memory at the same time. The computer runs one programming job until it reaches a point at which it needs access to some slow peripheral device such as a printer. If the printer is not busy, the computer will print out the produced results. If the printer is busy, the data to be printed is stored on a magnetic disk. The computer can then start another programming job while it waits for the printer to become available. When the printer becomes available, the computer can print out the results from the first program and then return to the second program. To further reduce the burden on the computer, some computers have separate circuitry that takes care of copying output data from magnetic disks to the printer. Multiprogramming improves the efficiency of the computer by keeping it busy more of the time, but it still does not allow the user to interact easily with the computer.

TIMESHARE AND MULTITASKING SYSTEMS

A further improvement in computer access is *time-sharing.* Figure 2-5 shows a block diagram of one type of timeshare system. Several video terminals are connected to the computer through direct wires or through telephone lines. The terminal can be on the user's desk

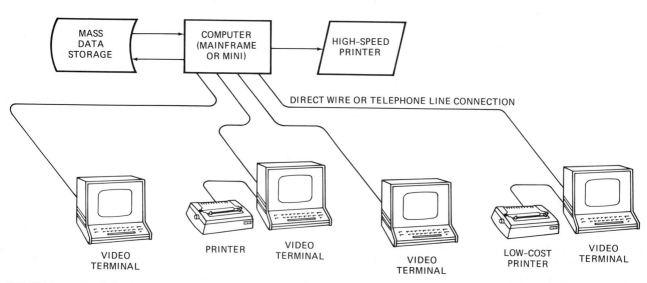

FIGURE 2-5 Block diagram of a computer timeshare system.

or even in his or her home. The rate at which a user usually enters data is very slow in comparison to the rate at which a computer can process the data. Therefore, the computer can serve many users by dividing its time among them in small increments. In other words, the computer works on user 1's program for perhaps a millisecond, works on user 2's program for a millisecond, then works on user 3's program for a millisecond, and so on until all the users have had a turn. In a few milliseconds the computer will get back to user 1 again and repeat the cycle. To each user it will appear as if he or she has exclusive use of the computer because the computer processes data as fast as it is entered. A timeshare system such as this allows several users to interact with the computer at the same time. Each user can get information from or store information in the large memory attached to the computer. Each user can have an inexpensive printer attached to his or her terminal or can direct program or data output to a high-speed printer attached directly to the computer.

An airline-ticket-reservation computer might use a timeshare system such as this to allow users from all over the country to access flight information and make reservations. A time-multiplexed, or time-sliced, system such as this can allow a computer to control many machines or processes in a factory. A computer is much faster than the machines or processes it controls. Therefore, it can check and adjust many pressures, temperatures, motor speeds, etc. before it needs to recheck the first one. A system such as this is often called a *multitasking system* because it appears to be doing many tasks at the same time.

Now let's take another look at our problem of computerizing the electronics company. A timeshare system seems to be a better idea than a batch system or even a multiprogramming system. We could put a powerful computer in some central location and run wires from it to video display terminals on each person's desk. Each user could then run the program needed to do his or her particular task. The accountant could run a ledger program, the secretary could run a word processor program, etc. Each user could access the computer's large data memory. Incidentally, a large collection of data stored in a computer's memory is often referred to as a *data base*. For a small company a system such as this might be adequate. However, there are at least two potential problems.

The first potential problem is, What happens if the computer is not working? The answer to this question is that everything grinds to a halt. In a situation where people have become dependent upon the computer, not much gets done until the computer is up and running again. The old saying about not putting all your eggs in one basket comes to mind here.

The second potential problem of the simple timeshare system is saturation. As the number of users increases, the time it takes the computer to do each user's task also increases. Eventually the computer's response time to each user becomes unreasonably long. People get very upset about the time they have to wait.

DISTRIBUTED PROCESSING, OR MULTIPROCESSING

A partial solution for the two potential problems of a simple timeshare system is to use a *distributed processor* system. Figure 2-6 shows a block diagram for such a system. The system has a powerful central computer with a large memory and a high-speed printer, as does the simple timeshare system described previously. However, in this system each user or group of users has a microcomputer instead of simply a video display terminal. In other words, each user station is an independent, functioning microcomputer with a CPU, ROM, RAM, and, probably, magnetic or optical disk memory. This means that a person can do many tasks locally on the microcomputer without having to use the large computer at all. Since the microcomputers are connected to the large computer with a network, however, a user can access the computing power, memory, or other resources of the large computer when needed.

Distributing the processing around to multiple computers or processors in a system has several advantages. First, if the large computer goes down, the local microcomputers can continue working until they need to access the large computer for something. Second, the burden on the large computer is reduced greatly, because much of the computing is done by the local microcomputers. Finally, the distributed-processor approach allows the system designer to use a local microcomputer best suited to the task it has to do.

Computerized Electronics Company: Overview

Distributed processing seems to be the best way to computerize our electronics factory. Engineers can each have personal computers on their desk. With these they can use available programs to design and test circuits. They can access the large computer if they need data from its memory. Through the telephone lines, the engineer with a personal computer can access data in the memories of other computers all over the world. The drafting people can have personal computers for simple work or large computer-aided design systems for more complex work. Completed work can be stored in the large computer memory. The accounting department can use personal computers with spreadsheet programs to work with financial data kept in the memory of the large computer. The warehouse supervisor can likewise use a personal computer with an inventory program to keep his or her own records and those in the large computer's memory updated. Corporate officers can have personal computers tied into the network. They then can interact with any of the other systems on the network. Salespeople can have portable personal computers that they can carry with them in the field. They can communicate with the main computer over the telephone lines using a modem. Secretaries doing word processing can use individual word processing units or personal computers. Since word processing is not a high-intensity use

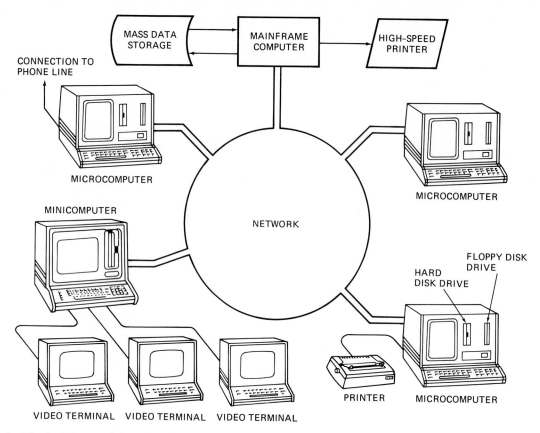

FIGURE 2-6   Block diagram of distributed processing computer system.

for a computer, several video display terminals for word processing can be connected to a local microcomputer, and this local microcomputer can be connected to the large computer through the network. Users can also send messages to each other over the network. The specifics of a computer system such as this will obviously depend on the needs of the individual company for which the system is designed.

SUMMARY AND DIRECTION FROM HERE

The main concepts that you should understand at this point are multiprogramming, timesharing, or multi-tasking, and distributed processing, or multiprocessing. As you work your way through the rest of this book, keep an overview of the computerized electronics company in the back of your mind. The goal of this book is to teach you how all the parts of a system such as this work, how the parts are connected together, and how the system is programmed at different levels.

The first step toward this goal will be a quick look at the different types of microprocessors available. We then discuss a specific microprocessor, the Motorola 68000, and the programming of a microcomputer built around a member of this microprocessor family, the Apple Macintosh. Next we discuss the hardware connections and timing of this microcomputer. From there we show how the microcomputer is interfaced to a wide variety of peripheral devices. And finally we cycle back to our computerized electronics company, the networks it uses, and the system programs it requires.

Common Microprocessor Types

MICROPROCESSOR EVOLUTION

A common way of categorizing microprocessors is by the number of bits with which their ALUs can work at a time. In other words, a microprocessor with a 4-bit ALU will be referred to as a 4-bit microprocessor, regardless of the number of address lines or the number of data bus lines that it has. The first microprocessor, as we use the term, was the Intel 4004, produced in 1971. It contained 2300 PMOS transistors. The 4004 was a 4-bit device intended to be used with some other devices in making a calculator. Some logic designers, however, saw that this device could be used to replace PC boards full of combinational and sequential logic devices. Also, the ability to change the function of a system by just changing the programming, rather than redesigning the hardware, was very appealing. These factors pushed the evolution of microprocessors.

In 1972 Intel came out with the 8008, which was capable of working with 8-bit words. The 8008, however, required 20 or more additional devices to form a functional CPU. In 1974 Intel announced the 8080, which had a much larger instruction set than the 8008 and required only two additional devices to form a functional CPU. Also, the 8080 used NMOS transistors, so it operated much faster than the 8008. The 8080 is referred to as a *second-generation micro-processor.*

Soon after Intel produced the 8080, Motorola came out with the MC6800, another 8-bit general-purpose CPU. The 6800 had the advantage that it required only a +5-V supply rather than the −5-V, +5-V, and +12-V supplies required by the 8080. For several years the 8080 and the 6800 were the top-selling 8-bit microprocessors. Some of their competitors were the MOS Technology 6502, used as the CPU in the Apple II microcomputer, and the Zilog Z80, used as the CPU in the Radio Shack TRS-80 microcomputer.

As designers found more and more applications for microprocessors, they pressured microprocessor manufacturers to develop devices with architectures and features optimized for doing certain types of tasks. In response to the expressed needs, microprocessors have evolved in three major directions during the last 10 years.

DEDICATED CONTROLLERS

One direction has been toward *dedicated controllers.* These devices are used to control "smart" machines such as microwave ovens, clothes washers, sewing machines, auto ignition systems, and metal lathes. Texas Instruments produced millions of their TMS-1000 family of 4-bit microprocessors for this type of application. In 1976 Intel introduced the 8048, which contains an 8-bit CPU, RAM, ROM, and some I/O ports, all in one 40-pin package. Other manufacturers have followed with similar products. These devices are often referred to as *microcontrollers.* Some currently available devices in this category, the Intel 8051 and the Motorola MC6801, for example, contain programmable counters and UARTS as well as a CPU, ROM, RAM, and I/O ports. A more recently introduced single-chip microcontroller, the Intel 8096, contains a 16-bit CPU, ROM, RAM, a UART, ports, timers, and a 10-bit analog to digital converter.

BIT-SLICE PROCESSORS

A second direction of microprocessor evolution has been toward *bit-slice processors.* For some applications general-purpose CPUs such as the 8080 and 6800 are not fast enough or their instruction set is not suitable. For such applications, several manufacturers produce devices that can be used to build a custom CPU. An example is the Advanced Micro Devices 2900 family. This family include 4-bit ALUs, multiplexers, sequencers, and other parts needed for custom-building a CPU. The term *slice* comes from the fact that these parts can be connected in parallel to work with 8-bit words, 16-bit words, or 32-bit words. In other words, a designer can add as many slices as needed for a particular application. Not only does the designer custom-design the hardware of the CPU, but also he or she custom-makes the instruction set for it using "microcode."

GENERAL-PURPOSE CPUs

The third major direction of microprocessor evolution has been toward general-purpose CPUs, which give a microcomputer most or all the computing power of earlier minicomputers. After Motorola came out with the MC6800, Intel produced the 8085, an upgrade of the 8080 requiring only a +5-V supply. Motorola then produced the MC6809, which has a few 16-bit instructions but is still basically an 8-bit processor. In 1978 Intel came out with the 8086, which is a full 16-bit processor. Some 16-bit microprocessors, such as the National PACE and the Texas Instruments 9900 family of devices, were available previously, but the market apparently wasn't ready. Soon after Intel came out with the 8086, Motorola came out with the 16-bit MC68000, and the 16-bit race was off and running. The 8086 and the 68000 work directly with 16-bit words instead of with 8-bit words, they can address a million or more bytes of memory instead of the 64K bytes addressable by the 8-bit processors, and they execute instructions much faster than the 8-bit processors. Also, these 16-bit processors have single instructions for functions that required a lengthy sequence of instructions on the 8-bit processors.

The evolution along this last path has continued to 32-bit processors that work with gigabytes (10^9 bytes) or terabytes (10^{12} bytes) of memory. Examples of these devices are the Intel 80386, the Motorola MC68020, and the National 32032.

Since we could not possibly describe in this book the operation and programming of even a few of the available processors, we confine our discussions primarily to one group of related microprocessors, the Motorola 68000, 68008, 68010, 68012, 68020, 68030, and 68040 family. Members of this family are very widely used in personal computers, business computer systems, and industrial control systems. Our experience has shown that learning the programming and operation of one family of microcomputers very thoroughly is much more useful than looking at many processors superficially. If you learn one processor family well, you will probably find it quite easy to learn another when you have to.

INTRODUCTION TO THE 68000, 68008, 68010, 68012, 68020, 68030, AND 68040 MICROPROCESSORS

The Motorola 68000 is a 16-bit microprocessor intended to be used as the CPU in a microcomputer. The term 16-*bit* means that its internal data paths are designed to work with 16-bit binary words. The 68000 has a 16-bit data bus, so it can read data from or write data to memory and ports either 16 bits at a time or 8 bits at a time. The 68000 has a 24-bit address bus, so it can address any one of 2^{24}, or 16,777,216, memory locations. Each of the 16,777,216 memory addresses of the 68000 represents a byte-wide location. Words are stored in two consecutive memory locations. The main point here is that the 68000 can read one complete instruction word (2 bytes) in one operation.

The 68008, on the other hand, reads from memory 1 byte at a time. The 68008 requires two read operations to access both bytes of an instruction word. Recall that Figure 2-2b showed the bytes in memory as accessed by a 68008 processor. Figure 2-2c showed how these same memory contents can be represented as words in memory using addresses that increase by 2 instead of by 1. In Figure 2-2c the initial addresses are $4000 and $4002, and the memory values are words rather than bytes. Figure 2-2b and 2-2c shows equivalent ways of representing the same memory contents. Note that Figure 2-2c shows a somewhat more compact representation. Figure 2-2c requires only 5 lines, whereas Figure 2-2b requires 10 lines.

The Motorola 68008 has the same ALU, the same registers, and the same instruction set as the 68000. The 68008 has a 20-bit address bus, so it can address any one of 1,048,576 bytes in memory. The 68008, however, has an 8-bit data bus, so it can read data from or write data to memory and ports only 8 bits at a time. The 68000, remember, can read or write either 8 or 16 bits at a time. To read a 16-bit word from two successive memory locations, the 68008 always has to do two read operations. Since the 68000 and the 68008 are almost identical, any reference we make to the 68000 in the rest of the book will also pertain to the 68008 unless we specifically indicate otherwise. This is done to make reading easier. The Motorola 68000, incidentally, is used as the CPU in the Apple Macintosh Personal Computer.

The Motorola 68010 is an improved version of the 68000, and the 68012 is an improved version of the 68010. The 68010 provides additional CPU state information, allowing virtual memory implementation as well as running at higher clock speeds than the 68000. (Virtual memory is discussed further in later chapters.) The 68012 includes a 30-bit address bus, allowing up to 1 gigabyte (Gbyte) of memory to be addressed (2^{30} equals 1 Gbyte, or 1,073,741,824 bytes).

The instruction set of the 68010 and the 68012 is a *superset* of the instruction set of the 68000. The term superset means that all the 68000 instructions will execute properly on a 68010 or on a 68012, but the 68010 and the 68012 have a few additional instructions. In other words, a program written for a 68000 or 68008 is upward-compatible to a 68010 or 68012, but a program written for a 68010 or for a 68012 may not execute correctly on a 68000 or 68008. In the instruction set descriptions in Chapter 6, we specifically indicate which instructions work only with the 68010 or 68012. The 68010 is used as the CPU in several microcomputers.

The Motorola 68020, 68030, and 68040 are advanced versions of the 68000 specifically designed for use as the CPU in a multiuser or multitasking microcomputer. The 68020 microcomputer runs with a faster clock speed than the 68010, and the 68030 is faster yet. 68000s may run at about 8-MHz clock speeds, the 68010, at 10 or 12 MHz, the 68020, at about 16 or 20 MHz, and the 68030, from 25 up to 33 MHz. Both the 68020 and the 68030 have full 32-bit address and data buses. Thus both can address up to 2^{32}, or 4 Gbytes, of memory. Both can access 8-bit, 16-bit, or 32-bit data in a single operation. The 68030 provides floating-point mathematical operations on real numbers directly within the CPU. This capability

is provided for the 68020 with the 68881 floating-point coprocessor chip. The 68030 also provides sophisticated memory-management capabilities directly on the CPU chip. These had previously been implemented on the 68851 memory-management chip. The 68020 CPU is used in the Hewlett Packard 9000/350 microcomputer and the 68030 is used in the Hewlett Packard 9000/370 microcomputer.

The 68040 is even faster than the 68030. 68040s can run with 50-MHz clocks and can be thought of as fasters 68030s that can also perform more complex operations. The 68040 CPU is used in the Hewlett Packard 9000/425 computer.

THE 68000 INTERNAL ARCHITECTURE

The three-instruction program section of this chapter describes how a CPU sends out addresses, control signals, and data to ports or memory and reads in instructions and data to internal registers. Before we can talk about how to write programs for the 68000, we need to discuss its specific internal features, such as registers, prefetch queue, and flags.

As shown by the block diagram in Figure 2-7, the major functional parts of the 68000 CPU are the memory and I/O interfaces, the prefetch queue, a bank of eight data accumulator registers, a bank of nine address registers, a program counter, an execution unit, a status register, an ALU, and a control unit. These parts are connected by three buses. Each bus is a group of signal lines that are logically used together and that are typically found together physically. The following sections describe each of these functional components.

THE MEMORY AND I/O INTERFACE

The memory interface connects the CPU to external memory—that is, to memory not on the CPU chip. This interface consists primarily of a set of address bus drivers and a set of data bus drivers. These drivers allow other chips to be connected to and driven directly by the CPU. They are called drivers because their outputs are strong enough (carry enough current) to drive the inputs of other integrated-circuit chips. Normally these drivers are connected to higher-power tristate latches for use on the longer lines that might run to many external memory chips. However in some cases, such as that of the URDA P68000 MDS, the CPU directly drives a few external memory chips.

The I/O interface on 68000 systems is the same as the memory interface. The I/O interface presents the address and data bus to the I/O devices. In the case of an I/O interface, the address lines and data lines are typically connected to one or several interface chips called parallel I/O ports. These I/O ports decode the address lines and, when enabled, latch the CPU output or the I/O device input. The data is said to be *latched* by the I/O port. This data is then, in turn, available to drive the I/O device or for the CPU to input.

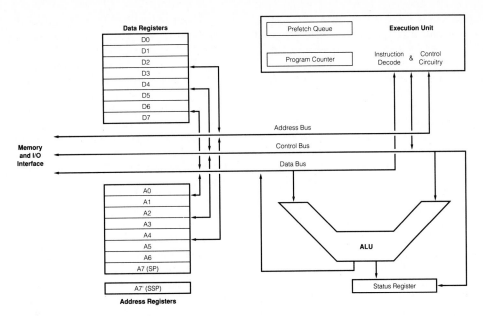

FIGURE 2-7   68000 CPU internal block diagram.

This method of I/O is called *memory-mapped* I/O because the CPU does not distinguish memory from I/O ports. The CPU accesses I/O ports in exactly the same manner and using exactly the same instructions as it uses to access memory. Figure 2-8 shows a *memory-map* picture for the URDA MDS. This picture shows where the URDA microprocessor development system has placed its RAM, ROM, and I/O ports in the CPU memory space. Notice that the I/O ports occupy a block of memory addresses in just the same manner as does the system RAM. The CPU can access these I/O ports using the same instructions as it uses to access RAM. The only difference is the actual memory addresses referenced.

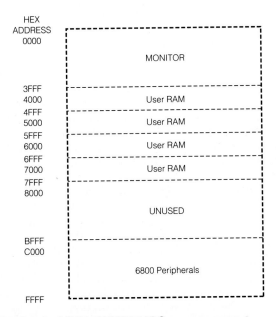

FIGURE 2-8   URDA P68000 MDS memory map.

THE EXECUTION UNIT

The execution unit of the 68000 tells the CPU from where to fetch instructions or data, decodes instructions, and executes instructions. Now take another look at the 68000 block diagram in Figure 2-7 to see what is contained in the execution unit, or EU. The EU contains *control circuitry,* which directs internal operations. A decoder in the EU performs *instruction decode,* the process of translating instructions fetched from memory into a series of actions that the EU carries out.

THE PROGRAM COUNTER

The program counter is a part of the EU; it stores a 32-bit binary value. This value is used as a memory address from which the next instruction will be fetched. The program counter is said to be a *pointer* into memory. Once an instruction word is fetched from memory, the program counter is automatically incremented to point to the next sequential memory location. The program counter is used in the CPU's basic process of instruction fetch from memory, instruction decode, instruction execution using control circuitry, and increment of the program counter. This process is repeated over and over by the CPU at very high speed.

THE PREFETCH QUEUE

To speed up program execution, the CPU fetches instructions ahead of time from memory. That is, while the CPU is interpreting one instruction, it is already fetching the next one from memory, and, in some cases, the next, the next, and so on. These instructions are said to be *prefetched* because they are fetched from memory before they are actually needed. The prefetched instruction bytes are held for the EU in a first in, first out group of registers called a *queue.* The CPU can be fetching instruction bytes while the

EU is decoding an instruction or while the EU is executing an instruction that does not require use of the buses. When the EU is ready for its next instruction, it simply reads the instruction from the queue already in the CPU. This is much faster than sending out an address to the system memory and waiting for memory to send back the next instruction byte or bytes. The process is analogous to the way a bricklayer's assistant fetches bricks ahead of time and keeps a queue of bricks lined up so that the bricklayer can just reach out and grab a brick when necessary. Except in the cases of JUMP and CALL instructions, where the queue must be dumped and then reloaded starting from a new address, this prefetch-and-queue scheme greatly speeds up processing. Fetching the next instruction while the current instruction executes is called *pipelining*.

This prefetch queue is a special form of *cache* memory. Cache memory is memory that is directly on the CPU chip in the case of a prefetch queue. Because it is directly on the CPU chip, it is much faster than the rest of the main memory chips. In general, cache memory is any memory that is faster and smaller than main memory and is normally used to bring often-used instructions and data "closer" to the CPU in terms of the time required for memory read and write.

The 68010 has a cache memory (prefetch queue) of only 3 words. The 68020 and 68030 provide increasingly larger caches (prefetch queues). The 68020 provides a 128-word cache and the 68030 has two 128-word caches, one for instructions and one for data. The 68040 has two 4096-byte caches, one for instructions and one for data.

THE DATA AND ADDRESS REGISTERS

Observe in Figure 2-7 that the CPU has 17 general-purpose registers, 8 labeled *data registers* and 9 labeled *address registers.* These registers can be used individually for temporary storage of 32-bit data. The data registers are sometimes called *accumulators.* The data registers can be used to perform arithmetic and logical operations on 32-, 16-, or 8-bit binary data values. The address registers are normally used to hold addresses that are usually 32-bit binary values in the 68000 family. Data can be moved freely among these data and address registers by using certain CPU instructions. Data can also be moved from external memory to the data registers and from the data registers to internal memory. These registers are sometimes called *internal memory* because they are storage locations internal to the CPU.

Most of the data contained by a 68000 system is organized in external memory as a list of sequential storage locations, each 1 byte long. These bytes of memory can be grouped into words, long words, and 8-byte and larger structures in memory. This grouping is both logical and physical. The CPU has certain restrictions on the way it accesses memory, and these restrictions usually are related to the grouping of memory bytes. For example, the CPU can access a full word of memory only if the address of the word is even. That

is, addresses 0, 2, 4, 6, . . . are fine, but trying to access a word of data starting with the byte at address 1, 3, 5, . . . will cause a CPU exception and report of a program error. Figure 2-9a shows how 68000-family memory bytes are grouped into data items. When we draw 68000 memory pictures, we will use pictures similar to Figure 2-9a.

A *stack* is a section of memory set aside to store data. The 68000 allows you to use any memory area as a stack. One type of stack seen commonly is the stack of trays in a cafeteria. New, clean trays are added to the stack by pushing them onto the top of the stack. Trays are pulled off the top of the stack by customers as they enter the cafeteria. Similarly, data is pushed onto the top of a memory stack to save it for later use, and data is pulled from the stack when it is used. The memory location where a word was most recently stored is called the *top of the stack.* Figure 2-9b shows this in diagram form. An address register is normally used to point to the top of the stack. A stack is a last in, first out data structure.

When the CPU performs certain operations using *subprogram* capabilities, one of two specific address registers is used as the top of a stack. The stack pointer (SP) and the supervisor stack pointer (SSP) are the address registers used by the CPU during subprogram execution. The SP is the same as address register seven (A7) and the SSP is the same as address register seven prime (A7'). We will see later why the SSP is called 7' rather than address register 8, as well as when each of the two stack registers is used.

The operation and use of the stack are discussed in more detail in Chapter 5.

THE ARITHMETIC LOGIC UNIT (ALU)

The CPU has a 32-bit *arithmetic logic unit,* or ALU, which can add, subtract, multiply, divide, AND, OR, XOR, increment, decrement, complement, or shift binary numbers. The ALU represents the basic computational engine of the CPU. The ALU accepts commands from the EU using the control circuitry. The ALU takes data from the data bus, manipulates it, and returns the results to the data bus.

THE STATUS REGISTER

A *flag* is a flip-flop that indicates some condition produced by the execution of an instruction or controls certain operations of the EU. The flip-flop stores 1 bit, which represents the flag value (0 or 1). These flags represent what Motorola literature calls *condition codes,* which contain information about the most recently performed operation or recently used operand. Many 68000 instructions use these condition-code flags when they are interpreted. A 16-bit *status register* in the CPU contains five active flags, or condition codes. Figure 2-10 shows the location of the condition codes in the status register. The condition codes are contained in the lower (user) byte of the status register.

Each condition code is set based on the last operation performed by the ALU. For example, a flip-flop called the *carry condition code,* or the *carry flag,* is

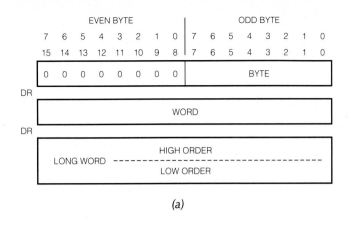

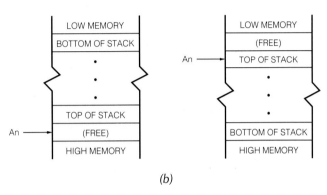

(a)

(b)

FIGURE 2-9 (a) 68000 standard data representations in memory with byte organization. (b) User stack organization.

set to 1 if the addition of two binary numbers produces a carry out of the MSB position. If no carry out of the MSB is produced by the addition, then the carry flag is 0. The EU thus effectively runs up a "flag" to tell you that a carry was produced. The flag is saved in the carry bit of the status register (the lowest bit, bit 0).

The five condition codes in this group are the *carry flag* (C), the *overflow flag* (V), the *zero flag* (Z), the *negative flag* (N), and the *extend flag* (X). The names of these flags should give you hints as to what condi-

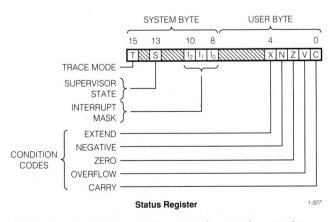

Status Register

1-927

FIGURE 2-10 68000 status register format showing bit positions of condition codes, state flags, and interrupt mask.

tions affect them. Certain 68000 instructions check these condition codes to determine which of two alternative actions should be done in executing the instruction.

The remaining byte in the status register is the system byte. This byte contains flags that are used to *control* certain operations of the processor. These flags are different from the five condition codes just described in the way they are set or reset. The five condition flags are set or reset by the EU based on the results of some arithmetic or logic operation. The *control flags* are deliberately set or reset with specific instructions you put in the program. The three control flags are the *trace mode bit* (T), which is used for single-stepping (tracing) through a program; the *interrupt mask* (I2, I1, and I0), which is used to allow or prohibit the interruption of a program; and the *supervisor state bit* (S), which specifies whether the CPU is executing in supervisor or user state.

The supervisor bit in the CPU can be either a 1 or a 0. If it is a 1, then the CPU is said to be in supervisor state. If it is a 0, then the CPU is said to be in user state. Because there are two states, the 68000 is often said to be a *dual-state CPU*. When we examine the CPU instructions in detail in Chapter 6, we will see that certain instructions behave differently, depending on whether the supervisor state bit is a 1 or a 0. These instructions are said to be *sensitive* instructions because they are sensitive to the state of the supervisor bit of the status register. The sensitive instructions are also called *privileged* instructions. They are privileged in that they generally function normally when the CPU is in supervisor state and they generally cause a CPU trap when the CPU is in user state. In effect, the user cannot execute these special instructions without dire consequences. In Chapter 7 we look more closely at exactly what a *trap* is and why the 68000 generates traps.

Later we discuss in detail the operation and use of the system byte of the status register.

THE DATA BUS, THE ADDRESS BUS, AND THE CONTROL BUS

A bus is a collection of signal lines that operate together to perform some common operation or that carry many signals whose functions are related. The 68000 CPU contains three main buses. These are the *data bus*, the *address bus*, and the *control bus*. The data bus is a collection of 16 data lines (32 lines in the 68020, 68030, and 68040). The lines of the data bus each contain signals that represent 1 bit of a data item. Taken together, all the data lines can carry one word (long word). The address bus is a collection of 32 lines, each of which represents 1 bit of a memory or I/O address. The control bus contains many lines, each used in some aspect of the control of the computer system. For example, one line may tell the external memory when to place data on the data bus, and another line may tell the ALU which of several operations to perform. Most of the control lines flow off the CPU chip through the memory and I/O interface; however, some are used only within the CPU.

INTRODUCTION TO PROGRAMMING THE 68000

Programming Languages

Now that you have an overview of the 68000 CPU, it is time to think about how it is programmed. To run a program, a microcomputer must have the program stored in binary form in successive memory locations. There are three language levels that can be used to write a program for a microcomputer.

MACHINE LANGUAGE

You can write programs simply as a sequence of the binary codes for the instructions you want the microcomputer to execute. The three-instruction program in Figure 2-2b is an example. This binary form of the program is referred to as *machine language* because it is the form required by the machine. However, it is difficult, if not impossible, for a programmer to memorize the thousands of binary instruction codes for a CPU such as the 68000. Also, it is very easy for an error to occur when working with long series of 1s and 0s. Using hexadecimal representation for the binary codes might help some, but there are still thousands of instruction codes to cope with.

ASSEMBLY LANGUAGE

To make programming easier, many programmers write programs in *assembly language*. They then translate the assembly language program to machine language so it can be loaded into memory and run. Assembly language uses two-, three-, or four-letter *mnemonics* to represent each instruction type. A mnemonic is just a device to help you remember something. The letters in an assembly language mnemonic are usually initials or a shortened form of the English word or words for the operation performed by the instruction. For example, the mnemonic for subtract is SUB, the mnemonic for negate is NEG, and the mnemonic for the instruction to copy data from one location to another is MOVE.

Assembly language statements are usually written in a standard form having four *fields*. Figure 2-11 shows an assembly language statement with the four fields indicated. The first field in an assembly language statement is the *label field*. A *label* is a symbol or group of symbols used to represent an address that is not specifically known at the time the statement is written. Labels are usually followed by a colon. Labels are not required in a statement; they are just inserted where they are needed. Later we show many uses of labels.

Instruction mnemonics are sometimes called *operation codes*, or *opcodes*. The *opcode field* of the instruction contains the mnemonic for the instruction to be performed. The ADD mnemonic in the example statement in Figure 2-11 indicates that we want the instruction to do an addition. The suffix .B on the mnemonic indicates that the operand size is 1 byte (8 bits). Chapter 6 describes the function of each 68000 instruction type and gives the opcodes for each. Chapter 6 also indicates when a special suffix is used and which forms are allowed.

The *operand field* of the statement contains the data, the memory address, the port address, or the name of the register on which the instruction is to be performed. *Operand* is just another name for the data item(s) acted on by an instruction. In the example instruction in Figure 2-11, there are two operands, 7 and D0, specified in the operand field. D0 represents data register zero, and 7 represents the number 7. This assembly language statement then says to add the number 7 to the contents of data register zero. By Motorola convention, the result of the addition will be put in the register or the memory location specified *after* the comma in the operand field. For the example statement in Figure 2-11, then, the result will be left in register D0. As another example, the assembly lan-

LABEL FIELD	OPCODE FIELD	OPERAND FIELD	COMMENT FIELD
NEXT:	ADD.B	#7,D0	Add correction

FIGURE 2-11 Assembly language program statement format.

guage statement ADD.L D0,D4, when converted to machine language and run, will add the contents of register D0 to the contents of register D4. The addition will use two long binary integers, each 32 bits in length. The result will be left in register D4.

Looking back at the example assembly language statement in Figure 2-11, observe the *comment field,* which starts with a semicolon. This field is very important. Comments do not become part of the machine language program. You write *comments* in a program to remind you of the function that this instruction or group of instructions performs in the program.

To summarize why we use assembly language, let's look a little more closely at the assembly language ADD statement. The general format of the 68000 ADD instruction is

ADD source,destination

The *source* can be a number written in the instruction, the contents of a specified register, or the contents of a memory location. The *destination* can be a specified register or a specified memory location. The source and the destination can both be memory locations in the same instruction.

A later section on 68000 addressing modes shows all the ways in which the source of an operand and the destination of the result can be specified. The point here is that the single mnemonic ADD, together with a specified source and a specified destination, can represent a great many 68000 instructions in an easily understandable form.

The question that may occur to you at this point is, If I write a program in assembly language, how do I get it translated into machine language, which can be loaded into the microcomputer and executed? There are two answers to this question. The first method of doing the translation is by working out the binary code for each instruction a bit at a time using the templates given in the manufacturer's data books. We show you how to do this in the next chapter. It is a tedious and error-prone task. The second method of doing the translation is with an *assembler.* An assembler is a program that can be run on a personal computer or *microcomputer development system.* It reads the assembly language instructions and generates the correct binary code for each. For developing all but the simplest assembly language programs, an assembler and other program-development tools are essential. We introduce you to these program development tools in the next chapter and describe their use throughout the rest of this book.

HIGH-LEVEL LANGUAGES

Another way of writing a program for a microcomputer is with a *high-level language* such as BASIC, FORTRAN, Modula II, C, or Pascal. These languages use program statements that are even more Englishlike than those of assembly language. Each high-level statement may represent many machine code instructions. An *interpreter program* or a *compiler program* is used to translate higher-level language statements to machine codes that can be loaded into memory and executed. Programs can usually be written more quickly in high-level languages than in assembly language because the high-level language works with bigger building blocks. However, programs written in a high-level language and interpreted or compiled execute more slowly than the same programs written in assembly language. Programs that involve a lot of hardware control, such as robots and factory-control systems, or programs that must run as quickly as possible are usually best written in assembly language. Programs that manipulate massive amounts of data, such as insurance company records, are usually best written in a high-level language. The decision of which language to use has recently been made more difficult because current assemblers allow the use of many high-level language features and some current high-level languages provide assembly language features.

OUR CHOICE

Throughout this book we use assembly language, for the most part, because we will be working very closely with hardware interfacing. Before we start teaching you assembly language programming in the next chapter, however, we want to give you an introduction to how the 68000 accesses data.

How the 68000 Accesses Immediate and Register Data

In a previous discussion of the 68000 CPU, we described how the 68000 accesses code bytes using a program counter (PC). We also described how the 68000 accesses the stack using SP and SSP. Before we can teach you assembly language programming techniques, we need to discuss some of the different ways that a 68000 can access the data on which it operates. The different ways that a processor can access data are referred to as its *addressing modes.* In assembly language statements the addressing mode is indicated by the way the instruction is written. The 68000 family offers 14 different addressing modes, which are listed in the next chapter. Here we will consider some of the basic addressing mode components, which can be combined to define the complex set of addressing modes provided. We will use the 68000 MOVE instruction to illustrate some of the 68000 addressing modes.

The MOVE instruction has the format

MOVE source,destination

When executed, this instruction copies a word or a byte from the specified source location to the specified destination location. The source can be a number written directly in the instruction, a specified register, or a memory location specified in one of up to 12 different ways. The destination can be a specified register or a memory location specified in any one of 8 different ways. The source and the destination can both be memory locations in the same instruction.

IMMEDIATE ADDRESSING MODE

Suppose in a program that you need to put the number $437B in register D0. The MOVE.W #$437B,D0 instruction can be used to do this. When it executes, this instruction will put the *immediate* hexadecimal number $437B in the lower 16 bits of register D0. This is referred to as the *immediate addressing mode* because the number to be loaded into register D0 will be put in two memory locations immediately following the code for the MOVE instruction. This is similar to the way the port address was put in memory immediately after the code for the input instruction in the three-instruction program in Figure 2-2b. In 68000 assembly language the pound sign, #, is used to indicate that immediate addressing is being used and the data value is immediately following the # in the assembly language representation.

A similar instruction, MOVE.B #$48,D3, could be used to move the 8-bit immediate number $48 into the lowest 8 bits of register D3. You can also write instructions to move an 8-bit immediate number into an 8-bit memory location or to move a 16-bit number into two consecutive memory locations. You can also move 32-bit data values into four consecutive memory locations, but we are not yet ready to show you how to specify these.

REGISTER DIRECT ADDRESSING MODE

Register direct addressing mode means that a register is the source of an operand for an instruction. The instruction MOVE.L D3,D2, for example, copies the contents of the 32-bit register D3 into the 32-bit register D2. Remember that the destination location is specified in the instruction after the source. Also note that the contents of D3 are just *copied* to D2, not actually moved. In other words, the previous contents of D2 are written over, but the contents of D3 are not changed. For example, if D2 contains $00002A84 and D3 contains $FFFF4971 before the MOVE.L D3,D2 instruction executes, then after the instruction executes, D2 will contain $FFFF4971 and D3 will still contain $FFFF4971. You can MOVE any 32-bit, 16-bit, or 8-bit portion of a register, but the 8-bit value will always be the lowest byte and the 16-bit value will always be the low word.

If you are using a *byte-type* operand, then use the .B suffix to the desired instruction mnemonic. Use .W for a *word-type* operand and .L for a *long-type* operand.

This is called *direct* addressing because the operand is found directly in a register. The CPU does not need to access external memory again to find the operand value; it is already directly in the CPU itself in a register.

How the 68000 Accesses Data in Memory

The 68000 memory is viewed by the 68000 CPU as a linear list of memory locations, each having an address, and each having some contents. The contents of RAM may be changed by the CPU, and the contents of ROM may not be changed. When accessing data from memory, the CPU will send an address to the memory chips, and the memory chips will return the data value that was in memory at the address specified. This is normally called accessing memory: the process of sending an address to memory and getting the data values back from memory. As we have seen, the 68000 can generate the addresses, which it sends to the memory in several different ways. Each way of generating an address is called a different addressing mode. We now look at the components of an addressing mode.

OVERVIEW OF MEMORY ADDRESSING MODE COMPONENTS

The addressing modes components described in the following sections are combined to specify the location of an operand in memory. Once all components have been considered, a value is generated that is considered to be the *effective address*, or EA, of the memory location where the data is stored. One component of an EA might be, for example, a *displacement*, or offset. In the instruction ADD.B #13(A0),D3, the source address is found by taking the value in register A0, adding the displacement value 13 to it, and using the result as the source operand EA. This final EA is what the CPU sends out to memory on the address bus.

INDIRECT ADDRESSING MODE

In the simplest memory addressing mode, the effective address is just a 32- or 16-bit number written in the instruction. The instruction MOVE.W ($4374),D0 is an example. The parentheses around the $4374 are shorthand for "the contents of the memory location(s) at." That is, $4374 is the address of the data, not the data itself. The data is in memory at location $4374.

Figure 2-12 shows how the operation is done. This addressing mode is called the *indirect* mode because the address, not the data, is found in the instruction. The data is in memory and must be accessed by the CPU with an additional memory cycle using the (indirect) address specified in the instruction. The CPU must access the data indirectly, with an address in the instruction, not directly from an internal CPU register itself. This address must then be used with the memory to determine the actual data value.

Indirect addressing can also use an address register to specify the address of the operand. For example, in the instruction MOVE.L (A0),D0 the source operand is the 4 bytes of data in memory at the location whose address is in register A0. Again, the instruction specifies the data indirectly by indicating where the address of the data can be found (in A0).

NOTE: When you are *hand coding* programs using direct addressing of the form just shown, make sure to put in the parentheses to remind you how to code the instruction. If you leave the parentheses out of an instruction such as MOVE.L ($4374),D0 you may code it as if it were the instruction as MOVE.L #$4374,D0. This will load the immediate number $4374 into D0, rather than load a word from memory at an address of $4374.

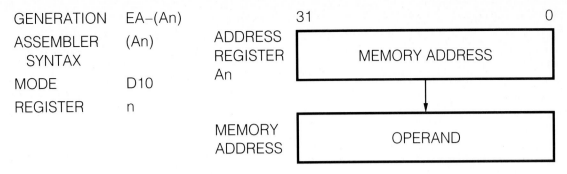

GENERATION	EA–(An)
ASSEMBLER SYNTAX	(An)
MODE	D10
REGISTER	n

FIGURE 2-12   68000 addressing mode diagram for indirect addressing.

CHECKLIST OF IMPORTANT TERMS AND CONCEPTS IN THIS CHAPTER

If there are terms or concepts in this list you do not remember, use the index to find them in the chapter.

Microcomputer, microprocessor

Hardware, software, firmware

Timeshare

Multitasking computer system

Distributed processing system

Multiprocessing

CPU

Memory, RAM, ROM

I/O ports

Address, data, and control buses

Control bus signals

ALU

Segmentation

CPU

Instruction prefetch queue, pipelining

Data and address registers, PC register, SP, SSP

EU

Status register

Condition codes

Flags

Machine language

Assembly language

Mnemonic, opcode, operand, label, comment, assembler

High-level language

Compiler

Effective address

Immediate addressing mode

Register direct addressing mode

Indirect addressing mode

REVIEW QUESTIONS AND PROBLEMS

1. Describe the sequence of signals that occurs on the address bus, the control bus, and the data bus when a computer fetches an instruction.

2. Describe the main advantages of a distributed processing computer system over a simple timeshare system.

3. What determines whether a microprocessor is considered an 8-bit, 16-bit, or 32-bit device?

4. a. How many address lines does 68000 have?
   b. How many memory addresses does this number of address lines allow the 68000 to access directly?

5. What is the main difference between the 68000 and the 68008?

6. a. Describe the function of the 68000 prefetch queue.
   b. How does the prefetch queue speed up process operation?

7. a. To what does the term memory-mapped I/O refer?
   b. What is an I/O port?

8. If the PC contains the value $143E and a one-word instruction is fetched from memory, decoded, and executed, what will the value of the PC be

after it is incremented to point to the next instruction?

9. What is the advantage of using a CPU register instead of a memory location for temporary data storage?

10. If the user stack pointer register, SP, contains $3000, what is the address of the top of the stack?

11. a. What is the advantage of using assembly language instead of writing a program directly in machine language?
    b. Describe the operation a 68000 will perform when it executes ADD.B D0,D1.

12. What types of programs are usually written in assembly language?

13. Describe the operation that a 68000 will perform when it executes each of the following instructions:

    a. MOVE.W #$03FF,D0
    b. MOVE.L ($00DB),D0
    c. MOVE.L D0,D3
    d. MOVE.B D4,D1

14. For each instruction in problem 13, indicate whether the source addressing mode is immediate, register direct, or indirect.

15. Write the 68000 assembly language statement that will perform the following operations:

    a. Load the number $7986 into register D0.
    b. Copy the contents of register D0 to register A3.
    c. Copy the contents of register A3 to register D3.
    d. Load the number $F3 into register D7.

16. Describe the difference between the instructions
    MOVE.W #$2437,D0 and MOVE.W ($2437),D0.

CHAPTER 3

68000 Family Assembly Language Programming—Introduction

The last chapter showed you the format for 68000 assembly language programs and introduced you to a few 68000 instructions. Developing a program, however, requires more than just writing a series of instructions. When you want to build a house, it is a good idea first to develop a complete set of plans for the house. With the plans you can see if the house has the rooms you need, if the rooms are efficiently placed, and if the house is structured so that you can easily add onto it if you want to.

Likewise, when you write computer programs, it is a good idea to start by developing a detailed plan or outline. A good outline helps you to break a large and seemingly overwhelming programming job into small modules, which can easily be written, tested, and debugged. The more time you spend organizing your programs, the less time it will take you to write and debug them. You should *never* start writing an assembly language program by just writing down instructions! In this chapter we show you how to develop assembly language programs in a systematic way.

OBJECTIVES

At the conclusion of this chapter, you should be able to

1. Write a task list, flowchart, or pseudocode for a simple programming problem.

2. Write, code or assemble, and run a very simple assembly language program.

3. Describe the use of program development tools such as editors, assemblers, linkers, locators, debuggers, and emulators.

4. Properly document assembly language programs.

PROGRAM DEVELOPMENT STEPS

Defining the Problem

The first step in writing a program is to think very carefully about the problem that you want the program to solve. In other words, ask yourself many times,

"What do I really want this program to do?" If you don't do this, you may write a great program, which works but does not do what you need it to do. As you think about the problem, it is a good idea to write exactly what you want the program to do and the order in which you want the program to do it. At this point you do not write down program statements, you just write the operations you want in general terms. The following list might be written for a simple programming problem:

1. Read temperature from sensor.

2. Add correction factor of +7.

3. Save result in a memory location.

For a program as simple as this, the three desired actions are very close to the eventual assembly language statements. For more complex problems, however, we develop a more extensive outline before writing the assembly language statements. The next section shows you some of the common ways of representing program operations in a program outline.

Representing Program Operations

The formula or sequence of operations used to solve a programming problem is often called the *algorithm* of the program. The following sections show you several ways of representing the algorithm for a program or program segment.

SEQUENTIAL TASK LISTS

Some programmers use just a *sequential list of the tasks,* such as the one in the preceding section, to show the algorithm for their programs. To give you a better idea of this form, we will show another slightly different example. Suppose that, instead of taking one data sample from the temperature sensor, we want to take in a data sample every hour for 24 hours, add 7 to each sample, and put each corrected value in a memory location. We could write a task list for this problem as follows:

1. Read data sample from temperature sensor.

2. Add 7 to value read in.

3. Store corrected value in memory location.

4. Wait 1 hr.

5. Read next sample from temperature sensor.

6. Add 7 to value read in.

7. Store corrected value in next memory location.

.

.

.

97. Read last data sample from temperature sensor.

98. Add 7 to value read in.

99. Store corrected value in next memory location.

As you can see, this direct form is not a very compact or efficient way of representing the operation of the program. A more efficient way of writing the sequential task list for this program is this:

Read a data sample from temperature sensor.

Add 7 to the value read in.

Store corrected value in memory location.

Wait 1 hr.

24 samples yet?

No, read next sample and process.

Yes, done.

The last three lines indicate that we want the program to do the read, add, store, and wait operations 24 times. Carefully written sequential task lists are often

quite close to the assembly language statements that will implement them, so you may find them useful. As you determine hardware details, such as port addresses for the system on which the program is to run, you can add this information to the appropriate task statement. The next section shows you a more graphic way of representing the algorithm of a program or program segment.

FLOWCHARTS

If you have done any previous programming in BASIC or in FORTRAN, you are probably familiar with *flowcharts*. Flowcharts use graphic shapes to represent different types of program operations. The specific operation desired is written in the graphic symbol. Figure 3-1 shows some of the common flowchart symbols. Plastic templates are available to help you draw these symbols if you decide to use them for your programs.

Figure 3-2 shows a flowchart for a program to read in 24 data samples from a temperature sensor at 1-hr intervals, add 7 to each, and store each result in a memory location. An *oval*, or *racetrack-shaped*, symbol labeled START is used to indicate the *beginning* of the program. A *parallelogram* is used to represent *input* or *output operations*. In this example we use it to indicate reading data from the temperature sensor. A *rectangular box symbol* is used to represent *simple operations* other than input and output operations. The box containing "add 7" in Figure 3-2 is an example.

A *rectangular box with double lines at each end* is often used to represent a *subroutine*, or *procedure* that will be written separately from the main program. When a set of operations must be done several times throughout a program, it is usually more efficient to write the series of operations once as a separate *subprogram* and then just use, or "call," this subprogram as it is needed. For example, suppose that there are several times in a program where you need to compute the square root of a number. Instead of writing the series of instructions for computing a square root each time you need it in the program, you can write the instruction sequence once as a subprogram and set it aside in some location in memory. You can then call

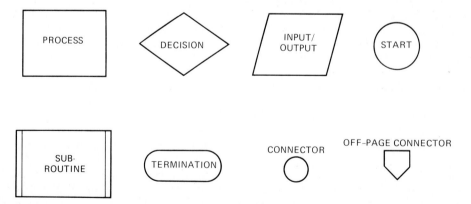

FIGURE 3-1 Flowchart symbols.

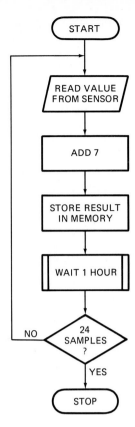

FIGURE 3-2 Flowchart for program to read in 24 data samples from a port, correct each value, and store each in a memory location.

this subprogram each time you need to compute a square root. In the flowchart in Figure 3-2 we use the double-ended box to indicate that the "wait 1 hr" operation will be programmed as a subroutine. Incidentally, the terms *subprogram*, *subroutine*, and *procedure* all have the same meaning. Chapter 5 shows how subroutines are written and used.

A *diamond-shaped* box is used in flowcharts to represent a *decision* point, or crossroad. Usually it indicates that some condition is to be checked at this point in the program and, if the condition is found to be *true*, one set of actions is to be done. If the condition is found to be *false*, then another set of actions is to be done. In the flowchart in Figure 3-2, the condition to be checked is whether 24 samples have been read in and processed. If 24 samples have not been read in and processed, the arrow labeled *No* in the flowchart indicates that we want the computer to jump back and execute the read, add, store, and wait steps again. If 24 samples have been read in, the arrow labeled *Yes* in the flowchart of Figure 3-2 indicates that all the desired operations have been done. The racetrack-shaped symbol at the bottom of the flowchart indicates the *end* of the program.

The two additional flowchart symbols in Figure 3-1 are *connectors*. If a flowchart column gets to the bottom of the paper but the entire program has not been represented, you can put a small circle with a

letter in it at the bottom of the column. You then start the next column at the top of the same piece of paper with a small circle containing the same letter. If you need to continue a flowchart on another page, you can end the flowchart on the first page with the five-sided off-page connector symbol containing a letter or number. You then start the flowchart on the next page with an off-page connector symbol containing the same letter or number.

For simple programs and program sections, flowcharts are a graphic way of showing the operational flow of the program. We will show flowcharts for many of the program examples throughout this book. However, flowcharts have several disadvantages. First, you can't write much information in the little boxes. Second, flowcharts do not present information in a very compact form. For more complex problems, flowcharts tend to become spread out over many pages. They are very hard to follow back and forth between pages. Third, and most important, with flowcharts the overall structure of the program tends to get lost in the details. The following section describes a more clearly *structured* and *compact* method of representing the algorithm of a program or program segment.

OVERVIEW OF STRUCTURED PROGRAMMING AND PSEUDOCODE

In the early days of computers, a single brilliant person might write even a large program single-handedly. The main concerns in this case were, Does the program work? and What do we do if this person leaves the company? As the number of computers increased and the complexity of the programs being written increased, large programming jobs were usually turned over to a team of programmers. In such cases the compatibility of parts written by different programmers became an important concern. During the 1970s it became obvious to many professional programmers that a systematic approach and standardized tools were absolutely necessary if team programming was to work.

One suggested systematic approach is called *top-down design*. In this approach a large programming problem is first broken down into major *modules*. The top level of the outline shows the relationship and function of these modules. This top level then presents a one-page overview of the entire program. Each of the major modules is broken down into still-smaller modules on following pages. The division is continued until the steps in each module are clearly understandable. Each programmer can then be assigned a module or set of modules to write for the program. Also, a person wanting to learn about the program later can start with the overview and work their way down to the level of detail they need. This approach is the same as drawing the complete plans for a house before starting to build it.

The opposite of top-down design is *bottom-up design*. In this approach each programmer starts writing low-level modules and hopes that all the pieces will eventually fit together. When completed, the result should be similar to that produced by the top-down design. Many modern programming teams use a combination of the two techniques. They do the top-down design and then build, test, and link modules starting from the smallest and working upward.

The development of standard programming tools was helped by the discovery that any desired program operation could be represented by three basic types of operation. The first type of operation is a *sequence*, which means simply doing a series of actions. The second basic type of operation is a *decision*, or *selection*, which means choosing between two alternative actions. The third basic type of operation is *repetition*, or *iteration*, which means repeating a series of actions until some condition is or is not present.

Based on this observation, the suggestion was made that all programmers use a set of three to seven standard *structures* to represent all the operations in their programs. Actually, only three structures—sequence, IF-THEN-ELSE, and WHILE-DO—are required to represent any desired program action, but three or four more structures derived from these often make programs clearer. If you have previously written programs in a structured language such as Pascal, then these structures are probably already familiar to you. Figure 3-3 uses flowchart symbols to represent the commonly used structures so you can more easily visualize their operations. In actual program documentation, however, Englishlike statements called *pseudocode* are used rather than the space-consuming flowchart symbols. Figure 3-3 also shows the pseudocode format and an example for each structure.

Each structure has only *one entry point* and *one exit point*. The output of one structure is connected to the input of the next structure. Program execution then proceeds through a series of these structures.

Any structure can be used within another. An IF-THEN-ELSE structure, for example, can contain a sequence of statements. Any place that the term *statement(s)* appears in Figure 3-3, one of the other structures could be substituted for it. The term statement(s) can also represent a subprogram or procedure that is called to do a series of actions.

STANDARD PROGRAMMING STRUCTURES

The structure shown in Figure 3-3a is an example of a simple sequence. In this structure the actions are simply written down in the desired order. An example is

Read temperature from sensor.

Add correction factor of +7.

Store corrected value in memory.

Figure 3-3b shows an IF-THEN-ELSE example of the decision operation. This structure is used to direct operation to one of two different actions based on some condition. An example is

IF temperature less than 70 degrees THEN
  Turn on heater
ELSE
  Turn off heater

The example says that if the temperature is below the thermostat setting, we want to turn the heater on. If the temperature is equal to or above the thermostat setting, we want to turn the heater off.

The IF-THEN structure shown in Figure 3-3c is the same as the IF-THEN-ELSE, except that one of the paths contains no action. An example of this is

    IF hungry THEN
  Get food.

The assumption for this example is that if you are not hungry, you will just continue on with your next task.

The WHILE-DO structure in Figure 3-3d is one form of repetition. It is used to indicate that you want to do some action or sequence of actions as long as some condition is present. This structure represents a *program loop*. The example in Figure 3-3d is

WHILE money lasts DO
  Eat supper out.
  Go to movie.
  Take a taxi home.

This example shows a sequence of actions you might do each evening until you ran out of money. Note that in this structure, the condition is checked *before* the action is done the first time. You certainly would want to check how much money you have before eating out.

Another useful structure derived from the WHILE-DO structure is the REPEAT-UNTIL structure shown in Figure 3-3e. You use this structure to indicate that you want the program to repeat some action or series of actions until some condition is present. A good example of the use of this structure is the programming problem we used in the discussion of flowcharts:

REPEAT
  Get data sample from sensor.
  Add correction of +7.
  Store result in a memory location.
  Wait 1 hr.
UNTIL 24 samples taken.

Compare the space required by the pseudocode representation for the desired action with the space required by the flowchart representation shown in Figure 3-2. The space advantage of pseudocode should be obvious.

As indicated previously, the REPEAT-UNTIL structure is derived from the WHILE-DO. In other words, any problem that can be represented by a REPEAT-UNTIL can also be represented by a properly written WHILE-DO. The example in Figure 3-3e could be written as follows:

WHILE NOT 24 samples DO
  Read data sample from temperature sensor.

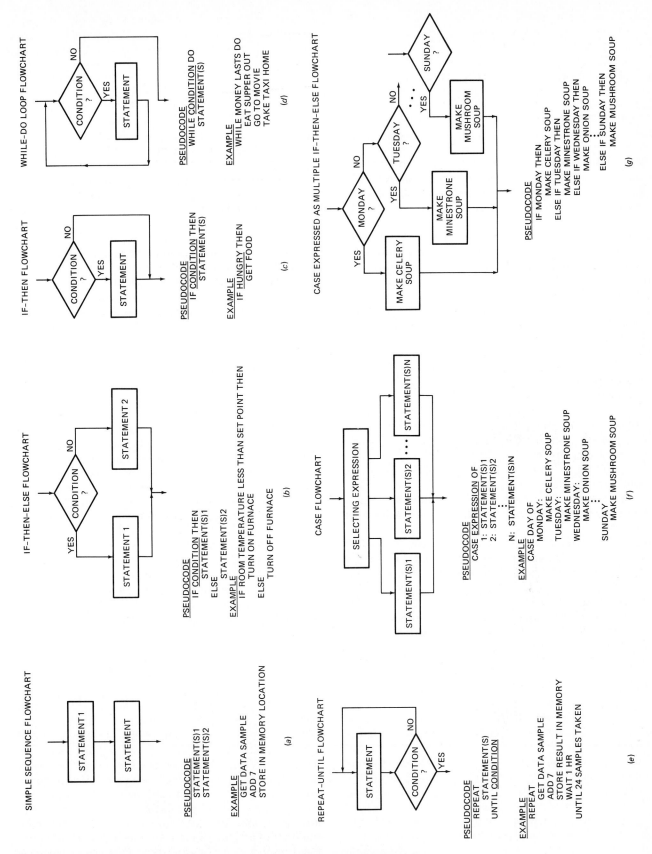

FIGURE 3-3 Standard program structures. (*a*) SEQUENCE. (*b*) IF-THEN-ELSE. (*c*) IF-THEN. (*d*) WHILE-DO. (*e*) REPEAT-UNTIL. (*f*) CASE. (*g*) CASE expressed as multiple IF-THEN-ELSE.

Add correction factor of +7.
Store result in memory location.
Wait 1 hr.

Note that the REPEAT-UNTIL structure indicates that the condition is first checked *after* the statement or statements are performed. In other words, a REPEAT-UNTIL structure indicates that the action or series of actions will always be done at least once. If you don't want this to happen, then use the WHILE-DO, which indicates that the condition is checked before any action is taken. As we show later, the structure you use makes a difference in the actual assembly language program you write to implement it.

The WHILE-DO and REPEAT-UNTIL structures contain a simple IF-THEN-ELSE decision operation. However, since this decision is an *implied* part of these two structures, we don't indicate the decision separately in them.

Another form of the repetition operation that you might see in high-level language programs is the FOR-DO loop. This structure has the form

FOR COUNT = 1 TO N DO
    statement
    statement

In assembly language we usually implement this type of operation with a REPEAT-UNTIL structure, so we have not included a sample of it.

The CASE structure shown in Figure 3-3f is a compact way of representing a choice among several alternative actions. The choice is determined by testing some quantity. The example in Figure 3-3f best shows how this is used. This everyday example describes the desired actions for a cook in a restaurant. The pseudocode is just a summary of the thinking he or she might go through. The cook or the computer checks the value of the variable called "day" and selects the appropriate actions for that day. Each of the indicated actions, such as "Make celery soup," is itself a sequence of actions that could be represented by the structures we have described.

The CASE structure is really just a compact way to represent a complex IF-THEN-ELSE structure. To illustrate this, Figure 3-3g also shows how the soup-cook example can be represented as a series of IF-THEN-ELSE structures. Note that in this example the last IF-THEN has no ELSE after it because all the possible days have been checked. You can, if you want, add the final ELSE to the IF-THEN-ELSE chain to send an error message if the data does not match any of the choices. The CASE structure does contain the final ELSE, however. The CASE form is more compact for documentation purposes, and some high-level languages such as Pascal allow you to implement it directly. However, the IF-THEN-ELSE structure gives you a much better idea of how you write an assembly language program section that chooses between several alternative actions.

Throughout the rest of this book we show you how to use these structures to represent program actions and how to implement these structures in assembly language.

SUMMARY OF PROGRAM STRUCTURE REPRESENTATION FORMS

Writing a successful program does not consist of just writing down a series of instructions. You must first think carefully about what you want the program to do and how you want the program to do it. Then you must represent the structure of the program in some way that is very clear to you and to anyone else who might have to work on the program. If the structure is well developed, it is usually not a difficult step to write the actual programming language statements that implement it.

One way of representing program operations is with a sequential task list. For initial thinking and simple programming problems, this technique works well. For more complex programming problems, a sequential list may become very messy because it has little real structure or standardization. Another way of representing program operations is with flowcharts. Flowcharts are a very graphic representation, and they are useful for short program segments, especially those that deal directly with hardware. However, flowcharts use a great deal of space. Consequently, the flowchart for even a moderately complex program may take up several pages. It often becomes difficult to follow program flow back and forth between pages. Also, since there are no agreed-upon structures, a poor programmer can write a flowchart that jumps all over the place and is even more difficult to follow.

A third way of representing the operations you want in a program is with a top-down design approach and standard program structures. The overall program problem is first broken into major functional modules. Each of these modules is broken into smaller and smaller modules, until the steps in each module are obvious. The algorithms for the whole program and for each module are each expressed with a standard structure. Only three basic structures, sequence, IF-THEN-ELSE, and WHILE-DO, are needed to represent any needed program action or series of actions. However, other useful structures, such as IF-THEN, REPEAT-UNTIL, FOR-DO, and CASE, can be derived from these basic three. A structure can contain another structure of the same type or of one of the other types. Each structure has only one entry point and one exit point. These programming structures may seem restrictive, but using them usually results in program representations that are easy to understand and for which it is easy to write the programs. A program written in a structured manner is easier to debug and is much more understandable to someone else who has to work on it. Furthermore, a program representation developed with structured programming techniques can be implemented easily in assembly language or in a high-level language such as Modula II or C.

Finding the Right Instruction

After you get the structure of a program worked out and recorded, the next step is to determine the instruction statements required to do each part of the program. Since the examples in this book are based on the 68000 family of microprocessors, now is a good time to give you an overview of the instructions the 68000 has for you to use.

You do not usually learn a new language by studying its dictionary from cover to cover. It is more productive first to learn a few very useful words and then to learn how to put together simple sentences. You can learn more words as you need them to express more complex thoughts. Chapter 6 contains a dictionary of all the 68000 instructions, with detailed descriptions and examples for each. You can use this as a reference as you write programs. Here we simply list the 68000 instructions in *functional* groups, with single-sentence descriptions, so that you can see the types of instructions that are available to you. As you read through this section, do not expect to understand all the instructions. When you start writing programs, you will probably use this section to determine the type of instruction and Chapter 6 to get the instruction details as you need them. After you have written a few programs, you will remember most of the basic instruction types and can just look up an instruction in Chapter 6 to get any additional details you need. Chapter 4 shows in detail how to use the *move, arithmetic, logical,* and *jump* instructions. Chapter 5 shows how to use the *call* instructions and the *stack*.

As you skim through the following overview of the 68000 instructions, see if you can find the instructions needed to do the "read temperature sensor value from a port, add +7, and store result in memory" example program.

Data Movement Instructions

OPERATIONS FOR MOVEMENT OF MEMORY AND REGISTER CONTENTS

MOVE—Copy bytes from memory or register to memory or register. This is the most commonly used general byte-moving instruction.

MOVEA—Copy the address of the source into the destination.

MOVEM—Copy CPU registers into memory or memory to registers.

MOVEP—Copy data to alternate bytes of memory, as when moving to an 8-bit peripheral device from a 16-bit bus.

MOVEQ—Copy the following data bytes into the destination register.

EXG—Exchange the contents of two registers.

OPERATIONS FOR ADDRESS MANIPULATION

LEA—Load the effective address of the source into the address register specified in the destination field.

PEA—Push the effective address onto the specified stack.

OPERATIONS FOR STACK MANAGEMENT

LINK—Create a link on the system stack between a calling main program and a called subroutine. See Chapter 6 for a description of what a link is.

UNLK—Remove the link between a subroutine and the program that called it.

Integer Arithmetic Instructions

ADDITION INSTRUCTIONS

ADD—Add two registers or two memory locations that contain integer values.

ADDA—Add an offset or index to an address register.

ADDI—Add the immediately following data to the destination.

ADDQ—Add a small value to the destination and do it quickly.

ADDX—Add using the sign-extend bit.

SUBTRACTION INSTRUCTIONS

SUB—Subtract byte from byte, word from word, or long word from long word.

SUBA—Subtract an offset from an address register.

SUBI—Subtract the immediately following data from the destination.

SUBQ—Subtract a small value from the destination.

SUBX—Subtract using the extend bit.

NEG—Negate the specified location.

NEGX—Negate using the extend bit.

COMPARISON INSTRUCTIONS

CMP—Compare the two integer operands by subtracting one from the other.

CMPA—Compare two addresses.

CMPI—Compare a register with the immediately following data.

CMPM—Compare two stacks' memory locations.

CLR—Clear a register by placing the value 0 in it.

EXT—Sign-extend a register by copying the sign bit.

MULTIPLICATION INSTRUCTIONS

MULS—Multiply the signed source times the signed destination and store the signed result in the destination.

MULU—Multiply unsigned values.

DIVISION INSTRUCTIONS

DIVS—Divide signed 16-bit values, producing a 16-bit result and a 16-bit remainder.

DIVU—Unsigned integer divide.

Logical Operation Instructions

LOGICAL INSTRUCTIONS

AND—Logically AND each bit of two operands.

ANDI—Logically AND each bit of an operand with the immediately following data.

EOR—Logically EXCLUSIVE-OR (XOR) each bit of an operand with a register.

EORI—Logically XOR each bit of an operand with the immediately following data.

OR—Logically OR each bit of an operand with a register.

ORI—Logically OR with immediate data.

NOT—Invert each bit of a byte, word, or long word.

TST—Set the CPU condition codes based upon an operand's value by subtracting 0 from the operand.

Shift and Rotate Instructions

ARITHMETIC SHIFT INSTRUCTIONS

ASL—Arithmetic shift left a byte, word, or long word.

ASR—Arithmetic shift right an operand a specified number of bits.

LOGICAL SHIFT INSTRUCTIONS

LSL—Logical shift left a byte, word, or long word.

LSR—Logical shift right an operand a specified number of bit positions.

ROTATE INSTRUCTIONS

ROL—Rotate a data register left.

ROR—Rotate a data register right.

ROXL—Rotate left using the extend bit.

ROXR—Rotate right using the extend bit.

SWAP—Swap the two words of a long-word data register.

Bit-manipulation Instructions

BCHG—Test a data bit and change it in one instruction.

BCLR—Test a bit and clear it.

BSET—Test and set a bit in one instruction.

BTST—Test a bit and set the zero-condition code to the same value.

Binary-coded Decimal Instructions

ABCD—Add two binary-coded decimal values.

NBCD—Negate a BCD value.

SBCD—Subtract two BCD values.

If you aren't tired of instructions, continue skimming through the rest of the list. Don't worry if the explanation is not clear to you, because we explain these instructions in detail in later chapters.

Program Control Instructions

BRANCH INSTRUCTIONS

The letters cc in the Bcc, DBcc, and Scc instructions represent one of 15 available condition-code tests, including CC, CS, EQ, GE, GT, HI, LE, LS, LT, MI, NE, PL, VC, and VS. Also, the Scc instruction can use the T or F condition codes. For example, the instruction BEQ represents the Bcc instruction testing the condition code EQ. (Is the zero bit set?) BEQ indicates branch if the zero bit is set.

Bcc—Branch and start executing instructions from a different address if the specified condition code is true.

DBcc—Decrement a register and branch on condition code.

Scc—Set a byte to all 0s or all 1s, depending on a condition code.

BRA—Branch always.

BSR—Branch to subroutine, leaving a return address on the stack.

JUMP INSTRUCTIONS

JMP—Jump to a new location and begin executing instructions there.

JSR—Jump in a subroutine fashion, leaving a return address on the stack.

NOP—No operation, do nothing for one instruction.

RETURNS

RTS—Return from a subroutine using the address on the top of the stack.

RTD—Return from subroutine and deallocate memory from the top of the stack.

RTR—Return from a subroutine and restore the CPU condition codes from the top of the stack.

System Control Instructions

Some system control operations are "normal" instructions that have special operands. For example, a MOVE to the status register is a privileged instruction and hence a system control instruction. Instruction forms such as MOVE that have already been listed are not mentioned again here.

PRIVILEGED INSTRUCTIONS

MOVEC—Move one of the CPU's internal control registers to one of the working registers or vice versa.

MOVES—(68010/68012) Move bytes from another address space into the current address space, as indicated by internal control registers.

RESET—Assert the RESET line controlling external devices for 124 clock cycles.

RTE—Return from an exception and restore the CPU status register.

STOP—Load the status register with the immediately following data and stop the CPU.

TRAP-GENERATING INSTRUCTIONS

BKPT—Execute a breakpoint-acknowledge bus cycle to allow an external debugger to take control here.

CHK—Check a data register against upper and lower bounds and trap if it is out of bounds.

ILLEGAL—Simulate an illegal instruction and generate a trap.

TRAP—Cause a trap using the vector number specified.

TRAPV—Cause a trap if the overflow condition code is set.

Multiprocessor Instructions

TAS—Test and set the byte operand in one indivisible operation. This can be used to synchronize multiple CPUs in the same system.

Now that you have glanced through an overview of the 68000 instruction set, let's see if you found the instructions needed to implement the "read sensor, add +7, and store result in memory" example program. The MOVE instruction can be used to read the temperature value from an A/D converter connected to a memory-mapped I/O port. The MOVEP instruction could also be used, but for this example it was not selected. Often alternative instructions may be used to perform similar operations.

The ADDQ instruction can be used to add the correction factor of +7 to the value read in. The ADD or the ADDI instruction could be used but would not be optimal in this case. Finally, the MOVE instruction can be used to copy the result of the addition to a memory location. A major point here is that breaking the programming problem into a sequence of steps makes it easy to find the instruction or small group of instructions that will perform each step. The next section shows you how to write the actual program using these instructions.

Writing a Program

INITIALIZATION INSTRUCTIONS

After finding the instructions needed to do the main part of your program, there are a few additional instructions you need to determine before you actually write your program. The purpose of these additional instructions is to *initialize* various parts of the system, such as address registers, flags, and programmable port devices. An address register, for example, must be loaded with the address in memory where the memory-mapped I/O port is. Another address register must be loaded with the address in memory where the final, corrected sensor reading is to be saved.

If you are using the stack in your program, then you must include an instruction to load the stack pointer register with the address of the top of the stack. Most microcomputer systems contain several programmable peripheral devices, such as ports, timers, and controllers. You must include instructions that send control words to these devices to tell them the function you want them to perform. Also, you usually need to include instructions that set or clear the control flags, such as the interrupt enable flag and the direction flag.

The best way to approach the initialization task is to make a checklist of all the registers, programmable devices, and flags in the system on which you are working. Then you can mark the ones you need for a specific program and determine the instructions needed to initialize each part. An initialization list for a 68000-based system, such as the URDA MDS prototyping board, might look like the following.

Initialization List

User stack pointer register

Initialize user status register

Initialize interrupt vectors

Initialize breakpoint locations

Determine available memory

Clear data memory

Initialize beeper

Initialize serial ports

Initialize keyboard controller

Initialize LED display

Show start-up message

Initialize data variables

Reset/clear flags

Clear/set interrupt enable

As you can see, the list can become quite lengthy, even though we have not included all the devices a system might commonly have. Now let's see how you put all these parts together to make a program.

A STANDARD PROGRAM FORMAT

In this section we show you the form your programs should have if you are going to construct the machine codes for each instruction by *hand*. A later section of this chapter will show you the additional parts you need to add to the program if you are going to use an *assembler* to produce the binary codes for the instructions.

To help you format your programs, *assembly language coding sheets* such as the one shown in Figure 3-4 are available. The *address* column is used for the address or the offset of a code byte or data byte. The actual code bytes or data bytes are put in the *data/code* column. A *label* is a name that represents an address referred to in a jump or call instruction. A label is put in the *label* column and is followed by a colon (:) if it used by a jump or call instruction in the same code segment. The *opcode* column contains the mnemonics for the instructions. The *operand* column contains the registers, memory locations, or data acted upon by the instructions. The *comment* column gives you space to describe the function of the instruction for future reference.

Figure 3-4 shows how the instructions for the "read temperature, add +7, store result in memory" program can be written in sequence on a coding sheet. We discuss here the operation of these instructions to the extent needed. If you want more information about any of these, detailed descriptions of the *syntax* (assembly language grammar) and operation of each of these instructions are given in Chapter 6.

The first line at the top of the coding form in Figure 3-4 does not represent an instruction. It simply indicates that we want to set aside a memory location to store the result. This location must be in available RAM so that we can write to it. Address $4200 is an available RAM location on the URDA MDS prototyping board, for example. Next, we decide where in memory we want to start putting the code bytes for the instructions of the program. Again, on the URDA MDS prototyping board, addresses $4000 and above are available RAM; by using the ORG instruction, we chose to start the program at address $4000.

The first operation we want to do in the program is to initialize two address registers. The MOVEA instruction is used to move an address into an address register. First, the address of the memory-mapped I/O port is moved into A0. This address is assumed to be $4100 for this example. Second, the address of the memory location where the final corrected result is to be stored is placed in address register A1. Both instructions use an immediate addressing mode, meaning that the address to be placed in the address register immediately follows the MOVEA instruction word. In the first case the immediate address is $4100, and in the second the address is $4200.

The next three instructions (the third, fourth, and fifth) actually perform the desired read, correct, and save operations. The third instruction in this example is a MOVE instruction, which moves 1 byte from the memory location pointed to by A0 into the low-order byte of data register 0 (i.e., D0). This accomplishes the desired read from the memory mapped I/O port. Notice that with the Motorola architecture, most I/O port operations look exactly like memory operations. The next instruction, ADDQ, adds the desired correction factor to the byte value just read. Because the correction factor is small (7 in this case), the ADDQ instruction will be faster than an ADDI or ADD instruction. The fifth instruction in this example is another MOVE instruction. This time the move is from the low-order byte of register D0 into the memory location pointed to by A1. Recall that A1 has already been initialized to point to the desired memory location.

The RTS instruction at the end of the program will cause the 68000 to stop executing the instructions of your program and return control to the *monitor* or *system program*. You can then use *system commands* to look at the contents of registers and memory locations or run another program. Without an instruction such as this at the end of the program, the 68000 would fetch and execute the code bytes for your program, and then it would go on fetching meaningless bytes from memory and trying to execute them as if they were code bytes.

The next major section of this chapter shows you how to construct the binary codes for these and other 68000 instructions so that you can assemble and run the programs on a development board such as the URDA MDS. First, however, we want to use Figure 3-4 to make an important point about writing assembly language programs.

DOCUMENTATION

In a previous section of this chapter we stressed the point that you should do a lot of thinking and carefully write the algorithm for a program before you start writing instruction statements. You should also document the program itself, so that its operation is clear to you and to anyone else who needs to understand it.

Each page of the program should contain the name of the program, the page number, the name of the programmer, and perhaps a version number. Each program or procedure should have a heading block that

| PROGRAMMER | A.L. Rood | | | SHEET | 1 | OF | 1 |

| PROGRAM TITLE | READ TEMPERATURE & CORRECT | | | | 8/26/91 |

ABSTRACT: This program reads in a temperature value from a sensor connected to a port at address $4100, adds a correction factor of +7 to the value read in, and then stores the result in a reserved memory location.

SUBROUTINES: None called.
REGISTERS: A0,A1,D0
MEMORY: $4200 – Data; $4000–$4013 – Code

ADDRESS	DATA/CODE	LABELS	MNEM.	OPERAND(S)	COMMENTS
$4200					result mem.
			ORG	$4000	start code
$4000	207C		MOVEA.L	#$4100,A0	point A0
2	0000				at I/0 port
4	4100				
6	227C		MOVEA.L	#$4200,A1	point A1
8	0000				at result
A	4200				memory loc.
C	1010		MOVE.B	(A0),D0	read temp
E	5E00		ADDQ.B	#7,D0	read temp
10	1280		MOVE.B	D0,(A1)	add correct.
12	4E75		RTS		to caller

FIGURE 3-4 Assembly language program on standard coding form.

contains an *abstract* describing what the program is supposed to do, which procedures it calls, which registers it uses, which ports it uses, which flags it affects, the memory used, and any other information that will make it easier for another programmer to interface with the program.

Comments should be used generously to describe the specific function of an instruction or group of instructions. Not every statement needs an individual comment. Comments should not just repeat the instruction mnemonic.

We cannot overemphasize the importance of clear, concise documentation in your programs. Experience has shown that even a short program that you wrote a month ago without comments may not be at all understandable to you now.

CONSTRUCTING THE MACHINE CODES FOR 68000 INSTRUCTIONS

This section shows you how to construct the binary codes for 68000 instructions. Most of the time you will probably let an assembler do this for you, but it is useful to understand how the codes are constructed. If you have a 68000-based prototyping board (such as the URDA 68000 MDS) available, knowing how to hand code instructions will enable you to code, enter, and run simple programs as you work your way through the 68000 instruction set examples in the next chapters.

Instruction Templates

To code the instructions for 8-bit processors such as the 6802, all you have to do is look up the hexadecimal code for each instruction on a simple chart. For the 68000 the process is not quite as simple. Here's why. There are 8 ways to specify the destination addressing mode of an instruction such as MOVE. The destination can also involve any one of 8 data registers. Each of the 64 possible destinations can be used with byte, word, or long-word data. The MOVE instruction source operand can use any one of 12 addressing modes and any one of 8 address registers. Furthermore, some of the MOVE instruction forms require extra words of immediate data specifying an absolute address or an index. Because there is such a large number of possible codes for the 68000 instructions, it is impractical to list them all in a simple table. Instead, we use a *template* for each basic instruction type and fill in bits within this template to indicate the desired addressing mode, data type, etc. In other words, we build up the instruction codes on a bit-by-bit basis.

The code templates for all the 68000 instructions are shown in Appendix B. As a first example of how to use these templates, we will build the code for the ADDQ.B #7,DO instruction from our example program. Figure 3-5a shows the template for this instruction. Note that 2 bytes are required for the instruction. The upper 4 bits of the upper byte (bits 15, 14, 13, and 12) tell the 68000 that this is an "add quick" instruction. Bits 11,

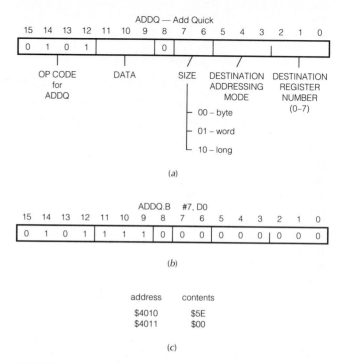

FIGURE 3-5   Coding template for 68000 ADDI instruction. (*a*) Template. (*b*) Example. (*c*) Hex codes in sequential memory locations.

10, and 9 contain the actual value to add, which must be 7 or less to fit in the 3 bits allowed. This instruction is called add quick because the value to add is contained in the instruction itself, so the add can be performed very quickly, without another memory or data access to get the value to add. Bit 8 is always set to 0. Bits 7 and 6 tell whether to add to a byte, a word, or a long word. For our example, make bit 7 a 0 and bit 6 a 0 to indicate a byte add. Make bit 7 a 0 and bit 6 a 1 to indicate a word add, and make bit 7 a 1 and bit 6 a 0 to indicate a long-word add. Bits 5 through 0 are used to specify the destination operand. That is, bits 5 through 0 indicate to what the 68000 is supposed to add 7. These 6 bits are found by looking them up in the *effective address encoding summary* of Figure 3-8. Bits 5, 4, and 3 tell what addressing mode to use. For the example instruction, we want the 68000 to add 7 directly to the value in data register 0. This is called *data register direct* addressing in the Motorola documentation. According to the table of Figure 3-8, the binary value 000 is used to indicate data register direct addressing. Make bit 5 a 0, bit 4 a 0, and bit 3 a 0. Bits 2, 1, and 0 specify the data register to use when the addressing mode is data register direct. In this case the register number is binary 000, so set bit 2 to 0, bit 1 to 0, and bit 0 to 0. Figure 3-5b shows the ADDQ template with all bits filled in. When the program is loaded into memory to be run, the first instruction byte will be put in one memory location and the second instruction byte will be put in the next. Figure 3-5c shows this in hexadecimal form as $E4, $05.

To illustrate further how these templates are used, we show several examples with the simple MOVE instruction. We then construct the codes for the example program in Figure 3-4. Other examples are shown as needed in the following chapters. Figure 3-6 shows the coding template or format for 68000 instructions that MOVE data from a register to a register, from a register to a memory location, from a memory location to a register, or from a memory location to a memory location. Note that at least 2 code bytes are required for the instruction.

The upper 2 bits of the first byte are an opcode that indicates the general type of instruction. These bits should both be set to 0 to tell the 68000 to perform a MOVE operation. Notice that the ADDQ opcode requires 4 bits, binary 0101, but the first 2 bits are not binary 00. The size field of the MOVE template uses bits 13 and 12. The MOVE instruction encodes the size differently than does the ADDQ instruction. Compare Figures 3-5*a* and 3-6 and note that the byte and word sizes are encoded differently.

The remaining 12 bits of the MOVE instruction are used to specify a source operand and a destination operand. Each operand requires 6 bits to specify. The 6 bits give the same type of information for the source and the destination operands, even though they are arranged slightly differently. Three bits are used to specify an effective addressing mode and 3 bits are used to specify the register number to use. The addressing mode implies whether an address register, a data register, or no register is to be used.

The 6 bits that specify the source operand in the MOVE instruction are arranged differently than are the 6 bits that specify the destination operand. The mode bits and the register number bits are swapped. The source requires 3 mode bits then 3 register number bits, whereas the destination requires 3 register numbers bits and then 3 mode bits. This ordering of bits is easiest for the CPU to process in an efficient manner.

The addressing mode portions of the MOVE instruction specify how the 68000 will compute the addresses

Addressing Modes	Syntax
Register Direct Addressing	
Data Register Direct	Dn
Address Register Direct	An
Absolute Data Addressing	
Absolute Short	xxx.W
Absolute Long	xxx.L
Program Counter Relative Addressing	
Relative with Offset	d_{16}(PC)
Relative with Index Offset	d_8(PC,Xn)
Register Indirect Addressing	
Register Indirect	(An)
Postincrement Register Indirect	(An)+
Predecrement Register Indirect	–(An)
Register Indirect with Offset	d_{16}(An)
Indexed Register Indirect with Offset	d_8(An,Xn)
Immediate Data Addressing	
Immediate	#xxx
Quick Immediate	#1-#8
Implied Addressing	
Implied Register	SR/USP/SP/PC

NOTES:
DN   = Data Register
An   = Address Register
Xn   = Address or Data Register used as Index Register
SR   = Status Register
PC   = Program Counter
SP   = Stack Pointer
USP = User Stack Pointer
( )   = Effective Address
d_8 = 8-Bit Offset (Displacement)
d_{16} = 16-Bit Offset (Displacement
#xxx = Immediate Data

FIGURE 3-7   Motorola MC68000 effective addressing modes and their assembly language syntax.

of the operands it requires. The 68000 provides 14 different addressing modes, but not all are available in all parts of all instructions. Figure 3-6 shows which addressing modes can be used for the source and the destination operands of the MOVE instruction. The following briefly describes each of the addressing modes available on the 68000 (see Figure 3-7). Please refer to Figures 3-8 and 3-9 as you read these descriptions.

1. *Data Register Direct.* In this addressing mode, the desired data value is held in one of the data

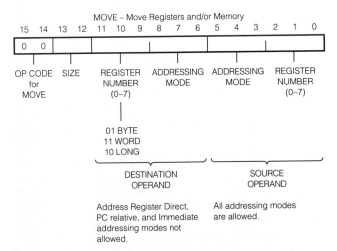

FIGURE 3-6   Coding template for 68000 instructions which MOVE data between registers, between a register and a memory location, or between memory locations.

Addressing Mode	Mode	Register
Data Register Direct	000	Register Number
Address Register Direct	001	Register Number
Address Register Indirect	010	Register Number
Address Register Indirect with Postincrement	011	Register Number
Address Register Indirect with Predecrement	100	Register Number
Address Register Indirect with Displacement	101	Register Number
Address Register Indirect with Index	110	Register Number
Absolute Short	111	000
Absolute Long	111	001
Program Counter with Displacement	111	010
Program Counter with Index	111	011
Immediate	111	100

FIGURE 3-8   Motorola MC68000 effective addressing mode encoding summary.

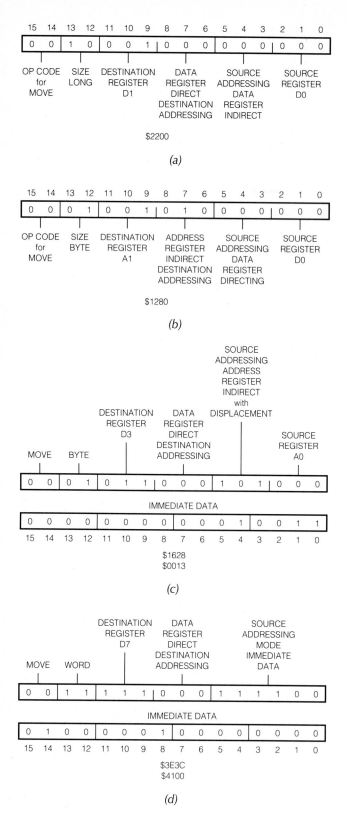

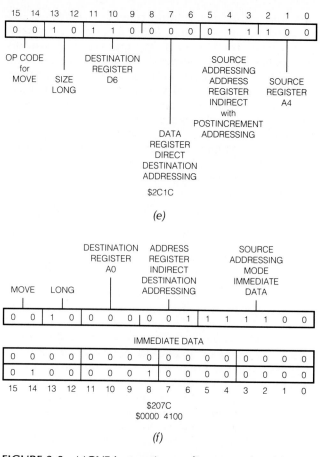

FIGURE 3-9 MOVE instruction coding examples. (a) MOVE.L D0,D1. (b) MOVE.B D0,(A1). (c) MOVE.B $13(A0),D3. (d) MOVE.W #$4100,D7. (e) MOVE.L (A4)+,D6. (f) MOVEA.L #$4100,A0.

registers. The data does not have a memory address but rather is associated with a register number between 0 and 7.

2. *Address Register Direct.* In this addressing mode the desired data value is held in one of the address registers. The data does not have a memory address but rather is associated with a register number between 0 and 7.

3. *Address Register Indirect.* In this addressing mode the address of the desired data value is held in one of the address registers. The value of the address register is used as a memory address, and the data value at that memory address is the desired operand. The address register is said to point to the desired memory location. Here indirect means that the address register does not directly contain the data value desired; instead, it contains the memory address of the desired data. The 68000 will use this address indirectly to find the desired data value by sending the address to system RAM and receiving the desired data value back from the RAM. In assembly language, parentheses are used to indicate *indirection*, which means that we do not want the value in a register; rather, we want the value in memory whose address is in that register. For example, (A1) is used to indicate address register indirect addressing, where address register 1 contains the address of the desired data in memory.

4. *Address Register Indirect with Postincrement.* This addressing mode is the same as the address register indirect mode except that the address register is incremented following the memory access, which loads the desired data. For example (A1)+ means A1 contains an address that is to be used to access the desired data, and after the data is moved to the destination, A1 has 1, 2, or 4 added to it, depending on whether the instruction operates on byte, word, or long data. This addressing mode is useful when manipulating stacks in memory. Stacks are explained in detail in later chapters.

5. *Address Register Indirect with Predecrement.* This addressing mode is the same as the address register indirect addressing mode except that the address register is decremented before the desired data is moved. For example −(A1) in byte mode means subtract 1 from the value in A1 and use the resulting value as the memory address of the desired data byte.

6. *Address Register Indirect with Displacement.* In this addressing mode the specified displacement is added to the specified address register, and the resulting value is used as the memory address of the desired data. The displacement is a 16-bit value, which is placed in the word in memory immediately following the instruction word. For example, #$4100(A0) means add hex 4100 to the value in A0 and use the result as the memory address of the desired data. This addressing mode can be used to access variables a given distance above or below the current top of a stack or stack mark.

7. *Address Register Indirect with Index.* In this addressing mode the index register can be any one of the data or address registers. This addressing mode also uses a displacement, as described in the previous addressing mode, but it uses an 8-bit displacement rather than a 16-bit displacement. The desired memory address is computed by adding the value in the index register to the value in the specified address register and then adding the displacement to the result and using this final value as the memory address of the desired value.

This addressing mode may sound very complex, but it is useful for manipulating tables of data as they are represented in computer memory. The index register can contain a row number or offset, and the displacement can be used to skip over a header in front of the table. The header might contain the table's name, for example. That is, #$100(D1,A0) means add the value in D1 to the value in A0, add hex 100 to the result, and use that as the memory address of the desired data.

8. *Absolute Short.* In this addressing mode the address of the desired data is placed in the word in memory following the instruction word. This ad-

dressing mode can only access the first 2^{16}, or 65,536, bytes of memory.

9. *Absolute Long.* In this addressing mode the address of the desired data is placed in the two words (long word) immediately following the instruction word in memory. In Motorola terms, this addressing mode requires two words of extension.

10. *Program Counter with Displacement.* This addressing mode is the same as the address register indirect addressing mode except that the program counter is used in place of an address register.

11. *Program Counter with Index.* This addressing mode is the same as the address register indirect with index except that the program counter is used in place of an address register. This and the previous addressing mode are useful when writing code that is position-independent. Position independent code can be moved about in memory yet still operate properly.

12. *Immediate Data.* In the immediate data addressing mode, the desired data itself is placed in memory immediately following the instruction word. If the desired data values are known beforehand, then this addressing mode can be used; separate data memory does not need to be reserved and addressed to move the desired data to the destination.

The last two addressing modes are not shown in Figure 3-8 because they are used only in certain special instructions. When these last two modes are used, the instruction opcode will say which of the two modes is required. These last two special modes are as follows.

13. *Immediate Quick Data.* In the immediate quick addressing mode, the data itself is stored in the same word in memory as the instruction. Since the instruction requires many of the word's bits to represent the desired operation, the immediate quick data must be represented in only 3 bits. This means that the immediate data value must be between 0 and 7.

14. *Implicit Reference.* Implicit reference is different from the preceding addressing modes in that addressing is not really required. The instruction ANDI.W #$0700,SR directs that the value 0700 hexadecimal should be logically ANDed together with the status register. The status register is the destination. It does not have a memory address associated with it. The destination address is implicit in the instruction encoding.

Several of these addressing modes require an additional value, either a displacement value or an immediate data value. When the MOVE instruction requires an additional value, that value is placed in memory immediately following the MOVE instruction word. These extra words are called *extension words.* For example, using absolute short addressing requires a 16-bit, or 1-word, extension. Absolute long requires two words of extension. A MOVE instruction with an absolute long source addressing mode and an absolute long destination addressing mode requires 1 plus 2 plus 2, or 5, words of memory. Two words are used for each absolute long extension and 1 word is used for the MOVE instruction itself.

Figure 3-8 shows how the register bits of an effective addressing mode do not always contain a register number. Some addressing modes such as absolute long do not use a register and therefore do not require a register number. These addressing modes all have the mode bits set to binary 111. These modes use the register number bits to specify which one among these special addressing modes to use.

MOVE Instruction Coding Examples

All the examples in this section use the MOVE instruction template in Figure 3-6. As you read through these examples, it is a good idea to keep track of the bit-by-bit development on a separate paper for practice.

MOVE.L D0,D1

The MOVE.L D0,D1 instruction will copy all 32 bits of register D0 into register D1. The instruction will require only one word of memory. The upper 2 bits will be binary 00. The size of the operand is long, so the next 2 bits will be binary 10, according to Figure 3-6. Both the source and destination are using data register direct addressing, encoded with a mode field of binary 000. The source register number is binary 000 and the destination register number is binary 001. Bits 11 through 6 indicate the destination register number and then the mode, so they will be binary 00 1000. Bits 5 through 0 specify the source register number and then the mode and will be set to binary 000000. Figure 3-9a shows that the final result of putting this all together is binary 0010 0010 0000 0000, or $2200.

MOVE.B D0,(A1)

The MOVE.B D0,(A1) instruction will copy 8 bits from the low byte of register D0 into the byte in memory whose address is in register A1. The MOVE opcode is binary 00 and the size is byte encoded as binary 01. The source addressing mode is data register direct encoded binary 000. The destination addressing mode is address register indirect, encoded binary 010. The source register number is binary 000, and the register used in the destination is address register number binary 001. Figure 3-9b shows how this instruction's encoding is put together to form $1280.

MOVE.B $13(A0),D3

The MOVE.B $13(A0),D3 instruction will move 1 byte of data into the low byte of data register 3. The source of the byte is the memory location whose address is equal to $13 plus the value in address register 0. The destination addressing mode is data register direct.

The source addressing mode is address register indirect with displacement. The displacement is $13 in this case; it is stored in the word in memory immediately following the MOVE instruction word. Figure 3-9c shows the 2 words as binary and as hexadecimal values.

MOVE.W #$4100,D7

The MOVE.W #$4100,D7 instruction moves one word of data directly from the instruction into the low word of data register 7. The destination addressing mode is data register direct. The source addressing mode is immediate data. The source specifies the actual data itself rather than specifying a memory address where the data is to be found. Since no address register is used, the bits in the instruction that normally specify the source register number are used to tell which of the special addressing modes to use. The addressing mode bits are binary 111, as with all the special modes, and the register number bits are binary 100, indicating the immediate data addressing mode. That is, the address specified is absolute and is 1 word long. The move operation itself is a word move, encoded binary 11. The opcode is 00, as with all MOVE instructions. See Figure 3-9d.

MOVE.L (A4)+,D6

The MOVE.L (A4)+,D6 instruction moves a long word (4 bytes) from the memory location whose address is in A4 into data register number 6. Address register is then incremented. Since the instruction data size is long, the address register has the value 4 added to it to perform the increment. The source addressing mode is address register indirect with postincrement, encoded as binary 011. The increment happens after the move. The destination addressing mode is data register direct. See Figure 3-9e.

MOVEA.L #$4100,A0

The MOVEA.L #$4100,A0 instruction moves 1 long word from the instruction itself into address register 0. Since the destination is an address register, the value being moved is an address. The MOVEA (move effective address) form of the MOVE instruction must be used to move addresses into address registers. Figure 3-9f shows how this instruction is encoded. Refer to the coding template for the MOVEA instruction found in Appendix B when encoding this instruction.

Coding the Example Program

As with the previous examples, it is a good idea to follow the bit-by-bit development of the instruction codes on a separate piece of paper for practice.

MOVEA.L #$4100,A0

The MOVEA.L #$4100,A0 instruction moves the value $4100 into address register number 0. The value is sign extended, so the value of A0 will be $00004100 after the instruction is executed. From Appendix B the opcode field is binary 00. The size is word, which is encoded as binary 11 for MOVEA. The destination register number is binary 000. The source addressing mode is immediate word data, which is encoded as binary 111100. For MOVEA, bits 8 through 6 are always binary 001. The final encoding for this is shown in Figure 3-9f.

MOVEA/L #$4200,A1

The MOVEA/L #$4200,A1 instruction is exactly the same as the previous instruction except that the destination register is A1 instead of A0, and the source immediate data is $4200 instead of $4100. There are only two bits in this encoding that differ from the previous instruction encoding.

MOVE.B (A0),D0

The MOVE.B (A0),D0 instruction moves 1 byte of data from the memory location whose address is in A0 into register D0. In our example the address $4100 has been placed in A0 by one of the preceding instructions. This address is presumed to be the address that corresponds to an I/O port, where we can read a temperature value from a sensor. The opcode encoding is binary 00 and the byte size encoding is binary 01. The destination addressing mode is data register direct, encoded as binary 000 using a data register number of binary 000. The source addressing mode is address register indirect, encoded as binary 010 using address register number binary 000. The full encoding of this instruction is $1010.

ADDQ.B #7,D0

The ADDQ.B #7,D0 instruction adds 7 to data register D0. It has been discussed in detail in previous sections. The instruction encoding is shown in Figure 3-5.

MOVE.B D0,(A1)

The MOVE.B D0,(A1) instruction moves 1 byte from register D0 to the memory location whose address is in register A1. The register was initialized previously to contain the address $4200. This is the memory address where the corrected temperature is to be saved. The source addressing mode is data register direct using D0, and the destination addressing mode is address register indirect using register A1. See if you can verify that the final instruction encoding is $1280.

SUMMARY OF HAND CODING THE EXAMPLE PROGRAM

Figure 3-4 shows the example program with all the instruction codes in sequential order as you would write them so that you could load the program into memory and run it. Codes are in HEX to save space.

A Few Words about Hand Coding

If you have to hand code 68000 assembly language programs, here are a few tips to make your life easier.

First, check your algorithm very carefully to make sure that it really does what it is supposed to do. Second, initially write just the assembly language statements and comments for your program. You can check the table in Appendix B to determine how many bytes each instruction takes so you know how many blank lines to leave between instruction statements. You may find it helpful to insert 3 or 4 NOP instructions after every 9 or 10 instructions. The NOP instruction doesn't do anything but kill time. However, if you accidentally leave out an instruction in your program, you can replace the NOPs with the needed instruction. This way you don't have to rewrite the entire program after the missing instruction.

After you have written the instruction statements, recheck very carefully to make sure you have the right instructions to implement your algorithm. Then, work out the binary codes for each instruction and write them in the appropriate places on the coding form.

Hand coding is laborious for long programs. When writing long programs, it is much more efficient to use an assembler. The next section of this chapter shows you how to write your programs so you can use an assembler to produce the machine codes for the instructions.

WRITING PROGRAMS FOR USE WITH AN ASSEMBLER

If you have a 68000 assembler available, you should learn to use it as soon as possible. Besides doing the tedious task of producing the binary codes for your instruction statements, an assembler also allows you to refer to data items by name rather than by numerical addresses. As you should soon see, this greatly reduces the work you have to do and makes your programs much more readable. In this section we show you how to write your programs so that you can use an assembler on them. The assemblers used for the programs in this book were the Raven® RV68k cross assembler for the 68000 CPU running on the IBM PC and the Consulair® MAC68000 assembler for the 68000 CPU running on the Apple Macintosh personal computer. A cross assembler is an assembler that runs on one computer but assembles code for another computer's CPU. If you are using another assembler, some features may be slightly different, so consult the manual for the assembler you are using.

Program Format

The best way to approach this section seems to be to show you a simple, but complete, program written for an assembler and explain the function of the various parts. By now you are probably tired of the "read temperature, add +7, and store result in memory" program, so we will use another example.

Figure 3-10 shows a 68000 assembly language program that multiplies two 16-bit binary numbers, with a 32-bit binary result. If you have a development

```
;   This program multiplies two 16-bit words in
;   the memory locations called MULTIPLICAND and
;   MULTIPLIER.  The result is stored in the memory
;   location called PRODUCT.
;
;PORTS USED               : none
;PROCEDURES USED          : none
;REGISTERS USED           : D0,D1
;
; Start code here
        ORG     $4000            ; Memory location where code is to start
        ABS_SHORT                ; use short addresses in absolute mode

        MOVE.W  (MULTIPLICAND),D0    ; get one word from memory
        MOVE.W  (MULTIPLIER),D1      ; get second word, the multiplier
        MULS    D1,D0                ; multiply signed 16-bit integers
                                     ; result is 32-bits long in D0
        MOVE.L  D0,(PRODUCT)         ; store result into memory

        RTS                          ; return to whoever called me

; End of code section

; Start the data here
        ORG     $4100            ; Memory location where data is to start

MULTIPLICAND:   DC.W    $204A        ; multiplicand value in memory
                                     ; location, stated in hex
MULTIPLIER:     DC.W    $3B2A        ; multiplier value
PRODUCT:        DC.L    0            ; initially the product's memory
                                     ; location will contain 0
; End of data
        END
```

FIGURE 3-10   Assembly language source program to multiply two 16-bit binary numbers to give a 32-bit result.

system or a computer with a 68000 assembler to work on, this is a good program for you to key in, assemble, and run in order to become familiar with the operation of your system. If you are working on a prototyping board such as the URDA MDS, you can construct the binary codes for each of the instructions, load the program into the onboard RAM, and run the program. In any case, you can use the structure of this example program as a model for your own programs.

In addition to program instructions, the example program in Figure 3-10 contains directions to the assembler. These directions to the assembler are commonly called *assembler directives* or *pseudo-operations*. A section at the end of Chapter 6 lists and describes a large number of the available assembler directives. Here we discuss the basic assembler directives you need to get started writing programs. We introduce more of these directives as we need them in the next two chapters.

ORG Directive

The ORG, or *origin*, directive is used to specify the origin in memory of the code or data that follows. The ORG directive is used only with the Raven 68000 cross assembler for the IBM PC. The ORG mnemonic should be followed by a space or spaces and then a number. This number is the memory address where the assembly language instructions that follow will be placed when the program is loaded into memory. The Raven cross assembler generates absolute code. By this we mean that the code contains absolute memory addresses and must be loaded into memory exactly where those addresses indicate.

The Consulair MAC68000 assembler, on the other hand, is a relative assembler, which generates relocatable code. The Consulair assembler does not use the ORG directive. The MAC68000 code can be placed anywhere in the 68000's memory—but only after it is properly linked and located in relation to the memory addresses where it will actually be loaded. The processes of linking and locating are discussed in greater detail later in this chapter.

Data and Address Naming Directives—EQU, DC, and DS

Programs work with three general categories of data—constants, variables, and addresses. The value of a constant does not change during the execution of the program. The number 7 is an example of a constant you might use in a program. A variable is the name given to a data item that can change during the execution of a program. The current temperature of an oven is an example of a variable. Addresses are referred to in many instructions. You may, for example, load an address into a register or jump to an address.

Constants, variables, and addresses used in your programs can be given names. This allows you to refer to them by name rather than having to remember or calculate their value each time you refer to them in an instruction. In other words, if you give names to constants, variables, and addresses, the assembler can use these names to find the desired data item or address when you refer to it in an instruction. Specific directives are used to give names to constants and variables in your programs. Labels are used to give names to addresses in your programs.

THE EQU DIRECTIVE

The EQU, or *equate*, directive assigns a name to constants used in your programs. The statement CORRECTION EQU $07 in a program such as our previous example tells the assembler to insert the value $07 every time that it finds the name CORRECTION in a program statement. In other words, when the assembler reads the statement ADD #CORRECTION,D0, it will automatically code the instruction as if you had written it ADD $07,D0. Here's the advantage of using an EQU directive to declare constants at the start of your program. Suppose that you use the correction factor of +$07 a total of 23 times in your program. Now the company for which you work changes brands of temperature sensor, and the new correction factor is +$09. If you used the number $07 in the 23 instructions that contain this correction factor, then you will have to go through the entire program, find each instruction that uses the correction factor, and update the value. Murphy's Law being what it is, you are likely to miss one or two of these, and the program won't work correctly. If you used an EQU at the start of your program and then referred to CORRECTION by name in the 23 instructions, all you have to do is change the value in the EQU statement from $07 to $09 and reassemble the program. The assembler will automatically insert the new value of $09 in all 23 instructions.

> NOTE: In large programs consisting of modules assembled separately, constants must be declared in each module. The assembler has no way of remembering an EQU value from one module when it assembles another module.

DC.B, DC.W, AND DC.L DIRECTIVES

The DC.B, DC.W, and DC.L (*declare constant*) directives are used to assign names to variables in your programs. The DC.B directive after a name specifies that the data is of *type byte*. The program statement OVEN_TEMPERATURE DC.B 27, for example, declares a variable of type byte and gives it the name OVEN_TEMPERATURE. DC.W is used to specify that the data is of *type word* (16 bits), and DC.L is used to specify that the data is of *type long word* (32 bits). If a number is written after the DC.B, DC.W, or DC.L, the data item will be *initialized* with that value when the program is loaded from disk into RAM. The statement CONVERSION_FACTORS DC.B $27,$48,$32,$69 will declare a data item of 4 bytes and initialize the 4 bytes with the specified 4 values. Note that data variables that are changed during the program should also be initialized with program instructions so that the program can be rerun from the start without reloading it to initialize variables. Figure 3-10 shows three more examples of naming and initializing data items.

The first example, MULTIPLICAND DC.W $204A, declares a data word named MULTIPLICAND and initializes that data word with the value $204A. What this means is that the assembler sets aside two successive memory locations and assigns the name MULTIPLICAND to the first location. As you will see, this allows us to access the data in these memory locations by name. The MULTIPLICAND DC.W $204A statement also indicates that when the final program is loaded into memory to be run, these memory locations will be loaded with (initialized to) $204A. Since this is a Motorola microprocessor, the first address in memory will contain the high byte of the word, $20, and the second memory address will contain the low byte of the word, $4A.

If the program's data is eventually put in ROM or EPROM, then MULTIPLICAND will function as a constant, because it cannot be changed during program execution. However, if the data is eventually put in RAM, then MULTIPLICAND can function as a variable because a new value could be written into those memory locations during program execution.

The second data declaration example in Figure 3-10, MULTIPLIER DC.W $3B2A, sets aside storage for a word in memory and gives the starting address of this word the name MULTIPLIER. When the program is loaded, the first memory address will be initialized with $3B, and the second memory location will be initialized with $2A.

The third data declaration example in Figure 3-10, PRODUCT DC.L 0, sets aside storage for 1 long word in memory and gives the starting address of the first byte the name PRODUCT. The 0 part of the statement tells the assembler to initialize the two words to all zeros. When we multiply two 16-bit binary numbers, the product can be as large as 32 bits. Therefore, we must set aside this much space to store the product. We could have used the DC.W directive to declare PRODUCT as 2 words or the DC.B directive to declare PRODUCT as 4 bytes. Since, in the program, we move the result to PRODUCT in one long-word MOVE instruction, it is more convenient to declare PRODUCT as 1 long word.

Figure 3-11 shows how the data for MULTIPLICAND, MULTIPLIER, and PRODUCT are actually arranged in memory starting from the base of the ORG $4100 address. Addresses in Figure 3-11 start small and grow larger as we move down the page. Reading down, in

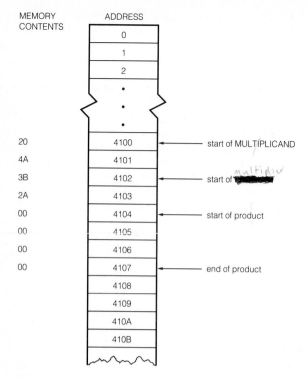

MEMORY CONTENTS	ADDRESS	
	0	
	1	
	2	
	•	
	•	
	•	
20	4100	← start of MULTIPLICAND
4A	4101	
3B	4102	← start of multiplier
2A	4103	
00	4104	← start of product
00	4105	
00	4106	
00	4107	← end of product
	4108	
	4109	
	410A	
	410B	

FIGURE 3-11   Data arrangement in memory for multiply program.

terms of increasing memory addresses, the values in memory appear as they would when written. On Intel CPUs the byte order is reversed, so Intel pictures often are drawn with memory addresses decreasing as we move down the page.

THE DS DIRECTIVE

The DS.B, DS.W, and DS.L (*define storage*) directives tell the assembler to reserve a block of storage area. For example the directive BLOCK_1 DS.B 1000 will reserve a block of 1000 bytes of storage, and BLOCK_1 will be the symbolic address (the name) of the first byte of this block of storage. The block of data might be used to store 1000 temperature readings. This is much more convenient than attempting to use a DC.B directive followed by 1000 zeros. The DS.W and DS.L directives reserve blocks of words and long words, respectively.

Types of Numbers You Can Use in Data Statements

All the previous examples of DC.B, DC.W, and DC.L declarations use hexadecimal numbers, as indicated by a "$" before the number. You can, however, put in a number in any one of several other forms. In each case, you must tell the assembler which form you use.

BINARY %

For example, when you use a binary number in a statement, you put a "%" before the string of 1s and 0s to let the assembler know that you want the number to be treated as a binary number. The statement TEMP_

MAX DC.B %01111001 is an example. If you want to put in a negative binary number, write the number in its 2's complement sign-and-magnitude form.

OCTAL

To indicate that you want a number to be evaluated as base-8, or octal, put a "0" before the string of octal digits. The statement OLD_COMPUTER DC.W 017341 is an example.

NOTE: The Raven cross assembler does not support octal notation.

DECIMAL

The assembler treats a number with no identifying letter after it as a decimal number. In other words, if you forget to put a $ before a number that you want the assembler to treat as hexadecimal, the assembler will treat it as a decimal number. The assembler automatically converts a decimal number in a statement to binary so the value can be loaded into memory. The statement TEMPERATURE_MAX DC.B 49 is an example. If you indicate a negative number in a data declaration statement, the assembler will convert the number to its 2's complement sign-and-magnitude form. For example, given the statement TEMP_MIN DC.B −20, the assembler will insert the binary value 11101100, which is the 2's complement representation for −20 decimal.

HEXADECIMAL

As shown in several previous examples, a hexadecimal number is indicated by a $ before the hexadecimal digits (for example, MULTIPLIER DC.W $3B2A).

ASCII

ASCII characters can be put in data declaration statements by enclosing them in quotation marks. For example, the statement BOY_1 DC.B 'ALBERT' tells the assembler to set aside six memory locations named BOY_1. It also tells the assembler to put the ASCII code for A in the first memory location, the ASCII code for L in the second, the ASCII code for B in the third, etc. The assembler will automatically determine the ASCII codes for the letters or numbers within the quotes.

NOTE: ASCII is normally used only with the DC.B directive.

DECIMAL REAL AND HEXADECIMAL REAL

Decimal and hexadecimal real are used to represent noninteger numbers such as 3.14159. We discuss how these are used in Chapter 11.

Accessing Named Data with Program Instructions

Now that we have shown you how the data structure is set up, let's look at how program instructions access this data. Find the instruction MOVE.W (MULTIPLI-CAND),D0 in the code section of the program in Figure 3-10. This instruction, when executed, will copy a word from memory to the D0 register. When the assembler reads through this program the first time, it will automatically calculate the address of each of the named data items. Referring to Figure 3-11, you can see that the address of MULTIPLICAND is $4100. This is because MULTIPLICAND is the first data item declared after the ORG $4100 directive. When the assembler reads the program the second time to produce the binary codes for the instructions, it will insert this address as part of the binary code for the instruction MOVE.W (MULTIPLICAND),D0. Since we know that the address of MULTIPLICAND is $4100, we could have written the instruction as MOVE.W ($4100),D0. However, there would be a problem if we later changed the program by adding another data item before MULTIPLICAND but after the ORG $4100 directive because the address of MULTIPLICAND would be changed. Therefore, we would have to remember to go through the entire program and correct the address in all instructions that access MULTI-PLICAND. If you use a name to refer to each data item as shown, the assembler will automatically calculate the correct address of that data item for you and insert this address each time you refer to it in an instruction.

To summarize how this works, then, the instruction MOVE.W (MULTIPLICAND),D0 is an example of absolute addressing, where the absolute address is represented by a name. For instructions such as this, the assembler will automatically calculate the address of the named data item and insert this value as part of the binary code for the instruction.

The next instruction in the program in Figure 3-10 is another example of absolute addressing using a named data item. The instruction MOVE.W (MULTI-PLIER),D1 moves the word named MULTIPLIER from memory into register D1. This operates just as does the previous MOVE instruction, except that the assembler will calculate the address of MULTIPLIER as $4102.

The next instruction, MULS D1,D0, multiplies the low word of D1 times the low word of D0 and places the resulting 32-bit product into D0.

The next instruction in the program in Figure 3-10, MOVE.L D0, (PRODUCT), copies the long-word result from D0 to memory. The highest byte of D0 will be copied to a memory location named PRODUCT. The second-highest byte of D0 will be copied to the next-higher address, which we can refer to as PRODUCT + 1. The second-lowest byte of the product will go into PRODUCT + 2, and the lowest byte will go into PROD-UCT + 3.

Figure 3-11 shows how the two words of the product are put in memory. Note that the higher byte of a word is always put in the lower memory address.

This example program should show you that if you are using an assembler, names are a very convenient way of specifying the direct address of data in memory.

Naming Addresses—Labels

Names representing addresses are called *labels*. They are written in the label field of an instruction statement or a directive statement. We have seen labels used before with the DC and DS directives to name variable memory locations. Another major use of labels is to represent the destination for jump and call instructions. Suppose, for example, we want the 68000 to jump back to some previous instruction over and over. Instead of computing the numerical address to which we want to jump, we put a label next to the instruction to which we want to jump and write the jump instruction as JMP label. Here is a specific example.

```
NEXT: MOVE.B ($4100),D0    ; Get data sample from
                           ; port.
    .                      ; Process data value
                           ; read in.
    .

    JMP NEXT               ; Get next data value
                           ; and process.
```

If you use a label to represent an address as shown in this example, the assembler will automatically calculate the address that needs to be put in the code for the jump instruction. The next two chapters show many examples of the use of labels with jump and call instructions.

We will now discuss some other parts of the example program that you will need to use in your programs.

The ABS_LONG and ABS_SHORT Directives

The ABS_LONG and ABS_SHORT, or *absolute long* and *absolute short*, directives are used only with the Raven cross assembler. These directives tell the assembler whether to use long or word (short) addresses in absolute addressing modes. ABS_LONG directs the assembler to generate 32-bit (long) absolute addresses. ABS_SHORT directs the assembler to generate 16-bit (short, or word) absolute addresses.

The END Directive

The END directive, as the name implies, tells the assembler to stop reading. Any instructions or statements that you write after the END directive will be ignored. An END directive is required in each assembly language program.

ASSEMBLY LANGUAGE PROGRAM DEVELOPMENT TOOLS

Introduction

For all but the very simplest assembly language programs, you will probably want to use some type of *microcomputer development system* and *program development tools* to make your work easier. Such systems range from units such as the Intel Series IV Microprocessor Development System shown in Figure 3-12 to the ubiquitous IBM PC. These systems usually contain several hundred kilobytes of RAM, a keyboard, a video display, floppy and/or hard disk drives, a printer, and perhaps an emulator. The following sections give you an introduction to several common program development tools that you use with these systems. Most of these tools are programs that you run to perform some function on the program you are writing. You will have to consult the manuals for your system to get the specific details for it, but this section should give you an overview of the steps involved in developing an assembly language microcomputer program using a system. An accompanying laboratory manual guides you through the use of some of these tools with the URDA MDS board and either the IBM PC or the Apple Macintosh PC.

Editor

An *editor* is a program that, when run on a system, lets you type in the assembly language statements for your program. Examples of editors are ALTER, which runs on INTEL systems, EDLIN, which runs on IBM PCs, and Wordstar, which runs on most systems. The main function of an editor is to help you construct your assembly language program in just the right format so that the assembler will translate it correctly to machine language. Figure 3-10 shows an example of the format you should use when typing in your program. This form of your program is called the *source program.* The actual position of each field on a line is not important, but you must put the fields of each statement in the correct order, and you must leave at least one blank between fields. Whenever possible, we like to line the fields up in columns so that it is easier to read the program.

As you type in your program, the editor stores the

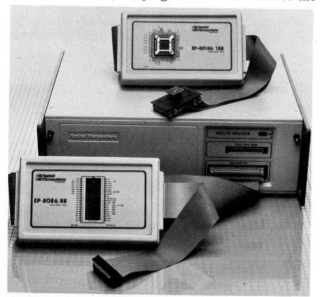

FIGURE 3-12   Photograph of Intel Services IV Microprocessor Development System. (*Intel Corp.*)

ASCII codes for the letters and numbers in successive RAM locations. If you make a typing error, the editor will let you back up and correct it. If you leave out a program statement, the editor will let you move everything down and insert the line. This is much easier than working with pencil and paper, even if you type very slowly.

When you have typed in all your program, you then copy it from memory to a file on a floppy or hard magnetic disk. This file, such as the one in Figure 3-10, is called a *source file.* If you later find that your program contains errors, you can use the editor to load the source file back into RAM and make the needed corrections in the source program.

Assembler

An *assembler* program is used to translate assembly language mnemonics to the correct binary code for each instruction. The assembler will read the source file of your program from the disk where you saved it after editing. An assembler usually reads your source file more than once. On the first pass through the source program, the assembler finds everything. It determines the displacement of named data items and the offset of labels and puts this information in a *symbol table.* On a second pass through the source program, the assembler produces the binary code for each instruction and assigns addresses to each.

The assembler generates two files on the floppy or hard disk. The first file is called the *object file.* The object file contains the binary codes for the instructions and information about the addresses of the instructions. This file contains the information that will eventually be loaded into memory and executed. The second file generated by the assembler is called the *assembler list file.* Figure 3-13 shows the assembler list file for the source program in Figure 3-10. This file contains the assembly language statements, the binary codes for each instruction, and the offset for each instruction. You usually send this file to a printer so that you will have a printout of the entire program to work with when you are testing and troubleshooting the program. The assembler listing will also indicate any typing or syntax (assembly language grammar) errors you made in typing in your source program.

> NOTE: The assembler will not tell you if you made a programming error. You usually have to run the program to find these. To correct the errors indicated on the listing, you use the editor to reedit your source program and save the corrected source program on disk. You then reassemble the corrected source program. It may take several times through the edit-assemble loop before you get all the syntax errors out of your source program.

Now let's take a look at some of the information given on the assembler listing. The leftmost column in the listing gives the addresses of data items and the addresses of code bytes as they will be loaded into

```
1:                                          ;
2:                                          ;   Figure 3-10
3:                                          ;
4:                                          ;   This program multiplies two 16-bit words in
5:                                          ;   the memory locations called MULTIPLICAND and
6:                                          ;   MULTIPLIER. The result is store in the memory
7:                                          ;   location called PRODUCT.
8:                                          ;
9:                                          ;PORTS USED              :  none
10:                                         ;PROCEDURES USED  :  none
11:                                         ;REGISTERS USED          :  D0,D1,D0
12:                                         ;
13:                                         ;   Start code here
14:  00004000                              ORG      $4000                          ;  Memory location where code is to start
15:
16:  00004000  207C  0000  4101            MOVEA.L  #PRODUCT,A0                    ;  address of memory to save product
17:  00004006  303C  4100                  MOVE.W   #MULTIPLICAND,D0              ;  get one word from memory
18:  0000400A  323C  4102                  MOVE.W   #MULTIPLIER,D1               ;  get second word, the multiplier
19:  0000400E  C1C1                        MULS     D1,D0                          ;  multiply signed 16-bit integers
20:                                                                                ;  result is 32-bits long in D0
21:  00004010  2080                        MOVE.L   D0,(A0)                       ;  store result into memory
22:
23:  00004012  4E75                        RTS                                    ;  return to whoever called me
24:
25:                                         ;   End of code section
26:
27:                                         ;   Start the data here
28:  00004100                              ORG      $4100                          ;  Memory location where data is to start
29:
30:  00004100  204A                        MULTIPLICAND:      DC.W    $204A        ;  multiplicand value in memory
31:                                                                                ;  location, stated in hex
32:  00004102  3B2A                        MULTIPLIER:        DC.W    $3B2A        ;  multiplier value
33:  00004104  0000  0000                  PRODUCT:  DC.L    0                     ;  initially the product's memory
34:                                                                                ;  location will contain 0
35:                                         ;   End of data
36:  00004108                              END
Symbol Name                     Attribute       Hex          Decimal
MULTIPLICAND.....................LABEL          00004100     16640
MULTIPLIER.......................LABEL          00004102     16642
PRODUCT .........................LABEL          00004104     16644
Obj bytes: 28D/0000001CH
End assembly.  Lines: 36  Errors: 0
```

FIGURE 3-13   Assembler listing for example program in Figure 3-10.

memory. Note that the Raven RV68k assembler generates absolute physical addresses. The Consulair MAC68000 assembler, on the other hand, does not generate absolute addresses. On the Macintosh, a linker or locator will do this later. On the MAC68000 listing, the addresses shown are relative. Also note that the MOVE (MULTIPLICAND),D0 statement is assembled by the MAC68000 assembler with some blanks after the basic instruction code. This is done because the absolute address where MULTIPLICAND starts is not known at the time the program is assembled.

The trailer section of the listing in Figure 3-13 gives some additional information about the names used in the program. The statement

PRODUCT . . . LABEL 00004104 16644

for example, tells you that MULTIPLICAND is a label that corresponds to memory address $00004104, which is equal to decimal 16644.

Linker

A *linker* is a program used to join together several object files into one large object file. When writing large programs, it is usually much more efficient to divide the large program into smaller *modules*. Each module can be individually written, tested, and debugged.

When all the modules work, they can be linked together to form a large, functioning program. Also, the object modules for useful programs—a square root program, for example—can be kept in a *library file* and linked into other programs as needed.

The linker produces a *link file*, which contains the binary codes for all the combined modules. The linker also produces a *link map* file, which contains the address information about the linked files. The linker, however, does not assign absolute addresses to the program; it assigns only relative addresses starting from zero. This form of the program is said to be *relocatable* because it can be put anywhere in memory to be run. If you are going to run your program on a system such as the Apple Macintosh, you can just load the link file into memory and run it. If you are going to run your program on a system such as the URDA MDS, then you must use a *locator program* to assign absolute addresses to the linker file.

Locator

A *locator* is a program used to assign the specific addresses at which the object code is to be loaded into memory. A locator program that comes with the IBM PC DOS is called EXE2BIN. Here's how you proceed if you want to produce a program with absolute addresses that you can download to an URDA MDS from an

IBM PC. First, build a source (.ASM) file using the EDLIN or perhaps the WORDSTAR editor; for example, you can create the source file EX1.ASM. Assemble the source file with the Raven RV68k assembler using, for example, RV68K EX1. Once the assembly completes the file, EX1.OBJ will have been created. This object (.OBJ) file contains the absolute binary codes corresponding to the EX1.ASM program.

On the Apple Macintosh, follow this procedure to produce a program with absolute addresses that you can download to an URDA MDS. Use the editor provided with the MAC68000 assembler system to create an assembly language file—for example, Exl.Asm. Using the transfer menu, select the assembler and assemble the file to create a relocatable file Exl.Rel. A linker control file, Exl.Link, is also created by the assembler. Select and open the linker control file, Exl.Link. The linker will produce the final application code as file Exl using the relocatable file Exl.Rel. The Exl file can be downloaded into the URDA MDS.

In most systems a single program performs both the link and the locate functions.

Debugger

If your program requires no external hardware or requires only hardware accessible directly from your system, then you can use a *debugger* to run and debug your program. A debugger is a program that allows you to load your object code program into system memory, execute the program, and troubleshoot, or debug, it. The debugger allows you to look at the contents of registers and memory locations after your program runs. It allows you to change the contents of registers and memory locations and rerun the program. Some debuggers allow you stop execution after each instruction so you can check or alter memory and register contents. A debugger also allows you to set a *breakpoint* at any point in your program. When you run the program, the system will execute instructions up to this breakpoint and stop. You can then examine register and memory contents to see if the results are correct at that point. If the results are correct, you can move the breakpoint to a later point in the program. If the results are not correct, you can check the program up to that point to find out why they are not correct. The debugger tools can help you isolate a problem in your program. Once you find the problem, you can then cycle back and correct the algorithm, if necessary. You then use the editor to correct your source program, reassemble the corrected source program, relink, and run the program again.

Microprocessor prototyping boards such as the URDA MDS contain a debugger program in ROM. On boards such as this, the debugger is commonly called a *monitor program* because it lets you monitor program activity. The URDA MDS monitor program, for example, lets you enter and run programs, single-step through programs, examine register and memory contents, and insert breakpoints. The MACDB® and MACSbug® programs, used with the Apple Macintosh, allow you to do the same functions and also provide a trace function, which shows you the contents of all the registers after each instruction executes.

Emulator

Another way to run your program is with an *emulator*. An emulator is a mixture of hardware and software. It is generally used to test and debug the hardware and software of an external system such as the prototype of a microprocessor-based instrument. Part of the hardware of an emulator is a multiwire cable, which connects the host system to the system being developed. A plug at the end of the cable is plugged into the prototype in place of its microprocessor. Through this connection the software of the emulator allows you to download your object-code program into RAM in the system being tested and run it. As with a debugger, an emulator allows you to load and run programs, examine and change the contents of registers, examine and change the contents of memory locations, and insert breakpoints in the program. The emulator also takes a "snapshot" of the contents of registers, activity on the address and data bus, and flags as each instruction executes. The emulator stores this *trace data,* as it is called, in a large RAM. You can do a printout of the trace data to see the results that your program produced on a step-by-step basis.

Another powerful feature of an emulator is the ability to use either system memory or the memory on the prototype for the program you are debugging. In a later chapter we discuss in detail the use of an emulator in developing a microprocessor-based product.

Summary of the Use of Program Development Tools

Figure 3-14 shows in diagram form the order in which you will use the program development tools we have described. The first and most important step is think very carefully what you want the program to do and how you want the program to do it. Next, use an editor to create the source file for your program. Assemble the source file with the assembler. If the assembler list file indicates any errors in your program, use the editor to correct these errors. Cycle through the edit-assemble loop until the assembler tells you on the listing that it found no errors. If your program consists of several modules, then use the linker to join their object modules together into one large object module.

NOTE: On some systems, such as the Apple Macintosh, you must use the linker even if your program has only one module.

If your system requires it, use the locate program to specify where in memory you want your program to be put. Your program is now ready to be loaded into memory and run. If your program does not interact with any external hardware other than that connected

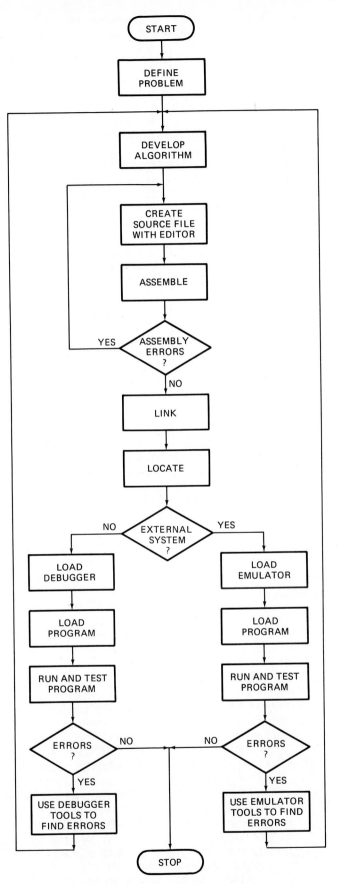

FIGURE 3-14   Program development algorithm.

directly to the system, then you can use the system debugger to run and debug your program. If your program is intended to work with external hardware, such as the prototype of a microprocessor-based instrument, then you will probably use an emulator to run and debug your program. We discuss and show the use of these program development tools throughout the rest of this book, but this section should give you an overview.

CHECKLIST OF IMPORTANT TERMS AND CONCEPTS IN THIS CHAPTER

If there are terms in this list you do not remember, use the index to find them in the chapter.

Algorithm

Sequential task list

Flowcharts and flowchart symbols

Structured programming

Pseudocode

Top-down and bottom-up design

Sequence, repetition, and decision operations

IF-THEN-ELSE, IF-THEN, WHILE-DO, REPEAT-UNTIL, and CASE structures

68000 instruction types

Mnemonics

Initialization list

Standard program format

Documentation

Instruction template

    Opcode
    Size
    Mode
    Register number

Effective addressing modes

Assembler

Assembler directives: ORG, EQU, DC, DS, ABS_LONG, ABS_SHORT, and END

Named data items

Development tools

Editor

Linker

    Library file
    Link files
    Link map
    Relocatable locator

Debugger, monitor program

Emulator, trace data

1. List the major steps in developing an assembly language program.

2. What is the main advantage of a top-down design approach to solving a programming problem?

3. Why is it necessary to develop a detailed algorithm for a program before writing any assembly language instructions?

4. a. What are the three basic structure types used when writing programs?
   b. What is the advantage of using only these structures when writing the algorithm for a program?

5. A program is like a recipe. Use a flowchart or pseudocode to show the algorithm for the following recipe. The operations in it are sequence and repetition. Instead of implementing the resulting algorithm in assembly language, implement it in your microwave and use the result to help you get through the rest of the book.

   Peanut Brittle

1 c sugar	1 tsp butter
0.5 c white corn syrup	1 tsp vanilla
1 c unsalted peanuts	1 tsp baking soda

   1. Put sugar and syrup in 1.5-q casserole (with handle) and stir until thoroughly mixed.
   2. Microwave on *high* for 4 min.
   3. Add peanuts and stir until thoroughly mixed.
   4. Microwave on *high* for 4 min. Add butter and vanilla, stir until well mixed, and microwave on *high* for 2 min more.
   5. Add baking soda and gently stir until the mixture is light and foamy. Pour mixture onto nonstick cookie sheet and let it cool for 1 h. When cool, break into pieces. Makes 1 lb.

6. Use a flowchart or pseudocode to show the algorithm for a program that gets a 1-byte number from a memory location, subtracts $20 from it, and outputs $01 to a port at address $3A00 if the result of the subtraction is greater than $25.

7. Given the register contents in Figure 3-15, answer the following questions.
   a. From what address will the next instruction be fetched?
   b. What is the address for the top of the stack?

8. Describe the operation and results of each of the following instructions, given the register contents shown in Figure 3-15. Include in your answer the physical address or register from which each in-

REGISTER	CONTENTS
D0	0000 0001
D1	7004 3333
D2	0000 0002
D3	1010 1010
D4	0000 0004
D5	FFFF FFFF
D6	FFFF FFFE
D7	0000 0007
A0	0000 4108
A1	0000 4104
A2	0000 4102
A3	0000 4100
A4	0000 4FF0
A5	0000 4200
A6	0000 4100
USP A7	0000 7EB0
SSP A7'	0000 7EB0
SR	0072
PC	0000 4000

MEMORY ADDRESS	CONTENTS
4100	0102 0304
4104	0506 0708
4108	090A 0B0C
410C	0D0E 0F10
4110	1112 1314

FIGURE 3-15   68000 register and memory contents for problem 10.

struction will get its operands and the physical address or register in which each instruction will put the result. Use the instruction descriptions in Chapter 6 to help you. Assume that the following instructions are independent, not sequential, unless they are listed together under a single letter.

a.	MOVE.L A3,D1	b.	MOVE.B −(A3),D6
c.	ADDQ.W #1,D0	d.	MOVE.L D0,(A7)+
e.	MOVE.W D6,A1	f.	ADD.L D2,D4
g.	MULS #13,D1	h.	SUBI.L #FE31,D0
i.	DIVU D0,D1	j.	SUB.B D0,D1
k.	OR.W #FF00,D3	l.	NOT.L D1
m.	ROL #1,D0	n.	AND.W #0000,D4
o.	MOVE.W #16(D0,A1),D1	p.	ROR.B #3,D1
q.	AND.B D2,(A0)	r.	MOVEA.L (A3)+,A2
s.	MOVE.B #EF,D1		

9. See if you can spot the grammatical (syntax) errors in the following instructions (use Chapter 6 to help you).
   a. MOVE D0,D1
   b. MOVE.B #FFE0097,A0
   c. ADDQ.W A3,134
   d. MOVE.L #3G6(A0),D3
   e. ADDA.W #4000,A2

10. Show the results that will be in the affected registers or memory locations after each of the following groups of instructions execute. Assume that each group of instructions starts with the register and memory contents shown in Figure 3-15. (Use Chapter 6.)
    a. ADD.L #4444,D0

    MOVE.B D0,D6
    b. MOVE.W #1234,D7
    ROR #4,D7
    c. MOVEA.L.W #$4000,A0
    MOVE.L A0,D5
    SUB.L #0111,D2
    ADDI.W #1,D2
    MOVE.B D2,(A0)
    d. ADDQ.L #7,D3
    NOP

11. Write the 68000 instruction that will perform the indicated operation. Use the instruction overview in this chapter and the detailed descriptions in Chapter 6 to help you.
    a. Copies A0 to D0.
    b. Loads $43 into D3.
    c. Increments the contents of D2 by 1.
    d. Copies SP to D2.
    e. Adds $07 to D0.
    f. Multiplies D3 times D2.
    g. Copies D3 to a memory location at displacement $5C from register A2 using D1 as an index.
    h. Decrements D2 by 1.
    i. Rotates the MSB of A5 into the LSB position.
    j. Copies D3 to a memory location whose address is in A3 with a displacement of $4000.
    k. Masks the lower 4 bits of D0.
    l. Sets the MSB of D0 to a 1 but does not affect the other bits.
    m. Inverts the lower 4 bits of D0 but does not affect the other bits.

12. Construct the binary code for each of the following 68000 instructions.
    a. MOVE.L A3,D7
    b. MOVE.B −(A0),D3
    c. ADD.W #4013,D0
    d. SUB.B #$FF,D1
    e. MOVE.L #9(A0),D3
    f. ROR.W D0,D3
    g. NOP
    h. AND.L D7,D3
    i. MULS D2,D4
    j. MOVEA.L #$4100,D7

13. Describe the function of each assembler directive and instruction statement in the following short program.

```
; pressure read program

PRESSURE_PORT EQU        $0400 ; pressure sensor
                               ; connected to port at
                               ; memory location
                               ; $0400
CORRECTION    EQU        $07   ; current correction
                               ; factor, 07
              ORG        $4000 ; start of program
              MOVEA.L    DATA_HERE,A0
              MOVE.B     (A0),D0
              MOVE.B     PRESSURE_PORT,D1
              ADDQ.B     #CORRECTION,D1
              MOVE.B     D1,PRESSURE
              ORG        $4100 ; data start
PRESSURE      DC.B       0     ; storage for pressure
              END
```

14. Describe how an assembly language program is developed and debugged using system tools such as editors, assemblers, linkers, locators, emulators, and debuggers.

15. Write the pseudocode representation for the flowchart in Figure 3-14.

CHAPTER

68000 Assembly Language Programming Techniques

The purpose of this chapter is to show you how some of the standard program structures described in the last chapter are implemented in 68000 assembly language, how these structures are used to solve some common programming problems, and how some of the 68000 instructions work.

OBJECTIVES

At the conclusion of this chapter, you should be able to

1. Write flowcharts or pseudocode for simple programming problems.

2. Write 68000 assembly language programs to solve IF-THEN, IF-THEN-ELSE, and multiple IF-THEN-ELSE-type programming problems.

3. Implement WHILE-DO and REPEAT-UNTIL program structures in 68000 assembly language.

4. Describe the operation of selected data transfer arithmetic, logical, jump, and loop instructions.

5. Use direct and indirect addressing modes to access data in your programs.

6. Describe a systematic approach to debugging a simple assembly language program using debugger, monitor, or emulator tools.

MORE PRACTICE WITH SIMPLE SEQUENCE PROGRAMS

This section describes in detail some slightly more complex programs that involve only the execution of a sequential list of instructions.

Converting Two ASCII Number Codes to Packed BCD

This problem involves the operations of masking and merging. Values can be combined in many useful ways by masking using the AND instruction and merging using the OR instruction. In this example we examine the masking and merging operations in detail.

Defining the Problem and Writing the Algorithm

If you type a 9 on the keyboard of an ASCII-encoded computer terminal, the 8-bit ASCII code sent to the computer will be 0011 1001 binary, or $39. If you type a 5 on the keyboard, the code sent to the computer will be 0011 0101 binary or $35, the ASCII code for 5. The ASCII codes for the numbers 0 through 9 are $30 through $39. As you can see, the lower nibble of the ASCII codes contains the 4-bit BCD code for the number represented by the ASCII code. For many applications we want to convert the ASCII code coming in from the terminal to its simple BCD equivalent. We can do this by simply replacing the 3 in the upper nibble of the byte with four 0s. For example, suppose we read in 0011 1001 binary, or $39, the ASCII code for 9. If we replace the upper 4 bits with 0s, we are left with 0000 1001 binary, or $09. The lower 4 bits contain 1001 binary, the BCD code for 9. Numbers represented as one BCD digit per byte are referred to as *unpacked BCD*. If two BCD digits are put in a byte, this form is referred to as *packed BCD*. Figure 4-1 shows examples of ASCII, unpacked BCD, and packed BCD. When we want to store BCD numbers in memory, the packed form is obviously more efficient because it has two BCD digits in each byte memory location. The problem we are going to work on here is how to convert two numbers from ASCII code form to unpacked BCD and then pack the two BCD digits into 1 byte. Figure 4-1 shows the steps in numerical form.

```
ASCII                          5        0011 0101  =  $35
ASCII                          9        0011 1001  =  $39

UNPACKED BCD                   5        0000 0101  =  $05
UNPACKED BCD                   9        0000 1001  =  $09

UNPACKED BCD                   5        0101 0000  =  $50
moved to upper nibble
PACKED BCD                     59       0101 1001  =  $59
```

FIGURE 4-1   ASCII, unpacked BCD, and packed BCD examples.

The algorithm for this problem can be stated simply:

Convert first ASCII number to unpacked BCD.
Convert second ASCII number to unpacked BCD.
Move first BCD nibble to upper nibble position in byte.
Pack 2 BCD nibbles in 1 byte.

This sequence doesn't look much like an assembly language program, and it shouldn't. The algorithm at this point should be general enough that it could be implemented in any programming language or on any machine. Once you are reasonably sure of your algorithm, then you can start thinking about the architecture and instructions of the specific microcomputer on which you plan to run the program. Now let's show you how we get from the algorithm to the assembly language program for it.

SETTING UP THE DATA STRUCTURE

One of the first things for you to think about in this process is the data with which the program will be working. You need to ask yourself questions such as

1. Will the data be in memory or in registers?

2. Is the data of type byte, type word, or perhaps type double word (long)?

3. How many data items are there?

4. Does the data represent only positive numbers, or does it represent positive and negative (signed) numbers?

5. For more complex problems you might ask how the data is structured. For example, is the data in an array or in a record?

Let's see how you can implement this algorithm in 68000 assembly language. Although it does not show in the algorithm, we know from a discussion in Chapter 3 that we should start the program with a list of initialization instructions. Start by putting this checklist at the top of the paper. At this point you may not know exactly which parts on the checklist will have to be initialized, but the presence of the list will remind you that it has to be done.

The Data Structure and Initialization List

For this example program let's assume that the first ASCII code entered is in the low byte of register D0, and the second ASCII code entered is in the low byte of register D1. Since we are not using memory for data in this program, we do not need to declare any data. In a real application this program would probably be a subroutine or a part of a larger program.

Choosing Instructions

Next look at the major actions that you want the program to perform other than moving data from one place to another. Look through the instruction summary in Chapter 3 and the instruction details in Chapter 6 to find the instructions that perform the operations you desire. Sometimes several instructions will be required to perform a complex operation. In this case you should try to break the complex operation into its smaller components until each component can be performed with one or two instructions.

Masking with the AND Instruction

The first operation in the algorithm is to convert a number in ASCII form to its unpacked BCD equivalent. This is done by replacing the upper 4 bits of the ASCII byte with four 0s. The 68000 AND instruction can be used to do this operation. Remember from basic logic or from the review in Chapter 1 that when a 1 or a 0 is ANDed with a 0, the result is always a 0. ANDing a bit with a 0 is called *masking* that bit, because the previous state of the bit is hidden, or masked. To mask 4 bits in a word, then, all you do is AND each bit you want to mask with a 0. Remember, a bit ANDed with a 1 is not changed.

According to the description of the AND instruction in Chapter 6, the instruction has the format AND source, destination. The instruction ANDs each bit of the specified source with the corresponding bit of the specified destination and puts the result in the specified destination. The source can be any data register or a memory location specified in one of those 15 different ways. The destination can be a register or a memory location. The source and the destination must both be bytes, they must both be words, or they must both be longs. The source and the destination cannot both be memory locations in an instruction.

For this example the first ASCII number is in the low byte of register D0, so we can just AND an immediate number with this register to mask the desired bits. The upper 4 bits of the immediate number should be 0s because these correspond to the bits we want to mask in D0. The lower 4 bits of the immediate number should be 1s because we want to leave these bits unchanged. The immediate number, then, should be 0000 1111 binary, or $0F. The instruction to convert the first ASCII number is AND.B #$0F,D0. When this instruction executes, it will leave the desired unpacked BCD in D0. Figure 4-2, p. 72, shows how this will work for an ASCII number of $35 initially in D0.

For the next action in the algorithm, we want to perform the same operation on a second ASCII number in register D1. The instruction AND.B #$0F,D1 will do this for us. After this instruction executes, D1 will contain the unpacked BCD for the second ASCII number.

MOVING A NIBBLE WITH THE ROTATE INSTRUCTION

The next action in the algorithm is to move the 4 BCD bits in the first unpacked BCD byte to the upper nibble position in the byte. We need to do this so that the 4 BCD bits are in the correct position for packing with the second BCD nibble. Take another look at Figure 4-1

ASCII 5	0 0 1 1	0 1 0 1
MASK	0 0 0 0	1 1 1 1
RESULT	0 0 0 0	0 1 0 1

FIGURE 4-2 Effects of ANDing with 1s and 0s.

to help you visualize this. What we are effectively doing here is swapping the nibbles of the low byte of D0. The 68000 does not have a specific instruction to swap the nibbles in a byte. However, if you think of the operation that we need to do as shifting or rotating the BCD bits 4 bit positions to the left, this will give you a good idea which instruction will do the job for you. The 68000 has several varieties of rotate and shift instructions. For now let's look at the rotate instructions. There are two instructions, ROL and ROXL, that rotate the bits of a specified operand to the left. Figure 4-3 shows in diagram form how these two work. For ROL each bit in the specified register or memory location is rotated a specified number of bit positions to the left. The bits that rotate out of the MSB are rotated around into the LSB position. The old MSB is also copied to the carry flag, C. For the ROXL instruction each bit of the specified register or memory location is also rotated to the left. However, the bit that was in the MSB position is moved to the extend bit, and the bit that was in the extend bit is moved into the LSB position. As indicated by the X in the middle of the mnemonic, the extend bit is in the rotated loop when the ROXL instruction executes. The ROXL instruction moves each MSB into the carry condition code, as does the ROL instruction. With the ROXL instruction the MSB also goes to the extend bit.

In the example program we really don't want the contents of the extend flag rotated into our operand, so the ROL instruction seems to be the one we want. If you consult the ROL instruction description in Chapter 6, you will find that the instruction has the format ROL count, destination. The destination can be a register or a memory location. If the destination is a memory location, then only a 1-bit rotate is performed. The count can be an immediate number specified directly in the instruction, or the count can be a number previously loaded into a data register. The instruction ROL.L #3,D0, for example, will rotate the contents of D0 3 bit positions to the left, using all 32 bits of D0. In this case we use the instruction ROL.B #4,D0 to do the rotation. When it executes, this instruction will auto-

matically rotate the low byte of register D0 4 bit positions to the left.

Now that we have determined the instructions needed to mask the upper nibbles and the instructions necessary to move the first BCD digit into position, the only thing left is to pack the upper nibble in D1 and the lower nibble in D0 into the same byte.

COMBINING BYTES OR WORDS WITH THE ADD OR THE OR INSTRUCTION

You can't use a standard MOVE instruction to combine 2 bytes into 1 byte, as we need to do here. The reason is that the MOVE instruction copies an operand from a specified source to a specified destination. The previous contents of the destination are lost. You can, however, use an ADD or an OR instruction to pack the two BCD nibbles.

The ADD instruction adds the contents of a specified source to the contents of a specified destination and leaves the result in the specified destination. For the example program here, the instruction ADD.B D1,D0 can be used to combine the two BCD nibbles. In this case we know that D1 has 0s in its lower 4 bits and D0 has 0s in its upper 4 bits; therefore, the ADD will cause no bit carries and will yield the desired result of merging the two nibbles. Take a look at Figure 4-1 to help you visualize this addition. For the general case of merging two registers, however, the OR instruction is more often used.

If you look up the OR instruction in Chapter 6, you will find that it has the format OR source, destination. This instruction ORs each bit in the specified source with the corresponding bit in the specified destination. The result of the ORing is left in the specified destination. Remember from basic logic or the review in Chapter 1 that ORing a bit with a 1 always produces a result of 1. ORing a bit with a 0 leaves the bit unchanged. To set a bit in a word to a 1, then, all you have to do is OR that bit with a word that has a 1 in that bit position and 0s in all the other bit positions. This is similar to the way the AND instruction is used to clear bits in a word to 0s. See the OR instruction description in Chapter 6 for examples of this.

For the example program here we use the instruction OR.B D1,D0 to pack the two BCD nibbles. Bits ORed with 0s will not be changed. Bits ORed with 1s will become or stay 1s. Again look at Figure 4-1 to help you visualize this operation.

SUMMARY OF BCD PACKING PROGRAM

Figure 4-4 shows the complete program for producing a packed BCD byte from two ASCII bytes. Work your way through this to make sure you understand how each part works. In this program we use the AND instruction to zero (mask) unwanted bits in the ASCII bytes. Any bit ANDed with a 0 will become or remain a zero. Any bit ANDed with a 1 will remain the same. We use the ROL instruction to rotate a nibble from the lower nibble position to the higher nibble position. Finally,

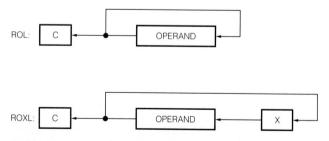

FIGURE 4-3 ROL instruction and RCL instruction operations for byte operands.

```
; 68000 PROGRAM
; ABSTRACT          : Program to produce a packed BCD byte from
;                     two ASCII-encoded digits.
;                     The first ASCII digit (5) is located in the low
;                     byte of D0, and the second ASCII digit (9) is located
;                     in the low byte of D1.
;
; REGISTERS USED:   D0, D1
; PORTS USED     :  none used
; PROCEDURES     :  none used
;
;                   alr 11-88
;

        ORG     $4000               ; start the code at memory address $4000

        MOVE.B  #'5',D0             ; load first ASCII digit into D0
        MOVE.B  #'9',D1             ; load second ASCII digit into D1
        AND.B   D0,$0F              ; mask upper 4 bits of first digit
        AND.B   D1,$0F              ; mask upper 4 bits of second digit
        ROL.B   #4,D0               ; rotate D0 4 bit positions left
        OR.B    D1,D0               ; combine nibbles, result in D0

        RTS                         ; return to whoever called me

        END
```

FIGURE 4-4   68000 assembly language program to produce packed BCD from two ASCII characters.

we use the OR instruction to combine the two BCD nibbles in 1 byte. Any bit ORed with a 1 will become or remain a 1. Any bit ORed with a 0 will remain the same as it was.

Finding the Average of Two Numbers

The next example problem deals with more traditional arithmetic, addition and division. Such details as handling the carry after an addition (if there was one) are discussed.

DEFINING THE PROBLEM AND WRITING THE ALGORITHM

A common need in programming is to find the average of two numbers. Suppose, for example, we know the maximum temperature and the minimum temperature on one day and we want to determine the average temperature. The sequence of steps we go through to do this might look something like the following.

Add maximum temperature and minimum temperature.

Divide sum by 2 to get average temperature.

Let's assume for this example that the data is all in memory, the data is of type byte, and that the data represents only positive numbers in the range 0 to $0FF. The bottom part of Figure 4-5, p. 74, shows how you might set up the data structure for this program. It

is very similar to the data structure for the multiply example in the last chapter. HI_TEMP is declared as a variable of type byte and initialized with a value of $92. In an actual application, the value in HI_TEMP would probably be put there by another program which reads the output from a temperature sensor. The statement LO_TEMP DC.B $52 declares a variable of type byte and initializes it with the value $52. The statement AV_TEMP DS.B 1 sets aside a byte location to store the average temperature but does not initialize the location to any value. When the program executes, it will write a value to this location.

INITIALIZATION CHECKLIST

Now that you have the data structure set up, let's start thinking about the instructions that we can use to perform the actions we want on this data. For this example program the only parts you have to initialize are the two working registers D0 and D1. These registers are initialized to 0 in preparation for later operations.

CHOOSING INSTRUCTIONS

Next look at the major actions that you want the program to perform other than moving data from one place to another. You want the program to add 2 byte-type numbers together, so scan through the instruction groups in Chapter 3 to determine which 68000 instruction will do this for you. The ADD instruction is the obvious choice in this case. ADD.B is

```
; 68000 PROGRAM
; ABSTRACT        : This program averages two temperatures named
;                   HI_TEMP and LO_TEMP and puts the results in
;                   the memory location AV_TEMP
;
; REGISTERS USED:  D0, D1, D2
; PORTS USED     :  none used
; PROCEDURES     :  none used
;
;                  alr 11-88
;

; start the code here
;

        ORG      $4000            ; start the code at memory address $4000

        CLR.L    D0               ; clear working registers D0
        CLR.W    D1               ;  and D1

        MOVE.B   (HI_TEMP),D0     ; get first temperature

        ADD.B    (LO_TEMP),D0     ; add in second temperature

        ; There may have been a carry, so move the carry bit to the
        ; bit 8 of D0 (i.e. the low bit of the second byte).

        MOVE.W   SR,D2            ; move condition codes to the lower portion
                                  ;  of D2 from the status register
        ANDI.B   #$01,D2          ; mask off all but the carry bit (bit 0)
        LSL.W    #8,D2            ; shift bit over one byte (8 bit positions)
        OR.W     D2,D0            ; move carry bit into the sum

        MOVE.B   #$02,D1          ; average by dividing by 2, since
                                  ; there are 2 values to be averaged

        DIVU     D1,D0            ; perform division
                                  ; quotient -> lower word of D0
                                  ; remainder -> upper word of D0

        MOVE.B   D0,(AV_TEMP)     ; save average in memory

        RTS                       ; return to whoever called me
; start the data here
;

HI_TEMP        DC.B    $92        ; max temp storage (try $F0 here
LO_TEMP        DC.B    $52        ; low temp storage  and $40 here also!)
AV_TEMP        DS.B    1          ; put average here

        END
```

FIGURE 4-5   68000 program to average two temperatures.

also clear, since both temperatures are byte values. Now find and read the detailed discussion of this instruction in Chapter 6. From this discussion you can determine how the instruction works and see if it will do the necessary job. From the discussion of the ADD instruction, you should find that the ADD instruction has the format ADD source, destination. A byte (word or long) from the specified source is added to a byte (word or long) in the specified destination. (Note that you cannot directly add a byte to a word or a long or add a word to a long.) The result, in any case, is put in the specified destination. The source can be an immediate number, a register, or a memory location. The destination can be a register or a memory location. The source and the destination cannot both be memory locations in a single instruction. This means that you have to move one of the operands from memory to a register before you can do the ADD. Another point to consider here is that if you add two 8-bit numbers, the sum can be larger than 8 bits. Adding $F0 and $40, for example, gives $130. The 8-bit destination will contain $30, and the carry will be held in the carry condition code, C (bit 0 of the status register). What this means is that you must collect the parts of the result in a location large enough to hold all 9 bits. The lower 16 bits of a data register are good choices. Before using the register, however, you should clear the bits to all 0s so bits 10 through 16 of the final result will be 0. To summarize, then, you need to clear the lower 16 bits of some data register such as D0, move one of the numbers you want to add into that data register, add the other number from memory to it, and move any carry produced by the addition to the upper half of the 16-bit register containing the result.

Now let's see how you can do this with program instructions. Take a look now at the first five instruction statements of the example program in Figure 4-5. The first instruction, ORG $4000, is an assembler directive telling the assembler to assemble this code at an address of origin equal to $4000. The next two instructions clear the two working registers, D0 and D1. In particular, we are interested in ensuring that the upper byte of the lower word of D1 and all the upper bits of D0 are all cleared to 0s.

Next we move the first operand into D0 using a MOVE.B instruction. We can now use the ADD.B instruction to bring the second temperature from memory and add it directly to the first temperature now held in register D0. Note that the name of the memory location holding the second temperature, LO_TEMP, is used in the ADD instruction instead of the actual hex address of the temperature. This makes the program much more readable and easier to understand. The assembler will convert LO_TEMP to the correct address value when it assembles the program (i.e., when the assembler translates the program from assembly language to machine language).

Following the ADD, we have the sum of the two temperatures in D0; the carry bit has been set, depending on whether or not the addition resulted in a carry.

Now that we have done the addition, the next thing to do is get the carry bit where we want it. We would like to get the contents of the carry condition code into the least significant bit of the upper byte of the lower word of D0—that is, into bit 8 of D0 (remember that bits are numbered by Motorola starting with bit 0). First, a copy is made of the status register in D2. This is accomplished with a MOVE.W SR,D2 instruction, moving one word from the status register to register D2.

NOTE: The 68010 uses the instruction MOVE.W CCR,D2 to access the condition-code portion of the status register.

Moves to and from the status register are always word-size moves.

Next the upper bits (bits 1–7) of D2 are all masked to 0s, leaving only the carry bit unchanged. This masking operation is the same as that of the previous example; this time, however, the mask is different. Here the mask is $01, clearing all but bit 0 (the LSB). In the previous example the mask was $0F, clearing only the upper 4 bits (bits 4–7).

The carry bit is then shifted over 8 bit positions so that it ends up in the low bit of the upper byte of the low word of D2 (that is, bit 8 of D2). This is similar to the rotate in the previous example except that here the operand size is word, so that the low 16 bits of D2 are rotated; and the rotation shifts D2 by 8 bit positions. The carry bit is then ORed as a word with the sum in D0. The OR operation leaves the lower byte and the upper 7 bits of D0 unchanged, but bit 8 ends up equal to the carry bit. If there was a carry, then the carry bit was a 1 and so bit 8 will also be a 1; if there was no carry, then the carry bit was a 0 and so bit 8 will be a 0.

We are also relying on the fact that the upper byte of D0 was cleared to 0 at the start of the program during initialization. We know the low bits of D2 will contain 0s because the left-shift operation shifts in 0s on the right as the register is shifted left (see Chapter 6). The result of all this is that the carry bit ends up in bit 8 of D0, which is what we set out to do. The end result is that the lower word of D0 has the correct 9-bit sum in bits 0–8 of register D0.

The next major action in our algorithm is to divide the sum of the two temperatures by 2. Look at the instruction groups in the last chapter to see if the 68000 has a divide instruction. You should find that it has two divide instructions, DIVS and DIVU. DIVU is for dividing unsigned numbers, and DIVS is used for dividing signed binary numbers. Since we are dividing unsigned binary numbers in this example, look up the DIVU instruction in Chapter 6 to find out how DIVU works. The DIVU instruction can be used to divide a 32-bit number in any data register by a specified 16-bit number in a register or in a memory location. After the division a 16-bit quotient is left in the lower word of the destination data register, and a 16-bit remainder is left in the upper word of the destination data register. There is a problem if the quotient is too large to fit in the indicated destination. In a later chapter we discuss what to do about this problem. Fortunately, for this example the data is such that the problem will not arise, since the sum is at most 9 bits and our divisor is 2.

As you can see, we already have the sum of the two temperatures positioned in register D0 ready for the DIVU operation. Before we can do the DIVU operation, however, we have to get the divisor, $02, into a register or memory location to satisfy the requirements of the DIVU instruction. A simple way to do this is with the

MOVE.B #$02,D1 instruction, which loads the immediate number $02 into register D1. Now we can do the divide operation with the instruction DIVU D1,D0. We know the upper bits of D0 and D1 are all 0s because we cleared all 32 bits of D0 and the upper 6 bits of D1 to 0s in the initialization part of the program. The 16-bit quotient from the division will be left in the lower word of register D0. All we have left to do is to copy the quotient to the memory location we set aside for the average temperature. The instruction MOVE.B D0, (AV_TEMP) will copy the low byte of D0 to this memory location. We can be sure the average fits in 8 bits because the original temperatures were both 8-bit values. Take another look at Figure 4-5 to see how these instructions are added on to the previous instructions.

Often, other more efficient or simpler methods will be used to accomplish the addition and division of problems similar to that of this program. For example, simply using a 16-bit addition when we know both operands are only 8 bits will allow us to ignore any carry (since no 16-bit carry is possible if the operands are only 8 bits). The particular division we are performing, unsigned division by 2, may be performed in some cases by a simple and efficient logical right shift of 1 bit position.

NOTE: We could have used the remainder in the upper word of register D0 to round the average temperature, but that would have made the program more complex than desired for this example.

SUMMARY: CONVERTING AN ALGORITHM TO ASSEMBLY LANGUAGE

The first step in converting an algorithm to assembly language is to set up and declare the data structure with which the algorithm will be working. Then write down the instructions required for initialization at the start of the code section. Next, determine the instructions required to implement the major actions in the algorithm and how the data must be positioned for these instructions. Finally, insert the MOVE or other instructions required to get the data in the correct position.

A Few Comments about the 68000 Arithmetic Instructions

The 68000 has instructions to add, subtract, multiply, and divide. It can operate on signed or unsigned binary numbers or BCD numbers. Rather than put a lot of arithmetic examples at this point in the book, we show arithmetic examples with each arithmetic instruction description in Chapter 6. The description of the MULU instruction in Chapter 6, for example, shows how unsigned binary numbers are multiplied. Also, we show other arithmetic examples as needed throughout the rest of the book. If you need to do some arithmetic operations on the 68000, you should examine the instructions to perform the basic addition (ADD), sub-

traction (SUB), multiplication (MULS, MULU), and division (DIVS, DIVU) operations given in Chapter 6. Notice as well the faster immediate versions ADDI and SUBI.

If you are adding BCD numbers, you also need to look up the add BCD (ABCD), subtract BCD (SBCD), and negate BCD (NBCD) instructions.

CONDITION CODES AND JUMPS

Introduction

The real power of a computer comes from its ability to repeat a sequence of instructions *as long as* some condition exists, repeat a sequence of instructions *until* some condition exists, or choose one of two or more sequences *if* some condition exists.

Condition codes (often called *flags*) indicate whether a condition is present or not. *Jump* and *Branch* instructions are used to tell the computer what sequence of actions to take based on the condition indicated by the condition codes. The condition codes are stored as bits in the lower byte of the status register. Certain instructions examine the condition codes and behave differently according to the values of the codes. Other instructions set or clear these codes depending on the results of numerical operations. In this section we discuss the 68000 condition codes and the 68000 jump and branch instructions. Later we will show with examples how the IF-THEN, WHILE-DO, and REPEAT-UNTIL structures are implemented and used.

The 68000 Condition Codes

The 68000 has five condition codes. They are the *carry* code (C), the *overflow* code (V), the *zero* code (Z), the *negative* code (N), and the *extend* code (X). Chapter 1 shows numerical examples of the conditions indicated by these flags. Chapter 2 shows where the codes are stored in the CPU status register (refer to Figure 2-9). Here we review these conditions and show how some of the important 68000 instructions affect these codes.

THE CARRY AND EXTEND CONDITION CODES WITH ADD, SUBTRACT, AND COMPARE INSTRUCTIONS

If the addition of two 8-bit numbers produces a sum greater than 8 bits, the carry flag will be set to a 1 to indicate a carry into the next bit position. Likewise, if the addition of two 16-bit numbers produces a sum greater than 16 bits, then the carry flag will be set to a 1 to indicate that a final carry was produced by the addition. Similarly, if the addition of two 32-bit numbers produces a sum greater than 32 bits, the carry flag will be set to a 1 to indicate a carry into the next bit position. In these cases the extend bit is set to the same value as the carry bit.

During subtraction the carry flag functions as a borrow flag. If the bottom number in a subtraction is larger than the top number, then the carry/borrow flag will be set to indicate that a borrow was needed to perform the subtraction. The extend bit is set to the same value as the carry bit.

The 68000 compare instruction has the format CMP source, destination. The source can be an immediate number, a register, or a memory location. The destination can be a register or a memory location. Source and destination cannot both be memory locations in the same instruction. The comparison is done by subtracting the contents of the specified source from the contents of the specified destination. Condition codes are updated to reflect the result of the comparison, but neither the source nor the destination are changed. If the source operand is greater than the specified destination operand, then the carry/borrow flag will be set to indicate that a borrow was needed to do the comparison (subtraction). If the source operand is the same size as or smaller than the specified destination operand, then the carry/borrow flag will not be set after the compare. If the two operands are equal, the zero flag will be set to a 1 to indicate that the result of the compare (subtraction) was all 0s. Here is an example and summary of this for your reference.

CMP.B D0,D1

Condition	C	Z
D0 > D1	1	0
D0 < D1	0	0
D0 = D1	0	1

The compare instruction is very important because it allows you to easily determine whether one operand is greater than, less than, or the same size as another operand.

THE OVERFLOW CONDITION CODE

The flag for the overflow condition code will be set if the result of a signed operation is too large to fit in the number of bits available to represent it. To remind you of what overflow means, here is an example. Suppose you add the 8-bit signed number 0111 0101 (+117 decimal) and the 8-bit signed number 0011 0111 (+55 decimal). The result will be 1010 1100 (+172 decimal), which is the correct binary result in this case but is too large to fit in the 7 bits allowed for the magnitude in an 8-bit signed number. For an 8-bit signed number, the 1 in the most significant bit indicates a negative number. As a signed number, the 8-bit sum 1010 1100 is interpreted as −84 decimal. The true sum, +172 decimal, requires at least 9 bits to be represented as a signed binary number. The overflow flag will be set after this operation to indicate that the result of the addition has overflowed into the sign bit.

THE ZERO-CONDITION CODE WITH INCREMENT, DECREMENT, AND COMPARE INSTRUCTIONS

As the name implies, the zero-condition code will be set to a 1 if the result of an arithmetic or logic operation is zero. For example, if you subtract two equal numbers, the zero code will be set to indicate that the result of the subtraction is zero. If you AND two words together and the result contains no 1s, the zero code will be set to indicate that the result was all 0s.

There are a few other very useful instructions besides the more obvious arithmetic and logic instructions that affect the zero-condition code. One of these is the compare instruction, CMP, which we discussed previously with the carry flag. As shown there, the zero code will be set to a 1 if the two operands compared are equal.

Another important instruction that affects the zero code is the decrement and branch instruction, Dcc. This instruction will decrement—or, in other words, subtract 1 from—a number in a specified register or memory location. If, after decrementing, the content of the register or memory location is zero, the zero flag will be set. In addition, if the DEQ (decrement and branch if EQual to zero) form of the decrement instruction is used, the instruction will also cause a branch to occur.

Here's a preview of how this is used with the BNZ form of the decrement and branch. BNZ branches if the result of the decrement is Not equal to Zero. Suppose that we want to repeat a sequence of actions nine times. To do this we first load a register with the number $09 and execute the sequence of actions. We then decrement the register and look at the zero flag to see if the register is down to zero yet. If the zero flag is not set, then we know that the register is not yet down to zero, so the 68000 automatically branches and goes back and executes the sequence of instructions again. The following sections will show many specific examples of how this is done.

THE NEGATIVE CODE

When you need to represent both positive and negative numbers for a 68000, you use 2's complement sign-and-magnitude form, as described in Chapter 1. In this form the MSB of the byte or word is used as a sign bit. A 0 in this bit indicates that the number is positive. A 1 in this bit indicates that the number is negative. The remaining 7 bits of a byte, the remaining 15 bits of a word, or the remaining 31 bits of a long word are used to represent the magnitude of the number. For a positive number the magnitude will be in standard binary form. For a negative number, the magnitude will be in 2's complement form. After an arithmetic or logic instruction executes, the negative condition code will be a copy of the most significant bit of the destination byte, the destination word, or the destination long word. If the signed result is negative, the MSB will be a 1 and the negative condition code will be a 1. If the signed result is positive, the MSB will be a 0 and the negative condition code will also be a 0.

In addition to its use with signed arithmetic operations, the sign flag can be used to determine if an operand has been decremented beyond zero. Decrementing $00, for example, will give $FF. Since the MSB of $FF is a 1, the sign flag will be set.

The 68000 Unconditional Jump Instruction

Normally, when a 68000 is done executing an instruction it will next start executing the instruction in the next-highest addressed memory word. This sequential march through memory from low addresses to high addresses is the normal operating method of the 68000. Jump instructions can be used to tell the 68000 to start fetching its instructions from some new location instead of the next-highest addressed location. Figure 4-6 shows in diagram form how a jump instruction affects the program execution flow. Remember, the 68000 increments the program counter (PC) as it executes in order to step through the instructions in memory. The 68000 JMP instruction places a new value specified as part of the JMP instruction into the PC. This causes the next instruction to be fetched from the new location specified in the PC. The 68000 JMP instruction always causes a jump to occur. This is referred to as an *unconditional* jump. The 68000 also has an unconditional branch instruction, BRA (BRanch Always). This instruction operates in the same manner as the JMP instruction except that only the low 16 bits of the PC are changed. This means that the BRA instruction can branch only within the near-

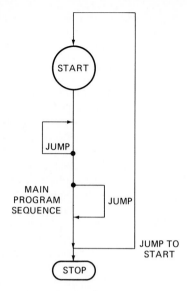

FIGURE 4-6 Change in program flow that can be caused by jump instructions.

JMP   Jump   JMP
(M68000 Family)

Operation: Destination Address ▶ PC

**Assembler
Syntax:**   JMP ⟨ea⟩

Attributes: Unsized

Description: Program execution continues at the effective address specified by the instruction. The addressing mode for the effective address must be a control addressing mode.

Condition Codes:
   Not affected.

Instruction Format:

15	14	13	12	11	10	9	8	7	6	5 4 3	2 1 0
0	1	0	0	1	1	1	0	1	1	EFFECTIVE ADDRESS MODE	REGISTER

Instruction Fields:
   Effective Address field — Specifies the address of the next instruction. Only control addressing modes are allowed as shown:

Addressing Mode	Mode	Register	Addressing Mode	Mode	Register
Dn	—	—	(xxx).W	111	000
An	—	—	(xxx).L	111	001
(An)	010	reg. number:An	#⟨data⟩	—	—
(An)+	—	—			
−(An)	—	—			
(d$_{16}$,An)	101	reg. number:An	(d$_{16}$,PC)	111	010
(d$_8$,An,Xn)	110	reg. number:An	(d$_8$,PC,Xn)	111	011

MC68020, MC68030, AND MC68040 ONLY

Addressing Mode	Mode	Register	Addressing Mode	Mode	Register
(bd,An,Xn)∗	110	reg. number:An	(bd,PC,Xn)∗	111	011
([bd,An,Xn],od)	110	reg. number:An	([bd,PC,Xn],od)	111	011
([bd,An],Xn,od)	110	reg. number:An	([bd,PC],Xn,od)	111	011

∗Can be used with CPU32.

(a)

FIGURE 4-7   68000 (a) JMP and (b) BRA instructions (p. 79). (*continued*)

Operation: PC + d ♦ PC

**Assembler
Syntax:**   BRA ⟨label⟩

Attributes: Size = (Byte, Word, Long*)
*(MC68020/MC68030/MC68040 only)

Description: Program execution continues at location (PC) + displacement. The
PC contains the address of the instruction word of the BRA instruction plus
two. The displacement is a twos complement integer that represents the relative
distance in bytes from the current PC to the destination PC. If the 8-bit displacement field in the instruction word is zero, a 16-bit displacement (the word
immediately following the instruction) is used. If the 8-bit displacement field
in the instruction word is all ones ($FF), the 32-bit displacement (long word
immediately following the instruction) is used.

Condition Codes:
Not affected.

Instruction Format:

15	14	13	12	11	10	9	8	7	6	5	4	3	2	1	0
0	1	1	0	0	0	0	0				8-BIT DISPLACEMENT				
16-BIT DISPLACEMENT IF 8-BIT DISPLACEMENT = $00															
32-BIT DISPLACEMENT IF 8-BIT DISPLACEMENT = $FF															

Instruction Fields:
8-Bit Displacement field — Twos complement integer specifying the number
of bytes between the branch instruction and the next instruction to be executed.
16-Bit Displacement field — Used for a larger displacement when the 8-bit
displacement is equal to $00.
32-Bit Displacement field — Used for a larger displacement when the 8-bit
displacement is equal to $FF.

NOTE

A branch to the immediately following instruction automatically uses
the 16-bit displacement format because the 8-bit displacement field
contains $00 (zero offset).

FIGURE 4-7 (*continued*)   (*b*)

est 64 Kbytes of memory. The JMP instruction affects the entire 32 bits of the PC and can jump to anywhere in memory (any of the 4 Gbytes possible). A branch is a jump that can go only a relatively short distance in memory. A jump can go anywhere in memory.

The 68000 also has a large collection of conditional branch instructions that cause a branch based on whether some condition is present or not. In this section we discuss how the unconditional jump instruction operates. In a later section we discuss the operation of the conditional branch instructions.

Unconditional Jump/Branch Instructions—JMP, BRA

The 68000 has two forms of unconditional jump/ branch instruction, JMP and BRA. Figure 4-7, pp. 78 and 79, shows the names and instruction coding templates for these two instructions. The JMP instruction places a new 32-bit value in the PC and thereby causes a jump to the address specified by the new PC value. Since a full 32 bits are used, the jump can be to any memory location the 68000 can address.

The BRA instruction uses a signed 16-bit displacement, which is added to the current contents of the PC. A signed 16-bit displacement means that the jump can

be to a location anywhere from +32,767 to −32,768 bytes from the current PR address. A positive displacement usually means you are jumping ahead in the program, and a negative displacement usually means you are jumping "backward" in the program.

One advantage of a branch-type instruction, such as BRA, is that the destination address is specified *relative* to the current PC value (which will be the address of the instruction after the branch instruction). Since the BRA instruction in this case does not contain an absolute address, the program can be loaded anywhere in memory and it will still run correctly. A program that can be loaded anywhere in memory to be run is said to be *relocatable*. Relocatable programs can be moved from one place in memory to another, which is often called *relocating the program*, and will still run correctly in any of the locations. You should try to write your programs so that they are relocatable.

Notice in the coding information of Figure 4-7 that the BRA instruction can also accept an 8-bit displacement. If 8 bits are used, then the range of the BRA must be within +128 to −127 bytes of the current PC value (the next instruction address). If you are using an assembler, it will determine which size displacement to use when it assembles the program.

The JMP instruction allows you to specify the target

address (the one to which you are jumping) in any of seven ways. The target address can be in an address register, it can be immediate data in the instruction, or it can be defined as a combination of displacement, PC, and index register. An index register is either an address or a data register. The target address can also be specified as the combination of an address register and a displacement and possibly an index register.

JMP AND BRA EXAMPLES

Suppose that in a program you want to keep executing an instruction or group of instructions over and over again. Figure 4-8 shows how the JMP instruction can be used to do this. In this program the label BACK followed by a colon is used to give a name to the address to which we want to jump back. When the assembler reads this label, it will make an entry in its symbol table as to where it found the label. Then, when the assembler reads the JMP instruction and finds the name BACK, it will have remembered the address of BACK. This address will be part of the code for the instruction. Even if you are not using an assembler, you should use labels to indicate jump destinations so that you can easily see them. The NOP instruction used in the program in Figure 4-8 does nothing except fill space. We used it in this example to represent the instructions that we want to loop through over and over. We also use it to represent the instructions after the JMP-BACK loop. Actually, the way this program is written, the 68000 will never get to the instructions after the JMP instruction. Can you see why? The answer is that once the 68000 gets into the JMP-BACK loop, it can get out only if the power is turned off, an interrupt occurs, or the system is reset. In most programs one of the instructions we have represented with a NOP would be a conditional jump instruction, which would get execution out of the loop when the specified condition occurred.

Now let's see how the binary code for the JMP instruction in Figure 4-8 is constructed. The jump is to a label, BACK. The effective addressing mode selected is absolute long, encoded as 11 1001 binary. The target address as indicated in the symbol table at the bottom of Figure 4-8 is $0000 4000. The instruction encoding using the template from Figure 4-7 is $4EF9 0000 4000; this includes the 32-bit absolute address of BACK.

Figure 4-9, p. 82, contains another simple example program to show how you can jump ahead over a group of instructions in a program using the branch always instruction, BRA. Here again we use a label to give a name to the address to which we want to branch. We also use NOP instructions to represent the instructions that we want to skip over and the instructions that continue after the branch. Now let's see how this BRA instruction is coded.

When the assembler reads through the source file for this program, it will find the label "THERE" after the BRA mnemonic. Then the assembler reads on through the rest of the program. When the assembler finds the specified label, it calculates the displacement (the dis-

tance) from the word after the BRA instruction to the label. Here's how you calculate the displacement to put in the instruction.

NOTE: An assembler automatically does this for you, but you should still learn how it is done to help you in troubleshooting.

The numbers in the left column of Figure 4-9 represent the address of each code byte. These are the numbers that will be in the program counter as the program executes. After the 68000 fetches an instruction word, it automatically increments the program counter, PC, to point to the next instruction word. The displacement in the BRA instruction will be added to the offset of the next in-line word after the BRA instruction word. In this case the PC will contain $4002 after the BRA instruction word is fetched. The offset in the BRA instruction is $000A. Adding the offset to the PC value yields $400C, which is the value given for the label "THERE" in the symbol table at the bottom of Figure 4-9. This is the correct target address for the branch. The assembler defaults to the long addressing mode of BRA and provides a 16-bit displacement. Chapter 6 shows the different ways some different assemblers can be made to use the shorter 8-bit displacement. The curious reader is referred to the ABS_SHORT assembler directive and the alternative ".S" suffix. The final BRA encoding, as indicated in Figure 4-9, is $6000 000A.

If the displacement of the BRA is negative (backward in the program), then it must be expressed in 2's complement form before it can be written in the instruction code template. In Chapter 1 we showed how to convert to and from 2's complement signed-magnitude form and the decimal equivalent.

SUMMARY OF UNCONDITIONAL JMP AND BRA

The 68000 has two types of unconditional jump instructions. The type you will probably use most often in your programs is the BRA instruction because the BRA instruction produces relocatable code. A label followed by a colon is used to give the destination address a name for both of these jump types. For the branch instruction, BRA, an 8-bit or 16-bit displacement contained in the instruction is added to the contents of the program counter to produce the destination address. This type of jump can be to an address in the range of −127 bytes to +128 bytes for an 8-bit displacement. An address in the range of −32,768 bytes to +32,767 bytes from the current PC contents can be reached using a 16-bit displacement. A jump backward in the program is usually represented by a negative displacement, which is coded in the instruction in its 2's complement sign-and-magnitude form.

The direct JMP instruction can use either a 16-bit or 32-bit absolute address to replace the PC. Alternatively, an address register or combination of registers and displacements can be used in a JMP instruction. We will see in later examples how these more complex JMP addressing modes can be useful.

```
 1:
 2:                                          ;  68000 PROGRAM
 3:                                          ;  ABSTRACT                    :  This program illustrates a "backward" jump
 4:                                          ;
 5:                                          ;  REGISTERS USED              :  DO
 6:                                          ;  PORTS USED                  :  none used
 7:                                          ;  PROCEDURES                  :  none used
 8:                                          ;
 9:                                          ;                                 air 3-88
10:                                          ;
11:
12:   00004000                                  ORG              $4000
13:
14:   00004000 5680           BACK:  ADDQ.L           #3,DO          ;  add 3 to total
15:
16:   00004002 4E71                  NOP                             ;  dummy instructions
17:   00004004 4E71                  NOP                             ;  to represent those
18:   00004006 4E71                  NOP                             ;  instructions jumped
19:   00004008 4E71                  NOP                             ;  back over
20:
21:   0000400A 4EF9 0000 4000        JMP              BACK           ;  loop back through
22:                                                                  ;  series of instructions
23:
24:   00004010 4E71                  NOP                             ;  dummy instructions to
25:   00004012 4E71                  NOP                             ;  represent continuation
26:                                                                  ;  after loop
27:
28:   00004014 4E75                  RTS
29:
30:   00004016                       END
```

Symbol Name	Attribute	Hex	Decimal
BACK..........................	LABEL	00004000	16384

Obj bytes: 22D/00000016H

End assembly.   Lines: 30   Errors: 0

FIGURE 4-8   Program demonstrating "backward" JMP.

```
 1:
 2:                                    ; 68000 PROGRAM
 3:                                    ; ABSTRACT      : This program illustrates a "forward" jump
 4:                                    ;
 5:                                    ; REGISTERS USED:  D0
 6:                                    ; PORTS USED    :  none used
 7:                                    ; PROCEDURES    :  none used
 8:                                    ;
 9:                                    ;              alr 3-88
10:                                    ;
11:
12: 00004000                              ORG      $4000
13:
14: 00004000 6000 000A                    BRA      THERE          ; skip over a series
15:                                                               ; of instructions
16:
17: 00004004 4E71                         NOP                     ; dummy instructions
18: 00004006 4E71                         NOP                     ; to represent those
19: 00004008 4E71                         NOP                     ; instructions skipped
20: 0000400A 4E71                         NOP                     ; over
21:
22: 0000400C 303C 0000       THERE:  MOVE.W  #$0000,D0            ; zero accumulator before addition
23:
24: 00004010 4E71                         NOP                     ; dummy instructions to
25: 00004012 4E71                         NOP                     ; represent continuation
26:                                                               ; of execution
27:
28: 00004014 4E75                         RTS
29:
30: 00004016                              END
```

Symbol Name	Attribute	Hex	Decimal
THERE	LABEL	0000400C	16396

Obj bytes: 22D/00000016H

End assembly. Lines: 30 Errors: 0

FIGURE 4-9   Program demonstrating "forward" JMP.

The 68000 Conditional Branch Instructions

As we stated previously, much of the real power of a computer comes from its ability to choose between two courses of action based on whether some condition is present or not. In the 68000 the five condition codes indicate the conditions that are present after an instruction. The 68000 conditional branch instructions look at the state of a specified code or codes to determine whether a branch (a short jump) should be made or not. Figure 4-10 shows the mnemonics for the 68000 conditional branch instructions. The conditional branch instructions are branch conditionally (Bcc) and decrement and branch conditionally (DBcc). The actual assembly language instructions are generated by replacing cc with one of the condition mnemonics from Figure 4-10. For example, BVS GO is the assembly language instruction to branch if the overflow condition code bit is set to location "GO." Branch

Bcc   **Branch Conditionally**   **Bcc**
                              (M68000 Family)

Operation: If (condition true) then PC + d $\blacktriangleright$ PC

**Assembler
Syntax:**   Bcc ⟨label⟩

Attributes: Size = (Byte, Word, Long*)
                     *(MC68020/MC68030/MC68040 only)

Description: If the specified condition is true, program execution continues at
                     location (PC) + displacement. The PC contains the address of the instruction
                     word of the Bcc instruction plus two. The displacement is a twos complement
                     integer that represents the relative distance in bytes from the current PC to the
                     destination PC. If the 8-bit displacement field in the instruction word is zero, a
                     16-bit displacement (the word immediately following the instruction) is used.
                     If the 8-bit displacement field in the instruction word is all ones ($FF), the 32-
                     bit displacement (long word immediately following the instruction) is used.
                     Condition code cc specifies one of the following conditions:

CC	carry clear	0100	$\overline{C}$
CS	carry set	0101	C
EQ	equal	0111	Z
GE	greater or equal	1100	$N \cdot V + \overline{N} \cdot \overline{V}$
GT	greater than	1110	$N \cdot V \cdot \overline{Z} + \overline{N} \cdot \overline{V} \cdot \overline{Z}$
HI	high	0010	$\overline{C} \cdot \overline{Z}$
LE	less or equal	1111	$Z + N \cdot \overline{V} + \overline{N} \cdot V$
LS	low or same	0011	$C + Z$
LT	less than	1101	$N \cdot \overline{V} + \overline{N} \cdot V$
MI	minus	1011	N
NE	not equal	0110	$\overline{Z}$
PL	plus	1010	$\overline{N}$
VC	overflow clear	1000	$\overline{V}$
VS	overflow set	1001	V

Condition Codes:
Not affected.

Instruction Format:

15	14	13	12	11	10	9	8	7	6	5	4	3	2	1	0
0	1	1	0	CONDITION				8-BIT DISPLACEMENT							
16-BIT DISPLACEMENT IF 8-BIT DISPLACEMENT = $00															
32-BIT DISPLACEMENT IF 8-BIT DISPLACEMENT = $FF															

Instruction Fields:
   Condition field — The binary code for one of the conditions listed in the table.
   8-Bit Displacement field — Twos complement integer specifying the number
      of bytes between the branch instruction and the next instruction to be exe-
      cuted if the condition is met.
   16-Bit Displacement field — Used for the displacement when the 8-bit displace-
      ment field contains $00.
   32-Bit Displacement field — Used for the displacement when the 8-bit displace-
      ment field contains $FF.

NOTE

A branch to the immediately following instruction automatically uses
the 16-bit displacement format because the 8-bit displacement field
contains $00 (zero offset).

"High" and "low" refer to the relationship of two signed values;
"greater" and "less" refer to the relationship of two signed values.

FIGURE 4-10   68000 conditional JMP instructions.

if minus is BMI GO and branch if plus is BPL GO. Decrement and branch if zero is DBEQ.

Next to each mnemonic in Figure 4-10 is a brief explanation of the mnemonic. Note that the terms *above* and *below* are used when you are working with unsigned binary numbers. The 8-bit unsigned number 1100 0110 is above the 8-bit unsigned number 0011 1001, for example. The terms *greater than* and *less than* are used when you are working with signed binary numbers. The 8-bit signed number 0011 1001 is greater than (more positive) than the 8-bit signed number 1100 0110, which represents a negative number. Also shown in Figure 4-10 is the instruction encoding for this branch condition. In the right column of each table half in Figure 4-10 is an indication of the condition-code expression that will cause the 68000 to do the branch. If the specified flag conditions are not present, the 68000 will just continue on to the next instruction in sequence. In other words, if the branch condition is not met, the conditional branch instruction will effectively function as a NOP. Suppose, for example, we have the instruction BCS SAVE, where SAVE is the label at the destination address. If the carry flag is set, this instruction will cause the 68000 to branch to the instruction at the SAVE: label. If the carry flag is not set, the instruction will have no effect other than taking up a little processor time.

The conditional branch instructions are usually used after arithmetic or logic instructions. Very commonly they are used after compare instructions. For this case the compare instruction syntax and the conditional branch instruction syntax are such that a little trick makes it very easy to see what will cause a jump to occur. Here's the trick. Suppose that you see the instruction sequence

```
CMP.B   D1, D0
BGE     HEATER_OFF
```

in a program and you want to determine what these instructions do. The CMP instruction compares the low byte in register D0 with the low byte in register D1 and sets condition codes according to the result. A previous section showed you how the carry and zero flags are affected by a compare instruction. According to Figure 4-10 the BGE instruction says "branch if greater or equal" to the label HEATER_OFF. The question now is, Will it jump if D0 is greater than D1, or will it jump if D1 is greater than D0? You could determine how the condition codes will be affected by the compare and use Figure 4-10 to answer the question. However, an easier way is to remember that the destination is always the key register and is always the basis for comparison. If the destination is D0, as in this case, then the condition will test as the statement "branch if D0 is greater than or equal to D1." Always say the destination first in a statement like this, and the meaning of the sequence will immediately be clear. Notice that the statement mixes the compare and the branch instruction meanings in a way that makes the intended result obvious. As you write your own programs, thinking of a conditional sequence in this way

should help you to choose the right conditional jump instruction. The next sections show you how we use conditional and unconditional jump instructions to implement some of the standard program structures and solve some common programming problems.

IF-THEN, IF-THEN-ELSE, and MULTIPLE IF-THEN-ELSE PROGRAMS

IF-THEN Programs

Remember from Chapter 2 that the IF-THEN structure has the format

```
IF condition THEN
    action
    action
```

This structure says that IF the stated condition is found to be true, the series of actions following THEN will be executed. IF the condition is false, execution will skip over the actions after the THEN and proceed with the next mainline instruction.

The simple IF-THEN is implemented with a conditional jump instruction. In some cases an instruction to set condition codes is needed before the conditional jump instruction. Figure 4-11a uses a program fragment to show one way to implement the simple IF-THEN structure. In this program we first compare D1 with D0 to set the required condition codes. If the zero code is set after the comparison, indicating that D1 is equal to D0, the BEQ instruction will cause execution to jump to the MOVE.B #$07,D2 instruction labeled THERE. If D1 is not equal to D0, then the three NOP instructions after the BEQ instruction will be executed before the MOVE.B #$07,D2 instruction.

The implementation in Figure 4-11a will work well for a short sequence of instructions after the conditional branch instruction. However, if the sequence of instructions is very lengthy, there is a potential problem. Remember from the discussion of conditional branches in the last chapter that a conditional branch can only be to a location in the range of −32,768 bytes to +32,767 bytes from the address after the conditional branch instruction. A very long sequence of instructions after the conditional branch instruction may put the label out of range of the conditional branch instruction. If you are absolutely sure that the destination label will not be out of range, then use the instruction sequence shown in Figure 4-11a to implement an IF-THEN structure. If you are not sure if the destination will be in range, Figure 4-11b shows an instruction sequence that will always work. In this sequence the conditional branch instruction only has to branch over the JMP instruction. The JMP instruction used to get to the label THERE can jump to anywhere in memory. Note that you have to change the conditional jump instruction from BEQ to BNE in this second version. The price you pay for not having to worry whether the destination is in range is an extra jump instruction.

```
              CMP.L    D0,D1              ; compare to set flags
              BEQ      THERE              ; if equal then skip correction

              NOP                         ; NOPs represent correction
              NOP                         ; instructions
      THERE:  MOVE.B   #$07,D2            ; load count


      ;
                                (a)


              CMP.W    D0,D1              ; compare to set flags
              BNE      FIX                ; if not equal do correction
              JMP      THERE
      FIX:    NOP                         ; NOPs represent correction
              NOP                         ; instructions
              NOP
      THERE:  MOVE.B   #$07,D2            ; load count


      ;
              END
                                (b)
```

FIGURE 4-11   IF-THEN implementations. (a) Conditional jump destinations closer than ±128 bytes. (b) Conditional jump destinations further than ±128 bytes.

By now you are probably thinking that this IF-THEN structure looks very familiar. It should, because a simple IF-THEN is part of the WHILE-DO and REPEAT-UNTIL structures. In the discussions of WHILE-DO and REPEAT-UNTIL structures later in this chapter, look for the simple IF-THEN as a building block used to help construct the more complex structures.

IF-THEN-ELSE Programs

The IF-THEN-ELSE structure is used to indicate a choice between two alternative courses of action. Figure 3-3b shows the flowchart and pseudocode for this structure. Basically the structure has the format

```
IF condition THEN
    action
    action
ELSE
    action
    action
```

This is a different situation than the simple IF-THEN, because here either one series of actions or another series of actions is done before going on with the next mainline instruction. An example will show how we implement this structure.

Suppose that in the computerized factory we discussed in Chapter 2 we have a 68000 microcomputer that controls a printed-circuit-board-making machine.

Part of the job of this 68000 is to check a temperature sensor and turn on a green lamp or a yellow lamp, depending on the value of the temperature it reads in. If the temperature is below 30°C, we want to turn on a yellow lamp to tell the operator that the solution is not up to temperature. If the temperature is greater than or equal to 30°C, we want to light a green lamp. With a system such as this the operator can visually scan all the lamps on the control panel until he or she sees all green lamps. When all the lamps are green, the operator can push the GO button to start making boards. The yellow lamp lets the operator know that this part of the machine is working, but the temperature is not yet up to 30°C.

Figure 4-12, p. 86, shows two ways—flowcharts and pseudocode—to represent the algorithm for this problem. The difference between the two is simply a matter of whether we make the decision based on the temperature being below 30°C or we make the decision based on the temperature being greater than or equal to 30°C. The two approaches are equally valid, but your choice determines which conditional jump instruction you choose. Figure 4-13a (pp. 87–88) shows the 68000 assembly language implementation of the algorithm in Figure 4-12a.

For this program segment, assume that we read the temperature in from an A/D converter connected to input port $C015. Also assume that the control for the yellow lamp is connected to bit 0 of port $C014 and the control for the green lamp is connected to bit 1 of port

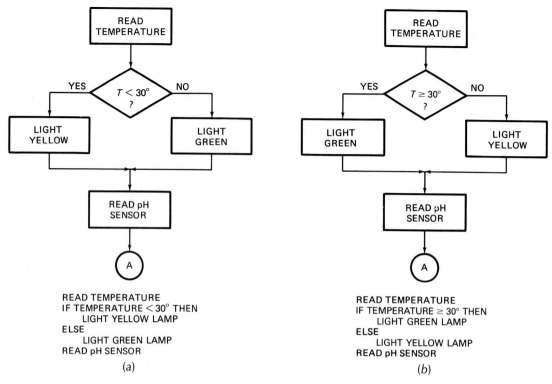

FIGURE 4-12 Flowcharts and pseudocode for two ways of expressing algorithm for PC-board-making machine. (a) Temperature below 30° test. (b) Temperature above 30° test.

$C014. A 1 sent to a bit position of port $C014 turns on the lamp connected to that line, and a 0 turns it off. After we read the data in from the port, we compare it with our setpoint value of 30°C. If the input value is below 30°C, then we jump to the instructions that turn on the yellow lamp. If the temperature is greater than or equal to 30°C, we jump to the instructions that turn on the green lamp. Note that we have implemented this algorithm in such a way that the BLT instruction will always be able to reach the label YELLOW.

To actually turn on a lamp, we load a 1 in the appropriate bit of register D0 with a MOVE.B instruction and send the byte to the lamp-control port, $C014. The instruction sequence MOVE.B #$01,D0; MOVE.B D0,($C014), for example, will light the yellow lamp by sending a 1 to bit 0 of port $C014.

Figure 4-13b (pp. 88–89) shows another equally valid assembly language program segment to solve our problem. This one uses a branch if greater or equal instruction, BGE, at the decision point and switches the order of the actions. This program more closely follows the second algorithm statement in Figure 4-12b. Perhaps you can see from these examples why two programmers may write very different programs to solve even very simple programming problems.

Multiple IF-THEN-ELSE Implementation

In the preceding section we showed how to implement and use the IF-THEN-ELSE structure, which chooses between two alternative courses of action. In many situations we want a computer to choose one of several alternative actions based on the value of some variable read in or on a command code entered by a user. To choose one alternative from several, we can *nest* IF-THEN-ELSE structures. The result has the following form:

```
IF condition THEN
    action
    action
ELSE IF condition THEN
        action
        action
    ELSE
        action
        action
```

It is important to note in this structure that the last ELSE is part of the IF-THEN just before it. Figure 3-3g showed a flowchart and pseudocode for a soup-cook example using this structure. The soup-cook example, however, is too messy to implement here. Therefore, while the PC board machine from the last section is still fresh in your mind, we will expand that example to show you how a multiple IF-THEN-ELSE is implemented.

Suppose that we want to have three lamps on our PC-board-making machine. We want a yellow lamp to indicate that the temperature is below 30°C, a green

```
1:
2:                              ; 68000 Program section for PC board making machine
3:                              ;
4:                              ; ABSTRACT      : This program section reads the temperature of a cleaning
5:                              ;                 bath solution and lights one of two lamps according to
6:                              ;                 the temperature read.  If the temp is below 30 degrees
7:                              ;                 Celcius, a yellow lamp will be turned on.  If the temp is
8:                              ;                 above or equal to 30 degrees, a green lamp will be turned
9:                              ;                 on.
10:                             ;
11:                             ; REGISTERS USED:  A0, D0
12:                             ; PORTS USED    :  $C016 as a control port for the lamp port
13:                             ;                  $C015 as a temperature input port
14:                             ;                  $C014 as a lamp control output (yellow=bit 0, green= bit 1)
15:                             ; PROCEDURES    :  none used
16:                             ;
17:                             ;              alr 12-88
18:                             ;
19:
20: 00004000                          ORG      $4000              ; start the code at memory address $4000
21:
22:                             ; initialize port $C014 as an output port for lamp output
23: 00004000 13FC 0000 0000           MOVE.B   #$00,($C016)       ; set for direction initialization
         C016
24: 00004008 13FC 00FF 0000           MOVE.B   #$FF,($C014)       ; all bits in port for output
         C014
25: 00004010 13FC 0004 0000           MOVE.B   #$04,($C016)       ; set for I/O
         C016
26:                             ; initialization complete
27:
28: 00004018 1039 0000 C015           MOVE.B   ($C015),D0         ; read temp from sensor on input port
29: 0000401E 0C00 001E               CMPI.B   #30,D0             ; compare temp to 30 degrees C
30: 00004022 6C00 0008               BGE      GREEN              ; if temp < 30 go light yellow lamp
31: 00004026 4EF9 0000 403C          JMP      YELLOW             ; elso go light green lamp
32:
33: 0000402C 103C 0002       GREEN:   MOVE.B   #$02,D0            ; load code to light green lamp
34: 00004030 13C0 0000 C014          MOVE.B   D0,($C014)         ; send code to light green lamp
35: 00004036 4EF9 0000 4046          JMP      EXIT               ; go to next mainline instruction
36:
37: 0000403C 103C 0001       YELLOW:  MOVE.B   #$01,D0            ; load code to light yellow lamp
38: 00004040 13C0 0000 C014          MOVE.B   D0,($C014)         ; send code to light yellow lamp
39:
40: 00004046 2079 0000 C016  EXIT:    MOVEA.L  $C016,A0           ; next mainline instruction
41:
42: 0000404C 4E75                    RTS                         ; return to whoever called me
43:
44: 0000404E                        END
```

(a) *(continued on p. 88)*

FIGURE 4-13   Assembly language program segments for PC-board-making
machine decisions. (a) Version for below 30° *(continued on p. 88)*. (b) Version
for above 30° (pp. 88–89).

```
Symbol Name                      Attribute    Hex        Decimal

EXIT. . . . . . . . . . . . . . . LABEL      00004046    16454
GREEN . . . . . . . . . . . . . . LABEL      0000403C    16444
YELLOW. . . . . . . . . . . . . . LABEL      0000402C    16428


Obj bytes: 78D/0000004EH


End assembly.  Lines: 43  Errors: 0
```

(a)

```
Symbol Name                      Attribute    Hex        Decimal

EXIT. . . . . . . . . . . . . . . LABEL      00004046    16454
GREEN . . . . . . . . . . . . . . LABEL      0000402C    16428
YELLOW. . . . . . . . . . . . . . LABEL      0000403C    16444


Obj bytes: 78D/0000004EH


End assembly.  Lines: 44  Errors: 0
```

(b) (continued on p. 89)

FIGURE 4-13 (*continued*)

lamp to indicate that the temperature is greater than or equal to 30°C but below 40°C, and a red lamp to indicate that the temperature is at or above 40°C. Figure 4-14, p. 90, shows three ways to indicate what we want to do here. The first way, in Figure 4-14a, simply indicates the desired action next to each temperature range. You may find this form very useful in visualizing problems where the alternatives are based on the range of a variable. Don't miss the ASCII-to-hexadecimal problem at the end of the chapter for some practice with this. Once you get the problem defined in this list form, you can easily convert it to a flowchart or pseudocode. When writing the flowchart or the pseudocode, it is best to start at one end of the overall range and work your way to the other. For example, in the flowchart in Figure 4-14b, we start by checking if the temperature is below 30°. If the temperature is not below 30°, then it must be above or equal to 30°, and you do not have to do another test to determine this. You then check if the temperature is below 40°. If the temperature is above or equal to 30° but below 40°, then you know that the temperature is in the green-lamp range. If the temperature is not less than 40°, then you know that the temperature must be greater than or equal to 40°. In other words, two carefully chosen tests will direct execution to one of the three alternatives.

Figure 4-15, pp. 91–92, shows how we can write a program for this algorithm in 68000 assembly language. In the program we first initialize port $C014 as an output port. We then read in the temperature from an A/D converter connected to port $C015. We compare the temperature read in with the first setpoint value, 30° ($1E). If the temperature is less than 30°, the branch if lower than (BLT) instruction will cause a jump to the label YELLOW. If the jump is not taken, we know the temperature is greater than or equal to 30°C, so we go on to the CMPI.B #$28,D0 instruction to see if the temperature is less than the second setpoint, 40° ($28). The BLT GREEN instruction will cause a branch

```
 1:                            ; 68000 Program section for PC board making machine
 2:                            ;
 3:                            ; ABSTRACT      : This program section reads the temperature of a cleaning
 4:                            ;                 bath solution and lights one of two lamps according to
 5:                            ;                 the temperature read.  If the temp is below 30 degrees
 6:                            ;                 Celcius, a yellow lamp will be turned on.  If the temp is
 7:                            ;                 above or equal to 30 degrees, a green lamp will be turned
 8:                            ;                 on.
 9:                            ;
10:                            ; REGISTERS USED:  A0, D0
11:                            ; PORTS USED    :  $C016 as a control port for the lamp port
12:                            ;                  $C015 as a temperature input port
13:                            ;                  $C014 as a lamp control output (yellow=bit 0, green= bit 1)
14:                            ; PROCEDURES    :  none used
15:                            ;
16:                            ;              alr 12-88
17:                            ;
18:
19: 00004000                            ORG      $4000          ; start the code at memory address $4000
20:
21:                            ; initialize port $C014 as an output port for lamp output
22: 00004000 13FC 0000 0000            MOVE.B   #$00,($C016)   ; set for direction initialization
         C016
23: 00004008 13FC 00FF 0000            MOVE.B   #$FF,($C014)   ; all bits in port for output
         C014
24: 00004010 13FC 0004 0000            MOVE.B   #$04,($C016)   ; set for I/O
         C016
25:                            ; initialization complete
26:
27: 00004018 1039 0000 C015            MOVE.B   ($C015),D0     ; read temp from sensor on input port
28: 0000401E 0C00 001E                 CMPI.B   #30,D0         ; compare temp to 30 degrees C
29: 00004022 6D00 0008                 BLT      YELLOW         ; if temp < 30 go light yellow lamp
30: 00004026 4EF9 0000 403C            JMP      GREEN          ; elso go light green lamp
31:
32: 0000402C 103C 0001       YELLOW:   MOVE.B   #$01,D0        ; load code to light yellow lamp
33: 00004030 13C0 0000 C014            MOVE.B   D0,($C014)     ; send code to light yellow lamp
34: 00004036 4EF9 0000 4046            JMP      EXIT           ; go to next mainline instruction
35:
36: 0000403C 103C 0002       GREEN:    MOVE.B   #$02,D0        ; load code to light green lamp
37: 00004040 13C0 0000 C014            MOVE.B   D0,($C014)     ; send code to light green lamp
38:
39: 00004046 2079 0000 C016  EXIT:     MOVEA.L  $C016,A0       ; next mainline instruction
40:
41: 0000404C 4E75                      RTS                     ; return to whoever called me
42:
43: 0000404E                           END
```

(b) (continued from p. 88)

FIGURE 4-13 *(continued)*

to the label GREEN if the temperature is less than 40° ($28). If the jump is not taken, we know that the temperature must be at or above 40°C, so we just go ahead and turn on the red lamp.

For this program we assume that the lines that control the three lamps are connected to port $C014. The yellow lamp is connected to bit 0, the green is connected to bit 1, and the red is connected to bit 2. We turn on a lamp by outputting a 1 to the appropriate bit of port $C014. The instruction sequence MOVE.B

TEMPERATURE

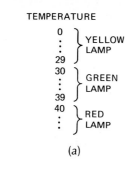

0
⋮   } YELLOW
29   LAMP
30
⋮   } GREEN
39   LAMP
40   } RED
⋮   LAMP

(a)

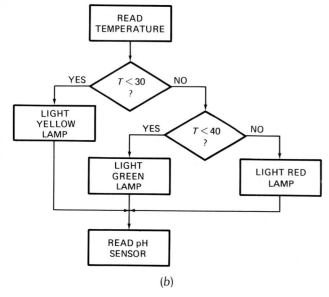

(b)

```
READ TEMPERATURE
IF TEMPERATURE < 30° THEN
    LIGHT YELLOW LAMP
ELSE IF TEMPERATURE < 40° THEN
    LIGHT GREEN LAMP
    ELSE LIGHT RED LAMP
READ pH SENSOR
```

(c)

FIGURE 4-14 Algorithm for three-light PC-board-making machine. (a) Condition list. (b) Flowchart. (c) Pseudocode.

#$02,D0; MOVE.B D0,($C014), for example, will turn on the green lamp by sending a 1 to bit 1 of port $C014.

SUMMARY OF IF-THEN-ELSE IMPLEMENTATION

Conditional branch instructions and instructions that set condition codes for them are used to implement IF-THEN-ELSE structures. A single IF-THEN-ELSE structure is used to choose one of two alternative series of actions. IF-THEN-ELSE structures can be linked to choose one of three or more alternative series of actions. As shown in Figure 3-3g, linked IF-THEN-ELSE structures are one way to implement the CASE structure. The algorithm for the PC board machine lamps program in the preceding section example could have been expressed as follows:

CASE temperature OF
  < 30   : light yellow lamp
  ≥ 30 and < 40   : light green lamp
  ≥ 40   : light red lamp

This CASE structure would be implemented in the same way as the program in Figure 4-15 (pp. 91–92). However, expressing the algorithm for the problem as linked IF-THEN-ELSE structures makes it much easier to see how to implement the algorithm in assembly language. Later, we show you another way to implement some CASE situations using a *jump table*.

WHILE-DO Implementation and Example

Remember from the discussion in Chapter 3 that the WHILE-DO structure has the form

WHILE some condition is present DO
    action
    action

An important point about this structure is that the condition is checked *before* any action is done. In industrial control applications of microprocessors, there are many cases where we want to do this. The following very simple example will show you how to implement this structure in 68000 assembly language.

DEFINING THE PROBLEM AND WRITING THE ALGORITHM

Suppose that in controlling a chemical process we want to bring the temperature of a solution up to 100°C before going on to the next step in the process. If the solution temperature is below 100°, we want to turn on a heater and wait for the temperature to reach 100°. If the solution temperature is at or above 100°, then we want to go on with the next step in the process. The WHILE-DO structure fits this problem because we want to check the condition (temperature) before we turn on the heater. We don't want to turn on the heater if the temperature is already high enough because we might overheat the solution.

Figure 4-16, p. 92, shows a flowchart and the pseudocode of an algorithm for this problem. The first step in the algorithm is to read in the temperature from a sensor connected to a port. The temperature read in is then compared with 100°. These two parts represent the condition-checking part of the structure. If the temperature is at or above 100°, execution will exit the structure and do the next mainline action, turn off the heater. If the heater is already off, it will not do any harm to turn it off again. If the temperature is less than 100°, the heater will be turned on and the temperature rechecked. Execution will stay in this loop while the temperature is below 100°. Incidentally, it will not do any harm to turn the heater on if it is already on. When the temperature reaches 100°, execution will exit the structure and go on to the next mainline action, turning off the heater.

```
1:                            ; 68000 Program section for PC board making machine
2:                            ;
3:                            ; ABSTRACT     : This program section reads the temperature of a cleaning
4:                            ;                 bath solution and lights one of two lamps according to
5:                            ;                 the temperature read.  If the temp is below 30 degrees
6:                            ;                 Celcius, a yellow lamp will be turned on.  If the temp
7:                            ;                 is >= 30 and < 40 degrees, a green lamp will be turned on.
8:                            ;                 Temps >= 40 degrees will turn on a red lamp.
9:                            ;
10:                           ; REGISTERS USED:  A0, D0
11:                           ; PORTS USED    :  $C016 as a control port for the lamp port
12:                           ;                  $C015 as a temperature input port
13:                           ;                  $C014 as a lamp control output (yellow = bit 0,
14:                           ;                            green = bit 1, red = bit 2)
15:                           ; PROCEDURES    :  none used
16:                           ;
17:                           ;         alr 1-89
18:                           ;
19:
20: 00004000                          ORG      $4000        ; start the code at memory address $4000
21:
22:                           ; initialize port $C014 as an output port for lamp output
23: 00004000 13FC 0000 0000           MOVE.B   #$00,($C016)      ; set for direction initialization
             C016
24: 00004008 13FC 00FF 0000           MOVE.B   #$FF,($C014)      ; all bits in port for output
             C014
25: 00004010 13FC 0004 0000           MOVE.B   #$04,($C016)      ; set for I/O
             C016
26:                           ; initialization complete
27:
28: 00004018 1039 0000 C015           MOVE.B   ($C015),D0 ; read temp from sensor on input port
29: 0000401E 207C 0000 C011           MOVEA.L  #$C011,A0  ; point A0 at output port
30: 00004024 0C00 001E              CMPI.B   #$1E,D0    ; compare temp to 30 degrees C
31: 00004028 6D00 0016              BLT      YELLOW     ; if temp < 30 go light yellow lamp
32: 0000402C 0C00 0028              CMPI.B   #$28,D0    ; compare with 40 degrees
33: 00004030 6D00 001A              BLT      GREEN      ; if temp < 40 go light green lamp
34: 00004034 103C 0004     RED:     MOVE.B   #$04,D0    ; temp >= 40 so load code to light red lamp
35: 00004038 2080                  MOVE.L   D0,(A0)    ; send code to light red lamp
36: 0000403A 4EF9 0000 4052          JMP      EXIT       ; go to next mainline instruction
37:
38: 00004040 103C 0001     YELLOW:  MOVE.B   #$01,D0    ; load code to light yellow lamp
39: 00004044 2080                  MOVE.L   D0,(A0)    ; send code to light yellow lamp
40: 00004046 4EF9 0000 4052          JMP      EXIT       ; go to next mainline instruction
41:
42: 0000404C 103C 0002     GREEN:   MOVE.B   #$02,D0    ; load code to light green lamp
43: 00004050 2080                  MOVE.L   D0,(A0)    ; send code to light green lamp
44: 00004052 207C 0000 C016  EXIT:  MOVEA.L  #$C016,A0  ; next mainline instruction
45: 00004058 1010                  MOVE.B   (A0),D0    ; read ph sensor
46: 0000405A 4E75                  RTS                 ; return to whoever called me
47:
48: 0000405C                          END
```

FIGURE 4-15 Assembly language program for three-light PC-board-making
machine (*continued on p. 92*).

Symbol Name	Attribute	Hex	Decimal
EXIT.	LABEL	00004052	16466
GREEN	LABEL	0000404C	16460
RED	LABEL	00004034	16436
YELLOW.	LABEL	00004040	16448

Obj bytes: 92D/0000005CH

End assembly. Lines: 48 Errors: 0

FIGURE 4-15 (*continued*)

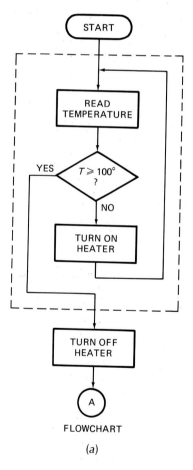

FLOWCHART

(a)

READ TEMPERATURE
WHILE TEMPERATURE < 100° DO
TURN HEATER ON
TURN HEATER OFF

PSEUDOCODE

(b)

FIGURE 4-16   Flowchart (a) and pseudocode (b) for heater-control problem.

IMPLEMENTING THE ALGORITHM IN ASSEMBLY LANGUAGE

Figure 4-17, pp. 93–96, shows one way to write the assembly language for this example. We have assumed for this example that the temperature sensor inputs an 8-bit binary value for the Celsius temperature to port $C015. We have also assumed that the heater control output is connected to the MSB of port $C014. (Incidentally, these port addresses are two of the available ports on an URDA® MDS board.) A 1 sent to the MSB of port $C014 turns the heater on.

Recall from Chapter 2 that the 68000 uses memory-mapped I/O. This means that the CPU accesses I/O ports using the same instructions as it uses to access main memory. The hardware outside the CPU determines where memory and where I/O devices appear in the memory address space. The 68000 CPU does reserve the 256 bytes of memory from $00000000 to $00000100 for interrupt vectors used during CPU startup and during unusual or exceptional situations. The term *port* refers to a data path to an I/O device that appears to the CPU at a particular location in its address space. A port is often referred to as the port at that particular address—for example, the port at $C014.

The 68000 presents a 32-bit address bus and a 16-bit data bus. The data bus must go to and from I/O devices, so the 68000 can access a word-wide (16-bit) I/O port. The 68000 is also often connected to 8-bit, or byte-wide, I/O devices. These devices can be mapped into the memory space such that each port on the I/O device has an even address and sits in the low byte of a 68000 CPU word. The 68000 provides a special instruction for this case, the MOVEP instruction (move peripheral data). MOVEP is unique in that it allows a block of data to be moved from the high bytes of words only or from the low bytes only.

These devices can also be mapped as in the URDA MDS such that successive byte-wide ports on the I/O device appear as successive bytes to the 68000, appearing alternately as low and then high bytes of

68000 CPU words. Normal 68000 MOVE instructions work perfectly well for this type of I/O. In fact, the only way for someone reading your program to tell whether the CPU is accessing I/O or variables in memory is through the comments you place in the source code.

The 68000 can access as many I/O ports as it can memory locations. For the 68000 this means that, in theory, 2^{24} or 16 Mbytes can be addressed (the other 8 address lines are not brought "off chip" on the 68000). The 68020, 68030, and 68040 have pins to bring out all 32 address lines. The 68010 presents only 24 address lines.

Most common devices used as ports for microcomputers can be used for input or output. When the power is first applied to these devices, they are in the input mode. If you want to use one of these devices as output ports, you must send the device a control word that switches the device to output mode. Chapter 9 and later chapters describe in detail how you initialize programmable port devices, but to give you an introduction, we show you here how to initialize one of the ports in a 6821 on an URDA MDS for use as an output port. To specify the function of one of these programmable devices, you send a control word to a register inside the device. You can find the control word format for each type of device in the manufacturer's data book. For one of the 6821s on an URDA board, the address of the control register that controls port $C014 in the device is $C016. To initialize all 8 bits of port $C014 as outputs, first the command byte $00 is sent to the control port address $C016. This tells the I/O device to listen on the I/O port at $C014 for a directional bit vector telling it which bits should be inputs and which should be outputs. The instruction MOVE.B #$00, ($C016) accomplishes this in Figure 4-17a, pp. 93–94. The direction bit vector is then written directly to the I/O port using the instruction MOVE.B#$FF,($C016). Finally, the control byte

#$04 is written to the control register telling it to put the port at address $C014 back into normal I/O mode. The instruction for performing this is MOVE.B #$04,($C016). It is to the port address $C014 that we will output a byte to turn the heater on or off.

After we input the data from the temperature sensor in Figure 4-17a, we compare the value read with 100 ($64). The BGE instruction after the compare can be read as branch to the label HEATER_OFF if D0 is greater than or equal to 100. Note that we used the branch if greater or equal instruction rather than a branch if equal instruction. Can you see why? To see the answer, visualize what would happen if we had used a BEQ instruction and the temperature of the solution were 101°. On the first check the temperature would not be equal to 100°, so the 68000 would turn on the heater. The heater would not be turned off until meltdown.

If the heater temperature is below 100°, we turn on the heater by loading a 1 in the MSB of D0 and outputting this value to the MSB of port $C014. We then do an unconditional JMP back to check the temperature again.

When the temperature is at or above 100°, we load a 0 in the most significant bit of D0 and output this to port $C014 to turn off the heater. Here we could have sent the byte directly using MOVE.B #$80,($C014). Note that the action of turning off the heater is outside the basic WHILE-DO structure. This is shown by the dotted box in the flowchart in Figure 4-16a and by the indentation in the pseudocode in Figure 4-16b.

SOLVING A POTENTIAL PROBLEM OF CONDITIONAL JUMP INSTRUCTIONS

In the example program in Figure 4-17a we used the conditional jump instruction BGT to help implement the WHILE-DO structure. Conditional branch instructions have a potential problem, of which you should

Symbol Name	Attribute	Hex	Decimal
HEATER_OFF.	LABEL	00004036	16438
TEMP_IN	LABEL	00004018	16408

Obj bytes: 66D/00000042H

End assembly. Lines: 39 Errors: 0

(a)   (continued)

FIGURE 4-17 Assembly language program for heater-control problem. (a) First approach (pp. 93–94). (b) Improved version (pp. 95–96).

```
1:                                          ; 68000 Program
2:                                          ;
3:                                          ; ABSTRACT      : This program turns a heater off if the temperature equals
4:                                          ;                 100 degrees or more, and turns the heater on if the
5:                                          ;                 temperature is below 100 degrees.
6:                                          ;
7:                                          ; REGISTERS USED: D0
8:                                          ; PORTS USED    : $C016 as a control register for the heater port
9:                                          ;                 $C015 for temperature data input
10:                                         ;                 $C014 MSB for heater control output
11:                                         ; PROCEDURES    : none used
12:                                         ;
13:                                         ;                     alr 10-88
14:                                         ;
15:
16: 00004000                                        ORG     $4000           ; start the code at memory address $4000
17:
18:                                         ; initialize port $C014 as an output port for lamp output
19: 00004000 13FC 0000 0000                         MOVE.B  #$00,($C016)    ; set for direction initialization
         C016
20: 00004008 13FC 00FF 0000                         MOVE.B  #$FF,($C014)    ; all bits in port for output
         C014
21: 00004010 13FC 0004 0000                         MOVE.B  #$04,($C016)    ; set for I/O
         C016
22:                                         ; initialization complete
23:
24: 00004018                                TEMP_IN:
25: 00004018 13C0 0000 C015                         MOVE.B  D0,($C015)      ; read in temperature data
26: 0000401E 0C00 0064                              CMPI.B  #100,D0         ; if temp >= 100
27: 00004022 6C00 0012                              BGE     HEATER_OFF      ; go turn heater off
28:
29: 00004026 103C 0080                              MOVE.B  #$80,D0         ; load code for heater on
30: 0000402A 13C0 0000 C014                         MOVE.B  D0,($C014)      ; turn heater on
31: 00004030 4EF9 0000 4018                         JMP     TEMP_IN         ; go and read temperature again
32:
33: 00004036                                HEATER_OFF:
34: 00004036 103C 0000                              MOVE.B  #$00,D0         ; load code for heater off
35: 0000403A 13C0 0000 C014                         MOVE.B  D0,($C014)      ; turn heater off
36:
37: 00004040 4E75                                   RTS                     ; return to whoever called me
38:
39: 00004042                                        END
```

(a)   (continued)

FIGURE 4-17 (continued)

become aware at this point. *All the conditional branch instructions are 8- or 16-bit-type branches.* This means that a conditional jump can only be to a location within the range of $-32,768$ bytes to $+32,767$ bytes from the instruction after the conditional jump instruction. This limit on the range of the jump posed no problem for the example program in Figure 4-17a because we were jumping to a location only 8 bytes ahead in the program. Suppose, however, that the instructions for turning off the heater required 100,000 bytes of memory. The HEATER—OFF label

would then be outside the range of the BGT instruction. This will normally not happen on the URDA MDS because it is a small system running small programs.

Figure 4-17b, pp. 95–96, shows how you can change the instructions slightly to solve the problem without changing the basic overall WHILE-DO structure. In this example we read the temperature in as before and compare it to 100 ($64). We then use the branch if less than instruction, BLT, to branch to the program section that turns on the heater. This instruction, together with the CMP instruction, says branch to the label

```
 1:
 2:                            ; 68000 Program
 3:                            ;
 4:                            ; ABSTRACT     : This program turns a heater off if the temperature equals
 5:                            ;                100 degrees or more, and turns the heater on if the
 6:                            ;                temperature is below 100 degrees.
 7:                            ;
 8:                            ; REGISTERS USED:  D0
 9:                            ; PORTS USED    :  $C016 as a control register for the heater port
10:                            ;                  $C015 for temperature data input
11:                            ;                  $C014 MSB for heater control output
12:                            ; PROCEDURES    :  none used
13:                            ;
14:                            ;                     alr 10-88
15:                            ;
16:
17: 00004000                            ORG      $4000           ; start the code at memory address $4000
18:
19:                            ; initialize port $C014 as an output port for lamp output
20: 00004000 13FC 0000 0000            MOVE.B   #$00,($C016)        ; set for direction initialization
              C016
21: 00004008 13FC 00FF 0000            MOVE.B   #$FF,($C014)        ; all bits in port for output
              C014
22: 00004010 13FC 0004 0000            MOVE.B   #$04,($C016)        ; set for I/O
              C016
23:                            ; initialization complete
24:
25: 00004018                   TEMP_IN:
26: 00004018 13C0 0000 C015            MOVE.B   D0,($C015)      ; read in temperature data
27: 0000401E 0C00 0064                 CMPI.B   #100,D0         ;
28: 00004022 6D00 0008                 BLT      HEATER_ON       ; if temp < 100 go
29:                                                             ;    turn heater ON
30: 00004026 4EF9 0000 403C            JMP      HEATER_OFF      ; temp >= 100 so go
31:                                                             ;    turn heater OFF
32:
33: 0000402C                   HEATER_ON:
34: 0000402C 103C 0080                 MOVE.B   #$80,D0         ; load code for heater on
35: 00004030 13C0 0000 C014            MOVE.B   D0,($C014)      ; turn heater on
36: 00004036 4EF9 0000 4018            JMP      TEMP_IN         ; go and read temperature again
37:
38: 0000403C                   HEATER_OFF:
39: 0000403C 103C 0000                 MOVE.B   #$00,D0         ; load code for heater off
40: 00004040 13C0 0000 C014            MOVE.B   D0,($C014)      ; turn heater off
41:
42: 00004046 4E75                      RTS                      ; return to whoever called me
43:
44: 00004048                           END
```

(b)   (continued)

FIGURE 4-17 (continued)

HEATER—ON if D0 is less than 100. If the temperature is at or above 100, the BLT instruction will act like a NOP, and the 68000 will go on to the JMP HEATER—OFF instruction. Changing the conditional jump instruction and writing the program in this way means that the destination for the conditional branch instruction is always just two instructions away. Therefore, you know that the destination will always be reachable. Except for very time-critical program sections, you may want to write conditional branch in-

Symbol Name	Attribute	Hex	Decimal
HEATER_OFF	LABEL	0000403C	16444
HEATER_ON.	LABEL	0000402C	16428
TEMP_IN.	LABEL	00004018	16408

Obj bytes: 72D/00000048H

End assembly.   Lines: 44   Errors: 0

(b)

FIGURE 4-17 (continued)

REPEAT-UNTIL IMPLEMENTATION AND EXAMPLES

Remember from the discussion in Chapter 3 that the REPEAT-UNTIL structure has the form

REPEAT
  action
  action
   .
   .
   .

UNTIL some condition is present

An important point about this structure is that the action or series of actions is done once before the condition is checked. Compare this with the WHILE-DO structure.

The following examples will show you how you can implement the REPEAT-UNTIL with 68000 assembly language and introduce you to some more assembly language programming techniques.

Waiting for a Strobe Signal

DEFINING THE PROBLEM AND WRITING THE ALGORITHM

Many systems that interface with a microcomputer output data on parallel-signal lines and then output a separate signal to indicate that valid data is on the parallel lines. The data-ready signal is often called a strobe. An example of a strobed data system such as this is an ASCII-encoded computer-type keyboard. Figure 4-18 shows how the parallel data lines and the strobe line from such a keyboard are connected to ports of a microcomputer. When a key is pressed on the keyboard, circuitry in the keyboard detects which key is pressed and sends the ASCII code for that key out on the eight data lines connected to port $C014. After the data has had time to settle on these lines, the circuitry in the keyboard sends out a key-pressed strobe, which lets you know that the data on the eight lines is valid. We have connected this strobe line to the LSB of port $C015. A strobe can be an active high signal or an

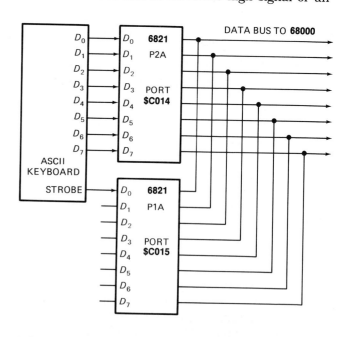

FIGURE 4-18   ASCII-encoded keyboard with strobe connected to microcomputer ports.

struction sequences in this way so that you don't have to worry about the potential problem. The disadvantages of this approach are the time and memory space required by the extra JMP instruction.

active low signal. For the example here, assume that the strobe signal goes high when a valid ASCII code is on the parallel data lines.

If we want to read the data from this keyboard, we can't do it at just any time. We must wait for the strobe to go high so that we know that the data we read will be valid. Basically what we have to do is look at the strobe signal and test it over and over until it goes high. Figure 4-19a shows how we can represent this operation with a flowchart and Figure 4-19b shows the pseudocode. We want to repeat the read strobe and test loop until the strobe is found to be high. Then we want to exit the loop and read in the ASCII code byte. Note that, as shown by the dotted box in the flowchart and the indentation in the pseudocode, the read ASCII data action is not part of the basic REPEAT-UNTIL structure.

IMPLEMENTING THE ALGORITHM WITH ASSEMBLY LANGUAGE

Figure 4-19c (pp. 97–98) shows the 68000 assembly language to implement this algorithm. To read in the key-pressed strobe signal, we first load the address of the port to which it is connected into register A0. Then

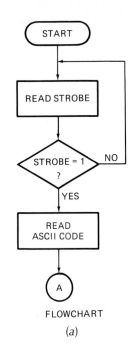

FLOWCHART

(a)

```
REPEAT
    READ KEYPRESSED STROBE
UNTIL STROBE = 1
READ ASCII CODE FOR KEY PRESSED

            PSEUDOCODE
```

(b)

FIGURE 4-19 Flowchart, pseudocode, and assembly language for reading ASCII code when a strobe is present. (a) Flowchart. (b) Pseudocode. (c) Assembly language program (continued on p. 98).

```
 1:                              ; 68000 Program
 2:                              ;
 3:                              ; ABSTRACT      : This program reads an ASCII code when a strobe signal
 4:                              ;                  is sent from a keyboard
 5:                              ;
 6:                              ; REGISTERS USED:  A0, D0
 7:                              ; PORTS USED    :  $C015 - strobe signal input port
 8:                              ;                  $C014 - ASCII data input port
 9:                              ; PROCEDURES    :  none used
10:                              ;
11:                              ;                          alr 10-88
12:                              ;
13: 00004000                        ORG      $4000
14:
15: 00004000 207C 0000 C015        MOVEA.L  #$C015,A0     ; point A0 at strobe port
16: 00004006                   LOOK_AGAIN:
17: 00004006 1010                  MOVE.B   (A0),D0       ; read keyboard strobe
18: 00004008 0200 0001             ANDI.B   #$01,D0       ; mask extra bits and
19: 0000400C 0C00 0000             CMPI.B   #$00,D0       ; set flags
20: 00004010 6700 FFF4             BEQ      LOOK_AGAIN    ; strobe low, keep looking
21:
22: 00004014 103C C011             MOVE.B   #$C011,D0     ; read in ASCII code
23:
24: 00004018 4E75                  RTS                    ; return to whoever called me
25: 0000401A                       END
```

(c)   (continued)

```
Symbol Name                          Attribute   Hex        Decimal

LOOK_AGAIN. . . . . . . . . .        LABEL       00004006   16390


Obj bytes: 26D/0000001AH


End assembly.  Lines: 25  Errors: 0
```

(c)

FIGURE 4-19 (continued)

we use the normal move instruction, MOVE.B (A0),D0, to read the strobe data into D0. This input instruction copies a byte of data from port $C015 to the low byte of register D0. However, we care only about the LSB of the byte, because that is the one to which the strobe is connected. We would like to find out if this bit is a 1. We will show you three ways to do this.

The first way, shown in Figure 4-19c, is to AND the byte in D0 with the immediate number $01. Remember that a bit ANDed with a 0 becomes a 0 (is masked). A bit ANDed with a 1 is not changed. If the LSB is a 0, then the result of the ANDing will be all 0s. The zero flag, Z, will be set to a 1 to indicate this. If the LSB is a 1, the zero flag will not be set to a 1 because the result of the ANDing will still have a 1 in the least significant bit. The branch if equal to zero instruction, BEQ, will check the state of the zero flag and, if it finds the zero flag set, will branch to the label LOOK_AGAIN. If the BEQ instruction finds the zero flag not set (indicating that the LSB was a 1), it passes execution on to the next sequential instruction, which reads in the ASCII data.

Another way to check the LSB of the strobe word is with the BTST instruction instead of the AND instruction. The 68000 BTST instruction has the format BTST source, destination. The BTST instruction sets the zero condition code, Z, depending on the value of the specified bit of the destination operand. The source operand specifies the bit number. If the destination is a data register, then the source is used modulo 32; otherwise the source bit number is used modulo 8, testing 1 bit of a byte operand. In the example program in Figure 4-19c, the ANDI.B #$01,D0 and CMPI.B #$00,D0 could both be replaced by a single BTST #1,D0 instruction.

Still another way to check the LSB of the strobe byte is with a rotate instruction. If we rotate the LSB into the carry flag, we can use a branch if carry or branch if not carry instruction to control the loop. For this example program, we can use either the ROR instruction or the ROXR instruction. Assuming that we choose the ROR instruction, the check and branch instruction sequence would look like this.

```
LOOK_AGAIN: MOVE.B  (A0),D0        ; read strobe byte
            ROR.B   #1,D0          ; Rotate LSB into
                                   ;  carry
            BCC     LOOK_AGAIN     ; If LSB = 0,
                                   ; keep looking
```

For your programs you can use the way of checking a bit that seems easiest in a particular situation.

To read the ASCII data, we can use the instruction MOVE.B ($C014),D0. We will normally read the strobe port many times for each one time we read the ASCII key data port. In this program example, we have loaded the address of the strobe port into an address register and kept it in the CPU during successive strobe read and test cycles. The ASCII data address, on the other hand, has the address of the port right in the instruction. As the listings show, the former case takes only 2 bytes for the instruction MOVE.L (A0),D0, whereas the MOVE.L ($C014),D0 instruction takes 6 bytes using long addressing. On the other hand, the former case requires an additional initialization instruction (MOVEA.L #$C015,A0).

The main purpose of the preceding section was to show you how you can use a conditional branch instruction to make the 68000 REPEAT a series of actions UNTIL the flags indicate that some condition is present. The following section shows another example of implementing the REPEAT-UNTIL structure. This example also shows you how a register-based addressing mode is used to access data in memory.

Operating on a Series of Data Items in Memory

In many programming situations we want to perform some operation on a series of data items stored in successive memory locations. We might, for example, want to read in a series of data values from a port and put the values in successive memory locations. A series of data values of the *same type* stored in successive memory locations is often called an *array*. Each value in the array is referred to as an *element* of the array. For our example program here, we want to add an inflation factor of $03 to each price in an eight-element array of prices. Each price is stored in a byte location as packed BCD (two BCD digits per byte). The prices, then, are in the range of 1¢ to 99¢. Figure 4-20a and Figure 4-20b show a flowchart and the pseudocode for the operations that we want to perform. Follow through with whichever form you feel more comfortable.

We read one of the BCD prices from memory, add the inflation factor to it, and copy the new value back to the array, replacing the old value. After that, a check is made to see if all the prices have been operated on. If they haven't, then we loop back and operate on the next price. The two questions that may occur to you at this point are, How are we going to indicate in the program which price we want to operate on, and how are we going to know when we have operated on all of the prices? To indicate which price we are operating on at a particular time, we use a register as a pointer. To keep track of how many prices we have operated on, we use another register as a counter. The example program in Figure 4-20c, p. 100, shows one way in which our algorithm for this problem can be implemented in assembly language.

The example program in Figure 4-20c uses several assembler directives. Let's review the function of these before describing the operation of the program instructions. The ORG directives are used to tell the assembler where to locate the program ($4000) and the data ($4100) in memory. The END directive lets the assembler know that it has reached the end of the program. Now let's discuss the data structure for the program.

The statement COST DC.B $20, $28, $15, $26, $19, $27, $16, $29 in the program tells the assembler to set aside successive memory locations for an eight-element array of bytes. The array is given the name COST. When the assembled program is loaded into memory to be run, the eight memory locations will be loaded with the eight values specified in the DC.B statement. The statement PRICES DC.B $36, $55, $27, $42, $38, $41, $29, $59 sets up another eight-element array of bytes and gives it the name PRICES. The eight memory locations will be loaded with the specified values when the assembled program is loaded into memory. Figure 4-21, p.102, shows how these two arrays will be arranged in memory. Note that the name of the array is associated with the address of the first element of the array.

The first three instructions, MOVEA.L PRICES,A1, MOVE.W #$0008,D1, and MOVE.B #$03,D2, initialize A1 to point to the array of prices, D1 to contain the starting value of the loop counter, and D2 to contain the correction factor. These are all stored in CPU registers so that the following loop can execute as fast as possible with as few references to external memory as possible. The MOVEA instruction moves an effective address into A1. We say that A1 is then a *pointer* to an element in the array PRICES. We will soon show you how this pointer is used to step through the array element by element. The counter register, D1, is loaded with the number of prices in the array, $08. We use this register as a counter to keep track of how many prices we have operated on. After we operate on each price, we decrement the counter by 1. When the counter reaches 0, we know that we have operated on all the prices. The data register D2 is used to hold the offset value, $03, so that it remains in the CPU during the loop.

The MOVE.B (A1),D0 instruction copies one of the prices from memory to the register D0. The next instruction, ABCD D2,D0, adds the immediate number $03, which we have previously placed in D2, to the contents of the low byte of register D0. The addition will be performed using BCD arithmetic.

The next instruction, MOVE.B D0,(A1)+, moves the resulting byte from data register D0 back to memory at

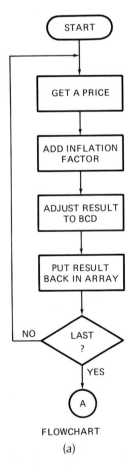

FLOWCHART

(a)

FIGURE 4-20 Adding a constant to a series of values in memory. (a) Flowchart. (b) Pseudocode. (c) Assembly language program (p. 100). (d) Assembly language program to add profit factor (p. 101).

```
REPEAT
    GET A PRICE FROM ARRAY
    ADD INFLATION FACTOR
    ADJUST RESULT TO CORRECT BCD
    PUT RESULT BACK IN ARRAY
UNTIL ALL PRICES ARE INFLATED

        PSEUDOCODE

            (b)
```

(continued on p. 100)

```
; 68000 Program
; ABSTRACT       : This program adds an inflation factor to a series
;                  of prices in memory.  It copies the new price
;                  over the old price.
; REGISTERS USED:  A1 ... pointer to array of prices
;                  D0 ... one price
;                  D1 ... loop counter
;                  D2 ... correction factor
; PORTS USED     : None
; PROCEDURES     : None used
;
;                          alr 10-88
;----------code segment-------------
        ORG        $4000              ; start code here

        MOVEA.L    PRICES,A1          ; initialize A1 as array pointer
        MOVE.W     #$0008,D1          ; initialize counter
        MOVE.B     #$03,D2            ; initialize inflation correction factor

DO_NEXT:
        MOVE.B     (A1),D0            ; copy a price to D0
        ABCD       D2,D0              ; add inflation factor
                                      ;    using BCD arithmetic
                                      ;    operand size is assumed to be BYTE
        MOVE.B     D0,(A1)+           ; copy result back to memory and
                                      ;    increment A1 to point to the next price
        DBGE       D1,DO_NEXT         ; if not last, go get next

        RTS                           ; return to whoever called me

; data follows:
;----------data segment-------------
        ORG        $4100

COST   DC.B        $20, $28, $15, $26, $19, $27, $16, $29
PRICES DC.B        $36, $55, $27, $42, $38, $41, $29, $59

        END
```

(c)   (continued)

FIGURE 4-20 (continued)

the same location from which it was originally loaded. However, this time the address register A1 is incremented (i.e., 1 is added to it) to point to the next byte in memory, which is also the next element in the PRICES array. Recall that this is using the address register indirect with postincrement addressing mode. Because the "+" is after the (A1), you can tell that the increment happens after the move-memory reference.

The DBGE D1, D0_NEXT instruction decrements the loop counter, and if the counter is still greater than or equal to 0, it branches back to start another cycle through the loop. The decrement and branch instruction allows construction of simple, efficient loops in 68000 assembly language.

The RTS instruction returns control back to the URDA MDS monitor program. We look at the RTS instruction in detail in the next chapter.

Using a pointer to access data items in memory is a powerful technique that you will want to use in your programs. Figure 4-20d shows another example. Here we want to add a profit of 15¢ to each element of an array called COST and put the result in the corresponding element in an array called PRICES. We first initialize A1 as a pointer to the first element in the PRICES array and A2 as a pointer to the first element in the cost array using MOVEA.L instructions. The instruction MOVE.B (A2)+,D0 will copy the first cost value into D0. The pointer to the cost array in A2 is automatically incremented to point to the next element in the array. This is implied by the + after the (A2). This is the same as in the previous example. The profit factor in D2 is added to the element using an ABCD instruction. The result is then put into the array of prices using MOVE.B D0,(A1)+ instruction. Again, the MOVE.B instruction uses the autoincrement addressing mode (indicated by the +), which automatically increments the pointer in A1 to point to the next element in the prices array.

Using a pointer to access data items in memory is a powerful technique that you will want to use in your programs. The 68000 has several address registers that can be used as pointers to data in memory.

```
; 68000 Program
; ABSTRACT       : This program adds a profit factor to each element
;                  in a COST array and puts the result in an array
;                  called PRICES
; REGISTERS USED: A1 ... pointer to array of PRICES
;                 A2 ... pointer to array of COSTs
;                 D0 ... one price
;                 D1 ... loop counter
;                 D2 ... profit factor
; PORTS USED     : None
; PROCEDURES     : None used
;
;                             alr 10-88
;--------code segment----------------
          ORG    $4000              ; start code here

          MOVEA.L PRICES,A1         ; initialize A1 as PRICES array pointer
          MOVEA.L COST,A2           ; initialize A2 as COST array pointer
          MOVE.W  #$0008,D1         ; initialize counter
          MOVE.B  #PROFIT,D2        ; initialize profit factor


DO_NEXT:
          MOVE.B  (A2)+,D0          ; copy a cost to D0 and
                                    ;   increment A2 to point to next cost

          ABCD    D2,D0             ; add profit factor
          MOVE.B  D0,(A1)+          ; copy result back to PRICES array and
                                    ;   increment A1 to point to the next price

          DBGE    D1,DO_NEXT        ; if not last, go get next

          RTS                       ; return to whoever called me

; data follows:
;--------data segment----------------
          ORG    $4100              ; start data here

PROFIT    EQU    $15

COST      DC.B   $20, $28, $15, $26, $19, $27, $16, $29
PRICES    DS.B   8

          END
```

(d)

FIGURE 4-20 (continued)

Figure 4-22, p. 102, summarizes all the ways you can tell the 68000 to calculate an effective address and a physical address for accessing data in memory. In all cases the effective address is generated as a 32-bit value, which is generated by combining zero, one, or two registers with a displacement or possibly an absolute address held in the instruction stream itself. Typically, address registers are used to hold pointers. These pointers may have an offset added to them in the form of a displacement in the instruction or as a value held in a data register.

The simplest addressing mode is still absolute addressing, where the instruction contains the absolute address itself. The fastest is normally the address register indirect mode(s), where the desired address is held in a CPU address register. The most complex modes involve an address register, an index register (a data or address register), and a displacement encoded directly in the instruction.

The instruction MOVE.B #100(A0,D1),D0 is an example of this last, complex addressing mode. Here the instruction source uses address register indirect with index addressing. This mode always uses an 8-bit displacement (which can be 0). Figure 4-23, p. 103, shows an example of why you might want this type of complex addressing. Here we have an array of records, each holding the information about one patient for a hospital. Each record in the array contains the name, address, and other important information. Let us assume that here each record is 120 ($78) bytes long and consists of 6 strings, each 20 bytes long. Let's assume that the array starts at location $4100 in memory. The register A0 is used to hold the address of the start of the entire array, assumed here to be $4100. The register D1 is used as index register, which holds the distance from the beginning of the array to the start of

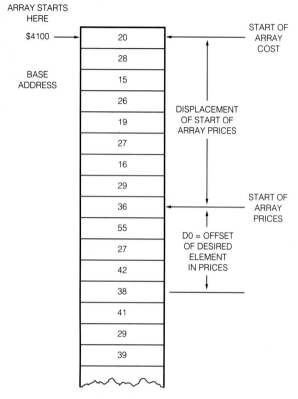

FIGURE 4-21   Data arrangement in memory for "inflate prices" program.

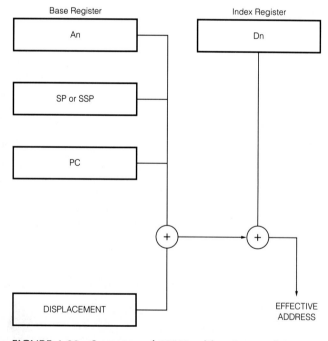

FIGURE 4-22   Summary of 68000 addressing modes.

this record. Its value should be equal to the index of the array element we want (counting from 0) times the size of each array element. In this case we are interested in record 1, which begins immediately after record 0. Record 0 takes 120 characters, so D1 should contain 1 × 120 = 120 ($78). If we are interested in array element 2, then D1 should contain 2 × 120 = 240. The constant displacement, 100 in this instruction, contains the displacement from the beginning of the record to the part of the record (the field) of interest. Here we are interested in the last field (the sixth), which holds the amount this patient owes the hospital. This string (here $0.00) starts at a byte displacement of 100 bytes from the start of the record. Putting this all together, the effective address is computed by adding the value in A0 ($4100) to the value in D1 (120 = $78) to the displacement (100 = $64). The final effective address is $41DC, which is correct, as Figure 4-23 demonstrates.

In general, operand effective addresses can either be encoded directly in the instruction itself, as an absolute address or as a register number, or be implicit in the instruction itself. An implicit address is one that is implied but not stated. For example, the JMP instruction affects the PC, but the instruction does not specifically mention the PC, only the target address which is to become the new PC value. The PC is an implicit operand of the JMP instruction.

Summary of REPEAT-UNTIL Implementation

The preceding sections have shown two examples of implementing the REPEAT-UNTIL structure. In the first example we repeated a series of actions until a condition was found to be present. Specifically, we kept looking and testing until we found a strobe signal high. In the second, we used a conditional branch instruction to check the condition of a flag and make the decision whether to repeat the series of actions or not.

In the second REPEAT-UNTIL example we introduced the concept of using a register as a pointer to a data element in an array. We also showed in this example how to make a program repeat a sequence of instructions a specific number of times. To do this we load the desired number of repeats in a register or memory location. Each time we execute the series of instructions, we decrement this counter by 1. When the count in the register is decremented to 0, the zero flag will be set. Again, we use a decrement and conditional branch instruction to manage the counter and perform the loopback branch each time it is called for.

The need for performing a sequence of actions a specified number of times in a program is so common that some programming languages use a specific structure to express it. This structure, derived from the basic WHILE-DO, is called the FOR-DO. It has the form

FOR count = 1 to count = n DO
   action
   action

```
                For simplicity the array PATIENTS is an array
                of records where each record contains 6 fields
                and each field is 20 bytes long (the data in some
                fields does not take all 20 bytes, but the field
                still reserves all 20 bytes)



                            The name PATIENTS represents the address
                            of the start of the array in memory

      PATIENTS                          ; array of patient records starts here

      A0 holds array ----->  $4100      RECORD 0
      base address                        TV N. BEER
      = $4100                             1324 Down Street
                                          Portland, OR 97219
                                          2/15/45
                                          247 lb
                                          $327.56


      D1 holds offset ---->             RECORD 1
      of desired record        $4178      IM A. RUNNER
      within the array         $418B      13733 S.W. Knaus Rd
      = index * record-size    $41A0      Oswego, OR 97304
      = 1 * 120 = $78          $41B4      6/30/41
                               $41C8      145 lb
      displacement ------->    $41DC      $0.00
      holds offset of desired
      field within the record
      = 100 = $64
      (base + offset + displacement
       = $4100 + $78 + $64
       = $41DC = address of desired
         field with desired record
         within array)

                            $41F0    RECORD 2
                                       . . .
```

FIGURE 4-23 Use of double-indexed addressing mode.

where *n* is the number of times we want to do the sequence of actions. In assembly language you will usually implement this by loading *n* into a register and counting it down, as shown in Figure 4-20c.

The common need to repeat a sequence of actions a specified number of times also led the designers of the 68000 to give it a group of instructions that make this easier for you. These instructions are the LOOP instructions, which we discuss in the next section.

68000 Loop Instruction Operation

As the last example demonstrated, efficient 68000 loops can be constructed using the decrement and branch conditionally instructions, forms of the DBcc

instruction. The 68000 also has a Bcc instruction, as we have seen, to construct branches independent of a decrementing counter. Figure 4-24, p. 104, also shows that the 68000 has an Scc instruction which sets or clears an operand depending on a particular condition code. We could have used Scc for the first example problem in this chapter.

The decrement and conditional branch instructions are useful for implementing the REPEAT-UNTIL structure for those special cases where we want to perform a series of actions a fixed number of times *or* until the zero flag changes state. These instructions incorporate two operations in each instruction; therefore, they are somewhat more efficient than using single instructions to do the same job. In the next section we

INSTRUCTION	OPERAND SYNTAX	OPERAND SIZE	OPERATION
CONDITIONAL			
Bcc	<LABEL>	8, 16	IF CONDITION TRUE, THEN PC + d → PC
DBcc	Dn, <LABEL>	16	IF CONDITION FALSE, THEN Dn – 1 → Dn IF Dn≠ – 1, THEN PC + d → PC
Scc	<EA>	8	IF CONDITION TRUE, THEN 1's → DESTINATION; ELSE 0's → DESTINATION

FIGURE 4-24 68000 Program Control Instructions.

introduce you to instruction timing and show how the DBGE instruction can be used to produce a delay between the execution of instructions.

INSTRUCTION TIMING AND DELAY LOOPS

The rate at which 68000 instructions are executed is determined by a crystal-controlled clock with a frequency of a few megahertz. Each instruction takes a certain number of clock cycles to execute. The MOVE.B immediate-data, data-register instruction, for example, requires 8 clock cycles to execute, and the NOP instruction requires 4 clock cycles. The BNZ instruction requires 10 clock cycles if it does the jump and only 8 clock cycles if it doesn't do the jump. A set of tables in Appendix A shows the number of clock cycles required by each instruction. This table shows, for example, that the NOP instruction takes 4 cycles, indicated by 4(1/0). The (1/0) indicates that one memory read and no memory writes are required. The NOP instruction requires only one memory read to access the instruction code word itself. If we were running with slow memory that required more than 4 cycles to perform a read, then the (1/0) would tell us how much extra time would be required. We can ignore the (1/0) for now, since the URDA MDS memory runs without requiring more than 4 cycles per read. The CPU does not require wait cycles to wait for the memory to catch up. Using the numbers in this table, you can calculate how long it takes to execute an instruction or series of instructions. For example, if we are running a 68000 with a 3.579-MHz clock, then each clock cycle takes 1/3.579 MHz, or 0.28 μs. An instruction that takes 4 clock cycles then will take 4 clock cycles × 0.28 μs/clock cycle, or 1.12 μs to execute.

A common programming problem is the need to introduce a delay between the execution of two instructions. For example, we might want to read a data value from a port, wait 1 μs, and then read the port again. A later chapter will show you can use interrupts to mark off time intervals. Here we show you how to use a program loop to do it.

The basic principle is to execute an instruction or series of instructions over and over until the desired time has elapsed. Figure 4-25a shows a program we might use to do this. The MOVE.B #N, D0 instruction loads the D0 register with the number of times we want to repeat the delay loop (we have left this as N for now). Shortly, we show you how to calculate the number N

for a desired amount of delay. The NOP instructions next in the program are not required. The KILL_TIME label could be right in front of the LOOP instruction. In this case, only the LOOP instruction would be repeated. We put the NOPs in to show you how you can get more delay by extending the time it takes to execute the loop. The DBGE D0, KILL_TIME instruction will decrement D0 and, if D0 is not down to zero yet, do a jump to the label KILL_TIME. The program then will execute the two NOP instructions and the DBGE instruction over and over until D0 is counted down to zero. The number in D0 will determine how long this takes. Here's how you determine the value to put in D0 for a given amount of delay.

First, you calculate the number of clock cycles needed to produce the desired delay. If you are running your 68000 with a 3.579-MHz clock, then the time for each clock cycle is 1/3.579 MHz, or 0.28 μs. Now, suppose that you want to create a delay of 1 ms, or 1000 μs, with a delay loop. If you divide the 1000 μs desired by the 0.28 μs per clock cycle, you get the number of clock cycles required to produce the desired delay. For this example, then, you need a total of 3571 (1000/0.28) clock cycles to produce the desired delay.

The next step is to write the number of clock cycles

```
            MOVE.W  #N,D0            8              = C0
KILL_TIME:  NOP                      4
            NOP                      4
            DBGE    D0,KILL_TIME    10    = 18 = CL
                                    /14
```
(a)

$$C_T = C_0 + N(C_L) + 4$$

$$N = \frac{C_T - C_0 - 4}{C_L} = \frac{3571 - 8 - 4}{18} = 198 = \$0C6$$

(b)

FIGURE 4-25   Delay loop program and calculations. (a) Program. (b) Calculations.

required for each instruction next to that instruction, as shown in Figure 4-25a. Then look at the program to determine which instructions are executed only once. The number of clock cycles for these instructions will contribute to the total only once. Instructions that enter only once in the calculation are often called *overhead*. We will represent the number of cycles of overhead with the symbol C_O. In Figure 4-25a the only instruction which executes just once is MOVE.W #N, D0, which takes 8 clock cycles. For this example, then, C_O is 8.

Now determine how many clock cycles are required for the loop. The two NOPs in the loop require a total of 8 clock cycles. The DBGE instruction requires 10 clock cycles if it does the jump back to KILL_TIME, but it requires 14 clock cycles when it exits the loop. For all but the very last time through the loop, it will require 10 clock cycles for the DBGE instruction. Therefore, you can use 10 as the number of cycles for the DBGE instruction and compensate later for the fact that for the last time it uses 4 more cycles. For the example program, the number of cycles per loop, C_L, is 8 + 10, or 18. The total number of clock cycles delayed by the loop is equal to the number of times the loop executes multiplied by the time per loop. To be somewhat more accurate, you can add the 4 extra cycles that were used when the last DBGE instruction executed. The total number of clock cycles required for the example program to execute is $C_O + N(C_L) + 4$. Set this equal to the number of clock cycles of delay you want, 3571 for this example, and solve the result for N. Figure 4-25b shows how this is done. The resultant value for N is 198 decimal, or $0C6. This is the number of times you want the loop to repeat, so this is the value of N that you will load into D0 before entering the loop.

With the simple relationship shown in Figure 4-25b you can determine the value of N to put in a delay loop you write, or you can determine the time a delay loop written by someone else will take to execute.

If you can't get a long-enough delay by counting down a single register or memory location, you can nest delay loops. The following is an example of this nesting:

```
                                  ; number of states
        MOVE.W   #COUNT1,D0       ; 8
CNTDN1: MOVE.W   #COUNT2,D1       ; 8 × COUNT1
CNTDN2: DBGE     D1,CNTDN2        ; ((10 × COUNT2) + 4)×COUNT1
        DBGE     D0,CNTDN1        ; 10 × COUNT1 + 4
        . . .
```

The principle here is to load D1 with COUNT2 and count D1 down COUNT1 times. To determine the number of states that this program section will take to execute, observe that the DBGE D1,CNTDN2 instruction will execute COUNT2 times for each count of D0. The total number of states then is COUNT1 times the number of states of the COUNT2 loop plus the states for the DBGE D0,CNTDN1 and the MOVE.W #COUNT2,D1 instructions. The total wait, then, is (in clock cycles): 8 + (8 × COUNT1) + [(10 × COUNT2) + 4] × COUNT1 + (10 × COUNT1) + 4. The best way to

approach getting values for the two unknowns, COUNT1 and COUNT2, is to choose a value such as $0100 for COUNT2 and then solve for the value of COUNT1. A couple of tries should get reasonable values for both COUNT1 and COUNT2. Delay loops are a very common application of the REPEAT-UNTIL structure. The next section describes how to perform some operations on strings using the 68000. String operations frequently use REPEAT-UNTIL structures.

Some 68000 String Manipulation Examples

INTRODUCTION AND OPERATION

A *string* is a series of bytes or words stored in successive memory locations. Often a string consists of a series of ASCII character codes. When you use a word processor or text-editor program, you are actually creating a string of this sort as you type in characters. One important feature of a word processor is the ability to move a sentence or group of sentences from one place in the text to another. Doing this involves moving a string of ASCII characters from one place in memory to another. The 68000 can do this efficiently using pointers and the MOVE instruction. Another important feature of most word processors is the ability to search through the text looking for a given word or phrase. The 68000 compare instruction, CMP, allows you to do this easily. Let's see how these string operations are constructed from the base 68000 instructions.

MOVING A STRING

Suppose that we have a string of ASCII characters in successive memory locations starting at address $4200 in the data area, and we want to move this string to an offset of $4400 in the data area. Figure 4-26a shows the basic pseudocode for this operation.

```
REPEAT
    MOVE BYTE FROM SOURCE STRING TO DESTINATION STRING
UNTIL ALL BYTES MOVED
```
(a)

```
INITIALIZE SOURCE POINTER - A0
INITIALIZE DESTINATION POINTER - A1
INITIALIZE COUNTER - D0
```

```
REPEAT
    COPY BYTE FROM SOURCE TO DESTINATION
      and INCREMENT SOURCE POINTER - A0
      and INCREMENT DESTINATION POINTER - A1
    DECREMENT COUNTER
UNTIL ( D0 = 0 )
```
(b)

(continued)

FIGURE 4-26 Program for moving a string from one location to another in memory. (a) First-version pseudocode. (b) Expanded-version pseudocode. (c) Assembly language.

```
LENGTH    EQU       80

          LEA       SOURCE,A0        ; INITIALIZE SOURCE POINTER, A0
          LEA       DEST,A1          ; INITIALIZE DESTINATION POINTER, A1
          MOVE.W    #LENGTH,D0       ; INITIALIZE COUNTER, D0

LOOP:                                ; REPEAT
          MOVE.B    (A0)+,(A1)+      ;    COPY BYTE FROM SOURCE TO DESTINATION
                                     ;    INCREMENT SOURCE POINTER, A0
                                     ;    INCREMENT DESTINATION POINTER, A1
          DBGT      D0,LOOP          ;    DECREMENT COUNTER
                                     ; UNTIL D0 = 0



SOURCE    DS.B      100
DEST      DS.B      100

          END
```
(c)

FIGURE 4-26 (continued)

When we start thinking about how we can implement this algorithm in assembly language, several points come to mind. We need a pointer to the source string to keep track of which string element we are moving at a given time. This is the same reason we needed a pointer in the price-fixing program in Figure 4-20c. We use an address register—for example, A0—for this pointer. A0 will hold the address of the byte that we are moving at a given time. We also need a pointer to the location to which we are moving string elements. Again, any other address register, such as A1, will suffice. Here the register A1 is used to hold the address of the location to which a byte is being moved at a given time. Another need is for a counter to keep track of how many string bytes have been moved so we can determine when we have moved all the string. We use the register D0 as a counter for this string operation example. Having these pieces in mind, we can expand the pseudocode for the problem, as shown in Figure 4-26b, p. 105. We often describe an algorithm in general terms at first and then expand sections as needed to help us see how the algorithm is implemented in a specific language. In the expanded version in Figure 4-26b you can see that we need to initialize the two pointers and the counter. The REPEAT-UNTIL loop consists of moving a byte while incrementing the pointers to point to the source and destination for the next byte and then decrementing the counter and branching, depending on whether all the bytes have been moved. As you examine the code in Figure 4-26c, notice that the pseudocode of Figure 4-26b actually appears word for word as comments in the assembly language program. This good technique links your assembly language code to your most detailed pseudocode and helps ensure that you have implemented all the pseudocode somewhere in your assembly language program.

Figure 4-26c shows the program instructions to move the string of bytes. The first three instructions in the program initialize the two string pointer registers, here A0 and A1, and the counter register, here D0. D0 will function as a counter to keep track of how many string bytes have been moved at any given time. In this case the two LEA instructions operate the same as would two MOVEA instructions, loading effective addresses into A0 and A1. The MOVEA instruction is somewhat more flexible and the LEA instruction is somewhat faster in execution. The instruction MOVE.B (A0)+,(A1)+ actually moves 1 byte from where A0 is pointing to where A1 is pointing and increments both A0 and A1 to point to the next byte in the source string and destination data area. The DBGT D0,LOOP instruction decrements the counter, D0, and tests it to see if all the bytes have been moved. The branch back to move another byte will be taken if the counter is still greater than 0. Here we are moving the string 1 byte at a time. If we know that the string is of even length, then it would be faster to move the string 1 word (2 bytes) at a time using the MOVE.W (A0)+, (A1)+ instruction. In this case we must remember that the count in D0 is now a word count, not a byte count.

USING THE COMPARE STRING BYTE TO CHECK A PASSWORD

For this program example suppose that we want to compare a password entered by a person who wants to use the computer with the correct password stored in memory. If the passwords do not match, we want to sound an alarm. If the passwords match, we want to continue on with the mainline program. Figure 4-27 shows how we might represent the algorithm for this with a flowchart and with pseudocode. Note that we want to terminate the REPEAT-UNTIL when either the compared bytes do not match or when we are at the end of the string. We then use an IF-THEN structure to sound the alarm if the compared strings were not equal at any point. If the strings match, the IF-THEN just directs execution on to the main program.

To implement this algorithm in assembly language, we probably would first expand the basic structures as we did for the previous string example in Figure 4-26. Figure 4-27c shows how we might do this expansion. The first action in the expanded algorithm is to initialize the port device for output. We need to have an output port because we will turn on the alarm by outputting a 1 to the alarm-control circuit. You can see that we need a pointer to each string and a counter to keep track of how many string elements have been compared. If you use A0 and A1 for the pointers and D0 for the counter, then the 68000 compare instruction, CMP, will implement the comparison. MOVE instructions and the DBGT can be used to implement the rest of the operations within the REPEAT-UNTIL structure.

Figure 4-28, p. 108, reviews some old concepts, introduces a few new ones, and shows how this program can be done in assembly language. First let's look at the data structure for this program. The statement PASSWORD DC.B 'FAILSAFE' sets aside 8 bytes of memory and gives the first memory location the name PASSWORD. This statement also initializes the eight memory locations with the ASCII codes for the letters FAILSAFE. The single quotes around FAILSAFE tell the assembler to put the ASCII codes for the letters of this word in successive memory locations. For FAIL-SAFE the ASCII codes will be $46, $41, $49, $4C, $53, $41, $46, and $45. The statement INPUT_WORD DS.B 8 will set aside eight memory locations and assign the name INPUT_WORD to the first location. The DS.B tells the assembler not to initialize these eight locations, but just reserve the memory area for data. We assume that another program section will

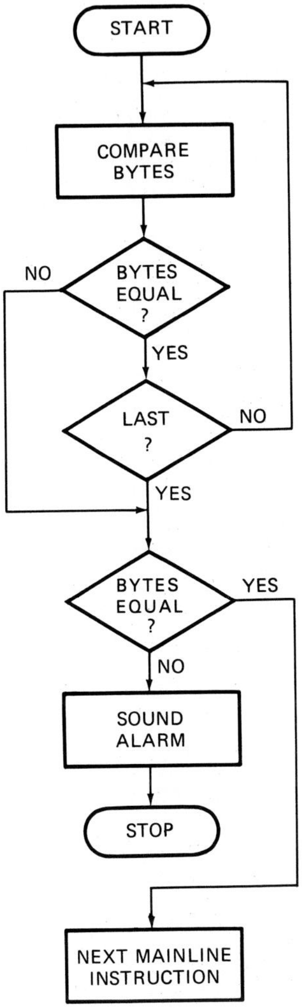

(a)

```
REPEAT
    COMPARE SOURCE BYTE WITH DESTINATION BYTE
UNTIL (BYTES NOT EQUAL) OR (END OF STRING)
IF BYTES NOT EQUAL THEN
    SOUND ALARM
    STOP
DO NEXT MAINLINE INSTRUCTION
```

(b)

```
INITIALIZE PORT DEVICE FOR OUTPUT
INITIALIZE SOURCE POINTER - A0
INITIALIZE DESTINATION POINTER - A1
INITIALIZE COUNTER - D0
REPEAT
    GET SOURCE BYTE
    INCREMENT SOURCE POINTER
    GET DESTINATION BYTE
    INCREMENT DESTINATION POINTER
    COMPARE SOURCE BYTE WITH DESTINATION BYTE
    EXIT LOOP IF BYTES NOT EQUAL
    DECREMENT COUNTER
UNTIL (D0 = 0)
IF STRING BYTES NOT EQUAL THEN
    SOUND ALARM
    STOP
DO NEXT MAINLINE INSTRUCTION
```

(c)

FIGURE 4-27 Flowchart and pseudocode for comparing strings program. (a) Flowchart. (b) Initial pseudocode. (c) Expanded pseudocode.

```
; 68000 Program
; ABSTRACT       : This program inputs a password and sounds an
;                  alarm if the password is incorrect.
; REGISTERS USED: A1 ... pointer to correct password string
;                 A2 ... pointer to user input string
;                 D0 ... one character from password string
;                 D1 ... one character from user string
;                 D2 ... loop counter
; PORTS USED     : $C014 - alarm output port
;                  $C016 - control port to configure alarm port
; PROCEDURES     : None used
;
;                        alr 1-89
        ORG     $4000           ; start code at $4000

                                ; INITIALIZE PORT DEVICE FOR OUTPUT
        MOVE.B  #$00,($C016)    ;   set for direction initialization
        MOVE.B  #$FF,($C014)    ;   all bits in port for output
        MOVE.B  #$04,($C016)    ;   set for I/O
        LEA     PASSWORD,A0     ; INITIALIZE SOURCE POINTER, A0
        LEA     INPUT_WORD,A1   ; INITIALIZE DESTINATION POINTER, A1
        MOVE.W  #$0008,D2       ; INITIALIZE COUNTER, D0

REPEAT:                         ; REPEAT
        MOVE.B  (A0)+,D0        ;   GET SOURCE BYTE & INCREMENT SOURCE POINTER
        MOVE.B  (A1)+,D1        ;   GET DEST. BYTE and INCREMENT DEST. POINTER
        CMP.B   D0,D1           ;   COMPARE SOURCE BYTE WITH DESTINATION BYTE
        BNE     SOUND_ALARM     ;     if characters do not match, go sound alarm
        DBGT    D2,REPEAT       ;   DECREMENT COUNTER
                                ; UNTIL (STRING BYTES NOT EQUAL) OR (D0 = 0)
        JMP     OK              ;   the two strings are equal, jump to
                                ;   next mainline instruction
SOUND_ALARM:
        BEQ     OK              ; IF STRING BYTES NOT EQUAL THEN
        MOVE.B  #1,($C011)      ;   SOUND ALARM
        STOP    #99             ;   STOP and leave 3 in the SR

OK:     NOP                     ; DO NEXT MAINLINE INSTRUCTION
        RTS                     ;   return to whoever called me

; data follows:
        ORG     $4200           ; start data at $4200

PASSWORD     DC.B       'FAILSAFE'
INPUT_WORD   DS.B       8

        END
```

FIGURE 4-28 Assembly language program for comparing strings.

load these locations with ASCII codes read from the keyboard.

Now let's look at the code segment section of the program. The first three statements initialize the port at $C014 as an output port. The next three instructions initialize the string pointers A0 and A1, and the counter D0, just as in the last example.

The next two instructions get 1 byte from each of the strings to be compared, the source string 'FAILSAFE' and the user's input string. The two instructions also increment the string pointers A0 and A1 to point to the next bytes in the two strings.

The CMP.B instruction will compare the bytes just accessed and set the condition codes accordingly. If the 2 bytes are not equal, then the BNE instruction will branch to the SOUND_ALARM code; otherwise the BNE will have no effect. The DBGT instruction is executed if we "fall through" the BNE instruction—that is, if the 2 bytes are equal. The DBGT instruction decrements the string counter. If there are more bytes to compare (the counter is still greater than 0), then the DBGT branches back to the REPEAT label and another pair of string bytes is compared. If the counter has counted down to zero, then we know that the two strings are equal because each pair of string bytes was equal. In this case we fall through the DBGT instruction to the JMP instruction. The JMP instruction skips the SOUND_ALARM section of code and goes on to the next mainline instruction.

Notice that we do not have to check again whether the strings were equal at the SOUND_ALARM code section. If we managed to get there, then the strings were not the same. Nonetheless we have included the BEQ test for equality of the last bytes compared in order to maintain a correspondence to our pseudocode. Once again, notice that the pseudocode is actually repeated in the comments of the assembly langúage program so we can be sure that we have encoded the pseudocode completely.

For this example we assume that the alarm control is connected to the least significant bit of port $C014 and that a 1 output to this bit turns on the alarm. The MOVE.B #1, ($C014) sends a 1 to the LSB of port $C014. This turns on the alarm. Finally, the STOP #7 instruction stops the computer. An interrupt or reset will be required to get it started again. The value 7 will be left in the status register to tell us what happened if we examine the SR once the CPU is restarted. Since the user did not guess the correct password, it seems appropriate to stop the CPU; however, in a real-world case we might let the user try again.

As the preceding examples show, string operations are very easy to implement using the normal 68000 MOVE, CMP, and DBcc instructions. Some of the programming problems at the end of the chapter will give you some practice with these. The next section here gives you some hints on how to debug the programs that you write.

DEBUGGING ASSEMBLY LANGUAGE PROGRAMS

So far in this book we have tried to show you the tools and techniques used to write assembly language programs. By now you should be writing some programs of your own, so we need to give you a few hints on how to debug your programs if they don't work correctly the first time you try to run them.

The first technique you use when you hit a difficult-to-find problem in either hardware or software is the *5-minute rule.* This rule says, "You get 5 min to freak out and mumble about changing vocations; then you have to cope with the problem in a systematic manner." What this means is step back from the problem, collect your wits, and think out a systematic series of steps to find the problem. We have seen many technicians waste a lot of valuable time randomly poking and probing to try and find the cause of a problem. Here is a list of additional techniques you may find useful in writing and debugging your programs.

1. Very carefully define the problem you are trying to solve with the program and work out the best algorithm you can.

2. If the program consists of several parts, write, test and debug each part individually; then add parts one at a time.

3. If a program or program section does not work, first recheck the algorithm to make sure it really does what you want it to. You might have someone else look at it also. Another person may quickly spot an error you have overlooked 17 times.

4. If the algorithm seems correct, check to make sure that you have used the correct instructions to implement the algorithm. It is very easy to accidentally switch the operands in an instruction. You might, for example, write down the instruction MOVE.B D0,D1 when the instruction you really want is MOVE.B D1,D0. Sometimes it helps to work out on paper the effect that a series of instructions will have on some sample numbers. These predictions on paper can later be compared with the actual results produced when the program section runs.

5. If you are hand coding your programs, this is the next place to check. It is very easy to get a bit wrong when you construct the 68000 instruction codes. Also, remember when constructing instruction codes containing addresses or displacements that the low byte of the address or displacement is coded in before the high byte.

6. If you don't find a problem in the algorithm, instructions, or coding, now is the time to use debugger, monitor, or emulator tools to help you localize the problem. You could use these tools right from the start, but by doing this it is easy to get lost in chasing bits and not see the bigger picture of what is causing the program to fail. For short program sections, the debugger or monitor *trace* and *single-step* functions may help you determine where the program is not doing what you want it to do. The MACDB® debugger trace command displays the contents of the registers after each instruction executes. After you run to a breakpoint, then you can use the dump-memory command to examine the contents of the memory. The URDA MDS board's single-step command executes one instruction and then stops execution. You can then use the examine register and examine memory commands to see if registers and memory contain the correct data at that point. If the results are correct at that point, you can use the trace or single-step command to execute the next instruction. Once you have localized the problem to one or two instructions, it is usually not too hard to find out what is wrong. See the accompanying laboratory manual instructions for using these functions.

7. For longer programs, the single-step approach can be somewhat tedious. Breakpoints are often a faster technique to narrow the source of a problem to a small region. Most debuggers, monitors, and emulators allow you to specify both a starting address

and an ending address in their RUN command. The MACDB monitor RUN command, for example, has the format RUN address, breakpoint address. When you give this command, execution will start at the address specified first in the command and stop when it reaches the address specified in the second position in the command. After the program runs to a breakpoint, you can use the examine register and examine memory commands to check the results at that point. Here's how we use breakpoints.

Instead of running the entire program, specify a breakpoint so that execution stops some distance into the program. You can then check to see if the results are correct at this point. If they are, you can run the program again with the breakpoint at a later address and check the results at that point. If the results are not correct, you can move the breakpoint to an earlier point in the program, run it again, and check that the results in registers and memory are correct.

Suppose, for example, you write a program such as the price-fixing program in Figure 4-20c and it does not give the correct results. The first place to put a breakpoint might be at the address of the ABCD D2,D0 instruction. Incidentally, the instruction at the address where you put the breakpoint does not get executed in most systems. After the program runs to this breakpoint, you check to see if the data registers and address registers were correctly initialized. You can also see if the first price got copied into D0. If the program works correctly to this point, you can run it again with the breakpoint at the address of the DBGE D1, DO_NEXT instruction. After the program executes to this breakpoint, you can check D0 to see if the addition produced the results you predicted. If the 68000 is working at all, it will almost always do operations such as this correctly, so recheck your predictions if you disagree with it. You can check the pointer in A1 to see if it is pointing at the next price, and you can check the count in D1 to see if it has been decremented as it should be. Also, you can check to see if the adjusted price got put back in memory. If you have not found the problem by now, the problem may be in the DBGE D1, DO_NEXT instruction. Perhaps you accidentally put the DO_NEXT label next to the ABCD D2,D0 instruction instead of next to the MOVE.B (A1),D0 instruction. Or, if you are hand coding, perhaps you calculated the displacement for the DBGE instruction incorrectly.

It helps your frustration level if you make a game of thinking where to put breakpoints to track down the little bug that is messing up your program. With a little practice you should soon develop an efficient debugging algorithm of your own using the specific tools available on your system.

CHECKLIST OF IMPORTANT TERMS AND CONCEPTS IN THIS CHAPTER

If there are terms or concepts in this list, you do not remember, use the index to find them in the chapter.

Defining a problem

Setting up a data structure

Making an initialization checklist

Masking and moving nibbles—using AND and OR instructions

Packed and unpacked BCD numbers

Conditional flags: C, V, Z, N, X

Jump and branch instructions
   Unconditional
   Conditional

Relocatable

Conditional branches

Memory-mapped port input/output

Addressing modes
   Immediate
   Indirect
   Indexed with displacement

Loop-building instructions

Delay loop—clock cycles

String operations using normal instructions

Debugging
   Break points
   Trace
   Single-step

REVIEW QUESTIONS AND PROBLEMS

1. Describe the operation and results of each of the following instructions, given the register contents shown in Figure 4-29. Include in your answer the physical address or register from which each instruction will get its operands and the physical address or register into which each instruction will put the result. Indicate the size of the data items affected as well. Use the instruction descriptions in Chapter 6 to help you. Assume that the instructions below are independent, not sequential, unless listed together under a letter.

```
a.  ROL.B D0,(A0)        b.  MOVE.W (A4),D3
c.  MOVE.B
    #02(A5,D0),D2        d.  ADD.B D0,(A1)
e.  JMP #4010            f.  JMP (A0)
g.
                         MOVE.L  #00000008,D1
    NEXT:                MOVE.B  (A0)+,D0
                         ADD.B   #02,D0
```

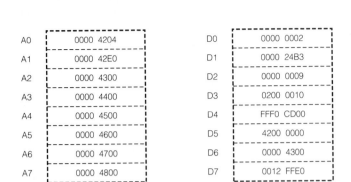

FIGURE 4-29   Figure for Chapter 4 problems.

```
                MOVE.B    D0,(A3)+
                DBGT      D1,NEXT
h.              MOVE.L    #12C2,D0
     COUNT_DOWN: DBGT     D0,COUNT_DOWN
i.              MOVE.L    #40,D2      ;length of STRING_1

MVSTR:          MOVE.L    (A4)+,(A5)+  ;move four bytes
                DBGT      D2,MVSTR
```

2. Construct the binary codes for the instructions of problems 1(a)–(f).

3. Predict the state of the five 68000 condition code flags (bits) after each of the following instructions or group of instructions executes. Use the register contents shown in Figure 4-29. Assume all flags are reset to 0 before the instructions execute. Use the detailed instruction descriptions in Chapter 6 to help you.
   a. MOVE.L D0,D3   b. AND.W D2,D3
   c. ADD.L   #−2,D0   d. OR.B   D6,D7

4. See if you can find any errors in the following instructions or groups of instructions.
   a. CNTDOWN: MOVE.B #−3,D0
                DBEQ DO,CNTDOWN
   b. ADD.B   #03402110,D0
   c. JMP   (D0)
   d. ADDI.L D0,D2
   e. DIVS   A2,D0

5. a. Write an algorithm for a program that adds a byte number from one memory location to a byte from the next memory location, puts the sum in a third memory location, and saves the state of the carry flag in the least significant bit of a fourth memory location. Mask the upper 7 bits of the memory location where the carry is stored.
   b. Write a 68000 assembly language program for this algorithm. (Hint: Use a rotate instruction to get the carry flag state into the LSB of a register or memory location.)
   c. What additional instructions would you have to add to this program so that it correctly adds 2 BCD bytes?

For each of the following programming problems, draw a flowchart or write the pseudocode for an algorithm to solve the problem. Then write a 68000 assembly language program to implement the algorithm. If you have a 68000 system available, enter and assemble your source program; then load the object code for the program into memory so you can run and test it. If the program does not work correctly, use the approach described in the last section of this chapter to help you debug it.

6. Convert a packed BCD byte to two ASCII characters for the two BCD digits in the byte. For example, given a BCD byte containing $57 (01010111 binary), produce the two ASCII codes $35 and $37.

7. Compute the average of 4 bytes stored in an array in memory.

8. Compute the average of any number of bytes in an array in memory. The number of bytes to be added is in the first byte of the array.

9. Add a 5-byte number in one array to a 5-byte number in another array. Put the sum in another array. Put the state of the carry flag in byte 6 of the array that contains the sum. The first value in each array is the LSB of that number.

10. A 68000-based process-control system outputs a measured Fahrenheit temperature to a display on its front panel. You need to write a short program that converts the Fahrenheit temperature to Celsius so that the system can be sold in Europe. The relationship between Fahrenheit and Celsius is $C = \frac{5}{9}(F - 32)$. The Fahrenheit temperature will always be in the range of 50° to 250°. Round the Celsius value to the nearest degree.

11. An ASCII keyboard outputs parallel ASCII + parity to port $C015 of an URDA board. The keyboard also outputs a strobe to the LSB (bit 0) of port $C013 (see Figure 4-18). When you press a key, the keyboard outputs the ASCII code for the pressed key on the 8 parallel lines and outputs a strobe pulse high for 1 ms. You want to poll the strobe over and over until you find it high. Then you want to read in the ASCII code, mask the parity bit (bit 7), and store the ASCII code in an array in memory. Next you want to poll the strobe over and over again until you find it low. When you find the strobe has gone low, check to see if you have read in ten characters yet. If not, then go back and wait for the strobe to go high again. If 10 characters have been read in, stop.

12. a. Write a delay loop that produces a delay of 500 μs on a 68000 with a 4.77-MHz clock.
    b. Write a short program that outputs a 1-kHz square wave on bit 0 of port $C015. The basic principle here is to output a high, wait 500 μs (0.5 ms), output a low, wait 500 μs, output a

high, etc. Remember that before you can output to a port device, you must first initialize it as in Figure 4-13a. If you connect a buffer such as that shown in Figure 8-25 and a speaker to bit 0 of the port, you will be able to hear the tone produced.

13. a. Move a string containing your name in the form Charlie T. Tuna from one string location in memory to a new string location named NEW—HOME, which is just above the initial location.

   b. Move the string containing your name up four addresses in memory. Consider whether the pointers should be incremented or decremented after each byte is moved in order to keep any needed byte from being written over. (*Hint:* Initialize A2 with the value of A1 + 4.)

14. Scan a string of 80 characters looking for a carriage return ($0D). If a carriage return is found, put the length of the string up to the carriage return in D0. If no carriage return is found, put $50 (80 decimal) in D0.

15. Given a string containing your name in the form Charlie T. Tuna, put the characters in a second string called LAST—FIRST in the order Tuna Charlie T.

16. Suppose, as part of a program, we had to convert each byte of the machine code program to ASCII codes for the two nibbles in the byte. In other words, a byte of $7A has to be sent as $41, the ASCII code for A, and $37, the ASCII code for 7. Once you separate the nibbles of the byte, this conversion is a simple IF-THEN-ELSE situation. Write an algorithm and assembly language program section which does the needed conversion.

17. A common problem when reading a series of ASCII characters from a keyboard is the need to filter out those codes that represent the hex digits 0−9 and A−F, and to convert those ASCII codes to the hex digits they represent. For example, if we read in $34, the ASCII code for 4, we want to mask the upper 4 bits to leave 04, the 8-bit hex code for 4. If we read in $42, the ASCII code for B, we want to add 09 and mask the upper 4 bits to leave 0B, the 8-bit code for hex B. If we read in an ASCII code that is not in the range of $30−$39 or $41−$46, then we want to load an error code of $FF instead of the hex value of the entered character. Figure 4-30 shows the desired action next to each range of ASCII values. Write an algorithm and an assembly language program which implements these actions. (*Hint:* A nested IF-THEN-ELSE structure might be useful.)

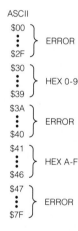

FIGURE 4-30 ASCII chart for problem 4-17.

CHAPTER

Subroutines and Macros

The last chapter showed you how quite a few of the 68000 instructions work and how jump instructions are used to implement IF-THEN-ELSE, WHILE-DO, and REPEAT-UNTIL structures. The major point of this chapter, however, is to show you how to write and use *subroutines* (sometimes called procedures or subprograms). A final section of the chapter shows you how to write and use assembler MACROs.

OBJECTIVES

At the conclusion of this chapter, you should be able to

1. Write a 68000 assembly language program that calls a subroutine.

2. Describe how a stack is initialized and used in 68000 assembly language programs that call subroutines.

3. Write and use an assembler MACRO.

In many programs where we want to choose between two or more alternative series of actions, each of the series of actions is quite lengthy. In many programs we want to perform some series of operations at several points in an algorithm. In these cases we write each series of actions as a subroutine and call this subprogram when it is needed. The next major section of this chapter shows you how to write and use subroutines. Subroutines and coroutines are types of procedures; we will not discuss coroutines in this text, but the reader is encouraged to investigate them once subroutines are well understood.

WRITING AND USING SUBROUTINES

Introduction

Whenever we have a series of instructions that we want to execute several times in a program, we write the series of instructions as a separate subprogram. We can then call this subprogram each time we want to execute that series of instructions. This saves us from having to write the series of instructions over and over

each time we want it to execute in the program. To be consistent with the Motorola literature, we use the term *subroutine* when referring to called subprograms. A subroutine is called using a jump to subroutine code and using a special type of jump that leaves a return address and can be returned from. The transfer of control to the subroutine is accomplished using a JSR (jump to subroutine) instruction, and the return from the subroutine to the mainline program is accomplished using an RTS (return from subroutine) instruction.

There is another major reason for using subroutines in programs. Recall from Chapter 2 the *top-down-design* approach to solving a programming problem. In this approach the problem is carefully defined and then the overall job is broken down into modules. Each of these modules is broken down into smaller modules. The process is continued until the algorithm for each module is clearly obvious. Figure 5-1, p. 114, shows how this hierarchy of modules can be represented in diagram form. A diagram such as this is often called a *hierarchy chart*. The point of all this is to break a large problem down into manageable-sized pieces that can be individually written, tested, and debugged. The individual modules are usually written as subroutines and called from a mainline program, which implements the highest level of the hierarchy. An added advantage of this approach is that a person can read the mainline program to get an overview of what the program does and then work his or her way down into the subroutines to see the amount of detail needed at a particular point. Now that you know what subroutines are used for, we will give you an overview of how they work.

Figure 5-2a, p. 114, shows in diagram form how program execution goes from the mainline to a subroutine and back to the mainline. A JSR instruction in the mainline loads the program counter with the starting address of the subroutine. The next instruction fetched, then, is the first instruction of the subroutine. At the end of the subroutine a return instruction, RTS, sends execution back to the next instruction after the JSR in the mainline program. The RTS instruction does this by loading the program counter with the address of the next instruction after the RTS instruction. As shown in Figure 5-2b, p. 114, a subroutine can

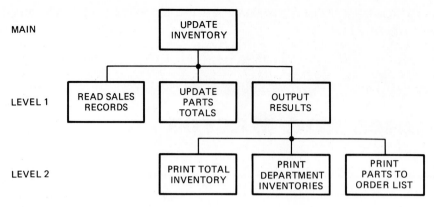

FIGURE 5-1 Hierarchical chart for inventory update program.

call another subroutine. This is called *nesting* subroutines. Nested subroutines are used to implement the hierarchy of modules we described in the preceding paragraph. In the case of nested subroutines, an RTS instruction at the end of the lower level subroutine returns execution to the higher-level subroutine. A second RTS instruction at the end of the higher-level subroutine returns execution to the mainline program.

The question that may occur to you at this point is, If a subroutine can be called from anywhere in a program, how does the RTS instruction know where to return execution? The answer to this question is that when a JSR instruction executes, it automatically stores the return address in a special section of memory called the *stack*. A later section introduces you to how 68000 stacks work. For now let's take a closer look at the 68000 JSR, RTS, and BSR instructions.

The 68000 JSR, BSR, and RTS Instructions

Jump to subroutine (JSR) and branch to subroutine (BSR) are the two forms of subroutine call instructions provided by the 68000. The BSR instruction can be used only when the called subroutine is within the 64K region of memory around the BSR instruction. This is because the BSR instruction uses an 8-bit or 16-bit displacement. The JSR instruction uses an absolute 32-bit address. BSR can be used to construct relocat-

able code because it uses displacements rather than absolute addresses. The RTS instruction can be used to return from both BSR and JSR subroutine calls.

THE JSR INSTRUCTION

The 68000 JSR instruction performs two operations when it executes. First, it stores the address of the instruction after the JSR instruction on the stack. This address is called the *return* address because it is the address to which execution will return after the subroutine executes.

The second operation of the JSR instruction is to change the contents of the program counter to contain the starting address of the subroutine. Figure 5-3, pp. 115–16, shows the coding formats for the 68000 JSR, BSR, and RTS instructions. The difference between the two subroutine calls is in the way they tell the 68000 to get the starting address for the subroutine. The JSR instruction gets the starting address of the subroutine from the 32 bits following the instruction. This is the 32-bit absolute address of the subroutine and will be loaded into the program counter directly.

THE BSR INSTRUCTION

The second form of subroutine call is branch to instruction (BSR). This form of subroutine call gets the starting address of the subroutine by adding the displacement in the last 8 bits of the instruction or from

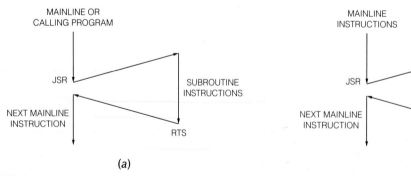

(a)   (b)

FIGURE 5-2 Program flow to and from subroutines. (a) Single subroutines. (b) Nested subroutines.

the 16 bits following the instruction. The BSR instruction takes less memory than does the JSR instruction if the subroutine address (or displacement) is considered. However, the BSR instruction has a shorter *reach* than does the JSR instruction, which means that the BSR instruction is limited to calling subroutines that are within +128 to −127 bytes (for an 8-bit displacement) or within −32,768 bytes to +32,767 bytes (for a 16-bit instruction) of the BSR instruction. The JSR instruction, on the other hand, can call anywhere in the 68000's 4 Mbytes of memory; the JSR can reach farther across memory to call a subroutine.

THE RTS INSTRUCTION

As we described in the previous section, when the 68000 performs a subroutine call, it saves the program counter value for the instruction after the JSR or BSR instruction on the stack. A return from subroutine (RTS) instruction at the end of the subroutine copies this value from the stack back to the program counter. This then returns execution to the mainline program. Both the JSR and the BSR instructions save a 32-bit return address on the stack, so both can be returned from by an RTS instruction. Now let's look at the stack where the return addresses are saved.

68000 Stacks

A *stack* is a section of memory set aside for storing values. The *system stack* is a particular stack used by the 68000 CPU to store return addresses. The system stack can also be used to save the contents of registers for the mainline program while a subroutine executes. A third use of the system stack is to hold data or addressess that will be acted upon by a subroutine. The system stack is pointed to by address register A7.

JSR
Jump to Subroutine
(M68000 Family)
JSR

Operation: SP − 4 ♦ Sp; PC ♦ (SP)
Destination Address ♦ PC

Assembler Syntax: JSR ⟨ea⟩

Attributes: Unsized

Description: Pushes the long-word address of the instruction immediately following the JSR instruction onto the system stack. Program execution then continues at the address specified in the instruction.

Condition Codes:
Not affected.

Instruction Format:

15	14	13	12	11	10	9	8	7	6	5	4	3	2	1	0
0	1	0	0	1	1	1	0	1	0	EFFECTIVE ADDRESS					

EFFECTIVE ADDRESS: MODE | REGISTER

Instruction Fields:
Effective Address field — Specifies the address of the next instruction. Only control addressing modes are allowed as shown:

Addressing Mode	Mode	Register
Dn	—	—
An	—	—
(An)	010	reg. number:An
(An)+	—	—
−(An)	—	—
(d16,An)	101	reg. number:An
(d8,An,Xn)	110	reg. number:An

Addressing Mode	Mode	Register
(xxx).W	111	000
(xxx).L	111	001
#⟨data⟩	—	—
(d16,PC)	111	010
(d8,PC,Xn)	111	011

MC68020, MC68030, AND MC68040 ONLY

Addressing Mode	Mode	Register
(bd,An,Xn)∗	110	reg. number:An
([bd,An,Xn],od)	110	reg. number:An
([bd,An],Xn,od)	110	reg. number:An

Addressing Mode	Mode	Register
(bd,PC,Xn)∗	111	011
([bd,PC,Xn],od)	111	011
([bd,PC],Xn,od)	111	011

∗Can be used with CPU32.

(a)

FIGURE 5-3   68000 JSR, BSR, and RTS instruction formats. (a) JSR. (b) BSR. (c) RTS. (*continued on p. 116*)

BSR
Branch to Subroutine
(M68000 Family)
BSR

Operation: SP − 4 ▶ SP; PC ▶ (SP); PC + d ▶ PC

Assembler
Syntax: BSR ⟨label⟩

Attributes: Size = (Byte, Word, Long*)
*(MC68020/MC68030/MC68040 only)

Description: Pushes the long word address of the instruction immediately following the BSR instruction onto the system stack. The PC contains the address of the instruction word plus two. Program execution then continues at location (PC) + displacement. The displacement is a twos complement integer that represents the relative distance in bytes from the current PC to the destination PC. If the 8-bit displacement field in the instruction word is zero, a 16-bit displacement (the word immediately following the instruction) is used. If the 8-bit displacement field in the instruction word is all ones ($FF), the 32-bit displacement (long word immediately following the instruction) is used.

Condition Codes:
Not affected.

Instruction Format:

15	14	13	12	11	10	9	8	7	6	5	4	3	2	1	0
0	1	1	0	0	0	0	1	8-BIT DISPLACEMENT							
16-BIT DISPLACEMENT IF 8-BIT DISPLACEMENT = $00															
32-BIT DISPLACEMENT IF 8-BIT DISPLACEMENT = $FF															

Instruction Fields:
8-Bit Displacement field — Twos complement integer specifying the number of bytes between the branch instruction and the next instruction to be executed.
16-Bit Displacement field — Used for a larger displacement when the 8-bit displacement is equal to $00.
32-Bit Displacement field — Used for a larger displacement when the 8-bit displacement is equal to $FF.

NOTE

A branch to the immediately following instruction automatically uses the 16-bit displacement format because the 8-bit displacement field contains $00 (zero offset).

(b)

RTS
Return from Subroutine
(M68000 Family)
RTS

Operation: (SP) ▶ PC; SP + 4 ▶ SP

Assembler
Syntax: RTS

Attributes: Unsized

Description: Pulls the program counter value from the stack. The previous program counter value is lost.

Condition Codes:
Not affected.

Instruction Format:

15	14	13	12	11	10	9	8	7	6	5	4	3	2	1	0
0	1	0	0	1	1	1	0	0	1	1	1	0	1	0	1

(c) FIGURE 5-3 (continued)

Any of the address registers can be used by the programmer to manipulate a stack. The 68000 CPU automatically uses A7 during JSR, BSR, and RTS instructions.

Remember from Figure 2-7 that the 68000 actually has two system stack registers, or A7 registers. One is used when the CPU is in supervisor state—that is, when the supervisor state bit of the status register (recall Figure 2-9) is a 1. When the supervisor state bit is set to a 0, then the user stack pointer is used. The supervisor stack pointer is referred to as A7', and the user stack pointer is called just A7. The supervisor state system stack pointer, A7', is used automatically by the CPU to store return addresses when the CPU is in supervisor state. When the CPU is in user state, register A7 is used. For our purposes using the URDA® MDS, we will always assume that we are in supervisor state. We will simply refer to register A7 and not make a distinction between A7 and A7'. When we discuss interrupts later in the text, you will see why we have chosen to operate always in supervisor state and never in user state.

When we write an instruction such as MOVEA.L STACK_TOP, A7, the CPU will use the appropriate system stack pointer, depending on whether the CPU is in supervisor or user state. We will never actually write A7', which is the A7 implied if the CPU is in supervisor state. In fact, an instruction such as MOVEA.L STACK_TOP, A7 can refer to the user A7 during one execution (when the supervisor status bit is 0) and to the supervisor A7 (A7') during another execution if the CPU supervisor status bit is set to a 1.

Figure 5-9 shows the pieces you need to add to your programs to declare a system stack and initialize A7. We have shown in Figure 5-4 how you should format all this for an assembler. If you are not using an assembler, then you should use the same format but put the desired numbers in place of the names we have used. The URDA MDS will automatically initialize both A7 and A7' to point to $7EB0. Figure 5-4 shows how to change A7 to point to a stack area in memory that we have declared for ourselves. The stack can reside anywhere in memory, provided register A7 is pointed to the area we choose.

When the 68000 is first powered on, it loads an initial value into A7 from memory location 0 and it loads an initial value into the PC from memory location 4. In a normal 68000 system these values are hard coded into ROM so that the system will always power up successfully (assuming the RAM is also operating properly).

Looking at Figure 5-4, there are two things being accomplished. The first is setting A7 to point to the top of the memory area reserved for the stack, and the second is reserving the stack memory area. The MOVEA.L STACK_TOP,A7 instruction moves the address of the top of the stack memory area into A7. If the CPU is in user state when this instruction executes, then the user stack pointer is used. If the CPU is in supervisor state, then the supervisor stack pointer is used. It is not until the program actually runs that the CPU can determine which version of A7 to use.

The instruction STACK_HERE: DS.W 40 requests the assembler to set aside an area of 40 words. This area will be used as the system stack, so it is called STACK_HERE. The instruction STACK_TOP: DS.W 0 is rather unusual in that it requests the assembler to set aside words of memory—but to set aside 0 words! The real intent of this instruction is to tell the assembler that the top of the previous array is to be given the name STACK_TOP. This allows us to use the symbolic name for the top of the stack in our MOVEA.L STACK_TOP,A7 instruction, which tells us more about what is really going on than would the alternate form MOVEA.L $00004050,A7.

Since the system stack will grow down (as shown in Figure 5-5, p. 118), we want to initialize the stack pointer (A7) to point to the top of the stack, not the bottom. The bottom of the stack has the lowest address and is called STACK_HERE. The top of the stack has the highest address and is called STACK_TOP. In the fashion of normal predecrement addressing and

```
;68000 Program fragment showing the initialization of the user stack
;
        MOVEA.L STACK_TOP,A7          ; load address STACK_HERE into
                                      ; A7 which is also the user stack.
                                      ; Subroutine calls will now leave
                                      ; return addresses starting at
                                      ; STACK_HERE and working down.
;       . . .
STACK_HERE: DS.W    40                ; declare a forty byte memory
                                      ; storage area.
STACK_TOP:  DS.W    0     ─────────>  ; the top of the stack is at the
                                      ; high memory address. DS.W 0
                                      ; implies do not reserve memory,
                                      ; but make symbolic name for top
                                      ; address of previous array.
```

FIGURE 5-4   Required program additions when using a stack.

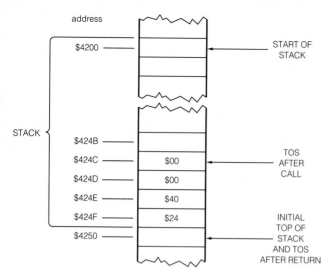

FIGURE 5-5 Stack diagram showing how the return address is pushed on the stack by JSR.

68000 stack usage, the stack top actually points to the next memory location above the stack. The stack top must be decremented before it is used.

Examine Figure 5-5. As with normal Motorola documentation, addresses start with the lowest addresses at the top of the figure and grow larger as you go down the page. This is opposite to the conventions normally used in Intel literature. The STACK_TOP is actually drawn at the bottom of the figure. It is called the stack top because when a JSR is performed, the return address is pushed onto the stack using predecrement addressing (recall Figure 5-3). The stack pointer moves up the figure (or down through memory) from higher to lower addresses. This may seem a bit confusing, but it goes back to the way the 68000 stores multibyte values. A 4-byte integer (a long value) is stored with the MSB in the low memory address. When we draw memory from low addresses to high addresses, the 4-byte number can be read from top to bottom in a normal fashion. In Figure 5-5 assume that a JSR has been executed with return address $00004024. We can read the return address directly at the "top" of the stack just by reading down the figure. If memory was drawn in the opposite direction (low addresses at the bottom), then we would have to reverse the bytes mentally when we read a number.

It is possible to create stacks on the 68000 that start at low memory and work to higher memory using the postincrement addressing mode and any of the address registers. However, whenever a JSR or RTS instruction is used, it automatically assumes we have a stack that grows down in memory from high addresses to low addresses.

Looking again at Figure 5-5, notice the locations of STACK_HERE and STACK_TOP, with 40 words ($50 bytes) of memory reserved. We decided to start the data at address $4200 for the purposes of this figure. The diagram also shows how the return address would be stored on the stack if a JSR were used with a return

address of $00004024. Return addresses are always 4 bytes (a full 32 bits); to emphasize this, we write them here as 8-digit hex values. The 4-byte return address is saved on the stack and the stack top is moved down in memory 4 bytes. When another JSR is executed, the next return address is placed below the $00004024 and the stack top moves down again. In this example we have tried to create a stack that is no larger than will be needed for the program at hand. Here 40 words are considered enough for simple programming examples.

When dealing with Motorola-style memory pictures, two simple rules will help keep things straight. The first is that memory reads from low to high addresses as you look down the page. Thus you can read numbers directly from the pictures, reading down as we normally do with written English. The second rule is that system stacks are drawn backward. On the system stack, the top of the stack is at the high address, which is drawn at the bottom of the page. The bottom of the stack is at the low address, which is drawn at the top of the page. Fortunately, however, even when reading multibyte numbers from the stack, the numbers are read in the normal fashion from top to bottom of the page. When we talk about *down* in 68000 terms, we mean toward lower addresses. *Up* means toward higher addresses. This is true even though in Motorola memory drawings, low addresses are at the top and high addresses are at the bottom of the page.

The next section shows how the pieces we have discussed are put in an example program that calls a subroutine. We also use this example to show you how the stack functions during a subroutine call and return.

A Subroutine Call and Return Example

Previous sections introduced you to the 68000 JSR and RTS instructions and showed you how to set up a stack. Here we use a program example to show you how subroutines are written and to dig more deeply into how the stack operates.

DEFINING THE PROBLEM AND WRITING THE ALGORITHM

Delay loops such as the one shown in Figure 4-25 are often written as subroutines so that they can be called from anywhere in a program. Suppose that we want to have a program that reads 100 data words from a port at 1-ms intervals, masks the upper 4 bits of each word, and puts each result in an array in memory. Before you read on, see if you can write a flowchart or pseudocode for this problem. Now compare your results with those in Figure 5-6a or Figure 5-6b. It is hoped that you recognized this problem as a REPEAT-UNTIL situation.

The next step is to expand the algorithm to take into account the specific architectural features of the 68000 that we will use to implement the algorithm. Figure 5-6c shows one way to do this expansion. We know that we need a pointer to the array and a counter to keep track of how many values we have put in the

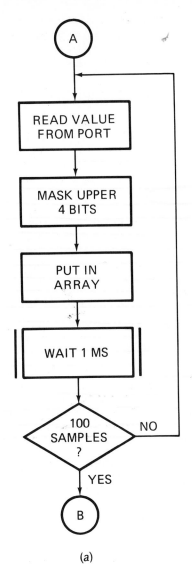

(a)

```
DATA SAMPLES PROGRAM
REPEAT
        GET DATA SAMPLE FROM PORT
        MASK UPPER 4 BITS
        PUT IN ARRAY
        WAIT 1 ms
UNTIL   100 samples taken
```

(b)

```
INITIALIZE POINTER TO ARRAY, A0
INITIALIZE COUNTER, D0

REPEAT
        READ PORT
        MASK UPPER 4 BITS
        PUT IN ARRAY, A0
        INCREMENT POINTER, A0
        CALL WAIT_1MS SUBROUTINE
        DECREMENT COUNTER, D0
UNTIL COUNTER = 0

WAIT_1MS   SUBROUTINE
        LOAD COUNT VALUE
        REPEAT
                DECREMENT COUNT VALUE
        UNTIL COUNT = 0
```

(c)

FIGURE 5-6   Algorithm for data samples at 1-ms intervals. (a) Flowchart. (b) Pseudocode. (c) Expanded pseudocode.

array. Therefore, we initialize these at the start. After we read in each value and put it in the array, we increment the pointer so that it points to the next location in the array. We then decrement the counter to indicate that we have taken another sample and call the WAIT_1MS subroutine. Note that the algorithm for the subroutine is done separately from that for the main program. As we discussed in the introduction to subroutines, the flow of the mainline program is much clearer if much of the detail is put in separate subroutines. Upon returning from the delay subroutine, we repeat the series of instructions if our sample counter is not yet down to zero.

For the delay subroutine we simply load a number in a register or memory location and decrement the number until it is down to zero. Note that even this expanded algorithm is general enough that it could be implemented on almost any microprocessor.

THE 68000 ASSEMBLY LANGUAGE PROGRAM

Figure 5-7, p. 120, shows the assembly language program for our expanded algorithm. This program reviews some of the concepts from previous chapters and demonstrates some new ones from this chapter. The program is a little longer than our previous examples, but don't let this overwhelm you. A large part of the program is simply initializing everything. Read through this program and see how much of it you can remember and/or figure out before you read our explanations in the following paragraphs. Deciphering a program written by someone else is an important skill to develop.

Let's start by examining the data declarations at the bottom of the program. We are placing the data sections of the example programs after the code sections. The operation of the URDA® MDS requires that the code of user programs start at address $4000. This is also the start of RAM on the URDA MDS, so the data must be placed at some address greater than $4000. We are not required to place the data after the code; however, in order to maintain a relationship similar to what actually occurs in RAM on the MDS the data is placed after the code.

The first data declaration PRESSURES: DS.W 100 requests that the assembler set aside 100 words of

```
; 68000 Program
; ABSTRACT       : This program takes in data samples from a port at 1
;                  ms intervals, masks the upper 4 bits of each sample,
;                  and puts each masked sample in successive locations
;                  in an array.
; REGISTERS USED: A0 ... pointer to array of pressure samples
;                 A2 ... pointer to pressure port
;                 D0 ... one sample
;                 D1 ... sample loop counter
;                 D2 ... 1 ms wait loop counter
; PORTS USED     : $C011 - input port for data samples
; PROCEDURES     : None used
;
;                        alr 10-88
PRESSURE_PORT   EQU     $C011      ; PRESSURE_PORT is the symbolic name for
                                   ;   the address of the pressure port

        ORG     $4000              ; start the code at $4000

; Mainline code
        LEA     STACK_TOP,A7       ; initialize user stack pointer to stack top
        LEA     PRESSURES,A0       ; initialize pressure reading array pointer
        LEA     PRESSURE_PORT,A2
        MOVE.B  #100,D1            ; initialize sample loop counter

NEXT_VALUE:
        MOVE.W  (A2),D0            ; read the pressure port
        ANDI.W  #$0FFF,D0          ; mask off upper 4 bits
        MOVE.W  D0,(A0)+           ; store data word in array and increment
                                   ;   array pointer to point to next word
        JSR     WAIT_1MS           ; delay of 1 ms
        DBGT    D1,NEXT_VALUE      ; decrement counter and repeat if greater
                                   ;   than 0
        RTS                        ; return to whoever called me

; Procedure to wait 1 ms
WAIT_1MS:
        MOVE.W  #$23F2,D2          ; load delay count
HERE:
        DBGT    D2,HERE            ; decrement count until <= 0
        RTS                        ; return to whoever called me

;-----------------------------
        ORG     $4200              ; start the data at $4200

PRESSURES:   DS.W   100           ; set up array of 100 words
STACK_HERE:  DS.W   40            ; set stack length of 40 words
STACK_TOP:   DS.W   0             ; the stack top is at the high address

        END
```

FIGURE 5-7 Assembly language program to read in 100 samples of data at
1-ms intervals.

memory and label the address of the first word with the name PRESSURES. In some cases we may also want to initialize all these 100 words to 0s. In such cases we could use a DC.W declaration. It really doesn't matter

what values are initially in these locations, because the program is going to write values in them. However, with later examples we may want to initialize arrays such as this to all 0s so that during debugging we can tell if the program wrote any values to these locations.

Next, we declare a stack 40 words, or $50 bytes, in length (40 × 2 = 80 = $50) and name the top of the stack. Recall that the statement STACK_TOP: DC.W 0 gives a name to the next address after the highest address in the stack we have set up. As described in the previous section, we can then access this location by name when we initialize the stack pointer.

Now let's work our way through the main program and the subroutine. The first task in most programs is initialization, and in this example we initialize four registers. The statement LEA STACK_TOP,A7 initializes the system stack pointer, as discussed in the previous section. The statement LEA PRESSURES,A0 initializes the register A0 as a pointer to the first location in the array PRESSURES. LEA performs the same operation as MOVEA.L. The third register initialized is one to point to the pressure port. Any address register that is not already in use will do; we have chosen A2. The statement LEA PRESSURE_PORT,A2 does this for us. We chose to use the register D1 as a sample counter, so we use the statement MOVE.B #100,D1 to initialize D0 with the number of samples we want to store.

As indicated by the PRESSURE_PORT EQU $C011 statement at the top of the program, the pressure sensor is connected to a port at address $C011. Notice how much more understandable it makes a program when we use a name such as PRESSURE_PORT in an instruction rather than $C011, the numerical port address. If you are working with an assembler, use EQU statements to do this. We label the top of our loop NEXT_VALUE:, although you may not realize that we need the label until you get to the bottom of the mainline program and consider what needs to be done there. The first real operation, then, is to read the pressure port. This program assumes that the port does not need to be initialized because all we are going to do is read from it. Since we have conveniently placed the address of the pressure port into register A2, all we have to do is MOVE.B (A2),D0 to read the pressure. That is, we move 1 word from the location to which A2 points (address register indirect addressing) into the low word of register D0.

When we get the pressure value into D0, we mask out the upper 4 bits with the ANDI.W #$0FFF,D0 instruction. We want to do this because the A/D converter to which the pressure sensor is connected is a 12-bit unit. The upper 4 bits of the 16-bit port are not connected to anything and may pick up random-noise signals. To prevent noise signals on the upper 4 bits from getting put in memory with our data, we mask these bits out by ANDing them with 0s. The instruction MOVE.W D0,(A0)+ will copy the data word from register D0 to the memory location pointed to by A0. Further, this instruction will increment A0 by a word (that is, it will add 2) to point to the next word in the array of saved pressure readings.

To produce the desired delay between samples, we call the WAIT_1MS subroutine using a JSR instruction. Putting a name in front of the subroutine allows us to call the subroutine by name. For the example in Figure 5-7, we named the subroutine WAIT_1MS to remind us of the function of the subroutine. Inside the subroutine we produce the desired delay by loading a number into register D2 with the MOVE.W #$23F2,D2 instruction and count the number down to 0 with the HERE: DBGT D2,HERE instruction. The DBGT instruction, remember, decrements D2 by 1 and jumps to the specified label if D0 is greater than 0. Since we put the label on the DBGT instruction, the DBGT instruction will simply execute over and over until D2 reaches 0. The RTS instruction at the end of the subroutine will return execution to the next instruction after the JSR in the mainline of the program. The JSR instruction copied the desired value for the program counter to the stack before going to the subroutine. The RTS instruction copies this value from the stack back to the program counter. If you are hand coding a program such as this, make sure to use the correct form of the RTS instruction. After we briefly discuss the rest of the mainline program, we will show you what happens to the stack and stack pointer as the return address is copied to and from the stack.

Back in the mainline, we need to get ready for reading the next data value. A0 already points to the location where we want to put the next data word because we used postincrement addressing. Since each address represents a byte and we are storing words, the CPU had to increment the pointer by 2 to point to the next storage word. We decrement the sample counter in D2 with the instruction DBGT D2,NEXT_VALUE. This instruction also tests D2; if it is equal to or less than 0, control passes through the DBGT instruction to the HALT instruction. If D2 is not yet counted down to 0, we need to go back to the top of the program and read in another pressure value. This is why we labeled the top of the program (after the initialization). The DBGT instruction will cause a branch back to NEXT_VALUE if the counter in D2 is greater than 0. Now let's see what happens to the stack and the stack pointer during all of this.

More Stack Operation and Use

STACK OPERATION DURING A JSR AND RTS

To show how the stack operates during a JSR and RTS, we will use some specific numbers with the example program in Figure 5-7. For that program we start the stack at address $4200, since we have an ORG $4200 just before the data declarations. The stack pointer, A7, will be initialized with $4200. We declared a stack length of 40 decimal, or $28, words with the DC.W 40 statement. These $28 words will occupy the $50 memory locations from $4200 to $424F. Figure 5-8, p. 122, shows this in diagram form. Remember, when we write words to the stack, we put the first byte at the highest address. For our example the first byte will be written at address $424F. As we write other bytes to the stack, they are written at lower addresses. In other words, the stack fills from the top down in terms of memory addresses and from the bottom up in the stack picture.

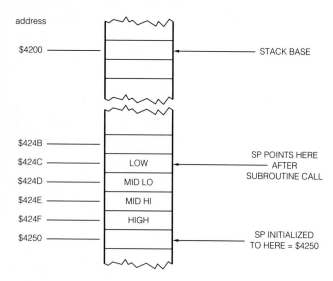

address

$4200 ———— ———— STACK BASE

$424B ————
$424C ———— LOW ———— SP POINTS HERE
                                  AFTER
$424D ———— MID LO   SUBROUTINE CALL
$424E ———— MID HI
$424F ———— HIGH
$4250 ———— ———— SP INITIALIZED
                              TO HERE = $4250

FIGURE 5-8   Stack diagram for JSR.

We use the stack pointer to keep track of where the last word was written to the stack. The location pointed to by the stack pointer at any time is called the *top of the stack*. In the program we initialized the stack pointer to STACK_TOP, the next even address above our actual stack, with the LEA STACK_TOP,A7 instruction. The actual value of STACK_TOP will be $4250.

After the 68000 fetches the JSR instruction from the prefetch queue in the execution unit, it automatically increments the program counter to $00004024, the offset of the next instruction after the JSR. The left columns of Figure 5-7 show that the address of the DBGT instruction is $00004024, which is immediately after the JSR instruction. The program counter then contains the address to which we want execution to return after the subroutine is completed. When the JSR instruction in our example program executes, the 68000 first decrements the stack pointer by 4. Then it copies the return address in the program counter to the memory location now pointed to by the stack pointer. If the stack pointer contained $4250 before being decremented, then after being decremented by 4, it will contain $424C. The highest byte of the program counter will be placed in location $424C, the next byte in $424D, and the next in $424E, and the low byte of the program counter will be copied to address $424F. This follows the Motorola convention of putting the lower byte of a word at the higher address in memory. Figure 5-8 shows these 4 bytes labeled as PC HIGH, PC MID HI, PC MID LO, and PC LOW. After the JSR instruction executes, the stack pointer is left pointing to address $424C. This location is now the top of the stack (TOS).

When the RTS instruction at the end of the subroutine in the example program executes, the 68000 copies the return address from the TOS to the program counter. This is accomplished using postincrement address register indirect addressing. Since the TOS was at $424C, the long word from addresses $424C through $424F will be copied to the program counter. After it copies the long word from the TOS to the

program counter, the 68000 increments the stack pointer by 4. For our example here, it will increment the stack pointer from $424C to $4250. The stack pointer is now back where it was before the JSR instruction executed. Note that the return address is still present in memory because the RTS instruction simply copied it to the program counter and incremented the stack pointer over it.

We could have used a BSR instruction in place of the JSR because the subroutine is very close in memory to the mainline program. The BSR and RTS interaction would be identical to that just described for the JSR and RTS combination. The only difference implied by the BSR is in the way the target address of the subroutine is encoded. A JSR uses an absolute 32-bit address, whereas a BSR uses an 8-bit or a 16-bit displacement (the assembler will decide whether to use an 8-bit or a 16-bit displacement).

As we mentioned previously, the stack can also be used to save the contents of registers while a subroutine executes and to hold data on which the subroutine is to act. The next section shows you how we do this.

USING −(A7) AND (A7)+ TO SAVE REGISTER CONTENTS

In the example program in Figure 5-7 we used register D1 to keep track of how many data samples we had taken in. After each data sample was taken in, we decremented register D1 and, using the DBGT instruction, determined whether to take another sample or to halt. We might have wanted instead to use register D2 to keep track of the number of samples taken if, for example, we were using D1 to keep a running sum of the sample readings (and perhaps all the other data registers D3–D7 were also being used already). We couldn't use D2 for this in the program because D2 is used in the subroutine. Any value we put in D2 in the mainline program would be written over by the MOVE.W #$23F2,D2 instruction in the subroutine. It is very common to want to use registers both in the mainline program and in a subroutine without the two uses interfering with each other. Even with eight general-purpose data registers, we run out of registers when performing complex tasks. The 68000 addressing modes and stacks make it easy to save and restore register contents. This allows us to use the same register for different purposes in subroutines. In particular, the predecrement and postincrement addressing modes can be combined nicely in a manner very similar to the way the CPU uses these modes during JSR and RTS processing.

The predecrement addressing mode, −(A7), decrements the stack pointer and copies the contents of the specified register or memory location to memory at the new TOS location. This operation is often called a *push* operation, or pushing the value onto the stack. The classic example of a stack data structure is the stack of trays in the cafeteria, where you take trays out of the stack and new trays are moved up by a big spring underneath the stack. You push trays onto the stack by placing them on top of the top tray in the stack and pushing the stack down. The MOVE.L D2,−(A7) instruction will decrement the stack pointer by 4 and copy the contents of register D2 to the stack where the stack pointer now points. This instruction is said to push D2 onto the stack, saving it there. This instruction then can be used to save the contents of D2 while a subroutine executes. The next question is, How do we get the saved value back when we want it?

The postincrement addressing mode, (A7)+, copies a value from the stack to the specified register or memory location and increments the stack pointer appropriately. If a byte is moved, A7 is incremented by 1; if a word is moved, A7 is incremented by 2; and if a long word is moved, then A7 is incremented by 4. This operation is commonly called a *pop* operation, or popping a value off the stack. The instruction MOVE.L (A7)+,D2 moves a 4-byte value from the stack into D2 and then increments the stack pointer, A7, by 4. After a pop, the stack pointer will point to the next value on the stack.

You can push any of the address or data registers or a value from a memory location specified by one of the 12 addressing modes in Figure 3-8. You can pop a value from the stack to any of the data registers or to a memory location specified in any one of the 8 data-alterable addressing modes.

When you push several registers on the stack using −(A7), you have to remember to pop them off using +(A7) in the reverse order from which you pushed them on. This is because the stack functions in a *last in, first out* manner. As mentioned earlier, an everyday example of this type of operation is the spring-loaded plate stacks seen in some restaurants and cafeterias. The last plate pushed on the stack is the first one popped off. Figure 5-9a should help you visualize how this works for the 68000. It shows a sequence of pushes you might use to save registers at the start of a subroutine called MULTO. Figure 5-9b shows how the instructions MOVE.L D0,−(A7), MOVE.L D1,−(A7), and MOVE.L D2,−(A7) put the contents of registers

D0, D1, and D2 on the stack. The first entry in the stack is the copy of the program counter put there by the JSR instruction that called the subroutine. Following this are words from registers D0, D1, and D2. Figure 5-9b shows words in memory rather than bytes. This is a more compact form when everything pushed on the stack is pushed as either words or long words. After all these are pushed on the stack, the stack pointer is left pointing at the location in the stack where D2 was pushed.

When we want to restore the saved values to the registers at the end of the subroutine, we first pop D2 because it was the last register pushed on the stack. So the first instruction in restoring the registers will be MOVE.L (A7)+,D2. After D2 is popped, the stack pointer will be left pointing at the location where D1 is stored. Therefore, we pop D1 next using MOVE.L (A7)+,D1. We continue popping until all the registers are restored. The RTS instruction then copies the return address from the stack to the instruction pointer to return execution to the main program. It is very important to keep the number of pushes equal to the number of pops or keep the stack balanced in some other way so that the RTS instruction finds the correct word to put in the program counter. If you do not keep the pushes and pops exactly matched, then the RTS instruction will most likely use some bogus value as a return address, and typically the CPU will generate a bus error and halt! This bogus value will be one of the saved register contents if you forget one of the pop operations and will be data that was sitting above the stack if you put in too many pop operations.

Some programmers like to push and pop registers in the mainline or calling program rather than in the subroutine, as we did in Figure 5-9a. This approach has the advantage that you can push only those registers that you care about saving each time you call the subroutine. The disadvantages of this approach are that the pushes and pops clutter up the mainline program and you may decide to use another register at

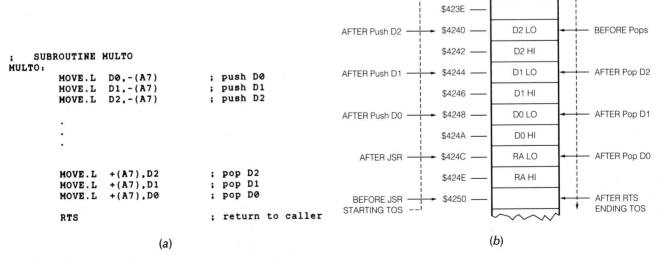

```
;   SUBROUTINE MULTO
MULTO:
        MOVE.L  D0,-(A7)        ; push D0
        MOVE.L  D1,-(A7)        ; push D1
        MOVE.L  D2,-(A7)        ; push D2
        .
        .
        .
        MOVE.L  +(A7),D2        ; pop D2
        MOVE.L  +(A7),D1        ; pop D1
        MOVE.L  +(A7),D0        ; pop D0

        RTS                     ; return to caller
```

(a)

(b)

FIGURE 5-9   Using push and pop operations. (a) Instruction sequence. (b) Effect on stack and stack pointer.

some point in the program and forget to add a push for it. We like to push any registers used in a subroutine directly in the subroutine. This way we always know that the subroutine can be called from anywhere in the program without losing the contents of any registers. Another advantage of this approach is that you have to write the pushes and pops only once. A disadvantage is that in a situation where all the pushes are not needed, the subroutine may take a little longer to run.

Passing Parameters to and from Subroutines

Often when we call a subroutine we want to make some data values or addresses available to the subroutine. Likewise, we often want a subroutine to make some processed data values or addresses available to the main program. These address or data values passed back and forth between the mainline and the subroutine are commonly called *parameters*. These values are also commonly called the *arguments* to the subroutine. There are three major ways of passing parameters to and from a subroutine. Parameters can be passed in *registers*, they can be passed in *dedicated memory locations*, or they can be passed in *stack locations*. In the following sections we use three versions of a simple program to show you how each of these methods work.

DEFINING THE PROGRAMMING PROBLEM

A common programming need is to convert a packed BCD number such as 4596 to its binary or hexadecimal equivalent. The hexadecimal equivalent of BCD 4596 is $11F4, for example. There are several ways to do this conversion, but to us the easiest is based on using the value of each placeholder or digit in the BCD number. Figure 5-10 shows the names and values for each digit in a 4-digit BCD number such as 4596. When we write a number such as this, it means that we have a total of 4 thousands + 5 hundreds + 9 tens + 6 units. To determine the value of this number in hexadecimal, we just multiply the number in each digit position by the value of that digit position in hexadeci-

mal and add the results. The right-hand side of Figure 5-10 shows how this works. The units position has a value of 1 in hex, so multiplying this by 6 units gives $0006. The tens position has a value of 10, or $A. Multiplying this value by 9, the number of tens, gives $005A. The hex value of the hundreds position is $64. When we multiply this value by 5, the number of hundreds, we get $01F4. When we multiply the hex value of the thousands position, $03E8, by 4 (the number of thousands), we get $0FA0. Adding the results for the 4 digits gives $11F4, which is the hex equivalent of 4596 BCD. You can use this method to convert a BCD number with any number of digits to its binary equivalent, but to conserve space here we will do it just for a 2-digit BCD number.

The algorithm for this program then is the simple sequence of operations:

Separate nibbles.

Save the lower nibble (don't need to multiply by 1).

Multiply the upper nibble by $A.

Add the lower nibble to result of the multiplication.

We want to implement this program as a subroutine that can be called from anywhere in a mainline program. For our first version we pass the BCD number to the subroutine in a register.

PASSING PARAMETERS IN REGISTERS

Figure 5-11 shows our first version of a subroutine to convert a 2-digit packed BCD number to its hex (binary) equivalent. The BCD number is passed to the subroutine in register D0, and the hex equivalent is passed back to the calling program in register D0. We start the subroutine by pushing the registers we use in the subroutine. Notice that we don't need to push and pop register D0 because we are using it to pass a value to the subroutine and expecting the subroutine to pass a different value back to the calling program in it.

It is hoped that the functions of the rest of the instructions in the subroutine are reasonably clear

```
4596        =       (4 x 1000) + (5 x 100) + (9 x 10) + (6 x 1)


1000    = $3E8    therefore    4000  =  4 x $3E8  = $0FA0

 100    = $64     therefore     500  =  5 x $64   = $1F4

  10    = $A      therefore      90  =  9 x  $A   = $5A

   1    = $1      therefore       6  =  6 x  $1   = $6


4596    =                                           $11F4
```

FIGURE 5-10   BCD-to-HEX or BCD-to-binary algorithm.

```
;  68000 Program and Subroutine for BCD to HEX conversion
;
;  ABSTRACT           : This program uses a subroutine to convert BCD
;                       numbers into HEX (binary).  It shows how to
;                       use register D0 to pass parameters to the subroutine.
;
;  REGISTERS USED:  D0
;  PORTS USED     :  none
;  PROCEDURES     :  BCD_HEX
;
;                 alr 1-89
;
    ORG          $4000            ; start the code at memory address $4000

    MOVE.B    (BCD_INPUT),D0      ; get the BCD value
    JSR       BCD_TO_HEX          ; call the subroutine
    MOVE.B    D0,(HEX_VALUE)      ; save the HEX value

    RTS

;-----------------------------
;SUBROUTINE:          BCD_TO_HEX          ( BCD_value )
;PARAMETERS:          incoming - D0 - the BCD value
;                     outgoing - D0 - the HEX value
;
;SAVES:                  saves, uses, and restores D1 and D2
BCD_TO_HEX:
    ;save registers
    MOVE.L    D1,-(A7)          ; push registers D1 and D2
    MOVE.L    D2,-(A7)          ;    in this order
    ;initialization
    CLR.L     D1
    CLR.L     D2
    ; perform the BCD to binary conversion
    MOVE.B    D0,D1             ; make a copy of the BCD value
    ANDI.B    #$0F,D0           ; isolate lower BCD digit in D0
    ROL.B     #4,D1             ; rotate high order BCD digit into low
                                ;     order position
    ANDI.B    #$0F,D1           ; isolate upper BCD digit in
                                ;     low nibble of D0
    MOVE.B    #$0A,D2           ; move conversion factor into D2
    MULU      D2,D1             ; leave result in D1 (we know it is <160)
    ADD.W     D1,D0             ; add up the two BCD digit values
    ; restore the registers to their value before this subroutine
    MOVE.L    (A7)+,D2          ; pop registers D1 and D2
    MOVE.L    (A7)+,D1          ;    in opposite order from when saved
    RTS                         ; return to whoever called me

; start data here
    ORG          $4200

BCD_INPUT    DS.B      1        ; storage for BCD value
HEX_VALUE    DS.B      1        ; storage for binary value

    END
```

FIGURE 5-11 Example program passing parameters in registers.

from the comments with them. We first make a copy of the BCD value in D1 so we have two copies to work on. We then mask the upper nibble of one and save it in D0. Since multiplying this nibble by 1 would not change its value, we are done with it for now. We mask the lower nibble of the other copy (in D1) of the BCD and rotate this nibble into the lower nibble position of the byte so we can multiply it correctly. When we multiply this nibble by the digit weight of $0A, the result is left in register D1. However, since the result can never be greater than 8 bits, we can disregard the carry flag and any overflow conditions. Finally, we add the lower nibble we saved in D0 to the result in D1 to get the hex total. The desired result is left in D0. Before returning to the main program we pop the registers we pushed at the start of the subroutine, remembering to pop them in the reverse order from which we pushed them.

The main program for this example is very simple. We just get the BCD value from memory (assuming some other program has stored it there). Then we call the subroutine using a JSR, with the BCD value in D0. On return from the subroutine, the hex value is in D0, and we can save this into memory for some later program to operate on. Then we simply return control back to the URDA MDS monitor program using an RTS instruction.

USING GENERAL MEMORY TO PASS PARAMETERS

For cases where we have to pass only a few parameters to and from a subroutine, registers are a convenient way to do it. However, in cases where we need to pass a large number of parameters to a subroutine or in cases where we don't want to use registers, we use memory. This memory may be a dedicated section of general memory or part of the stack. The following example shows a very simple case using dedicated memory locations.

Figure 5-12a shows a fragment of a program that uses another version of our BCD_TO_HEX subroutine. In this version the number to be converted is stored in a dedicated memory location named BCD_INPUT, and the hex result is returned from the subroutine to a dedicated memory location called HEX_VALUE.

In the subroutine we push all the registers used in the subroutine. This time D0 is included, since it is used in the subroutine but is no longer used for passing parameters. The main program may be using D0 for some other purpose. In the initialization we also clear D0 to all 0s just to be sure D0 is "clean" for subsequent operations. We then copy the BCD number into D0 with the MOVE.B (BCD_INPUT),D0 instruction. From here on, the subroutine is the same as the previous version until we reach the point where we want to pass the hex result back to the calling program. Here we use the MOVE.B D0,(HEX_VALUE) instruction to copy the result to the dedicated memory location we set aside for it. To complete the subroutine, we pop the registers (in reverse order) and return to the main program.

The approach used in Figure 5-12a works in this case, but it has a severe limitation. Can you see what it is? This subroutine will always look to the memory location named BCD_INPUT to get its data and always put its result in the memory location called HEX_VALUE. In other words, the way it is written we can't easily use this subroutine to convert a BCD number in some other memory location. We would have to get the BCD value out of that other memory location, place it into BCD_INPUT, and then get the result from HEX_VALUE after the subroutine and place it where we wanted. The main program and the subroutine must agree as to the exact memory locations or this method won't work.

PASSING PARAMETERS USING POINTERS

A parameter-passing method that overcomes the disadvantage of using data item names directly in a subroutine is to pass the subroutine a pointer to the desired data. Figure 5-12b, p. 128, shows one way to do this. In the main program, before we call the subroutine, we use the MOVEA.L BCD_INPUT,A0 instruction to set up register A0 as a pointer to the memory location BCD_INPUT. We also use the MOVEA.L HEX_VALUE,A1 instruction to set up register A1 as a pointer to the memory location named HEX_VALUE. In the subroutine the MOVE.B (A0),D0 instruction will copy the byte pointed to by A0 into D0. Likewise, the instruction MOVE.B D0,(A1) later in the subroutine will copy the byte from D0 to the memory location pointed to by A1.

This second approach, which actually uses a combination of registers and memory, is more versatile because you can pass the subroutine pointers to data anywhere in memory. You can pass pointers to individual values or pointers to arrays or strings. If you don't want to use registers to pass the pointers, you can use memory locations dedicated specifically to holding the pointers. In that case the subroutine will first fetch the pointer and then use it to access the desired data.

For many of your programs you will probably use registers or a combination of registers and general memory to pass parameters to subroutines. However, for more complex programs, such as those that allow several users to timeshare a system, we use the stack to pass parameters to and from subroutines.

PASSING PARAMETERS USING THE STACK

To pass parameters to a subroutine using the stack, we push them on the stack somewhere in the mainline program before we call the subroutine. Instructions in the subroutine then read these parameters from the stack. Likewise, parameters to be passed back to the calling program are written to the stack by instructions in the subroutine and read off the stack by instructions in the mainline. A simple example will show you how this works.

Figure 5-13a, p. 129, has a version of our BCD-to-hex subroutine that uses the stack for passing the BCD number to the subroutine and for passing the hex value back to the calling program. To save space here

```
;  68000 Program and Subroutine for BCD to HEX conversion
;
; ABSTRACT        : This program uses a subroutine to convert BCD numbers
;                   into HEX (binary).  It shows how to use dedicated memory
;                   locations to pass parameters to the subroutine.
; not shown       : Register A7 is presumed to be a valid stack pointer
; REGISTERS USED: none
; PORTS USED      : none
; PROCEDURES      : BCD_HEX
;
;                alr 1-89
;
        ORG        $4000            ; start the code at memory address $4000

        JSR        BCD_TO_HEX       ; call the subroutine

        RTS
;-------------------------
;SUBROUTINE:       BCD_TO_HEX      ( BCD_value )
;PARAMETERS:       incoming - BCD_INPUT
;                  outgoing - HEX_VALUE
;
;SAVES:                    saves, uses, and restores D1 and D2
BCD_TO_HEX:
        ;save registers
        MOVE.L    D0,-(A7)         ; save registers D0, D1, and D2
        MOVE.L    D1,-(A7)         ;    in this order
        MOVE.L    D2,-(A7)
        ;initialization
        CLR.L     D0
        CLR.L     D1
        CLR.L     D2
        MOVE.B    (BCD_INPUT),D0 ; get the BCD input value from the
                                 ;    dedicated memory location BCD_INPUT
        ; perform the BCD to binary conversion
        MOVE.B    D0,D1            ; make a copy of the BCD value
        ANDI.B    #$0F,D0          ; isolate lower BCD digit in D0
        ROL.B     #4,D1            ; rotate high order BCD digit into low
                                   ;    order position
        ANDI.B    #$0F,D1          ; isolate upper BCD digit in low nibble of D0
        MOVE.B    #$0A,D2          ; move conversion factor into D2
        MULU      D2,D1            ; leave result in D1 (we know it is <160)
        ADD.W     D1,D0            ; add up the two BCD digit values
        MOVE.B    D0,(HEX_VALUE) ; save the result in dedicated memory
        ; restore the registers to their value before this subroutine
        MOVE.L    (A7)+,D2         ; restore registers D0, D1, and D2
        MOVE.L    (A7)+,D1         ;    in opposite order from when saved
        MOVE.L    (A7)+,D0
        RTS                        ; return to whoever called me

; start data here
        ORG        $4200

BCD_INPUT      DS.B      1         ; storage for BCD value
HEX_VALUE      DS.B      1         ; storage for binary value
        END
```

(a)   (continued on p. 128)

FIGURE 5-12 Example program passing parameters in named memory
locations. (a) Named memory location only. (b) More versatile approach using
pointers to named memory locations (p. 128).

```
; 68000 Program and Subroutine for BCD to HEX conversion
;
; ABSTRACT        : This program uses a subroutine to convert BCD numbers
;                   into HEX (binary).  It shows how to use pointers
;                   to pass parameters to the subroutine.
; not shown       : Register A7 is presumed to be a valid stack pointer
; REGISTERS USED: A0, A1
; PORTS USED      : none
; PROCEDURES      : BCD_HEX
;
;                alr 1-89
;
        ORG        $4000            ; start the code at memory address $4000

        MOVEA.L    BCD_INPUT,A0     ; load pointer to first parameter
        MOVEA.L    HEX_VALUE,A1     ; load pointer to second parameter
        JSR        BCD_TO_HEX       ; call the subroutine

        RTS
;----------------------------------
;SUBROUTINE:        BCD_TO_HEX       ( BCD_value )
;PARAMETERS:        incoming - A0 - pointer to BCD input value
;                   outgoing - A1 - pointer to the HEX value
;
;SAVES:             saves, uses, and restores D1 and D2
BCD_TO_HEX:
        ;save registers
        MOVE.L     D0,-(A7)         ; save registers D0, D1, and D2
        MOVE.L     D1,-(A7)         ;    in this order
        MOVE.L     D2,-(A7)
        ;initialization
        CLR.L      D0
        CLR.L      D1
        CLR.L      D2
        MOVE.B     (A0),D0          ; get the BCD input value from where A0 points
        ; perform the BCD to binary conversion
        MOVE.B     D0,D1            ; make a copy of the BCD value
        ANDI.B     #$0F,D0          ; isolate lower BCD digit in D0
        ROL.B      #4,D1            ; rotate high order BCD digit into low
                                    ;    order position
        ANDI.B     #$0F,D1          ; isolate upper BCD digit in low nibble of D0
        MOVE.B     #$0A,D2          ; move conversion factor into D2
        MULU       D2,D1            ; leave result in D1 (we know it is <160)
        ADD.W      D1,D0            ; add up the two BCD digit values
        MOVE.B     D0,(A1)          ; save the result where A1 points
        ; restore the registers to their value before this subroutine
        MOVE.L     (A7)+,D2         ; restore registers D0, D1, and D2
        MOVE.L     (A7)+,D1         ;    in opposite order from when saved
        MOVE.L     (A7)+,D0
        RTS                         ; return to whoever called me

; start data here
        ORG        $4200
BCD_INPUT   DS.B       1            ; storage for BCD value
HEX_VALUE   DS.B       1            ; storage for binary value
        END
```

(b)

FIGURE 5-12 (continued)

we assume that previous instructions in the mainline set up a stack segment, initialized the stack segment register, and initialized the stack pointer. We also assume that previous instructions in the mainline have left the BCD number in D0. In the mainline fragment in Figure 5-13a, we copy D0 to the stack with the MOVE.W D0,−(A7) instruction. Here we are pushing a full word to keep the stack aligned on even-word

```
;  68000 Program and Subroutine for BCD to HEX conversion
;
; ABSTRACT          : This program uses a subroutine to convert BCD numbers
;                     into HEX (binary).  It shows how to use a stack
;                     to pass parameters to the subroutine.
; not shown         : Register A7 is presumed to be a valid stack pointer
; REGISTERS USED: A0, A1
; PORTS USED        : none
; PROCEDURES        : BCD_HEX
;
;                     alr 1-89
;
        ORG         $4000               ; start the code at memory address $4000
        ;   .
        ;   .       assume arguement (number to convert) is in D0
        ;   .
        MOVE.W      D0,-(A7)            ; move parameter to stack
        JSR         BCD_TO_HEX          ; call the subroutine
        MOVE.W      (A7)+,D0            ; get return value from stack
        ;   .
        ;   .
        ;   .

        RTS
;------------------------
;SUBROUTINE:        BCD_TO_HEX          ( BCD_value )
;PARAMETERS:        the BCD input value was placed on the stack by the
;                   calling routine
;SAVES:             Saves, uses, and restores D0, D1, and D2
BCD_TO_HEX:
        ;save registers
        MOVE.L      D0,-(A7)            ; save registers D0, D1, and D2
        MOVE.L      D1,-(A7)            ;    in this order
        MOVE.L      D2,-(A7)
        ;initialization
        CLR.L       D1
        CLR.L       D2
        MOVE.B      20(A7),D0           ; get the BCD input value from where the
                                        ;    caller put it on the stack
        ; perform the BCD to binary conversion
        MOVE.B      D0,D1               ; make a copy of the BCD value
        ANDI.B      #$0F,D0             ; isolate lower BCD digit in D0
        ROL.B       #4,D1               ; rotate high order BCD digit into low
                                        ;    order position
        ANDI.B      #$0F,D1             ; isolate upper BCD digit in low nibble of D0
        MOVE.B      #$0A,D2             ; move conversion factor into D2
        MULU        D2,D1               ; leave result in D1 (we know it is <160)
        ADD.W       D1,D0               ; add up the two BCD digit values
        MOVE.B      D0,#20(A7)          ; save the result where A1 points
        ; restore the registers to their value before this subroutine
        MOVE.L      (A7)+,D2            ; restore registers D0, D1, and D2
        MOVE.L      (A7)+,D1            ;    in opposite order from when saved
        MOVE.L      (A7)+,D0
        RTS                             ; return to whoever called me

; start data here
        ORG         $4200
BCD_INPUT   DS.B        1               ; storage for BCD value
HEX_VALUE   DS.B        1               ; storage for binary value
        END
```

(a)   (continued)

FIGURE 5-13 Example program passing parameters on the stack. (a) Assembly
language program. (b) Stack diagram (p. 130).

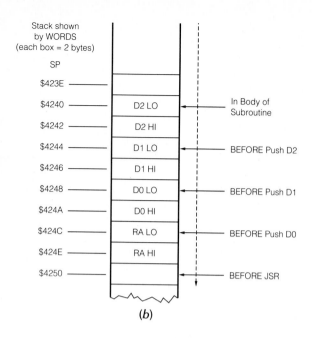

Stack shown
by WORDS
(each box = 2 bytes)

SP

Address	Value	
$423E		
$4240	D2 LO	← In Body of Subroutine
$4242	D2 HI	
$4244	D1 LO	← BEFORE Push D2
$4246	D1 HI	
$4248	D0 LO	← BEFORE Push D1
$424A	D0 HI	
$424C	RA LO	← BEFORE Push D0
$424E	RA HI	
$4250		← BEFORE JSR

(b)

FIGURE 5-13 (continued)

boundaries. In a more complex example the BCD number or a pointer to it would probably be put on the stack by a different mechanism, but the important point for now is that the parameter is on the stack for the subroutine to access. The JSR instruction in the mainline decrements the stack pointer by 4, copies the return address on the stack, and loads the program counter with the starting address of the subroutine. MOVE.L Dn,−(A7) instructions at the start of the subroutine save all the registers used in the procedure on the stack. Before discussing any more instructions, let's take a look at the contents of the stack after these pushes.

Figure 5-13b shows how the values pushed on the stack will be arranged. Note that the BCD value is in the stack at a higher address than the return address. After the registers are pushed on the stack, the stack pointer is left pointing to the stack location where D2 is stored. The question now is, How can we easily access the parameter that seems buried in the stack? One way is to add 20 to the stack pointer with an ADD instruction so the stack pointer points to the word we want from the stack. A MOVE.W (A7)+,D0 instruction could then be used to copy the desired word from the stack to D0. However, for a variety of reasons that we will explain later, we would like to be able to access the parameter without changing the contents of the stack pointer.

The design of the 68000 makes it very easy to do this. Remember from Chapter 2 that the 68000 has an "address register indirect with displacement" addressing mode. With this addressing mode we can access a value 20 bytes above the top of the stack without changing the stack pointer value. This is how

we use indirect with displacement addressing in our example program here. We write what we want directly using the instruction MOVE.W #20(A7),D0. This instruction says move the word value that is at the address 20 bytes above where A7 points into D0. That is, the displacement is 20 and the address register is A7; add 20 to the value in A7 and get the word from the resulting address (just where we left the BCD value on the stack). This instruction does not change the value in A7; the addition is done in a temporary internal area in the CPU and does not change A7.

Once we have the BCD number copied from the stack into D0, the instructions which convert it to hex are the same as those in the previous versions. When we want to put the hex value back in the stack to return it to the calling program, we again use address register indirect with displacement addressing. The instruction MOVE.W D0,#20(A7) will copy D0 to a stack location 20 addresses higher than that where A7 is pointing. This, of course, is the same location we used to pass the BCD number to the subroutine. After we pop the registers and return to the calling program, the registers will all have the values they had before the JSR instruction executed. D0 will contain the original BCD number, and the stack pointer will be pointing to the hex value now at the top of the stack. In the mainline we can now pop this hex value into a register with an instruction such as MOVE.W (A7)+,D0.

Whenever you are using the stack to pass parameters, it is very important to keep track of what you have pushed on the stack and where the stack pointer is at each point in a program. We have found that diagrams such as the one in Figure 5-13b are very helpful in doing this. One potential problem to watch for when using the stack to pass parameters is stack overflow. Stack overflow means that the stack fills up and overflows the memory space you set aside for it. To see how this can easily happen if you don't watch for it, consider the following. Suppose that we use the stack to pass 4 word parameters to a subroutine but that we take only 1 word parameter back off the stack in the calling program. Figure 5-14 shows a stack diagram for this situation. Before a JSR instruction the four parameters to be passed to the subroutine are pushed on the stack. During the subroutine the parameter to be returned is put in the stack location previously occupied by the fourth input parameter. After the RTS instruction at the end of the subroutine executes, the stack pointer will be left pointing at this value. Now assume we pop this value into a register. The MOVE.W instruction will copy the value to a register and increment the stack pointer by 2. The stack pointer now points to the third word we pushed to pass to the subroutine. In other words, the stack pointer is six addresses lower than it was when we started this process. Now suppose that we call this subroutine many times in the course of the mainline program. Each time we push 4 words on the stack but pop only 1 word off, the stack pointer will be left six addresses lower than it was before the process. The top of the stack will keep being moved downward. When the stack pointer gets down to $4040, or right into the bottom of

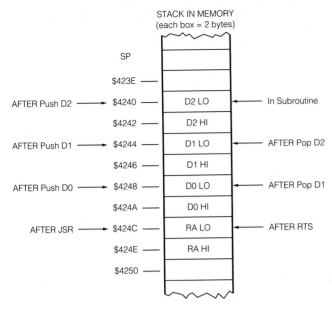

FIGURE 5-14   Stack diagram showing cause of stack overflow.

your code, it starts to overwrite your code with stack return addresses and parameters. Pretty soon your entire program has been written over (commonly called being "stomped on" by the stack)! This is what we mean by the term *stack overflow*. *Stack underflow* can occur if you keep trying to pop more values than you push in your main program and the top of the stack goes through its intended bottom, typically chewing up other data. If the subroutine itself mismatches pushes and pops, then the program can abort quickly, as described in the previous section. In brief, make sure you match your pushes and pops or very bad things will usually result!

The cure for this potential problem is to use your stack diagrams to help you keep the stack balanced. You need to keep the number of pops equal to the number of pushes or in some other way make sure the stack pointer gets back to its initial location.

For this example we could use an ADDI.L #6,A7 instruction after the pop to get the stack pointer back up the additional six addresses to where it was before we pushed the four parameters on the stack.

Summary of Passing Parameters to and from Subroutines

You can pass parameters between a calling program and a subroutine using registers, dedicated memory locations, or the stack. The method you choose depends largely on the specific program. There are no hard rules, but here are a few guidelines. For simple programs with just a few parameters to pass, registers are usually the easiest to use. For passing arrays or other data structures to and from subroutines, you can use registers to pass pointers to the start of these data structures. As we explained previously, passing point-

ers to the subroutine is a much more versatile method than having the subroutine access the data structure directly by name.

For subroutines in a multiuser-system program, subroutines that will be called from a high-level language program, or subroutines that call themselves, parameters should be passed on the stack. When writing programs that pass parameters on the stack, you should use stack diagrams such as the one in Figure 5-13*b* to help you keep track of where everything is in the stack at a particular time. The following section will give you some additional guidance in regard to when to use the stack to pass parameters, and it will give you some additional practice following the stack and stack pointer as a program executes.

Reentrant and Recursive Subroutines

The terms *reentrant* and *recursive* are often used in microprocessor manufacturers' literature but are seldom illustrated with examples. Here we try to give these terms some meaning for you. Sooner or later you have to write reentrant subroutines, particularly when using interrupt-service routines, so read that section carefully. You will seldom have to write a recursive subroutine, so the main points to find in that section are the definition of the term and the operation of the stack as a recursive subroutine operates.

REENTRANT SUBROUTINES

The 68000 has a signal input that allows a signal from some external device to interrupt the normal program execution sequence and call a specified subroutine. In our electronics factory, for example, a temperature sensor in a flow-solder machine could be connected to the interrupt input. If the temperature got too high, the sensor would send an interrupting signal to the 68000. The 68000 would then stop whatever it was doing and go to a subroutine that would take whatever steps were necessary to cool down the solder bath. This procedure is called an *interrupt-service routine*. Chapter 8 discusses 68000 interrupts and interrupt-service routines in great detail, but it is appropriate to introduce the concept here.

Suppose that the 68000 was in the middle of executing a multiply subroutine when the interrupt signal occurred and that we also need to use the multiply subroutine in the interrupt-service subroutine. Figure 5-15, p. 132, shows the program execution flow we want for this situation. When the interrupt occurs, execution goes to the interrupt-service routine. The interrupt-service routine then calls the multiply subroutine when it needs it. The RTS instruction at the end of the multiply subroutine returns execution to the interrupt-service routine. A special return instruction at the end of the interrupt-service routine returns execution to the multiply subroutine, where it was executing when the interrupt occurred. When an interrupt occurs, the 68000 saves the return address of the next instruction to execute in the interrupted program, and it also saves the contents of the status

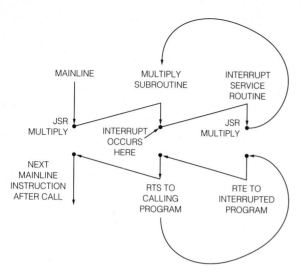

FIGURE 5-15 Program execution flow for reentrant subroutine.

be restored by pop instructions in the ISR before returning to complete the first execution.

A second method of making the BCD_TO_HEX subroutine reentrant is to pass pointers to the data items in registers as we did in the program in Figure 5-12b. Again, anything in registers will be saved by push operations and restored by pop operations when the subroutine is called by the interrupt-service routine.

Usually at this point someone remembers that the 68000 allows you to push the contents of a memory location on the stack and asks, Why can't I just save the contents of BCD_INPUT on the stack with a push BCD_INPUT operation? You can do this, but if an interrupt occurs after you have entered the subroutine but before this instruction occurs, you still have the problem.

The third way to make the BCD_TO_HEX subrou-

register. The special return from the interrupt-service routine instruction restores the status register (which contains all the condition codes) and then uses the saved return address to return to the interrupted program at the correct instruction. The RTE (return from exception) instruction is discussed in more detail in Chapter 8. The multiply subroutine must be written so that it can be interrupted, used, and "reentered" without losing or writing over anything. A subroutine that can function in this way is said to be *reentrant*.

To be reentrant, a subroutine must save all registers used in the subroutine. Also, to be reentrant, a program should use only registers or the stack to hold parameters. To see why this second point is necessary, let's take another look at the program in Figure 5-12a. This program uses the named variables BCD_INPUT and HEX_VALUE. The procedure BCD_TO_HEX accesses these two directly by name. Now, suppose that the 68000 is in the middle of executing the BCD_TO_HEX subroutine and an interrupt occurs. Further suppose that the interrupt-service routine loads some new value in the memory location named BCD_INPUT and calls the BCD_TO_HEX subroutine again. The initial value in BCD_INPUT has now been written over. If the interrupt occurs before the first execution of the subroutine has a chance to read in this value, the value will be lost forever. When execution returns to BCD_TO_HEX after the interrupt-service routine, the value used for BCD_INPUT will be that put there by the interrupt-service routine instead of the desired initial value. There are several ways we can handle the parameters so that the subroutine BCD_TO_HEX is reentrant.

The first is to simply pass the parameters in registers as we did in the program in Figure 5-16. If this form of the subroutine is called by an interrupt-service routine (often termed an *ISR*), all the variables will be saved by push instructions at the start of the ISR, and they will

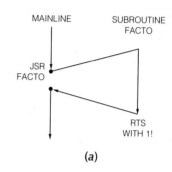

(a)

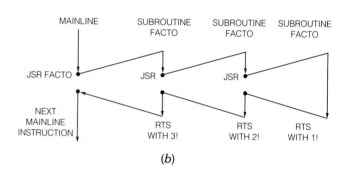

(b)

```
SUBROUTINE FACTO
IF N = 1
        FACTORIAL = 1
        RTS
ELSE
        REPEAT
            DECREMENT N
            JSR FACTO
        UNTIL N = 1
        MULTIPLY (N - 1)! x PREVIOUS N
        RTS
```

(c)   (continued)

FIGURE 5-16 Algorithm for program to compute factorial for a number N between 1 and 9. (a) Flow diagram for N = 1. (b) Flow diagram for N = 3. (c) Pseudocode. (d) Flowchart (p. 133).

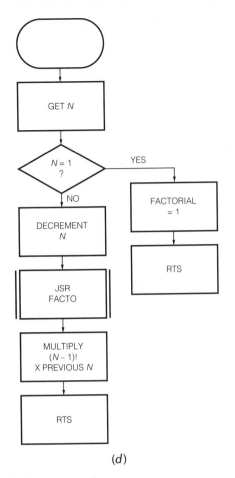

FIGURE 5-16 (continued)

(d)

tine reentrant is by passing parameters on the stack, as we did in the version in Figure 5-13. In this version the mainline pushes the BCD number on the stack and then calls the subroutine. The subroutine pushes registers on the stack and accesses the BCD number relative to where the stack pointer ends up. If an interrupt occurs, the interrupt-service routine will push on the stack the BCD number it wishes to convert and call BCD_TO_HEX. This BCD number will be pushed on the stack at a different location from the first BCD number that was pushed. Since everything is saved on the stack no matter where the interrupt occurs, the first execution of the subroutine will produce correct results when it is reentered.

If you are writing a subroutine that you may want to call from a program in a high-level language such as Pascal, PL/M, or C, then you should definitely use the stack for passing parameters because that is how these languages do it. Check the manual for the high-level language to determine the parameter-passing conventions for that language.

RECURSIVE SUBROUTINES

A recursive subroutine is a subroutine that calls itself. This seems simple enough, but you wonder why we would want a subroutine to call itself. Certain types of problems, such as choosing the next move in a com-

puter chess program, can best be solved with a recursive subroutine. Recursive subroutines (often referred to by the more general term *recursive procedures*) are used to work with complex data structures called *trees*. It is unlikely that you will have to write a recursive subroutine because most of the programming problems that you are likely to encounter can be solved with a simple WHILE-DO or REPEAT-UNTIL approach. You should, however, know what the term means when you encounter it. For those of you who wish to know more about how a recursive subroutine works, we have included an example in the following sections.

Most of the examples of recursive subroutines that we could think of are too complex to show here. Therefore, to show you how recursion works, we have chosen a simple problem that could be solved without recursion.

RECURSIVE SUBROUTINE EXAMPLE—ALGORITHM

The problem we have chosen to solve is to compute the factorial of a given number in the range of 1 to 9. The factorial of a number is the product of the number and all of the positive integers less than the number. For example, 5 factorial is equal to $5 \times 4 \times 3 \times 2 \times 1$. The word factorial is often represented with an exclamation point. We therefore write 5 factorial as 5!.

What we want to do here is write a recursive subroutine that will compute the factorial of a number N, which we pass to it on the stack, and pass the factorial back to the calling program on the stack. The basic algorithm can be expressed very simply as: IF N = 1 THEN factorial = 1, ELSE factorial = N × (factorial of N − 1). This says that if the number we pass to the subroutine is 1, the subroutine should return the factorial of 1, which is 1. If the number we pass is not 1, then the subroutine should multiply this number by the factorial of the number minus 1. Here is where the recursion comes in. Suppose we pass a 3 to the subroutine. When the subroutine is first called, it has the value of 3 for N, but it does not have the value for the factorial of $N − 1$ that it needs to do the multiplication indicated in the algorithm. The subroutine solves this problem by calling itself to compute the needed factorial of $N − 1$ (that is, of 3 − 1 = 2). It calls itself over and over until the factorial of $N − 1$ that it has to compute is the factorial of 1.

Figure 5-16 shows several ways to represent this process. In the program flow diagram in Figure 5-16a, you can see that if the value of N passed to the subroutine is 1, then the subroutine simply loads 1 in the stack location reserved for N! and returns to the calling program. If the number passed to the subroutine is some number other than 1, Figure 5-16b shows the program flow that will occur. If we call the procedure with $N = 3$, the subroutine will call itself to compute $(N − 1)!$, or 2!. It will then call itself again to compute the value of the next $N − 1$ factorial, or 1!. Since 1! is 1, the subroutine will return this value to the program that called it. In this case the program that called it was a previous execution of the same subroutine that needed this value to compute 2! Given this value it will compute 2! (as $2 \times 1 = 2$) and return the value to the program that called it. Here again the program that called it was a previous execution of the same subroutine that needed 2! to compute the factorial of 3. Given the factorial of 2, this call of the procedure can now compute the factorial of 3 (as $3 \times 2 = 6$) and return to the program that called it. For the example here, the return will be to the mainline program.

Figure 5-16c shows how we can represent this algorithm in slightly expanded pseudocode. Use the program flow diagram in Figure 5-16b to help you see how execution continues after the return when $N = 1$ and $N = 3$. Can you see that if N is initially 1, the first return will return execution to the instruction following JSR FACTO in the mainline? If the initial N was 3, for example, this return would return execution back to the instruction after the call in the subroutine. Likewise, the return after the multiply can send execution back to the next instruction after the call or back to the mainline if the final result has been computed.

Figure 5-16d shows a flowchart for this algorithm. Note that the flowchart shows the same ambiguity about the place to which the return operations send execution.

ASSEMBLY LANGUAGE RECURSIVE FACTORIAL SUBROUTINE

Figure 5-17a shows a 68000 assembly language subroutine that computes the factorial of a number in the range of 1 to 9. To save space we have not included instructions to return an error message if the number passed to the subroutine is out of this range. Figure 5-17b, p. 136, uses a stack diagram to show how the stack will be affected if this subroutine is called with an N of 3. When working your way through a recursive subroutine or any subroutine that uses the stack extensively, a stack diagram such as this is absolutely necessary to keep track of everything.

The first parts of the program are some housekeeping chores we described in previous examples. We have declared a stack of 200 words with a label at the top of the stack. We have also declared a memory location to contain the N of which we are to compute the factorial and initialized N to 3. The first instruction in the mainline program initializes the stack pointer. Next we load the number whose factorial we want into D0 and push the value on the stack where the subroutine will access it. Now we are ready to call the subroutine, which we have given the name FACTO.

At the start of the subroutine we save all the registers used in the subroutine on the stack. The subroutine uses D0, D1, and D2. In this case we have used the move multiple registers instruction, MOVEM, in place of three normal MOVE instructions. Move multiple registers is a special instruction that makes saving and restoring registers fast and easy. Refer to Chapter 6 for a more detailed description. In this example the MOVEM instruction takes a register list that looks like

D0–D2. This says to save registers D0 through D2. This single instruction produces the same results as did the three regular MOVE instructions of the previous example. The MOVEM at the end of the subroutine uses postincrement addressing and restores registers D0 through D2, just as the three regular MOVE instructions did in the previous example. MOVEM is smart enough to restore the registers in the correct order (the opposite from that saved), even though the register lists look identical. As part of the initialization we clear register D1 for later use and place a long 1 in D2.

Take a look at Figure 5-17b to see what is on the stack at this point. Note that the value of N is buried 20 addresses up the stack from where the stack pointer was left after D2 was pushed. To access this buried value, we use the same address register indirect with displacement addressing mode that we used in the previous example. The instruction MOVE.L #20(A7),D0 gets N from the stack. If the value of N read in is 1, then the factorial is 1. We want to put $00000001 in the stack location we reserved for the result, restore the registers, and return to the mainline program. Follow this path through the program in Figure 5-17a. Note how the MOVE.L D0,#20(A7) instruction is used to load a value to a location buried in the stack. When the incoming argument is equal to 1, we simply return the same 1 that was sent to FACTO. After all, the 1s are the same as both are 32 bits long.

Now let's see what happens if the number passed to FACTO is a 3. The CMP.L D2,D0 and BEQ IS1 instructions determine that N is not 1 and allow execution to pass through the BEQ to the MOVE.L D0,D1 instruction. According to the algorithm we are going to find the value of $N!$ by multiplying N times the value of $(N - 1)!$. We will be calling FACTO again to find the value of $(N - 1)!$. The SUB.L D2,D0 instruction computes $N - 1$ and the MOVE.L D0,–(A7) instruction places that value onto the stack. The value of $(3 - 1)!$ will be returned in this location.

When we call FACTO now to compute the value of $(N - 1)!$, the registers will again be pushed on the stack. Take another look at Figure 5-17b to see what is on the stack at this point. The value of $N - 1$ that we need is again buried 20 addresses up in the stack. This is no problem because the MOVE.L #20(A7),D0 instruction will allow us to access the value. We started with $N = 3$ for this example, so the value of $N - 1$ that we read in at this point is 2. Since this value is not 1, execution will again fall through the BEQ test. We decrement N by 1 to get $N - 1$, which is now 1. We push this value on the stack and call FACTO to compute the factorial of 1.

After pushing all the registers on the stack, FACTO reads this 1 from the stack with the MOVE.L #20(A7),D0 instruction. When the CMP.L D2,D0 instruction in FACTO finds that the number passed to it is 1, FACTO returns this value of 1 in the same place on the stack where the original 1 was passed to it. Look at the stack diagram in Figure 5-17b to see where these 4 bytes are in the stack. FACTO will then do a return to the next instruction after the JSR instruction that called it.

```
; 68000 Program Factorial
;
; ABSTRACT       : This program computes the factorial of a number
;                  between 1 and 9
; REGISTERS USED: A7, D0
; PORTS USED     : none
; PROCEDURES     : BCD_HEX
;
;                  alr 7-88
        ORG      $4000              ; start the code at memory address $4000

        MOVEA.L  #STACK_TOP,A7      ; initialize stack top
        MOVE.L   (NUMBER),D0        ; get number to compute factorial
        MOVE.L   D0,-(A7)           ; move number to stack
        JSR      FACTO              ; call the subroutine to compute the factorial
        MOVE.L   (A7)+,D0           ; get the factorial result off the stack

        NOP                         ; simulate next mainline instructions
        NOP                         ; ...
        STOP
;-------------------------------------
;SUBROUTINE:      FACTO ( number )
;                 Recursive subroutine to compute the factorial of a number
;                 Incoming parameter is a long unsigned integer on the stack
;PARAMETERS:      A7, D0
;PORTS USED:      none
FACTO:
        ;save registers
        MOVEM.L  D0-D2,-(A7)   ; save registers D0, D1, and D2
        ;initialization
        CLR.L    D1
        MOVE.L   #1,D2              ; amount to subtract each recursion
        MOVE.L   20(A7),D0         ; get the number from the stack
        ; perform the FACTORIAL computation
        CMP.L    D2,D0             ; IF the number is equal to 1
        BEQ      IS1               ;    THEN go return the same 1
        MOVE.L   D0,D1             ;    ELSE save a copy of number in D1
        SUB.L    D2,D0             ;         compute number-1 in D0
        MOVE.L   D0,-(A7)          ;         push number-1 onto the stack
        JSR      FACTO             ;         call FACTO(number-1)
        MOVE.L   (A7)+,D0          ;         get the result
        MULU     D1,D0             ;         compute FACTO(number-1)*number
IS1:    MOVE.L   D0,#20(A7)        ;         return result to stack
        ; restore the registers to their value before this subroutine
        MOVEM.L  (A7)+,D0-D2   ; restore registers D0, D1, and D2
        RTS                        ; return to whoever called me

; start data here
        ORG      $4200
STACK_HERE  DS.B    $200      ; the user stack
STACK_TOP   DS.B    0         ; the initial top of the stack
NUMBER      DC.L    3         ; the number to compute the factorial of
        END
```

(a)

(continued on p. 136)

FIGURE 5-17   Recursive subroutine to calculate factorial of number between 1 and 9. (a) Assembly language. (b) Stack diagram showing contents of stack for $N = 3$ (p. 136).

In this case FACTO was called from a previous execution of FACTO, so the return will be to the MOVE.L (A7)+,D0 instruction after JSR FACTO. This instruction copies the last computed $(N - 1)!$ from the stack to D0 so that we can multiply it by N. Restricting the allowed range of N for this example means that we have to do only a 16-bit by 16-bit multiply. Since N is presumed to be 9 or less, we know a 16-bit by 16-bit multiply will not overflow. We could increase the allowed range of N by simply setting aside larger spaces in the stack for factorials and including instructions to multiply larger numbers. In this example the MULU D1,D0 instruction multiplies the $(N - 1)!$ in D0 by the previous N from the stack. The 32-bit product is left in D0. Execution then flows into the MOVE.L D0,#20(A7) instruction, which copies this product to the stack locations where the incoming N (2 in this case) used to be. Now take a look at the stack diagram in Figure 5-17b to see where this value gets put and where the stack pointer is at this time. The next operation we do in the subroutine is pop the registers and return.

To see where we are returning, take another look at Figure 5-17b. We are returning with 2! in the stack, so we still need one more computation to produce the desired 3!. Therefore, the return is again to the MOVE.L (A7)+,D0 instruction after JSR in FACTO. The instructions after this will multiply 2! times 3 to produce the desired 3! and copy 3! to the stack, as described in the preceding paragraph. Since we have done all the required computations, this time the return will be to the mainline program. The desired result, 3!, will be in the memory location we reserved for it in the stack, overwriting the original value of N passed into FACTO on the JSR from the main program. We can access this result with a normal pop addressing mode (address register indirect with postincrement) when we need the value in the mainline.

If you can work your way through the flow of the stack and the stack pointer in this example program, you should have a good understanding of how the stack is used.

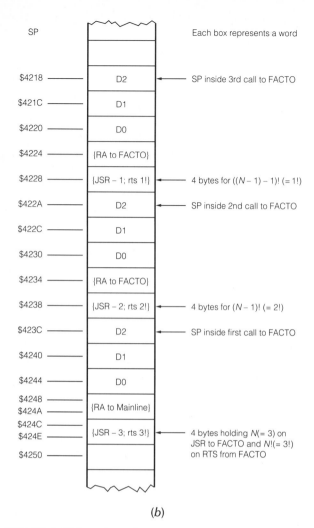

SP

Each box represents a word

$4218 —— D2 ←— SP inside 3rd call to FACTO

$421C —— D1

$4220 —— D0

$4224 —— {RA to FACTO}

$4228 —— {JSR – 1; rts 1!} ←— 4 bytes for ((N – 1) – 1)! (= 1!)

$422A —— D2 ←— SP inside 2nd call to FACTO

$422C —— D1

$4230 —— D0

$4234 —— {RA to FACTO}

$4238 —— {JSR – 2; rts 2!} ←— 4 bytes for (N – 1)! (= 2!)

$423C —— D2 ←— SP inside first call to FACTO

$4240 —— D1

$4244 —— D0

$4248 ——
$424A —— {RA to Mainline}

$424C ——
$424E —— {JSR – 3; rts 3!} ←— 4 bytes holding N(= 3) on JSR to FACTO and N!(= 3!) on RTS from FACTO

$4250 ——

(b)

FIGURE 5-17 (continued)

Accessing a Subroutine and Data in a Separate Assembly Module

As we have discussed previously, the best way to write a large program is as a series of modules. Each module can be individually written, assembled, tested, and debugged. Working modules can then be linked together. The previous section showed you how to access a subroutine in the same assembly module as your JSR instruction. Here we show you how to write your programs so that they can access data or subroutines in another assembly module. By another assembly module, we mean that the source code for the subroutine is in a different text file than that of the main program. The two files are assembled at different times; the resulting object code files are then linked together to create one executable file.

This example uses the Consulair® Assembler for the Apple Macintosh®. In order for a linker to be able to access data or a subroutine in another assembly module correctly, there are two major types of information that you must give the assembler. We will give you an overview of these four and then show with a program example how you actually write them.

In the assembly module that contains the calling program, you must use the XREF directive to tell the assembler the names of any subroutines or data items that are in other assembly modules. In the assembly module containing the subroutine, you must use the XDEF directive to tell the assembler the names of any labels or data items for which it must look in another assembly module.

PROBLEM DEFINITION AND ALGORITHM DISCUSSION

The subroutine in the following example program was written to solve a small problem we encountered when writing the program for a microprocessor-controlled medical instrument. Here's the problem.

In the program we add a series of values read in from an A/D converter. The sum is an unsigned number of between 24 and 32 bits. We needed to scale this value by dividing it by 10. This seems easy because the 68000 DIVU instruction will divide a 32-bit unsigned binary number by a 16-bit binary number. The quotient from the division, remember, is put in the low word of a data register—e.g., D0—and the remainder is put in the high word of the same register. However, if the quotient is larger than 16 bits, as it will be for our scaling, the quotient will not fit in 16 bits. In this case the 68000 will automatically respond in the same way that it would if you tried to divide a number by zero. We will discuss the details of this response in Chapter 8. For now it is enough to say that we don't want the 68000 to make this response. The simple solution we came up with is to do the division in two steps in such a way that we get a 32-bit quotient and a 16-bit remainder.

Our algorithm is a simple sequence of actions very similar to those used in the way we were taught to do long division. We will first describe how this works with decimal numbers and then we will show how it works with 32-bit and 16-bit binary numbers. Figure 5-18a shows an example of long division of the decimal number 433 by the decimal number 9. The 9 won't divide into the 4, so we put a 0 (or nothing) in this digit position of the quotient. We then decide if 9 divides into 43. It fits 4 times, so we put a 4 in this digit position of the quotient and subtract 4 × 9 from 43. The remainder of 7 now becomes the high digit of the 73, the next number into which we try to divide 9. After we find that 9 fits 8 times and subtract 9 × 8 from 73, we are left with a final remainder of 1. Now let's see how we do this with large binary numbers.

As shown in Figure 5-18b we first divide the 16-bit divisor into a 32-bit number made up of a word of all 0s and the high word of the dividend. This division gives us the high word of the quotient and a remainder. The remainder becomes the high word of the dividend for the next division, just as it did for the decimal division. We move the low word of the original dividend in as the low word of this dividend and divide by the 16-bit divisor again. The 16-bit quotient from this division is the low word of the 32-bit quotient we want. The 16-bit final remainder can be used to round the quotient or be discarded, depending on the application.

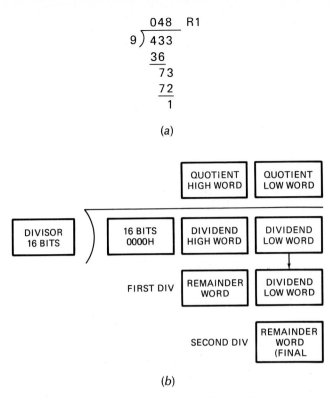

$$
\begin{array}{r}
048 \ \text{R1} \\
9 \overline{)\ 433} \\
36 \\
\hline
73 \\
72 \\
\hline
1
\end{array}
$$

(a)

FIRST DIV

SECOND DIV

(b)

FIGURE 5-18   Algorithm for smart divide subroutine.
(a) Decimal analogy. (b) 68000 approach.

THE ASSEMBLY LANGUAGE PROGRAM

Figure 5-19a, p. 138, shows the mainline of a program that calls the subroutine shown in Figure 5-19b, p. 139, implementing our division algorithm. We wrote these two as separate assembly modules so that we could show you what you need to add to each module in order for the modules to be linkable. Let's look closely at these added parts before we discuss the actual division subroutine.

The first added part of the program to look at is the statement XDEF SMART_DIVIDE in the subroutine module in Figure 5-19b. This statement is necessary to tell the assembler that the subroutine SMART_DIVIDE will be accessed from some other assembly module or modules. Essentially what we are doing here is telling the assembler to put the address of SMART_DIVIDE in a special table, where it can be accessed when the program modules are linked. Whenever you want a named subroutine to be accessible from another assembly module, you must declare it as an "eXternally accessible DEFinition." At the end of the assembler listing in the table, note that SMART_DIVIDE is global. This is the assembler's way of telling you that it can be accessed from other modules by the linker.

The other side of this coin is that, when you need to access a subroutine, a label, or a named data item in another module, you must use the XREF directive to tell the assembler that the label or data item is not in the present module—that is, you will be making an eXternal REFerence to something defined in another module (file). In the example program of Figure 5-19a,

the statement XREF SMART_DIVIDE tells the assembler that we will be accessing a label or subroutine defined in some other assembly module. For this example we will be accessing our subroutine, SMART_DIVIDE. As you can see in the table at the end of the assembler listing in Figure 5-19a (p. 138), SMART_DIVIDE is identified as an external label.

Now that we have explained the use of XDEF and XREF, let's work our way through the rest of the program. At the start of the mainline we initialize the stack pointer register, as described in previous example programs. Before calling the SMART_DIVIDE subroutine, we copy the dividend and divisor from memory to some registers. The dividend and the divisor are passed to the subroutine in these registers. As we explained in a previous section, if we pass parameters to a subroutine in registers, the subroutine does not have to refer to specific named memory locations. The subroutine is then more general and can more easily be called from any place in the mainline program. We then call the subroutine.

In the subroutine we first save the working registers that will be used by the subroutine. We then check to see if the divisor is zero with a TST.L D0 instruction. If the divisor is zero, the BEQ instruction will send execution to the label ERROR_EXIT. There we set the carry flag with MOVE.W #$01,CCR as an error indicator and return to the mainline program. If the divisor is not zero, then we go on with the division. To understand how we do the division, remember that the 68000 DIVU instruction divides the 32-bit number in a data register by the 16-bit number in a specified data register or memory location. It puts a 16-bit quotient in the low bits of the destination data register and a 16-bit remainder in the high bits of the same register. According to our algorithm in Figure 5-19b, we want to put $0000 in the high bits of the dividend and move the upper 16 bits into the low bits of the dividend for our first DIVU operation. MOVE.W D0,D2 saves a copy of the low word of the dividend for future reference. LSR.L #8,D0 and LSR.L #8,D0 shift the upper bits of the dividend into the lower bit positions and place 0s in the upper bit positions. We would like to have used a shift count of 16, but 8 is the largest immediate shift count allowed, so we used two 8-bit shifts to achieve the 16-bit shift desired. After the first DIVU instruction executes, the low 16 bits of D0 will contain the high word of the 32-bit quotient we want as our final answer. We save this in D3 with the MOVE.W D0,D3 instruction so that we can use D0 for the second DIVU operation.

The remainder from the first DIV operation was left in register D0's upper bits. As shown by the diagram in Figure 5-19b, this is right where we want it for the second DIVU operation. All we have to do now, before we do the second DIVU operation, is to use the MOVE.W D2,D0 instruction to get the low word of the original dividend back into D0. After the second DIVU instruction executes, the 16-bit quotient will be in D0. This word is the low word of our desired 32-bit quotient. We just leave this word in D0 to be passed back to the mainline. The upper bits of D0 contain the remain-

```
; 68000 Program 32 / 16 bit division
;
; ABSTRACT      : This program divides a 32-bit number by a 16-bit number
;                 to give a 32-bit quotient and a 16 bit remainder.  This
;                 program produces the correct result even if the quotient
;                 is larger than can be represented in 16-bits.
; REGISTERS USED: A7 ... the user stack pointer
;                 D0 the dividend on call to divide, quotient on return
;                 D1 the divisor on call to divide, the remainder on return
; PORTS USED    : none
; SUBROUTINES   : SMART_DIVIDE .. the smart division subroutine itself
;
;                 alr 8-51
;
        ORG      $4000          ; start the code at memory address $4000

        MOVEA.L  #STACK_TOP,A7  ; initialize stack top

; Place the parameters for the subroutine in the desired registers
; where they can be conveniently accessed.
;
        MOVE.L   (DIVIDEND),D0  ; get the dividend to pass to SMART_DIVIDE
        MOVE.L   (DIVISOR),D1   ; get the divisor to pass to SMART_DIVIDE

        JSR      SMART_DIVIDE   ; call the subroutine to perform the division

; Upon return from the subroutine the carry condition code will be set
; if some problem occurred during the division.  In this case, go and
; stop the CPU.  If the division went OK (CC cleared) then get the
; parameters from the registers (the quotient and remainder) and place
; them into memory in the designated locations.  The user can check these
; memory locations to see what the result of the division was.
;
        BNC      SAVE_ALL       ; if there was no error, go save the results
        JMP      STOP           ; otherwise, just go stop

; Save the results from the division back into memory
;
SAVE_ALL:
        MOVE.L   D0,(QUOTIENT)  ; save the quotient in memory
        MOVE.L   D1,(REMAINDER) ; save the remainder in memory
        RTS                     ; return to the monitor program
                                ; This in' the 'normal' program flow
                                ; back to the whoever called this main
                                ; program.

; The carry bit was set which means an error occurred.
; for now, just halt the processor and leave a status code (3)
; to use when debugging the situation.
;
STOP:   NOP                     ; the program could attempt to take some
                                ; corrective action here; such as printing a
                                ; message for the user and then returing to the
                                ; monitor program.

        HALT,#3                 ; halt the CPU with a 3 in the status register


;---------end of main program---------------------------
```

(a)

FIGURE 5-19 Assembly language program to divide a 32-bit number by a
16-bit number and return a 32-bit quotient. (a) Mainline program module.
(b) Subroutine module.

der, which we move to D1 with a MOVE.L D0,D1 instruction. We then shift this remainder right into the lower 16 bits, creating the final remainder value to be passed back to the mainline program in D1. After the first DIVU operation, we saved the high word of our 32-bit quotient in D3. We now use two shift-left instructions to move this into the upper 16 bits of D3 and shift 0s into the lower 16 bits. We mask off the remainder (upper 16 bits) in register D0. We then merge the upper 16 bits of the final quotient back with the lower 16 bits using an OR.L D3,D0 instruction, leaving the result in D0 to be passed back to the mainline program. We know the carry flag is clear because the OR instruction always clears the carry flag.

Back in the mainline we check the carry flag with the BCS instruction. If the carry flag is set, we know that the divisor was 0, no division was done, and there

```
;***************************************************
; subroutine: SMART_DIVIDE
; incoming parameters:    D0 - dividend; D1 - divisor
; returning parameters:   D0 - quotient; D1 - remainder
;                         CC - set if division failed
SMART_DIVIDE:
        ;save registers
        MOVE.L  D2,-(A7)        ; save registers D2 and D3
        MOVE.L  D3,-(A7)

        TST.L   D0              ; if the dividend is 0
        BEQ     ERROR_EXIT      ;   then go error exit
        MOVE.W  D0,D2           ; make a copy of the dividend low 16 bits
        LSR.L   #16,D0          ; logical shift upper bits of dividend into lower
                                ;   positions, 0s are shifted into the upper bits
        DIVU.L  D1,D0           ; divide D1 into D0 and leave the remainder and
                                ;   quotient in D0, we know there will be no
                                ;   overflow because D0 is not 0, and D0 is
                                ;   really only 16-bits long
        MOVE.L  D0,D3           ; save the division results
        MOVE.W  D2,D0           ; move the low 16 bits of the dividend back into
                                ;   D0, merging them with the remainder from the
                                ;   previous division in the upper bits of D0
        DIVU    D1,D0           ; perform second division, again we know there
                                ;   can not be any overflow
        MOVE.L  D0,D1           ; copy the result to D1
        LSR.L   #16,D1          ; logical shift the remainder into position
        LSL.L   #16,D3          ; move high order bits of quotient into place
                                ;   for combination with the low order bits
                                ;   the low bits of D3 are filled with 0s
        AND.L   #0000FFFF,D0    ; remove remainder from D0
        OR.L    D3,D0           ; combine upper and lower bits of quotient
        JMP     EXIT

ERROR_EXIT:
        MOVE.B  #$01,CCR        ; set the carry flag and clear the rest
EXIT:   MOVE.L  (A7)+,D3        ; restore registers D3 and D2
        MOVE.L  (A7)+,D2
        RTS                     ; return to whoever called me
;------------------------
; start data here
        ORG     $4200
STACK       DS.W    $256        ; the user stack
STACK_TOP   DS.W    0           ; the initial top of the stack
DIVIDEND    DC.L    $8C72403B   ; the dividend
DIVISOR     DC.W    $5692       ; the divisor
QUOTIENT    DS.L    1           ; memory for the quotient
REMAINDER   DS.W    1           ; memory for the remainder
        END
```

(b)

FIGURE 5-19 (continued)

is no result to put in memory. If the carry flag is not set, then we know that a valid 32-bit quotient was returned in D0 and a 16-bit remainder was returned in D1. Finally, we copy this quotient and this remainder to some named memory locations we set aside for them.

Writing and Debugging Programs Containing Subroutines

The most important point in writing a program containing subroutines is to approach the overall job very systematically. We carefully work out the overall structure of the program and break it down into modules that can easily be written as subroutines. We then write the mainline program so that we know what each subroutine has to do and how parameters can be most easily passed to each subroutine. To test this mainline we simulate each subroutine with a few instructions that simply pass test values back to the mainline. Some programmers refer to these "dummy" subrou-

tines as *stubs*. If the structure of the mainline seems reasonable, we then develop each subroutine and replace the dummy with it. The advantage of this approach is that you have a structure on which to hang the subroutines. If you write the subroutines first, you have the problem of trying to write a mainline to connect all the pieces together. This can get messy.

Now, suppose that you have approached a program as we suggested, and the program doesn't work. Probably the best tools to help you localize a problem to a small area are breakpoints. Run the program to a breakpoint just before a JSR instruction to see if the correct parameters are being passed to the subroutine. Put a breakpoint at the start of the subroutine to see if execution ever gets to the subroutine. Move the breakpoint to a later point in the subroutine to determine if the subroutine found the parameters passed from the mainline. Use a breakpoint just before the RTS instruction to see if the subroutine produced the correct results and put these results in the correct locations to pass them back to the mainline program. Inserting breakpoints at key points in your program is much more effective in locating a problem than random poking and experimenting.

WRITING AND USING ASSEMBLER MACROS

Macros and Subroutines Compared

Whenever we need to use a group of instructions several times throughout a program, there are two ways we can avoid having to write the group of instructions each time we want to use it. One way is to write the group of instructions as a separate subroutine. We can then just call the subroutine whenever we need to execute that group of instructions. A big advantage of using a subroutine is that the machine codes for the group of instructions in the subroutine have to be put in memory only once. Disadvantages of using a subroutine are the need for a stack and the overhead time required to call the subroutine and return to the calling program.

When the repeated group of instructions is too short or not appropriate to be written as a subroutine, we use a macro. A macro is a group of instructions we bracket and name at the start of our program. Each time we "call" the macro in our program, the assembler will insert the defined group of instructions in place of the call. In other words, the macro call is like a shorthand expression that tells the assembler, "Every time you see a macro name in the program, replace it with the group of instructions defined as that macro at the start of the program." An important point here is that the assembler generates machine codes for the group of instructions each time the macro is called. Replacing the macro with the instructions it represents is commonly called *expanding* the macro. Since the generated machine codes are right *in-line* with the rest of the program, the processor does not have to go off to a subroutine and return. Therefore, using a macro avoids the overhead time involved in calling and returning from a subroutine. A disadvantage of generating in-line code each time a macro is called is that this may make the program take up more memory. The following examples should help you see how to define and call macros. For these examples we use the syntax of the Macintosh-style macros of the Consulair assembler for the Apple Macintosh. If you are developing your programs on some other machine, consult the assembly language programming manual for your machine to find the macro definition and calling formats for it.

Defining and Calling a Macro without Parameters

For our first example suppose that we are writing a 68000 program that has many complex subroutines. At the start of each subroutine we want to save the flags and all the registers by pushing them on the stack. At the end of each subroutine we want to restore the flags and all the registers by popping them off the stack. Each subroutine would normally contain a series of push instructions (MOVEs and MOVEM) at the start and a series of pop instructions (MOVEs and MOVEM) at the end. Typing in these lists of push and pop instructions is tedious and prone to error. Reading them is confusing and inefficient. We could write a subroutine to do the pushing and another subroutine to do the popping. However, this adds more complexity to the program and is therefore not appropriate. Two simple macros will solve the problem for us.

Here's how we write a macro to save the registers and condition codes:

```
MACRO  PUSH_ALL =
   MOVEM.L  D0-D3,-(A7)
   MOVE.W   CCR,D0
   MOVE.L   D0,-(A7)
   |
```

The MACRO PUSH_ALL statement identifies the start of the macro and gives the macro a name. The vertical bar (|) marks the end of the macro.

Now, to call the macro in one of our procedures we simply put in the name of the macro, just as we would an instruction mnemonic. The start of a procedure that does this might look as follows:

```
BREATH_RATE:
   PUSH_ALL
   MOVE.L PATIENT_PARAMETERS,D0
   MOVE.L #60,D2
      .
      .
      .
```

When the assembler assembles this program section, it will replace PUSH_ALL with the instructions that it represents and insert the machine codes for these instructions in the object code version of the program. As you can see from the example here, using a macro makes the source program much more readable because the source program does not have the long series of MOVE instructions cluttering it up.

The preceding example showed how a macro can be used as simple shorthand for a series of instructions. The real power of macros, however, comes from being able to pass parameters to them when you call them. The next section shows you how and why this is done.

Passing Parameters to Macros

Most of us have received computer printed letters of the form:

Dear MR. HALL,
   We are pleased to inform you that you may have won up to $1,000,000 in the *Publishers Clearing Barn* sweepstakes. To find out if you are a winner, MR. HALL, return the gold card to *Publish-*

ers Clearing Barn in the enclosed envelope before OCTOBER 22, 1992. You can take advantage of our special offer of three years of *Publishers Clearing Barn* for only $24.95 by putting an X in the YES box on the gold card. If you do not wish to take advantage of this offer, which is one-third off the newsstand price, mark the NO box on the gold card.

Thank you,

A letter such as this is an everyday example of the concept of a macro with parameters. The basic letter (macro) is written with dummy words in place of the addressee's name, the reply date, and the cost of a 3-yr subscription. Each time the macro that prints the letter is called, new values for these parameters are passed to the macro. The result is a "personal" letter.

In assembly language programs we can likewise write a generalized macro with dummy parameters. Then when we call the macro, we can pass it the actual parameters needed for the specific application.

Suppose, for example, we are writing a word processor program. A frequent need in a word processor program is to move strings of ASCII characters from one place in memory to another. The 68000 MOVE and DBcc instructions can be used to do this. Remember from the discussion of the string operations in Chapter 4, however, that in order for the MOVE instruction to work correctly, you first have to load A0 with the address of the source start, A1 with the address of the destination start, and D0 with the number of bytes or words to be moved. We can define a macro to do all this as follows.

```
MACRO  MOVE_ASCII  NUMBER,SOURCE,DESTINATION =
       MOVE.L  #NUMBER,D0    ; Number of characters to be
                             ;   moved in D0
       LEA     SOURCE,A0     ; Point A0 at ASCII source
       LEA     DESTINATION,A1 ; Point DI at ASCII
                             ;   destination
@1     MOVE.B  (A0)+,(A1)+   ; Copy ASCII string to new
       DBGT    D0,@1         ;   location
```

Notice that again we have an equals sign between the MACRO statement and the body of the macro. The words NUMBER, SOURCE, and DESTINATION in this macro are called *dummy variables*. When we call the macro, values from the calling statement will be put in the instructions in place of the dummies. If, for example, we call this macro with the statement

```
MOVE_ASCII $03D,BLOCK_START,BLOCK_DEST,
```

the assembler will expand the macro as follows.

```
       MOVE.L  #$03D,D0      ; Number of characters to be
                             ;   moved in D0
       LEA     BLOCK_START,A0 ; Point A0 at ASCII
                             ;   destination
       LEA     BLOCK_DEST,A1 ; Point DI at ASCII
                             ;   destination
@1     MOVE.B  (A0)+,(A1)+   ; Copy ASCII string to new
       DBGT    D0,@1         ;   location
```

The label @1 is a local label. That means that it has meaning only in the area around where it occurs. This allows us to use the macro many times without having a duplicate label, or doubly defined label (an assembler error). The local label has meaning only between the two closest normal labels, so when we use the macro several times there must be a normal label in the source code between the uses. This will usually be the case without special work on our part.

We do not have space here to show you very much of what you can do with macros. Read through the assembly language programming manual for your system to find more details about working with macros.

Summary of Subroutines versus Macros

SUBROUTINE

Accessed by JSR or BSR call instructions and RTS return instruction during program execution.

Machine code for instructions put in memory only once.

Parameters passed in registers, memory locations, or stack.

MACRO

Accessed during assembly with name given to macro when defined.

Machine code generated for instructions each time called.

Parameters passed as part of statement that calls macro.

CHECKLIST OF IMPORTANT TERMS AND CONCEPTS IN THIS CHAPTER

If there are terms or concepts in this list you do not remember, use the index to find them in the chapter.

Subroutine

Procedure

JSR and BSR instructions

RTS instruction

Nested subroutines

Subroutine call

Jump to subroutine

Branch to subroutine

Return from subroutine

Stack
  Top of stack
  Stack pointer

Push and pop operations

Predecrement and postincrement addressing

Parameter, parameter passing

Stack overflow

Reentrant and recursive subroutines

Interrupt

Interrupt-service routine

Separate assembly modules (files)

Macro

REVIEW QUESTIONS AND PROBLEMS

1. Show the 68000 instruction or group of instructions that will do the following.
   a. Initialize the stack pointer to $43F0.
   b. Call a near subroutine named FIXIT.
   c. Save D0 and A0 at the start of a subroutine and restore them at the end of the subroutine.
   d. Return from a subroutine, restore A0 and D0, and automatically increment the stack pointer as needed.

2. a. Use a stack map to show the effect of each of the following instructions on the stack pointer and on the contents of the stack.

```
        MOVEA.L    843FC, A7
        MOVE.L     D0,-(A7)
        JSR        MULTO
        MOVE.L     (A7)+,D0
MULTO:
        MOVE.L     A0,-(A7)
        MOVE.L     A1,-(A7)
        .
        .
        .
        MOVE.L     (A7)+,A1
        MOVE.L     (A7)+,A0
        RTS
```

   b. What effect would it have on the execution of this program if the MOVE.L (A7)+,A0 instruction in the subroutine was accidentally left out? Describe the steps you would take in tracking down this problem if you did not notice it in the program listing.

3. Show the binary codes for the following instructions.
   a. JSR (A0)
   b. JSR #04(A2,D2)
   c. The instruction that will call a subroutine $98 addresses higher in memory than the JSR instruction.
   d. An instruction that returns execution to a mainline program and increments the stack pointer by 4.

4. a. List three methods of passing parameters to a subroutine. Give the advantage and disadvantage of each method.
   b. Define the term *reentrant* and explain how you must pass parameters to a subroutine so that it is reentrant.

5. a. Write a subroutine that produces a delay of 3.33 ms when run on a 68000 with an 8-MHz clock.
   b. Write a mainline program that uses this subroutine to output a square wave on bit 0 of a port at $C015.

6. Write a subroutine that converts a 4-digit BCD number passed in D0 to its binary equivalent. Use the algorithm in Figure 5-10.

7. The 68000 MULU instruction allows you to multiply a 16-bit number by a 16-bit binary number to give a 32-bit result. In some cases, however, you may need to multiply a 32-bit number by a 32-bit number to give a 64-bit result. With the MULU instruction and a little adding, you can easily do this. Figure 5-20 shows in diagram form how to do it. Each letter in the diagram represents a 16-bit number. The principle is to use MULU to form partial products and add these partial products together as shown. Write an algorithm for this multiplication and then write the 68000 assembly language program for the algorithm.

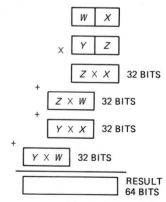

FIGURE 5-20   32-bit by 32-bit multiply method for problem 5-7.

8. Calculating the factorial of a number, which we did with a recursive subroutine in Figure 5-17a, can easily be done with a simple REPEAT-UNTIL structure of the following form:

(a)

IF N = 1 THEN

    FACTORIAL = 1

ELSE

    FACTORIAL = 1

    REPEAT

        FACTORIAL = FACTORIAL × N

        DECREMENT N

    UNTIL N = 0

Write a 68000 subroutine that implements this algorithm for an N between 1 and 8.

9. Write an assembler macro that will restore, in the correct order, the registers saved by the macro PUSH_ALL in this chapter.

10.   *a.* Show how you would tell the assembler to make the label BINADD available to other assembly modules.

    b. Show how you would tell the assembler to look for a byte-type data item named CONVERSION_FACTOR in a different assembly module.

This chapter consists of two major sections. The first section is a dictionary of all of the 68000/68008/68010 instructions. For each instruction we give a detailed description of its operation, the correct syntax for the instruction, the condition codes affected by the instruction, and the allowable addressing modes for each of the instruction's operands. Also, numerical examples are shown for those instructions where appropriate. The binary coding templates for the instructions are shown alphabetically in a table in Appendix B. Putting the codes together in a table makes it easier to find codes if you are hand coding a program.

The second major section of this chapter is a dictionary of commonly used 68000 assembler directives. The directives described here are a common subset of those defined by the Raven® cross assembler, which runs on the IBM PC, and those defined by the Consulair Corporation 68000 assembler, which runs on an Apple Macintosh®. If you are using some other assembler, it probably has similar capabilities, but the names may be different.

You will probably use this chapter mostly as a reference to get the details of an instruction or directive as you write programs of your own or decipher someone else's programs. However, you should skim through the chapter at least once to get an overview of the material contained here. You should not try to absorb all the chapter at once. Most of the instructions described here are used and discussed in various example programs throughout the book.

OBJECTIVES

At the conclusion of this chapter, you should be able to

1. Summarize the addressing modes available on the Motorola 68000 CPU.

2. Describe the instruction set of the 68000.

3. Describe the assembler directives available for a typical symbolic assembler program.

ADDRESSING TERMINOLOGY

The 68000 family provides 14 different addressing modes. Of these, the *implicit modes* (usually referring to the status register, SR, or to the condition code register, CCR) are usually distinguished and described individually when they occur. As shown in Figure 3-8, 12 addressing modes occur normally in many of the following instructions. These will commonly be called *all* the addressing modes (or "any addressing mode is allowed"). In the descriptions that follow, several other terms will be used as shorthand for certain subsets of the addressing modes. In particular, there are four terms that can be combined to refer to subsets of the addressing modes. These terms are *data, memory, alterable,* and *control.* The term data refers to modes that can be used to name data operands. Address register direct, for example, is not a data-addressing mode because it refers to an address register, not a data register. The term memory refers to addressing modes that can address memory. Therefore, data register direct and address register direct are not memory-addressing modes. The term alterable refers to addressing modes that address something that can be altered, or modified. So, for example, immediate data is not alterable, and immediate addressing is not an alterable addressing mode. Finally, the term control is used to refer to addressing modes that do not require a size to be associated with them. For example, address register indirect, as used with the jump to subroutine instruction, does not require a size to be associated with it because it specifies an address to jump to rather than a size of data to move. Thus address register indirect can be a control addressing mode. Address register indirect with postincrement does require a size because the instruction must know whether to increment by 1 (for a byte), by 2 (for a word), or by 4 (for a long). Hence, address register indirect with postincrement is not a control addressing mode.

These four terms are often combined in pairs to yield common subsets of the 12 allowable addressing modes. The usages that occur in the following descriptions are explained in a little more detail as they occur.

Data-alterable addressing modes refer to those modes containing data that can be altered (immediate data, for example, cannot be altered). The data alterable addressing modes include data register direct (Dn), address register indirect ((An)), address register indirect with predecrement (−(An)), address register indirect with postincrement ((An)+), address register indirect with displacement ((d$_{16}$,An)), address register indirect with index ((d$_8$,An,Xn)), absolute word ((xxx).W), and absolute long ((xxx).L). Another way to think of it is that data alterable addressing includes any addressing mode *except* address register direct, immediate, and PC relative modes.

Data-addressing modes include all 12 addressing modes except address register direct. That is, data-addressing modes include 11 of the 12 modes, with address register direct being the one mode not included.

Control addressing modes include any of the 12 modes except data register direct, address register direct, postincrement, predecrement, and immediate addressing modes. Thinking of this in the positive sense, control addressing modes include address register indirect, address register indirect with displacement, address register indirect with index, absolute word, absolute long, program counter relative with displacement, and program counter relative with index. The control modes are those allowed in the jump to subroutine instruction (JSR), for example. In the JSR these modes are used to change the flow of control in the program.

Control alterable addressing modes are similar to the control addressing modes except that the PC relative modes are not included. So the control alterable addressing modes include only address register indirect, address register indirect with displacement, address register indirect with index, absolute word, and absolute long. In some sense the PC relative addressing modes are not alterable, so they are not included.

Memory alterable addressing modes include all the modes except register direct (address or data register), immediate, and PC relative (with displacement or with index). That is, memory alterable addressing modes include all the address register indirect modes (normal, postincrement, predecrement, with displacement, and with index) and the absolute modes (word and long).

Last but not least, the *memory addressing modes* include all the modes that can be used to refer to memory, or every mode except the register direct modes.

INSTRUCTION DESCRIPTIONS

ABCD Instruction—Add Decimal with Extend: ABCD Dy,Dx or ABCD −(Ax),−(Ay)

The ABCD instruction adds the source operand to the destination operand and places the result back in the destination operand. The addition is performed using BCD arithmetic. The extend bit is used during the addition to allow carries into this addition from a lower-digit addition carry and to send a carry from this byte addition to the next-higher digit. The operation is a byte operation only. Both the source operand and the destination operand must be data registers, or they must both be memory locations accessed using the address register indirect with predecrement addressing mode.

Following the operation, the carry bit is set if a decimal carry was generated and is cleared if there was no carry. The extend bit is set equal to the carry bit. The zero bit is cleared if the result is nonzero and is unchanged otherwise. The zero bit is normally cleared via programming before a series of BCD additions (a multiple-precision operation) and tested once following all the additions. This allows convenient testing after decimal additions of BCD values represented as several BCD digits.

EXAMPLES

```
ABCD D0,D1        ; Add the two BCD digits in D0
                  ; to the two BCD digits in
                  ; D1 and place the result
                  ; in D1.
ABCD −(A3),−(A2)  ; Add the BCD digits in
                  ; the memory pointed
                  ; at by A3 to the BCD
                  ; digits pointed at by
                  ; A2. Decrement each
                  ; pointer before
                  ; accessing the BCD
                  ; digits. Store the
                  ; result in the memory
                  ; location pointed at
                  ; by A2.
```

ADD Instruction—Add: ADD Source, Destination

The ADD instruction adds a number from some source to a number from some destination and puts the result in the specified destination. The source may be an immediate number, a register, or a memory location, as specified by any of the 12 addressing modes shown in Figure 3-8. The destination may be a register or a memory location specified by any one of the alterable addressing modes in Figure 3-8. Both the source and the destination can be data registers, but at least one *must* be a data register. Thus, the source and the destination in an instruction cannot both be memory locations. The source and the destination must be of the same type. In other words, they must both be byte locations, they must both be word locations, or they must both be long locations. If you want to add a byte to a word, you must copy the byte to a word location and fill the upper byte of the word with zeros before adding. Flags affected are X, N, Z, V, C.

ADD.B ($4204),D0   ; Add byte from address $4204
                                   ; to contents of D0

ADD.L D0,D3   ; Add the long contents of D0 to
                                   ; the long contents of D3 and
                                   ; store the result in D3.

ADD.W (A4)+,D3   ; Add the word contents of
                                   ; memory pointed to by A4 to
                                   ; the contents of D3 and store
                                   ; the result in D3. A4 is
                                   ; incremented following the
                                   ; operation.

ADD.W D2,−(A2)   ; Add the word contents of D2
                                   ; to the word in memory
                                   ; pointed at by A2, and store
                                   ; the result back into the
                                   ; same memory location. A2 is
                                   ; decremented before the
                                   ; operation.

ADDA Instruction—Add Address: ADDA Source, Destination

The ADDA instruction adds together two address registers or a source address value and a destination address register and places the result in an address register. The source operand can be any register, immediate data, or a memory location using any addressing mode. The destination must be an address register. The operation size must be word or long (byte operations are not allowed). Condition codes are *not affected* by this instruction. Address arithmetic is signed binary arithmetic. If the operation is of size word, then the source operand is sign-extended to a long operand and the addition is performed using all 32 bits of the destination address register.

EXAMPLES

ADDA.W #$1004,A0   ; Add offset $1004
                                  ; to contents of A0

ADDA.L A0,A3   ; Add the long contents of D0
                                  ; to the long contents of D3
                                  ; and store the result in D3.

ADDI Instruction—Add Immediate: ADDI Source, Destination

The ADDI instruction is used to add data values held in the instruction itself to some destination. The data in the instruction is called *immediate data* and may be of byte, word, or long size. The immediate data is placed in memory immediately following the instruction code word. If the immediate data is of size byte, then a byte is skipped to keep the instruction code on word boundaries.

All condition codes are affected. Condition codes are set to reflect the result of the add immediate operation.

Only data-alterable addressing modes are allowed in the destination field.

EXAMPLES

ADDI.B #$74,D0   ; Add immediate byte $74 to
                               ; contents of D0

ADDI.L #$123489AB,(A4)
                               ; Add the long contents of D0
                               ; to the long contents of
                               ; D3 and store the result
                               ; in D3.

ADDQ Instruction—Add Quick: ADDQ Source, Destination

ADDQ is a faster way to add if the source operand is in the range 1 to 8. With such a small operand, the operand value itself can be coded in the single-instruction code word and the add can be performed with only a one-word memory reference. This is the instruction of choice for adding small values. The destination can be accessed using any alterable addressing mode.

All the condition codes are affected by this operation. Each code is set or cleared according to the results of the addition operation.

EXAMPLES

ADDQ.B #$7,D0   ; Add quick $7 to contents of D0

ADDQ.L #1,($4206)   ; Add 1 to the long contents
                                  ; at memory address $4206

ADDX Instruction—Add Extended: ADDX Source, Destination

The ADDX instruction adds a source operand to a destination operand using binary addition and the extend bit. Both operands must be data registers or both must use the predecrement address register indirect addressing mode. All condition codes are affected by the operation and are set according to the addition results. This operation is particularly useful for high-precision (multibyte) arithmetic. Operands must be byte, word, or long.

EXAMPLES

ADDX.B D1,D0
                                  ; Add extended byte D1 to D0

ADDX.W −(A2),−(A1)
                                  ; Add extended the word
                                  ; contents of the memory A2 points at to the
                                  ; value where A1 points. Decrement both
                                  ; address registers (by 2) before the memory
                                  ; reference. Return the result to the
                                  ; original location A1 points to.

AND Instruction—AND Corresponding Bits of Two Operands: AND Source, Destination

The AND instruction ANDs each bit in a source byte, word, or long with the same-number bit in a destination byte, word, or long. The result is put in the specified destination. The contents of the specified source are not changed. The result for each bit position follows the truth table for a two-input AND gate. In other words, a bit in the specified destination is a 1 only if that bit is a 1 in both the source and the destination operands. Therefore, a bit can be masked (reset to 0) by ANDing it with 0.

The source operand can be accessed using any data-addressing mode (i.e., anything but address register direct). The destination can use any alterable addressing mode. However, one of the operands must be a data register. V and C are always cleared; X is not affected. Z is set if the result is 0 and N is set if the most significant bit of the result is set and is cleared otherwise. Operand size is byte, word, or long.

EXAMPLES

```
AND.B D2,D0   ; AND the low byte of D2 with the
              ; low byte of D0 and store the
              ; result in the low byte of D0.
AND.L #$40(A2),D3
              ; AND the long contents of
              ; memory where A2 + 40
              ; points to D3.
```

ANDI Instruction—AND Immediate the Corresponding Bits of Two Operands: AND Source, Destination

The ANDI instruction will AND immediate a value in the word(s) following the instruction code word to a value specified by a data-alterable destination-addressing mode. Condition codes are set as for the AND instruction. That is, V and C are cleared, X is not affected, and Z and N are set according to the value of the result of the AND operation. Operand size is byte, word, or long. If the operand size is byte, then the immediate data is padded with one additional byte to keep the instruction on even word boundaries.

It is also possible to ANDI to the CCR in order to set or clear one or several condition codes.

EXAMPLES

```
ANDI.B #$0F,D0   ; AND low byte of D0 with $0F.
                 ; This will "mask off" the
                 ; high nibble.
ANDI.W #$FF00,D2
                 ; AND $FF00 with the low word of
                 ; D2. This will mask the low
                 ; byte of D2 to all 0s.
```

```
ANDI.B #$01,CCR  ; AND immediate the value $01 to
                 ; the CCR. This will clear
                 ; all the condition codes
                 ; except the carry bit, which
                 ; will be left as it was.
```

ASL and ASR Instructions—Arithmetic Shift Left (Right): ASL Source, Destination; ASR Source, Destination

The ASL and ASR instructions shift the destination operand left (right). The shift is arithmetic, meaning that for left shifts 0s are moved into the low end of the destination. For right shifts the sign bit is copied and shifted into the upper bits. The carry and extend bits are filled with the last bit shifted out of the left (right) of the destination. The shift count is specified as an immediate value in the instruction for counts in the range 1 to 8. For larger counts the shift count must be loaded into a data register, which is then specified as the source operand. If the destination is a memory location, then the shift count is presumed to be 1 and only one operand is used (the destination operand). Operand size can be byte, word, or long. Only memory-alterable addressing modes may be used, with a word size required and a 1-bit shift count implied (no other count allowed).

The condition codes N and V are set according to the result of the shift. V is set if the most significant bit is changed anytime during the shift operation. X is set equal to the last bit shifted out of the operand. If the shift count is 0, then X is not affected. C is set equal to the last bit shifted out of the operand. If the shift count is 0, then C is cleared.

EXAMPLES

```
ASL.B D1,D2   ; Arithmetic shift D2 left by
              ; the count in D1 (module 64).
ASR.W #3,D7   ; Shift D7 right 3 bit positions.
ASL.W (A4)    ; Shift the memory location pointed
              ; at by A4 1 bit left. Memory
              ; shifts must be word and use a
              ; 1-bit count.
ASL.L #2,D0   ; Arithmetic shift left D0 by 2
              ; bit positions. This has the
              ; same effect as multiplying by 4.
```

Bcc Instruction—Branch Conditional: Bcc Destination

The Bcc instruction means branch conditionally to destination. This is actually a short form for 14 different instructions. The instructions are explained in more detail in Figure 4-10. The instructions are shown here by example:

```
BCC there   ; branch to "there" if carry clear (0)
BCS there   ; branch to "there" if carry set (1)
```

```
BEQ there    ; branch to "there" if equal to 0
BGE there    ; branch to "there" if greater or equal to 0
BGT there    ; branch to "there" if greater than 0
BHI there    ; branch to "there" if higher than 0
BLE there    ; branch to "there" if less than or equal
               to 0
BLS there    ; branch to "there" if lower than or the
               same as 0
BLT there    ; branch to "there" if less than 0
BMI there    ; branch to "there" if minus
BNE there    ; branch to "there" if not equal to 0
BPL there    ; branch to "there" if plus
BVC there    ; branch to "there" if oVerflow clear (0)
BVS there    ; branch to "there" if oVerflow set (1)
```

Rather than including all 14 instructions in the manuals, Motorola literature normally lumps these 14 instructions together with one opcode and form. The instructions differ only in which condition code they check. Figure 4-10 shows the actual bit-combination equation used to compute the condition given the five main condition codes.

You may wonder why oVerflow, with a capital V? V is the overflow bit in the condition-code portion of the status register, just as with Carry (the C bit) and Zero (the Z condition-code bit).

Higher than and lower than refer to signed values, whereas greater than and less than refer to unsigned values. For example, using 8-bit values, $F8 is lower than $04, but $F8 is greater than $04. That is, when viewed as signed decimal values, −8 is less than 4, but when viewed as unsigned decimal values, 248 is greater than 4. Plus refers to just the N condition code, or "plus is not negative." The instruction may use an 8-bit displacement, giving a range of +128 to −127 bytes, size byte, or it may use a 16-bit displacement, giving a range of +32,768 to −32,767 bytes, size word. The Raven cross assembler uses absolute long and absolute short to control this size.

The condition codes are not affected.

EXAMPLE

```
BEQ there    ; Branch if Z condition code set
             ; (= 1) to "there"—that is, if the
             ; last operation produced a zero.
```

BCHG Instruction—Bit Test and Change: BCHG Source, Destination

The BCHG instruction tests a bit in the destination operand and changes the bit in one indivisible operation. The value of the old bit is saved in the Z condition code, and the bit is inverted. If the bit is a 1, it is set to 0, and if it is a 0, it is set to 1. The source specifies the bit number to test and must be either an immediate bit count or a data register. The bit numbering is modulo 32, so that bit 32 = bit 64 = bit 96 and so on. The destination may be specified using any data-alterable addressing mode. The Z bit is set if the bit tested is 1 and is cleared otherwise. The other condition codes are not affected.

EXAMPLES

```
BCHG D2,(A1)   ; Test and change the bit
               ; in memory pointed at by A1
               ; using the bit number in D2.
BCHG #17,D0    ; Test and change bit 17 of D0.
```

BCLR Instruction—Bit Test and Clear: BCLR Source, Destination

The BCLR instruction tests a bit in the destination operand and clears the bit in one indivisible operation. The value of the old bit is saved in the Z condition code, and the bit is cleared (set to 0). The source specifies the bit number to test and must be either an immediate bit count or a data register. The bit numbering is modulo 32, so that bit 32 = bit 64 = bit 96 and so on. The destination may be specified using any data-alterable addressing mode. The Z bit is set if the bit tested is 1 and is cleared otherwise. The other condition codes are not affected.

EXAMPLES

```
BCLR D3,(A1)   ; Test and clear the bit
               ; in memory pointed at by A1
               ; using the bit number in D3.
BCHG #11,D0    ; Test and clear bit 11 of D0.
```

BRA Instruction—Branch Always: BRA Destination

The BRA instruction means branch to the destination always. This is the 68000 unconditional branch operation. The destination is specified as a label in assembly language. In the machine code bits the destination is specified using an 8-bit or a 16-bit address displacement, which is added to the program counter. The instruction uses one code word if the destination can be reached using an 8-bit displacement (+128 to −127 bytes). The instruction uses two code words if it includes a 16-bit displacement. An assembler will normally determine which displacement size to use. The condition codes are not affected.

This instruction can be thought of as a branch conditional instruction where the condition is always true.

EXAMPLE

```
BRA there    ; Branch to there always
```

BSET Instruction—Bit Test and Set: BSET Source, Destination

The BSET instruction tests a bit in the destination operand and sets the bit (= 1) in one indivisible operation. The value of the old bit is saved in the Z condition code, and the bit is set (set = 1). The source specifies the bit number to test and must be either an immediate bit count or a data register. The bit numbering is modulo 32, so that bit 32 = bit 64 = bit 96 and so on. The destination may be specified using any data-alterable addressing mode. The Z bit is set if the bit tested was 1 and cleared otherwise. The other condition codes are not affected.

EXAMPLES

```
BSET D2,(A3)  ; Test and set the bit
              ; in memory pointed at by A3
              ; using the bit number in D2.
BSET #1,D0    ; Test and set bit 1 of D0.
```

BSR Instruction—Branch to Subroutine: BSR Destination

The BSR instruction branches to the subroutine indicated in the destination. The destination address is specified as an 8-bit or a 16-bit displacement, which is added to the program counter. A 32-bit return address is saved on the system stack (A7) for use by a subsequent RTS instruction. The condition codes are not affected.

This is a short form of the subroutine call that uses 1 or 2 words. The JSR instruction uses 3 words. A BSR uses 1 word if the displacement is an 8-bit value and 2 words if the displacement is a 16-bit value. Normally the assembler will determine automatically which size displacement to use.

EXAMPLE

```
BSR print_it  ; Branch to subroutine called
              ; "print_it".
```

BTST Instruction—Bit Test: BTST Source, Destination

The BTST instruction tests a bit in the destination operand but does not change the bit. The value of the bit is saved in the Z condition code, and the bit is not affected. The source specifies the bit number to test and must be either an immediate bit count or a data register. The bit numbering is modulo 32, so that bit 32 = bit 64 = bit 96 and so on. The destination may be specified using any data-alterable addressing mode. The Z bit is set if the bit tested was 1 and cleared otherwise. The other condition codes are not affected.

EXAMPLES

```
BCHG D2,(A1)  ; Test the bit in
              ; memory pointed at by A1
              ; using the bit number in D2.
BCHG #7,D3    ; Test bit 7 of D3.
```

CHK Instruction—Check Against Bounds: CHK Source, Destination

The CHK instruction performs an operation similar to the compare instruction, except that the instruction will generate a CPU exception (a *trap*) if the comparison fails. The trap will cause the CPU to transfer control to an exception-handling routine at an address specified by address 24 ($00000018). That is, the CPU will get an address from memory at address $00000018 and load that address into the program counter.

The general use of this instruction is in array manipulation, where the programmer is concerned with overflow or underflow. Rather than do a comparison (with a CMP instruction), the CHK instruction will actually cause a conditional jump to exception handler. Hence the programmer does not have to perform a conditional branch, as is required after a compare instruction. The exception handler can take some action to correct the situation, such as making the array bigger by allocating more memory and then adjusting the bounds register and returning to the mainline program. Alternatively, the exception handler could abort the mainline program and request assistance from the user.

The CHK instruction compares a source operand word (normally considered the *bounds* register) against a data register. The source value can be addressed in any data-alterable addressing mode and may come from a register or from memory. The operation size is always word. The destination must be a data register, whose value is not changed. If the bounds value (source operand) is greater than the destination data register or if the data register value is less than 0, a CHK-type CPU exception is generated, and control is transferred to the CHK exception-handling routine. The data register would normally have a working index value used to index into the array. The data register is presumed to contain a 2's complement integer. The instruction is tailored to checking array bounds, since a double comparison is made to the upper bound (source operand) and to the lower bound (0).

The Z, V, and C condition codes are left with undefined values after the operation. X is not affected. N is set if the data register was less than 0, is cleared if the data register is greater than the source value (upper bound), and is undefined otherwise. In other words, the exception-handling routine can use the N bit to determine which comparison failed, but the mainline cannot rely on the N bit being set in any particular manner.

EXAMPLES

```
CHK #4(A4),D0     ; Check D0 (the index register)
                  ; against the array boundary
                  ; pointed at by A4 offset by 4.
                  ; If the test fails, then trap
                  ; and let handler fix things.
MOVE.B #0(A2,D0),D2
                  ; Get the value from array
                  ; element whose index is
                  ; in D0 and base address
                  ; is in register A2.
```

CLR Instruction—Clear: CLR Destination

The CLR instruction clears the destination operand to all 0 bits. The operation size can be byte, word, or long. The destination operand can be specified by any data-alterable addressing mode (that is, any mode except immediate, PC relative, and address register direct). The Z condition code bit is always set to 1. The N, V, and C condition code bits are always cleared to 0. The X bit is not affected.

EXAMPLES

```
ADD.B #$74,D0   ; Add immediate byte $74 to
                ; contents of D0.
ADD.L D0,D3     ; Add the long contents of D0 to
                ; the long contents of D3 and
                ; store the result in D3.
```

CMP Instruction—Compare: CMP Source, Destination

This instruction compares a byte from the specified source with a byte from the specified destination, a word from a specified source with a word from a specified destination, or a long word from a specified source to a long word in a specified destination. The source can be an immediate number, a register, or a memory location specified by one of the 12 addressing modes shown in Figure 3-8. The destination must be a data register. The comparison is actually done by subtracting the source byte, word, or long word from the destination using temporary internal CPU registers. The destination data register is not changed. The X condition code is not affected. The N, Z, V, and C bits are affected according to the results of the comparison operation. That is, C is set if a borrow is generated by the subtraction and cleared otherwise. N is set for a negative result and cleared otherwise, Z is set if the result is zero (that is, the two operands were equal) and cleared otherwise, and V is set if an overflow is generated and cleared otherwise.

EXAMPLES

```
CMP.B D3,D0      ; Compare the low byte of D0 to
                 ; the low byte of D3.
CMP.L ($4200),D2 ; Compare the long contents of
                 ; the memory at address
                 ; $4200 to the long value in
                 ; D2.
```

CMPA Instruction—Compare Address: CMPA Source, Destination

The CMPA form of compare is used when the destination is an address register. Normally, the assembler will automatically convert a CMP to a CMPA if necessary. The operand size must be word or long. See the CMP instruction.

EXAMPLES

```
CMPA.L A3,A0      ; Compare A3 to A0.
CMPA.W ($4200),A2 ; Compare the word value
                  ; at memory address $4200
                  ; to the word address in
                  ; A2.
```

CMPI Instruction—Compare Immediate: CMPI Source, Destination

The CMPI form of compare is used when the source is immediate data. Normally, the assembler will automatically convert a CMP to a CMPI if necessary. The destination may be specified using any data-alterable addressing mode. See the CMP instruction.

EXAMPLES

```
CMPI.B #$74,D0
    ; Compare D0 to the constant $74.
CMPI.L #$12345678,(A2)+
    ; Compare the
    ; immediate long value $12345678 to the long
    ; value pointed at by A2 and increment A2 (by 4)
    ; after the comparison.
```

CMPM Instruction—Compare Memory: CMPM Source, Destination

The CMPM form of compare is used for memory-to-memory comparisons. Normally, the assembler will automatically convert a CMP to a CMPM if necessary. Both operands must be specified using the address register indirect with postincrement addressing mode. See the CMP instruction.

EXAMPLE

```
CMPM.L (A1)+,(A2)+   ; Compare the long value
                     ; pointed at by A1 to the
                     ; long value pointed at
                     ; by A2. Increment both
                     ; registers (by 4) after
                     ; the comparison.
```

DBcc Instruction—Decrement and Branch Conditionally: DBcc Source, Destination

The DBcc instruction is one of the basic looping *primitives* of the 68000 family. It is normally used to implement the REPEAT-UNTIL control structure. For example, a count is decremented until it reaches 0 using DBGT, decrement and branch if greater than. For each count a series of instructions performs some operation, such as adding an inflation factor to a data value in an array.

The lowercase c's in DBcc are normally replaced by one of 14 different condition tests. For example, replacing cc with GT yields the DBGT instruction. Thus DBcc really represents 14 types of branches. See the description for the Bcc instruction.

The condition codes are not affected.

```
DBGE D0,there
        ; Decrement D0 and branch to "there"
        ; if the result is greater than or
        ; equal to 0.
DBEQ D1,loop1
        ; Decrement D1 and branch to "loop1"
        ; if the result is equal to 0.
```

DIVS Instruction—Divide Signed: DIVS Source, Destination

The DIVS instruction divides the destination operand by the source operand and places the quotient in the lower word of the destination. It places the remainder in the high word of the destination operand. The division is performed using 2's complement signed binary arithmetic. The operation presumes a 32-bit dividend (destination operand) and a 16-bit divisor (source operand). The result is a 16-bit quotient and a 16-bit remainder. The destination must be a data register. The source can be specified in any data-alterable addressing mode. The condition codes are set according to the result of the division. The X bit is not affected.

If the source operand (divisor) is 0, then a CPU trap is generated, and control is transferred to the zero divide exception service routine, whose address is stored at address $014. If overflow is detected and set before the completion of the instruction, the operands are not modified.

EXAMPLE

```
DIVS #−311,D0   ; Divide D0 by the constant
                ; −311.
```

DIVU Instruction—Divide Unsigned: DIVU Source, Destination

DIVU performs a division using unsigned binary division. Otherwise, the instruction operates as described in the previous DIVS discussion.

EXAMPLE

```
DIVS #311,D0   ; Divide D0 by the constant
               ; 311.
```

EOR Instruction—Exclusive OR Logical: EOR Source, Destination

Each bit of the source operand is combined with the corresponding bit of the destination operand using the exclusive-OR operation, and the result is placed back into the corresponding bit of the destination. The resulting bit is a 1 only when exactly one of the two initial bits is 1 (that is, 1 and 0 or 0 and 1). If both bits are initially 0 or both are initially 1, then the resulting bit is a 0. The source must be a data register and the destination must use a data-alterable addressing mode. The operands can be of size byte, word, or long. The V and C condition codes are both cleared. The X condition code is not affected. Z is set if the result has all bits equal 0 and cleared otherwise. The N condition code is set equal to the MSB of the result.

EXAMPLE

```
EOR.W D0,D3   ; Exclusive-OR the low word of
              ; register D0 with D3 and
              ; put the result back in D0.
```

EORI Instruction—Exclusive-OR Immediate: EORI Source, Destination

Each bit of the source operand is combined with the corresponding bit of the destination operand using the exclusive-OR operation and the result is placed back into the corresponding bit of the destination. The resulting bit is a 1 only when exactly one of the two initial bits is 1 (that is, 1 and 0 or 0 and 1). If both bits are initially 0 or both are initially 1, then the resulting bit is a 0. The source must be immediate data and the destination must use a data-alterable addressing mode. The immediate data follows the instruction opcode word in memory. If the operand size is byte or word, then 1 additional word of immediate data is required. If the operand size is long, then 2 additional words are required. If the operand size is byte, then the lower byte of the immediate data word contains the byte of immediate data. The operands can be of size byte, word, or long. The V and C condition codes are both cleared. The X condition code is not affected. Z is set if the result has all bits equal 0 and cleared otherwise. The N condition code is set equal to the MSB of the result.

This instruction can also be used to exclusive-OR a byte of immediate data with the condition-code register (EORI to CCR), thereby affecting the condition codes, or with the status register to set the CPU status. The EORI to SR instruction is a privileged instruction. It can be executed only while in the supervisor state of the CPU (that is, when the supervisor bit of the status register is equal to 1). If the CPU is in user state when the EORI to SR is attempted, a CPU trap will occur. EORI to SR is always of size word, and EORI to CCR is always of size byte.

EXAMPLES

```
EORI.W #FFFF,SR   ; Change all the bits of the
                  ; status register. That is,
                  ; if a bit is a 0,
                  ; set it to 1; if it is a 1, set it to 0.
```

```
EORI.B #01,SR   ; Change the carry condition
                ; code bit. If it is a 1, set it to 0; if
                ; it is a 0, set it to 1.
```

EXG Instruction—Exchange Register Contents: EXG Source, Destination

The EXG instruction exchanges the contents of any two registers. The exchange can be between two data registers, two address registers, or one address and one data register. The operand size is always long (32 bits). The condition codes are not affected.

EXAMPLES

```
EXG D0,D3   ; Exchange D0 and D3.
EXG A0,A3   ; Exchange A0 and A3.
EXG A0,D3   ; Exchange A0 and D3.
```

EXT Instruction—Sign-Extend a Data Register: EXT Destination

The EXT instruction sign-extends a data register from a byte to a word (size word) or from a word to a long (size long). The sign bit of the operand is copied into the upper bits of the word (or long). The V and C condition codes are always cleared. The X condition code is not affected. The N and Z condition codes are set according to the value of the sign-extended result.

EXAMPLES

```
EXT.W D4   ; Sign extend D4 from a byte
           ; to a word.
EXT.L D3   ; Sign extend D3 from a word
           ; to a long.
```

Illegal Instruction—Cause an Illegal Instruction Trap: ILLEGAL

The ILLEGAL instruction causes an illegal instruction trap. The current program counter value (which will be pointing at the instruction following the ILLEGAL instruction) is pushed on the supervisor system stack. The status register is pushed on the supervisor stack, and the program counter is loaded with the illegal instruction vector. The illegal instruction vector is found at memory address $010. This type of trap will occur if any illegal instruction pattern is encountered. The ILLEGAL instruction is normally used to test the trap-handling routine. Bit patterns other than the ILLEGAL instruction pattern ($8AFC) are normally reserved for future instructions in future 680x0 CPUs.

The condition codes are not affected.

EXAMPLE

```
ILLEGAL   ; Cause an illegal instruction trap.
```

JMP Instruction—Jump Unconditionally to the Destination Address: JMP Destination

The JMP instruction performs the standard unconditional jump operation. The destination can be specified using any control addressing mode (that is, not address or data register direct, postincrement or predecrement, or immediate addressing). The 32-bit address found at the specified effective address is loaded into the program counter. The condition codes are not affected.

Since the JMP instruction uses a 32-bit transfer address, any of the 68000's memory can be reached and jumped to by the JMP instruction.

EXAMPLES

```
JMP there   ; Jump to the address
            ; represented by the label
            ; "there."
JMP (A3)    ; Jump to the location pointed
            ; at by register A3.
```

JSR Instruction—Jump to Subroutine: JSR Destination

The JSR instruction jumps to a subroutine. It also saves the program counter on the A7 stack and loads the program counter with the destination value. The destination can be specified using any control addressing mode ((An), d(An,Xi), Abs.W, ABS.L, d(PC), or d(PC,Xi)). The condition codes are not affected.

This instruction uses a 32-bit destination address so it can jump to anywhere in memory. BSR can be used when an 8- or 16-bit displacement is acceptable.

EXAMPLES

```
JSR ADD_CORRECTION
            ; Call the subroutine
            ; ADD_CORRECTION. Save
            ; a 32-bit return address
            ; on the system stack.
JSR #$1200(PC)
            ; Call the subroutine that
            ; is $1200 bytes beyond the
            ; current program counter—
            ; i.e., add $1200 to the PC.
```

LEA Instruction—Load Effective Address: LEA Source, Destination

The LEA instruction computes an effective address and loads that address into a CPU address register. The operand size is always long (32 bits). The condition codes are not affected.

In most instructions the effective address would automatically be used to access one of the operands from memory. The LEA instruction provides access to the effective address itself rather than the operand at which it points.

EXAMPLES

LEA PRICES,A2
   ; Load A2 with the address
   ; PRICES.
LEA #$20(A2,D0),A1
   ; Load the address that is
   ; the value of A2 plus the
   ; value of D0 plus the
   ; constant $20 into A1.
   ; A2 would normally be the address of the base of
   ; a data structure (an array of records). D2
   ; would contain the offset of the current record
   ; in the array, and $20 is the offset to the value
   ; of interest in the current record of the array.

LINK Instruction—Link and Allocate Stack Space: LINK Source, Destination

The link this instruction creates is a *link* on the stack. The link separates the stack space reserved for one subroutine from that reserved for another subroutine. The link connects (links) the two subroutines and contains the base address of the calling subroutine's reserved memory on the system stack. The base address is normally stored by a program in an address register specified by the source operand. The value of the address register is pushed onto the system stack (the link itself); then the system stack pointer (A7) is decremented. The new system stack pointer value is loaded into the address register. This is the base address of the called subroutine's reserved memory. This link is part of the subroutine connection made by a typical high-level language compiler.

By *allocate* we mean reserve some space on the stack. This is performed by adding a value (the displacement contained in the destination operand). The system stack then has the displacement added to it. In normal usage this displacement is negative and is the negative of the number of bytes of memory to reserve on the stack for the called subroutine. The destination operand is 16 bits long (sign extended and added to the stack pointer), so the subroutine can reserve up to 32,766 bytes of memory (using a displacement of −32,766). The displacement should normally be even so that the stack is always *word aligned*. Word aligned means that the stack is on a word boundary rather than pointing at the middle of a word.

The LINK instruction pushes the current address register value onto the stack (incrementing the stack in the process). It then places the stack value into the address register and adds the displacement to the stack pointer.

In more abstract terms, the address of the calling subroutine's reserved memory is saved on the system stack. Then the address of the called subroutine's reserved memory area is loaded as the new subroutine's reserved memory area base address, and the called subroutine's memory is reserved on the stack.

The source operand must be an address register. The destination operand must be a 16-bit signed integer

constant. The condition codes are not affected. The link instruction is normally used in conjunction with the UNLK instruction.

EXAMPLE

LINK A3,$100 ; Link using A3 as the base
                ; register and allocate $100
                ; bytes of memory on the system
                ; stack.

LSL and LSR Instructions—Logical Shift Left (Right): LSL Source, Destination; LSR Source, Destination

The LSL and LSR instructions shift the destination operand left (right). The shift is logical, meaning that for left shifts 0s are moved into the low end of the destination and for right shifts 0s are shifted into the upper bits. The carry and extend bits are filled with (set equal to) the last bit shifted out of the left (right) of the destination. The shift count is specified as an immediate value in the instruction for counts in the range 1 to 8. For larger counts the shift count must be loaded into a data register, and that data register must be used as the source operand. If the destination is a memory location, then the shift count is presumed to be 1, and there is only one operand (the destination). Operand size can be byte, word, or long. Only memory-alterable addressing modes may be used, with a word size required and a 1-bit shift count implied (no other count allowed).

The condition codes N and V are set according to the result of the shift. V is set if the MSB is changed anytime during the shift operation. X is set equal to the last bit shifted out of the operand. If the shift count is 0, then X is not affected. C is set equal to the last bit shifted out of the operand. If the shift count is 0, then C is cleared.

EXAMPLES

LSL.B D1,D2 ; Logical shift D2 left by
            ; the count in D1 (module 64).
LSR.W #3,D7 ; Shift D7 right 3 bit positions.
LSL.W (A4)   ; Shift the memory location pointed
           ; at by A4 one bit left. Memory
           ; shifts *must* be word and use a
           ; 1-bit count.
LSL.L #2,D0 ; Logical shift D0 left by 2
           ; bit positions. This has the
           ; same effect as multiplying by 4.

MOVE Instruction—Move Data: MOVE Source, Destination

The MOVE instruction is the real workhorse instruction of the 68000. It is generally used to move data. The instruction can move data to and from the CPU registers, to and from RAM, from ROM, to and from memory-mapped I/O ports, and, in general, anywhere within the main system where data might be useful.

The MOVE instructions transfer a word or byte of data from some source to a destination. The destination can be a register or a memory location. The source can be a register, a memory location, or an immediate number. The source can use any of the twelve 68000 addressing modes shown in Figure 3-8. The destination can use any data-alterable addressing mode. The source and destination in an instruction cannot both be memory locations. The source and destination in a MOVE instruction must both be of type byte, they must both be of type word, or they must both be of type long.

The V and C condition codes are always cleared. X is not affected. N and Z are set according to the value actually moved.

This instruction can also be used to move a word of immediate data to from the condition-code register (MOVE to CCR), thereby affecting the condition codes, or to move a word of immediate data to the status register to set the CPU status. The upper byte of data is ignored during a MOVE to CCR instruction. The MOVE to SR instruction is a privileged instruction. It can be executed only while in the supervisor state of the CPU (that is, when the supervisor bit of the status register is equal to 1). If the CPU is in user state when the MOVE to SR is attempted, a CPU trap will occur. MOVE to SR is always of size word, and MOVE to CCR is always of size word.

MOVE can also be used to move the contents of the CCR or SR from the CPU status register to an effective address. Only data-alterable addressing modes are allowed. MOVE from SR is a privileged instruction that can be executed only in supervisor state (without generating a CPU trap).

When in supervisor state, the move instruction can be used to move an address to the user stack pointer (USP) from an address register or to an address register from the USP. This is a privileged instruction.

EXAMPLES

MOVE.W D0,D1	; Move a word from D0 ; to D1.
MOVE.B (A3),D3	; Move a byte from ; where A3 points to ; D2.
MOVE.L #$100(A2,D3),D2	; Move from the base ; address in A2 using ; the index in D3 and ; an offset of $100.
MOVE.L D0,$20(A2)	; Move a long from D0. ; to memory where A2 ; points offset by 20.
MOVE.W #$00FF,CCR	; Move $00FF to the ; CCR. The upper byte ; is ignored.
MOVE.W SR,D0	; Move the SR to D0.
MOVE.L A2,USP	; Move A2 to the user ; stack pointer.

MOVEA Instruction—Move Effective Address: MOVEA Source, Destination

MOVEA is the form of MOVE used when the destination is an address register. The operand size is always long. Also see the MOVE instruction description.

EXAMPLES

MOVEA.L #$100(PC),A2	; Move the address in the ; program counter plus ; $100 into A2.

MOVEM Instruction—Move Multiple Registers: MOVEM Register List, Destination; MOVEM Source, Register List

The MOVEM instruction moves the listed registers to or from memory. This instruction is very useful when you want to save the contents of several registers so that they can be used and then restored to their previous values. This operation is typically used when a subroutine is called and when a subroutine returns. MOVEM accepts a register list as the source operand and an effective address (control-alterable or predecrement modes) as the destination operand, or MOVEM accepts an effective address as the source operand (only control-alterable modes and postincrement modes) and a register list as the destination operand. The register list is encoded in the instruction as a bit map, which is located in the word immediately following the instruction code word.

MOVEM can also be used to provide the fastest 68000 memory-to-memory move by MOVEMing from memory to the CPU registers and then MOVEMing from the CPU registers to memory. Because many registers can be used in one MOVEM pair, the CPU has to fetch only 2 instructions (4 instruction words) in order to move up to 64 bytes (16 long words). Normally at least 16 MOVE.L instructions would be required, which would imply fetching and interpreting at least 16 code words. Using MOVEM, only 4 instruction code words need be fetched and interpreted to move 16 long words.

MOVEM operand size can be word or long. The condition codes are not affected.

EXAMPLES

MOVEM.L D0−D3,−(A7)	; Save D0, D1, and D2 on ; the system stack.
MOVEM.L D0−D7/A0−A7,−(A7)	; Save all the CPU ; registers on the system stack using a push ; (that is, predecrement the stack pointer before ; each register value is saved).
MOVEM.L (A7)+,D0−D7/A0−A7	; Restore all the

```
                                    ; CPU registers by popping them off the system
                                    ; stack.
                    MOVEM.W D0–D2,(#$4210)
                                    ; Save the low words of
                                    ; registers D0, D1, and D2 in memory at address
                                    ; $4210.
```

MOVEP Instruction—Move Peripheral Data: MOVEP Source, Destination

Move peripheral data performs a special kind of move, in which alternate bytes in memory are moved rather than consecutive bytes. That is, every other byte is moved from a data register to a series of memory-mapped I/O ports (or to memory) or to a data register from every other memory byte. The operation can be either word or long. Bytes are transferred starting with the MSB of the data register for long operands and starting with the high-order byte of the low word of the data register if the operand size is word.

The general idea is that many peripherals use 8-bit-wide I/O ports but use several of these ports. It is often easiest to implement these byte-wide ports using all even bytes of the 68000 word-wide data bus. In this case the I/O ports appear at even addresses, which alternate bytes in 68000 memory (only the even byte addresses (or odd) are used). Using MOVEP, 2 or 4 bytes can be moved to such an I/O device using a single instruction. This can save time and instruction memory space.

The condition codes are not affected. Only the address register indirect with displacement addressing mode is allowed. Either the source or the destination must be a data register.

EXAMPLE

```
MOVEP.L D0, #$10(A3)
            ; Move bytes of data from D0
            ; to where A3 points plus $10.
            ; First byte goes to A3+$10,
            ; second to A3+$12, etc.
```

MOVEQ Instruction—Move Quick: MOVE Source, Destination

Move quick is a faster way to move if the source operand is an 8-bit immediate value. With such a small operand, the operand value itself can be coded in a single instruction code word and the move can be performed with only 1 instruction word memory reference. This is the instruction of choice for moving small constant values. The destination must be a data register. The operand is sign extended to 32 bits. The operand size is always long, even though the immediate data is only 1 byte in size.

The V and C condition codes are always cleared. The X condition is not affected. N is set if the data is negative and cleared otherwise. Z is set if the data is 0 and cleared otherwise.

EXAMPLE

```
MOVEQ #$7,D0   ; Move quick $7 to D0.
```

MULS Instruction—Multiply Unsigned Bytes, Words, or Longs: MULS Source, Data Register

The MULS instruction multiplies the destination operand by the source operand and places the result in the destination. The division is performed using 2's complement signed binary arithmetic. The operation presumes two 16-bit operands. The result is a 32-bit product. The destination must be a data register. The source can be specified in any data-alterable addressing mode. The N and Z condition codes are set according to the result of the division. The X bit is not affected. V and C are always cleared.

EXAMPLES

```
MULS #–311,D0   ; Multiply D0 by the constant
                ; –311.
MULS D2,D1      ; Multiply the low word of D2
                ; by the low word of D1 and
                ; place the long result in D1.
```

MULU Instruction—Multiply Unsigned Bytes, Words, or Longs: MULU Source, Data Register

MULU performs a multiply using unsigned binary division. Otherwise the instruction operates as described in the preceding MULS discussion.

EXAMPLES

```
MULU #311,D0    ; Divide D0 by the constant
                ; 311.
MULU D2,D1      ; Multiply the low word of D2
                ; by the low word of D1 and
                ; place the long result in D1.
                ; Use unsigned arithmetic.
```

NBCD Instruction—Negate Decimal with Extend: NBCD Destination

The NBCD instruction negates the BCD (binary-coded decimal) byte in a data register. The negation is accomplished by subtracting the data register value from 0. The extend bit is subtracted from the result. If the extend bit is set (to 1), this operates as though there had been a borrow from a previous byte negation. The destination must use one of the data-alterable addressing modes. Operand size is always byte, and type is always BCD (decimal).

The N and V condition code bits are undefined following the operation. The C bit is set if a decimal borrow is generated and cleared otherwise. The X bit is set the same as the carry bit (C). The Z bit is cleared if the result is nonzero and is unchanged otherwise.

Normally the Z bit would be cleared before a multibyte BCD (decimal) negate and checked when all the bytes have been negated.

EXAMPLES

NBCD D0   ; Negate the low byte of D0
                  ; assuming D0 has a BCD value in
                  ; it.
NBCD #$100(A3)   ; Negate the byte pointed at by
                  ; address register A3 and a
                  ; displacement of $100.

NEG Instruction—Negate: NEG Destination

The NEG instruction negates a binary 2's complement signed value. The negation is performed by subtracting the destination operand from 0. The result is stored in the destination. The destination can be specified using any data-alterable addressing mode. The operand size can be byte, word, or long.

The condition codes are set according to the result of the subtraction.

EXAMPLES

NEG.B D2   ; Negate the low byte of D2.
NEG.L (A3)+   ; Negate the long word to which A3
              ; points
              ; and increment A3 (by 4)
              ; following the negation.

NEGX Instruction—Negate with Extend: NEGX Destination

The NEGX instruction operates as does the NEG instruction, except that the extend bit is subtracted from the negated result. The extend bit is normally set if there is a borrow from a previous NEGX instruction. This is particularly useful when performing multiple-precision arithmetic (using several bytes, words, or longs).

The V condition-code bit is set if an overflow is generated and cleared otherwise. The N code is set if the result is negative and cleared otherwise. The C bit is set if a binary borrow is generated and cleared otherwise. The X bit is set the same as the carry bit (C). The Z bit is cleared if the result is nonzero and is unchanged otherwise. Normally the Z bit would be cleared before a multibyte (word or long) binary negate and checked when all the bytes have been negated.

EXAMPLE

NEGX.B (A2)+   ; Negate the byte pointed at by
               ; A2 and then increment A2.
               ; Use the extend bit during
               ; negation (i.e., subtract it
               ; afterward).

NOP Instruction—Perform No Operation: NOP

The NOP instruction simply uses up four clock periods and increments the program counter to point to the next instruction. NOP affects no flags. The NOP instruction can be used to increase the delay of a delay loop, as shown in Figure 4-20. It can also be used to hold a place in a program for instructions that will be added later.

EXAMPLE

NOP   ; Do nothing for four cycles
NOP   ; and another four
NOP

NOT Instruction—Invert Each Bit of Operand: NOT Destination

The NOT instruction inverts each bit (forms the 1's complement of) the byte, word, or long at the specified destination. The destination can be a byte, word, or long operand. The destination must be specified using a data-alterable addressing mode.

The V and C condition codes are always cleared. X is not affected. N and Z are set according to the result of the operation.

EXAMPLES

NOT.W D0   ; Complement contents of the low
            ; word of register D0.
NOT.L (A3) ; Complement the long contents of
            ; memory where A3 points.

OR Instruction—Logically OR Corresponding Bits of Two Operands: OR Source, Destination

The OR instruction ORs each bit in a source byte, word, or long with the same-number bit in a destination byte, word, or long. The result is put in the specified destination. The contents of the specified source will not be changed. The result for each bit position will follow the truth table for a two-input OR gate. In other words, a bit in the specified destination will be a 1 if that bit is a 1 in either the source or the destination operand or both. The bit in a specified destination will be a 0 only when corresponding bits in both the source and destination are 0s. Therefore, a bit can be set to 1 by ORing it with 1.

The source operand can be accessed using any data-addressing mode (i.e., anything but address register direct). The destination can use any alterable addressing mode. However, one of the operands must be a data register. V and C are always cleared. X is not affected. Z is set if the result is 0, and N is set if the MSB of the result is set and cleared otherwise. Operand size is byte, word, or long.

```
OR.B D2,D0        ; OR the low byte of D2 with the
                  ; low byte of D0 and store the
                  ; result in the low byte of D0.
OR.L #$40(A2),D3  ; OR the long contents of
                  ; memory where A2 + 40
                  ; points to D3.
```

ORI Instruction—Logically OR Corresponding Bits of Two Operands: ORI Source, Destination

The ORI instruction immediately ORs a value in the word(s) following the instruction code word to a value specified by a data alterable destination addressing mode. Condition codes are set as for the OR instruction. That is, V and C are cleared, X is not affected, and Z and N are set according to the value of the result of the OR operation. Operand size is byte, word, or long. If the operand size is byte, then the immediate data is padded with one additional byte to keep the instruction on even word boundaries.

It is also possible to ORI to the CCR in order to set or clear one or several condition codes. It is also possible to ORI to the status register to affect the CPU status. ORI to SR is a privileged instruction. That is, if an ORI to SR is attempted while in user state of the CPU (when the supervisor state bit is a 0), then a CPU trap is generated and control transfers to an exception-handling routine.

EXAMPLES

```
ORI.B #$F0,D0
          ; OR the low byte of D0 with $F0. This
          ; will set the upper nibble to all 1s
          ; and leave the lower nibble unchanged.
ORI.W #$FF00,D2
          ; OR the low word of D2 with $F0. This
          ; will set the upper byte to all 1s
          ; and leave the lower byte unchanged.
ORI.B #$01,CCR
          ; OR immediate the value $01 with the
          ; CCR. This will set the carry bit and
          ; leave the other condition codes unchanged.
```

PEA Instruction—Push Effective Address: PEA Destination

The PEA instruction computes an effective address and pushes that address onto the system stack (A7). The stack is decremented (by 4) after the effective address is saved on the stack. The operand size is always long (32 bits). The condition codes are not affected.

In most instructions the effective address would automatically be used to access one of the operands from memory. The PEA instruction provides access to the effective address itself rather than the operand at which it points.

```
PEA PRICES
          ; Push the address PRICES
          ; onto the system stack.
PEA #$20(A2,D0)
          ; Push the address that is
          ; the value of A2 plus the value
          ; of D0 plus the constant $20.
          ; A2 normally is the address of the base of
          ; a data structure (an array of records). D2
          ; contains the offset of the current record
          ; in the array, and $20 is the offset to the value
          ; of interest in the current record of the array.
```

RESET Instruction—Reset External Device: RESET

The 68000 CPU has a control line that goes from the CPU to external I/O devices and is used to reset those devices to their power-on state. This line is called the *reset* line. The RESET instruction places a 1 on this line for a time long enough to reset the I/O devices. The condition codes are not affected.

EXAMPLE

```
RESET    ; Pull on the reset line
         ; to reset I/O devices external
         ; to the CPU.
```

ROL and ROR Instructions—Rotate (Without Extend) Left or Right: ROL Source, Destination; ROR Source, Destination

The ROL (ROR) instruction rotates the destination operand left (right). The rotation is circular, meaning that for left shifts the bits that rotate out of the right end of the destination are copied back into the low end of the destination. For right shifts the bits rotated out of the right end of the destination are copied back into the left end of the destination. The carry bit is filled, set with the last bit rotated out of the left (right) of the destination. The rotate count is specified as an immediate value in the instruction for counts in the range 1 to 8. For larger counts the shift count must be loaded into a data register, which is then specified as the source operand. If the destination is a memory location, then the rotate count is presumed to be 1, and only one operand is used (the destination operand). Operand size can be byte, word, or long. Only memory-alterable addressing modes may be used, with a word size required and a 1-bit rotate count implied (no other count allowed).

The condition codes N and V are set according to the result of the rotate. V is set if the MSB is changed anytime during the shift operation. X is not affected. C is set equal to the last bit rotated out of the operand. If the rotate count is 0, then C is cleared.

```
ROL.B D1,D2   ; Rotate D2 left by
              ; the count in D1.
ROR.W #3,D7   ; Rotate D7 right 3 bit positions.
ROL.W (A4)    ; Rotate the memory location
              ; pointed at by A4 one bit left.
              ; Memory rotates MUST be word and
              ; use a 1-bit count.
ROL.L #2,D0   ; Rotate left D0 by 2
              ; bit positions.
```

ROXL and ROXR Instructions—Rotate with Extend Left or Right: ROXL Source, Destination; ROXR Source, Destination

Rotate with extend is similar to the rotate instruction, except that the extend bit is included in the rotation. That is, with a left rotate the bits rotated out of the left end of the operand are copied into the extend bit, and the extend bit is copied into the right end of the operand.

EXAMPLES

```
ROXL.B D1,D2   ; Rotate D2 left by
               ; the count in D1, including the
               ; extend bit in the rotation.
ROXR.W #3,D7   ; Rotate D7 right 3 bit positions
               ; using the extend bit as well.
```

RTE Instruction—Return from Exception: RTE

When an exception occurs, the address where the CPU is currently operating is pushed onto the system stack. The status register is also pushed onto the stack. This leaves one word more on the stack than is pushed when a normal jump to subroutine is executed. The extra word is the status register. After the address and status register are pushed, a new program counter value is accessed from the low-memory area according to what type of exception occurred (e.g., divide by 0 or privilege violation). This address is the address of an exception handler, often called an *exception service routine*. The routine is like a subroutine except that it is not called from some mainline program; it is called when a CPU exception occurs. This same type of operation happens in response to a CPU interrupt from some external device. An interrupt is a kind of exception in some sense.

When the exception-handling routine has completed its operation, which normally involves "fixing" the problem which caused the exception, then control may be transferred back to the code that was executing when the exception (or interrupt) occurred. However, a normal return from subroutine will not work properly because the return from subroutine uses only a return address from the stack. The saved status register would be left clogging up the stack. Therefore, the 68000 provides a special type of return instruction

used to return from an exception. This instruction is the RTE instruction. RTE is used to return from an exception (or interrupt) and RTS is used to return from a subroutine.

The RTE instruction pops one word from the stack, places it in the status register, and then pops a return address from the stack and places it in the program counter, which causes control to return to the interrupted code. The condition codes are modified according to the new status register. The instruction is unsized.

Because the RTE instruction affects the entire status register, it is a privileged instruction. That is, the CPU must be in supervisor state for the proper execution of this instruction (i.e., the supervisor state bit of the status register is a 1). If the CPU is in user state, then a CPU trap occurs (an exception occurs).

EXAMPLE

```
RTE   ; Restore status register and return from
      ; exception-handling routine.
```

RTR Instruction—Return and Restore Condition Codes: RTR

RTR is a form of RTE in which only the condition-code portion of the status register is affected. RTR is, therefore, not a privileged instruction. RTR is used to return from an exception handler or interrupt-service routine when in the user (or supervisor) state of the CPU. The condition codes are set according to the word popped from the system stack. The upper byte of the status register is not affected.

EXAMPLE

```
RTR   ; Return and restore condition codes.
```

RTS Instruction—Return from Subroutine: RTS

The RTS instruction is the most common method of returning to a calling mainline program. This instruction is a companion instruction to the JSR and BSR instructions. Control is passed to a subroutine using a JSR and control is returned to the mainline program using an RTS instruction.

The instruction operates by popping a long-word address off the system stack and placing that address in the program counter. The address is presumed to have been pushed onto the stack by a JSR (or BSR) instruction. The system stack pointer is postincremented (by 4) after the return address is popped off. The condition codes are not affected.

EXAMPLE

```
RTS   ; Return from this subroutine
      ; to the mainline program after the
```

```
; JSR (or BSR) instruction that
; made the call.
```

SBCD Instruction—Subtract Decimal with Extend: SBCD Source, Destination

The SBCD instruction subtracts the source operand to the destination operand and places the result back in the destination operand. The subtraction is performed using BCD arithmetic. The extend bit is used during the addition to allow borrows for the subtraction from a higher-digit subtraction and to send a borrow from the byte subtraction to the next-lower digit. The operation is a byte operation only. Both the source operand and the destination operand must be data registers, or they must both be memory locations accessed using the address register indirect with predecrement addressing mode.

Following the operation, the carry bit is set if a decimal borrow was generated and is cleared if there was no borrow. The extend bit is set equal to the carry bit. The zero bit is cleared if the result is nonzero and is unchanged otherwise. The zero bit is normally cleared via programming before a series of BCD subtractions (a multiple-precision operation) and tested once following all the subtractions. This allows convenient testing after decimal subtractions of BCD values represented as several BCD digits.

EXAMPLES

```
SBCD D0,D1        ; Subtract the two BCD digits
                  ; in D0 from the two BCD
                  ; digits in D1 and place the
                  ; result in D1.
SBCD -(A3),-(A2)  ; Subtract the BCD digits in
                  ; the memory pointed
                  ; at by A3 from the BCD
                  ; digits pointed at by
                  ; A2. Decrement each
                  ; pointer before
                  ; accessing the BCD
                  ; digits. Store the
                  ; result in the memory
                  ; location pointed at
                  ; by A2.
```

Scc Instruction—Set According to Condition: Scc Destination

Scc sets according to some condition. This is actually a short form for 14 different instructions. The instructions are explained in more detail in Figure 4-10. The instructions are shown here by example:

```
SCC D0   ; Set D0 to 1s if carry clear (0).
SCS D0   ; Set D0 to 1s if carry set (1).
SEQ D0   ; Set D0 to 1s if equal to 0.
SGE D0   ; Set D0 to 1s if greater than or equal to 0.
SGT D0   ; Set D0 to 1s if greater than 0.
```

```
SHI D0   ; Set D0 to 1s if higher than 0.
SLE D0   ; Set D0 to 1s if less than or equal to 0.
SLS D0   ; Set D0 to 1s if lower than or same as 0.
SLT D0   ; Set D0 to 1s if less than 0.
SMI D0   ; Set D0 to 1s if minus.
SNE D0   ; Set D0 to 1s if not equal to 0.
SPL D0   ; Set D0 to 1s if plus.
SVC D0   ; Set D0 to 1s if oVerflow clear (0).
SVS D0   ; Set D0 to 1s if oVerflow set (1).
```

Rather than including all 14 instructions in the manuals, Motorola literature normally lumps these 14 instructions together with one opcode and form. The instructions differ only in which condition-code combination they check. Figure 4-10 shows the actual bit-combination equation used to compute the condition-code combination given the five main condition codes.

You may wonder why oVerflow, with a capital V? V is the overflow bit in the condition-code portion of the status register, just as with Carry (the C bit) and Zero (the Z condition code bit).

Higher than and lower than refer to signed values, whereas greater than and less than refer to unsigned values. For example, using 8-bit values, $F8 is lower than $04, but $F8 is greater than $04. That is, when viewed as signed decimal values, −8 is less than 4, but when viewed as unsigned decimal values, 248 is greater than 4. Plus refers to just the N condition code, or "plus is not negative." The instruction may use an 8-bit displacement, giving a range of +128 to −127 bytes, size byte, or it may use a 16-bit displacement, giving a range of +32,768 to −32,767 bytes, size word. The Raven cross assembler uses absolute long and absolute short to control this size.

The destination must be specified using any data-alterable addressing mode. The condition codes are not affected.

EXAMPLE

```
SEQ (A3)   ; Set the byte A3 points at to all
           ; 1s if the zero condition code is
           ; set; otherwise set the byte to
           ; all 0s.
```

STOP Instruction—Stop the CPU: STOP Destination

When the STOP instruction is executed, the CPU moves the immediate data from the destination operand into the entire status register and halts. Execution of the CPU is stopped and does not continue. This is a privileged instruction. If it is executed while the CPU is in user mode (the supervisor bit of the SR is 0), then a trap is generated and control transfers to the privilege violation exception handler.

The condition codes are set according to the immediate data in the destination operand.

STOP #7   ; Stop the CPU and place 7 in
          ; the status register ($0007)

SUB Instruction—Subtract: SUB Source, Destination

The SUB instruction subtracts a number from some source from a number from some destination and puts the result in the specified destination. The source may be an immediate number, a register, or a memory location, as specified by any of the 12 addressing modes shown in Figure 3-8. The destination may be a register or a memory location specified by any one of the alterable addressing modes in Figure 3-8. Both the source and the destination can be data registers, but at least one *must* be a data register. Thus, the source and the destination in an instruction cannot both be memory locations. The source and the destination must be of the same type. In other words, they must both be byte locations, they must both be word locations, or they must both be long locations. If you want to subtract a byte from a word, you must copy the byte to a word location and fill the upper byte of the word with zeros before subtracting (or sign-extend the byte using the EXT instruction). Flags affected are X, N, Z, V, C.

EXAMPLES

SUB.B ($4204),D0   ; Subtract byte at address $4204
                   ; from the contents of D0.
SUB.L D0,D3   ; Subtract the long contents of
                   ; D0 from the long contents of
                   ; D3 and store the result in
                   ; D3.
SUB.W (A4)+,D3   ; Subtract the contents of
                   ; memory pointed to by A4 from
                   ; the contents of D3 and store
                   ; the result in D3. A4 is
                   ; incremented following the
                   ; operation.
SUB.W D2,−(A2)   ; Subtract the word contents of
                   ; D2 from the word in memory
                   ; pointed at by A2, and store
                   ; the result back into the
                   ; same memory location. A2 is
                   ; decremented before the
                   ; operation.

SUBA Instruction—Subtract Address: SUBA Source, Destination

The SUBA instruction subtracts two address registers or a source address value and a destination address register and places the result in an address register. The source operand can be any register, immediate data, or a memory location using any addressing mode.

The destination must be an address register. The operation size must be word or long (byte operations are not allowed). Condition codes are *not affected* by this instruction. Address arithmetic is signed binary arithmetic. If the operation is of size word, then the source operand is sign-extended to a long operand and the addition is performed using all 32 bits of the destination address register.

EXAMPLES

SUBA.W #$1004,A0   ; Subtract offset $1004
                   ; from the contents of A0.
SUBA.L A0,A3   ; Subtract the long contents of
                   ; A0 from the long contents
                   ; of A3 and store the result
                   ; in A3.

SUBI Instruction—Subtract Immediate: SUBI Source, Destination

The SUBI instruction is used to subtract data values held in the instruction itself from some destination. The data in the instruction is called immediate data and may be of byte, word, or long size. The immediate data is placed in memory immediately following the instruction code word. If the immediate data is of size byte, then a byte is skipped to keep the instruction code on word boundaries.

All condition codes are affected. Condition codes are set to reflect the result of the subtract immediate operation. Only data-alterable addressing modes are allowed in the destination field.

EXAMPLES

SUBI.B #$74,D0
       ; Subtract immediate byte $74
       ; from the contents of D0.
SUBI.L #$123489AB,(A4)
       ; Subtract the long contents
       ; of D0 from the long
       ; contents of D3 and store
       ; the result in D3.

SUBQ Instruction—Subtract Quick: SUBQ Source, Destination

SUBQ is a faster way to subtract if the source operand is in the range 1 to 8. With such a small operand, the operand value itself can be coded in the single-instruction code word and the subtraction can be performed with only a 1-word memory reference. This is the instruction of choice for subtracting small values. The destination can be accessed using any alterable addressing mode.

All the condition codes are affected by this operation. Each code is set or cleared according to the results of the addition operation.

```
SUBQ.B #$7,D0      ; Subtract quick $7 from
                   ; the contents of D0.
SUBQ.L #1,($4206)  ; Subtract 1 from the long
                   ; contents at memory
                   ; address $4206.
```

SUBX Instruction—Subtract Extended: SUBX Source, Destination

Subtract a source operand from a destination operand using binary addition and the extend bit. Both operands must be data registers or both must use the predecrement address register indirect addressing mode. All condition codes are affected by the operation and are set according to the addition results. This operation is particularly useful for high-precision (multibyte) arithmetic. Operands must be byte, word, or long.

EXAMPLES

```
SUBX.B D1,D0
     ; Subtract extended byte D1
     ; from D0.
SUBX.W −(A2),−(A1)
     ; Subtract the extended word
     ; contents of the memory at which A2 points from
     ; the value where A1 points. Decrement both
     ; address registers (by 2) before the memory
     ; reference. Return the result to the
     ; original location to which A1 points.
```

SWAP Instruction—Swap Register Halves: SWAP Data Register

The SWAP instruction exchanges the lower and upper words of a data register. The operand size is always word and the destination operand must always be a data register.

The V and C condition codes are always cleared. The X bit is not affected. N is set if the MSB of the result is set and cleared otherwise. The Z bit is set if the 32-bit result is 0 and cleared otherwise.

EXAMPLE

```
SWAP D3   ; Swap the upper and lower words of
          ; data register 3.
```

TAS Instruction—Test and Set in One Operation: TAS Destination

Test and set is the basic semaphore operation of the 68000 CPU. A semaphore is a bit or byte used to synchronize several processors or several processes. The idea behind a semaphore is that when set, it represents a lock on some area of memory. When cleared, the area of memory or other resource is not locked—i.e., it is available for use. The test and set instruction allows a program to examine a semaphore (test one) and set the semaphore in one indivisible operation. If the semaphore is already set, then the resource is already locked to some other processor or process. In this case the N bit is set to indicate that the semaphore is already locked. Then the program must wait until the resource is unlocked. Normally, the program would wait a predetermined time and then test the semaphore again. If the semaphore is not set, then it will be set by the TAS instruction and the bit will be clear, indicating that the resource is available and is now locked to the program that just executed the TAS.

If the test and set were two separate instructions (a TST and a MOVE), then some other processor or program might get control and lock the resource between the TST and the set (MOVE). The reason that the TAS must be indivisible is so that no other processor or program will come in between the operations. This instruction can be used to ensure that the semaphore is used properly.

The V and C condition codes are always cleared. The X bit is not affected. The Z and N bits are set according to the high bit of the destination byte. The destination's high bit is set to 1 by the operation. The destination can be specified using any data-alterable addressing mode.

EXAMPLE

```
TAS (A3)+   ; Test and set the byte pointed
            ; at by A3 and increment A3
            ; following the operation.
```

TRAP Instruction—Cause a CPU Trap: TRAP Vector Number

The TRAP instruction generates a CPU trap, which causes a transfer of control to an exception-handling routine. The routine is specified by the low 4 bits of the immediate data in the destination operand. These bits specify which of 16 possible exception handlers are called. The addresses of these routines are kept in 68000 memory from $000 to $0BF, each address being 4 bytes long. For example the vector number 0 implies that the vector address starts at memory location $080, vector 1 starts at $084, and so on.

The instruction operates by pushing the current program counter value on the system stack (the return address) and then pushing the status register on the system stack. The specified address (vector) is loaded from the appropriate memory location and loaded into the program counter. This has the effect of transferring control to the desired trap service routine. The trap handler will later use the RTR or RTE instruction to return control back to the mainline instruction.

The condition codes are not affected.

```
TRAP #3   ; Cause a CPU trap and use
          ; exception vector number
          ; 3 (at address $08C).
```

TRAPV Instruction—Cause a CPU Trap on Overflow: TRAPV

The TRAPV instruction causes a CPU trap if the overflow condition code is set. The current PC is pushed on the system stack, followed by the status register. The PC is loaded with the address from the TRAPV location ($01C). Also see the TRAP instruction. The condition codes are not affected.

This instruction can be used to transfer control to an overflow-handling routine if an overflow has occurred.

EXAMPLE

```
TRAPV   ; Cause a CPU trap if an
        ; overflow has occurred.
```

TST Instruction—Test an Operand: TST Destination

With the TST instruction, the destination operand is tested and the N and Z condition codes are set according to its value. The V and C condition code bits are always cleared, and X is not affected. Only data-alterable addressing modes are allowed. The operand size can be byte, word, or long.

EXAMPLES

```
TST.W D0     ; Test the low word of D0 and
             ; set the N and Z condition
             ; codes according to their values.
TST.L (A3)+  ; Test the long word pointed at
             ; by A3 and increment A3 (by
             ; 4) following the test.
```

UNLK Instruction—Unlink the Stack by Loading New Stack Pointer: UNLK Address Register

See the LINK instruction description for an explanation of what a *link* is and what it is used for. The UNLK instruction is used in conjunction with the LINK instruction to create and remove links on the system stack. The LINK instruction is used when a subroutine is called, and the UNLK instruction is used when the subroutine returns. The UNLK instruction operates by loading the stack pointer from the address register specified as the destination operand and then loading that address register with a value popped from the new system stack.

EXAMPLE

```
UNLK A3   ; Remove the link from the stack,
          ; deallocating stack memory, load
          ; a new stack pointer value from the
          ; address register A3, and load a
          ; new reserved memory base
          ; address from the stack into A3.
```

ASSEMBLER DIRECTIVES

The words defined in this section are directions to the assembler; they are not instructions for the 68000. The assembler directives described here are a common subset of those defined for the Raven® cross assembler, which runs on the IBM PC, and the Consulair® Corporation 68000 assembler, which runs on an Apple Macintosh. If you are using some other assembler, it probably has similar capabilities, but the names may be different.

ABS_LONG, ABS_SHORT—Absolute Long, Absolute Short: ABS_LONG; ABS_SHORT

The absolute long and absolute short directives, used only by the Raven cross assembler, tell the assembler to use either 32-bit (long) or 16-bit (short) addresses when assembling instructions with absolute addresses in them. The Consulair assembler for the Macintosh uses .L and .S suffixes to indicate long or short absolute addresses.

EXAMPLES

```
ABS_SHORT    ; Use short addressing.
BLT smaller  ; Branch to location
             ; "smaller"
             ; if less than; use a 16-bit
             ; address so smaller must be
             ; within this 64K area.
ABS_LONG     ; Change to long addressing.
BGT larger   ; If greater; branch to
             ; location "larger." Use
             ; 32-bit addressing so
             ; larger can be anywhere in
             ; this 4-Gbyte area.
```

DC—Define Constant: DC Data list

The DC directive is used to define a byte, word, or long-type variable or to set aside one or more storage locations of type byte, word, or long in memory. The statement CURRENT_TEMPERATURE DC.B $42, for example, tells the assembler to reserve 1 byte of memory for a variable named CURRENT_TEMPER-ATURE and to put the value $42 in that memory location when the program is loaded into memory to be run. Refer to Chapter 3 for further discussion of the DC directive and to Chapter 4 for a discussion of how you can access variables named with a DC in your programs. Here are a few more examples of DC statements.

EXAMPLES

PRICES DC.B $49, $98, $29
    ; Declare an array of 3 bytes
    ; named PRICES and initialize
    ; the 3 bytes as shown.
NAME_HERE DC.B 'THOMAS'
    ; Declare an array of 6 bytes
    ; and initialize with ASCII
    ; codes for letters in THOMAS.

DS—Define Storage: DS Constant

The DS directive is used to declare a variable of type long, word, or byte. The memory for the variable is not initialized. The constant specifies the number of bytes, words, or longs to reserve.

EXAMPLES

X1 DS.L 30   ; Reserve 30 bytes of memory and
    ; call the first byte X1.

END—End Program

The END directive is put after the last statement of a program to tell the assembler that this is the end of the source program file. The assembler will ignore any statements after an END directive, so you should make sure to only use one END directive at the very end of your program.

EXAMPLE

END

EQU—Equate

EQU is used to give a name to some value or symbol. Each time the assembler finds the given name in the program, it will replace the name with the value or symbol you equated with that name. If, for example, you write the statement CORRECTION_FACTOR EQU $03 at the start of your program and later in the program you write the instruction statement ADDI.B CORRECTION_FACTOR,D0, when it codes this instruction statement, the assembler will code it as if you had written the instruction ADDI.B $03,D0. The advantage of using EQU in this manner is that if CORRECTION_FACTOR is used 27 times in a program and you want to change the value, all you have to do is change the EQU statement and reassemble the program. The assembler will automatically put in the new

value each time it finds the name CORRECTION_FACTOR. If you had used $03 instead of EQU, then you would have to find and change all 27 instructions yourself. Here are some more examples.

EXAMPLES

STRING_START EQU (A4)
    ; Give name to (A4).
MAXIMUM EQU 100
    ; The symbolic name MAXIMUM
    ; is equal to the constant
    ; 100.

EVEN—Align on Even Memory Address: EVEN

As the assembler assembles a section of data declarations or instruction statements, it uses a location counter to keep track of how many bytes it is from the start of a segment at any time. The EVEN directive tells the assembler to increment the location counter to the next even address if it is not already at an even address.

The Consulair assembler uses .ALIGN instead of EVEN to request word or long-word alignment in memory.

The 68000 can read a word from memory in one bus cycle if the word is at an even address. If the word starts on an odd address, the 68000 must do two bus cycles to get the 2 bytes of the word. Therefore, a series of words can be read much more quickly if they are on even addresses. When EVEN is used in a data segment, the location counter will simply be incremented to the next even address if necessary. The code segment is always word-aligned (even) in 68000 instruction streams.

EXAMPLES

DC.B 1   ; Declare 1 byte with the constant
    ; 1 in it.
EVEN   ; Move to the next even address
    ; (i.e., skip over 1 byte).

INCLUDE—Include Additional Source Code File: INCLUDE File Name

The INCLUDE directive tells the assembler to read source statements from another file. In effect, the file specified as the operand for INCLUDE is inserted into the current source file at the point of the INCLUDE statement.

EXAMPLE

INCLUDE "SUBONE.ASM"
    ; Add the
    ; source file SUBONE.ASM

```
                        ; to the program at this
                        ; point.
```

LIST, NOLIST—Create an Output Listing

The Consulair assembler uses .NoList, .ListToFile, and .ListToDisp. These directives tell the assembler to turn off (on) the listing of source statements in the listing file. This can be useful if you have a long sequence of instructions that you already know are correct and that you do not want to see listed.

EXAMPLES

```
LIST      ; Turn on listing.
NOLIST    ; Turn off listing.
NOP
NOP       ; Don't care to see these NOPS
NOP       ; in the listing.
NOP
NOP
LIST      ; Turn listing back on.
```

ORG—Specify an Address of Origin for the Program: ORG Address Constant

The ORG statement is used during absolute assembly to tell the assembler what address to start assembling the code into. When assembling code that will later be linked to specific addresses, ORG is not required. ORG is used only in the Raven assembler.

EXAMPLE

```
ORG $4000   ; Start assembling code at address
            ; $4000.
```

XDEF, XREF—Define External, Reference External: XDEF Symbol; XREF Symbol

The XDEF and XREF directives are provided only by the Consulair assembler. The Raven cross assembler uses RORG to provide similar capability.

The XDEF directive tells the assembler the symbol that follows is defined here and may be referred to by some other program module. The XREF directive tells the assembler the symbol is not defined here but is defined elsewhere (in some other module). The XREF directive states that the symbol is referenced here but not defined here.

EXAMPLES

```
XDEF ADD_SUBR
    ; The ADD_SUBR routine is
    ; defined here and referenced elsewhere. The
    ; XREF goes with the subroutine code in the
    ; subroutine code module.
XREF ADD_SUBR
    ; The ADD_SUBR routine is
    ; referenced here but defined elsewhere.
    ; The XREF
    ; directive goes in the main program and tells the
    ; assembler that the code for the subroutine is in a
    ; different module.
```

CHECKLIST OF IMPORTANT TERMS AND CONCEPTS IN THIS CHAPTER

Assembler directives

Addressing terminology

Data-addressing modes
Memory-addressing modes
Alterable addressing modes
Control-addressing modes
Data-alterable addressing modes

Instruction source

Instruction destination

REVIEW QUESTIONS AND PROBLEMS

1. List the data-alterable addressing modes. List the control-alterable addressing modes.

2. If you want to store a value in a CPU register into a memory location, which instruction(s) could you use?

3. What is the difference between the CMP and the CMPI instructions?

4. Why does the CPU have an ILLEGAL instruction? For what can the instruction be used?

5. Why is the MOVEM instruction faster for moving several registers from the CPU to memory than simply using several MOVE instructions?

6. What can the MOVE instruction do that the MOVEM instruction cannot?

7. Show how you could combine several MOVE instructions to perform the same operation as the SWAP instruction. What are the differences between a single SWAP and the MOVE instruction sequence?

8. What is the difference between the DIVS and DIVU instructions?

9. How are assembler directives different from the normal CPU instructions?

10. Try to guess which instruction is the most frequently used instruction in "normal" assembly language code. Why do you think this instruction is used most?

11. Which assembler directive would you use to mark the end of your assembly language source program?

12. Describe the function of the ORG assembler directive.

CHAPTER 7

68000 System Connections, Timing, and Troubleshooting

In Chapter 2 we showed that a microcomputer consists of a CPU, memory, and ports. We also showed in Chapter 2 that these parts are connected by three major buses, the address bus, the control bus, and the data bus. For Chapters 3 through 6, however, we made little mention of the hardware of a microcomputer because we were concerned in these chapters, for the most part, with how a microcomputer is programmed. In this chapter we come back to take a closer look at the hardware of a microcomputer.

OBJECTIVES

At the conclusion of this chapter, you should be able to

1. Draw a diagram showing how RAMs, ROMs, and I/O ports are added to a 68000 CPU to make a simple microcomputer.

2. Describe how addresses are sent out on the 68000 data bus.

3. Describe the signal sequence on the buses as a simple 68000-based microcomputer fetches and executes an instruction.

4. Describe how address-decoding circuitry gives a specific address to each device in a system and makes sure only one device is enabled at a time.

5. Calculate the required access time for a memory device or port to work correctly in a 68000 microcomputer system.

6. List a series of steps you might take to troubleshoot a malfunctioning microcomputer system that once worked.

68000 HARDWARE OVERVIEW

In previous chapters we worked with what is often called the *programmer's model* of the 68000. This model shows features such as internal registers, number of address lines, and number of data lines that we need in order to be able to program the device. Now we will look at the hardware model of the 68000 so that we

can show how a microcomputer system is built around it. We also discuss the hardware connections for a 68008. A later chapter shows the hardware connections for the 68020, 68030, and 68040 microprocessors.

68000 Input and Output Signals

To get started, let's take a look at the pin diagram for the 68000 in Figure 7-1. Don't be overwhelmed by all those pins with strange mnemonics next to them. You don't need to learn the detailed functions of all these at once. We describe and show the use of these different pins throughout the next few chapters as needed. When you need to refresh your memory of the function of a particular pin, consult the index to find the section where that particular pin or signal is described in detail. For reference, the complete data sheet showing all of the pin descriptions is shown in Appendix A.

Look first at the dual-in-line package, which is quite common in Figure 7-1. Notice that V_{CC} is on pins 14 and 49, whereas ground is on pins 16 and 53. Next find the clock input labeled CLK on pin 15. A 68000 requires a clock signal from some external, crystal-controlled clock generator to synchronize internal operations in the processor. Different versions of the 68000 have maximum clock frequencies ranging from 8 MHz to 12.5 MHz. Notice in Figure 7-1 that the 16-bit data bus is carried on pins D0–D15. Remember from previous chapters that the 68000 has a 24-bit address bus. The astute reader will notice that only pins A1–A23 exist. What happened to address line A0? The lowest-order bit of the address is represented by the $\overline{UDS}$ and $\overline{LDS}$ pins (upper and lower data strobes). The 23 bits can address 8 megawords of memory, which is equal to 16 Mbytes, since each word consists of 2 bytes.

Figure 7-2 shows the 68000 pins grouped into logical collections, depending on the pin's function. The data and address buses are shown on the upper right. The actual pin locations and numbers were shown in Figure 7-1. The directions of the arrows indicate whether the signals on the pins represent information moving into or out of the 68000 CPU. The address bus is actually a three-state bus, where each bit can be a 0, a 1, or "floating," where the CPU does not drive the

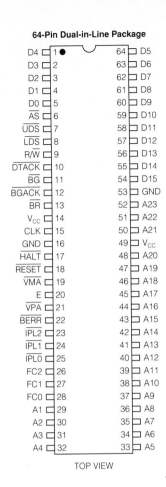

64-Pin Dual-in-Line Package

D4	1	64	D5
D3	2	63	D6
D2	3	62	D7
D1	4	61	D8
D0	5	60	D9
$\overline{AS}$	6	59	D10
$\overline{UDS}$	7	58	D11
$\overline{LDS}$	8	57	D12
$R/\overline{W}$	9	56	D13
$\overline{DTACK}$	10	55	D14
$\overline{BG}$	11	54	D15
$\overline{BGACK}$	12	53	GND
$\overline{BR}$	13	52	A23
V_{CC}	14	51	A22
CLK	15	50	A21
GND	16	49	V_{CC}
$\overline{HALT}$	17	48	A20
$\overline{RESET}$	18	47	A19
$\overline{VMA}$	19	46	A18
E	20	45	A17
$\overline{VPA}$	21	44	A16
$\overline{BERR}$	22	43	A15
$\overline{IPL2}$	23	42	A14
$\overline{IPL1}$	24	41	A13
$\overline{IPL0}$	25	40	A12
FC2	26	39	A11
FC1	27	38	A10
FC0	28	37	A9
A1	29	36	A8
A2	30	35	A7
A3	31	34	A6
A4	32	33	A5

TOP VIEW

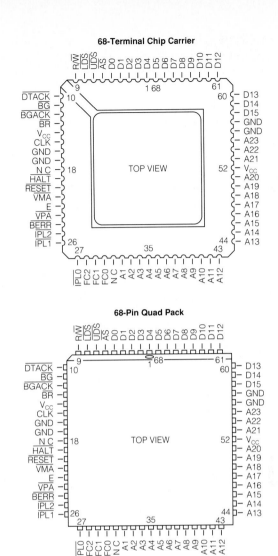

68-Terminal Chip Carrier

TOP VIEW

68-Pin Quad Pack

TOP VIEW

FIGURE 7-1 68000 pin diagram. (*Reprinted with permission of Motorola Inc.*)

value of the bus. The data bus is also a tristate bus, but it can either send or receive data. The CPU can be the source of the data going out of it, or it can be the destination for the data going into it.

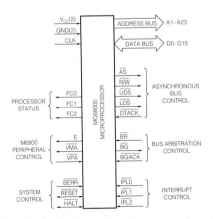

FIGURE 7-2 Input and output signals. (*Reprinted with permission of Motorola Inc.*)

Figure 7-2 also shows the power lines (V_{CC}), the ground lines (GND), and the clock line (CLK). The remaining pins are grouped into the processor state lines, the M6800 peripheral control lines, the system control lines, the asynchronous bus control lines, the bus arbitration control lines, and the interrupt control lines. Each of these groups of lines is discussed briefly here. Most are revisited in later chapters in more detail. During these discussions the term *low* is generally used to indicate the presence of a logical 0 on the line. The *active* state of a line is a high voltage for some lines and a low voltage for other lines. Table 7-1, p. 168, shows the real active state for each line. In the discussion, however, the terms *assert* or *assertion* (e.g., we can assert $\overline{UDS}$ by making it have a low voltage) and *negate* or *negation* are often used. The names actually carry the correct condition in them. For example, the upper data strobe line is labeled $\overline{UDS}$ (that is, "UDS bar"), not just UDS, because when we assert the upper data strobe, we give it a low voltage (i.e., a 0). This makes $\overline{UDS}$ true and UDS false. Another way to think of this is that if we want to access the

TABLE 7-1
68000 SIGNAL SUMMARY (Reprinted with permission of Motorola Inc.)

Signal Name	Mnemonic	Input/Output	Active State	Hi-Z On $\overline{\text{HALT}}$	Hi-Z On $\overline{\text{BGACK}}$
Address Bus	A1-A23	Output	High	Yes	Yes
Data Bus	D0-D15	Input/Output	High	Yes	Yes
Address Strobe	$\overline{\text{AS}}$	Output	Low	No	Yes
Read/Write	R/$\overline{\text{W}}$	Output	Read-High Write-Low	No	Yes
Upper and Lower Data Strobes	$\overline{\text{UDS}}$, $\overline{\text{LDS}}$	Output	Low	No	Yes
Data Transfer Acknowledge	$\overline{\text{DTACK}}$	Input	Low	No	No
Bus Request	$\overline{\text{BR}}$	Input	Low	No	No
Bus Grant	$\overline{\text{BG}}$	Output	Low	No	No
Bus Grant Acknowledge	$\overline{\text{BGACK}}$	Input	Low	No	No
Interrupt Priority Level	$\overline{\text{IPL0}}$, $\overline{\text{IPL1}}$, $\overline{\text{IPL2}}$	Input	Low	No	No
Bus Error	$\overline{\text{BERR}}$	Input	Low	No	No
Reset	$\overline{\text{RESET}}$	Input/Output	Low	No[1]	No[1]
Halt	$\overline{\text{HALT}}$	Input/Output	Low	No[1]	No[1]
Enable	E	Output	High	No	No
Valid Memory Address	$\overline{\text{VMA}}$	Output	Low	No	Yes
Valid Peripheral Address	$\overline{\text{VPA}}$	Input	Low	No	No
Function Code Output	FC0, FC1, FC2	Output	High	No[2]	Yes
Clock	CLK	Input	High	No	No
Power Input	V_{CC}	Input	—	—	—
Ground	GND	Input	—	—	—

NOTES:
1. Open drain
2. Function codes are placed in high-impedance state during HALT for R9M, T6E, and BF4 mask sets

upper byte of a word, we want to assert the upper data strobe signal. To do this we should place a 1 on the upper data strobe control line, but that means we should place a low voltage on the $\overline{\text{UDS}}$ pin of the 68000. This is exactly what Table 7-1 tells us needs to be done, because $\overline{\text{UDS}}$ is active low.

ASYNCHRONOUS BUS CONTROL

The bus control lines include the address strobe line ($\overline{\text{AS}}$), the read/write line (R/$\overline{\text{W}}$), the upper and lower data strobes ($\overline{\text{UDS}}$ and $\overline{\text{LDS}}$), and the data transfer acknowledge line ($\overline{\text{DTACK}}$). These lines are used to synchronize and control the address bus and data bus operation. The 68000's normal addressing mode is an *asynchronous* mode in that the bus timing is regular, but not fixed. For example, a bus read operation by the CPU can take any number of clock cycles, depending on how fast the system RAM or I/O devices are. The CPU will not go on processing following a read until the reader (which may be RAM or some I/O device) sends a transfer complete acknowledgment using the $\overline{\text{DTACK}}$ line. Table 7-2 shows how the upper and lower data strobes in combination with the read/write line indicate when data is valid on which bits of the data bus. $\overline{\text{DTACK}}$ is used to indicate that the appropriate data bits have been successfully read. For example, when the $\overline{\text{UDS}}$ and $\overline{\text{LDS}}$ lines are both low and R/$\overline{\text{W}}$ is also low, then a word write is occurring. There is valid data

in all 16 bits of the data bus. When the I/O device has finished reading the word of data, it should set $\overline{\text{DTACK}}$ low. The 68000 can also provide a *synchronous* mode of operation using its M6800 peripheral control lines.

M6800 PERIPHERAL CONTROL LINES

Systems built using Motorola 6800 series peripheral device controllers typically require synchronous operation. In a synchronous system the CPU grinds on at its own speed, and it is up to the rest of the devices to keep up. In such systems all chips are synchronized to the system clock and must operate in fixed numbers of clock cycles for the system to operate properly. Devices of this type often cannot be conveniently configured to use the $\overline{\text{DTACK}}$ line to indicate when a read is complete. The peripheral control lines, Enable (E), valid peripheral address (VPA), and valid memory address (VMA), provide synchronous control of the bus for interfacing 68000 class CPUs to 6800 class peripheral devices. These lines are discussed in more detail in later examples.

SYSTEM CONTROL LINES

The system control lines, bus error ($\overline{\text{BERR}}$), reset ($\overline{\text{RESET}}$), and halt ($\overline{\text{HALT}}$) are used to start and stop the system. Halt is a bidirectional line that will cause the CPU to stop its operation at the completion of the

TABLE 7-2
DATA STROBE CONTROL OF DATA BUS (Reprinted with permission of Motorola Inc.)

$\overline{UDS}$	$\overline{LDS}$	R/$\overline{W}$	D6-D15	D0-D7
High	High	—	No Valid Data	No Valid Data
Low	Low	High	Valid Data Bits 8-15	Valid Data Bits 0-7
High	Low	High	No Valid Data	Valid Data Bits 0-7
Low	High	High	Valid Data Bits 8-15	No Valid Data
Low	Low	Low	Valid Data Bits 8-15	Valid Data Bits 0-7
High	Low	Low	Valid Data Bits 0-7*	Valid Data Bits 0-7
Low	High	Low	Valid Data Bits 8-15	Valid Data Bits 8-15*

*These conditions are a result of current implementation and may not appear on future devices.

current bus cycle. When halted, the CPU asserts the halt line. The reset line is used by the CPU to reset external devices. The reset line can be used to reset the CPU so that the CPU begins its start-up processing. If both the halt and reset lines are asserted, then an entire system reset is performed. When the CPU resets external devices as a result of executing a RESET instruction, the CPU internal state is not affected. The bus error line can be used to cause a CPU bus error exception and initiate error handling by the bus error service routine. Typically, this line is tied to external time-out circuitry so that if an I/O device does not respond within some reasonable length of time (determined by the hardware designer), the bus error line is asserted and the CPU can handle the error and continue processing. Otherwise, with an asynchronous bus, if some I/O device is unable to respond, then the entire system is stopped because the CPU cannot proceed without a $\overline{DTACK}$ (or bus error). If a second bus error occurs while the CPU is attempting to service the first bus error, then the CPU will halt. This is called a *double bus error condition.*

PROCESSOR STATUS

The processor status lines consist of three function code lines (FC0, FC1, and FC2), which tell the outside world what the CPU is doing. The function codes give the CPU state and the type of bus cycle being performed. Table 7-3, p. 170, shows the encoding used. For example, if FC2 and FC1 are both low (0) and FC0 is high (1), then the CPU is in user state and the bus cycle is accessing data. The read/write line indicates whether a read or a write is being performed.

INTERRUPT-CONTROL LINES

The interrupt-control lines are three input lines ($\overline{IPL0}$, $\overline{IPL1}$, and $\overline{IPL2}$) that encode the interrupting device's priority level. Signals can be applied to these inputs to cause the 68000 to interrupt the program it is executing and go execute a specified interrupt-service routine. We might, for example, connect a temperature sensor from a steam boiler to the interrupt inputs on a 68000. If the boiler gets too hot, then it will assert the interrupt inputs. This will cause the 68000 to stop executing its current program and execute a routine we wrote to turn off the fuel supply to the boiler. At the end of the interrupt-service routine we can return to executing the interrupted program. Chapter 8 describes in detail the operation and uses of interrupts.

The CPU will not acknowledge an interrupt which is of lower priority than its current interrupt mask level (specified in the CPU status register). If the CPU interrupt mask is set to 3, for example, then interrupts from devices with priority level 3 and lower will not be recognized. Interrupts from devices with interrupt priority levels of 4, 5, 6, or 7 will be acknowledged as quickly as possible. Interrupt level 7 is used for a *nonmaskable* interrupt, which is always acknowledged at the next instruction cycle. Since the boiler will explode if it gets too hot, we had better connect the boiler sensor so that it sets $\overline{IPL0}$, $\overline{IPL1}$, and $\overline{IPL2}$ to a 7 (i.e., to binary 111, all 1s) when the temperature gets critical. Interrupt level 7 will assure that the CPU finds time to call the interrupt-service routine and turn off the boiler fuel.

BUS ARBITRATION CONTROL LINES

In a simple 68000 system the 68000 CPU controls the operation of the system buses using its various bus control lines. In some more complex systems, however, there may be several 68000 family devices using the same bus. Clearly, they cannot all control the bus at once. In such systems one device controls the bus (the *system controller*); however, there is a mechanism whereby that device can give up control of the opera-

TABLE 7-3

TABLE 7-3
68000 CPU FUNCTION CODE OUTPUTS
(Reprinted with permission of Motorola Inc.)

Function Code Output			
FC2	FC1	FC0	Cycle Type
Low	Low	Low	(Undefined, Reserved)
Low	Low	High	User Data
Low	High	Low	User Program
Low	High	High	(Undefined, Reserved)

Function Code Output			
FC2	FC1	FC0	Cycle Type
High	Low	Low	(Undefined, Reserved)
High	Low	High	Supervisor Data
High	High	Low	Supervisor Program
High	High	High	Interrupt Acknowledge

pins on a 68000, we will take a closer look at what is happening on the buses during a read operation and during a write operation.

Basic Signal Flow on 68000 Buses

Figure 7-3 shows, in flowchart form, the activities of the CPU (bus master) and the memory (slave) during a byte-read operation. Figure 7-4 shows, in timing diagram form, the activities on the 68000 buses during word- and byte-read operations. Don't be overwhelmed by all the lines on this diagram. Their meanings should become clear to you as we work our way through the diagram.

68000 BUS ACTIVITIES DURING A READ MACHINE CYCLE

Follow along in Figure 7-3. First, the CPU asserts the read/write line to indicate a read is going to occur. The function code lines are set to indicate that a user data or a supervisor data operation will occur (depending on the CPU status register supervisor bit state). The upper 23 bits of the address are placed on the address lines and the address strobe ($\overline{AS}$) is asserted. The upper or lower data strobe is also asserted, depending on the address. If the address is even (i.e., bit A0 is a 0), then the lower data strobe is asserted; otherwise $\overline{UDS}$ is asserted. The memory and I/O devices then decode the address. Whichever device is addressed places the data on the data bus, using the upper and lower data strobes to determine whether to use the upper or the lower byte of the data bus. The device (or memory) then asserts

tion of the buses and allow some other device to take over control. The process of passing the bus typically involves a form of electronic arbitration in which several devices determine which will be the new bus controller. The bus arbitration control lines are used to pass bus control to other devices and perform bus arbitration when many devices are competing for control. We look in more detail at such complex multiprocessor systems in Chapter 12.

Now that you have an overview of most of the major

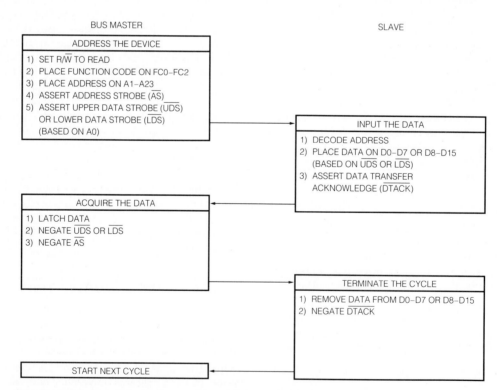

FIGURE 7-3   68000-byte read-cycle flowchart. (*Reprinted with permission of Motorola Inc.*)

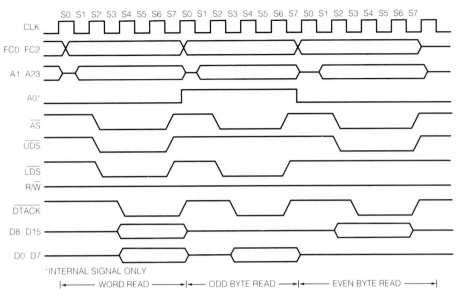

FIGURE 7-4 68000 word- and byte-read cycle timing diagram. (*Reprinted with permission of Motorola Inc.*)

$\overline{\text{DTACK}}$ to indicate that the data has been placed on the bus. The CPU then latches the data, recording it in internal memory areas called *buffers*, or *latches*. The CPU negates $\overline{\text{UDS}}$ or $\overline{\text{LDS}}$ (whichever was used for the transfer). The CPU negates $\overline{\text{AS}}$, indicating that the address bus is no longer in use. The I/O device or memory then stops driving the data bus; that is, it removes that data from the bus and negates $\overline{\text{DTACK}}$. The CPU then starts the next bus cycle. We can trace this entire operation in another manner using the timing diagram of Figure 7-4.

The first line to look at in Figure 7-4 is the *clock waveform* at the top (CLK). This represents the crystal-controlled clock signal sent to the 68000 from an external clock generator device, as shown at the top left of Figure 7-2. One cycle of this clock is referred to as a *state*. A state is measured from the falling edge of one clock pulse to the falling edge of the next clock pulse. S0 in the figure is state 0, S1 is state 1, and so on. The diagram shows the states numbered relative to the start of the machine cycle. Three machine cycles are shown: One word-read cycle is represented by the first seven states, S0–S7, in Figure 7-4; the next cycle is an odd-byte read represented by the second group of states S0–S7; and the third group of states S0–S7 is an even-byte-read bus cycle. As we discussed in Chapter 4, each instruction requires a certain number of states to execute. The total time it takes the 68000 to fetch and execute an instruction is called an *instruction cycle*. An instruction cycle consists of one or more *machine cycles*. A machine cycle represents a basic bus operation, such as reading a byte from memory or writing a word to a port. To summarize, then, an instruction cycle is made up of machine cycles, and a machine cycle is made up of states. Here we examine the activities that occur on the buses during a read machine cycle.

Let's start at the left of the diagram by examining the activities during a word-read operation. During S0 of a read machine cycle, a 68000 first asserts the function code and address signals. This gives these lines time to settle so that later uses of the lines will yield clean, reproducible results. The FC0–FC2 and A1–A23 lines are shown as two lines that cross. This is because the signals may be going low or going high for the read cycle. That is, the address bits may include both 0s and 1s. The point where the two waveforms cross indicates the time at which the signal becomes valid for this machine cycle. Note that the address line signals are not guaranteed to be valid until the start of state S1. The function code lines, on the other hand, are valid by the end of S0. Likewise, in the rest of the timing diagram, crossed lines are used to represent the time when information on a line or group of lines is changed. Incidentally, the best way to analyze a timing diagram such as this one is to think of time as a vertical line moving from left to right across the diagram. With this technique you can easily see the sequence of activities on the signal lines as you move your imaginary time line across the waveforms.

During S1 the address lines become valid (stable enough for use). During S2 the $\overline{\text{AS}}$, $\overline{\text{UDS}}$, and $\overline{\text{LDS}}$ lines are asserted, indicating a valid address and data desired on both the upper and lower bytes of the data bus. Notice also that the read/write line (R/$\overline{\text{W}}$) is assumed to be asserted throughout the entire operation. The buses are now ready, and the I/O device or memory (the *slave* device) should be preparing to provide the data. S3 is the first opportunity that the device has to provide the data. If the device is fast, then it can provide the data immediately. When the data is on the bus and valid, the slave device will assert $\overline{\text{DTACK}}$, telling the CPU that the data is valid. The CPU latches the data during S5 and S6, remembering it internally to the CPU. During S7 the CPU negates $\overline{\text{AS}}$, $\overline{\text{UDS}}$, and $\overline{\text{LDS}}$, the device negates $\overline{\text{DTACK}}$, and the cycle is completed. If the device were very slow, then additional states would be inserted after S3 and before S4, with the $\overline{\text{DTACK}}$ assertion coming only when the device was providing valid data.

Now, referring to Figure 7-4 again, find the D0–D7 waveform marked off near the bottom of the diagram. The addressed memory location or I/O port must put valid data on the data bus as soon as possible once it recognizes that it is being addressed. The diagram shows the data lines being asserted (with a mix of 0s and 1s) during S3. Suppose, for example, that we are addressing a ROM. ROMs typically have an access time of a few hundred nanoseconds. In other words, after we apply an address to a ROM, it will be a few hundred nanoseconds before we will see valid data on the outputs of the ROM. If the access time for a ROM in a system is longer than the access time shown in Figure 7-4, then there will not be valid data on the bus during S3. The 68000 waits until $\overline{\text{DTACK}}$ is asserted, which might not be until some later state. There might be additional clock cycles between states S2 and S3 if $\overline{\text{DTACK}}$ is not asserted immediately after S2. In this case the diagram shows $\overline{\text{DTACK}}$ asserted immediately after S2, in S3.

A later section of this chapter shows you how to calculate how long a particular ROM, RAM, or port device will take to respond in terms of wait states, which the CPU will have to insert automatically in a given 68000 system. For now, however, we just need you to understand the concept so you know that a 68000 can accommodate a slow device. In a machine cycle, the 68000 will insert one or more wait states between S2 and S3 in that machine-read cycle as necessary, waiting for $\overline{\text{DTACK}}$ to be asserted. What we have done by inserting the WAIT states is to freeze the action on the buses for one or more clock cycles. This gives the addressed device extra clock cycle times to put out valid data. If, for example, we want to use a slower (cheaper) ROM in a system, we can add a simple circuit that asserts $\overline{\text{DTACK}}$ only after the device has placed valid data on the data bus.

On most real systems, buffers such as 8286s are connected on the data bus. For a very small system these buffers are not needed, but as more devices are added to a system, they become necessary. Here's why. Most of the devices such as ROMs and RAMs used around microprocessors have MOS inputs, so on a dc basis they don't require much current. However, each input or output added to the system data bus, for example, acts as a capacitor of a few picofarads connected to ground. In order to change the logic state on these inputs from low to high, all this added capacitance must be charged. To change the logic state to a low, the capacitance must be discharged. If we add more than a few devices on the data bus lines, the 68000 outputs cannot supply enough current drive to charge and discharge the circuit capacitance rapidly. Therefore, we add high-current drive buffers to do the job.

We must be able to float the outputs of buffers used on the data bus so that they do not interfere with other activities on these lines. For example, we certainly don't want data bus buffer outputs enabled onto the bus during a write by some external device.

The middle third and the right third of Figure 7-4 show the timing of an odd-byte write and an even-byte write. These two show the same activity as the activity during a word-read cycle except for the $\overline{\text{UDS}}$, $\overline{\text{LDS}}$, and data lines. The $\overline{\text{LDS}}$ line is asserted during an odd-byte-read cycle and the $\overline{\text{UDS}}$ line is asserted during the even-byte-read cycle. The byte is read onto D0–D7 of the data bus during an odd-byte-read cycle and onto D8–D15 during an even-byte-read cycle.

68000 BUS ACTIVITIES DURING A WRITE MACHINE CYCLE

Now that we have analyzed the 68000 bus activities for a read machine cycle, let's take a look at the timing diagram for a write machine cycle. Figure 7-5 shows a flowchart of the activity flow during a byte-write cycle. Figure 7-6 shows the signal timing for word and byte writes. The two figures should look familiar to you because they are very similar to the read cycle figures (7-3 and 7-4).

Follow the discussion by referring to Figure 7-5. First, the bus master, the 68000 CPU in most cases, places the CPU function code onto lines FC0–FC2. In this case the function code lines will indicate a user data write or a supervisor data write. The CPU then places the desired write address onto the address bus (lines A1–A23) and asserts the address strobe ($\overline{\text{AS}}$). The R/$\overline{\text{W}}$ line is set to indicate a write (R negated, which is the same as W asserted, which is the same as $\overline{\text{W}}$ negated). The data is placed onto the data bus lines D0–D7 for a low-byte write (odd address) or lines D8–D15 for a high-byte write (even address). The appropriate data strobe is then asserted, $\overline{\text{UDS}}$ for the upper byte (even) and $\overline{\text{LDS}}$ for the lower byte (odd). The bus master (68000 CPU) then waits for the slave device (for example, the RAM). The slave decodes the address to be sure that it is the device being addressed. The data is stored from lines D0–D7 if $\overline{\text{LDS}}$ is asserted or from lines D8–D15 if $\overline{\text{UDS}}$ is asserted. Once the data has been saved in the RAM, $\overline{\text{DTACK}}$ is to acknowledge that the data byte has been written into the RAM (or other device). The CPU then negates $\overline{\text{UDS}}$ or $\overline{\text{LDS}}$, depending on which was used. The address strobe, $\overline{\text{AS}}$, is negated, the data is removed from the data bus, and the data bus drivers are floated. The CPU sets R/$\overline{\text{W}}$ to read. Finally, the device negates $\overline{\text{DTACK}}$, indicating that it has completed its operation and the machine cycle is completed.

Now follow along in the center of Figure 7-6. Let's assume that an odd-byte write is occurring, so we look at the middle group of states (S0–S7) in Figure 7-6.

During S0 of the write machine cycle, the 68000 asserts the function code lines, address lines, and the W line (i.e., negates R/$\overline{\text{W}}$). The address lines are stable by S1, as is $\overline{\text{W}}$. During S1, $\overline{\text{AS}}$ is asserted and stabilized by S2. During S2, the data is placed on the bus and the data is stabilized by S3. During S3, $\overline{\text{LDS}}$ is asserted, since we are looking at an odd-byte write. The data is

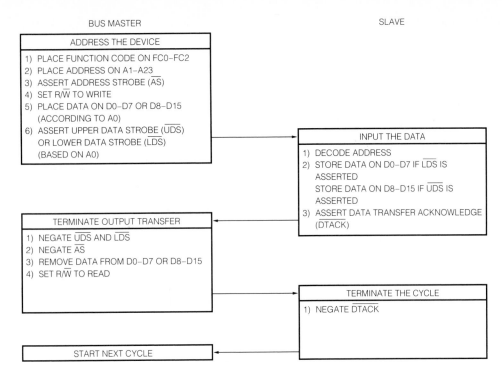

BUS MASTER

ADDRESS THE DEVICE
1) PLACE FUNCTION CODE ON FC0–FC2
2) PLACE ADDRESS ON A1–A23
3) ASSERT ADDRESS STROBE ($\overline{AS}$)
4) SET R/$\overline{W}$ TO WRITE
5) PLACE DATA ON D0–D7 OR D8–D15
   (ACCORDING TO A0)
6) ASSERT UPPER DATA STROBE ($\overline{UDS}$)
   OR LOWER DATA STROBE ($\overline{LDS}$)
   (BASED ON A0)

SLAVE

INPUT THE DATA
1) DECODE ADDRESS
2) STORE DATA ON D0–D7 IF $\overline{LDS}$ IS
   ASSERTED
   STORE DATA ON D8–D15 IF $\overline{UDS}$ IS
   ASSERTED
3) ASSERT DATA TRANSFER ACKNOWLEDGE
   ($\overline{DTACK}$)

TERMINATE OUTPUT TRANSFER
1) NEGATE $\overline{UDS}$ AND $\overline{LDS}$
2) NEGATE $\overline{AS}$
3) REMOVE DATA FROM D0–D7 OR D8–D15
4) SET R/$\overline{W}$ TO READ

TERMINATE THE CYCLE
1) NEGATE $\overline{DTACK}$

START NEXT CYCLE

FIGURE 7-5 68000-byte write-cycle flowchart. (*Reprinted with permission of Motorola Inc.*)

FIGURE 7-6 68000 word- and byte-write cycle timing diagram. (*Reprinted with permission of Motorola Inc.*)

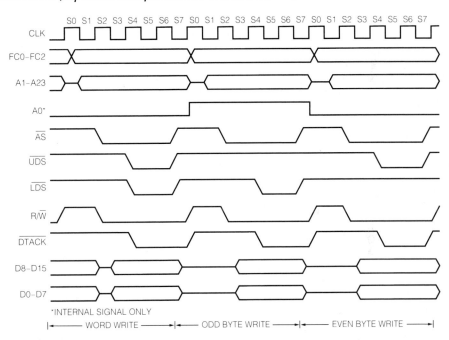

latched by the device (e.g., by the RAM) and $\overline{DTACK}$ is asserted during S3, stabilizing by S4. The CPU negates $\overline{AS}$ during S6 and negates $\overline{LDS}$ during S6. The device negates $\overline{DTACK}$ during S6; by S7 these control lines have stabilized and the machine cycle is complete. The bus is then ready to begin another machine cycle.

If the device is slow and requires several cycles to read the data bus, then wait states will be introduced between S3 and S4. The device will not assert $\overline{DTACK}$ during S4 but will wait until it has successfully latched the data before asserting $\overline{DTACK}$. The CPU will wait until $\overline{DTACK}$ is asserted before it begins the process of terminating the data transfer and removing the data

from the bus. Therefore, if we have a memory or port device which needs more time to absorb the data from the data bus, we can use some external hardware to hold off $\overline{DTACK}$ until the device has gotten the data off the data bus and saved it. Delaying $\overline{DTACK}$ will cause the 68000 to insert one or more WAIT states in the machine cycle, thus giving the addressed device more time to absorb the data.

Work your way across the timing diagrams for the read and write machine cycles in Figures 7-4 and 7-6 until you feel that you understand the sequence of activities that occur. Understanding them well will make later sections easier to understand.

68000 Bus Activities During a Read-Modify-Write Machine Cycle

The 68000 provides one more type of machine cycle, which combines the read and write cycles. This read-modify-write cycle is executed by the CPU as one indivisible operation that cannot be interrupted by external devices. This type of cycle is typically used for synchronizing multiple CPUs or for performing locking of a resource where the user wants access to the resource (e.g., a section of RAM) without any other user or device being able to access it. As was mentioned in the TAS instruction description, this indivisible operation helps support data base locking as well as multiple processor synchronization.

Figures 7-7 and 7-8 show the read-modify-write cycle, first in flowchart form and then in signal timing diagram form. Read through these two figures and notice that they are really a combination of the two cycles already discussed, the read and the write machine cycles. Notice that the read-modify-write cycle takes a minimum of 20 states (S0–S19) and may require more if a slow device and wait states are added.

ANALYZING A SMALL SYSTEM: THE URDA® MDS

The previous sections showed how a 68000 provides I/O pins, which are used as an address bus, a data bus,

and a control bus. A small number of other devices can be connected directly to these pins. As mentioned in the previous section, if we desire to connect more than a few devices to these buses, we must add bus drivers, separate chips with greater power capabilities than the CPU chip itself. In this major section of the chapter we discuss how the CPU lines can be connected with ROM, RAM, ports, and other devices to form a system. The system we use for this discussion is the *URDA Microprocessor Development System*, the *URDA P68000 Microlab®*, a 68000-based unit available from University Development and Research Associates suitable for building the prototypes of small microcomputer-based instruments.

Figure 7-9 shows a photograph of the URDA MDS board. From the photograph you can see that, in addition to the microcomputer ICs, the board has a hexadecimal keypad, some seven-segment displays, and a pair of 50-pin connectors for adding more ROM, RAM, ports, or other circuitry. A monitor program in ROM on the board allows you to enter, execute, and debug machine code programs using the onboard hex keypad or an external CRT terminal connected to the serial port on the board. The board comes with 4 Kbytes of RAM. The board also has two 8-bit parallel ports that you can program to be inputs or outputs. To get a better idea of the hardware functions on the board and the devices used to implement these functions, let's look at the detailed block diagram of the URDA MDS in Figure 7-10, p. 176.

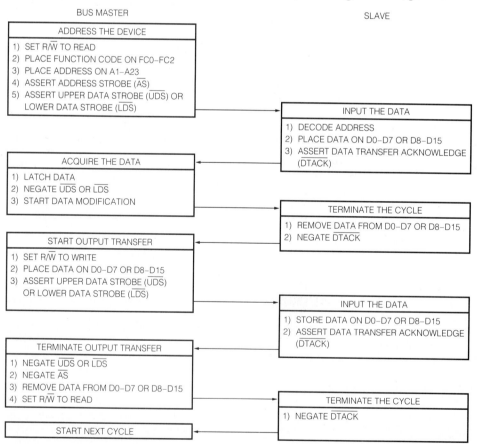

FIGURE 7-7 68000 read-modify-write cycle flowchart. (*Reprinted with permission of Motorola Inc.*)

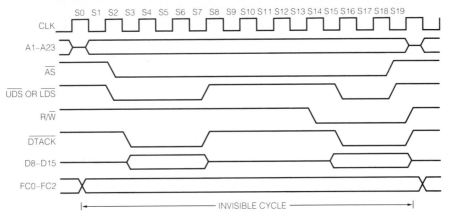

FIGURE 7-8   68000 read-modify-write cycle timing diagram. (*Reprinted with permission of Motorola Inc.*)

Whenever you are approaching a system that is new to you, it is a good idea to study the detailed block diagram of the system carefully before you start digging into the actual schematics. The schematics for even a small system such as this are sometimes spread over many pages. Without the overview that the block diagram gives, it is very difficult for you to see how all the schematic pieces fit together.

The first parts to look at in Figure 7-10 are the 68000 CPU and the *clock generator*. Note that the MDS has a 3.579545-MHz crystal connected to it. The crystal is connected to a 74LS14 IC, which is in turn connected to the 68000 CPU.

Notice also that there are no bus drivers or bus latches other than those on the CPU chip. The CPU chip itself can drive several other ICs to build a small system such as this. If we had a bigger system with more ICs, we might need to include separate, higher-power bus driver ICs. In this system the internal 68000 buses are actually the same "wires" as used on the main PC board external to the CPU IC itself. This makes the system very easy to deal with conceptually.

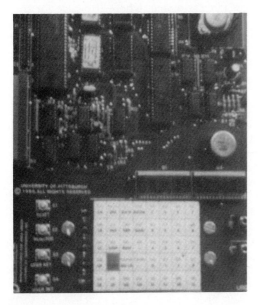

FIGURE 7-9   The URDA MDS.

There is no difference between the internal 68000 CPU buses and the external PC board-level buses. The 68000 CPU is by far the largest IC in physical dimensions, being more than 3 in. long and $\frac{3}{4}$ in. wide in its most common dual-in-line package (see Figure 7-1).

The RAMs and ROMs in the block diagram connect to all three buses and are each composed of two physical ICs. There may be more RAM and ROM ICs in more complex systems. The URDA MDS can have additional RAM added to it by means of an external PC board connected to the two connectors at the right side of the diagram. The two connectors in the block diagram represent a general ability to expand the MDS. URDA makes other add-on boards, including a serial interface and a floating-point coprocessor card. Most systems need a serial port so they can communicate with CRT terminals, MODEMS, PCs, and other devices that require data to be sent and received in serial form. The URDA MDS product family uses a Motorola MC68681 as a *serial port*. The 68681 is a type of USART, or *universal synchronous/asynchronous receiver transmitter*. Chapter 14 discusses the initialization and use of the 68681. For now, just think of this device as two registers. One is a shift register, which accepts a parallel byte you give it and sends it out, bit by bit, on a single data line. The other register is a control register, to which you send bytes of data to configure and command the USART. For example, to select the desired frequency from the available speeds, one sends the control register commands to select a specific *baud rate*, which is the way of specifying the rate at which data bits are shifted in or out of a serial device. Baud rate for a device such as the 68681 is defined as 1 over the time per bit (in seconds). If the time per bit is 3.33 ms, for example, then the baud rate is 300 baud. Common baud rates for serial data transmission are 300, 600, 1200, 2400, 9600, and 19,200.

The I/O ports on the URDA MDS are used to control the LED display and the keyboard. The URDA MDS *system port* is one of two I/O ports in the block diagram in Figure 7-10. The system port is used to control the display and the keyboard. On the URDA MDS, two PIAs (programmable interface adapters) at the top right give the system *programmable* parallel

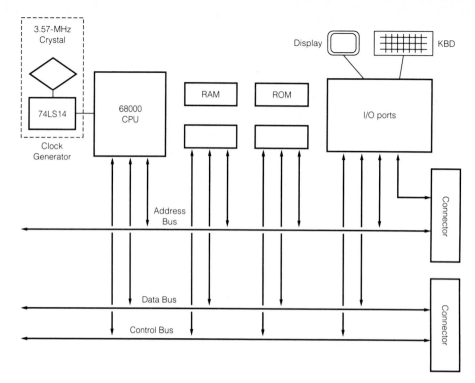

FIGURE 7-10   Basic 68000 system block diagram.

ports, one the system port and the other the user port. The term programmable in this case means that as part of your program, you can send the port a *control byte,* as described for the serial device. The user ports are for the experimenter to use in any way desired. On the upper right of the PC board itself are two 6821 PIAs, which act as the two primary I/O ports in the URDA MDS.

One of the most important things not shown in Figure 7-10 is exactly how all these devices are connected on the PC board itself. Which pins are connected by PC board traces to which other pins, and why? Figure 7-11, the schematic for the URDA MDS, answers the first part of the question. The schematic shows exactly which pins are to be connected. The ICs shown on the schematic are labeled to correspond to labeling on the PC board itself. Also, the schematic indicates the expected IC part numbers for most of the ICs. The schematic does not show exactly where the ICs are placed on the PC board. The actual location information is normally shown on a layout diagram, which shows exactly how the physical ICs are "laid out" on the PC board so that they can all be interconnected. Additionally, a loading diagram can be used to indicate how ICs are to be loaded into specific sets of holes or sockets on the PC board.

The second part of the question is much more difficult to explain. In the remainder of this and the next section we examine the question of why we should connect the system in a particular way.

Perhaps the first key piece of information needed in answering the question Why? is the expected placement of the various devices in the address space of the 68000 CPU. Recall that the address space on a 68000 is 16 Mbytes (or 8 megawords) and uses addresses 0 to $FFFFFF. Normally, ROMs are used in the lowest absolute addresses, starting at address 0, because the devices at the low 256 addresses must provide exception vectors and the power-on stack location for the 68000 CPU. ROMs are some of the most common and reliable devices that can be implemented by low-cost ROM ICs or by user-programmable EPROM or EEPROM ICs. Two EPROMs, 2732s, are used on the URDA MDS. They can be programmed to point back into the expected RAM address space, where the code for the actual exception handling and start-up routines would reside. The URDA 2732s are located at absolute addresses $000000 to $0001FFF, a range of 4 Kbytes. However, they are connected such that one of the 2-Kbyte 2732s hold all the upper (even) bytes and the other 2732 holds all the lower (odd) bytes. Since the 68000 has a 16-bit data bus, the two 8-bit EPROMs can work in parallel to provide all 16 bits of data as quickly as possible.

The URDA MDS does not use the upper 8 bits of the address bus. Address pins A16–A23 are not used. Therefore, we will normally use only 16 bits, or 4 hex digits, to describe URDA MDS addresses. Thus the EPROMs are said to be located at addresses $0000 to $1FFF.

The RAMs represent the changeable storage for the computer where programs will be placed and executed. The RAMs occupy addresses $4000 to $4FFF, 4 Kbytes of address space. In the URDA MDS, two 6116 ICs are used, each providing 2 Kbytes of RAM (16 Kbits). The RAMs are also used in pairs in a typical 68000 system

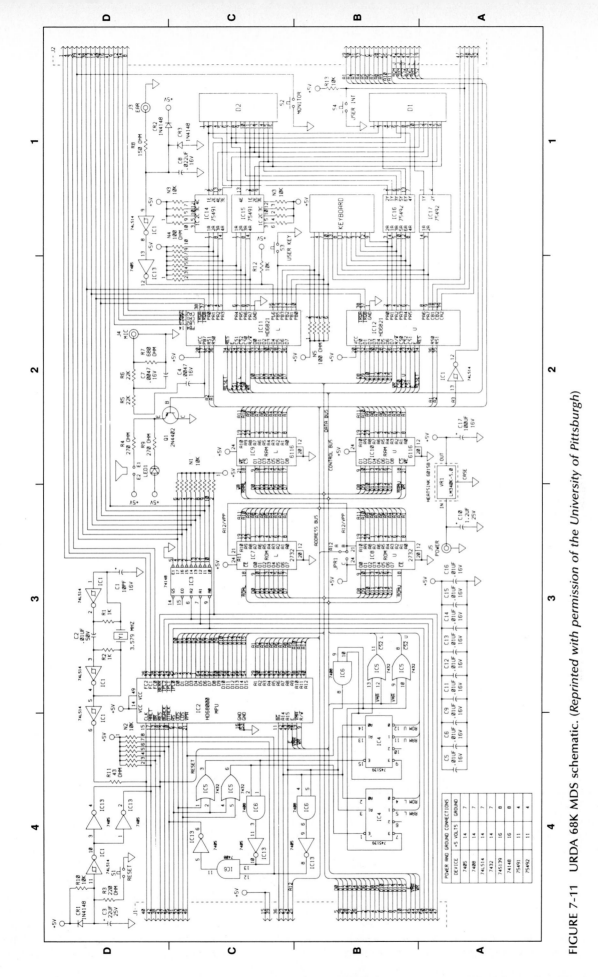

FIGURE 7-11 URDA 68K MDS schematic. (*Reprinted with permission of the University of Pittsburgh*)

so that they can operate in parallel and each provide 1 byte of a full word of data.

Finally, we have already mentioned the connectors on the right side of the block diagram in Figure 7-10. On the URDA MDS, there are actually only sets of posts to which a connector can be attached (i.e., the "male" portions of the connector pair). These connectors can be used for add-on boards from URDA or for experimentation by the owner or student.

A Look at the URDA MDS Schematic

Now that you have seen an overview of the URDA MDS, the next step is to take a close look at Figure 7-11, which shows the actual schematic for the board. At first this maze of lines may seem overwhelming to you, but if you use the *5-minute rule* and then approach the schematic one part at a time, you should have no trouble understanding it. The schematic simply shows greater detail for each of the parts of the block diagram that we discussed in the preceding sections of the chapter.

At this point we want to make clear that it is not the purpose of this chapter to make you an expert on the circuit connections of an URDA MDS board. We use parts of this schematic to demonstrate some major concepts such as address decoding and to show how the parts are connected together to form a small, but real, system. Even if you do not have an URDA MDS board, you can learn a great deal about how a 68000 system functions from these schematics. This schematic is actually quite simple as the industry goes. One often encounters multipage schematics, such as those typical for any PC or sophisticated microprocessor-based board or product.

Before getting started on the next major concept, we discuss some of the symbols used on most microprocessor system schematics. The first thing that we want to look at in the schematics is the numbers across the top and bottom and the letters along the sides. These are called *zone coordinates*. You use these coordinates to identify the location of a part or connection on the schematic just as you might use similar coordinates on a road map to help you locate Bowers Avenue.

For example, on the schematic find the CPU IC, which is in zone B3. To find the CPU IC, first move across the row of the schematic labeled B until you come to the column labeled 3. This zone is small enough that you should easily be able to find where the CPU IC is. It is the largest IC on the schematic and is labeled IC2, then MC68000, and then MPU (microprocessing unit). For practice, try finding the RAMs in zones B2 and B3 and the clock crystal in zone D2.

The next point to look at on the schematic is the numbers on the ICs. In addition to a part number such as MC68000, each IC has a number of the form ICn where n is a number. For example the CPU is labeled IC2. This second number is used to help locate the IC on the printed circuit board. The number is usually silk-screened on the board next to the corresponding

IC. Usually IC numbers are sequential and start from the upper left corner of the component side of a board. There may be several ROMs on the board, but only one will be labeled IC7. Notice that several logic gates on the board may have the same IC number, since often a single IC will provide more than one gate. For example, IC5 provides four NAND gates, two shown in zone B3 and two in zone C4.

Other devices often found on microprocessor boards are *resistor packs*. You can find an example in zone C4 of the schematic, labeled N2. As you can see from the schematic, this device contains seven 10-KΩ resistors. Resistor packs may physically be thin vertical, rectangular wafers, or they may be in packages similar to small ICs. The advantages of resistor packs are that they take up less PC board space and are easier to install than individual resistors. The function of this resistor pack connection is to assert the lines to which they are tied. For example, notice that $\overline{BGACK}$ is tied to +5 V through a resistor in the resistor pack. What this means is that $\overline{BGACK}$ is always asserted. The same is true for $\overline{RES}$, and the rest of the lines tied to the resistor pack without additional circuitry.

Some other symbols to look at in the schematics are the structures with labels such as J2 and P1. You can find examples of these in zones C7 and B7 of schematic sheet 1. These symbols are used to indicate *connectors*. The number in the rectangular box specifies the pin number on the connector to which a signal goes. The letter P stands for *plug*. A connector is considered a plug if it plugs into something else. In the case of the URDA MDS, the connector labeled P1 is the printed circuit board edge connector. The letter J next to a connector stands for *jack*. A connector is considered a jack if something else plugs into it. On the URDA MDS board, the jacks J1 and J2 are 50-pin connectors into which you can plug ribbon cable connectors. These jacks allow the address bus, data bus, control bus, and parallel ports to be connected to additional circuitry.

One more point to notice on the URDA MDS schematic is the capacitors on the power supply inputs shown in zone A3. As you can see there, the schematic shows a large number of 0.01-μF capacitors in parallel with a 1.2-μF capacitor. Most systems have *filtering* such as this on their power lines. You may wonder what is the use of putting all these small capacitors in parallel with one that is obviously many times larger. The point of this is that the large capacitor filters out, or *bypasses,* low-frequency noise on the power lines, and the small capacitors, spread around the board, bypass high-frequency noise on the power supply lines. Noise is produced on the power supply lines by devices switching from one logic state to another. If this noise is not filtered out with bypass capacitors, it may become large enough to disturb system operation.

Glance through the URDA MDS schematic to get an idea of where various parts are located and to see what additional information you can pick up from the notes on them. In the next section of this chapter we discuss how microcomputer systems address memory and ports. As part of the discussion, we cycle back to the schematic to see how the URDA MDS does it.

ADDRESSING MEMORY AND PORTS IN MICROCOMPUTER SYSTEMS

68000 Addressing and Address-decoding Concepts

While examining the block diagram of the URDA MDS board earlier in this chapter, we mentioned that a key to understanding the system interconnections is an understanding of the memory map, which shows to which memory addresses each device responds. The circuitry that implements the memory map performs *address decoding*. One function of the address-decoding interconnections is to produce a signal that enables the ROM, RAM, or port device that you want enabled for a particular address. A second, related function of an address decoder is to make sure that only one device at a time is enabled to put data on the data bus lines. If more than one IC tries to put data on the data bus at the same time, the result will almost always be garbage on the bus.

It seems that every microcomputer system does address decoding in a different way from every other system. Therefore, rather than memorizing the method used in one particular system, it is important that you understand the concept of address decoding. You can then figure out any system you have to work on.

68000 MEMORY BLOCKS

The 68000 memory and I/O address space form one huge linear list of addresses. In this address space certain address ranges will normally be reserved for RAM, certain address ranges will be for ROM, and certain address ranges will be for I/O ports. The block diagram of Figure 7-10 shows the RAM, ROM, and I/O ports connected in parallel to the three buses, but it does not show how the system prevents the RAM from operating at the same time as the ROM and the I/O ports. The signals that do this normally run in the control bus. These signals are generated by some address-decoding hardware, with one or more ICs connected to allow exactly one of the RAM, ROM, or I/O ports to operate at one time.

The address decoding hardware, the *decoder*, will normally use the CPU address lines to determine which of the memory or I/O devices to enable in a given cycle. The address the CPU puts on the address bus determines which device will be enabled. If the address is in the range reserved for ROM, then the ROM will be enabled by the address decoder, and the RAMs and I/O ports will be disabled. Similarly, if the address is one of those in the ROM's address space, the decoder will enable the ROM and not the RAM or the I/O ports. Each of these reserved address ranges is called a *memory block*, which is a block of consecutive addresses reserved for use by a particular type of device. On any given memory cycle, exactly one memory block will be enabled by the address decoder.

68000 MEMORY BANKS

The 68000 has a 24-bit address bus, so it can address 2^{24}, or 16,777,216, addresses. Each address repre-

sents a stored byte. As you know from previous chapters, when you write a word to memory with an instruction such as MOVE.W D0,($437A), the word is actually written into two consecutive memory addresses. The high byte of the word is written into the specified memory address, $437A, and the low byte of the word is written into the next higher address, $437B. To make it possible to read or write a word with one machine cycle, the memory for a 68000 is set up as two "banks" of up to 8,388,608 bytes each.

One memory bank contains all the bytes with even addresses such as 00000, 00002, and 00004. The data lines of this bank are connected to the lower eight data lines, D0–D7, of the 68000. The other memory bank contains all the bytes that have odd addresses, such as 00001, 00003, and 00005. The data lines of this bank are connected to the upper eight data lines, D8–D15, of the 68000. Address line A0 is used as part of the enabling for memory devices in the banks. On a 68000, address line A0 is encoded using the upper and lower data strobe lines, $\overline{UDS}$ and $\overline{LDS}$. A memory device in the lower bank will be enabled when $\overline{LDS}$ is asserted, as it will for any even address. A device in the high bank will be enabled when $\overline{UDS}$ is asserted, as it is for any odd address. Address lines A1–A23 are used to select the desired memory device in the bank and address the desired byte in that device. On word operations both $\overline{UDS}$ and $\overline{LDS}$ are asserted.

If you read a byte from or write a byte to an even address, such as $00000, A0 will be asserted low, $\overline{LDS}$ will be asserted low, and $\overline{UDS}$ will not be asserted. The lower bank will be enabled and the upper bank will be disabled. A byte will be transferred to or from the addressed location in the low bank on D0–D7. For an instruction such as MOVE.B D0,(0000), the 68000 will automatically transfer the byte of data from the lower data bus lines to the low byte of register D0. You just write the instruction and the 68000 takes care of getting the data in the right place.

Now, if you read a word from memory into D0 and you use an instruction such as MOVE.W D0,(0000) to read a word from memory into D0, both $\overline{UDS}$ and $\overline{LDS}$ will be asserted low. Therefore, both banks will be enabled. The high byte of the word will be transferred from address $00000 to the 68000 on D0–D7. The low byte of the word will be transferred from address $00001 to the 68000 on D8–D15. Remember, the 68000 memory is set up in banks so that words, which have their high byte at an even address, can be transferred to or from the 68000 in one bus cycle. On the 68000, word memory references must be word-aligned. That is, the addresses used in word memory references must be even. If they are not, a CPU exception will be generated and the CPU will call the address error exception–handling routine. When programming a 68000, then, it is important to start an array of data words on an even address. If you are using the Raven® PC cross assembler, the EVEN directive is used to do this. If you are using the Macintosh® Consulair® assembler, the .ALIGN directive is used to do this.

When you use an instruction such as MOVE.B D0,(1) to access just a byte at an odd address, A0 will be high,

$\overline{UDS}$ will be asserted low, and $\overline{LDS}$ will not be asserted. Therefore, the low bank will be disabled, and the high bank will be enabled. The byte will be transferred from memory address $00001 in the high bank to the 68000 on lines D8–D15. The 68000 will automatically transfer the byte of data from the higher eight data lines to the low byte of register D0. Note that address $00001 is actually the first location in the upper bank.

A memory bank is a collection of one or more ICs that can be enabled at the same time as other banks of memory. Think of the two 68000 banks as the banks of a river: You can fish from one side or the other side or even (if there are two of you) both sides at the same time. A *memory block*, on the other hand, is a collection of consecutive addresses that must be enabled to the exclusion of other memory blocks. The RAMs cannot be enabled at the same time as the ROMs or the I/O ports; they are all in different memory blocks.

ROM ADDRESS DECODING

Now that you have an overview of address decoding and of the 68000 memory banks, let's look at some examples of how all this might be put together in a small system. The URDA MDS schematic in Figure 7-11 shows the circuit connections for the EPROMs and EPROM decoder. The 2732 EPROMs shown in zones B3 and C3 are 4K × 8 devices. One of the EPROMs has its eight data outputs connected in parallel to system data lines D0–D7. This EPROM gives 4 Kbytes of storage in the lower memory bank. The other EPROM has its data outputs connected in parallel on system data lines D8–D15 to give 4 Kbytes of storage in the upper bank of ROM. Twelve address lines are needed to address the 4 Kbytes in each device. Therefore, system address lines A1–A12 are connected to each EPROM. Remember that we can't use A0 for this because, as we described in the last section, it is used in enabling the lower bank.

The URDA address decoder is 74LS139-based (see zone B4). The 74LS139 decoder output is connected to the 2732 chip enable input. This allows the decoder to enable or disable the EPROMs. The output labeled 0 inside the IC box is also labeled $\overline{ROM}$ U or $\overline{ROM}$ L outside the box. Further notice that the $\overline{ROM}$ U and $\overline{ROM}$ L lines are connected to the 2732 EPROMs' chip enable ($\overline{CE}$) input. What this implies is that the ROMs will be in memory block 0.

RAM ADDRESS DECODING

To give you another example of memory address decoding, we now discuss briefly the RAM decoding of the URDA MDS board. The URDA MDS schematic in Figure 7-11 shows the circuit for the system RAM (in B2 and C2) and RAM decoder (in B4). Let's look at this schematic to see what we can learn from it.

First, look at the input and output lines on the 6116 static RAM devices. From the fact that each device has eight data lines, you can conclude that the devices store bytes. The fact that each device has 11 address inputs, A1–A11, indicates that each one stores 2^{11}, or 2048, bytes. To store words, two 6116s are enabled in parallel. Each 6116 represents one memory bank. The enable inputs to the RAMs are connected to the decoder output lines labeled 1, so they are in memory block 1. The labels 5 and 11 on the $\overline{RAM}$ U and $\overline{RAM}$ L lines are IC pin numbers, not function labels. The 1 label inside the IC box indicates the function.

URDA MDS PORT ADDRESSING AND PORT DECODING

In a previous chapter we described *memory-mapped input/output*. In a system with memory-mapped I/O, port devices are accessed in exactly the same manner as memory devices such as RAM and ROM. The system normally determines how an I/O port is addressed and selected using address decoders as if they were memory devices. The main advantage of memory-mapped I/O is that any instruction that refers to memory can theoretically be used to read from or write to a port. The single instruction ADD.B D0,($1209) could be used to read a byte from a port and add the byte read in to register D0. The disadvantage of memory-mapped I/O is that the ports occupy part of the system memory space. This space is then not available for storing data or instructions.

The URDA MDS uses 6821s as I/O ports. These are enabled and disabled using connections similar to those described for the RAMs and ROMs. Take a look now at the 74LS139-based address decoder to see if you can determine what conditions might enable the I/O port 6821s. Things are a bit more complex because the CPU $\overline{VPA}$ (valid peripheral address) line is gated with the decoder output to create the 6821 enable inputs ($\overline{CS2}$ U and $\overline{CS2}$ L).

Address Decoding in the URDA MDS

In this section we look in more detail at the URDA MDS decoding circuitry, how it operates, and how it creates the memory blocks and banks described before.

As mentioned already, the URDA MDS uses a 74LS139 decoder as the basis for building its memory blocks and banks. The 74LS139 provides two 1-of-4 decoders. The URDA MDS uses these two decoders to perform address decoding for each of the two memory banks. Each of the two decoders is used to separate the address space into four memory blocks, one for RAM, one for ROM, one for I/O ports, and one for future expansion. Note that the 74LS139 decoder has one unused output, which can be used as part of the enabling for devices added to the system by add-on boards from URDA or built by the experimenter during prototyping.

THE URDA SYSTEM ROM DECODER

To start, look at Figure 7-12. This figure shows how two EPROMs can be connected in parallel on a common address bus and common data bus. From just looking at the schematic you can see that these EPROMs output bytes of data because each has eight outputs connected to the system data bus. The number of address lines connected to each device gives you an

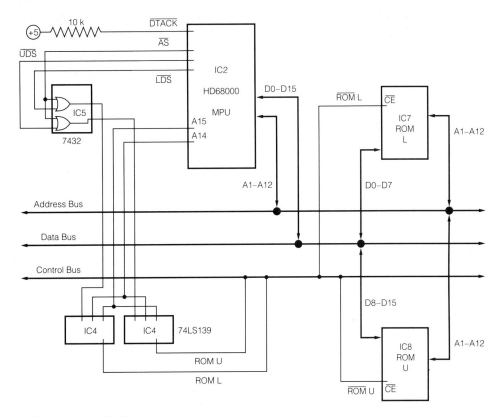

FIGURE 7-12 Parallel ROMs with decoder.

indication of how many bytes are stored in it. Each EPROM has 12 address lines (A1–A12) connected to it. Therefore, the number of bytes stored in the device is 2^{12}, or 4096. If you have trouble with this, think of how many bits a counter must have to count the 4096 states from 0 to 4095 decimal, or $0000 to $3FFF.

Note that each 2732 in Figure 7-12 has a chip select ($\overline{CS}$) input. When this input is asserted low, the addressed byte in a device will be output on the data bus. To get meaningful data from the EPROMs, we need to make sure that the $\overline{CS}$ input of only one device at a time is low. In the circuit in Figure 7-12, this is done by the 74LS139.

The 74LS139 contains two 1-of-4 decoders. These are shown in separate boxes in Figure 7-12 even though the actual IC uses only one package. The two boxes representing the two decoders are distinguished from each other by the pin numbers written on the schematic. If the first decoder in the 74LS139 is enabled asserting its enable input ($\overline{E}$), then only one output of the decoder will be asserted at a time. The output that will be asserted is determined by the 2-bit address applied to the A1 and A0 select inputs. For example, if the address is 00, then the 0 output will be asserted, and all the other outputs will be high. If the address is 10, then only the 2 output will be asserted.

Examining the line connected to the enable input should reveal that the input is connected to the output of an OR gate (in a 7432 IC), which combines the $\overline{LDS}$ (lower data strobe) and $\overline{AS}$ (address strobe) control lines coming out of the 68000 MPU. Thus, the decoder

is enabled when the address strobe and the lower data strobe are both asserted. Hence, this decoder is used to enable the lower byte ROM. The upper bytes of ROM are enabled by a decoder whose $\overline{E}$ input is connected to the AND combination of $\overline{AS}$ and $\overline{UDS}$ (the upper data strobe).

To determine the addresses of ROMs, RAMs, and ports in a system, a good approach in many cases is to use a worksheet such as that in Figure 7-13, p. 182. To make one of these worksheets, write the address bits and the binary weight of each address bit across the top of the paper, as shown in the figure. To make it easier to convert binary addresses to hex, it helps if you mark off the address lines in groups of four, as shown. Next, draw vertical lines that mark off the two address lines that connect to the decoder-select inputs (A0 and A1). For the decoding shown in Figure 7-12, address lines A15 and A14 are connected to the A1 and A0 inputs of the decoder, respectively, so mark off columns A15 and A14. Since we are using A15 and A14 only to decode for the EPROMs, we show the four possible combinations of these 2 bits as the four possible *memory blocks*.

Now, under each address bit write the logic level that must be on that line to address the first location in the first EPROM. To address the first location in any of the EPROMs, the A1 through A12 address lines must all be low, so put a 0 under each of these address bits on the worksheet. To enable the EPROM 0, the select inputs of the decoder must be all 0s. Since address lines A15 and A14 are connected to the inputs of the decoder and

Block		Hex Digit				Hex Digit				Hex Digit				Hex Digit			
		2^{16} A15	2^{14} A14	2^{13} A13	2^{12} A12	2^{11} A11	2^{10} A10	2^9 A9	2^8 A8	2^7 A7	2^6 A6	2^5 A5	2^4 A4	2^3 A3	2^2 A2	2^1 A1	2^0 A0
1	Start	0	0	0	0	0	0	0	0	0	0	0	0	0	0	0	0
	End	0	0	1	1	1	1	1	1	1	1	1	1	1	1	1	1
2	Start																
	End																
3	Start																
	End																
4	Start																
	End																

FIGURE 7-13 Address decoder worksheet showing address decoding for two 2732s in Figure 7-12.

the EPROM-enable input is connected to output line 0, the EPROM will be enabled only when both A15 and A14 are 0. Write 0s under address bits A15 and A14. We are left with A13 and A0 not yet filled in.

A0 tells whether a byte is even or odd. In terms of memory organized into words, A0 determines whether the byte is a low byte or a high byte. Notice that the $\overline{UDS}$ and $\overline{LDS}$ lines from the CPU are used in conjunction with the $\overline{AS}$ line to enable the EPROM decoders. The $\overline{UDS}$ and $\overline{LDS}$ lines encode the value of A0. So, if $\overline{UDS}$ is asserted, then the "high" decoder will be enabled, which will, in turn, enable the *high*-byte EPROM. If both $\overline{UDS}$ and $\overline{LDS}$ are asserted (a full word operation), then both decoders will be enabled and both EPROMs will, in turn, be enabled. If only $\overline{LDS}$ is asserted, then only the *low*-byte EPROM will be enabled. For our address decoder worksheet, we will consider the two EPROMs to be in one memory block, since they both work in lockstep providing alternate bytes in memory—one the high bytes and one the low bytes. Notice, finally that data lines D0 to D7 come from the low-byte EPROM and data lines D8 to D15 come from the high-byte EPROM.

A13 is not used in connection with the EPROMs. What this means is that the EPROMs will be addressed when A13 is a 0 and when it is a 1. What this has the effect of doing is duplicating the ROM address space, with one copy occurring where A13 is 0 and the other where A13 is a 1. The 2732 bits are used twice and can be accessed with an A13 value of either 1 or 0. Looking at the completed worksheet, then, the 2732 EPROMs are said to be *overlapped*, occupying both the space $0000 to $1FFF and the space $2000 to $3FFF.

2764 EPROMs provide 8 Kbytes each of memory (64 Kbits) instead of the 4 Kbytes (32 Kbits) that 2732s provide. If the system used 2764 EPROMs instead of 2732 EPROMs, then A13 would be an input to the EPROMs and there would not be this duplication of EPROM memory space.

You can now read the starting address of EPROMs directly from the worksheet as $0000. The highest address in the EPROMs is that address where A0–A13

are all 1s. If you put a 1 under each of these bits, as shown on the worksheet, you can see that the ending address for the EPROMs is $3FFF. Remember that A15 and A14 have to be low to select the EPROMs. A15 has to be low to enable the decoder. The address range of EPROM 0 is said to be $0000 to $3FFF, a 16-Kbyte block. Draw a horizontal line below the highest EPROM address, $3FFF, to indicate the end of the EPROM memory block. We explain shortly why the RAMs are shown in the second memory block.

These EPROMs are put at the low address in memory on the URDA MDS board because, after a RESET, the 68000 goes to address $0000 to get the address of its first instruction. Since we want the URDA MDS to execute its monitor program after we press the RESET button, we put the address of the monitor routine in location $0000 of the EPROM. We also normally put the monitor routine itself in EPROM.

Some people like to think of address lines A14 and A15 as "counting off" 16-Kbyte blocks of memory. If you think of the address lines as the outputs of a 16-bit counter, you can see how this works. The end address for each EPROM has all 1s in address bits A1–A13. When you increment the address to access the next byte in memory, these bits all go to 0, and a 1 rolls over into bits A14 and A15. This increments the count in these 3 bits by 1 and enables the next highest 16-Kbyte memory block. The count in these bits goes from binary 00 to 11.

THE URDA SYSTEM RAM DECODER

The system in Figure 7-7 contains only ROM. In most systems we want to have ROM, RAM, and ports. To give you more practice with basic address decoding, we will now show you how the same decoders work with the RAM in the system.

Suppose that we want to add two 2K × 8 RAMs to the system, and we want the first RAM to start at address $4000, just above the EPROMs, which end at address $3FFF. The URDA board uses 6116 static RAMs. The R/$\overline{W}$ line from the 68000 will be connected to the *write enable* ($\overline{WE}$) input of the 6116s to tell the RAMs whether a read or a write is occurring. The 6116s have one *chip enable* input ($\overline{CE}$), which will be connected in some fashion to the address decoder. Let's look more closely at how the address decoder is connected and why.

To start, use another worksheet (as in Figure 7-14), just like the one of Figure 7-13. Addressing one of the 2048 bytes (2^{11}) in each RAM requires 11 address lines, A1–A11. These lines will be connected directly to each RAM. Since we are decoding using address lines A14 and A15, we can use the same 74LS139 as we used for the EPROMs. You may ask how we decided to use A15 and A14 as the basis for partitioning memory into blocks. In general, this is a matter of tuning for the particular system the designer has in mind. By using A15 and A14, we get 16-Kbyte memory blocks, which the URDA MDS designers felt would be enough EPROM and RAM as a maximum allowed in the base system. Having made this decision, the connection scheme can be based on A15 and A14. The RAM chip enable inputs are connected to the A1 output of the 74LS139 decoder. This means that the RAMs can be enabled only when A15 and A14 are binary 01. On the next available line of the worksheet, write 0 and 1 as the values of bits A15 and A14, respectively, if the RAMs are to be accessed.

As with the EPROM lines, the first location of the RAMs will be accessed when A1–A11 are all 0s, and the last location will be accessed when A1–A11 are all 1s. Also, as with the EPROMs, the A0 bit is encoded on $\overline{UDS}$ and $\overline{LDS}$. Both byte-wide RAM ICs will operate when a word operation occurs, and only one will operate for a byte operation. We will consider the two RAMs to be in the same memory block because they provide alternate bytes in memory, as did the EPROMs. The first byte will come from the low EPROM when A0 is 0 and the last will come from the high EPROM when A0 is 1. Finally, notice that from the RAM's viewpoint, both A12 and A13 are not used. This means that the RAMs will be enabled for all combinations of A12 and A13—that is, for binary 00, 01, 10, and 11. Using 16-Kbit (2-Kbyte) RAMs, the RAM memory space is overlapped four times. This is often called "folding"

the memory space into four copies at $4000–$4FFF, $5000–$5FFF, $6000–$6FFF, and $7000–$7FFF. A reference to the address $410C will be the same as a reference to $510C, to $610C, and to $710C. This is actually fairly wasteful of the memory address space, but it makes address decoding much simpler. After filling in A12 and A13 as 00 for the low address and 11 for the high address, you will be able to read the address of the RAM memory block directly from the worksheet of Figure 7-14. The RAM is at memory addresses $4000 to $7FFF.

If you apply the read or write timing signal analysis to the connections of Figure 7-12, you will notice that $\overline{DTACK}$ is always asserted. This avoids requiring any sophisticated timing circuitry to assert it. However, this implies that the RAMs and ROMs must always have data ready as soon as the MPU is ready to accept it. In effect, the system will be running synchronously at full speed.

A System Port Decoder

The URDA MDS uses 6821 ICs as system and user I/O ports. These ports contain data bits that can be used either to control peripheral devices or to read data from peripheral devices. The 6821 is a peripheral interface adapter that contains buffers, I/O bus drivers, and control circuitry. Figure 7-15, p. 184, shows a block diagram of the internal structure of a 6821. The device provides two 8-bit-wide bidirectional I/O ports along with control circuitry to cause system interrupts. Interrupt circuitry is discussed in the next chapter.

Figure 7-16, p. 185, shows how two 6821s are connected to the system in the URDA MDS using the same 74LS139 that provides address decoding for the ROMs and RAMs. The chip select control line ($\overline{CS2}$) is tied to the third output of the two address-decoding 74LS139s. Recall that A15 and A14 are used as inputs to the decoders. Therefore, the 6821 PIAs will be selected only when A15 and A14 are both 1s (i.e., when A15 and A14 are binary 11, which equals 3 decimal). The other chip select lines, CS0 and CS1, are

Block		Hex Digit				Hex Digit				Hex Digit				Hex Digit			
		2^{15}	2^{14}	2^{13}	2^{12}	2^{11}	2^{10}	2^9	2^8	2^7	2^6	2^5	2^4	2^3	2^2	2^1	2^0
		A15	A14	A13	A12	A11	A10	A9	A8	A7	A6	A5	A4	A3	A2	A1	A0
1	Start	0	0	0	0	0	0	0	0	0	0	0	0	0	0	0	0
	End	0	0	1	1	1	1	1	1	1	1	1	1	1	1	1	1
2	Start	0	1	0	0	0	0	0	0	0	0	0	0	0	0	0	0
	End	0	1	1	1	1	1	1	1	1	1	1	1	1	1	1	1
3	Start																
	End																
4	Start																
	End																

FIGURE 7-14   Address decoder worksheet for two 2-Kbyte RAMs starting at address $4000.

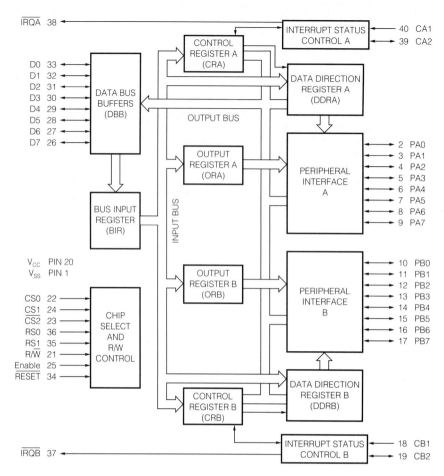

FIGURE 7-15 MC6821 internal block diagram. (*From Motorola Inc. datasheet*)

tied high so that they are always asserted. Figure 7-17 shows the entire URDA memory map as a collection of the EPROM, RAM, and I/O port memory blocks. A memory map such as the one in Figure 7-17 is a convenient way to summarize where each device is located in the system address space.

Figure 7-18, p. 186, shows an address decoder worksheet for the I/O ports similar to those for the EPROMs (Figure 7-13) and RAMs (Figure 7-14). Address bits A15 and A14 must both be 1s to assert decoder line 3 and enable the I/O port PIAs. Fill in 1s in the columns for A15 and A14. Examine Figure 7-16 and notice that the only other address lines connected to the PIAs are A2 and A1. Further notice that A2 and A1 are connected to the register select lines of the PIAs (RS1 and RS0). Table 7-4, p. 185, shows which PIA register is selected by each combination of register select lines. If both A2 and A1 are 0s when RS1 and RS0 are 0s, then peripheral register A or data direction register A will be selected. The data register will be selected if bit 2 of control register A is 0; otherwise the peripheral register will be set. If A2 and A1 are binary 01, then control register A will be selected. If A2 and A1 are 11, then control register B will be selected. If A2 and A1 are 10, then RS1 and RS0 will be 10 and either the data direction register or the peripheral data register will be selected, depending on the value of bit 2 of control

register B. Table 7-1 shows why the particular I/O port initialization used in previous chapters' examples works.

Completing the worksheet of Figure 7-18, for address lines A2 and A1 fill in 0s for the low address of the I/O memory block and 1s for the high address. Address line A0 is used implicitly, as with the ROM and RAM decoding, because $\overline{\text{UDS}}$ and $\overline{\text{LDS}}$ are used to enable the decoders. The low-byte decoder enables the low PIA and the high-byte decoder enables the high PIA. The two PIAs can also be used in parallel, as can the RAMs and ROMs. This style of connection means that all even addresses refer to one PIA (the high one) and all odd addresses all refer to the other PIA (the low one).

The remaining address lines, A3–A13, are not connected during I/O space decoding. The values used on these lines do not matter. They can be either 0s or 1s and have the same effect. For example, to access the control register for the upper PIA port A, the address $C012 could be used as well as $DF12 or $DF12. Fill in 0s for the low address used to access the PIAs and 1s for the highest address. Keep in mind that the PIA memory map will be folded over throughout this space.

The 6821 connection also involved using the special capabilities of the 6800 to provide MC6800 peripheral control using the valid peripheral address ($\overline{\text{VPA}}$) and valid memory address ($\overline{\text{VMA}}$) lines instead of the normal $\overline{\text{DTACK}}$. The $\overline{\text{VPA}}$ input to the 68000 is asserted

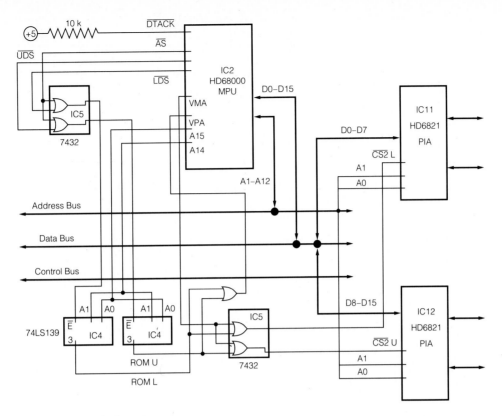

FIGURE 7-16   Parallel ports with decoder.

FIGURE 7-17   Memory map for URDA MDS board.

BLOCK		HEX ADDRESS	Block FUNCTION
1	START	$0000	ROM
	END	$3FFF	
2	START	$4000	RAM
	END	$7FFF	
3	START	$8000	(not used)
	END	$BFFF	
4	START	$C000	I/O ports
	END	$FFFF	

TABLE 7-4
6821 INTERNAL ADDRESSING
(From Motorola Inc. datasheet)

RS1	RS0	Control Register Bit		Location Selected
		CRA-2	CRB-2	
0	0	1	X	Peripheral Register A
0	0	0	X	Data Direction Register A
0	1	X	X	Control Register A
1	0	X	1	Peripheral Register B
1	0	X	0	Data Direction Register B
1	1	X	X	Control Register B

X = Don't Care

Block		Hex Digit				Hex Digit				Hex Digit				Hex Digit			
		2^{15} A15	2^{14} A14	2^{13} A13	2^{12} A12	2^{11} A11	2^{10} A10	2^{9} A9	2^{8} A8	2^{7} A7	2^{6} A6	2^{5} A5	2^{4} A4	2^{3} A3	2^{2} A2	2^{1} A1	2^{0} A0
1	Start	0	0	0	0	0	0	0	0	0	0	0	0	0	0	0	0
	End	0	0	1	1	1	1	1	1	1	1	1	1	1	1	1	1
2	Start	0	1	0	0	0	0	0	0	0	0	0	0	0	0	0	0
	End	0	1	1	1	1	1	1	1	1	1	1	1	1	1	1	1
3	Start																
	End																
4	Start	1	1	0	0	0	0	0	0	0	0	0	0	0	0	0	0
	End	1	1	1	1	1	1	1	1	1	1	1	1	1	1	1	1

FIGURE 7-18   Address decoder worksheet for two MC6821 PIAs.

whenever A15 and A14 are both 1s—in other words, whenever an I/O port memory reference is made. The CPU then uses $\overline{VMA}$ to control timing for synchronous MC6800 family devices such as the MC6821. $\overline{VMA}$ is used in conjunction with the 74LS139 decoder output 3 to enable the PIA ICs.

Recall that a decoder that translates memory addresses to chip select signals for port devices is called *memory-mapped I/O*. In this system a port will be written to or read from in the same way as any other memory location. The advantage of memory-mapped I/O is that any instruction that references memory can be used to input data from or output data to ports. In a system such as this, for example, the single instruction ADD.B D0,($C014) could be used to input a byte of data from the port at address $C014 and add the byte to register D0. The disadvantage of memory-mapped I/O is that some of the system memory address space is used up for ports and is therefore not available for memory.

You can use memory-mapped I/O with any microprocessor, but some microprocessors—such as those of the Intel 8086 family—allow you to set up separate address spaces for input ports and for output ports. You access ports in these separate address spaces directly with the IN and OUT instructions. Having separate address spaces for input and output ports is called *direct I/O*. The advantage of direct I/O is that none of the system memory space is used for ports. The disadvantage is that only the specialized IN and OUT instructions can be used to input or output data. Since 68000 family processors all use memory-mapped I/O, we do not mention direct I/O again.

Notice that in several of the preceding discussions we indicated that some address lines were not used. This is sometimes called *incomplete decoding*. In contrast, URDA could have built a system using *complete decoding*, in which all the address lines played a part in selecting a device and one of its internal ports or registers. Complete decoding often creates a system with better expansion capabilities because more smaller memory blocks are provided. In a completely decoded system each memory block is fully used or is available for future use.

Using incomplete decoding as we have, there are few memory blocks and each memory block is consumed, even though the entire block may not have been needed. Remember that two 6116 RAMs required only 4 Kbytes of address space, but we gave them 16 Kbytes and simply wasted 12 Kbytes as additional addresses to which the RAMs respond. The RAM memory space of 16 Kbytes was folded into four identical 4-Kbyte chunks. Incomplete decoding is, however, the easiest to implement in real hardware. On the URDA MDS we did not have to connect A13 to the RAM, ROM, I/O ports, or to the address decoder. This saves expense and time in construction of the URDA MDS and dollars in its cost to the student.

How the 68008 Microprocessor Accesses Memory and Ports

Now that we have shown in detail how the 68000 accesses memory and port devices, we can show you how the 68008 does it.

The instruction set of the 68008 is identical to that of the 68000, and the registers of the two are the same. There are two major differences between the two devices. First, the 68008 provides only 20 address lines, whereas the 68000 provides 24 lines. Thus the 68008 can address only 2^{20}, or 1,048,576, bytes. Second, and most important, the 68008 memory is not divided into two banks as the 68000 memory is. The 68008 has only an 8-bit data bus, D0–D7. All the memory devices and ports in a 68008 system are connected onto these eight lines. The 68008 memory then functions as a single bank of up to 1,048,576 bytes. Figure 7-19 shows this structure. This single-bank structure means that a 68008 cannot read a word from or write a word to memory in one machine cycle, as the 68000 can. The 68008 can read or write only bytes, so the 68008 must always do two machine cycles to read or write a word. Address lines A0–A19 are used with some decoders to select a desired byte in memory.

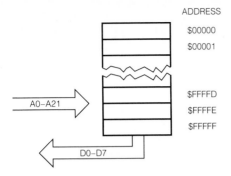

ADDRESS

$00000
$00001

A0–A21

$FFFFD
$FFFFE
$FFFFF

D0–D7

FIGURE 7-19   68008 memory structure.

Because the 68008 is designed around an 8-bit data bus, it does not need to distinguish between upper and lower data bytes. The 68008 does not use $\overline{UDS}$ and $\overline{LDS}$, but rather provides an A0 pin and a single data strobe line ($\overline{DS}$).

The 68008 was created primarily to accommodate simpler, smaller designs where multiple memory banks, a 16-bit data bus, or large memories are not required. Most of the currently available memory devices and I/O devices are designed for 8-bit microprocessors, which have 8-bit data buses. The 68008 was designed with an 8-bit data bus so that it would interface more easily with 8-bit memory devices and I/O devices.

68000 TIMING PARAMETERS

In previous sections of this chapter we used generalized timing waveforms such as that in Figure 7-4. These diagrams are sufficient to show the sequence of activities on the 68000 buses. However, they are not detailed enough to determine, for example, whether a memory device is fast enough to work in a given 68000 system. To allow you to make precise timing calculations, manufacturer's data books give detailed timing waveforms and the lists of timing parameters for each microprocessor. Complete timing information for the 68000 is contained in the data sheet in the appendix. Figures 7-20a and 7-21, pp. 188 and 190, respectively, show some of these for the 68000.

As you look at Figure 7-20a, remember the 5-minute rule. Most of the time there are only a very few of these parameters that you need to worry about. In most systems, for example, you don't need to worry about the clock signal parameters, because a 74LS14 hex inverted with Schmidt trigger inputs and a crystal will be used to produce the clock signal. The Schmidt trigger inputs of the 74LS14 transform the crystal output into a clean clock signal.

The edges of the clock signal cause operations in the 68000 to occur; therefore, as you can see in Figure 7-20, the clock waveform is used as a reference for other times. The timing values for when the 68000 puts out $R/\overline{W}$ addresses, function codes, and control signals, for example, are all specified with reference to

an appropriate clock edge.

As we mentioned earlier, one of the main things for which you use these diagrams and parameters is to find out whether a particular memory or port device is fast enough to work in a system with a given clock frequency. Here's an example of how you do this.

First, you look up the access times for the 2732 EPROM in the appropriate data book. According to an Intel data book, the 2732 has a maximum address to output access time, t_{ACC}, of 450 ns. This means that if the 2732 is already enabled and its output buffers turned on, it will put valid data on its outputs no more than 450 ns after an address is applied to the address inputs. The 2732 data sheet also gives a chip enable to output access time, t_{CE}, of 450 ns. This means that if an address is already present on the address inputs of the 2732 and the output buffers are already enabled, the 2732 will put valid data on its outputs no later than 450 ns after the $\overline{CE}$ input is asserted low. A third parameter given for the 2732 in the data book is an output enable to output time, t_{OE}, of 120 ns maximum. This means that if the device already has an address on its address inputs and its $\overline{CE}$ input is already asserted, valid data will appear on the output pins at most 120 ns after the $\overline{OE}$ pin is asserted low.

Now that you have these three parameters for the 2732, the next step is to check if each one of these times is short enough for the device to work with a 3.579-MHz 68000. In other words, does the 2732 put out valid data soon enough after it is addressed and enabled to satisfy the requirements of the 68000? Or do we need to hook up some delay circuitry to $\overline{DTACK}$ to cause the CPU to insert wait states during EPROM access? To determine this you need to look at both the 68000 timing parameters and how the 2732 is addressed and enabled on the URDA MDS board. Notice that the upper right corner of Figure 7-20 and times 1–5 characterize the clock and its component times.

To make it easier for you to find the important parameters for these calculations, in Figure 7-20b, p. 189, we show a simplified version of the timing diagram of Figure 7-20a. You should try to do this simplification mentally whenever you are faced with a complex timing diagram. Remove or ignore the lines and times that will not be used. As shown by the timing diagram in Figure 7-20b, the 68000 sends out $\overline{AS}$, $\overline{UDS}$, and/or $\overline{LDS}$ and an address during S0 and S1 of the machine cycle. Note on the A0–A23 lines of the timing diagram that the 68000 outputs this information within a time labeled "6" after the falling edge of the clock at the start of S1. Figure 7-22, pp. 191–92, shows that time 6 is the time for t_{CLAV}, where t_{CLAV} stands for *time from clock low to address valid*. According to the data sheet shown in Figure 7-22, in the 8-MHz column the maximum value of this time is 70 ns. For 4 Mhz this value would be doubled, to 140 ns. For a 3.579-MHz clock, this time would be (8/3.579) × 70 = 156 ns. Now look further to the right on the A0–A23 lines. You should see that valid data must arrive at the 68000 from memory at time labeled "27" before the falling edge of the clock at the end of S6. Timing parameter 27 in Figure 7-22 is listed as t_{DICL},

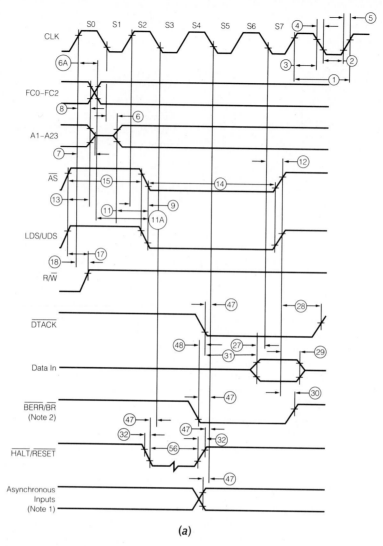

FIGURE 7-20 (a) 68000 read-cycle timing diagram. (b) Simplified version of
68000 read-cycle timing diagram. (*Reprinted with permission of Motorola Inc.*)
(*continued*)

which stands for *time data in must be valid before
clock goes low.* The data sheet gives a value of 15 ns
for this parameter as a minimum. Converting to the
time for a 3.579-MHz clock yields 34 ns.

The time between the end of the t_{CLAV} interval and the
start of the t_{DICL} interval is the time available for getting
the address to the memory and for the t_{ACC} of the
memory device. You can determine this time by subtracting t_{CLAV} and t_{DICL} from the time for three clock
cycles (end of S0 to end of S6). With a 3.579-MHz clock,
each clock cycle is 279 ns. Three clock cycles then
total 837 ns. Subtracting a t_{CLAV} of 156 ns and a t_{DICL} of
34 ns leaves 647 ns available for getting the address to
the 2732 and for its t_{ACC}. To help you visualize these
times, Figure 7-23a, p. 193, shows this operation in
simplified diagram form.

Now, as we told you in a previous paragraph, the
2732 has a maximum t_{ACC} of 450 ns. Since this 450 ns
is less than the 647 ns available, you know that the t_{ACC}
of the 2732 is acceptable for the URDA MDS operating
with a 3.579-MHz clock. You still, however, must
check if the values of t_{CE} and t_{OE} for the 2732 are
acceptable.

If you look at the URDA MDS schematic, you should
see that the $\overline{CE}$ inputs of the 2732s are connected to
either $\overline{ROM}$ U or to $\overline{ROM}$ L. $\overline{ROM}$ L and $\overline{ROM}$ U are
generated from the $\overline{AS}$, $\overline{UDS}$, and $\overline{LDS}$ lines. The
timing for these signals is similar to that for the
addresses in the preceding section. There are two main
differences. First, the $\overline{AS}$ and $\overline{UDS}$ lines are asserted

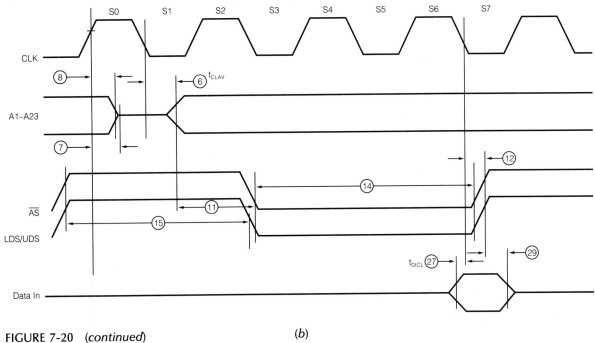

FIGURE 7-20   (continued)   (b)

low in the middle of S2 and continue to be asserted for a time labeled "14" (t_{SL}). Looking at Figure 7-20 you can tell that the data must be ready (data_in starts) two full clock cycles after the $\overline{AS}$ and $\overline{UDS}/\overline{LDS}$ signals are asserted. This gives a starting time window of 558 ns. The second difference is that the $\overline{AS}$ and $\overline{UDS}/\overline{LDS}$ signals are passed through gates and an address decoder. If you look at the URDA MDS schematic, you should see that the address decoding circuitry that enables the 2732 passes the $\overline{AS}$ signal and the A14−A15 address information from the 68000 through a 7432 NAND gate, through a 74LS139 decoder, and through another 7432 NAND gate. Looking these up in a data catalog, you should find that the 74LS139 causes a maximum delay of 40 ns and the 7432 causes a maximum propagation delay of 15 ns before the enable signal gets to the 2732s. The propagation delay of the 74LS139s and 7432s must be subtracted from 558 ns to determine how much time is actually available for the t_{CE} of the 2732. Subtracting 70 ns (15 ns + 40 ns + 15 ns) from 558 ns leaves 488 ns for the t_{CE} of the 2732. Since the maximum t_{CE} of the 2732 is 450 ns, you know that this parameter is also acceptable for an URDA MDS operating with a 3.579-MHz clock. Figure 7-23b shows this diagramatically.

The final parameter to check is t_{OE} of the 2732. According to the URDA MDS schematics, the $\overline{G}$ (output enable) signal is tied low. This means that the output buffers are always enabled on the 2732s. Therefore, we know that t_{OE} will not hinder the 2732 operation. When the system power is turned on, $\overline{G}$ will be asserted, which implies the output buffers will be powered up and enabled. The buffers will be configured to drive the data bus 120 ns after power on and will stay enabled until the system is powered down. The 2732s will operate only when the main $\overline{E}$ is asserted. Whenever the chip is enabled, however, the 2732s will attempt to output data to the bus. This is fine for EPROMs and ROMs. If you accidentally try to write to the EPROMs because of a programming error, the EPROMs will not change. If you accidentally write to the EPROMs, both the EPROMs and the CPU will try to put data on the data bus. The data on the bus will be garbage, but neither the CPU nor the EPROMs will be harmed. Since no other device will be using the bus, there will be no harm done and the operation will be one big NOP, except for the effect on the CPU status bits.

The output buffer-enabling line will normally be connected to the R/$\overline{W}$ CPU line. Since the EPROMs should be read from but are not normally written to, the connection is not necessary. However, if we look at the RAM, then the direction of the I/O buffers is very important. A write will change the RAM contents.

You have now checked all three 2732 parameters and found that all three are acceptable for an URDA MDS operating on a 3.579-MHz clock. No wait states need to be inserted when these devices are accessed, so extra circuitry connected to $\overline{DTACK}$ is not necessary. No additional wait states need to be introduced to slow the CPU while the memory devices catch up. Thus, from the EPROM's point of view, $\overline{DTACK}$ can be asserted constantly.

Look up the 6116 in a data book and perform a timing analysis like the one just given to verify that the 6116 is fast enough to operate in the URDA MDS with a 3.579-Mhz clock. Use the timing diagram from Figure 7-21 to find the necessary write cycle times.

TROUBLESHOOTING A SIMPLE 68000-BASED MICROCOMPUTER

Now that you have some knowledge of the software and the hardware of a microcomputer system, we can start

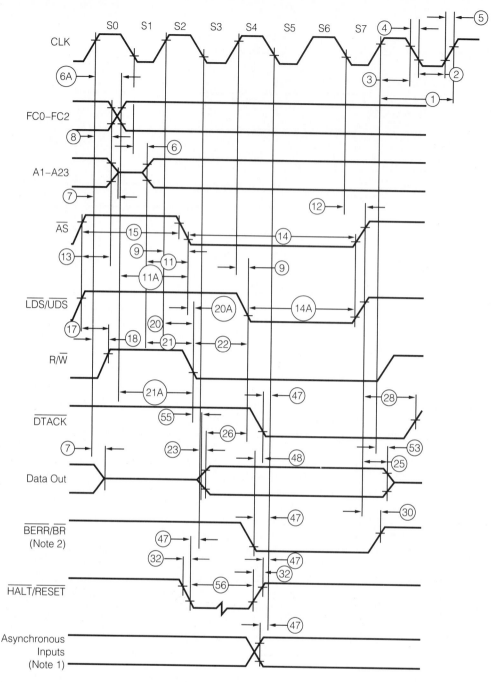

FIGURE 7-21   68000 write-cycle timing diagram. (*Reprinted with permission of Motorola Inc.*)

teaching you how to troubleshoot a simple microcomputer system such as an URDA MDS board. For this section assume that the microcomputer- or microprocessor-based instrument previously worked. Later sections of this book will describe how the prototype of a microprocessor-based instrument is developed.

The following sections describe a series of steps that we have found effective in troubleshooting various microcomputer systems. The first point to impress on your mind about troubleshooting a microcomputer is that a systematic approach is almost always more effective than random poking, probing, and hoping. You don't, for example, want to spend 2 h troubleshooting a system and finally discover the problem is that the power supply is putting out only 3 V instead of 5 V. Use the following list of steps or a list of your own each time you have to troubleshoot a microcomputer.

1. *Identifying the Symptoms.* Make a list of the symptoms that you find or those that a customer describes to you. Find out, for example, whether the symptom is present immediately or whether

Num.	Characteristic	Symbol	8 MHz		10 MHz		12.5 MHz		Unit
			Min	Max	Min	Max	Min	Max	
1	Clock Period	t_{CYC}	125	250	100	250	80	250	ns
2	Clock Width Low	t_{CL}	55	125	45	125	35	125	ns
3	Clock Width High	t_{CH}	55	125	45	125	35	125	ns
4	Clock Fall Time	t_{Cf}	—	10	—	10	—	5	ns
5	Clock Rise Time	t_{Cr}	—	10	—	10	—	5	ns
6	Clock Low to Address Valid	t_{CLAV}	—	70	—	60	—	55	ns
6A	Clock High to FC Valid	t_{CHFCV}	—	70	—	60	—	55	ns
7	Clock High to Address, Data Bus High Impedance (Maximum)	t_{CHADZ}	—	80	—	70	—	60	ns
8	Clock High to Address, FC Invalid (Minimum)	t_{CHAFI}	0	—	0	—	0	—	ns
9[1]	Clock High to $\overline{AS}$, $\overline{DS}$ Low	t_{CHSL}	0	60	0	55	0	55	ns
11[2]	Address Valid to $\overline{AS}$, $\overline{DS}$ Low (Read)/ $\overline{AS}$ Low (Write)	t_{AVSL}	30	—	20	—	0	—	ns
11A[2,7]	FC Valid to $\overline{AS}$, $\overline{DS}$ Low (Read)/ $\overline{AS}$ Low (Write)	t_{FCVSL}	60	—	50	—	40	—	ns
12[1]	Clock Low to $\overline{AS}$, $\overline{DS}$ High	t_{CLSH}	—	70	—	55	—	50	ns
13[2]	$\overline{AS}$, $\overline{DS}$ High to Address/FC Invalid	t_{SHAFI}	30	—	20	—	10	—	ns
14[2,5]	$\overline{AS}$, $\overline{DS}$ Width Low (Read)/$\overline{AS}$ Low (Write)	t_{SL}	240	—	195	—	160	—	ns
14A[2]	$\overline{DS}$ Width Low (Write)	t_{DSL}	115	—	95	—	80	—	ns
15[2]	$\overline{AS}$, $\overline{DS}$ Width High	t_{SH}	150	—	105	—	65	—	ns
16	Clock High to Control Bus High Impedance	t_{CHCZ}	—	80	—	70	—	60	ns
17[2]	$\overline{AS}$, $\overline{DS}$ High to R/$\overline{W}$ High (Read)	t_{SHRH}	40	—	20	—	10	—	ns
18[1]	Clock High to R/$\overline{W}$ High	t_{CHRH}	0	70	0	60	0	60	ns
20[1]	Clock High to R/$\overline{W}$ Low (Write)	t_{CHRL}	—	70	—	60	—	60	ns
20A[8]	$\overline{AS}$ Low to R/$\overline{W}$ Valid (Write)	t_{ASRV}	—	20	—	20	—	20	ns
21[2]	Address Valid to R/$\overline{W}$ Low (Write)	t_{AVRL}	20	—	0	—	0	—	ns
21A[2,7]	FC Valid to R/$\overline{W}$ Low (Write)	t_{FCVRL}	60	—	50	—	30	—	ns
22[2]	R/$\overline{W}$ Low to $\overline{DS}$ Low (Write)	t_{RLSL}	80	—	50	—	30	—	ns
23	Clock Low to Data Out Valid (Write)	t_{CLDO}	—	70	—	55	—	55	ns
25[2]	$\overline{AS}$, $\overline{DS}$ High to Data Out Invalid (Write)	t_{SHDOI}	30	—	20	—	15	—	ns
26[2]	Data Out Valid to $\overline{DS}$ Low (Write)	t_{DOSL}	30	—	20	—	15	—	ns
27[6]	Data in to Clock Low (Setup Time on Read)	t_{DICL}	15	—	10	—	10	—	ns
28[2,5]	$\overline{AS}$, $\overline{DS}$ High to $\overline{DTACK}$ High	t_{SHDAH}	0	245	0	190	0	150	ns
29	$\overline{AS}$, $\overline{DS}$ High to Data in Invalid (Hold Time on Read)	t_{SHDII}	0	—	0	—	0	—	ns
30	$\overline{AS}$, $\overline{DS}$ High to $\overline{BERR}$ High	t_{SHBEH}	0	—	0	—	0	—	ns
31[2,6]	$\overline{DTACK}$ Low to Data in (Setup Time)	t_{DALDI}	—	90	—	65	—	50	ns
32	$\overline{HALT}$ and $\overline{RESET}$ Input Transition Time	$t_{RHr,f}$	0	200	0	200	0	200	ns
33	Clock High to $\overline{BG}$ Low	t_{CHGL}	—	70	—	60	—	50	ns
34	Clock High to $\overline{BG}$ High	t_{CHGH}	—	70	—	60	—	50	ns
35	$\overline{BR}$ Low to $\overline{BG}$ Low	t_{BRLGL}	1.5	90 ns +3.5	1.5	80 ns +3.5	1.5	70 ns +3.5	Clk. Per.

FIGURE 7-22   68000 system timing requirements: V_{CC} = 5.0 V dc ± 5%; GND = 0 V dc; $T_A = T_L$ to T_H (continued on p. 192). (*Reprinted with permission of Motorola Inc.*)

the system must operate for a while before it shows up. If someone else describes the symptoms to you, check them yourself or have that person demonstrate the symptoms to you. This allows you to check if the problem is with the machine or with how the person is attempting to use the machine.

2. *Making a Careful Visual and Tactile Inspection.* This step is good for preventive maintenance as well as for finding a current problem. Check for components that have been or are excessively hot. When touching components to see if any are too hot, do it gently, because a bad IC can get hot enough to give a nasty burn if you keep your finger on it too long.

Check to see that all ICs are firmly seated in their sockets and that the ICs have no bent pins. Vibration can cause ICs to work loose in their sockets. A bent pin may make contact for a while, but after heating, cooling, and vibration, it may no longer make contact. Also, inexpensive IC sockets may oxidize with age and no longer make good contact.

Check for broken wires and loose connectors. A

Num.	Characteristic	Symbol	8 MHz		10 MHz		12.5 MHz		Unit
			Min	Max	Min	Max	Min	Max	
36[9]	$\overline{BR}$ High to $\overline{BG}$ High	'BRHGH	1.5	90 ns +3.5	1.5	80 ns +3.5	1.5	70 ns +3.5	Clk. Per.
37	$\overline{BGACK}$ Low to $\overline{BG}$ Low	'GALGH	1.5	90 ns +3.5	1.5	80 ns +3.5	1.5	70 ns +3.5	Clk. Per.
37A[10]	$\overline{BGACK}$ Low to $\overline{BR}$ High	'GALBRH	20	1.5 Clocks	20	1.5 Clocks	20	1.5 Clocks	ns
38	$\overline{BG}$ Low to Control, Address. Data Bus High Impedance ($\overline{AS}$ High)	'GLZ	—	80	—	70	—	60	ns
39	$\overline{BG}$ Width High	'GH	1.5	—	1.5	—	1.5	—	Clk. Per.
40	Clock Low to $\overline{VMA}$ Low	'CLVML	—	70	—	70	—	70	ns
41	Clock Low to E Transition	'CLET	—	70	—	55	—	45	ns
42	E Output Rise and Fall Time	'Er,f	—	25	—	25	—	25	ns
43	$\overline{VMA}$ Low to E High	'VMLEH	200	—	150	—	90	—	ns
44	$\overline{AS}$, $\overline{DS}$ High to $\overline{VPA}$ High	'SHVPH	0	120	0	90	0	70	ns
45	E Low to Control, Address Bus Invalid (Address Hold Time)	'ELCAI	30	—	10	—	10	—	ns
46	$\overline{BGACK}$ Width Low	'GAL	1.5	—	1.5	—	1.5	—	Clk. Per.
47[6]	Asynchronous Input Setup Time	'ASI	20	—	20	—	20	—	ns
48[3]	$\overline{BERR}$ Low to $\overline{DTACK}$ Low	'BELDAL	20	—	20	—	20	—	ns
49[11]	$\overline{AS}$, $\overline{DS}$ High to E Low	'SHEL	−70	70	−55	55	−45	45	ns
50	E Width High	'EH	450	—	350	—	280	—	ns
51	E Width Low	'EL	700	—	550	—	440	—	ns
53	Clock High to Data Out Invalid	'CHDOI	0	—	0	—	0	—	ns
54	E Low to Data Out Invalid	'ELDOI	30	—	20	—	15	—	ns
55	R/$\overline{W}$ to Data Bus Driver	'RLDBD	30	—	20	—	10	—	ns
56[4]	$\overline{HALT}$ $\overline{RESET}$ Pulse Width	'HRPW	10	—	10	—	10	—	Clk. Per.
57	$\overline{BGACK}$ High to Control Bus Driven	'GABD	1.5	—	1.5	—	1.5	—	Clk. Per.
58[9]	$\overline{BG}$ High to Control Bus Driven	'GHBD	1.5	—	1.5	—	1.5	—	Clk. Per.

NOTES

1 For a loading capacitance of less than or equal to 50 picofarads, subtract 5 nanoseconds from the value given in the maximum columns.
2 Actual value depends on clock period.
3 If #47 is satisfied for both $\overline{DTACK}$ and $\overline{BERR}$, #48 may be 0 nanoseconds.
4 For power up, the MPU must be held in $\overline{RESET}$ state for 100 ms to allow stabilization of on-chip circuitry. After the system is powered up, #56 refers to the minimum pulse width required to reset the system.
5 #14, #14A, and #28 are one clock period less than the given number for T6E, BF4, and R9M mask sets.
6 If the asynchronous setup time (#47) requirements are satisfied, the $\overline{DTACK}$ low-to-data setup time (#31) requirement can be ignored. The data must only satisfy the date-in clock-low setup time (#27) for the following cycle.
7 For T6E, BF4, and R9M mask set #11A timing equals #11, and #21A equals #21. #20A may be 0 for T6E, BF4, and R9M mask sets.
8 When $\overline{AS}$ and R/$\overline{W}$ are equally loaded (±20%), subtract 10 nanoseconds from the values given in these columns.
9 The processor will negate $\overline{BG}$ and begin driving the bus again if external arbitration logic negates $\overline{BR}$ before asserting $\overline{BGACK}$.
10 The minimum value must be met to guarantee proper operation. If the maximum value is exceeded, $\overline{BG}$ may be reasserted.
11 The falling edge of S6 triggers both the negation of the strobes ($\overline{AS}$ and $\overline{xDS}$) and the falling edge of E. Either of these events can occur first depending upon the loading on each signal. Specification #49 indicates the absolute maximum skew that will occur between the rising edge of the strobes and the falling edge of the E clock.

FIGURE 7-22   (continued)

thin film of dust may form on printed circuit board edge connectors and prevent them from making dependable contact. The film can be removed by gently rubbing the edge connector fingers with a clean, nonabrasive pencil eraser. If the microcomputer has ribbon cables, check to see if they have been moved around or stressed. Ribbon cables usually have small wires that are easily broken. If you suspect a broken conductor in a ribbon cable, you can later make an electrical check to verify your suspicions.

3. *Checking the Power Supply.* From the manual for the microcomputer, determine the power supply voltages. Check the supply voltage(s) directly on the appropriate pins of some ICs to make sure the voltage is actually getting there. Check with a scope to make sure the power supplies do not have excessive noise or ripple. One microcomputer that we were called on to troubleshoot had very strange symptoms caused by 2-V_{p-p} ripple on the 5-V supply.

4. *Making a Signal Roll Call.* The next step is to make a quick check of some key signals around the CPU of the microcomputer. If the problem is a bad IC, this can help point you toward the one that is bad. First, check if the clock signal is present and at the right frequency. If it is not, perhaps the clock generator IC is bad. If the microcomputer has a

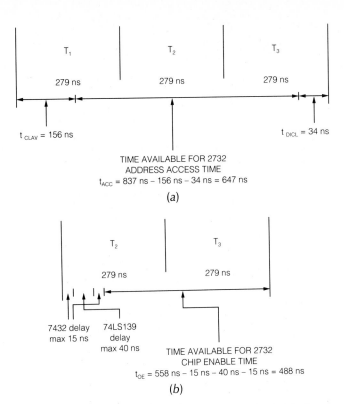

T_1 T_2 T_3

279 ns   279 ns   279 ns

$t_{CLAV} = 156$ ns $t_{DICL} = 34$ ns

TIME AVAILABLE FOR 2732
ADDRESS ACCESS TIME
$t_{ACC} = 837$ ns $- 156$ ns $- 34$ ns $= 647$ ns

(a)

T_2 T_3

279 ns   279 ns

7432 delay
max 15 ns

74LS139
delay
max 40 ns

TIME AVAILABLE FOR 2732
CHIP ENABLE TIME
$t_{OE} = 558$ ns $- 15$ ns $- 40$ ns $- 15$ ns $= 488$ ns

(b)

FIGURE 7-23 Calculations of 68000 times available for 2732 EPROM access. (a) Time for t_{ACC}. (b) Time for t_{CE}.

clock but doesn't seem to be doing anything, use an oscilloscope to check if the CPU is putting out control signals such as R/$\overline{W}$, $\overline{UDS}$, and $\overline{AS}$. Also, check the least significant data bus lines to see if there is any activity on the buses. If there is no activity on these lines, a common cause is that the CPU is stuck in a wait, hold, halt, or reset condition by the failure of some TTL devices. To check this out, use the manual to help you predict what logic level should be on each of the CPU input control signals for normal operation. The $\overline{RES}$ input of the 68000, for example, should be high for normal operation. If an external logic gate fails and holds $\overline{RES}$ low, the 68000 will constantly be reset, and the buses will be held constant. If the 68000 $\overline{HALT}$ input is held high, the 68000 bus activity will stop. Connecting a scope probe to these lines will pull them to ground, so you will see them as lows.

If there is activity on the buses, use an oscilloscope to see if the CPU is putting out control signals such as R/$\overline{W}$ and $\overline{AS}$. Also check with your oscilloscope to see if select signals are being generated on the outputs of the ROM, RAM, and port decoders as the system attempts to run its monitor or basic program. If no select signals are being produced, then the address-decoding circuitry may be bad or the CPU may not be sending out the correct addresses.

After a little practice you should be able to work through the previously described steps quite quickly. If you have not located the problem at this point, the next step for a system with its ICs in sockets is to systematically substitute known good ICs for those in the nonworking system.

5. *Systematically Substituting ICs.* The easiest case of substitution is that where you have two identical microcomputers, one that works and one that doesn't, and the ICs of both units are in sockets. For this case you can use the working system to test the ICs from the nonworking system. The trick here is to do this in such a way that you don't end up with two systems that do not work! Here's how you do it.

First of all, *do not remove or insert any ICs with the power on!* With the power off, remove the CPU from the good system and put it in a piece of conductive foam. Plug the CPU from the bad system into the now-empty socket on the good board and turn on the power. If the good system still works, then probably the CPU is good. Turn off the power and put the CPU back in the bad system. If the good system does not work with the CPU from the bad system, then the CPU is probably bad. Remove it from the good system and bend the pins so that you know it is bad. If the CPU seems bad, you can try replacing it with the CPU you removed from the good system. If you do this, however, it is important to keep track of where each IC came from. To do this mark each IC from the good system with a wide-tip, water-soluble marking pen. The good system can then be rebuilt by simply putting back all the marked ICs. The marks on the ICs can easily be removed with a damp cloth.

The procedure from here on is to keep testing ICs from the bad system until you find all the bad ICs. Make sure to turn the power off before you remove or insert any ICs. Be aware that more than one IC may be bad. It is not unusual, for example, that an ac power surge will wipe out several devices in a system. You can work your way out from the CPU to address latches, buffers, decoders, and memory devices. Often the specific symptoms point you to the problem group of ICs without your having to test every IC in the system. If, for example, the system accesses ROM but doesn't access RAM, suspect the RAM decoder. If a system uses buffers on the buses, suspect these devices. Buffers are high-current devices and they often fail.

6. *Troubleshooting a System with Soldered-in ICs.* The approach described in the preceding paragraphs works well if the system ICs are all in sockets and you have two identical systems. However, since sockets add to the cost and unreliability of a system, many small systems put only the CPU and ROMs in sockets. This makes your troubleshooting work harder, but not impossible.

Again, if you have two identical systems, one that works and one that doesn't work, you can attempt to run the monitor or basic system program on each and compare signals on the two. A missing or wrong signal may point you to the bad IC or ICs.

If the system works enough to read some instructions from ROM and execute them, you can replace the monitor or basic system ROM with one containing diagnostic programs that test RAM and I/O devices. A RAM test routine, for example, might attempt to write all 1s to each RAM location and then read the memory location to see if the data was written correctly to that location. If the data read back is not correct, the diagnostic program can stop and in some way indicate the address to which it could not write. If a write of all 1s is successful, then the test routine will try to write all 0s to each memory location. A port test routine might initialize a port for output and then write alternating 1s and 0s to the port over and over again. With an oscilloscope you can then see if the port device is being enabled and if the data is getting to the output of the port device. Another port-test routine might try to read a byte of data in from a port over and over so that you can again see if the device is being enabled and if the data is getting through the device to the system data bus. The technique of using program routines to test hardware is a very important one that you will use many times when you are working with microcomputer systems.

Now, suppose that you have localized the problem to a few ICs that are soldered in. If the problem is one that occurs when the unit gets hot, you might try spraying some Freon spray on the ICs, one at a time, to see if you can determine which one has a problem. If this does not find the bad IC or the problem is not heat-related, you next replace these ICs one at a time until the system works correctly. The point we want to stress here is that the cost of these few ICs is probably much less that the cost of the time it would take you to determine just which IC is bad if you do not have specialized test equipment.

To remove an IC from a printed circuit board, *do not* attempt to desolder pins with a hand-held solder "slurper." Modern multilayer printed circuit boards are quite fragile, and these tools can slip and knock a trace right off the board. Instead, use cutters with narrow tips to cut all the leads of the IC next to the body. Since you are going to throw it out anyway, you don't care if you destroy the IC. With the body of the IC out of the way, you can then gently heat each pin individually and use needle-nose pliers to remove it from the PC board. If the hole fills with solder, heat it gently and insert a small wooden toothpick until the solder cools. After you replace each IC, power up the system and see if it now works.

The techniques described in the preceding sections will enable you to troubleshoot many microcomputer systems with a minimum of test equipment. However, specialized test equipment is available to speed up the process and help find complex problems. The following sections describe two of these instruments.

7. *Using a Logic Analyzer to Troubleshoot a Micro-*

computer System. A *logic analyzer* is an instrument that allows you to see what is happening on up to 64 signal lines at once. With a logic analyzer you can, for example, see the signals on the address bus, data bus, and control bus of a microcomputer. Figure 7-24 shows a picture of a Tektronix 318 logic analyzer, and Figure 7-25, p. 195, shows a block diagram of a simple logic analyzer.

Pods with small clip leads are used to get the signals into the analyzer. Since logic analyzers are used to detect and display only 1s and 0s, a comparator is put on each input. The reference input of the comparator is set for the logic threshold of the devices in the system. The signals out of the comparators to the rest of the analyzer are then clearcut 1s or 0s.

The analyzer takes "snapshots" of the logic levels on each of the data inputs and stores these samples in an internal RAM. Different analyzers store between 256 and 1024 samples for each input channel. A *clock* signal tells the analyzer how often to take samples. As shown by the block diagram in Figure 7-25, some external signal can be used to clock the analyzer. If you are using an analyzer to look at 68000 address and data lines, for example, you could use $\overline{AS}$ as a clock signal. The analyzer will then take a sample each time the 68000 puts out an address and pulses $\overline{AS}$. The samples stored in the analyzer memory will then represent the sequence of addresses output by the 68000 after some specified *trigger*. As another example, you could clock the analyzer on R/$\overline{W}$ from a 68000. After a specified trigger, the analyzer will take a sample each time the 68000 does a read operation. In this case the samples stored in the analyzer memory will represent the sequence of data words read in from memory or from ports.

To make precise timing measurements with an analyzer, you can tell an analyzer to take a sample

FIGURE 7-24 Tektronix 318 logic analyzer. (*Tektronix Inc.*)

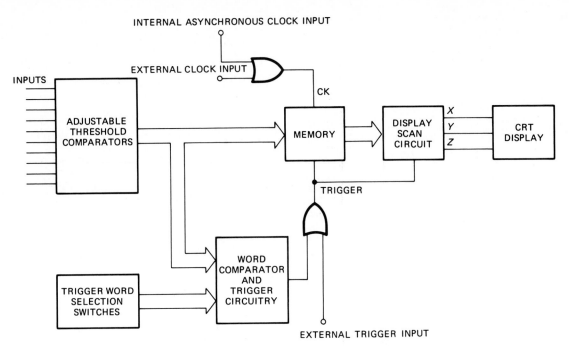

INTERNAL ASYNCHRONOUS CLOCK INPUT

EXTERNAL CLOCK INPUT

INPUTS

ADJUSTABLE
THRESHOLD
COMPARATORS

CK

MEMORY

DISPLAY
SCAN
CIRCUIT

X
Y
Z

CRT
DISPLAY

TRIGGER

WORD
COMPARATOR
AND
TRIGGER
CIRCUITRY

TRIGGER WORD
SELECTION
SWITCHES

EXTERNAL TRIGGER INPUT

FIGURE 7-25   Logic analyzer block diagram.

each time a pulse from an internal clock oscillator occurs. If, for example, you set the frequency of the internal clock to 50 MHz, the analyzer will take a sample every 20 ns.

If the analyzer is receiving either an internal or an external clock, it will be continuously taking samples of the input data and storing these samples in the internal RAM. A *trigger* signal tells the analyzer when to display the samples stored in the RAM. As shown by the block diagram in Figure 7-25, some external signal can be used to trigger the analyzer, or the trigger signal can come from a word recognizer in the analyzer. The word recognizer compares the binary word on the input signal lines with a word you set with switches or a keyboard. When the two words match, the word recognizer sends out a trigger signal. Since the analyzer is continuously taking samples, you can set the analyzer for a *pretrigger* display, a *center-trigger* display, or a *posttrigger* display. For an analyzer that displays 256 samples, pretrigger means that the display will show the 256 samples that were taken just before the trigger occurred. For center-trigger mode, 128 samples taken before the trigger and 128 samples taken after the trigger will be displayed. Posttrigger mode means that the analyzer will take 256 more samples after the trigger and display them.

Figure 7-26, p. 196, shows some of the formats in which a logic analyzer can display the samples stored in its RAM. The series of displayed data samples is often called a *trace*. The timing diagram format in Figure 7-26a is most useful when making time measurements with an internal clock. A binary listing such as that in Figure 7-26b is useful for

seeing the actual pattern of 1s and 0s on signal lines, but a hexadecimal listing such as that in Figure 7-26c makes it easier to recognize if a microcomputer is putting out addresses in the right sequence. Some analyzers, such as the Tektronix 318, allow you take a series of samples from a functioning system, store these samples in a second memory in the analyzer, and then compare these samples with a series taken from a nonfunctioning system. The dual listing in Figure 7-26c is an example of this. This feature is quite helpful.

Now that you have an overview of how a logic analyzer works, here's a few hints on how to use one for troubleshooting a 68000 microcomputer.

Connect the analyzer data inputs to the address and data bus lines from the CPU. For a 68000, connect the external clock input of the analyzer to the 68000 $\overline{\text{DTACK}}$ pin. Look at a 68000 timing diagram such as the one in Figure 7-20 to see at which edge of the $\overline{\text{DTACK}}$ signal valid addresses are present on the buses. Set the analyzer to clock on this edge. Set the analyzer to trigger on address $0000, the first address output by the 68000 after a reset. Set the analyzer display format for pretrigger display. Tell the analyzer to do a trace and press the 68000 system reset button. The display on the analyzer should show you the sequence of addresses output after a reset. Use the system monitor listing to see if the displayed sequence is correct. If it is not, look for address bits that should change but don't. A common failure mode for buffers is that an input or an output will short to V_{CC} or to ground, which prevents that line from changing.

If the address sequence seems reasonable, connect the analyzer external clock input to the 68000

(a)

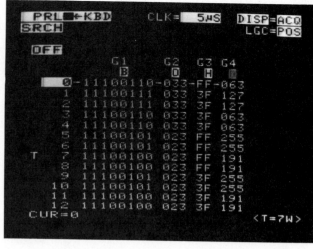

(b)

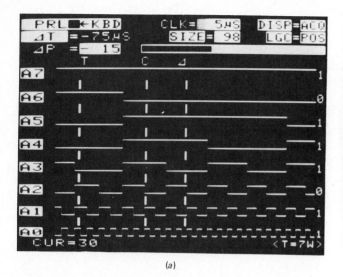

(c)

FIGURE 7-26   Logic analyzer display formats. (*Tektronix Inc.*)

R/$\overline{W}$ pin. Set the analyzer to clock on the positive edge of this signal. Set the format for posttrigger display. Tell the analyzer to do a trace, and push the system-reset button. The display on the analyzer should show the data transferred on D0–D15. Again, use the monitor program listing to see if instruction bytes are coming in correctly. To help with this, some analyzers allow you to display the instruction mnemonic that corresponds to the bytes read in. If the data sequence is not correct, again check for stuck bits.

We obviously can't describe here all the ways to use a logic analyzer. If you have one, consult the manual to learn some of the finer points of its use. The point here was to show you how to use the analyzer as a "window" into what's going on in a system. By carefully choosing the signals you look at, the signal you clock on, and the word you trigger on, you can usually solve difficult problems. For

this reason, a logic analyzer is a valuable tool when developing a new microcomputer-based product. However, it is important for you to have a perspective of when to use an analyzer in troubleshooting simple systems that previously worked. Most of the time you can use the techniques described in previous sections to find and fix a problem in less time than it would take you to connect up the logic analyzer and figure out the trace display. If you have an analyzer, however, don't hesitate to use it when the simple techniques don't seem to be getting you anywhere.

8. *Other Microcomputer Troubleshooting Equipment.* A logic analyzer is a very powerful troubleshooting tool, but to use it effectively you need some detailed knowledge and a program listing for the system that you are trying to troubleshoot. If you are working as a repair technician and have to repair several different types of microcomputer systems with poor documentation from which to work, most analyzers are not too useful. To make your life easier in this case, "smart" instruments such as the Fluke 9010A Microsystem Troubleshooter have been created.

As you can see from the picture of the 9010A in Figure 7-27, it has a keyboard, a display, and an "umbilical" cable with an IC plug on the end. The unit also contains a minicasette tape recorder. For troubleshooting, the 9010A is used as follows.

The microprocessor in a fully functioning unit is removed, and the plug at the end of the cable is inserted in its place. The learn function of the 9010A is then executed. This function finds and maps ROM, RAM, and I/O registers that can be written into and read from. It also computes signatures (checksums) for blocks of ROM. All these parameters are stored in the 9010A's RAM and/or on a minicassette tape. The microprocessor on a malfunctioning unit is then removed and the plug at the end of the umbilical cable is inserted in its place. An automatic test function is then executed.

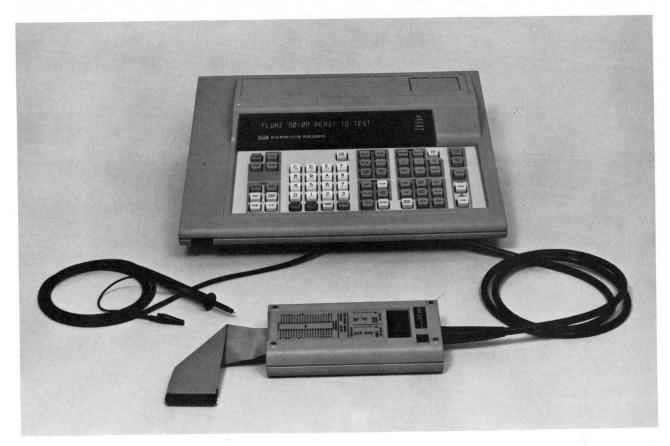

FIGURE 7-27　Fluke 9010A microsystem troubleshooter.
(*John Fluke Mfg. Co., Inc.*)

In this mode the 9010A tests the buses, RAM, ROM, ports, power supply, and clock on the malfunctioning system. Any problem found, such as stuck nodes or adjacent trace short circuits, is indicated on the display. The results of this test give some good hints as to the source of the problem. Because of its built-in intelligence, the 9010A can be programmed to do other tests as well.

The point of an instrument such as the 9010A is that with it, you do not have to be intimately familiar with the programming language and hardware details of a simple microcomputer system in order to troubleshoot it.

CHECKLIST OF IMPORTANT TERMS AND CONCEPTS IN THIS CHAPTER

If there are terms or concepts in this list you do not remember, use the index to find them in the chapter.

Pin functions of 68000
V_{CC} R/$\overline{W}$
CLK
$\overline{AS}$
$\overline{HALT}$
$\overline{UDS}$

$\overline{LDS}$
$\overline{DTACK}$
RES

Asynchronous bus control lines

M6800 peripheral control lines

System control lines

Processor status lines

Interrupt control lines

Bus arbitration control lines

68000 RESET response

Synchronous and asynchronous systems

Small and complex 68000 systems

68000 timing diagram interpretation

State, instruction cycle, machine cycle, wait state, DTACK signal

Bus activities during read/write

Bidirectional buffer

General functions
74LS139

68681
6116
6821

URDA MDS schematic
   Zones
   Plugs
   Jacks
   Resistor packs

Address decoding
   ROM decoding
   RAM decoding
   Port decoding

Memory-mapped I/O

Direct I/O

68000 memory banks

Timing parameters: t_{CLAV}, t_{DICL}

68000 typical clock frequencies

Troubleshooting steps for a simple 68000-based microcomputer

Logic analyzer
   Clock signal
   Trigger
   Trace

REVIEW QUESTIONS AND PROBLEMS

1. For what are the 68000 processor status pins used? The asynchronous bus control pins? The system control pins?

2. How can the 68000 operate properly with RAM and ROM and yet not have an A0 pin?

3. What is the purpose of the $\overline{DTACK}$ signal in a 68000 system? The $\overline{BERR}$ signal?

4. Describe the sequence of events on the 68000 data/address bus, the $\overline{AS}$ line, the $\overline{UDS}/\overline{LDS}$ line, and the R/$\overline{W}$ line as the 68000 fetches an instruction word.

5. What logic levels will be on the 68000 R/$\overline{W}$ and $\overline{AS}$ lines when the 68000 is doing a write to a memory location? A read from a port?

6. What is the major difference between a 68000 operating synchronously and a 68000 operating asynchronously?

7. Describe the response a 68000 will make when its RESET ($\overline{RES}$) input is asserted low.

8. Why are buffers often needed on the address, data, and control buses in a microcomputer system?

9. *a.* How is a 68000 forced to add a wait state?
   b. At what point in a machine cycle does a 68000 enter a wait state?
   c. How long is a wait state?
   d. How many wait states can be inserted?
   e. Why would you want the 68000 to insert a wait state?

10. What is the function of the 68000 R/$\overline{W}$ signal?

11. What does an arrow labeled with a number (often going from a transition on one signal waveform to another transition) tell you?

12. What are the functions of the UDS and LDS lines of the 68000 CPU?

13. How does a register pack look on a schematic?

14. Describe the two purposes of address decoders in microcomputer systems.

15. A memory device has 15 address lines connected to it and 8 data outputs. What size words and how many words does the device store?

16. Briefly describe the function of the 6821, 74LS139, and 6116 devices in the URDA MDS.

17. A group of signal lines on a schematic is said to be in zone C4. What is the meaning of this?

18. What is the difference between a connector identified with a J and a connector identified with a P?

19. Describe the purpose of the many small capacitors connected between V_{CC} and ground on microcomputer printed circuit boards.

20. A 74LS139 decoder has its two SELECT inputs connected to A14 and A13 of the system address bus. It does not use A15 (presume that A15 is 0). $\overline{AS}$ and $\overline{UDS}/\overline{LDS}$ are combined using a NAND gate, then combined with R/$\overline{W}$ using and AND gate, and then connected to the enable line ($\overline{E}$). Use an address decoder worksheet to determine what four ROM address blocks the decoder outputs will select. Why would R/$\overline{W}$ be used as one of the enables on the ROM decoder?

21. Show a memory map for the ROMs in problem 20.

22. Use an address decoder worksheet to help you draw a circuit to show how another 74LS139 can be connected to select one of four 1-Kbyte RAMs starting at address $8000.

23. Why are there actually many addresses that will select one of the port devices connected to the address decoder in Figure 7-16?

24. Describe memory-mapped I/O and direct I/O. Give the main advantage and main disadvantage of each.

25. *a.* Why is the 68000 memory set up as two byte-wide banks?

b. What logic levels (0 or 1) would you find on $\overline{UDS}$ and $\overline{LDS}$ if a 68000 is writing a byte to address $4274? Writing a word to $4274?

c. Can the 68000 write a word to address $4373?

26. Does the circuitry on the URDA MDS make sure that you cannot accidentally write a byte or word to EPROM?

27. Why is some EPROM put at the low address space in a 68000 system?

28. Describe how the 68008 memory is configured. Why doesn't the 68008 need $\overline{UDS}$ and $\overline{LDS}$ signals?

29. By referring to the 68000 timing diagrams in Figure 7-20 and parameters in Figure 7-22, determine each of the following for a 68000 system with a 12.5-MHz clock:
a. The minimum clock period
b. The maximum time between CLK going high and R/$\overline{W}$ going high
c. The maximum time for which memory must hold data on the data bus after CLK goes low at the end of S6.
d. The maximum time for which the 23 address bits will be valid after the clock goes low in S0.

30. The 27128-25 is a 16K × 8 EPROM with a t_{ACC} of 250 ns max, a t_{CE} of 250 ns max, and a t_{OE} of 100 ns max. Will this device work correctly without wait states in an 8-MHz 68000 system with circuit connections, such as those in the URDA MDS schematics? Assume the NAND gates have a propagation delay of 15 ns and the decoder has a delay of 40 ns.

31. List the major steps you would take to troubleshoot a microcomputer system such as the URDA MDS that previously worked. Assume all ICs are in sockets.

32. Why is it important to check power supplies with an oscilloscope?

33. Describe how you can keep from mixing up ICs from a good system with those from a bad system when substituting one for the other.

34. Write a 68000 routine to test the system RAM in addresses $4000–$4FFF.

35. Write a test routine to output alternating 1s and 0s to port $C014 over and over. With this routine running, you could check with an oscilloscope to see if the port device is being enabled and is outputting data.

36. Describe the symptoms that an URDA MDS would show for each of the following problems.
a. Pin 9 of IC4 in zone B3 of the schematic is stuck high.
b. The reset key is stuck on.
c. None of the outputs of IC7 in zone C3 of the schematic ever goes low.
d. Pin 8 of IC2 in zone C3 of the schematic is stuck low.

37. Draw a block diagram of a simple logic analyzer and briefly describe how it operates. Include in your answer the function of the CLOCK and the function of the trigger.

38. What clock do you use for a logic analyzer when you want to make detailed timing measurements?

39. On what signal and what edge of that signal would you clock a logic analyzer and on what word would you trigger to see the following in a 68000 system?
a. The sequence of addresses output after a RESET
b. The sequence of instructions read in after a RESET
c. Both the addresses sent out and the words read in

40. Most logic analyzers have a clock qualifier input. If this input is used, the logic analyzer will not respond to a clock signal unless a specified logic level is on the qualifier input. You might, for example, connect the ROM L to the clock qualifier input and set it for a low to see a trace of low-byte data read from memory. What clock qualifier would you use to see a trace of only data read in from ports?

41. How is it possible for a logic analyzer to display data that occurred before the trigger?

CHAPTER

Interrupts and Interrupt-Service Routines

Most microprocessors allow normal program execution to be interrupted by some external signal or by a special instruction in the program. When a microprocessor is interrupted, it stops executing its current program and calls a routine that "services" the interrupt. At the end of the interrupt-service routine, execution is usually returned to the interrupted program. This chapter shows you how the 68000 family members respond to interrupts, how to write interrupt-service routines, and how interrupts are used in a variety of applications.

OBJECTIVES

At the conclusion of this chapter, you should be able to

1. Describe the interrupt response of a 68000 family processor.

2. Initialize a 68000 interrupt-vector (pointer) table.

3. Write interrupt-service routines.

4. Describe the operation of an 8254 programmable counter/timer and write the instructions necessary to initialize an 8254 for a specified application.

5. Describe the operation of an 8259A priority-interrupt controller and write the instructions needed to initialize an 8259A for a specified application.

68000 INTERRUPTS AND INTERRUPT RESPONSES

Overview

Interrupts provide a mechanism whereby the CPU can stop what it is currently doing (executing the mainline program) and do some processing required by a special external or internal event. As an analogy, suppose you are in the basement building a bookcase and the phone rings. Typically, you put down your hammer or saw and run up the stairs, trying to get to the telephone before the person who is calling hangs up. Once you finish talking on the phone, you go back downstairs,

pick up the hammer again, and continue your construction where you left off. The phone interrupted your task, you serviced the interrupt (i.e., answered the phone), and then you went back to your task, resuming it at just the point where you left it, even in the middle of hammering in a nail.

As a different example, suppose the mail arrives while you are building your bookshelf. Normally you won't leave things immediately but will wait until you come to a normal break in your work, possibly when the bookshelf is finished. Then you go get the mail. The mail arrival does not generate an interrupt because it does not require immediate attention. It can wait in the mailbox until you are ready to get it. This latter case corresponds to a polled I/O, where you check the mailbox for mail at your convenience. The phone corresponds to an interrupt I/O, where you have to answer the phone within a short amount of time or the calling party will hang up and you won't get the phone call. With a computer, polled I/O can be used when the I/O events do not require immediate attention—that is, when you can afford to wait for the event, doing nothing but watching for it. Interrupt I/O services higher-priority events that require the CPU's immediate attention.

A 68000 *exception* happens when some abnormal condition occurs that requires the CPU's immediate processing attention. An exception causes the CPU to stop executing the program from which it is currently operating and to begin executing an exception-handling routine. 68000 exceptions can be generated by either internal or external causes. An exception caused externally is usually termed a *hardware interrupt*. An exception caused internally is sometimes called a *software interrupt*. We will frequently use the terms interchangeably. When they need to be distinguished, the differences will be explicitly noted.

The externally generated interrupts can occur because of bus errors (asserting $\overline{BERR}$), because of reset requests, or because a device asserts a combination of the $\overline{IPL0}$, $\overline{IPL1}$, and $\overline{IPL2}$ lines. The third case, in which some external device attempts to cause a CPU exception by asserting an interrupt line, is often used as the "restricted" definition of an interrupt.

At the end of each instruction cycle, the 68000 checks to see if any interrupts have been requested. If an interrupt has been requested, the 68000 responds to the interrupt by stepping through the following series of major actions.

1. It saves the current value of the status register internally, asserts the S bit (placing the CPU in supervisor state), and clears the T bit, stopping CPU instruction tracing.

2. It determines the interrupt- (exception) vector number. That is, it determines what caused the interrupt and where the exception-handling routine is.

3. It decrements the stack pointer by 3 words and pushes the current program counter and the saved status register onto the supervisor stack.

4. It fetches the new PC value from the indicated vector address and starts execution at this new address. This has the effect of transferring control to the start of the subroutine you wrote to respond to the interrupt.

To summarize these steps, the 68000 saves the status register, asserts the S bit, and clears the T bit. It then determines the vector number to use, stacks the PC and SR, and fetches the new PC from the indicated vector location. This, in effect, causes a subroutine call to the interrupt-service routine (ISR). Figure 8-1 shows this in diagram form. Note that an RTE instruction at the end of the interrupt-service procedure returns execution to the main program. Recall that the RTE is similar to the RTS instruction, with the additional feature that it restores the status register as well as returning to the mainline. This is necessary to ensure that the mainline program is not affected by the operation of the ISR. Figure 8-2 shows the contents of the supervisor stack after the interrupt occurs and is recognized, during the execution of the ISR.

The address of the ISR is pulled from a designated part of 68000 memory. This special part of memory starts at address $0000 and contains a series of 4-byte addresses. The addresses are organized such that the CPU knows which address to use for each type of exception or interrupt. The table contains ISR addresses. The starting address of an interrupt-service routine

FIGURE 8-2 68000 exception stack order (groups 1 and 2).

stored in this table is often called the *interrupt vector* or the *exception vector*, and the table itself is then referred to as the *exception vector table*. Sometimes these interrupt vectors are called *interrupt pointers*.

Table 8-1, p. 202, shows how the 256 exception vectors are arranged in the memory table. Each long-word interrupt vector is identified by a number from 0 to 255. The first vector contains the address the CPU uses to start execution when a reset occurs (for example, at power-on of the system) This vector is really a two-part vector containing a long-word address that is loaded into the stack register (A7) and a long-word address that is the actual reset transfer address (loaded into the PC at reset). Table 8-1 indicates when the following vectors are used. For example, when a divide by 0 exception occurs, the CPU uses the address in vector 5 as the address of the 0-divide exception-handling routine. Vectors 6 and 7 are used for exceptions caused by the CHK and TRAPV instructions. Vectors 10 and 11 are intended to be used by software emulation routines. In multiprocessor systems instructions beginning with binary 1010 and 1111 are executed by the coprocessors (e.g., a floating-point coprocessor). When the coprocessors are not present, the main 68000 can emulate the coprocessor instructions using routines at addresses specified by vectors 10 and 11. Some vector numbers are reserved for future use, as indicated in Table 8-1.

The 68000 has three interrupt lines ($\overline{IPL0}$, $\overline{IPL1}$, and $\overline{IPL2}$), which allow external devices to interrupt at any of seven interrupt levels (the eighth level is the no-interrupt level). These seven levels of interrupts can each be serviced by a different routine. The ISR addresses are located at vectors 25 through 31. Vectors 32 through 47 are used by the TRAP instruction. Recall that the TRAP instruction uses a 4-bit trap number argument encoded in the instruction. TRAP 1 uses vector 32, TRAP 2 uses vector 33, and so on for the 16 vectors provided. Finally, vectors 64 through 255 are for user-interrupt vectors. These are accessed by devices that tell the CPU which vector number to use as part of the interrupt-acknowledgment cycle. The interrupting device will cause an interrupt and then tell the 68000 which vector to use by providing a vector number to the 68000.

When the 68000 responds to an interrupt, it automatically goes to the specified location in the interrupt-pointer table to get the starting address of the interrupt-service routine.

Now that you have an overview of how the 68000 responds to interrupts, we can show in detail how one of these interrupts works.

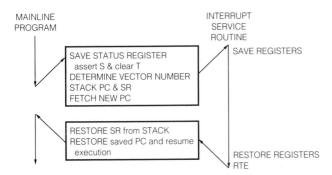

FIGURE 8-1 68000 exception response.

TABLE 8-1
68000 EXCEPTION VECTOR TABLE

Vector Number(s)	Address			Assignment
	Dec	Hex	Space	
0	0	000	SP	Reset Initial SSP
—	4	004	SP	Reset Initial PC
2	8	008	SD	Bus Error
3	12	00C	SD	Address Error
4	16	010	SD	Illegal Instruction
5	20	014	SD	Zero Divide
6	24	018	SD	CHK Instruction
7	28	01C	SD	TRAPV Instruction
8	32	020	SD	Privilege Violation
9	36	024	SD	Trace
10	40	028	SD	Line 1010 Emulator
11	44	02C	SD	Line 1111 Emulator
12*	48	030	SD	(Unassigned, Reserved)
13*	52	034	SD	(Unassigned, Reserved)
14*	56	038	SD	(Unassigned, Reserved)
15	60	03C	SD	Uninitialized Interrupt Vector
16-23*	64	04C	SD	(Unassigned, Reserved)
	95	05F		—
24	96	060	SD	Spurious Interrupt
25	100	064	SD	Level 1 Interrupt Autovector
26	104	068	SD	Level 2 Interrupt Autovector
27	108	06C	SD	Level 3 Interrupt Autovector
28	112	070	SD	Level 4 Interrupt Autovector
29	116	074	SD	Level 5 Interrupt Autovector
30	120	078	SD	Level 6 Interrupt Autovector
31	124	07C	SD	Level 7 Interrupt Autovector
32-47	128	080	SD	TRAP Instruction Vectors
	191	0BF		—
48-63*	192	0C0	SD	(Unassigned, Reserved)
	255	0FF		—
64-255	256	100	SD	User Interrupt Vectors
	1023	3FF		—

*Vector numbers 12, 13, 14, 16 through 23, and 48 through 63 are reserved for future enhancements by Motorola. No user peripheral devices should be assigned these numbers.

A 68000 Interrupt Response Example—Type 5: Zero Divide

Probably the easiest 68000 exception to understand is the divide by zero exception, identified as *type 5* in Table 8-1. We use a type 5 interrupt to show you in detail how a 68000 interrupt works and how to write a routine to service an interrupt.

First of all, let's refresh your memory about how the 68000 DIVS and DIVU instructions work. The 68000 DIV instructions allow you to divide a 32-bit binary number in the destination data register by a 16-bit binary number in the specified source effective address. The 16-bit result (quotient) from this division will be left in the lower half of the destination register. The 16-bit remainder will be left in the upper 16 bits of the destination register. The DIVS instruction operates

on signed numbers, and the DIVU instruction operates on unsigned numbers.

If the quotient from the division is too large to fit in 16 bits, the result of the division will be meaningless. In this case, the overflow bit is usually set and the operands are unchanged. However, a special case of this is where an attempt is made to divide a 32-bit number by 0 (i.e., the source operand is 0). The result of dividing by 0 is infinity (actually undefined), which is somewhat too large to fit in 16 bits. Whenever the source operand of a DIVS or DIVU instruction is 0, the 68000 will do a type 5 trap (zero divide).

The type 5 response proceeds as follows. The 68000 first saves the status register internally to the CPU. It clears the S bit and sets the T bit in the status register. It determines the interrupt vector to use (in this case, vector 5). It then copies the PC and the saved status

```
INITIALIZATION LIST

REPEAT
        get INPUT_VALUE
        divide by scale factor
        IF result valid THEN
                store result as scaled value
        ELSE store zero
    UNTIL all values scaled
```

(a)

```
Save registers
Set error flag
Restore registers
Return to mainline
```

(b)

FIGURE 8-3   Algorithm for divide by zero program example. (a) Mainline program. (b) Interrupt-service routine.

register to the stack. The 68000 then gets the starting address of the exception-handling routine from the type 5 locations in the exception vector table. As you can see in Figure 8-2, it gets the new value for PC from addresses $0020 through $0023. After the starting address of the routine is loaded into the PC, the 68000 fetches and executes the first instruction of the service routine.

At the end of the interrupt-service routine, an RTE instruction will be used to return execution to the interrupted program, restoring the status register in the process. The RTE instruction pops the stored value of the status register off the stack and increments the stack pointer by 2. This restores the status register of the interrupted mainline program, including the condition codes, as they were before the exception occurred. It then pops the stored value of the PC off the stack and increments the stack pointer by 4. To summarize, then, RTE returns execution to the interrupted program and restores the status register to the state it was in before the interrupt. Now that we have described the type 5 response, we can show you how to write a program to handle this interrupt.

A 68000 Interrupt Program Example

DEFINING THE PROBLEM AND WRITING THE ALGORITHM

Instead of jumping directly into the program, let's use this example to review how you go about writing any program.

As described in Chapter 3, you start by carefully defining the problem that you want it to perform. Part of this step is to determine the amount and types of data with which the program is to work.

For the example program here, we have four word-sized hexadecimal values stored in memory. We want to divide each of these values by a word-type scale factor to give a word-type scaled value. If the result of the division is valid, we want to put the scaled value in an array in memory. If the result of the division is invalid (too large to fit in the 16-bit result register), we want to put the unscaled value in the array for that scaled value. If the division fails (i.e., division by zero) we want to put the best approximation to infinity we can in the array of scaled values. We will use $FFFF as the closest we can find to infinity. Figure 8-3 shows the algorithm for this program in pseudocode. As shown in Figure 8-3a, the mainline part of this program gets each 16-bit value from memory in turn and divides that value by the scale factor. If the result of the division is too large to fit in the 16-bit quotient area of the destination data register, then the 68000 will leave the destination operand unaffected. If the divisor is 0, then the 68000 will do a type 5 trap immediately after the divide instruction finishes.

Figure 8-3b shows the algorithm for our type 5 exception service routine. The main function of this routine is to set a *flag* that will be checked by the mainline program. The flag in this case is not one of the flags in the 68000 status register. The flag here is a bit in a memory location we set aside for this purpose. In the actual program we give this memory location the name BAD_DIV_FLAG. At the end of the exception service routine, we return to the interrupted mainline program.

After the division in the mainline program, we check to see if the result of the division is valid. If the result is good, we store it in the correct place in the scaled values array in memory. If the result is bad, we leave $FFFF (our approximation of infinity) in that place in the scaled values array. To decide if a result is valid or not, we check the BAD_DIV_FLAG. If the division had a zero divisor, then the 68000 will have done a type 5 trap, and our exception service routine will have set the BAD_DIV_FLAG to a 1. If the result of the division is valid, then the 68000 will not do the trap, and the BAD_DIV_FLAG will be 0.

The sequence of operations is repeated until all the values have been scaled. We use a register to keep track of which input value is being operated on at a particular time and another register to keep track of the scale factor we wish to use.

WRITING THE INITIALIZATION LIST

After you have worked out the data structure and the algorithm for a program, the next step is to make an initialization list such as the one shown in Chapter 3. Here is a list for this program.

1. Set up a stack to store the return address, since we are essentially calling a subroutine, when the trap occurs.

2. Initialize the exception vector table. In other words, the starting address of our type 5 interrupt-service routine must be put in the proper location.

3. Initialize a pointer to the start of the data to be scaled, a counter to keep track of how many values we have scaled, and a pointer to the start of the array where we want to put the scaled values.

The second step deserves some explanation. The trap 5 exception vector is in memory at location $0020. Unfortunately, this location is in the EPROM in the URDA® MDS (and in most 68000 systems). We cannot change the values in the EPROMs without taking them out of the MDS, erasing them, and reprogramming them. This cannot be done by a program. Fortunately, the system designers of the URDA MDS have adopted a

scheme that involves *indirection* through a RAM jump table for all the key exception vectors. This is done specifically to allow us to change the values of these exception vectors, as we want to do in this case.

Figure 8-4 shows what we mean by indirection. Rather than having the 68000 exception vectors point directly to the exception-handling routines, they are instead pointed to a set of indirection routines that, in turn, use a set of vectors stored in RAM. The 68000 exception vector addresses are fixed, and the vectors themselves are encoded in EPROM (or ROM). They are often called *hard vectors* because they cannot be changed by software. The RAM vector table contents are called *soft vectors* because they can be changed by software. They actual flow of control is indicated by the solid arrows in Figure 8-4. When the zero-divide exception occurs, the 68000 CPU accesses the vector stored in memory location $0020. This vector points to a small indirection routine. The routine gets a vector from the soft vector table in RAM and uses it. The actual code for the indirection routine is

```
ZERO_DIV_VEC:
    MOVE.L   ZERO_DIV_PTR,-(A7)
    RTS
```

The MOVE.L instruction gets the soft vector from RAM and pushes it onto the stack. The RTS instruction transfers control to a routine pointed at by the soft vector. This can also be done by a routine such as

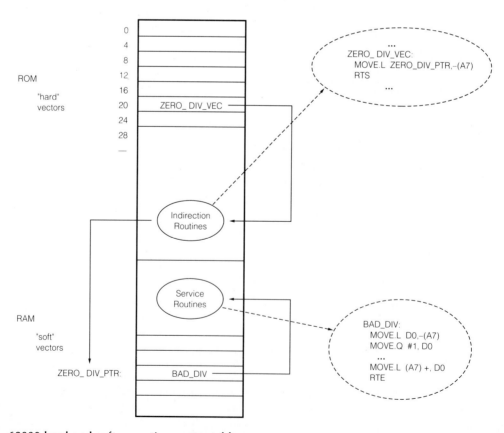

FIGURE 8-4 68000 hard and soft exception vector tables.

```
ZERO_DIV_VEC:
   MOVE.L  ZERO_DIV_PTR,A0
   JMP     (A0)
```

However, this routine mashes the contents of A0 and is, therefore, not really suitable. We don't want to mash the mainline program's A0, since that might make the mainline program operate incorrectly.

This type of indirection through a soft RAM-based vector table is typical in 68000 development systems to achieve flexibility in exception handling. The actual location of the soft vector table varies from system to system. For the URDA MDS the zero-divide soft vector location is $7FC4. In the program of Figure 8-5, this address is specified in an EQU pseudo instruction.

```
; 68000 Program
; ABSTRACT        : This program scales some data values by division.
;
; REGISTERS USED: A0 ... pointer to array of data values
;                 A1 ... pointer to array of scaled data values
;                 D0 ... one value
;                 D1 ... sample loop counter
; PORTS USED      : none
; PROCEDURES      : BAD_DIV, a division by 0 exception handler
;
;                        alr 3-89

ZERO_DIV_PTR    EQU     $7FC4
                ORG     $4000                   ; start the code at $4000

; Mainline code
;
;        INITIALIZATION LIST
;
        LEA     STACK_TOP,A7    ; initialize user stack pointer to top of stack

        LEA     BAD_DIV,A0              ; get address or exception handler
        MOVE.L  A0,D0
        MOVE.L  D0,(ZERO_DIV_PTR)      ; place into soft vector table

        LEA     INPUT_VALUES,A0 ; initialize data array pointer
        LEA     SCALED_VALUES,A1
        MOVE.B  #3,D1                  ; initialize sample loop counter
;
;        REPEAT
;
;
NEXT_VALUE:
;        get INPUT_VALUE
         CLR.L          D0
         MOVE.W         (A0)+,D0
;        divide by scale factor
         DIVU           D1,D0
;        IF result valid THEN
         CMPI.B         #$01,(BAD_DIV_FLAG)
         BEQ            BAD
;            store result as scaled value
             MOVE.W D0,(A1)+
             JMP    SKIP1
;        ELSE store zero
BAD:         MOVE.W         #$FFFF,(A1)+
;        UNTIL all values scaled
SKIP1:  MOVE.B  #0,(BAD_DIV_FLAG)      ; reset the division by 0 flag
        DBGT    D1,NEXT_VALUE          ; dec counter and loop if > 0
;
        NOP                             ; continue with mainline program
        NOP
;        ...
```

(a)   (continued)

FIGURE 8-5   68000 assembly language program for divide by zero example.
(a) Mainline. (b) Exception service routine, p. 206.

205

```
;- - - - - - - - - - - - - - - - -
; Division by 0 exception handling routine
BAD_DIV:
;         Save   registers
          MOVE.L  D0,-(A7)
;         Set error flag
          MOVEQ   #1,D0
          MOVE.B  D0,(BAD_DIV_FLAG)
;         Restore registers
          MOVEM.L (A7)+,D0
;         Return to mainline
          RTE                        ; return to the interrupted program


;----------------------------
          ORG     $4200              ; start the data at $4200

;                                    ; declare input data values
INPUT_VALUES:   DC.W    $35,$855,$2011,$1359
SCALED_VALUES:  DS.W    4          ; room for scaled data values
BAD_DIV_FLAG:   DC.B    0          ; bad division flag (set by exception handler)
STACK_HERE:     DS.W    40         ; set stack length of 40 words
STACK_TOP:      DS.W    0          ; the stack top is at the high address

          END
```

(b)

FIGURE 8-5 (continued)

ASSEMBLY LANGUAGE PROGRAM AND EXCEPTION HANDLING ROUTINE

Once you have the algorithm and the initialization list for a program, the next step is to start writing the instructions for the program, so now let's look at the assembly language program for this problem.

Figure 8-5 shows our 68000 assembly language program for the mainline and for the type 5 interrupt-service routine. You can use many of the parts of these when you write your own interrupt programs.

First, examine the data declarations at the end of the program. The input values are words, so we use a DC.W directive to declare these four values. The scaled values will also be words, so we use the DS.W directive to set aside four locations for these. As the program executes, the results will be written into these locations. We will be using the loop counter as our scale factor for this example. It will be held in a data register and counted down from 3 to 0. We don't need a memory location for this. This means that the scaling will use a different scale factor for each input value. We reserve a byte for the bad division flag using a DC.B directive. Finally, the stack area is reserved in the normal fashion using a DS.W 40 directive to declare the memory area of 40 words and a DS.W 0 directive to associate a label with the top of the stack.

At the start of the mainline program in Figure 8-5, we use an EQU declaration to define the address of the soft exception vector for the zero-divide exception. This will be used later in the program when we set up the vector to point to our exception-handling routine. We then declare the program starting address as $4000. Part of the 68000 exception response is essentially a call to the exception service routine. In any program that calls a subroutine (or causes one to be called by causing a trap), we have to set up a stack to store the return address and parameters passed to and from the routine. The next section of the main program initializes a stack segment called STACK_HERE. It also initializes the stack pointer to the next location above the stack with the statement LEA STACK_TOP,A7. Remember from the examples in Chapter 5 that this label is used to initialize the stack pointer to the next location after the top of the stack.

The rest of the program initialization involves setting up an address register to point to the input array (A0) and a second address register to point to the scaled value array (A1). The last part of the initialization loads the initial value of our loop counter to its starting value, 3. We will count this value down to 0 and scale each input value accordingly, so the last scaling operation will cause a zero-divide exception.

The next three instructions are needed to place the address of the BAD_DIV routine in the type 5 location in the soft exception vector table. Recall from the previous discussion that we cannot change the low memory EPROM hard vector values, but we can change the high-memory RAM vector values. First we load up the address of the bad division exception-handling routine using an LEA BAD_DIV,A0 instruction. We then move the address into a data register so that we can store it back into memory at the soft zero-divide exception vector location. The type 5 trap soft vector is at location $7FC4. Since we have declared the symbol BAD_DIV_PTR to be equal to $7FC4, we can use the symbol when setting up the vector. The instruction MOVE.L D0,ZERO_DIV_PTR makes it easier to remember what is happening than does the instruction MOVE.L D0,$7FC4. It may make things simpler if you think of the soft vectors as the "real" vectors and forget about the hard vectors for now.

Finally, everything is initialized, and we get to the operations we set out to do. First, we clear all 32 bits of a data register. This makes sure that the upper 16 bits of the data register are 0s, in preparation for a 32-bit by 16-bit division. The statement MOVE.W (A0)+,D0 gets a 16-bit input value while leaving the upper 16 bits of D0 still 0s. This instruction also increments A0 to point to the next input value, ready for the next time through this loop. The DIVU D1,D0 instruction divides the 32-bit number in D0 by the 16-bit number in D1. Recall that we are using D1 both as the loop counter and as the scaling factor. The 16-bit quotient from this division will be put in the low bits of D0, and the 16-bit remainder will be put in the high bits of D0. If the quotient is too large to fit in D0, then the 68000 will automatically set the overflow bit in the status register and leave D0 unchanged. This is the behavior we want for this case. If the divisor is 0, then the 68000 cannot perform a division; instead it causes a type 5 trap. For our program here, the 68000 will push the flags on the stack (by pushing a copy of the status register), set the S bit and clear the T bit, and push the return address on the stack. It will then go to address $014 to get the PC value for the zero-divide exception handler. This will transfer control to the indirection routine (recall Figure 8-4), which in turn will get the address of the soft type 5 exception vector, push it on the stack, and transfer control to it using an RTS instruction. Control will then transfer to the start of BAD_DIV, the routine we wrote to service a type 5 exception. It will next execute the BAD_DIV routine. Now let's look at the exception service routine (Figure 8-5) and see how it works.

An important operation to do at the start of any interrupt-service routine is to push on the stack any registers that you are going to use in the routine. You can then restore these registers by popping them off the stack just before returning to the interrupted program. The interrupted program will then resume with its registers as they were before the interrupt. The status register has already been pushed onto the stack and will be restored by the final RTE routine. This ensures that the mainline program's status flags are not changed. In our routine here, we save D0. The point is that an interrupt-service routine should be written so that it can be used at any point in a program. By saving the interrupted program's D0 and restoring D0 after using it, this interrupt-service routine can be used in a program section that is already using D0 for some purpose of its own.

Finally, we get to the whole point of this routine with the MOVEQ #1,D0 and MOVE.B D0,(BAD_DIV_FLAG) instructions. These instructions set the LSB of the memory location that we set aside with a DC.B directive at the end of the program. This bit will be tested by the mainline program following the division to see if an error occurred.

To complete the routine, we pop the saved registers off the stack (in this case just D0) and return to the interrupted program. The RTE instruction, remember, is different than the regular RTS instruction in that it pops the status register and the return address off the stack.

Now let's look back in the mainline to see what it does with this BAD_DIV_FLAG. Immediately after the DIVU instruction, the mainline checks to see if the BAD_DIV_FLAG is set by comparing it with $01. If the BAD_DIV_FLAG was set by the type 5 exception service routine, then a jump is made to the MOVE.W #$FFFF,(A1)+ instruction. This instruction copies our approximation to infinity to the memory location in SCALED_VALUES pointed to by A1 and increments A1 to point to the next scaled value location. This is the bad-division case.

If BAD_DIV_FLAG was not set by a type 5 exception, the "normal" good-division case, then the scaled value (the result of the division) is put in the memory location in SCALED_VALUES and a jump is made to the MOVE.B #0,(BAD_DIV_FLAG) instruction, which resets the BAD_DIV_FLAG. Since this jump passes over the MOVE.W #$FFFF,(A1)+ instruction, the infinity result will not be copied into one of the locations in SCALED_VALUES. Notice that in both the good- and bad-division cases, the BAD_DIV_FLAG is reset to 0 to be ready to start the next loop.

After putting the scaled value or infinity in the array and resetting the flag, we get ready to operate on the next input value. The DBGE D1,NEXT_VALUE instruction decrements D1 by 1, and, if D1 is greater than or equal to 0, it causes the 68000 to jump to the specified label, NEXT_VALUE.

The preceding section has shown you how to set up an exception vector table entry, how to write an exception service routine, and how the 68000 responds to a type 5 exception. This exception causes the mainline program to interrupt its normal processing and service the exception condition. We call this an *exception-handling routine* to conform to Motorola literature, but the reader should recognize that this is really a special type of an interrupt condition. Often the service routine will be called an *interrupt-service routine* even though it is servicing a CPU exception instead of an external device interrupt signal. The term *exception* is meant to imply that something other than the normal is occurring (e.g., a division by 0), and some special CPU attention is required.

Now we can discuss some of the other types of 68000 interrupts.

68000 Exception Types and Priorities

The preceding sections used the type 5 exception as an example of how the 68000 handles exceptions. In this section we discuss in detail the different ways an 68000 can be interrupted and how the 68000 responds to different types of exceptions. We discuss these in order, starting with type Z (zero divide), so that you can easily find a particular discussion when you need to refer back to it. However, as you read through this section you should not attempt to learn all the details of all the kinds of interrupts at once. Read through the different kinds to get an overview, and then focus on the details of the hardware-caused exceptions such as bus errors, the software interrupts produced by the TRAP and CHK instructions, and the hardware interrupt produced by applying a signal to the IPL0, IPL1, and IPL2 input pins.

Table 8-2 shows the different types of 68000 CPU exceptions organized into three groups. Let's examine each group in more detail. Refer also to Table 8-1 to recall the memory location of the exception vector for each type of exception.

GROUP 2: TRAP, TRAPV, CHK, AND ZERO DIVIDE

As we described in the preceding section, the 68000 will automatically do a type 5 trap if the divisor of a DIVU operation or a DIVS operation is 0. For a type 5 exception the 68000 pushes a copy of the status register on the stack, sets the S bit and clears the T bit, and pushes the return address (PC) on the stack. It then gets the vector for the start of the exception service routine from address $014 in the exception vector table and transfers control to the indicated address.

Since the 68000 zero-divide response is automatic and cannot be disabled in any way, you have to account for it in any programs where you use the DIVS or DIVU instructions. One way to do this is to make sure the divisor is never 0. We showed one way to do this in a program in Chapter 5. In that example you may remember we first made sure the divisor was not 0 by testing it for 0 and then did the division only when the divisor was not 0.

Another way to account for the 68000 zero-divide response is to simply write an exception service routine that takes a desired action when an invalid division occurs. The advantage of this approach is that you don't have the overhead of a more complex division routine in your mainline program. The 68000 auto- matically does the checking and does the exception routine only if there is a problem. Remember that when using any exceptions with the 68000, you must in some way load the starting address of the exception service routine in the (hard or soft) exception vector.

The CHK, TRAP, and TRAPV instructions can also cause CPU traps to occur. The CHK instruction is used to check an array index to see if it is below 0 or above the top bound of an array. If the index is out of bounds, then a type 6 trap occurs. The CPU behavior is just the same as that for the zero-divide trap except that the sixth exception vector is used instead of the fifth. The CHK instruction is useful when manipulating arrays where the array index needs to be checked often, but we do not want to complicate the mainline program code with a lot of comparisons and conditional branches.

The TRAP instruction always causes a CPU exception, but the vector number it uses depends on the instruction encoding. Any of 16 different exception vectors can be used, depending on the value of the TRAP destination operand. For example a TRAP #4 instruction would use vector 35 at memory location $08C.

The traps in group 2 are often called software interrupts because they are caused by the expected actions of a normal CPU instruction. One important use of software interrupts is to call desired subroutines or procedures from many different programs in a system. The basic input-output system in a 68000 or other computer often uses the TRAP instruction for this. The Basic Input-Output System, or BIOS, typically is a collection of routines in ROMs. Each routine performs some specific function, such as reading a character from the keyboard, writing some characters to the CRT, or reading some information from a disk. BIOS routines are called with TRAP instructions. Each TRAP vector is assigned to a specific BIOS routine.

The main advantage of calling subroutines in this way is that you don't need to worry about the absolute address where the subroutine actually resides and trying to link the subroutine into your program. All you have to know is the trap type for the routine and the format for the parameters you need to pass to the routine. Figure 8-6 shows an example program that sends a string of characters to a printer using a BIOS-like TRAP #3 instruction to call the printer driver routine. The driver is called using a trap exception.

The TRAPV instruction is used as a trap when the overflow bit of the status register is set. That is, it is useful to check for an overflow occurrence. Again, we might use it instead of a test and branch in the mainline program. The TRAPV instruction uses the exception vector from vector location 7 (address $01C).

The 68000 overflow flag, V, will be set if a signed result of an arithmetic operation on two signed numbers is too large to be represented in the destination register or memory location. For example, if you add the 8-bit signed number 0110 1100 (108 decimal) and the 8-bit signed number 0101 0001 (81 decimal), the signed result will be 1011 1101 (189 decimal). This is

TABLE 8-2
68000 EXCEPTION GROUPING AND PRIORITY

Group	Exception	Processing
0	Reset Address Error Bus Error	Exception processing begins within two clock cycles
1	Trace Interrupt Illegal Privilege	Exception processing begins before the next instruction
2	TRAP, TRAPV, CHK, Zero Divide	Exception processing is started by normal instruction execution

```
;  68000 Program
;  ABSTRACT       : This program sends a string of characters to a
;                 : printer using a print driver exception handler at
;                 : TRAP vector number 3.  The printer initialization
;                 : routine is at TRAP vector 2.
;
;  REGISTERS USED: A0 ... pointer to array of characters
;                  D0 ... one character
;                  D1 ... character sent return flag from driver
;                  D2 ... string character counter
;  PORTS USED    : none
;  PROCEDURES    : BAD_DIV, a division by 0 exception handler
;
;                        alr 3-89
CHAR_COUNT         EQU     27

         ORG        $4000              ; start the code at $4000
; Mainline code
;
;          INITIALIZATION LIST
;
;
;
;
         MOVE.B     #0,D0              ; load printer index to initialize
         TRAP       #2                 ; cause CPU exception and call TRAP handler #2

         LEA        STACK_TOP,A7       ; initialize user stack pointer to top of stack
         LEA        MESSAGE,A0         ; initialize data array pointer
         MOVE.B     CHAR_COUNT,D2      ; initialize sample loop counter
AGAIN:
         MOVE.B     (A0)+,D0           ; get character to print (& increment pointer)
         TRAP       #3                 ; invoke printer driver
         CMPI.B     #1,D1              ; if character not printed then D1=1
         BNE        NEXT

         ORI.W      #$0001,SR          ; set carry flag to indicate message not sent
         JMP        EXIT

NEXT:    DBGE       D1,AGAIN           ; go send next char if not done with string
         ANDI.W     #$FFFE,SR          ; clear carry flag to indicate char sent
EXIT:
         NOP                           ; continue with mainline program
         NOP
;        ...
         RTS


;----------------------
         ORG        $4200              ; start the data at $4200

;                                      ; declare data values
MESSAGE:           DC.B     'HELLO THERE, HOW ARE YOU?'
MESSAGE_END:       DC.B     $0D,$0A ; return and line feed

STACK_HERE:        DS.W     200        ; set stack length of 200 words
STACK_TOP:         DS.W     0          ; the stack top is at the high address

         END
```

FIGURE 8-6 68000 assembly language program for outputting characters to a printer.

the correct result for the sum of unsigned binary numbers, but it is not the correct signed result. For signed operations, the 1 in the most significant bit of the result indicates that the result is negative and in 2's complement form. The result then actually represents −67 decimal, which is obviously not the correct result of adding +108 and +89.

There are two major ways to detect and respond to an

overflow error in a program. One way is to put the branch if overflow set instruction, JVS, immediately after the arithmetic instruction. If the overflow flag is set as a result of the arithmetic operation, execution will branch to the address specified in the JVS instruction. At this address you can put an error routine that responds to the overflow in whatever way you want.

The second way of detecting and responding to a overflow error is to put the *trap on overflow* instruction, TRAPV, immediately after the arithmetic instruction in the program. If the overflow flag is not set when the 68000 executes the TRAPV instruction, the instruction will simply function as a NOP. However, if the overflow flag is set, indicating an overflow error, the 68000 will do a *type 7* trap after it executes the TRAPV instruction.

When the 68000 does a type 7 trap, it saves the status register internally, sets the S bit and clears the T bit, pushes the saved status register value onto the stack, pushes the PC on the stack, and then gets a new execution address from vector 7 at memory location $01C and loads the new address as the PC value. Instructions in the exception service routine then perform the desired response to the error condition. The service routine might, for example, set a "flag" in a memory location as we did in the BAD_DIV routine in Figure 8-5. The advantage of using the TRAPV and type 7 exception approach is that the error routine is easily accessible from any program. Calling programs don't need to know the address or name of the exception service routine; they need to know only enough to use the TRAPV instruction.

GROUP 1: TRACE, INTERRUPT, ILLEGAL, PRIVILEGE

In a section of Chapter 3 on debugging assembly language programs, we discussed the use of the single-step feature present in some monitor programs and debugger programs. When you tell a system to single step, it will execute one instruction and stop. You can then examine the contents of registers and memory locations. If they are correct, you can tell the system to execute the next instruction. In other words, when in single-step mode, a system will stop after it executes each instruction and wait for further direction from you. The 68000 trace flag (the T bit in the status register) and trace exception response make it quite easy to implement a single-step feature in a 68000-based system.

If the 68000 trace flag, T, is set, the 68000 will automatically do a type 9 trap after each instruction executes. When the 68000 does a type 9 trap, it behaves similarly to when a zero-divide trap occurs. It pushes a copy of the status register on the stack, sets the supervisor state bit (S) and clears the trace mode bit (T), and pushes the PC value for the next instruction on the stack. It then gets the value of the trace exception vector for the start of the type 9 exception service routine from address $024, and it uses this address as the location of the trace exception service routine. Another term for the service routine is the

trace *handler*, or the trace exception-handling routine. Notice that the trace bit is cleared, so that when the trace handler itself executes, it does not trap after each instruction. When the handler is done executing, it should execute an RTE instruction, which will restore the status register (with the T bit set) and then trap again after the next instruction.

The tasks involved in implementing single stepping, then, are to (1) set the trace mode flag (the T bit in the status register), (2) write a trace exception service routine, which saves all registers on the stack where they can later be examined or perhaps displayed on the CRT, and (3) load the starting address of the type 9 exception service routine into address $024 (or, more likely, into the soft vector address in RAM). The actual single-step routine will depend a great deal on the system on which it is to be implemented. We do not have space here to show you the different ways to do this. The trace mode bit is normally set or cleared using an OR to SR instruction or an AND to SR instruction, where the T bit is set or cleared. Recall that the T bit is bit 15 of the status register.

Note again that since the trace mode flag is reset when the 68000 does a type 9 trap, the single-step mode will be disabled during the exception service routine.

A *privilege* trap (type 8) occurs when an attempt is made to execute a privileged instruction while the CPU is in user state. This is done to provide some protection from other users in a multiuser system. Only the operating system should be running in supervisor state. User programs should run in user state. Recall from the instruction descriptions in Chapter 6 that the privileged instructions are STOP, RESET, RTE, MOVE to SR, AND immediate to SR, EOR immediate to SR, OR immediate to SR, and MOVE USP. Basically, any instruction that could change the supervisor state bit in the CPU is privileged. Remember that when an exception occurs, the CPU sets the S bit, placing the CPU in supervisor state. This means that if a user-mode program attempts to execute a privileged instruction, the CPU will automatically perform a type 8 trap and transfer control to the supervisor mode privilege violation exception service routine. That routine would then typically throw the user program out of the machine and tell the user he or she tried to execute a privileged instruction. That is, the user tried to break the operating system's and CPU's security mechanism, which is forbidden.

A third group 1 exception occurs when the CPU encounters an instruction bit pattern that it does not recognize. This causes an *illegal instruction* trap. This can happen if a hand-assembled program was incorrectly hand assembled. Another way this can happen is if you try to execute your data. Since the bit pattern does not represent an instruction known to the CPU, the CPU has no option but to trap and request that an exception service routine figure out what to do. Typically, the service routine will tell you that you tried to execute garbage for instructions and will throw your program out of the machine (i.e., stop its execution). The line 1010 and line 1111 emulation exceptions are special cases of the illegal instruction trap, each of which has its own exception vector. The illegal instruction trap uses vector 4.

One use of the illegal instruction interrupt is to implement a breakpoint function in a system. In Chapter 4 we described the use of breakpoints in debugging assembly language programs. We hope that you have been using them in debugging your programs. When you insert a breakpoint, the system executes the instructions up to the breakpoint and then saves the contents of registers on the stack. Depending on the system, the register contents will be displayed on the CRT, or they can be checked with an examine register command. Unlike the single-step feature, which stops execution after each instruction, the breakpoint feature executes all the instructions up to the inserted breakpoint and then stops execution.

When you tell some 68000 systems to insert a breakpoint at some point in your program, they actually do it by temporarily replacing the instruction word at that address with $4AFC, the 68000 code used to force an illegal instruction trap. When the 68000 executes this ILLEGAL instruction, it pushes the status register on the stack, resets S and sets T, and pushes the PC value for the next mainline instruction on the stack. The 68000 then gets the vector value of the start of the illegal instruction exception service routine from the vector at address $010. A breakpoint exception service routine usually saves all the registers' contents on the stack. Depending on the system, it may then send the register contents to the CRT display and wait for the next command from the user, or in a simple system it may just return control to the user. In this case an examine register command can be used to check if the register contents are correct at that point in the program. When the breakpoint is completed, the illegal instruction code word is replaced with the original mainline code word, the return address saved in the stack is decremented by 2, and the exception-handling routine performs an RTE back to the interrupted mainline program. The return address saved on the stack is incremented to ensure that the mainline codeword replaced by the illegal instruction is actually executed and not skipped over.

The fourth group 1 exception condition is the *interrupt* proper. This is probably the most interesting and most often-used exception that occurs in 68000 systems. Interrupts are caused by input/output (I/O) devices, which assert some of the 68000 lines. The I/O devices, sometimes called *peripheral* devices, or just *peripherals*, consist of everything from disc drives, printers, and keyboards to simple sensors that detect power failure. The devices interrupt the 68000 because they need its attention for some reason, typically because the CPU is expected to read (input) some data or write (output) some data.

The 68000 has three interrupt pins. Normally, none of these is asserted. If any or all of these pins are asserted, then the CPU will be interrupted. The exception vector selected will depend on the combination of interrupt lines asserted and the use of the $\overline{VPA}$ line. The three interrupt lines, $\overline{IPL0}$, $\overline{IPL1}$, and $\overline{IPL2}$, are used to encode the *priority* of the interrupt as well as to signal that an interrupt is requested. Seven is the highest priority. A priority 6 interrupt is also called a *level* 6 interrupt. A level 7 interrupt has higher priority than a level 6 interrupt, level 6 is higher priority than level 5, and so on. The CPU status register has a 3-bit *interrupt mask,* which encodes the CPU priority. The interrupt priority must be higher than the CPU priority for an interrupt to occur. If the CPU priority is higher than or equal to the interrupt priority, then the interrupt will not be acknowledged. If the CPU priority is higher than or equal to the interrupt priority, then the CPU will not recognize the interrupt and will cause neither an exception nor transfer to the interrupt-service routine. In this way the CPU can protect itself from an interrupt if the programmer chooses. A level 7 interrupt is the one case that breaks this rule. If a level 7 interrupt is requested (all three interrupt lines asserted) and the CPU is at priority level 7 (or any lower priority level), then the interrupt will still occur. A level 7 interrupt is called a *nonmaskable interrupt* because it cannot be masked out at any CPU priority.

A common use of the level 7 interrupt is to save program data in the case of a system power failure. Some external circuitry detects when the ac power to the system fails and sends an interrupt signal to the interrupt input. Because of the large-filter capacitors in most power supplies, the dc system power will remain for perhaps 50 ms after the ac power is gone. This is more than enough time for a level 7 interrupt service routine to copy program data to some RAM that has a battery backup power supply. When the ac power returns, program data can be restored from the battery-backed RAM and the program can resume execution where it left off. A practice problem at the end of the chapter gives you a chance to write a simple ISR for this task.

Interrupt processing proceeds in a fashion similar to any other exception processing. The status register contents are saved, the S bit is asserted, and the T bit is not asserted. The CPU priority level is set equal to the interrupt level. Setting the CPU priority equal to the interrupt level prevents the same interrupt from causing an infinite loop of interrupt acknowledges while the interrupt line continues to be asserted. In effect the CPU automatically protects itself from further interrupts at the same or lower levels until the interrupt-service routine changes the CPU priority level. The easy way to change the CPU priority level is by using an ORI to SR instruction to move the CPU priority level up (ORing to the interrupt mask in the status register) or ANDI to SR instruction to move the CPU priority down.

Since the $\overline{IPL0}$, $\overline{IPL1}$, and $\overline{IPL2}$ lines are level activated, the interrupt signal must remain present until it is recognized by the 68000. The RTE instruction at the end of the interrupt-service routine restores the status register to the condition it was in before the ISR by popping the status register off the stack. This will reenable the interrupt inputs. If a high-level signal is still present on the IPL input lines, it will cause the 68000 to be interrupted again. If we do not want the

68000 to be interrupted again by the same input signal, we have to use external hardware to make sure the interrupt signals are made low again before we reenable interrupts with the ANDI to SR instruction or before the end of the interrupt-service routine.

During interrupt processing the 68000 will normally get an interrupt-vector number from the interrupt device. Figure 8-7 shows a flowchart for the interrupt acknowledge, vector number acquisition, and start of interrupt processing. Figure 8-8 shows the signal-timing diagram for these operations. These diagrams are similar to those for the 68000 read and write processing examined in Chapter 7. First the CPU compares the interrupt level with the status register to see if the interrupt should be acknowledged. If the interrupt level is higher (or is level 7), the CPU places the interrupt level on A1, A2, and A3 to tell the I/O device which interrupt level it is acknowledging. The CPU sets the function code lines to interrupt acknowledge (FC0, FC1, and FC2 to binary 111). The CPU asserts the address strobe line ($\overline{AS}$) and asserts both data strobe lines ($\overline{UDS}$ and $\overline{LDS}$). $\overline{LDS}$ is asserted, but no data is read from the upper data byte (D8–D15). The I/O device then provides 1 byte, which is the vector number, on D0–D7 and asserts the $\overline{DTACK}$ line. The CPU reads and saves the vector number and negates the data strobes and the address strobe. The I/O device negates $\overline{DTACK}$, and the CPU is ready to continue normal exception servicing.

The status register is pushed onto the supervisor stack, and the PC is pushed onto the stack. The interrupt-vector number is used to determine which exception vector address to use. The indicated exception vector (interrupt-service-routine address) is accessed, and interrupt servicing begins in the ISR code.

The interrupt-vector number tells the 68000 which address in the exception vector table to use. Referring again to Table 8-1, notice that the user interrupt uses exception vectors 64 through 255, which start at address $100 and continue to address $3FC. The I/O device provides 1 byte of data, which encodes the vector number to use. If $\overline{BERR}$ is asserted during the

interrupt-vector-number read cycle, then it is assumed that the interrupt was *spurious* and the spurious exception vector—number 24 at address $060—is used.

The $\overline{VPA}$ line is used in data transfer with 6800 family peripherals, and it is also used during the interrupt-acknowledge cycle to cause *autovectoring*. (The Motorola 6800 family is Motorola's 8-bit CPU and I/O processor line of ICs.) If $\overline{VPA}$ is asserted while the processor is fetching the vector number, then the 68000 assumes autovectoring is being requested; rather than using one of the user-interrupt vectors, the 68000 will use the interrupt-autovector exception vector that corresponds to the priority level of the interrupt. This provides seven different exception vectors (numbers 25 through 31), which can be used without having to provide an interrupt-vector number. This speeds up operation and makes the connection simpler. If only seven or fewer different devices are used, then they can each be connected at a different priority level and each can use a different autovector exception vector. If there are more than seven I/O devices, then the system designer has at least two options. One option is to use an external interrupt controller to connect several devices at the same priority level. The other option is to use I/O device controllers, which adhere to 6800 family conventions and provide their own interrupt vectors. Which design makes most sense depends on the specific types and number of devices. We will examine an external interrupt controller, the Intel 8259A, in detail later in this chapter.

GROUP 0—RESET. ADDRESS ERROR, BUS ERROR

Finally we come to the group 0 exceptions. These are the most severe exceptions and generally indicate a major problem or a critical exception. When the reset line is asserted, the external hardware is requesting a radical event—start over! When an address error occurs, the CPU again is in a very serious condition. It has an address with which it cannot deal, such as an odd address where a word operation has been request-

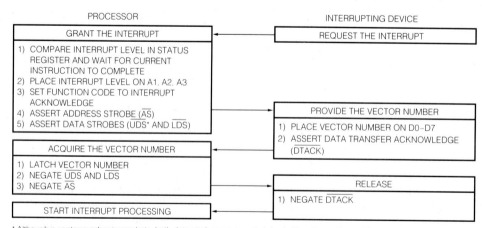

FIGURE 8-7   68000 interrupt-acknowledge processing flowchart.

FIGURE 8-8
68000 interrupt-acknowledge
signal-timing diagram.

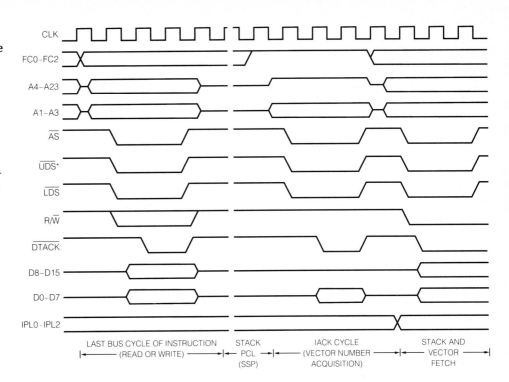

*Although a vector number is one byte, both data strobes are asserted due to the microcode used for exception processing. The processor does not recognize anything on data lines D8 through D15 at this time.

ed (the 68000 can't do it during normal operation). A bus error indicates that some I/O device or memory is simply not responding. These are serious problems from the CPU's viewpoint, and help from an exception-handling routine is required.

During group 0–type exceptions, the CPU pushes more information onto the system stack than it does for group 1 and 2 exceptions. This additional information consists of four additional words of data, including the relevant access address, the instruction register, and some status bits describing the operation that was occurring when the exception occurred (R/W̄, I/N, and function code). Figure 8-9 shows the organization and order of information pushed during a group 0 exception. The program counter and status register are the same as we saw during the group 1 and 2 exceptions. The access address was the effective address being used by the CPU when the exception occurred. Depending on the addressing mode in use by the particular instruction being executed, the effective address

may be any valid combination of register values, memory values, and instruction code displacements or addresses. The instruction register contains the code word on which the CPU was operating internally when the exception occurred. The R/W̄ bit indicates whether a read or a write was occurring. A 1 implies a read. The I/N bit indicates whether or not the CPU was processing an instruction. A 1 indicates that it was not, which typically means the CPU was fetching a new instruction to execute. The function code bits indicate the state of the FC0, FC1, and FC2 CPU status lines when the exception occurred. This information is not sufficient to restart the interrupted operation, but it is very useful in debugging the situation.

When a type 0 trap occurs, the CPU will begin exception processing within two clock cycles, terminating the operation currently in process if necessary. The status register is copied internally, the supervisor state is entered, and tracing is suppressed (S bit asserted, T bit off). The appropriate vector number is gener-

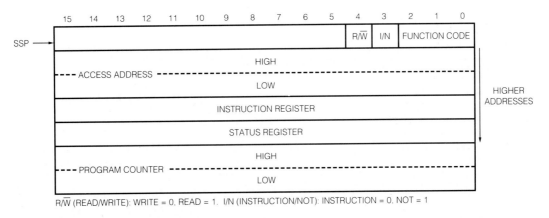

FIGURE 8-9 Exception stack order (group 0).

ated (2 for bus error, 3 for address error, and 0 for reset). The program counter is pushed on the supervisor stack, followed by the status register. The instruction register (internal to the CPU) is pushed on the stack, followed by the access address. Finally the R/W, I/N, and function code bits are pushed as a word of data. The CPU then accesses the desired exception vector, loads the new address into the PC, and begins executing the exception-handling routine.

If a second bus error occurs during the exception-acknowledgment processing for a bus error or an address error, then the CPU halts. This is called a *double bus error*. Only the $\overline{RESET}$ pin can restart a halted processor.

A bus error is caused by the $\overline{BERR}$ line. Normally external logic will assert the bus error line when it wishes the CPU to execute a bus error trap. In a 68000 system, such hardware would be used in memory space where there are no I/O or memory devices. The hardware's purpose would be to prevent the CPU from waiting forever if it referenced an address where there was no device to assert $\overline{DTACK}$ or $\overline{VPA}/\overline{VMA}$.

An address error occurs when the CPU attempts to reference a word or long-word data operand or an instruction word using an odd address. An address error can be thought of as an internally generated bus error.

The reset exception is a special case. A reset is used to indicate a catastrophic event that requires a restart of the system. Restart processing aborts the current operation in such a manner that it cannot be restarted. The current bus cycle is aborted. The S bit is asserted, moving the CPU to supervisor state. The T bit is cleared, turning tracing off. The vector number 0 is generated. The processor is forced to priority level 7 (i.e., the status register priority interrupt mask is set to binary 111). Nothing is saved on the stack. A new stack pointer is loaded from vector number 1 (address $004). A new PC is loaded from exception vector 0 (address $000), and processing starts in the reset exception service routine.

Note that the $\overline{RESET}$ instruction does not cause the reset exception trap but does assert the $\overline{RESET}$ line to reset external devices. The $\overline{RESET}$ is a bidirectional signal that can be used by the CPU to reset I/O devices and by external hardware to reset the CPU.

PRIORITY OF 68000 INTERRUPTS

As you read through the preceding discussions of the different exception types, you may have wondered what happens if two or more exceptions occur at the same time. The answer is that the highest-priority exception will be serviced first, and then the next-highest-priority exception will be serviced. Table 8-2 shows the priorities of the 68000 exceptions. Group 0 exceptions have the highest priority, and within group 0 the reset exception has the highest priority, followed by the bus error and then the address error exception. Group 1 has higher priority than group 2. Group 1 is ordered internally as indicated in Table 8-2. Since only one

instruction can be executing at a time, there is no priority implied among the group 2 exceptions.

Group 2 and group 1 exceptions begin processing at the normal completion of the current instruction. Privilege violation and illegal instruction are detected before the execution of the offending instruction. Group 0 exception processing aborts the current operation and begins within two clock cycles. The priority relationship between two exceptions determines which is taken or taken first. Some examples will show you what these priorities actually mean.

As a first example, suppose a bus error occurs during the processing of a TRAP instruction. The bus error takes precedence and will be processed first. The TRAP instruction processing is aborted.

As another example, suppose an interrupt request occurs during the processing of an instruction when the T bit is set. Suppose also that the CPU priority is lower than that of the interrupt, so that the interrupt is acknowledged. In this case the trace exception has priority and is processed first. Before instruction processing resumes in the trace exception handler, however, the interrupt will be acknowledged and the interrupt exception will be processed, with normal instruction processing commencing in the interrupt-service routine.

Now that we have shown you the different types of 68000 exceptions and how the 68000 responds to each, we will show you a few examples of how the 68000 hardware interrupts are used. Other applications of interrupts are shown throughout the rest of the book.

HARDWARE INTERRUPT APPLICATIONS

Hardware and Software Considerations when Using Interrupts

HARDWARE

Whenever you are going to do a task with an interrupt, there are some important hardware points for you to consider. Among these are the following:

1. How many interrupt inputs does the microprocessor have?

2. Do these inputs require active high, active low, or edge-active signals to assert them?

3. Do the interrupt inputs have priorities?

4. Is external hardware required to insert a restart instruction or interrupt type, or is this done automatically when the CPU responds to the interrupt?

SOFTWARE

Among the software considerations when you are going to use an interrupt are the following:

1. What instructions are required to unmask/enable the interrupt input you want to use?

2. How is the stack pointer initialized?

3. Does the CPU automatically save flags and register contents when it responds to the interrupt, or do you have to use push instructions at the start of the routine to do this?

4. How can data required by the interrupt-service routine be accessed no matter where in the main program the interrupt occurs?

5. What instructions are required at the end of the routine to restore main program flags and registers, enable interrupts, and return to the interrupted mainline program?

SIMPLE INTERRUPT DATA INPUT

One of the most common uses of interrupts is to relieve a CPU of the burden of polling. In Chapter 4 we showed you how ASCII characters can be read in from an encoded keyboard on a polled basis. Figure 4-18 shows the circuit connections, and Figure 4-19 shows the algorithm and program for this. To refresh your memory, polling works as follows.

The strobe, or data-ready, signal from some external device is connected to an input port line on the microcomputer. The microcomputer uses a program loop to read and test this port line over and over until the data-ready signal is found to be asserted. The microcomputer then exits the polling loop and reads in the data from the external device. Data can also be output on a polled basis.

The disadvantage of polled input or output is that while the microcomputer is polling the strobe or data-ready signal, it cannot easily be doing other tasks. In systems where the microcomputer must be doing many tasks, polling is a waste of time, so interrupt input and output is used. In this case the data-ready, or strobe, signal is connected to an interrupt input on the microcomputer. The microcomputer then goes about doing its other tasks until it is interrupted by a data-ready signal from the external device. An interrupt-service routine can read in or send out the desired data and, when finished, return execution to the interrupted program.

For our example here we will connect the key-pressed strobe to the interrupt inputs of the 68000 on an URDA MDS. We will use autovectoring because it does not require an external hardware device to insert the exception vector number.

Refer to the 68000 schematic (Figure 7-11), which shows a 74148 multiplexer IC (IC3 in C3) connected to the IPL inputs to the CPU. The inputs I0–I7 of the 74148 can be used to cause autovectored interrupts on the 68000. Interrupt autovectors 2–5 are used by the two 6821s on the MDS, so we will use interrupt autovector 1 for this example. When only input I1 of the 74148 is asserted, the multiplexer IC in turn asserts $\overline{IPL0}$ and does not assert $\overline{IPL1}$ and $\overline{IPL2}$.

Figure 8-10 shows how we modified the circuitry of Figure 4-18 for our example here. We have no longer connected the key strobe line to a status bit to be polled

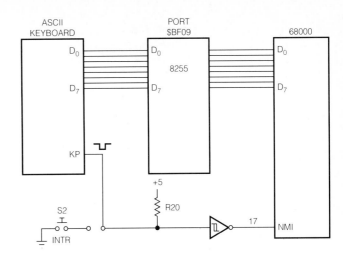

FIGURE 8-10 Circuit modifications for URDA MDS interrupt input.

by the CPU. Instead we have connected the key strobe output to the 74148 I1 input. The 74148 output is, in turn, connected to the CPU $\overline{IPL0}$ line (as well as other lines). When a key on the ASCII keyboard is pressed, the keyboard circuitry sends out the ASCII code for the pressed key on its eight parallel data lines, and it asserts the key-pressed strobe line. The key-pressed strobe assertion causes the I1 input of the 74148 to be asserted, which causes the CPU's $\overline{IPL0}$ line to be asserted. This causes the 68000 to do a group 1 interrupt. Now let's look at the hardware and software considerations for this interrupt example.

The hardware considerations for this example are quite simple. The $\overline{IPL0}$ input requires a sustained low signal for assertion; with the circuit connections shown in Figure 8-10, this will be produced when a key on the ASCII keyboard is pressed. Since we are using only one interrupt here, we are not concerned about priorities. In response to its $\overline{IPL0}$ input being asserted and if the CPU priority level is 0 (i.e., the CPU interrupt priority mask in the status register is 000), the 68000 automatically does a group 1 interrupt response. No external hardware is needed to insert the interrupt type.

The software considerations require a little more thought, but their answers are very similar to those for the divide by 0 example in a previous section. At the start of the mainline we need to load address $7FF4 with the soft vector table address of the level 1 interrupt-service routine. Since any interrupt response uses the stack, we need to set up a stack. Assuming that we are going to read in the ASCII characters from the keyboard and put them in an array in memory, we need to set up a data area for the array. In the actual code section of the mainline, we need to initialize the stack pointer. Figure 8-11, pp. 216–17, shows the instructions for doing all this. Another important thing to do in the start of the mainline program is to initialize a pointer to the start of the array, where the ASCII characters will be put as they are read in. The state-

```
; 68000 PROGRAM TO READ CHARACTERS FROM A KEYBOARD
; ABSTRACT         : The mainline of this procedure initializes the interrupt
;                  : table with the address of the procedure that reads the
;                  : characters from a keyboard on an interrupt basis.
;
; REGISTERS USED: A0 ... used to place KEYBOARD ISR address
; PORTS USED     : none in mainline
; PROCEDURES     : KEYBOARD - ISR to read characters from Keyboard
;
;                          alr 3-89
          ORG      $4000              ; start the code at $4000
;
;         INITIALIZATION
;
          LEA      STACK_TOP,A7       ; initialize user stack pointer to top of stack

; store address for the KEYBOARD routine at address $7FF4.  This
; address will be used by the ROM monitor as the user level 1 interrupt
; service routine indirect address (i.e. the address of the KEYBOARD
; ISR will be found at address $7FF4).

          LEA      KEYBOARD,A0        ; get the address of the KEYBOARD ISR
          MOVE.L   A0,($7FF4)         ; save that address at $7FF4

          ANDI.W   #$F8FF,SR          ; enable interrupts (set mask to 000)

; simulate larger program
HERE:     BRA      HERE               ; loop forever

;----------------------------
          ORG      $4200              ; start the data at $4200

STACK_HERE:    DS.W    200            ; set stack length of 200 words
STACK_TOP:     DS.W    0              ; the stack top is at the high address
ASCII_STRING:  DS.B    100            ; storage for characters
ASCII_POINTER: DC.L    ASCII_STRING   ; pointer to start of char storage
CHARCNT:       DC.B    100            ; read 100 characters
KEYDONE:       DC.B    0              ; done flag (initially false = 0)
```

(a)   (continued)

FIGURE 8-11   Reading characters from an ASCII keyboard on an interrupt
basis. (a) Initialization and mainline. (b) Interrupt-service routine, p. 217.

ment ASCII_POINTER DC.L ASCII_STRING in the data segment in Figure 8-11 sets aside a long-word location in memory and initializes that location with the address of the start of the array we declared to put the ASCII characters in. In the interrupt-service routine we get this pointer, use it to store a character, and increment it to point to the next location in the array. Since this pointer is stored in a named memory location, it can be accessed easily by the ISR, no matter when the interrupt occurs in the mainline program.

Next we enable interrupts by setting the CPU priority to 0 using an AND to SR instruction. Finally, the HERE: BRA HERE instruction at the end of the mainline program simulates a complex mainline program that the 68000 might be executing. The 68000 will execute this instruction over and over until an interrupt occurs. When an interrupt occurs, the 68000 will service the interrupt and then return to execute the HERE: JMP HERE instruction over and over again until the next interrupt.

Figure 8-11 also shows the interrupt-service routine for this example. The comments for the ISR express its algorithm fairly clearly. After saving A0, D0, and D1 on the stack, we check to see if all characters have been read. If CHARCNT is zero, then we do not read in any characters. If CHARCNT is not zero, we copy the array pointer from its named memory location, ASCII_POINTER, to A0. We then read in the ASCII character from the port to which the keyboard is connected and mask the parity bit of the ASCII character. The MOVE.B D1,(A0)+ instruction next copies the ASCII character to the memory location pointed to by A0 and increments A0 to point to the next available location. To get the pointer ready for the read and store operation, we store the incremented pointer back into memory at the ASCII_POINTER location. Finally, our work done, we restore D1, D0, and A0 and return to the mainline program.

Sitting in a HERE: JMP HERE loop waiting for an interrupt signal may not seem like much of an im-

```
;------------------------
; Subroutine: KEYBOARD
; ABSTRACT       : This interrupt service routine reads in ASCII characters
;                : from an encoded keyboard on an interrupt basis and
;                : stores them in a buffer in memory.
;
; REGISTERS USED: A0 ... pointer to current location in buffer
;                : D0 ... character count
;                : D1 ... the current character
; PORTS USED     : $C014 as the input port for the keyboard input
; PROCEDURES     : none used
;
            ORG      $4100                  ; start KEYBOARD ISR at $4100
KEYBOARD:
            MOVEM.L  D0-D1/A0,-(A7)         ; save D0,D1, and A1

            CMPI.B   #0,(CHARCNT)           ; see if all characters read in
            BEQ      EXIT                   ; leave if all done

            MOVE.B   (CHARCNT),D0           ; get character count
            LEA      (ASCII_POINTER),A0     ; get the current string pointer
            MOVE.B   D1,($7FF4)             ; read in a character
            ANDI.B   #$7F,D1                ; mask off the parity bit
            MOVE.B   D1,(A0)+               ; move character to buffer and increment
                                            ;   pointer
            MOVE.L   A0,(ASCII_POINTER)     ; save incremented pointer in memory
            SUBQ.B   #1,D0                  ; decrement counter
            MOVE.B   D0,(CHARCNT)           ; save decremented counter in memory
            BNE      NOTDONE                ; if (read all 100 chars)
            MOVE.B   #$01,(KEYDONE)         ;    set last character flag
            JMP      EXIT                   ; else
NOTDONE:
            MOVE.B   #$00,(KEYDONE)         ;    clear flag (not done)

EXIT:
            MOVEM.L  (A7)+,D0-D1/A0         ; restore D0,D1, and A1

            RTE                             ; return from exception to the interrupted
                                            ; program, restore the status register

            END
```

(b)

FIGURE 8-11 (continued)

provement over polling the key-pressed strobe. However, in a more realistic program the 68000 would be doing many other tasks between keyboard interrupts. With polling, the 68000 would not easily be able to do these other tasks.

USING INTERRUPTS FOR COUNTING AND TIMING COUNTING

As a simple example of the use of an interrupt input for counting, suppose that we are using a 68000 to control a printed-circuit-board-making machine in our computerized electronics factory. Further suppose that we want to detect each finished board as it comes out of the machine and to keep a count of finished boards so that we can compare this count with the number of boards fed in. This way we can determine if any boards were lost in the machine.

To do this count on an interrupt basis, all we have to do is detect when a board passes out of the machine and send an interrupt signal to an interrupt input on the 68000. The interrupt-service routine for that input can simply increment the board count stored in a named memory location.

To detect a board coming out of the machine, we use an infrared LED, a phototransistor, and two conditioning gates, as shown in Figure 8-12, p. 218. The LED is positioned over the track where the boards come out, and the phototransistor is positioned below the track. When no board is between the LED and the phototransistor, the light from the LED will strike the phototransistor and turn it on. The collector of the phototransistor will then be low, as will the interrupt input to the 74148, and the IPL lines on the 68000 will not be asserted. When a board passes between the LED and the phototransistor, the light will not reach the phototransistor, and it will turn off. Its collector will go high, as will the signal to the 74148; in turn, the $\overline{IPL0}$ input to the 68000 will be asserted. The 74LS14 Schmitt trigger inverters are necessary to turn the slow rise-time signal from the phototransistor collector into a

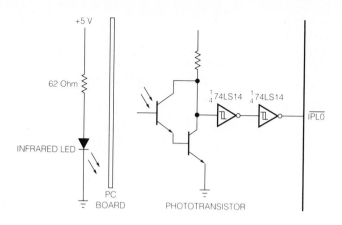

FIGURE 8-12   Circuit for optically detecting presence of an object.

signal that meets the risetime requirements of the 74148 input. When the 68000 senses that the $\overline{IPL0}$ line is being asserted, it automatically does an interrupt response. As we mentioned before, all the interrupt-service routine has to do in this case is increment the board count in a named memory location and return to running the machine. This same technique can be used to count people going into a stadium, cows coming in from the pasture, or just about anything else you might want to count.

TIMING

In Chapter 4 we showed how a delay loop could be used to set the time between microcomputer operations. In that example we used a delay loop to let us take in data samples at 1-ms intervals. The obvious disadvantage of a delay loop is that while the microcomputer is stuck in the delay loop, it cannot easily be doing other useful work. In many cases a delay loop would be waste of the microcomputer's valuable time. For most microcomputer timing, an interrupt approach is much more efficient.

Suppose, for example, that in our 68000-controlled printed-circuit-board machine we need to check the pH of a solution approximately every 4 min. If we used a delay loop to count off the 4 min, either the 68000 wouldn't be able to do much else, or we would have to do some difficult calculations to figure out at what points in the program to check the pH.

To solve this problem, all we have to do is connect a simple 1-Hz pulse source to an interrupt input, as shown in Figure 8-13. This 555 timer circuit is not very accurate, but it is inexpensive, and it is good enough for this application. We connected the timer output to the 68000 interrupt input (through the 74148), as you might do to demonstrate this concept on an URDA MDS board. The 555 timer will send an interrupt signal to the 68000 $\overline{IPL0}$ input approximately once every second. If we simply count the number of

interrupts that occur, we will then know how many seconds have passed.

Here's how the programming is done for this application. In the mainline we set aside a memory location for the seconds' count and initialize that location to the number of seconds that we want to count off. In this case we want 4 min, which is 240 decimal, or $F0, seconds. Each time the 68000 receives an interrupt from the 555 timer, it executes the interrupt service routine for the level 1 interrupt. In this ISR we decrement the seconds' count in the named memory location and test to see if the count is down to zero yet. If the count is zero, we know that 4 min have elapsed, so we reload the seconds' count memory location with $F0 and call the routine that reads the pH of the solution and takes appropriate action if the pH is not correct. If the seconds' count is not zero, execution

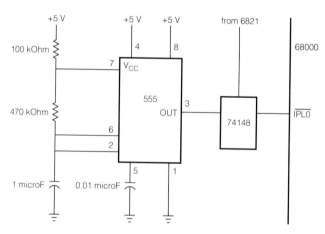

FIGURE 8-13   Inexpensive 1-Hz pulse source for interrupt timing.

simply returns to the mainline program until the next interrupt from the 555 or from some other source occurs. To help you visualize how this works, Figure 8-14 shows the algorithm for this mainline and ISR. The advantage of this interrupt approach is that the interrupt-service routine takes only a few microseconds of the 68000's time once every second. The rest of the time, the 68000 is free to run the mainline program.

USING AN INTERRUPT TO PRODUCE A REAL-TIME CLOCK

Another application using a 1-Hz interrupt input might be to generate a real-time clock of seconds, minutes, and hours. The time from this clock can then be displayed and/or printed out on time cards, etc. To generate the clock a 1-Hz signal is applied to an interrupt input. A seconds' count, a minutes' count, and an hours' count are kept in three successive memory locations. When an interrupt occurs, the seconds' count is incremented by 1. If the seconds' count is not equal to 60, then execution is simply returned to the mainline program. If the seconds' count is equal to 60, then the seconds' count is reset to zero, and the minutes' count is incremented by 1. If the minutes' count is not 60, then execution is simply returned to the mainline. If the minutes' count is 60, then the minutes' count is reset to 0, and the hours' count is incremented by 1. If the hours' count is not 13, then execution is simply returned to the mainline. If the hours' count is equal to 13, then it is reset to 1 and execution is returned to the mainline. A problem at the end of the chapter asks you to write the algorithm and program for this real-time clock.

The interrupt-service routine for the real-time clock can easily be modified to keep track of other time measurements as well, such as the 4-min timer shown in the preceding example. In other words, the single interrupt-service routine can be used to keep track of several different time intervals. By counting a different number of interrupts or applying a different frequency signal to the interrupt input, this technique can be used to time many different tasks in a microcomputer system.

GENERATING AN ACCURATE TIME BASE FOR TIMING INTERRUPTS

The 555 timer that we used for the 4-min timer described before was accurate enough for that application, but for many applications, it is not. For more precise timing we usually use a signal derived from a crystal-controlled oscillator such as the processor clock signal. The processor clock signal is stable, but it is obviously too high in frequency to drive a processor interrupt input directly. Therefore, it is divided down with an external counter device to an appropriate frequency for the interrupt input. Most microcomputers have a counter device such as the Intel 8253 or 8254, which can be programmed with instructions to divide an input frequency by any desired number. Besides acting as programmable frequency dividers, these devices have many important uses in microcomputer systems. Therefore, the next section describes how an 8254 operates, how an 8524 can easily be added to an URDA MDS board, and how an 8254 is used in a variety of interrupt applications. In the next section we also use the 8254 discussion to show you the general procedure for initializing any of the pro-

```
INITIALIZE
        INTERRUPT POINTER TABLE
        STACK AND STACK SEGMENT POINTER
        DATA SEGMENT
        SECONDS COUNT TO 240 DECIMAL
WAIT FOR INTERRUPT
```

(a)

```
SAVE REGISTERS
DECREMENT SECONDS COUNT
IF SECONDS COUNT = 0 THEN
        RELOAD SECONDS COUNT WITH 240 DECIMAL
        CALL pH READ PROCEDURE
        RESTORE REGISTERS
        RETURN TO MAINLINE
ELSE RESTORE REGISTERS
        RETURN TO MAINLINE
```

(b)

FIGURE 8-14 Algorithm to read pH at 4-min intervals. (a) Initialization and mainline. (b) Interrupt-service routine.

grammable peripheral devices we discuss in later chapters.

A Software Programmable Timer/Counter: the Intel 8253 and 8254

Because of the many tasks for which they can be used in microcomputer systems, it is very important that you understand programmable timer/counters. As you read through the following sections, pay particular attention to the applications of this device in systems and the general procedure for initializing a programmable device such as the 8254. Read lightly through the discussions of the different counter modes to become aware of the types of problems that the device can solve for you. You can later dig into the details of these discussions when you have a specific problem to solve.

Another important point to make to you here is that the discussions of various devices throughout the rest of this book are not intended to replace the manufacturers' data sheets for the devices. Many of the programmable peripheral devices we discuss are so versatile that each requires almost a small book to describe all the details of its operations. The discussions here are intended to introduce you to the devices, show you what they can be used for, and show you enough details about them so that you can do some real jobs with them. After you become familiar with using a device in some simple applications, you can read the data sheets to learn about further features of the devices.

Basic 8253 and 8254 Operation

The Intel 8253 and 8254 each contain three 16-bit counters, which can be programmed to operate in several different modes. The 8253 and 8254 devices are pin-for-pin compatible, and they are nearly identical in function. The major differences are as follows:

1. The maximum input clock frequency for the 8253 is 2.6 MHz, and the maximum clock frequency for the 8254 is 8 MHz (10 MHz for the 8254-2).

2. The 8254 has a *read-back* feature, which allows you to latch the count in a counter and the status of the counter at any point. The 8253 does not have this read-back feature.

To simplify reading of this section, we refer only to the 8254. However, you can assume that the discussion also applies to the 8253 except where we specifically state otherwise.

As shown by the block diagram of the 8254 in Figure 8-15, the device contains three 16-bit counters. In some ways these counters are similar to the TTL presettable counters we reviewed in Chapter 1. The big advantage of these counters, however, is that you can load a count in them, start them, and stop them with instructions in your program. The device is then said

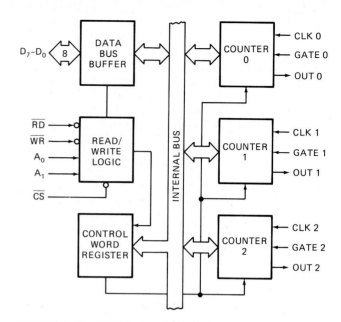

FIGURE 8-15   8254 internal block diagram. (*Intel Corporation*)

to be *software programmable*. To program the device you send count bytes and control words to the device, just as you would send data to a port device.

If you look along the left side of the block diagram in Figure 8-15, you will see the signal lines used to interface the device to the system buses. A little later we show how these are actually connected in a real system. The main points for you to note about the 8254 at the moment are that it has an 8-bit interface to the data bus, it has a $\overline{CS}$ input, which is asserted by an address decoder when the device is addressed, and it has two address inputs, A0 and A1, to allow you to address one of the three counters or the control word register in the device.

The right side of the 8254 block diagram in Figure 8-15 shows the counter inputs and outputs. You can apply a signal of any frequency from dc to 8 MHz (2.6 MHz for the 8253) to the counter clock inputs, labeled CLK in the diagram. The GATE inputs on each counter allow you to start or stop that counter with an external hardware signal. If the GATE input of a counter is high (1), then the counter is enabled for counting. If the GATE input is low, the counter is disabled. The resultant frequency or pulse from each counter appears on its OUT pin. Now let's see how a programmable peripheral device such as the 8254 is connected in a system.

SYSTEM CONNECTIONS FOR AN 8254 TIMER/COUNTER

An 8254 is a very useful device to have in a microcomputer system, but, in order to keep the cost down, the URDA MDS was not designed with one on the board. For an actual example of how an 8254 is connected in a system, we show you here how to add one to an URDA MDS board. If you use wire-wrap headers for connectors J1 and J2, the circuitry shown can easily be wire wrapped on a prototyping board connected to the URDA MDS board. URDA makes an add-on product for the MDS specifically for this purpose.

Figure 8-16 shows the circuit connections for adding an 8254 and 8259A(s) to an URDA MDS board. We discuss the 8259A priority interrupt controller, or PIC,

in the last section of this chapter. Analyzing the circuit in Figure 8-16 should help refresh your memory on address decoding.

The 74LS138 in Figure 8-14 is used to produce chip select ($\overline{\text{CS}}$) signals for the 8254, the 8259A, and any other I/O devices we might want to add. We will look first at the circuitry around this device to determine

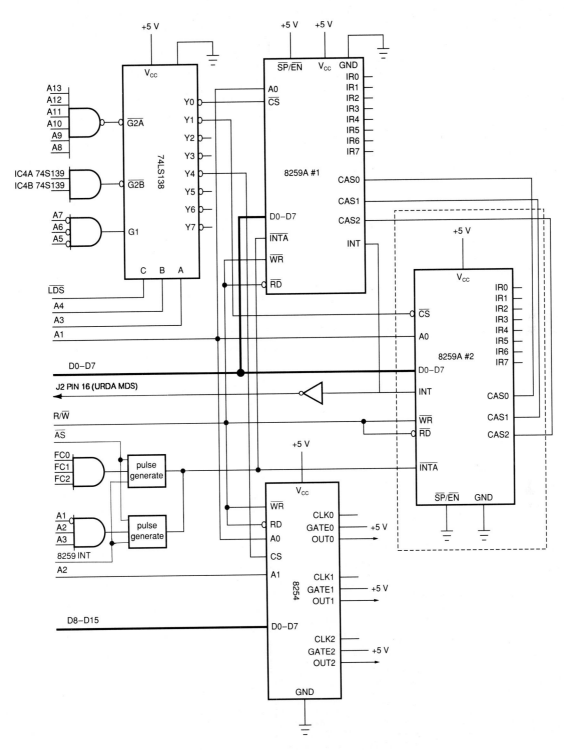

FIGURE 8-16   Circuit showing how to add an 8254 and 8259A(s) to an URDA MDS board.

the system base address that selects each device. The 74LS138 is a three-input and eight-output version of the 74LS139, with which we dealt in detail in the last chapter. The 74S139 has two inputs and four outputs, but the general operating philosophy of the two devices is the same. The inputs are used to select one of the outputs. At most one output will be active at a time. The input connections cause the address decoding we desire in our system. Let's look at the 74LS138 connections in more detail.

In order for any of the outputs of the 74LS138 to be asserted, the G1, $\overline{G2A}$, and $\overline{G2B}$ enable inputs must all be asserted. The G1 input will be asserted (high) if system address lines A5, A6, and A7 are all low. The $\overline{G2A}$ input will be asserted (low) if system address lines A8–A13 are all high. As shown by the truth table in Figure 8-17, these two inputs then will be asserted for a system base address of $BF00. The $\overline{G2B}$ input of the 74LS138 will be asserted (low) if the 74LS139 lines are low, as they will be for a port read or write operation involving the third address block. Here we are using the address decoding on the main URDA MDS to condition the address decoding being performed by the 74LS138.

Now, remember from Chapter 7 that only one of the Y outputs of the address decoder (74LS138 or 74S139) will ever be asserted at a time. For a 74LS138, the output asserted is determined by the 3-bit binary code applied to the A, B, and C select inputs. In the circuit in Figure 8-16 we connected system address line A0 to the C input, address line A4 to the B input, and address line A3 to the A select input. The truth table in Figure 8-17 shows the system base addresses that will enable each of the 74LS138 Y outputs. As you will see a little later, system address lines A1 and A2 are used to select internal parts of the 8254 and 8259.

We connected A0 to the C input so that half of the Y outputs will be selected by even addresses and half of the Y outputs will be selected by odd addresses. We did this so that we can equalize loading on the two halves of the data bus as we add peripheral devices such as the 8254 and 8259A. To see how this works, note that the peripheral devices have only eight data lines. For an odd-addressed device, we connect these data lines to the upper eight data lines of the system, and for an even-addressed device, we connect these to the lower eight data lines of the system. By alternating between odd and even selected outputs as we add peripheral devices, we equalize loading on the bus as desired.

As shown by the truth table in Figure 8-17, the system base address of the added 8254 is $BF01. Other connections to the 8254 are the system R/$\overline{W}$ line, used to enable the 8254 for reading or writing; eight data lines, used to send control words, status bytes, and count values between the CPU and the 8254; and system address lines A1 and A2, used to select the control register or one of the three counters in the 8254. Next we will show you how to initialize an 8254 to do some useful work for you.

INITIALIZING A PROGRAMMABLE PERIPHERAL DEVICE—THE 8254

When the power is first turned on, programmable peripheral devices such as the 8254 are usually in

BLOCK	HEX DIGIT 2^{15} 2^{14} 2^{13} 2^{12} A15 A14 A13 A12	HEX DIGIT 2^{11} 2^{10} 2^{9} 2^{8} A11 A10 A9 A8	HEX DIGIT 2^{7} 2^{6} 2^{5} 2^{4} A7 A6 A5 A4	HEX DIGIT 2^{3} 2^{2} 2^{1} 2^{0} A3 A2 A1 A0	Y OUTPUT Selected	SYSTEM BASE ADDR	DEVICE
1 START	0 0 0 0	0 0 0 0	0 0 0 0	0 0 0 0			
END	0 0 1 1	1 1 1 1	1 1 1 1	1 1 1 1			
2 START	0 1 0 0	0 0 0 0	0 0 0 0	0 0 0 0			
END	0 1 1 1	1 1 1 1	1 1 1 1	1 1 1 1			
3 START	1 0 0 0	0 0 0 0	0 0 0 0	0 0 0 0			
	1 0 1 1	1 1 1 1	0 0 0 0	0 x x 0	0	BF00	8259A #1
	1 0 1 1	1 1 1 1	0 0 0 0	1 x x 0	1	BF08	8259A #2
	1 0 1 1	1 1 1 1	0 0 0 1	0 x x 0	2	BF10	
	1 0 1 1	1 1 1 1	0 0 0 1	1 x x 0	3	BF18	
	1 0 1 1	1 1 1 1	0 0 0 0	0 x x 1	4	BF01	8254
	1 0 1 1	1 1 1 1	0 0 0 0	1 x x 1	5	BF09	
	1 0 1 1	1 1 1 1	0 0 0 1	0 x x 1	6	BF11	
	1 0 1 1	1 1 1 1	0 0 0 1	1 x x 1	7	BF19	
END	1 0 1 1	1 1 1 1	1 1 1 1	1 1 1 1			
4 START	1 1 0 0	0 0 0 0	0 0 0 0	0 0 0 0			
END	1 1 1 1	1 1 1 1	1 1 1 1	1 1 1 1			

FIGURE 8-17 Truth table for 74LS138 address decoder in Figure 8-16.

undefined states. Before you can use them for anything, you have to initialize them in the *mode* you need for your specific application. Initializing these devices is not usually difficult, but it is very easy to make errors if you do not do it in a very systematic way. To initialize any programmable peripheral device, you should work your way through the following series of steps.

1. Determine the system base address for the device. You do this from the address decoder circuitry or the address decoder truth table. From the truth table in Figure 8-17, the system base address of the 8254 in our example here is $BF01.

2. Use the device data sheet to determine the internal addresses for each of the control registers, ports, timers, status registers, etc., in the device. Figure 8-18a shows the internal addresses for the three counters and the control word register for the 8254. A0 in this table represents the A0 input of the device and A1 represents the A1 input of the device. Note in the schematic in Figure 8-16 that we connected system address line A1 to the A0 input and system address line A2 to the A1 input of the 8254. Among other reasons, we did this because—as described before—we wanted to use system address line A0 (LDS) as an input to the address decoder.

3. Add each of the internal addresses to the system base address to determine the system address of each part of the device. You need to do this so that you know to what address to send control words, timer values, etc. Figure 8-18b shows the system addresses for the three timers and the control register of the 8254 we added to the URDA MDS board. Note that the addresses are all odd.

4. In the data sheet for the device, look up the format of the control word(s) that you have to send to the device to initialize it. For different devices, inciden-

tally, the control word(s) may be referred to as command words or mode words. To initialize the 8254, you send a control word to the control register for each counter that you want to use. Figure 8-19 shows the format for the 8254 control word.

5. The next step is to construct the control word required to initialize the device for your specific application. You construct this control word on a bit-by-bit basis. We have found it helpful to actually draw the eight small boxes as shown at the top of Figure 8-19 so that we don't miss any bits. (An easy way to draw the eight boxes is to draw a long rectangle, divide it in half, divide each resulting half in two, and, finally, divide each resulting quarter in two.) To help keep track of the meaning of each bit of a control word, write the meaning of each bit under that bit. A little later we show you how to do this for an 8254 control word. Documentation of this sort is very valuable when you are

A_1	A_0	SELECTS
0	0	COUNTER 0
0	1	COUNTER 1
1	0	COUNTER 2
1	1	CONTROL WORD REGISTER

(a)

SYSTEM ADDRESS				8254 PART
B	F	0	1	COUNTER 0
B	F	0	3	COUNTER 1
B	F	0	5	COUNTER 2
B	F	0	7	CONTROL REG

(b)

FIGURE 8-18   8254 internal addresses and system addresses. (a) Internal. (b) System.

D_7	D_6	D_5	D_4	D_3	D_2	D_1	D_0
SC1	SC0	RW1	RW0	M2	M1	M0	BCD

SC — SELECT COUNTER:

SC1	SC0	
0	0	SELECT COUNTER 0
0	1	SELECT COUNTER 1
1	0	SELECT COUNTER 2
1	1	READ-BACK COMMAND (SEE READ OPERATIONS)

RW — READ/WRITE:

RW1	RW0	
0	0	COUNTER LATCH COMMAND (SEE READ OPERATIONS)
0	1	READ/WRITE LEAST SIGNIFICANT BYTE ONLY.
1	0	READ/WRITE MOST SIGNIFICANT BYTE ONLY.
1	1	READ/WRITE LEAST SIGNIFICANT BYTE FIRST, THEN MOST SIGNIFICANT BYTE.

M — MODE:

M2	M1	M0	
0	0	0	MODE 0 — INTERRUPT ON TERMINAL COUNT
0	0	1	MODE 1 — HARDWARE ONE-SHOT
X	1	0	MODE 2 — PULSE GENERATOR
X	1	1	MODE 3 — SQUARE WAVE GENERATOR
1	0	0	MODE 4 — SOFTWARE TRIGGERED STROBE
1	0	1	MODE 5 — HARDWARE TRIGGERED STROBE

BCD:

0	BINARY COUNTER 16-BITS
1	BINARY CODED DECIMAL (BCD) COUNTER (4 DECADES)

NOTE: DON'T CARE BITS (X) SHOULD BE 0 TO INSURE COMPATIBILITY WITH FUTURE INTEL PRODUCTS.

FIGURE 8-19   8254 control word format. (*Intel Corporation*)

trying to debug a program or modify an old program for some new application.

6. Finally, you send the control word(s) you have made up to the control register address for the device and send the starting count to the counter registers. Now, let's take a closer look at the 8254 control word format to see how you make up one of these words.

A separate control word must be sent for each counter that you want to use in the device. However, according to Figure 8-18a, the 8254 has only one control register address. The trick here is that the control words for all three counters are sent to the same address in the device. You use the upper 2 bits of each control word to tell the 8254 which counter you want that control word to initialize. For example, if you are making up a control word for counter 0 in the 8254 you make the SC1 bit of the control word a 0 and the SC0 bit a 0. Later we will explain the meaning of the read-back command specified by a 1 in each of these bits.

Next let's look at the bit labeled BCD in the control word. The 16-bit counters in the 8254 are down counters. This means that the number in a counter will be decremented by each clock pulse. You can program the 8254 to count down a loaded number in BCD (decimal) or in binary. If you make the D0 bit of the control word a 0, then the counter will treat the loaded number as a pure binary number. In this case the largest number that you can load in is $FFFF. If you make the D0 bit of the control word a 1, then the largest number you can load in the counter is $9999, and the counter will count a loaded number down in decimal (BCD). Actually, because of the way the 8254 counts, the "largest" number you can load in for both cases is 0000, but thinking of $FFFF and $9999 makes it easier to remember the difference between the two modes.

Now let's take a brief look at the mode bits (M2, M1, and M0) in the control word format in Figure 8-17. The binary number you put in these bits specifies the effect that the GATE input will have on counting and the waveform that will be produced on the OUT pin. For example, if you specify mode 3 for a counter by putting 011 in these 3 bits, the counter will be put in square-wave mode. In this mode the output will be high for half of the loaded count and low for the second half of the loaded count. When the count reaches zero, the original count is automatically reloaded and the countdown is repeated. The waveform on the OUT pin in this mode will then be a square wave with a frequency equal to the input clock frequency divided by the count you wrote to the counter. A little later we will discuss and show applications for some of the six different modes. First let's finish looking at the control word bits and see how you send the control word and a count to the device.

The RW1 and RW0 bits of the control word are used to specify how you want to write a count to a counter or to read the count from a counter. If you want to load a 16-bit number into a counter, you put 1s in both of these bits in the control word you send for that counter. After you send the control word, you send the low byte of the count to the counter address and then send the high byte of the count to the counter address. In a later paragraph we show an example of the instruction sequence to do this. In cases where you want to load a new value only in the low byte of a counter, you can send a control word with 01 in the RW bits and then send the new low byte to the counter. Likewise, if you want to load only a new high byte value in the counter, you can send a control word with 10 in the RW bits and then send the new high byte to the counter.

You can read the number in one of the counters at any time. The usual way to do this is first to latch the current count in some internal latches by sending a control word with 00 in the RW bits. Send another control word with 01, 10, or 11 in the RW bits to specify how you want to read out the bytes of the latched count. Then read the count from the counter address.

Now, for a specific example, suppose that we want to use counter 0 of the 8254 in Figure 8-16 to produce a stable 110.8-kHz square-wave signal for a UART clock by dividing down the 3.579-MHz CLK signal available on the URDA MDS board. To do this we first connect the URDA MDS CLK signal to the CLK input of counter 0 and tie the GATE input of counter 0 high to enable it for counting. To produce 110.8 kHz from 3.579 MHz, we have to divide by 32 decimal, so this is the value that we will eventually load into counter 0. First, however, we have to determine the system addresses for the device, make up the control word for counter 0, and send the control word.

As shown in Figure 8-18b, the system address for the control register of this 8254 is $BF07. This is where we will send the control word. For our control word we want to select counter 0, so we make the SC1 and SC0 bits both 0s. We want the counter to operate in square-wave mode. This is mode 3, so we make the mode bits of the control word 011. Since we want to divide by 32 decimal, we tell the counter to count down in decimal by making the BCD bit of the control word a 1. This makes our life easier, because we don't have to convert the 32 to binary or hex. Finally, we have to decide how we want to load the count into the counter. Since the count that we need to load in is less than 99, we have to load only the lower byte of the counter. According to Figure 8-19, the RW1 bit should be a 0 and the RW0 bit should be a 1 for a write to only the lower byte (LSB). The complete control word then is 0001 0111 in binary. Here are the instructions to send the control word and count to counter 0 of the 8254 in Figure 8-16. Note how the bits of the control word are documented.

```
MOVE.B #%00010111,D0
        ; Control word for counter 0
    ; read/write LSB only, mode 3, BCD
```

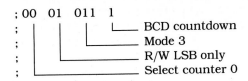

```
;  00   01   011   1
;                 └─────── BCD countdown
;             └────────── Mode 3
;         └────────────── R/W LSB only
;   └──────────────────── Select counter 0
```

```
LEA $BF07,A0      ; Point at 8254 control
                  ;   register
MOVE.B D0,(A0)    ; Send control word
MOVE.B #$32,D0    ; Load lower byte of count
LEA $BF01,A0      ; Point to counter 0 count
                  ;   register
MOVE.B D0,(A0)    ; Send count to count register
```

Note that since we set the RW bits of the control word for the read/write LSB only, we do not have to include instructions to load the MSB of the counter. Programmed in this way, the 8254 will automatically load 0s in the upper byte of the counter.

If you need to load a count that is larger than 1 byte, make the RW bits in the control word both 1s. Send the lower byte of the count as shown before. Then send the high byte of the count to the count register by adding the instructions

```
MOVE.B #HIGH_BYTE_OF_COUNT,D0
                  ; Load MSB of count
MOVE.B D0,(A0)    ; Send MSB to count
                  ;   register
```

Note that the high byte of the count is sent to the same address as the low byte of the count. For each counter that you want to use in an 8254, you repeat the preceding series of six or eight instructions with the control word and count for the mode that you want. Before going on with this chapter, review the six initialization steps shown at the start of this section to make sure they are firmly fixed in your mind. In the next section we discuss and show some applications of the different modes in which an 8254 counter can be operated, but we do not have space there to show all the steps for each of the modes.

8254 Counter Modes and Applications

As we mentioned previously, an 8254 counter can be programmed to operate in any one of six different modes. The Intel data book uses timing diagrams such as those in Figure 8-20 to show how a counter functions in each of these modes. Since all of these waveforms may not be totally obvious to you at first glance, we will work our way through some of them to show you how to interpret them. We will also show some uses of the different counter modes.

MODE 0—INTERRUPT ON TERMINAL COUNT

First read the Intel notes at the bottom of Figure 8-20; then take a look at the top set of waveforms in the figure. For this first example, the GATE input is held high so the counter is always enabled for counting. The

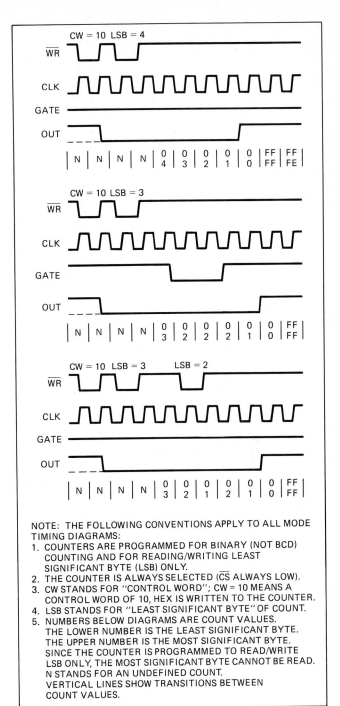

NOTE: THE FOLLOWING CONVENTIONS APPLY TO ALL MODE TIMING DIAGRAMS:
1. COUNTERS ARE PROGRAMMED FOR BINARY (NOT BCD) COUNTING AND FOR READING/WRITING LEAST SIGNIFICANT BYTE (LSB) ONLY.
2. THE COUNTER IS ALWAYS SELECTED (CS ALWAYS LOW).
3. CW STANDS FOR "CONTROL WORD"; CW = 10 MEANS A CONTROL WORD OF 10, HEX IS WRITTEN TO THE COUNTER.
4. LSB STANDS FOR "LEAST SIGNIFICANT BYTE" OF COUNT.
5. NUMBERS BELOW DIAGRAMS ARE COUNT VALUES. THE LOWER NUMBER IS THE LEAST SIGNIFICANT BYTE. THE UPPER NUMBER IS THE MOST SIGNIFICANT BYTE. SINCE THE COUNTER IS PROGRAMMED TO READ/WRITE LSB ONLY, THE MOST SIGNIFICANT BYTE CANNOT BE READ. N STANDS FOR AN UNDEFINED COUNT. VERTICAL LINES SHOW TRANSITIONS BETWEEN COUNT VALUES.

MODE 0

FIGURE 8-20   8254 mode 0 example timing diagrams. (*Intel Corporation*)

first dip in the waveform, labeled $\overline{\text{WR}}$, represents the control word for the counter being written to the 8254. CW = 10 over this dip indicates that the control word written is $10. According to the control word format in Figure 8-19, this means that counter 0 is being initialized for binary counting, mode 0, and a read/write of only the LSB. After the control word is written to the control register, the output pin of counter 0 will go low. The next dip in the $\overline{WR}$ waveform represents a count of 4 being written to the count register of counter 0. Before this count can be counted down, it must be transferred from the count register to the actual counter. If you look at the count values shown under the OUT waveform in the timing diagram, you should see that the count of 4 is transferred into the counter by the next clock pulse after $\overline{WR}$ goes high. Each clock pulse after this will decrement the count by 1. When the counter transitions to zero, the OUT pin will go high. If you write a count N to a counter in mode 0, the OUT pin will go high after $N + 1$ clock pulses have occurred. Note that the counter decrements from 0000 to $FFFF on the next clock pulse unless you load some new count into the counter. If the OUT pin is connected to an active high interrupt input of the processor, then the processor will be interrupted when the counter reaches zero (terminal count).

The second set of waveforms in Figure 8-20 shows that if the GATE input is made low, the counter value will be held. When the GATE input is made high again, the counter continues to decrement by 1 for each clock pulse. The third set of waveforms in Figure 8-20 shows that if a new count is written to a counter, the new count will be loaded into the counter on the next clock pulse. Following clock pulses will decrement the new count until it reaches zero.

As an example of the use of this mode, suppose that as one of its jobs we want to use an available 68000 to control some parking lot signs around our electronics factory. The main parking lot can hold 1000 cars. When it is full, we want to turn on a sign that directs people to another available lot. To detect when a car enters the lot, we can use an optical sensor such as the one shown in Figure 8-12. Each time a car passes through, this circuit will produce a pulse. We could connect the signal from this sensor to an interrupt input and have the processor count interrupts, as we did for the printed-circuit-board-making machine in a previous example. However, the less we burden the processor with trivial tasks such as this, the more it is available to do complex work for us. Therefore, we let a counter in an 8254 count cars and interrupt the 68000 only when it has counted 1000 cars.

We connect the output from the optical sensor circuit to the CLK input of, say, counter 1 of an 8254. We tie the GATE input of counter 1 to +5 V so it will be enabled for counting. We connect the OUT pin of counter 1 to an interrupt input on the 68000.

In the mainline program we initialize counter 1 for mode 0, BCD counting, and read/write LSB and then MSB with a control word of 0111 0011 binary. We want the counter to produce an interrupt after 1000 pulses from the sensor, so we send a count of 999 decimal to the counter. The reason that we want to send 999 instead of 1000 is that, as shown in Figure 8-20, the OUT pin will go high $N + 1$ clock pulses after the count value is written to the counter. Since we initialized the counter for read/write LSB and then MSB, we send $99 and then $09 to the address of counter 1. Note that we initialized the counter for BCD

counting, so we can just send the count value as a BCD number instead of having to convert it to hex.

The service routine for this interrupt will contain instructions that turn on the parking-lot-full sign, close off the main entrance, and return to the mainline program. For this example we don't worry that the counter decrements from 0000 to $FFFF because the counter will not receive any more interrupts after we shut the gate.

MODE 1—HARDWARE RETRIGGERABLE ONE-SHOT

The basic principle of a *one-shot* is that when a signal is applied to the trigger input of the device, its output will be asserted. After a fixed amount of time, the output will automatically return to its unasserted state. For a TTL one-shot such as the 74LS122, the time that the output is asserted is determined by the time constant of a resistor and a capacitor connected to the device. For an 8254 counter in one-shot mode, the time that the output is asserted low is determined by the frequency of an applied clock and a count loaded into the counter. The advantage of the 8254 approach is that the output pulse width can be changed under program control, and if a crystal-controlled clock is used, the output pulse width can be very accurately specified.

Figure 8-21 shows some example timing waveforms for an 8254 counter in mode 1. Let's take a look at the top set of waveforms. Again, the first dip in the $\overline{WR}$ waveform represents the control word of $12 being sent to the 8254. Use Figure 8-19 to help you determine how this control word initializes the device. You should find that a control word of $12 programs counter 0 for binary count, mode 1, read/write LSB and then MSB. When the control word is written to the 8254, the OUT pin goes high.

The second dip in the WR waveform represents writing a count to the counter. Note that because the GATE input is low, the counter does not start counting down immediately when the count is written, as it does in mode 0. For mode 1 the GATE input functions as a trigger input. When the GATE/trigger input is made high, the count will be transferred from the count register to the actual counter on the next clock pulse. Each following clock pulse will decrement the counter by 1. When the counter reaches zero, the OUT pin will go high again. In other words, if we load a value of N in the counter and we trigger the device by making the GATE input high, the OUT pin will go low for a time equal to N clock cycles. The output pulse width is then N times the period of the signal applied to the CLK input. Incidentally, the dashed sections of the GATE waveforms in Figure 8-21 mean that the GATE/trigger input signal can go low again anytime during that time interval.

The second set of waveforms in Figure 8-21 demonstrates what is meant by the term *retriggerable*. If another trigger pulse comes before the previously loaded count has been counted down to zero, the original count will be reloaded on the next clock pulse. The

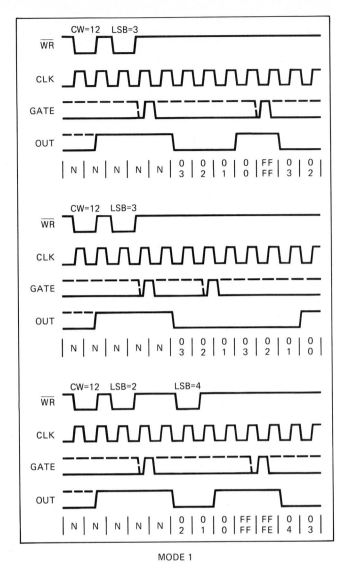

MODE 1

FIGURE 8-21   8254 mode 1 example timing diagrams.
(*Intel Corporation*)

60-Hz line frequency, a pulse will be produced every 16.66 ms. Now what we want to do here is to load the counter with a value such that the counter will always be retriggered by the power line pulses before the countdown is completed. As shown by the second set of waveforms in Figure 8-21, the OUT pin will then stay low and not send an interrupt signal to the $\overline{\text{IPL0}}$ input of the 68000. If the ac power fails, no more pulses come in to the 8254 trigger input. The trigger input will be left high, and the countdown will be completed. The 8254 OUT pin will then go high and interrupt the 68000.

To determine the counter value for this application, just calculate the number of input clock pulses required to produce a countdown time longer than 16.66 ms, such as 18 ms. If we use the 3.579-MHz CLK signal on an URDA MDS board, 20 ms requires 64,776 cycles of CLK, so this is the number we would load in the 8254 counter. Since this number is too large to load in as a BCD count, we load it in as $FD08, and in the control word we tell the 8254 to count the number down in binary.

MODE 2—TIMED INTERRUPT GENERATOR

In a previous section we described how a real-time clock of seconds, minutes, and hours could be kept in three memory locations by counting interrupts from a 1-Hz pulse source. We also described how the 1-Hz interrupts could be used to measure off other time intervals. The difficulty with using a 1-Hz interrupt signal is that the maximum resolution of any time measurement is 1 s. In other words, if you use a 1-Hz signal, you can measure times only to the nearest second. To improve the resolution of time measurements, most microcomputer systems use a higher-frequency signal, such as 1 kHz for a real-time clock interrupt. With a 1-kHz interrupt signal, the time resolution is then 1 ms. An 8254 counter operating in mode 2 can be used to produce a stable 1-kHz signal by dividing down the processor clock signal.

Figure 8-23 shows the waveforms for an 8254 counter operating in mode 2. Let's look at the top set of waveforms first. The two dips in the $\overline{\text{WR}}$ waveform represent a control word and the LSB of a count being written to the count register. The next clock pulse after the count is written will transfer the count from the count register to the actual counter. Since the GATE input is high, succeeding clock pulses will count down this value until it reaches 1. When the count reaches 1, the OUT pin, which was previously high, will go low. The falling edge of the next clock pulse will cause the OUT pin to go high again and the original count to again be loaded into the counter. Successive clock pulses will cause the countdown and load cycle to repeat over and over. If the counter is loaded with a number *N*, the OUT pin will go low for one clock cycle every *N* input clock pulses. The frequency of the output waveform then will be equal to the input clock frequency divided by *N*.

For a specific example, suppose that we want to produce a 1-kHz signal for a real-time clock from an

countdown will then start over and continue until another trigger occurs or until the count reaches zero. If trigger pulses continue to come before the count is decremented to zero, the OUT pin will remain low.

The bottom set of waveforms in Figure 8-21 shows that if you write a new count to a count register while the OUT pin is low, the new count will not be loaded into the counter and counted down until the next trigger pulse occurs.

For an example of the use of mode 1, we will show you how to make a circuit that produces an interrupt signal if the ac power fails. This circuit could be connected to the $\overline{\text{IPL0}}$ input of a 68000 to vector to an ISR that saves parameters in battery-backed RAM when the ac power fails. Figure 8-22, p. 228, shows a circuit that uses an optical coupler (LED and a phototransistor packaged together) to produce logic-level pulses at power line frequency. The 74LS14 inverters sharpen the edges of these pulses so that they can be applied to the GATE/trigger input of an 8254. For a

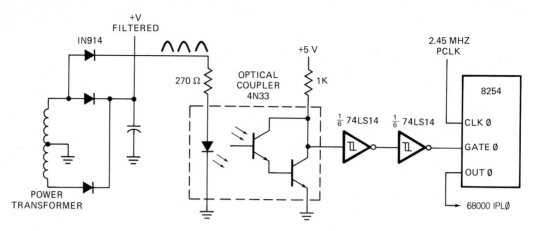

FIGURE 8-22 Circuit to produce logic-level pulses at power line frequency.

8-MHz processor clock signal. To do this we connect the processor clock signal to the CLK input on one of the 8254 counters and tie the GATE input of that counter high. We initialize that counter for BCD counting, mode 2, and read/write LSB and then MSB. Since we want to divide the 8 MHz by 8000 decimal to get 1 kHz, we then write $00 to the counter as the LSB and $80 to the counter as the MSB.

A question that may occur to you at this point is, How do I count seconds if the interrupts are coming in every millisecond? The answer is that you set aside a memory location as a milliseconds' counter and initialize that location with 1000 decimal ($3E8). The interrupt-service routine decrements this count each time an interrupt occurs and checks to see if the count is down to zero yet. If the count is not zero, then execution is simply returned to the mainline. If the count is down to zero, 1000 interrupts (1 s) have passed. Therefore, the milliseconds' counter location is reloaded with $3E8, and the seconds-minutes-hours procedure is called to update the count of seconds. In a similar way the 1-kHz interrupt-service routine can measure off several different time intervals that are multiples of 1 ms.

The middle set of mode 2 waveforms in Figure 8-23 demonstrates that if the GATE input is made low while the counter is counting, counting will stop. If the GATE input is made high again, the original count will be reloaded into the counter by the next clock pulse. Succeeding clock pulses will decrement the loaded count.

The bottom set of mode 2 waveforms in Figure 8-23 shows that if a new count is written to the count register, this new count will not be transferred to the counter until the previously loaded count has been decremented to 1.

MODE 3—SQUARE-WAVE MODE

If an 8254 counter is programmed for mode 3 and an even number is written to its count register, the waveform on the OUT pin will be a square wave. The frequency of the square wave will be equal to the frequency of the input clock divided by the number written to the count register. If an odd number is written to a counter programmed for mode 3, the output waveform will be high for one more clock cycle than it is low, so the waveform will not be quite symmetrical. Figure 8-24 shows some example waveforms for mode 3. By now these waveforms should look quite familiar to you.

The top set of waveforms shows that after a control word is written to the control register and a count is written to the count register, the count is transferred to the counter on the next clock pulse. As shown by the count sequence under the OUT waveform, each additional clock pulse decrements the counter by 2. When the count is down to 2, the OUT pin goes low and the original count is reloaded. The OUT pin stays low while the loaded count is again counted down by 2s. When the count is down to 2, the OUT pin goes high again and the original count is again loaded into the counter. The cycle then repeats.

The center set of waveforms in Figure 8-24 shows what happens if an odd number is written to the count register. As you can see from this waveform, the number of clock cycles for each waveform is still equal to the number loaded into the count register. However, as we mentioned before, the clock is high for one more clock cycle than it is low.

The bottom set of waveforms in Figure 8-24 shows that counting stops if the gate is made low at any time. After the GATE input is made high again, the original count will be loaded by the next clock pulse.

Mode 3 can be used for any case where you want a repetitive square-wave-type signal. In a previous section we showed how an 8254 counter operating in mode 3 can be used to generate the baud-rate clock for a USART such as the 8251A. Mode 3 can also be used to generate interrupt pulses for a real-time clock, as we described for mode 2.

Another use of 8254 counters operating in mode 3 is as programmable audio tone generators. For this application a high-frequency clock such as the 3.579-MHz CLK signal on an URDA MDS board is connected to the counter CLK input, the GATE input is tied high, and the OUT pin is connected to an audio buffer such as that shown in Figure 8-25. This simple buffer allows

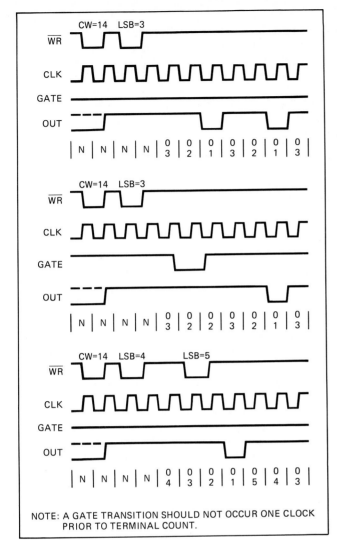

NOTE: A GATE TRANSITION SHOULD NOT OCCUR ONE CLOCK
PRIOR TO TERMINAL COUNT.

MODE 2

FIGURE 8-23 8254 mode 2 example timing waveforms.
(*Intel Corporation*)

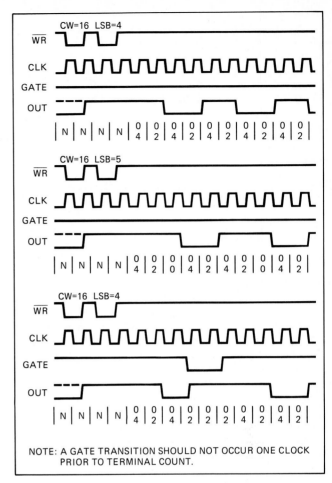

NOTE: A GATE TRANSITION SHOULD NOT OCCUR ONE CLOCK
PRIOR TO TERMINAL COUNT.

MODE 3

FIGURE 8-24 8254 mode 3 example timing waveforms.
(*Intel Corporation*)

the outputs of several counters to be added together if
desired and supplies the current required to drive a
small speaker.

As an example of this application, suppose that you
want to produce a 440-Hz tone that is a musical A from
the 3.579-MHz CLK signal. Dividing the CLK signal by
8139 will give the desired 440 Hz. Therefore, you
simply send a control word that programs a counter for
mode 3, read/write LSB and then MSB, and BCD
counting. You then write the LSB of $39 and the MSB
of $81 to the counter. If you want to change the
frequency, all you have to do is write a new count to the
count register. With a few programmable counters and
some relatively simple programming, you can play your
favorite songs.

MODE 4—SOFTWARE-TRIGGERED STROBE

This mode and mode 5 are often confused with mode 1,
but there is an obvious difference. Mode 1 is used to

produce a low-going pulse that is N clock pulses wide.
If you look at the top set of waveforms for mode 4 in
Figure 8-26, p. 230, you should see that mode 4
produces a low-going pulse *after* $N + 1$ clock pulses.
For mode 4 the output pulse is low for the time of one
input clock pulse and then returns high. In other
words, in mode 4 a counter produces a low-going strobe
pulse $N + 1$ clock cycles after a count is written to the

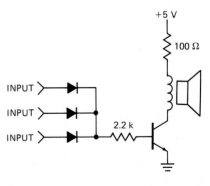

FIGURE 8-25 Audio speaker buffer for 8254 timer
output or port.

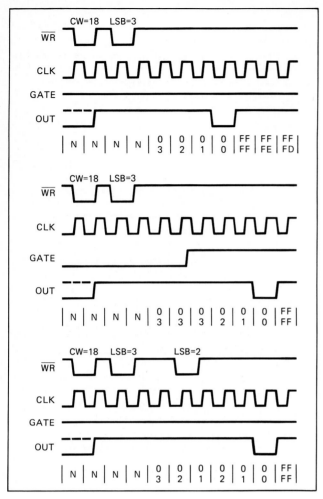

MODE 4

FIGURE 8-26   8254 mode 4 example timing waveforms. (*Intel Corporation*)

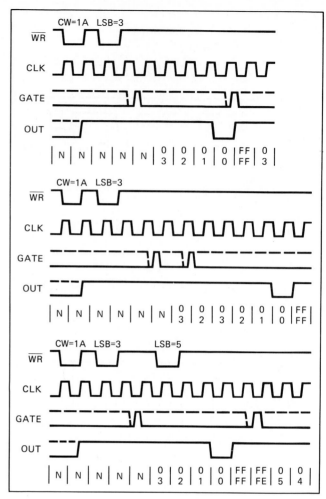

MODE 5

FIGURE 8-27   8254 mode 5 example timing waveforms. (*Intel Corporation*)

count register. Mode 4 is referred to as *software-triggered* because it is the writing of the count to the count register that starts the process. Note that after the loaded count is counted down, the counter decrements to $FFFF and then continues to decrement from there.

Mode 4 can be used in a case where you want to send out some parallel data on a port and then, after some delay, send out a strobe signal to let the receiving system know that the data is available.

MODE 5—HARDWARE-TRIGGERED STROBE

Mode 5 is used where we want to produce a low-going strobe pulse some programmable time interval after a rising-edge trigger signal is applied to the GATE input. This mode is very useful when we want to delay a rising-edge signal by some amount of time.

Figure 8-27 shows some example waveforms for a counter operating in mode 5. For a start let's look at the top set of waveforms. As usual we write a control word and the desired count to a counter. As shown by the count sequence under the OUT waveform, however,

the count is not transferred to the counter until the GATE (trigger) input is made high. When the trigger input is made high, the count will be transferred to the counter on the next clock pulse. Succeeding clock pulses will decrement the counter. When the counter reaches zero, the OUT pin will go low for one clock pulse time. The OUT pin will go low $N + 1$ clock pulses after the trigger input goes high.

The second set of waveforms in Figure 8-27 shows that if another trigger pulse occurs during the count-down time, the original count will be reloaded on the next clock pulse and the countdown will start over. The OUT pin will remain high until the count is finally counted down. If trigger pulses continue to come before the countdown is completed, the OUT pin will continue to stay high. Therefore you can use a counter in mode 5 to produce a power-fail signal, as we showed in the discussion of mode 1. Note that for mode 5, however, the OUT pin will be high if the power is on and will go low when the power fails.

The bottom set of waveforms in Figure 8-27 shows that if a new count is written to a counter, the new count will not be loaded into the counter until a new trigger pulse occurs.

USING A NONSYSTEM CLOCK WITH 8254 IN MODES 2 AND 3

If we are applying a signal that is not derived from the system clock to the CLK input of an 8254 (not 8253), then a small note in the Intel data sheet indicates that the GATE input of a counter must be pulsed low just after the count is written to the counter. An easy way to do this is to connect the GATE input of the counter to an otherwise unused output port pin. We can then pulse the GATE by outputting a low and then outputting a high to that port pin.

READING THE COUNT FROM AN 8254 COUNTER

For many counter applications we want to be able to read the current count in the counter. Suppose, for example, that we are using an 8254 counter to count the cars coming into a parking lot, as we did in our example for mode 0. In that case we used the counter to produce an interrupt when the parking lot was full so we could shut the gate. Now further suppose that as part of a traffic flow study, we want to find out how many cars have come into the lot by 7:30 A.M. An interrupt-driven real-time clock routine can, at 7:30 A.M., call a routine that reads in the current count from the counter. Since the counter was initially loaded with 1000 decimal and is being counted down as cars come in, we can simply subtract the current count from 1000 to determine how many cars have come in.

The counters in an 8254 have latches on their outputs. When you read the count from a counter, what you are actually reading is the data on the outputs of these latches. These latches are normally enabled during counting so that the latch outputs just follow the counter outputs. If you try to read the count while the counter is counting, the count may change between reading the LSB and the MSB. This may give you a strange count. To read a correct count, you must in some way stop the counting or latch the current count on the output of the latches. There are three major ways of doing this.

The first is to stop counting by turning off the clock signal or making the GATE input low with external hardware. This method has the disadvantages that it requires external hardware and that a clock pulse occurring while the clock is disabled will obviously not be counted.

The second way of reading a stable value from a counter is to latch the current count with a counter latch command and then read the latched count. A counter is latched by sending a control word to the control register address in the 8254. If you look at the format for the 8254 control word in Figure 8-19, you should see that a counter latch command is specified by making the RW1 and RW0 bits both 0. The SC1 and SC0 bits specify which counter we want to latch. The lower 4 bits of the control word are don't cares for a counter latch command word, so we usually make

them 0s for simplicity. As an example, here is the sequence of instructions you would use to latch and read the LSB and MSB from counter 1 of the 8254 in Figure 8-16. We assume that the counter was already programmed for read/write LSB and then MSB when the device was initialized. If the counter was programmed for only LSB or only MSB, then only that byte can be read.

```
MOVE.B #%01000000,D0
                ; Counter latch command for
                ;   counter 1
LEA $BF07,A0    ; Point at 8254 control
                ;   register
MOVE.B D0,(A0)  ; Send latch command
LEA $BF03,A0    ; Point at counter 1 address
CLR.W D0        ; Clear area for count
MOVE.B (A0),D0  ; Read LSB of latched count
MOVE.B (A0),D1  ; Read MSB of latched count
ROL.W #8,D1     ; Rotate into MSB position
OR.W D1,D0      ; Count now in D0
```

Notice that the byte-ordering differences between Intel and Motorola have affected us in this example. Because we are connecting an Intel counter to a Motorola CPU, the bytes occur in what seems like a backward order. The program code has to accept the low-order byte first and then the high-order bit, so that the high-order byte must be shifted left and ORed with the low-order byte. If we were using a Motorola peripheral, then it would typically send the MSB first and then the LSB.

When a counter latch command is sent, the latched count is held until it is read. When the count is read from the latches, the latch outputs again follow the counter outputs.

The third method of reading a stable count from a counter is to latch the count with a read-back command. This method is available in the 8254 but not in the 8253. It is essentially an enhanced version of the counter latch command approach described in the preceding paragraphs.

Figure 8-28 shows the format for the 8254 counter read-back command word. It is sent to the same address as other control words are for a particular 8254. The 1s in bits D7 and D6 identify this as a read-back command word. To latch the count on a counter, you

A0, A1 = 11 $\overline{CS}$ = 0 $\overline{RD}$ = 1 $\overline{WR}$ = 0

D7	D6	D5	D4	D3	D2	D1	D0
1	1	COUNT	STATUS	CNT 2	CNT 1	CNT 0	0

D_5: 0 = LATCH COUNT OF SELECTED COUNTERS(S)
D_4: 0 = LATCH STATUS OF SELECTED COUNTER(S)
D_3: 1 = SELECT COUNTER 2
D_2: 1 = SELECT COUNTER 1
D_1: 1 = SELECT COUNTER 0
D_0: RESERVED FOR FUTURE EXPANSION; MUST BE 0

FIGURE 8-28   8254 read-back control word format.

put a 0 in bit D5 of the control word and put a 1 in the bit position that corresponds to that counter in the control word. The advantage of this control word is that you can latch one, two, or all three counters by putting 1s in the appropriate bits. Once a counter is latched, the count is read, as shown in the preceding example program. After being read, the latch outputs again follow the counter outputs.

If a read-back command word with bit D4 = 0 is sent to an 8254, the status of one or more counters will be latched on the output latches. Consult the Intel data sheet for further information on this latched status.

The preceding sections have shown how 8254 counters can be used to do a wide variety of tasks around microcomputers. Many of these applications produce an interrupt signal, which must be connected to an interrupt input on the microprocessor. In the next section we show how a priority interrupt controller device, the Intel 8259A, is used to service multiple interrupts.

Multiple Interrupts and the 8259A Priority Interrupt Controller

Previous sections of this chapter have shown how interrupts can be used for a variety of applications. In a small system, for example, we might read ASCII characters in from a keyboard on an interrupt basis; count interrupts from a timer to produce a real-time clock of seconds, minutes, and hours; or detect several emergency or job-done conditions on an interrupt basis. Each of these interrupt applications requires a separate interrupt input. If we are working with a 68000, we do not have a problem because the 68000 has seven levels of interrupt inputs. In larger systems, however, we may wish to connect more than seven I/O devices to the CPU. For example, we may be operating a 10-story parking garage and want to handle each parking level differently. There aren't 10 different interrupt levels, so we must find a way to allow several devices to use the same level. For applications where we have interrupts from multiple sources using one interrupt level, we use an external device called a *priority interrupt controller,* or PIC, to "funnel" the interrupt signals into one interrupt level input on the processor. In this section we show how a common PIC, the Intel 8259A, is connected in a 68000 system, how it is initialized, and how it is used to handle interrupts from multiple sources.

8259A OVERVIEW AND SYSTEM CONNECTIONS

To show you how an 8259A functions in a 68000 system, we first need to review how the 68000 interrupt inputs work. Remember from an earlier discussion that if the 68000 interrupt mask (the status register CPU priority bits) is set to 0 and any of the interrupt inputs are asserted, the 68000 will do the following:

1. Save a copy of the status register internally.

2. Set the S bit and clear the T bit.

3. Determine the exception vector number to use.

4. Push the status register and return address on the stack.

The CPU also sends out the acknowledged interrupt level on its A1, A2, and A3 pins. During user-interrupt processing, the CPU gets the exception vector number from the interrupting I/O device. In other cases, the CPU will use autovectoring, during which the exception vector number is determined by the interrupt level being used by the I/O device. Once the return address has been stacked, the CPU will access the appropriate exception vector and load that address into the PC. This causes the 68000 to begin to execute the interrupt-service routine.

Now if you look at the internal block diagram of the 8259A in Figure 8-29, I think you will begin to see how it fits into the interrupt operation. First notice the 8-bit data bus and control signal pins in the upper left corner of the diagram. The data bus allows the 68000 to send control words to the 8259A and read a status word from the 8259A. The $\overline{RD}$ and $\overline{WR}$ inputs control these transfers when the device is selected by asserting its chip select ($\overline{CS}$) input low. The 8-bit data bus also allows the 8259A to send interrupt-vector numbers to the 68000. Next notice the eight interrupt inputs labeled IR0–IR7 on the right side of the diagram. If the 8259A is properly enabled, an interrupt signal applied to any one of these inputs will cause the 8259A to assert its INT output pin high. If this pin is connected to the interrupt pins of a 68000 and if the 68000 interrupt mask is cleared, then this high signal will cause the previously described interrupt response.

The INT pin can be connected to the 68000 using a 74148 to multiplex the desired interrupt level onto the three 68000 interrupt inputs, as is done on the URDA MDS. The eight interrupt inputs on the 8259A thus become subpriorities of the original 68000 interrupt level. For example, if the INT line is connected to the 74148 I1 line, then the IR0 input will be the highest-priority device of the level one 68000 interrupt. IR1 would be the next-highest priority, and IR7 would be the lowest. One easy way to think of it is that the IR0 line represents priority level 1.7, IR1 is level 1.6, and so on, with IR7 at level 1.0. If the 8259A were connected to the 79148 I5 (68000 priority level 5), then IR0 would be priority 5.7, IR1 would be level 5.6, and so on. In this way the 68000 can have devices connected at any of 7 × 8, or 56, different priority levels. Notice that since we are connecting an Intel PIC to a Motorola CPU, there is a slight conflict in terms. The Motorola terminology uses level 7 as the highest priority and Intel uses level 7 as the lowest. Aside from this complication, things are pretty straightforward.

The $\overline{INTA}$ input of the 8259A is connected to the A1, A2, and A3 outputs of the 68000 (see Figure 8-16). The 8259A uses the first pulse from the 68000 to do some activities that depend on the mode in which it is programmed. When it receives the interrupt acknowl-

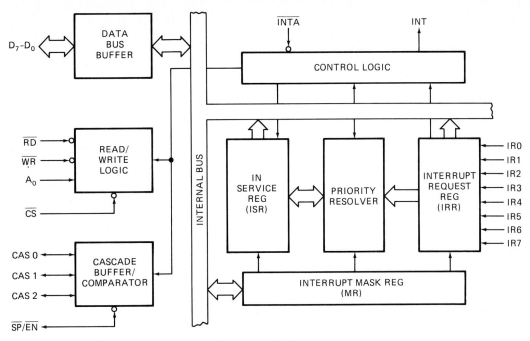

FIGURE 8-29 8259A internal block diagram. (*Intel Corporation*)

edge from the 68000 function codes, the 8259A outputs an interrupt vector on the 8-bit data bus, as shown in Figures 8-7 and 8-8. The interrupt vector that it sends to the 68000 is determined by the IR input that received an interrupt signal and by a number you send the 8259A when you initialize it. The point here is that the 8259A "funnels" interrupt signals from up to eight different sources into a single 68000 interrupt level, and it sends the 68000 a specified interrupt-vector number for each of the eight interrupt inputs.

At this point you might wonder what would happen if interrupt signals appear at, for example, IR2 and IR4 at the same time. In the *fixed-priority mode* in which the 8259A is usually operated, the answer to this question is quite simple. In this mode the IR0 input has the highest priority (most importance), the IR1 input the next highest, and so on down to IR7, which has the lowest priority. What this means is that if two interrupt signals occur at the same time, the 8259A will service the one with the highest priority first assuming that both inputs are unmasked (enabled).

Now let's look again at the block diagram of the 8259A in Figure 8-29 so we can explain in more detail how the device will respond to multiple interrupt signals. In the block diagram, note the four boxes labeled *interrupt request register* (IRR), *interrupt mask register* (IMR), *in-service register* (ISReg), and priority resolver. The operation of these four functional blocks is quite logical.

The interrupt mask register is used to disable (mask) or enable (unmask) individual interrupt inputs. Each bit in this register corresponds to the interrupt input with the same number. You unmask an interrupt input by sending a command word with a 0 in the bit position that corresponds to that input.

The IRR keeps track of which interrupt inputs are asking for service. If an interrupt input is unmasked and has an interrupt signal on it, then the corresponding bit in the interrupt request register will be set.

The ISReg keeps track of which interrupt inputs are currently being serviced. For each input that is currently being serviced, the corresponding bit will be set in the ISReg. An example will show how the priority resolver acts as a judge in the middle of all this.

Suppose that IR2 and IR4 are unmasked and that an interrupt signal comes in on the IR4 input. Since IR4 is unmasked, bit 4 of the IRR will be set. The priority resolver will detect that this bit is set and see if any action needs to be taken. To do this it checks the bits in the ISReg to see if a higher-priority input is being serviced. If a higher-priority input is being serviced, as indicated by a bit being set for that input in the ISReg, then the priority resolver will take no action. If no higher-priority interrupt is being serviced, then the priority resolver will activate the circuitry that sends an interrupt signal to the 68000. When the 68000 responds with an interrupt acknowledge, the 8259A will send the interrupt type that we specified for the IR4 input when we initialized the device. The 68000 will use the vector number it receives to find and execute the interrupt-service routine we wrote for the IR4 interrupt.

Now, suppose that an interrupt signal arrives at the IR2 input of the 8259A while the 68000 is executing the IR4 service routine. Since we assumed for this example that IR2 was unmasked, bit 2 of the IRR will be set. The priority resolver will detect that this bit in the IRR is set and make a decision whether to send another interrupt signal to the 68000. To make the decision, the priority resolver looks at the ISReg. If a higher-priority bit in the ISReg is set, then a higher-priority interrupt is being serviced. The priority resolver will wait until the higher-priority bit in the ISReg is reset before sending an interrupt signal to the 68000 for the new interrupt input. If the priority resolver finds that the new interrupt has a higher priority than that of the highest-priority interrupt currently being serviced, it will set the appropriate bit in the ISReg and activate the circuitry that sends a new interrupt signal to the 68000. For our example here, IR2 has a higher priority than IR4, so the priority resolver will set bit 2 of the ISR and activate the circuitry that sends a new interrupt signal to the 68000. If the 68000 interrupt input was reenabled with an AND to SR instruction at the start of the IR4 service routine, as shown in Figure 8-30a, then this new interrupt signal will interrupt the 68000 again. When the 68000 sends out a second interrupt acknowledge in response to this interrupt, the 8259A will send it the type number for the IR2 service routine. The 68000 will use the received type number to find and execute the IR2 service routine.

At the end of the IR2 routine, we send the 8259A a command word that resets bit 2 of the ISReg register so that lower-priority interrupts can be serviced. After that, an RTE instruction at the end of the IR2 routine

sends execution back to the interrupted IR4 routine. At the end of the IR4 routine, we send the 8259A a command word that resets bit 4 of the ISReg so that lower-priority interrupts can be serviced. An RTE instruction at the end of the IR4 routine returns execution to the mainline program. This all sounds very messy, but it is really just a special case of nested subroutines. Incidentally, if the IR4 routine did not reenable the interrupt input with an AND to SR instruction, as shown in Figure 8-30b, the 68000 would not respond to the IR2-caused INT signal until it finished executing the IR4 routine. We can't describe all the possible cases, but the main point here is that the 68000 and the 8259A can be programmed to respond to interrupt signals from multiple sources in almost any way you want them to. Now, before we show you how to initialize and write programs for an 8259A, we will show you more about how it is connected in microcomputer systems.

8259A SYSTEM CONNECTIONS AND CASCADING

Figure 8-16 shows how an 8259A can be added to an URDA MDS board. As shown by the truth table in Figure 8-17, the 74LS138 address decoder will assert the $\overline{CS}$ input of the 8259A when an I/O base address of $BF00 is on the address bus. The A0 input of the 8259A is used to select one of two internal addresses in the device. This pin is connected to system address line A1, so the system addresses for the two internal addresses are $BF00 and $BF02. The eight data lines of the 8259A are always connected to the lower half of the 68000 data bus because the 68000 expects to receive interrupt types on these lower eight data lines. $\overline{RD}$ and $\overline{WR}$ are connected to the system R/W line. The function code lines from the 68000 are connected to $\overline{INTA}$ on the 8259A, such that only the interrupt-acknowledge CPU function will pulse $\overline{INTA}$. The interrupt request signal (INT) from the 8259A is connected to the interrupt input of the 68000 using the 74148. Just the multipurpose $\overline{SP}/\overline{EN}$ pin is tied high because we are using only one 8259A in this system. Since we are not cascading any slave 8259As on the IR inputs, the cascade lines (CAS0, CAS1, and CAS2) can be left open. The eight IR inputs are available for interrupt signals. Unused IR inputs should be tied to ground so that a noise pulse cannot accidentally cause an interrupt. In a later section we will show you how to initialize this 8259A, but first we need to show you how more than one 8259A can be added to a system.

The dashed box on the right side of Figure 8-16 shows how another 8259A could be added to the URDA MDS system to give 15 interrupt inputs. If needed, an 8259A could be connected to each of the 8 IR inputs of the original 8259A to give a total of 64 interrupt inputs if needed. Note that since we are using only one 68000 interrupt level, only one of the 8259A INT pins is connected to the 74148 I1 pin. The 8259A connected directly into the 74148 I1 pin is referred to as the *master*. The INT pin from the other 8259A connects into an IR input on the master. This secondary, or

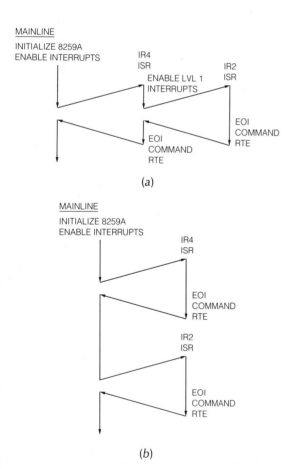

(a)

(b)

FIGURE 8-30   8259A and 68000 program flow for IR4 interrupt followed by IR2 interrupt. (a) Response with interrupts enabled in IR4 procedure. (b) Response with interrupts not enabled in IR4 procedure.

cascaded, device is referred to as a *slave*. Note that the interrupt-acknowledge signal from the 68000 goes to both the master and to the slave devices.

Each 8259A has its own addresses, so that command words can be written to it and status bytes read from it. For the cascaded 8259A in Figure 8-16, the two system I/O addresses will be $BF08 and $BF0A.

The cascade pins (CAS0, CAS1, and CAS2) from the master are connected to the corresponding pins of the slave. For the master these pins function as outputs, and for the slave device they function as inputs. A further difference between the master and the slave is that on the slave the $\overline{SP/EN}$ pin is tied low to let the device know that it is a slave.

Briefly, here is how the master and the slave work when the slave receives an interrupt signal on one of its IR inputs. If that IR input is unmasked on the slave and if that input is a higher priority than any other interrupt level being serviced in the slave, then the slave will send an INT signal to the IR input of the master. If that IR input of the master is unmasked and if that input is a higher priority than any other IR inputs currently being serviced, then the master will send an interrupt signal to the 68000 interrupt inputs. If the 68000 interrupts are enabled, the 68000 will go through its level 1 interrupt-service routine and send out two interrupt-acknowledge pulses to both the master and the slave. The slave ignores the first interrupt-acknowledge pulse. When the master receives the first interrupt acknowledge (generated by the A1, A2, and A3 outputs), it outputs a 3-bit slave identification number on the CAS0, CAS1, and CAS2 lines. (Each slave in a system is assigned a 3-bit ID as part of its initialization). Sending the 3-bit ID number enables the slave. When the slave receives the second interrupt acknowledge from the 68000, the slave will send the desired interrupt-type number to the 68000 on the eight data lines.

If an interrupt signal is applied directly to one of the IR inputs on the master, the master will send the desired interrupt type to the 68000 when it receives the second interrupt acknowledge from the 68000.

Now that we have given you an overview of how an 8259A operates and how 8259As can be cascaded, the initialization command words for the 8259A should make some sense to you.

INITIALIZING AN 8259A

Earlier in this chapter, when we showed you how to initialize an 8254, we listed a series of steps you should go through to initialize any programmable device. To refresh your memory of these very important steps, we will work quickly through them again for the 8259A.

The first step in initializing any device is to find the system base address for the device from the schematic or from a memory map for the system. In order to have a specific example here, we will use the 8259A shown in Figure 8-16. The base address for the 8259A in this system is $BF00.

The next step is to find the internal addresses for the device. For an 8259A the two internal addresses are

selected by a high or a low on the A0 pin. In the circuit in Figure 8-16, the A0 pin is connected to system address line A1, so the internal addresses correspond to 0 and 2.

Next you add the internal addresses to the base address for the device to get the system address for each internal part of the device. The two system addresses for this 8259A, then, are $BF00 and $BF02.

Now look at Figure 8-31*a*, p. 236, for the format of the command words that must be sent to this device to initialize it. The sight of all of these command words may seem overwhelming at first, but taken one at a time they are quite straightforward. To help you see which initialization control words are needed for various 8259A applications, Figure 8-31*b*, p. 236, shows this in flowchart form. According to this flowchart, an ICW1 and an ICW2 must be sent to any 8259A in the system. If the system has any slave 8259As (cascade mode), then an ICW3 must be sent to the master, and a different ICW3 must be sent to the slave. If the system is a 68000 system or if you want to specify certain special conditions, then you have to send an ICW4 to the master and to each slave. Now let's look at the formats for the different ICWs.

The first thing to notice about the ICW formats in Figure 8-31*a* is that the bit labeled A0 on the left end of each of these is not part of the actual command word. This bit tells you the internal address to which the control word must be sent. The A0 = 0 next to ICW1, for example, tells you that ICW1 must be sent to internal address 0, which for our 8259A corresponds to system address $BF00.

The next step in the initialization procedure is to make up the control words. The LSB of ICW1 tells the 8259A whether it needs to look for an ICW4 or not. For this type of connection the 68000 will be *emulating* an 8086 system. That is, the 8259A will be led to believe that it is connected to an 8086 (even though we know it is really connected to a 68000). We do this because we want the 8259A to use an 8-bit vector number rather than a 16-bit vector address. Recall that the 68000 expects an 8-bit vector number between 64 and 255 for user-interrupt vectors. Since we are using the device in a 68000 system emulating an 8086 system, we need to send ICW4. Therefore we make bit D0 a 1. We want to use only one 8259A for now, so we make bit D1 a 1. When used with a 68000 emulating an MCS80, bit D2 is a don't care, so we make it a 0. Bit D3 is used to specify level-triggered mode or edge-triggered mode. In level-triggered mode, service will be requested whenever a high level is present on an IR input. In edge-triggered mode a signal on an IR input must go from low to high and stay high until serviced. We usually use the edge-triggered mode because this prevents a square-wave trigger from causing multiple interrupts. Making bit D3 a 0 does this. Bit D4 should be a 1. For operation in a 68000 system, bits D5, D6, and D7 are don't cares, so we make them 0s for simplicity. The ICW1 for our example here, then, is 0001 0011.

In a 68000 system ICW2 is used to tell the 8259A the type number to send in response to an interrupt signal

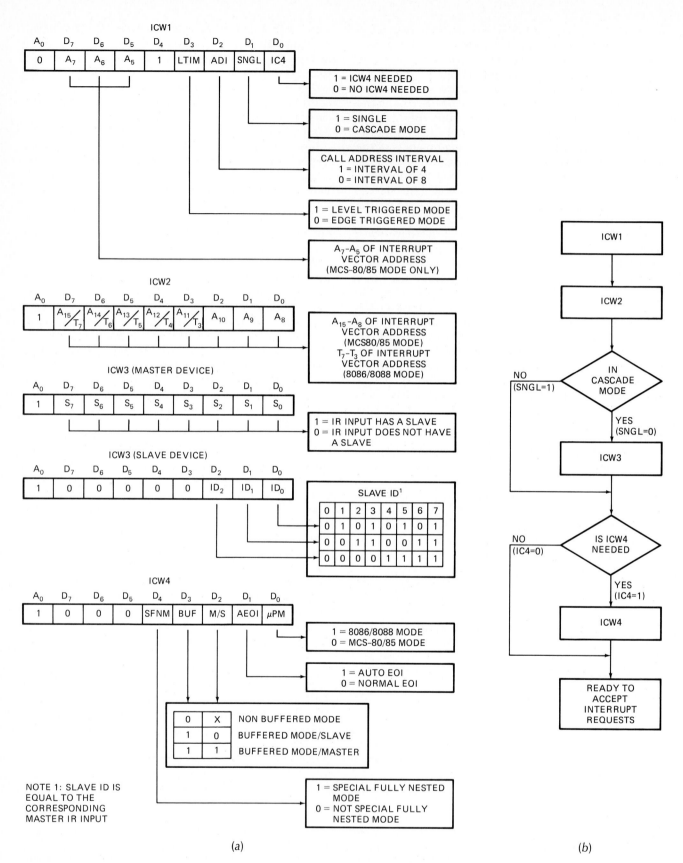

FIGURE 8-31   8259A initialization command word formats and sending order.
(a) Formats. (b) Sending order and requirements. (Intel Corporation)

on the IR0 input. In response to an interrupt signal on some other IR input, the 8259A will automatically add the number of the IR input to this base number and send the result to the 68000 as the type number for that input. Because 68000 interrupt types 0–63 are either dedicated or reserved, type 64 (decimal) is the lowest-type number available for us to use. If we send the 8259A an ICW2 of 0100 0000 binary or 64 decimal, the 8259A will send this number as the type to the 68000 in response to an IR0 interrupt. For an IR1 input, the 8259A will send 0100 0001 binary or 65 decimal, and so on for the other IR inputs. In any ICW2 you send the 8259A, the lowest 3 bits must always be 0s, because the 8259A automatically supplies these bits to correspond to the number of the IR input.

Since we are not using a slave in our example, we don't need to send an ICW3. If you are using a slave 8259A in a system, you have to send an ICW3 to the master to tell it which IR inputs have slaves. The master has to be told this so that it knows for which IR

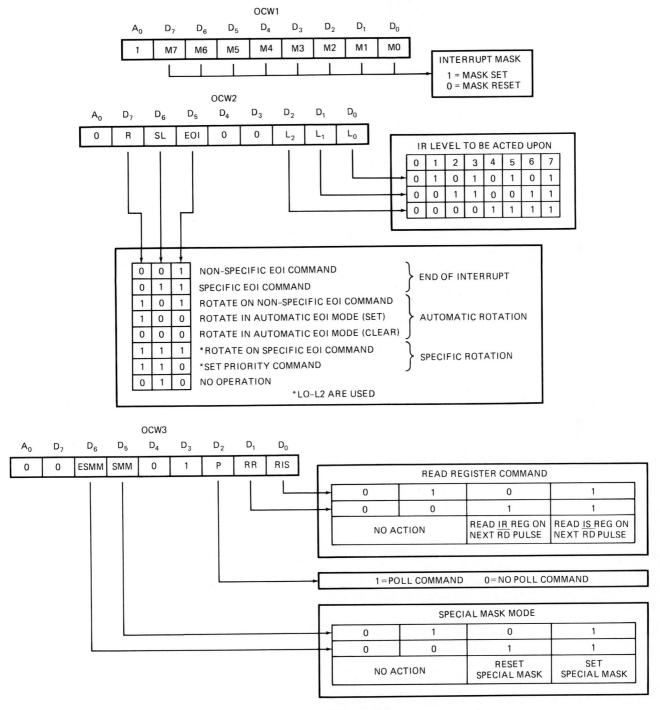

FIGURE 8-32   8259A operational command words. (*Intel Corporation*)

input signals it has to send out a slave ID number on the CAS0, CAS1, and CAS2 lines. You have to send an ICW3 to a slave 8259A to give it an ID number. The ID number you give a slave is equal to the IR input of the master to which its INT output is connected. When the master sends out an ID number on the CAS lines, the slave will recognize its ID number and output the desired vector number to the 68000 when it receives an interrupt-acknowledge pulse.

For our example here, the only reason we need to send an ICW4 is to let the 8259A know that it is emulating an MCS80 system. We do this by making bit D0 of the word a 0. Another interesting bit in this command word is D1, the automatic end-of-interrupt bit. If this bit is set in ICW4, the 8259A will automatically reset the ISReg bit for the interrupt input that is being responded to when the second interrupt acknowledge pulse is received. The effect of this is that the 8259A will then be able to respond to an interrupt signal on a lower-priority IR input. In other words, a lower-priority interrupt input could then interrupt a higher-priority routine. Since we don't want automatic end of interrupt, the ICW4 for our example here is 0000 0001.

In addition to the initialization command words shown in Figure 8-31a, the 8259A has a second set of command words called *operation command words*, or OCWs. These are shown in Figure 8-32, p. 237. An OCW1 must be sent to an 8259A to unmask any IR inputs to which you want it to respond. For our example here, let's assume that we want to use only IR2 and IR3. Since a 0 in a bit position of OCW1 unmasks the corresponding IR input, we put 0s in these two bits and

1s in the rest of the bits. Our OCW1 then is 1 1111 0011.

OCW2 is mainly used to reset a bit in the ISReg. This is usually done at the end of the interrupt-service procedure, but it can be done at any time in the procedure. The effect of resetting the IRS bit for an interrupt level is that once the bit is reset, the 8259A can then respond to interrupt signals of the same or lower priority. In small systems we usually use the nonspecific *end-of-interrupt* (EOI) command word. The OCW2 for this is 0010 0000. When the 8259A receives this OCW, it will automatically reset the ISReg bit for the IR input currently being serviced. If you want to reset a specific ISReg bit, you can send the 8259A an OCW2 with 011 in bits D7, D6, and D5 and the number of the ISReg bit you want to reset in the lowest 3 bits of the word. You can also use OCW2 to tell the 8259A to rotate the priorities of the IR inputs so that after an IR input is serviced, it drops to the lowest priority. If you are interested, consult the Intel data sheet for more information on this and on the use of OCW3.

Now that we have made up the required ICWs and OCWs, the next step is to write the instructions to send these command words to the 8259A.

Figure 8-33 contains a 68000 assembly language program that shows how to initialize an 8259A and combines many of the concepts of this chapter. You can use this program as a pattern for writing programs that service several interrupts. The purpose of this program is to initialize the URDA MDS system in Figure 8-16 for generating a real-time clock of seconds, minutes, and hours from a 1-kHz interrupt signal and

```
; 68000 PROGRAM FRAGMENT
; ABSTRACT        :   TO SHOW INITIALIZATION OF INTERRUPT JUMP TABLE
;                 :   8259A, AND COUNTER 0 OF 8254
;
; REGISTERS USED: A0 ... used to place ISR addresses
; PORTS USED      : $BF00 ... 8259A control
;                 : $BF02 ... ICW2 address
;                 : $BF07 ... 8254 control
;                 : $BF01 ... 8254 counter 0 data
; PROCEDURES      : KEYBOARD - ISR to read characters from Keyboard
;                 : CLOCK - ISR to service the 1hz clock interrupt
;
;                          alr 8-89
        ORG     $4000              ; start the code at $4000
;
;       INITIALIZATION
;
        LEA     STACK_TOP,A7       ; initialize user stack pointer to top of stack

; store addresses for the KEYBOARD and CLOCK routines at addresses
; $7FD4 and $7FD0 (in the soft exception vector table in RAM)

        LEA     KEYBOARD,A0        ; get the address of the KEYBOARD ISR
        MOVE.L  A0,($7FD4)         ; save that address in the RAM jump table

        LEA     CLOCK,A0           ; get the address of the KEYBOARD ISR
        MOVE.L  A0,($7FD0)         ; save that address in the RAM jump table
```

FIGURE 8-33 Assembly language program showing initialization of 68000, 8259A, and 8254 for real-time clock and keyboard-interrupt procedures (*continued*).

```
; initialize 8259A
        MOVE.B  #%00010011,($BF00)   ; edge triggered, single, ICW4

        LEA     $8002,A0             ; ICW2 address
        MOVE.B  #%01000000,(A0)      ; type 64 is first 8259A type
        MOVE.B  #%00000001,(A0)      ; set (68000) MCS80 mode
        MOVE.B  #%11111010,(A0)      ; unmask IR0 and IR1

; initialize 8254 counter 0 for 1 kHz output
;  8254 command word for counter 0, LSB then MSB,
;  square wave, BCD
        MOVE.B  #%00010011,($BF07)   ; counter 0 command word
        MOVE.B  #$79,($BF07)         ; count LSB of $79
        MOVE.B  #$35,($BF07)         ; count MSB of $35

; enable interrupts for 68000
        ANDI.W  #%1111100011111111,SR

; wait for interrupt
HERE:
        JMP     HERE
;------------------------
; Subroutine: KEYBOARD
;
KEYBOARD:
        ; ...                        ; keyboard subroutine instructions

        MOVE.B  #%00100000,($BF00)   ; OCW2 for non-specific EOI
                                     ; sent to indicate end of interrupt

        ; ...                        ; keyboard subroutine instructions
        RTE                          ; return from exception to the interrupted
                                     ; program, restore the status register
;------------------------
; Subroutine: CLOCK
;
CLOCK:
        ; ...                        ; clock subroutine instructions

        MOVE.B  #%00100000,($BF00)   ; OCW2 for non-specific EOI
                                     ; sent to indicate end of interrupt

        ; ...                        ; clock subroutine instructions
        RTE                          ; return from exception to the interrupted
                                     ; program, restore the status register

;------------------------
        ORG     $4300                ; start the data at $4200

STACK_HERE:  DS.W    200             ; set stack length of 200 words
STACK_TOP:   DS.W    0               ; the stack top is at the high address

SECONDS:     DC.B    0
MINUTES:     DC.B    0
HOURS:       DC.B    0

INT_COUNT:   DC.W    $3E8            ; 1 kHz interrupt counter
KEY_BUF:     DS.B    100             ; Buffer for 100 ASCII characters

        END
```

FIGURE 8-33   (continued)

for reading ASCII codes from a keyboard on an interrupt basis. This program assumes that the 3.579-MHz CLK signal on the board is connected to the CLK input of 8254 counter 0, the GATE input of the 8254 counter 0 is tied high, and the OUT pin of counter 0 is connected to the IR0 input of the 8259A. The program further assumes that the key-pressed strobe from the ASCII keyboard is connected to the IR2 input of the 8259A.

The data declarations for our program set aside some memory locations for seconds' count, minutes' count, hours' count, and 100 characters read in from the keyboard. We also set aside a word of memory filled with the constant $3E8 (1000 decimal), which will be used during our 1-kHz count (1000 decimal), which will be used during our 1-kHz count (1000 ms = 1 s). Also, as part of the data area we set up a stack of 200 words.

At the start of the mainline program, we initialize the stack pointer register. We will be using interrupt vector 64 for a real-time clock, and vector 66 will point at the start of the routine that reads ASCII codes from the keyboard. We will not be using a type 65 interrupt in this program. The next four instructions are needed to place the addresses of the clock and keyboard-interrupt service routines in the type 64 and type 66 locations in the soft exception vector table. Later we initialize the 8259A so that type 64 corresponds to its IR0 input and type 66 corresponds to its IR2 interrupt.

We then initialize the 8259A with the command words we worked out before, with the exception of the ICW2. We have chosen type 64 to correspond to an IR0 interrupt so the new ICW2 will be 0100 0000. Note that those command words shown with a 0 as the A0 bit in Figures 8-31 and 8-32 are sent to system address $BF00, and those command words shown with a 1 as the A0 bit are sent to system address $BF02.

The next section of the mainline program initializes counter 0 of the 8254 for mode 2, BCD countdown, and read/write LSB and then MSB. To produce a 1-kHz signal from the 3.579-MHz CLK, we then write a count of 3579 to counter 0. This will not give exactly 1 kHz, but it is as close as we can get with this particular input clock frequency. The CLK frequency for this board was not chosen to make a 1-kHz real-time clock. Larger systems usually have two or more crystal-controlled oscillators to accommodate both baud-rate generation and real-time clock generation.

Finally, after the timer is initialized, we enable the 68000 interrupt input with the ANDI.W to SR instruction so that the 68000 will respond to interrupt signals from the 8259A and wait for an interrupt with the HERE: JMP HERE instruction.

For the two interrupt-service routines, we show just the skeletons and the end-of-interrupt instructions. We leave it to you to write the actual routines. Remember from a previous discussion that when the 8259A responds to an IR signal, it sets the corresponding bit in the ISReg. This bit must be reset at some time during or at the end of the interrupt-service routine so that the priority resolver can respond to future interrupts of the same or lower priority. At the end of our interrupt-

service routines, we do this by sending an OCW2 to the 8259A. The OCW2 of 0010 0000 that we send tells the 8259A to reset the ISReg bit for the IR level that is currently being serviced. This is a nonspecific end-of-interrupt instruction.

This chapter has introduced you to interrupts and some interrupt applications. The following chapters show you more of this, because much of the interfacing discussed there is done on an interrupt basis.

CHECKLIST OF IMPORTANT TERMS AND CONCEPTS IN THIS CHAPTER

If there are terms or concepts in this list you do not remember, use the index to help you find them in the chapter.

Interrupt (INT)

Interrupt priority levels 0-7

Interrupt pins
$\overline{IPL0}$
$\overline{IPL1}$
$\overline{IPL2}$

Nonmaskable interrupts—level 7

Software interrupts—TRAP

Interrupt-service routine

Interrupt type

Exception vector, exception pointer

Exception vector table, interrupt pointer table

Divide by 0 exception—type 5

Trace interrupt—type 9

Breakpoints

Autovectoring of interrupts

Group 2 exceptions
TRAP
TRAPV
CHK
Zero divide

Group 1 exceptions
Trace
Interrupt
Illegal instruction
Privilege violation

Group 0 exceptions
Reset
Address error
Bus error

Software interrupts—type 32–47

User interrupts—type 64–255

BIOS

Edge-activated interrupt input

Level-activated interrupt input

Interrupt priority

Hardware interrupts

Software programmable

Programmable timer/counter device 8253, 8254

Internal addresses

Control words, command words, mode words

8259A priority interrupt controller
   Fixed priority
   In-service register (ISReg)
   Priority resolver
   Interrupt request register (IRR)
   Interrupt mask register (IMR)

REVIEW QUESTIONS AND PROBLEMS

1. List and describe in general terms the steps a 68000 will take when it responds to an exception.

2. Describe the purpose of the 68000 exception vector table.

3. What addresses in the exception vector table are used for a type 5 exception?

4. The starting address for a type 5 exception service routine is $4178. Show where this address should be placed in the hard exception vector table. Show where it should be placed in the soft exception table.

5. Address $0108 in the interrupt jump table contains $4224, and address $010C contains $0440. To what exception types do these locations correspond? What are the starting addresses for the interrupt-service routines?

6. Briefly describe the condition or conditions that cause the 68000 to perform each of the following types of exceptions: TRAPV, CHK, zero divide, trace, and user interrupt.

7. Why is it necessary, at the start of an interrupt-service routine, to push all registers used in the routine and to pop them at the end of the routine?

8. Why must you use an RTE instruction rather than the regular RTS instruction at the end of an interrupt-service routine?

9. Show the assembler directives and instructions you would use to initialize the soft exception vector table for a type 5 routine called DIV_0_ERROR and a type 15 routine called POWER_FAIL.

10. Describe the main use of the 68000 type 9 (trace) trap. Show the assembly language instructions necessary to set the 68000 T bit in the status register.

11. In a system that has battery-backed RAM for saving data in case of a power failure, the stack is often put in the battery-backed RAM. This makes it easy to save registers and critical program data. Assume that the battery-backed RAM is in the address range of $8000–$8FFF. Write a 68000 power failure interrupt-service routine that

   Sets an external battery-backed flip-flop connect-

ed to bit 0 of the port at $C014 to indicate that a power failure has occurred.

Saves all registers on the stack.

Saves the stack pointer value for the last entry at location $8000.

Saves the contents of memory locations $0400–05FF after the saved stack pointer value at the start of the battery-backed memory. (A string-move-type operation might be useful for this.)

Halts.

When the power comes back on, the startup routine can check the power fail flip-flop. If the flip-flop is set, the start-up routine can copy the saved data back into its operating locations and initialize the stack pointer value from address $8000. Using this value it can restore the pushed registers and return execution to where the power fail interrupt occurred. This is called a *warm start*. If we don't want it to do a warm start, we can reset the flip-flop with an external RESET key so the system does a start from scratch, or a *cold start*.

12. Why is the 68000 interrupt mask (CPU priority level) automatically set to level 7 when the 68000 is RESET? How are the 68000 interrupt inputs enabled to respond to interrupts? What instruction can be used to disable (mask) the interrupt inputs? Why is the interrupt mask (CPU priority level) automatically set to the level of the current interrupt as part of the response to an interrupt? How are the interrupts automatically reenabled at the end of an interrupt-service routine?

13. Describe the response a 68000 will make if it receives a level 7 interrupt signal during a division operation that produces a divide by 0 trap.

14. The data outputs of an 8-bit A/D converter are connected to bits D0–D7 of port $BFF9 and the end-of-conversion signal from the A/D converter is connected to the $\overline{IPL0}$, $\overline{IPL1}$, and $\overline{IPL2}$ inputs of a 68000 (i.e., to interrupt level 7). Write a simple mainline program and an interrupt-service routine that reads in a byte of data from the converter. If the MSB of the data is a 0, indicating the value is in range, add the byte to a running total kept in two successive memory locations. If the

MSB of data is 1, showing that the value is out of range, ignore the input. After 100 samples have been totaled, divide by 100 to get the average, store this average in another reserved memory location, and reset the total to zero.

15. Write the algorithm and the program for an interrupt-service routine that turns on an LED connected to bit D0 of a port at $C014 on for 25 s and off for 25 s. The routine should also turn a second LED connected to bit D1 of port $C014 on for 1 min and off for 1 min. Assume that a 1-Hz interrupt signal is connected to the level 1 interrupt inputs of a 68000 and that a high on a port bit turns on the LED connected to it.

16. Write the algorithms for a mainline program and an interrupt-service routine that generate a real-time clock of seconds, minutes, and hours in three memory locations using a 1-Hz signal applied to the level 1 interrupt inputs of a 68000. Then write the assembly language programs for the mainline and the ISR. If you are working on an URDA MDS board, there is a routine in Figure 9-33 that you can add to your program to display the time on the data and address field LEDs of the board. You can use this routine without understanding the details of how it works. To display a word on the data field, simply put the word in the D1 register, put $00 in D0, and call the subroutine. To display a word on the address field, put the word in D1, put $01 in D0, and call the subroutine.

17. In Chapter 5 we discussed using breakpoints to debug programs containing subroutines. List the sequence of locations at which you would put breakpoints in the example program in Figure 8-11 to debug it if it did not work when you loaded it into memory.

18. Suppose that we add another 8254 to the URDA MDS add-on circuitry shown in Figure 8-16 and that the $\overline{CS}$ input of the new 8254 is connected to the Y5 output of the 74LS138 decoder.

   a. What will be the system base address for this added 8254?
   b. To which half of the 68000 data bus should the eight data lines from this 8254 be connected?
   c. What will be the system addresses for the three counters and the control word register in this 8254?
   d. Show the control word you would use to ini-

tialize counter 1 of this device for read/write LSB and then MSB, mode 3, and BCD count-down.

   e. Show the sequence of instructions you would use to write this control word and a count of 356 decimal to the counter.
   f. Assuming the GATE input is high, when does the counter start counting down in mode 3?
   g. Assuming initialization as in parts d and f and that 712 kHz is applied to the CLK input of counter 1 in mode 3, describe the frequency, period, and duty cycle of the waveform that will be on the OUT pin of the counter.
   h. Describe the effect that a control word of 1001 0000 sent to this 8254 will have.

19. Show the instructions you would use to initialize counter 2 of the 8254 in Figure 8-16 to produce a 1.2-ms wide STROBE pulse on its OUT pin when it receives a trigger input on its GATE input.

20. Show the instructions needed to latch and read a 16-bit count from counter 1 of the 8254 in Figure 8-16.

21. Describe the sequence of actions that an 8259A and a 68000, as connected in Figure 8-16, will take when the 8259A receives an interrupt signal on its IR2 input. Assume only IR2 is unmasked in the 8259A and that the 68000 interrupt inputs have been enabled with an ANDI to SR instruction.

22. Describe the use of the CAS0, CAS1, and CAS2 lines in a system with a cascaded 8259A.

23. Describe the response that an 8259A will make if it receives an interrupt signal on its IR3 and IR5 inputs at the same time. Assume fixed priority for the IR inputs. What response will the 8259A make if it is servicing an IR5 interrupt and an IR3 interrupt signal occurs?

24. Why is it necessary to send an end-of-interrupt (EOI) command to an 8259A at some time in an interrupt-service routine?

25. Show the sequence of command words and instructions that you would use to initialize an 8259A with a base address of $FF10 as follows: edge-triggered, only one 8259A, (68000 emulating an) MCS80 system, interrupt-type 40 corresponds to IR0 input, normal EOI, nonbuffered mode, not special fully nested mode, IR1 and IR3 unmasked.

CHAPTER 9

Digital Interfacing

The major goal of this chapter and the next is to show you much of the interface circuitry and software needed to control a complex machine such as our printed-circuit-board-making machine or a medical instrument with a microprocessor. We try to show enough detail in each topic so that you can build and experiment with some real circuits and programs. Perhaps you can use some of this to control appliances around your house or solve some problems at work.

OBJECTIVES

At the conclusion of this chapter, you should be able to

1. Describe simple input and output, strobed input and output, and handshake input and output.

2. Initialize a programmable parallel port device such as the 6821 for simple input or output and for handshake input or output.

3. Interpret the timing waveforms for handshake input and output operations.

4. Describe how phonemes are sent to a speech synthesizer on a handshake basis.

5. Describe how parallel data is sent to a printer on a handshake basis.

6. Show the hardware connections and the programs that can be used to interface keyboards to a microcomputer.

7. Show the hardware connections and the programs that can be used to interface alphanumeric displays to a microcomputer.

8. Describe how an 8279 can be used to refresh a multiplexed LED display and scan a matrix keyboard.

9. Initialize an 8279 for a given display and keyboard format.

10. Show the circuitry used to interface high-power devices to microcomputer ports.

11. Describe the hardware and software needed to control a stepper motor.

PROGRAMMABLE PARALLEL PORTS AND HANDSHAKE INPUT/OUTPUT

Throughout the program examples in the preceding chapters, we have used port devices to input parallel data to the microprocessor and to output parallel data from the microprocessor. Most of the available port devices such as the 6821 on the URDA® MDS board contain two or three ports that can be programmed to operate in one of several different modes. The different modes allow you to use the device for many common types of parallel data transfer. First, we discuss some of these common methods of transferring parallel data, and then we show how the 6821 is initialized and used in a variety of I/O operations.

Methods of Parallel Data Transfer

SIMPLE INPUT AND OUTPUT

When you need to get digital data from some simple switch such as a thermostat into a microprocessor, all you have to do is connect the switch to an input port line and read the port. The thermostat data is always present and ready, so you can read it at any time.

Likewise, when you need to output data to a simple display device such as an LED, all you have to do is connect the input of the LED buffer on an output port pin and output the logic level required to turn on the light. The LED is always there and ready, so you can send data to it at any time. The timing waveform in Figure 9-1a, p. 244, represents this situation. The crossed lines on the waveform represent the time at which a new data byte becomes valid on the output lines of the port. The absence of other waveforms indicates that this output operation is not directly dependent on any other signals.

SIMPLE STROBE I/O

In many applications valid data is present on an external device only at a certain time, and it must be read in at that time. An example of this is the ASCII-encoded keyboard shown in Figure 4-13. When a key is pressed on the keyboard, circuitry on the keyboard sends out the ASCII code for the pressed key on eight parallel data lines. The keyboard circuitry then sends

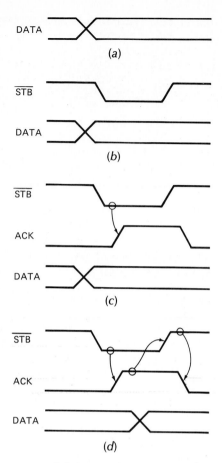

FIGURE 9-1 Parallel data transfer. (a) Simple output.
(b) Simple strobe I/O. (c) Single-handshake I/O.
(d) Double-handshake I/O.

out a strobe signal on another line to indicate that valid
data is present on the eight data lines. As shown in
Chapter 3, you can connect this strobe line to an input
port line and poll it to determine when you can input
valid data from the keyboard. Another alternative,
described in Chapter 8, is to connect the strobe line to
an interrupt input on the processor and have an
interrupt-service routine read in the data when the
processor receives an interrupt. The point here is that
this transfer is time dependent. You can read in data
only when a strobe pulse tells you that the data is valid.

Figure 9-1b shows the timing waveforms that represent this type of operation. A sending device, such as a
keyboard, outputs parallel data on the data lines and
then outputs an $\overline{STB}$ (strobe) signal to let you know
that valid data is present.

For low rates of data transfer, such as from a keyboard to a microprocessor, a simple strobe transfer
works well. However, for high-speed data transfer, this
method does not work because there is no signal that
tells the sending device when it is safe to send the next
data byte. In other words, the sending system might
send data bytes faster than the receiving system could
read them. To prevent this problem, a *handshake* data
transfer scheme is used.

SINGLE-HANDSHAKE I/O

Figure 9-1c shows some example timing waveforms for
a *handshake data transfer* from a peripheral device to
a microprocessor. The peripheral outputs some paral-
lel data and sends an $\overline{STB}$ signal to the microprocessor.
The microprocessor detects the asserted $\overline{STB}$ signal on
a polled or interrupt basis and reads in the byte of data.
The microprocessor then sends an acknowledge signal, ACK, to the peripheral to indicate that the peripheral can send the next byte of data. From the viewpoint
of the microprocessor, this operation is referred to as a
handshake, or strobed, input.

These same waveforms might represent a handshake output from a microprocessor to a parallel printer. In this case, the microprocessor outputs a character
to the printer and asserts an $\overline{STB}$ signal to the printer
to tell the printer, "Here is a character for you." When
the printer is ready, it answers back with the ACK
signal to tell the microprocessor, "I got that one, send
me another." We show you much more about printer
interfacing in a later section.

The point of this handshake scheme is that the
sending device or system cannot send the next data
byte until the receiving device or system indicates with
an ACK signal that it is ready to receive the next byte.

DOUBLE-HANDSHAKE DATA TRANSFER

For data transfers where even more coordination is
required between the sending system and the receiving
system, a *double handshake* is used. Figure 9-1d
shows some example waveforms for a double-handshake input from a peripheral to a microprocessor.
Perhaps it will help you to follow these waveforms by
thinking of them as a conversation between two people. In these waveforms each signal edge has meaning.
The sending device asserts its $\overline{STB}$ line low to ask,
"Are you ready?" The receiving system raises its ACK
line high to say, "I'm ready." The peripheral device
then sends the byte of data and raises its $\overline{STB}$ line high
to say, "Here is some valid data for you." After it has
read in the data, the receiving system drops its ACK
line low to say, "I have the data, thank you, and I await
your request to send the next byte of data."

For a handshake output of this type, from a microprocessor to a peripheral, the waveforms are the same,
but the microprocessor sends the $\overline{STB}$ signal and the
data and the peripheral sends the ACK signal. In a later
section we show how this type of handshake is used to
transfer phoneme bytes from a microprocessor to a
speech-synthesizer device.

For handshake data transfer, a microprocessor can
determine when it is time to send the next data byte on
a polled or on an interrupt basis. We usually use the
interrupt approach because it makes better use of the
processor's time. The $\overline{STB}$ or ACK signals for these
handshake transfers can be produced on a port pin by
instructions in the program. This method, however,
tends to use too much processor time. Therefore, port
devices such as the 6821 have been designed so that
they can be programmed to manage the handshake
operation automatically. For example, the 6821 can be

programmed to receive an $\overline{STB}$ signal from a peripheral automatically, send an interrupt signal to the processor, and send the ACK signal to the peripheral at the proper times. The following sections show you how to connect, initialize, and use a 6821 for a variety of applications.

6821 Internal Block Diagram and System Connections

Figure 9-2 shows the internal block diagram of the 6821. Along the right side of the diagram you can see that the device has 16 I/O lines. Port A can be used as an 8-bit input port or as an 8-bit output port. Likewise, port B can be used as an 8-bit input port or as an 8-bit output port. In fact, the ports can be used so that some of the lines are input lines and at the same time other

lines in an 8-bit port are output lines. The data direction registers for each port tell which lines are used in which direction (as inputs or as outputs). We discuss the different modes for these lines in detail a little later.

Along the left side of the diagram you see the usual signal lines used to connect the device to the system buses. Eight data lines allow you to write data bytes to a port or the control register and to read bytes from a port or the status register under the control of the R/$\overline{W}$ line. The register select inputs, RS0 and RS1, allow you selectively to access one of the two ports or control registers. The internal addresses for the device are port A, 00; port B, 01; control A, 10; and control B, 11. Asserting the chip select inputs of the 6821 enables it for reading or writing. The CS0, CS1, and $\overline{CS2}$ inputs will be connected to the output of the address decoder circuitry to select the device when it is addressed.

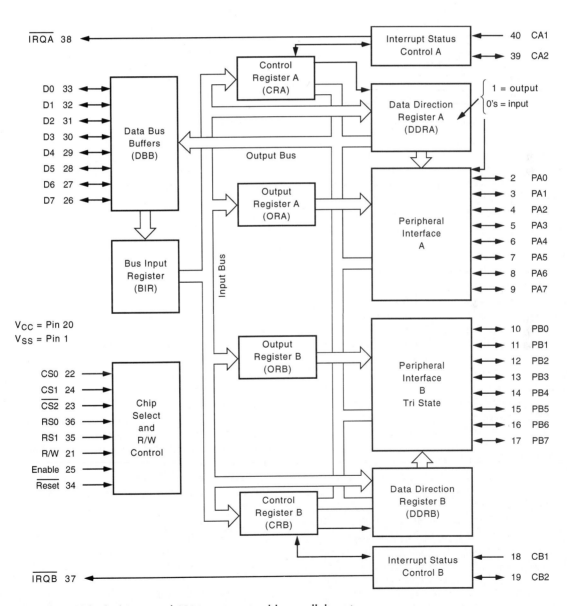

FIGURE 9-2 Internal block diagram of 6821 programmable parallel port device.

The 6821 control registers are also used to control data register versus data direction register addressing (more about this in the next section), to control interrupt or handshake behavior, and to control the type of triggering to be used with I/O devices. Each port has its own control register so that the two ports can be configured to operate in the same manner or in different manners. That is, the ports are truly independently configurable and operable I/O channels.

The CA1 and CA2 (CB1 and CB2 for port B) lines are used to carry interrupt signals from the I/O devices to and from the 6821. The $\overline{IRQA}$ ($\overline{IRQB}$ for port B) lines carry interrupt signals back from the 6821 to the 68000. These interrupt-control lines are probably the most complex of the 6821 controls and are discussed in some detail later in this chapter.

The RESET input of the 6821 is connected to the system reset line so that, when the system is reset, all the port lines are initialized as input lines. This is done to prevent destruction of circuitry connected to port lines. If port lines were initialized as outputs after a power-up or reset, the port might try to output into the output of a device connected to the port. The possible argument between the two outputs might destroy one or both of them. Therefore, all the programmable port devices initialize their port lines as inputs when reset.

We discussed in Chapter 7 how two 6821s are connected in the URDA MDS. Look at Figure 7-6 (URDA MDS schematic) to refresh your memory about these connections. Note that one of the 6821s is connected to the lower half of the 68000 data bus, and the other 6821 is connected to the upper half of the data bus. This is done so that a byte can be transferred by enabling one device, or a word can be transferred by enabling both devices at the same time. According to the truth table for the I/O port address decoder in Figure 7-15, the 6821 on the lower half of the data bus will be enabled for a base address of $C010, and the other 6821 will be enabled for a base address of $C014.

Another point to notice in Figure 7-6 is that system address line A1 is connected to the 6821 RS0 inputs, and system address line A2 is connected to the 6821 RS1 input. With these connections, the system addresses for the two data and control registers in the lower 6821 will be $C010, $C011, $C012, and $C013, as shown in Figure 7-15. Likewise, the system addresses for the upper 6821 data registers and control registers are $C014, $C015, $C016, and $C017.

6821 Internal Addressing

Figure 9-3 summarizes how the different internal registers of the 6821 are addressed. As described in the previous section, the 6821 has six internal registers: two 8-bit data registers, two 8-bit data direction registers, and two 8-bit control registers. The 6821 has only two register address lines, the register select lines RS0 and RS1. Since two address lines can encode only four different combinations, the reader may wonder how the lines can be used to address any of six internal registers. The answer lies in a common trick used in

RS1	RS0	Control Register Bit CR A-2	CR B-2	Location Selected
0	0	1	X	Peripheral Register A
0	0	0	X	Data Direction Register A
0	1	X	X	Control Register A
1	0	X	1	Peripheral Register B
1	0	X	0	Data Direction Register B
1	1	X	X	Control Register B

X = Don't Care

FIGURE 9-3   6821 internal addressing.

smaller ICs to keep the number of address pins down. This trick involves using two of the address combinations to address the two control registers. As shown in Figure 9-3, when RS0 and RS1 are both 1s, control register B is selected. Data written to the 6821 data lines (D0–D7) will go into control register B. If RS0 and RS1 are 0 and 1, respectively, then control register A is addressed. Data written to the data bus (D0–D7) is sent to control register A. The other two possible values for RS0 and RS1, 00 binary and 10 binary, are used to address the remaining four registers, with one of the bits in the control register used to tell which of the remaining four registers is addressed.

Looking at Figure 9-3 notice that if the control register bit 2 is a 1, then a peripheral data register is selected. If the control register bit 2 is a 0, then a data direction register is selected. So, for example, if RS0 and RS are both 0s, then port A is selected. If bit 2 of control register A is a 0, then the data direction register is selected. If bit 2 of control register A is a 1, then the peripheral data register is selected. Similarly, if RS0 and RS1 are binary 10, then port B is being addressed, and control register B bit 2 determines whether the data register or the data direction register is being addressed. Bit 2 in the control registers is called the *data direction register (DDR) access* bit. Port A's control register bit 2 is a DDRA access bit (the data direction register access bit for port A). Similarly, Port B's control register bit 2 is called the DDRB access bit.

If you think about how things must occur when addressing internal registers on a 6821, you soon realize that first you have to address a control register and set the data direction register access bit. Then and only then will you be sure what the bit is set to, and you can address the data register (bit 2 set to 1) or the data direction register (bit 2 set to 0).

Constructing and Sending 6821 Control Words

Figure 9-4 shows the formats for the two 6821 control words. Notice that the format of the two control words is identical. The only difference is that one is used to control port A and the other is used to control port B.

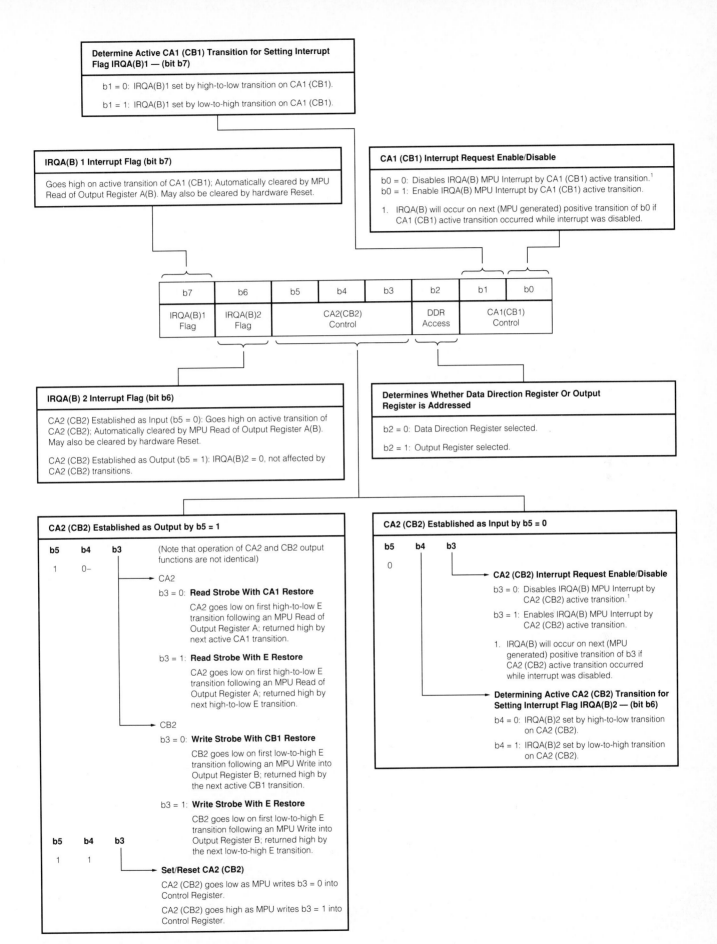

FIGURE 9-4 6821 control word formats.

Controlling the 6821 at its simplest amounts to writing the appropriate control words to the appropriate control registers, possibly writing to the direction registers, and then reading and/or writing data to or from the data registers.

The two control registers each contain 6 bits, which can be read or written by the 68000 (bits 0–5). Bits 6 and 7 of the control registers are read only for the 68000 and are modified by external interrupts occurring on the CA1 and CA2 lines (CB1 and CB2 for port B).

Figure 9-4 also shows what the bits in the two larger bit fields (CA2 control and CA1 control) of the control word are used for. Figure 9-4 shows how bits 0 and 1 of the control word affect the operation of the interrupt inputs CA1 or CB1. Figure 9-4 shows how bit 5 of the control word determines how to interpret the meaning of bits 3 and 4. If bit 5 is set to 0, then CA2 (or CB2 for the port B control word) is established as an input, and Figure 9-4 shows how to interpret bits 3 and 4. If bit 5 is a 1, then CA2 (CB2) is established as an input, and Figure 9-4 shows how to interpret bits 3 and 4.

As usual, making up a control word consists of figuring out what to put in the eight small boxes, 1 bit at a time. As an example for this device, suppose that you want to initialize the upper 6821 port B in Figure 7-6 as follows: no interrupts, data register selected, and CA2 used as an output to control the I/O device. The 6821 can be used in the simplest output without handshake mode, in a simple handshake mode, or in a pulse strobed mode. Assume for this example we want to use simple I/O with no handshake (i.e., we may not even have the 6821 CA1 line connected to the I/O device).

Figure 9-5a shows the control word that will program the 6821 in this way. The figure also shows how you should document any control words you make up for use in your programs. Using Figure 9-4a, work your way through this word to make sure you see why each bit has the value it does.

As we said previously, the control register address for the upper 6821 port B is $C016. To send a control word, you load the control word into the low byte of D0 with a MOVE.B #$04,D0 instruction, point A0 at the port address with the MOVEA.L $C016,A0 instruction, and send the control word to the 6821 control register with the MOVE.B D0,(A0) instruction.

Figure 9-5b shows the code you might actually use to initialize the 6821's control and data direction registers. We have seen this code before in the examples in previous chapters. Notice that first we write to the control register to set the data direction access bit. We then write to the data direction register. Then we write the control word we want for normal operation to the control register. Finally, we can write data to the data register and the 6821 will send that data to the I/O device. Notice that we care about the DDRA access bit (bit 2) only when we first write to the control register, because we know we will write to the register again immediately to set the DDRA access bit back to the data register. However, we do care that the interrupts are not accidentally enabled when we make the first control register write, since we don't want to cause an unintentional interrupt of the 68000 by the 6821. We learn more about interrupts later.

6821 Handshake Application Examples

INTERFACING TO A MICROCOMPUTER-CONTROLLED LATHE

All the machines in the machine shop of our computer-controlled electronics factory operate under microcomputer control. One example of these machines is a lathe that makes bolts from long rods of stainless steel. The cutting instructions for each type of bolt that we need to make are stored on $\frac{3}{4}$-in.-wide paper or metal tape. Each instruction is represented by a series of holes in the tape. A tape reader pulls the tape through

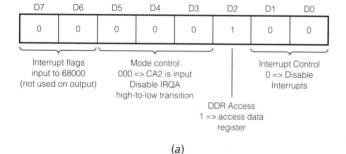

(a)

```
MOVEA.L    #$C014,A2    ; Point A2 at data register
                        ;   (or data direction register)
MOVEA.L    #$C016,A3    ; Point A3 at control register
MOVE.B     #$00,(A3)    ; Bit D2=0 implies access
                        ;   data direction register
                        ;   interrupts disabled
MOVE.B     #$FF,(A2)    ; Make all bits of port outputs
MOVE.B     #$04,(A3)    ; Bit D2=1 implies access data reg,
                        ;   interrupts disabled
```

(b)

FIGURE 9-5   Control word examples for 6821. (a) Mode-set control word. (b) Control register bit-set control word to set bit 3.

an optical or mechanical sensor to detect the hole patterns and convert these to an 8-bit parallel code. The microcomputer reads the instruction codes from the tape reader on a handshake basis and sends the appropriate control instructions to the lathe. The microcomputer must also monitor various conditions around the lathe. It must, for example, make sure the lathe has cutting lubricant oil, is not out of material to work on, and is not jammed up in some way. Machines that operate in this way are often referred to as *computer numerical control, or CNC, machines.*

Figure 9-6 shows in diagram form how two 6821s might be used to interface a microcomputer to the tape reader and lathe. In the next chapter we show you some of the actual circuitry needed to interface the port pins of the 6821s to the sensors and the high-power motors of the lathe. For now we want to talk about initializing the 6821s for this application and analyze the timing waveforms for the handshake input of data from the tape reader.

First you want to make up the control word to initialize the 6821s in the correct modes for this application. To do this, start by making a list showing how you want each port pin or group of pins to function. Then put in the control word bits that implement those pin functions. For our example here, the lower 6821 port A needs to be initialized for handshake input, because instruction codes have to be read in from the tape reader on a handshake basis. The upper 6821 port B needs to be initialized for simple output. No handshaking is needed here because this port is

being used to output simple on or off control signals to the lathe.

The upper 6821 port A bits D0, D1, and D2 are used for simple input of sensor signals from the lathe. The lower port B bit D2 functions as the stop/go signal for the transfer from the tape reader connected to the lower 6821 port A. Port B, bit D2 is used for output of the STOP/GO signal to the tape reader. The rest of the bits in the lower 6821 port B and the upper 6821 port A are not used for this example.

Figure 9-7a, p. 250, shows the control words to initialize the 6821s for these pin functions. These words are sent to the control register addresses as shown previously. Now let's talk about how the program for this machine might operate and how the handshake data transfer actually takes place.

After initializing everything, the system would probably read the upper 6821 port A bits D0, D1, and D2 to check if the lathe is ready to operate. For any 6821 mode you read port A by simply doing an input from the port A address. Be sure, however, that the control register is configured to address the data port (not the data direction register) and that the corresponding bit in the data direction register is a 0, meaning the bit is an output from the 6821 to the I/O device. Then the microprocessor would output a start command to the tape reader on the lower 6821 port B bit D2. This is done with another simple output to the port data register. Figure 9-7b, p. 250, shows the code to initialize the 6821s and start the tape reader. When the tape reader receives the go command, it will start the handshake data transfer to the 6821. Let's work our way through the timing waveforms in Figure 9-8, p. 250, to see how the data transfer takes place.

The 6821 CRA is programmed with CA1 enabled and active on the falling edge and CA2 as an output of read strobe with E restore. The tape reader sends a $\overline{STB}$ signal to the CA1 input and a byte of data to port A. The 6821 then sends an interrupts request ($\overline{IRQA}$) to the CPU. The CPU performs an interrupt service routine that reads the data from port A of the 6821. The RD signal going high causes the $\overline{IRQA}$ signal from the 6821 to return high. The CA2 output goes low following the falling edge of the E signal after the read. As programmed, the CA2 signal returns high just after the next high-to-low edge of the E signal. CA2 returning high is a signal to the tape reader that it can send the next byte of data. This is shown by the dashed section on the right side of the data waveform in Figure 9-8. Secondly, if the interrupt signal output has been enabled, the rising edge of the $\overline{STB}$ signal will cause the lower 6821 to output an interrupt request signal to the microprocessor on line $\overline{IRQB}$. If interrupt is not enabled, the 68000 CPU must poll the lower 6821 port B D0 bit in order to know when the tape reader has sent a byte of data.

In the interrupt case the processor response to the interrupt request will be to go to an interrupt-service routine that reads in the byte of data latched in the lower 6821 port A. In the polled case the 68000 sits in a loop reading the lower 6821 port B and waiting for bit

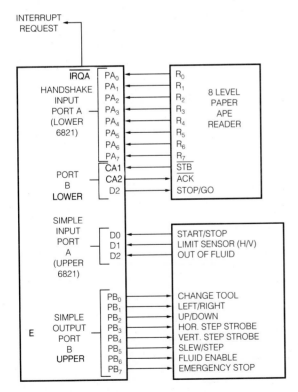

FIGURE 9-6 Interfacing a microprocessor to a tape reader and lathe.

D7	D6	D5	D4	D3	D2	D1	D0	
0	0	0	0	0	1	0	0	Lower 6821 Port A
0	0	0	0	0	1	0	0	Lower 6821 Port B
0	0	0	0	0	1	0	0	Upper 6821 Port A

(a)

```
MOVE.B      #$00,($C016)    ; Bit D2=0 implies access
                            ;   data direction register
                            ;   interrupts disabled
MOVE.B      #$FF,(A2)       ; Make all bits of port outputs
MOVE.B      #$04,(A3)       ; Bit D2=1 implies access data reg,
                            ;   interrupts disabled
```

(b)

FIGURE 9-7   (a) Control word to initialize the 6821 for interface with tape reader and lathe. (b) 68000 code to initialize and start the tape reader.

D0 to go high (i.e., to be set to a 1 by the tape reader); then the 68000 can read the data from port A. When the R/$\overline{W}$ signal from the microprocessor goes low for this read of port A, the 6821 will automatically reset its interrupt request signal on $\overline{IRQB}$. This is done so that a second interrupt cannot be caused by the same data byte transfer. When the processor raises its R/$\overline{W}$ signal high again at the end of the read operation, the lower 6821 drops its acknowledge signal on port B, bit D1, low again. The acknowledge going low again is the signal to the tape reader that the data transfer is complete and that it can send the next byte of data. The time between when the lower 6821 sends the interrupt request signal and when the processor reads the data byte from port A depends on when the processor gets around to servicing that interrupt. The point here is that this time doesn't matter. The tape reader will not send the next byte of data until it detects that the acknowledge signal has gone low again. The transfer cycle will then repeat for the next data byte.

After the processor reads in the lathe-control instruction byte from the tape reader, it will decode this instruction and output the appropriate control byte to the lathe on the upper 6821 port B. The tape reader then sends the next instruction byte. If the instruction tape is made into a continuous loop, the lathe will keep making the specified parts until it runs out of material. The unused bits of the lower 6821 port B could be connected to a mechanism that loads in more material so the lathe can continue.

Figure 9-9 shows the 68000 code for this type of handshaking operation. In this application the 68000 actually performs the handshaking itself and is responsible for manipulating all the handshake signals itself, by writing to the appropriate 6821 port data register bits. It is also possible to connect the 6821 using the $\overline{IRQA}$ and CA1 lines such that part of the handshaking is done automatically by the 6821. In the next example we show how this is done. The 68000 direct handshake method is slower and does not use the full functionality of the 6821. However, it is conceptually simpler and is more flexible in terms of timing requirements. When following through the next example, try to map the 68000 handshake operations

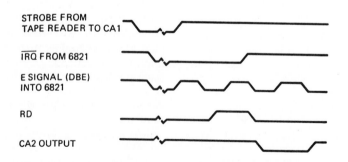

FIGURE 9-8   Timing waveforms for 6821 handshake data input from a tape reader.

```
MOVE.B    #$04, ($C013)          ; Initialize lower 6821 Port A
MOVE.B    #$04, ($C017)          ; Initialize lower 6821 Port B
MOVE.B    #$04, ($C012)          ; Initialize upper 6821 Port A

END
```

FIGURE 9-9   Control register to set to enable interrupt request outputs for handshake modes.

into the equivalent operations as handled by the 6821 internal logic. The mysterious parts of the next example can best be understood by referring back to this simple direct example.

The microcomputer-controlled lathe we have described here is a small example of automated manufacturing. The advantage of this approach is that it relieves humans of the drudgery of standing in front of a machine, continually making the same part, day after day. It is hoped that society can find more productive use for the human time made available.

A Speech Synthesizer Interface—6821 Handshake Output

Many microprocessor-based products now recognize spoken commands and speak to you. In Chapter 13 we discuss in detail several methods of producing human speech under microprocessor control. For our example here we chose the *Votrax SC-01A phoneme speech synthesizer* because it is relatively inexpensive, it is easy to program, and it interfaces easily with a microprocessor port on a handshake basis. You may want to build up the circuit shown here and give your programs a voice. The circuit can be connected to one of the 6821s on an URDA® MDS board if you have one of these available.

SC-01A OPERATION AND CIRCUIT CONNECTIONS

Figure 9-10*a*, p. 252, shows how an SC-01A speech synthesizer IC can be connected to a 6821. The SC-01A uses *phonemes* to produce speech. Phonemes are the individual sounds in words. By linking phonemes, you can produce any word. To produce words, phrases, or even sentences, the microcomputer simply has to output a series of phonemes to the SC-01A with the proper timing. A 6-bit binary code sent to the P0–P5 inputs of the SC-01A determines which of its 64 phonemes it will output. An additional 2 bits sent to the SC-01A's I1 and I2 inputs determine the inflection of the sounded phoneme. Appendix C shows the 64 phoneme codes and the phoneme sequence for some example words. To sound a phoneme you send the phoneme and inflection codes for that phoneme and then assert the STB input of the SC-01A high. The SC-01A will then assert its acknowledge/request ($\overline{A/R}$) line low to tell you that it received the phoneme, and it will sound the phoneme. The time required to sound a phoneme ranges from 47 ms to 250 ms. When the SC-01A finishes sounding the phoneme, it will raise its

$\overline{A/R}$ line high again to indicate that it is ready for the next phoneme. The variable time it takes to sound a phoneme means that you have to send phonemes to the SC-01A on a handshake basis. You could poll the $\overline{A/R}$ line to determine when the SC-01A is ready for the next phoneme (as in the last example), but because of the relatively long time between requests, it is much more reasonable to service the device on an interrupt basis. A 6821 port operating in handshake mode easily manages the required STB, $\overline{A/R}$ and interrupt signals, so these lines are connected to the appropriate bits of the 6821 ports for this mode. Before we go on to the 6821 operation and timing waveforms, here are a few more points about the circuit connections.

The LM380 in Figure 9-10*a* is an audio amplifier, which amplifies the signal from the SC-01A so that it can drive a speaker. The resistors and capacitors connected to pins 15 and 16 of the SC-01A determine the internal clock frequency. This clock frequency determines the pitch of the phoneme. You can adjust the 10-kΩ potentiometer to get a frequency of about 680 kHz on pin 16 or until you like the pitch of the sounded phonemes. The 74C906 open-drain CMOS buffers, between the 6821 PA6–PA7 pins and the I1–I2 pins, convert the 0–5-V-range signals from the 6821 to the 0–12-V-range signals required by the SC-01A inputs. Likewise, the 74C906 buffer on the $\overline{A/R}$ output of the SC-01A converts the 0–12-V-range signal from the SC-01A to the 0–5-V-range signal required by the 6821. The STB signal to the SC-01A must come at least 450 ns after the phoneme and inflection codes arrive at the device. The 20-kΩ resistor and the 100-pF capacitor between the two 74C906 buffers on the STB line produce the required delay for this signal. The transistor after the second buffer inverts the CB2 signal from the 6821 so it has the correct polarity for the SC-01A STB input. It is often necessary to "massage" the handshake strobe signal so that it meets the timing requirements of the receiving device. In our next application example, the printer interface, we show you another way to do this.

PHONEME TRANSFER TIMING WAVEFORMS

Figure 9-10*b*, p. 252, shows the timing waveforms for a handshake output data transfer to the SC-01A. Here's how this works.

When the SC-01 is first powered up, it raises its $\overline{A/R}$ output high to indicate that it is ready for a phoneme. This causes the 6821 to send an interrupt signal to the processor. In response to the interrupt request, the processor executes an interrupt-service routine, which writes a phoneme and an inflection code to port A of the 6821. The left edge of the waveforms in Figure 9-10*b* represents the start of the phoneme write operation. During this write operation the R/$\overline{W}$ from the 68000 will go low. When the 6821 detects this low, it will automatically reset its interrupt request output on pin $\overline{IRQB}$. A little later you will see how this was set. Now, when the R/$\overline{W}$ signal from the 68000 goes high, the phoneme and inflection codes will be present on the output of the 6821. R/$\overline{W}$ being at a high state

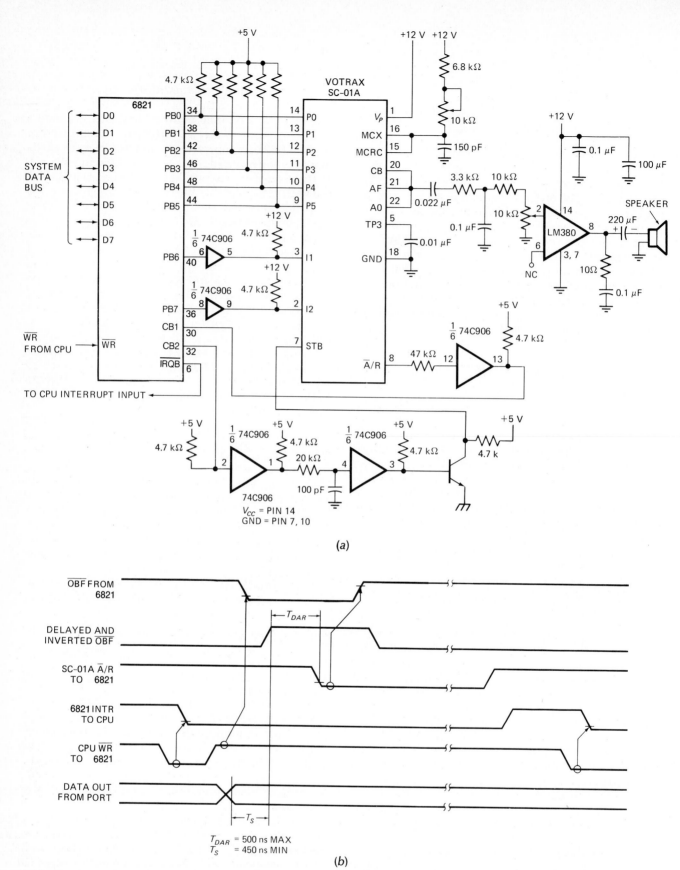

FIGURE 9-10   (a) Connection of a Votrax SC-01A speech synthesizer to a 6821 for handshake output of phonemes. (b) Timing waveforms for transfer of a phoneme from 6821 to SC-01A on handshake basis. (*Courtesy Votrax Incorporated*)

causes the 6821 automatically to assert its output buffer full (OBF) signal low on line CA1. This signal, inverted and delayed 450 ns by the buffer circuit, arrives at the STB input of the SC-01A. This signal edge says to the SC-01A, "Here is a phoneme for you." In response, the SC-01A drops its $\overline{A}/R$ output low to say, "I got the phoneme, thank you." When this falling edge arrives at the 6821 CA2 input, the 6821 automatically raises its OBF signal high again. This edge essentially asks the SC-01A, "May I send you another phoneme?" After the SC-01A finishes sounding the phoneme (47–250 ms later) it raises its $\overline{A}/R$ line high again to say, "Send me the next phoneme." When the 6821 CA1 input receives the rising edge of this $\overline{A}/R$ signal, it automatically raises the interrupt request signal on line $\overline{IRQA}$ high if that signal has been enabled. If the 68000 interrupt input being used is enabled, the 68000 will execute the interrupt-service routine that writes a phoneme to port A of the 6821. Writing a phoneme to the 6821 will cause the 6821 interrupt request output on $\overline{IRQA}$ to be automatically reset. The handshake sequence then repeats for this phoneme.

6821 INITIALIZATION FOR HANDSHAKE OUTPUT

In order to have specific addresses, let's assume the SC-01A is connected to the upper 6821 on an URDA MDS board. As shown in Figure 7-15, the port addresses for this device are port A control register, $C012; port A data register, $C010; port B control register, $C016; and port B data register, $C014. Now let's make up the mode control word to send to the 6821.

We want to use port B as a handshake port, so we initialize it by putting 101 binary in bits b5, b4, and b3. To initialize the port A data register for output, we put a 0 in bit b2, write $00 to the data direction register using address $C010, and then put a 1 in bit b2 to use $C010 for the data register. Since bits b7 and b6 are read-only, it doesn't matter what we put in them, so we can put 0s there to fill in the control word. We will be using interrupts in this example with the interrupt on the high-to-low transition, so set b1 to 0 (high-to-low transition) and set b0 to 1 (enable interrupts). Figure 9-11 shows the resultant control word. We send this mode control word to the control register at address $C012.

PROGRAM NOTES FOR SC-01A MAINLINE AND INTERRUPT-SERVICE ROUTINE

The major tasks you have to do for the mainline here are as follows:

1. Set up a table containing the sequence of phoneme codes you want to send. Make the last code in the table the no-sound phoneme, $FF, so that you can easily determine when all of the phoneme codes have been sent. As you read out the codes from the table, you can then compare each with this *sentinel* value to see if you have reached the end of the table.

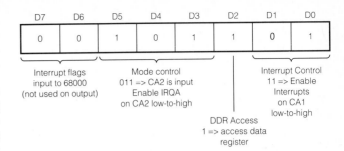

FIGURE 9-11   6821 control words for Votrax SC-01A interface. (a) Mode control word for port A, mode 1. (b) Bit set/reset control word to enable port A interrupts.

2. Initialize, in a memory location, a pointer to the start of the phoneme table.

3. Initialize the interrupt-pointer table to point to the start of the interrupt-service routine.

4. Enable the interrupts in the 68000.

5. Initialize the 6821 and enable the 6821 interrupt request output. When the SC-01A is ready for the next phoneme, the 6821 will send an interrupt signal to the 68000.

The 68000 interrupt-service routine must get the table pointer from memory, use the pointer to get the next phoneme from the table, and send the phoneme to the 6821. The service routine should then compare the phoneme code to the sentinel value of $FF. If the phoneme code is equal to $FF, then the routine can simply return to the interrupted program. If the code is not $FF, then the routine should increment the table pointer to point to the next phoneme, store the pointer back in memory, and do an RTE.

We leave the actual assembly language program for you to write as an exercise at the end of the chapter.

Parallel Printer Interface—Another Handshake Output Example

For most common printers such as the HP Thinkjet printer, the Epson FX-80, and the NEC 8023, the data to be printed is sent to the printer as ASCII characters on eight parallel lines. The printer receives the characters to be printed and stores them in an internal RAM buffer. When the printer detects a carriage-return character ($0D), it prints out the first row of characters from the print buffer. When the printer detects a second carriage return, it prints out the second row of characters. The process continues until all the desired characters have been printed.

Transfer of the ASCII codes from a microcomputer to a printer must be done on a handshake basis because the microcomputer can send characters much faster than the printer can print them. The printer must in some way let the microcomputer know that its buffer is full and that it cannot accept any more characters until it prints some out. A common standard for interfacing with parallel printers is the *Centronics Parallel Standard*, named for the company that developed it. In the following sections we show you how a Centronics parallel interface works and how to implement it with a 6821.

CENTRONICS INTERFACE PIN DESCRIPTIONS AND CIRCUIT CONNECTIONS

Centronics-type printers usually have a 36-pin interface connector. Figure 9-12 shows the pin assignments and descriptions for this connector as it is used in the Epson printers. Some manufacturers use 1 or 2

pins differently, so consult the manual for your specific printer before connecting it up as we show here.

Thirty-six pins may seem like a lot of pins just to send ASCII characters to a printer. The large number of lines is caused by the fact that each data and signal line has its own individual ground-return line. For example, as shown in Figure 9-12, pin 2 is the LSB of the data character sent to the printer, and pin 20 is the ground return for this signal. The reason for the individual ground returns is to reduce the chance of picking up electrical noise in the lines. If you are making an interface cable for a parallel printer, these

SIGNAL PIN NO.	RETURN PIN NO.	SIGNAL	DIRECTION	DESCRIPTION
1	19	STROBE	IN	STROBE pulse to read data in. Pulse width must be more than 0.5 μs at receiving terminal. The signal level is normally "high"; read-in of data is performed at the "low" level of this signal.
2	20	DATA 1	IN	These signals represent information of the 1st to 8th bits of parallel data respectively. Each signal is at "high" level when data is logical "1" and "low" when logical "0."
3	21	DATA 2	IN	
4	22	DATA 3	IN	
5	23	DATA 4	IN	
6	24	DATA 5	IN	
7	25	DATA 6	IN	
8	26	DATA 7	IN	
9	27	DATA 8	IN	
10	28	ACKNLG	OUT	Approximately 5 μs pulse; "low" indicates that data has been received and the printer is ready to accept other data.
11	29	BUSY	OUT	A "high" signal indicates that the printer cannot receive data. The signal becomes "high" in the following cases: 1. During data entry. 3. In "offline" state. 2. During printing operation. 4. During printer error status.
12	30	PE	OUT	A "high" signal indicates that the printer is out of paper.
13	—	SLCT	OUT	This signal indicates that the printer is in the selected state.
14	—	AUTO FEED XT	IN	With this signal being at "low" level, the paper is automatically fed one line after printing. (The signal level can be fixed to "low" with DIP SW pin 2-3 provided on the control circuit board.)
15	—	NC		Not used.
16	—	OV		Logic GND level.
17	—	CHASIS-GND	—	Printer chasis GND. In the printer, the chassis GND and the logic GND are isolated from each other.
18	—	NC	—	Not used.
19-30	—	GND	—	"Twisted-Pair Return" signal; GND level.
31	—	INIT	IN	When the level of this signal becomes "low" the printer controller is reset to its initial state and the print buffer is cleared. This signal is normally at "high" level, and its pulse width must be more than 50 μs at the receiving terminal.
32	—	ERROR	OUT	The level of this signal becomes "low" when the printer is in "Paper End" state, "Offline" state and "Error" state.
33	—	GND	—	Same as with pin numbers 19 to 30.
34	—	NC	—	Not used.
35				Pulled up to +5 Vdc through 4.7 k-ohms resistance.
36	—	SLCT IN	IN	Data entry to the printer is possible only when the level of this signal is "low." (Internal fixing can be carried out with DIP SW 1-8. The condition at the time of shipment is set "low" for this signal.)

Notes: 1. "Direction" refers to the direction of signal flow as viewed from the printer.
2. "Return" denotes "Twisted-Pair Return" and is to be connected at signal-ground level.
When wiring the interface, be sure to use a twisted-pair cable for each signal and never fail to complete connection on the return side. To prevent noise effectively, these cables should be shielded and connected to the chassis of the system unit.
3. All interface conditions are based on TTL level. Both the rise and fall times of each signal must be less than 0.2 μs.
4. Data transfer must not be carried out by ignoring the ACKNLG or BUSY signal. (Data transfer to this printer can be carried out only after confirming the ACKNLG signal or when the level of the BUSY signal is "low.")

FIGURE 9-12 Pin connections and descriptions for Centronics-type parallel interface to Hewlett-Packard Thinkjet printer.

ground-return lines should be connected together and to ground only at the microcomputer end of the cable, as shown in Figure 9-12. While we are talking about grounds, note that pin 16 is listed as logic ground and pin 17 is listed as chassis ground. In order to prevent large noise currents from flowing in the logic ground wire, these wires should be connected together only in the microcomputer. (This precaution is necessary whenever you connect any external device or system to a microcomputer.)

The rest of the pins on the 36-pin connector fall into two categories, signals sent to the printer to tell it what operation to do and signals from the printer that indicate its status. The major control signals to the printer are $\overline{\text{INIT}}$ on pin 31, which tells the printer to perform its internal initialization sequence and $\overline{\text{STB}}$ on pin 1, which tells the printer, "Here is a character for you." Two additional input pins, pin 14 and pin 36, are usually taken care of inside the printer.

The major status signals output from the printer are the following:

1. The $\overline{\text{ACKNLG}}$ signal on pin 10, which, when low, indicates that the data character has been accepted and the printer is ready for the next character.

2. The BUSY signal on pin 11, which is high if for some reason, such as being out of paper, the printer is not ready to receive a character.

3. The PE signal on pin 12, which goes high if the out-of-paper switch in the printer is activated.

4. The SLCT signal on pin 13, which goes high if the printer is selected for receiving data.

5. The $\overline{\text{ERROR}}$ signal on pin 32, which goes low for a variety of problem conditions in the printer.

Figure 9-13 shows the timing waveforms for transferring data characters to an Epson parallel interface printer using the basic handshake signals. Here's how this works.

Assuming the printer has been initialized, you first check the BUSY signal pin to see if the printer is ready to receive data. If this signal is low, indicating the printer is ready (not busy), you send an ASCII code on

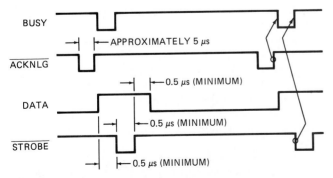

FIGURE 9-13   Timing waveforms for transfer of a data character to a Centronics-type parallel printer such as the IBM-PC or Epson printer. (*IBM Corporation*)

the eight parallel data lines. After at least 0.5 μs you assert the $\overline{\text{STB}}$ signal low to tell the printer a character has been sent. The $\overline{\text{STB}}$ signal going low causes the printer to assert its BUSY signal high. After a minimum time of 0.5 μs, the $\overline{\text{STB}}$ signal can be raised high again. Note that the data must be held valid on the data lines for at least 0.5 μs after the $\overline{\text{STB}}$ signal is made high.

When the printer is ready to receive the next character, it asserts its $\overline{\text{ACKNLG}}$ signal low for about 5 μs. The rising edge of the $\overline{\text{ACKNLG}}$ signal tells the microcomputer that it can send the next character. The rising edge of the $\overline{\text{ACKNLG}}$ signal also resets the BUSY signal from the printer. BUSY being low is another indication that the printer is ready to accept the next character. Some systems use the $\overline{\text{ACKNLG}}$ signal for the handshake, and some systems use the BUSY signal. Now let's see how you can do this handshake printer interface with a 6821.

MC6821 CONNECTIONS AND INITIALIZATION

Figure 9-14, p. 256, shows the circuit for connecting the Centronics parallel printer signals to a 6821. We show here the pin connections for the J2 connector on the URDA MDS board so you can easily add this interface if you are working with one.

For this interface circuitry, 74LS07 open-collector buffers are used on the signal and data lines from the 6821. The 6821 outputs do not have enough current drive to charge and discharge the capacitance of the connecting cable fast enough. Pull-up resistors for the open-collector outputs are built into the printer.

Port B is used for the handshake output data lines. Therefore, as shown in Figure 9-3, line $\overline{\text{IRQB}}$ functions as the interrupt request output to the 68000. The $\overline{\text{ACKNLG}}$ signal from the printer is connected to the 6821 CB1 input. The CB2 signal from the 6821 does not have the right timing parameters for this handshake, so CB2 is left unconnected. For this application the $\overline{\text{STB}}$ input of the printer is connected to bit PA4 of port A. The $\overline{\text{STB}}$ signal is generated by a bit write of this pin.

The four printer status signals are connected to port A so the program can read them in, determine the condition of the printer, and send the appropriate messages to the CRT if the printer is not ready.

Finally, the $\overline{\text{INIT}}$ input of the printer is connected to bit PA5 so that the printer can be reinitialized under program control. Now let's look at the 6821 control words for this application.

Figure 9-15, p. 256, shows the control word to initialize port B for handshake output and port A for input. The upper four bits of port B are initialized as outputs. Figure 9-15 also shows the control word bits necessary to enable the interrupt request signal on line $\overline{\text{IRQB}}$ for the handshake.

THE PRINTER DRIVER PROGRAM

Routines that input data from or output data to peripheral devices such as disc drives, MODEMs, and printers are often called *I/O drivers*. Here we show you one

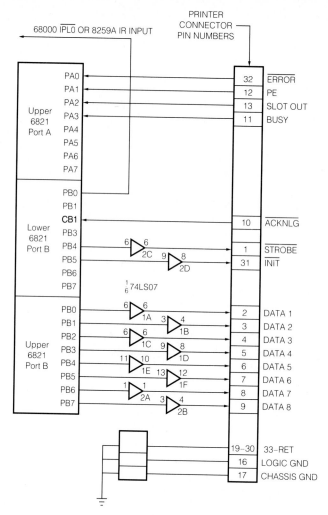

PRINTER
CONNECTOR
PIN NUMBERS

Upper 6821 Port A
PA0
PA1
PA2
PA3
PA4
PA5
PA6
PA7

32	ERROR
12	PE
13	SLOT OUT
11	BUSY

Lower 6821 Port B
PB0
PB1
CB1
PB3
PB4
PB5
PB6
PB7

10	ACKNLG
1	STROBE
31	INIT

$\frac{1}{6}$74LS07

Upper 6821 Port B
PB0
PB1
PB2
PB3
PB4
PB5
PB6
PB7

2	DATA 1
3	DATA 2
4	DATA 3
5	DATA 4
6	DATA 5
7	DATA 6
8	DATA 7
9	DATA 8

19–30	33–RET
16	LOGIC GND
17	CHASSIS GND

FIGURE 9-14 Circuit for interfacing Centronics-type parallel input printer to a 6821 on an URDA MDS board.

way to write the driver routine for our parallel printer interface.

The first point to consider when writing any I/O driver is whether to do it on a polled or on an interrupt basis. For the parallel Centronics interface here, the maximum data transfer rate is about 1000 characters/second. This means that there is a little less than 1 ms

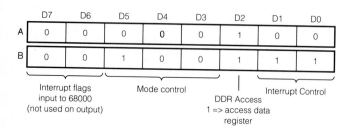

	D7	D6	D5	D4	D3	D2	D1	D0
A	0	0	0	0	0	1	0	0
B	0	0	1	0	0	1	1	1

Interrupt flags input to 68000 (not used on output)

Mode control

DDR Access 1 => access data register

Interrupt Control

FIGURE 9-15 6821 control words for printer interface.

between transfers. If characters are sent on an interrupt basis, many other program instructions can be executed while waiting for the interrupt request to send the next character. Also, when the printer buffer gets full, there will be an even longer time during which the processor can be working on some other job while waiting for the next interrupt. This is another illustration of how interrupts allow the computer to do several tasks "at the same time." For our example here, assume that the interrupt request from IRQB of the 8255A is connected to the interrupt input of the 68000, as shown in Figure 7-15 (the URDA MDS schematic), so that a clock interrupt, a keyboard interrupt, and the printer interrupt can all be serviced in turn.

Figure 9-16a shows the steps you need in the mainline to initialize everything and "call" the printer driver to send a string of ASCII characters to the printer.

At the start of the mainline, some named memory

```
Mainline Algorithm for printer driver

Initialization

        set up control block

                word for storing pointer to ASCII string

                word for number of characters in string

        enable 68000 interrupts

        mode set control words to 6821

        send STROBE high to printer

        initialize printer (pulse init low)

To send ASCII string

        read printer status from port

        if error then

                send error message

                exit

        set print status done bit

        load starting address of string into pointer store

        load length of string into character counter

        enable 6821 IRQA output

        wait for interrupt
```

(a)

FIGURE 9-16   Algorithm for printer mainline and interrupt-based printer driver routine. (a) Mainline steps. (b) Printer driver routine steps, p. 258.

locations are set aside to store parameters needed for transfer of data to the printer. The memory locations set aside for passing information between the mainline and the driver routine are often called a *control block*. In the control block a named location is set aside for a pointer to the address of the ASCII character that is currently being sent. Another memory location is set aside to store the number of characters to be sent. The number in this location will function as a counter so you know when you have sent all the characters in the buffer. Instead of using this *counter approach* to keep track of how many characters have been sent, the *sentinel method* we described for handshake output to the SC-01A in Figure 9-10 could have been used. With the sentinel approach you put a *sentinel* character in memory after the last character to be sent out. MS-DOS, for example, uses a $ character ($24) as a sentinel character for some of its drivers. As you read each character in from memory, you compare it with the sentinel value. If it matches, you know all the characters have been sent. The sentinel approach and the counter approach are both widely used, so you should be familiar with both.

To get the hardware ready to go, you need to initialize

Printer Driver Interrupt Service Routine Algorithm

```
save registers

get pointer to string

get ASCII character from buffer

send character to printer

wait 1 microsecond

send STROBE low

wait 1 microsecond

send STROBE high

increment pointer to string

put pointer back in pointer store

decrement character count

if character count = 0 then

        disable 6821 interrupt request output

restore registers

return from interrupt service routine
```

(b)

FIGURE 9-16   (continued)

the 68000 by unmasking its interrupt inputs. This enables 68000 interrupts. Next the 6821 must be initialized by sending it the control word sequence shown earlier. A bit write to the control word of the 6821 then makes the STB signal to the printer high because this is its unasserted level. To make sure the printer is internally initialized, you pulse the INIT line to the printer low for a few microseconds.

When you are actually ready to print some characters in a program, you first read the printer status from port A and check if the printer is selected, not out of paper, and not busy. In a more complete program you could send a specific error message to the display indicating the type of error found. The program here just sends a general error message. If no printer error condition is found, you load the starting address of the string of ASCII characters into the control block location you set aside for this and load the number of

characters to be sent in the reserved location in the control block. Finally, you enable the interrupt request pin on the 6821. Note that you do not enable this interrupt until you are actually ready to send data. A high on the ACKNLG line from the printer causes the 6821 to output an interrupt request signal to the 68000. This interrupt request signal goes to the processor and causes it to go to the interrupt-service routine.

Figure 9-16b shows the algorithm for the interrupt-service routine (ISR) that services this interrupt and actually sends the characters to the printer. After pushing some registers, the 68000 interrupts are enabled so that higher-priority interrupts can interrupt this ISR. The string address pointer is then read in from the control block and used to read a character in from the buffer to D0. The character in D0 is then output to port B of the 6821. From here on the program follows the timing diagram in Figure 9-13. After sending the character, the program waits at least 0.5 μs, asserts the STROBE input low, waits at least another 0.5 μs and raises the STROBE line high again. The data byte will be latched on the port B output pins until the next character is sent, so the data hold parameter in the timing diagram is satisfied. Sending of the character is now complete, so the next step is to get ready to send another character.

To do this the buffer pointer is incremented by 1, and the incremented value is put back in the control block location. The character counter in the control block is then decremented. If the character counter is not down to zero, there are more characters to send, so the 68000 ISR causes everything to be popped off the stack, and execution is returned to the interrupted program. If the character counter is down to zero, all the characters have been sent, so the interrupt request output of the 6821 is disabled with a bit set/reset control word to prevent further interrupt requests from there. This interrupt source will remain disabled until you want to send another buffer of characters to the printer. Execution then exits from the ISR. The 68000 pops the saved registers and does an RTE.

Figures 9-17 and 9-18, pp. 260-62, show the pertinent parts of the mainline program and the printer driver routine. The preceding discussion of the algorithms and the comments with the instructions should make most of these reasonably clear if you work your way through them one step at a time. You have seen many of the pieces in previous programs. One part of the program that we do want to expand and clarify is the generation of the $\overline{STB}$ signal with bit PB4.

In the speech synthesizer example in a preceding section, we used external hardware to "massage" the CA1 signal from the 6821 so it matched the timing and polarity requirements of the receiving device. Here we generate the strobe directly under software control.

In the mainline we make the $\overline{STB}$ signal on PB4 high by executing a bit write to the control register of the 6821. In the printer driver routine a character is sent to the printer with the MOVE.B D0,(A1) instruction. According to the timing diagram in Figure 9-13, we then want to wait at least 0.5 μs before asserting the $\overline{STB}$ signal low. This is automatically done in the program because the instructions required to assert the strobe low take longer than 0.5μs. The bit write instruction requires at least eight clock cycles, and the MOVE.B instruction requires at least eight clock cycles to execute. Assuming a 4-MHz clock (0.25-μs period) these two instructions take 4 μs to execute, which is more than required. The URDA MDS actually has a 3.57-MHz clock, which is slightly slower.

Again referring to the timing diagram in Figure 9-13, the $\overline{STB}$ time low must also be at least 0.5 μs. The bit-write instruction takes eight or more clock cycles and the byte-write instruction takes eight or more clock cycles. With a 4-MHz clock, this totals 4 μs, which again is more than enough time for $\overline{STB}$ low. In this case creating the $\overline{STB}$ signal with software does not use much of the processor's time, so this is an efficient way to do it.

INTERFACING A MICROPROCESSOR TO KEYBOARDS

Keyboard Types

When you press a key on your computer, you are activating a switch. There are many different ways of making these switches. Here's an overview of the construction and operation of some of the most common types.

MECHANICAL KEYSWITCHES

In mechanical switch keys, two pieces of metal are pushed together when you press the key. The actual switch elements are often made of a phosphor-bronze alloy with gold plating on the contact areas. The keyswitch usually contains a spring to return the key to the nonpressed position and perhaps a small piece of foam to help damp out bouncing. Mechanical switches are relatively inexpensive, but they have several disadvantages. First, they suffer from *contact bounce*. A pressed key may make and break contact several times before it makes solid contact. Second, the contacts may become oxidized or dirty with age so they no longer make a dependable connection. Higher-quality mechanical switches typically have a rated lifetime of about 1 million keystrokes.

MEMBRANE KEYSWITCHES

Membrane keyswitches are really just a special type of mechanical switch. They consist of a three-layer plastic or rubber sandwich, as shown in Figure 9-19a, p. 263. The top layer has a conductive line of silver ink running under each row of keys. The middle layer has a hole under each key position. The bottom layer has a conductive line of silver ink running under each column of keys. When you press a key, you push the top ink line through the hole to contact the bottom ink line. The advantage of membrane keyboards is that they can be made as very thin, sealed units. They are often used on cash registers in fast-food restaurants, on medical instruments, and in other messy applications. The lifetime of membrane keyboards varies over a wide range.

CAPACITIVE KEYSWITCHES

As shown in Figure 9-19b, p. 263, a capacitive keyswitch has two small metal plates on the PC board and another metal plate on the bottom of a piece of foam. When you press the key, the movable plate is pushed closer to the fixed plate. This changes the capacitance between the fixed plates. Sense-amplifier circuitry detects this change in capacitance and produces a logic-level signal that indicates a key has been pressed. The big advantage of a capacitive switch is that it has no

```
; 68000 Printer-driver program
; ABSTRACT          : This program sets up the 6821 (PIA) on an URDA MDS
;                   : board so that a message in a buffer can be sent to a
;                   : Printer.  The mainline sets up a control block and
;                   : initializes all variables.
;
; PORTS USED        : URDA MDS ports upper 6821 port A - $C014 data
;                   :                                   - $C016 control
;                   :                    upper 6821 port B - $C015 data
;                   :                                   - $C017 control
; PROCEDURES        : PRINT_IT uses to output characters
;
;                             alr 9-89
;
;---------------------------------
; defines for I/O port addresses
UPPERA_CNTL         EQU       $C016
UPPERA_DATA         EQU       $C014
UPPERB_CNTL         EQU       $C012
UPPERB_DATA         EQU       $C010
LOWERB_CNTL         EQU       $C017
LOWERB_DATA         EQU       $C015

        ORG       $4200               ; start the data at $4200

STACK_HERE:         DS.W      200     ; set stack length of 200 words
STACK_TOP:          DS.W      0       ; the stack top is the high address
MESSAGE_1:          DC.B      "This is the message from the printer driver"
                    DC.B      $0D,$0A,$0D    ; return and line-feed for printer
PRINT_DONE:         DC.B      0
POINTER:            DC.L      MESSAGE_1      ; pointer to MESSAGE_1
COUNTER:            DC.B      0              ; counter for length of message 1
PRINTER_ERROR:      DC.B      0

;---------------------------------
        ORG       $4000               ; start the code at $4000
;
;         INITIALIZATION
;
        LEA       STACK_TOP,A7        ; initialize user stack pointer to top of stack

; store address for the PRINT_IT routine at address $7FF4.  This
; address will be used by the ROM monitor as the user level 1 interrupt
; service routine indirect address (i.e. the address of the printer
; driver will be found at address $7FF4).

        LEA       PRINT_IT,A0         ; get the address of the KEYBOARD ISR
        MOVE.L    A0,($7FF4)          ; save that address at $7FF4

; enable the 68000 interrupt
        ANDI.W    #$F8FF,SR           ; enable interrupts (set mask to 000)
; initialize the upper 6821
        MOVE.B    #$00,(UPPERB_CNTL)      ; address data direction register
        MOVE.B    #$FF,(UPPERB_DATA)      ; all bits inputs
        MOVE.B    #$04,(UPPERB_CNTL)      ; address data register
        MOVE.B    #$00,(UPPERA_CNTL)      ; address data direction register
        MOVE.B    #$31,(UPPERA_DATA)      ; PB0, PB4, and PC5 output, others
                                          ;   inputs
        MOVE.B    #$04,(UPPERA_CNTL)      ; address data register
        MOVE.B    #$00,(LOWERB_CNTL)      ; address data direction register
        MOVE.B    #$00,(LOWERB_DATA)      ; all bits outputs
        MOVE.B    #$04,(LOWERB_CNTL)      ; address data register
```

FIGURE 9-17   68000 assembly language mainline instructions for printer driver
example.   (*continued*)

```
; send strobe high to printer with bit set on upper PB4
        BSET    #4,(UPPERB_DATA)
; initialize printer - pulse INIT low on upper PB5
        BSET    #5,(UPPERB_DATA)
        BCLR    #5,(UPPERB_DATA)

; read printer status from upper port A, status OK - D0 = XXXX0101
; PA3-BUSY=0, PA2-SLCT=1, PA1-PE=0, PA0-ERROR=1
        MOVE.B  #$00,(PRINTER_ERROR)    ; printer OK so far
        MOVEA.L UPPERA_DATA,A1          ; point to upper A data register
        MOVE.B  (A1),D0                 ; get status of printer
        CMP.B   #$05,D0                 ; is status OK?
        JEQ     SEND_IT                 ; send it if OK
; printer not ready, try once more after waiting 20 ms.
        MOVE.W  #$16EA,D0               ; load count for 20 ms
PAUSE:  DBGT    D0,PAUSE                ; and wait
        MOVE.B  (A1),D0                 ; get status of printer
        CMP.B   #$05,D0                 ; is status OK?
        JEQ     SEND_IT                 ; send it if OK
        MOVE.B  #$01,(PRINTER_ERROR)    ; set error code
        BRA     FIN                     ; not ready so terminate send

;set up pointer to message storage and say print not done yet
SENDIT: MOVEA.L MESSAGE_1,A1
        MOVE.L  A1,D1
        MOVE.L  D1,(POINTER)
        MOVE.B  #$00,(PRINT_DONE)
        MOVE.B  #MESSAGE_LENGTH,(COUNTER)

; enable 6821 IRQB interrupt request line
        MOVE.B  #$1F,(UPPERA_DATA)

; wait for an interrupt from the printer
WT:     BRA     WT
FIN:    NOP
```

FIGURE 9-17 (*continued*)

mechanical contacts to become oxidized or dirty. A small disadvantage is the specialized circuitry needed to detect the change in capacitance. Capacitive keyswitches typically have a rated lifetime of about 20 million keystrokes.

HALL EFFECT KEYSWITCHES

A Hall effect keyswitch is another type of switch that has no mechanical contact. It takes advantage of the deflection of a moving charge by a magnetic field. Figure 9-19c, p. 263, attempts to show you how this works. A reference current is passed through a semiconductor crystal between two opposing faces. When a key is pressed, the crystal is moved through a magnetic field that has its flux lines perpendicular to the direction of the current flow in the crystal. (Actually, it is easier to move a small magnet past the crystal.) Moving the crystal through the magnetic field causes a small voltage to be developed between two of the other opposing faces of the crystal. This voltage is amplified and used to indicate that a key is pressed. Hall effect keyboards are more expensive because of the more complex switch mechanisms, but they are very dependable and have typical rated lifetimes of 100 million or more keystrokes.

Keyboard Circuit Connections and Interfacing

In most keyboards the keyswitches are connected in a matrix of rows and columns, as shown in Figure 9-20a, p. 264. We will use simple mechanical switches for our examples here, but the principle is the same for other types of switches. Getting meaningful data from a keyboard such as this requires doing three major tasks:

1. Detect a key-press.
2. Debounce the key-press.
3. Encode it (produce a standard code for the pressed key).

The three tasks can be done with hardware, software, or a combination of the two, depending on the application. We will first show you how they can be done with software, as might be done in a microprocessor-based grocery scale, where the microprocessor is not pressed for time. Later we describe some hardware devices that do these tasks.

```
;************************************************************
; INTERRUPT SERVICE ROUTINE FOR PRINTER (DRIVER PROGRAM)
; ABSTRACT:        This Interrupt Servie Routine outputs a character
;                  from a buffer to a printer.  If no characters
;                  are left in the buffer then the interrupts to the
;                  68000 are disabled.
; SUBROUTINES:  None
; PORTS:           USES URDA MDS lower 6821 port B to send characters
;                  and Upper 6821 port A for control lines
; REGISTERS USED:        D0 - character holder
;                        D1 -
;                        A1 - pointer to printer I/O data port
;                        A2 - pointer to message buffer
;                        A3 - pointer to printer I/O control port
;                  destroys no registers (saves and restores all used)
;
PRINT_IT:
        MOVEM.L  [A1-A2,D0-D1],-(A7)     ; save registers
        MOVEA.L  #$C013,A1               ; pointer to lower A data register
        MOVEA.L  #$C014,A3               ; pointer to upper B data register
        MOVEA.L  (POINTER),A2            ; pointer to message
        MOVE.B   (A2)+,D0                ; get a character
; send printer a strobe on upper PA4 (low then high)
        BCLR     #4,(A3)                 ; clear (low = 0)
        BSET     #4,(A3)                 ; set (high = 1)
; increment pointer and decrement counter
        MOVE.L   (POINTER),D1            ; get pointer
        ADDI.L   #1,D1                   ; one byte increment
        MOVE.L   D1,(POINTER)            ; return to memory
        MOVE.B   (COUNTER),D1            ; get counter
        SUBI.B   #1,D1                   ; decrement
        MOVE.B   D1,(COUNTER)            ; return to memory
        BGE      NEXT                    ; wait for next character?

; no more characters - disable 6821 in request
        MOVE.B   #$00,(UPPERB_CNTL)      ; disable interrupts from 6821
        MOVE.B   #$01,(PRINT_DONE)       ; printing is done

NEXT:
        MOVEM.L  (A7)+,[A1-A2,D0-D1]     ; restore registers
        RTE
        END
```

FIGURE 9-18   68000 assembly language subroutine instructions for printer driver example.

Software Keyboard Interfacing

CIRCUIT CONNECTIONS AND ALGORITHM

Figure 9-20a, p. 264, shows how a hexadecimal keypad can be connected to a couple of microcomputer ports so the three tasks can be done as part of a program. The rows of the matrix are connected to four output port lines. The column lines of the matrix are connected to four input port lines. When no keys are pressed, the column lines are held high by the pull-up resistors to +5 V. The main principle here is that pressing a key connects a row to a column. If a low is output on a row and a key in that row is pressed, then the low will appear on the column that contains that

key and can be detected on the input port. If you know the row and the column of the pressed key, you then know which key was pressed and can make up any code you want to represent that key. Figure 9-20b, p. 264, shows a flowchart for a subroutine to detect, debounce, and produce the hex code for a pressed key.

The first step is to output 0s to all the rows. Next the columns are read and checked over and over until the columns are all high. This is done to make sure a previous key has been released before looking for the next one. In standard keyboard terminology this is called *two-key lockout*. Once the columns are found to be all high, the program enters another loop, which waits until a low appears on one of the columns,

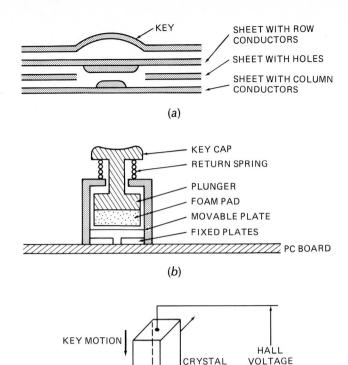

FIGURE 9-19 Keyswitch types. (a) Membrane.
(b) Capacitive. (c) Hall effect.

indicating a key has been pressed. This loop does the detect task for us. A simple 20-ms delay procedure then does the debounce task.

After the debounce time, another check is made to see if the key is still pressed. If the columns are all high, then no key is pressed, and the initial detection was just a noise pulse or a light brushing past a key. If any of the columns are still low, then the assumption is made that it is a valid key-press.

The final task is to determine the row and column of the pressed key and convert this row and column information to the hex code for the pressed key. To get the row and column information, a low is output to one row and the columns are read. If none of the columns are low, the pressed key is not in that row, so the low is rotated to the next row, and the columns are checked again. The process is repeated until a low on a row produces a low on one of the columns. The pressed key is in the row that is low at that time. The byte read in from the input port will contain a 4-bit code that represents the row of the pressed key and a 4-bit code that represents the column of the pressed key. As we show later, this row-column code can easily be converted to hex using a lookup table.

Figure 9-21, pp. 265-66, shows the assembly language program for this subroutine. The detect, debounce, and row-detect parts of the program follow the flowchart very closely and should be easy for you to follow. Work your way down through these parts until you reach the ENCODE label; then continue with the discussion here.

CODE CONVERSION

There are two major ways of converting one code to another in a program. The ENCODE portion of this program uses a *compare* technique, which is important for you to learn, so we will discuss this portion in detail. In a later section on keyboard interfacing with hardware, we show you the other major code-conversion technique, which we call *add and point*.

After the row that produces a low on one of the columns is found, execution jumps to the label EN-CODE. The MOVE.B (A0),D0 instruction here reads the row and column codes in from the input port. This 8-bit code read in represents the key pressed. All that has to be done now is to convert this 8-bit code to the simple hex code for the key pressed. For example, if you press the D key, you want to exit from the procedure with $0D in D0.

The conversion is done with the lookup table declared with DC.B directives at the top of Figure 9-21. This table contains the 8-bit key-pressed codes for each of the 16 keys. Note that the codes are put in the table in order for the hex code they represent. The principle of the conversion technique we use here is to compare the row and column code read in with each of the values in the table until a match is found. We use a counter to keep track of how far down the table we have to go to find a match for a particular input code. When a match is found, the counter will contain the hex code for the key pressed.

In the program in Figure 9-21, we use the D1 register as the counter and as a pointer to one of the codes in the table. To start we load a count of $000F in D1 with the MOVE.B #$000F,D1 instruction. The CMP.B TABLE[D1],D0 after this compares the code at offset [D1] in the table with the row and column code in D0. D1 contains $000F, and the code in the table at this offset is the row and column code for the F key. If we get a match on this first compare, we know the F key was pressed, and D1 contains the hex code for this key. The hex code in D1 is copied to D0 to pass it back to the calling program, and D1 is loaded with $00 to tell the calling program this was a valid key-press and a return was made to the calling program.

If we don't get a match on the first compare, we decrement D1 to point to the code for the E key in the table and do another compare. If a match occurs this time, the E key was the key pressed, and the hex code for that key, $0E, is in D1. If we don't get a match on this compare, we cycle through the loop until we get a match or until the row and column code for the pressed key has been compared with all of the values in the table. As long as the value in D1 is zero or above, the DBGE TRY_NEXT instruction will cause execution to go back to the compare instruction. If no match is found in the table, D1 will decrement from 0 to $FFFF. Execution will then fall through to an instruction that

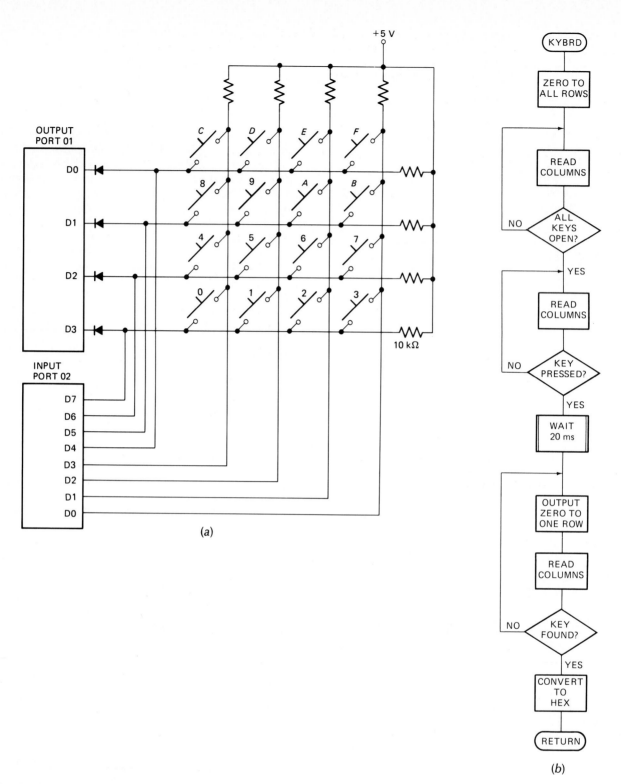

FIGURE 9-20 Detecting a matrix keyboard key-press, debouncing it, and encoding it with a microcomputer. (a) Port connections. (b) Flowchart for subroutine.

```
;  68000 Program to scan and decode a 16 switch keypad
;  ABSTRACT          : This program initializes the ports below and then
;                    : calls a subroutine to input an 8-bit value from
;                    : a 16-switch keypad and decodes it.
;
;  PORTS USED        : URDA MDS ports upper 6821 port A - $C014 data output
;                    :                                  - $C016 control
;                    :                   upper 6821 port B - $C015 data input
;                    :                                  - $C017 control
;  PROCEDURES        : Calls KEYBRD to scan and decode 16-switch keypad
;  REGISTERS         : Uses D0 and A1 (and status register condition codes)
;
;                              alr 9-89
;
;-------------------------------------
; defines for I/O port addresses
UPPERA_CNTL         EQU       $C016
UPPERA_DATA         EQU       $C014
UPPERB_CNTL         EQU       $C012
UPPERB_DATA         EQU       $C010

           ORG      $4200               ; start the data at $4200

STACK_HERE:         DS.W      200       ; set stack length of 200 words
STACK_TOP:          DS.W      0         ; the stack top is the high address
TABLE:              DC.B      $77,$7B,$7D,$7E,$B7,$BB,$BD,$BE
;                             0    1    2    3    4    5    6    7
                    DC.B      $D7,$DB,$DD,$DE,$E7,$EB,$ED,$EE
;                             8    9    A    B    C    D    E    F

;-------------------------------------
           ORG      $4000               ; start the code at $4000
;
;          INITIALIZATION
;
           LEA      STACK_TOP,A7        ; initialize user stack pointer to top of stack

; initialize ports
           MOVE.B   #$

; initialize the upper 6821 port A output, port B input
           MOVE.B   #$00,(UPPERB_CNTL)     ; address data direction register
           MOVE.B   #$FF,(UPPERB_DATA)     ; all bits inputs
           MOVE.B   #$04,(UPPERB_CNTL)     ; address data register
           MOVE.B   #$00,(UPPERA_CNTL)     ; address data direction register
           MOVE.B   #$00,(UPPERA_DATA)     ; all bits outputs
           MOVE.B   #$04,(UPPERA_CNTL)     ; address data register

           JSR      KEYBRD
           NOP
           NOP

; program will continue here with other tasks

;*******************************************************************
; SUBROUTINE KEYBRD
; ABSTRACT:          Subroutine gets a code from a 16-switch keypad and decodes
;                    it.  It returns the code for the keypress in D0 and D1=$00.
;                    If there is an error in the keypress then it returns D1=$01.
; SUBROUTINES:       None
; PORTS USED         : URDA MDS ports upper 6821 port A - $C014 data output
;                    :                                  - $C016 control
;                    :                   upper 6821 port B - $C015 data input
;                    :                                  - $C017 control
; INPUTS             : Keypress from port
; OUTPUTS            : keypress code in D0 and error message in D1
```

FIGURE 9-21 Assembly language instructions for keyboard detect, debounce, and encode subroutine. (*continued*)

```
;   REGISTERS       : Destroys D0 and D1
;      Save/Restore: A1 - output port data register address
;                   : A2 - input port data register address
;                   : D2 - loop counter
;
KEYBRD:
        MOVEM.L  [A1-A2,D2],-(A7)      ; save registers
        MOVEA.L  #UPPERA_DATA,A1       ; pointer to lower A data register
        MOVEA.L  #UPPERB_DATA,A2       ; pointer to upper B data register
        MOVE.B   #$00,(A1)             ; send 0's to all rows
; read columns
WAIT_OPEN:
        MOVE.B   (A2),D0
        AND.B    #$0F,D0               ; mask row bits
        CMP.B    #$0F,D0               ; wait until no keys pressed
        JNZ      WAIT_OPEN

; Read columns for keypress
WAIT_PRESS:
        MOVE.B   (A2),D0               ; read column
        AND.B    #$0F,D0               ; mask row bits
        CMP.B    #$0F,D0               ; see if keypressed
        JEQ      WAIT_PRESS

; Debounce keypress
        MOVE.W   #$16EA,D1             ; delay of 20 ms
DELAY:  DBGE     D1,DELAY
        MOVE.B   (A2),D0               ; read columns
        AND.B    #$0F,D0
        CMP.B    #$0F,D0               ; see if key still pressed
        JEQ      WAIT_PRESS

; Initialize row mask with bit 0 low
        MOVE.B   #$FE,D2

NEXT_ROW:
        MOVE.B   D2,(A1)               ; put a low on one row
        MOVE.B   (A2),D0               ; read columns and check for low bit
        AND.B    #$0F,D0               ; mask out row code
        CMP.B    #$0F,D0               ; check for low in a column
        BNE      ENCODE                ; found column, now encode it
        ROL.B    #1,D2                 ; rotate mask
        BRA      NEXT_ROW              ; look at next row

; Encode the row/column information
ENCODE: MOVEA.L  $TABLE,A1
        MOVE.B   #$0F,D2               ; set up D2 as a counter
        MOVE.B   (A2),D0               ; read row and column from port
TRY_NEXT:
        CMP.B    (A1,D2),D0            ; compare row/col code with table
        BEQ      DONE
        DBGE     D2,TRY_NEXT           ; decrement counter to point to
                                       ;   next table entry (fall through if
                                       ;   not in table)
        MOVE.B   #$01,D1               ; error code
        BRA      EXIT

DONE:   MOVE.B   #$00,D1               ; code for good keycode in D0
EXIT:

        MOVEM.L  (A7)+,[A1-A2,D2]        ; restore registers
        RTS

        END
```

FIGURE 9-21   (continued)

loads an error code of $01 in D1. We then return to the calling program. The calling program will check D1 on return to determine if the contents of D0 represent the code for a valid key-press.

ERROR TRAPPING

The concept of detecting some error condition such as "no match found" is called *error trapping*. Error trapping is a very important part of real programs. Even in this simple program, think what might happen with no error trap if two keys in the same row were pressed at exactly the same time. A column code with two lows in it would be produced. This would not match any of the row and column codes in the table. After all the values in the table were checked, D1 would be decremented to $FFFF and D0 would then be compared with a value in memory at offset $FFFF. The cycle would continue until, by chance, the value in a memory location matched the row and column code in AL. The contents of D1 at that point would be passed back to the calling routine. The chances are 1 in 256 that this would be the correct value. Since these are not very good odds, it is advisable to put error traps in your programs whenever there is a chance for the program to go off to "never-never land" in this way. The error/no-error code can be passed back to the calling program in a register as shown, in a dedicated memory location, or on the stack.

Keyboard Interfacing with Hardware

The previous section described how you can connect a keyboard matrix to a couple of microprocessor ports and perform the three interfacing tasks with program instructions. For systems where the CPU is too busy to be bothered doing these tasks in software, an external device is used to do them. One example of an MOS device that can do this is the General Instruments AY-5-2376, which can be connected to the rows and columns of a keyboard switch matrix. The AY-5-2376 independently detects a key-press by cycling a low down through the rows and checking the columns, just as we did in software. When it finds a key pressed, it waits a debounce time. If the key is still pressed after the debounce time, the AY-5-2376 produces the 8-bit code for the pressed key and sends it out to, for example, a microcomputer port on eight parallel lines. To let the microcomputer know that a valid ASCII code is on the data lines, the AY-5-2376 outputs a strobe pulse. The microcomputer can detect this strobe pulse and read in the ASCII code on a polled basis, as we showed in Figure 4-14, or it can detect the strobe pulse on an interrupt basis, as we showed in Figure 8-9. With the interrupt method the microcomputer doesn't have to pay any attention to the keyboard until it receives an interrupt signal, so this method uses very little of the microcomputer's time. The AY-5-2376 has a feature called *two-key rollover*. This means that if two keys are pressed at nearly the same time, each key will be detected, debounced, and converted to ASCII. The ASCII code for the first key and a strobe signal for it will be sent out; then the ASCII code for the second key and a strobe signal for it will be sent out. Compare this with two-key lockout, which we described previously in the software method of keyboard interfacing.

CONVERTING ONE KEYBOARD CODE TO ANOTHER

Suppose that you are building up a simple microcomputer to control the heating, watering, lighting, and ventilation of your greenhouse. As part of the hardware, you buy a high-quality, fully encoded keyboard at the local electronics surplus store for a few dollars. When you get the keyboard home you find that it works perfectly but that it outputs EBCDIC codes instead of the ASCII codes that you want. Here's how you use the 68000 looping instructions to solve this problem easily.

First look at Table 1-2, which shows the ASCII and EBCDIC codes. The job you have to do here is convert each input EBCDIC code to the corresponding ASCII code. One way to do this is to use the compare technique described previously for the hex-keyboard example. For that method you first put the EBCDIC codes in a table in memory in the order shown in Table 1-2 and set up a register as a counter and pointer to the end of the table. Then enter a loop that compares the EBCDIC character in D0 with each of the EBCDIC codes in the table until a match is found. The counter is decremented after each compare so that when a match is found, the count register contains the desired ASCII code. This compare technique works well, but for this conversion it will, on the average, have to do 64 compares before a match is found. Thus the compare technique is often too time-consuming for long tables. There is another method that is much faster: using a *hash table*.

The first step in the new method is to make up in memory a table that contains all the ASCII codes. You can use the DC.B assembler directive to do this. Since EBCDIC code is an 8-bit code, the table will require 256 memory locations. The trick here is to put each ASCII code in the table at a displacement equal to the value of the EBCDIC character from the start of the table. For example, the EBCDIC code for uppercase A is $C1, so at offset $C1 in the table you put the ASCII code for uppercase A, $41, as shown in Figure 9-22, p. 268.

To do the actual conversion, you simply load the D1 register with the address of the start of the table, load the EBCDIC character to be converted in the A0 register, and do an indexed MOVE indirect instruction. When the 68000 executes the MOVE.B (A0,D1),D0 instruction, it internally adds the EBCDIC value in D1 to the starting address of the table in A0. Because of the way the table is made up, the result of this addition will be a pointer to the desired ASCII value in the table. The 68000 uses this pointer to copy the desired ASCII character from the table to D0. D1 is called the *hash code* for the desired ASCII character.

The advantage of this technique is that, no matter where in the table the desired ASCII value is, the conversion requires only execution of two loads and

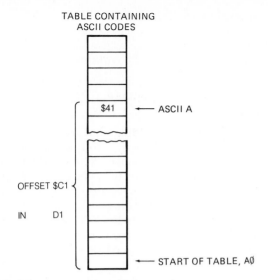

TABLE CONTAINING
ASCII CODES

$41 ← ASCII A

OFFSET $C1

IN   D1

← START OF TABLE, AØ

FIGURE 9-22   Memory table setup for converting EBCDIC keycodes to ASCII equivalent.

one move-indexed indirect instruction. It may occur to you at this point to wonder why, if this method is so fast, we didn't use it for the hex keypad conversion described earlier. The answer is that since the row and column code from the hex keypad is an 8-bit code, the lookup table for the hash code method would require 256 memory locations. Of these 256 memory locations, only 16 would actually be used. This would be a waste of memory, so the compare method is a better choice. It is important for you to become familiar with both code conversion methods so that you can use the one that best fits a particular application.

DEDICATED MICROPROCESSOR KEYBOARD ENCODERS

Most computers and computer terminals now use detached keyboards with built-in encoders. Instead of using a hardware encoder device such as the AY-5-2376, these keyboards use a dedicated microprocessor. Figure 9-23 shows the encoder circuitry for the IBM PC capacitive-switch matrix keyboard. The 8048 microprocessor used here contains an 8-bit CPU, a ROM, some RAM, three ports, and a programmable timer/counter. A program stored in the on-chip ROM performs the three keyboard tasks and sends the code for a pressed key out to the computer. To cut down the number of connecting wires, the key code is sent out in serial form rather than in parallel form. Some keyboards send data to the computer in serial form using a beam of infrared light instead of a wire.

Note in Figure 9-23 the sense amplifier to detect the change in capacitance produced when a key is pressed. Also note that the 8048 uses a tuned LC circuit rather than a more expensive crystal to determine its operating clock frequency.

One of the major advantages of using a dedicated microprocessor to do the three keyboard tasks is pro-

grammability. Special-function keys on the keyboard can be programmed to send out any code desired for a particular application. By simply plugging in an 8048 with a different lookup table in ROM, the keyboard can be changed from outputting ASCII characters to outputting some other character set.

The IBM keyboard, incidentally, does not send out ASCII codes but instead sends out a hex "scan" code for each key when it is pressed and a different scan code when that key is released. This double-code approach gives the system software maximum flexibility because a program command can be implemented either when a key is pressed or when it is released.

INTERFACING TO ALPHANUMERIC DISPLAYS

Many microprocessor-controlled instruments and machines need to display letters of the alphabet and numbers to give directions or data values to users. In systems where a large amount of data needs to be displayed, a CRT is usually used to display the data. In a later chapter we show you how to interface a microcomputer to a CRT. In systems where only a small amount of data needs to be displayed, simple digit-type displays are often utilized. There are several technologies used to make these digit-oriented displays, but we have space here to discuss only the two major types. These are *light-emitting diodes* (LEDs) and *liquid-crystal displays* (LCDs). LCD displays use very low power, so they are often used in portable, battery-powered instruments. LCDs however, do not emit their own light; they simply change the reflection of available light. Therefore, for an instrument that is to be used in dim light conditions, you have to include a light source for the LCDs or use LEDs, which emit their own light. Starting with LEDs, the following sections show you how to interface these two types of displays to microcomputers.

Interfacing LED Displays to Microcomputers

Alphanumeric LED displays are available in three common formats. For displaying only numbers and hexadecimal letters, simple seven-segment displays such as that shown in Figure 1-6a are used. To display numbers and the entire alphabet, 18-segment displays, such as that shown in Figure 9-24a, p. 270, or 5 × 7 dot-matrix displays, such as that shown in Figure 9-24b, p. 270, can be used. The seven-segment type is the least expensive, most commonly used, and easiest to interface, so we will concentrate first on how to interface this type. Later we will show the modifications needed to interface to the other types.

STATIC AND MULTIPLEXED DISPLAYS CIRCUITS

Figure 9-25, p. 270, shows a circuit you might use to drive a single seven-segment, common-anode display. For a common-anode display, a low is applied to a segment to turn it on. When a BCD code is sent to the

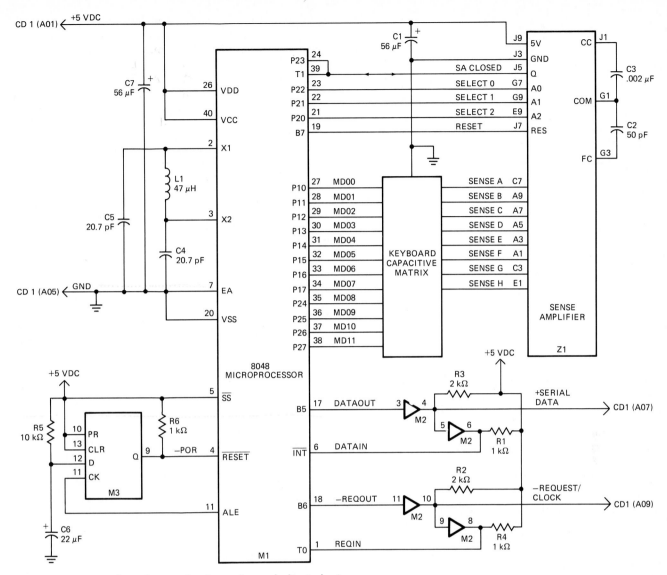

FIGURE 9-23 Keyboard scan circuitry using a dedicated microprocessor.
(*Courtesy IBM Corporation*)

inputs of the 7447, it outputs lows on the segments required to display the number represented by the BCD code. This circuit connection is referred to as a *static display* because current is being passed through the display at all times. Note that current-limiting resistors are required in series with each segment. Here's how you calculate the value of these resistors.

Each segment requires a current of between 5 and 30 mA to light. Let's assume you want a current of 20 mA. The voltage drop across the LED when it is lit is about 1.5 V. The output low voltage for the 7447 is a maximum of 0.4 V at 40 mA, so assume that it is about 0.2 V at 20 mA. Subtracting these two voltage drops from the supply voltage of 5 V leaves 3.3 V across the current-limiting resistor. Dividing 3.3 V by 20 mA gives a value of 168 Ω for the current-limiting resistor. The voltage drops across the LED and the output of the 7447 are not exactly predictable, and the exact current through the LED is not critical as long as we don't

exceed its maximum rating. Therefore, a standard value of 150 Ω is reasonable.

The circuit in Figure 9-25, p. 270, works well for driving just one or two LED digits. However, there are problems if you want to drive, for example, eight digits. The first problem is power consumption. For worst-case calculations, assume that all eight digits are displaying the digit 8 so all seven segments are lit. Seven segments times 20 mA per segment gives a current of 140 mA per digit. Multiplying this by eight digits gives a total current of 1120 mA, or 1.12 A for the eight digits! A second problem of the static approach is that each display digit requires a separate 7447 decoder; each uses perhaps another 13 mA. The current required by the decoders and the LED displays might be several times the current required by the rest of the circuitry in the instrument.

To solve the problems of the static display approach, we use a *multiplex method*. A circuit example is the

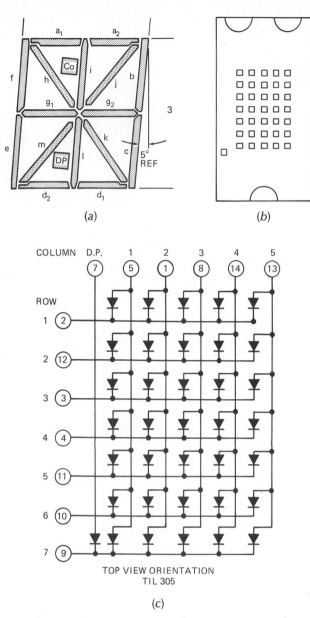

FIGURE 9-24 Eighteen-segment and 5 × 7 matrix LED displays. (a) 18-segment display. (b) 5 × 7 dot-matrix display format. (c) 5 × 7 dot-matrix circuit connections.

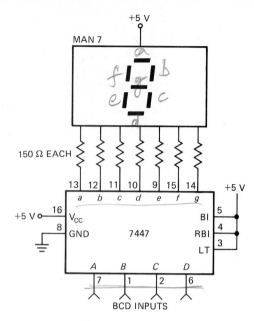

FIGURE 9-25   Circuit for driving single seven-segment LED display with 7447.

easiest way to explain to you how this multiplexing works. Figure 9-26 shows a circuit you can add to a couple of microcomputer ports to drive some common-anode LED displays in a multiplexed manner. Note that the circuit has only one 7447 and that the segment outputs of the 7447 are bused to the segment inputs of all the digits. The question that may occur to you on first seeing this is, Aren't all the digits going to display the same number? The answer is that they would if all of the digits were turned on at the same time. The trick of multiplexing displays is that the segment information is sent out to all the digits on the common bus, but only one display digit is turned on at a time. The PNP transistor in series with the common anode of each digit acts as an on-and-off switch for that

digit. Here's how the multiplexing process works.

The BCD code for digit 1 is first output from port B to the 7447. The 7447 outputs the corresponding seven-segment code on the segment bus lines. The transistor connected to digit 1 is then turned on by outputting a low to that bit of port A. (Remember, a low turns on a PNP transistor.) All the rest of the bits of port A should be high to make sure no other digits are turned on. After 1 or 2 ms, digit 1 is turned off by outputting all highs to port A. The BCD code for digit 2 is then output to the 7447 on port B, and a word to turn on digit 2 is output on port A. After 1 or 2 ms, digit 2 is turned off, and the process is repeated for digit 3. The process is continued until all the digits have had a turn. Then digit 1 and the following digits are lit again in turn. We leave it to you as an exercise at the end of the chapter to write a procedure that is called on an interrupt basis every 2 ms to keep these displays refreshed with some values stored in a table.

With eight digits and 2 ms per digit, you get back to digit 1 every 16 ms, or about 60 times per second. This refresh rate is fast enough that, to your eye, the digits will each appear to be lit all the time. Refresh rates of 40 to 200 times a second are acceptable.

The immediately obvious advantages of multiplexing the displays are that only one 7447 is required and only one digit is lit at a time. We usually increase the current per segment to between 40 and 60 mA for multiplexed displays so that they will appear as bright as they would if not multiplexed. Even with this increased segment current, multiplexing provides a large saving in power and parts.

NOTE: If you are calculating the current-limiting resistors for multiplexed displays, make sure

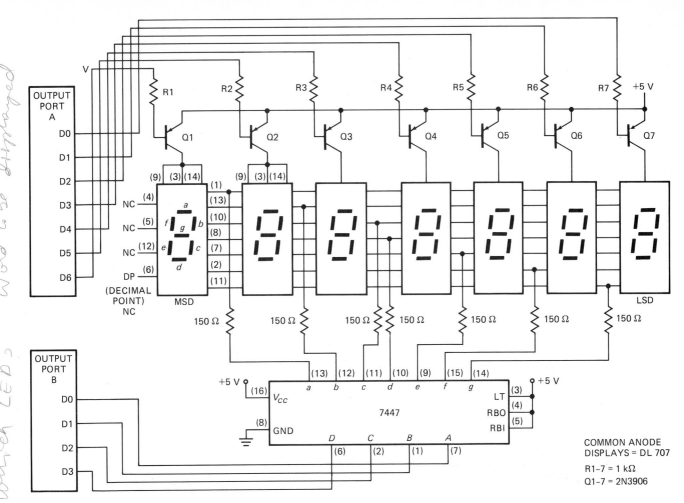

Handwritten margin notes: *Word to be displayed* / *which LED?*

FIGURE 9-26 Circuit for multiplexing seven-segment displays with a microcomputer.

to check the data sheet for the maximum current rating for the displays you are using.

A disadvantage of the software multiplexing approach shown here is that it puts an additional burden on the CPU. Also, if the CPU gets involved in doing some lengthy task that cannot be interrupted to refresh the display, only one digit of the display will be left lit. An alternative approach to interfacing multiplexed displays to a microcomputer is to use a *dedicated display controller,* such as the Intel 8279, which independently keeps displays refreshed and scans a matrix keyboard. In the next section we show you how an 8279 is connected in a circuit, discuss how the 8279 operates, and show you how to initialize an 8279.

Display and Keyboard Interfacing with the 8279

8279 CIRCUIT CONNECTIONS AND OPERATION OVERVIEW

Figure 9-27a, p. 272, shows how an 8279 can be used to connect two multiplexed seven-segment displays

and a hex keypad to an URDA MDS. The displays here are common anode, and each digit has a PNP transistor switch between its anode and the +5-V supply. A logic low is required to turn on one of these switches. Note the 22-μF capacitor between +5 V and ground at the top of the schematic. This is necessary to filter out transients caused by switching the large currents to the LEDs off and on. The segments of each digit are all connected on a common bus. Since these are common-anode displays, a low is needed to turn on a segment.

The drive for the digit-switch transistors comes from a 7445 BCD-to-decimal decoder. This device is also known as a one-of-ten-low decoder. When a 4-bit BCD code is applied to the inputs of this device, the output corresponding to that BCD number will go low. For example, when the 8279 outputs 0100 or BCD 4, the 7445 output labeled 04 will go low. In the mode used for this circuit, the 8279 outputs a continuous BCD count sequence from 0000 to 1111 over and over. This causes a low to be stepped from output to output of the 7445 in ring-counter fashion, turning on each LED digit in turn. Only one output of the 7445 will ever be low at a time, so only one LED digit will be turned on at a time.

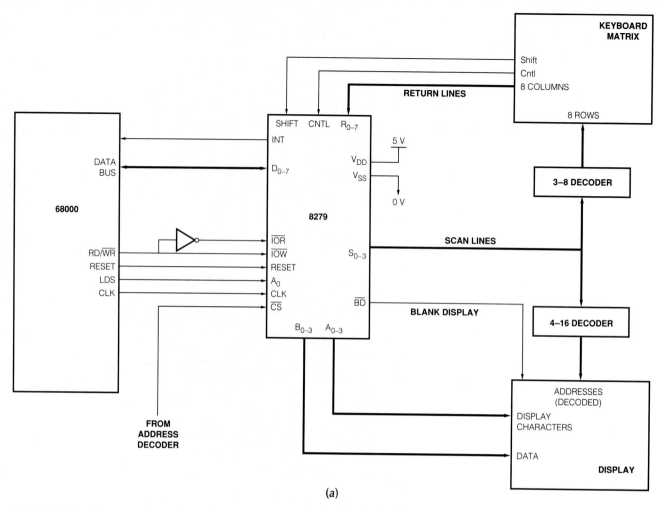

(a)

FIGURE 9-27 (a) Circuit connections for two seven-segment displays and a hex keypad connected to an URDA MDS. (b) 8279 display refresh timing and keyboard scan timing. (*Intel Corporation*)

The segment bus lines for the displays are connected to the A3–A0 and B3–B0 outputs of the 8279 through some high-current buffers in the ULN2003A. Note that the 22-Ω, current-limiting resistors in series with the segment lines are much smaller in value than those we calculated for the static circuit in Figure 9-25. There are two reasons for this. First, there is a drop of an additional few tenths of a volt across the transistor switch on each anode. Second, when multiplexing displays we pass a higher current through the displays so that they appear as bright as they would if not multiplexed. Here's how the 8279 keeps these displays refreshed.

When you want to display some letters or numbers, you write the seven-segment codes for the letters or numbers that you want displayed to a 16-byte RAM inside the 8279. The 8279 then automatically cycles through the process we described previously for sending these codes in sequence to the displays. Figure 9-27b shows the operation in timing diagram form. The 8279 first outputs the BCD number for the first digit to the 7445 on the SL0–SL3 lines (Figure 7-6, sheet 7) to turn on the first one of the digit driver

transistors. The lines S0 and S1 in Figure 9-27 represent the SL0 and SL1 lines. The 8279 then outputs the seven-segment code for the first digit on the A3–A0 and B3–B0 lines. This lights the first digit with the desired pattern. After 490 μs the 8279 outputs a code on the A and B lines that turns off all the segments. For the circuit in Figure 7-6, sheet 7, this blanking code will be all 1s ($FF). The display is blanked here to prevent "ghosting" of information from one digit to the next when the digit strobe is switched to the next digit. While the displays are blanked, the 8279 sends out the BCD code for the next digit to the 7445 to enable the digit-2 driver transistor. It then sends out the seven-segment code for digit 2 on the A and B lines. This then lights the desired pattern on digit 2. After 490 μs the 8279 blanks the display again and goes on to digit 3. The 8279 steps through all the digits and then returns to digit 1 and repeats the cycle. Since each digit requires about 640 μs, the 8279 gets back to digit 1 after about 5.1 ms for an 8-digit display and back to digit 1 after about 10.3 ms for a 16-digit display. The time it takes to get back to a digit again is referred to as the *scan time*.

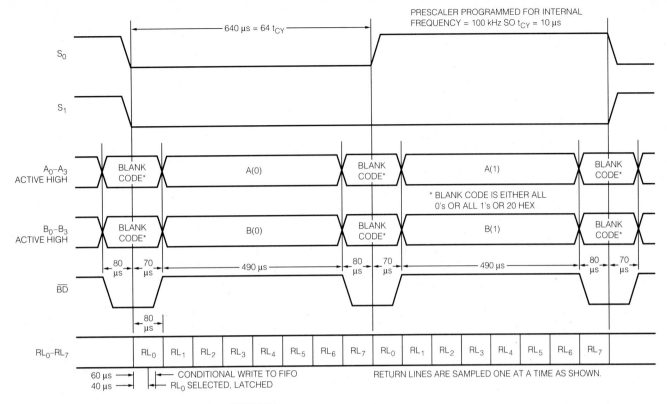

PRESCALER PROGRAMMED FOR INTERNAL
FREQUENCY = 100 kHz SO t_{CY} = 10 μs

* BLANK CODE IS EITHER ALL
0's OR ALL 1's OR 20 HEX

CONDITIONAL WRITE TO FIFO
RL_0 SELECTED, LATCHED
RETURN LINES ARE SAMPLED ONE AT A TIME AS SHOWN.

*NOTE: SHOWN IS ENCODED SCAN LEFT ENTRY
S_2-S_3 ARE NOT SHOWN BUT THEY ARE SIMPLY S_1 DIVIDED BY 2 AND 4

(b)

FIGURE 9-27 (continued)

The point is that once you load the seven-segment codes into the internal RAM in the 8279, it automatically keeps the displays refreshed without your having to do anything else in the program. As we will show later, the 8279 can be connected and initialized to refresh a wide variety of displays.

The 8279 can also automatically perform the three tasks for interfacing to a matrix keyboard. Remember from previous discussions that the three tasks involve putting a low on a row of the keyboard matrix and checking the columns of the matrix. If any keys are pressed in that row, a low will be present on the column that contains the key because pressing a key shorts a row to a column. If no low is found on the columns, the low is stepped to the next row and the columns are checked again. If a low is found on a column, then after a debounce time, the column is checked again. If the keypress was valid, a compact code representing the key is constructed. Take a look at the circuit in Figure 9-27a to see how an 8279 can be connected to do this.

When connected as shown in Figure 9-27a, the 74LS156 functions as a one-of-eight-low decoder. In other words, if you apply 011, the binary code for 3, to its inputs, the 74LS156 will output a low on its 2Y3 output. Remember from the discussion of 8279 display refreshing that the 8279 is outputting a continuous counting sequence from 0000 to 1111 on its SL0–SL3 lines. This count sequence applied to the inputs of the 74LS156 will cause it to step a low along its outputs.

The 74LS156 then puts a low on one row of the keyboard at a time.

The column lines of the keyboard are connected to the return lines, RL0–RL7, of the 8279. As a low is put on each row by the scan-line count and the 74LS156, the 8279 checks these return lines one at a time to see if any of them are low. The bottom line of the timing waveforms in Figure 9-27 shows when the return lines are checked. If the 8279 finds any of the return lines low, indicating a key-press, it waits a debounce time of about 10.3 ms and checks again. If the key-press is still present, the 8279 produces an 8-bit code that represents the key pressed. Figure 9-28, p. 274, shows the format for the code produced. Three bits of this code represent the number of the row in which it found the pressed key, and another 3 bits represent the column of the pressed key. For interfacing to full typewriter keyboards, the shift and control keys are connected to pins 36 and 37, respectively, of the 8279. The upper 2 bits of the code produced represent the status of these two keys.

After the 8279 produces the 8-bit code for the pressed key, it stores the word in an internal 8-byte *FIFO* (first in, first out) RAM. When you start reading codes from the FIFO, the first code you read out will be that for the first key pressed. The FIFO can store the codes for up to eight keys before overflowing.

When the 8279 finds a valid key-press, it does two things to let you know about it. It asserts its interrupt request pin, IRQ, high, and it increments a FIFO count

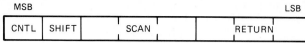

MSB   LSB

| CNTL | SHIFT | SCAN | RETURN |

SCANNED KEYBOARD DATA FORMAT

FIGURE 9-28   Format for data word produced by 8279 keyboard encoding.

in an internal status register. You can connect the IRQ output to an interrupt input and detect when the FIFO has a character for you on an interrupt basis, or you can simply check the count in the status word to determine when the FIFO has a code ready to be read. The point here is that once the 8279 is initialized, you don't need to pay any attention to it until you want to send some new characters to be displayed or until it notifies you that it has a valid key-pressed code for you in its FIFO. Now that you have an overview of how the 8279 functions, we will show you how to initialize an 8279 to do all these wondrous things and more.

INITIALIZING AND COMMUNICATING WITH AN 8279

As we have shown before, the first step in initializing a programmable device is to determine the system base address for the device, the internal addresses, and the system addresses for the internal parts. As an example here, we will use the 8279 in Figure 7-29a. Figure 8-15b shows that the system base address for this device is $BF10. The 8279 has only two internal addresses, which are selected by the logic level on its A0 input, pin 21. If the A0 input is low when the 8279 is selected, then the 8279 is enabled for reading data from it or writing data to it. A0 being high selects the internal control/status registers. For the circuit in Figure 9-27a, the A0 input is connected to system address line A1. Therefore, the data address for this 8279 is $BF10 and the control/status address is $BF11.

After you have figured out the addresses for a device, the next step is to look at the format for the control word(s) you have to send to the device to make it operate in the mode you want. Figure 9-29 shows the format for the 8279 control words as they appear in the Intel data book. After you use up your 5-minute-rule time, we will help you decipher these.

A question that may occur to you when you see all of these control words is, If the 8279 only has one control register address, how am I going to send it all these different control words? The answer to this is that all the control words are sent to the same control register address, $BF11 for this example. The upper 3 bits of each control word tell the 8279 which control word is being sent. A pattern of 010 in the upper 3 bits of a control word, for example, identifies that control word as a "Read FIFO/Sensor RAM" control word. This is similar to the trick used to connect address the 6821, except that more registers are accessed through one 68000 address. (Here eight of them, versus two for the 6821 data and data direction registers, are accessed.)

The first control word you send to initialize the 8279 is the *keyboard/display mode set* word. Keep Figure 9-29 handy as we discuss this and the other control words. The bits labeled DD in the control word specify first of all whether you have 8 digits or 16 digits to refresh. If you have 8 or fewer displays, make sure to initialize for 8 digits so the 8279 doesn't spend half of its time refreshing nonexistent displays. The DD bits in this control word also specify the order in which the characters in the internal 16-byte display RAM will be sent out to the digits. In the left entry mode, the seven-segment code in the first address of the internal display RAM will be sent to the leftmost digit of the display. If you want to display the letters AbCd on the four leftmost digits of an 8-digit display, then you put the seven-segment codes for these letters in the first four locations of the display RAM, as shown in Figure 9-30a, p. 276. Codes put in higher addresses in the display RAM will be displayed on following digits to the right. In the right entry mode, the first code sent to the display RAM is put in the lowest address. This character will be displayed on the rightmost digit of the display. If a second character is written to the display RAM, it will be put in the second location in the RAM, as shown in Figure 9-30b, p. 276. On the display, however, the new character will be displayed on the rightmost digit, and the previous character will be shifted over to the second position from the right. This is the way that the displays of most calculators function as you enter numbers.

Now let's look at the KKK bits of the mode-set control word. The first choice you have to make here if you are using the 8279 with a keyboard is whether you want *encoded scan* or *decoded scan*. You know that for scanning a keyboard or turning on digit drivers, you need a pattern of stepping lows. In encoded mode the 8279 puts out a binary count sequence on its SL0–SL3 scan lines, and an external decoder such as the 7445 is used to produce the stepping lows. If you have only four digits to refresh, you can program the 8279 in decoded mode. In this mode the 8279 directly outputs stepping lows on the four scan lines. The second choice you have to make for this control word is whether you want *two-key lockout* or *N-key rollover*. In the two-key mode one key must be released before another key-press will be detected and processed. In the *N-key rollover mode*, if two keys are pressed at nearly the same time, both key-presses will be detected and debounced, and their codes will be put in the FIFO in the order the keys were pressed.

In addition to being used to scan a keyboard, the 8279 can also be used to scan a matrix of switch sensors such as the metal strips and magnetic sensors you see on store windows and doors. In sensor matrix mode, the 8279 scans all the sensors and stores the condition of up to 64 switches in the FIFO RAM. If the condition of any of the switches changes, an IRQ signal is sent out to the processor. An interrupt-service procedure can then sound an alarm and turn the dogs loose. The return lines of the 8279 can also function as a strobed input port in much the same way as the 8255A we described earlier.

Keyboard/Display Mode Set

Code: MSB `0 0 0 D D K K K` LSB

Where DD is the Display Mode and KKK is the Keyboard Mode.

DD

0 0	8 8-bit character display — Left entry
0 1	16 8-bit character display — Left entry*
1 0	8 8-bit character display — Right entry
1 1	16 8-bit character display — Right entry

For description of right and left entry, see Interface Considerations. Note that when decoded scan is set in keyboard mode, the display is reduced to 4 characters independent of display mode set.

KKK

0 0 0	Encoded Scan Keyboard — 2 Key Lockout*
0 0 1	Decoded Scan Keyboard — 2-Key Lockout
0 1 0	Encoded Scan Keyboard — N-Key Rollover
0 1 1	Decoded Scan Keyboard — N-Key Rollover
1 0 0	Encoded Scan Sensor Matrix
1 0 1	Decoded Scan Sensor Matrix
1 1 0	Strobed Input, Encoded Display Scan
1 1 1	Strobed Input, Decoded Display Scan

Program Clock

Code: `0 0 1 P P P P P`

All timing and multiplexing signals for the 8279 are generated by an internal prescaler. This prescaler divides the external clock (pin 3) by a programmable integer. Bits PPPPP determine the value of this integer which ranges from 2 to 31. Choosing a divisor that yields 100 kHz will give the specified scan and debounce times. For instance, if Pin 3 of the 8279 is being clocked by a 2 MHz signal, PPPPP should be set to 10100 to divide the clock by 20 to yield the proper 100 kHz operating frequency.

Read FIFO/Sensor RAM

Code: `0 1 0 AI X A A A`   X = Don't Care

The CPU sets up the 8279 for a read of the FIFO/Sensor RAM by first writing this command. In the Scan Keyboard Mode, the Auto-Increment flag (AI) and the RAM address bits (AAA) are irrelevant. The 8279 will automatically drive the data bus for each subsequent read ($A_0 = 0$) in the same sequence in which the data first entered the FIFO. All subsequent reads will be from the FIFO until another command is issued.

In the Sensor Matrix Mode, the RAM address bits AAA select one of the 8 rows of the Sensor RAM. If the AI flag is set (AI = 1), each successive read will be from the subsequent row of the sensor RAM.

Read Display RAM

Code: `0 1 1 AI A A A A`

The CPU sets up the 8279 for a read of the Display RAM by first writing this command. The address bits AAAA select one of the 16 rows of the Display RAM. If the AI flag is set (AI = 1), this row address will be incremented after each following read *or write* to the Display RAM. Since the same counter is used for both reading and writing, this command sets the next read *or write* address and the sense of the Auto-Increment mode for both operations.

Write Display RAM

Code: `1 0 0 AI A A A A`

The CPU sets up the 8279 for a write to the Display RAM by first writing this command. After writing the command with $A_0 = 1$, all subsequent writes with $A_0 = 0$ will be to the Display RAM. The addressing and Auto-Increment functions are identical to those for the Read Display RAM. However, this command does not affect the source of subsequent Data Reads; the CPU will read from whichever RAM (Display or FIFO/Sensor) which was last specified. If, indeed, the Display RAM was last specified, the Write Display RAM will, nevertheless, change the next Read location.

Display Write Inhibit/Blanking

Code: A B A B `1 0 1 X IW IW BL BL`

The IW Bits can be used to mask nibble A and nibble B in applications requiring separate 4-bit display ports. By setting the IW flag (IW = 1) for one of the ports, the port becomes marked so that entries to the Display RAM from the CPU do not affect that port. Thus, if each nibble is input to a BCD decoder, the CPU may write a digit to the Display RAM without affecting the other digit being displayed. It is important to note that bit B_0 corresponds to bit D_0 on the CPU bus, and that bit A_3 corresponds to bit D_7.

If the user wishes to blank the display, the BL flags are available for each nibble. The last Clear command issued determines the code to be used as a "blank." This code defaults to all zeros after a reset. Note that both BL flags must be set to blank a display formatted with a single 8-bit port.

Clear

Code: `1 1 0 C_D C_D C_D C_F C_A`

The C_D bits are available in this command to clear all rows of the Display RAM to a selectable blanking code as follows:

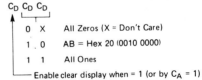

C_D C_D C_D		
0 X		All Zeros (X = Don't Care)
1 0		AB = Hex 20 (0010 0000)
1 1		All Ones

Enable clear display when = 1 (or by C_A = 1)

During the time the Display RAM is being cleared ($\sim$160 μs), it may not be written to. The most significant bit of the FIFO status word is set during this time. When the Display RAM becomes available again, it automatically resets.

If the C_F bit is asserted ($C_F = 1$), the FIFO status is cleared and the interrupt output line is reset. Also, the Sensor RAM pointer is set to row 0.

C_A, the Clear All bit, has the combined effect of C_D and C_F; it uses the C_D clearing code on the Display RAM and also clears FIFO status. Furthermore, it resynchronizes the internal timing chain.

End Interrupt/Error Mode Set

Code: `1 1 1 E X X X`   X = Don't care.

For the sensor matrix modes this command lowers the IRQ line and enables further writing into RAM. (The IRQ line would have been raised upon the detection of a change in a sensor value. This would have also inhibited further writing into the RAM until reset).

For the N-key rollover mode — if the E bit is programmed to "1" the chip will operate in the special Error mode. (For further details, see Interface Considerations Section.)

FIGURE 9-29   8279 command word formats and bit descriptions. (*Intel Corporation*)

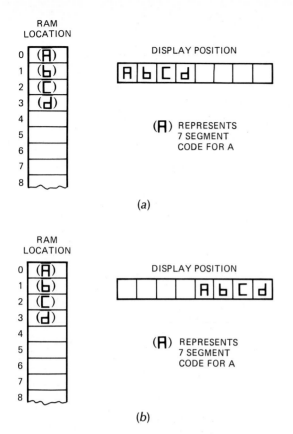

RAM LOCATION

0   (A)
1   (b)
2   (C)
3   (d)
4
5
6
7
8

DISPLAY POSITION

| A | b | C | d | | | | |

(A) REPRESENTS
7 SEGMENT
CODE FOR A

(a)

RAM LOCATION

0   (A)
1   (b)
2   (C)
3   (d)
4
5
6
7
8

DISPLAY POSITION

| | | | | A | b | C | d |

(A) REPRESENTS
7 SEGMENT
CODE FOR A

(b)

FIGURE 9-30   8279 RAM and display location relationships. (a) Left entry. (b) Right entry.

The URDA MDS in the following driver routine initializes the 8279 for eight-character display, left entry, encoded scan, and two-key lockout. See if you can determine the mode-set control word for these conditions. You should get 0000 0000.

The next control word you have to send the 8279 is the *program clock word*. The 8279 requires an internal clock frequency of 100 kHz. A programmable divider in the 8279 allows you to apply some available frequency such as the 3.579 MHz CLK signal to its clock input and divide this frequency down to the needed 100 kHz. The lower 5 bits of the program clock control word simply represent the binary number by which you want to divide the applied clock. For example, if you want to divide the input clock frequency by 24, you send a control word with 001 in the upper 3 bits and 11000 in the lower 5 bits.

The final control word needed for basic initialization is the *clear* word. You need to send this word to tell the 8279 what code to send to the segments to turn them off while the 8279 is switching from one digit to the next. (Refer to Figure 9-27 and its discussion.) In addition to telling the 8279 what blanking character to use during refresh, this control word can be used to clear the display RAM and/or the FIFO at any time. For now we are concerned only with the first function. The lower two bits, labeled C_D in Figure 9-29, specify the desired blanking code. The required code will depend on the hardware connections in a particular system.

For the URDA MDS, a high from the 8279 turns on a segment, so the required blanking code is all 0s. Therefore you can put 0s in the two C_D bits. The resultant control word is 1100 0000.

The three control words described so far take care of the basic initialization. However, before you can send codes to the internal display RAM, you have to send the 8279 a *write display RAM* control word. This word tells the 8279 that data later sent to the data address should be put in the display RAM, and it tells the 8279 where in the display RAM to put the data byte sent in. Refer to Figure 9-29 for the format of this word. The 8279 has an internal 4-bit pointer to the display RAM. You use the lower 4 bits of this control word to initialize the pointer to the location where you want to write a data byte in the RAM. If you want to write a data byte to the first location in the display RAM, you put 0000 in these bits. If you put a 1 in the autoincrement bit, labeled AI in the figure, the internal pointer will be automatically incremented to point to the next RAM location after each data byte is written. To start loading characters in the first location in the RAM and selecting autoincrement, the control word is 1001 0000.

Figure 9-31 shows the sequence of instructions to send the control words we have developed here to an 8279 connected to an URDA MDS board. Also shown are some instructions to send a seven-segment code to the first location in the display RAM. Note that the control words are all sent to the control address, $BF11, and the character going to the display RAM is sent to the data address, $BF10. Also note that the D0 bit of the byte sent to the display RAM corresponds to segment output B0, and D7 of the byte sent to the display corresponds to segment output A3. This is important to know when you are making up a table of seven-segment codes to send to the 8279.

You now know how to initialize an 8279 and send characters to its display RAM. Two additional points we need to show you are how to read key-pressed codes from the FIFO and how to read the status word. In order to read a code from the FIFO, you first have to send a *read FIFO/sensor RAM* control word to the 8279 control address. Figure 9-29 shows the format for this word. For a read of the FIFO RAM, the lower 5 bits of the control word are don't cares, so you can just make them 0s. You send the resultant control word, 0100 0000, to the control register address and then do a read from the data address. The bottom section of Figure 9-31 shows this.

Now, suppose that the processor receives an interrupt signal from the 8279 indicating that one or more valid key-presses have occurred. The question then occurs, How do we know how many codes to read from the FIFO? The answer to this question is that we read the status register from the control register address before we read the FIFO. Figure 9-32 shows the format for this status word. The lowest 3 bits of the status word indicate the number of valid characters in the FIFO. You can load this number into a memory location and count it down as you read in characters. Incidentally, if more than eight characters have been entered in the FIFO, only the last eight will be kept. The

```
;       INITIALIZATION

        MOVEA.L #$BF10,A1        ; Point at 8279 control register
        MOVE.B  #$00,(A1)        ; Mode set word for left entry,
                                 ;   encoded scan, 2-key lockout
                                 ;   sent to 8279 control port
        MOVE.B  #$38,(A1)        ; Clock word for divide by 24
        MOVE.B  #$A0,(A1)        ; Clear display char is all zeros

;       ...
;
;       SEND SEVEN SEGMENT CODE TO DISPLAY RAM

        MOVEA.L #$BF10,A1        ; Point at 8279 control register
        MOVE.B  #$90,(A1)        ; Write display RAM, first location
                                 ;   auto increment to 8279
        MOVEA.L #$BF09,A1        ; Point at 8279 control register
        MOVE.B  #$6F,(A1)        ; Send seven segment display code for 9
        MOVE.B  #$5B,(A1)        ; Send seven segment display code for 2

;       ...
;
;       READ KEYBOARD CODE FROM FIFO

        MOVEA.L #$BF10,A1        ; Point at 8279 control register
        MOVE.B  #$40,(A1)        ; Control word for read FIFO RAM
        MOVEA.L #$BF09,A1        ; Point at 8279 data register
        MOVE.B  (A1),D0          ; Read FIFO RAM

        END
```

FIGURE 9-31   68000 instructions to initialize an URDA MDS connected to an 8279, write to display RAM, and read FIFO RAM.

error-overrun bit, labeled 0 in the status word, will be set to tell you characters have been lost.

Characters can be read from the 8279 on a polled basis as well as on an interrupt basis. To do this you simply read and test the status word over and over again until bit 0 of the status word becomes a 1. The URDA MDS uses this method to tell when the FIFO holds a key-pressed code.

URDA MDS Display Driver Routine

Figure 9-33, p. 278, shows a 68000 assembly language routine to display the contents of register D0 on the new LED display connected to the MDS using an 8279. This routine assumes the 8279 has already been initialized, as shown in the first part of Figure 9-31. If D0 is zero when this routine is called, the contents of D1 will be displayed on the data field LEDs. If D0 is not zero, then the contents of D1 will be displayed on the address field LEDs. There are two main points for you to see in this routine. The first is the sending of the write display RAM control word to the 8279 so we can write to the desired locations in the display RAM. Note that, for the data field, we write a control word of $90, which tells the 8279 to put the next data word sent into

the first location in the display RAM. Since the 8279 is initialized for left entry, the first location should correspond to the leftmost display digit. However, if you look at Figure 9-27a you will see that digit 1 (leftmost as far as the 8279 is concerned) is actually the rightmost on the board. This means that, for the URDA MDS, the position of a seven-segment code in the display RAM corresponds to its position in the display starting from the right! All you have to do is send the seven-segment code for a number you want to display in a particular digit position to the corresponding location in the display RAM.

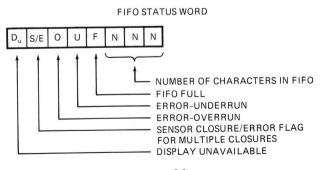

FIGURE 9-32   8279 status word format.

```
; 68000 SUBROUTINE TO DISPLAY DATA ON LEDs CONNECTED TO URDA MDS USING 8279
; ABSTRACT          : This subroutine displays characters on the display
;                   : connected to the URDA MDS via an 8279.  The data is sent
;                   : to this subroutine in the following manner:
;                   :         D0 = 00 implies use data field
;                   :         D0 = 01 implies use address field
;
; PORTS USED    : None
; SUBROUTINES   : None
; REGISTERS     : Uses A2 - 8279 control/data register pointer
;               :       A3 - Pointer to seven-seg table
;               :       D2 - Seven-seg table index
;-------------------------------
; defines for I/O port addresses
CONTROL_ADDR    EQU     $BF10
DATA_ADDR       EQU     $BF09

        ORG     $4200               ; start the data at $4200
STACK_HERE:  DS.W   200             ; set stack length of 200 words
STACK_TOP:   DS.W   0               ; the stack top is the high address
SEVEN_SEG:   DC.B   $77,$7B,$7D,$7E,$B7,$BB,$BD,$BE
;                    0    1    2    3    4    5    6    7
             DC.B   $D7,$DB,$DD,$DE,$E7,$EB,$ED,$EE
;                    8    9    A    b    C    d    E    F
;-------------------------------
        ORG     $4100
        MOVEM.L D2/A2-A3,-(A7)          ; save registers
        MOVEA.L CONTROL_ADDR,A2 ; point at 8279 control register
        CMPI.B  #$00,D0                 ; see if data field requested
        BEQ     DATFLD                  ; yes, go load control word for data
        MOVE.B  #$94,D0                 ; no. load address field control word
        BRA     SEND                    ; go send control word
DATFLD: MOVE.B  #$90,D0                 ; control word for data field
SEND:   MOVE.B  D0,(A2)                 ; send to 8279
        MOVEA.L SEVEN_SEG,A3            ; point at seven_seg table
        MOVEA.L DATA_ADDR,A2            ; point at data register
        MOVE.B  D0,D2                   ; get copy of low nibble to display
        ANDI.B  #$0F,D2                 ; mask upper nibble
        MOVE.B  0(A3,D2),D2             ; translate lower nibble to 7-seg code
        MOVE.B  D2,(A2)                 ; send to 8279 display RAM
        MOVE.B  D0,D2                   ; get another copy of low nibble
        ROL.B   #4,D2                   ; rotate high nibble into low position
        ANDI.B  #$0F,D2                 ; mask nibble
        MOVE.B  0(A3,D2),D2             ; translate upper nibble to 7-seg code
        MOVE.B  D2,(A2)                 ; send to 8279 display RAM
        ROR.W   #8,D0                   ; rotate bytes to get at upper 2 digits
        MOVE.B  D0,D2                   ; get copy of upper byte
        ANDI.B  #$0F,D2                 ; mask upper nibble
        MOVE.B  0(A3,D2),D2             ; translate lower nibble to 7-seg code
        MOVE.B  D2,(A2)                 ; send to 8279 display RAM
        MOVE.B  D0,D2                   ; get another copy of upper byte
        ROL.B   #4,D2                   ; rotate high nibble into low position
        ANDI.B  #$0F,D2                 ; mask nibble
        MOVE.B  0(A3,D2),D2             ; translate upper nibble to 7-seg code
        MOVE.B  D2,(A2)                 ; send to 8279 display RAM
        MOVEM.L (A7)+,D2/A2-A3          ; restore registers
        RTS                             ; return to caller

        END
```

FIGURE 9-33   Subroutine to display contents of D0 register on URDA MDS
LED displays.

The second important part of the display routine at which to take a close look is the instructions that convert the four hex nibbles in the D1 register to the corresponding seven-segment codes for sending to the display RAM. To do this conversion, we first shuffle and mask to get each nibble into a byte by itself. We then use a lookup table and the move indexed indirect instruction to do the actual conversion. Note that when making up seven-segment codes for the URDA MDS board example, a high turns on a segment, bit D0 of a display RAM byte represents the "a" segment, bit D6 represents the "g" segment, and bit D7 represents the decimal point. Work your way through this section as a review of using this move indexed indirect to perform a simple hash table lookup.

INTERFACING TO 18-SEGMENT AND DOT-MATRIX LED DISPLAYS

In the preceding examples we used an 8279 to refresh some seven-segment displays. The seven-segment codes for each digit were stored in successive locations in the display RAM. To display ASCII codes on 18-segment LED displays, you can store the ASCII codes for each digit in the display RAM. (Remember that the A lines are driven from the upper nibble of the display RAM and the B lines are driven by the lower nibble). An external ROM is used to convert the ASCII codes to the required 18-segment codes and send them to the segment drivers. Strobes for each digit driver are produced, just as they are for the seven-segment displays in Figure 7-6. The refreshing of each digit then proceeds just as it does for the seven-segment displays.

Refreshing 5 × 7 dot-matrix LED displays is a little more complex, because instead of lighting an entire digit, you have to refresh one row or one column at a time in each digit. Think of how you might do this for one 5 × 7 matrix that has its row drivers connected to one port and its column drivers connected to another port. To display a letter on this matrix, you send out the code for the first column to the row drivers and send a code to the column drivers to turn on that column. After a millisecond or so, you turn off the first column, send out the code for the second column, and light the second column. You repeat the process until all the columns have been refreshed and then cycle back to column 1 again. You could use additional ports to drive additional digits, but the number of ports required soon gets too large. To reduce the number of ports required, inexpensive external latches can be used to hold the row codes for each digit. You then write the row codes for the first columns of all the digits to these latches. The columns of all the digits are connected in parallel, so when you output a code to turn on the first column, the first column of each digit will be lit with the code stored in its row latch. The process is repeated for each column until all columns are refreshed and then started over again.

To further simplify interfacing multidigit dot-matrix LED displays to a microcomputer, Beckman Instruments, Hewlett-Packard, and several other companies make large integrated display/driver devices that re-

quire you to send only a series of ASCII codes for the characters you want displayed and one or two strobe signals for each character sent.

Liquid-Crystal Display Operation and Interfacing

LCD OPERATION

Liquid-crystal displays are created by sandwiching a thin (10- to 12-μm) layer of a liquid-crystal fluid between two glass plates. A transparent, electrically conductive film or backplane is put on the rear glass sheet. Transparent sections of conductive film in the shape of the desired characters are coated on the front glass plate. When a voltage is applied between a segment and the backplane, an electric field is created in the region under the segment. This electric field changes the transmission of light through the region under the segment film.

There are two commonly available types of LCD: *dynamic scattering* and *field effect*. The dynamic scattering type scrambles the molecules where the field is present. This produces light characters on a dark background, similar to those you might see in etched glass. Field-effect types use polarization to absorb light where the electric field is present. This produces dark characters on a silver-gray background.

To turn on the segment, most LCDs require a voltage of 2 or 3 V between the backplane and a segment. You can't, however, just connect the backplane to ground and drive the segments with the outputs of a TTL decoder, as we did the static LED display in Figure 9-25! The reason for this is that LCDs rapidly and irreversibly deteriorate if a steady dc voltage of more than about 50 mV is applied between a segment and the backplane. To prevent a dc buildup on the segments, the segment-drive signals for LCDs must be square waves with a frequency of 30 to 150 Hz. Even if you pulse the TTL decoder, it still will not work because the output low voltage of TTL devices is greater than 50 mV. CMOS gates are often used to drive LCDs.

Figure 9-34*a*, p. 280, shows how two CMOS gate outputs can be connected to drive an LCD segment and backplane. Figure 9-34*b*, p. 280, shows typical drive waveforms for the backplane and for the ON and the OFF segments. The OFF (in this case unused) segment receives the same drive signal as the backplane. There is never any voltage between them, so no electric field is produced. The waveform for the ON segment is 180° out of phase with the backplane signal, so the voltage between this segment and the backplane will always be positive. The logic for this is quite simple, because you have to produce only two signals, a square wave and its complement. To the driving gates the segment-backplane sandwich appears as a somewhat leaky capacitor. The CMOS gates can easily supply the current required to charge and discharge this small capacitance.

Older and/or inexpensive LCD displays turn on and off too slowly to be multiplexed in the way we multiplex LED displays. At 0°C some LCDs may require as much

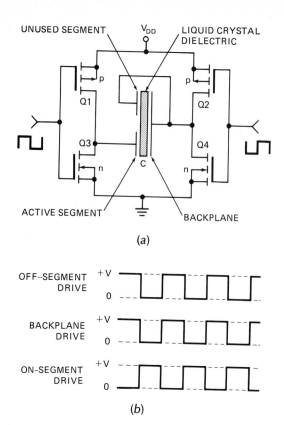

FIGURE 9-34   LCD drive circuit and drive waveforms.
(a) CMOS drive circuits. (b) Segment- and backplane-
drive waveforms.

as 0.5 s to turn on or off. To interface to these types we use a nonmultiplexed driver device. Newer LCDs can turn on and off faster. To reduce the number of connecting wires when interfacing to these, we use a *triplex* technique. The following sections show you brief examples of each of these.

Interfacing a Microcomputer to Nonmultiplexed LCD Displays

Figure 9-35 shows how an Intersil ICM7211M can be connected to drive a 4-digit, nonmultiplexed, seven-segment LCD display such as you might buy from your local electronics surplus store. The 7211M inputs can be connected to port pins or directly to microcomputer buses, as shown. For our example here we have connected the $\overline{CS}$ inputs to the Y2 output of the 74LS138 port decoder that we showed you how to add to an URDA MDS board in Figure 8-14. According to the truth table in Figure 8-15, the device will then be addressable as ports with a base address of $BF10. URDA MDS system address line A2 is connected to the digit-select input (DS2) and system address line, A1, is connected to the DS1 input. This gives digit 4 a system address of $BF10. Digit 3 will be addressed at $BF12, digit 2 at $BF14, and digit 1 at $BF16. The data inputs are connected to the lower four lines of the URDA MDS data bus. The oscillator input is left open.

To display a character on one of the digits, you simply put the 4-bit hex code for that digit in the lower 4 bits of the D0 register and output it to the address of that digit. The ICM7211M converts the 4-bit hex code to the required seven-segment code. The rising edge of the $\overline{CS}$ input signal causes the seven-segment code to be latched in the output latches for the addressed digit. The internal oscillator automatically generates the segment and backplane drive waveforms shown in Figure 9-34b.

INTERFACING TO TRIPLEXED LCD DISPLAYS

With many microcomputer-based instruments, we want to display letters as well as numbers. To do this we usually use 18-segment digits such as the one shown in Figure 9-24a. For 18-segment LED digits, we simply bus all the segment inputs and multiplex the displays as described previously. Current LCD digits, however, cannot be multiplexed in the same way because of their slow switching response time. To reduce the connections required for a set of LCD digits, a compromise approach called *triplexing* has been devised. For triplexing, each digit is built as a matrix of six rows and three columns. Each digit has a 6-bit latch to hold the 6-bit row code for the segments in a column. The row codes are sent to all of the latches and the columns of each digit turned on. After a period of time, the row codes for the second column are sent out to the latches. The first column is turned off and the second column is turned on. After a period of time the row codes for the third columns are sent out to digits and the third columns are turned on. At any given time one of the three columns in each display is activated, which is the source of the term triplexing. Since only three columns ever need to be refreshed, no matter how many digits are connected, the switching rates are much lower than they are for the LED multiplexing method. The Intersil ICM7233 is an example of a device that contains all the circuitry needed to drive four triplexed, 18-segment LCD digits. It can be connected directly to a microcomputer bus, as we showed for the ICM7211M in Figure 9-35. To display a series of characters, all you have to do is output a 6-bit ASCII code for each character to the appropriate digit address in the device. A demonstration kit containing two 7233s, eight 18-segment LCD displays, and a PC board is available from Intersil if you want to add this type of display to something you are building.

INTERFACING MICROCOMPUTER PORTS TO HIGH-POWER DEVICES

As shown for the 6821 in Figure 9-36, the output pins on programmable port devices can typically source only a few tenths of a milliamp from the +5-V supply and sink only 1 or 2 mA to ground. If you want to control some high-power devices, such as lights, heaters, solenoids, and motors, with your microcomputer, you need to use interface devices between the port pins

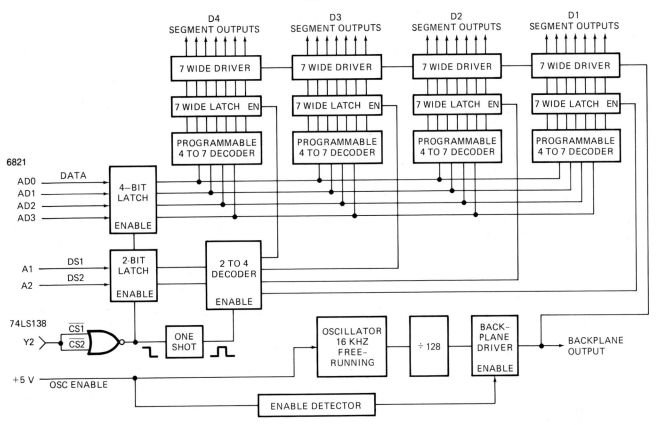

FIGURE 9-35   Circuit for interfacing four LCD digits to an URDA MDS bus
using Intersil ICM7211M.

INTEGRATED CIRCUIT BUFFERS

and the high-power device. This section shows you a few of the commonly used devices and techniques.

One approach to buffering the outputs of port devices is with TTL buffers, such as the 7406 hex inverting and 7407 hex noninverting. In Figure 9-14, for example, we show using 74LS07 buffers on the lines from ports to a printer. In an actual circuit the 6821 outputs to the computer-controlled lathe in Figure 9-6 should also have buffers of this type. The 74LS06 and 74LS07 have open-collector outputs, so you have to connect a pull-up resistor from each output to +5 V. Each of the buffers in a 74LS06 or 74LS07 can sink as much as 40 mA to ground. You could then drive an LED with each

D.C. CHARACTERISTICS
$T_A = 0°C$ to $70°C$, $V_{CC} = +5$ V ±5%; GND = 0V

SYMBOL	PARAMETER	MIN.	MAX.	UNIT	TEST CONDITIONS
V_{IL}	INPUT LOW VOLTAGE	−0.5	0.8	V	
V_{IH}	INPUT HIGH VOLTAGE	2.0	V_{CC}	V	
V_{OL} (DB)	OUTPUT LOW VOLTAGE (DATA BUS)		0.45	V	$I_{OL} = 2.5$ mA
V_{OL} (PER)	OUTPUT LOW VOLTAGE (PERIPHERAL PORT)		0.45	V	$I_{OL} = 1.7$ mA
V_{OH} (DB)	OUTPUT HIGH VOLTAGE (DATA BUS)	2.4		V	$I_{OH} = -400$ μA
V_{OH} (PER)	OUTPUT HIGH VOLTAGE (PERIPHERAL PORT)	2.4		V	$I_{OH} = -200$ μA
I_{DAR}[1]	DARLINGTON DRIVE CURRENT	−1.0	−4.0	mA	$R_{EXT} = 750$ Ω; $V_{EXT} = 1.5$ V
I_{CC}	POWER SUPPLY CURRENT		120	mA	
I_{IL}	INPUT LOAD CURRENT		±10	μA	$V_{IN} = V_{CC}$ TO 0V
I_{OFL}	OUTPUT FLOAT LEAKAGE		±10	μA	$V_{OUT} = V_{CC}$ TO 0V

NOTE 1: AVAILABLE ON ANY 8 PINS FROM PORT B AND C.

FIGURE 9-36   6821 dc operating characteristics.

output by simply connecting the LED and a current-limiting resistor in series between the buffer output and +5 V.

Buffers of this type have the advantage that they come six to a package, and they are easy to apply. For cases where you need a buffer on only one or two port pins, you may use discrete transistors.

TRANSISTOR BUFFERS

Figure 9-37 shows some transistor circuits you can connect to microprocessor port lines to drive LEDs or small dc lamps. We will show you how to determine quickly the part values to put in these circuits for your particular application. First, determine how much current you need to flow through the LED, lamp, or other device. For our example here, suppose that we want 20 mA to flow through an LED. Next determine whether you want a logic high on the output port pin to turn on the device or whether you want a logic low to turn on the device. If you want a logic high to turn on the LED, then use an NPN circuit. Now look through your transistor collection to find an NPN transistor that can carry the required current, has a collector-to-emitter breakdown voltage (VBCEO) greater than the applied supply voltage, and can dissipate the power generated by the current flowing through it. We usually keep some inexpensive 2N3904 NPNs and some 2N3906 PNPs on hand for low-current switch applications such as this. Some alternatives are the 2N2222 NPN and the 2N2907 PNP. When you decide what transistor you are going to use, look up its current gain, h_{FE}, on a data sheet. If you don't have a data sheet, assume a value of 50 for the current gain of a small-signal transistor

such as these. Remember, current gain—or beta, as it is commonly called—is the ratio of collector current to the base current needed to produce that current. To produce a collector current of 20 mA in a transistor with a beta of 50 requires a base current of 20 mA/50, or 0.4 mA. To drive this buffer transistor, then, the output port pin has to supply only 0.4 mA.

A look at the V_{OH}(PER) specification of the 6821 in Figure 9-36 shows that a 6821 peripheral port pin can source only 200 μA (0.2 mA) of current and still maintain a legal TTL-compatible output voltage of 2.4 V. When you see this specification, you may at first think the port output will not be able to drive the transistor. However, the outputs can source more than 0.2 mA, but if they source more than 0.2 mA, the output high voltage will drop below 2.4 V. You don't care about the output high voltage dropping below 2.4 V except in the unlikely case that you are trying to drive a logic gate input off the same port pin as the transistor. The IDAR specification in Figure 9-36 indicates that port B and port C pins can source at least 1.0 mA, but when doing so the output voltage may be as low as 1.5 V. Let's assume an output voltage of 2.0 V for calculating the value of our current-limiting resistor, R_b. The value of this resistor is not very critical as long as it lets through enough base current to drive the transistor. The base of the NPN transistor will be at about 0.7 V when the transistor is conducting, and the output port pin will be at least 2.0 V. Dividing the 1.3 V across R_b by the desired current of 0.4 mA gives an R_b value of 3.25 kΩ. A 2.7-kΩ or 3.3-kΩ resistor will work fine here.

For the PNP circuit in Figure 9-37b, the output port pin can easily supply the needed drive current. The V_{OL}(PER) specification in Figure 9-36 shows that an output pin can sink at least 1.7 mA and still have an output low voltage no greater than 0.45 V. R_b in Figure 9-37b has about 4 V across it. Dividing this voltage by the required 0.4 mA gives an R_b value of 10 kΩ.

When you need to switch currents larger than about 50 mA on and off with an output port line, a single transistor does not have enough current gain to do this dependably. One solution to this problem is to connect two transistors in a Darlington configuration. Figure 9-38 shows how we might do this to drive a small solenoid-controlled valve that controls the flow of a chemical into our printed-circuit-board-making machine or a small solenoid in the print heads of a dot-matrix printer. For the case of the printer solenoid, when a current is passed through the coil of the solenoid, a print wire is forced out. The print wire hits the ribbon against the paper and produces a dot on the paper.

The dotted lines around the two transistors in Figure 9-38 indicate that both devices are contained in the same package. Here's how this configuration works. The output port pin supplies base current to transistor Q1. This base current produces a collector current beta times as large in Q1. The collector current of Q1 becomes the base current of Q2 and is amplified by the current gain of Q2. The result of all this is that the device acts as a single transistor with a current gain of

(a)

(b)

FIGURE 9-37 Transistor buffer circuits for driving LED from 6821 port pin. (a) NPN. (b) PNP.

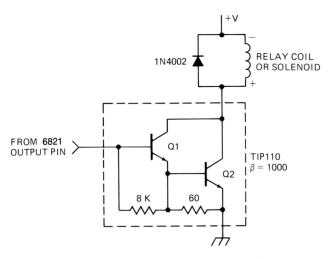

FIGURE 9-38 Darlington transistor used to drive relay coil or solenoid.

beta Q1 × beta Q2 and a base-emitter voltage of about 1.4 V. The internal resistors help turn off the transistors. The TIP110 device we show here has a minimum beta of 1000 at 1 A. If we assume that we need 400 mA to drive the solenoid, then the worst-case current that the output port pin must supply is about 400 mA/1000, or 0.4 mA, which it can easily do. If the drive current required for the Darlington is too high for the port output, you can add a resistor from the transistor base to +5 V to supply the added current. The output can easily sink the added current when the output is in the low state. Also, another transistor could be added as a buffer between the output pin and the Darlington input. Note that since the V_{BE} of the Darlington is about 2 V, no R_b is needed here. How let's check out the power dissipation.

According to the data sheet for the TIP110, it comes in a TO-220 package, which can dissipate up to 2 W at an ambient temperature of 25°C with no heat sink. With 400 mA flowing through the device, it will have a collector-emitter saturation voltage of about 2 V. Multiplying the current of 400 mA times the voltage drop of 2 V gives us a power dissipation of 0.8 W for our circuit here. This is well within the limits for the device. A rule of thumb that we like to follow is: If the calculated power dissipation for a device such as this is more than half of its 25°C no-heat-sink rating, mount the device on the chassis or a heat sink to make sure it will work on a hot day. If mounted on the appropriate heat sink, the device will dissipate 50 W at 25°C.

One more important point to mention about the circuit in Figure 9-38 is the reverse-biased diode connected across the solenoid coil. You must remember to put in this diode whenever you drive an inductive load such as a solenoid, relay, or motor. Here's why. The basic principle of an inductor is that it fights against a change in the current through it. When you apply a voltage to the coil by turning on the transistor, it takes a while for the current to start flowing. This does not cause any major problems. However, when you turn off the transistor, the collapsing magnetic field in the

inductor keeps the current flowing for a while. This current cannot flow through the transistor because it is off. Instead, this current develops a voltage across the inductor with the polarity shown by the + and − signs on the coil in Figure 9-38. This induced voltage, sometimes called inductive "kick," will usually be large enough to break down the transistor if you forget to put in the diode. When the coil is conducting, the diode is reverse-biased, so it doesn't conduct. However, as soon as the induced voltage reaches 0.7 V, this diode turns on and supplies a return path for the induced current. The voltage across the inductor is clamped at 0.7 V, which saves the transistor.

Figure 9-39 shows how a power MOSFET transistor can be used to drive a solenoid, relay, or motor winding. Power MOSFETs are several times more expensive than bipolar Darlingtons, but they have the advantage that they require only a voltage to drive them. The Motorola IRF130 shown here, for example, requires a maximum gate voltage of only 4 V for a drain current of 8 A. Note that a diode is required across the coil here also.

INTERFACING TO AC POWER DEVICES

To turn 110-V, 220-V, or 440-V ac devices on and off under microprocessor control, we usually use *mechanical or solid-state relays*. The control circuitry for both types of relay is electrically isolated from the actual switch. This is very important because if the 110-V ac line gets shorted to the V_{CC} line of a microcomputer, it usually bakes most of the microcomputer's ICs. Figure 9-40a, p. 284, shows a picture of a mechanical relay. This relay has both normally open and normally closed contacts. When a current is passed through the coil of the relay, the switch arm is pulled down, opening the top contacts and closing the bottom set of contacts. The contacts are rated for a maximum current of 25 A, so this relay could be used to turn on a 1- or 2-horsepower motor or a large electric heater in one of the machines in our electronics factory. When driven from a 12-V supply, the coil requires a current of about 170 mA. The circuit shown in Figure 9-38 could easily drive this relay coil from a microcomputer port line.

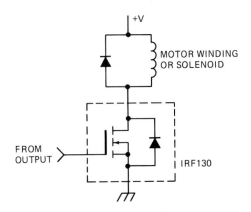

FIGURE 9-39 Power MOSFET circuit for driving solenoid or motor winding.

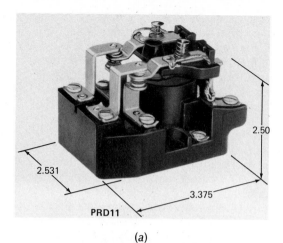

2.50

2.531

3.375

PRD11

(a)

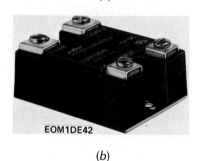

EOM1DE42

(b)

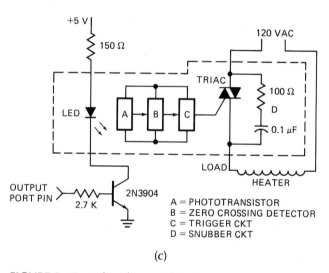

+5 V

150 Ω

120 VAC

TRIAC

LED   A → B → C

100 Ω

D

0.1 μF

LOAD

HEATER

OUTPUT
PORT PIN   2.7 K   2N3904

A = PHOTOTRANSISTOR
B = ZERO CROSSING DETECTOR
C = TRIGGER CKT
D = SNUBBER CKT

(c)

FIGURE 9-40   Relays for switching large currents.
(a) Mechanical. (b) Solid-state. (*Potter and Brumfield*)
(c) Block diagram of the circuitry in the device and its
connection.

Mechanical relays, sometimes called contactors, are available to switch currents from milliamps up to several thousand amps. However, mechanical relays have several serious problems. When the contacts are opened and closed, arcing takes place between the contacts. This causes the contacts to oxidize and pit, just as the points in your car do with age. As the contacts become oxidized, they make a higher-resistance contact and may get hot enough to melt. Another

disadvantage of mechanical relays is that they can switch on or off at any point in the ac cycle. Switching on or off at a high-voltage point in the ac cycle can cause a large amount of electrical noise called *electromagnetic interference*, or EMI. The solid-state relays discussed next avoid these problems to a large extent.

Figure 9-40b shows a picture of a solid-state relay that is rated for 25 A at 25°C if mounted on a suitable heat sink. Figure 9-40c shows a block diagram of the circuitry in the device and its connection from an output port to an ac load.

The input circuit is essentially an LED and a current-limiting resistor. To turn the device on, you simply turn on the buffer transistor, which pulls the required 11 mA through the internal LED. The light from the LED is focused on a phototransistor connected to the actual output-control circuitry. Since the only connection between the input and the output is a beam of light, there are several thousand volts of isolation between the input circuitry and the output circuitry.

The actual switch in a solid-state relay is a triac, which conducts in either direction when triggered. The zero-voltage detector makes sure that the triac is triggered only when the ac line voltage is very close to one of its zero-voltage crossing points. If you output a signal to turn on the relay, the relay will not actually turn on until the next time the ac line voltage crosses zero. Triacs automatically turn off when the current through them drops below a small value, called the *holding current*. If the control signal is on, the trigger circuitry will automatically retrigger the triac for each half-cycle. If you send a signal to turn off the relay, it will actually turn off the next time the ac current drops to zero. Zero-point switching eliminates most of the EMI that would be caused by switching the triac on at high-voltage points in the ac cycle.

Solid-state relays then have the advantages that they produce less EMI, have no mechanical contacts to arc, and are easily driven from microcomputer ports. Their disadvantages are that they are more expensive than an equivalent mechanical relay and there is a voltage drop of a couple of volts across the triac when it is on. Another potential problem with solid-state relays occurs when driving a large inductive load such as a motor. Remember from basic ac theory that voltage waveform leads the current waveform in an ac circuit with inductance. A triac turns off when the current through it drops to near zero. In an inductive circuit the voltage waveform may be at several tens of volts when the current is at zero. When the triac is conducting, it has perhaps 2 V across it. When the triac turns off, the voltage across the triac quickly jumps to several tens of volts. This large dV/dT may possibly turn on the triac at a point at which you don't want it turned on. To keep the voltage across the triac from changing too rapidly, an *RC snubber* circuit is connected across the triac, as shown in Figure 9-40c. A system in the next chapter uses a solid-state relay to control an electrical heater.

INTERFACING A MICROCOMPUTER TO A STEPPER MOTOR

A unique type of motor useful for moving things in small increments is the stepper motor. If you have a dot-matrix printer such as the Epson FX-80, look inside and you will probably see one small stepper motor that is used to advance the paper to the next line position and another small stepper motor that is used to move the print head to the next character position. You might look also for a small device containing an LED and a phototransistor, which detects when the print head is in the "home" position. Stepper motors are also used to position the read/write head over the desired track of a hard or floppy disk and to position the pen on X-Y plotters.

Instead of rotating smoothly around and around as most motors do, stepper motors rotate, or "step," from one fixed position to the next. Common step sizes range from 0.9° to 30°. A stepper motor is stepped from one position to the next by changing the currents through the fields in the motor. The two common field connections are referred to as *two-phase* and *four-phase* connections. We discuss *four-phase steppers* here because their drive circuitry is much simpler.

Figure 9-41 shows a circuit you can use to interface a small four-phase stepper such as the Superior Electric MO61-FD302, IMC Magnetics Corp. Tormax 200, or a similar, nominal 5-V unit to four microcomputer port lines. If you build up this circuit, bolt some small heat sinks on the MJE2955 transistors and mount the 10-W resistors where you aren't likely to touch them.

Since the 7406 buffers are inverting, a high on an output-port pin turns on current to a winding. Figure 9-41b shows the switching sequence to step a motor such as this clockwise, as you face the motor shaft, or counterclockwise. Here's how this works. Suppose that SW1 and SW2 are turned on. Turning off SW2 and turning on SW4 will cause the motor to rotate one step of 1.8° clockwise. Changing to SW4 and SW3 on will cause the motor to rotate another 1.8° clockwise.

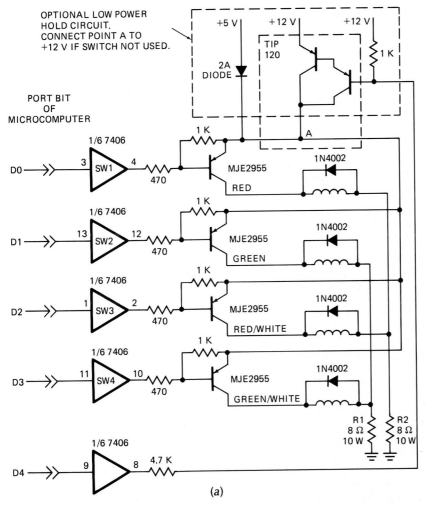

STEP	SWITCH				
	SW4	SW3	SW2	SW1	CW
1	0	0	1	1	
2	1	0	0	1	
3	1	1	0	0	
4	0	1	1	0	
1	0	0	1	1	CCW

1 = SWITCH ON

(b)

EIGHT-STEP INPUT SEQUENCE
(HALF-STEP MODE)

STEP	SW4	SW3	SW2	SW1
1	OFF	OFF	ON	ON
2	OFF	OFF	OFF	ON
3	ON	OFF	OFF	ON
4	ON	OFF	OFF	OFF
5	ON	ON	OFF	OFF
6	OFF	ON	OFF	OFF
7	OFF	ON	ON	OFF
8	OFF	OFF	ON	OFF
1	OFF	OFF	ON	ON

(c)

FIGURE 9-41 Four-phase stepper motor interface circuit and stepping waveforms. (a) Circuit. (b) Full-step drive signal order. (c) Half-step drive signal order.

Changing to SW3 and SW2 on will cause another step. After that, changing to SW2 and SW1 again will cause another step clockwise. You can repeat the sequence until the motor has rotated as many steps clockwise as you want. To step the motor counterclockwise, you simply work through the switch sequence in the reverse direction. In either case the motor will be held in its last position by the current through the coils. Figure 9-41c shows the switch sequence that can be used to rotate the motor half-steps of 0.9° clockwise or counterclockwise.

A close look at the switch sequence in Figure 9-41b shows an interesting pattern. To take the first step clockwise from SW2 and SW1 being on, the pattern of 1s and 0s is simply rotated 1 bit position around to the right. The 1 from SW1 is rotated around into bit 4. To take the next step, the switch pattern is rotated one more bit position. To step counterclockwise the switch pattern is rotated left 1 bit position for each step desired. Suppose that you initially load 0011 0011 into D0 and output this to the switches. Duplicating the switch pattern in the upper byte of D0 will make stepping easy. To step the motor clockwise, you just rotate this pattern right 1 bit position and output it to the switches. To step counterclockwise, you rotate the switch pattern left 1 bit position and output it. After you output one step code, you must wait a few milliseconds before you output another step command, because the rate at which the motor can step is limited. Maximum stepping rates for different types of steppers vary from a few hundred steps per second to several thousand steps per second. To achieve high stepping rates, the stepping rate is slowly increased to the maximum; then it is decreased as the desired number of steps is approached.

As a stepper motor steps to a new position, it tends to oscillate around the new position before settling down. A common software technique for damping out this oscillation is to first send the pattern to step the motor toward the new position. When the motor has rotated part of the way to the new position, a word to step the motor backward is output for a short time. This is like putting the brakes on. The step-forward word is then sent again to complete the step to the next position. The timing for the damping command must be determined experimentally for each motor and load.

Before we go on, here are a couple of additional points about the circuit in Figure 9-41a, in case you want to add a stepper to your robot or some other project. First of all, don't forget the clamp diodes across each winding to save the transistors from inductive kick. Second, we need to explain the function of the current-limiting resistors, R1 and R2. The motor we used here has a nominal voltage rating of 5.5 V. This means that we could have designed the circuit to operate with a voltage of about 6.5 V on the emitters of the driver transistors (5.5 V for the motor plus 1 V for the drop across the transistor). For low stepping rates, this would work fine. However, for higher stepping rates and more torque while stepping, we use a higher supply voltage and current-limiting resistors, as shown. The point of this is that by adding series

resistance, we decrease the L/R time constant. This allows the current to change more rapidly in the windings. For the motor we used, the current per winding is 0.88 A. Since only one winding on each resistor is ever on at a time, 6.5 V/0.88 A gives a resistor value of 6.25 Ω. To be conservative we used 8-Ω, 10-W resistors. The optional transistor switch and diode connection to the +5-V supply are used as follows. When not stepping, the switch to +12 V is off, so the motor is held in position by the current from the +5-V supply. Before you send a step command, you turn on the transistor to +12 V to give the motor more current for stepping. When stepping is done, you turn off the switch to +12 V and drop back to the +5-V supply. This cuts the power dissipation.

In small printers such as the IBM PC parallel printer, a dedicated microprocessor is used to control the various operations in the printer. In this case the microprocessor has plenty of time to control the print-head and line-feed stepper motors in software as we described earlier. For applications where the main microcomputer is too busy to be bothered with controlling a stepper directly, a simple one-chip microcomputer or a device such as the Cybernetic Microsystems CY525 stepper controller is used.

OPTICAL MOTOR SHAFT ENCODERS

In order to control the machines in our electronics factory, the microcomputers in these machines often need information about the position, direction of rotation, and speed of rotation of various motor shafts. The microcomputer, of course, needs this information in digital form. The circuitry that produces this digital information from each motor for the microcomputer is called a *shaft encoder*. There are two basic types of shaft encoder, *absolute* and *incremental*. Here's how these two types work.

Absolute Encoders

Absolute encoders attach a binary-coded disk such as the one shown in Figure 9-42 on the rotating shaft. Light sections of the disk are transparent, and dark sections are opaque. An LED is mounted on one side of each track, and a phototransistor is mounted on the other side, opposite the LED. Outputs from the four phototransistors produce one of the binary codes shown in Figure 9-42. The phototransistor outputs can be conditioned with Schmitt trigger buffers and connected to a microcomputer port. Each code represents an absolute angular position of the shaft in its rotation. With a 4-bit disk, 360° are divided into 16 parts, so the position of the shaft can be determined to the nearest 22.5°. With an 8-bit disk the position of the disk can be determined to the nearest 360°/256, or 1.4°.

Observe that the codes in Figure 9-42 do not follow a normal binary count sequence. The codes here follow a sequence called a *Gray code*. Using Gray code reduces the size of the largest possible error in reading the

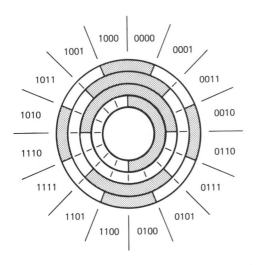

FIGURE 9-42 Gray-code optical-encoder disk used to determine angular position of a rotating shaft.

shaft position to the value of the LSB. If the disk used straight binary code, the largest possible error would be the value of the most significant bit. Look at the parallel listings of binary and Gray codes in Table 1-1 to help you see why this is the case.

To start, assume we did have a binary disk and the disk was rotating from position 0111 (7) to position 1000 (8). Now suppose that the detectors pick up the change to 000 on the least significant 3 bits but don't pick up the change to 1 on the most significant bit. The output code would then be 0000 instead of the desired 1000. This is an error equal to the value of the MSB. Now, while this is fresh in your mind, look across the table at the same position change for the Gray-code encoder. The Gray code for position 7 is 0100 and the Gray code for position 8 is 1100. Note that only one bit changes for this transition. If you look at the Gray-code table closely, you will see that this is the case for all the transitions. What this means is that if a detector fails to pick up the new bit value during a transition, the resulting code will always be the code for the preceding position. This represents an error equal to the value of the LSB.

If you need to construct a Gray-code table for more than 4 bits, a handy method is to observe the pattern of 1s and 0s in Table 1-1 and just extend it. The LSB column starts with a 0 and then has alternating groups of two 1s and two 0s. The second-most significant column starts with two 0s and then has alternating groups of four 1s and four 0s. The third column starts with four 0s and has alternating groups of eight 1s and eight 0s. By now you should see the pattern. Try to figure out the Gray code for the decimal number 16. You should get 1 1000.

Absolute encoding using a Gray-code disk has the advantage that each position is represented by a specific code that can be read in directly by the microcomputer. Disadvantages are the multiple detectors needed, the multiple lines required, and the difficulty keeping track of position during multiple rotations.

Incremental Encoders

An incremental encoder produces a pulse for each increment of shaft rotation. Figure 9-43 shows the Rhino XR-2 robot arm, which uses incremental encoders to determine the position and direction of rotation for each of its motors. For this encoder, a metal disk with two tracks of slotted holes is mounted on each motor shaft. An LED is mounted on one side of each track of holes, and a phototransistor is mounted opposite the LED on the other side of the disk. Each phototransistor produces a train of pulses as the disk is rotated. The pulses are passed through Schmitt trigger buffers to sharpen their edges.

The two tracks of slotted holes are 90° out of phase with each other, as shown at the top of Figure 9-44, p. 288. Therefore, as the disk is rotated, the waveforms shown at the bottom of Figure 9-44 will be produced by the phototransistors for rotation in one direction. Rotation in the other direction will shift the phase of the waveforms 180° so that the B waveform leads the A waveform by 90° degrees instead of lagging it by 90°. Now the question is, How do you get position, speed and direction information from these waveforms?

You can determine the speed of rotation by simply counting the number of pulses in the time between two interrupts, as we described in Chapter 8. Each track has 6 holes, so 6 pulses will be produced for each revolution. Some simple arithmetic will give you the speed in revolutions per minute (rpm).

You can determine the direction of rotation with hardware or with software. For the hardware approach, connect the A signal to the D input of a D flip-flop and the B signal to the clock input of the flip-flop. The rising edge of the B signal will clock the level of the A signal at that point through the flip-flop to its Q output. If you look at the waveforms in Figure 9-44, you should see that the Q output will be high for rotation in the direction shown. You can convince yourself that the Q output will be low for rotation in the other direction. To determine the direction of rotation

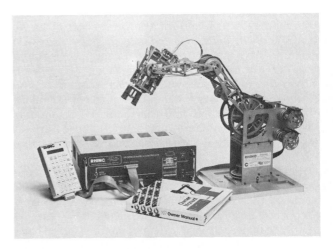

FIGURE 9-43 Rhino XR robotics system. (*Courtesy Rhino Robots Incorporated*)

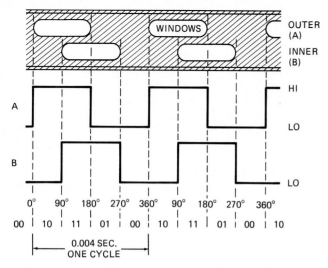

FIGURE 9-44   Optical-encoder disk slot pattern and output waveforms.

more directly, you can detect the rising edge of the B signal on a polled or an interrupt basis and then read the A signal. As shown in the waveforms, the A signal being high represents rotation in one direction, and the A signal being low represents rotation in the opposite direction.

To determine the position of the motor shaft, you simply keep track of how many holes the motor has moved from some "home" position. On the Rhino robot arm a small mechanical switch on each axis is activated when the arm is in its starting, or home, position. When you turn on the power, the motor controller/driver box automatically moves the arm to this home position. To move the arm to some new position, you calculate the number of holes each motor must rotate to get the arm to that position. For each motor you then send the controller a command that tells it in which direction to rotate that motor and how many holes to rotate it. The controller will drive the motor the specified number of holes in the specified direction. If you then manually rotate the encoder wheel or a heavy load moves the arm and rotates the encoder disk, the controller will detect the change in position of the disk and drive the motor back to its specified position. This is an example of digital *feedback control*, which is easily done with a microcomputer. The Rhino controller uses an 8748 single-chip microcomputer to interpret and carry out the commands you send it. Commands are sent to the controller in the serial ASCII form described at the start of Chapter 13.

Incidentally, you may wonder at this point why the designers of the Rhino arm did not use stepper motors such as those we described in a previous section. Stepper motors are much more expensive than the simple dc motors used; if a stepper motor is forced back a step, there is no way to know about it and correct for it unless you have an external encoder; and the dc

motor-encoder approach better demonstrates the method used in large commercial robots.

In the Rhino robot arm each motor drives its section of the arm through a series of gears. Gearing the motor down reduces the force that the motor has to exert and makes the exact position of the motor shaft less critical. Therefore, for the Rhino, six sets of slots in the encoder disk are sufficient. However, for applications where a much more accurate indication of shaft position is needed, a self-contained shaft encoder such as the Hewlett-Packard HEDS-5000 is attached to the motor shaft. These encoders have two track-encoder disks with 500 tiny radial slits per track. The waveforms produced are the same as those shown for the Rhino encoder in Figure 9-44, but at a much higher frequency for the same motor speed.

Optical encoders, in their many different forms, are an important part of a large number of microcomputer-controlled machines.

CHECKLIST OF IMPORTANT TERMS AND CONCEPTS IN THIS CHAPTER

If there are terms and concepts in this list you do not remember, use the index to find them in the chapter.

Simple input and output

Simple strobe I/O

Single-handshake I/O

Double-handshake data transfer

6821 initialization of ports A and B
    Handshake mode
    Strobed mode
    Interrupt mode
    Mode definition control word
    Set/reset control word

Computer numerical control (CNC) machines

VOTRAX SC-01A speech synthesizer
    Phoneme

Centronix parallel standard
    I/O driver
    Control block
    Counters and sentinels

Keyswitches
    Mechanical
    Capacitive
    Hall effect

Debounce key-press

Two-key lockout, two-key rollover

Code conversion
    Compare
    Add and point
    Error-trapping
    Hash code method

LED

    Static display
    Multiplexed display
    Dedicated display controller
    Scan time

8279

    FIFO
    Encoded and decoded scan
    Keyboard/display mode-set control word
    Clear control word
    Write display control word

LCD

    Dynamic scattering
    Field effect

    Backplane
    Triplexing

Relays
    Mechanical
    Solid state
    Electromagnetic interference
    Zero-point switching
    RC snubber circuit

Four-phase stepper motor

Shaft encoder, absolute and incremental

Digital feedback control

REVIEW QUESTIONS AND PROBLEMS

1. Why must data be sent to a printer on a hand-shake basis?

2. For the double-handshake data transfer in Figure 9-1d:
   a. Indicate which signal is asserted by the sender and which signal is asserted by the receiver.
   b. Describe the meaning of each of the signal transitions.

3. Why are the port lines of programmable port devices automatically put in the input mode when the device is first powered up or reset?

4. A 6821 has a system base address of $C010. What are the system addresses for the two port-control and data registers for this 6821?

5. a. Show the mode-set control words needed to initialize an 6821 as follows:

   Port A: handshake input

   Port B: handshake output

   b. Show the bit writes needed to enable the port A interrupt request and the port B interrupt request.
   c. Show the assembly language instructions you would use to send these control words to the 6821 in problem 4.
   d. Show the additional instruction you need if you want the handshake to be done on an interrupt basis through the $\overline{\text{IRQA}}$ output of the lower 6821 in Figure 7-6.

6. Describe the exchange of signals between the tape reader, 6821, and 68000 in Figure 9-6 as a byte of data is transferred from the tape reader to the microprocessor.

7. Why is it more efficient to send phonemes to the SC-01A speech synthesizer in Figure 9-10a on an interrupt basis than on a polled basis?

8. If you have an SC-01A speech IC connected to your system, as shown in Figure 9-10a, write the mainline program and the interrupt-service routine to send phonemes to the SC-01A. The mainline can terminate with the HERE: BRA HERE instruction, so that it simply waits for interrupts from the 6821. Use the phoneme table in the appendix to help you make up the table of phonemes for your message.

9. When connecting peripheral devices such as printers and terminals to a computer, why is it very important to connect the logic ground and the chassis ground together only at the computer?

10. Describe the function and direction of the following signals in a Centronics parallel printer interface.

   a. $\overline{\text{STB}}$
   b. ACKNLG
   c. BUSY
   d. $\overline{\text{INIT}}$

11. Modify the printer driver procedure in Figure 9-17 so that it stops sending characters to the printer when it finds a sentinel character of $03, instead of using the counter approach.

12. Would the software method of generating the STROBE signal to the printer in Figure 9-17 still work if you try to run the program with an 8-MHz 68000? A 50-MHz 68030?

13. Show the instructions you would use to read the status byte from the 6821 in problem 5.

14. Describe the three major tasks needed to get meaningful information from a matrix keyboard.

15. Describe how the "compare" method of code conversion in Figure 9-21 works.

16. Why is error trapping necessary in real programs?

Describe how the error trap in the program in Figure 9-21 works.

17. Assume the rows of the circuit shown in Figure 9-45 are connected to ports $C014 and the 74148 is connected to port $C015 of an URDA MDS board. The 74148 will output a low on its $\overline{GS}$ output if a low is applied to any of its inputs. The way the keyboard is wired, the $\overline{A2}$, $\overline{A1}$, and $\overline{A0}$ outputs will have a 3-bit binary code for the column in which a low appears. Use the algorithm and discussion of Figure 9-21 to help you write a routine that detects a key-press, debounces the key-press, and determines the row number and column number of the pressed key. The routine should then combine the row code, column code, shift bit and control bit into a single byte in the form control, shift, row code, column code. The MOVE indexed indirect instruction can then be used to convert this code byte to ASCII to return to the calling program. (*Hint:* Use DC.B directive to make up table of ASCII codes.) Why is the hash code approach more efficient than the compare technique for this case?

NOTE: For test purposes, the keyboard matrix can be simulated by building the diodes, resistors, and 74148 on a prototyping board and using a jumper wire to produce a key press.

18. *a.* Calculate the value of the current-limiting resistor needed in series with each segment of a seven-segment display driven by a 7447 if we want 40 mA per segment.

b. Approximately how much current is being pulsed through each LED segment on the URDA MDS board?

19. *a.* Write the algorithm for a subroutine that refreshes the multiplexed LED displays shown in Figure 9-26. Assume the routine will be called every 2 ms by an interrupt signal to the 68000.

b. Write the assembly language instructions for the display refresh subroutine. Since this routine is called on an interrupt basis, all display parameters should be kept in named memory locations. If you have time, you can add the circuitry shown in Figure 9-26 to your microcomputer so you can test your program.

20. Figure 9-46 shows a circuit for an 8 × 8 matrix of LEDs that you can add to a couple of ports on your microcomputer to produce some interesting displays. The principle here is to output a 1 to port B for each LED you want turned on in the top row and then output a 1 to the D0 bit of port A to turn on that row. After 2 ms, you output the pattern you want in row 2 to port B and a 1 to bit 1 of port A to turn on the second row. The process is repeated until all rows are done and then started over.

The row patterns can be kept in a table in memory. If you want to display a sequence of letters, you can display the contents of one table for a few seconds, then switch to another table containing the second letter. Using the rotate instruction, you can produce some scrolled displays. (*Hint:* The writing required to build the LED matrix can be reduced by using an IC 5 × 7 dot-matrix LED display such as the Texas Instruments TIL305.

Write the algorithm and program for an interrupt-service routine (called every 2 ms) to refresh these displays.

21. You are assigned the job of fixing several URDA MDS boards with display problems. For each of the problems listed, describe a possible cause of the problem and tell where you would look with an oscilloscope to check out your theory. Use the circuit on sheet 7 of Figure 7-6 to help you.

a. The segment never lights.

b. The leftmost digit of the data field never lights.

c. All the displays show dim 8s.

22. *a.* Show the command words and assembly language instructions necessary to initialize an 8279 at address $C080 and $C082 as follows:

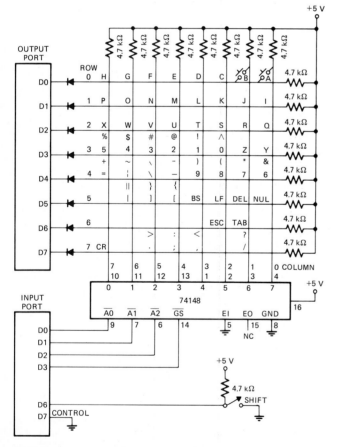

FIGURE 9-45 Interface circuitry for unencoded matrix keyboard for problem 17.

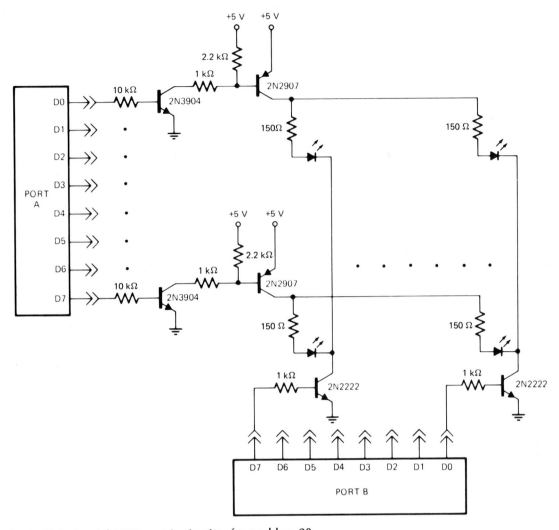

FIGURE 9-46 Eight by eight LED matrix circuitry for problem 20.

16 character display, left entry, encoded-scan keyboard, N-key rollover.

1-MHz input clock divided to 100 kHz

Blanking character $FF

b. Show the 8279 instructions necessary to write $99 to the first location in the display RAM and autoincrement the display RAM pointer.

c. Show the assembly language instructions necessary to read the first byte from the 8279 FIFO RAM.

d. Determine the seven-segment codes you would have to send to the URDA MDS 8279 to display the word HELP on the data field display. Remember that D0 of the byte sent equals B0 and D7 of the byte sent equals A3.

e. Show the sequence of instructions you can send to the 8279 of the URDA MDS board to blank the entire display.

23. Write a subroutine that polls the LSB of the 8279

status register on the URDA MDS board until it finds a key pressed and then reads the key-pressed code from the FIFO RAM to D0 and returns.

24. Why must the backplane and segment-line signals be pulsed for LCD displays?

25. Draw a circuit you could attach to a 6821 port B pin to drive a 1-A solenoid valve from a +12-V supply. You want a high on the port pin to turn on the solenoid.

26. Why must reverse-biased diodes always be placed across inductive devices when you are driving them with a transistor?

27. What are the major advantages and disadvantages of mechanical relays and solid-state relays?

28. a. How is electrical isolation between the control output and the output circuitry achieved in a solid-state relay?

b. Describe the function of the zero-crossing

detector used in better-quality solid-state relays.

    c. Why is a snubber circuit required across the TRIAC of a solid-state relay when driving inductive loads?

29. Write the algorithm and the program for a 68000 subroutine to drive the stepper motor shown in Figure 9-41. Assume the desired direction of rotation is passed to the procedure in D0 (D0 = 1 = clockwise; D0 = 0 = counterclockwise) and the number of steps is passed to the subroutine in D1. Also assume full-step mode as shown in Figure 9-41b. Don't forget to delay 20 ms between step commands!

30.   a. Why is Gray code, rather than straight binary code, used on many absolute-position shaft encoders?

    b. If a Gray-code wheel has six tracks and each track represents 1 binary bit, what is its angular resolution?

31.   a. Look at the encoder disk on the Rhino arm in Figure 9-43. Do the waveforms in Figure 9-44 represent clockwise or counterclockwise rotation of the motor shaft as seen from the gear end of the motor, which is what you care about?

    b. Assume the A signal shown in Figure 9-44 is connected to bit D0 of an input port and the B signal is connected to bit D1 of port C014. Write a routine that determines the direction of rotation and passes a 1 back in D0 for clockwise and a 0 back in D0 for counterclockwise rotation.

    c. The dc motors, such as those on the Rhino arms, are rotated clockwise by passing a current through them in one direction and rotated counterclockwise by passing a current through them in the opposite direction. Assume you have a motor controller that responds to a 2-bit control word as follows:

00 = hold   01 = rotate clockwise
11 = hold   10 = rotate counterclockwise

Write the algorithm and program for a routine to rotate a motor; the number of holes is passed to the procedure in D1 and the direction of rotation is determined by the value in D0 (D0 = 1 = clockwise, D0 = 0 = counterclockwise).

CHAPTER
Analog Interfacing and Industrial Control

10

In order to control the machines in our electronics factory, medical instruments, or automobiles with a microcomputer, we need to determine the values of variables such as pressure, temperature, and flow. There are usually several steps in getting an electrical signal that represents the values of these variables and converting the electrical signals to a digital form that the microcomputer understands.

The first step involves a *sensor*, which converts the physical pressure, temperature, or other variable to a proportional voltage or current. The signals from most sensors are quite small, so they must next be amplified and perhaps filtered. This is usually done with some type of operational-amplifier (op-amp) circuit. The final step is to convert the signal to digital form with an A/D converter. In this chapter we review some op-amp circuits commonly used in these steps, show the interface circuitry for some common sensors, and discuss the operation and interfacing of A/D converters. We also discuss the interfacing of D/A converters and show how all these pieces are put together in a microcomputer-based scale and a machine-control system.

OBJECTIVES

At the conclusion of this chapter, you should be able to

1. Recognize several common op-amp circuits, describe their operations, and predict the voltages at key points in each.

2. Describe the operation and interfacing of several common sensors used to measure temperature, pressure, flow, etc.

3. Draw circuits showing how to interface D/A converters with any number of bits to a microcomputer.

4. Define D/A data sheet parameters such as resolution, settling time, accuracy, and linearity.

5. Describe briefly the operation of flash, successive approximation, and ramp A/D converters.

6. Draw circuits showing how A/D converters of various types can be interfaced to a microcomputer.

7. Write programs to control A/D and D/A converters.

8. Describe how feedback is used to control variables such as pressure, temperature, flow, and motor speed.

9. Describe the operation of a time-slice factory control system.

REVIEW OF OPERATIONAL-AMPLIFIER CHARACTERISTICS AND CIRCUITS

Basic Operational Amplifier Characteristics

Figure 10-1a, p. 294, shows the schematic symbol for an operational amplifier commonly called an op amp. Here are the important points for you to remember about the basic op amp. First, the pins labeled +V and −V represent the power supply connections. The voltages applied to these pins will usually be +15 V and −15 V or +12 V and −12 V. The op amp also has two signal inputs. The amplifier amplifies the difference in voltage between these two inputs by 100,000 or more. The input labeled with a − sign is called the *inverting input* and the one labeled with the + sign is called the *noninverting input*. The + and − on these inputs have nothing to do with the power supply voltages. These signs indicate the phase relationship between a signal applied to that input and the result that the signal produces on the output. If, for example, the noninverting input is made more positive than the inverting input, the output will move in a positive direction, which is in phase with the applied input signal. Now let's see how far the output changes for a given input signal and see how an op amp is used as a comparator.

Op-amp Circuits and Applications

OP AMPS AS COMPARATORS

We said previously that the op amp amplifies the difference in voltage between its inputs by 100,000 or more. (The number is variable with temperature and from device to device.) Suppose that you power an op amp with +15 V and −15 V, tie the inverting input of the op amp to ground, and apply a signal of +0.01 V dc

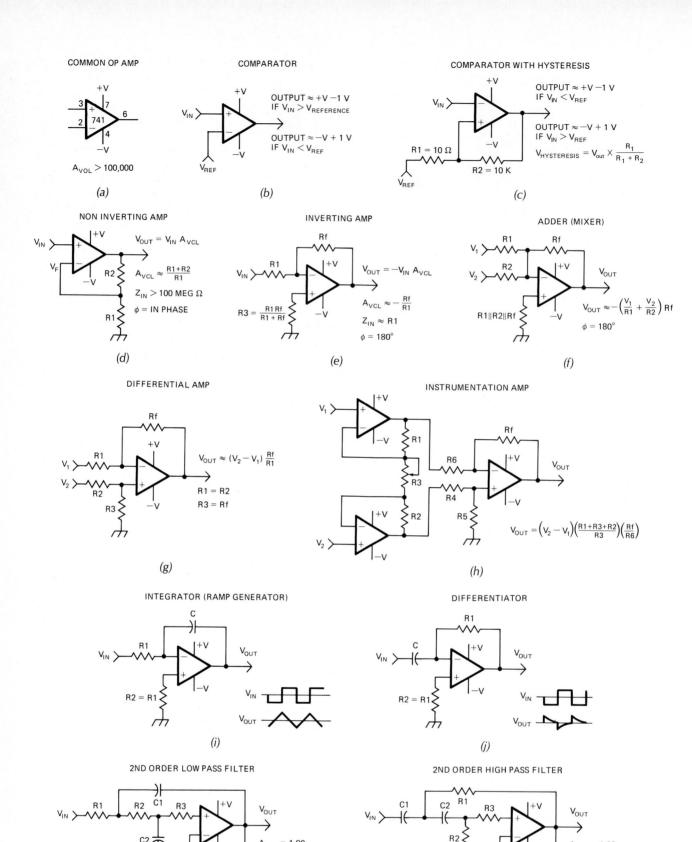

FIGURE 10-1   Overview of commonly used op-amp circuits. (*a*) Common op amp. (*b*) Comparator. (*c*) Comparator with hysteresis. (*d*) Noninverting amp. (*e*) Inverting amp. (*f*) Adder (mixer). (*g*) Differential amp. (*h*) Instrumentation amp. (*i*) Integrator (ramp generator). (*j*) Differentiator. (*k*) Second-order low-pass filter. (*l*) Second-order high-pass filter.

to the noninverting input. The op amp will attempt to amplify this signal by 100,000 and produce the result on its output. An input signal of 0.01 V times a gain of 100,000 predicts an output voltage of 100 V. The op-amp output, however, can go positive only to a voltage that is a volt or two less than the positive supply voltage, perhaps 13 V, so this is as far as it goes. Now suppose that you apply a signal of -0.01 V to the noninverting input. The output will now try to go to -100 V as fast as it can. The output, however, can go only to about -13 V, so this is where it stops.

In this circuit the op amp effectively compares the input voltage with the voltage on the inverting input and gives a high or low output depending on the result of the comparison. If the input is more than a few microvolts above the reference voltage on the inverting input, the output will be high ($+13$ V). If the input voltage is a few microvolts more negative than the reference voltage, the output will be low (-13 V). An op amp used in this way is called a *comparator*. Figure 10-1b shows how a comparator is usually labeled. The reference voltage applied to the inverting input does not have to be ground (0 V). An input voltage can be compared to any voltage within the input range specified for the particular op amp.

As you will see throughout this chapter, comparators have many applications. We might, for example, connect a comparator to a temperature sensor on the boiler in our electronics factory. When the voltage from the temperature sensor goes above the voltage on the reference input of the comparator, the output of the comparator will change state and send an interrupt signal to the microprocessor controlling the boiler. Commonly available comparators, such as the LM319, have TTL-compatible outputs, which can be connected directly to microcomputer port or interrupt inputs.

Figure 10-1c shows another commonly used comparator circuit. Note in this circuit that the reference signal is applied to the noninverting input, and the input voltage is applied to the inverting input. This connection simply inverts the output state from those in the previous circuit. Note also in Figure 10-1c the positive-feedback resistors from the output to the noninverting input. This feedback gives the comparator a characteristic called *hysteresis*. Hysteresis means that the output voltage changes at a different input voltage when the input is going in the positive direction than it does when the input voltage is going in a negative direction. If you have a thermostatically controlled furnace in your house, you have seen hysteresis in action. The furnace, for example, may turn on when the room temperature drops to 65°F and then not turn off until the temperature reaches 68°F. Hysteresis is the difference between the two temperatures. Without hysteresis, the furnace would rapidly be turning on and off if the room temperature were near 68°F. Another situation where hysteresis saves the day is the case in which you have a slowly changing signal with noise on it. Hysteresis prevents the noise from causing the comparator output to oscillate as the input signal gets close to the reference voltage.

To determine the amount of hysteresis in a circuit such as that in Figure 10-1c, assume $V_{REF} = 0$ V and $V_{OUT} = 13$ V. A simple voltage-divider calculation will tell you that the noninverting input is at about 13 mV. The voltage on the inverting input of the amplifier will have to go more positive than this before the comparator will change states. Likewise, if you assume V_{OUT} is -13 V, the noninverting input will be at about -13 mV, so the voltage on the inverting input of the amplifier will have to go below this to change the state of the output. The hysteresis of this comparator is then $+13$ mV to -13 mV, or a total of 26 mV.

NONINVERTING AMPLIFIER OP-AMP CIRCUIT

When operating in open-loop mode (no feedback to the inverting input), an op amp has a very high, but unpredictable, gain. This is acceptable for use as a comparator but not for use as a predictable amplifier. Figure 10-1d shows one way negative feedback is added to an op amp to produce an amplifier with stable, predictable gain. First of all, notice that the input signal in this circuit is applied to the noninverting input, so the output will be in phase with the input. Second, note that a fraction of the output signal is fed back to the inverting input. Now, here's how this works.

To start, assume that V_{IN} is 0 V, V_{OUT} is 0 V, and the voltage on the inverting input is 0. Now, suppose that you apply a $+0.01$-V dc signal to the noninverting input. Since the 0.1-V difference between the two inputs will be amplified by 100,000, the output will head toward 100 V as fast as it can. However, as the output goes positive, some of the output voltage will be fed back to the inverting input through the resistor divider. This feedback to the inverting input will decrease the difference in voltage between the two inputs. To make a long story short, the circuit quickly reaches a predictable balance point, at which the voltage on the inverting input (V_{IN}) is very, very close to the voltage on the noninverting input (V_F). For a 1.0-V dc output, this equilibrium voltage difference might be about 10 μV. If you assume that the voltages on the two inputs are equal, then predicting the output voltage for a given input voltage is simply a voltage-divider problem: $V_{OUT} = V_{IN}(R1 + R2)/R1$. If R2 is 99 k$\Omega$ and R1 is 1 kΩ, then $V_{OUT} = V_{IN} \times 100$. For a 0.01-V input signal, the output voltage will be 1.00 V. The closed-loop gain, A_{VCL}, for this circuit is equal to the simple resistor ratio, $(R1 + R2)/R1$.

To see another advantage in feeding some of the output signal back to the inverting input, let's see what happens when the load connected to the output of the op amp changes and draws more current from the output. The output voltage will temporarily drop because of the increased load. Part of this drop will be fed back to the inverting input, increasing the difference in voltage between the two inputs. This increased difference will cause the op amp to drive its output to correct for the increased load. Feedback that causes an amplifier to oppose a change on its output is called *negative feedback*. Because of the negative feedback, the op amp will work day and night to keep its output stabilized and its two inputs at nearly the same voltage! This is probably the most important point you need to know in order to analyze or troubleshoot an op-amp circuit with negative feedback. Draw a box around this point in your mind so you don't forget it.

The noninverting circuit we have just discussed is used mostly as a *buffer*, because it has a very high *input impedance* (Z_{IN}) and will, therefore, not load down a sensor or some other device you connect to its input. Bipolar transistor-input op amps have input impedances greater than 100 MΩ. Some op amps, such as the National LF356, have an FET input stage, so their input impedance is 10^{12} Ω.

INVERTING AMPLIFIER OP-AMP CIRCUIT

Figure 10-1*e* shows a somewhat more versatile amplifier circuit using negative feedback. Note that in this circuit the noninverting input is tied to ground with a resistor and the signal you want to amplify is sent to the inverting input through a resistor. The output signal will therefore be 180° out of phase with the input signal. Resistor Rf supplies the negative feedback that keeps the two inputs at nearly the same voltage. Since the noninverting input is tied to ground, the op amp will sink or source current to hold the inverting input also at 0 V. In this circuit the inverting input point is referred to as *virtual ground* because the op amp holds it at ground. The voltage gain of this circuit is also determined by the ratio of two resistors. The A_{VCL} for this circuit at low frequencies is equal to $-Rf/R1$. You can derive this for yourself by just thinking of the two resistors as a voltage divider with V_{IN} at one end, 0 V in the middle, and V_{OUT} on the other end. The minus sign in the gain expression simply indicates that the output is inverted from the input. The input impedance (Z_{IN}) of this circuit is approximately R1 because the op amp holds one end of this resistor at 0 V.

One additional characteristic we need to recall about op-amp circuits before going on to other op-amp circuits is *gain-bandwidth product*. As we indicated previously, an op amp may have an open-loop dc gain of 100,000 or more. At higher frequencies the gain decreases until, at some frequency, the open-loop gain drops to 1. Figure 10-2*a* shows an open-loop voltage gain versus frequency graph for a common op amp such as a 741. The frequency at which the gain is 1 is referred to on data sheets as the *unity-gain bandwidth*, or the *gain-bandwidth product*. A common value for this is 1 MHz. The bandwidth of an amplifier circuit with negative feedback times the low-frequency closed-loop gain will be equal to this value. For example, if an op amp with a gain-bandwidth product of 1 MHz is used to build an amplifier circuit with a closed-loop gain of 100, the bandwidth of the circuit (f_C) will be about 1 MHz/100, or 10 kHz, as shown in Figure 10-2*b*.

OP-AMP ADDER CIRCUIT

Figure 10-1*f* shows a commonly used variation of the inverting amplifier described in the previous section.

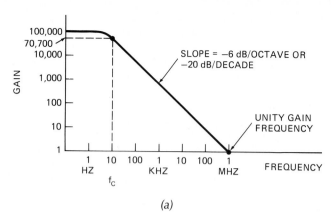

(a)

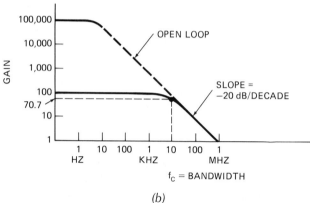

(b)

FIGURE 10-2 (a) Open-loop gain versus frequency response of 741 op amp. (b) Gain versus frequency response of 741 op-amp circuit with closed-loop gain of 100.

This circuit adds together, or mixes, two or more input signals. Here's how it works.

Remember from the previous discussion with the inverting circuit that the op amp holds the inverting input at virtual ground. The input voltage V_1 produces a current through R1 to this point. The input voltage V_2 causes a current through R2 to this point. The two currents add together at the virtual ground, which is commonly called the *summing point* for this circuit. The sum of the two currents is pulled through resistor Rf by the op amp to hold the inverting input at zero volts. The output voltage is then equal to the sum of the currents times the value of Rf, or (V_1/R1 + V_2/R2) × Rf. A circuit such as this is used to mix audio signals and to sum binary-weighted currents in a D/A converter. An adder can have several inputs.

SIMPLE DIFFERENTIAL-INPUT AMPLIFIER CIRCUIT

As we show later, many sensors have two output signal lines with a dc voltage of several volts on each signal line. The dc voltage present on both signal lines is referred to as a *common-mode signal*. The actual signal you need to amplify from these sensors is the few-millivolt difference between them. If you try to use a standard inverting or noninverting amplifier circuit to do this, the large dc voltage will be amplified along with the small difference voltage you need to amplify.

Figure 10-1g shows a simple circuit, which, for the most part, solves this problem without using coupling capacitors to block the dc. The analysis of this circuit is beyond the space we have here, but basically the resistors on the noninverting input hold this input at a voltage near the common-mode voltage. The amplifier holds the inverting input at the same voltage. If the resistors are matched carefully, the result is that only the difference in voltage between V_2 and V_1 will be amplified. The output will be a single line that contains only the amplified difference. We say that the common-mode signal has been *rejected*.

AN INSTRUMENTATION AMPLIFIER CIRCUIT

Figure 10-1h shows an op-amp circuit used in applications needing a greater rejection of the common-mode signal than is provided by the simple differential circuit in Figure 10-1g. The first two op amps in this circuit remove the common-mode voltage and the last op amp converts the result from a differential signal to a signal referenced to ground. Instrumentation amplifier circuits such as this are available in single packages.

AN OP-AMP INTEGRATOR CIRCUIT

Figure 10-1i shows an op-amp circuit that can be used to produce linear-voltage ramps. A dc voltage applied to the input of this circuit will cause a constant current of $V_{IN}/R1$ to flow into the virtual-ground point. This current flows onto one plate of the capacitor. In order to hold the inverting input at ground, the op-amp output must pull the same current from the other plate of the capacitor. The capacitor is then getting charged by the constant current $V_{IN}/R1$. Basic physics tells you that the voltage across a capacitor being charged by a constant current is a *linear ramp*. Note that because of the inverting amplifier connection, the output will ramp negative for a positive input voltage. Also note that some provision must be made to prevent the amplifier output from ramping into *saturation*.

The circuit is called an integrator because it produces an output voltage proportional to the integral, or "sum," of the current produced by an input voltage over a period of time. The waveforms in Figure 10-1i show the circuit response for a pulse-input signal.

AN OP-AMP DIFFERENTIATOR CIRCUIT

Figure 10-1j shows an op-amp circuit that produces an output signal proportional to the rate of change of the input signal. With the input voltage to this circuit at zero or some other steady dc voltage, the output will be at zero. If a new voltage is applied to the input, the voltage across the capacitor cannot change instantly, so the inverting input will be pulled away from 0 V. This will cause the op amp to drive its output in a direction to charge the capacitor and pull the inverting input back to zero. The waveforms in Figure 10-1j show the circuit response for a pulse-input signal. The time required for the output to return to zero is determined by the time constant of R1 and C.

OP-AMP ACTIVE FILTERS

In many control applications we need to filter out unwanted low-frequency or high-frequency noise from the signals read in from sensors. This could be done with simple RC filters, but *active filters* using op amps give much better control over filter characteristics. There are many different filter configurations using op amps. The main points we want to recall here are the meanings of the terms *low-pass* filter, *high-pass* filter, and *band-pass* filter and how you identify the type when you find one in a circuit you are analyzing.

A low-pass filter amplifies or passes through low frequencies, but at some frequency determined by circuit values, the output of the filter starts to decrease. The frequency at which the output is down to 0.707 of the low-frequency value is called the *critical frequency*, or *breakpoint*. Figure 10-3a shows a graph of gain versus frequency for a low-pass filter with the

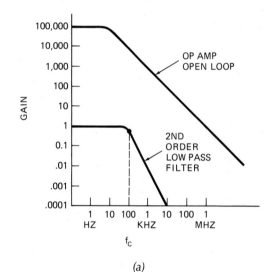

(a)

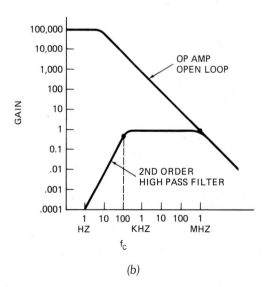

(b)

FIGURE 10-3 Gain versus frequency response for second-order low-pass and high-pass filters. (a) Low-pass. (b) High-pass.

critical frequency (f_C) labeled. Note that above the critical frequency, the gain drops off rapidly. For a first-order filter such as a single R and C, the gain decreases by a factor of 10 for each increase of 10 times in frequency (−20 dB/decade). For a second-order filter the gain decreases by a factor of 100 for each increase of 10 times in frequency.

Figure 10-1k shows a common circuit for a second-order low-pass filter. The way you recognize this as a low-pass filter is to look for a dc path from the input to the noninverting input of the amplifier. If the dc path is present, as it is in Figure 10-1k, you know that the amplifier can amplify dc and low frequencies. Therefore, it is a low-pass filter with a response such as that shown in Figure 10-3a.

For contrast look at the circuit for the second-order high-pass filter in Figure 10-1l. Note that in this circuit the dc component of an input signal cannot reach the noninverting input because of the two capacitors in series with that input. Therefore, this circuit will not amplify dc and low-frequency signals. Figure 10-3b shows the graph of gain versus frequency for a high-pass filter such as this. Note that the gain-bandwidth product of the op amp limits the high-frequency response of the circuit.

For the low-pass circuit in Figure 10-1k, the gain for the flat part of the response curve is 1, or unity, because the output is fed back directly to the inverting input. At the critical frequency, f_C, the gain will be 0.707, and above this frequency the gain will drop off. The critical frequency for the circuit is determined by the equation next to the circuit. The equation assumes that R1 and R2 are equal and that the value of C1 is twice the value of C2. R3 is simply a damping resistor. The positive feedback supplied by C1 is the reason the gain is down to only 0.707 at the critical frequency rather than down to 0.5 as it would be if we simply cascaded two simple RC circuits.

For the high-pass filter, the gain for the flat section of the response curve is also 1. Assuming that the two capacitors are equal and the value of R2 is twice the value of R1, the critical frequency is determined by the formula shown next to Figure 10-1l. Again, R3 is for damping.

A low-pass filter can be put in series with a high-pass filter to produce a band-pass filter, which lets through a desired range of frequencies. There are also many different single amplifier circuits that will pass or reject a band of frequencies.

Now that we have refreshed your memory about basic op-amp circuits, we will next discuss some of the different types of sensors you can use to determine the values of temperatures, pressures, position, etc.

SENSORS AND TRANSDUCERS

It would take a book many times the size of this one to describe the operation and applications of all the different types of available sensors and transducers. What we want to do here is introduce you to a few of these

and show how they can be used to get data for microcomputer-based instruments in, for example, our electronics factory.

Light Sensors

One of the simplest light sensors is a light-dependent resistor such as the Clairex CL905 shown in Figure 10-4a. A glass window allows light to fall on a zigzag pattern of cadmium sulfide or a cadmium solenoid whose resistance depends on the amount of light present. The resistance of the CL905 varies from about 15 MΩ when in the dark to about 15 kΩ when in a bright light. Photoresistors such as this do not have a very fast response time and are not stable with temperature, but they are inexpensive, durable, and sensitive. For these reasons they are usually used in applications where a measurement of the amount of light does not need to be precise. The devices on top of street lights that turn them on when it gets dark, for example, contain a photoresistor, a transistor driver, and a mechanical relay, as shown in Figure 10-4b. As it gets dark, the resistance of the photoresistor goes up. This increases the voltage on the base of the transistor, until, at some point, it turns on. This turns on the transistor driving the relay, which in turn switches on the lamp.

Another device used to sense the amount of light present is a photodiode. If light is allowed to fall on a specially constructed silicon diode, the reverse-leakage current of the diode increases linearly as the amount of light falling on it increases. A circuit such as that shown in Figure 10-5 can be used to convert this small leakage current to a proportional voltage. Note that in

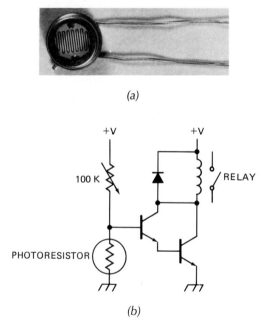

(a)

(b)

FIGURE 10-4 (a) Cadmium sulfide photocell (*Clairex Electronics*). (b) Light-controller relay circuit using a photocell.

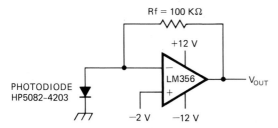

FIGURE 10-5 Photodiode circuit to measure infrared light intensity.

this circuit a negative reference voltage is applied to the noninverting input of the amplifier. The op amp will then produce this same voltage on its inverting input, reverse-biasing the photodiode. The op amp will pull the photodiode leakage current through Rf to produce a proportional voltage on the output of the amplifier. For a typical photodiode such as the HP 5082-4203 shown, the reverse-leakage current varies from near 0 μA to about 100 μA, so with the 100-kΩ Rf, an output voltage of about 0 V to 10 V will be produced. The circuit will work without any reverse bias on the diode, but with the reverse bias, the diode responds faster to changes in light. An LM356 FET input amplifier is used here because it does not require an input-bias current.

A photodiode circuit such as this might be used to determine the amount of smoke being emitted from a smokestack. To do this, a gallium arsenide infrared LED is put on one side of the smokestack, and the photodetector circuit is put on the other. Since smoke absorbs light, the amount of light arriving at the photodetector is a measure of the amount of smoke present. An infrared LED is used here because the photodiode is most sensitive to light wavelengths in the infrared region.

Still another useful light-sensitive device is a solar cell. Common solar cells are simply large, very heavily doped, silicon P-N junctions. Light shining on the solar cell causes a reverse current to flow, just as in the photodiode. Because of the large area and the heavy doping in the solar cell, however, the current produced is milliamps rather than microamps. The cell functions as a light-powered battery. Solar cells can be connected in a series-parallel array to produce a solar power supply.

Light meters in cameras, photographic enlargers, and our PC-board-making machine use solar cells. The current from the solar cell is a linear function of the amount of light falling on the cell. A circuit such as that in Figure 10-5 can be used to convert the output current to a proportional voltage. Because of the larger output current, we decrease Rf to a much smaller value, depending on the output current of the cell. We also connect the noninverting input of the amplifier to ground because we don't use reverse biasing with solar cells. The frequency response to light (spectral response) of solar cells has been tailored to match the output of the sun. Therefore, they are ideal in photographic applications where we want a signal propor-

tional to the total light from the sun or from an incandescent lamp.

Temperature Sensors

Again, there are many types of temperature sensors. The two types we discuss here are semiconductor devices, which are inexpensive and can be used to measure temperatures over the range of −55°C to 100°C, and thermocouples, which can be used to measure very low temperatures and very high temperatures.

SEMICONDUCTOR TEMPERATURE SENSORS

The two main types of semiconductor temperature sensors are temperature-sensitive voltage sources and temperature-sensitive current sources. An example of the first type is the National LM35, for which we show the circuit connections in Figure 10-6a, p. 300. The voltage output from this circuit increases by 10 mV for each degree Celsius that its temperature is increased. By connecting the output to a negative reference voltage (V_S) as shown, the sensor will give a meaningful output for a temperature range of −55°C to +150°C. You adjust the output to 0 V for 0°C. The output voltage can be amplified to give the voltage range you need for a particular application. In a later section of this chapter, we show another circuit using the LM35 temperature sensor. The accuracy of this device is about 1°C.

Another common semiconductor-temperature sensor is a temperature-dependent current source such as the Analog Devices AD590. The AD590 produces a current of 1 μA/K. Figure 10-6b, p. 300, shows a circuit that converts this current to a proportional voltage. In this circuit the current from the sensor (I_T) is passed through approximately a 1-kΩ resistor to ground. This produces a voltage that changes by 1 mV/K. The AD580 is a precision voltage reference used to produce a reference voltage of 273.2 mV. With this voltage applied to the inverting input of the amplifier, the amplifier output will be at 0 V for 0°C. The advantage of a current-source sensor is that voltage drops in long connecting wires do not have any effect on the output value. If the gain and offset are carefully adjusted, the accuracy of the circuit in Figure 10-6b is ±1°C using an AD590K part.

THERMOCOUPLES

Whenever two different metals are put in contact, a small voltage is produced between them. The voltage developed depends on the types of metals used and the temperature. Depending on the metals, the developed voltage increases between 7 μV and 75 μV for each degree Celsius increase in temperature. Different combinations of metals are useful for measuring different temperature ranges. A thermocouple junction made of iron and constantan, commonly called a type J thermocouple, has a useful temperature range of about −184°C to +760°C. A junction of platinum and an alloy of platinum and 13% rhodium has a useful range of 0°C

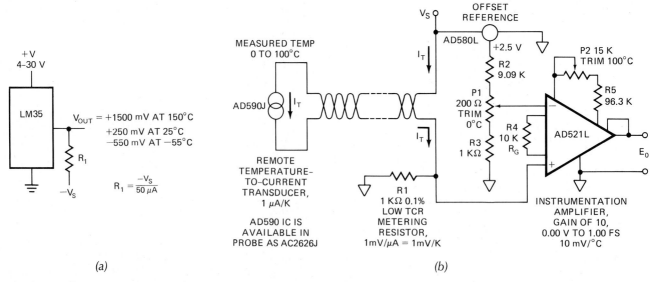

(a)

(b)

FIGURE 10-6 Semiconductor temperature-sensor circuits. (a) LM35
temperature-dependent voltage source. (b) AD590 temperature-dependent
current source. (*Analog Devices Incorporated*)

to about 1600°C. Thermocouples can be made small, rugged, and stable; however, they have three major problems that must be overcome.

First of these is the fact that the output is very small and must be amplified a great deal to bring it up into the range where it can, for example, drive an A/D converter. Second, in order to make accurate measurements, a second junction made of the same metals must be included in the circuit as a reference. Adding this second junction is referred to as a *cold-junction compensation*. Figure 10-7 shows a circuit to amplify the output of a thermocouple and provide cold-junction compensation for a type J thermocouple.

The first thing to notice in the circuit is that the reference junction is connected in the reverse direction

from the measuring junction. This is done so that the output connecting wires are both constant. The thermocouples formed by connecting these wires to the copper wires going to the amplifier will then cancel out. The resultant output voltage will be the difference between the voltages across the two thermocouples. If we simply amplify the output of the two thermocouples, however, there is a problem if the temperature of both thermocouples is changing. The problem is that it is impossible to tell which thermocouple caused a change in output voltage. One cure for this is to put the reference junction in an ice bath or a small oven to hold it at a constant temperature. This solution is usually inconvenient, so instead a circuit such as that in Figure 10-7 is used to compensate electronically for changes in the temperature of the reference junction.

As we discussed in a previous section, the AD590 shown here produces a current proportional to its temperature. The AD590 is attached to the reference thermocouple so that they are both at the same temperature. The current from the AD590, when passed through the resistor network, produces a voltage that compensates for changes in the reference thermocouple with temperature. The output amplifier for this circuit is a differential amplifier such as that shown in Figure 10-1g or the instrumentation amplifier shown in Figure 10-1h.

The third problem with thermocouples is that their output voltages do not change linearly with temperature. This can be corrected with analog circuitry that changes the gain of an amplifier according to the value of the signal. However, when a thermocouple is used with a microcomputer-based instrument, the correction can easily be done using a lookup table in ROM. An A/D converter converts the voltage from the thermocouple to a digital value. The digital value is then

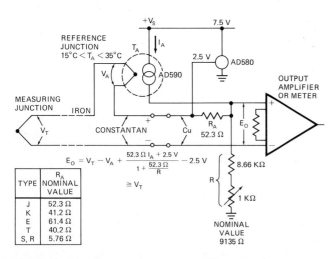

FIGURE 10-7 Circuit showing amplification and cold-junction compensation for thermocouple. (*Analog Devices Incorporated*)

used as a pointer to a ROM location that contains the correct temperature for that reading.

For use in industrial environments, circuitry such as that in Figure 10-7 is usually packaged in durable modules and mounted on racks in metal cabinets. Figure 10-8, p. 302, shows some of the Analog Devices 3B series signal-conditioning modules on a rack-mount panel. The 3B37, for example, is a thermo-couple-amplifier module with built-in cold-junction compensation. The silver probe in front of the unit is a common type of thermocouple. This rack unit is constructed so that you can plug in the modules you need for a given application. Modules such as these usually have both a voltage output and a current output. Sending a signal as a current has the advantage that the signal amplitude is then not affected by resistance, induced-voltage noise, or voltage drops in a long connecting line. A common range of currents used to represent analog signals in industrial environments is 4 mA to 20 mA. A current of 4 mA represents a zero output, and a current of 20 mA represents the full-scale value. The reason that the current range is offset from zero is so that a current of zero is left to represent an open circuit. The current can be converted to a proportional voltage at the receiving end by simply passing it through a resistor.

Force and Pressure Transducers

To convert force or pressure (force/area) to a proportional electrical signal, the most common methods are *strain gages* and *linear variable differential transformers* (LVDTs). Both these methods involve moving something. This is why we refer to them as *transducers* rather than as sensors. Here's how strain gages work.

STRAIN GAGES AND LOAD CELLS

A strain gage is a small resistor whose value changes when its length is changed. It may be made of thin wire, thin foil, or semiconductor material. Figure 10-9a, p. 303, shows a simple setup for measuring force or weight with strain gages. One end of a piece of spring steel is attached to a fixed surface. A strain gage is glued on the top of the flexible bar. The force or weight to be measured is applied to the unattached end of the bar. As the applied force bends the bar, the strain gage is stretched, increasing its resistance. Since the amount that the bar is bent is directly proportional to the applied force, the change in resistance will be proportional to the applied force. If a current is passed through the strain gage, then the change in voltage across the strain gage will be proportional to the applied force.

Unfortunately, the resistance of the strain-gage elements also changes with temperature. To compensate for this problem, two strain-gage elements mounted at right angles, as shown in Figure 10-9b, p. 303, are often used. Both the elements will change resistance with temperature, but only element A will change resistance appreciably with applied force. When these two elements are connected in a balanced-bridge configuration, as shown in Figure 10-9c, any change in resistance of the elements due to temperature will have no effect on the differential output of the bridge. However, as force is applied, the resistance of the element under strain will change and produce a small differential output voltage. The full-scale differential output voltage is typically 2 or 3 mV per volt of applied voltage. For example, if 10 V is applied to the bridge, the full-load-output voltage will only be 20 or 30 mV. This small signal can be amplified with a differential amplifier or an instrumentation amplifier. The Analog Devices 3B16 module shown in Figure 10-8 provides a 10-V excitation voltage and amplification for the differential output signal for a strain-gage bridge.

Strain-gage bridges are used in many different forms to measure many different types of force and pressure. If the strain-gage bridge is connected to a bendable beam structure, as shown in Figure 10-9a, the result —called a *load cell*—is used to measure weight. Figure 10-10, p. 303, shows a 10-lb load cell that might be used in a microprocessor-controlled delicatessen scale or postal scale. Larger versions can be used to weigh barrels being filled or even trucks.

If a strain-gage bridge is mounted on a movable diaphragm in a threaded housing, the output of the bridge will be proportional to the pressure applied to the diaphragm. If a vacuum is present on one side of the diaphragm, then the value read out will be a measure of the absolute pressure. If one side of the diaphragm is open, then the output will be a measure of the pressure relative to atmospheric pressure. If the two sides of the diaphragm are connected to two other pressure sources, then the output will be a measure of the differential pressure between the two sides. Figure 10-11, p. 303, shows a National LX1602D pressure transducer, which measures pressures in the range of 0 to 15 lb/in². A transducer such as this might be used to measure blood pressure in a microcomputer-based medical instrument.

LINEAR VARIABLE DIFFERENTIAL TRANSFORMERS (LVDTs)

An LVDT is another type of transducer often used to measure force pressure or position. Figure 10-12, p. 303, shows the basic structure of an LVDT. It consists of three coils of wire wound on the same form and a movable iron core. An ac excitation signal of perhaps 20 kHz is applied to the primary. The secondaries are connected so that the voltage induced in one opposes the voltage induced in the other. If the core is centered, then the induced voltages are equal and they cancel, so there is no net output voltage. If the coil is moved off center, coupling will be stronger to one secondary coil, so that coil will produce a greater output voltage. The result will be a net output voltage. The phase relationship between the output signal and the input signal is an indication of which direction the core moved from the center position. The amplitude of the output signal is linearly proportional to how far the core moves from the center position.

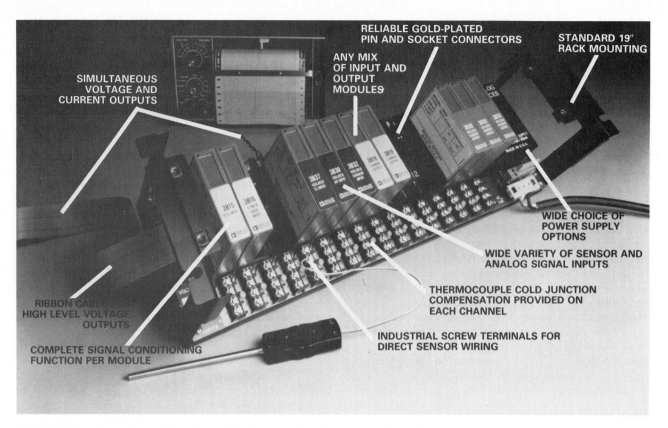

FIGURE 10-8   Packaging of signal-conditioning circuitry for use in industrial environments. (*Analog Devices Incorporated*)

An LVDT can be used directly in this form to measure displacement or position. If you add a spring so that a force is required to move the core, then the voltage out of the LVDT will be proportional to the force applied to the core. In this form the LVDT can be used in a load cell for an electronic scale. Likewise, if a spring is added and the core of the LVDT is attached to a diaphragm in a threaded housing, the output from the LVDT will be proportional to the pressure exerted on the diaphragm. We do not have space here to show the ac interface circuitry required for an LVDT.

Flow Sensors

If we are going to control the flow rate of some material in our electronics factory, we need to be able to measure it. Depending on the material, flow rate, and temperature, we use different methods.

One method used is to put a paddle wheel in the flow, as shown in Figure 10-13a, p. 304. The rate at which the paddle wheel turns is proportional to the rate of flow of a liquid or gas. An optical encoder can be attached to the shaft of the paddle wheel to produce digital information as to how fast the paddle wheel is turning.

A second common method of measuring flow is with a *differential-pressure transducer,* as shown in Figure 10-13b, p. 304. A wire mesh or screen is put in the pipe

to create some resistance. Flow through this resistance produces a difference in pressure between the two sides of the resistance. The pressure transducer gives an output proportional to the difference in pressure between the two sides of the resistance. In the same way that the voltage across an electrical resistor is proportional to the flow of current through the resistor, the output of the pressure transducer is proportional to the flow of a liquid or gas through the pipe.

Other Sensors

As we mentioned previously, the number of different types of sensors is very large. In addition to the types we have discussed, there are sensors to measure pH, concentration of various gases, thickness of materials, and just about any thing else you might want to measure. Often you can use commonly available transducers in creative ways to solve a particular application problem you have. Suppose, for example, that you need to determine accurately the level of a liquid in a large tank. To do this you could install a pressure transducer at the bottom of the tank. The pressure in a liquid is proportional to the height of the liquid in the tank, so you could easily convert a pressure reading to the desired liquid height. The point here is to check out what is available and then be creative.

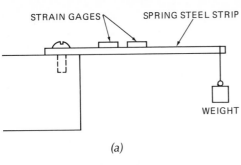

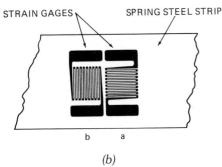

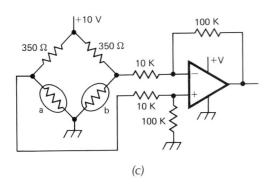

FIGURE 10-9   Strain gauges used to measure force. (a) Side view. (b) Top view (expanded). (c) Circuit connections.

FIGURE 10-10   Photograph of load-cell transducer used to measure weight. (*Transducers, Incorporated*)

FIGURE 10-11   National LX1602D pressure transducer. (*Sensym, Inc.*)

D/A CONVERTER OPERATION, INTERFACING, AND APPLICATIONS

In the previous sections of this chapter, we discussed how we use sensors to get electrical signals proportional to pressure, temperature, etc. and how we use op amps to amplify and filter these electrical signals. The next logical step would be to show you how we use an A/D converter to get these signals into digital form, with which a microcomputer can work. However, since D/A converters are simpler and several types of A/D converter have D/As as part of their circuitry, we discuss D/As first.

D/A CONVERTER OPERATION AND SPECIFICATIONS OPERATION

The purpose of a D/A converter is to convert a binary word to a proportional current or voltage. To see how this is done, let's look at the simple op-amp circuit in Figure 10-14, p. 304. This circuit functions as an adder. Since the noninverting input of the op amp is grounded, the op amp will work day and night to hold

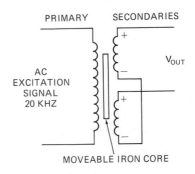

FIGURE 10-12   LVDT structure.

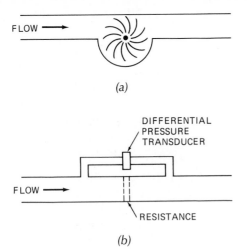

FIGURE 10-13   Flow sensors. (a) Paddle wheel. (b) Differential pressure.

the inverting input also at 0 V. This point, remember, is referred to as a virtual ground, or summing point. When one of the switches is closed, a current will flow from −5 V (V_{REF}) through that resistor to the summing point. The op amp will pull the current on through the feedback resistor to produce a proportional output voltage. If you close switch D0, for example, a current of 0.05 mA will flow into the summing point. In order to pull this current through the feedback resistor, the op amp must put a voltage of 0.05 mA × 10 kΩ, or 0.5 V, on its output. If you also close switch D1, it will send another 0.1 mA into the summing point. In order to pull the sum of the currents through the feedback resistor, the op amp has to output a voltage of 0.15 mA × 10 kΩ, or 1.5 V.

The point here is that the binary-weighted resistors produce-binary weighted currents, which are summed by the op amp to produce a proportional output voltage. The binary word applied to the switches produces a proportional output voltage. Technically, the output voltage is "digital" because it can have only certain fixed values, just as the display on a digital voltmeter can. However, the output simulates an analog signal, so we refer to it as analog. Switch D3 in Figure 10-14 represents the most significant bit, because closing it produces the largest current. Note that since V_{REF} is negative, the output will go positive as switches are closed.

As you see here, the heart of a D/A converter is a set of binary-weighted current sources, which can be switched on or off according to a binary word applied to the converter's inputs. Since these current sources are usually inside an IC, we don't need to discuss the different ways the binary-weighted currents can be produced. As shown in Figure 10-14, a simple op-amp circuit can be used to convert the sum of the currents to a proportional voltage if needed.

D/A CHARACTERISTICS AND SPECIFICATIONS

Figure 10-15 shows the circuit for an inexpensive, IC D/A converter with an op-amp circuit as a current-to-voltage converter. We will use this circuit for our discussion of D/A characteristics.

The first characteristic of a D/A converter is *resolution*, which is determined by the number of bits in the input binary word. A converter with eight binary inputs, such as the one in Figure 10-15, has 2^8, or 256, possible output levels, so its resolution is 1 part in 256. As another example, a 12-bit converter has a resolution of 1 part in 2^{12}, or 4096. Resolution is sometimes expressed as a percentage. The resolution of an 8-bit converter is about 0.39 percent.

The next D/A characteristic to determine is the *full-scale output voltage*. For the converter in Figure 10-15 the current for all the switches is supplied by V_{REF} through R14. The current output from pin 4 of the D/A is pulled through R0 to produce the output voltage. The formula for the output voltage is shown under the

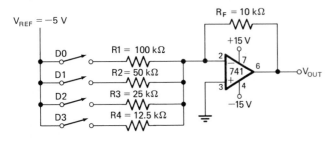

FIGURE 10-14   Simple 4-bit D/A converter.

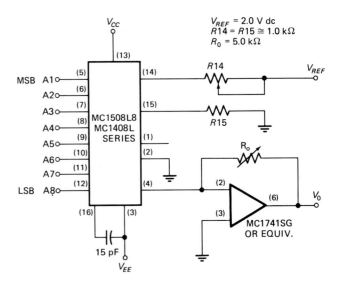

Theoretical V_0

$$V_0 = \frac{V_{REF}}{R14}(R_0)\left\{\frac{A1}{2} + \frac{A2}{4} + \frac{A3}{8} + \frac{A4}{16} + \frac{A5}{32} + \frac{A6}{64} + \frac{A7}{128} + \frac{A8}{256}\right\}$$

ADJUST V_{REF}, R14 OR R_0 SO THAT V_0 WITH ALL DIGITAL INPUTS AT HIGH LEVEL IS EQUAL TO 9.961 V

$$V_0 = \frac{2\,V}{1\,k\Omega}(5\,k\Omega)\left\{\frac{1}{2} + \frac{1}{4} + \frac{1}{8} + \frac{1}{16} + \frac{1}{32} + \frac{1}{64} + \frac{1}{128} + \frac{1}{256}\right\}$$

$$= 10\,V\left\{\frac{255}{256}\right\} = 9.961\,V$$

FIGURE 10-15   Motorola MC1408 8-bit D/A with current-to-voltage converter.

circuit in Figure 10-15. In the equation the term A1, for example, represents the condition of the switch for that bit. If a switch is closed, allowing a current to flow, put a 1 in that bit. If a switch is open, put a 0 in that bit. As we also show in Figure 10-15, if all the switches are closed, the output will be (10 V)(255/256), or 9.961 V. Even though the output voltage can never actually get to 10 V, this is referred to as a 10-V *output converter*. The maximum output voltage of a converter will always be the value of one significant bit less than the named value. As another example of this, suppose that we have a 12-bit, 10-V converter. The value of one LSB will be (10 V)/4096, or 2.44 mV. The highest voltage out of this converter when it is properly adjusted will then be (10.0000 − 0.0024) V, or 9.9976 V.

Several different binary codes, such as *straight binary*, BCD and *offset binary*, are commonly used as inputs to D/A converters. We show examples of these codes in a later discussion of A/D converters.

The accuracy specification for a D/A converter is a comparison between the actual output and the expected output. It is specified as a percentage of the full-scale output voltage or current. If a converter has a full-scale output of 10 V and [+/-]0.2 percent accuracy, then the *maximum error* for any output will be 0.002 × 10.00 V, or 20 mV. Ideally, the maximum error for a D/A converter should be no more than $\pm\frac{1}{2}$ of the value of the LSB.

Another important specification for a D/A converter is *linearity*. Linearity is a measure of how much the output ramp deviates from a straight line as the converter is stepped from no switches on to all switches on. Ideally, the deviation of the output from a straight line should be no greater than $\pm\frac{1}{2}$ of the value of the LSB to maintain overall accuracy. However, many D/A converters are marketed that have linearity errors greater than that. National Semiconductor, for example, markets the DAC1020, DAC1021, DAC1022 series of 10-bit resolution converters. The linearity specification for the DAC1020 is 0.05 percent, which is appropriate for a 10-bit converter. The DAC1021 has a linearity specification of 0.10% and the DAC1022 has a specification of 0.20%. The question that may occur to you at this point is, What good is it to have a 10-bit converter if the linearity is equivalent only to that of an 8- or 9-bit converter? The answer to this question is that for many applications, the resolution given by a 10-bit converter is needed for small-output signals, but it doesn't matter if the output value is somewhat nonlinear for large signals. The price you pay for a D/A converter is proportional not only to its resolution, but also to its linearity specification.

Still another D/A specification to look for is *settling time*. When you change the binary word applied to the input of a converter, the output will change to the appropriate new value. The output, however, may overshoot the correct value and "ring" for a while before finally settling down to the correct value. The time the output takes to get within $\pm\frac{1}{2}$ LSB of the final value is called settling time. As an example, the National DAC1020 10-bit converter has a typical settling time of 500 ns for a full-scale change on the output. This

specification is important, because if a converter is operated at too high a frequency, it may not have time to settle to one value before it is switched to the next.

D/A Applications and Interfacing to Microcomputers

D/A converters have many applications besides those where they are used with a microcomputer. In a compact-disk audio player, for example, a 13- or 14-bit D/A converter is used to convert the binary data read off the disk by a laser to an analog audio signal. Most speech-synthesizer ICs contain a D/A converter to convert stored binary data for words into analog audio signals. Here, however, we are primarily interested in the use of a D/A converter with a microcomputer.

The inputs of the D/A circuit (A1–A8) in Figure 10-15 can be connected directly to a microcomputer output port. As part of a program, you can produce any desired voltage on the output of the D/A. Here are some ideas as to what you might use this circuit for.

As a first example, suppose that you want to build a microcomputer-controlled tester that determines the effect of power supply voltage on the output voltage of some IC amplifiers. If you connect the output of the D/A converter to the reference input of a programmable power supply or simply add the high-current buffer circuit shown in Figure 10-16 to the output of the D/A, you have a power supply that you can vary under program control. To determine the output voltage of the IC under test as you vary its supply voltage, connect the input of an A/D converter to the IC output, and connect the output of the A/D converter to an input port of your microcomputer. You can then read in the value of the output voltage on the IC.

Another application for which you might use a D/A and a power buffer is to vary the voltage supplied to a small resistive heater under program control. Also, the speed of small dc motors is proportional to the amount of current passed through them, so you could connect a small dc motor on the output of the power buffer and control the speed of the motor by the value you output to the D/A. Note that without feedback control, the

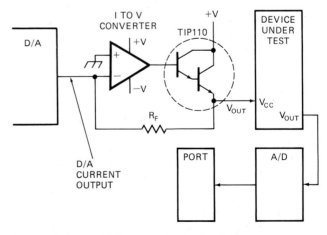

FIGURE 10-16   High-power buffer for D/A output.

speed of the motor will vary if the load changes. Later we show you how to add feedback control to maintain constant motor speed under changing loads.

So far we have talked about using an 8-bit D/A with a microprocessor. Interfacing an 8-bit converter involves simply connecting the inputs of the converter to an output port; for some D/As, it means simply connecting it to the buses, as you would a port device. Now, suppose that for some application you need 12 bits of resolution, so you need to interface a 12-bit converter. If you are working with a system that has an 8-bit data bus, your first thought might be to connect the lower 8 inputs of the 12-bit converter to one output port and the upper 4 inputs to another port. You could send the lower 8 bits with one write operation and the upper 4 bits with another write operation. However, there is a potential problem with this approach that is caused by the time between the two writes. Suppose, for example, that you want to change the output of a 12-bit converter from 0000 1111 1111 to 0001 0000 0000. When you write the lower 8 bits, the output will go from 0000 1111 1111 to 0000 0000 0000. When you write the upper 4 bits, the output will then go back up to the desired 0001 0000 0000. The point here is that for the time between the two writes, the output will go to an unwanted value. In many systems this could be disastrous. The cure for this problem is to put latches on the input lines. The latches can be loaded separately and then strobed together to pass all 12 bits to the D/A converter at the same time.

Many currently available D/A converters contain built-in latches to make this easier. Figure 10-17a shows a block diagram of the National DAC1230- and DAC1208-type 12-bit converters. Note the internal latches and the register. The DAC1230 series of parts has the upper 4 input bits connected to the lower 4 bits so that the 12 bits can be written with two write operations from an 8-bit port or data bus, such as that of the 68008 microprocessor. The DAC1208 series of parts has the upper 4 data inputs available separately so they can be connected directly to the bus in a system that has a 16-bit data bus, as shown in Figure 10-17a. If, for example, you want to connect up a DAC1208 converter to an URDA® MDS board, you can simply connect the DAC1208 data inputs to the lower 12 data bus lines, connect the $\overline{CS}$ input to an address decoder output, connect the $\overline{WR1}$ input to the system RD/$\overline{WR}$ line, and tie the $\overline{WR2}$ and $\overline{XFER}$ inputs to ground. The BYTE1/$\overline{BYTE2}$ input is tied high. You then write words to the converter just as if it were a 16-bit port. The timing parameters for the DAC1208 are acceptable for a 68000 operating with a clock frequency of 4 MHz or less. For higher 68000 clock frequencies, you would have to add a one-shot or other circuitry that inserts a wait state each time you write to the D/A. Here are a few notes about the analog connections for these devices.

These D/A converters require a precision voltage reference. The circuit in Figure 10-17b uses a −10.000-V reference. The D/A converters have a current output, so we use an op amp, as shown, to convert

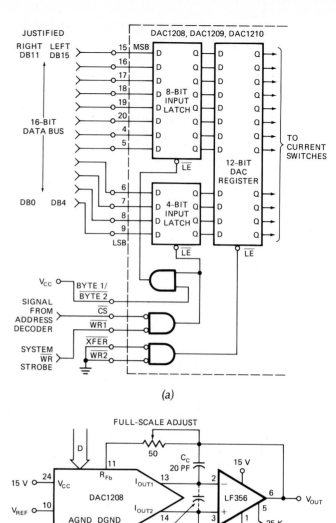

$$V_{OUT} = -(I_{OUT1} \times R_{Fb}) = \frac{-V_{REF}(D)}{4096} \text{ FOR } 0 \leqslant D \leqslant 4095$$

(b)

FIGURE 10-17   (a) National DAC1208 12-bit D/A input block diagram showing internal latches. (b) Analog circuit connections.

the output current to a proportional voltage. An FET-input amplifier is used, because the input-bias current of a bipolar input amp might affect the accuracy of the output. The DAC1208 and DAC1230 have built-in feedback resistors, which match the temperature characteristics of the internal current-divider resistors, so all you have to add externally is a 50-Ω resistor for "tweaking" purposes. With a −10.000-V reference, as shown, the output voltage will be equal to (the digital-input word/4096) × (+10.000 V). Note that the D/A has both a digital ground and an analog ground. To avoid getting digital noise in the analog portions of the circuit, these two should be connected together only at the power supply.

A/D CONVERTER TYPES, SPECIFICATIONS, AND INTERFACING

A/D Converter Types

The function of an A/D converter is to produce a digital word that represents the magnitude of some analog voltage or current. The specifications for an A/D converter are very similar to those for a D/A converter. The resolution of an A/D converter refers to the number of bits in the output binary word, so an 8-bit converter has a resolution of 1 part in 256. Accuracy and linearity specifications have the same meanings for an A/D converter as we described previously for a D/A converter. Another important specification for an A/D converter is its *conversion time*. This is simply the time it takes the converter to produce a valid output binary code for an applied input voltage. When we refer to a converter as *high speed*, we mean it has a short conversion time. There are many different ways to do an A/D conversion, but we have space here to review only three commonly used methods, which represent a wide variety of conversion times.

PARALLEL COMPARATOR A/D CONVERTER

Figure 10-18 shows a circuit for a 2-bit A/D converter using *parallel comparators*. A voltage divider sets reference voltages on the inverting inputs of each of the comparators. The voltage at the top of the divider chain represents the full-scale value for the converter. The voltage to be converted is applied to the noninverting inputs of all the comparators in parallel. If the input voltage on a comparator is greater than the reference voltage on the inverting input, the output of the comparator will go high. The outputs of the comparators then give us a digital representation of the voltage level of the input signal. With an input voltage

of 2.6 V, for example, the outputs of comparators A1 and A2 will be high.

The major advantage of a parallel, or *flash*, A/D is its speed of conversion, which is simply the propagation delay time of the comparators. The output code from the comparators is not a standard binary code, but it can be converted with some simple logic. The major disadvantage of a flash A/D is the number of comparators needed to produce a result with a reasonable amount of resolution. The 2-bit converter in Figure 10-18 requires three comparators. To produce a converter with N bits of resolution, you need $2^N - 1$ comparators. In other words for an 8-bit conversion, you need 255 comparators, and for a 10-bit flash converter, you need 1023 comparators. Single-package flash converters are available from TRW for applications where the high speed is required, but they are relatively expensive. Devices are available that can do an 8-bit conversion in 20 nS.

DUAL-SLOPE A/D CONVERTERS

Figure 10-19a, p. 308, shows a functional block diagram of a *dual-slope* A/D converter. This type of converter is often used as the heart of a digital voltmeter because it can give a large number of bits of resolution at a low cost. Here's how the converter in Figure 10-19 works.

To start, the control circuitry resets all the counters to zero and connects the input of the integrator to the input voltage to be converted. If you assume the input voltage is positive, then this will cause the output of the integrator to ramp negative, as shown in Figure 10-19b, p. 308. As soon as the output of the integrator goes a few microvolts below ground, the comparator output will go high. The comparator output being high enables the AND gate and lets the 1-MHz clock into the counter chain. After some fixed number of counts, the control circuitry switches the input of the integrator to a negative reference voltage and resets all the counters to zero. With a negative input voltage the integrator output will ramp positive, as shown in Figure 10-19b. When the integrator output crosses 0 V, the comparator output will drop low and shut off the clock signal to the counters. The number of counts required for the integrator output to get back to zero is directly proportional to the input voltage. For the circuit shown in Figure 10-19a, an input signal of +1 V, for example, produces a count of 1000 counts. Because the resistor and the capacitor on the integrator are used for both the input voltage integrate and the reference integrate, small variations in their values with temperature do not have any effect on the accuracy of the conversion.

Complete slope-type A/D converters are readily available in single IC packages. One example is the Intersil ICL7136, which contains all of the circuitry for a $3\frac{1}{2}$-digit A/D converter and all of the interface circuitry needed to drive a $3\frac{1}{2}$-digit LCD display. Another example is the Intersil ICL7135, which contains all of the circuitry for a $4\frac{1}{2}$-digit A/D converter and has a multiplexed BCD output. Note that because of the usual use of this type of converter, we often express its

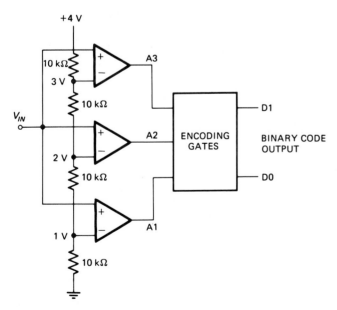

FIGURE 10-18   Parallel comparator A/D converter.

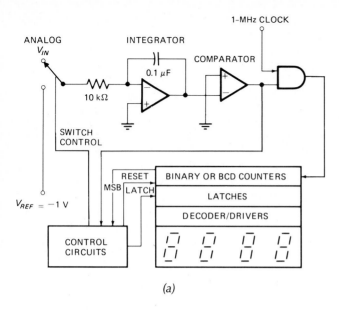

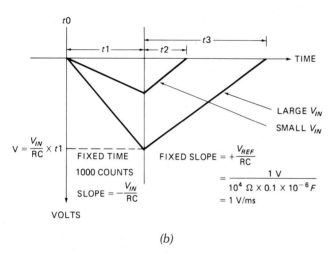

(a)

(b)

FIGURE 10-19   Dual-slope A/D converter. (a) Circuit. (b) Integrator output waveform.

resolution in terms of a number of digits. The full-scale reading for a $3\frac{1}{2}$-digit converter is 1999, so the resolution corresponds to about 1 part in 2000. A two-chip set, the Intersil ICL8068 and ICL7104-16, contains all the circuitry for a slope-type 16-bit binary-output A/D converter.

The main disadvantage of slope-type converters is their slow speed. A $4\frac{1}{2}$-digit unit may take 300 ms to do a conversion.

SUCCESSIVE-APPROXIMATION A/D CONVERTERS

Figure 10-20 shows a circuit for an 8-bit *successive-approximation* converter that uses readily available parts. The heart of this converter is a successive-approximation register (SAR) such as the MC14549, which functions as follows.

On the first clock pulse at the start of a conversion cycle, the SAR outputs a high on its MSB to the MC1408 D/A converter. The D/A converter and the

amplifier convert this to a voltage and apply it to one input of a comparator. If this voltage is higher than the input voltage on the other input of the comparator, the comparator output will go low and tell the SAR to turn off that bit because it is too large. If the voltage from the D/A converter is less than the input voltage, then the comparator output will be high, which tells the SAR to keep that bit on. When the next clock pulse occurs, the SAR will turn on the next most significant bit to the D/A converter. Based on the answer this produces from the comparator, the SAR will keep or reset this bit. The SAR proceeds in this way on down to the LSB, adding each bit to the total in turn and using the signal from the comparator to decide whether to keep that bit in the result. Only eight clock pulses are needed to do the actual conversion here. When the conversion is complete, the binary result is on the parallel outputs of the SAR. The SAR sends out an end-of-conversion (EOC) signal to indicate this. In the circuit in Figure 10-20, the EOC signal is used to strobe the binary result into some latches, where it can be read by a microcomputer. If the EOC signal is connected to the start-conversion (SC) input as shown, then the converter will do continuous conversions. Note in the circuit in Figure 10-20 that the noninverting input of the op amp on the 1408 D/A converter is connected to -5 V instead of to ground. This shifts the analog input range from -5 V to +5 V instead of 0 V to +10 V, so that sine-wave and other ac signals can be input directly to the converter to be digitized.

The National ADC1280 is a single-chip 12-bit successive-approximation converter, which does a conversion in about 22 μs. Datel and Analog Devices have several 12-bit converters with conversion times of about 1 μs.

Several commonly available successive-approximation A/D converters have analog multiplexers on their inputs. The National ADC0816, for example, has a 16-input multiplexer. This allows one converter to digitize any one of 16 input signals. You specify the input channel you want to digitize with a 4-bit address you apply to the address inputs of the device. An A/D converter with a multiplexer on its inputs is often called a *data acquisition system*, or DAS. Later in this chapter we show an application of a DAS in a factory control system.

Before we go on to discuss A/D interfacing, we need to make a few comments about common A/D output codes.

A/D OUTPUT CODES

For convenience in different applications, A/D converters are available with several different, somewhat confusing output codes. The best way to make sense out of these different codes is to see them all together with representative values, as shown in Figure 10-21, p. 310. The values shown here are for an 8-bit converter, but you can extend them to any number of bits.

For an A/D converter with only a positive input range (*unipolar*), a straight binary code or inverted binary code is usually used. If the output of an A/D

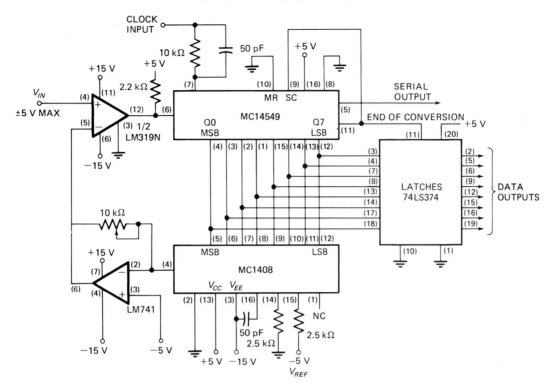

FIGURE 10-20   Successive-approximation A/D converter circuit.

converter is going to drive a display, then it is convenient to have the output coded in BCD. For applications where the input range of the converter has both a negative and a positive range (*bipolar*), we usually use offset binary coding. As you can see in Figure 10-21 the values of 0000 0000 to 1111 1111 are simply shifted downward so that 0000 0000 represents the most negative input value and 1000 0000 represents an input value of zero. This coding scheme has the advantage that the 2's complement representation can be produced by simply inverting the most significant bit. Some bipolar converters output the digital value directly in 2's complement form.

Interfacing Different Types of A/D Converters to Microcomputers

INTERFACING TO PARALLEL COMPARATOR A/D CONVERTERS

In any application where a parallel comparator converter is used, the converter is most likely going to be producing digital output values much faster than a microcomputer could possibly read them in. Therefore, separate circuitry is used to bypass the microprocessor and load a set of samples from the converter directly into a series of memory locations. The microprocessor can later perform the desired operation on the samples. Bypassing the microprocessor in this way is called *direct memory access*, or DMA. The basic principle of DMA is that an external controller IC tells the microprocessor to float its buses. When the microprocessor does this, the DMA controller takes control

of the buses and allows data to be transferred directly from the A/D converter to successive memory locations. We discuss DMA in detail in the next chapter.

INTERFACING TO SLOPE-TYPE A/D CONVERTERS

Most of the commonly available slope-type converters were designed to drive seven-segment displays in, for example, a digital voltmeter. Therefore, they usually output data in a multiplexed BCD or seven-segment form. Figure 10-22 shows how you can connect the multiplexed BCD outputs of an inexpensive $3\frac{1}{2}$-digit slope converter, the MC14433, to a microprocessor port. In the section of the chapter where Figure 10-22 is located, we use this converter as part of a microcomputer-based scale. The BCD data is output from the converter on lines Q0–Q3. A logic high is output on one of the digit strobe lines, DS1–DS4, to indicate when the BCD code for the corresponding digit is on the Q outputs. The MC14433 converter shown in Figure 10-23 outputs the BCD code for the most significant digit and then outputs the BCD code for the most significant digit and then outputs a high on the DS1 pin. After a period of time it outputs the BCD code for the next most significant digit and outputs a high on the DS2 pin. After all 4 digits have been put out, the cycle repeats.

To read in the data from this converter, the principle is simply to poll the bit corresponding to a strobe line until you find it high, read in the data for that digit, and put the data in a reserved memory location for future reference. After you have read the BCD code for one digit, you poll the bit that corresponds to the strobe line

VALUE	10 VOLTS FULL SCALE	BINARY (BIN)	COMPLEMENTARY BINARY (CB)	INVERTED BINARY (IB)	INVERTED COMPLEMENTARY BINARY (ICB)
+FS −1 LSB	9.9609	1111 1111	0000 0000		
+½ FS	5.0000	1000 0000	0111 1111		
+½FS −1 LSB	4.9609	0111 1111	1000 0000		
+1 LSB	0.0391	0000 0001	1111 1110		
ZERO	0.0000	0000 0000	1111 1111	0000 0000	1111 1111
−1 LSB	−0.0391			0000 0001	1111 1110
−½ FS + 1 LSB	−4.9609			0111 1111	1000 0000
−½ FS	−5.0000			1000 0000	0111 1111
− FS + 1 LSB	−9.9609			1111 1111	0000 0000

UNIPOLAR BINARY CODED DECIMAL CODES

VALUE	10 VOLTS FULL SCALE	BINARY CODED DECIMAL (BCD)	COMPLEMENTARY BINARY CODED DECIMAL (CBCD)	INVERTED BINARY CODED DECIMAL (IBCD)	INVERTED COMPLEMENTARY BINARY CODED DECIMAL (ICBCD)
+ FS −1 LSB	9.9	1001 1001	0110 0110		
+½ FS	5.0	0101 0000	1010 1111		
+1 LSB	0.1	0000 0001	1111 1110		
ZERO	0.0	0000 0000	1111 1111	0000 0000	1111 1111
−1 LSB	−0.1			0000 0001	1111 1110
−½ FS	−5.0			0101 0000	1010 1111
−FS +1 LSB	−9.9			1001 1001	0110 0110

BIPOLAR BINARY CODES

VALUE	10 VOLTS FULL SCALE RANGE	OFFSET BINARY (OB)	COMPLEMENTARY OFFSET BINARY (COB)	TWO'S COMPLEMENT (TC)
+FS	5.0000			
+FS −1 LSB	4.9609	1111 1111	0000 0000	0111 1111
+1 LSB	0.0391	1000 0001	0111 1110	0000 0001
ZERO	0.0000	1000 0000	0111 1111	0000 0000
−1 LSB	−0.0391	0111 1111	1000 0000	1111 1111
−FS +1 LSB	−4.9609	0000 0001	1111 1110	1000 0001
−FS	−5.0000	0000 0000	1111 1111	1000 0000

FIGURE 10-21   Common A/D output codes.

for the next digit until you find it high, read the code for that digit, and put it in memory. Repeat the process until you have the data for all the digits. The A/D converter in Figure 10-23 is connected to do continuous conversions, so you can call the procedure to read in the value from the A/D converter at any time.

Frequency counters, digital voltmeters, and other test instruments often have multiplexed BCD outputs available on their back panels. With the connections and procedure we have just described, you can use these instruments to input data to your microcomputer.

INTERFACING A SUCCESSIVE-APPROXIMATION A/D CONVERTER

Successive-approximation A/D converters usually have outputs for each bit. The code output on these lines is usually straight binary or offset binary. You can simply connect the parallel outputs of the converter to the required number of input port pins and read the converter output in under program control. In addition to the data lines, there are two other successive-approximation A/D converter signal lines you need to interface to the microcomputer for the data transfer. The first of these is a START CONVERT signal, which you output from the microcomputer to the A/D to tell it to do a conversion for you. The second signal is a STATUS signal, which the A/D converter outputs to indicate that the conversion is complete and that the word on the outputs is valid. Here are the program steps you use to get a data sample from the converter.

First you pulse the START CONVERT high for a minimum of 100 ns. You then detect the STROBE signal going low on a polled or interrupt basis. Next, you read in the digitized value from the parallel outputs of the converter. In a later section of this chapter we show a detailed example of this for the ADC0808 converter.

If you are working with a personal computer such as the IBM PC, there are available a wide variety of multichannel A/D and D/A converter boards that plug directly into the bus connectors of these machines.

A MICROCOMPUTER-BASED SCALE

So far in this book we have shown you how a lot of the pieces of a microcomputer system function. Now it's time to show you how some of these pieces are put together to make a microcomputer-based instrument. The first instrument we have chosen is a "smart" scale such as you might see at the checkout stand in your local grocery store.

Overview of Smart-Scale Operation

Figure 10-22 shows a block diagram of our smart scale. A load cell converts the applied weight of, for example, a bunch of carrots, to a proportional electrical signal. This small signal is amplified and converted to a digital value, which can be read in by the microprocessor and sent to the attached display. The user then enters the price per pound with the keyboard and this price per pound is shown on the display. When the user presses the compute key on the keyboard, the microprocessor multiplies the weight times the price per pound and shows the result on the display. After holding the price display long enough for the user to read it, the scale goes back to reading in the weight value and displaying it. To save the user from having to type the computed price into the cash register, an output from the scale could be connected directly into the cash register circuitry. A speech synthesizer, such as the Votrax SC-01A we described in Chapter 9, could be attached to tell the customer the weight, price per pound, and total price.

Smart scales such as this have many applications other than weighing carrots. A modified version of this scale is used in company mail rooms to weigh packages and calculate the postage required to send them to different postal zones. The output of the scale can be connected to a postage meter, which then automatically prints out the required postage sticker. Another application of smart scales is to count coins in a bank or gambling casino. For this application the user simply enters the type of coin being weighed. A conversion

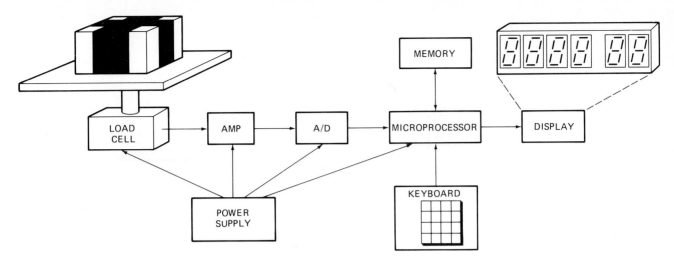

FIGURE 10-22   Block diagram of microcomputer-based smart scale.

factor in the program then computes the total number of coins and the total dollar amount. Still another application of a scale such as this is in packaging items for sale. Suppose, for example, that we are manufacturing wood screws and that we want to package 100 of them per box. We can pass the boxes over the load cell on a conveyer belt and fill them from a chute until the weight—and therefore the count—reaches some entered value. The point here is that the combination of intelligence and some simple interface circuitry gives you an instrument with as many uses as you can imagine.

Smart-Scale Input Circuitry

Figure 10-10 shows a picture of the Transducers, Inc. Model C462-10#-10P1 strain-gage load cell we used when we built this scale. We added a piece of plywood to the top of the load cell to keep the carrots from falling off. This load cell has an accuracy of about 1 part in 1000, or 0.01 lb over the 0- to 10-lb range for which it was designed.

As shown in Figure 10-23, p. 312, the load cell consists of four 350-Ω resistors connected in a bridge configuration. A stable 10.00-V excitation voltage is applied to the top of the bridge. With no load on the cell, the outputs from the bridge are at about the same voltage, 5 V. When a load is applied to the bridge, the resistance of one of the lower resistors will be changed. This produces a small differential output voltage from the bridge. The maximum differential output voltage for this 10-lb load cell is 2 mV per volt of excitation. With a 10.00-V excitation, as shown, the maximum differential-output voltage is then 20 mV.

To amplify this small differential signal, we use a National LM363 instrumentation amplifier. This device contains all the circuitry shown for the instrumentation amplifier in Figure 10-1h. The closed-loop gain of the amplifier is programmable for fixed values of 5, 100, and 500 with jumpers on pins 2, 3, and 4. We have jumpered it for a gain of 100 so that the 20-mV

maximum signal from the load cell will give a maximum voltage of 2.00 V to the A/D converter input. A precision voltage divider on the output of the amplifier divides this signal in half so that a weight of 10.00 lb produces an output voltage of 1.000 V. This scaling simplifies the display of the weight after it is read into the microprocessor. The 0.1-μF capacitor between pins 15 and 16 of the amplifier reduces the bandwidth of the amplifier to about 7.5 Hz. This removes 60 Hz and any high-frequency noise that might have been induced in the signal lines.

The MC14433 A/D converter used here is an inexpensive dual-slope device intended for use in $3\frac{1}{2}$-digit digital voltmeters, etc. Because the load cell changes slowly, a fast converter isn't needed here. The voltage across an LM329, 6.9-V precision reference diode is amplified by IC4 to produce the 10.00-V excitation voltage for the load cell and a 2.000-V reference for the A/D. With a 2.000-V reference voltage, the full-scale input voltage for the A/D is 2.000 V. Conversion rate and multiplexing frequency for the converter are determined by an internal oscillator and R11. An R11 of 300 kΩ gives a clock frequency of 66 kHz, a multiplex frequency of 0.8 kHz, and about four conversions per second. Accuracy of the converter is ±0.05% and ±1 count, which is comparable to the accuracy of the load cell. In other words, the last digit of the displayed weight may be off by 1 or 2 counts. As we described in a previous section, the output from this converter is in multiplexed BCD form.

An Algorithm for the Smart Scale

Figure 10-24, p. 312, shows the flowchart for our smart scale. Note that, as indicated by the double-ended boxes in the flowchart, most major parts of the program are written as procedures. The output of the A/D is in multiplexed BCD form, as we described in the section on slope-converter interfacing. Therefore, each strobe has to be polled until it goes high, and then the BCD code for that digit can be read in.

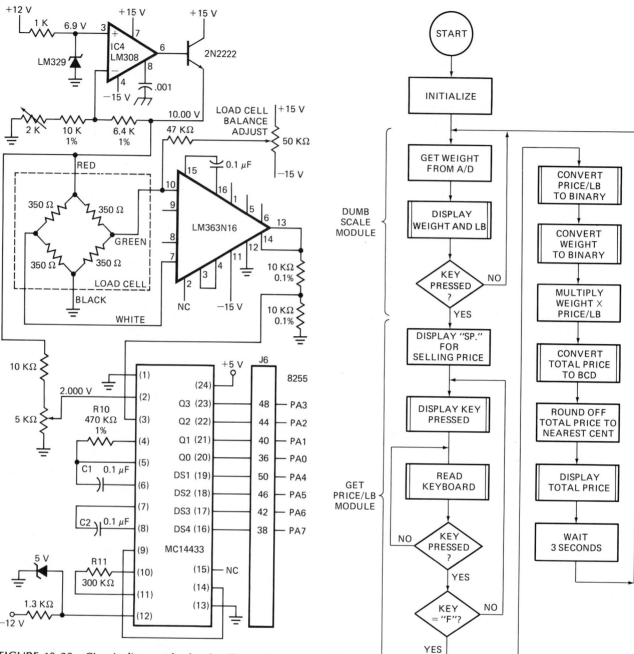

FIGURE 10-23 Circuit diagram for load-cell interface circuitry and A/D converter for smart scale.

FIGURE 10-24 Flowchart for a smart-scale program.

The BCD values read in from the converter are stored in four memory locations. A display procedure accesses these values and sends them to the address field display of the URDA MDS. The letters LB are displayed in the data field. After the weight is displayed, a check is made to see if any keys have been pressed by the user. If a key has been pressed, the letters SP, which represent selling price, are displayed in the address field. Keycodes are read from the 8279 as entered and displayed on the data field display. Keys can be pressed until the desired price per pound shows on the display. The price per pound entered by a user is assembled in a series of memory locations. When a nonnumeric key

is pressed, it is assumed that the entered price per pound is correct, and the program goes on to compute the total price.

Computing the price involves multiplying the weight in BCD form times the price per pound in BCD form. It is not easy to do a BCD × BCD multiply directly, so we took an alternate route to get there. Both the weight and the price per pound are converted to binary. The two binary numbers are then multiplied. The binary result of the multiplication is converted to BCD, rounded to the nearest cent, and displayed in the data field. The letters PR are displayed in the address field. After a few seconds the program goes back to reading and displaying weight over and over, until a key is pressed.

The Microprocessor-based Scale Program

Figure 10–25, pp. 314-20, shows the complete program for our microprocessor-based scale. It is important for you not to be overwhelmed by a multipage program such as this. If you use the 5-minute rule and work your way through this program one module at a time, you should pick up some more useful programming techniques and subroutines for your toolbox.

Three 4-byte buffers set up at the start of the program are used to store the unpacked BCD values of the weight, the price per pound, and the computed total price. These values will be used by the display procedure. Instead of using the display procedure we showed you in Figure 9-33, we used a more versatile procedure here that can display a few letters as well as hex digits. The SEVEN_SEG table in the data segment contains the seven-segment codes for hex digits and these letters. In the display procedure, you will see how these codes are accessed. After initializing everything the program polls the digit strobe for the MSD from the A/D converter. Since this A/D converter is a $3\frac{1}{2}$-digit unit, the MSD can be only a 0 or a 1. The value for this digit is sent in the third bit (bit 2) of the 4-bit digit read in. If this bit is a 1, then 01 is loaded into the buffer location. If the bit is a 0, then the value that will access the seven-segment code for a blank (14H) is loaded into the buffer location. Each of the other digit strobes is then polled in turn, and the values for those digits are read in. When all the BCD digits for the weight are in the WEIGHT_BUFFER, the display procedure is called to show the weight on the address field.

To use this display subroutine, you first load a 0 or a 1 into D0 to specify data field or address field and a 1 or a 0 in D1 to specify a decimal point in the middle of the display, or no decimal point. You then load A1 with the offset of a buffer containing codes for the digits to be displayed. A program loop in the display subroutine uses the MOVE with offset instruction and the SEVEN_SEG table to convert these codes to the required seven-segment values and send the values to the 8279 display RAM. Note how a 1 is ORed into the seven-segment code for digit 3 when a 1 is put in D1 before the JSR. For displaying the weight, A1 is simply loaded with the offset of WEIGHT_BUFFER, D0 is loaded with 01 to display the weight in the address field, and D1 loaded with 01 to insert a decimal point at the appropriate place.

To display the letters LB in the data field, A1 is loaded with the offset of the string named LB, and the display subroutine is called. Again, the MOVE with offset instruction loop converts the codes from the LB string to the required seven-segment codes and sends them out to the 8279 display RAM. The codes in the string named LB represent the offsets from the start of the SEVEN_SEG table for the desired seven-segment codes. For example, the seven-segment code for a P is at offset $12 in the SEVEN_SEG table. Therefore, if you want to display a P, you put $12 in the appropriate location in the character string in memory. The MOVE instruction will then use the value $12 to access the seven-segment code for P in the SEVEN_SEG table.

After displaying the weight, the program reads the 8279 status register to see if the operator has pressed a key to start entering a price per pound. If no key has been pressed or if a nonnumeric key has been pressed, the program simply goes back and reads the weight again. If a number key has been pressed, the weight is removed from the address field and the letters SP are displayed there. The number entered is put in the SELL_PRICE buffer and displayed on the rightmost digit of the data field. The program then polls the 8279 status register until another keypress is detected. If the pressed key is a numeric key, then the code(s) for the previously entered number(s) will be shifted one location in the buffer to make room for the new number. The new number is then put in the first location in the buffer so that it will be displayed in the rightmost digit of the display. In other words, previously entered numbers are continuously shifted to the left as new numbers are entered. If a mistake is made, the operator can simply enter a 0 followed by the correct price per pound.

If the pressed key is not a numeric key, then this is the signal that the displayed price per pound is correct and that the total price should now be computed. Before the weight and the price per pound can be multiplied, they must each be put in packed BCD form and converted to binary. The PACK subroutine converts four unpacked BCD digits in a memory buffer pointed to by A0 to a 4-digit packed result in D0. This subroutine simply involves some masking and moving nibbles. Conversion of the packed weight and the packed price per pound is done by the CONVERT2BIN subroutine. The algorithm for this subroutine is explained in detail in Chapter 5.

For the 68000 a single MULU instruction does the 16 × 16 binary multiply to produce the total price. Earlier processors required a messy subroutine to do this. After the multiplication, the total price is in binary form, which is not the form needed for the display subroutine. The subroutine BINCVT is used to convert the binary total price to packed BCD form. Here's how this procedure works.

In a binary number, each bit position represents a power of 2. An 8-bit binary number, for example, can be represented as

$$b7 \times 2^7 + b6 \times 2^6 + b5 \times 2^5 + b4 \times 2^4 + b3 \times 2^3 + b2 \times 2^2 + b1 \times 2^1 + b0$$

This can be shuffled around and expressed as

$$\text{binary number} = (((((2b7 + b6)\,2 + b5)\,2 + b4)\,2 + b3)\,2 + b2)\,2 + b1)\,2 + b0$$

where b7 through b0 are the values of the binary bits. If we start with a binary number and do each operation in the nested parentheses in BCD with the aid of a decimal-adjust operation, the result will be the BCD number equivalent to the original binary number.

```
; 68000 PROGRAM FOR SMART SCALE
;
; PORTS:        Uses input port upper 6821 Port B - control - $C016
;                                              data    - $C014
;               8279 Port at - control - $BF10
;                              data     - $BF09
; SUBROUTINES: READ_KEY, PACK, EXPAND, CONVERT2BIN, BINCVT

; First, the data:
;               ORG      $4300           ; for the Consulair Cross-assembler

STACK_HERE:     DS.W     200             ; reserve 200 words for the stack
STACK_TOP:      DS.W     0               ; stack top is high address
WEIGHT_BUFFER:  DS.B     4               ; Space for unpacked BCD weight
SELL_PRICE:     DS.B     4               ; Space for unpacked price/pound
PRICE_TOTAL:    DS.B     4               ; Space for total price to display
BINARY_WIEGHT:  DC.W     0               ; Space for converted wieght
LB:             DC.B     $0B,$10,$14,$14 ; b, L, blank, blank
S_P:            DC.B     $12,$11,$14,$14 ; P, S, blank, blank
PR:             DC.B     $13,$12,$14,$14 ; r, P, blank, blank

SEVEN_SEG:      DC.B     $3F, $06, $5B, $4F, $66, $6D, $7D, $07
;                         0    1    2    3    4    5    6    7
                DC.B     $7F, $6F, $77, $7C, $39, $5E, $79, $71
;                         8    9    A    b    C    d    E    F
                DC.B     $38, $6D, $73, $50, $00, $76
;                         L    S    P    r  blank  H
;----------------------------------------------------
; start code
;               ORG      $4000           ; for the Consulair Cross-assembler
START:  LEA     STACK_TOP,A7             ; initialize user stack pointer

; Iinitialize 8279
        LEA     $BF10,A1                 ; point to 8279 control address
        MOVE.B  #$00,(A1)                ; configure 8279 for 8 character display
                                         ;    left entry encoded scan, 2-key lockout
        MOVE.B  #$38,(A1)                ;    clock word for divide by 24
        MOVE.B  #$C0,(A1)                ;    clear display character is all 0's

; Initialize upper 6821 port B for output
        MOVE.B  #$00,(#$C016)            ; write to cntl reg to addr direction reg
        MOVE.B  #$FF,(#$C014)            ; all bits input from D/A
        MOVE.B  #$04,(#$C016)            ; address data register

; Dumb scale start
RDWT:   CLR.L   (#WEIGHT_BUFFER)         ; zero out wieght buffer
        CLR.L   (#SELL_PRICE)            ; zero out price/pound buffer

; Get weight from A/D converter and display
        MOVEA.L #WEIGHT_BUFFER,D1
        ADDA.L  #3,D1
        MOVE.L  D1,A1                    ; point to MSD of weight buffer
DS1:    MOVE.B  (#$C014),D0              ; read A/D to check strobe bit
        BTST    #4,D0                    ; test MSD strobe bit
        BZR     DS1                      ; loop and read A/D again if
                                         ;   MSD strobe bit not set
        MOVE.B  (#$C014)                 ; read A/D to get digit
        AND.B   #$0F,D0                  ; mask out strobe bits
        BTST    #3,D0                    ; see if MSD in bit 3 is a one
        BNZ     LOAD1                    ; Yes, go load $01 in buffer
        MOVE.B  #$14,D0                  ; No, load code for a blank
        BRA     NXTCHR
LOAD1:  MOVE.B  #$01,D0
NXTCHR: MOVE.B  D0,(A1)-                 ; save MSD code in weight buffer
                                         ;   and decrement pointer to point to
                                         ;   next lower digit
```

FIGURE 10-25   Assembly language program for smart scale. (pp. 314-20)

```
DS2:      MOVE.B    (#$C014),D0    ; read A/D to check MSD bit
          BTST      #5,D0          ; test digit 2 strobe bit
          BZR       DS2            ; loop and read A/D again if
                                   ;   MSD strobe bit not set
          MOVE.B    (#$C014)       ; read A/D to get digit
          AND.B     #$0F,D0        ; mask out strobe bits
NXTCHR:   MOVE.B    D0,(A1)-       ; save digit 2 code in weight buffer
                                   ;   and decrement pointer to point to
                                   ;   next lower digit

DS3:      MOVE.B    (#$C014),D0    ; read A/D to check MSD bit
          BTST      #6,D0          ; test digit 3 strobe bit
          BZR       DS3            ; loop and read A/D again if
                                   ;   MSD strobe bit not set
          MOVE.B    (#$C014).      ; read A/D to get digit
          AND.B     #$0F,D0        ; mask out strobe bits
NXTCHR:`  MOVE.B    D0,(A1)-       ; save digit 3 code in weight buffer
                                   ;   and decrement pointer to point to
                                   ;   next lower digit

DS4:      MOVE.B    (#$C014),D0    ; read A/D to check MSD bit
          BTST      #7,D0          ; test digit 4 strobe bit
          BZR       DS4            ; loop and read A/D again if
                                   ;   MSD strobe bit not set
          MOVE.B    (#$C014)       ; read A/D to get digit
          AND.B     #$0F,D0        ; mask out strobe bits
NXTCHR:   MOVE.B    D0,(A1)        ; save digit 4 code in weight buffer

; Display weight on URDA MDS LEDs
          MOVEA.L   #WEIGHT_BUFFER,A1    ; point at stored weight
          MOVE.B    #$01,D0              ; specifies use address field
          MOVE.B    #$01,D1              ; specifies use decimal point
          JSR       DISPLAY              ; call the display subroutine
          MOVEA.L   #LB,A1               ; point at Lb string
          MOVE.B    #$00,D0              ; specifies use data field
          MOVE.B    #$00,D1              ; specifies no decimal point
          JSR       DISPLAY              ; call display subr for Lb label

; Check to see if key has been pressed
          MOVE.B    (#$BF10),D0    ; read 8279 FIFO status
          BTST      #1,D0          ; see if FIFO has keycode
          JNZ       GETKEY         ; Yes, go read it
          BRA       RDWT           ; No, go get weight and display
GETKEY:   MOVE.B    #$40,D0        ; Control word to read FIFO
          MOVE.B    D0,(#$BF10)    ; Send to 8279
          MOVE.B    (#$BF09),D0    ; Read code from FIFO (through 8279
                                   ;   data register)
          CMP.B     #$09,D0        ; Check if legal keycode (number)
          BLE       D0,OK          ; Go on if below or equal 9
          BRA       RDWT           ; Else ignore, read weight again

; Read in and display price/pound

OK:       MOVEA.L   #SELL_PRICE,A1 ; point at price per pound buffer
          MOVE.B    #$00,D0        ; specify data field for display
          MOVE.B    #$01,D1        ; specify decimal point
          JSR       DISPLAY        ; Call display subr to show price per pound
          MOVEA.L   #S_P,A1        ; point at SP string
          MOVE.B    #$01,D0        ; specify address field
          MOVE.B    #$00,D1        ; specify no decimal point
          JSR       DISPLAY

NXTKEY:   JSR       READ_KEY       ; Wait for next keypress
          CMP.B     #$09,D0        ; See if more price or command
          BGT       COMPUTE        ; Go compute total price if not above 9
          CLR.L     D1             ; Clear D1 in preparation for shift price
          MOVE.L    (A1),D1        ; Get old selling price per pound
          ROL.L     #8,D1          ; Shift contents of buffer
          MOVE.B    D0,D1          ; Insert new digit
```

(continued)

```
        MOVE.L   D1,(A1)              ; Return shifted price with new digit
                                      ;   to sell price buffer
        MOVE.B   #$00,D0              ; Specify data field
        MOVE.B   #$01,D1              ; Specify decimal point
        JSR      DISPLAY              ; Call display routine to show new price
        BRA      NXTKEY               ; Keep reading and displaying shifted keys
                                      ;   until command key pressed

; Compute total price
COMPUTE:
        MOVEA.L  #WEIGHT_BUFFER,A1    ; point at weight buffer
        MOVE.B   (A1+3),D0            ; get MSD
        CMPI.B   #$14,D0              ; see if MSD = 0
        JNZ      NOTZER
        MOVE.B   #$00,D0
        MOVE.B   D0,(A1+3)            ; Yes, was = 0 so load blank
                                      ;   instead of 0 (strip MSD 0)
NOTZER: JSR      PACK                 ; pack BCD weight into word
        JSR      CONVERT2BIN          ; Convert to 16-bit binary in D0
        MOVE.B   D0,(BINARY_WEIGHT)   ; and save in memory
        MOVEA.L  #SELL_PRICE,A1       ; point at price per pound for pack
        JSR      PACK                 ; Pack BCD price into D0 for convert
        JSR      CONVERT2BIN          ; Convert price to 16-bit binary
                                      ;   in D0
        MOVE.W   (BINARY_WEIGHT),D1   ; weight in D1, price in D0
        MULU     D1,D0                ; 32-bit product in D0
        JSR      BINCVT               ; Packed BCD price in D1

; Round off price to nearest cent and display
        CMP.B    #$49,D1              ; See if low digits > $49
        BGE      ADD1                 ; If greater, add 1 to upper digits
        CLR.B    D2                   ; Else add 0, Clear low byte of D2
        BRA      START_ADD
ADD1:   MOVE.B   #$01,D2
START_ADD:
        LSR.L    #8,D1                ; Shift over result (eliminate
                                      ;   cents digits)
        ABCD     D2,D1                ; Add carry (or 0 if wasn't one)
        MOVE.B   D1,D3                ; Save result temporarily
        CLR.B    D2                   ; Clear for next add (in case there
                                      ;   was another carry out)
        LSR.L    #8,D1                ; Shift over result
        ABCD     D2,D1                ; Add with extend (carry)
        MOVE.B   D1,D4                ; save result temporarily
        LSR.L    #8,D1                ; Shift over result
        ABCD     D2,D1                ; Add with extend (carry)
        ; now that the additions are completed, move the pairs of BCD
        ; digits back into D1
        LSL.L    #8,D1                ; move MSD back over
        MOVE.B   D4,D1                ; restore next two digits
        LSL.L    #8,D1                ; move over
        MOVE.B   D3,D1                ; restore digits (only 6 left)
        ; now prepare for and call the EXPAND subroutine to unpack
        ; the BCD digits
        LEA      #PRICE_TOTAL,A1      ; point at price total buffer
        JSR      EXPAND               ; convert to unpacked BCD
        MOVE.B   #$00,D0              ; Display total price on data
        MOVE.B   #$01,D1              ; field with decimal point
        JSR      DISPLAY
        LEA      #PR,A1               ; point at price/lb string
        MOVE.B   #$01,D0              ; and display in address field
        MOVE.B   #$00,D1              ; without decimal point

; Delay a few seconds
        MOVE.W   #$FFFF,D0            ; Count down from $FFFF as a delay
CNTDN1: MOVE.W   #$000A,D1            ; and for each count, count down $A
CNTDN2: DBGE     D1,CNTDN2
        DBGE     D0,CNTDN1
```

```
; go read next weight
        BRA     RDWT                    ; Jump back to dumb scale program
                                        ;   start

;************************************************************************
;*************** subroutines use in smart scale program **************
; SUBROUTINE  READ_KEY
; ABSTRACT       reads the URDA Keyboard attached via an 8279 - subroutine
;                polls the status register until it finds a key pressed.
;                It then reads the keypressed code from the FIFO RAM into
;                D0 and returns.
; REGISTERS USED:        Destroys D0 - returns character read in D0
;
READ_KEY:
        MOVE.L  A1,-(A7)                ; save A1 on the stack
        LEA     #$BF10,A1               ; point at 8279 control register
NO_KEY: MOVE.B  (A1),D0                 ; get FIFO status; LSB high if key pressed
        BTST    #0,D0                   ; test LSB
        JZR     NO_KEY                  ; poll until bit is high
        MOVE.B  $#40,D0                 ; control word for read FIFO
        MOVE.B  (A1),D0                 ; send to 8279
        LEA     #$BF09,A1               ; point at 8279 data register
        MOVE.B  (A1),D0                 ; read character from FIFO RAM
        MOVE.L  (A7)+,A1                ; restore A1 from stack
        RTS                             ; return to calling routine

;************************************************************************
; SUBROUTINE DISPLAY
; ABSTRACT       This subroutine displays characters on the display
;                connected to the URDA MDS via an 8279.  The data is sent
;                to this subroutine in the following manner:
;                INCOMING Parameters:
;                        A1 -- pointer to buffer containing the 7-seg
;                              codes of the 4 characters to be displayed
;                        D0 = 0 implies use data field
;                        D0 = 1 implies use address field
;                        D1 = 0 implies no decimal point
;                        D1 = 1 implies decimal point between second
;                              and third digit
; REGISTER USAGE (all saved and restored)
;                A2 - 8279 control/data register pointer
;                A3 - pointer to seven-seg table
;                D2 - digit loop counter
;                D3 - temporary index for BCD to seven seg translation
;

DISPLAY:
        MOVEM.L [A2,A3,D2,D3],-(A7)     ; save working registers on stack
        LEA     #$BF10,A2               ; point at 8279 control register
        CMP.B   #$00,D0                 ; see if data field required
        JZR     DATFLD                  ; yes, load cntl wd for data field
        MOVE.B  #$94,D0                 ; no, load cntl wd for addr field
        BRA     SEND                    ; go send control word to 8279
DATFLD: MOVE.B  #$90,D0                 ; load control word for data field
SEND:   MOVE.B  D0,(A2)                 ; send control word to 8279
        LEA     #$BF09,A2               ; point to 8279 display RAM
        MOVE.B  #4,D2                   ; counter for number of characters
        LEA     #SEVEN_SEG,A3           ; pointer to seven seg codes
AGAIN:  MOVE.B  (A1)+,D3               ; get character to be displayed
        MOVE.B  (A3,D3),D0              ; get seven seg code to display
        CMP.B   #$02,D2                 ; see if digit that gets decimal pt
        BNE     MORE                    ; no go send digit
        CMP.B   #$01,D1                 ; yes, see if decimal pt specified
        BNE     MORE                    ; no, go send character
        OR.B    #$80,D0                 ; yes, OR in decimal point
MORE:   MOVE.B  D0,(A2)                 ; send seven-seg code to 8279
                                        ;   display RAM
        DBGT    D2,AGAIN                ; decrement digit counter and loop
                                        ;   to send another if > 0   (continued)
```

```
        MOVEM.L  -(A7),[A2,A3,D2,D3]     ; restore saved registers from stack
        RTS                              ; return to calling routine

;************************************************************************
; SUBROUTINE PACK
; ABSTRACT      This subroutine converts four unpacked BCD digits pointed
;               to by A1 to four packed BCD digits in D0
;
; DESTROYS  D0
;
PACK:   MOVE.L  D1,-(A7)         ; save D1

        CLR.L   D0               ; clear D0 for result
        MOVE.B  (A1)+,D0         ; get first digit
        MOVE.B  (A1)+,D1         ; get second digit
        LSL.L   #4,D0            ; shift first digit left to make room
        AND.B   $0F,D1           ; ensure top of D1 digit is clear
        AND.B   D1,D0            ; merge in second digit
        LSL.L   #4,D0            ; shift digits left to make room
        MOVE.B  (A1)+,D1         ; get third digit
        AND.B   $0F,D1           ; ensure top of D1 digit is clear
        AND.B   D1,D0            ; merge in third digit
        LSL.L   #4,D0            ; shift digits left to make room
        MOVE.B  (A1)+,D1         ; get fourth digit
        AND.B   $0F,D1           ; ensure top of D1 digit is clear
        AND.B   D1,D0            ; merge in fourth digit

        MOVE.L  (A7)+,D1         ; restore D1
        RTS                      ; return to routine which called me

;************************************************************************
; SUBROUTINE:   EXPAND
; ABSTRACT      This subroutine expands a packed BCD number in D0
;               to four unpacked BCD digits in a buffer pointed to by A1
;
EXPAND: MOVE.L  D1,-(A7)         ; save D1 on stack

        MOVE.B  D0,D1            ; make a copy of low digits
        AND.B   #$0F,D1          ; strip upper digit away
        MOVE.B  D1,(A1)+         ; place in unpacked BCD buffer (digit 1)
        LSR.W   #4,D0            ; shift digits over 1 digit (four bits)
        MOVE.B  D0,D1            ; make a copy of low digits
        AND.B   #$0F,D1          ; strip upper digit away
        MOVE.B  D1,(A1)+         ; place in unpacked BCD buffer (digit 2)
        LSR.W   #4,D0            ; shift digits over 1 digit (four bits)

        MOVE.B  D0,D1            ; make a copy of low digits
        AND.B   #$0F,D1          ; strip upper digit away
        MOVE.B  D1,(A1)+         ; place in unpacked BCD buffer (digit 3)
        LSR.W   #4,D0            ; shift digits over 1 digit (four bits)

        MOVE.B  D0,D1            ; make a copy of low digits
        AND.B   #$0F,D1          ; strip upper digit away
        MOVE.B  D1,(A1)+         ; place in unpacked BCD buffer (digit 4)

        MOVE.L  (A7)+,D1         ; restore D1 from stack
        RTS                      ; return to calling routine

;************************************************************************
; SUBROUTINE:   CONVERT2BIN
; ABSTRACT:     This subroutine converts a four-digit BCD number in
;               D0 into its BINARY (HEX) equivalent.  It returns the
;               result in register D0.
; SAVES:        D1 - BCD value saved
;               D2 - multiplier constant
;               D3 - digit 3
;               D4 - digit 2
;               D5 - digit 1
```

(continued)

```
; DESTROYS:      D0 - return with binary value in it
;
CONVERT2BIN:
          MOVEM.L  [D1-D5],-(A7)    ; save working registers D1-D5

          MOVE.L   D0,D1            ; make a copy of incoming BCD value
          CLR.L    D0               ; clear D0 for binary result
          MOVE.B   D1,D5            ; place lower 2 digits in D5
          ANDI.B   #$0F,D5          ; strip upper digit
          CLR.W    D4               ; clear D4 for digit
          MOVE.B   D1,D4            ; place another copy of lower digits in D4
          LSR.W    #4,D4            ; shift so just has digit 2
          LSR.L    #8,D1            ; shift down two upper digits
          MOVE.B   D1,D3            ; make copy of upper digits
          ANDI.W   #$0F,D3          ; strip so just digit 3 in D3
          LSR.L    #4,D1            ; shift uppermost digit into low four bits
          MOVE.B   D1,D0            ; put MSD in D0
          MOVE.L   #$0A,D2          ; put 10 multiplier in D2
          MULU     D2,D0            ; digit4 * 10 in D0
          ADD.L    D3,D0            ; add in next most significant digit
          MULU     D2,D0            ; ((digit4 * 10) + digit3) * 10 in D0
          ADD.L    D4,D0            ; add in next most significant sigit
          MULU     D2,D0
          ; (((digit4 * 10) + (digit3 * 10) + digit2) *10 in D0
          ADD.L    D5,D0            ; add in LSD to get final result
          ; ((((digit4 * 10) + (digit3 * 10) + digit2) *10) + digit1  in D0


          MOVEM.L  (A7)+,[D1-D5]    ; restore working registers D1-D5
          RTS                       ; return to calling routine

;*****************************************************************************
; SUBROUTINE BINCVT
; ABSTRACT       This subroutine converts a 24-bit binary number in D0
;                to a packed BCD equivalent in D0
; INPUT:         D0 - 24-bit binary number
; OUTPUT:        D0 - packed BCD equivalent
; USES and SAVE/RESTORES:      D1 - number of bits in value for CNVT1
;                              D2 -
;                              D3 -
;                              D4 -
;                              D5 -
;                              D6 - uses as workspace in CNVT1
; CALLS:         CNVT1 - extract two BCD digits from the binary input (D0)
; DESTROYS:      D0
;
BINCVT:
          MOVEM.L  [D1-D6],-(A7)    ; save working registers D1-D6

          MOVE.L   #24,D1           ; 24-bit binary value (send to CNVT1)
          JSR      CNVT1            ; extract two digits
          MOVE.B   D1,D3            ; save two resulting digits

          MOVE.L   #24,D1           ; 24-bit binary value (send to CNVT1)
          JSR      CNVT1            ; extract two digits
          MOVE.B   D1,D4            ; save two resulting digits

          MOVE.L   #24,D1           ; 24-bit binary value (send to CNVT1)
          JSR      CNVT1            ; extract two digits
          MOVE.B   D1,D5            ; save two resulting digits

          MOVE.L   #24,D1           ; 24-bit binary value (send to CNVT1)
          JSR      CNVT1            ; extract two digits

          CLR.L    D0               ; clear D0 for result
          MOVE.B   D1,D0            ; two MSDs
          LSR.L    #8,D0            ; shift over to make room for next 2 digits
          MOVE.B   D5,D0            ; merge in next two MSDs        (continued)
```

```
        LSR.L    #8,D0            ; shift over
        MOVE.B   D4,D0            ; merge in next two digits
        LSR.L    #8,D0            ; shift over
        MOVE.B   D3,D0            ; merge in two LSDs

        MOVEM.L  (A7)+,[D1-D6]    ; restore working registers D1-D6
        RTS                       ; return to calling routine

;************************************************************************
; SUBROUTINE CNVT1
; ABSTRACT       Extract two BCD digits from the incoming binary number in
;                D0, leave D0 as the new value less the BCD equivalent.
;                On incoming D1 indicates the number of bits in the incoming
;                value, return the two digits in the low byte of D1
;
CNVT1:
CNVT2:  CLR.L    D6               ; clear D as workspace and clear carry
        DBGT     D1,CONTINUE      ; decrement bit count and return if 0
        RTS                       ; return to calling routine

CONTINUE:
        ROL.L    #1,D0            ; rotate left 1 bit
        ASLX.B   #1,D6            ; double BCD digit being built and add
                                  ;   extend bit (carry)
        ; decimal adjust here

        CMP.B    #99,D6           ; carry from D6:
        BNC      CNVT2
        ADD.L    #$80,D0          ; add back into binary
        SUB.W    #$80,D6          ; remove from BCD working value
        BRA      CNVT2

        END
```

FIGURE 10-25   (end)

The subroutine in Figure 10-25 produces two BCD digits of the result at a time by calling the subroutine CNVT1. Figure 10-26 shows a flowchart for the operation of CNVT1. The main principle here is to shift the 24-bit number left 1 bit position so the MSB goes into the carry flip-flop and then add this bit to twice the previous result. We use a decimal-adjust operation to keep the result of the addition in BCD format. If the decimal-adjust produces a carry, we add this carry back into the shifted 24-bit number in D2 so that it will be propagated into higher BCD digits. After each run of CNVT1 (24 runs of CNVT2), D2 will be left with a binary number that is equal to the original binary number minus the value of the two BCD digits produced. You can adapt this subroutine to work with a different number of bits by simply calling CNVT1 more or fewer times and by adjusting the count loaded into D1 to be 1 more than the number of binary bits in the number to be converted. The count has to be 1 greater because of the position of the decrement in the loop. The temperature-controller routine in Figure 10-25 shows another example of this conversion.

The least significant two digits of the BCD value for the total price returned by BINCVT in D1 represent tenths and hundredths of a cent. If the value of these two BCD digits is greater than $49, then the carry produced by the compare instruction and the next two higher BCD digits in D2 are added to D1. This must be done in a data register, because the decimal-adjust operations, used to keep the result in BCD format, work only on an operand in a data register. Any carry from these two BCD digits is propagated on to the upper two digits of the result in D2. After this rounding, the packed BCD for the total price is left in D1.

In order for the display subroutine to be able to display this price, it must be converted to unpacked BCD form and put in four successive memory locations. Another "mask and move nibbles" subroutine called EXPAND does this. The DISPLAY subroutine is then called to display the total price on the data field. The DISPLAY subroutine is called again to display the letters PR in the address field.

Finally, after delaying a few seconds to give the operator time to read the price, execution returns to the "dumb-scale" portion of the program and starts over.

A question that may occur to you when reading a long program such as this is, How do you decide which parts of the program to keep in the mainline and which parts to write as subroutines? There is no universal agreement on the answer to this question. The general guidelines we follow are to write a program section as a subroutine if it is going to be used more than once in

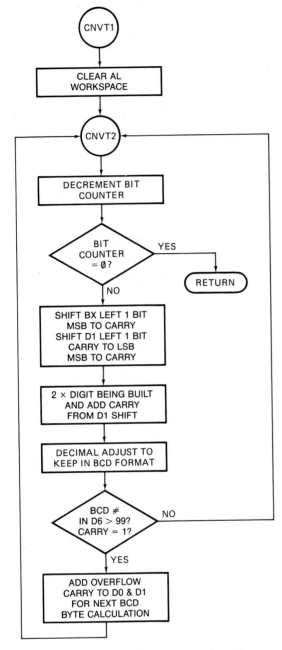

FIGURE 10-26 Flowchart for CNVT1 subroutine.

A MICROCOMPUTER-BASED INDUSTRIAL PROCESS-CONTROL SYSTEM

Overview of Industrial Process Control

An area in which microprocessors and microcomputers have had a major impact is in *industrial process control*. Process control involves first measuring system variables such as motor speed, temperature, the flow of reactants, the level of a liquid in a tank, the thickness of a material, etc. The system is then adjusted until the value of each variable is equal to a predetermined value for that variable called a *set point*. The system controller must maintain each variable as closely as possible to its set-point value, and it must compensate as quickly and accurately as possible for any change in the system, such as an increased load on a motor. A simple example will show the traditional approach to control of a process variable and explain some of the terms used in control systems.

The circuit in Figure 10-27 shows one approach to controlling the speed of a dc motor. Attached to the shaft of the motor is a dc generator, or *tachometer*, which puts out a voltage proportional to the speed of the motor. The output voltage is typically a few volts per thousand revolutions per minute. A fraction of the output voltage from the tachometer is fed back to the inverting input of the power amplifier driving the motor. A positive voltage is applied to the noninverting input of the amplifier as a set point. When the power is turned on, the motor accelerates until the voltage fed back from the tachometer to the inverting input of the amplifier is nearly equal to the setpoint voltage. Using negative feedback to control a system such as this is often called *servo control*. A control loop of this type keeps the motor speed quite constant for applications where the load on the motor does not change much. Some hard-disk-drive motors and high-quality phonograph turntables use this method of speed control.

the program; it is reusable (could be used in other programs); it is so lengthy (more than 1 page) that it clutters up the conceptual flow of the main program; or it is an essentially independent section. The disadvantage of using too many subroutines is the time and overhead required for each subroutine call. As you write more programs, you will arrive at a balance that feels comfortable to you. The following section shows you another long program example that was written in a highly modular manner so that it can easily be expanded. This example should further help you see when and how to use subroutines.

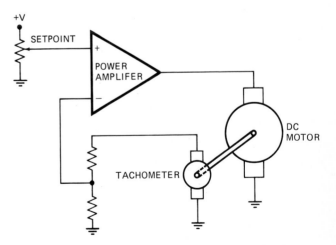

FIGURE 10-27 Circuit for controlling speed of a dc motor using feedback from tachometer.

For applications in which the load and/or set point changes drastically, there are several potential problems. The first of these, overshoot when you change the set point, is shown in Figure 10-28a. In this case the variable—motor speed, for example—overshoots the new set point and bounces up and down for a while. The time it takes the bouncing to settle within a specified error range or error band is called the *settling time.* This type of response is referred to as *underdamped* and is similar to the response of a car with bad shock absorbers when it hits a bump. Figure 10-28b shows the opposite situation, where the system is overdamped, so that it takes a long time for the variable to reach the new set point.

Another problem of any control system is *residual error.* Figure 10-28c shows the response of a control system such as the motor-speed controller in Figure 10-27 when more load is added to the motor. When the increased load is first added, the motor slows down, so the voltage out of the tachometer decreases. This increases the voltage difference between the amplifier inputs and causes the amplifier output to increase. Increased amplifier output increases the speed of the motor and, thereby, the output from the tachometer. When the system reaches equilibrium, however, there

is some noticeable difference between the set point and the voltage fed back from the tachometer. It is this difference, or residual, error that is amplified by the gain of the amplifier to produce the additional drive for the motor. For stability reasons, the gain of many control systems cannot be too high. Therefore, even if you adjust the speed of a motor, for example, to be exactly at a given speed for one load, when you change the load there will always be some residual error between the set point and the actual output.

To help solve these problems, circuits with more complex feedback are used. Figure 10-29 shows a circuit that represents the different types of feedback commonly used. First note in this circuit that the output power amplifier is an adder with four inputs. The current supplied to the summing point of the adder by the set-point input produces the basic output drive current. The other three inputs do not supply any current unless there is a difference between the set point and the feedback voltage from the tachometer. Amplifier 1 is another adder, whose function is to compare the set-point voltage with the feedback voltage from the tachometer. Let's assume the two input resistors, R1 and R2, are equal. Since the set-point voltage is negative and the voltage from the tachometer is positive, there will be no net current through the feedback resistor of the amplifier if the two voltages are equal in magnitude. In other words, if the speed of the motor is at its set-point value, the output of amplifier 1 will be zero, and amplifiers 2, 3, and 4 will contribute no current to the summing junction of the power amp.

Now, suppose that you add more load on the motor, slowing it down. The tachometer voltage is no longer equal to the set-point voltage, so amplifier 1 now has some output. This error signal on the output produces three types of feedback to the summing junction of the power amp.

Amplifier 1 produces simple dc feedback proportional to the difference between the set point and the tachometer output. This is exactly the same effect as the voltage divider on the tachometer output in Figure 10-27. *Proportional feedback,* as this is called, will correct for most of the effects of the increased load, but as we discussed before, there will always be some residual error.

The cure for residual error is to use some *integral feedback.* Amplifier 3 in Figure 10-29 provides this type of feedback. Remember from a previous discussion that this circuit produces a ramp on its output whenever a voltage is applied to its input. For the example here, the integrator will ramp up or ramp down as long as there is any error signal present on its input. By ramping up and down just a tiny bit about the set point, the integrator can eliminate most of the residual error. Too much integral feedback, however, will cause the output to oscillate up and down.

A third type of feedback, called *derivative feedback,* is produced by amplifier 4 in Figure 10-29. Integral feedback discussed in the previous paragraph is slow because the error signal must be present for some time before the integrator has much output. Derivative

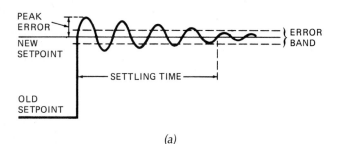

(a)

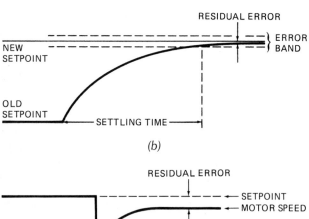

(b)

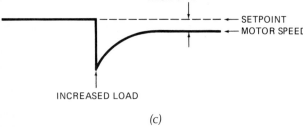

(c)

FIGURE 10-28   Overshoot and undershoot of system when set point or load is changed. (*a*) Overshoot. (*b*) Undershoot. (*c*) Load change.

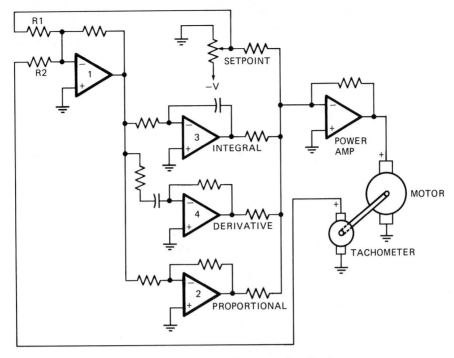

FIGURE 10-29   Circuit showing proportional, integral, and derivative feedback control.

feedback is a signal proportional to the rate of change of the error signal. If the load on the system is suddenly changed, the derivative amplifier circuit will give a quick shot of feedback to try and correct the error. When the error signal is first applied to the differentiator circuit, the capacitor in series with the input is not charged, so it acts as a short circuit. This initially lets a large current flow, so the amplifier has a sizable output. As the capacitor charges, the current decreases, so the feedback from the differentiator decreases. Too much derivative feedback can cause the system to overshoot and oscillate.

The point here is that by using a combination of some or all of these types of feedback, a given feedback-controlled system can be adjusted for optimum response to changes in load or set point. Process-control loops that use all three types of feedback are called *proportional-integral-derivative-* (PID-) control loops. Because process variables change much more slowly than the microsecond operation of a microcomputer, a microcomputer with some simple input and output circuitry can perform all the functions of the analog circuitry in Figure 10-29 for several PID loops.

Figure 10-30, p. 324, shows a block diagram of a microcomputer-based process-control system. DASs convert the analog signals from various sensors to digital values that can be read in and processed by the microcomputer. A keyboard and display in the system allow the user to enter set-point values and to read the current values of process variables. Relays, D/A converters, solenoid valves, and other actuators are used to control process variables under program direction.

A programmable timer in the system determines the rate at which control loops get serviced.

Microcomputer-based process-control systems range from a small programmable controller such as the one shown in Figure 10-31, p. 324, which might be used to control one or two machines on a factory floor, to a large minicomputer used to control an entire fractionating column in an oil refinery. To show you how these microcomputer-based control systems work, here's an example system you can build and experiment with.

A 68000-BASED PROCESS-CONTROL SYSTEM

Program Overview

Figure 10-32, p. 325, shows in flowchart form one way in which the program for a microcomputer-based control system with eight PID loops can operate. After power is turned on, a mainline or *executive program* initializes ports, initializes the timer, and initializes process variables to some starting values. The executive program then sits in a loop waiting for a user command from the keyboard or a clock "tick" from the timer. Both the keyboard and the clock are connected to interrupt inputs.

When the microcomputer receives an interrupt from the timer, it goes to a subroutine that determines whether it is time to service the next control loop. The interrupt-service routine does this by counting interrupts in the same way as the real time clock we

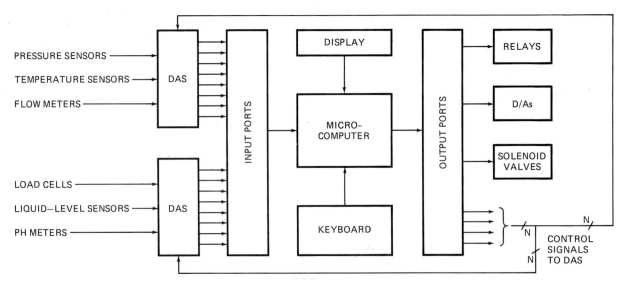

FIGURE 10-30 Block diagram of microcomputer-based process-control system.

described in Chapter 8. For example, if you program the timer to produce a pulse every 1 ms and you want the controller to service another loop every 20 ms, you can simply have the interrupt-service routine count 20 interrupts before going on to update the next loop. Once you have counted down 20 interrupts, the program then falls into a decision structure that determines which loop is to be updated next. Every 20 ms, a new loop is updated in turn, so with eight loops, each loop gets updated every 160 ms. Note that each loop is serviced at a regular interval instead of simply updating all eight loops, one loop right after another. This is done so that the timing for each loop is independent of the timing for the other loops. A change in the internal timing for one loop then will not affect the timing in the other loops. This system is one type of *time-slice* system, because each loop gets a 20-ms "slice" of time.

The routines that actually update each control loop are independent of each other. For our example system here, we have space to show the implementation of only one loop, the control of the temperature of a tank of liquid in our PC-board-making machine, for instance. You could write other, similar control-loop procedures to control pH, flow, light-exposure timing, motor speed, etc. Figure 10-32c shows the flowchart for our temperature-controller loop. We explain how this works after we have a look at the hardware for the system.

Hardware for Control System and Temperature Controller

To build the hardware for this project, we started with an URDA MDS board and added an 8254 programmable timer and an 8259A priority interrupt controller, as shown in Figure 8-14. The timer is initialized to produce 1-kHz clock ticks. The 8259A provides interrupt inputs for the clock-tick interrupts and for keyboard interrupts. We built the actual temperature-sensing and detecting circuitry on a separate prototyping board and connected it to some ports on the URDA MDS with a ribbon cable. Figure 10-33, p. 326, shows the added circuitry.

The temperature-sensing element in the circuit is an LM35 precision Celsius temperature sensor. The voltage between the output pin and the ground pin of this device will be 0 V at 0°C and will increase by 10 mV for each increase of 1°C above that. The 300-kΩ resistor connecting the output of the LM35 to −15 V allows the output to go negative for temperatures below 0°C. (If you are operating with ±12-V supplies, use a 240-kΩ resistor.) This makes the circuit able to measure temperatures over the range of −55°C to +150°C. For our

FIGURE 10-31 Photograph of Texas Instrument's programmable controller for up to eight PID loops.

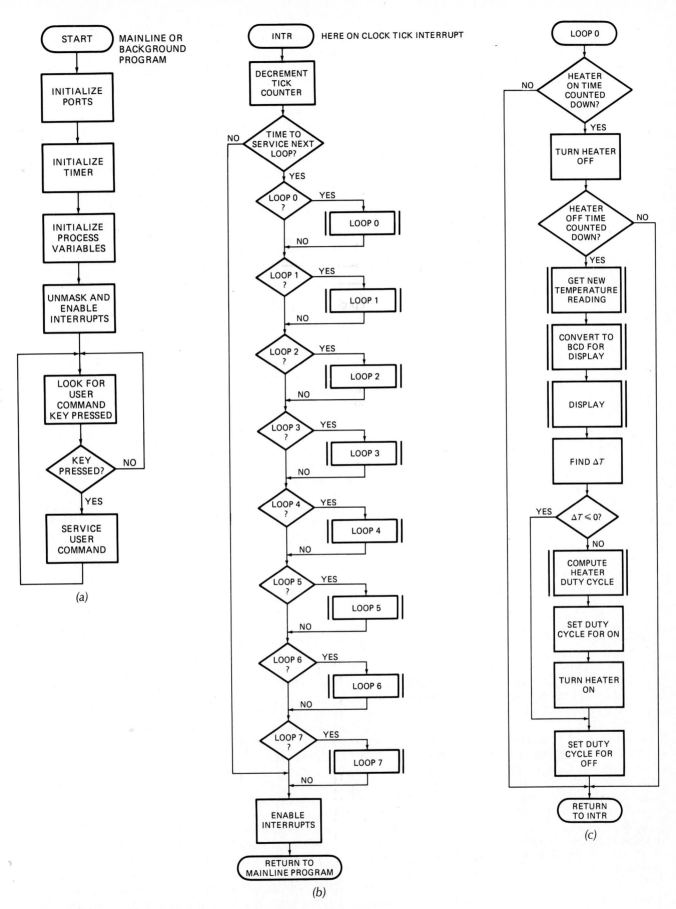

FIGURE 10-32   Flowchart for microcomputer-based process-control system.
(a) Mainline or executive. (b) Loop selector. (c) Temperature-control loop.

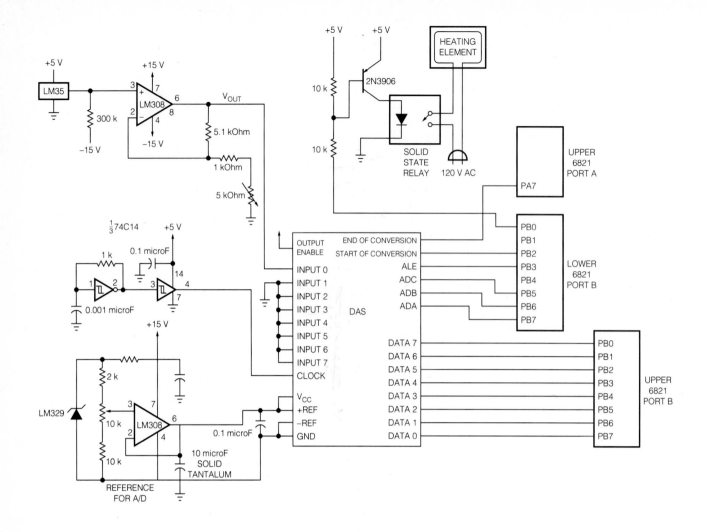

FIGURE 10-33 Temperature-sensing and heater-control circuitry for microcomputer-based controller.

application here, we use only the positive part of the output range, but we thought you might find this circuit useful for some of your other projects. An LM308 amplifies the signal from the sensor by 2 so that the signal uses a greater part of the input range of the A/D converter. This improves the noise immunity and resolution.

The ADC0808 A/D converter used here is an eight-input DAS. You tell the device which input signal you want digitized with a 3-bit address you send to the ADC, ADB, and ADA inputs. This eight-input device was chosen so that other control loops could be added later. Some Schmitt-trigger inverters in a 74C14 are connected as an oscillator to produce a 300-kHz clock for the DAS. The voltage drop across an LM329 low-drift zener is buffered by an LM308 amplifier to produce a V_{CC} and a V_{REF} of 5.12 V for the A/D converter. With this reference voltage, the A/D converter will have 256 steps of 20 mV each. Since the temperature sensor signal is amplified by 2, each degree Celsius of

temperature change will produce an output change of 20 mV, or one step on the A/D converter. This gives us a resolution of 1°C, which is about equal to the typical accuracy of the sensor. The advantage of using V_{REF} as the V_{CC} for the device is that this voltage will not have the switching noise that the digital V_{CC} line has. The control inputs and data outputs of the A/D converter are simply connected to URDA MDS ports, as shown.

Figure 10-34 shows the timing waveforms and parameters for the ADC0808. Note the sequence in which control signals must be sent to the device. The 3-bit address of the desired input channel is first sent to the multiplexer inputs. After at least 50 ns, the ALE input is sent high. After another 2.5 μs the START CONVERSION input is sent high and then low. Then the ALE input is brought low again. When you detect the END-OF-CONVERSION signal from the A/D converter going high, you can then read in the 8-bit data value which represents the temperature.

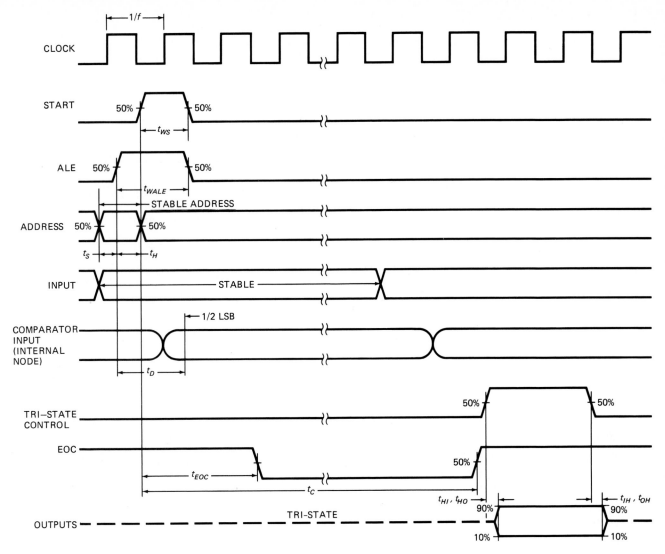

FIGURE 10-34   Timing waveforms for the ADC0808 data acquisition system.

To control the power delivered to the heater, we used a 25-A, 0-V turn-on, solid-state relay such as the Potter and Brumfield unit described in Chapter 9. With this relay we can control a 120- or 240-V-ac-powered hot plate or immersion heater. The heater is pulsed on and off under program control. The duty cycle of the pulses determines the amount of heat put out by the heater.

For very low power applications, a D/A converter and a power amplifier could be used to drive the heater. However, in high-power applications this is not very practical, because the power amplifier dissipates as much or more power than the load. For example, when driving a 5000-W heater, the amplifier will dissipate 5000 W or more. The D/A converter approach has the added disadvantage that it cannot directly use the available ac line voltage.

The driver transistor on the input of the solid-state relay serves three purposes: It supplies the drive for the relay, isolates the port pin from the relay, and holds the relay in the off position when the power is first turned on. Port pins, remember, are in a floating state after a reset. Now that you know how the hardware is connected, we can explain how the program for this system works.

The Controller System Program

THE MAINLINE OR EXECUTIVE SECTION

Figure 10-35, pp. 328–33, shows the assembly language program for our controller system. Refer to the flowchart in Figure 10-32 as you work your way through this program. The mainline or executive part of the program starts by initializing port $C014 for output, the 8259A to receive interrupt inputs from the timer and the keyboard, and the 8254 to produce a 1-kHz square wave from its counter 0. We have described these operations in detail previously, so we won't dwell on them here. We also initialize some process variables, which we explain later when they will have more meaning. After enabling the 68000

```
;  68000 PROGRAM FOR CONTROLLER SYSTEM - MODULE 1
;
; ABSTRACT           This program services eight process control loops on a
;                    rotating basis.  It is written to run on a system similar
;                    to the URDA MDS board.
;                    Timing for the control loop is generated on an interrupt basis
;                    by an 8254 timer.  Control loop 0 in the program controls
;                    the temperature of a water bath.
;
; PORTS USED         Uses Upper PIA port A ($C016) as output
;                    bit 7 = heater, bits 6,3 = not connected,
;                    bit 5 = start conversion, bit 4 = ALE,
;                    bits 2,1,0 = channel address
;                    Uses Upper PIA port B ($C012) as input
;                    Uses Lower PIA port B ($C017) as end-of-conversion input fr A/D
; SUBROUTINES        Calls: CLOCK_TICK - interrupt service routine
;                           KEYBOARD   - interrupt service routine (empty)
;-------------------------------
; defines for I/O port addresses
CONTROL_ADDR      EQU      $BF10
CONTROL2_ADDR     EQU      $BF12
DATA_ADDR         EQU      $BF09
CNTL_8254         EQU      $BD07
COUNT1_8254       EQU      $BD01
UPPERA_CNTL       EQU      $C016
UPPERA_DATA       EQU      $C014
UPPERB_CNTL       EQU      $C012
UPPERB_DATA       EQU      $C010
LOWERB_CNTL       EQU      $C017
LOWERB_DATA       EQU      $C015

        ORG       $4700               ; start the data at $4200
STACK_HERE:       DS.W     200         ; set stack length of 200 words
STACK_TOP:        DS.W     0           ; the stack top is the high address

COUNTER:          DC.B     0           ; counter for number of interrupts
TIMEHI:           DC.B     0           ; heater relay - time on
TIMELO:           DC.B     0           ; heater relay - time off
LOOPNUM:          DC.B     0           ; temp storage for loop counter
CURTEMP:          DC.B     0           ; current temperature
SETPOINT:         DC.B     0           ; setpoint termperature

LOOP_ADDR_TABLE:
                  DC.L     LOOP0
                  DC.L     LOOP1
                  DC.L     LOOP2
                  DC.L     LOOP3
                  DC.L     LOOP4
                  DC.L     LOOP5
                  DC.L     LOOP6
                  DC.L     LOOP7


SEVEN_SEG:        DC.B     $77,$7B,$7D,$7E,$B7,$BB,$BD,$BE
;                          0   1   2   3   4   5   6   7
                  DC.B     $D7,$DB,$DD,$DE,$E7,$EB,$ED,$EE
;                          8   9   A   b   C   d   E   F
;-------------------------------
        ORG       $4100
```

(a)

FIGURE 10-35   68000 assembly language program for process-control system.
Mainline module 1. Interrupt-service routine. Loop service routines. Utility routines.
(Continued on pp. 329–33.)

```
; initialize stack pointer
        LEA        STACK_TOP,A7

; define the addresses for the interrupt service routines
        LEA        CLOCK_TICK,A0          ; get ISR address for clock
        MOVE.L     A0,($7FF4)             ; save the address in transfer table
        LEA        KEYBOARD,A0            ; get ISR address for KBD
        MOVE.L     A0,($7FFA)             ; save the address in transfer table

; initialize ports
        MOVE.B     #$00,(UPPERA_CNTL)     ; address data direction register
        MOVE.B     #$00,(UPPERA_DATA)     ; all bits output
        MOVE.B     #$00,(UPPERB_CNTL)     ; address data direction register
        MOVE.B     #$FF,(UPPERB_DATA)     ; all bits input
        MOVE.B     #$00,(LOWERB_CNTL)     ; address data direction register
        MOVE.B     #$FF,(LOWERB_DATA)     ; all bits input

; initialize 8259A
        MOVE.B     #%00010011,(CONTROL_ADDR)   ; edge triggered, single, ICW4
        MOVE.B     #%01000000,(CONTROL2_ADDR)  ; type 64 is first 8259 type (IR0)
        MOVE.B     #%00000001,(CONTROL2_ADDR)  ; ICW4, 8086 mode
        MOVE.B     #%11111110,(CONTROL2_ADDR)  ; ICW4, 8086 mode

; initialize 8254 counter 0 for 1-kHz output
;  8254 command word for counter 0, LSB them MSB, square wave, BCD
        MOVE.B     #%00110111,(CNTL_8254)  ; send counter 0 command word
        MOVE.B     #$58,(COUNT1_8254)      ; send LSB of count
        MOVE.B     #$24,(COUNT1_8254)      ; send MSB of count

; initialize variables
        MOVE.B     #$3C,(SETPOINT)        ; initialize final temp of 60 deg
        MOVE.B     #$14,(COUNTER)         ; initialize time counter
        MOVE.B     #$00,(LOOPNUM)         ; start at first loop
        MOVE.B     #$01,(TIMELO)
        MOVE.B     #$01,(TIMEHI)
        MOVE.B     #$00,(CURTEMP)

; enable interrupt input of 68000
        ANDI.W     #$F8FF,SR              ; enabler interrupts (set mask to 000)

HERE:
        NOP
        NOP                               ; if required can put more
        NOP                               ;  instructions here
        NOP
        BRA HERE                          ; loop forvere waiting for interrupts
;        :                                ; return to caller
        RTS


;----------------------------------------------------------------------
;68000 INTERRUPT SERVICE ROUTINE TO SERVICE PROCESS CONTROL LOOPS
;
;ABSTRACT:       This routine calls 1 of 8 process control loops on a
;                rotating basis.
;PORTS USED:     none
;SUBROUTINES:    calls LOOP0,LOOP1,LOOP2,LOOP3,LOOP4,LOOP5,LOOP6,LOOP7
;REGISTERS:      save all
;
CLOCK_TICK:                          (b)
```

(continued)

```
            MOVEM.L  A0/D0-D4,-(A7)               ; save registers

            SUBI.B   #1,(COUNTER)                 ; decrement interrupt counter
            BNE      EXIT2                        ; not zero yet, go wait
            MOVE.B   #20,(COUNTER)                ; if zero, reset counter to 20
            MOVE.L   #0,D2                        ; load D2 with number of loop to svc
                                                  ;    this should be the loop# * 4
            MOVE.B   (LOOPNUM),D2                 ;    as saved last time through
            LEA      LOOP_ADDR_TABLE,A0           ; get address of loop jump table
            JSR      0(A0,D2)                     ; go service that loop
            ADDI.L   #4,D2                        ; point to next loop address
            CMPI.L   #$20,D2                      ; is this the last loop?
            BNE      EXIT2                        ; no, exit
            MOVE.B   #0,(LOOPNUM)                 ; yes, get back to first loop
EXIT2:      MOVE.B   #%00100000,D0                ; OCW2 for nonspecific EOI
            MOVE.B   D0,(CONTROL_ADDR)            ; send to 8279

            MOVEM.L  (A7)+,A0/D0-D4               ; restore registers
            RTE


;------------------------------------------------------------------
;DUMMY INTERRUPT SERVICE ROUTINE TO SERVICE KEYBOARD
;

KEYBOARD:
;         ...                                     ; keyboard routine instructions

            MOVE.B   #%00100000,D0                ; OCW2 for non-specific EOI
            MOVE.B   D0,(CONTROL_ADDR)            ; send OCW2 for end of interrupt
                                                  ;   to 8279

            RTE

;------------------------------------------------------------------
;68000 ROUTINE TO SERVICE TEMPERATURE CONTROLLER
;
;ABSTRACT:      This ISR services the temperature controller
;REGISTERS:     Destroys none
;PORTS:         Uses Upper A port as output port to turn on heater with
;               bit 7.
;CALLS:         DISPLAY, A_D_READ, BINCVT

LOOP0:
            MOVEM.L  D0-D3,-(A7)                  ; save registers

            SUBI.B   #1,(TIMEHI)                  ; decrement time for heater on
            BNE      EXIT                         ; return to interrupt svc routine
            ;  fall through to here if TIMEHI was just decremented to 0 (i.e.
            ;  if the heater has been on long enough)
            MOVE.B   #1,(TIMEHI)                  ; reset time high to fall through value
                                                  ;    so next time decrement will yield 0
            MOVE.B   #$B0,D0                      ; turn heater off bit
            MOVE.B   D0,(UPPERA_DATA)             ; send to heater control port
            SUBI.B   #1,(TIMELO)                  ; decrement time for heater off
            BNE      EXIT                         ; return to interrupt svc routine
            ; fall through to here if TIMELO was just decremented to 0 (i.e. the
            ; heater has been off long enough)
            MOVE.B   #$00,D3                      ; load cahnnel address (0)
            JSR      A_D_READ                     ; do A/D conversion (get temperature)
            MOVE.B   D0,(CURTEMP)                 ; save current temperature
```

(c)

```
;                :          D1 = data to display (BCD value)
; PORTS USED    : None
; SUBROUTINES   : None
; REGISTERS     : Uses A2 - 8279 control/data register pointer
;                :      A3 - Pointer to seven-seg table
;                :      D2 - Seven-seg table index
;-------------------------------
DISPLAY:
        MOVEM.L D2/A2-A3,-(A7)          ; save registers
        MOVEA.L CONTROL_ADDR,A2 ; point at 8279 control register
        CMPI.B  #$00,D0                 ; see if data field requested
        BEQ     DATFLD                  ; yes, go load control word for data
        MOVE.B  #$94,D0                 ; no. load address field control word
        BRA     SEND                    ; go send control word
DATFLD: MOVE.B  #$90,D0                 ; control word for data field
SEND:   MOVE.B  D0,(A2)                 ; send to 8279
        MOVEA.L SEVEN_SEG,A3            ; point at seven_seg table
        MOVEA.L DATA_ADDR,A2            ; point at data register
        MOVE.B  D1,D2                   ; get copy of low nibble to display
        ANDI.B  #$0F,D2                 ; mask upper nibble
        MOVE.B  0(A3,D2),D2             ; translate lower nibble to 7-seg code
        MOVE.B  D2,(A2)                 ; send to 8279 display RAM
        MOVE.B  D1,D2                   ; get another copy of low nibble
        ROL.B   #4,D2                   ; rotate high nibble into low position
        ANDI.B  #$0F,D2                 ; mask nibble
        MOVE.B  0(A3,D2),D2             ; translate upper nibble to 7-seg code
        MOVE.B  D2,(A2)                 ; send to 8279 display RAM
        ROR.W   #8,D0                   ; rotate bytes to get at upper 2 digits
        MOVE.B  D1,D2                   ; get copy of upper byte
        ANDI.B  #$0F,D2                 ; mask upper nibble
        MOVE.B  0(A3,D2),D2             ; translate lower nibble to 7-seg code
        MOVE.B  D2,(A2)                 ; send to 8279 display RAM
        MOVE.B  D1,D2                   ; get another copy of upper byte
        ROL.B   #4,D2                   ; rotate high nibble into low position
        ANDI.B  #$0F,D2                 ; mask nibble
        MOVE.B  0(A3,D2),D2             ; translate upper nibble to 7-seg code
        MOVE.B  D2,(A2)                 ; send to 8279 display RAM
        MOVEM.L (A7)+,D2/A2-A3          ; restore registers
        RTS                            ; return to caller


;---------------------------------------------------------------------
;68000 SUBROUTINE   TO CONTROL A/D CONVERTER
;
;PORTS:          Upper port B is input from A/D
;                Upper port A bit 7 = heater, bit 5 = start conversion
;                          bit 4 = ALE,    BITS 2,1,0 - channel address
;                Lower port A bit 0 = end of conversion
;INPUTS:         Channel Address for A/D in D0
;OUTPUTS:        A/D data in D0
;REGISTERS:      Destroys D0

A_D_READ:
        MOVEM.L D1-D2,-(A7)             ; save registers

        MOVE.B  $80,D1                  ; control for heater off
        OR.B    D3,D1                   ; combine with channel address
        MOVE.B  D1,(UPPERA_DATA)        ; send to output port (heater cntl)
        MOVE.B  $90,D1                  ; send ALE, keep heater on
        OR.B    D3,D1                   ; keep channel address on
        MOVE.B  D1,(UPPERA_DATA)        ; send to output port (heater cntl)
```

(d)

```
              JSR      BINCVT                    ; convert to BCD
              MOVE.W   D0,D1                     ; data to diaply
              MOVE.B   #$00,D0                   ; use data register of display
              JSR      DISPLAY
              CLR.W    D0
              CLR.W    D1                        ; clear registers for sub and divide
              MOVE.B   (CURTEMP),D0              ; get current temperature
              MOVE.B   (SETPOINT),D1             ; get setpoint temp to compare to
              SUB.B    D0,D1                     ; see if temp less than setpoint
              BGE      DONE                      ; heater off if above or equal setpoint
              MOVE.B   #$64,D1                   ; compute new TIMELO
              DIVU     D0,D1                     ; 64/temp
              MOVE.B   D0,(TIMELO)               ; save new low time
              MOVE.B   #4,(TIMEHI)               ; set TIMEHI for 4 loops on
              MOVE.B   #0,D0
              MOVE.B   D0,(UPPERA_DATA)          ; turn heater on
              BRA      EXIT
DONE:         MOVE.B   #1,(TIMEHI)               ; fall through value for time high
              MOVE.B   #$7F,(TIMELO)             ; long off value for time low
EXIT:

              MOVEM.L  (A7)+,D0-D3               ; restore  registers
              RTS

; Dummy Loops here
LOOP1:
;                      :                ; instructions for this loop
                       RTS


LOOP2:
;                      :                ; instructions for this loop
                       RTS


LOOP3:
;                      :                ; instructions for this loop
                       RTS


LOOP4:
;                      :                ; instructions for this loop
                       RTS


LOOP5:
;                      :                ; instructions for this loop
                       RTS


LOOP6:
;                      :                ; instructions for this loop
                       RTS


LOOP7:
;                      :                ; instructions for this loop
                       RTS


;-------------------------------------------------------------------
; 68000 SUBROUTINE TO DISPLAY DATA ON LEDs CONNECTED TO URDA MDS USING 8279
; ABSTRACT        : This subroutine displays characters on the display
;                 : connected to the URDA MDS via an 8279.  The data is sent
;                 : to this subroutine in the following manner:
;                 :       D0 = 00 implies use data field
;                 :       D0 = 01 implies use address field
```

(e)

```
              MOVE.B   $B0,D1                    ; start of conversion command
              OR.B     D3,D1                     ; keep channel address on
              MOVE.B   D1,(UPPERA_DATA)          ; send to output port (heater cntl)
              MOVE.B   $80,D1                    ; turn off ALE and start
              OR.B     D3,D1                     ; keep channel address on
              MOVE.B   D1,(UPPERA_DATA)          ; send to output port (heater cntl)
EOCL:         MOVE.B   (LOWERB_DATA),D1          ; get end of conversion bit
              ROXR.B   #1,D1                     ; rotate into carry bit
              BCS      EOCL                      ; loop if carry set (conv not started)
EOCR:         MOVE.B   (LOWERB_DATA),D1          ; get end of conversion bit
              ROXR.B   #1,D1                     ; rotate into carry bit
              BCC      EOCR                      ; loop if carry clr (conv not complete)
              MOVE.B   D1,(UPPERB_DATA)          ; read data from A/D

              MOVEM.L  (A7)+,D1-D2               ; restore registers
              RTS

;-------------------------------------------------------------------------
;SUBROUTINE TO CONVERT FROM 8-BIT BINARY TO PACKED BCD
;
;ABSTRACT:        Converts an 8-bit binary number in D1 to packed binary
;                 in D1
;                     D0 - bit counter for loop control
;                     D1 - input binary, output BCD
;                     D2 - temp for saving copy of binary
;                     D3 - temp for construction of BCD
;INPUTS:          D1 - 8-bit binary number
;OUTPUTS:         D1 - Packed BCD result

BINCVT:
              MOVEM.L D2-D3,-(A7)                ; save registers and flags

              MOVE.L  #9,D0                      ; bit counter for 8 bits
              MOVE.B  D1,D2                      ; save a copy of the binary input
              MOVE.B  #0,D3                      ; clear D2 for use as a buffer
CNVT2:        CLR.B   D4                         ; clear D4 and carry
              DBNE    D0,GO_ON                   ; decrement bit counter and loop
                                                 ; if more bits to do
              BRA     HOME                       ; otherwise we're done (go home)
GO_ON:        ROXL.B  #1,D1                      ; MSB from D2 into carry bit
              MOVE.B  D3,D1                      ; move BCD digit being built into D1
              ABCD    D1,D1                      ; double D1 and add carry from D2 shift
              MOVE.B  D1,D3                      ; put back in D3 for next time around
              BRA CNVT2:                         ; continue conversion
HOME:         MOVE.B  D3,D1                      ; BCD in D1 for return

              MOVEM.L +(A7),D2-D3                ; restore registers

              RTS

              END
```

(f)

interrupt input with an AND to SR instruction, the program then enters a loop and waits for an interrupt from the user via the keyboard or from the timer. The keyboard interrupt-service routine would normally contain a command recognizer and subroutines to implement each of the commands, similar to the way the URDA MDS monitor program is structured. Due to space limitations, we do not show here the implemen-tation of the keyboard interrupt-service routine that allows the user to change set points, stop a process, or examine the value of process variables at any time.

THE CLOCK-TICK INTERRUPT HANDLER

The next part of the program to discuss is the inter-rupt-service routine that counts clock ticks and decides which process-control loop to service. At the start of this routine, we simply decrement an interrupt counter kept in a memory location. In the initialization this counter was set to 20 decimal, or $14. If the counter is not down to zero, execution is simply returned to the wait loop. If the tick counter is now down to zero, the clock-tick counter is reset to 20, and one of the loop subroutines is called to service the next loop. It is important that this clock-tick routine be reentrant, because if one of the loop subroutines takes more than the time between clock ticks (1 ms), the routine will be reentered before its first use is completed. The procedure is made reentrant by pushing all registers used in the routine and by immediately resetting the clock-tick counter to 20. If a loop subroutine takes longer than 1 ms and the clock-tick routine is called again, it will just decrement the tick counter and return to the interrupted loop subroutine.

The method used here to call the desired loop subroutine is an important programming technique. It uses a *call table* to efficiently implement the CASE or nested IF-THEN-ELSE programming structure described in Chapter 3. Here's how it works.

To keep track of which loop should be serviced next, we use a variable called LOOPNUM in memory. During initialization, LOOPNUM is loaded with $00. When it is time to service the first loop, the value in LOOPNUM is loaded into D0. The JSR (A0,D0) instruction then gets a subroutine address from a table called LOOP_ADDR_TABLE in memory. A0 functions as a pointer to the desired address in the table. D0 functions as the offset in the table to the desired subroutine address. For the first access D0 is zero, so the first address in the table is used.

Take a look at how the table of subroutine addresses is set up with DC.L directives at the start of module 2 in Figure 10-35. The names LOOP0, LOOP1, LOOP2, etc. are the names of the subroutines to service each of the loops. When this program module is linked and loaded into memory, the program counter pointer addresses for each of the subroutines will be loaded into the table.

When execution returns from one of the loop subroutines, 4 is added to LOOPNUM so that execution will go to the next loop in sequence the next time the tick counter is counted down to zero. LOOPNUM must be incremented by 4 because each address in the call table uses 4 bytes. If all loops have been serviced, LOOPNUM is set back to 0 so LOOP0 will be serviced again. Now let's look at the actual temperature-control loop.

THE TEMPERATURE-CONTROLLER SUBROUTINE

As we said previously, the amount of heat output by the heater is controlled by the duty cycle of a pulse waveform sent to the solid-state relay. The time on for the output waveform to the solid-state relay is determined by counting down a value called TIMEHI. The time off for this waveform is determined by counting down a value called TIMELO. At start-up the mainline program initializes TIMEHI and TIMELO to $01, so that the first time the LOOP0 subroutine is called, both

of these are decremented to 0 and execution falls through to the A/D conversion subroutine. This needs to be done so that we have a temperature value to use for computing the duty cycle.

The number of the A/D channel that we want to digitize is passed to the A/D conversion subroutine in the D0 register. The subroutine then sends out this channel number to the A/D converter and generates the control waveforms shown in Figure 10-34 under software control. The binary value for the temperature is returned in D0.

Upon return, the binary value of the temperature is stored in a memory location called CURTEMP for future reference. For testing purposes we want to display the temperature on the address field of the URDA MDS display. To do this we convert the binary value for the temperature to a BCD value using a reduced version of the binary-to-BCD subroutine from the scale program earlier in this chapter and the display routine from Chapter 9. After displaying the current temperature, it is then compared with the set-point temperature to see if the heater needs to be turned on. If the temperature is at or above the set point, TIMEHI is loaded with the fall-through value and TIMELO, with a large number.

If the temperature is below the set point, we call the subroutine DUTY_CYCLE, which computes the correct values for TIMEHI and TIMELO based on the difference between the set point and the current temperature. A complex PID algorithm might be used for this subroutine in a precision system. For our example here, however, we have used simple proportional feedback. To further simplify the calculations, a fixed value of 4 was used for TIMEHI. The thinking for the value of TIMELO then goes as follows. If the difference in temperature is large, then TIMELO should be small so the heater is on for a longer duty cycle. If the difference in temperature is small, then the value of TIMELO should be large so the heater has a short duty cycle. Experimentally, we found that a good first approximation for our system was (difference in temperature × TIMELO) = 100 decimal ($64). For example, if the difference in temperature is 20° ($14), then $64/$14 gives a value of 5 for TIMELO. The values for TIMEHI and TIMELO are returned in their named memory locations. Upon return to the main loop routine, we send a control word that turns on the heater. Execution then jumps to EXIT.

When execution returns to loop 0 again after 160 ms, TIMEHI will be decremented. If TIMEHI did not decrement to 0, then execution simply adjusts a few things and returns. If TIMEHI is 0 after the decrement, the heater is turned off, and TIMELO is decremented. TIMELO is then decremented every time loop 0 is serviced (every 160 ms) until TIMELO reaches 0. When TIMELO gets counted down to 0, a new A/D conversion is done, and a new feedback value for TIMELO is recalculated.

An important point here is that the part of the program that determines the feedback is separate from the rest of the program, so it can easily be altered without changing any of the rest of the program. All that need to be changed in this routine are the value of TIMEHI, the value of TIMELO, and the rate at which these change in response to a difference in temperature to produce proportional, integral, and derivative feedback control.

TEMPERATURE-CONTROLLER RESPONSE

The dotted line in Figure 10-36 shows the temperature versus time response of our system with traditional thermostat control, which is often called *on-off control*, or "bang-bang" control. As you can see, the temperature overshoots the set point by a great deal and then oscillates around the set point temperature. The solid line in Figure 10-36 shows the response of the system operating with our temperature-controller program. The initial overshoot was caused by the large thermal inertia of the hotplate we used. The overshoot and the residual error of about 1° could be eliminated by using a more complex feedback algorithm. This example should make you aware of the advantages of computer feedback control.

Robotics

In recent years the term *robot* has become a "buzzword" in the media and in many people's minds. Science fiction movies have helped us form an image of robots as mobile, rational companions. Robots, however, have many forms, and in operation they are simply special cases of feedback-control systems, such as we described in the previous section. This is why we have not included a chapter dedicated just to robotics. The Rhino robot arm shown in Figure 9-43, for example, uses optical encoders to detect the position of its different joints, motors (actuators) to move each joint to a desired position, and a microcomputer to control the motors based on feedback from the sensors. In large industrial robots such as those that weld or spray-paint cars, the sensors used may also include vision, and the actuators may be hydraulic or pneumatic, but the control principle is the same. Feedback from the various sensors is used to control the output to the actuators.

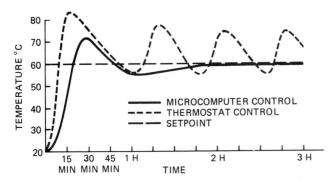

FIGURE 10-36 Temperature versus time response for a thermostat-controlled and a microcomputer-controlled heater.

Most of you have probably used some simple robots around your home without realizing it. One example is an electric garage-door opener, which opens or closes when you tell it to and then stops when a sensor indicates that it is closed or open as desired. Other examples are an automatic clothes washer, a clothes dryer, and a microwave oven with a temperature probe.

The next major section of this chapter is a discussion of how you develop the prototype of a microcomputer-based instrument such as the smart scale or the control system we discussed in the preceding sections.

DEVELOPING THE PROTOTYPE OF A MICROCOMPUTER-BASED INSTRUMENT

The first step in developing a new instrument is to define, very carefully, exactly what you want the instrument to do. The next step is to decide which parts of the instrument you want to do in hardware and which parts you want to do in software. You can then decide how you want to do each of these.

For the software, you will break the overall programming job into modules that can be individually tested and debugged, as we have described previously. For the hardware, there are several different approaches you can take.

Using a Microcomputer Prototyping Board

One approach is to use a commercially available microcomputer prototyping board such as the URDA MDS we used for the examples in this chapter. An advantage of this approach is that it gives you the basic CPU, RAM, ROM, and ports already tested. You can then easily add any needed timers, priority interrupt controllers, and other interface circuitry. Some of the available prototyping boards, such as the URDA MDS, have onboard monitor programs that let you load and execute your programs. The major advantage of this approach is that it allows you quickly to get a prototype up and running and to see if the instrument is feasible. If the instrument is feasible, you can then design a custom hardware board that exactly fits your needs.

Computer-Aided-Design Approach

Another approach to creating the needed hardware for the prototype is with a *computer-aided-design*, or CAD, system. This system may be a large and powerful engineering workstation such as those made by Mentor Graphics Corporation or simply an IBM PC–type computer with programs such as the PCAD system from Personal CAD Systems, Inc., Electronic Design Automation Division. The programs on these systems allow you, first of all, easily to design and draw a schematic for your hardware. You can just select the schematic symbol for a part you want to use by number from a large library of common devices in a disk file and bring it on to your CRT screen. You can use a mouse to move the symbol into position and to draw signal lines connecting it to other symbols. You can move the device around as needed, and the connecting signal lines will follow.

When you get the schematic drawn up, you can then use another program in the CAD system to *simulate* the operation of the circuit. By simulate, we mean to "run" the circuit in software. This helps you to find out if the signals are connected correctly and if timing parameters are acceptable. If the circuit passes simulation, you can make a printout of the schematic on a printer or plotter.

The next step is to design a printed-circuit board for your circuit. Another program in the CAD system will, with a little help from you, produce the artwork for the printed-circuit board. Some systems will even produce the control tape for the machine that automatically drills the required holes in the printed-circuit board. The time is not too far away when the engineering workstation will be connected directly to the printed-circuit-board-making machine, the machine that gets parts from the warehouse, the machine that stuffs the parts in the PC board, and the machine that does the initial functional tests on the board. This concept, incidentally, is called *computer-integrated manufacturing,* or CIM; the industry seems to be headed in the direction of CIM, but it isn't quite there yet. Therefore, you still have some work to do when you get the prototype PC board back.

After you "stuff" the board with the required parts, you can power it up and check for hot or otherwise unhappy components. If there are no apparent problems, you can test the board. Probably the best tool for testing the board is an emulator.

Using an Emulator

Figure 3-12 shows a picture of an Applied Microsystems ES 1800 emulator, which works with the IBM PC and other compatible computers. Several other companies make similar emulators. The hardware of an emulator consists of control circuitry, memory to store the trace data after each instruction executes, and an "umbilical" cable with a plug at the end of it. To use the emulator you remove the microprocessor from the prototype unit and insert the plug at the end of the umbilical cable in its place. The emulator contains a microprocessor that will actually run your test programs under control of the emulator. The emulator then gives you a window into the operation of the circuitry on the prototype under control of a development system or PC.

The software of the emulator is similar to a powerful monitor program or debugger program. You can use the emulator commands and the system memory to test each part of the prototype. For example, you can write a short program to test the RAM in the prototype, load this program into the system RAM, and run the program under emulator control. To help with debugging, emulators allow you to set breakpoints, examine and change the contents of registers and memory locations, and do a trace that shows the contents of

registers after each instruction executes. Some emulators have an additional pod like those used on logic analyzers so that you can do a trace of the sequence of hardware signals on a group of lines to check timing.

An important point here is that, just as we stressed with building programs, the fastest way to get a prototype debugged and operating is by doing one small part at a time. Because problems tend to interact, trying to debug too large a section at a time can be frustrating and time consuming. Therefore, remove all but the basic CPU group ICs for your first test; then keep adding, testing, and debugging one section at a time. As you get a hardware section working, you can, if you want, write and debug the software module that uses or drives that hardware module. To give you a better idea of how to do this development process, we briefly describe the steps we went through to develop the process-control system discussed earlier in this chapter.

A Product Development Example

For our process-control demonstration system, we started with an URDA MDS board because we wanted to make only one unit and because we did not have CAD equipment and a PC-board-making machine. For the controller we needed a timer to produce 1-kHz clock ticks and a priority interrupt controller to handle keyboard and clock-tick interrupts. We added these two devices and some address decoder circuitry to the URDA MDS shown in Figure 8-14 and tested this circuitry with an emulator. To do this we wrote a short program that wrote a byte to the starting address for the timer over and over again. We ran this program with the emulator, and with a scope we checked to see if the $\overline{CS}$ input of the timer was getting asserted. It was, so we knew that the address-decoding circuitry was working correctly. We then connected the 3.579-MHz CLK signal to the clock inputs of all three timers in the 8254 and wrote the instructions needed to initialize the three timers for 1-kHz square-wave output. Even though we needed only one timer here, it was very little additional work to check the other two for future reference. The timers worked the first time, so we went on to the 8259A PIC.

Testing the 8259A was a little more complex because we had to provide an interrupt signal, initialize the 8259A, initialize the interrupt-vector table in low RAM, and provide a location for execution to go to when the PIC received an interrupt. We used the 1-kHz clock tick from the timer as the interrupt signal to the 8259A. For 8259A initialization and the interrupt jump table initialization, we used the instructions in the mainline program in Figure 10-35. For the test interrupt-service routine we actually used a real-time clock and display subroutine that we developed for examples in previous chapters. We used these so that we could see if the interrupt mechanism was working correctly by watching the displays on the URDA MDS count off seconds. This again shows the advantage of writing programs as separate, reusable modules. In the program in Figure 10-35, note that we initialize the 8259A before we initialize and start the timer. When we first wrote a test program to test an 8259A and an 8254, we did this in the reverse order. When we ran the test program with the emulator, the system would accept only one interrupt and then hang up. We did a trace with the emulator and found that execution was returning from the interrupt-service routine to the wait loop in the mainline program properly, but it was not recognizing the next interrupt. Careful reading of the 8259A data sheet showed us that we had to initialize the 8259A *before* we started sending it interrupt signals, or it would not respond correctly to the nonspecific EOI command that we used at the end of the interrupt-service routine to reset the 8259A's in-service register.

After the interrupt mechanism was working correctly, we wrote the interrupt-service routine that implements the decision structure shown in Figure 10-32b. Initially, we made all eight loops dummy loops to test the basic structure. By inserting breakpoints with the emulator, we were able to see if execution was getting to each of the eight loops. When all this was working, we went on to build and test the temperature-control section.

For the temperature-control section, we first built the analog circuitry and tested it. Then we wrote a small program to read the temperature from the A/D converter and display the result on the URDA MDS displays. Initially, then, the loop 0 subroutine simply read in the temperature, displayed it in binary (hex) form, and returned. This worked the first time, so we went on to add the binary-to-BCD conversion routine and run the result with the emulator. This was a previously written and tested module, so that when it was added, the result worked fine.

Next we added a couple of instructions to turn the heater on during one execution of loop 0 and turn the heater off during the next time through loop 0. We then used an oscilloscope to check that the solid-state relay was getting turned on and off correctly.

Finally, we added the actual duty cycle and control instructions and sat back waiting for the system to heat a big container of water for tea.

The actual development cycle will obviously be somewhat different for every instrument developed. The main points here are to develop and test both the hardware and software in small modules. To speed up the debugging process, take the time to learn to use all or most of the power of the emulator and system you are working with.

DIGITAL FILTERS

A section at the start of this chapter showed how op amps can be used to build high-pass and low-pass filter circuits. Filtering of a signal can also be done by taking samples of the signal with an A/D converter, performing mathematical operations on the samples from the A/D converter, and outputting the result to a D/A converter. This approach, referred to as a *digital filter*, can easily produce a response curve that is difficult, if not impossible, to produce with analog circuitry. This digital approach has the further advantage that the filter response can be changed under program control. Digital filters are used in speech synthesizers, satellite image-enhancement systems, and many other applications.

There are two basic types of digital filter, the *finite-impulse response*, or FIR, type, and the *infinite-impulse response*, or IIR, type. The basic principle of a digital filter is to operate on the samples as a function of time rather than as a function of frequency, as the analog filter does.

Figure 10-37a shows a functional diagram of the operation of an FIR-type filter. The box containing Z^{-1} represents a delay of one sample interval. Circles containing an X represent a multiplication operation, and the letters to the left of each circle represent the number by which the term will be multiplied. Y0 represents the value of the current sample from the A/D, Y1 represents the value of the previous sample from the A/D, and Y2 represents the value of the sample before that. Here's how this works. The output value, V, at any time is produced by summing together the (current sample × some number (coefficient)) + (the previous sample × some coefficient) + (the sample before that × some coefficient), etc. To do all this with a microprocessor involves simple operations of saving previous samples, multiplying, and adding. The Intel 2920 microprocessor, which was specifically designed for this type of operation, contains an A/D converter, D/A converter, and an architecture and instruction set that works with the 25-bit numbers required for accurate filter response.

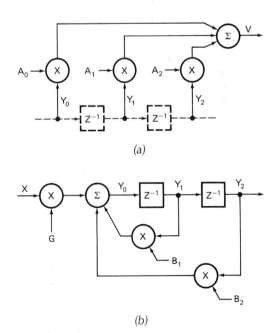

(a)

(b)

FIGURE 10-37   FIR and IIR digital filter principles. (a) FIR. (b) IIR.

Figure 10-37b shows a functional diagram for an IIR digital filter. Here again the blocks containing Z^{-1} represent a delay of one sample time. The value of the current sample from the A/D converter is represented by the X at the left of the diagram. The Y0 point represents the output from the microprocessor to the D/A converter. Note that for an IIR filter, it is this output value that is saved to be used in computing feedback terms for future samples. In the FIR type, remember, the samples from the A/D converter were saved directly for future use. The output for an IIR type is produced by summing (the current sample × a calculated coefficient) + (the previous output value × a calculated coefficient) + (the output value before that × a calculated coefficient), etc. The coefficients for both the FIR- and the IIR-type filters are usually calculated using a computer program. FIR filters are easier to design, but they may require many terms to produce a given filter response. IIR filters require fewer stages, but they have to be carefully designed so that they do not become oscillators.

A new type of filter called a *switched-capacitor filter* implements digital filtering for simple filter responses without the need for the A/D and D/A converter. An example is the National MF10. In this type of filter, an input signal is sampled on a capacitor. The signal is passed on to other capacitors and fractions of the outputs from these capacitors are summed to produce an analog output signal directly. Switched capacitor filters are less expensive, but they do not give the degree of programmability that the microprocessor-based filters do.

CHECKLIST OF IMPORTANT TERMS AND CONCEPTS IN THIS CHAPTER

If there are terms or concepts in this list you do not remember, use the index to find them in the chapter.

Op amp

Comparator

Hysteresis

Noninverting amplifier

Inverting amplifier
    Virtual ground

Gain-bandwidth product

Unity-gain bandwidth

Adder circuit—summing point

Differential amplifier
    Common-mode signal
    Common-mode rejection

Instrumentation amplifier

Op-amp integrator circuit
    Linear ramp
    Saturation

Op-amp differentiator

Op-amp active filters
    Low-pass filter
    High-pass filter
    Band-pass filter
    Critical frequency or break point
    Sound-order low-pass filter
    Second-order high-pass filter

Light sensor
    Photodiode
    Solar cell

Temperature-sensitive voltage sources

Temperature-sensitive current sources

Thermocouples
    Type J thermocouple
    Cold-junction compensation

Force and pressure transducers
    Strain gage
    LVDT
    Load cell

Flow sensors
    Paddle wheel
    Differential pressure transducer

D/A converters
    Binary weighted
    Resolution
    Full-scale output voltage
    Maximum error
    Linearity
    Settling time

A/D converters
    Conversion time
    Parallel comparator A/D converter
    Dual-slope A/D converter
    Successive-approximation A/D converter
    Data acquisition system

A/D output codes
    Unipolar binary code
    Unipolar BCD code
    Bipolar binary code

Direct-memory access

Set point

Servo control

Settling time—underdamped, overdamped

Residual error

Proportional integral derivative control loop (PID)

Data acquisition system (DAS)

Time slice

On-off control

Robotics

Digital filters
   Finite-impulse response (FIR)
   Infinite-impulse response (IIR)

Computer-integrated manufacturing (CIM)

Emulator

Switched-capacitor filter

Computer-aided design
   Simulation

REVIEW QUESTIONS AND PROBLEMS

1. *a.* A comparator circuit such as the one in Figure 10-1*b* is powered by ±15 V, the inverting input is tied to +5 V, and the noninverting input is at +5.3 V. About what voltage will be on the output of the comparator?

   b. An amplifier circuit, such as the one in Figure 10-1*d*, has an R1 of 10 kΩ and an R2 of 190 kΩ. Calculate the closed-loop voltage gain for the circuit and the V_{OUT} that will be produced by a V_{IN} of 0.030 V. What voltage would you measure on the inverting input? What would be the gain of the circuit if R2 = 0 Ω?

   c. An amplifier circuit, such as the one in Figure 10-1*e*, is built with an R1 of 15 kΩ and an Rf of 75 kΩ. Calculate the closed-loop voltage gain for the circuit and the output voltage for an input voltage of 0.73 V. What voltage will you always measure on the inverting input of this circuit?

   d. A differential amplifier, such as the one in Figure 10-1*g*, is built with R1 = R2 = 100 kΩ and Rf = R3 = 1 MΩ. V1 is 4.9 V and V2 = 5.1 V. Calculate the output voltage and polarity.

   e. Describe the main advantage of the instrumentation amplifier in Figure 10-1*h* over the simple differential amplifier in Figure 10-1*g*.

   f. If the amplifier used in the circuit in part *b* has a gain-bandwidth product of 1 MHz, what will be the closed-loop bandwidth of the circuit?

2. Draw a circuit showing how a light-dependent resistor can be connected to a comparator so the output of the comparator changes state when the resistance of the LDR is 10 kΩ.

3. For the photodiode amplifier circuit in Figure 10-5, what voltage will you measure on the inverting input of the amplifier? Why is it important to use an FET input amplifier for this circuit? Which direction are electrons flowing through the photodiode?

4. In what application might you use a temperature-dependent current device such as the AD590 rather than a temperature-dependent voltage device such as the LM35?

5. Why must thermocouples be cold-junction compensated in order to make accurate measurements? How can the nonlinearity of a thermocouple be compensated for?

6. Why are strain gages usually connected in a bridge configuration? Why do you use a differential amplifier to amplify the signal from a strain-gage bridge?

7. Calculate the full-scale output voltage for the simple D/A converter in Figure 10-14.

8. What is the resolution of a 13-bit D/A converter? If the converter has a full-scale output of 10,000 V, what is the size of each step? What will be the actual maximum output voltage of this converter? What accuracy should this converter have to be consistent with its resolution?

9. Why must a 12-bit D/A converter have latches on its inputs if it is to be connected to 8-bit ports or an 8-bit data bus?

10. Describe the operation of a "flash"-type A/D converter. What are its main advantages and disadvantages?

11. For the dual-slope A/D converter in Figure 10-19, what will be the displayed count for an input voltage of 2.372 V? What is the resolution of a 4.5-digit slope-type A/D converter expressed in bits?

12. How many clock cycles does a 12-bit successive-approximation A/D converter take to do a conversion on a 0.1-V input signal? On a 5-V input signal? How does this compare with the number of clock cycles required for a 12-bit dual-slope type?

13. *a.* Assume the inputs of the MC1408 D/A converter in Figure 10-20 are connected to an output port on your microcomputer board and the output of the comparator is connected to bit D0 of an input port. Write the algorithm for a subroutine to do an A/D conversion by outputting an incrementing count to the output port.

   b. Write an algorithm for a subroutine to do the conversion by the successive-approximation method. Which method will produce a faster result? If the hardware is available, write the programs for these algorithms and compare the times by watching the comparator output with an oscilloscope.

14. Show the detailed algorithm for the subroutine you would use to read in the data from a multi-

plexed BCD output A/D converter such as the MC14433 in Figure 10-23 and assemble the value in a 16-bit register for display.

15. The data sheet for an A/D converter indicates that its output is in offset binary code. If the converter is set up for a range of -5 V to $+5$ V and the output code is 01011011, what input voltage does this represent? How could you convert this code to 2's-complement form after you read the code into your microcomputer?

16. Write a subroutine to round a 32-bit BCD number in D0 to a 16-bit BCD number in D1.

17. For the scale circuitry in Figure 10-23, what voltage should you measure on the inverting input of the LM308 amplifier? What voltages should you measure on the two inputs of the LM363 amplifier with no load on the scale? What voltage should you measure on the output of the LM363 with no load on the scale?

18. The section of the scale program following the label NXTKEY in Figure 10-35 moves some bytes around in memory. Rewrite this section of the program using the 68000 MOVEM instruction to do the move operations. Which version seems more efficient in this case?

19. Describe how feedback helps hold the value of some variable, such as a motor speed, constant. Refer to Figure 10-27 in your explanation.

20. What problem in a control loop does integral feedback help solve? Why is derivative feedback sometimes added to a control loop?

21. What is the major advantage of a microcomputer-controlled loop over the analog approach shown in Figure 10-29?

22. Suppose that you want to control the speed of a small dc motor, such as the one in Figure 10-27, with LOOP 1 of our microcomputer-based process controller.
    a. Show how you would connect the output from the motor's tachometer to the system in Figure 10-33. Also show how you would connect an 8-bit D/A to control the current to the motor.
    b. Write a flowchart for the LOOP 1 subroutine to control the speed of the motor.
    c. Describe how a lookup table could be used to determine the feedback value.

23. Describe the major difference in how the feedback is produced in an FIR digital filter and how it is produced in an IIR filter.

24. When developing a prototype, why is it very important to build, test, and debug both software and hardware in small modules?

CHAPTER 11

DMA, DRAMs, Cache Memories, Coprocessors, and EDA Tools

The major objective of the first six chapters of this book was to introduce you to structured programming and to writing 68000 assembly language programs. Chapters 7 through 10 introduced you to the hardware of a minimal 68000 system, showed you how to interface a microcomputer to a wide variety of input and output devices, and finally demonstrated how all these pieces are put together to build a simple microcomputer-based instrument or control system. The major goal of the remaining chapters in the book is to show you the hardware and software of larger microcomputer systems.

As an example of what we mean by a larger system, look at Figure 11-1, which shows the component side of the main microprocessor board, or *motherboard,* for an Apple Macintosh® II. As you can see, the board contains a 68020 microprocessor, ROM, and a large block of dynamic RAM. The 68020 is a newer member of the 68000 family that is compatible with the 68000 but also includes some additional capabilities. We have chosen the Mac II for discussions in this chapter because it represents a large 68000 family system, which includes a 68881 floating-point processor. Finally, note the system-expansion connectors in the upper left corner of Figure 11-1. These connectors allow you to plug in additional boards that give the system the specific interface functions you need. For example, you may want to add a disk-controller board, a serial-port board, a CRT-controller board, a board with additional memory, an A/D-D/A board, or a board that allows your MAC to function as a logic analyzer. This "open-system" approach lets you easily customize the system for your application and your financial state.

In later chapters we discuss the operation of peripheral boards such as CRT-controller boards, disk drive–controller boards, and serial communication boards, which plug into these expansion connectors.

The first goal of this chapter is to show you how the circuitry on a microcomputer motherboard such as the one in Figure 11-1 works. A second goal of this chapter is to show you how computer-based tools are used to design, test, debug, and produce the hardware and software for a board such as this.

OBJECTIVES

At the conclusion of this chapter, you should be able to

1. Show how a 68020 is connected with a controller device for operation in a large system.

2. Show how a direct-memory-access (DMA) controller device can be connected in a 68020 system, and describe how a DMA data transfer takes place.

3. Describe how large banks of dynamic RAM can be connected in a system.

4. Describe how a cache memory is used to reduce the number of wait states required in a system that has a large dynamic RAM main memory.

5. Describe how automatic error-detecting and correcting circuitry works with memories.

6. Show how a coprocessor can be connected to a 68020.

7. Describe how a 68020 and a 68881 cooperate during the execution of a program that contains instructions for each.

8. Write a simple assembly language program for a 68881.

9. Describe how schematic capture programs, simulator programs, and other computer-based tools are now used to develop a microcomputer system.

INTRODUCTION

The Apple Macintosh family of computers has three form factors. The original Macintosh had a compact form factor. This Mac had a relatively small "footprint"—about 12 in. by 9 in.—and was about 15 in. tall. It had a relatively small (9-in. diagonal) black and white screen. Several years ago Apple introduced Macintosh computers in an "open" form factor, similar to that of the IBM PC. These open Macs, consisting of a main box containing the Mac electronics and a separate monitor and keyboard, look very much like IBM PCs. The new Macs have I/O slots for expansion cards

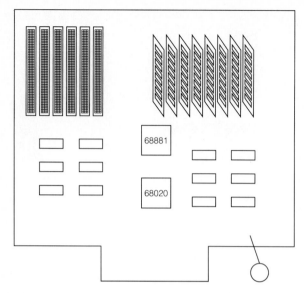

FIGURE 11-1 Component layout diagram for Apple Macintosh.

similar to the IBM PC. Finally, Apple introduced the portable Macintosh. The portable Mac is similar in appearance to a small briefcase or a large notebook. The original Macintosh used the 68000 CPU, but more recent Macintosh computers use the 68020 (Mac II and Mac SE/20) or the 68030 (Mac IIx and Mac SE/30). We discuss these CPUs in detail in later chapters. For now suffice it to say that they are faster, more powerful versions of the 68000 family. They can run 68000 programs and also have additional, enhanced instruction sets.

We will use the Apple Macintosh SE/20 for some of the system examples in this chapter. The Mac SE/20 demonstrates well the concepts of DMA, DRAM interface, and coprocessors that we want to teach here. The Macintosh, however, uses some custom ICs for its RAM and DMA access. These chips are nonstandard, and we will, in general, not discuss them in detail. Rather, we will at times focus on some of the industry standard ICs that perform the same functions (for example, in IBM PCs and more normal 68000 family-based technical workstations such as the Apollo DN4500). When we discuss industry-standard DMA controllers, we will indicate which of the Macintosh ICs perform the same functions in Mac systems.

To give you a more detailed idea of where we are going in this chapter and how it relates to what you have learned in previous chapters, let's take a look at Figure 11-2, which shows a block diagram of circuitry on a Macintosh II motherboard. As you look at this diagram, you should see many familiar parts and a few new ones. Start on the left side of the diagram and work your way across it from the 68020 CPU and the custom priority-interrupt controller (called "GLUE" here). Over the 68020 main processor, note the auxiliary 68881 math coprocessor.

The next vertical line of devices to the right in Figure 11-2 consists of the address bus buffers, the data bus

buffers, and the custom bus-controller chip. As we explain later, a bus-controller chip is required to generate control bus signals when the 68020 is operated in a large-scale system. The buses from these devices go across the drawing and connect to the NuBus peripheral board connectors so the 68020 can communicate with the boards in the peripheral expansion slots as well as with the ROM, RAM, and ports on board. Incidentally, the layout of the newer Macintosh models is very similar to this layout.

Now find the ROM in the lower center, the keyboard logic and other features in the middle, and the dynamic RAM in the middle right. Finally, take a look at the column of devices that contains the DMA controller.

The major parts of this circuit that are new to you are the DMA section, the dynamic RAM section and its associated parity check/generator logic, and the auxiliary processor. In the following sections of the chapter, we discuss each of these types of circuitry in detail.

First, however we explain what we mean when we say that a 68020 is operating in multimaster mode, because many of the circuits shown in this chapter and the following chapters use the devices in this mode.

THE 68020 MULTIMASTER MODE

Figure 11-3a, p. 344, shows the pin diagram of the 68020. Normally, the 68020 controls when devices use the main system data and instruction buses. The 68020 sends enable signals to devices when they are supposed to read from or write to the buses. It is possible, however, for the 68020 to give up control of the main system buses and allow other ICs to control the flow of information on those buses. A typical example of this is the way a direct memory access controller operates. When the 68020 is used in a system with a DMA controller, the 68020 is said to be operating in a multimaster mode.

Figure 11-3b shows the circuit connections for a typical complex, multimaster 68020 system. Figure 11-3c shows the state of the FC0, FC1, and FC2 lines; these control which device is actually operating as the bus master. In a multimaster system these three lines are used to synchronize the different bus masters.

Now we show you some of the ways that a microprocessor can timeshare its buses.

DIRECT MEMORY ACCESS (DMA) DATA TRANSFER

DMA Overview

Up to this point in the book we have used program instructions to transfer data from ports to memory or from memory to ports. However, for some applications, such as transferring data bytes to memory from a magnetic or optical disk, the data bytes are coming from the disk faster than they can be read in with program instructions. In a case such as that, we use a dedicated hardware device called a *direct memory*

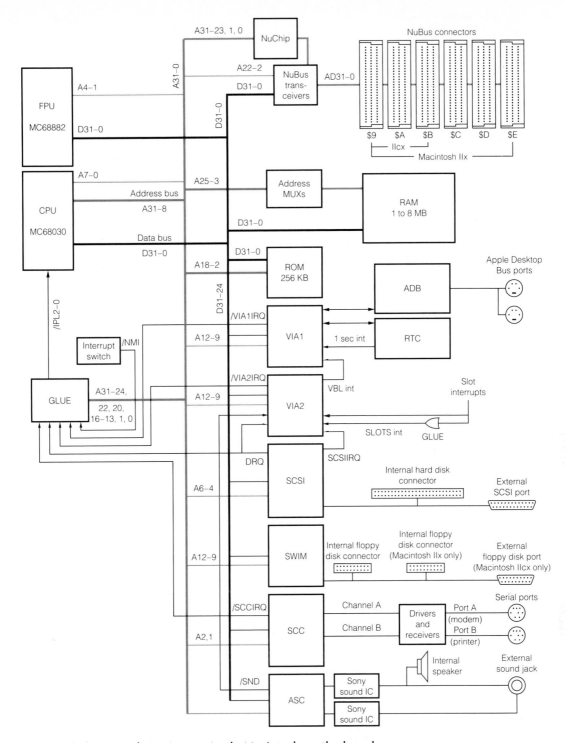

FIGURE 11-2 Block diagram of circuitry on Apple Macintosh motherboard.

access (DMA) controller to manage the data transfer. The DMA controller temporarily borrows the address bus, data bus, and control bus from the microprocessor and transfers the data bytes directly from the disk controller to a series of memory locations. Because the data transfer is handled totally in hardware, it is much faster than it would be if done by program instructions. A DMA controller can also transfer data from memory to an I/O port. Some DMA devices can even do memo-ry-to-memory transfers to implement fast block trans-fers. Here's an example of how a common DMA con-troller is connected and used in a 68020 system.

Circuit Connections and Operation of the Intel 8237 DMA Controller

We chose the 8237 DMA controller as the example for this section because it is a commonly used device.

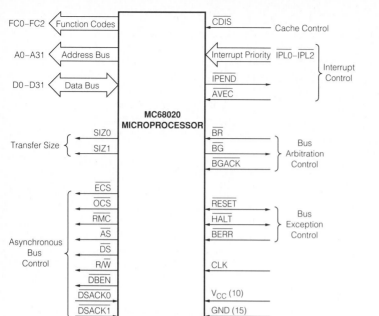

(a)

FC2	FC1	FC0	Cycle Type
0	0	0	(Undefined, Reserved)*
0	0	1	User Data Space
0	1	0	User Program Space
0	1	1	(Undefined, Reserved)*
1	0	0	(Undefined, Reserved)*
1	0	1	Supervisor Data Space
1	1	0	Supervisor Program Space
1	1	1	CPU Space

* Address space 3 is reserved for user definition, while 0 and 4 are reserved for future use by Motorola.

(c)

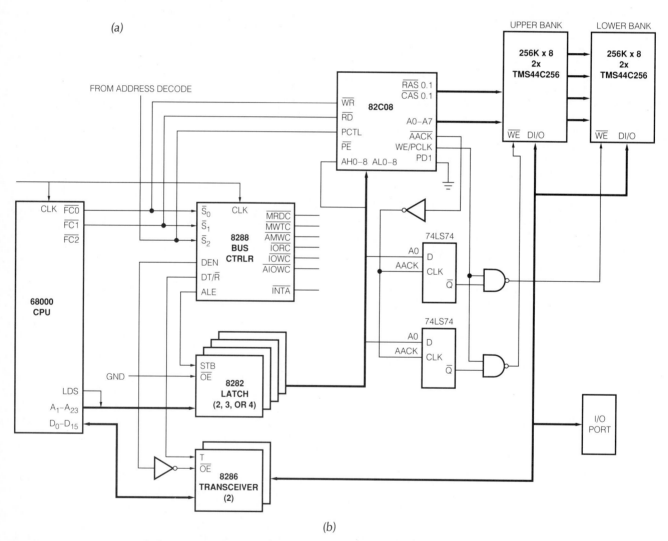

(b)

FIGURE 11-3   68000 revisited. (*a*) 68000 pin diagram. (*b*) Circuit showing 68000 connections for a complete system. (*c*) FC0, FC1, and FC2 codes for 68000 machine cycles.

Before we dig into the actual connections and operation of an 8237 circuit, however, let's take a look at the block diagram in Figure 11-4 to get an overview of how a DMA transfer takes place. The main point to keep in mind here is that the microprocessor and the DMA controller timeshare the use of the address, data, and control buses. The three switches in the middle of the block diagram attempt to show how control of the buses is transferred.

When the system is first turned on, the switches are in the up position, where the buses are connected from the microprocessor to system memory and peripherals. We initialize all the programmable devices in the system and go on executing our program until we need, for example, to read a file from a disk. To read a disk file we send a series of commands to the smart disk-controller device, telling it to find and read the desired block of data from the disk. When the disk controller has the first byte of data from the disk block ready, it sends a DMA request, DREQ, signal to the DMA controller. If that input (channel) of the DMA controller is unmasked, the DMA controller will send a bus request, BREQ, to the microprocessor BREQ input. The microprocessor will respond to this input by floating its buses and sending out a bus-grant (BGRA) signal to the DMA controller. When the DMA controller receives the BGRA signal, it sends out a bas-grant-acknowledge (BGACK) signal back to the CPU. The DMA controller then sends a control signal that throws the three bus switches down to their DMA position. This disconnects the processor from the buses and connects the DMA controller to the buses.

When the DMA controller gets control of the buses, it sends out the memory address where the first byte of data from the disk controller is to be written. Next the DMA controller sends a DMA-acknowledge (DACK0) signal to the disk-controller device to tell it to get ready

to output the byte. Finally, the DMA controller asserts both the MEMW and the IOR lines on the control bus. Asserting the MEMW signal enables the addressed memory to accept data written to it. Asserting the IOR signal enables the disk controller to output the byte of data from the disk on the data bus. The byte of data is then transferred directly from the disk controller to the memory location without passing through the CPU or the DMA controller.

> NOTE: For this type of transfer the disk controller chip select input does not have to be enabled by the port address decoding circuitry as it does for normal reading from and writing to registers in the device. In fact, the normal port-decoding circuitry is disabled during DMA operations to prevent the combination of IOR and the output memory address from turning on unwanted ports.

When the data transfer is complete, the DMA controller unasserts its hold-request signal to the processor and releases the buses. The switches in Figure 11-4 are effectively thrown back up to the CPU position. This lets the processor take over the buses again until another DMA transfer is needed. The processor continues executing from where it left off in the program.

A DMA transfer from memory to the disk controller proceeds in a similar manner except that the DMA controller asserts the memory-read control (MEMR) signal and the output-write control (IOW) signal. DMA transfers may be done a byte at a time or in blocks.

Now, to give you more practice working your way through actual microprocessor circuits, let's look at Figure 11-5, p. 347, to see some of the circuitry we might add to a 68020 system so that we can do DMA

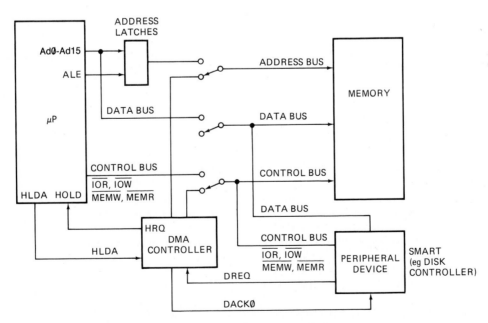

FIGURE 11-4 Block diagram showing how a DMA controller operates in a microcomputer system.

transfers to and from a disk controller. This circuitry is simply a more detailed version of the block diagram in Figure 11-4.

The first thing to do in analyzing this schematic is to identify the major devices and relate their function, where possible, to the block diagram. The 8237 is, of course, the DMA controller, and the 8272 is the floppy-disk controller. We discuss the operation of a disk controller more in Chapter 13, but for now all you need to know about it is the overview of how it interacts with the 8237, as we described previously. The 8282s in this circuit are octal latches with three-state outputs. They are used here to latch address output from either the 68020 or from the DMA controller. These devices are controlled by AE from the 68020 and by AEN and ADSTB from the DMA controller.

When the power is first turned on, the address-enable (AEN) signal from the DMA controller is low. Devices U1, U2, and U4 are then enabled, and the AE signal from the 68020 goes to the strobe inputs of all three devices. When the 68020 sends out an address and an address strobe signal, these three devices will grab the address and send it out on the address bus lines, A31–A0. This is just as would be done in a simpler 68000 system. Now, when the DMA controller wants to take over the bus, it asserts its AEN output high. This does several things. First, it disables device U1 so that the address lines A7–A0 no longer come from the 68020 bus. The 8237 directly outputs the lower 8 bits of the memory address for the DMA transfer.

Secondly, AEN, going high, switches the strobe multiplexer so that the strobe for device U2 comes from the address strobe output of the 8237. To save pins, the 8237 outputs the upper 8 bits of the memory address for the DMA transfer on its data bus pins and asserts its ADSTB output high to let you know that this address is present there. At the start of a DMA transfer, then, memory address bits A15–A8 will be sent out by the 8237 and latched on the outputs of U2.

Still another effect of AEN going high is to switch the source of address bits A31–A16 from device U4 to device U3. The DMA controller does not send out these address bits during a DMA transfer, so you have to produce them in some other way. You can either hard-wire the inputs of U3 to ground or +5 V to produce a fixed value for these bits, or you can connect these inputs to an output port so you can specify these address bits under program control.

Finally, AEN going high switches the source of the control bus signals from the outputs of the control bus decoder circuitry to the control bus signal outputs of the DMA controller. This is necessary because, during a DMA transfer, the 8237 generates the required control bus signals, such as MEMW and IOR. Incidentally, the NOR gate decoder circuitry in the upper right corner of the schematic is necessary to produce processor control bus signals compatible with those from the 8237.

The final part of the circuit in Figure 11-5 to analyze consists of the two 8286 octal bus transceivers. The disk controller has only an 8-bit data bus output. If we connected these eight lines on the lower eight data bus lines of the 68020 system, the DMA controller could transfer bytes only to even addresses. Likewise, if we connected the disk-controller data outputs on the upper eight data lines of the 68020 system, the DMA controller could transfer bytes only to odd addresses in memory. To solve this problem, we connect the two 8286s as a switch, which can route data to or from the disk controller from or to either odd or even addresses in memory. If you work through the glue logic, you should see that A0 determines which half of the data bus is connected to the eight data pins of the disk controller. MEMW determines whether the buffers are set to transfer data to or from the disk controller. Now let's look more closely at the signal flow and timing for this circuit.

A DMA Transfer Timing Diagram

Figure 11-6 shows the sequence of signals that take place for a DMA transfer in a system such as that in Figure 11-5. Keep a copy of Figure 11-5 handy as you work your way through these waveforms. The labels we have added to each signal should help you. We will pick up where the 8237 asserts AEN high and gains control of the buses. After the 8237 gains control of the bus, it sends out the lower 8 bits of the memory address on its A7–A0 pins and the upper 8 bits of the memory address on its DB0–DB7 pins. The 8237 pulses ADSTB high to latch these address bits in the 8282 and then removes these address bits from the data bus. At about the same time the 8237 sends a DACK signal to the disk controller to tell it to get ready for a data transfer.

Now that everything is ready, the 8237 asserts two control bus signals to enable the actual transfer. For a transfer from memory to the disk controller, it will assert MEMR and IOW. For a transfer from the disk controller to memory, it will assert MEMW and IOR. Note that the 8237 does not have to put out an I/O address to enable the disk controller for this transfer. When programmed in DMA mode, the disk controller needs only IOR or IOW to be asserted to enable it for the transfer. Also note that the 8237 will not output a new address on A8–A15 when a second transfer is done unless those bits have to be changed. This saves time during multiple-byte transfers.

When the programmed number of bytes have been transferred, the DMA controller pulses its end-of-process (EOP) pin low, unasserts its hold request to the 68020, and drops its AEN signal low. This releases the buses back to the 68020. Now that you have an idea how an 8237 is connected and operates in a system, we will give you an overview of what is involved in initializing it.

8237 Initialization Overview

Initializing an 8237 is not difficult, but it does require a fairly large number of bytes. We do not have space here

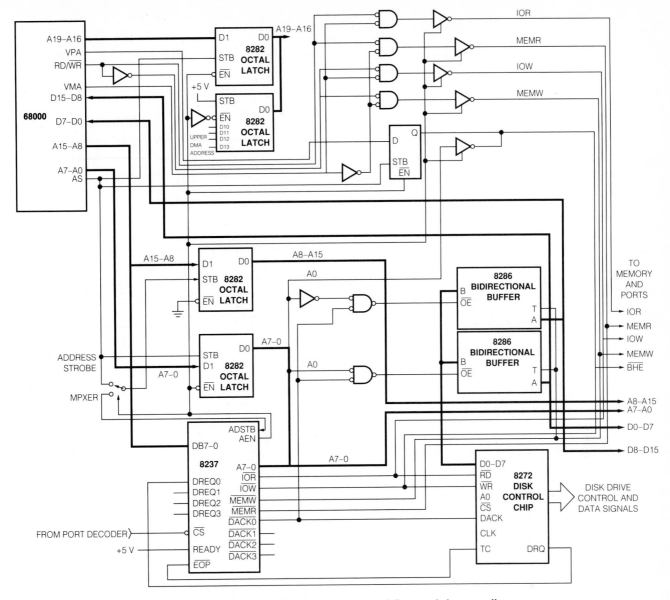

FIGURE 11-5 Schematic for 68000 system with DMA controller and floppy-disk controller.

to show you a complete initialization, but here is an overview.

The 8237 is connected in a system as a port device, so you write initialization words to it just as you would to any other port device. Incidentally, several 8237s can be cascaded in a master-slave arrangement to give more input channels, and each device must be initialized.

As shown by the pin labels on the 8237 in Figure 11-5, the 8237 has four DMA request inputs, or *channels,* as they are commonly called. For each channel you need to send a command word that specifies the general operation, mode words, the starting memory address, and the number of bytes to be transferred. Each channel of the 8237 can be programmed to transfer a single byte for each request, to transfer a block of bytes for each request, or to keep transferring bytes until it receives a wait signal on the EOP input/

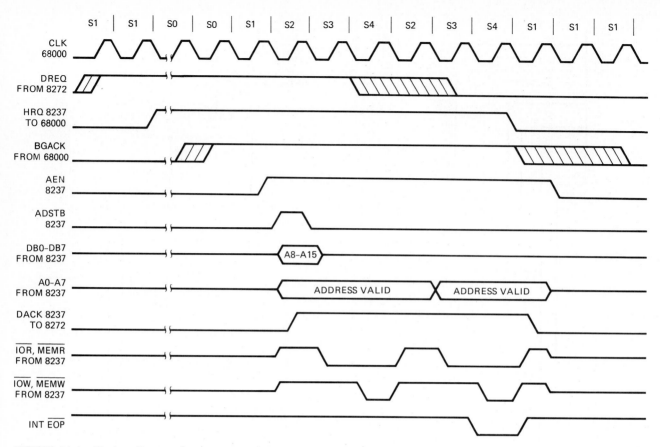

FIGURE 11-6   Timing diagram for DMA transfer.

output. Consult the data sheet in an Intel data book to get the details of each command word.

Now that you know how DMA works in a microcomputer, the next block of circuitry to talk about is the RAM section.

INTERFACING AND REFRESHING DYNAMIC RAMs

Review of Dynamic RAM Characteristics

For small systems such as the URDA® MDS, where we only need a few kilobytes of RAM, we usually use static RAM devices because they are very easy to interface to. For larger systems where we want several hundred kilobytes or megabytes of memory, we use dynamic RAMs, often called DRAMs. Here's why.

Static RAMs store each bit in an internal flip-flop, which requires four to six transistors. In DRAMs a data bit is stored as a charge or no charge on a tiny capacitor. All that is needed in addition to the capacitor is a single transistor switch to access the capacitor when a bit is written to it or read from it. The result of this is that DRAMs require much less power per bit, and many more bits can be stored in a given-size chip. This makes the cost per bit of storage much less. The disadvantage of DRAMs is that each stored data bit must be refreshed every 2 to 8 ms because the charge

stored on the tiny capacitors tends to change due to leakage. When activated by an external signal, the refresh circuitry in the device checks the voltage level stored on each capacitor. If the voltage is greater than $V_{CC}/2$, then that location is charged to V_{CC}. If the voltage is less than $V_{CC}/2$, then that location is discharged to 0 V. Let's take a look at a typical DRAM to see how we read, write, and refresh it. Figure 11-7(a) and (b) shows the pins on a Macintosh used to control the RAMs. Refer back to this figure while reading the following discussion.

Figure 11-8a, p. 349, shows an internal block diagram for a Texas Instruments TMS44C256 CMOS DRAM. This device is a 256K × 4 device, so it stores 262,144 words of 4 bits each in its 20-pin package. You can connect two of these in parallel to store bytes or four in parallel to store 16-bit words. Since DRAMS are almost always connected in parallel, several companies now produce DRAM modules such as the TI TM4256FL8 256K × 8 device shown in Figure 11-8b. The 30-pin single-in-line package (SIP) takes much less PC board space than the equivalent DIPs.

According to the basic rules of address decoding, 18 address lines should be required to address one of the 256K, or 2^{18}, words stored in the MT44C256 DRAM. The diagram in Figure 11-8a, however, shows only nine address inputs, A0–A8. The trick here is that to save pins, DRAMs usually multiplex in the address one-half at a time. A look at the timing diagram for a

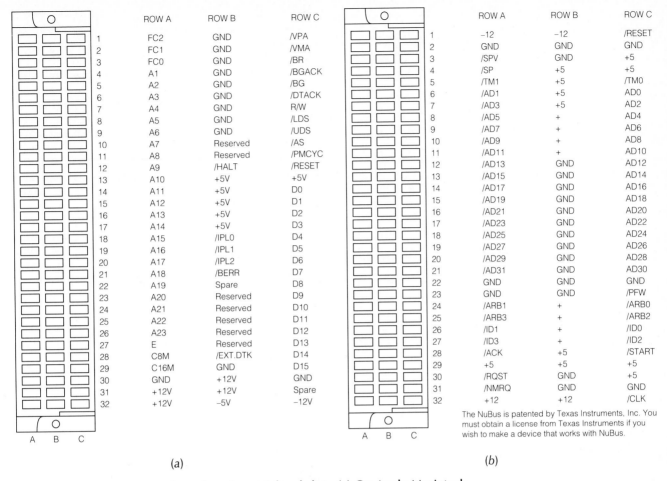

	ROW A	ROW B	ROW C			ROW A	ROW B	ROW C
1	FC2	GND	/VPA		1	–12	–12	/RESET
2	FC1	GND	/VMA		2	GND	GND	GND
3	FC0	GND	/BR		3	/SPV	GND	+5
4	A1	GND	/BGACK		4	/SP	+5	+5
5	A2	GND	/BG		5	/TM1	+5	/TM0
6	A3	GND	/DTACK		6	/AD1	+5	AD0
7	A4	GND	R/W		7	/AD3	+5	AD2
8	A5	GND	/LDS		8	/AD5	+	AD4
9	A6	GND	/UDS		9	/AD7	+	AD6
10	A7	Reserved	/AS		10	/AD9	+	AD8
11	A8	Reserved	/PMCYC		11	/AD11	+	AD10
12	A9	/HALT	/RESET		12	/AD13	GND	AD12
13	A10	+5V	+5V		13	/AD15	GND	AD14
14	A11	+5V	D0		14	/AD17	GND	AD16
15	A12	+5V	D1		15	/AD19	GND	AD18
16	A13	+5V	D2		16	/AD21	GND	AD20
17	A14	+5V	D3		17	/AD23	GND	AD22
18	A15	/IPL0	D4		18	/AD25	GND	AD24
19	A16	/IPL1	D5		19	/AD27	GND	AD26
20	A17	/IPL2	D6		20	/AD29	GND	AD28
21	A18	/BERR	D7		21	/AD31	GND	AD30
22	A19	Spare	D8		22	GND	GND	GND
23	A20	Reserved	D9		23	GND	GND	/PFW
24	A21	Reserved	D10		24	/ARB1	+	/ARB0
25	A22	Reserved	D11		25	/ARB3	+	/ARB2
26	A23	Reserved	D12		26	/ID1	+	/ID0
27	E	Reserved	D13		27	/ID3	+	/ID2
28	C8M	/EXT.DTK	D14		28	/ACK	+5	/START
29	C16M	GND	D15		29	+5	+5	+5
30	GND	+12V	GND		30	/RQST	GND	+5
31	+12V	+12V	Spare		31	/NMRQ	GND	GND
32	+12V	–5V	–12V		32	+12	+12	/CLK

The NuBus is patented by Texas Instruments, Inc. You must obtain a license from Texas Instruments if you wish to make a device that works with NuBus.

(a)

(b)

FIGURE 11-7   Pin names and numbers for peripheral slots. (a) On Apple Macintosh Plus motherboard. (b) On Apple Macintosh SE motherboard.

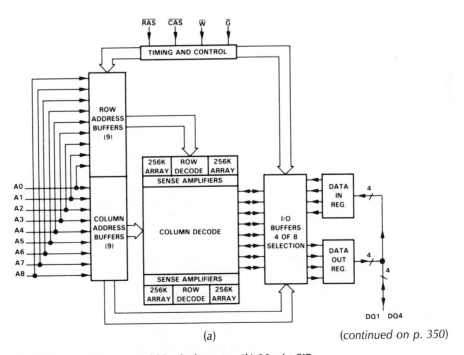

(a)

(continued on p. 350)

FIGURE 11-8   TMS44C256 DRAM. (a) Functional block diagram. (b) 30-pin SIP diagram (p. 349). (c) Read cycle timing (p. 350). (Texas Instruments Inc.)

DMA, DRAMS, CACHE MEMORIES, COPROCESSORS, AND EDA TOOLS   **349**

TM4258FL8...L SINGLE-IN-LINE PACKAGE
(TOP VIEW)

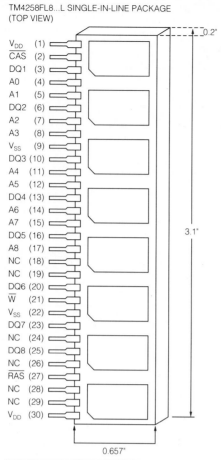

PIN NOMENCLATURE TM4258FL8	
A0-A8	Address Inputs
$\overline{CAS}$	Column-Address Strobe
DQ1-DQ8	Data In/Data Out
NC	No Connection
$\overline{RAC}$	Row-Address Strobe
V_{DD}	5-V Supply
V_{SS}	Ground
$\overline{W}$	Write Enable

(b)

FIGURE 11-8 (continued)   (continued on p. 351)

read operation in Figure 11-8c should help you to see how this works.

To read a word from a bank of dynamic RAMs, a DRAM-controller device or other circuitry asserts the write-enable (W) pin of the DRAMs high to enable them for a read operation. It then sends the upper half of the address, called the *row address*, or *page address*, to the nine address inputs of the DRAMs. The controller then asserts the row-address-strobe (RAS) input of the DRAM low to latch the row address in the DRAM. After the proper timing interval, the controller removes the row address and outputs the lower half of the address, called *column address*, to the nine address inputs of the DRAMs. The controller then asserts the column-address-strobe (CAS) inputs of the DRAMs low to latch the column address in the DRAMs. After a propagation delay, the data word from the addressed memory cells will appear on the data outputs of the DRAMs.

The timing diagram for a write cycle is nearly the same except that after it sends out the column address and CAS, the controller asserts the write-enable input low to enable the DRAMs for writing and asserts a signal, which is used to gate the data to be written onto the data inputs of the DRAMs.

To refresh a row in a DRAM, the row address is applied to the address inputs and the RAS input is pulsed low. For this particular device, each row must be refreshed at least once every 8 ms. The refresh can be done in either a burst mode or in a distributed mode. In the burst mode all 512 rows are addressed and pulsed with a RAS strobe, one right after the other every 8 ms. In the distributed mode a row is addressed and pulsed after every 8/512 ms, or 15.6 μs. In a particular system you use the mode that will least interfere with the operation of the system. Now that the operation of dynamic RAMs is fresh in your mind, we will show you how you interface banks of DRAMs to a 68020.

Overview of Interfacing DRAMs to a Microprocessor

As perhaps you can see from the preceding discussion, the main tasks you have to do to interface a bank of DRAMs to a microprocessor are the following:

1. To multiplex the two halves of the address into each device with the appropriate RAS and CAS strobes.

2. To provide a read/write control signal to enable data into or out of the devices.

3. To refresh each row at the proper interval.

4. To assure that a read or write operation and a refresh operation do not take place at the same time.

There are many ways to do these tasks. For a start let's look at how they are done in a 68000-based microcomputer.

Using an 82C08 DRAM Controller IC

In high-performance systems where we want DRAM refreshing to take up a minimum amount of the processor's time, we usually use a dedicated device that handles all the refreshing chores without tying up the microprocessor or its buses, as the DMA approach does. An example of this type of device is the Intel 82C08. Figure 11-9, p. 352, shows, in block diagram form, how an 82C08 can be connected with a 68000 in maximum mode to refresh and control 512 Kbytes of dynamic RAM. The 82C08 takes care of all the addressing and refresh tasks.

The memories here are the 256K × 4 devices shown in Figure 11-8a. As usual for a 68000 system, the memory is set up as two byte-wide banks. In this system each bank has two DRAM devices, so each bank has 256 Kbytes.

read cycle timing

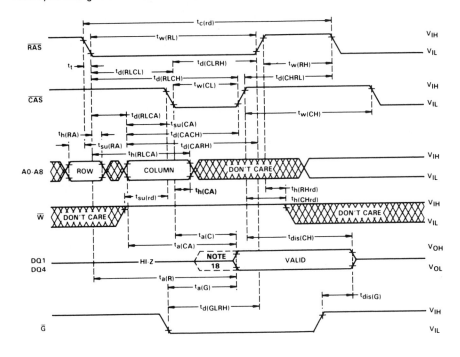

NOTE 18: Output may go from high impedance to an invalid data state prior to the specified access time.

(c)

FIGURE 11-8 (continued)

One important point to observe here is that the status signals from the 68000, FC0–FC2, are connected directly to the control inputs of the 82C08. The 82C08 decodes these status signals to produce the read and write signals needed for the DRAMs. This advanced decoding means that, except when a refresh cycle is in progress, the 68000 will be able to read a byte or word from the DRAMs without WAIT states.

If you look closely at the 82C08 in Figure 11-9, you should find the port enable input, PE. This input is asserted low to request access to the DRAM. If the 82C08 is not involved in a refresh operation when PE is asserted low, the 82C08 will multiplex the address from the address bus into the DRAMs with the appropriate RAS and CAS strobes. The 82C08 will also send out an AACK signal, which clocks the 74LS74 flip-flops to transfer the A0 and BHE signals to the two memory banks. For a read operation, the addressed byte or word will then be output on the data bus to the 68000. For a write operation, the byte or word on the data bus will be written to the addressed locations in the DRAMs.

The output of an address decoder is connected to the PE input to assert it for the desired range of addresses. Because the DRAM banks in the circuit in Figure 11-9 are so large, the address decoding is very simple. Each bank in the circuit contains 256 Kbytes. Since 256K = 2^{18}, 18 address lines are required to address one of the bytes in a bank. In most systems we connect system address lines A1–A18 to the 82C08 address inputs, and the 82C08 multiplexes these signals into the DRAMs, nine at a time. Address line A0 is used along with the BHE signal to select the desired bank(s). This leaves only the A19 system address line unaccounted for. If we connect the A19 address line directly to the PE input of the 82C08, then PE will be asserted whenever the 68000 outputs a memory address with A19 low. In other words, the PE input will be asserted when the 68000 outputs any address between $00000 and $7FFFF.

NOTE: The status signals from the 68000 are decoded in the 82C08, so it knows whether an address is intended for memory or an I/O port.

The address decoder here is simply an inverter that connects A19 to the PE input. This connection puts the RAM in the upper part of the 68000 address range, which is appropriate because for a 68000, we want ROMs containing the startup program to be at the bottom of the address range.

The next point to consider in the system in Figure 11-9 is how the controller arbitrates the dispute that occurs if the CPU tries to read from or write to memory while the controller is doing a refresh cycle. If the 82C08 in Figure 11-9 happens to be in the middle of a refresh cycle when the 68000 tries to read a DRAM location, the 82C08 will hold its AACK high until it is finished with the refresh cycle. With the connections shown in Figure 11-9, this will cause the 68000 to insert one or more WAIT states while the 82C08 finish-

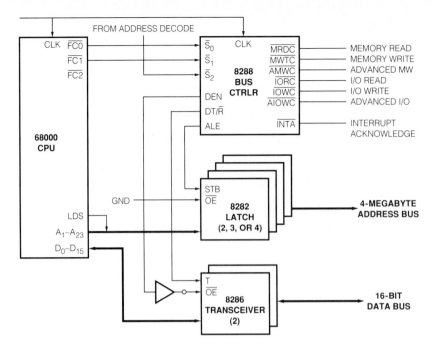

FIGURE 11-9 The 68000 microcomputer system using DRAM controller.

es its refresh cycle. In this system, then, the occasional access conflict is arbitrated by the DRAM controller. Inserting a wait state now and then slows the 68000 down less than the other DMA approaches.

Another interesting feature of the system in Figure 11-9 is the battery backup circuitry. In Chapter 8 we discussed the use of a 68000 interrupt-service routine to save program data in the case of a power failure. In the few milliseconds between the time the ac power goes off and the time the dc power drops below operating levels, an interrupt-service routine copies program data to a block of CMOS static RAM, which has a battery backup power supply. When the system is repowered, the saved data is copied back into the main RAM, and processing takes up where it left off. In larger systems there may not be time enough to copy all the important data to another RAM, so we simply use a battery backup for the entire DRAM array.

In this circuit we used CMOS DRAMs because when these devices are not being accessed for reading, writing, or refreshing, they take only microwatts of power. During battery backup of the DRAMs, they must still be refreshed, so the 82C08 DRAM controller is also connected to the battery power.

When the power supply voltage drops below a specified level, the PFO pin on the MAXIM 691 supervisor device sends a signal to the 68000. The interrupt-service routine saves parameters so the program can restart correctly when power returns and then sends a signal to the power down detect (PDD) input of the 82C08. In response to this signal the 82C08 switches from the high-frequency system clock to a lower-frequency clock signal from the CMOS crystal oscillator. Reducing the clock frequency decreases the amount of current required by the DRAMs and by the

82C08 to perform refresh operations. Also, by using the CMOS oscillator, the high-current 8284 system clock generator does not need to be kept running.

When the power returns, the MAX691 generates a power-on-reset signal, RESET, with the correct timing for the 68000. If a low is output to the PDD input of the 82C08 as part of the startup sequence, the 82C08 will automatically switch to using the system clock and operate normally for read, write, and refresh operations.

For the backup battery we use nickel-cadmium or some other type that can stand the continuous recharging and supply the needed current. The diodes in the circuit prevent the power supply output and the battery from fighting with each other.

In applications where the entire system must be kept running during an ac power outage, we use a noninterruptible power supply, or NPS. These power supplies contain large batteries, charging circuitry, and circuitry needed to convert the battery voltage to the voltages needed by the microcomputer.

Dynamic RAM Timing in Microcomputer Systems

In Chapter 7 we showed you how to determine if a memory device such as a ROM or RAM is fast enough to operate in a synchronous 68000 system with a given clock frequency. To make these calculations for a ROM or for an SRAM, you use its access times. For DRAMs, however, the limiting time is the read cycle time, t_{RD}. Here's why.

If you take a close look at the read cycle timing diagram for the TMS44C256 in Figure 11-8c, you should see that valid data will be present on the output for a time $t_{a(R)}$ after RAS goes low. For the fastest current version of the device, this time is about 100 ns. Before another row in the device can be accessed, however, the RAS input has to be made high and held high for a time labeled $t_{w(RH)}$. This time of about 80 ns is required to precharge the DRAM so that it is ready to accept the next row address. (Reading data from a storage location in a row discharges that location somewhat and the internal circuitry in the DRAM "precharges" the location again before it allows access to another row).

The precharge time effectively adds to the access time, so the time before a data bit from another row can be available on the output is considerably longer than the access time. The total time from the start of one read cycle to the start of the next is identified in Figure 11-8c as $t_{c(rd)}$. For the fastest version of the TMS44C256, the access time is only 100 ns, but the $t_{c(rd)}$ is 190 ns. For applications where the data words are rapidly being read from random rows, it is this $t_{c(rd)}$, then, that limits the rate that words from random rows can be read. Let's see how this time fits in a microprocessor read cycle.

As shown in Figure 7-19, a 68000 requires four clock cycles for each memory access. If the 68000 is operated with a 10-MHz clock (100 ns per clock), a memory access cycle will take 400 ns. This means that if you are willing to pay the price, you can get DRAMs that will operate without wait states in a microcomputer using a 10-MHz 68000. However, as we discuss in Chapter 14, later-generation processors such as the 68030 require only two clock cycles for a memory access, and they are typically operated with a clock signal of 25 MHz or more. These factors drastically decrease the time available for memory access. If currently available DRAMs are used as the main memory in a microcomputer that has a clock frequency greater than about 15 MHz, one or more wait states must usually be inserted in every DRAM read or write cycle. However, the low cost per bit of DRAMs make them attractive enough that several methods have been developed so they can be used without having to insert wait states in every memory access cycle. While the characteristics of DRAMs are fresh in your mind, we introduce you to some of these techniques.

Page Mode and Static Column Mode DRAM Systems

Two of the most commonly used techniques to reduce the number of wait states needed with DRAMs are the page mode method and the static column method. Here's how they work.

Remember from our discussion of DRAMs in a previous section that a precharge time is required each time a new row (page) is accessed in a DRAM. This precharge time is the reason that the typical read and write cycle times are so much longer than the access times for DRAMs. If successive data words are read from or written to locations in the same page (row), however, no precharge time is required. Also, if successive data words are read from the same page, the row address is the same, so a new row address does not have to be sent out and strobed in with a RAS signal. With the proper DRAM controller, these two factors make it possible to read data from a page or write data to a page without wait states. Some timing diagrams should help you see this.

Figure 11-10a shows the read timing waveforms for a Texas Instruments TMS44C256 DRAM that can be used for page mode access. For the first access in a row (page), the DRAM controller carries out a normal row address (RAS), column address (CAS) sequence of signals. If the next address the controller sends out is in the same row, an external comparator will send a signal to DRAM controller. In response to this "same-row" signal, the DRAM controller will hold RAS low, send out just the column address to the A0–A8 inputs of the DRAMs, and pulse CAS low. As long as the microprocessor continues to access memory locations in the same page (row), the controller will simply hold RAS low, send out the column part of the addresses to the DRAMs, and pulse CAS low for each new column address. These accesses within a page then are much faster because they require no row address and RAS time and because they require no precharge time.

To determine if a memory access is within the same page, a device such as the SN74ALS6310 is connected to the address bus. This device holds the page part of the previous address in a register and compares it to the page part of the new address. If the two address parts are the same, the 6310 signals the DRAM controller to do a page mode access such as that shown in Figure 11-10a. If the previous page address and the current page address are different, the controller will do a normal RAS and CAS access.

Figure 11-10b shows the read timing waveforms for a Texas Instruments TMS44C257 DRAM that is designed for static column mode operation. During the first access in a row, the DRAM controller carries out a normal row address (RAS), column address (CAS) sequence of signals. If the next address the controller sends out is in the same row, an external comparator will signal the DRAM controller. In response to this same-row signal the DRAM controller will hold RAS and CAS low and send out just the column address to the A0–A8 inputs of the DRAMs. As long as the microprocessor continues to access memory locations in the same page (row), the controller will simply hold RAS and CAS low and send out the column part of the addresses to the DRAMs. The static column mode is more difficult to implement than page mode, but it is faster than the page mode because it does not require CAS strobes and the associated setup and hold times.

In a high-speed microprocessor system, the static column decode technique can reduce the average number of wait states per memory access from two or three to perhaps 0.8. This is a considerable improvement, but it is not as much of an improvement as can be gained by using a cache system.

enhanced page-mode read cycle timing

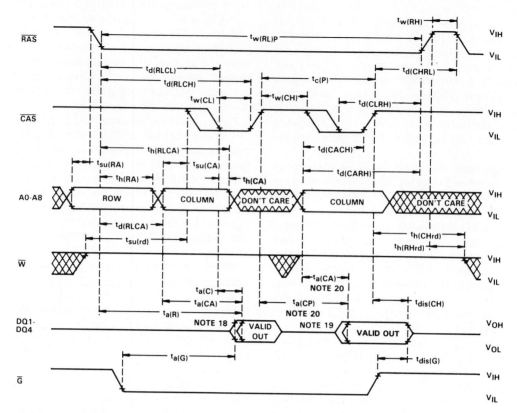

NOTES: 18. Output may go from high impedance to an invalid data state prior to the specified access time.
　　　　19. A write cycle or read-modify-write cycle can be mixed with the read cycles as long as the write and read-modify-write timing specifications are not violated.
　　　　20. Access time is $t_{a(CP)}$ or $t_{a(CA)}$ dependent.

(a)

static column decode mode read cycle timing

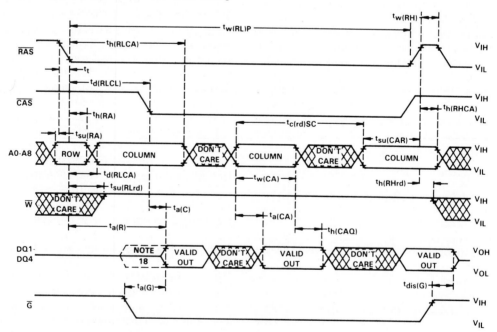

NOTE 18: Output may go from high impedance to an invalid data state prior to the specified access time.

(b)

FIGURE 11-10   TMS44C256 DRAM. (a) Page mode read cycle operation.
(b) Static column read cycle operation. (*Texas Instruments Inc.*)

Cache Mode DRAM Systems

INTRODUCTION

Traditionally the term *cache*, which is pronounced "cash," refers to a hiding place where you put provisions for future use. As we describe how a cache memory system is implemented in a microcomputer, perhaps you can see why the term is used here.

Figure 11-11 shows in block diagram form how a simple cache memory system is implemented in a 68020-based microcomputer system. In Chapter 15 we discuss the details of the 68020 microprocessor, but for this discussion all you need to know is that the 68020 has a 32-bit data bus and a 32-bit address bus. A 32-bit address bus allows the 68020 to address up to 4 Gbytes of memory, and a 32-bit data bus allows the 68020 to read or write 4 bytes in parallel.

The cache in a system such as this consists of perhaps 32 or 64 Kbytes of high-speed SRAM. The main memory consists of a few megabytes or more of slower but cheaper DRAM. The general principal of a cache system is that code and data sections currently being used are copied from the DRAM to the high-speed SRAM cache, where they can be accessed by the processor with no wait states. A cache system takes advantage of the fact that most microcomputer programs work with only small sections of code and data at a particular time. The fancy term for this is *locality of reference*. Here's how the system works.

When the microprocessor outputs an address, the cache controller checks to see if the contents of that address have previously been transferred to the cache. If the addressed code or data word is present in the cache, the cache controller enables the cache memory to output the addressed word on the data bus. Since this access is to the fast SRAM, no wait states are required.

If the addressed word is not in the cache, the cache controller enables the DRAM controller. The DRAM controller then sends the address on to the main memory to get the data word. Since the DRAM main memory is slower, this access requires one or two wait states. However, when a word is read from main memory, it not only goes to the microprocessor, it is also written to the cache. If the processor needs to access this data word again, it can then read the data directly from the cache with no wait states. The percentage of accesses where the microprocessor finds the code or data word it needs in the cache is called the *hit rate*. Current systems have average hit rates greater than 90 percent.

For write-to-memory operations most cache systems use a posted-write-through method. If the cache controller determines that the addressed word is present in the cache, the controller will write the new word to the cache with no wait states and signal the 68020 that the write is complete. The controller will then write the data word to main memory. This write to the main memory is transparent to the main processor unless the main memory is still involved in a previous write operation.

To keep track of which main memory locations are currently present in the SRAM cache, the cache controller uses a cache directory. For the Intel 82385 cache controller shown in Figure 11-11, the cache directory RAM is contained in the controller. Each location in the cache is represented by an entry in the directory. The exact format for the directory entry depends on the particular cache scheme used. The three basic cache schemes are direct mapped, two-way set associative, and fully associative. We don't have time here to do a detailed discussion of these three caching schemes, but we give you an introduction to each so you will understand the terms if you see them in a computer magazine article or advertisement. We discuss cache systems further in Chapter 15.

A DIRECT-MAPPED CACHE

Figure 11-12*a* shows a block diagram of how a direct-mapped 32-Kbyte cache can be implemented in a 68020 system with an 82385 controller. As we said before, a 68020 has a 32-bit address bus, so it can address 2^{32} bytes, or about 4 Gbytes, of memory. The

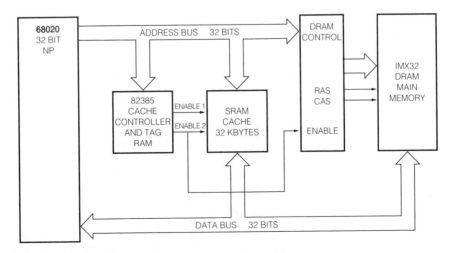

FIGURE 11-11   68020 microcomputer RAM memory system using high-speed SRAM cache.

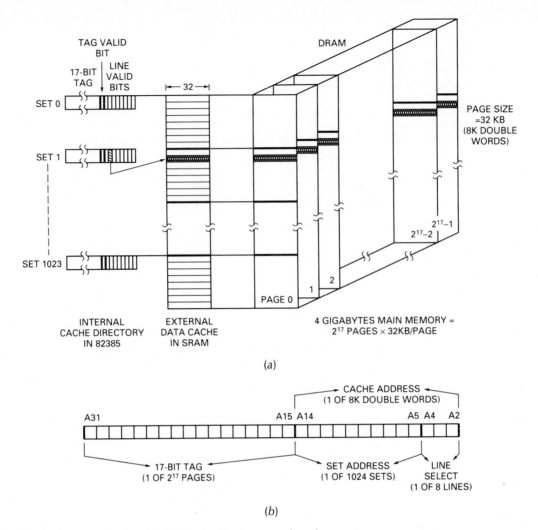

FIGURE 11-12 Cache organization for 32-Kbyte direct-mapped cache.
(a) Block diagram. (b) Use of 32-bit address by cache controller.

68020 also has a 32-bit data bus, so it can read up to 4 bytes at a time from memory. A group of 4 parallel bytes is commonly referred to as a *line*.

The cache memory for the 68020 system in Figure 11-12a is set up to hold 8K 4-byte lines, or a total of 32 Kbytes. The 8K lines in the cache are organized as 1024 sets of 8 lines each. The cache controller treats the 4 Gbytes of main memory as 2^{17}, or 131,072, pages of 32 Kbytes each. Each page in main memory then is the same size as the cache.

The term direct mapped here means that a particular numbered line from a page in main memory will always be copied to that same numbered line in the cache. For example, if line 1 from page 0 is in the cache, it will be stored in line 1 of the cache. If line 1 from page 131,070 is in the cache, it will be stored in line 1 of the cache. The cache directory on the left side of Figure 11-12a is used to keep track of which lines from the main memory currently have copies in the cache. As you can see, the directory contains a 26-bit entry for each set of 8 lines in the cache. The upper 17 bits of a directory entry are called a *tag*. The tag in a

directory entry identifies the main memory page that a line or set of lines in the cache duplicate. Each directory entry also contains a tag valid bit and eight line valid bits (one for each line in the set). Here's how the 82385 uses this directory during a read operation.

When the 68020 sends out a 32-bit address to read a word from memory, address lines A15–A31 represent a main memory page, address lines A5–A14 identify the set containing a desired line, and address lines A2–A4 identify the number of the line in the set containing the desired word. Figure 11-2b shows this in diagram form. The cache controller first uses address bits A5–A14 to select the directory entry for the set that contains the addressed line. Then it compares the upper 17 bits of the address from the 68020 with the 17-bit tag stored in the directory entry. If the two are equal, the controller checks the tag valid bit to see if the tag is current. If the tag valid bit is set, the controller checks the line valid bit for the line addressed by address 4. If the tag matches and is valid and the line is valid, the line is in the cache. This is a cache *hit*. In this case the controller will apply address bits A2–A14 to the cache memory and enable the cache memory to output the addressed word on the data bus.

If the upper 17 bits of address from the 68020 are not the same as the tag in the directory, the tag bit is not valid, or the line bit for the addressed line is not valid, the read operation is a cache *miss*. In this case the 82385 will send the complete address from the 68020 along to the DRAM controller. The DRAM controller will cause the main memory to output the addressed line on the data bus. When this line appears on the data bus, the 82385 will enable the cache memory so that the line gets written to the cache as well as going to the 68020. The 82385 will also update the cache directory to indicate that this line is now in the cache. If this line or any part of it is needed again, it can be read directly from the cache.

When the 68020 writes a word to memory, the 82385 grabs the address and the data word and then signals the 68020 that the transfer is complete. The controller then enables the main memory so that the word is written to the correct address in the main memory. If the data word is present in the cache, it is also written to the cache. This *posted write* process does not require any wait states unless the memory is still busy with a previous write.

A TWO-WAY SET-ASSOCIATIVE CACHE SYSTEM

One difficulty with the direct-mapped cache approach is that if a program happens to use the same numbered line from two memory pages at the same time, it will be swapping the two lines back and forth between main memory and the cache as it executes. This swapping back and forth is called *thrashing*. A scheme that helps avoid thrashing is the two-way set-associative cache approach shown in Figure 11-13a, p. 358. In this approach two separate caches and two separate cache directories are set up so that the same lines from two different pages can be cached at the same time. Each cache is half the size of the direct-mapped cache we discussed in the previous section, so the controller treats memory as 262,144 pages of 4096 lines each. To identify one of these 262,144 pages, the tag in each cache directory entry contains 18 bits. Each directory entry in this system also contains a tag valid bit, eight line valid bits, and a least recently used bit, or LRU. Here's how this system works during a read operation.

When the 68020 outputs an address, the 82385 controller uses address bits A5–A13 to select the appropriate entry in each cache directory. It then compares the upper 18 bits of the address from the 68020 with the tag in each of the selected directory entries. If one of the tags matches, the controller checks the tag valid bit in that directory entry. The controller also checks the line valid bit for the line specified by address bits A2–A4. If these bits are set, the controller outputs address bits A2–A13 to the cache associated with that directory and enables the cache to output the desired word on the data bus.

If the addressed data word is found in cache A, the LRU bit in the directory entry is set to indicate that cache A was the most recently used. If the data word is found in cache B, the LRU bit will be set to indicate that cache B was the most recently used. This mechanism is used to determine which cache should be used to hold a new line that is read in from main memory. When a read operation produces a cache miss, the 82385 will send the address and control signals to the main memory to read a line containing the desired word. When this line comes down the data bus, the 82385 will write it to the least recently used cache and update the corresponding directory entry. If the controller finds that the tag for a read operation is correct but a line valid bit is invalid, it will read the line from main memory and write it in the cache whose directory contains the tag. This assures that adjacent lines from a page in main memory end up in the same cache.

For a write operation this two-way set-associative cache approach uses the same posted write-through method we described earlier. The controller always writes an output data word to the main memory, and if the word is present in one of the caches, the controller also updates the word in the cache.

Because of the two tag RAMs and the associated circuitry, this approach is somewhat more complex to implement, but it usually produces a better hit rate than a direct-mapped cache.

A FULLY ASSOCIATIVE CACHE SYSTEM

Still another type of cache that you may hear mentioned is the fully associative type. In this type a 4-byte block or line from main memory can be written in any location in the cache. Figure 11-14, p. 359, shows in block diagram form how this works.

The system has a 32-bit address bus, so it can address 4 Gbytes of memory. This corresponds to 1 Gbyte of 4-byte lines. Since 1 Gbyte is equal to 2^{30}, a 30-bit tag is required to identify each block or line stored in the cache. Each entry in the directory then must contain 30 bits for the tag plus any additional bits used to keep track of how recently the line was used.

A fully associative cache has the advantage that it can hold the same numbered lines from several different pages at the same time. It has the disadvantage, however, that the upper 30 bits of each memory address sent out by the microprocessor must be compared with all the tags in the directory to see if that line is present in the cache. This can be a time-consuming process. Also, when a fully associative cache is full, some algorithm must be used to determine which line to overwrite when a new line must be brought in from main memory. The most common algorithm replaces the least recently used line with the new line. The 82385, incidentally, is not designed to work with a fully associative cache system.

SUMMARY

The key point for you to remember about a cache is that by keeping the currently used code and data in a

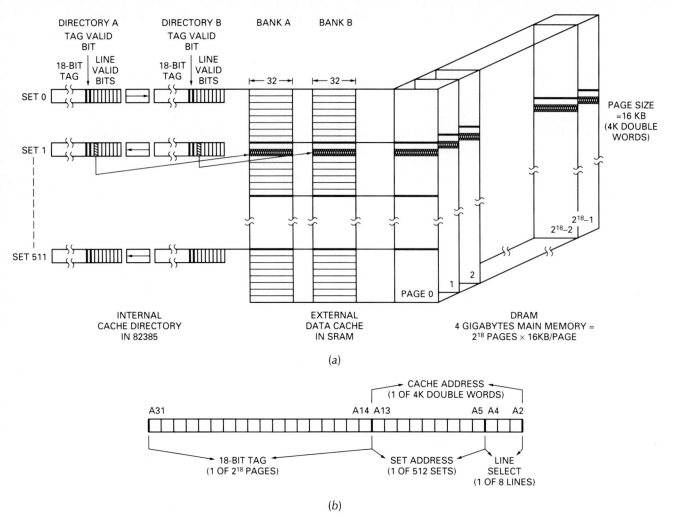

FIGURE 11-13   Two-way set-associative cache for 32-bit address bus system.
(a) Block diagram. (b) Use of 32-bit address by cache controller.

high-speed SRAM cache, the processor can use relatively inexpensive DRAM for its large main memory and still operate with few wait states. A cache controller device such as the 82385 automatically keeps the cache and the cache directory updated, so the process is essentially invisible to the microprocessor and to an executing program.

Error Detecting and Correcting in DRAM Arrays

PARITY GENERATION AND CHECKING

Data read from DRAMs is subject to two types of errors, hard errors and soft errors. *Hard errors* are caused by permanent device failure. This may be caused by a manufacturing defect or simply random breakdown in the chip. *Soft errors* are one-time errors caused by a noise pulse in the system or, in the case of dynamic RAMs, perhaps an alpha particle or some other radiation causing the charge to change on the tiny capacitor

where a data bit is stored. As the size of a RAM array increases, the chance of a hard or a soft error increases sharply. This increases the probability that the entire system will fail. It seems unreasonable that one fleeting alpha particle could cause an entire system to fail. To prevent or at least reduce the chances of this kind of failure, we add circuitry that detects and in some cases corrects errors in the data read out from DRAMs. There are several ways to do this, depending on the amount of detection and correction needed.

The simplest method for detecting an error is to use a parity bit. This is the method used in the IBM PC. In this type of system and in many others, each DRAM memory bank is 9 bits wide. Eight of these bits make up the data byte being stored, and the ninth bit is a parity bit that is used to detect errors in the stored data. A 74LS280 parity generator-checker circuit generates a parity bit for each byte and stores it in the ninth location as each byte is written to memory. When the 9 bits are read out, the overall parity is checked by the parity generator-checker circuit. If the

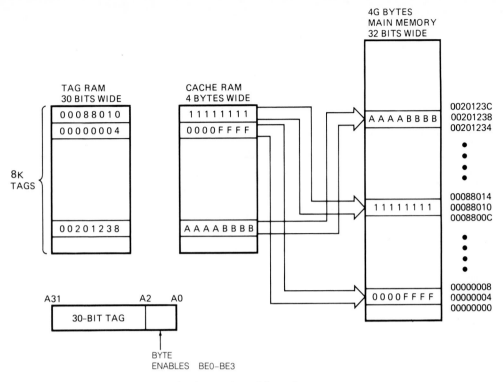

FIGURE 11-14 Fully associative 32-Kbyte cache for 32-bit address bus system.

parity is not correct, an error signal is sent to the NMI logic to interrupt the processor. When you first turn on the power to the microcomputer or warm boot it by pressing keys, one of the self-tests that it performs is to write byte patterns to all the RAM locations and check if the byte read back and the parity of that byte are correct. If any error is found, an error message is displayed on the screen so you don't try to load and run programs in defective RAM.

Detecting Errors and Correcting Circuits

One difficulty with a simple parity check is that two errors in a data word may cancel each other. A second problem with the simple parity method is that it does not tell you which bit in a word is wrong so that you can correct the error. More complex error detecting-correcting codes (ECCs), often called *Hamming codes* (after the man who did some of the original work in this area), permit you to detect multiple-bit errors in a word and to correct at least one bit error.

Special ICs can be used to implement this. For example, a TI 74AS632 error-detecting and -correcting (EDAC) device can be connected in the data path between a 32-bit microprocessor and 16-Mbyte DRAM main memory. The EDAC is connected in parallel with the DRAM refresh controller and in series with the SRAM cache. Here's how the EDAC device works.

When a data word is sent from the microprocessor to memory, it also goes to the EDAC. As the data word is read in by the EDAC, several encoding or check bits are generated and written in memory, along with the data word. As shown in Figure 11-15b, the number of encoding bits required, K, is determined by the size of the data word, M, and the degree of detection or correction desired. The total number of bits required for a data word, N, is equal to M + K. For example, 5 encoding bits are required to detect and correct a single-bit error in a 16-bit data word, so a total of 21 bits have to be stored for each 16-bit word. To detect or correct a 1-bit error and detect 2 wrong bits in a 32-bit word requires 7 encoding bits, or a total of 39 bits. The encoding bits, incidentally, are not just tacked on to one end of the data word as a parity bit is. They are interspersed in the data word.

When the processor reads a data word from memory, the data word and the check bits from memory go to the EDAC. The EDAC calculates the check bits for the data word read out from memory and XORs these check bits with the check bits that were stored in memory with the data word. The result of this XOR operation is called a *syndrome word*. The syndrome word is decoded to determine if the data word has no errors, a single-bit error, or multiple-bit errors.

If the data word contains no errors, the 74AS632 EDAC will simply output the data word to the processor on the data bus. If the data word contains a single-bit error, the EDAC device uses the syndrome word to determine which bit is incorrect and simply inverts that bit to correct the bit. The EDAC then outputs the corrected data word to the processor on the data bus. If the data word contains multiple-bit errors, the EDAC device asserts a signal, which is usually connected to

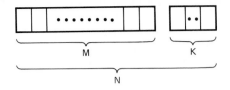

	SINGLE CORRECT/ SINGLE DETECT		SINGLE CORRECT/ DOUBLE DETECT	
K	$\leq M \leq$		$\leq M \leq$	
4	4	11	1	3
5	12	26	4	10
6	27	57	11	25
7	58	120	26	56
8	121	245	57	119

FIGURE 11-15   Hamming code data bits and encoding bits and number of encoding bits required for desired degree of detection/correction.

an interrupt input on the processor. In the case of a multiple-bit error, the programmer must decide what action to take and write the appropriate interrupt-service routine.

The 74AS632 EDAC can also work with the 74ALS6301 DRAM controller to remove errors in stored data words during refresh operations as well as during normal read operations. This process is called scrubbing. Correcting errors during each refresh operation decreases the chance of multiple-bit errors accumulating between read operations.

For more information on DRAM error detecting and correcting, consult the data sheets for error-detecting and -correcting devices such as the Intel 8206, the Texas Instruments 74AS632, or the National DP8402A.

In the next section of this chapter, we show you how a second processor can directly share the address, data, and control buses with the main processor in a microcomputer. Processors that share the local buses in this way are referred to as *coprocessors*. The example we use for this section is a Motorola 68881 math coprocessor. As shown in Figure 11-2, the Apple Macintosh II has one of these devices.

A COPROCESSOR—THE 68881 MATH COPROCESSOR

Overview

Many microcomputer programs, such as those used for scientific research, engineering, business, and graphics, need to make mathematical calculations, such as computing the square root of a number, the tangent of a number, or the log of a number. Another common need is to do arithmetic operations on very large and very small numbers. There are several ways to do all this.

One way is to write the number-crunching part of the program in a high-level language such as FORTRAN, compile this part of the program, and link in I/O modules written in assembly language. The difficulty with this approach is that programs written in high-level languages tend to run considerably more slowly than programs written in assembly language.

Another way is to write an assembly language program that uses the normal instruction set of the processor to do the arithmetic functions. Reference books that contain the algorithms for these are readily available. Our experience has shown that it is often time-consuming to get from the algorithm to a working assembly language program.

Still another approach is to buy a library of floating-point arithmetic object modules from the manufacturer of the microprocessor with which you are working or from an independent software house. In your program you just declare a function needed from the library as external, call the function as required, and link the library object code files for the functions to the object code for your program. This approach spares you the labor of writing all the functions.

In an application where you need to do a calculation as quickly as possible, however, all the previous approaches have a problem. The architecture and instruction sets of general-purpose microprocessors such as the 68000 are not designed to do complex mathematical operations efficiently. Therefore, even highly optimized number-crunching programs run slowly on these general-purpose machines. To solve this problem, special processors with architectures and instruction sets optimized for number crunching have been developed. An example of this type of number-crunching processor is the Motorola 68881 math processor. A 68881 is used in parallel with the main microprocessor in a system, rather than serving as a main processor itself. Therefore, it is referred to as a *coprocessor*. The major principle here is that the main microprocessor—a 68020, for example—handles the general program execution, and the 68881 coprocessor handles specialized math computations. A 68881 instruction may perform a given mathematical computation 100 times faster than the equivalent sequence of 68000 instructions.

An important point that we need to make is that the 68881 is an actual processor with its own specialized instruction set. Instructions for the 68881 are written in a program as needed, interspersed with the 68000/68020 instructions. To you, the programmer, adding a 68881 to the system simply makes it appear that you have suddenly been given a whole new set of powerful math instructions to use in writing your programs. When your program is assembled, the opcodes for the 68881 instructions are put in memory right along with the codes for the 68020 or 68000 instructions. As the 68020 or 68000 fetches instruction bytes from memory and puts them in its queue, the 68881 also reads these instruction bytes and puts them in its internal queue. The 68881 decodes each instruction that comes into its queue. When it decodes an instruction from its queue and finds that it is a 68000 instruction, the 68881 simply treats the instruction as a NOP. Likewise, when the 68020 or 68000 decodes an instruction from its queue and finds that it is a 68881 instruction, the 68020 simply treats the instruction as a NOP or, in some cases, reads a data word from memory for the 68881. The point here is that each processor decodes all the instructions in the fetched instruction byte stream but executes only its own instructions. The first question that may occur to you is, How do the two processors recognize 68881 instructions? The answer is that all the 68881 instruction codes have 1011 as the most significant bits of their first code byte.

To start our discussion of the 68881, we will show you the data types and internal architecture and programming of a 68881; then we will describe how a 68881 is connected and functions in a system. If you have a Mac II, you can run our example 68881 program or your own 68881 programs.

68881 Data Types

Figure 11-16 shows the formats for the different types of numbers with which the 68881 is designed to work. The three general types are binary integer, packed decimal, and real. We discuss and show examples of each type individually.

BINARY INTEGERS

The first three formats in Figure 11-16 show different-length binary integer numbers. These all have the same basic format that we have been using to represent signed binary numbers throughout the rest of the book. The most significant bit is a sign bit, which is 0 for positive numbers and 1 for negative numbers. The other 15 to 63 bits of the data word in these formats represent the magnitude of the number. If the number is negative, the magnitude of the number is represented in 2's complement form. Zero, remember, is considered a positive number in this format, because it has a sign bit of 0. Also note in Figure 11-16 the range of values that can be represented by each of the three

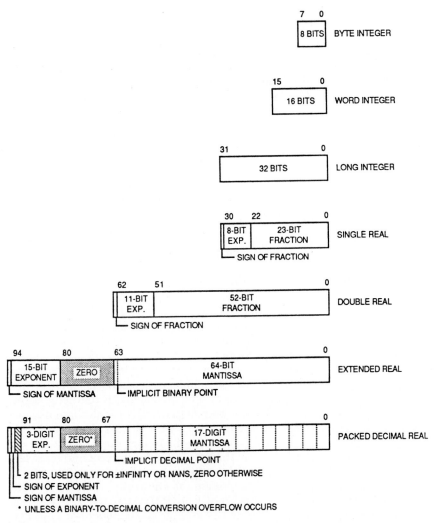

FIGURE 11-16   68881 data formats.

integer lengths. When you put numbers in this format in memory for the 68881 to access, you put the least-significant byte in the highest address.

PACKED DECIMAL NUMBERS

The second type of 68881 data format to look at in Figure 11-16 is the packed decimal. In this format a number is represented as a string of 18 BCD digits, packed 2 per byte. The most significant bit is a sign bit which is 0 for positive numbers and 1 for negative numbers. The bits indicated with an X are don't cares. This format is handy for working with financial programs. Using this format you can represent a dollar amount as large as $9,999,999,999,999,999.99, which is probably about what the national debt will be by the year 2000. Again, when you are putting numbers of this type in memory locations for the 68881 to access, the least significant byte goes in the highest address.

REAL NUMBERS

Before we discuss the 68881 real-number formats, we need to talk a little about real numbers in general.

So far the computations we have shown in this book have used signed integer numbers or BCD numbers. These numbers are referred to as fixed-point numbers because they contain no information as to the location of the decimal point or binary point in the number. The decimal or binary point is always assumed to be to the right of the least significant digit, so all numbers are represented in this form as whole numbers with no fractional part. A weight of 9.4 lb, for example, is stored in a memory location simply as 1001 0100 BCD or 0101 1110 binary. A price of $0.29 per pound is stored in a memory location as 0010 1001 in BCD or 0001 1101 in binary. When the binary representation of the weight is multiplied by the price per pound to give the total price, the result is 1010 1010 0110 binary, or 2726 decimal. To give the desired display of $2.73, the programmer must round the result and keep track of where to put the decimal point. For simple numbers such as these from the scale program in Chapter 10, it is not too difficult to do this. However, for a great many applications we need a representation that automatically keeps track of the position of the decimal or binary point for us. In other words we need to be able to represent numbers that have both an integer part and a fractional part. Such numbers are called real numbers, or floating-point numbers.

There are several different formats for representing real numbers in binary form. The basic principle of all these, however, is to use one group of bits to represent the digits of the number and another group of bits to represent the position of the binary point with respect to these digits. This is very similar to the way numbers are represented in scientific notation, so as a lead-in we will refresh your memory about scientific notation.

To convert the number 27,934 to scientific notation, you move the decimal point four digit positions to the left and multiply the number by 10^4. The result, 2.7934×10^4, is said to be in scientific notation. As another example, you convert 0.00857 to scientific notation by moving the decimal point three digit positions to the right and multiplying by 10^{-3}, giving 8.57×10^{-3}. The process of moving the decimal point to a position just to the right of the most significant, non-zero digit is called *normalizing* the number. In these examples you can see the digit part, sometimes called the *significand,* or the *mantissa,* and the exponent part of the representation. When you are working with a calculator or computer, the number of digits you can store for the significand determines the accuracy, or precision, of the representation. In most cases the real numbers with which you work in your computer will be approximations because to represent a number such as π "accurately" would require an infinite number of digits. The point here is that more digits give more precision—or, in other words, a better approximation.

The number of digits you can store for the exponent of a number determines the range of magnitudes of numbers you can store in your computer or calculator. The sign of the exponent indicates whether the magnitude of the number is greater than 1 or less than 1. The sign of the significand, or mantissa, indicates whether the number itself is positive or negative. Now let's see how you represent real numbers in binary form so the 68881 can digest them.

First, let's look at the short-real format shown in Figure 11-16. This format, which uses 32 bits to represent a number, is sometimes referred to as single-precision representation. In this format 23 bits are used to represent the magnitude of the number, 8 bits are used to represent the magnitude of the exponent, and 1 bit is used to indicate whether the number is negative or positive. The magnitude of the number is normalized so that there is only a single 1 to the left of the binary point. The 1 to the left of the binary point is not actually present in the representation; it is simply assumed to be there. This leaves more bits for representing the magnitude of the number. You can think of the binary point as being between the bits numbered 22 and 23. The exponent for this format is put in an offset form, which means that an offset of 127 ($7F) is added to the 2's complement value of the exponent. This is done so that the magnitude of two numbers can be compared without having to do arithmetic on the exponents first. The sign bit is 0 for positive numbers and 1 for negative numbers. To help make this clear to you, we will show you how to convert a decimal number to this format.

We chose the number 178.625 for this example because the fractional part converts exactly, and therefore we don't have to cope with rounding at this point. The first step is to convert the decimal number to binary, giving 1011 0010.101, as shown in Figure 11-17. Next normalize the binary number so that only a single 1 is to the left of the binary point and represent the number of bit positions you had to move the binary point as an exponent, as shown in Figure 11-17. The result at this point is 1.0110 0101 01E7. If you now add the bias of 127 ($7F) to the exponent of 7, you get the biased exponent value of $86 that you need for the

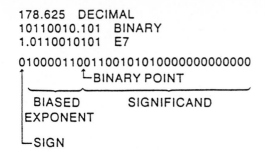

```
178.625   DECIMAL
10110010.101   BINARY
1.0110010101   E7

01000011001100101010000000000000
         └─BINARY POINT
    ┌──────────────┴──────────────┐
    │ BIASED          SIGNIFICAND
    │ EXPONENT
    │
    └─SIGN
```

FIGURE 11-17   Converting a decimal number to short-real format.

short-real representation. The final line in Figure 11-17 shows the complete short-real result. For the significand you put in the binary bits to the right of the binary point. Remember, the 1 to the left of the binary point is assumed. The biased exponent value of 86H, or 1000 0110 binary, is put in as bits 23 through 30. Finally, since the number is positive, a 0 is put in bit 31 as the sign bit. The complete result is then 0100 0011 0011 0010 1010 0000 0000 0000, or $4332A000, which is lengthy but not difficult to produce.

The long-real format shown in Figure 11-16 uses 64 bits to represent each number. This format is often referred to as *double-precision representation*. This format is basically the same as that of the short-real, except that it allows greater range and accuracy because more bits are used for each number. For long-real, 52 bits are used to represent the magnitude of the number. The number is again normalized so that only a single 1 is to the left of the binary point. You can think of the binary point as being between the bits numbered 51 and 52. The 1 to the left of the binary point is not actually put in as one of the 64 bits. For this format, 11 bits are used for the exponent, so the offset added to each exponent value is 1023 decimal, or $3FF. The most significant bit is the sign bit. Our example number of 178.625 will be represented in this long-real or double-precision format as $4066 5400 0000 0000. Note in Figure 11-16 the range of numbers that can be represented with this format. This range should be large enough for most of the problems you want to solve with a 68881.

The final format in Figure 11-16 to discuss is the temporary-real format, which uses 80 bits to represent each number. This is the format to which all numbers are converted by the 68881 as it reads them in, and it is the format in which the 68881 works with numbers internally. The large number of bits used in this format reduces rounding errors in long chain calculations. To understand what this means, think of multiplying 1234 × 4567 in a machine that can store only the upper 4 digits of the result. The actual result of 5,635,678 is truncated to 5,635,000. If you then divide this by 1234 to get back to the original 4567, you instead get 4566 because of the limited precision of the intermediate number.

As you can see in Figure 11-16, the temporary-real format has a sign bit, 15 bits for a biased exponent, and 64 bits for the significand. The offset or bias added to the exponent here is 16,383 decimal, or $3FFF. A major difference in the significand for this format from that for short-reals and long-reals is that the 1 to the left of the binary point after normalization is included as bit 63 in the significand. To express our example number of 178.625 in this form, then, we convert it to binary and normalize it as before to give 1.0110 0101 01E7. This gives us the upper bits of the significand directly as 101 1001 0101. We simply add enough 0s on the right of this to fill up the rest of the 64 bits reserved for the significand. To produce the required exponent, we add the bias value of $3FFF to our determined value of 7. This gives $4006, or 100 0000 0000 0110 binary as the value for the exponent. The sign bit is a 0 because the number is positive. Putting all these pieces together gives $4006 B2A0 0000 0000 0000 as the temporary-real representation of 178.625.

The 68881 Internal Architecture

Figure 11-18, p. 364, shows an internal block diagram of the 68881. As we discuss in detail later, the 68881 connects directly to the address, data, and status lines of the 68020 so that it can track and decode instructions fetched by the 68020 host. The 68881 has a control-word register and a status register. Control words are sent to the 68881 by writing them to a memory location and having the 68881 execute an instruction that reads in the control word from memory. Likewise, to read the status word from a 68881, you have it execute an instruction that writes the status word to memory, where you can read or check it with a 68020 instruction. Figure 11-19, p. 364, shows the formats for the 68881 control and status words. Take a look at these now so you have an overview of the meaning of the various bits of these words. We will discuss the meaning of most of these bits as we work our way through the following sections. Figure 11-20, p. 365, shows the 68881 programmer's model.

The 68881 works internally with all numbers in the 80-bit temporary-real format (represented with 96 bits) which we discussed in the preceding paragraphs. To hold numbers being worked on, the 68881 has a register stack of eight 80-bit registers labeled FP0–FP7 in Figure 11-18. These are general-purpose registers for floating-point operations similar to the 68000's date registers, D0–D7.

68881 Instruction Set

68881 INSTRUCTION FORMATS

Before we work our way through the list of 68881 instructions, we will use one simple instruction to show you how 68881 instructions are written, how they operate, and how they are coded. The instruction

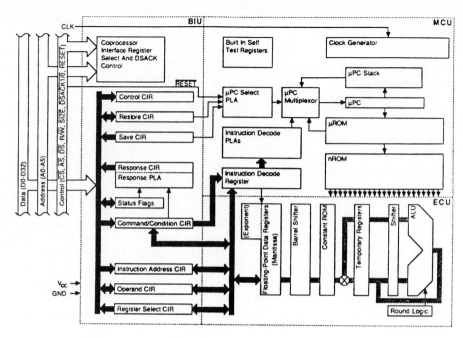

FIGURE 11-18   68881 internal block diagram. (*Motorola, Inc.*)

we have chosen to use as an example here is the FADD instruction.

All the 68881 mnemonics start with an F, which stands for floating point, the form in which the 68881 works with numbers internally. If you look in the Motorola data book, you will see this instruction represented as FADD.f <ea>,FPn and FADD.X FPm,Pn. This cryptic representation means that the instruction can be written in two different ways.

As an example, the instruction FADD.f CORREC-TION_FACTOR,FP0 will add a real number from the memory location named CORRECTION_FACTOR to the number in floating-point register FP0. Another example, the instruction FADD FP0,FP1 will add the number in register FP0 to the number in FP1 and store the result in FP1.

Coding 68881 Instructions

Common 68000 family assemblers accept 68881 mnemonics and an assembler is the only practical way to produce codes for 68881 programs. However, to give you a feeling for how they are coded, we show a simple example.

Figure 11-21, p. 366, shows the coding template for the FADD instruction as well as the binary code for the example instruction FADD FP0,FP1. The R/M bit indicates whether the operation is register to register or (= 0) or memory to register (= 1). In this case the operation is register to register, so the R/M bit is set to 0. Since R/M is 0, the effective address mode and register (first word bits 6−0) are all set to 0. The source floating-point register is FP0 (i.e., 000) and the destination is floating-point register FP1 (i.e., 001). This yields a final encoding of $F20000A2.

68881 Instruction Descriptions

The 68881 instruction mnemonics all begin with the letter F, which stands for floating point and distinguishes the 68881 instructions from 68020 instruc-

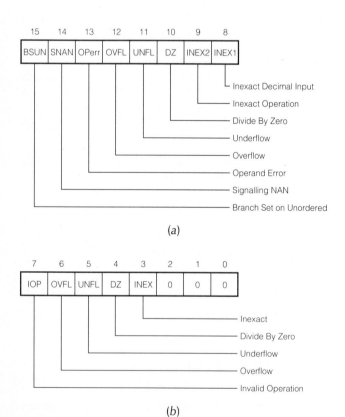

(a)

15	14	13	12	11	10	9	8
BSUN	SNAN	OPerr	OVFL	UNFL	DZ	INEX2	INEX1

- Inexact Decimal Input
- Inexact Operation
- Divide By Zero
- Underflow
- Overflow
- Operand Error
- Signalling NAN
- Branch Set on Unordered

(b)

7	6	5	4	3	2	1	0
IOP	OVFL	UNFL	DZ	INEX	0	0	0

- Inexact
- Divide By Zero
- Underflow
- Overflow
- Invalid Operation

FIGURE 11-19   68881 control and status word formats. (*a*) Control. (*b*) Status.

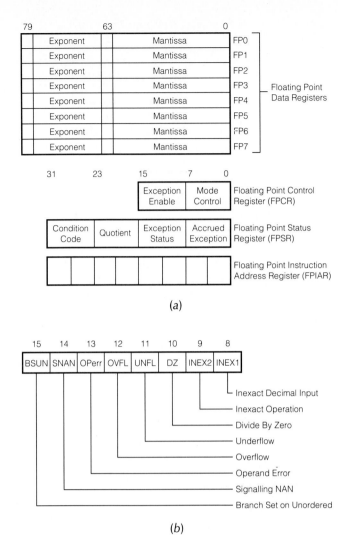

FIGURE 11-20 (a) 68881 data register and control diagram. (b) 68881 exception condition enable register.

If the 68881 detects an error condition, usually called an *exception*, while it is executing an instruction, it will set the appropriate bit in its status register. After the instruction finishes executing, the status register contents can be transferred to memory with another 68881 instruction. You can then use 68020 instructions to check the status bits and decide what action to take if an error has occurred. Figure 11-19b shows the format of the 68881 status word. The lowest 6 bits are the exception status bits. These bits will all be 0s if no errors have occurred. In the instruction descriptions in the appendix, the first letter of each exception type is used to indicate the status bits affected by each instruction.

If you send the 68881 a control word that unmasks the exception interrupts, as shown in Figure 11-19a, the 68881 will also send out a hardware-interrupt signal when an error occurs. This signal can be used to send the 68020 directly to an exception-handling routine.

Here are the 68881 instructions in alphabetical order.

FABS—Floating absolute value.

FACOS—Floating arccosine function.

FADD—Floating add.

FASIN—Floating arcsine function.

FATAN—Floating arctangent function.

FATANH—Floating hyperbolic arctangent function.

FBcc—Branch on floating-point condition.

FCMP—Floating compare.

FCOS—Floating cosine function.

FCOSH—Floating hyperbolic cosine function.

FDBcc—Test floating-point condition, decrement, and branch.

FDIV—Floating-point divide.

FETOX—e^x function.

FETOXM1—$e^x - 1$ function.

FGETEXP—Get exponent.

FGETMAN—Get mantissa.

FINT—Get integer part.

FINTRZ—Get integer part, round to zero.

FLOG10—Logarithm, base 10.

FLOG2—Logarithm, base 2.

FLOGN—Logarithm, base e (natural log).

FLOGNPI—Logarithm $(x + 1)$, base e.

FMOD—Modulo remainder.

FMOVE (control register)—Move floating-point control register.

tions. If you mentally remove the F as you read the mnemonic, it makes it easier to connect the mnemonic and the operation performed by the instruction. Here we briefly describe each of the 68881 instructions so that you can use some of them to write simple programs. As you read through these instructions the first time, don't try to absorb them all, or you probably won't remember any of them. Concentrate first on the instructions you need to get operands from memory into the 68881, simple arithmetic instructions, and the instructions you need to get results copied back from the 68881 to memory where you can use them. Then work your way through the example program in the next section. After that, read through the instructions again and pay special attention to the transcendental instructions, which allow you to perform trigonometric and logarithmic operations.

Only a brief description of each instruction is shown here. The MC68881 data book provides more detail and shows the coding templates and clock cycles for each instruction.

FADD Instruction
Floating Add

Syntax: FADD.f <ea>,FPn
FADD.X FPm,FPn

Description

The FADD instruction adds an operand to a floating point data register.

Exceptions								Data Formats						
BSUN	SNAN	OPERR	OVFL	UNFL	DZ	INEX1	INEX2	Byte	Word	Long	Sgl	Dbl	Ext	Pack
0	•	•	•	•	0	•	•	•	•	•	•	•	•	•

BSUN	Cleared.
SNAN	Set if source operand is an SNAN. Cleared otherwise.
OPERR	Set if adding + infinity to − infinity. Cleared otherwise.
OVFL	Set if overflow occurred. Cleared otherwise.
UNFL	Set if underflow occurred. Cleared otherwise.
DZ	Cleared.
INEX1	May be set if memory operand is a packed decimal number. Cleared otherwise.
INEX2	Set if result is inexact. Cleared otherwise.

Numerical Results

Destination		Source					
		In Range		Zero		Infinity	
		+	−	+	−	+	−
In Range	+	Add		Add		+ infinity	− infinity
	−						
Zero	+	Add		+ 0.0 0.0		+ infinity	− infinity
	−			0.0 − 0.0			
Infinity	+	+ infinity		+ infinity		+ infinity NAN(OPERR)	
	−	− infinity		− infinity		NAN(OPERR) − infinity	

Exception bits that are always set by a combination of operand ranges are indicated in parentheses. Adding + zero to + zero or − zero to − zero produces + zero in RN, RZ, and RP rounding modes, and − zero in RM mode.

FIGURE 11-21   68881 FADD coding templates.
(*Reprinted with permission of Motorola, Inc.*)

(*continued*)

FMOVE (data register)—Move floating-point data register.

FMOVECR—Move constant to floating-point data register.

FMOVEM (control register)—Move multiple floating-point control registers.

FMOVEM (data register)—Move multiple floating-point data registers.

FMUL—Floating-point multiply.

FNEG—Floating-point negate.

FNOP—Floating-point no operation.

FREM—IEEE remainder.

FRESTORE (privileged)—Restore coprocessor state.

FSAVE (privileged)—Save coprocessor state.

FSCALE—Scale exponent.

FScc—Test floating-point condition and set condition code.

FSGLDIV—Floating-point divide (single precision).

FSGLMUL—Floating-point multiply (single precision).

Valid Addressing Modes

Syntax	Mode	Reg	Valid
Dn*	000	Dn	•
An	001	An	
(An)	010	An	•
(An)+	011	An	•
−(An)	100	An	•
(d16,An)	101	An	•
(d8,An,Xn)	110	An	•
(bd,An,Xn)	110	An	•
([bd,An,Xn],od)	110	An	•
([bd,An],Xn,od)	110	An	•

Syntax	Mode	Reg	Valid
xxx.W	111	000	•
xxx.L	111	001	•
#<data>	111	100	•
(d16,PC)	111	010	•
(d8,PC,Xn)	111	011	•
(bd,PC,Xn)	111	011	•
([bd,PC,Xn],od)	111	011	•
([bd,PC],Xn,od)	111	011	•

* Valid only for byte, word, long, or single data types

Instruction Format

15	14	13	12	11	10	9	8	7	6	5	4	3	2	1	0
1	1	1	1	0	0	1	0	0	0	Mode			Register		
0	R/M	0	Source Spec			Dest Register			0	1	0	0	0	1	0

Bit 14 (R/M) of the extension word determines whether the operation is register to register (R/M = 0) or memory to register (R/M = 1). The effective address field (bits 5–0 of the first instruction word) is valid only if the R/M bit is a 1. For the register-to-register form (R/M = 0), the effective address field should be zeros.

The Source Spec field (bits 12–10 of the extension word) indicates the register number for the register-to-register form (R/M = 0) or the operand format for the memory-to-register form (R/M = 1). The encoding for this field is

Value	Suffix	Data Type
000	.L	Longword (32-bit) Integer
001	.S	Single Precision Real
010	.X	Extended Precision Real
011	.P	Packed Decimal Real
100	.W	Word (16-bit) Integer
101	.D	Double Precision Real
110	.B	Byte (8-bit) Integer
111		(Reserved)

FIGURE 11-21   (continued)

FSIN—Floating sine function.

FSINCOS—Simultaneous sine and cosine functions.

FSINH—Floating hyperbolic sine function.

FSQRT—Floating square root.

FSUB—Floating subtract.

FTAN—Floating tangent function.

FTANH—Floating hyperbolic tangent function.

FTENTOX—10^x.

FTRAPcc—Trap on floating-point condition.

FTST—Floating test.

FTWOTOX—2^x.

A 68881 Example Program—Pythagoras Revisited

As you may remember from geometry, the Pythagorean theorem states that the hypotenuse (longest side) of a right triangle squared is equal to the sum of the square of one of the other sides and the square of the remaining side. This is commonly written as $C^2 = A^2 + B^2$. For this example program we want to solve for the hypotenuse, C, so we take the square root of both sides of the equation, which gives $C = \text{square\_root}(A^2 + B^2)$.

Figure 11-22 shows a simple 68881 program you can use to compute the value of C for given values of A and B. As you examine this program, notice how similar it looks to the 68000 code we have seen in previous chapters. The FMOVE instructions look very much like the MOVE instructions except that they have the F in their instruction mnemonic and they use .X as their instruction mnemonic suffix. Also, the FMOVE instructions operate on floating-point registers as well as on memory address, whereas the MOVE instructions operate on the normal 68000 data registers as well as memory locations. Both instruction types use the same addressing conventions and notation.

At the start of the program we set aside some named memory locations to store the values of the three sides of our triangle. For this example we assume that some other routine has already placed the values of the triangle's two sides in memory and that this other routine is wanting the resulting hypotenuse value to be placed back into memory. Remember, the only way you can pass numbers to and from the 68881 is by using 68881 instructions to read the numbers from memory locations or write the numbers to memory locations. In this section of the example program, the statement

SIDE_A DS.B 12 tells the assembler to set aside six words in memory where the value of one of the sides of the triangle will be placed by the calling program. Likewise, the statement SIDE_B DS.B 12 tells the assembler to set aside six words for the value of the second side of the triangle. The statement HYP DS.B 12 reserves a six-word space for the result of our computation (HYP is short for hypotenuse). The calling program is assumed to place the values of the two sides, A and B, into the appropriate memory locations before calling this routine. If A is 3.0 and B is 4.0, then when the program is finished, the HYP locations will contain the real representation for 5.0.

You would normally write the actual code section of this program as a subroutine so that you could call it as needed. To make it simple here, we have written it without worrying about saving and restoring registers as we would normally do in a properly written subroutine. We start by loading the addresses of the values of the two triangle sides into two address registers. To perform the actual computation, we start at the inside of the equation and work our way outward. The FMOVE (A0),FP0 instruction brings in the value of the first side. Next we bring SIDE_B into FP1 with the FMOVE (A1),FP1 instruction. FMUL FP0,FP0 multiplies FP0 by FP0 and puts the result back in FP0, so

```
;68881 PROGRAM
;ABSTRACT:   FLOATING POINT COPROCESSOR EXAMPLE PROGRAM
;            This program calculates the hypotenuse of a right
;            triangle, given SIDE A and SIDE B.
;INPUT:  Incoming 96-bit values in SIDE_A and SIDE_B
;OUTPUT: Result (hypotenuse) in HYP as 96-bit value

SIDE_A          DS.B 12                 ; Set aside 96 bits for SIDE_A value
SIDE_B          DC.B 12                 ; Set aside 96 bits for SIDE_B value
HYP             DC.B 12                 ; 96 bits for the resulting value
                                        ;   (the hypotenuse)

START:          LEA     SIDE_A,A0       ; Address of SIDE_A value
                LEA     SIDE_B,A1       ; Address of SIDE_B value

                FMOVE.X (A0),FP0        ; load SIDE_A value into floating
                                        ;   point register 0
                FMOVE.X (A1),FP1        ; load SIDE_B value into floating
                                        ;   point register 1

                FMUL.X  FP0,FP0         ; (SIDE_A * SIDE_A)
                FMUL.X  FP1,FP1         ; (SIDE_B * SIBE_B)
                FADD.X  FP0,FP1         ; (SIDE_A*SIDE_A)+(SIDE_B*SIDE_B)
                FSQRT.X FP1,FP1         ; Square Root((A*A)+(B*B))
                                        ;   with result to floating point
                                        ;   register 1


                LEA     HYP,A0
                FMOVE.X FP1,(A0)        ; Store hypotenuse back into
                                        ;   memory at location HYP

                RTS

                END
```

FIGURE 11-22   68881 program to compute the hypotenuse of a right triangle.

FP0 = A². The value of B is in FP1, so we can square it with the FMUL FP1,FP1 instruction. FP1 now contains B² and FP0 now contains A². We add these together and leave the result in FP0 with the FADD instruction. FSQRT takes the square root of the contents of FP0 and leaves the results in FP0. Finally, we load the address of the memory location for the result, HYP, and use an FMOVE instruction to move the result into that memory location.

This program might be more complex in two areas. First, we assumed that the 68881 was already initialized and ready to perform the desired long-real operations. We could have added instructions to write control words to the various control registers (shown in Figure 11-19). Second, we did not check to see if there were any errors resulting from the floating-point operations (such as trying to take the square root of a negative number). We could have examined the exception status register (shown in Figure 11-20) to see if an exception condition had occurred. If there were no exceptions (errors), these status bits would all be 0's. If there were exceptions, then one or more bits would be 1's, indicating what type of exception had occurred.

Now that you know how it is programmed, let's look

at how a 68881 is connected in a system and how it works with a 68020 as it executes programs.

68881 Circuit Connections and Cooperation

Figure 11-23 shows the schematic for the Apple Macintosh II. We chose this schematic not only to show you how a 68881 is connected in a system with a 68020 microprocessor but also to show you another way in which schematics for microcomputers are commonly drawn.

In Figure 11-23 first note the numbers along the left and right edges of the schematic. These numbers indicate the other sheet(s) to which the signal goes. This is an alternative approach to the zone coordinates used in the schematics in Figure 7-8. In the schematic here the zone coordinates are not needed because all the input signal lines are extended to the left edge of the schematic, and all the output signal lines are run to the right edge of the schematic. If you see that an output signal goes to sheet 10, then it is a simple task to scan down the left edge of sheet 10 to find that signal. The wide connection lines in Figure 11-23 represent the address, data, and control buses. From

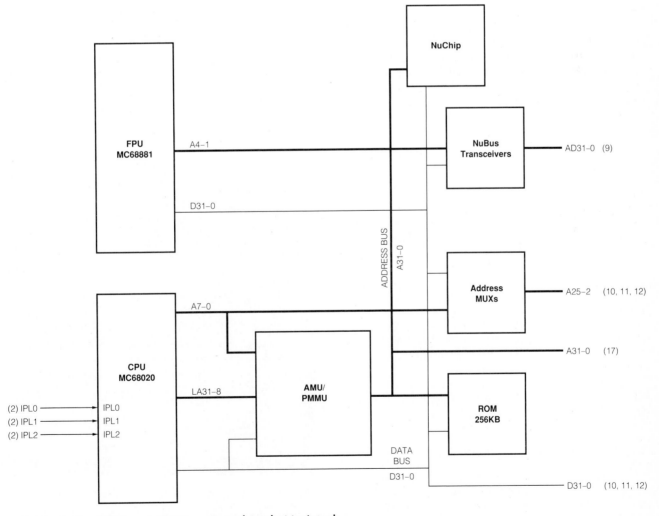

FIGURE 11-23   68000 and 68881 section of Apple Macintosh.

the pin descriptions for the major ICs, you know where these signals are produced. You can then scan along the bus to see where various signals get dropped off at other devices. On an actual schematic the buses are always expanded to individual lines where they enter or leave a schematic. Now let's look at how the 68881 and 68020 are connected.

The Apple system uses custom VLSI to manage the connections between the 68881 and the 68020, as it does for its DRAM connections. Most important to notice is that the 68020 function codes (FC0–FC2), address lines, and data lines all run directly to the 68881. This allows the 68881 to "watch" the 68020 instruction stream "looking" for 68881 instructions to execute.

COMPUTER-BASED DESIGN AND DEVELOPMENT TOOLS

In more and more companies the entire design, proto-typing, manufacturing, and testing process for an electronic product such as a microcomputer is being done with the help of a series of computer programs. The term *computer-aided engineering* (CAE) has been used in the past to describe the use of these tools, but now we commonly use the term *electronic design automation* (EDA) instead of the more general term CAE. The term EDA gives a better indication of the extent to which the currently available tools automate much of the design process. The following sections describe how a new microcomputer is designed and developed using design automation tools.

The Design Review Committee and Design Overview

The most important step in the design of any system is to think very carefully about what you want the system to do. In most companies a new product is now defined by a team consisting of design engineers, marketing or sales representatives, mechanical engineers, and pro-duction engineers. This team approach is necessary so that the product can be designed using the latest technology, manufactured and tested with minimal problems, and marketed successfully.

Once the specifications for the new product are agreed upon, the design engineers then think about how the circuit for it can be implemented. The next step in the design process is to partition the overall in-strument design into major functional blocks, or mod-ules. Each module can then be individually designed and tested or even assigned to different designers.

Initial Design and Schematic Generation

The next step in the design process is to analyze each functional block to determine how it can best be implemented. After working out the basic design of

each module, the design engineers draw a schematic for it. Until about 5 years ago they drew schematics on a large sheet of grid paper with a mechanical pencil and a plastic template. If they decided that a section of circuitry did not fit at a particular point on a schemat-ic, they erased the block of circuitry with an electric eraser and started over again. The process was very time-consuming and tedious.

Now engineers use a *schematic capture* program to draw schematics on an engineering workstation, such as the Apollo DN4500 shown in Figure 11-24. Using a computer to draw schematics has the same advantage over hand drawing that using a word processor has over using a standard mechanical typewriter. Since the schematic is drawn on the computer screen, you don't have to erase anything on paper. You can move symbols around on the screen with a mouse, change connecting wires, add or delete symbols, and print out the result on a printer or plotter when the schematic looks just the way you want it to. If you change your mind about some part of the schematic, you can just edit the drawing on the screen and do a new printout.

A further advantage of the computer-aided drafting approach is that you usually don't even have to draw the symbols! Most schematic capture programs have large library files containing common device symbols, complete with pin numbers and electrical characteris-tics. All you have to do when you want to put a particular IC on a schematic is to pull the symbol for it from a library file. Once you have the IC symbols for a circuit on the screen, you can use a mouse to draw the connecting wires between them and then add junc-

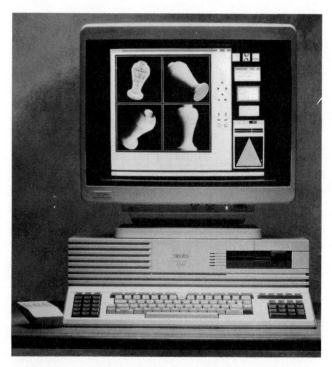

FIGURE 11-24　Apollo DN4500 workstation. (*Apollo Computers—HP Inc.*)

tions, connectors, labels, and the like to complete the drawing.

Schematic capture programs are available for most computers. The Ideaware programs from Mentor Graphics run on Hewlett Packard/Apollo engineering workstations such as the one shown in Figure 11-24. We used a workstation such as this and the Mentor Graphics Neted schematic capture program to draw the basic microcomputer system in Figure 11-25. Workstations such as this are used for designing large, complex digital systems or ICs. For small projects an IBM PC/AT or a Macintosh type computer is often used. Schematic capture programs for IBM PC-type computers include CapFast from Phase Three Logic, Draft from OrCAD Systems Corporation, Schema II+ from OMATION, Inc. and EE Designer II from Visionics. Schematic capture programs available for the Macintosh include Schematic from Douglas Electronics Inc. and LogicWorks from Capilano Computing Systems Ltd.

When the schematic design file is completed, it is processed by a program called a *design rule checker*, or *DRC*, which checks that there are no duplicate symbols, overlapped lines, or dangling lines. This step is similar to checking a text file with a spelling checker program.

After the schematic design file passes the DRC check, it is processed by a program called an *electrical rule checker*, or *ERC*, which checks for wiring errors such as two outputs connected together, an output connected to V_{CC}, etc.

When the schematic design file for a module passes the ERC test, a *netlist* program produces a netlist, or wiring list, for the design. A netlist is a file that lists all devices in the design and all the connections between devices.

Prototyping the Circuit—Simulation

After the design is polished, the next step is to prototype, or "breadboard," the circuit design to make sure the logic and timing in the circuit are correct. In the past this prototyping was usually done by soldering or wire wrapping the circuit on a prototype board of some type. Now, *software breadboarding* is more frequently used to test the operation of circuits or ICs. To do this a program called a *simulator* is used.

The simulator uses software *models* of the devices in the design to determine the response that the circuit will make to specified input signals. One big advantage of simulation, or software breadboarding, is that you don't have to order parts and wait for them to come in before you can test the operation of your design. Another big advantage of simulation is that you can change the design and resimulate the circuit in a matter of minutes to hours instead of waiting days for new parts to come in so you can modify a physical prototype and test it. Apollo Computer Corporation reportedly used simulation to cut several months from the prototype debug time for an engineering workstation such as the one shown in Figure 11-24.

Another advantage of simulation over traditional breadboarding is that you can simulate the circuit operation with worst-case timing parameters for all devices. This often pinpoints marginal timing problems that might not show up in a physical prototype because you can't vary the timing parameters of physical parts. In one actual situation, a timing problem did not show up in the wire-wrapped prototype but caused a 40 percent failure rate in the first production run of the instrument.

As we said before, a simulator program uses *models* of the devices in the circuit to determine the effect that specified input signals will have on the outputs of the circuit. Most models are just software descriptions of the characteristics of the devices. These descriptions are usually written in a high-level programming language such as Pascal or C. As a simple example, part of the model for a basic, three-input AND gate might look something like the following.

```
PROCEDURE ANDGATE ;
   CONST   TPLH = 15;
           TPHL = 10;
VAR IN1, IN2, IN3 : INTEGER ;
   DELAY, OUT : INTEGER ;
BEGIN
   IF (IN1 = 1) AND (IN2 = 1) AND (IN3 = 1)
      THEN BEGIN
         DELAY := TPLH
         OUT := 1;
      END
      ELSE BEGIN
         DELAY := TPHL
         OUT := 0
      END
END;
```

This model is very primitive, but it should give you the idea. The constants represent the characteristics of the specific device being simulated (TPLH and TPHL). The variables represent the input logic levels (IN1–IN3), the output logic level (OUT), and the time between a change on the input and the corresponding change on the output (DELAY). Some simulators refer to these characteristics as *properties*. The schematic symbol is really part of the model for a device, so when you draw a schematic with a schematic capture program, you are actually creating a design file that contains the logical and timing characteristics of each device as well as the schematic symbols and connections.

When you set up the simulator to do a simulation run, you specify the signals you want applied to the inputs at a particular time, just as you connect signal generators to the inputs of a physical circuit. The simulator uses the model to determine the effects that the specified input signals will have on the output and schedules the output to change appropriately after the delay time for that device. As you can see, the model for the three-input AND gate device tells the simulator program that if the input signals become all 1s, the

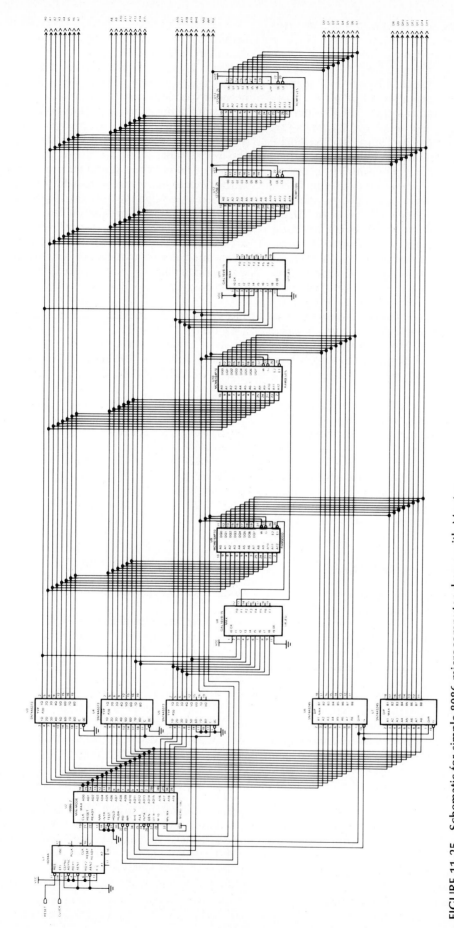

FIGURE 11-25   Schematic for simple 8086 microcomputer drawn with Mentor Graphic's Neted schematic capture program.

output should be scheduled to change to a 1 after 15 ns. If the inputs change to a case where they are not all 1s, the output should be scheduled to change to a 0 after 10 ns.

The smallest increment of time used by a simulator is called its *time step.* You can think of the time step as the time resolution of the simulator. For simulating TTL and CMOS circuits, simulators usually use a time step of 1 ns or 0.1 ns because the delay times for these devices are a few nanoseconds. An important point here is that the 0.1-ns time step is simulator time, not real time. The simulator may take 20 min to determine the effects that some input-signal changes produce on the outputs of a complex circuit. The physical circuit would respond to the same input changes in a real time of just a few nanoseconds. The simulator essentially exercises the circuit "in slow motion" and generates an output that represents, or simulates, the real-time operation of the circuit.

Now that you have an overview of how a simulator uses models, we need to talk briefly about some of the commonly used types of models. Three of these types are

Gate-level models

Behavioral models

Hardware models

As you may remember from a basic logic course, any digital circuit can be implemented with just basic gates. We didn't bother to show you, but even a complex device such as a 68020 or 68030 microprocessor can be modeled at the basic gate level for simulation. The difficulty with using gate-level models for complex devices is that simulation using these models requires a very long time. The reason for this is that the simulator must evaluate the effects of each signal change on all the intermediate circuit points (*nodes*) in the device.

If the complex device is a standard part, we usually know that all the internal circuitry works correctly, so we don't need to resimulate at the gate level of detail. To speed up the simulation of circuits containing complex devices, we often use *behavioral models.* Behavioral models simply describe the effects that input signals will have on the output signals and the signal delays between inputs and outputs. A behavioral model of a D flip-flop, for example, will indicate that 20 ns after a positive clock edge, the logic level on the D input will be transferred to the Q output if neither the preset nor the clear input is asserted. Behavioral models also contain properties such as setup times, hold times, and minimum pulse widths so the simulator can check for violations of these times by the signals propagating through the circuit. Sophisticated behavioral models such as the Smartmodels from Logic Automation Inc. give detailed error messages to pinpoint a timing problem instead of making you work your way through a logic-analyzer-type display to find the problem.

For simulating microprocessors, there are two types of behavioral models available. One type is called a *hardware verification model.* This type model is essentially a "black box," which will, for example, produce the correctly timed address and control bus signals for a memory-read cycle when given the proper *processor control language* (PCL) file. Hardware verification models are easy to use for checking system timing because all they need is a simple PCL file as a stimulus. However, hardware verification models do not allow simulation of actual microprocessor instructions. If we need this level of simulation, we use *full functional models,* which do allow the execution of instructions. The disadvantages of full functional models are that they operate more slowly than hardware verification models and you have to develop a file containing the actual object codes for the microprocessor instructions you want to execute.

In cases where a behavioral model of a device is not available and it is not practical to write a model or in cases where the simulation must interface with external circuitry at real time speeds, we use *hardware modeling.* In this approach the devices to be simulated are plugged into an external unit such as the Mentor Graphics Hardware Modeling System (HML) shown in Figure 11-26. When using a unit such as this, the simulator program sends stimulus signals to the external devices, reads back the responses of the external devices, and includes these responses in the simulation.

To develop complex systems such as the engineering workstation shown in Figure 11-24, we use *multilevel* simulators. An example of a multilevel simulator is Mentor Graphics QuickSim, which can simulate combinations of gate, behavioral, and hardware models. Quicksim runs on engineering workstations such as the one in Figure 11-24. Another useful, but somewhat less powerful, multilevel simulator is SUSIE from Aldec Corp. SUSIE runs on PC-type computers and is available to schools at a generous discount. Multilevel

FIGURE 11-26   Mentor Graphics HML box.

simulators such as this even allow the JEDEC files for PALs to be included in the simulation.

To simulate analog circuits, you can use an *analog circuit simulator* such as PSPICE from Microsim Corporation or Accusim from Mentor Graphics. For circuits such as A/D converters, which have both analog and digital circuitry, you can use *mixed-mode simulators* such as SABER from Analogy, Inc. or LSIM from Silicon Compiler Systems.

A Microcomputer Simulation Example

We drew the schematic for the basic 8086-based microcomputer in Figure 11-25 using Mentor Graphics Neted and Logic Automation Smartmodels. As you can see in the figure, the circuit uses SN74AS373s as address latches and SN74AS245s as data bus buffers. The ROM in this system consists of two I27256 EPROMS, one for the even bank and one for the odd bank. A lattice GAL16V8 EPLD is used as an address decoder for the ROMS. The RAM in this basic system consists of two MCM6164 static RAM devices, one for the even bank and one for the odd bank. A second lattice GAL16V8 EPLD is used as an address decoder for the RAMS. Off-page connectors go to a second sheet, which contains the ports, timers, etc. For this example we are interested only in the basic microprocessor and memory section of the system.

The Logic Automation Smartmodel for the 8086 processor in Figure 11-25 is a hardware verification type. As we said before, this type model allows us to verify that the signal connections, address decoding, and timing of the system are correct. To refresh your memory as to what is involved in the timing of a system such as this, look again at Figure 7-13.

As you can see in Figure 7-13a, the 68000 and memories essentially form a loop. To read a word from memory, the 68000 sends out address and control signals, and after some propagation delay the memory sends the data word back to the 68000. In order for the data word to be accepted by the 68000, it has to get back to the 68000 within a certain time period. In Figure 7-20 and the accompanying discussion, for example, we showed you how to determine if the address access time of a 2716 EPROM was fast enough for the device to work in a 3.57-MHz 68000 system.

When you use Smartmodels to simulate a system such as that in Figure 11-25, the simulator will automatically perform all the memory timing computations and give you an error message if it finds any timing violations. You can then redesign the circuit and re-simulate until you do not get error messages.

To simulate the circuit you have to give the simulator several types of information in addition to the basic netlist produced from the schematic. These additional parts are put in files, which the simulator will read out as it needs them. The process is really quite simple. Here is a list of the parts you need.

1. A fuse map or JEDEC file for each of the GAL16V8 EPLD address decoders. These can be produced

with a PAL programming tool such as ABEL from Data I/O. Figure 11-27a shows an ABEL source file for the U11 ROM decoder.

2. A memory image file for each of the memory de-

```
U11                DEVICE 'P16V8S';
A0,BHE,MIO         PIN 2,3,4;
A16,A17,A18,A19    PIN 6,7,8,9;
ROMF_EVEN, ROMF_ODD   PIN 19,18;
ROME_EVEN, ROME_ODD   PIN 17,16;

EQUATIONS

    !ROMF_EVEN = A19 & A18 & A17 &  A16 & !A0  & MIO;
    !ROMF_ODD  = A19 & A18 & A17 &  A16 & !BHE & MIO;
    !ROME_EVEN = A19 & A18 & A17 & !A16 & !A0  & MIO;
    !ROME_ODD  = A19 & A18 & A17 & !A16 & !BHE & MIO;
END rompal
```

(a)

```
0:100/88;
```

(b)

```
#include <i8086min.cmd>
    int i,addr;
main( )
(
    trace_on( );
    set_trace_level(1);
    addr = 0x0000;

    for (i=0; i<=16; i++)
    (
    write(1,addr,i);
    read(1,addr);
    idle(5);
    addr++;
    )
    addr = 0xf0000;
        i = 0;
    for (i=0; i<=16; i++)
    (
    read(2,addr);
    addr++;
    addr++;
    )
)
```

(c)

```
CLOCK PERIOD 125
FORCE CLOCK 0 0     -R
FORCE CLOCK 1 62.5 -R
FORCE RESET 0 0
FORCE RESET 1 1000
```

(d)

FIGURE 11-27 Files required for simulating microcomputer circuit in Figure 11-25. (a) ABEL source file for PAL address decoder. (b) Memory image file. (c) Processor control file. (d) Simulator stimulus file.

vices. These are simple text files which essentially initialize the memory devices with known contents so you will know if data is read back correctly. Figure 11-27b shows a memory image file that will initialize the first $100 locations of a memory device with $88.

3. A processor control (PCL) file, which tells the simulator the bus operations you want the processor to perform. For Logic Automation Smartmodels, this file is written in C. Figure 11-27c shows an example of a PCL file for our 8086 system. The instructions in the first block write bytes to a sequence of RAM locations starting at address $0000. After it is written, each byte is read back. The results from this part after the simulation is run help us determine if the address decoding, control signals, and timing are correct for the RAM part of the circuit. The next block in Figure 11-27c reads data words from a series of ROM locations to verify the address decoding, control signals, and timing of the ROM section of the circuit. If we were also simulating programable peripheral devices, we would include a section in the PCL file to initialize the devices and exercise their functions.

4. A stimulus file, which tells the simulator what signals to apply to the signal inputs of the system so that it runs through the operations in the PCL file. Figure 11-27d shows an example. The first three statements generate an 8-MHz clock for the external clock input of the 8284 clock generator. The next two statements generate a RESET signal. Note that the numbers such as 125, 62.5, and 1000 in these statements represent times in nanoseconds.

Once you have generated the necessary files, all you have to do is run the simulation. Figure 11-28 shows the screen messages produced as Quicksim is invoked and run on our microcomputer system design. As you can see, Quicksim first loads the required files in memory. When the Quicksim prompt appears, we execute the stimulus file in Figure 11-27d with DO MICRO.DO command. Then we run the simulator for 1,000,000 time units of 1 ns with the RUN 100000 command.

When the simulator started running, it immediately gave an error message indicating that we did not hold the RESET input of the 8086 low for the four clock periods required by the manufacturer's specifications. The problem here is that in our force file shown in Figure 11-27d, we generated an 8-MHz clock on the external clock input of the 8284 clock generator, and held RESET low for 1000 ns, or eight of these clock cycles. However, the 8284 divides the external clock signal by 3 to produce the clock signal actually applied to the processor. This means that in actuality, our reset stimulus was holding the RESET input low only for a little more than two cycles of the clock applied to the 8086, rather than the required four. This is a good example of the intelligence built into the models.

When we discovered this error, we stopped the simulation, corrected the stimulus file, and ran the simulation again. The second time we ran the simulation it did not show the RESET error. As directed by the trace settings we put in the PCL file, the simulator produced a trace of each state as the 8086 wrote to and read from memory. The bottom few lines of Figure 11-28 show some examples of the type of information the trace gives you. Note that the first operations the simulator carries out are to write to and read back from RAM locations specified in the PCL file. A careful study of the trace shows that values were written to memory and read back correctly. This indicates that the address decoders are working correctly and that the circuit connections are correct. After we fixed the RESET problem described before, we ran the simulator again and got no significant timing warnings, so we felt reasonably sure the system would work correctly when we designed and built a PC board for it.

A very important point here is that it took only about 10 to 12 h to design the system in Figure 11-25, draw the schematic for the system, and completely simulate it. Perhaps you can see that when designing a more complex system such as the microcomputer system in Figure 11-15a, simulation is the only practical way to determine if all the timing requirements are met in the design.

Design for Test

Once a system has passed simulation, the next step is to design in some circuitry that allows the system to be tested easily when it goes to production. Many microcomputers now contain built-in self-test (BIST) circuitry so that the unit does a complete internal test each time the power is turned on. If the unit fails any test, it sends a message to the CRT.

After the test circuitry is added, the circuit is simulated again to make sure the added test circuitry has not adversely affected the operation of the circuit.

Printed-Circuit-Board Design

In past years we used a light table and large plastic sheets to develop the layout for a PC board. To produce "pads" for IC pins, transistor leads, resistor leads, etc., we stuck opaque "donuts" on the sheets. To produce traces between pads, we used opaque tape. The plastic sheets were photographed and the resulting films were used to produce the desired patterns of traces on copper-plated circuit boards.

Now we use automatic place-and-route programs such as Board Station from Mentor Graphics, Allegro from Valid Logic Systems, or Tango PCB from ACCEL Technologies, Inc., to lay out PC boards. These programs work with the netlist file and determine the best placement of components and the most efficient route for traces between components. The programs allow user interaction, so that specific paths can be optimized if needed. For example, in designing a PC board for a very high speed system, you might determine the

```
# Executing object named: '/idea/sys/lib/lsim_server.mod'
#   LOGIC SIMULATION SERVER V6.1_1.10 Monday, April 18, 1988 6:01:59 pm (PDT)
#   LAI Version: MG_A3_610_970_200  May 17, 1988
#   SmartModels: All pictorial, graphic, and audiovisual works, collective works
#                representations, compilations, and arrangements therof,
#                Copyright 1984-1988 Logic Automation Incorporated.
#
#   Note: Loading the PCL program from file "/user/doug/micro2/MICRO_OBJ".
#         Instance I$4(U2:I8086-2), sheet1 of micro2 at time 0.0
#
# ! Warning: Input pin MNMX is not allowed to change (will continue in MIN mode)
# !          Instance I$4(U2:I8086-2), sheet 1 of micro2 at time 0.0
#
#   Note: Loading the JEDEC file "/user/doug/micro2/U11.JED"
#         Instance I$62(U11:GAL16V8-15), sheet1 of micro2 at time 0.0
#         --- 173 fuses have been blown.
#
#   Note: Loading the JEDEC file "/user/doug/micro2/U8.JED"
#         Instance I$11(U8:GAL16V8-15), sheet1 of micro2 at time 0.0
#         --- 169 fuses have been blown.
#
#   Note: Loading the memory image file "/user/doug/micro2/RAM0EVEN"
#         Instance I$61(U10:MCM6164P70), sheet1 of micro2 at time 0.0
#         --- 257 values have been initialized.
#
#   Note: Loading the memory image file "/user/doug/micro2/RAM0ODD"
#         Instance I$41(U9:MCM6164P70), sheet1 of micro2 at time 0.0
#         --- 257 values have been initialized.
#
#   Note: Loading the memory image file "/user/doug/micro2/RAMFEVEN"
#         Instance I$63(U13:I27256-25), sheet1 of micro2 at time 0.0
#         --- 257 values have been initialized.
#
#   Note: Loading the memory image file "/user/doug/micro2/RAMFODD"
#         Instance I$15(U12:I27256-25), sheet1 of micro2 at time 0.0
#         --- 257 values have been initialized.
    VIEw Sheet
QuickSim>
    DO MICRO.DO
    RUN 100000
#
# ! Warning: RESET did not last 4 Clock Cycles.
# !               Instance I$4(U2:I8086-2), sheet1 of micro2 at time 1562.5
#
#   Trace: Trace is turned on
#               Instance I$4(U2:I8086-2), sheet1 of micro2 at time 4812.5
#
#   Trace: Trace level is now set to 1 (internal timing states shown)
#               Instance I$4(U2:I8086-2), sheet1 of micro2 at time 4812.5
#
#   Trace: CPU state T1
#               Instance I$4(U2:I8086-2), sheet1 of micro2 at time 4937.5
#
#   Trace: Write Memory (1-byte) location 00000 with 0000
#               Instance I$4(U2:I8086-2), sheet1 of micro2 at time 4937.5
#
#   Trace: CPU state T2
#               Instance I$4(U2:I8086-2), sheet1 of micro2 at time 5312.5
#
#   Trace: CPU state T3
#               Instance I$4(U2:I8086-2), sheet1 of micro2 at time 5687.5
#
#   Trace: CPU state T4
#               Instance I$4(U2:I8086-2), sheet1 of micro2 at time 6062.5
#
#   Trace: CPU state T1
#               Instance I$4(U2:I8086-2), sheet1 of micro2 at time 6437.5
#
#   Trace: Read Memory (1-byte) location 00000
#               Instance I$4(U2:I8086-2), sheet1 of micro2 at time 6437.5
```

FIGURE 11-28   Screen messages during simulator invocation and run.

actual signal delays from an initial layout attempt and then resimulate the system with these delays. If the resimulation shows a problem, you can manually alter the layout to solve the problem before going on.

The file produced by the PC-board layout program is sent to a laser printer to produce film negatives directly for each layer of the board. The negative is used to photographically produce the desired pattern on a copper-plated PC board. A chemical solution then etches copper from all the areas of the board except those where component pads, traces, ground planes, and power planes are desired. For a multilayer board, several individual boards are produced and then epoxied together under pressure to form a single board.

The board is then drilled under computer control. Finally the plated-through holes and other *vias* that connect traces on different layers are electrochemically added to the board.

After manufacture, the "bare" PC boards are tested with a computer-based tester to check for shorts and opens. On a prototype PC board, minor problems can often be solved by, for example, drilling out a plated-through hole that accidentally got shorted to a power plane. A jumper wire can be added to make a missed connection.

Case Design

Once the PC board, power supply, and display have been designed for an instrument, the mechanical engineer can design the case for the system. A program such as the Mentor Graphics Package Station can be used to do much of this design. This program allows the designer to draw a three-dimensional view of a case and the placement of components in the case. The Package Station program also allows a designer to determine the temperature that will be present at each location in the prototype case for a specified ambient temperature and airflow. This feature allows the designer to determine if the airflow is great enough, the placement of the PC board(s) in the case is reasonable, and perhaps if devices that produce a large amount of heat are placed too close together on a PC board. Here is another example of software breadboarding that saves much work and materials because, if a problem is found, you can simply go back to the computer screen and try a new design instead of producing a new physical box and trying it.

Developing the System Software

In addition to designing the hardware of a microcomputer, you also have to develop the BIOS software that allows programs to interact with the hardware. As we said earlier, the Logic Automation Hardware Verification model for a processor such as the 68000 allows you to include statements in a PCL file to initialize the programmable peripheral device models, write data to them, and read data from them. This, then, is a way to verify the address, operation, and timing of these devices. If a fully functional model is available for the microprocessor, you can write sections of actual code for the microprocessor and run the code as part of the simulation.

When a prototype PC board for the system becomes available, an emulator such as we described in Chapter 3 can be used to develop the more complex software procedures of the BIOS.

Production and Test

Once the prototype of a system is debugged and any necessary changes are made, the design is finalized and released to production. Many parts of the production, test, and troubleshooting of the instrument are done with the aid of computer programs.

Programs are available to generate a parts list from the netlist for a design. Other available programs direct a robot to collect the needed parts from the warehouse for the production run. A computer program running on an automatic tester tests the bare PC boards for shorts and opens before parts are inserted. Another program controls the machine that automatically places the components on the printed-circuit board. The machine that solders all the components on the board is probably controlled by a microcomputer program. Still another computer program controls the machine that automatically tests the finished PC boards. The program for this automatic test system uses test vectors, which were developed as part of the design process. If the product does not have a complete built-in self-test, the finished product is also tested with an automatic test system. The linking together of all the computer-based tools used in the production of a product is called computer-integrated manufacturing, or CIM.

CHECKLIST OF IMPORTANT TERMS AND CONCEPTS IN THIS CHAPTER

If there are terms or concepts in this list you do not remember, use the index to find them in the chapter.

Motherboard and system expansion slots

68020 large-scale system

DMA operation

DMA channel

DRAM
    RAS and CAS strobes
    Refresh: burst and distributed modes
    82C08 DRAM controller IC
    Error detecting and correcting
        Hard and soft errors
        Parity check
        Hamming codes and syndrome word
    Page mode read/write access
    Static column read/write access

Cache memory system
  Direct-mapped cache
  Two-way set-associative cache
  Fully associative cache

68881 math coprocessor
  Data types and terms
    Word, short, and long integers
    Packed decimals
    Short-, long-, and temporary-reals
  Fixed-point numbers
  Floating-point numbers
  Normalizing
  Significand, mantissa, exponent, biased exponent
  Single- and double-precision representation

Electronic design automation
  Schematic capture
  Simulation
    Gate-level model
    Behavioral model
    Hardware model
    Time step
    Stimulus file
  Design for test
  PC board layout
  Case design

Computer-integrated manufacturing

REVIEW QUESTIONS AND PROBLEMS

1. Why are microcomputers such as the Apple Macintosh designed with peripheral expansion slots instead of having functions such as a CRT controller designed into the motherboard?

2. Describe how the control bus signals are produced for a large-scale 68020 system.

3. Why is DMA data transfer faster than doing the same data transfer with program instructions?

4. Describe the series of actions that a DMA controller will perform after it receives a request from a peripheral device to transfer data from the peripheral device to memory.

5. Describe how the 20-bit memory address for a DMA transfer is produced by the circuit in Figure 11-5.

6. Sketch the sequence of signals that must occur to read a data word from a dynamic RAM such as the TMS44C256.

7. List the major tasks that must be done to support dynamic RAM in a microcomputer system.

8. How does a dynamic RAM controller, in a system such as that in Figure 11-9, arbitrate the dispute that occurs when the CPU attempts to read from or write to a bank of dynamic RAMs while the controller is doing a refresh cycle?

9. a. What timing parameter limits the rate at which data words can be read from random rows (pages) in a DRAM?
   b. Explain how page mode operation of a bank of DRAMs makes it possible for a microprocessor to read data words without wait states.
   c. What is the main difference between page mode operation and static column mode operation of a bank of DRAMs?

10. a. Describe how an SRAM cache reduces the average number of wait states required by a microprocessor that uses DRAM for its main memory.
    b. How does a cache controller keep track of which blocks from the main memory are present in the cache?
    c. With a direct-mapped cache system, what does each entry in the cache tag RAM represent?
    d. In a direct-mapped cache system, only one block with a particular number can be present in the cache at a time. How does a two-way set-associative cache overcome this problem?

11. Describe how parity is used to check for RAM data errors in microcomputers such as the Apple Macintosh. What is a major shortcoming of the parity method of error detection?

12. When using a Hamming code error detection/correction scheme for DRAMs, how many encoding bits must be added to detect and correct a single-bit error in a 64-bit data word?

13. In what ways are a standard microprocessor and a coprocessor different from each other?

14. a. Convert the decimal number 2435.5625 to binary, normalized binary, long-real, and temporary-real format.
    b. Why are most floating-point numbers actually approximations?

15. Using the example program in Figure 11-24 as a guide, write a 68881 program that computes the volume of a sphere. The formula is $V = \frac{4}{3}\pi R^3$.

16. a. Where does the 68881 coprocessor in Figure 11-23 get its instructions from?
    b. How does the main processor distinguish its instructions from those for the 68881 as it fetches instructions from memory?
    c. Describe how the 68881 and 68020 work together to load a long-real data item from memory to the 68881 ST.

d. How does the 68881 in Figure 11-23 signal the 68020 that it needs to use the buses?

17. a. Describe how a schematic is drawn using a schematic capture program.
b. What are the major advantages of the schematic capture approach over the traditional drafting approach?

18. a. What is meant by the term software breadboard?
b. Describe the major advantages of simulation over hardware prototyping.

c. What information does the simulation model for a device contain?
d. Briefly describe the steps involved in simulating a microcomputer such as the one in Figure 11-25.
e. What information does simulation give you about a circuit such as the one in Figure 11-25?

19. Briefly describe the sequence of steps in the electronic design automation method of designing, debugging, and producing an electronic product such as a microcomputer.

CHAPTER 12

C: A High-level Language for System Programming

In the last chapter we introduced you to the operation of the motherboard hardware of a typical microcomputer system. Before we discuss the operation of system peripherals such as CRTs, hard disks, and telecommunications links, we need to introduce you to the languages and tools that are now commonly used to write application- and system-level programs.

Up to this point in the book we have used assembly language for all the programming examples because we were working very close to the hardware. As we said earlier in the book, assembly language is appropriate for initializing peripheral devices, writing programs that manipulate a lot of hardware, or writing programs that have to execute very fast. It is very slow and tedious to write large system-level programs in assembly language, so we usually write major parts of these programs in a high-level language such as Pascal or C.

As you are probably aware, there are many different high-level languages. For the high-level language programming examples throughout the rest of this book, we use the C language. We chose C because it is very widely used in industry, it is a good stepping stone to a modern programming language called C++, which is used in some very large system programs, and it is very easy to learn if you are already familiar with 68000-type assembly language programming.

To develop a system-level program, the overall design is broken down into a group of modules. A decision is then made whether each module can be written in a high-level language or must be written in assembly language. The high-level modules are written, debugged, and compiled to produce object code files. Likewise, the assembly language modules are written, debugged, and assembled to object code files. All the object files are then linked together to produce an executable file that can be run. This is basically the same process we described in Chapter 5 for writing multimodule assembly language programs. In this chapter we first show you how to write some simple programs in C; we then will show you how to write programs that contain both high-level language modules and assembly language modules.

OBJECTIVES

At the conclusion of this chapter, you should be able to

1. Describe how the tools in an integrated programming environment are used to edit, compile, link, run, and debug C programs.

2. Describe the data types that are available in C.

3. Declare and initialize simple variables, arrays, and structures in C.

4. Implement standard programming structures such as if-then-else, switch (case), while-do, do-while, and for-do in C.

5. Declare, define, and call functions (procedures) in C programs.

6. Write C programs that implement simple algorithms.

7. Write simple programs that consist of C code and assembly language code.

INTRODUCTION—A SIMPLE C PROGRAM EXAMPLE

As we said before, it is very easy to learn the C programming language if you are already familiar with 68000 assembly language programming. To give you some feeling for how easy it is to make this transition and to give you an introduction to the general structure of a C program, we first show how the cost-price array example program in Figure 4-23 can be written in C.

If you look back at the program in Figure 4-23, you will see that this program adds a profit of 15 to each of eight costs. More specifically, the program reads in a value from an array called COST, adds a profit of 15 to the value read in, and puts the computed price in the corresponding element of an array called PRICES.

Figure 12-1a shows a simple C program that will perform basically the same operations and also write the results out on your computer screen. The first

380

```
/* COMPUTE THE SELLING PRICE OF 10 ITEMS */

#include <stdio.h>
#define PROFIT 15
#define MAX_PRICES 10
int cost[] = { 20,28,15,26,19,27,16,29,39,42 }; /* array of 10 costs */
int prices[10];                                  /* array to hold 10 prices */
int index;                                       /* variable to use as index */


main()
{
        for (index=0; index <MAX_PRICES; index++)  /* for loop to compute */
        prices[index] = cost[index] + PROFIT;      /* 10 prices */

        for (index=0; index <10; index++)  /* for loop to display results */
        printf("cost = %d, price = %d, \n", cost[index], prices[index]);

}
```

(a)

```
                    cost = 20, price = 35,
                    cost = 28, price = 43,
                    cost = 15, price = 30,
                    cost = 26, price = 41,
                    cost = 19, price = 34,
                    cost = 27, price = 42,
                    cost = 16, price = 31,
                    cost = 29, price = 44,
                    cost = 39, price = 54,
                    cost = 42, price = 57,
```

(b)

FIGURE 12-1   (a) Simple C program to add profit of 15 to each of 10 items.
(b) Printout of program results.

point to observe in this program is that any text enclosed between /* and */ is a comment, not part of the actual program. The next parts to look at in this program are the statements that define the data with which the program is going to work. The statement int cost[ ] = {20,28,15,26,19,27,16,29,39,42}; declares an array of 10 integers called cost and initializes the 10 elements of the array with the specified values. This corresponds to the COST DC.B 20, . . . statement in the program of Figure 4-23. The statement int prices[10]; declares an array of 10 integers called prices. Since no values are given, the elements of this array are not initialized. Note that the C program statements are terminated with semicolons.

Program lines that begin with a # are *preprocessor directives*. These lines do not generate any code; instead, they give instructions to the compiler. The #define PROFIT 15 line in Figure 12-1a, for example, tells the compiler to replace the name PROFIT with the constant 15 each time it finds PROFIT in the program. This is equivalent to the PROFIT EQU 15 line in the assembly language version in Figure 4-23. The #define MAX_PRICES 10 line in Figure 12-1a is another

example. As we pointed out in our earlier discussions of assembly language programming techniques, it is very important to define constants at the start of a program in this way rather than using "hard" numbers directly in the program. Then if you have to change a number, you simply have to change the value in the equ or the #define instead of finding and changing the value each place it occurs in the program. Note that we always use uppercase letters for constants such as PROFIT so that we can tell them from variables, which we put in lowercase letters.

The int index; statement in Figure 12-1a declares a variable called index. The int at the start of the statement indicates that the variable can have only integer values. This index will be used to point to the array element being processed at a particular time and to keep track of how many elements have been processed. Now that you have an overview of the data, let's take a look at the action part of the program.

All the action statements in C programs, even those in the mainline part of a program, are written in functions. In Pascal and some other languages, a function is the name given to a subroutine that returns some value(s) to the calling program. In C all subroutines are referred to as functions whether they return a value or not.

Every C program must have a function, usually called *main*, which is called when your program starts executing. Other functions are called from main as needed. As you can see, the main( ) function in Figure 12-1*a* contains a for structure and two statements. "Curly braces" ({ and }) are used to enclose the parts of a function. The parentheses after the name of the function are used to contain parameters and the names of variables that you want passed to the function. Later we will show you examples of how to do this. Empty parentheses after a function name mean that no parameters are being passed to the function.

The statement for (index=0; index <MAX_PRICES; index++) implements a for-do loop, which executes the statements contained in the second set of curly braces 10 times (index values of 0–9). The index++ term in the parentheses means that the value of index will be incremented each time through the loop. The prices[index] = cost[index] + PROFIT statement and the printf statement are also implemented each time through the loop.

As perhaps you can figure out, the prices[index] = cost[index] + PROFIT; statement reads an indexed location in the cost array, adds a PROFIT of 15 to the value read, and writes the result to the same indexed location in the prices array. Note how the variable index is used here to access the elements in each array and also to determine how many times the loop executes.

Each time through the loop, the printf statement calls the predefined printf( ) function, which sends the specified text and values to the screen. The parentheses after printf contain the parameters we are passing to the function. Characters enclosed in quotation marks inside the parentheses are printed out as written until a % is encountered. A % indicates that the value of a variable is to be inserted at that point. The name of that variable is included in a list of variables after the second " in the print statement. In this example, the first variable encountered after the second " is cost[index], so the value of this variable will be printed out after cost = is printed out. The d after the % tells the function to print the decimal value of cost[index]. When the function encounters the second %d in the parentheses, it will print the decimal value of prices[index], the next variable after cost[index] in the variables list. The /n in the statement stands for *newline* and tells the printf function to send a carriage return character and a linefeed character. This will move the cursor to the start of the next line down on the screen. Figure 12-1*b* shows the printout produced by the printf function when this program is run.

As you can see in Figure 12-1*a*, the printf function is not present in our program. The printf function is found in a library of input/output functions that comes with the program development software. The #include <stdio.h> at the start of the program tells the preprocessor part of the compiler that the prototype for the printf function is in a file called stdio.h. The linker will use this prototype to get the object code for the printf function from a library file and link it with the object code for our price.c program so that it will be part of the final executable file. In a later section we tell you more about predefined functions.

If you compare the number of statements in our C program with the number of statements needed to do the job in the assembly language version in Figure 4-23, you should immediately see one of the advantages of writing as many programs as possible in a high-level language. In the next section we discuss some software tools you can use to develop your own C programs. Then in the following sections we show you much more of the structure and syntax of the C language.

PROGRAM DEVELOPMENT TOOLS FOR C

To develop a C program you need an editor to create a source program such as the one in Figure 12-1*a*, a compiler to convert the source program to an object code file, a linker to link the various object code modules of your program into an executable (.exe) file, and a powerful debugger to help you get the program working correctly. For the examples in this section, we chose the Apple Think C® Integrated Development Environment, which has all these features and more. These tools run on Apple Macintosh® microcomputers. The term *Integrated Development Environment* means that you can access all the programming tools from one on-screen menu. We chose this Apple system because it is very powerful but easy to use. Other available tool sets are very similar, so you should have little trouble adapting the following discussion if you have some other set of programming tools.

The purpose of this section is not to make you an expert with these tools, but rather to show you enough about using tools such as these that you can enter, run, and experiment with the simple program examples in the later sections of the chapter. Even if you don't have tools such as these available, this section should show you how programs are developed in a modern programming environment and some of the features you should look for when you buy a tool set.

For the following discussions we assume your Apple tools and libraries are all installed in a hard disk directory (folder) named Think C, as described in the Think C manual. We further assume that your work disk is a floppy. Here's how you use these tools to develop a program such as the prices.c program in Figure 12-1*a*.

To bring up the Think C environment, you simply move your mouse over to the Think C icon and double click. After a short pause the main menu screen shown in Figure 12-2*a* will appear. The entries along the bottom of the screen identify often-used operations that you can do by simply clicking on the icon corresponding to the desired function. Each of the entries in the banner at the top of the display represents a pull-down menu of commands. To get to one of these

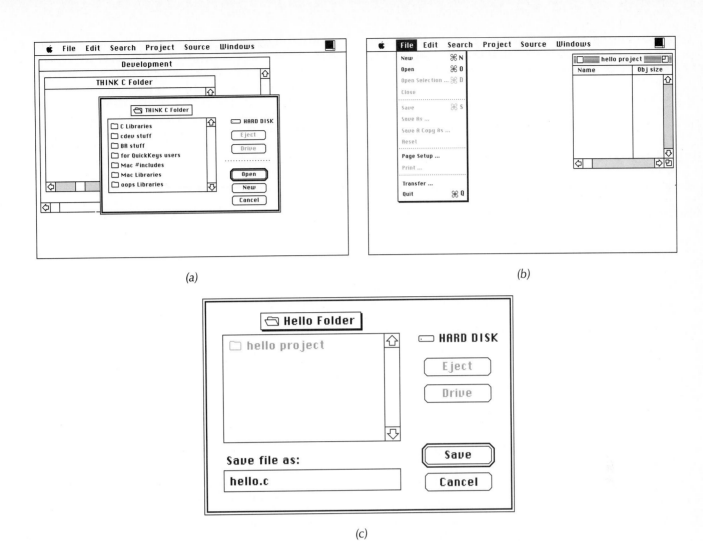

(a)

(b)

(c)

FIGURE 12-2   Apple Think C® integrated program-development screen
displays. (a) Main menu and edit window 2. (b) Options submenu.
(c) Directories submenu of options submenu.

menus, you first move the mouse onto the menu banner button and press the mouse button. Then you select the desired menu item from the menu that appears by using the arrow keys to move the highlighted box to the desired menu name and press the Enter key.

The first thing you have to do when you create a program is to tell the compiler, linker, etc., where to put the object and executable files they create. You can use a command in the menu to do this. If you prefer, you can allow the tools to create object and executable files using the standard, or "default," names. These names are created by adding standard suffixes to the name of the source code file in which your C code program resides. If you decide to use the default names (do so for this example), all you need to do is give your source code file a name. Use the File menu to do this. Figure 12-2b shows the menu that appears when you move to the File button and press the mouse key. The file pull-down menu will appear. Since we will be creating a new file for this example, select the Open

(new file) menu item by keeping the mouse button depressed and sliding the pointer down to the Open file menu item. This item will highlight. Release the mouse button to select Open (new) file. This is the familiar Macintosh menu-selection paradigm.

The next step in developing a program is to use the editor to enter the source text for the program. The large window in the center of the screen is the edit window where you enter text. If the blinking cursor is not already in this window, move the mouse into the window and press the mouse button to get the cursor there. Now type in your program as you would with any text editor. Note that—as in Figure 12-1a—we use spaces instead of tabs to format our programs. The reason for this is that the default tab setting of most printers is 8, and at this setting C programs do not usually fit easily on 8.5-in.-wide paper because too many tabs would be used, even in a simple program.

After you type in the source file, you need to save it on your work disk. To do this, you again use the File button in the banner menu. This time use the Save as menu item. A dialog box will appear, asking for the name of the new file. Enter the desired name (price.c). The ".c" suffix implies that this file will contain C source code statements.

The next step is to compile the program to generate the object file. To do this you select the Compile option from the Build pull-down menu.

If the compiler finds any errors, it will display a window with a flashing error message. When you press a key, the error messages will be displayed in the message window at the bottom of the screen. Figure 12-3 shows the error messages we produced when we intentionally left out the # sign in front of the include statement in price.c. A highlighted line in the source program indicates the statement that caused the error highlighted in the message window. To remedy this error, all we had to do was insert the missing # before the include directive. A major error such as this will cause many errors throughout the program, so when you find one of these it is a good idea to compile the program again before you start chasing down the other indicated errors.

To recompile the program all you have to do is use the Compile option from the Build pull-down menu again. Since we fixed the one error in the program, the compile is now successful. Once the compile is successful, you should always save your source file before continuing. Use the File menu and the Save menu items to do this. This is important, because if your program locks up the machine when you run it, your program will be lost.

The next step in developing a program is to generate an executable file that you can run. For this example the file will be given the name price.exe by the linker that generates it. There are two ways to generate the executable file. One is to assemble an assembly language program and the other is to compile a C program.

Now you can run your executable program file. This can be done simply by double clicking on the icon representing the executable file when the program has finished running.

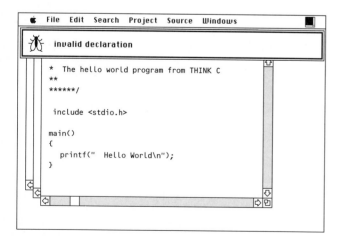

FIGURE 12-3 Compiler error messages generated by omitting # in #include<stdio.h> directive.

Suppose that your program doesn't work correctly the first time you run it. The Think C environment contains a powerful *source-level* debugger. A source-level debugger allows you to view your source program on the screen and single-step through it one statement at a time or run to a breakpoint you placed on a statement and watch the values of variables change as program statements execute. The debugger is integrated with the editor, compiler, and linker, so when you find an error, you can just go back to the edit window, fix the error, and then run the program again, all from the same main menu. In most cases this integrated approach is much more efficient than the independent-tools approach. Here's a short example of how you might watch the values of some variables change as you single-step your way through our example program, price.c.

NOTE: For this process to work as described, the program must have been just compiled and linked so the debugger has the needed "hooks."

As a first step let's assume that you want to observe the values of index, cost[index], and prices[index] change as you single-step through the program. You do this by putting a "watch," or "breakpoint," at the source line where you want to stop execution. This is explained in detail in the introductory programs in the Think C manual. Once the program breaks at the desired statement, you can move to the Data window and type in the name of the data variable you wish to examine. The value of the item will appear in the column next to the variable name.

If you find an error as you step through your program, you can just go back to the edit window and change the program.

Before we leave this section, there is one additional point we want to mention. Modern compilers such as the one in the Think C environment allow you to specify how you want the generated object code to be optimized. In its default mode, the compiler compiles your program to a binary instruction sequence that uses minimum memory. An alternative is to tell the compiler to produce code that is optimized for speed. You can also tell the compiler to make maximum use of registers to hold variables and to rearrange the code so that loops and other jumps are optimized.

We usually leave the compiler optimization in its default mode when debugging a program, and then when we know the program works correctly, we recompile it with speed, register, and jump optimizations on to produce the final version of the program. The reason we initially leave these optimizations off is that it is very difficult to step through a program that has been highly optimized unless you are familiar with the algorithms used by the compiler.

Now that you have an overview of the tools used to develop C programs, we will show you more of the structure and syntax of the C language so you can write some programs of your own.

PROGRAMMING IN C

Introduction

One reason it is easy to learn a second programming language is that you already know what features to look for. When you have to learn a new language, we suggest a "bottom-up" approach, roughly as follows.

1. First, explore the data types that are available in the language and how these data types are represented. In 68000 assembly language, for example, you have worked with bytes, words, double words, and ASCII characters.

2. Then look at how basic statements of such variable declarations are written in the language. The DC.B, DC.W, DC.L, DS.B, DS.W, and DS.L declaration statements are examples of this in 68000 assembly language.

3. Next, find out what logical, mathematical, and bit "operators" are available in the language. This is equivalent to looking at available 68000 instructions such as AND, ADD, INC, etc. It is best just to skim through these and pick out some commonly used ones. Don't try to remember them all the first time through.

4. Since you should always try to write programs in a structured way, the next step is to see how standard programming structures such as IF-THEN-ELSE, CASE, REPEAT-UNTIL, WHILE-DO, and FOR-NEXT are implemented in the language. Look for examples such as the 68000 assembly language examples we showed you in Chapter 4.

5. As we showed you in the previous chapters, most programs contain many subroutines, so next find out how subroutines are defined and called in the language and how parameters are passed to subroutines. Look for examples such as the assembly language examples we showed you in Chapter 5.

6. The final step in the discovery process is to use the new language to write some simple programs that you have written successfully in another language. Since the algorithms are already very familiar, all you have to do is determine the syntax needed to express the algorithms in the new language. You are really just translating each program from one language to another. The simple program in Figure 12-1a is an example of translating a familiar algorithm to C.

In the following sections we lead you through the C language along the path described in the preceding steps. If you have some C programming tools available, we suggest that you work your way through the exercises at the end of the chapter and those in the accompanying lab manual to develop some skill in C. Use Figure 12-4 with the lab exercise or watch values.

C Data Types

In the first 10 chapters of this book you worked with integer data types such as bytes, words, double words, and ASCII character codes. Then in Chapter 11 you met a variety of floating-point data types. Figure 12-5 shows the data types available in Turbo C, the number of memory bits used to store each type, and the range of values that can be represented by each type. You have met most of these data types before, so they should be readily understandable.

You use type char mostly for ASCII character codes. You use one of the six integer types to represent whole numbers according to the range needed. Likewise, you use one of the three floating-point types to represent real numbers, depending on the range of values you need for that variable. The C floating-point types shown in Figure 12-5 correspond to the three 68881 floating-point formats shown in Figure 11-18 and described in detail in the corresponding section of Chapter 11. Later in this chapter we show you how the 68881 floating-point Pythagoras program in Figure 11-22 can be written in C.

As in 68000 assembly language, C has short pointers and long pointers. You use a short (16-bit) pointer if you need to represent only the offset of a code or data word in a segment, and you use a long (32-bit) pointer if you need to represent data or code anywhere in memory. The *enumerated* data type shown as enum in Figure 12-5 is a user-defined type, which can have integer values. You probably won't use this type in your first programs.

Declaring and Initializing Simple Variables in C

CHAR VARIABLES

In your 68000 assembly language programs, you declared and initialized variables with DC.B, DC.W,

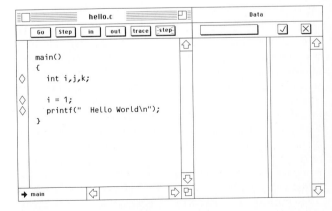

FIGURE 12-4 Debugger screen display showing watch values.

```
C data types, sizes, and ranges

type      subtype           size (bits)              range

char

          unsigned char     8                        0->255
          char              8                       -128->+127

enum                        16              -32,768->+32,767

int

          unsigned short    16                       0->65,535
          short             16              -32,768->+32,767
          unsigned int      16                       0->65,535
          int               16              -32,768->+32,767
          unsigned long     32                       0->4,294,967,295
          long              32     -2,147,483,648->+2,147,483,647

float

          float             32              3.4E-38->3.4E+38
          double            64              1.7E-308->1.7E+308
          long double       80              3.4E-4932->1.1E+4932

pointer

          short             16              -32,768->+32,767
          long              32     -2,147,483,648->+2,147,483,647
```

FIGURE 12-5   C data types and sizes.

DC.L, and DS statements. The example program in Figure 12-1a showed you a few examples of how you declare and initialize simple variables and arrays in a C program. In this and the following sections we show how to declare and initialize variables of all the different C types. To start, Figure 12-6 shows some examples of how you declare and initialize char-type variables.

The first five variable declarations in Figure 12-6 are all *extern*, which means that they are outside of any function. Variables declared outside any function are "global," so they can be accessed by any function in a program. If you declare a variable within a function, the variable is by default *automatic*, which means that it is "local" and can be accessed only within that function. For example, the declaration char command[15]; in Figure 12-6 is in function main, so the variable command is automatic and can be accessed only within main. When we show you how to declare and use functions, we will discuss in more detail how you decide whether to make a variable extern or automatic. The general rule is to declare variables inside of main unless they need to be accessible to other program modules. This avoids a conflict if a module written by some other programmer has a different variable with the same name as one in the main module. Now, let's take a closer look at the syntax of declaring and initializing char type variables.

As shown in Figure 12-5, a single char-type variable uses 1 byte of memory. A declaration such as char key declares a variable named key and reserves 1 byte of storage for it. If the declaration is outside of main, the variable will be initialized with a default value of 0.

The second char example in Figure 12-6 shows how you can declare a variable named yes and initialize the variable with the ASCII code for a lowercase y. Note that the ASCII character is enclosed in single quotes.

If you want to initialize a char variable with the ASCII code for a nonprinting character, you can enter a \, followed by the hex code for the character. The \x07 in the third char example initializes the variable bell with the ASCII code, which will sound a "bell" on your computer.

A char variable declaration such as one of the first three examples reserves space for just 1 byte, but the char message [20] example shows how you can declare an array of characters. In this case all 20 locations in the array are initialized with the default value of 0.

The char message[ ] = "Turn off the power"; statement in Figure 12-6 declares an array of characters

```
/*Examples of declaring and initializing char type variables*/

char key;   /*declare variable key but don't initialize      */

char yes = 's';   /* declare and initialize in one statement */

char bell = '\x07'; /*initialize with ASCII bell code */

char message[20];   /* message declared as array for 20 char-not init */

char err_mess[] = "Turn off the power";
        /*array of char initialized with specified string*/
main()
{
    char command[15]; /* automatic array for 15 char */
                      /* accessible only within main */

}
```

FIGURE 12-6   Declaring and initializing char variables in C.

and initializes the locations in the array with the ASCII codes for the characters enclosed in double quotes. Note that you use single quotes to initialize a single character variable, but you use double quotes to initialize the elements in an array of characters. We did not need to put a number in the [ ], because the compiler automatically counts the number of characters enclosed in the double quotes and allocates the required memory bytes. The array actually contains 1 more byte than the number of characters in the string because the compiler automatically inserts an ASCII null character, $00, as a sentinel after the last byte of the string. This sentinel character is used by many functions to identify the end of the string.

The declaration char command[15] in main in Figure 12-6 declares a 15-byte array of type char. As we said before, the declaration is in the routine main, so this array is automatic and can be accessed only in main. We did not initialize the array, so the locations in the command array will contain whatever random garbage happens to be in the memory locations set aside for the array. In some cases zeros get put in these locations, but you can't count on it, so you might tuck in a back corner of your mind that the default initialization for external arrays is 0 and the default initialization for automatic arrays is garbage.

INT VARIABLES

As shown in Figure 12-5, a simple INT variable uses 16 bits and can represent integers in the range −32,768 to +32,767. The example declarations in Figure 12-7 are all declared as simple int type, but you can replace the int at the start of any of these with one of the other int types shown in Figure 12-5 to get the range you need for a specific application.

As indicated by its comment, the first int example in Figure 12-7 declares an int-type variable named head-count, reserves a 16-bit word in memory for it, and leaves the location initialized with a default value of 0. Headcount is declared outside of main, so it is extern.

The second int example shows you how to initialize a variable to 10 decimal, and the third int example shows you how to initialize a declared variable with $FFFF. The 0x in front of the ffff tells the compiler that the ffff represents a hexadecimal number. Note that since type int represents a signed value, $ffff is actually equal to −1. If you want to declare a variable and initialize it with a value of +$ffff, you can use a statement such as "unsigned int hex_value = 0xffff;."

The int i = 10, j = 20, k = 30; example in Figure 12-7 shows how you can declare and initialize three or more variables of the same type in a single statement to make your program more compact.

The following two examples declare arrays. These examples should be very familiar to you from the program in Figure 12-1a. The int prices[10]; statement declares an array of 10 words and leaves the 10 locations uninitialized. The int cost[ ] = {20,28,15,26,19, 27,16,29,39,42}; declares an array of 10 words and initializes the 10 locations with the specified values. Note that you do not have to include the length of the array in the [ ] for the cost declaration, because the compiler counts the number of specified values and makes the array long enough to hold that number.

The last two int examples in Figure 12-7 show how to declare two- and three-dimensional arrays. A two-dimensional array consists of rows and columns. An instructor's grade roster is an example of a two-dimensional array. The rows represent the names of the students, and the columns represent the scores on tests, quizzes, and labs. The statement int test_scores[25][4]; declares a two-dimensional array that might be used to store four test scores for each of 25 students. The 25 in this declaration represents the number of rows and the 4 represents the number of columns. We did not initialize this array, because a

```
/* Examples of declaring and initializing int type variables */

int headcount; /* declare but don't initialize variable headcount */
                           /* headcount is extern */

main()
{
int index = 10; /* declare and initialize with 10 decimal */

int address = 0xffff; /* initialize with hex ffff */

int i=10, j=20, k=30; /* declare and init 3 int variables */

int prices[10]; /* array of 10 int, uninitialized */

int cost[]= {20,28,15,26,19,27,16,29,39,42};
        /* array of 10 int, initialized with values shown */

int test_scores[25][4];
        /* 2 dimensional array with 25 rows and 4 columns */

int av_temp[5][12][31]; /* Three dimensional array- pages, rows, columns*/

unsigned long population_1990; /* 32-bit unsigned integer */
}
```

FIGURE 12-7 Declaring and initializing int variables in C.

program that uses this array would probably prompt the instructor to enter the values for the array from the keyboard. To see how to initialize a two-dimensional array as part of the declaration, see the array declarations under the float type in Figure 12-8.

You can think of the three-dimensional array declared by the int av_temp[5][12][31]; statement in Figure 12-7 as consisting of 5 "pages" with 12 horizontal rows and 31 vertical columns on each page. This array represents the form in which the average temperature values for a 5-y period might be stored.

The program that uses this array would probably compute the value for each element in the array using maximum and minimum values entered by a friendly weatherperson. Later we show you how to access elements in multidimensional arrays such as this.

FLOAT VARIABLES

As shown in Figure 12-5, the three floating-point number types available in C are float, double, and long double. The basic format of float-type declarations is

```
/* Examples of declaring and initializing float type variables */

long double national_debt;              /* 80-bit floating point number */
                                        /* extern, anybody can access */
void main()
{
float side_a = 3.0, side_b = 4.0, side_c;  /* Init side_a and side_b, but not side_c*/
float max_min_temp[2] [7]=
    {{37.3,42.0,42.9,46.0,51.7,44.2,40.0},
     {29.4,32.2,30.1,34.2,37.2,36.1,32.3}}; /* declare and initialize 2 dimensional
                                        array of 2 rows and 7 columns */

}
```

FIGURE 12-8 Declaring and initializing float variables in C.

the same as that for int-type declarations, so we have just shown a couple of examples of this type in Figure 12-8. The first example again shows how you can declare and initialize several variables in a single statement. The second example shows how you can declare and initialize a two-dimensional array of real numbers. Note how the inner curly braces are used to set off the rows and the outer curly braces are used to enclose all the rows. The final float example in Figure 12-8 shows how to declare a long double–type variable. A new floating-point type will probably have to be created when the national debt becomes too large to be represented with a long double–type variable.

Declaring, Initializing, and Using Pointers in C

INTRODUCTION

People who have not worked with a 68000-type assembly language often have trouble understanding pointers when they are first learning C. By now you have several chapters of experience with 68000 assembly language pointer instructions such as MOVE.L (A2),D3 and MOVE.B D1,#102(A2,D4), so if we do our job well, you should have little trouble with C pointers.

To help you with the transition to C, we will not only show you how to declare and initialize pointers, we will show you how they are used in simple programs. To further help you, we will show the 68000 assembly language equivalents for some of the C examples we use. Read through this section until you thoroughly

understand it, because much of the power of the C language is based on the use of pointers.

A SIMPLE int POINTER

The first statement in the pointer example in Figure 12-9a declares an integer-type variable called headcount and initializes the variable with a value of 5. The second statement in this example declares a pointer named present and initializes the pointer with the address of the variable headcount. There are three points to remember from this example.

First, the type for a pointer is the type of the data pointed to. Second, the * in front of the name present in the declaration tells the compiler that present is a pointer. Third, the & in front of headcount is the "address of" operator. This operator tells the compiler that you want to initialize the pointer present with the address of the variable headcount. To summarize, then, this statement declares a pointer-type variable named present and initializes it with the address of the int variable called headcount.

To help you relate all this to your previous experience, the data segment in Figure 12-9b shows the 68000 assembly language equivalent for this C program. The assembly language was produced by using the MONITOR command from the Think C debug menu and then disassembling the contents of memory where the program was placed. The comments in the assembly language listing indicate the assembly language statements that correspond to specified C language statements. We examine such assembly lan-

```
/* declaring and initializing a simple int pointer */

#include <stdio.h>

main()
{
   int headcount = 5;   /* declare variable and initialize to 5 */
   int *present = &headcount;
                     /* declare pointer named present and initialize
                        the pointer with the address of headcount */

   printf(" headcount = %d \n &headcount = %p \n present = %p \n"
          " *present = %d \n &present = %p \n",
          headcount, &headcount, present, *present, &present );

   *present = *present + 10;

   printf(" headcount = %d \n &headcount = %p \n present = %p \n"
          " *present = %d \n &present = %p \n",
          headcount, &headcount, present, *present, &present );
}
```

(a)

FIGURE 12-9 (a) Declaring and initializing a simple int pointer. (b) Assembly language example of initializing and using int pointer. (c) Results produced by printf statement in Figure 12-9. (continued)

```
;   main()
;   {
        LINK      A6,#$FFFA

;   int headcount = 5;   /* declare variable and initialize to 5 */
        MOVEQ     #$05,D0
        MOVE.W    D0,$FFFE(A6)

;   int *present = &headcount;
;               /* declare pointer named present and initialize
;                       the pointer with the address of headcount */
        LEA       $FFFE(A6),A0
        MOVE.L    A0,$FFFA(A6)
        PEA       $FFFA(A6)

;   printf(" headcount = %d \n &headcount = %p \n present = %p \n"
;         " *present = %d \n &present = %p \n",
;       headcount, &headcount, present, *present, &present );
        MOVEA.L   $FFFA(A6),A0
        MOVE.W    (A0),-(A7)
        MOVE.L    $FFFA(A6),-(A7)
        PEA       $FFFE(A6)
        MOVE.W    $FFFE(A6),-(A7)
        PEA       $F372(A5)
        JSR       NV$3898                    ; 000E9B74
        LEA       $0014(A7),A7

;   *present = *present + 10;
        MOVEA.L   $FFFA(A6),A0
        MOVE.W    (A0),D0
        ADDI.W    #$000A,D0
        MOVEA.L   $FFFA(A6),A0
        MOVE.W    D0,(A0)
        PEA       $FFFA(A6)

;   printf(" headcount = %d \n &headcount = %p \n present = %p \n"
;         " *present = %d \n &present = %p \n",
;       headcount, &headcount, present, *present, &present );
        MOVEA.L   $FFFA(A6),A0
        MOVE.W    (A0),-(A7)
        MOVE.L    $FFFA(A6),-(A7)
        PEA       $FFFE(A6)
        MOVE.W    $FFFE(A6),-(A7)
        PEA       $F3C6(A5)
        JSR       NV$3866                    ; 000E9B74
        LEA       $0014(A7),A7

;   }

        UNLK      A6
        RTS
```

(b)

FIGURE 12-9   (continued)

```
headcount = 5
&headcount = 00176612
present = 5
*present = 00176612
&present = 0017660E


headcount = 15
&headcount = 00176612
present = 15
*present = 00176612
&present = 0017660E
```

(c)

FIGURE 12-9   (continued)

guage more closely in examples later in this chapter. For now, notice that the variables present and headcount are stored on the system stack and accessed as offsets from register A6, the stack mark register. Headcount is an integer, so D0 is used to manipulate it. D0 is loaded with 5 and stored into headcount using the MOVEQ and MOVE.W instructions. Present is an address, so its value is loaded using the LEA and PEA instructions. Remember that LEA means *load effective address* and PEA means *push effective address.*

Figure 12-9c shows the results produced by the printf statement in Figure 12-9a. Work your way carefully through these so you see the two ways of representing the value of headcount and the two ways of expressing the address of headcount in programs.

You can refer to the value of headcount directly by name or with the *present representation. When used in a program statement, the * in front of a pointer name means "the contents of the memory location pointed to by that pointer." The *present term in the printf statement then means the value of the variable pointed to by present. The standard programming jargon for using a * in front of a pointer to refer to the value pointed to by the pointer is *dereferencing the pointer.* As you can see in our example here, present points to headcount, so the value printed for *present is the same as that printed for headcount. The only confusion here is that in a pointer declaration, the * is used to indicate that the declared variable is a pointer, and in other program statements, the * indicates the value of the variable pointed to by the pointer named after the *. The * in this context means the same thing as the ( ) in an assembly language statement such as MOVE.B (A2),D0. Remember, we told you to read these ( ) as "the contents of the memory location(s) pointed to by the value in register A2."

The output of the printf function in Figure 12-9c also shows that you can represent the address where headcount is stored in two ways. One way is with the "address of" operator, &. The term &headcount is a shorthand way of saying "the address where the variable headcount is stored in memory." The second way to refer to the address of headcount is with the pointer, present. In the int *present = &headcount; statement, we declared present as a pointer and "pointed it" at

headcount. As shown by the printout, the value of present then is the same as the value of &headcount. Notice that the integer values are printed using the "%d," or decimal, format, whereas the pointers are printed using the "%p," or pointer, format.

Finally, in the printf output note the value produced by &present. This value represents the memory address where the compiler decided to store the pointer present. If you take another look at the assembly language equivalent of this program in Figure 12-9b, you can see how this corresponds to the address where present is stored on the stack.

Now that you know a little about C pointers, we want to take a moment to show you one reason why they are important.

When you call a C function you often want to pass parameters (arguments) to the function. For example, the statement printf("%d", sum); calls the printf function and passes it a variable called sum. What is actually passed to the function is a *copy* of the variable sum. The function then is given the value of the variable sum but is not given access to the actual variable itself. The technical term for this is *passing by value.* If only the value of a variable is passed to a function, then the function cannot modify the actual variable. For a function such as printf, this is no problem, because printf is not intended to change the values of variables.

However, if you call a function that is intended to change the value of a variable, you must pass the address of the variable to the function. The function can then use the address it receives to access and change the value of the variable. As an example of this, the C statement scanf("%d", &headcount); calls the predefined function scanf to read a decimal value from the keyboard and assign the value to a variable called headcount. The &headcount in this statement passes the address of headcount to scanf so that scanf can write the new value in headcount. If present has been previously declared and initialized as a pointer to headcount with int *present = &headcount; statement, then another way to write the scanf statement is scanf("%d", present);.

In a later section we discuss C functions in great detail, but to give you a head start you might remember the fact that when you call a C function to change the value of a variable, you must pass the address of the variable to the function instead of passing the value of the variable. The technical term for this is *passing by reference.* For a simple variable such as headcount, you can use &headcount to represent the address of the variable headcount. However, for many applications declaring a separate pointer is a much more versatile technique. In the following section we show you how to declare and use pointers with simple, one-dimensional arrays. Throughout the rest of the book we show many more examples of how you use pointers in programs.

USING POINTERS WITH int ARRAYS

The program in Figure 12-10a shows three different ways to add a profit to each of 10 costs from an array of ints. As in the example in Figure 12-1a, we first declare an int array called cost, initialize the cost array with 10 values, and declare an empty array of 10 elements to hold the computed prices. In the third line of declarations, we declare a simple variable called index and declare two pointers. The *cpntr = cost term declares a pointer called cpntr and initializes the pointer with the address of the first element in the array cost. The *ppntr = prices term in the third line declares a pointer called ppntr and initializes it with the address of the first element in the prices array. Now let's look at the three methods of accessing the elements in these arrays.

The first method shown in Figure 12-10a is the array-index method we showed you in Figure 12-1a. When we declare an array such as cost[ ], C treats the name cost as a pointer to the first element in the array. This pointer, however, is a constant, so it cannot be incremented to access the other elements in the array. To access the other elements in the array, we have to in some way add an index to cost. The term cost[index] in the array-index example in Figure 12-10a tells the compiler to generate the effective address by adding the

value of index to the address represented by the name cost. Likewise, the term prices[index] tells the compiler to generate the effective address of the variable by adding the value of index to the address represented by the name prices. The first time through the for loop, index will have a value of zero, so the first element in each array will be accessed when the cost[index] = prices[index] + profit; statement is executed. The second time through the for loop, index will have a value of 1, so the second element in each array will be accessed.

The method described for this C example is exactly the same method we used to access the array elements in the assembly language program in Figure 4-23. If you look back at that program, you will see that we loaded the index into D2, used the instruction MOVE.B #COST(A3,D2),D0 to copy an element from the cost array to D0, and used the instruction MOVE.B D0,#PRICES(A4,D3) to copy the computed price back to the indexed location in the PRICES array.

The second method of accessing the elements in the arrays uses the pointers cpntr and ppntr that we declared. The statement *ppntr = *cpntr + profit; says read the value pointed to by cpntr, add a profit of 15 to

```
/* COMPUTE THE SELLING PRICE OF 10 ITEMS */
#include <stdio.h>
#define PROFIT 15
#define MAX_PRICES 10

main()
{
    int cost[] = { 20,28,15,26,19,27,16,29,39,42 };
    int prices[10];
    int index, *cpntr = cost, *ppntr = prices;

        /* array index method */
        for (index=0; index <MAX_PRICES; index++)
        {
        prices[index] = cost[index] + PROFIT;
        printf("cost = %d, price = %d, \n", cost[index], prices[index]);
        }
    /* pointer method */
        for (index =0; index<MAX_PRICES; index++)
        {
                *ppntr = *cpntr + PROFIT;
                printf("cost = %d, price = %d,\n",*cpntr,*ppntr);
                cpntr++; ppntr++;
        }
    /* pointer arithmetic method */
        for (index =0; index<10; index++)
        {
                *(prices +index) = *(cost +index) + PROFIT;
                printf("cost = %d, price = %d, \n",
                 *(cost + index), *(prices + index));
        }
}
```

(a)

FIGURE 12-10 (a) C program that uses pointers to compute selling prices.
(b) 68000 assembly language equivalent of program in a. (continued)

```
; 68000 assembly language program to add profit to costs using pointers

;ABSTRACT: Program adds a profit factor to each element in a
;          COST array and puts the result in a PRICES array.

PROFIT   EQU      15         ; profit = 15 cents

COST:    DC.B     20,28,15,26,19,27,16,29,39,42
PRICES:  DS.B     10

CPNTR:   DC.L     COST
PPNTR:   DC.L     PRICES

START:   MOVEQ    #10,D1              ; loop counter
         MOVEA.L  (CPNTR),A2          ; load cost pointer into A2
         MOVEA.L  (PPNTR),A3          ; load prices pointer into A3

LOOP:    MOVE.B   (A2)+,D0            ; get cost
         ADDI.B   #PROFIT,D0          ; add profit factor
         MOVE.B   D0,(A3)+            ; save in prices

         DBGT     D1,LOOP             ; decrement counter and loop if still > 0

         RTS

         END
```

(b)

FIGURE 12-10 (continued)

the value, and write the result at the location pointed to by ppntr. In the initial declarations we initialized cpntr with the address of the first element in cost and ppntr with the address of the first element in prices. Therefore, the first execution of the for loop will read the first element in cost, perform the specified computation, and write the result in the first element of prices. The cpntr and ppntr pointers are variables, so they can be, for example, incremented, decremented, added to, or subtracted from, to access other elements in the arrays. The cpntr++; statement increments cpntr to point to the next element in cost, and the ppntr++; statement increments ppntr to point to the next element in prices.

NOTE: Cpntr and ppntr were declared as pointers to int type variables, so the compiler automatically generates instructions that increment the pointers as needed to access the next elements in the two arrays. Since int variables take 2 bytes, the compiler will generate instructions that add 2 to the value of cpntr and add 2 to the value of ppntr. The next time through the for loop, then, cpntr will point to the second element in cost and ppntr will point to the second element in prices. With this pointer method you do not need [index] to identify the desired elements in the arrays, because the pointers are incremented to point to the desired elements. The printf( ) statement in the pointer method example in Figure 12-10a also uses the *cpntr notation to represent the contents of the memory location(s) pointed to by

cpntr and *ppntr to represent the contents of the memory location pointed to by ppntr. We didn't bother to show you, but this second method produces the same printout as that shown in Figure 12-1b.

To help you further understand how this pointer version of the program works, Figure 12-10b shows how you could write it in 68000 assembly language. The program in Figure 12-10b actually generates machine code very close to that generated by the compiler for the C pointer example we have just discussed, except that it works with bytes instead of words and it obviously does not produce the code for the printf function.

In this assembly language example you can see that we first use a DC.L statement to declare and initialize a pointer to the first element in cost and another DC.L statement to declare and initialize a pointer to the first element in prices. Then in the code section of the program, we load CPNTR into A2 and PPNTR into A3 so we can use them to access the arrays. We use MOVE.B (A2)+,D0 to read in an element from cost and MOVE.B D0,(A3)+ to copy the result to prices. These instructions also increment the pointers so they point to the next elements in the arrays. We then decrement the loop counter in D1 and loop back to do the next add and store operations.

The third method of accessing the elements in the two arrays is the pointer arithmetic method shown in Figure 12-10a. As we said before, the name of an array such as cost is a pointer to the first element in the array. To access the other elements in the array you need to add an offset to the value of cost. One way to indicate this addition is with an expression such as cost[index] that we showed you in the first array access method. Another way to indicate this addition is with an expression such as (cost + index). Putting an * in front of this expression gives *(cost + index), which translates as "the value in memory pointed to by the sum of cost + index." The expression *(cost + index) is exactly equivalent to the expression cost[index], and the compiler generates the same code for each expression. Note that since cost is a pointer to an int-type array, the compiler generates instructions that add two times the value of index to cost when it translates the expression (cost + index).

Now that you have seen the three methods of accessing an array, you may wonder which one is best. Usually, you can use any of these methods. The array-index method is probably more intuitive when you are first learning about arrays, but most experienced C programmers use the direct pointer or the pointer arithmetic method because it generates considerably more efficient machine code. If for no other reason, you should use these last two methods in your programs so that you can easily follow them in other people's programs.

Another point we want briefly to make about the program in Figure 12-10a is the format in which the data is stored and manipulated. Cost is declared as type int, so according to Figure 12-5, 2 bytes are set aside for each element in cost. The compiler converts the decimal value supplied for each element to a 16-bit signed equivalent. When the program is loaded into memory to be run, these 16-bit signed values are loaded in the memory locations allocated for cost. When the program is run, the binary equivalent of 15 is added to each value from cost and the 16-bit signed result is put in the appropriate location in prices. The %d format specifiers in the printf( ) statement cause the printf function to convert the *cpntr and *ppntr values to their decimal equivalents before sending the values to the screen. The result is the decimal printout shown in Figure 12-1b. For reference, Figure 12-11 shows the formats for some of the specifiers you can use with printf, scanf, and other predefined functions.

A FLOAT POINTER EXAMPLE

By now you are probably getting tired of the cost-price example, but we will use it one more time to show you a few useful techniques that make the program more realistic.

Figure 12-12 shows the new, "improved" version. The first improvement is to make the program able to work with floating-point numbers instead of just integers. We did this by declaring the two arrays as type float instead of type int.

The second improvement is to make it easy to change the program so it can work with some number of values other than 10. Note how we use the preprocessor directive #define MAX_PRICES 10 at the start of

FORMAT SPECIFIER SYMBOL	PRINT
%d	decimal integer
%u	unsigned integer
%ld	long decimal integer
%p	pointer value
%f	floating point format
%6.2f	floating point format round off to two digits of decimal point, total of six digits
%e	exponential format floating point
%c	ASCII character for value
%s	string
%x or %X	hex value of integer

FIGURE 12-11 C format specifiers for use in printf, scanf, and other library functions.

the program to declare a constant called MAX_PRICES and then use MAX_PRICES in the for loops and every time we refer to the number of elements in the arrays. If we want to change the number of elements in the arrays, all we have to do is change the value of MAX_PRICES in the #define and recompile the program. The compiler will automatically replace each occurrence of MAX_PRICES with the new value. This shows the advantage of using defined constants instead of hard numbers in a program.

A third improvement in the program is to add a section that allows us to enter any desired values instead of using just the fixed values we put in cost for the previous examples. To do this we declare the array cost as shown, but we do not initialize the array with fixed values. After using the predefined function printf to send a prompt message to the user, we use another predefined function called scanf and a for loop to read in 10 values entered on the keyboard.

The actual code for the scanf function is contained in the library file. The #include <stdio.h> preprocessor directive at the start of the program tells the compiler to look in the file stdio.h for the prototype of the scanf( ) function. When the program is linked, the code for scanf( ) and printf( ) functions will be linked with the code for the rest of our program to generate the executable file.

The scanf("%f", cpntr) statement in the program calls the function and passes the parameters needed by the function. The scanf function needs to know what type of data we want it to read and where we want it to put the data. As with the printf function we used before, we use a format specifier to indicate the

```
/* float pointers and reading data from the keyboard */
#include<stdio.h>
#define MAX_PRICES 10
main ()
{
        float cost[MAX_PRICES], prices[MAX_PRICES];
        float *cpntr = cost, *ppntr = prices;
        int i;

        printf("Enter %d costs. After each cost press "
                    "space or enter.\n", MAX_PRICES);
        for(i=0; i < MAX_PRICES; i++)
        {
                scanf("%f", cpntr);
                cpntr++;
        }
        cpntr = cost;   /* reset cost pointer to start of array */
        for(i=0; i < MAX_PRICES; i++)
        {

                *ppntr = *cpntr + .25 * (*cpntr);
                printf("cost= %6.2f, price= %6.2f \n",*cpntr,*ppntr);
                cpntr++; ppntr++;
        }
}
```

FIGURE 12-12   Program using float pointers and the scanf function.

type of data we want it to read. In this program we want scanf to read floating-point values, so we pass a %f to scanf by putting it first in the ( ). As we said earlier, the scanf function requires that you pass it a pointer to tell it where to put the data read. We want the data values to be put in the cost array, so we pass the pointer cpntr, which we initialized with the starting address of the cost array. Each time through the for loop, cpntr will be incremented so that it points to the next element in cost.

This is a good time to show you why the type of each variable is important. According to Figure 12-5, a float-type variable uses 4 bytes of memory, so the elements of cost are at intervals of four in memory. Since cost is an array of floats, we declared cpntr as a type float pointer. When the compiler translates the cpntr++ statement, it automatically generates a 68000 instruction that adds 4 to the value of cpntr so it points to the next element in cost.

When this first section of the program runs, it sends the "Enter 10 costs . . ." message to the screen and waits for you to enter a value. After we enter a value and press the space bar or the Enter key, the program will put the value in the array and wait for us to enter the next value.

After all 10 values are read in, the cpntr pointer is reset to point at the start of the cost array with the cpntr = cost; statement, so we can process the 10 values read. To process the 10 values we use a for loop, as in the previous examples. Now let's see how we compute each cost.

In the previous examples we added a fixed profit of 15 to each cost, but this is not very realistic. A more realistic approach is to compute profit as a percentage of the cost and add the computed profit to the initial cost for each item. The statement *ppntr = *cpntr + 0.25*(*cpntr); does this. This statement says, "Get the cost pointed to by cpntr, multiply that value by 0.25, add the value pointed to by cpntr to the result, and write the result to the memory locations pointed to by ppntr. Note that the * symbol is used to represent the multiplication operation as well as to represent the contents of the memory location pointed to by a pointer. The meaning of an * in a statement is usually clear from its use.

After we compute each selling price, we call printf to display the entered costs and the computed prices on the screen. Since we want to print floating-point values, we use %f format specifiers. The 2 between the % and the f indicates that we want the values rounded to two digits to the right of the decimal point. This is appropriate for money values. The 6 between the % and the f indicates that the values will have a maximum of six digits, including the two to the right of the decimal point. This number is optional. Note that we use *cpntr to pass the current cost value to printf and *ppntr to pass the current price value to printf. We then increment the two pointers, cpntr and ppntr, so they point to the next locations in their arrays.

Now that you have some experience with int and float pointers, let's take a look at some char pointers, which work just a little bit differently.

CHAR POINTERS AND CHARACTER STRINGS

Some programming languages such as BASIC have a string data type, which is used for ASCII code sequences. In C you just use an array of type char to store strings. The last two examples in Figure 12-6 show how to declare char arrays. The next-to-last example in Figure 12-6 shows how you can initialize a char array with a desired string of ASCII codes. Remember that when you initialize a char array in this way, the compiler automatically includes a null character as a sentinel at the end of the string.

As with int and float arrays, the name of a char array is a pointer to the first element in the array, but again, this pointer is a constant, so it cannot be incremented, etc. It is often useful to declare a variable pointer to the start of a char array and use this pointer to access the array. Figure 12-13 shows how to declare char pointers and some of the different ways to work with character strings in C programs.

At the top of Figure 12-13 note that we can use the #define preprocessor directive to declare a constant string. Whenever the compiler finds the identifier exitmess, it will substitute the constant string "password incorrect." Since this string is a constant, it cannot be modified in the program.

The first char example in Figure 12-13 does several jobs. It declares a char-type pointer called greeting and sets aside 2 bytes of memory to store the pointer. It allocates 14 bytes of memory and initializes these bytes with the ASCII codes for the string "Good Morning" and a null character. Finally, it initializes the pointer greeting with the address of the first character in the string.

The printf("%s \n", greeting); statement in main shows how we can get this message printed out on the screen. To let printf know that we are passing it a string, we use the %s format specifier. To identify the string we want to send to the screen, we simply use the name of the pointer to the string. Note that we do not have to put an * in front of the name of the pointer, as we did for the float pointer in the printf( ) statement in Figure 12-11. For string operations the compiler assumes that the name of the pointer refers to the whole string. Since the pointer greeting initially points to the first element in the string, a term such as *greeting would refer only to the first element in the string rather than to the whole string. Don't overly complicate this. Just remember that we don't use an * in front of a pointer to a string unless we want to refer to just the first character in the string or individual elements in the string.

```
/* examples of declaring and using char type pointers */
#include <stdio.h>
#define exitmess "password incorrect"

main()
{
        char *greeting = "Good morning, ";
        /* pointer to type char location, initialized with string */

        char wakeup[20] = "Good morning\n";
        /* array of 20 char initialized with string shown */
        char *message; /* declare pointer named message,
                but allocate no storage */
        char name[20];

        printf("%s\n", exitmess);

        printf("%s\n", greeting);
        printf("%s\n", wakeup);

        message = "Hello there."; /* allocate storage and
                    load string into locations
                        starting where pointer message points */
        printf("The message is, %s\n", message);

        printf("Please type in your name and press the Enter key.\n");
        gets(name);
        printf("%s%s\n", greeting, name);
}
```

FIGURE 12-13   Declaring and using char type pointers.

The char wakeup[ ] = "Good morning.\n"; statement in Figure 12-13 declares an array of characters and initializes the elements of the array with the ASCII codes for the specified string. An ASCII null character, $00, will automatically be inserted as a sentinel at the end of the string. As we said before, the name of an array is a pointer to the first element in the array, so we can print this message with a statement such as printf("%s \n", wakeup). Note that again we do not have to use an * in front of wakeup to tell printf that we want to print the contents of a string named wakeup.

The char *message; declaration in Figure 12-13 declares a char-type pointer and sets aside a couple of memory locations for the pointer. However, this statement does not assign any value to the pointer, and it does not allocate any memory for storing a string. When the compiler reads the message = "Hello there."; statement in main, it will allocate some memory locations for the string "Hello there." and store the ASCII codes for the string in the allocated memory bytes. The compiler will also initialize the pointer named message with the starting address of the memory allocated for the string. Note again that we referred to the string simply with the name message. The compiler is smart enough to know that message refers to the entire string.

The char name[20]; statement in Figure 12-13 allocates 20 bytes of memory for an array of characters but does not initialize these bytes. The last three statements in main show how you can read a string in from the keyboard and put it in this array.

The printf( ) statement at the start of this section simply prompts the user to enter his or her name and press the Enter key. The second line in this section of the program uses the predefined function gets( ) to read characters entered on the keyboard. We tell gets( ) where to put the characters by passing it a pointer to some char type locations. In this example, name is a pointer to the array we declared, so we just pass name to gets( ) by including it in the ( ). Gets( ) keeps reading ASCII codes from the keyboard and putting them in the array until it reads the code for a carriage return. When it reads a carriage return, gets( ) puts a null character at the end of the stored string and returns to main. The final printf( ) statement sends the declared string "Good morning, " to the screen and then sends the string read in from the keyboard to the screen.

As you look at this last example, the question that may occur to you is, Why didn't we use the scanf( ) function that we illustrated in Figure 12-12 to read in the string? The answer to this is that scanf terminates when it finds a space, a tab, or a carriage return. The space between a first name and a last name then would terminate scanf, and only the first name would be read in and put in the array. The scanf function with a %s format specifier works fine if you want to read in only a single character or a single word.

Two important points to remember when working with character arrays or strings are the following:

1. Use just the name of the array or the name of the pointer to refer to the array. You don't need an * in front of the name unless you want to refer to just the first character in the array or individual elements in the string.

2. You must tell the compiler to allocate storage for a string with a statement such as char name[20]; before you can read in a string from the keyboard. You cannot just declare a pointer with char *message; and then gets(message); because the char *message; declaration doesn't allocate any space for the characters read from the keyboard. It just declares a pointer.

Now that you know how to declare different C data types, how to send messages to the screen, and how to read strings from the keyboard, you should be able to write some simple programs to entertain your friends. To make your programs more interesting, you need some more instructions in your toolbox. In the next sections we show you the different C "instructions," or operators, you can use to perform computations and the like in your programs.

C Operators

THE ASSIGNMENT OPERATOR

The assignment operator in C is simply the = sign. We have already used the assignment operator in the preceding program examples without bothering to give it a name. A statement such as side_a = 3.0;, for example, assigns a value of 3.0 to the variable side_a. This corresponds to an assembly language instruction such as MOVE.W #3,(side_a)

The = sign says "evaluate the expression to the right of the = and write the result in the variable to the left of the =." For example, the statement prices[index] = cost[index] +15; adds 15 to an element from the cost array and puts the result in the corresponding element in the prices array.

In 68000 assembly language you used MOVE instructions to copy the contents of one memory location to another. One way to do this in C is with a simple assignment statement. If you have two variables of the same type, such as maxval and curval, you can copy the value of curval to maxval with the statement maxval = curval;.

ARITHMETIC OPERATORS

Operation	Symbol	Examples
Addition	+	a = c + d;
Subtraction	−	a = c − d;
Multiplication	*	a = 4 * b;
Division	/	a = c/d;
Modulus	%	a = c%d; /* a = remainder of c/d */
Increment	++	index++; /* increment index by 1 */
		a = a + b++; / *postfix increment */
		/* add b to a, then inc b */

		a = a + ++b; /* prefix increment */ /* inc b, add result to a */
Decrement	--	count--; /* decrement count by one */ a = a - b--; /* postfix decrement */ /* subtract b from a, decrement b */ a = a + --b; /* prefix decrement */ /* decrement b, then add b to a */

BITWISE OPERATORS

Bitwise operators correspond to assembly language instructions such as AND, OR, XOR, NOT, ROL, and ROR. As with the assembly language instructions, they perform the specified operation on a bit-by-bit basis. The AND operator, for example, logically ANDs each bit of one operand with the corresponding bit of the other operand. For reference, here are the C bit operators and some examples of each.

Operation	Symbol	Examples
AND	&	a = a & b; /* each bit of b ANDed with corresponding bit in a, result in a */ a = a & 0xff; /* mask upper 8 bits of int a */
OR	|	a = a | b; /* each bit of b ORed with corresponding bit in a, result in a */ a = a | 0x8000; /* set MSB of int in a */
XOR	∧	a = a ∧ b; /* each bit in b is XORed with corresponding bit in a, result in a */ a = a ∧ 0x000f; /* invert low nibble int a */
NOT	~	a = ~a; /* invert bits in a, result in a */
Shift-left	<<	a = a << 4; /* shift bits in a 4 bit positions left around loop. This corresponds to 68000 assembly language sequence MOVEI.B #4,D0 ROL.W #a,D0*/
Shift-right	>>	a = a >> 8; /* shift bits in a 8 bit positions right around loop. This corresponds to 68000 assembly language sequence MOVEI.B #8,D0 ROR.W #a,D0 It effectively swaps the bytes of a if a is type int. */

COMBINED OPERATORS

Many experienced C programmers have a habit of trying to pack as much action as possible in a single program statement. This often makes the statement somewhat difficult to decipher. In the rest of the book we try to show you some of the more common shortcuts so that you can use them or at least recognize them when you see them. To start, we show how expressions using the operators in the previous sections are commonly written in shortened form. Again, the best way to do this seems to be with a list of examples, to which you can easily refer. Once you see the pattern of these, you will find them quite easy.

Operation	Standard Form	Combined Form
Addition	a = a + b;	a +=b;
Subtraction	a = a - b;	a -=b;
Multiplication	a = a * b;	a *=b;
Division	a = a/b;	a /=b;
Modulus	a = a%b;	a %=b;
AND	a = a&b;	a &=b;
OR	a = a|b;	a |=b;
XOR	a = a∧b;	a ∧=b;
Shift-left	a = a<<b	a <<=b;
Shift-right	a = a>>b	a >>=b;

RELATIONAL OPERATORS

Relational operators are used in expressions to compare the values of two operands. If the result of the comparison is true, then the value of the expression is 1. If the result of the comparison is false, then the value of the expression is 0. These comparisons are usually used to determine which of two actions to take. You will see many more examples in a later section, which discusses how the standard program structures are implemented in C, but a simple example here using the greater-than-or-equal-to operator should help you see how these are used.

In Chapter 4 we showed you how to implement an algorithm that turned on a light if the temperature in a printed-circuit-board-making machine was equal to or greater than a preset value. To implement this decision, we used a compare instruction and a conditional jump instruction. In C you might implement this action with a couple of statements such as:

```
if (current_temp >= run_temp)
    {
    heater(off);
    green_light(on);
    }
```

We assume here that the value of current_temp was read from an A/D converter by calling an assembly language subroutine before the if statement. (Later in the chapter we show you how to do this.) If the value of current_temp is not equal to or greater than the predeclared value of run_temp, then the comparison is false, and the statements in the curly braces will be skipped over. If the expression in ( ) evaluates to true, then the two statements in the curly braces will be executed. In the first of these statements we call a function called heater and pass it a value that will turn the heater off. Likewise, in the second statement we call a function called green_light and pass it a value that will turn on the green light. The heater and green_light functions would most likely call assembly language subroutine to manipulate the actual hardware.

Here is a list of the C relational operators. As you read each of these, mentally insert them in a statement such as "if (a == b) { }" to help you remember how they are used. Note that the == used here has a very different meaning from the single = used for assignment.

Operator	Symbol
Equal to	==
Not equal to	!=
Greater than	>
Greater than or equal to	>=
Less than	<
Less than or equal to	<=

LOGICAL OPERATORS

In the last section we showed you how the relational operators are used to choose between two actions in, for example, an IF-THEN-ELSE structure. The C logical operators allow you to include two or more conditions in a decision such as this. The three logical operators and the symbols which represent them are as follows.

Operator	Symbol	Examples
AND	&&	if(curtemp < maxtemp && curpress < maxpress) { green_light(on); } /* green light on only if both conditions true */
OR	||	if (curtemp > maxtemp || curpress > maxpress) { red_light(on); } /* red light on if either condition met */
NOT	!	if(!a) { statements; } /* do statements if a is false (= 0) skip over statements if a is true (=1) */

OPERATOR PRECEDENCE

In the preceding sections we have shown you most of the C operators. We show you the few remaining operators in later program examples, where they may

make more sense. The next topic we have to discuss here is the priority, or precedence, of the C operators. To properly evaluate or write an expression that has several operators, you have to know the order in which the operations are done. As an example of this, in the statement *prices = *cost + 0.25 * (*cost);, how did we know that the 0.25 would first be multiplied by *cost and then the result added to *cost? The answer to this is that the multiplication operator has a higher priority, or precedence, than the addition operator, so the multiplication is done before the addition.

As another simple example of this, suppose you have an expression such as a/b + c/d. From ordinary algebra you know that division also has a higher precedence than addition, so the two divisions will be done first, and then the results of the two divisions will be added together.

Shown here in descending order is the precedence of the C operators. For reference we have included some operators that we haven't discussed yet, so don't worry if you don't recognize every operator. To help you identify the different operators, we have included simple examples of each. In the paragraphs following this list, we show you some more examples to help fix the important ones in your mind.

NOTE: All the operators in a group have the same priority.

Operator	Example	
( )	4 * (9 + 2)	/* operation in parentheses done first */
[ ]	cost[3]	/* fourth element in array cost */
.	class.ssnmbr	/* pointer to ssnmbr member of structure */
->		/* indirect structure operator */
-	a = -23;	/* negation */
+	a = +28;	/* positive value */
~	a = ~a ;	/* invert each bit in a */
*	*cpntr	/* contents of location pointed to by cpntr */
&	&headcount	/* address of headcount */
++	index++	/* increment operator */
--	count--	/* decrement operator */ o7 3
sizeof	count = sizeof cost;	/* determine # of bytes in cost */
*	a * b	/* multiplication */
/	a/b	/* division */
%	a%b	/* modulus—remainder from division */
+	a + b	/* addition */
-	a - b	/* subtraction */
<<	a<<4	/* shift bits of a left 4 bit positions */

Operator	Example	
>>	a>>8	/* shift bits of a right 8 bit positions */
<	if(a<10)	/* less than */
>	if(temp>30)	/* greater than */
<=	if(a<=10)	/* less than or equal to */
>=	if(temp>=5)	/* greater than or equal to */
==	if(a==b)	/* relational equal */
!=	if(a!=b)	/* relational not equal */
&	a & 0xfff0	/* AND a with $fff0 to mask lowest nibble */
|	a | 0x8000	/* OR a with $8000 to set MSB */
∧	a ∧ 0x000f	/* XOR a with $000f to invert 4 LSBs
&&	if(condition 1 && condition 2)	/* both 1 AND 2 */
||	if(condition 1 || condition 2)	/* 1 OR 2 */

Simple assignment
=   a = 4;   /* simple assignment */
Combined assignment (see previous examples)
*= /= %= += −= <<= >>= &= |= ∧=

As we showed before, the precedence of C arithmetic operators is basically the same as in ordinary algebra, so you should have little trouble with these. In an expression such as 3 + 4 * a, the multiplication is done before the addition because multiplication has a higher precedence than addition. If you want the addition to be done first, you can write the expression as (3 + 4) * a. Parentheses have a higher precedence than multiplication, so any operation within parentheses will be done first. If there is any possibility of misinterpreting an expression, you should use parentheses to make it clear.

The only case where you may initially need a little help in understanding the precedence of operators is with the increment and decrement operators, so we will discuss these. If you use the increment operator, ++, in a simple statement such as index++;, you can write the ++ after index or in front of it. In other words, the statement ++index; and the statement index++; each increment the value of index by 1. When ++ or −− are used in more complex expressions, however, the placement of the operator is important.

In a statement such as Y = (a + ++b)/10; for example, the value of b is first incremented by 1, and the result is added to a. The sum of a and the incremented b is then divided by 10, and the result is assigned(copied) to the variable y. Incrementing or decrementing a variable before it is used in the expression is often referred to as a *prefix* operation.

If you write the statement as Y = (a + b++)/10;, the current value of b will be added to a. Next the result of this addition will be divided by 10 and assigned to Y. Finally, the value of b will be incremented by 1. Using a variable and then incrementing or decrementing it is often referred to as a *postfix* operation.

The simple rules here, then, are: Put the ++ or −− operator in front of the variable name if you want the variable incremented or decremented before it is used to evaluate the expression. Put the ++ or −− operator after the variable name if you want the current value of the variable used to evaluate the expression.

Statements such as those shown in the preceding paragraphs are usually quite straightforward, once you understand the prefix and postfix concept. Another situation where you will often see the increment and decrement operators is in a conditional expression such as while(a++ <20), which might be used at the start of a WHILE-DO structure. The ++ is after the variable a, so you know that the current value of a is used to evaluate the expression, and then a is incremented. The expression then says "compare the current value of a to 20 and then increment a. If the value of a is less than 20, do the statements following the while."

To see if you understand how this works, try interpreting the statement while(−−b >0) { }. The −− is before the variable b, so b is decremented, and the decremented value of b is compared with 0. If the decremented value is greater than 0, the statements following the while are executed. If the decremented value of b is equal to 0, execution will go to the next statement in the program after the while block.

Throughout the preceding discussions we have given you glimpses of how the standard programming structures are implemented in C. In the next section we take a closer look at these.

IMPLEMENTING STANDARD PROGRAM STRUCTURES IN C

As we tried to show you in Chapter 3, the most successful way to write any program is to solve the problem mentally, write the algorithm for the solution using the basic IF-THEN-ELSE, CASE, REPEAT-UNTIL, WHILE-DO, and FOR-DO structures shown in Figure 3-3, and finally translate the algorithm to an appropriate programming language. The C implementation of these structures is very close to the pseudocode for them, so the translation is usually quite easy. In this section we discuss each of these and show you more C programming techniques.

IF-THEN AND IF-THEN-ELSE IMPLEMENTATION
The general format of the if-then-else structure in C is

```
if(condition)
{
statement;
statement
}
else
{
statement;
statement;
}
```

Condition in this format represents some expression such as currtemp==maxtemp. If the condition expression evaluates to 1 or any nonzero value, the block of statements under the if will be executed. If the condition expression evaluates to 0, the block of statements under the else will be executed. The else block can be omitted if you want just an if-then instead of an if-then-else. Note that the curly braces are not needed for the case where the if block contains only one statement. Likewise, the curly braces are not needed in the else block if it contains only one statement.

The program section in Figure 12-14 shows a simple if-else structure and introduces you to getch( ), another predefined function that you will probably want to use in your programs. This example also gives you a little more practice with operator precedence.

At the start of the program we declare a char-type variable and give it the traditional name ch. After printing a couple of prompt messages, we use an if-else to determine a course of action based on the user's response. To evaluate an expression such as the if condition in Figure 12-14, you start with the innermost parentheses and work your way out. The getch( ) part of the if expression calls the predefined function getch( ). The getch( ) function sits in a loop until the user presses a key on the keyboard. When the user presses a key, getch( ) terminates and returns the ASCII code for the key pressed. In this example ch = getch( ) means that the returned ASCII value will be assigned (copied) to the variable named ch. This completes the action in the inner parentheses. The value produced by these actions is the ASCII code stored in ch.

The == 'n' next in the expression compares the value in ch with the ASCII code for a lowercase n. If the values are the same, the entire expression is true (evaluates to 1) and the statements in the if block are executed. If the value in ch is not equal to the value of the ASCII code for a lowercase n, the ‖ ch == 'N' part of

the expression compares the value of ch with the ASCII code for an uppercase N. Remember that the ‖ symbol represents the logical OR operation, so the overall expression is true if ch = n or ch = N. If the entered character is an N, the statements in the if block are executed. If the character is not an n or an N, the entire expression evaluates to 0, and statements in the else block will be executed.

NOTE: The expression for the if statement is evaluated from left to right, so (ch=getch( )) is done first, and the result is compared with 'n'. For the second comparison you just write ch = 'N', because ch already has the value read in from the keyboard. If we had used (ch = getch( ))== 'N' here, execution would sit in getch( ) until the user pressed another key! Incidentally, if we want the key pressed by the user to be echoed to the CRT, you can use the getche( ) function instead of the getch( ) function.

The exit( ); statement in the if block calls a predefined function, which terminates the program and returns control to the operating system.

In the else block we display a message to let the user know that something is happening; then we use the goto start statement to send execution to the beginning of the program. The goto statement in C corresponds to the unconditional JMP instruction in assembly language. As in assembly language, the name start represents a label that you place in front of the instruction statement to which you want execution to go. In C you write a : after the label, just as you do in assembly language. In this example we put the start label next to the first printf statement, just to show you how to write labels.

NOTE: The label for a goto must be in the same function as the goto statement.

```
#include <stdio.h>
main()
{
char ch;
start:   printf("Game over.\n");
         printf("Enter y to play another game, n to quit.\n");
         if ((ch = getch()) == 'N' || ch == 'n')
                {
                printf("Goodbye.\n");
                exit();
                }
         else
                {
                printf("Here we go again.\n");
                goto start;
                }
}
```

FIGURE 12-14   Basic if-else example.

Some structured programming purists say that you should never use even a single goto in a program. This attitude is probably a reaction to the way goto statements were abused in old BASIC programs. To many, however, using a simple goto to rerun the entire program is the clearest way to do it. In reality, even if you hide the action in some other structure, the compiler will usually generate an unconditional jmp instruction to implement the action.

The program fragment in Figure 12-14 has a minor problem. It thoroughly tests to see if the user entered an n or an N and exits if either of these was entered. However, if any other key is pressed, the else block statements start the game over again. Figure 12-15 shows how you can use a nested if-else structure to provide three alternative actions based on the key pressed. For an n or N, the statements in the first if block are executed. For a y or a Y, the statements in the second if block are executed. For any other key, the statements after the final else will be executed. In a later example we show you how a "real C programmer" might write this program segment to avoid the direct goto statement in the final else block.

MULTIPLE CHOICES—THE SWITCH STATEMENT

To implement algorithms with more than three choices, you can nest additional if-else sections, but often a more efficient way to do this is with the *switch* structure. The C switch structure is essentially the same as the CASE structure we showed you in Figure 3-3. The general format for the switch statement is

switch (variable)
{

case value1:
{
statements;
break;
}
case value2: statement(s); break;
case value3: statement(s); break;
default: statement; /* optional */

Variable in this statement must be some quantity such as an int or char that can be evaluated as an integer. Value1 in the first case line represents some value of the variable used to make the decision. After each case line you write the statement(s) you want executed if the variable has that value. If, for example, the value of variable is equal to value1, the statements after case value1: will be executed. The break statement at the end of this block of statements will cause execution to skip over the rest of the choices in the structure. If you leave out the break statement, the actions for the next case after the selected case will be executed. The optional default directive at the end of the switch structure allows you to specify the action(s) you want taken if the value of variable does not match any of the specified values.

Figure 12-16 shows how you might use the switch statement to implement a "command recognizer" in one of your programs. This example shows how a typical development environment might be implemented, like the one we discussed earlier in the chapter. The switch statement is used to implement an example main menu. To select the desired submenu, you then press the key that corresponds to the first letter in the name of the submenu. The choices are F,

```
        #include <stdio.h>
        main()
        {
                char ch;
                printf("Game over.\n");
prompt:         printf("Enter y to play another game, n to quit.\n");
                if ((ch = getch()) == 'N' || ch == 'n')
                        {
                        printf("Goodbye.\n");
                        exit();
                        }
                else if (ch == 'Y'|| ch == 'y')
                        {
                        printf("Here we go again.\n");
                        /* goto start; */
                        }
                else
                        {
                        ch = getchar(); /* clear buffer */
                        goto prompt;
                        }
        }
```

FIGURE 12-15   Nested if-else example.

```
#include<stdio.h>
main()
{
        char ch;
        ch=getchar();
        switch (ch) {
        case 'F':
        case 'f':  /* file_menu(); */ break;
        case 'e':  /* edit_window(); */ break;
        case 'r':  /* run_menu(); */ break;
        case 'c':  /* compile_menu(); */break;
        case 'p':  /* project_menu(); */ break;
        case 'o':  /* options_menu(); */ break;
        case 'd':  /* debug_menu(); */ break;
        case 'b':  /* break_menu(); */ break;
        default:   /* edit_window(); */ ;
        }

}
```

FIGURE 12-16   Example of C switch structure.

E, R, C, P, O, D, and B. Each of these options brings up a lower-level menu or carries out a command.

In the program in Figure 12-16 we use our new friend getch( ) to read a character from the keyboard. We then use a switch structure to evaluate the character and decide what action to take. To simplify the basic structure of this example, we call a function to implement each of the desired actions. Actually, for this example we show the function calls as comments, because we did not want to declare and define all these functions. When execution returns from the called function, the break statement at the end of that line will cause execution to skip to the next statement after the switch structure. If the key pressed by the user does not match any of the choices, the default: edit_ window( ); statement at the end of the block sends execution back to the edit operation. You can have only one value in each case evaluation, so if you want the program to accept lower- or uppercase letters, you have to put case lines in for each. The line case 'F': followed by the line case 'f': file( ); break;, for example, will call the file function if the user enters either a lower- or uppercase f. A more versatile alternative is to write a small function that converts all entered characters to lowercase before entering the switch structure. We leave this for you to do as an exercise at the end of the chapter.

THE WHILE AND DO-WHILE IMPLEMENTATIONS

In Chapter 3 we showed you how the while-do and the repeat-until structures are used to loop through a series of statements. In C these two structures are called the while and the do-while, respectively. The major difference between the two structures occurs when the exit test is done. For comparison, Figure 12-17 shows how the two are implemented in C.

As you can see, in the while loop in Figure 12-17a, the condition is evaluated before any statements are executed. If the condition expression initially evaluates to 0, execution will simply bypass the block of statements under while and go on with the rest of the program. In this case none of the statements in the while block will be executed. If the condition expression initially evaluates to a nonzero value, the statements in the while block will be executed once. Then the condition expression will be evaluated again, and if the result of the evaluation is still nonzero, the statements in the while block will be executed again. Looping will continue until the condition expression evaluates to 0.

The key point of a while loop is that the condition is

```
/* while format */

while(condition)
        {
        statement(s);
        }
```
                        (a)
```
/* do-while format */
do
        {
        statement(s);
        }
while(condition);
```
                        (b)

FIGURE 12-17   (a) Basic format of C while structure. (b) Basic format of C do-while structure.

tested before any statements are executed. In most cases this "look before you leap" approach is the best one, and most loop algorithms can be written in this way.

For those cases where you want the loop statements to be executed once before the condition is checked, C has the do-while structure shown in Figure 12-17b. In this structure the statements in the do-while block are executed once, and then the specified condition expression is evaluated. If the condition expression evaluates to 0, the do-while terminates and execution goes on to the rest of the program. With this structure, then, the statements in the do-while block will always be executed at least once. If the condition expression evaluates to a nonzero value after executing these statements, the statements in the do-while block will be executed again and the condition expression will be evaluated again. Looping will continue until the condition expression evaluates to 0. Note that in this structure there is a semicolon at the end of the while line.

Figure 12-18a shows how you can use a while loop to make a user enter a Y or an N in response to a prompt. This approach avoids using a goto such as the goto prompt; statement in Figure 12-15. The declaration statement for ch at the start of the program gives it a null value, so the first time the condition for the while statement is tested, the result is false. Therefore, the ch=getch(); statement part of the while is executed. When getch() returns a new value to ch, the condition expression for the while will be checked again. Execution will stay in this loop until getch() returns a y, Y, n, or N. After it exits the loop, execution goes to the if-else section of the program to determine the actions to take based on the value returned by getch() and assigned to ch.

Figure 12-18b shows how the same program section can be implemented as a do-while. In this example we did not need to give ch an initial value, because the ch=getch(); statement at the start of the do-while gives ch a value before any tests are made. The ch=getch() statement is repeated until the value of ch matches one of the values in the condition test part of the do while.

It is not obvious in the examples shown in Figure 12-18, but in most cases the while structure is a better choice than the do-while, because the condition is checked before any action is done.

THE FOR LOOP

As we have showed you in several previous program examples, a for loop can be used to do a sequence of statements a specified number of times. The general format of a for loop is

```
for (initialization(s); test; modify)
{
statement(s)
}
```

To refresh your memory, Figure 12-19 shows a simple example of a for loop. The initialization in this example assigns a value of 0 to the variable count. If you want to, you can include more than one initializa-

```
/* while example */
#include <stdio.h>
main()
{
char ch = 0x00;   /* assign initial value to ch */
while(ch!='n'&& ch!='N'&& ch!='y'&& ch!='Y')
        {
        printf("Enter y to play another game, n to quit.\n");
        ch=getch();
        }
if (ch=='n'|| ch=='N')
        {
        printf("Goodbye.\n");
        exit();
        }
else
        {
        printf("Here we go again.\n");
        /* goto start */
        }
}
```

(a)

FIGURE 12-18 (a) Example of C while structure. (b) Example of C do-while structure. (continued)

```
/* do-while example */
#include <stdio.h>
main()
{
        char ch;
        do
        {
        printf("Enter y to play another game, n to quit.\n");
        ch=getch();
        }
while(ch!='n'&& ch!='N'&& ch!='y'&& ch!='Y');
if (ch=='n'|| ch=='N')
        {
        printf("Goodbye.\n");
        exit();
        }
else
        {
        printf("Here we go again.\n");
        /* goto start */
        }
}
```

(b)

FIGURE 12-18   *(continued)*

tion here. You might, for example, include two initialization statements such as count=0; b=23; to initialize a variable called b with a value of 23 as well as initialize the loop variable count.

The test part of this example compares the value of count with the terminal value. If the value of count is not equal to the terminal value, the statements in the loop will be repeated.

The count++ in our example represents the "modify" part of the for. This is where you specify what you want to change each time around the loop so that the loop eventually terminates. In some C programs you may see more than one action statement in the modify section of the for( ). You might, for example, see something such as "count++, index=index+4;" in the modify section. These two statements will increment count by 1 and increment index by 4 each time through the loop. The authors' personal feeling is that the program is more readable if you put only the loop

variable initialization and loop variable modification in the for parentheses.

To give you a little more challenging example of a for loop and teach you more about arrays, the first part of the program in Figure 12-20a shows how you can use nested for loops to read maximum and minimum temperature values from the keyboard and put the values in a two-dimensional array. The last section of the program uses another for loop to compute the average temperature for each day and display all the results.

The int temps[7][3]; statement at the start of the program declares an array of seven rows and three columns. To help you visualize this, Figure 12-20b shows this array in diagram form. As you can see, there is one row for each of the seven days of the week. Also, there is one column for the daily maximum temperatures, one column for the daily minimum temperatures, and one column for the averages that will be calculated. The arrow looping through the array shows the sequence in which the array values are stored in memory. As you can see, the three elements in the first row are stored in the three lowest memory locations, the three elements in the next row are stored in the next three memory locations, etc.

The elements of the array are stored in sequence in memory, so you could access the elements in this array as if it were a one-dimensional array of 21 elements. In other words, you could set up a pointer to the first element in the array and then keep incrementing the pointer to access the other elements in the array. The problem with this method is that you lose the row and column information.

A much more versatile way to access the elements in this array is with row and column index values. The

```
#include<stdio.h>
int count;
main()
{
        int count;
        for (count=10; count>0; count--)
        {
        printf("%d\n ", count);
        }
        printf("blastoff!");
}
```

FIGURE 12-19   Example of simple count-down for loop.

index for an array starts from zero, so the term temps[0][0] is a way to refer to the element in the first row of the first column. Likewise, the term temps[0][1] is a way to refer to the element in the second column of the first row, and the term temps[6][2] is a way to refer to the value of the third element of the seventh row.

In the program in Figure 12-20*a* we use the variable *i* to index a desired row and the variable *j* to index a desired column in the array. The inner for loop in the program uses *j* to access the elements in a row. The first time the inner loop executes, it will put the value returned by scanf in the first element in the row. The second time the inner for loop executes, it will put the value returned by scanf in the second element in the row. Since the inner loop is set to terminate for *j* < 2,

```
/*Program to read max and min temperatures, then compute average */

#include <stdio.h>
int temps[7][3];
main()
{
        int i, j;
        for (i=0; i<7; i++)  /* read values entered */
            {
              printf("Enter max temp for day %d,"
                     "then min temp.\n", i+1);
              for(j=0; j<2; j++) /* read max, then min */
                scanf ("%d", (*(temps+i)+j));
            }
        for(i=0; i<7; i++) /* compute averages and print all values */
        {
        *(*(temps+i)+2) = (*(*(temps+i)+0) + *(*(temps+i)+1))/2;
        printf("For day %d max = %d min = %d av = %d \n",
          (i+1), *(*(temps+i)+j), *(*(temps+i)+1), *(*(temps+i)+2));
        }
}
```

(a)

(b)

(c)

FIGURE 12-20   (a) Program showing index method of accessing elements in two-dimensional array. (b) Two-dimensional array of seven rows and three columns used to store maximum, minimum, and average temperatures for 7 d. (*Note:* Arrow shows order that values are stored in memory going from lowest to highest memory address.) (c) Two-dimensional array shown as seven-element array of one-dimensional three-element arrays. (d, p. 407) Program in a rewritten using pointer notation. (e, p. 407) Results produced by program in a or d.

```
/*Program to read max and min temperatures, then compute average */

#include <stdio.h>
int temps[7][3];   /* extern so other modules can access */

main()
{
        int i, j;
        for (i=0;  i<7;  i++)
            {
                printf("Enter max temp for day %d,"
                        "then min temp.\n", i+1);
                for(j=0;  j<2;  j++) /* read max, then min */
                    scanf ("%d", &temps[i][j]);
            }
        j=0;   /* reset column index */
        for(i=0;  i<7;  i++)
        {
        temps[i][j+2] = (temps[i][j] + temps[i][j+1])/2;
        printf("For day %d max = %d min = %d av = %d \n",
                (i+1), temps[i][j], temps[i][j+1], temps[i][j+2]);
        }
}
```

(d)

```
For day 1 max = 98 min = 68 av = 83
For day 2 max = 89 min = 65 av = 77
For day 3 max = 87 min = 59 av = 73
For day 4 max = 90 min = 67 av = 78
For day 5 max = 86 min = 58 av = 72
For day 6 max = 79 min = 68 av = 73
For day 7 max = 83 min = 69 av = 76
```

(e)

FIGURE 12-20   *(continued)*

the inner loop will then terminate and execution will go back to the outer for loop.

The outer for loop uses i to access the desired row in the array. The first time through the outer loop $i = 0$, so the first row in the array will be accessed. The next time through the loop i has been incremented to 1, so the second row in the array will be accessed. This process is essentially the same as the nested delay loops that you met in earlier chapters.

The scanf function requires that you pass it a format specifier to tell it what type of data it will be reading and that you pass it the address of the location where you want the data put. You use the %d specifier to indicate that you want the data treated as a decimal value, and you use the term &temps[i][j] to pass the address of the desired element in the array to scanf. Remember that temps[i][j] is a way to refer to the value of an element in the array, so &temps[i][j] is a simple way to refer to the address of that element. Note that we use $i + 1$ for the value of the day instead of just i. An array index starts from zero, but we want the days to be numbered 1–7.

After all 14 temperature values are read in and put in the appropriate locations in the array, we use a single for loop to compute the average temperature for each day and put the computed results in the appropriate row of the third column in the array. The temps[i][j+2] = (temps[i][j] + temps[i][j+1])/2 statement shows how to add a constant to the j index value to access the different elements in a row. Likewise, in the last printf statement in Figure 12-20a, we add constants to the j index to access the three elements in a row. Textbooks often refer to this as *pointer arithmetic*.

Now that you know the array index method of accessing the elements in a two-dimensional array such as this, we briefly show you the direct pointer method, which is very commonly used by experienced C programmers. Even if you don't choose to use this pointer method yourself, you should understand it well enough to follow it in other people's programs.

As we said before, one way of thinking about the array temps[7][3] is as a two-dimensional array with seven rows and three columns. Another common way of thinking of the array named temps is as seven one-dimensional arrays of three elements each. In this view, shown in Figure 12-20c, temps[0] is the name of the first three-element array, temps[1] is the name of the second three-element array, and temps[6] is the name of the last three-element array.

The key to understanding how you work with this form is to remember that *the name of an array is a pointer to the first element in the array.* The name temps then is a pointer to the first element in the array of arrays. In this view the first element in the array is the subarray temps[0], so temps is a pointer to temps[0]. One way to represent this relationship in C syntax is temps = &temps[0]. The other way to represent this relationship is *temps = temp[0].

Now, temp[0] is the name of an array of three ints, so temp[0] is a pointer to the first element in the array temps[0]. You can refer to the value of the first element in temps[0] with the expression *temps[0]. This expression simply says "the value pointed to by the pointer temps[0]." In the last paragraph we showed you that *temps = temps[0], so with a little substitution, the expression *temps[0] can be written as **temps. The **temps expression, which is the pointer form we wanted, means "the contents of the memory location pointed to by the contents of the memory location pointed to by temps." This is easier to understand if you mentally put parentheses around *temps and think of it as a pointer to the first subarray, temps[0].

Thus the three equivalent ways to refer to the value of the first element in the first subarray of temps are

$$\text{temps[0][0]} = \text{*temps[0]} = \text{**temps}$$

The expression temps[0][0] is the two-dimensional-array method we showed you in Figure 12-20a. The expression *temps[0] takes advantage of the fact that temps[0] is a pointer to the first subarray and *temps[0] represents the value pointed to. The expression **temps is just an indirect way to point to temps[0] and then to the value pointed to by temps[0]. The two-dimensional-array form is probably the most intuitive, but most compilers convert it to the pointer form to produce the actual machine code. Therefore, many programmers write array expressions directly in the pointer form.

If you follow that **temps is a valid way to refer to the first element in the first subarray or row of temps, the question that may occur to you is, How do you access the other elements in the array using the pointer form? The answer to this question is that you add index values to the pointer to access the desired element. If you use i as the row or subarray index and j as the column index as we did in Figure 12-20a, then

$$\text{temps[i][j]} = \text{*(*(temps+i)+j)}$$

The *(temps+i) in the second expression points to the desired subarray. Adding j to this changes the value of the pointer to point to the desired element in the subarray. For reference, Figure 12-20d shows how the program in Figure 12-20a can be written using the pointer notation we have just shown you. If you work

your way through this example, you should be well on your way to understanding C pointers. Note that we used the numbers 0, 1, and 2 to index the desired column in the statement that computes the average and the printf statement. The +0 is not needed in the second term, but we included it to emphasize the position of the column index in the term. Figure 12-20e shows the results produced by either the program in 12-20a or the one in 12-20d.

C Functions

DECLARING, DEFINING, AND CALLING C FUNCTIONS

As we have told you many times before, often the best way to write a large program is to break it down into manageable modules and write each module as a function or a series of functions. The C functions we used in the preceding program examples are all "predefined." The code for these functions is contained in a library file. All you have to do to use one of these functions is to put #include<> at the start of your program to tell the compiler the name of the file that contains the prototype of the function, call the function by name, and in some cases pass some parameters to the function. Now we need to show you how to write and use your own C functions.

To create and use a function in a program, you must declare the function, define the function, and call the function. Figure 12-21a shows a template or model of how you do each of these, and Figure 12-21b shows a simple program example. To help you understand the terms in the templates, we suggest that you look at the corresponding parts in the example program as we discuss the templates. Don't worry about the details of the example program, because after we work through the templates, we will discuss the example program more thoroughly. The three templates in Figure 12-21a are shown in the order that they appear in programs, but we will discuss them in the order that you usually construct them as you write a program.

The first step in writing a function is to define the actual function. Functions are always defined outside of main( ), because you cannot define one function within another. To actually write the function, you will probably work from the inside out. In other words, you will probably first write the data declarations and the action statements that implement the algorithm for the body of the function. Note that the statement block for the function is enclosed in curly braces. After you write the body of the function, you can then decide what values have to be passed to the function and what value, if any, will be returned from the function to the calling program. When you arrive at these decisions you can write the header for the function.

As shown in Figure 12-21a, the function header starts with a type such as int, float, or char. The type in this case represents the type of the variable returned from the function to the calling program. A C function can return the value of only one variable to the calling

TEMPLATES FOR DECLARING, CALLING AND DEFINING C FUNCTIONS

DECLARATION (PROTOTYPE)

```
type          function_name(variable list);
  ^                          ^
```
type of data   type and formal parameter (dummy)
returned by function   name for each variable to be passed

CALL

```
main()
{
          function_name(actual arguments);
                          ^
```
                        names of variables or pointers
                        to be passed to function this call
```
}
```

DEFINITION

```
type      function_name(formal arguments)
  ^                     ^              ^
  :                     :        note: no ;
  :                     :
```
type of data   types and names of local
retured by   variables which correspond to
function   actual variables passed to function

```
     {
     statements;

     return(variable);
              ^
```
            name of variable returned to
            calling function
```
     }
```

(continued)

FIGURE 12-21   Declaring, calling, and defining C functions. (a) Template.
(b, p. 410) Examples in a program.

program. If the function does not directly return a value to the calling program, you give the function a type void.

After the function name you enclose in parentheses the type and name for each function variable that will receive values passed from the calling program. These variables declared in the function header are often called *formal arguments* or *formal parameters.* The trick here is that you usually use different names for particular variables in the calling program and in the function. This makes the function "generic," because you can then pass any variables of the same types to the function in place of the "local" variables declared in the function definition header. Later when we discuss the details of the example program in Figure 12-21b, you will better see how this works.

As an example of a function header, the function header int c2f(int c) in Figure 12-21b declares a function called c2f, which returns an int value and requires an int value to be passed to it. The int value passed to the function will be automatically assigned to the int variable called c in the function. Also in Figure 12-21b, the function header void get_temp(int*ptr) defines a function called get_temp that does not return a value but requires that a pointer to an int-type variable be passed to it. Note that function header lines do not have semicolons after them.

After you write the function definition, the next step is to declare the function by writing a *prototype* for the function. This declaration is equivalent to declaring a variable at the start of your program. Note in Figure 12-21a that the function prototype declaration at the

```
/* Declaring, calling, and defining functions */

#include<stdio.h>
int tempc, tempf;        /* external (global) variables */

int c2f(int c);   /* declare function c2f which returns an int value */

void get_temp(int *ptr); /* declare function which modifies a value
                pointed to, but does not directly return a value */
main()
{
        get_temp(&tempc);       /* call function get_temp.
                                get_temp writes directly to tempc */

        tempf = c2f(tempc);        /* call c2f function, pass value
                                of tempc to function. Returned value
                                assigned to tempf */

        printf("The temperature in Celsius is %d\n", tempc);
        printf("The temperature in Fahrenheit is %d\n",tempf);
}   /* end of main */

int c2f(int c)    /* define function c2f. Note no ; at end */
        {
        int f;      /* automatic (local) variable */
        f = 9*c/5 + 32;
        return (f);
        }

void get_temp(int *ptr)        /* define function get_temp */
        {
        printf("Please enter the Celsius temperature.\n");
        scanf("%d",ptr);
        }
```

(b)

FIGURE 12-21   *(continued)*

start of the program has the same format as the function definition header, but it is followed by a semicolon. This prototype lets the compiler know the name of the function and the types of data to be passed to the function. The compiler uses this information to make sure that the correct data types are passed to the function when it is called. In large programs the function prototypes are put in a separate header file and pulled into the program at compile time with a #include<> directive. This reduces the "clutter" at the start of the main program.

As shown in the CALL section of Figure 12-21a, you call a function with its name and a set of parentheses that enclose the name(s) of the variables being passed to the function. If no variables are passed to the function, you put the term void in the parentheses after the function name.

The variables named in the function call are commonly called *actual arguments*, or *actual parameters*. Remember from a previous discussion that when you pass a variable to a function in C, you pass just the

value of the variable—or, in other words, just a copy of the variable. If you want the function to be able to access and change the actual value of a variable, you must pass the function a pointer to the variable. Now that you have an overview of the three tasks, let's look a little closer at the example program in Figure 12-21b.

In this example program we first declare an int variable named tempc that will hold the value of a Celsius temperature entered by the user and an int variable called tempf that will hold the value of a Fahrenheit temperature calculated by a function in the program.

The int c2f(int c); statement next in the program is the function prototype declaration for the c2f function. As you should be able to tell from the statement, the c2f function returns an int value and expects to receive a single int value from the calling program. Before we look at the next function prototype, let's work our way through the call and execution of the c2f function.

We call the c2f function with the statement tempf = c2f(tempc); statement. This statement will pass the value of tempc to the function and assign the value returned by the function to tempf. This second effect is the same as you met earlier in statements such as ch = getch( ).

Note that the variable name tempc does not appear in the c2f function block. As we said before, the actual argument passed in the function call is given to the corresponding formal argument identified in the function header. In this case the only formal argument in the header is c, so the value of the actual argument tempc will be assigned to the variable c in the function. In a case where several arguments are being passed to the function, each actual argument will be assigned to the corresponding numbered formal argument.

In the c2f function we declare an additional int variable named f and then use the familiar formula to calculate the equivalent Fahrenheit temperature for the Celsius value passed to the function. The operator precedence rules we showed you earlier in the chapter tell you that c is first multiplied by 9, and the result is divided by 5. Then 32 is added to the quotient, and the result is assigned to the variable f. The return(f); statement at the end of the function returns execution to the calling program and passes back the value of f. As we said before, this value is assigned to tempf in the calling program. Incidentally, the parentheses after the return statement can contain any expression that evaluates to an int. You could, for example, write the return statement as return(9*c/5 + 32);. For your first programs, however, it is probably better to keep the action "spread out" as we did in the example so you can follow it more easily. Now let's work through the second function in Figure 12-21b.

The void get_temp(int*ptr); prototype declaration tells you that the function get_temp does not directly return a value and that the function expects to receive a pointer to an int-type variable when called. We call the function with the statement get_temp(&tempc), so the address of the variable tempc is passed to the function. In the get_temp function header, we declared a pointer named ptr with the (int *ptr) after the function name, so the address of tempc will be assigned to ptr when it is passed to the function. In other words, ptr = &tempc.

In the get_temp function we send a prompt message to the user and then use scanf to read the user's response. As you may remember from previous examples, the predefined scanf function requires a format specifier and a pointer to the location where you want it to put the data read from the keyboard. In this call to scanf, we pass ptr to it, so the result read from the keyboard will be written to the location pointed to by ptr. Since ptr= &tempc, the value read from the keyboard will be written to tempc. This function has no return statement because no value is returned to the calling program, but when the scanf("%d",ptr) call is finished, execution returns to the calling program.

Now that you know more about C functions, we need to talk again about the difference between variables declared in a function and variables outside any function.

EXTERN, AUTOMATIC, STATIC, AND REGISTER STORAGE CLASSES

Any variable or function declared in a program has two properties, which are sometimes referred to as *lifetime* and *visibility*, or *scope*. These terms are best explained by some examples. As we mentioned in an earlier section, variables declared outside of main are, by default, extern—or, in other words, global. This means that they are visible to or accessible from anywhere in the source file where they are defined or from other files that will be linked with that file. Extern variables are created in memory when the program is loaded and remain there, or "live," as long as the program is running. In Figure 12-21b tempc and tempf are examples of variables that are extern by default.

We also mentioned earlier that variables declared in a function are by default automatic. An automatic variable is local, which means that it is accessible or visible only within the function where it is declared. Each time you call a function that contains an automatic variable, a temporary storage space is allocated on the stack for that variable. When the function returns execution to the calling program, this storage space is deallocated. An automatic variable then lives only during the execution of the function block where it is declared. In Figure 12-21b the variables ptr, c, and f are examples of automatic variables.

Now, suppose that you want to declare a variable within a function so the whole world can't access it, but you want the variable to keep its value from one call of the function to the next. You can do this by putting the word *static* in front of the variable declaration. For example, if the declaration static int count; is located in a function, count will be visible only in the function but will hold its value all the time that the program is running. If you put the word static in front of a variable declaration that is outside of main, the effect is to make the variable accessible, or visible, only in the source file where it is declared.

Another useful storage class for variables is *register*. You might, for example, declare a variable in a function with a statement such as register int index;. The term register at the start of this declaration asks the compiler to assign this variable to one of the 68000 registers. The reason for doing this is that it is much faster to, for example, increment the contents of a register than it is to increment the contents of a memory location dynamically allocated to an automatic variable. If all registers are in use, the compiler will ignore the register storage request and treat the variable as a normal automatic variable.

Functions also have storage classes. By default functions are extern, or global. This means that they can be accessed from other files. To access a function from another file, you write a copy of the function prototype in that file and put the word extern in front of it.

If you give a function the storage class static, the function is accessible only from within the file where it is defined.

To summarize the different storage classes and their characteristics, Figure 12-22 shows examples of each. You can use these examples to help you decide which storage class to use for particular applications in your programs.

FUNCTIONS AND ARRAYS

One of the main reasons to learn about C pointers is so that you can use them with functions. As we said before, if you want a function to modify the value of a variable, you must pass the function a pointer to the variable. In Figure 12-21b we showed you how to pass a pointer to a simple variable and in Figure 12-12 we showed you how to pass an array pointer to the predefined scanf function. Now we need to show you how to pass array pointers to functions you write.

Figure 12-23 shows how you can declare, define, and call a function to add profit to costs instead of doing the operations in main, as we did in previous examples. The first section of main prompts the user and then calls scanf to read in 10 costs and put the 10 values in a float array called cost. Remember that scanf requires a format specifier and a pointer to where you want to put the value read. In Figure 12-12 we used a declared pointer as the argument for scanf, but here we use the expression (cost+i) as a pointer to the desired element in cost. Cost is a pointer to the first element in the array, and, as we explained earlier, (cost+i) is a pointer to element i in the array. When the compiler performs pointer arithmetic on the expression (cost+i), it automatically multiplies i times the number of bytes in the data type so that the computed pointer accesses the desired element.

After all the values are read into the cost array, we call the function add_profit to compute the selling price for each and print the results. The add_profit function is type void, because it does not return a value directly to main. The expression in the parentheses of the add_profit function header declares a float pointer called pp that will be used to receive a pointer to prices and a float pointer called cp that will be used to receive a pointer to cost. The header also declares an int that will receive the number of elements in the array. Here's why we declared these three.

The function reads a value from the array cost, computes the selling price, and puts the result in the array prices. Since we are changing values in the prices array, we have to pass the function a pointer to prices. For this simple example, however, we are not modifying the values in cost, so we did not actually have to pass a pointer to cost. The array cost could have been accessed directly from the function. (Remember, cost is declared outside of main, so it is extern and accessible globally.)

If you refer to cost directly in the function, then the function will work only with values from the array cost. We passed both the source and the destination pointers to the function so that the function will work with any array of costs and any array of prices. Likewise, we pass the number of elements in the array to the function. The for loop in the function uses this passed number instead of a fixed number to determine how many elements to process. The function then can process arrays with any number of elements up to the limit of int, which is +32,767.

In a more realistic program you might declare the arrays large enough to hold 1000 or more elements and then get the value for number by counting how many costs a user actually entered before entering an EOF character (Ctrl Z). The main point we are trying to make here is that by passing pointers and lengths to functions instead of directly named variables, you make the function more universally useful, or "portable."

Since the name prices is a pointer to the prices array and the name cost is a pointer to the cost array, the actual call of add_profit in Figure 12-23 passes prices to pp, cost to cp, and number to count.

The example we have just discussed shows you how to write a function that accesses two one-dimensional arrays. Figure 12-24 shows how you can declare, define, and call a function that accesses the elements in a two-dimensional array. Specifically, the function in this program converts each Celsius temperature in a two-dimensional array of temperatures to its Fahrenheit value. This program is simply an extension of the program in Figure 12-20a.

In Figure 12-24 the first for loop in main reads the maximum and minimum Celsius temperatures for 7 d and puts them in the first two columns of a 7 × 3 array.

```
VARIABLE EXAMPLE          LIFETIME    ACCESSIBILITY
int tempf;                program     all source files
static int tempc;         program     this file only
extern int book_total     program     defined in another file
int c2f(inc c);           program     all source files
static int f2c(intf)      program     this source file only

void main ()
{
int count;                block       block and sub blocks
                                      after declared
static int interrupt_cnt; program     block and sub blocks
                                      after declared
register int index        block       block and sub blocks
                                      after declared
```

FIGURE 12-22   Examples of variable and function storage classes.

```
/* C PROGRAM F12-23.C */

/* Passing array pointers to functions */

float cost[10], prices[10];              /* array declarations */
                                         /* function declaration or prototype */

void add_profit(float *pp, float *cp, int count);

void main ()
{
    int i;
    int number=10;
    printf("Enter %d costs. After each cost press enter.\n",number);

    for(i=0; i < number; i++)            /* read in costs */
      scanf("%f", (cost+i));

    add_profit(prices, cost, number); /* function call */
} /* end of main */


/* function definition */

void add_profit(float *pp, float *cp, int count)
    {
    int i;
    for(i=0; i < count; i++)
      {
      *(pp+i) = *(cp+i) + .25 * *(cp+i);
      printf("cost=%6.2f, price=%6.2f \n",*(cp+i),*(pp+i));
      }
    }
```

FIGURE 12-23   Program showing how to pass array pointers to functions.

The second for loop in main computes the average temperature for each day and writes the result in the third column of the appropriate row in the array.

Once all the Celsius values are in place, we call the function c2f to convert each Celsius value to its Fahrenheit equivalent and put the results in an array called ftemps. As with the previous example, we want to pass pointers to the two arrays and pass the length of the arrays so that the function is as versatile as possible.

The expression int ct[ ][3] in the c2f function header in Figure 12-24 shows one way to declare the pointer needed to receive a pointer to a two-dimensional array. The empty brackets between ct and [3] indicate that ct is a pointer to an array of three elements. When we call the c2f function, we pass ctemps as the actual argument. As shown in Figure 12-20c, the name ctemps is a pointer to the first three-element array, temps[0], so the call gives the c2f access to the first three-element array. In the c2f function, a nested for loop is used to access the elements in ctemps[0], ctemps[1], ctemps[2], etc.

In the same way the int ft[ ][3] expression in the c2f function header declares another pointer to an array of three elements. This formal parameter is used to receive a pointer to ftemps during the call. Incidentally, you can declare a pointer to a three-dimensional array with an expression such as float hrs_worked[ ][12] [31]. The trick here is to simply leave empty the first set of brackets after the array name.

Another method of declaring the formal argument for passing the ctemps pointer to the function is with the expression int (*ct)[3]. This expression likewise declares ct as a pointer to a three-element array. The parentheses around *ct are required to indicate that you are declaring a pointer to an array. The expression int *ct[3] declares an array of three pointers, which each point to int-type variables.

To summarize the operation of all this, the c2f(ctemps, ftemps, days) statement in Figure 12-24 calls the function. The ctemps in the function call passes a pointer to the ctemps array to the function pointer variable ct. The ftemps in the function call passes a pointer to the ftemps array to the function pointer variable ft. The days in the function call pass the value of the variable days to the function variable called rows. The procedure uses these passed values and a nested for loop to read an element from ctemps, compute the Fahrenheit equivalent, and write the result to the same element in ftemps. Note that since the number of rows is a variable in the function, the function can be called to process any number of three element arrays.

```
/* C PROGRAM F12-24.C */
/* Program to read max and min Celsius temperatures, compute average,
    convert all values to Fahrenheit, and display results */

#include <stdio.h>
int ctemps[7][3];
int ftemps[7][3];
void c2f(int ct[][3], int ft[][3], int rows);    /* function declaration */

void main()
{
    int days = 7;
    int i, j;                        /* note i and j separate variables in main and c2f */
    for (i=0; i<days; i++)
        {
          printf("Enter max Celsius temp for day %d,"
                "then min Celsius temp for day %d.\n", i+1,i+1);
          for(j=0; j<2; j++)                              /* read max, then min */
          scanf ("%d", &ctemps[i][j]);
          }

    for(i=0; i<days; i++)
    {
    ctemps[i][2] = (ctemps[i][0] + ctemps[i][1])/2; /* average */
    printf("Celsius temperatures for day %d: max = %d min = %d "
      "av = %d \n", (i+1), ctemps[i][0], ctemps[i][1], ctemps[i][2]);
    }
    c2f(ctemps,ftemps, days);              /* call c2f function */
    for(i=0; i<days; i++)
    printf("Fahrenheit temperatures for day %d: max = %d min = %d "
        "av = %d \n", i+1,
        ftemps[i][0], ftemps[i][1], ftemps[i][2]);
}  /* end of main */

    /* define c2f function */
void c2f(int ct[][3], int ft[][3], int rows)
    {
    int i, j;                        /* note these variables different from I,J in main */
    for(i=0; i < rows; i++)
        for(j=0; j<3; j++)
        ft[i][j] = 9*ct[i][j]/5 + 32;
    }
```

FIGURE 12-24   Program using pointers and functions with a two-dimensional array.

DECLARING AND USING POINTERS TO FUNCTIONS

In the preceding sections we have shown you how to declare pointers to simple variables and pointers to arrays. You can also declare and initialize a pointer to a function. This is an advanced technique and it is unlikely that you will use pointers to functions in your initial programs. However, we want to show you a couple of examples so that you will recognize them in someone else's programs. Here is how you could declare a pointer to the c2f function in Figure 12-21c and call the function using the pointer instead of using a direct call.

int c2f(int c); /* declare the function c2f */

int (*convert)(int c); /* declare a pointer to a
                            function */
convert = c2f; /* initialize the pointer to point to
                  c2f */
tempf = (*convert)(tempc); /* call c2f with pointer
                              and pass value of tempc
                              to the function */
int c2f(int c) /* c2f function definition header */

The basic function declaration and definition here are the same as those in Figure 12-21b. The second statement declares a pointer called convert that points to a function. The key to recognizing that convert is a pointer to a function is the double set of parentheses in the declaration. The int at the start of the declaration indicates that the function pointed to returns an int value. The int c in the second set of parentheses indicates that the function pointed to expects to receive an int value. The parentheses around the name of the function pointer are required to indicate that convert is a pointer to a function. The statement int *convert(int c);, which does not have these parentheses, declares a function that returns a pointer to an int value.

The tempf = (*convert)(tempc); statement calls the c2f function using the pointer called convert. The term *convert represents the contents of convert, which we initialized with the address of the c2f function. The value of tempc is passed to the function, and the int value returned by c2f is assigned to tempf.

Now that you know much more about functions, in the next section we take a closer look at some of the predefined functions available to you in libraries.

C Library Functions

INTRODUCTION

Throughout this chapter we have used predefined functions such as printf( ), scanf( ), and getch( ) in many of the example programs. The functions we have used are just a small sample of those available. C comes with library files containing over 450 predefined functions and macros. These library functions allow you to perform I/O operations with a variety of devices, dynamically allocate memory in a program, produce graphics displays, read from and write to disk files, perform complex mathematical computations, etc. For many applications you can use one of these predefined functions instead of writing your own function. The source code for all these functions is available, so if the predefined function does not quite fit your application, you can modify a copy of the source code for the function to produce a custom version that does.

The declarations, or prototypes, for the predefined functions are contained in files called *header files* or *include files*. These files have names such as stdio.h, string.h, math.h, graphics.h, and alloc.h. You use the preprocessor #include directive to tell the compiler which header files to search for the predefined functions you use in a program. The directive #include< stdio.h>, for example, tells the compiler to look in the header file called stdio.h to find the prototypes for functions such as printf( ), scanf( ), and getch( ).

The actual codes for the predefined functions are contained in library (.lib) files. When you call a function, the object code for the function is linked with the code for the rest of your program when the executable file is created.

In the following sections of the chapter we review the functions we have used previously and show some more functions and examples that you may find useful in your programs. In later chapters we show you how to use other predefined functions for graphics, disk file, and communications programs. To help you refer to the examples here, we have separated them according to the type of operation they perform. For discussions of all 450+ functions and macros, consult the C Reference Guide.

KEYBOARD INPUT FUNCTIONS

Function	Prototypes in stdio.h	
getch( )	int getch(void)	/* read char as soon as pressed */
getche( )	int getche(void)	/* read char and echo to CRT */
getchar( )	int getchar(void)	/* wait for <Enter>, read char */
gets( )	char *gets(char *s)	/* reads characters from keyboard until <Enter> and writes string to location pointed to by s. Reads spaces and tabs. */
scanf( )	int scanf(const char *format,[address, . . .)	/* scanf reads characters from the keyboard

until it reads a blank, a tab, or <Enter>. Data read in is formatted according to the format specifier in the call and written to the address passed in the call. The three dots after address indicate that the number of arguments to be passed to scanf is variable. This means that you can include several format specifiers and several addresses in one scanf call to read in multiple values. */

Scanf normally returns the number of values read and stored. If the first entered character that scanf reads cannot be converted to the specified format, scanf will not store the value, and it will return a value of 0. For example, if the scanf call statement contains a %f format specifier and you accidentally enter a T, scanf will terminate and return a 0.

The input loop in Figure 12-12 can be rewritten as follows to make sure that the pointer does not get incremented if no value was written to one of the elements in the array.

```
for(i=0;i<10; i++)
{
if(scanf("%f",cpntr))==0)
   {
   i--; /* correct index value */
   fflush(stdin); /* clear unread characters from
                     keyboard buffer */
   continue; /* skip rest of loop actions */
   }
else cpntr++;
}
```

The continue statement here will cause the cpntr++ to be skipped over in this trip through the loop if the value returned by scanf is zero.

NOTE: This cure does not work if an illegal character is entered in any but the first digit position.

OUTPUT FUNCTIONS

Function   Prototype in stdio.h

putchar( )   int putchar(int c) /* outputs passed
             character to screen. Returns −1 (EOF) if
             error.

puts( )   int puts(const char *s) /* Puts sends a null
             terminated string pointed to by s to the
             screen. If an error occurs, puts returns a
             value of −1 (EOF). For outputting simple
             strings, puts uses much less memory
             and time than printf. */

printf( )   int printf(const char
             *format,[argument, . . .]);

As shown by the many examples in the preceding programs, the format here consists of text and format specifiers. The arguments are a list of variables, one for each format specifier. The general form of the format specifier is as follows:

% flags width . precision [f, h, i, s] type
where

flags   = output justification, numeric signs and
             other
−   = left-justify printed digits
+   = print + or − sign in front of value
blank   = positive values start with blank instead
             of +
width   = total number of digits to print
precision   = number of digits left of decimal point
[f, h, i, s] = override default size of argument with
             f = floating point
             h = hexadecimal value
             i = short int
             s = string value
type   = conversion specifier as shown in Figure
             12-11

Consult the C Reference Manual for a complete explanation of the print controls in printf;

fprintf( ) int fprintf(FILE *stream, constant char
*format [,argument, . . .])

With the proper setup, fprintf( ) will send program output to the printer instead of to the CRT screen. As we discuss further in a later chapter, we often think of data going to or coming from a disk file as a "stream." The same term can be used to refer to data going to the CRT. The fprintf( ) function allows a stream of data to be sent to the printer. Figure 12-26 shows how this function can be used to send the output of our prices program to the printer.

Before you can call the fprintf( ) function you must use the predefined setmode( ) function to tell the compiler that you are going to send a text file to the printer. The 0004 in this call is a "handle" that identifies the printer, and the O_TEXT is a predefined term for text mode. The prototype for setmode( ) is in fcntl.h, so we put #include<fcntl.h> at the top of the program.

The fprintf( ) function call is the same as a call to printf, except that we include the term stdprn before the usual printf arguments. The term stdprn tells fprintf to direct the data stream to the standard printer device. Incidentally, the \f in the final fprintf statement is a formfeed character, which tells the printer to advance to the top of the next page.

STRING FUNCTIONS

Function   Prototype in string.h

strcat( )   char *strcat(char *dest, cons char *src) /*
             strcat( ) adds a copy of string pointed to
             by src to the string pointed to by dest.
             and returns a pointer to the start of the
             combined string. */

strchr( )   char *strchr(const char *s, int c); /* strchr
             scans a string pointed to by s for the first
             occurrence of C. Strchr returns a pointer
             to the first occurrence of c, or returns a
             null if c was not found in the string.*/

strlen( )   size_t strlen(const char *s); /* returns
             length of string pointed to by s */

strcmp( )   int strcmp(const char *s1, const char *s2);
             /* strcmp compares each character in s1
             with the corresponding character in s2;
             strcmp( ) returns 0 if the two strings are
             equal, a positive number if s1 is greater
             than s2, and a negative number if s2 is
             greater than s1. The stricmp( ) function
             is the same as strcmp( ), except that it
             ignores the case of the characters in the
             strings. Figure 12-25 shows how you
             can use the stricmp( ) function to
             implement an improved version of the
             password check program from Figure
             5-3. */

At the start of the program we declare the required character arrays and a counter. Then we prompt the user and use gets( ) to read the response. The while loop compares the value returned by stricmp with 0 to see if the entered password is correct. If the password is correct, execution exits the while loop and goes on to the if structure. If the entered password is incorrect, the while loop gives the user two more tries to enter the correct password before going on to the if structure.

If the value returned by stricmp( ) is equal to zero, execution will simply fall through the if structure and print the welcome message. If the user did not get the password correct in three tries, then the if structure prints a message, sounds an alarm, and exits. In a more realistic program you would probably call a function that locks up the machine at this point instead of doing a simple exit.

MATH FUNCTIONS

Function   Prototype in math.h

sqrt( )   double sqrt(double x); /* sqrt( ) returns the
             positive square root of x. If x is negative,
             sqrt returns zero.*

```
/* C PROGRAM F12-25.C   */
/* Sending program output to a printer */

#include <stdio.h>
#include <fcntl.h>

int cost[] = { 20,28,15,26,19,27,16,29,39,42 };   /* array of 10 costs */
int prices[10];                                     /* array to hold 10 prices */

void main()
{
    int index;
    setmode(0004, O_TEXT);
    for (index=0; index <10; index++)               /* for loop to compute */
    prices[index] = cost[index] + 15;               /* 10 prices */

    for (index=0; index <10; index++)               /* for loop to display results */
      fprintf(stdprn,"cost = %d, price = %d, \n",
                        cost[index], prices[index]);
    fprintf(stdprn,"\f");

}
```

FIGURE 12-25   Program using predefined string function to compare passwords.

We don't have space here to discuss the prototypes for the many 68881 type math functions found in math.h. However, to keep a promise we made earlier, Figure 12-27 shows how the Pythagoras program from Chapter 11 can be written in C.

Remember, this program calculates the value of the hypotenuse of a right triangle by taking the square root of the sum of the squares of the two legs. In the program in Figure 12-27 we call the predefined function sqrt() to take the square root. We pass sqrt a value equal to side_a squared + side_b squared. Sqrt returns the square root of the sum and assigns it to side_c. Note that we wrote a # include<math.h> directive at the start of the program to tell the compiler where to look for the prototype of the sqrt() function.

When the compiler compiles this program, it will use

```
/* C PROGRAM F12-26.C    */
/* Password program in C */
#include<stdio.h>
#include<string.h>
void main()
{
 char password[] = "failsafe";
 char input_word[8];
 int try = 0;
 printf("Please enter your password.\n");
 gets(input_word);
 while(stricmp(password,input_word) != 0 && try++ <2)
  {
  printf("Entered password is incorrect,try again.\n");
  gets(input_word);
  }
 if(stricmp(password,input_word) != 0)
  {
  printf("This computer does not know you!");
  /* alarm() *//* call ASM function to sound alarm */
  exit();
  }
 printf("Welcome, what can I do for you?");
}
```

FIGURE 12-26   Program using predefined fprintf function to send program output to a printer instead of to the CRT.

```
/* C PROGRAM F12-27.C */
/*PYTHAGORAS REVISITED */

#include <stdio.h>
#include <math.h>
void main (  )
{
   float side_a, side_b, side_c;
   side_a = 3.0;
   side_b = 4.0;

   side_c = sqrt (side_a * side_a + side_b * side_b);
   printf("side a = %2.2f side b = %2.2f
           side C = %2.2f\n", side_a, side_b, side_c);
}
```

FIGURE 12-27 C version of 68000 Pythagoras program in Figure 11-22.

the default mode of "emulator" for the instructions that act on floating-point numbers. When you run the program, a predefined function determines if your system contains a 68881. If a 68881 is present, the program will use 68881 instructions to implement floating-point operations in the program. If your system does not contain a 68881, the program will use floating-point library functions, which emulate the 68881 instructions.

Writing Programs That Contain C and Assembly Language

INTRODUCTION

The C language is very useful for writing user-interface programs, but code produced by a C compiler does not execute fast enough for applications such as drawing a complex graphics display on a CRT. Therefore, system programs are often written with a combination of C and assembly language functions. The main user interface may be written in C and specialized, high-speed functions written in assembly language. These assembly language functions are simply called from the C program as needed.

Also, when writing a program that is mostly assembly language, you may find it useful to call one of the predefined C functions to do some task that you don't want to take the time to implement in assembly language.

The main points you have to consider when interfacing C with assembly language are these:

1. How do you call a desired function?

2. How do you pass parameters to the called function?

3. How are parameters passed back to the calling program from the function?

4. How do you declare code and data in the function so that they are compatible with those in the calling program?

In the next section we answer these questions.

THE ASSEMBLY LANGUAGE EQUIVALENT OF A C PROGRAM

Figure 12-28a shows a simplified version of the temperature conversion program in Figure 12-21b and Figure 12-28b shows an edited version of the asm program produced from it. To make the program easier to follow, we have added the C statements as comments in the assembly language code. As with Figure 12-9, the assembly language was generated by using the MONITOR command on the DEBUG menu and having MacsBug disassemble the code directly from memory. Read the C program in Figure 12-28a, skim through the asm version in Figure 12-28b to see how much you can intuitively understand, and then come back to the discussion here to get more details. The analysis of this program should help you better understand some of the earlier discussions of passing arguments to functions and variable storage classes. The assembly language listing contains several columns, which indicate the memory address where the code was found, then the name of the routine the code represents (main or c2f), then the offset within the routine, and finally the assembly language itself.

The C program in Figure 12-28a calls our c2f function to compute the Fahrenheit equivalent of 25°C and calls the predefined printf function to display the result. You should use these same conventions when you write an assembly language function to be called from a C program. We will step through the assembly language instructions once and explain what each group of instructions is doing. As we told you in Chapter 5, the easiest way to keep track of the position of everything in the stack is with a simple stack map such as that in Figure 12-29. Follow what is on the stack using Figure 12-29 as we step through the program.

The first instruction in main is a LINK instruction, which creates a "stack mark" linking the area for the main routine with the routine that called it (the debugger executive in this case). Similarly, the c2f function starts with a LINK instruction. Looking at the stack diagram in Figure 12-29, the call to main leaves a return address (4 bytes) on the stack. The LINK

```
/* Temperature conversion function */

#include<stdio.h>
int tempc = 25, tempf;          /* external (global) variables */

int c2f(int c);   /* declare function c2f which returns an int value */

main()

        tempf = c2f(tempc);          /* call c2f function, pass value
                              of tempc to function. Returned value
                              assigned to tempf */
        printf("Celsius = %d, Fahrenheit = %d \n", tempc, tempf);
   /* end of main */

  int c2f(int c)    /* define function c2f. Note no ; at end */
        {
        int f;       /* automatic (local) variable */
        f = 9*c/5 + 32;
        return (f);
        }                                              (continued)
                              (a)
```

FIGURE 12-28   (a) Simplified version of Figure 12-21b. (b, p. 420) Assembly language equivalent of C program in a produced by C compiler.

A6,#$FFFC instruction then pushes the old value of A6 onto the stack and moves the value of A7 (the stack pointer) into register A6. The LINK instruction then subtracts 4 bytes from A7, which has the effect of reserving 4 bytes of memory on the stack. The LINK instruction works using a negative value to allocate memory, and $FFFC is equal to −4 decimal, which allocates 4 words of stack space. As indicated in Figure 12-29 these 4 words are used as space for the variables tempc and tempf. In the rest of the main routine, notice that the variables tempc and tempf are accessed using offsets from A6. The MOVEQ #$19,D0 and MOVE.W D0,$FFFE(A6) move 25 into D0 and then into tempc.

Looking at the next group of instructions, we can answer the question, How does C call an assembly language routine? The answer is surprisingly simple: the same way an assembly language routine calls another assembly language routine—that is, using a JSR instruction. In this case the instruction is JSR C2F. Notice that the C compiler uses all capital letters for the assembly language entry points.

The next point to consider here is how C passes arguments to a function. If you call an asm function from a C program, this is the way the arguments will be passed to the function. If you call a C function from an asm program, this is how you have to pass arguments to the C function.

C passes almost all arguments to functions by pushing them on the stack. The first instruction in the c2f calling group of instructions in main in Figure 12-28b pushes the value of tempc on the stack to pass to c2f. The instruction MOVE.W $FFFE(A6),−(A7) gets a copy of the value in tempc and pushes it onto the stack for c2f to use. As we said earlier, this call just passes a copy of ctemp to the function, so the function cannot change the actual value of ctemp. Remember, if you want a function to change the value of a variable, you pass the address of the variable to the function.

Once the function c2f returns, main has an ADDQ.L #$2,A7 instruction. This instruction has the effect of removing the argument space from the stack that was placed there by the MOVE.W instruction before the call to c2f. Finally, the MOVE.W D0,$FFFC(A6) instruction takes the return value from the function c2f and places it into tempf. By convention C functions always return their return values in register D0.

The next group of instructions represents the call to printf. First the arguments are pushed on the stack. By convention the arguments are pushed on the stack from right to left, in the reverse order from their order in the C function call. So, first tempf is printed (with a MOVE.W $FFFC(A6),−(A7)), then tmepc is pushed (with a MOVE.W $FFFE(A6),−(A7)), and, finally, the address of the printf string is pushed (with a PEA $F3FC(A5). Looking at the next two instructions, notice that the JSR NV$388E (which is actually the call to the printf routine) is followed by an ADDQ.L #$8,A7. This ADDQ.L 'removes' the arguments from the stack. After the call to printf, 8 bytes must be removed because 8 bytes were passed to printf (4 bytes for the two word arguments tempc and tempf; and 4 bytes for the address of the printf string argument "Celsius = %d, Fahrenheit = %d \n").

The last thing that main does is to free up the memory it used with an UNLK ("unlink") instruction. This instruction also restores A6 to the value it had when main was called. Finally, main uses an RTS to return to whomever called it.

```
                        ;      main()
                        ;      {
0EE258:  MAIN    +0000    LINK      A6,#$FFFC

                        ;         int tempc = 25, tempf;
0EE25C:  MAIN    +0004    MOVEQ     #$19,D0
0EE25E:  MAIN    +0006    MOVE.W    D0,$FFFE(A6)

                        ;         tempf = c2f(tempc);
0EE262:  MAIN    +000A    MOVE.W    $FFFE(A6),-A7
0EE266:  MAIN    +000E    JSR       C2F      0000    ; 000EE28E
0EE26A:  MAIN    +0012    ADDQ.L    #$2,A7
0EE26C:  MAIN    +0014    MOVE.W    D0,$FFFC(A6)

                        ;         printf("Celsius = %d, Farenheit = d \n", tempc ...
0EE270:  MAIN    +0018    MOVE.W    $FFFC(A6),-(A7)
0EE274:  MAIN    +001C    MOVE.W    $FFFE(A6),-(A7)
0EE278:  MAIN    +0020    PEA       $F3FC(A5)
0EE27C:  MAIN    +0024    JSR       NV$388E          ; 000F1B0A
0EE280:  MAIN    +0028    ADDQ.L    #$8,A7

                        ;      }
0EE282:  MAIN    +002A    UNLK      A6
0EE284:  MAIN    +002C    RTS


                        ;      int c2f(int c)
                        ;      {
                        ;         int c;
0EE28E:  C2F     +0000    LINK      A6,#$FFFE

                        ;         f = 9*c/5 + 32;
0EE292:  C2F     +0004    MOVE.W    $0008(A6),D0
0EE296:  C2F     +0008    MULS.W    #$0009,D0
0EE29A:  C2F     +000C    EXT.L     D0
0EE29C:  C2F     +000E    DIVS.W    #$0005,D0
0EE2A0:  C2F     +0012    ADDI.W    #$0020,D0
0EE2A4:  C2F     +0016    MOVE.W    D0,$FFFE(A6)

                        ;         return (f);
0EE2A8:  C2F     +001A    MOVE.W    $FFFE(A6),D0

                        ;      }
0EE2AC:  C2F     +001E    UNLK      A6
0EE2AE:  C2F     +0020    RTS
```

FIGURE 12-28 (continued)

Now let's look at how the function accesses the tempc value passed to it on the stack. The process here is the same one we introduced to you in Figure 5-17. Looking again at the stack diagram of Figure 12-29, notice that the JSR instruction pushed a 4-byte return address on the stack. The first instruction in c2f is a LINK instruction, just as was used in the main routine. The LINK instruction pushed the old value of A6. In this case the value of A6 was the one the main routine was using to remember where its variables (tempc and tempf) were on the stack. Register A6 is loaded with the stack pointer value (A7), and 2 bytes of memory are reserved on the stack (since the LINK second argument

is −2 decimal = $FFFE). A7, the stack pointer, is left pointing below the area for the c2f function, just in case c2f, in turn, wanted to call some other routine.

The next group of instructions in c2f computes the C expression 9*c/5 + 32. See if you can follow how this computation is done. The final value is left in D0. Remember that the arguments in the assembly language are in hexadecimal (e.g., $0020 = 32 decimal). Finally, the routine c2f places the return value in D0, which is the standard convention for C functions. That is, the computed value of f is returned to the calling program in register D0. Finally, c2f uses an UNLK instruction to free up the 2 bytes of memory it was

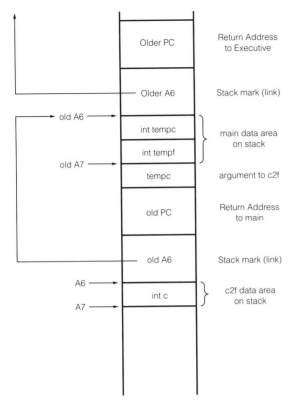

FIGURE 12-29 Stack map showing use of SP to access arguments passed to a function on the stack.

using for the variable c and uses an RTS to return to the routine which called it. Notice that the variable 'f' was never declared and hence no memory on the stack was reserved for it. It was a "temporary" variable whose value was created in D0 and then returned to the calling routine in D0.

If you look at the stack map in Figure 12-29 again, you should see that when execution returns to main from the function, A7 (the SP) will be pointing to the value of ctemps in the stack. The unlink instruction in main will "clean up" the stack by incrementing SP to its initial value. The UNLK instruction also restores A6 to its original value so that the calling routine can continue to use it. In this case the UNLK in c2f restores A6 to the value that main was using to access tempc and tempf.

Now that you have some ideas about how a C compiler "thinks," let's talk about how you can use this to write assembly language functions you can call from your C programs and how you can call C functions from your assembly language programs.

A PROGRAM WITH C AND ASSEMBLY LANGUAGE MODULES

Figure 12-28b shows you almost everything you need to know to interface C and assembly language and to make it a little clearer. Figure 12-30 shows a C pro-

gram that calls two assembly language functions and also shows the two assembly language functions. To show a C function call from assembly language, one of the assembly language functions calls the predefined C function, printf( ).

In the C program in Figure 12-30a, we put the term extern in the two function declarations to let the compiler know that these functions are in another source module. We then call the functions by name and pass any required arguments, just as we would call C functions.

In the assembly language part of the program in Figure 12-30b, we declare segments using the names shown in Figure 12-28b. Note that the assembly language names are all in capitals. This is required for compatibility with the C compiler conventions.

The c2f function in Figure 12-30b is the same as that produced by the compiler in Figure 12-28b. It is very common practice to write a function in C, compile the function to its assembly language equivalent, and then "hand optimize" the .asm equivalent for maximum efficiency in the specific application. As we will show you, the .asm file can be assembled and the resulting object file linked with the object file for the mainline program.

The show function in Figure 12-30b calls printf to display the Celsius temperature, the Fahrenheit temperature, and appropriate text. We declare the text in the data segment with a simple DC.B statement. The $0A at the end of the declaration represents a carriage return, and the $00 is a NULL character required as a terminator on the string. From the string you can see that we need to pass three arguments to printf, just as we did in Figure 12-28a. The three arguments are a pointer to the string, the value of tempc, and the value of tempf. The three push statements in Figure 12-30b put these arguments on the stack in reverse order as required by the C calling convention. When execution returns from printf, we add 8 to the stack pointer (A7) to increment it up over the three arguments we passed to printf.

A very important point to observe in Figure 12-30 is the use of the extern, XDEF, or XREF directives. In the C program we use the extern directive to tell the compiler that c2f and show are in another source module. In the assembly module in Figure 12-30b, we use the XDEF directive to make the functions c2f and show accessible to other source modules. Also in Figure 12-30b, use the XREF directive to tell the assembler that the variables tempf and tempc are defined in another source module.

As we told you in Chapter 5, the rules here are very simple. You declare a function or variable public in the module where it is defined if you want other modules to be able to access it. You use the extern or extrn directive to tell the assembler/compiler that a function or variable is located in some other source module.

Now that you know how to write C and assembly language modules that interface with each other, let's show you the more common way to mix C and assembly language.

```
/* C PROGRAM F12-30A.C */
/* Temperature conversion function */

#include<stdio.h>
int tempc = 25, tempf; /* external (global) variables*/
int extern c2f(int c); /* declare function c2f which */
                       /* returns an int value */
void extern show(void);/* function show is in
                          another module */
void main()
{
 tempf = c2f(tempc);  /* call c2f function, pass
                         value of tempc to function.
                         Returned value assigned
                         to tempf */

 show();
}/* end of main */
```

(a)

```
P_STRING          DC.B      "Celsius = %d, Farenheit = %d \n",$0A,$00

XDEF              PRINTF

XREF              C2F
XREF              SHOW
XREF              TEMPC
XREF              TEMPF

C2F:    LINK      A6,#$FFFE
        MOVE.W    $0008(A6),D0
        MOVE.W    #$0009,D0
        EXT.L     D0
        DIVS.W    #$0005,D0
        ADDI.W    #$0020,D0
        MOVE.W    D0,$FFFE(A6)
        MOVE.W    $FFFE(A6),D0
        UNLK      A6
        RTS

SHOW:   LINK      A6,#$0000
        MOVE.W    (TEMPF),-(A7)
        MOVE.W    (TEMPC),-(A7)
        PEA       P_STRING
        JSR       PRINTF
        ADDQ.L    #$8,A7
        UNLK      A6
        RTS
```

(b)

FIGURE 12-30   Program with C and assembly language modules. (a) C mainline
module. (b) Assembly language functions.

MIXING C AND ASSEMBLY LANGUAGE

If you are using the Think C environment, you may choose to place assembly language code directly in your C programs. This eliminates the necessity of worrying about separate compilation and assembly. In order to do this, all you need to know is how to use the *inline assembler*.

This is very easy. You simply have to use the asm statement in C. The asm statements looks like this:

```
asm {
    . . . /* assembly language instructions, one per
        line */
}
```

In this chapter we used your knowledge of assembly language to teach you much about the C programming language. Finally, we showed how you can write programs consisting of both C and assembly language modules. In the following chapters we show you some more examples of C programming in interesting applications.

CHECKLIST OF IMPORTANT TERMS AND CONCEPTS IN THIS CHAPTER

If there are terms or concepts in this list you do not remember, use the index to help you find them in the chapter.

Integrated program development environment

Compiler optimizations

C language

Variable types

Variable declarations

Simple pointers

Array pointers

Dereferencing a pointer

Passing a parameter by value

Passing a parameter by reference

Preprocessor directives

Assignment operator, =

Arithmetic operators, +, −, *, /, %, ++, −−

Bitwise operators, &, |, ∧, ~, <<, >>

Combined operators

Relational operators, ==, !=, >, >=, <, <=

Logical operators, &&, ||, !

Operator precedence

If-else

Switch and break statements

Goto statement

While and do-while loops

For loops

Function prototype, function declaration

Function definition

Function call

Formal arguments

Actual arguments

Return statement

Extern, automatic, static, and register storage classes

Lifetime and visibility of variables

Passing pointers to functions

Pointers to functions

Predefined library functions

Cleaning up the stack

REVIEW QUESTIONS AND PROBLEMS

1. *a.* What is the index value for the first element in the cost array in Figure 12-1*a*?
   b. Which element in the cost array is accessed by the term cost[index] during the second execution of the for loop?
   c. What is the purpose of the #include< stdio.h> line at the top of the program in Figure 12-1*a*?
   d. To what does the word printf in the statement in Figure 12-1*a* refer?

2. *a.* Describe the advantages of an integrated program environment over the separate tools approach.
   b. How does the C compiler let you know if it finds any errors when it compiles your program?
   c. What is meant by the term watch in the C environment?

3. Give the range of values that can be represented by each of the following C data types.
   a. Char
   b. Int
   c. Unsigned int
   d. Long
   e. Float

4. Write C declaration statements for each of the following variables:
   a. An integer named total_boards.
   b. A character named no, initialized with the ASCII code for lowercase n.
   c. A floating-point variable named body_temp, initialized with 98.6.
   d. A five-element integer array called scores.
   e. A six-element integer array called scores and initialized with the values 95, 89, 84, 93, and 92 (last element uninitialized).

f. A pointer called ptr, which points to the array declared in part *e.*

g. A two-dimensional character array called screen that has 25 rows and 40 columns.

h. A three-dimensional character array called screen_buffer that has 4 pages of 25 rows and 80 columns.

i. An integer called monitor_start, initialized with +$FE00.

j. A character pointer named answer.

k. A pointer named ptr initialized with the address of an integer variable called setpoint.

l. A pointer named wptr initialized with the start of the array and declared with the statement float net_weights[100];.

5. Describe the operation or sequence of operations performed by each of the following expressions:
   a. 5−4 * 7/9
   b. (a + 4) *17 − B/2 + 6
   c. x + y++
   d. x − −−Y
   e. count +=4;
   f. strobe_val & 0x0001
   g. y = a>>4;
   h. a = 4;
       b = 39%a;
   i. If(ch == 'Y' || ch == 'Y')
       goto start;

6. Write printf statements that do the following.
   a. Print the decimal value of an integer named count.
   b. Print a prompt message that tells the user to enter his or her weight.
   c. Print the value of a float variable named conversion_factor with 4 decimal places and a total of 10 digits.
   d. Print the value of a float variable called average_lunar_distance in exponential format.

7. Given the array declared by int nums[ ] = {45, 65, 38, 72};, write a program that computes the average and prints the result.

8. Use Figure 12-12 to help you write a program that does the following:

Declares a six-element array of integers.

Reads five test scores entered by a user into the array.

Computes the average of the five scores and puts the computed average in the sixth element in the array.

9. Write a program that does the following:

Declares an array for 25 characters.

Prompts the user to enter his or her name.

Reads an entered name into the array.

Determines the number of characters in the name.

Prints out appropriate text and the number of letters.

10. *a.* Write a program section that calls the predefined exit function if the user enters a q or a Q on the keyboard.
    b. Write a program that does the following:

Declares an array for up to 1000 characters.

Reads characters from the keyboard and puts them in the array until the array is full or until the user enters an EOF character(∧Z).

Prints a "buffer full" message if 1000 characters are entered.

Prints a "goodbye" message and exits to DOS if the EOF character is entered.

11. The character display on a CRT screen can be thought of as an array of 25 rows and 80 columns. Write a program that does the following:

Declares a character array of 25 rows and 80 columns.

Declares a character array initialized with your name.

Uses a nested for loop to write the ASCII code for a blank, $20, to each element in the array.

Writes your name in the array elements that approximately correspond to the center of the screen.

12. Use the array-index method as shown in Figure 12-20a to write a program that does the following:

Declares a two-dimensional array of seven rows and three columns.

Reads in the maximum and minimum temperatures for each of 7 d and puts the values in the array.

Computes the average temperature for each day and puts the result in the appropriate position in the third column of the array.

Computes the average maximum temperature for the week.

Computes the average minimum temperature for the week.

Computes the average temperature for the entire week.

Prints out the results with appropriate labeling.

13. Rewrite the program in problem 12 using pointer notation instead of array-index notation.

14. Explain the difference between formal arguments and actual arguments.

15. Write the declaration, definition, and call for a function that converts a Fahrenheit temperature to its Celsius equivalent. The formula is $F = 9C/5 + 32$.

16. Write a program that reads characters from the keyboard until an EOF (Ctrl Z) is entered, uses a function to detect and convert the ASCII codes for uppercase letters to their lowercase equivalents, and writes the codes in an array.

17. Given the array declared by int nums[ ] = 45, 65, 38, 72;, write a function that computes the average of the four values and passes the average back to the calling program to print out.

18. Rewrite the answer to problem 12 so that it uses a function to compute the desired averages and print the result.

19. Give the lifetime and accessibility of each of the variables and functions declared here.
    a. int scale_factor = 12;
    b. char *text;
    c. float tax(float income, float deductions);
    d. static double debts;
       main( )
       {
    e. static weight = 145;
    f. register count = 23;
    g. int tare;
       {

20. Extend problem 13 to read in two sets of row and column coordinates from a user, store these values, and then call a function that ORs each element in the array between the specified coordinates with 0×80.

21. What is the main advantage and the main disadvantage of using predefined C library functions?

22. Rewrite the Pythagoras program in Figure 12-27 so that it allows a user to enter values for side_a and side_b, does the computation, and sends the results to a printer.

23. What are the main points you have to consider when you want to write an assembly language function that will be called from a C program?

24. Describe the default memory model for the C compiler.

25. Briefly describe the process used to develop a program that consists of assembly language modules and C language modules.

26. Given the array declared with int screen[25][80];, write a C mainline that calls an assembly language function to write a $20 in the low byte of each element and $07 in the high byte of each element.

CHAPTER

Microcomputer System Peripherals

13

In the preceding chapters we discussed basic microcomputer systems and some of the programmable peripheral devices used in these systems. In this chapter we expand outward to discuss the hardware and software of system peripherals such as CRT displays, computer vision devices, disk drives, and printers.

OBJECTIVES

1. Describe how characters are produced on a CRT or an LCD screen.

2. Use OS calls to display a message on the CRT display of an Apple Macintosh compatible computer.

3. Describe how bit-mapped and vector graphic displays are produced on a CRT.

4. Describe how computer vision systems produce an image that can be stored in a digital memory.

5. Show in general terms the formats in which digital data is stored on magnetic and optical disks.

6. Describe the operation of disk-controller circuitry.

7. Use OS calls to open, read or write, and close disk files.

8. Describe the mechanism used in several common types of computer printers.

9. Describe how phoneme, formant filters, and linear predictive coding synthesizers produce human-sounding speech from a computer.

10. Describe the basic principle used in speech-recognition systems.

MICROCOMPUTER DISPLAYS

Currently there are several different technologies used by a microcomputer to display numbers, letters, and graphics. The most common types are the *cathode-ray tube* (CRT) and *liquid crystal display* (LCD). In Chapter 9 we discussed the operation of alphanumeric LCD displays and a little later in this chapter we show how

large LCD screens are interfaced to a microcomputer. For now, however, we want to discuss the operation and interfacing of CRT-type displays.

Basic CRT Operation

A CRT is a large, bottle-shaped vacuum tube. The picture tube used in a TV set is an example of a CRT. An electron gun at the rear of the tube produces a beam of electrons that is directed toward the front of the tube. The inside surface of the front of the tube is coated with a phosphor substance, which gives off light when it is struck by electrons. The color of the light given off is determined by the particular phosphor used. To produce color displays, as in a color TV set, dots of red-, blue-, and green-producing phosphors are put on the inside of the screen in triangle patterns. Separate electron beams are focused on the dots for each color phosphor. By altering the intensity ratio of the three beams, the three-dot triangle can be made to appear to be any desired color. Equal beam intensities produce white.

The most common method of producing images on the CRT screen is to sweep the electron beam(s) back and forth across the screen. When the beam reaches the right side of the screen, it is turned off (blanked) and retraced rapidly back to the left side of the screen to start over. If the beam is slowly swept from the top of the screen to the bottom of the screen as it is swept back and forth horizontally, the entire screen appears lighted. When the beam reaches the bottom of the screen, it is blanked and rapidly retraced back to the top to start over. A display produced in this way is referred to as a *raster* display. To produce an image the electron beams are turned on or off as they sweep across the screen. The trick here is to get the beam intensity, or *video information,* synchronized with the horizontal and vertical sweeping so that the display is stable.

Black-and-white TVs in the United States use a horizontal sweep frequency of 15,750 HZ and a vertical sweep frequency of 60 Hz. One sweep of the beam from the top of the screen to the bottom is called a *field.* Sixty fields per second are then swept out. To get better picture resolution and avoid flicker, TVs use *interlaced scanning.* As shown in Figure 13-1a, this means the

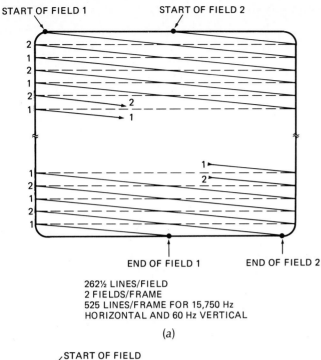

START OF FIELD 1 START OF FIELD 2

2
1
2
1
2
1

2
1

1
2

1
2
1
2
1

END OF FIELD 1 END OF FIELD 2

262½ LINES/FIELD
2 FIELDS/FRAME
525 LINES/FRAME FOR 15,750 Hz
HORIZONTAL AND 60 Hz VERTICAL

(a)

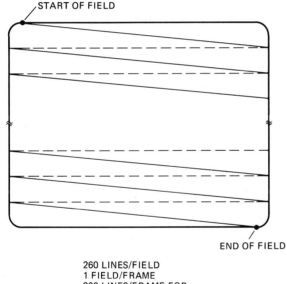

START OF FIELD

END OF FIELD

260 LINES/FIELD
1 FIELD/FRAME
260 LINES/FRAME FOR
15,600 Hz HORIZONTAL AND
60Hz VERTICAL

(b)

FIGURE 13-1   CRT scan patterns. (a) Interlaced. (b) Noninterlaced.

scan lines for one field are offset and interleaved with those of the next field. After every other field, the scan lines repeat. Therefore, two fields are required to make a complete picture, or frame. The frame rate is then 30 frames/s. The beam sweeps 262.5 times horizontally for each vertical sweep.

CRT units used for computer readouts usually have *noninterlaced scanning,* as shown in Figure 13-1b. In this case a horizontal sweep rate of 15,600 Hz and a vertical sweep rate of 60 Hz give 260 sweep lines/field.

The field rate and the frame rate are both 60 Hz in this case.

Whether the CRT you are using to display your programs is in a TV set, a video monitor, or a terminal, there are certain basic circuits required to drive the CRT: the vertical oscillator to produce the vertical sweep signal for the beam, the horizontal oscillator to produce the horizontal sweep signal for the beam, and the video amplifier to control the intensity of the electron beam. A unit that contains only this basic drive circuitry is referred to as a *video monitor.* A TV set contains the basic monitor functions plus RF and audio-decoding circuitry. A CRT *terminal* contains a keyboard, memory, communication circuitry, and (usually) a microprocessor to control all of these parts.

The basic CRT drive circuitry for a one-color, or *monochrome,* display requires three input signals to operate properly. It must have horizontal sync pulses to keep the horizontal oscillator synchronized and vertical sync pulses to keep the vertical oscillator synchronized. Also, it must have the video information for each point as the beam sweeps across the screen. All this must be synchronized so that a particular dot of video information is displayed at the same point on the screen during each frame. If you have seen a TV picture rolling or a TV picture with jagged horizontal lines in it, you have seen what happens if the horizontal, vertical, and video information are not synchronized.

When transmitted to a TV set or to a video monitor, the two sync signals and the video information are usually combined into a single signal called *composite video.* Figure 13-2 shows a typical TV-type composite video signal waveform. It is hard to show in a figure, but there is one vertical sync pulse for each of the 262.5 horizontal sync pulses. The video information is represented by the waveform sections between horizontal sync pulses. For these waveforms, a more positive voltage turns the beam off. Therefore, the beam will be *blanked* during the horizontal retrace time represented by the pulse on which the horizontal sync pulse sits. The beam will also be blanked during the vertical retrace time. Now let's see how we generate these three signals to display characters on a CRT screen.

Creating a Page of Monochrome Characters on a CRT

Characters or graphics are generated on a CRT screen as a pattern of light and dark dots. To generate these patterns, the electron beam is turned on and off as it sweeps across the screen. Figure 13-3 shows how this works. The round dots in the figure represent the beam on, and the empty square boxes represent the beam off. With this dot matrix we can produce a reasonable approximation to any letter or symbol. The more dots used for each character, the better the representation. Common dot-matrix sizes for a character are 5×7, 7×9, and 7×12. The dot patterns for each character we want to display are stored in a ROM called a *character-*

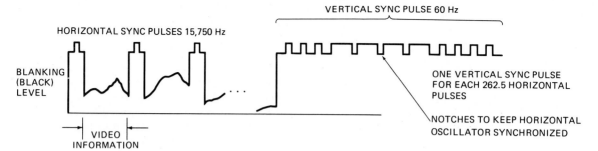

FIGURE 13-2 Composite video waveforms.

generator ROM. Figure 13-4 shows the matrix for a Motorola MC6571 character generator. The MC6571 uses a 7 × 9 matrix for the actual character, but it has extra dot rows to leave space between rows of characters and to allow lowercase letters to be dropped in the matrix to show descenders correctly. Each dot row in Figure 13-4 represents the pattern of dots for a horizontal scan line of the character. Figure 13-5 shows how the character generator is connected with some RAM, a shift register, and some counters to produce the signals required to display characters on a CRT. Here's how it works.

The ASCII or EBCDIC code for the characters to be displayed on the screen is stored in a RAM so that it can be changed when you want to display something new on the screen. This RAM is often referred to as the *display RAM,* or the *display refresh RAM.* The RAM must contain at least one byte location for each character to be displayed. A common display size is 25 rows of characters with 80 characters in each row. This display then requires about 2 Kbytes of display RAM. A character counter and a row counter are used to address the ASCII codes in this RAM.

To start the display in the upper left corner, the character counter and the row counter outputs are all 0s, so the ASCII code for the first character is addressed in the display RAM. The addressed code will be output from the ROM to the data inputs of the character-generator ROM. The outputs of a dot row counter are also applied to the character generator. With these two inputs the character generator will output the 7-bit dot pattern for one dot row in the character. For the first scan across the screen, the counter will output

0000, so the dot pattern output will be that for dot row 0000 of the character. The output from the character generator is in parallel form. In order to turn the beam on and off at the correct time as it sweeps across the screen, this dot pattern must be in serial form. A simple parallel-to-serial shift register is used to do this conversion. Note that the eighth data input of the shift register is tied to ground, so that there is always one dark dot, or *undot,* between characters. The high-frequency clock used to clock this shift register is called the *dot clock* because it controls the rate at which dot information is sent out to the video amplifier.

After the dots for the first scan line of the first character are shifted out, the character counter is incremented by 1. It then points to the ASCII code for the second character in the top row of characters in the display RAM. Therefore, the ASCII code for this second character will be output to the character-generator ROM. Since the dot line counter inputs to the ROM are still 0000, the ROM will output the dot pattern for the top scan line of the second character in the top row of characters on the screen. When all the dots for the top

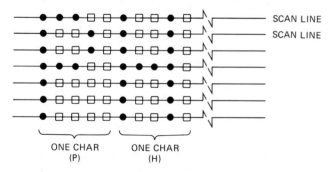

FIGURE 13-3 Producing characters on a CRT screen with dots.

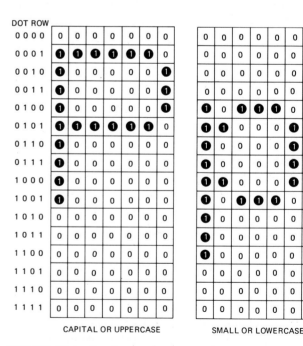

FIGURE 13-4 Dot format for Motorola MC6571 character-generator ROM.

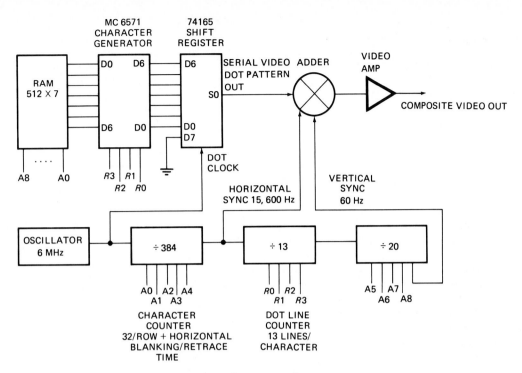

FIGURE 13-5   Block diagram of circuitry to produce dot-matrix character display on CRT.

scan line of this character are shifted out, the character counter will be incremented by 1 again, and the process will be repeated for the third character in the top row of characters. The process continues until the first scan line for all 80 characters in the top row of characters is traced out.

A horizontal sync pulse is then produced to cause the beam to sweep back to the left side of the screen. After the beam retraces to the left, the character counter is rolled back to zero to point to the ASCII code for the first character in the row again. The dot line counter is incremented to 0001 so that the character generator will now output the dot patterns for the second scan line of each character. After the dot pattern for the second scan line of the first character in the row is shifted out to the video amplifier, the character counter is incremented to point to the ASCII code for the second character in the display RAM. The process repeats until all the scan lines for one row of characters have been scanned.

The character row counter is then incremented by 1. The outputs of the character counter and the character row counter now point to the display RAM address where the ASCII code for the first character of the second row of characters is stored. The process we described for the first row is repeated for the second row of characters. After the second row of characters is swept out, the process goes on to the third row of characters, and then on to the fourth, and so on until all 25 rows of characters have been swept out.

When all the character rows have been swept out, the beam is at the lower right corner of the screen. The counter circuitry then sends out a horizontal sync

pulse to retrace the beam to the left side of the screen and a vertical sync pulse to retrace the beam to the top of the screen. When the beam reaches the top left corner of the screen, the whole *screen-refresh* process that we have described repeats. As we mentioned before, the entire screen must be scanned (refreshed) 30 to 60 times a second to avoid a blinking display. Now let's see what frequencies are involved in each major part of the circuitry.

CRT Display Timing and Frequencies

There are many different horizontal, vertical, and dot clock frequencies commonly used in raster-scan CRT displays. The horizontal sweep frequency is usually in the range of 15 to 30 kHz, the vertical sweep frequency is usually 50 or 60 Hz, and the dot clock frequency is usually 5 to 25 MHz. For our first specific example, we use the frequencies used in the IBM monochrome display adapter, which we use as a circuit example in a later section.

The IBM monochrome display adapter produces a display of 25 rows of 80 characters per row. Each character is produced as a 7 × 9 matrix of dots in a 9 × 14 dot space. This means that because clear space is left around each actual character, each character uses 9 dot spaces horizontally and 14 scan lines vertically. The active horizontal display area then is 9 dots/character × 80 characters/line, or 720 dots. The active vertical display area is 25 rows × 14 scan lines/row, or 350 scan lines.

According to the IBM Technical Reference Manual, the monochrome adapter uses a dot clock frequency of

16.257 MHz. This means that the video shift register is shifting out 16,257,000 dots/s. The manual also indicates that the board uses a horizontal sweep frequency of 18,432 lines/s. Multiplying 16,257,000 dots/s × 1/18,432 s/line tells you that the board is shifting out 882 dots/line. We just showed you that the active display area of a line is only 720 dots. The extra 162 dot times actually present are required to give the beam time to get from the right edge of the active display to the right edge of the screen, retrace to the left edge of the screen, and sweep to the left edge of the active display area. This large number of extra dot times is necessary because most monitors have a large amount of *overscan*. This means that the beam is actually swept far off the left and right sides of the screen so that the portion of the sweep actually displayed is linear.

The manual for the display adapter indicates that the frame rate is 50 Hz. In other words, the beam sweeps from the top of the screen to the bottom and back again 50 times/s. To see how many horizontal lines are in each frame, you can divide 18,432 lines/s by 50 frames/s to give 369 scan lines/frame. As we showed before, the active vertical display area is 350 lines, so this gives 19 extra scan line times for the beam to get to the bottom of the screen, retrace to the top of the screen, and get to the start of the active display area again. Note that the dot clock, horizontal sweep frequency, and vertical sweep frequency must all be related to each other so that the display is synchronized.

Another point we need to make here concerns the bandwidth required by a video amplifier or monitor to clearly display a given number of dots per line. For our example here, the dot clock frequency is 16.257 MHz. This means that the dot shift register is shifting out 16,257,000 dots/s. If we are shifting out alternating dots and undots, then the waveform on the serial output pin of the shift register will be a square wave with a frequency of half that of the dot clock, or 8.1285 MHz. In order to produce a clear display with this many dots per line, then, the video amplifier in the monitor connected to the display adapter must have a bandwidth of at least 8 MHz. In other words, the circuitry in the monitor must be able to turn on and off fast enough so that dots and undots don't smear together.

This bandwidth requirement is the reason that normal TV sets connected to computers cannot display high-resolution 80-character lines for word processing and similar applications. In order to filter out the sound subcarrier and the color subcarrier, the bandwidth of TV video amplifiers is limited to about 3 MHz. When using a TV as a readout device for a microcomputer, then, we usually limit the display to a smaller number of dots per character and to 40 characters/line. To summarize, a CRT monitor used for displaying characters or graphics should have a bandwidth greater than one-half the dot clock frequency. Next we show you how programmable CRT display controllers are used to produce a desired display.

A final point we want to make about CRT timing is how often the display refresh RAM has to be accessed.

As the circuitry scans one line of the display, it has to access a new character in RAM after each 9 dots are shifted out, assuming 9 dots horizontally per character. Dividing the dot clock frequency of 16.257 MHz by 9 dots/character tells you that characters are read from RAM at a rate of 1,806,333 characters/s, or 1 character every 553 ns!

CRT Controller ICs and Circuits

In addition to the chain of counters shown in Figure 13-5, a great deal of other circuitry is needed to produce horizontal blanking pulses, vertical blanking pulses, a cursor, scrolling, and highlighting for a CRT display. Several manufacturers offer CRT controller ICs that contain different amounts of the required circuitry. The two devices we discuss here are the Intel 8275 and the Motorola 6848.

THE INTEL 8275 CRT CONTROLLER

Figure 13-6 shows, in block diagram form, how an 8275 controller is connected with other circuitry to produce the drive signals for a CRT monitor. The 8275 contains a row counter that can be programmed for a display of 1 to 64 rows, a character counter that can be programmed for a display of 1 to 80 characters/row, and a scan line counter that can be programmed for 1 to 16 scan lines/character. The 8275 also has an 80-byte buffer to hold the ASCII characters for the row currently being displayed and an 80-byte buffer to hold the ASCII characters for the next row of characters to be displayed.

For the system in Figure 13-6 the page of characters to be displayed is stored in a buffer in the main microprocessor memory. While the 8275 is using the contents of one of its 80-byte buffers to refresh a row of characters on the screen, it fills the other 80-byte buffer from the main memory on a DMA basis. To do this, it sends a DMA request signal (DREQ) to the 8257 DMA controller. The DMA controller sends a DMA request signal to, for example, the $\overline{BR}$ (bus request) input of a 68000. When the 68000 sees the request signal, it floats its buses and sends a bus grant ($\overline{BG}$) signal. The 5287 then asserts the bus grant acknowledge ($\overline{BGACK}$) and begins direct bus access. As we described in Chapter 11, the DMA controller then sends out the memory address and control signals needed to transfer the characters from memory to the 8275 buffer. The DMA approach uses only a small percentage of the microprocessor's time and, since the *display page* is located in the main memory, new characters are easily written to it.

The character generator is left out of the controller so that a ROM for any desired character set can be used. The dot clock and the dot shift register are also external because of the high frequencies involved in that part of the circuit. The 8275 produces vertical and horizontal sync signals, but external circuitry is used to massage the timing of these signals to correspond with the video information from the dot shift register. Next we show you another CRT-controller approach.

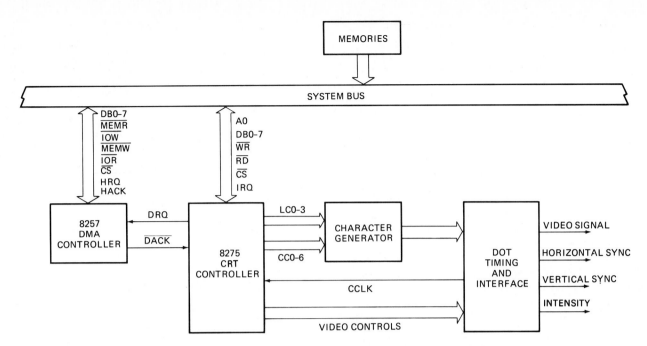

FIGURE 13-6   Block diagram showing connections of Intel 8275 CRT controller in a microcomputer system.

THE MOTOROLA 6845 CRT CONTROLLER

The 6845 CRT-controller chip performs most of the 8275 functions discussed in the previous section, but it interfaces with the display refresh RAM in a very different way. The 6845 is used in both the monochrome display adapter board and the color/graphics monitor adapter boards for the IBM PC, so we use some circuitry from these boards to show you how it works.

Figure 13-7 shows a block diagram for the IBM PC monochrome display adapter board. Take a look at this figure and see what parts you recognize from our previous discussions. You should quickly find the CRT controller, character generator, and dot shift register. Next, find the 2-Kbyte memory where the ASCII codes for the characters to be displayed are stored. To the right of this memory is another 2-Kbyte memory used to store an attribute code for each character. An attrib-

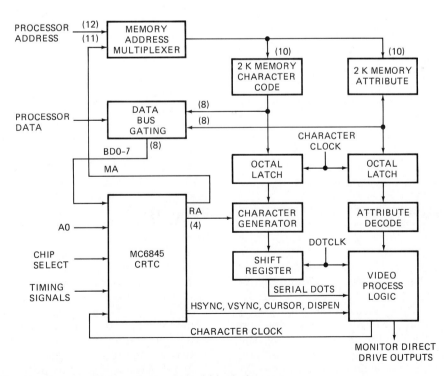

FIGURE 13-7   IBM monochrome display adapter board block diagram.

ute code specifies how the character is to be displayed —for example, with an underline or with increased or decreased intensity. As you may have observed, it is common practice to display a menu at reduced intensity so it does not distract from the main text on the screen.

Now observe that there is a multiplexer in series with the address lines going to the character and attribute memories. This is done so that either the CPU or the CRT controller can access the display refresh RAM. The 6845 has 14 address outputs, so it can address up to 16-Kbyte display and attribute locations. To keep the display refreshed, the 6845 sends out the memory address for a character code and an attribute code. The character clock signal latches the code from memory for the character generator and the attribute code for the attribute decode circuitry. The character clock also increments the address counter in the 6845 to point to the next character code in memory. The character clock transfers the next codes to the character generator and attribute decoder. The process cycles through all the characters on the page and then repeats. When you want to display some new characters on the screen, you simply have the CPU execute some instructions that write the ASCII codes for the new characters to the appropriate address in the display RAM. When the address-decoding circuitry detects a display RAM address, it produces a signal that toggles the multiplexers so that the CPU has access to the display RAM. The question that probably occurs to you at this point is, What happens if the 6845 and the CPU both want to access the display RAM at the same time? There are several solutions to this problem. One solution is to allow the CPU to access the RAM only during horizontal and/or vertical retrace times. Another solution is to interleave 6845 accesses and CPU accesses. This is how it is done in the IBM board. The character clock signal going to the 6845 and the multiplexers allows the CPU to access the RAM during one-half of the clock signal and allows the 6845 to access the RAM during the other half of the clock signal. If the CPU tries to access the display RAM during the controller's half of the character clock cycle, a not-ready signal from the CRT-controller board will cause the processor to insert wait states until the half of the character clock signal when it can access the display refresh RAM.

6845 INTERNAL REGISTERS AND INITIALIZATION

Figure 13-8 shows the pin diagram and labels for the 6845. We will take a brief look at these pin functions and then discuss the internal registers so we can show you how the device is initialized.

The functions of most of the pins should be easily recognizable to you from the block diagram in Figure 13-7. Ground is on pin 1, +5 V is on pin 20, and a reset input is on pin 2. The 6845 sends out the display RAM address of the character currently being scanned on the MA0–MA13 lines. On the RA0–RA4 pins, the 6845 sends out the number of the character scan line currently being scanned to the character generator. A character clock signal that changes state when it is

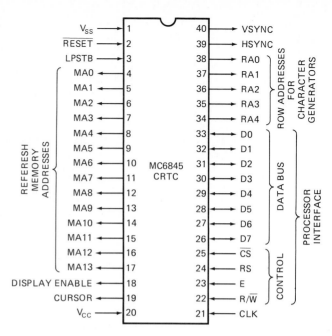

FIGURE 13-8   Motorola MC6845 CRT controller pin names.

time for the controller to access the next character in memory is connected to the 6845 CLK input. The horizontal and vertical sync output signals on pins 39 and 40 are produced by dividing down this CLK input signal. The 6845 has eight data inputs, D0–D7, which connect to the system data bus so that initialization words can be written to the device and status words read from the device, just as with any of the other peripheral devices we have discussed. The 6845 will be enabled for a read or write on its data bus when its $\overline{CS}$ input is asserted low. The $R/\overline{W}$ is asserted high for a read and low for a write. The processor clock—or a signal derived from it—is applied to the E input of the 6845 to synchronize data transfers in or out on the data lines. As seen from the processor, the 6845 has two internal addresses, a control address selected when RS is low and a data address selected when the RS input is high. We will tell you more about this after we talk briefly about the few remaining pins.

The cursor output pin will be asserted high when the controller is displaying the cursor. This signal can be combined with signals from the attribute decoder to cause the cursor to blink or to be highlighted, depending on attribute stored for the cursor location.

The display enable output pin will be asserted when the 6845 is scanning the active display area of the screen. This signal can be used to produce blanking pulses during horizontal and vertical retrace times. In a system that accesses the display RAM during retrace times, this signal can be used to tell the CPU when it can access the display RAM.

When the light pen strobe input, LPSTB, is made to go from low to high, the current refresh address will be latched in two registers inside the 6845.

The 6845 has a register bank of 19 registers that are used to set and to keep track of display counts during display refreshing. Figure 13-9 shows the function of each of these registers. Even if you are not going to be programming a 6845, it is worth taking a look at this figure so you have an idea of the types of parameters you specify for a CRT-controller chip such as the 6845.

The 6845 has only 2 internal I/O addresses that are selected by the RS input. When the RS input is low, the internal address register is selected. When the RS input is high, one of the 18 internal data registers is selected. In order to access one of the internal data registers, you first have to write the number (address) of that register to the address register with RS low and then write the data to the 6845 with RS high. RS is usually tied to a system address line so that you just write the address word to one address, perhaps $3B4, and the data word to another address, perhaps $3B5.

The standard way to initialize all of these parameters for a 6845 in a system is to use a program loop of the form

REPEAT
   Output a data register number to the 6845
      internal address register (RS = 0).
   Output parameter byte for that register to data
      register address (RS = 1).
UNTIL all required registers of the 18 are initialized.

RASTER-SCAN CRT GRAPHICS DISPLAYS

The previous section of this chapter showed you how a monochrome display of alphanumeric characters can be produced on a CRT screen. In this section we show you how we produce a picture or graphics display. The two major methods of producing a graphics display are the *bit-mapped raster-scan* approach and the *vector graphics* approach. We'll explore the raster approach first.

Figure 13-5 shows a block diagram of some simple circuitry that can be used to create a display of characters on a CRT screen by turning the electron beam on and off as it is scanned across the screen. Characters are produced as a series of dots and undots on the screen. The ASCII codes for the page of characters to be displayed are stored in a display refresh RAM. The dot patterns for each scan line of each character are stored in a character-generator ROM. Now, suppose that we leave the character generator out of this circuit and connect the outputs of the RAM directly to the inputs of the dot shift register. And further suppose that instead of storing the ASCII codes for characters in the RAM, we store the dot patterns we want for each eight dots of a scan line in successive memory locations. When a byte is read from the RAM and loaded into the

RS	Register number	Function
0	X	Holds number of data register to write to.
1	0	Total number of horizontal character times +1, including retrace.
1	1	Number of horizontal characters displayed.
1	2	Character number when horizontal-sync pulse is produced. Determines horizontal display position.
1	3	Width of horizontal-sync pulse in character times.
1	4	Total number of vertical character rows-1, including vertical retrace.
1	5	Adjusts vertical timing to get exactly 50 or 60 Hz.
1	6	Number of vertical character rows displayed.
1	7	Vertical row number when vertical-sync pulse produced. Controls vertical position on screen.
1	8	Sets controller for interlaced or non-interlaced scanning.
1	9	Number of horizontal scan lines-1 per character row.
1	10	Starting scan line for the cursor and cursor blink rate.
1	11	Ending scan line for the cursor.
1	12	Starting address (high byte) for character to be put out after vertical retrace. Determines which character row from buffer appears at top of screen. Change this value to scroll display.
1	13	Low byte of first row starting address.
1	14	High byte of current cursor address.
1	15	Low byte of current cursor address in display RAM.
1	16	High byte of display RAM address when LPSTR occurs.
1	17	Low byte of display RAM address when LPSTR occurs.

FIGURE 13-9   MC6845 internal register functions.

shift register, the stored dot pattern will be shifted out to the CRT beam and produce the desired pattern of dots for that section of a scan line on the screen. The next RAM byte will hold the dot pattern for the next 8 dots on a scan line, and so on. Operating in this mode, each bit location in memory corresponds to a dot location on the screen. The entire screen then can be thought of as a matrix of dots, which can be programmed to be on or off by putting a 1 or a 0 in the corresponding bit location in RAM. A graphics display produced in this way is known as a *bit-mapped raster-scan display*. Each dot or in some cases block of dots is called a *picture element*. Most people shorten this to *pixel* or *pel*. For our first example let's assume a pixel is one dot.

Now, suppose that we want a graphics display of 640 pixels horizontally by 200 pixels vertically. This gives a total of 200 × 640, or 128,000, dots on the screen. Since each dot corresponds to a bit location in memory, this means that we have to have at least 128,000 bits, or 16 Kbytes, of RAM to hold the pixel information for just one display screen. Compare this with the 2 Kbytes needed for each page of an 80 × 24 character display. As we show you a little later, producing a color graphics display with a large number of pixels increases the memory requirements even further.

Now that you have a picture of a raster graphics screen as a large matrix of dots, the question that may occur to you is, How do I draw a rocket ship or other picture on the screen? One method is to program each of the 128,000 dots to be on or off, as required to produce the desired display. This method works, but it is somewhat analogous to hand-printing copies of a long book, a very tedious process. To make your life easier, many graphics programs are now available. These programs allow you to create a complex graphics display, dump the display to a printer, store the display on a disk, or include the display in another program you are writing. These graphics programs contain graphics routines, or *primitives*, that allow you to draw lines, draw arcs, draw three-dimensional figures, shade in areas, set up "windows," and so on. Often these programs work with a *mouse*. A mouse in this case is a device that moves a cursor around the CRT screen when you move it around on the desk next to your computer. To draw a straight line between two points, for example, you move the cursor to the point on the screen where you want one end of the line and press a button on the mouse. You then move the cursor to the point on the screen where you want the other end of the line, and press a button on the mouse again. The graphics program then computes the coordinates for the other points on the line and puts 1s in the appropriate locations in the display RAM to draw in the line. By moving the cursor around on the screen and pressing buttons on the mouse at the appropriate times, you can quickly create some elaborate graphics displays. If you have not had a chance to play with a computer that has these graphics capabilities, go to your nearest computer store and experiment with a graphics program on the Apple Macintosh® or IBM PC.

CRT TERMINALS

Several times previously in this book we have used the term CRT terminal. You may have used a CRT terminal to communicate with a minicomputer or mainframe computer. In addition to the basic CRT drive circuitry, a terminal contains a keyboard so you can talk to it, the CRT refresh RAM and controller to keep the display refreshed, and a UART to communicate to and from a computer. Most CRT terminals now have one or more built-in microprocessors to coordinate keyboard, display, and communications functions. A major advantage of using a microprocessor instead of dedicated logic here is that key functions and communications parameters can be changed to match a given computer by simply typing a few keystrokes. A device from National Semiconductor, the NS456, contains a microprocessor-based CRT controller, a keyboard interface, a UART, and most of the other functions needed for a graphics/character CRT terminal.

RASTER-SCAN COLOR GRAPHICS

Monochrome graphics displays get boring after a while, so let's see how you can get some color in the picture.

To produce a monochrome display the inside of a tube is coated with a single phosphor, which produces the desired color light when bombarded with electrons from a single electron gun at the rear of the tube. To produce a color CRT display, red, green, and blue phosphors are applied to the inside of the tube, and three different phosphors are bombarded with three separate electron beams. One approach is to have dots of the three phosphors in a triangular pattern, as shown in Figure 13-10. The dots are close enough together so that to your eye they appear as a single dot. By changing the intensity ratio of the three beams, we

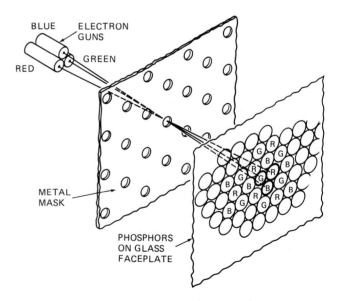

FIGURE 13-10   Three-color phosphor dot pattern used to produce color on a CRT screen.

can make the three-part dot appear any color we want, including black and white. If all three beams are off, the dot is, of course, black. If the beams are turned on in the ratio of 0.30 red, 0.59 green, and 0.11 blue, then the dot will appear white. The overall intensity of the three beams, often represented by the letter I or the letter Y, determines whether the dot will be a light or a dark shade of the color. Figure 13-11 shows 16 colors that can be produced simply by turning on or off different combinations of the red, blue, and green beams. A 1 in the I bit means that the overall intensity of the beam is increased to lighten the color, as shown. If we drive the color guns and the intensity with the output of a D/A converter instead of simply on or off signals, we can produce a much wider variety of colors. A 2-bit D/A converter on each of the color signals and the intensity signal, for example, gives 256 color variations. In order to produce a display with a large number of pixels and a large number of colors, a large memory is needed. As we discuss a common color graphics adapter in the next section, we show you some of the trade-offs involved in this.

The IBM PC Color/Graphics Adapter Board

As a real system example, we use the IBM PC color/graphics adapter board whose block diagram is shown in Figure 13-12.

This board again uses the Motorola MC6845 CRT-controller device to do the overall display control. It produces the sequential addresses required for the display refresh RAM, the horizontal sync pulses, and the vertical sync pulses, as we described in a previous section. The 16-Kbyte display refresh RAM is *dual-ported,* which means that it can be accessed by either the system processor or the CRT controller on a time-

I	R	G	B	COLOR
0	0	0	0	BLACK
0	0	0	1	BLUE
0	0	1	0	GREEN
0	0	1	1	CYAN
0	1	0	0	RED
0	1	0	1	MAGENTA
0	1	1	0	BROWN
0	1	1	1	WHITE
1	0	0	0	GRAY
1	0	0	1	LIGHT BLUE
1	0	1	0	LIGHT GREEN
1	0	1	1	LIGHT CYAN
1	1	0	0	LIGHT RED
1	1	0	1	LIGHT MAGENTA
1	1	1	0	YELLOW
1	1	1	1	HIGH INTENSITY WHITE

FIGURE 13-11 Sixteen colors produced by different combinations of red, blue, and green beams at normal and at increased intensity.

share basis, as we also described previously. A little later we show you how display information is stored in RAM for various display modes.

This adapter board can operate in either a character mode or in a graphics mode. In the character mode it uses a character-generator ROM and a single shift register (alpha serializer) to produce the serial dot information for display scan lines. When operating in a color/graphics mode, the board uses separate shift registers (graphics serializer) to produce the dot information for each of the color guns and for the overall intensity.

As you can see by the signals shown in the lower right corner of Figure 13-12, the adapter board is designed to drive either of the two common types of color monitor. One type, commonly called an RGB monitor, has separate inputs for each of the required signals: red, green, blue, intensity, horizontal sync, and vertical sync. The other type of color monitor is called a *composite color monitor* because all the required signals are combined on a single line. Color TV sets used as color monitors for computers require a composite video signal if they have a direct video input, or they require a radio-frequency signal modulated with the composite video signal if they do not have a direct video input. Later we show you how we produce a composite color video signal from the separate signals. Now let's look at how the display information is stored in the display refresh RAM for various display modes.

In the character, or alphanumeric, mode each character is represented by 2 bytes in the display refresh RAM in the format shown in Figure 13-13a. This is the same format as the monochrome adapter board. The upper byte contains the 8-bit ASCII code for the character to be displayed. The lower byte contains an attribute code, which you use to specify the character color (foreground) and the background color for the character. The intensity bit, I, in the attribute byte allows you to specify normal intensity or increased intensity for a character. The bit patterns used to produce different colors with the RGB and I bits are shown in Figure 13-13b. The B bit in the attribute byte allows you to specify that a character will be blinked. Only 4 Kbytes of the display RAM are needed to hold the character and attribute codes for an 80-character by 25-row display.

For displaying graphics, the adapter board can be operated in three different modes—low resolution, medium resolution, and high resolution. Higher resolution means more pixels in the display. We use these three modes to show you the trade-offs between number of colors, resolution, and memory requirements.

We often use the low-resolution mode when we are using a color TV set or a composite video monitor as a display device because this mode requires less video amplifier bandwidth than high-resolution modes. In this low-resolution mode each PEL is 2 dot times horizontally and 2 dot times vertically, so the picture is actually being made with larger blocks. The display consists of 100 rows of PELs with 160 PELs in each row. The total number of PELs is then 16,000. The

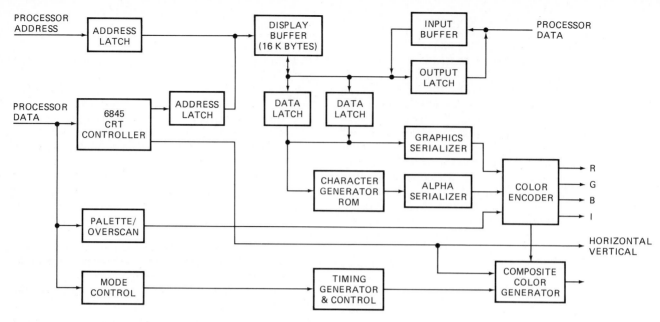

FIGURE 13-12 IBM PC color graphics adapter board block diagram.

color and intensity for each pixel is specified by the I, R, G, and B bits in the lower half of a byte in the display RAM. Since 4 bits are being used to specify color and intensity, a PEL can be any one of 16 colors. Because a byte is used to store the information for each PEL, all 16 Kbytes of the display RAM are used to display the 100 × 160 PEL display.

In the medium-resolution mode, each PEL is a single dot. The display consists of 200 rows of PELs with 320 PELs in each row, or a total of 64,000 PELs. The 16 Kbytes of display refresh RAM correspond to 16K × 8, or 128 Kbits. Dividing the number of PELs into the number of bits available for storage tells you that in

DISPLAY-CHARACTER CODE BYTE   ATTRIBUTE BYTE

7	6	5	4	3	2	1	0	7	6	5	4	3	2	1	0

(a)

ATTRIBUTE FUNCTION	ATTRIBUTE BYTE						
	7	6	5	4	3	2	1	0
	B	R	G	B	I	R	G	B
	FG	BACKGROUND				FOREGROUND		
NORMAL	B	0	0	0	1	1	1	1
REVERSE VIDEO	B	1	1	1	1	0	0	0
NONDISPLAY (BLACK)	B	0	0	0	1	0	0	0
NONDISPLAY (WHITE)	B	1	1	1	1	1	1	1

I = HIGHLIGHTED FOREGROUND (CHARACTER)
B = BLINKING FOREGROUND (CHARACTER)

(b)

FIGURE 13-13 Data storage formats for IBM color graphics board operating in alphanumeric mode. (a) Character byte and attribute byte. (b) Attribute byte format.

this mode there are only 2 bits per PEL available to store color information. With 2 bits we can specify only one of four colors for each PEL. As you can see, increasing the resolution of the display has reduced the number of colors that can be specified with a given amount of memory. Figure 13-14 shows the format in which the PEL information is stored in RAM bytes and the meaning of the bits in these bytes. The background color is selected by outputting a control byte through port $3D9 to the palette circuit shown on the left edge of Figure 13-12.

In the high-resolution graphics mode, the IBM color/graphics adapter board displays 200 rows of PELs with 640 PELs in each row, or a total of 128,000 PELs. Since the 16-Kbyte refresh RAM contains 128,000 bits, this corresponds to 1 bit per PEL. Therefore, you can specify for each bit only whether it is on or off. In other words, in this high-resolution mode you are limited to a black-and-white display, because there are no bits left to specify colors. Figure 13-15 shows the format in which PEL data is stored in display RAM bytes for high-resolution displays. Here again we want to point out that if you want to produce color graphics displays as part of your programs, the best approach is probably to buy one of the commercially available graphics packages. These programs allow you to produce the figures you want with a mouse or with drawing instructions rather than specifying the bit values for each pixel.

As you should see by now, the limiting factor for color graphics displays is the amount of memory you are willing to devote to the display. Some high-resolution displays used in engineering work stations have a display of 1000 PELs by 1000 PELs with 16 colors. A display such as this requires about 500 Kbytes of high-speed refresh RAM.

For each of the graphics formats discussed, data for a

	7	6	5	4	3	2	1	0
	C1	C0	C1	C0	C1	C0	C1	C0
	FIRST DISPLAY PEL		SECOND DISPLAY PEL		THIRD DISPLAY PEL		FOURTH DISPLAY PEL	

C1	C0	FUNCTION
0	0	DOT TAKES ON THE COLOR OF 1 of 16 PRESELECTED BACKGROUND COLORS
0	1	SELECTS FIRST COLOR OF PRESELECTED COLOR SET 1 OR COLOR SET 2
1	0	SELECTS SECOND COLOR OF PRESELECTED COLOR SET 1 OR COLOR SET 2
1	1	SELECTS THIRD COLOR OF PRESELECTED COLOR SET 1 OR COLOR SET 2

COLOR SET 1	COLOR SET 2
COLOR 1 IS GREEN COLOR 2 IS RED COLOR 3 IS BROWN	COLOR 1 IS CYAN COLOR 2 IS MAGENTA COLOR 3 IS WHITE

FIGURE 13-14 Data storage format for medium-resolution graphics mode of IBM PC color adapter board.

PEL is read from the display RAM and converted to separate R, G, B, and I signals. These signals, along with the horizontal and vertical sync signals, can be sent directly to an RGB-type monitor. Before they can be sent to a composite video-type monitor, however, the signals must be put together in a single signal. Here's how we do it.

Producing a Composite Color Video Signal

In order to produce a composite color signal from the R, G, B, and sync signals, we can't just add all the signals

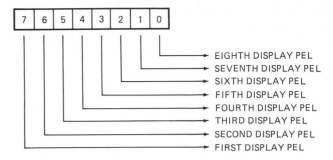

FIGURE 13-15 Data storage format for high-resolution graphics mode of IBM PC color graphics adapter board.

together. Instead, the approach we use is based on the NTSC standards for color television signals. Figure 13-16 shows in diagram form the somewhat complex method used to put the pieces together.

As a first step, the red, the green, and the blue signals are combined in the ratios shown to produce a signal proportional to the overall intensity, or *luminance*. If horizontal and vertical sync pulses are added to this signal, the result is a monochrome composite video signal identical to that we described earlier in this chapter. This signal will produce a monochrome display on either a monochrome monitor or a color monitor.

To develop the correct color signals, we pass the luminance signal through a 1.5-MHz low-pass filter and then an inverter. The filter is required to comply with FCC bandwidth rules if the signal is going to be sent out as part of a TV signal modulation. The inverted luminance signal, $-Y$, is then added to the red signal to produce $R - Y$, and it is added to the blue signal to produce $B - Y$. The reason we do this is probably not obvious to the casual observer, but this scheme reduces the number of separate signals that have to be sent. Here's how it works. The Y, $R - Y$, and $B - Y$ signals are sent as part of the color TV signal or as part of the composite video signal. In the receiver the Y signal is added to the $R - Y$ signal to reconstruct

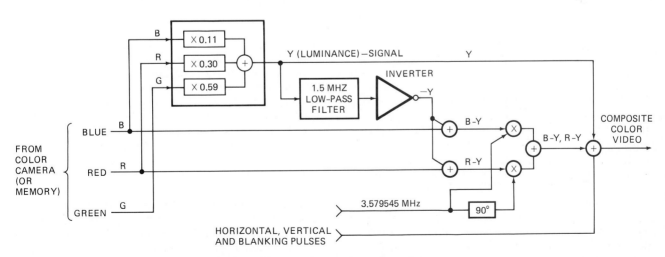

FIGURE 13-16 Block diagram of circuitry used to produce composite color video signal.

the red signal. The Y signal is added to the B − Y signal to reconstruct the blue signal. Since the Y signal is composed of red, green, and blue, the red signal and the blue signal are subtracted from the Y signal to reconstruct the green signal. Because of this, we don't have to send a separate green signal. Now that you have an idea about what is happening, let's continue the story to the point of a composite color video signal.

The key to the next step is a stable 3.579545-MHz signal produced by a crystal oscillator. The B − Y signal is used to modulate this signal, and the R − Y signal is used to modulate a portion of this 3-MHz signal, whose phase has been shifted by 90°. The two modulated 3.579545-MHz signals are then added together. The result is sometimes called the *chroma* signal, because it contains the color information.

To produce the composite color video signal, we simply add the horizontal sync pulses, the vertical sync pulses, the Y signal, and this chroma signal together, as shown in Figure 13-16. When the composite video monitor receives this signal, it will separate all the pieces again.

To produce a composite signal that can be fed into the antenna input of a color TV set, we usually use a chroma modulator device such as the Motorola MC1372 shown in Figure 13-17. This device produces the 3.579545-MHz color carrier frequency, and it produces the chroma signal from the R − Y and B − Y signals. The device also produces a radio-frequency carrier at the frequency for standard TV channel 3 or 4 and modulates this carrier signal with the Y, R − Y, B − Y, and sync information. When a color TV set receives this modulated signal, it demodulates the signal and separates the various parts. Because it has to filter out the remnants of the 3.579545-MHz color carrier frequency, the bandwidth of a composite color monitor or a color TV is limited to less than 3 MHz. As we explained in the section of the chapter on monochrome displays, this limits the resolution and makes it difficult to display 80-character lines or detailed graphics on these types of displays.

VECTOR-SCAN CRT DISPLAYS

A raster-scan CRT display scans the electron beam over the entire screen and turns the beam on and off to produce a light or dark spot at each point in the scan. For certain CRT display applications, such as computer-aided design workstations, where the display consists mostly of background and an array of straight lines, it seems wasteful to sweep the beam back and forth over the entire screen. Also, diagonal lines drawn on a raster-scan display look like stair steps if you look closely at them because of the rigid placement of the pixels on the screen.

A vector graphics scheme solves both of these problems by directly tracing out only the desired lines on the CRT. In other words, if we want a line connecting point *A* with point *B* on a vector graphics display, we simply drive the beam-deflection circuitry with a sig-

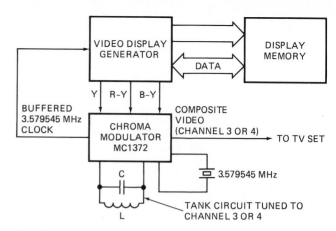

FIGURE 13-17 Motorola MC1372 used to produce color video signal compatible with a standard TV channel.

nal that causes the beam to go directly from point *A* to point *B*. If we want to move the beam from point *A* to point *B* without showing a line between the points, we can blank the beam as we move it. To draw a line on the CRT, then, we simply tell the beam how far to move and in what direction to move across the CRT. The name *vector graphics* comes from the fact that in physics a quantity that has magnitude and direction is called a vector.

The question that may occur to you at this point is, How do you tell the beam where to move on the screen? One way to direct the beam is by connecting a D/A converter to the horizontal deflection circuitry and another D/A converter to the vertical deflection circuitry. The values input to the two D/A converters then determine the position of the beam on the screen. If we use 10-bit D/A converters, then we can direct the beam to one of 1024 positions horizontally and one of 1024 positions vertically. This is equivalent to a 1K × 1K raster display in resolution. Color displays can be produced by using a three-beam, three-phosphor CRT and moving the three beams together, as we described for the raster-scan color display.

The next question that may occur to you is, If this scheme is so simple, why don't we use it for all CRT graphics displays? The answer is that a vector display works well where the information we want to display is mostly straight lines, but it does not work well for displays that have many curves and large shaded areas. When using a vector graphics system, we draw a circle, for example, by drawing many short vectors around in a circle. The circle is then made up of short line segments or points. The number of vectors you can draw on the screen is limited by the fact that you have to go back and redraw each vector 60 times a second to keep the display refreshed. Some current vector graphics systems can draw 150,000 short vectors 60 times a second, but for complex images you soon run out of vectors. The point here is that no one display technique or technology has all the marbles at this point in time. Here's another display technology that has some advantages for portable instruments and computers.

ALPHANUMERIC/GRAPHICS LCD DISPLAYS

In Chapter 9 we discussed how LCDs work and how they can be used to display numbers and letters as individual digits. To make a screen-type display, the liquid crystal elements are constructed in a large, X-Y matrix of dots. The elements in each row are connected together, and the elements in each column are connected together. An individual element is activated by driving both the row and the column containing that element. LCD elements cannot be turned on and off fast enough to be scanned one dot at a time in the way that we scan a CRT display. Therefore, we apply the data for one dot line of one character, or for an entire line, to the X axis of the matrix and activate that dot row of the matrix. For a graphics display we wait a short time; then we deactivate that dot row, apply the data for the next dot row to the X axis, and activate that dot row. We continue the process until we get to the bottom of the display and then start over at the top of the screen. For large LCD displays the matrix may divided into several blocks of perhaps 40 dot lines each. Since each block of dot rows can be refreshed individually, this reduces the speed at which each liquid crystal element must be switched in order to keep the entire display refreshed. Large LCD displays usually come with the multiplexing circuitry built in so that all you have to do is send the display data to the unit in the format specified by the manufacturer for that unit. We should soon see color LCD displays for use with computers.

COMPUTER VISION

For many applications we need a microcomputer to be able to "see" its environment or perhaps a part on which the machine it controls is working. As part of a microcomputer-controlled security system, for example, we might want the microcomputer to look down a corridor to see if any intruders are present. In an automated factory application we might want a microcomputer-controlled robot to look in a bin of parts, recognize a specified part, pick up the part, and mount the part on an engine being assembled. There are several mechanisms we can use to allow a computer to see. The first one we discuss uses sound waves.

Ultrasonic Vision

Bats "see" in the dark by emitting sound waves that are above the human hearing range, or *ultrasonic*. A bat sends out ultrasonic pulses, and based on the time it takes for echoes to return, determines how far it is from obstacles. Some Polaroid cameras use the same mechanism to determine the distance to an object being photographed. The camera then uses the dis-

tance information to focus the camera lens automatically.

The major parts of the rangefinder circuitry used in these cameras, including a printed-circuit board, are available as a kit from Polaroid Corporation, Ultrasonic Ranging Marketing, 1 Upland Road, Norwood, MA 02062. With one of these kits and some simple circuitry, you can add this type of vision to your microcomputer. Figure 13-18a shows a block diagram for the circuitry on the experimental board, and Figure 13-18b shows the major waveforms for one cycle of operation. A cycle starts when the VSW input is pulsed high. The transmitter section then sends out a "chirp" of 56 pulses through the transducer. The output is called a chirp because the 56 pulses step through four frequencies, 60 kHz, 57 kHz, 53 kHz, and 50 kHz, to avoid absorption problems that might occur with just one frequency. This transmission is represented by the XLG signal in Figure 13-18b.

After the pulses are sent out, the circuitry is switched so that the transducer functions as a receiver. When the echo of the sound waves returns to the transducer, it produces an analog electrical signal out of the transducer. A programmable gain amplifier amplifies this echo and converts it to a digital pulse, shown as the FLG signal in Figure 13-18b. The time it takes the ultrasonic signal to go out to the target and return is the time between the first rising edge of XLG and the rising edge of the FLG signal.

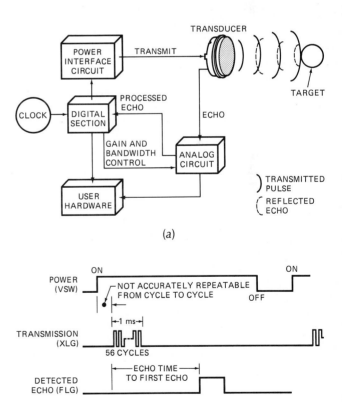

FIGURE 13-18 Polaroid ultrasonic rangefinder. (a) Block diagram of interface circuitry. (b) Major signal waveforms.

You can measure this time in any one of several ways. One way is to start a counter with the rising edge of XLG and stop the counter with the rising edge of FLG. The number left in the counter is then the number of clock pulses required for the signal to go out to the target and back. To get the total time for the trip, you can multiply the number of clock pulses counted by the period of the clock pulses. Divide this time by 2 to get the actual time to the target. Since sound travels at about 1 ft/0.888 ms, you can easily convert the transit time to an equivalent distance. An exercise in the laboratory manual that accompanies this book shows you how to do this.

A simple ultrasonic rangefinder such as we have described here could be mounted in a mobile robot. By scanning the rangefinder back and forth the robot could determine a clear path through a series of obstacles or detect when someone intrudes into its space. The rangefinder we described has a range of about 35 ft and a resolution of about $\frac{1}{8}$ in. when looking at a flat surface perpendicular to the sound waves. For applications where we need greater resolution or to recognize the shapes of objects, we use optical vision devices with our microcomputer.

Video Cameras and Computers

Cameras used in TV stations and for video recorders use a special vacuum tube called a *vidicon*. A light-sensitive coating on the inside of the face of the vidicon is swept horizontally and vertically by a beam of electrons. The beam is swept in the same way as the beam in a TV set displaying a picture is swept. The amount of beam current that flows when the beam is at a particular spot on the vidicon is proportional to the intensity of the light that falls on that spot. The output signal from the vidicon for each scan line is an analog signal proportional to the amount of light falling on the points along that scan line. This signal is represented by the waveform between the horizontal sync pulses in Figure 13-2. In order to get this analog video information into a digital form that can be stored and processed by a computer, we have to pass it through an A/D converter. For a color camera we need an A/D converter on each of the three color signals. Each output value from an A/D converter then represents a dot of the picture. The number of bits of resolution in the A/D converter will determine the number of intensity levels stored for each dot.

Standard video cameras and the associated digitizing circuitry are relatively expensive, so they are not cost effective for many applications. In cases where we don't need the resolution available from a standard video camera, we often use a CCD camera.

CCD Cameras

Charge-coupled devices, or CCDs, are constructed as long shift registers on semiconductor material. Figure 13-19 shows the structure for a CCD shift register section. As you can see, the structure consists simply

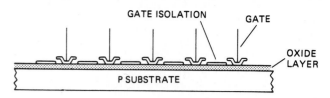

FIGURE 13-19 Basic structure of charge-coupled device used in CCD video cameras.

of a P-type substrate, an insulating layer, and isolated gates. If a gate is made positive with respect to the substrate, a *potential well* is created under that gate. This means if a charge of electrons is injected into the region under the gate, the charge will be held there. By applying a sequence of clock signals to the gates, this stored charge can be shifted along to the region under the next gate. In this way a CCD can function as an analog or a digital shift register.

To make an image sensor, several hundred CCD shift registers are built in parallel on the same chip. A photodiode is doped in under every other gate. When all the gates with photodiodes under them are made positive, potential wells are created. A cameral lens is used to focus an image on the surface of the chip. Light shining on the photodiodes causes a charge proportional to the light intensity to be put in each well that has a diode. These charges can be shifted out to produce the dot-by-dot values for the scan lines of a picture. Improved performance can be gained by alternating nonlighted shift registers with the lighted ones. Information for a scan line is shifted in parallel from the lighted register to the dark and then shifted out serially.

The video information shifted out from a CCD register is in discrete samples, but these samples are analog because the charge put in a well is simply a function of the light shining on the photodiode. To get the video information into a form that can be stored in memory and processed by a microcomputer, it must be passed through an A/D converter or in some way converted to digital. For many robot applications and surveillance applications a black-and-white image with no gray tones is all we need. In this case the video information from the CCD registers can simply be passed through a comparator to produce a 1 or a 0 for each dot of the image. CCD cameras have the advantages that they are smaller in size, more rugged, less expensive, and easier to interface to computer circuitry than vidicon-based cameras. Next we describe an inexpensive type of camera that produces digital video information directly.

OPTICRAM Cameras

Figure 13-20 shows a picture of the Micron Eye camera produced by Micron Technology in Boise, Idaho. This camera is relatively inexpensive, interfaces easily to common microcomputers, and has enough resolution for simple robot-type applications.

light. To use the dynamic RAM as an image sensor, then, we start by charging up all the cells to a logic 1 level. After some amount of time we read the logic level on each cell. A cell that still contains a logic 1 represents a dark spot, and a cell that has dropped to a logic 0 represents a light spot. The logic levels can be read out of the OPTICRAM and stored directly in a microcomputer memory for processing. The sensitivity of the camera to light can be adjusted by changing the time between when you charge up all the cells and when you read out the logic levels on the cells. For instance, for brighter light conditions, use a shorter time.

Available with the Micron Eye are PC boards that contain circuitry to interface the camera to common microcomputers such as the IBM PC, the APPLE computers, and the Commodore 64. With these boards installed you can display images on the CRT screen, adjust display parameters under program control, and save images on a disk. Once you get the bit pattern for an image into memory, you can then experiment with programs that attempt to recognize, for example, a square in the image.

Figure 13-21 shows an example of what a little vision can do for a robot. The Sumitomo Electric Company robot shown here can play an organ using both hands on the keys and both feet on the pedals. It can press up to 15 keys/s. The robot can play selections

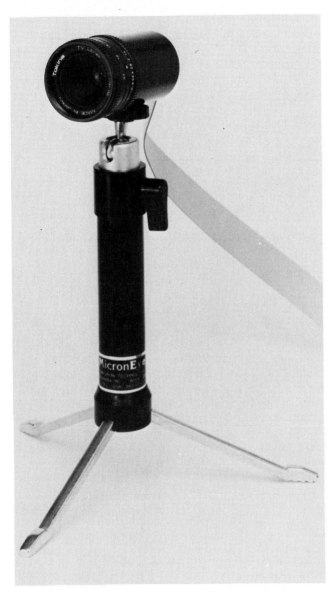

FIGURE 13-20 Micron Eye Optic RAM video camera with interface board for IBM PC. (*Micron Technology Inc.*)

The heart of this camera is a 64-Kbit dynamic RAM with a glass cover instead of the usual metal lid. A lens on the front of the camera is used to focus the image directly onto the surface of the dynamic RAM. Here's how it works.

The 65,536 storage cells of dynamic RAM are arranged in two arrays of 128×256 cells each. Each cell functions as a pixel. There is a dead zone of about 25 cell widths between the two arrays. If the two arrays are used together, this dead zone has to be taken into account.

Remember now that data is stored in dynamic RAMS as a charge on a tiny capacitor. Dynamic RAMS have to be refreshed because the charge gradually changes due to leakage. If you shine a light on a dynamic RAM cell, the charge changes faster than it would without the

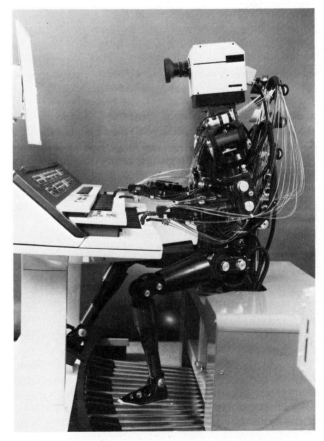

FIGURE 13-21 Organ-playing robot developed by Sumitomo Electric Company.

from memory when verbally told to do so. Using its vision, it can read and play songs from standard sheet music. The robot uses seventeen 16-bit microprocessors and fifty 8-bit controllers to control all its activities.

If you think about what is involved in recognizing complex visual shapes in all their possible orientations with a computer program, it should give you a new appreciation for the pattern-recognition capabilities of the human eye-brain system.

Another area where the human brain excels is in that of data storage. Only very recently have the devices used to store computer data approached the capacity of the human brain. In the next section we look at how some of these mass data-storage systems operate and how they are interfaced to microcomputers.

MASS DATA-STORAGE SYSTEMS

Since the ROM and RAM in a computer cannot possibly hold all the programs that we might want to run and all the data that we might want to analyze, a computer system needs some other form of data storage that can hold massive amounts of data, is nonvolatile, can be updated, and has a relatively low cost per bit of storage. The most common devices used for mass data storage are magnetic tape, floppy magnetic disks, hard magnetic disks, and optical disks. Magnetic tapes are used mostly for backup storage, because the access time to get to data stored in the middle of the tape is usually too long to be acceptable. Therefore, in our limited space here we concentrate on the three types of disk storage.

FLOPPY-DISK DATA STORAGE

Floppy Disk Overview

Figure 13-22 shows a picture of a typical floppy disk enclosed in its protective envelope. The common sizes for disks are 8, 5.25, and 3.5 in. The disk itself is made of Mylar and coated with a magnetic material. The Mylar disk is only a few thousandths of an inch thick—thus the name floppy. When the disk is inserted in a drive unit, a spindle clamps in the large center hole and spins the disk at a constant speed of perhaps 300 or 360 rpm.

Data is stored on the disk in concentric, circular tracks, rather than in a spiral track as on a phonograph record. A read/write head contacts the disk through the racetrack-shaped slot to read from or write to the disk. Figure 13-23 shows a diagram of a read/write head. In the write mode a current passing through the coil in the head creates a magnetic flux in the iron core of the head. A gap in the iron core allows the magnetic flux to spill out and magnetize the magnetic material on the disk. Once a region on the disk is

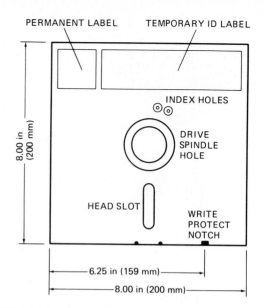

FIGURE 13-22   Floppy disk in protective envelope.

magnetized in a particular direction, it retains that magnetism. The polarity of the magnetized region is determined by the direction of the current through the coil. We say more about this later.

Data can be read from the disk with the same head. Whenever the polarity of the magnetism changes as the track passes over the gap in the read/write head, a small voltage, typically a few millivolts, is induced in the coil. An amplifier and comparator are used to convert this small signal to standard logic levels.

The write-protect notch in a floppy-disk envelope can be used to protect stored data from being written over, as can the knockout plastic tabs on audio tape cassettes. An LED and a phototransistor can indicate whether the notch is present and disable the write circuits if it is.

An index hole punched in the disk indicates the start of the recorded tracks. An LED and a phototransistor are used to detect when the index hole passes.

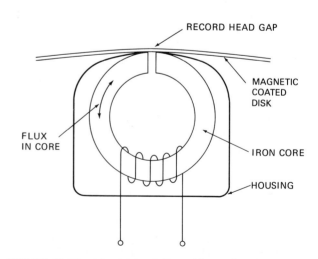

FIGURE 13-23   Magnetic-disk read/write head.

Disk Drive and Head Positioning

The motor used to spin the floppy disk is usually a dc motor whose speed is precisely controlled by negative feedback, as we described in Chapter 10. In most systems this speed will be held constant at all times. Typically it takes about 250 ms for the motor to start up after a start-motor command.

The most common method of positioning the read/write head over a desired track is with a stepper motor. A lead screw or a let-out-take-in steel band such as that shown in Figure 13-24 converts the rotary motion of the stepper motor to the linear motion needed to position the head over the desired track on the disk. As the stepper motor in Figure 13-24 rotates, the steel band is let out on one side of the motor pulley and pulled in on the other side. This slides the head along its carriage.

To find a given track, the motor is usually stepped to move the head to track zero near the outer edge of the disk. The motor is then stepped the number of steps required to move the head to the desired track. Typically, it takes a few hundred milliseconds to position the head over a desired track.

Once the desired track is found, the head must be pressed against the disk, or *loaded.* Typically, it takes about 50 ms to load the head and allow it time to settle against the disk.

Floppy-Disk Data Formats and Error Detection

As we said previously, floppy disks come in several standard sizes. Larger disks tend to have more data tracks than smaller disks, but there is no one standard number of tracks for any size disk. Eight-inch disks typically have about 77 tracks per side, 5.25-in. disks have about 40 tracks per side, and the new 3.5-in. disks in hard plastic envelopes have about 80 tracks per side. Single-sided drives record data tracks on only one side of the disk. Double-sided drives use two read/write heads to store data on both sides of the disk. The data tracks on floppy disks are divided into sectors. There are two different methods of indicating the start of sectors: *hard sectoring* and *soft sectoring.* Hard-sectored 8-in. disks typically have 32 additional index holes spaced equally around the disk. Each hole signals the start of a sector. The index hole photodetector is used to detect these sector holes.

Soft-sectored disks have only one index hole, which indicates the start of all of the tracks. The sector format is established by bytes stored on the track. Most newer systems use soft sectoring because it is more reliable than hard sectoring.

The actual digital data is stored on floppy disks in many different formats, so we can't begin to show you all of them. To give you a general idea, we will use an old standard, the IBM 3740 format, which is the basis of most current formats. Figure 13-25 shows how bytes are written to a track in this format.

In the 3740 format a track has three types of fields. An *index field* identifies the start of the track. *ID fields* contain the track and sector identification numbers for each of the 26 data sectors on the track. Each of the 26 sectors also contains a *data field,* which consists of 128 bytes of data plus two bytes for an error-checking code. As you can see, in addition to the bytes used to store data, many bytes are used for identification, synchronization, error checking, and buffering between sectors. One type of separator used here is called a *gap.* A gap is simply a region that contains no data. Gaps are provided to separate fields, so that the information stored in one field can be changed without altering an adjacent field.

Address marks shown at several places in this format are special bytes that have an extra clock pulse recorded along with their D2 data bits. Address marks are used to identify the start of a field. The four types of address mark are index, ID, data, and deleted data.

Two bytes at the end of the each ID field and 2 bytes at the end of each data field are used to store *checksums* or *cyclic redundancy characters.* These are used to check for errors when the ID and the data are read out. The data checksum, for example, is produced by adding up all the data bytes and keeping only the least significant 2 bytes of the result. These 2 bytes are then recorded after the data bytes. When the data is read, it is readded and the sum is compared with the recorded checksum bytes. If the two sums are equal, then the data was probably read out correctly. If the sums do not agree, then another attempt can be made to read the data. If after several tries the sums still do not compare, then a disk-read error can be sent out to the CRT.

Instead of using a checksum, most disk systems use the cyclic redundancy character, or CRC, method. There are actually several similar techniques using CRCs. Here's one way to give you the idea. To produce the 2 CRC bytes the 128 data bytes are treated as a single large binary number and are divided by a constant number. The 16-bit remainder from this division

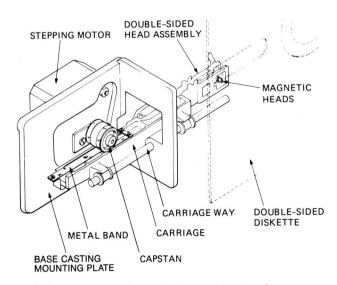

FIGURE 13-24 Head-positioning mechanism for floppy-disk-drive unit. (*Shugart Corporation*)

STEPPING MOTOR

DOUBLE-SIDED HEAD ASSEMBLY

MAGNETIC HEADS

CARRIAGE WAY

DOUBLE-SIDED DISKETTE

METAL BAND

CARRIAGE

BASE CASTING MOUNTING PLATE

CAPSTAN

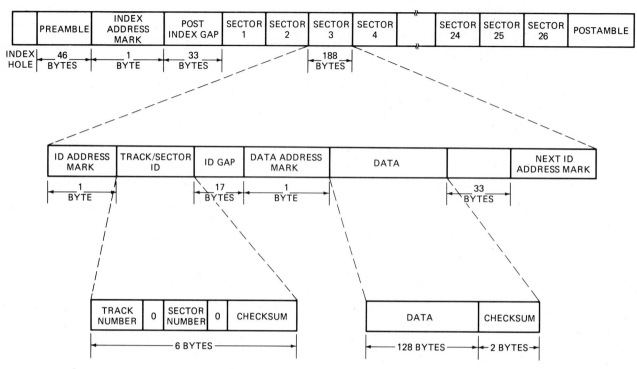

FIGURE 13-25   IBM 3740 floppy-disk soft-sectored track format (single density).

is written in after the data bytes as the CRC bytes. When the data bytes and the CRC bytes are read out, the CRC bytes are subtracted from the data string. The result is divided by the original constant.

Since the original remainder has already been subtracted, the result of the division should be zero if the data was read out correctly. Higher-quality systems usually write data to a disk and immediately read it back to see if it was written correctly. If an error is detected, then another attempt can be made. If 10 write attempts are unsuccessful, then the operator can be prompted to throw out the disk or the write can be directed to another sector on the disk.

The IBM 3740 format we have been describing is referred to as *single density.* An 8-in. disk in this format has one index track and 76 data tracks. Since each track has 26 sectors with 128 data bytes in each sector, the total is about 250 Kbytes. If we use both sides of the disk, we get about 500K bytes. To increase the storage capacity even further, most systems use *double-density* recording. Double-density recording uses a different clock and data bit pattern to pack twice as many sectors in a track. Now let's look at how data is actually recorded on floppy disks.

Recorded Bit Formats—FM and MFM

A 1 bit is represented on magnetic disks as a change in the polarity of the magnetism on the track. A 0 bit is represented as no change in the polarity of the mag-

netism. This form of recording is often called *nonre-turn-to-zero* (NRZ) recording, because the magnetic field is never zero on a recorded track. Each point on the track is always magnetized in one direction or the other. The read head produces a signal when it is passed over by a region where the magnetic field changes. As you read through the next section, keep in mind that what we show in the waveforms as a pulse simply represents a change in magnetic polarity on the disk.

Figure 13-26 shows how bits are stored on a disk track in single-density format. This format is often called *frequency-modulation,* FM, or F2F recording. Note that there is a clock pulse, C, at the start of each bit cell in this format. These pulses represent the basic frequency. A 1 is written in a bit cell by putting in a pulse, D, between the clock pulses; a 0 is represented by no pulse between the clock pulses. Putting in the data pulses modifies the frequency, which gives the name frequency modulation.

The recorded clock pulses are required to synchronize the read-out circuits. The actual distance—and therefore time—between data bits read from an outer track is longer than it is for data bits read from an inner track. A circuit called a *phase-locked loop* adjusts its frequency to that of the clock pulses and produces a signal that tells the read circuit when to check for a data bit. Recording clock information along with data information not only makes it possible to read data accurately from different tracks, but it also

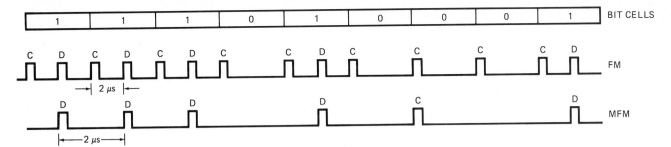

FIGURE 13-26   FM and MFM recording formats for magnetic disks.

reduces the chances of a read error caused by small changes in disk speed.

A disadvantage of standard F2F recording is that a clock pulse and the data bit are required to represent each data bit. Since bits can be packed only so close together on a disk track without interfering with each other, this limits the amount of data that can be stored on a track in this format. To double the amount of data that can be stored on a track, the *modified frequency-modulation,* or MFM, recording format (shown as the second waveform in Figure 13-26) is used. The basic principle of this format is that both clock pulses and 1 data pulses are used to keep the phase-locked loop and read circuitry synchronized. A clock pulse is not put in unless data pulses do not happen to come often enough in the data bytes to keep the phase-locked loop locked. Clock bits are put at the start of the bit cell and data bits are put in the middle of the bit cell time. However, a clock bit will be put in only if the data bit in the previous cell was a 0 and the data bit in the current bit cell is also a 0. Since this format has, in all cases, only one pulse per bit cell, a bit cell can be half as long, or, in other words, twice as many of them can be packed into a track. This is the way that double-density recording is achieved in the IBM PC and other common microcomputers. For a 5.25-in. double-density recorded disk, data bits will be read out at about 250,000 *bits*/s. Incidentally, a new disk-recording technology called *perpendicular,* or *vertical,* recording should allow four to eight times as much data to be put on a given-size disk. With perpendicular recording the tiny magnetic regions are oriented perpendicularly to the disk surface instead of parallel to it as they are for standard disks.

Now that we have shown you how digital data is stored on floppy disks, we show you the circuitry required to interface a floppy disk drive to a microcomputer.

A Floppy-Disk Controller—the Intel 8272A

As you can probably tell from the preceding discussion, writing data to a floppy disk and reading the data back requires coordination at several levels. One level is the motor and head-drive signals. Another level is the actual writing and reading at the bit level. Still another level is interfacing with the rest of the circuitry of a microcomputer. This coordination is a full-time job, so we use a specially designed floppy-disk controller to do it. As our example device here we use the Intel 8272A controller, which is equivalent to the NEC uPD675 controller used in the IBM PC. However, it is easier to find data sheets and application notes for the 8272A if you need further information.

8272 SIGNALS AND CIRCUIT CONNECTIONS

Figure 11-3 showed you how an 8272A controller can be connected in a 68000-based microcomputer system. Also in Chapter 11, we discussed in detail how data can be transferred to and from a floppy disk controller on a DMA basis. Now we want to take a closer look at the controller itself to show you the types of signals it produces and how it is programmed.

To start, take a look at the block diagram of the 8272A in Figure 13-27. The signals along the left side of the diagram should be readily recognizable to you. The data bus lines, RD/$\overline{WR}$, A0, RESET, and $\overline{CS}$ are the standard peripheral interface signals. The DRQ, $\overline{DACK}$, and INT signals are used for DMA transfer of data to and from the controller. To refresh your memory from Chapter 11, here's a review of how the DMA works. When a microcomputer program needs some data from the disk, it sends a series of command words to registers inside the controller. The controller then reads the data from the specified track and sector on the disk. When the controller reads the first byte of data from a sector, it sends a DMA request, or DRQ, signal to the DMA controller. The DMA controller sends a hold request signal to the HOLD input of the CPU. The CPU floats its buses and sends a hold-acknowledge signal to the DMA controller. The DMA controller then sends out the first transfer address on the bus and asserts the $\overline{DACK}$ input of the 8272 to tell it that the DMA transfer is underway. When the number of bytes specified in the DMA initialization has been transferred, the DMA controller asserts the TERMINAL COUNT input of the 8272. This causes the 8272 to assert its interrupt output signal, INT. The INT signal can be connected to a CPU or 8259A interrupt input to tell the CPU that the requested block of data has been read in from the disk to a buffer in memory. The process would proceed in a similar manner for a DMA write-to-disk operation.

Now let's work our way through the drive-control signals shown in the lower right corner of the 8272 block diagram in Figure 13-27. Reading through our

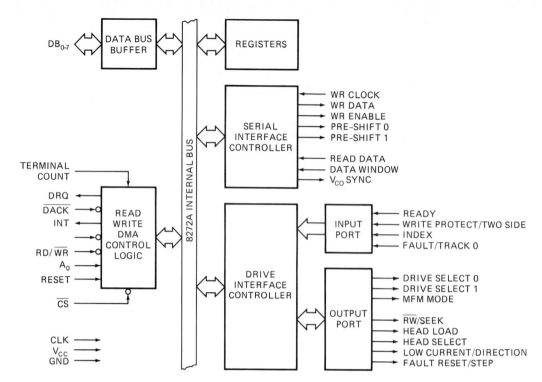

FIGURE 13-27   INTEL 8272A floppy-disk-controller block diagram.

brief descriptions of these signals should give you a better idea of what is involved in the interfacing to the disk-drive hardware. Note the direction of the arrow on each signal.

The READY input signal from the disk drive will be high if the drive is powered and ready to go. If, for example, you forget to close the disk-drive door, the READY signal will not be asserted.

The WRITE PROTECT/TWO SIDE signal indicates whether the write-protect notch is covered when the drive is in the read or write mode. When the drive is operating in track-seek mode, this signal indicates whether the drive is two-sided or one-sided.

The INDEX signal is pulsed when the index hole in the disk passes between the LED and phototransistor detector.

The FAULT/TRACK 0 signal indicates some disk-drive problem during a read/write operation. During a track-seek operation, this signal is asserted when the head is over track 0, the outermost track on the disk.

The DRIVE SELECT output signals, DS0 and DS1, from the controller are sent to an external decoder, which uses these signals to produce an enable signal for one to four drives.

The MFM output signal is asserted high if the controller is programmed for modified frequency modulation and low if the controller is programmed for standard frequency modulation (FM).

The RW/SEEK signal is used to tell the drive to operate in read/write mode or in track-seek mode. Remember, some of the other controller signals have different meanings in the read/write mode than they do in the seek mode.

The HEAD LOAD signal is asserted by the controller to tell the drive hardware to put the read/write head in contact with the disk. When interfacing to a double-sided drive, the HEAD SELECT from the controller is used along with this signal to indicate which of the two heads should be loaded.

During write operations on inner tracks of the disk, the LOW CURRENT/DIRECTION signal is asserted by the controller. Because the bits are closer together on the inner tracks, the write current must be reduced to prevent recorded bits from splattering over each other. When executing a seek-track command this signal pin is used to tell the drive whether to step outward towards the edge of the disk or inward towards the center.

The FAULT RESET/STEP output signal is used to reset the fault flip-flop after a fault has been corrected when doing a read or write command. When the controller is carrying out a track-seek command, this pin is used to output the pulses that step the head from track to track.

Now that we have led you quickly through the drive interface signals, let's take a look at the 8272A signals used to read and write the actual clock and data bits on a track. To help with this, Figure 13-28 shows a block diagram of the circuitry between these pins and the read/write head.

Remember from our discussion of FM and MFM recording that clock information is recorded on the track with the data information. We use the clock bits to tell us when to read the data bits. The VCO SYNC signal from the controller tells an external phase-locked-loop circuit to synchronize its frequency with that of the clock pulses being read off the disk. (In the case of MFM recording, the data bits are also part of

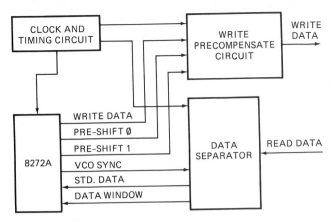

FIGURE 13-28 Block diagram of external circuitry used with Intel 8272A floppy-disk controller for reading and writing serial data.

the signal on which the PLL locks). The output from the phase-locked-loop circuitry is a DATA WINDOW signal. This signal is sent to the controller to tell it where to find the data pulses in the data stream coming in on the READ DATA input.

For writing pulses to the disk, the story is a little more complex. External circuitry supplies a basic WR CLOCK signal at a frequency of 500 kHz for FM and 1 MHz for MFM recording. The 8272 outputs the serial stream of clock bits and data bits that are to be written to the disk on its WR DATA pin. During a write operation, the 8272 asserts its WR ENABLE signal to turn on the external circuitry that actually sends this serial data to the read/write head. Data bits written in MFM on a disk will tend to shift in position as they are read out. A 1 bit, for example, will tend to shift toward an adjacent 0 bit. This shift can cause errors in readout unless it is compensated for. The PRE-SHIFT 0 and PRE-SHIFT 1 signals from the controller go to external circuitry that shifts bits forward or backward as they are being written. The bits are then in the correct position when read out.

8272 COMMANDS

The 8272 can execute 15 different commands. Each of these commands is sent to the data register in the controller as a series of bytes. Consult an 8272 data sheet to find the formats for these commands if you need them. After a command has been sent to the 8272, it carries out the command and returns the results to status registers in the 8272 and/or to the data register in the 8272. To give you an overview of the commands you can send to an 8272, we list them here with a short description for each.

SPECIFY—Initialize head load time, head step time, DMA/non-DMA.

SENSE DRIVE STATUS—Return drive status information.

SENSE INTERRUPT STATUS—Poll the 8272 interrupt signal.

SEEK—Position read/write head over specified track.

RECALIBRATE—Position head over track 0.

FORMAT TRACK—Write ID field, gaps, and address marks on track.

READ DATA—Load head, read specified amount of data from sector.

READ DELETED DATA—Read data from sectors marked as deleted.

WRITE DATA—Load head, write data to specified sector.

WRITE DELETED DATA—Write deleted data address mark in sector.

READ TRACK—Load head, read all sectors on track.

READ ID—Return first ID field found on track.

SCAN EQUAL—Compare sector of data bytes read from disk with data bytes sent from CPU or DMA controller until strings match. Set bit in status register if match.

SCAN HIGH OR EQUAL—Set flag if data string from disk sector greater than or equal to data string from CPU or DMA controller.

SCAN LOW OR EQUAL—Set flag if data string from disk sector is less than or equal to data string from CPU or DMA controller.

Working out a series of commands for a disk controller such as the 8272 on a bit-by-bit basis is quite tedious and time consuming. Fortunately, you usually don't have to do this, because in most systems, you can use higher-level procedures to read from and write to a disk. In the next section we show you some of the software used to interface to disk drives.

Disk-Drive Interface Software

There are several different software levels at which you can interact with a disk drive. One level is directly at the controller level. The next level up is at the BIOS level. A still-higher and easier-to-use level is at the operating system level, or OS level. Figure 13-29 shows this situation diagramatically. Figures like that of Figure 13-29 are often called *stack diagrams*, obviously because they look like a stack of boxes. The order of the stacking is important, however, because the order implies the calling sequences used between the layers. Where two of the stacked boxes meet is an *interface*. The implication is that the software routines in the upper box call the routines in the lower box (using them as subroutines), but the routines in the lower box

| OPERATING SYSTEM INTERFACE ROUTINES |
| BASIC I/O SYSTEM ROUTINES |
| CONTROLLER (DRIVER) ROUTINES |

FIGURE 13-29 Disk-access-routine stack diagram.

typically do not call routines in the upper box. In the following sections we examine both the IBM PC and PC-DOS and the Apple Macintosh and Macintosh operating system. Using the Apple Macintosh as an example we also show you in the following sections how to interface your programs with a disk drive using the Mac OS approach.

| Operating system interface routines |
| Basic I/O system routines |
| Controller (driver) routines |

Operating System (OS) Interfacing

DISK OPERATING SYSTEM (DOS) OVERVIEW

First of all, let's clarify some terms for you. An *operating system* is simply a program or collection of programs that allows you to format disks, execute other programs, create disk files, write data to files, read data from files, communicate with system peripherals such as modems and printers, etc. As we discuss in Chapter 14, some operating systems allow several users to share a CPU on a timeshare basis. The term *disk operating system*, or DOS, means that the operating system resides on a disk and is loaded into memory and executed when you turn on or reset the system. In common usage the acronym *DOS* has come to imply specifically the IBM PC disk operating system, PC-DOS. The term *file* in this case refers to a collection of related data accessible by name. The principle is the same as having a named file folder in an office file cabinet.

Using the OS to format disks, write files, and read files relieves you of the burden of keeping track of the individual tracks and sectors. The OS does all this for you. Now, before we show you how to use the OS procedure calls, we briefly show you how IBM's PC-DOS keeps track of where it puts everything.

Figure 13-30 shows the "housekeeping" information that IBM PC-DOS puts on the first track of a disk to keep track of where it puts data. The basic structure for these parts is put on a disk when it is formatted

with a DOS format command. As files are created and written to the disk, the relevant information for each file is put in the directory and tables.

The boot record in the first sector of the first track indicates whether the disk contains the DOS files needed to load DOS into RAM and run it. Loading DOS and running it is commonly referred to as *booting* the system.

The directory on the disk contains a 32-byte entry for each file. Let's take a quick look at the use of these bytes to get an overview of the information stored for each file.

Byte Number	(Decimal)
0–7	Filename
8–10	Filename extension
11	File attribute
	$01 Read only
	$02 Hidden file
	$04 System file
	$08 Volume label in first 11 bytes, not filename
	$10 File is a subdirectory of files in lower level of hierarchical file tree
	$20 File has been written to and closed
12–21	Reserved
22–23	Time the file was created or last updated
24–25	Date the file was created or last updated
26–27	Starting cluster number; DOS allocates space for files in *clusters* of one or more adjacent sectors in size
28–31	Size of the file in bytes

DOS uses the first *file allocation table*, or FAT, to keep track of which clusters on a disk are currently being used for each file and which clusters are still available. The FAT is part of the link between a filename and the actual track and sector numbers where that file is stored. The second FAT is simply a copy of the first, included for backup purposes.

Most current microcomputer operating systems— IBM PC DOS 2.1 and later versions, for example— allow you to set up a *hierarchical file structure*. In this structure you have one main, or *root*, directory which resides in the directory of the disk, as shown in Figure 13-30. This root directory can contain the names of program or data files. The root directory can also have the names of *subdirectories* of files. Each subdirectory can also refer directly to program or data files or it can refer to lower subdirectories. The point here is that this structure allows you to group similar files together and to avoid going through a long list of filenames to find a particular file you need. To get to a file in a lower-level directory, you simply specify the *path* to that file. The path is the series of directory names that you go through to get to that file.

| Boot record—variable size |
| First copy of file allocation table—variable size |
| Second copy of file allocation table—variable size |
| Root directory—variable size |
| Data area |

FIGURE 13-30   IBM PC DOS format for floppy disks.

Macintosh Operating System (OS) Overview

The Macintosh family of personal computers all have system ROMs that take control of the machine when power is first applied. These ROMs provide capabilities similar to those found in a typical BIOS. However, the Macintosh ROMs also provide higher-level capabilities found in a typical operating system. Referring to Figure 13-29, you can see why we call these "higher-level" capabilities. We do so because in the stack diagram that represents the layers of software, the OS is at a higher level (i.e., higher up in the diagram) than is the BIOS software.

The Macintosh also loads some of its operating system software from disk when the system is initialized. Nonetheless, we don't usually call the Mac OS a DOS because it does much more than just interface with the disk memory systems. The term DOS has the connotation of being a fairly simple OS that provides primarily disk interface services (especially loading other programs from the disk). Technically, nearly all the operating systems in common use today are disk-based in that they have some part of their code read from the disk at boot time.

The Macintosh operating system is also somewhat unusual in that it is implemented in an *object-oriented* style. By object-oriented we mean that the operating system is written as a collection of *objects* rather than just a collection of routines. An object is a collection of routines itself, but constructed in a special manner. Objects hide their internal data from other objects in the system. Objects communicate among themselves by sending each other messages (similar to routines calling other subroutines). The benefits of object-oriented programming include better modularization, which leads to better software reusability. As well, by having objects hide their internal data structures from each other, individual objects can be much simpler.

Polled Versus Event-driven I/O

Most of the program examples we have seen take a traditional flow-of-control approach to the mainline programming. The mainline program executes a sequence of instructions that accomplish a sequence of tasks. If the program wants to deal with I/O devices, then these I/O devices are accessed sequentially, often in a polled manner. Some of the later examples showed interrupt-driven programming. In these examples the mainline program initializes the I/O devices and then sits in a tight loop waiting for interrupts from the devices. The interrupts cause interrupt-service routines to be executed that perform the tasks desired of the system. These latter programs are examples of a simple type of *event-driven* programming. Rather than having the mainline program specify the exact sequence of events that will occur, the sequence is determined by the interrupts that occur. In one case a certain device (e.g., the disk) may interrupt first to say a sector is ready to be read; in another run the keyboard may interrupt first, saying a key has been pressed; and in yet another run the timer may interrupt first. In the Macintosh environment applications are normally written entirely in an event-driven manner. The mainline program first initializes devices (resources in Mac terminology) and then waits in an *event loop* for external (typically user-generated) events to occur. Once an event occurs, it is handled by the appropriate event-handling routine.

USING APPLE MACINTOSH OS CALLS IN YOUR PROGRAMS

As we said previously, an OS is largely a collection of routines that you can call from your programs, similar to the way you call BIOS subroutines. Many disk operating systems and earlier versions of PC DOS require you to construct a *file-control block*, or FCB, in order to access disk files from your programs. The format of a file-control block differs from system to system, but basically the FCB must contain, among other things, the name of the file, the length of the file, the file attribute, and information about the blocks in the file. Version 2.0 and later versions of PC DOS simplify calling DOS file routines by letting you refer to a file with a single 16-bit number. This number is called the *file handle*, or *token*. You simply put the file handle for a file you want to access in a register and call the DOS routine. DOS then constructs the FCB needed to access the file. The question that may occur to you at this point is, How do I know what the file handle is for a file I want to access on a disk? The answer is that to get the file handle for a disk file, you simply call a DOS routine that returns the file handle in a register. You can then pass the file handle to the routine that you want to call to access the file. PC DOS treats external devices such as printers, the keyboard, and the CRT as files for read and write operations. These devices are assigned fixed file handles by DOS.

When using the Macintosh OS to access disk files, handles are also used. First the programmer opens the file and, in return, gets a file handle from the operating system. That handle is then used to tell the OS which file to read and/or write. Finally, the handle is used to tell the OS which file to close.

When interfacing with the Macintosh OS from assembly language, we use methods very similar to those used when calling other assembly language routines. First we load certain registers and memory locations (e.g., the stack) with arguments we wish to pass to the OS. These arguments tell the OS about the details of the operation we would like it to perform for us. In the Mac OS we then cause a CPU TRAP using the vector corresponding to the operation we want to have performed. There are many references which list the traps available when using the Mac OS, but the *Inside Macintosh* (see the bibliography) series from Apple Computer is the recognized standard reference. Figure 13-31 shows an example assembly language program that interfaces to the disk and to the display on a Macintosh.

```
; Program fragment showing assembly language to Write to a file
; using a TRAP to the Operating System.
;
; C equivalent:
;                    WriteFile( refNum, p, num )
;                    int refNum;
;                    char p;
;                    long num;
;                    {
;                        int io;
;                        io = FSWrite( refNum, &num, p);
;                    }
;
        LINK      A6,#$FFFE       ; allocate 2 bytes on the stack
        CLR.W     -(A7)           ; set the word to 0
        MOVE.W    $0008(A6),-(A7) ; pass incoming parameter along (num)
        PEA       $000E(A6)       ; pass along parameter (string pointer, p)
        MOVE.L    $000A(A6),-(A7) ; pass along parameter (refNum)
        JSR       FSWrite         ; call the write routine
        MOVE.W    (A7)+,D0        ; get return value
        MOVE.W    D0,$FFFE(A6)    ; put in local variable (normally to
                                  ;   be tested for WriteFile failure)

        UNLK      A6
        RTS


; FSWrite actually traps to the Operating System
;
FSWrite:
        ST        D1              ; set D1 to 1 (this flags a Write)
        LINK      A6,$FFCE        ; allocate 34 byte on the stack
        LEA       $FFCE(A6),A0
        MOVE.L    $0008(A6),$0020(A0)
        MOVE.W    $0010(A6),$0018(A0)
        MOVEA.L   $000C(A6),A1
        MOVE.L    (A1),$0024(A0)
        CLR.W     $002C(A0)
        CLR.L     $002E(A0)
        TST.B     D1
        BNE.S     x$0006          ; 0012F9FC
        TRAP      $A002           ; Read
        BRA.S     x$0004          ; 0012F9FE
        TRAP      $A003           ; Write
        MOVE.W    D0,$0012(A6)
        MOVEA.L   $000C(A6),A1
        MOVE.L    $0028(A0),(A1)
        UNLK      A6
        MOVEA.L   (A7)+,A1        ; get return address from stack
        ADDA.W    #$000A,A7       ; move up stack pointer
        JMP       (A1)            ; return to calling routine
```

FIGURE 13-31   Instruction sequence fragments to access Macintosh disk and display.

RAM DISKS

Currently available for most microcomputers are programs that allow you to set aside an area of RAM in such a way that it appears to DOS as simply another disk drive. In an IBM PC that has two actual drives, A: and B:, the installed RAM disk becomes C:. You can copy files to and from this RAM disk by name just as you would for any other drive. Here's the point of this. Suppose you are using Wordstar to edit program files. Most of the time when you execute a Wordstar command, the system must go and get the code for that command from the Wordstar system disk and load it into memory before it can execute the command. This means you spend a lot of time waiting. If you load all the Wordstar files into the RAM disk, then they can be accessed much faster because there is no mechanical access time. The advantage of configuring the RAM as a disk drive is that the software then does not have to be altered to work from the RAM.

MAGNETIC HARD-DISK DATA STORAGE

The floppy disks that we discussed in the previous section have the advantage that they are relatively inexpensive and removable. The distance between tracks—and, therefore, the amount of data that can be stored on floppy disks—is limited to a large extent by the flexibility of the disks. The rate at which data can be read off a disk is limited by the fact that a floppy disk can be rotated at only 300 or 360 rpm. To solve these problems, we use a hard-disk system such as that shown in Figure 13-32.

The disks in a hard-disk system are made of a metal alloy, coated on both sides with a magnetic material. Hard disks are more dimensionally stable. This means that they can be spun at higher rpm and that tracks and the bits on the tracks can be put closer together. In most cases the hard disks are permanently fastened in the drive mechanism and sealed in a dust-free package, but some systems do have removable enclosed disks. Common hard-disk sizes are 3.5, 5.25, 8, 10.5, 14, and 20 in. To increase the amount of storage and drive, several disks may be stacked with spacers between. A read/write head is used for each disk surface. Current technology allows 3 to 10 Mbytes per 5.25-in. disk, 5 to 20 Mbytes per 8-in. disk, 30 to 50 Mbytes per 10-in. disk, and 40 to 100 Mbytes per 14-in. disk.

Rigid disks are rotated at 1000 to 3600 rpm. This high speed not only makes it possible to read and write data faster, it creates a thin cushion of air that floats the read/write head 10 μin. off the disk. Unless the head *crashes*, it never touches the recorded area of the disk, so wear is minimized. When data is not being read or written, the head is retracted to a *parking zone*, where no data is recorded. Hard disks must be kept in a dust-free environment, because the diameter of dust and smoke particles may be 10 times the distance the head floats off the disk. If dust does get into a hard disk system, the result will be the same as when a plane does not fly high enough to get over some mountains. The head will crash and perhaps destroy the data stored on the disk.

Hard-disk drives are often referred to as Winchesters. Legend has it that the name came from an early IBM dual-drive unit with a planned storage of 30 Mbytes/drive. The 30-30 configuration apparently reminded someone of the famous rifle, and the name stuck.

In some hard-disk drives, the read/write heads are positioned over the desired track by a stepper motor and a band actuator, as we described for the floppy-disk drive. Other hard-disk drives use a *linear voice coil* mechanism to position the read/write heads. This mechanism uses feedback control, such as we described in Chapter 10, to control the position of what is essentially a linear motor. The feedback system adjusts the position of the head over the desired track until the strength of the read signal is a maximum.

Most hard-disk drives record data bits on a disk track using the MFM method we described in the floppy-disk section of this chapter. As with floppy disks, there is no real standard for the format in which the data is recorded. Most systems format a track in a manner similar to that shown for floppy disks in Figure 13-25. The hard disk drive unit used in the IBM PC XT, for example, used two double-sided hard disks with 306 tracks on each disk surface. On disk drives with more than one recording surface, tracks are often referred to as *cylinders*, because if you mentally connect same-numbered tracks on the two sides of a disk or on different disks, the result is a cylinder. The cylinder number then is the same as the track number. On the PC XT hard disk, each track has 17 sectors with 512 bytes in each sector. This adds up to about 10 Mbytes of data storage. Data is read out at 5 M*bits*/s, which is about 10 times faster than the readout rate for double-density floppy disks.

To interface a hard-disk drive to a microcomputer system, we use a dedicated controller device such as the Intel 82064, which operates similarly to the 8272 floppy-disk controller we described previously in this chapter. An added feature of this controller is the ability to record either CRC words or error-correcting code words with each data sector.

From a software standpoint, writing files to and reading files from a hard disk is very similar to the same operations for a floppy disk. To DOS the hard disk appears for the most part as simply another drive. One difference is that a hard disk is often divided into *partitions*, so that groups of programs can be separated from each other. Partitions function essentially as separate disks. An operating system loaded from one partition, for example, cannot accidentally destruct another operating system stored in another partition.

FIGURE 13-32 Multiple-platter hard-disk memory system.

The only way to get to the other partition in many systems is to reboot the system into that partition.

Another term encountered in connection with hard disks is *file server*. A file server is a hard disk system that has its own CPU and operating system. The unit is usually a major part of a computer network. The function of the file server is to manage the access to and use of files stored on the disk by other systems on the network.

To prevent data loss in the event of a head crash, hard-disk files are backed up on some other medium, such as floppy disks or magnetic tape. The difficulty with using floppy disks for backup is the number of disks required. Backing up a 10-Mbyte hard disk with 360-Kbyte floppies requires 30 disks and considerable time shoving disks in and out. Many systems now use a high-speed magnetic tape system for backup. A typical streaming tape system, as these high-speed systems are often called, can dump or load the entire contents of a 10-Mbyte hard disk to a single tape in a few minutes. The next technology we discuss here, optical disks, can store even larger amounts of data on a single-drive unit than magnetic hard disks can.

OPTICAL-DISK DATA STORAGE

Optical disks are probably familiar to you from their use as laser video disks and compact audio disks. Higher-quality versions of the same type of disk can be used to store very large quantities of digital data for computers. One currently available unit, the Shugart Optimem 1000, for example, stores up to a total of 1 Gbyte (1000 Mbytes) of data on one side of a single 12-in. disk. This amount of storage corresponds to about 400,000 pages of text. In addition to their ability to store large amounts of data, optical disks have the advantages that they are relatively inexpensive, immune to dust, and, in most cases, removable. Also, since data is written on the disk and read off the disk with the light from a tiny laser diode, the read/write head does not have to touch the disk. The laser head is held in position above the disk, so there is no disk wear, and the head cannot crash and destroy the recorded data as it can with magnetic hard disks.

The actual drive and head-positioning mechanisms for optical-disk drives are very similar to those for magnetic hard-disk drives. A feedback system is used to precisely control the speed of the motor that rotates the disk. Some units spin the disk at a constant speed of 700 to 1200 rpm. Other systems, such as those based on the compact audio (CD) format, adjust the rotational speed of the disk so that the track passes under the head with a constant linear velocity. In this case the disk is rotated more slowly when reading outer tracks. Some optical-disk systems record data in concentric tracks as magnetic disks do. The CD disk systems and some other systems record data on a single spiral track as a phonograph record does. A linear voice-coil mechanism with feedback control is used to position the read head precisely over a desired track or section of the track. The head positioning

must be very precise, because the tracks on an optical disk are so close together. The 24-μin.-wide tracks on the Optimem 1000 disks, for example, are only 70 μin. between centers. This spacing allows 40,000 tracks to be put on the disk. For the Optimem 1000 the average access time to a track is 150 ms, and data is read out at 5 Mbits/s. The disk sizes currently available in different systems are 4.72 (the compact audio disk size), 5.25, 12, and 14 in. Optical-disk systems are available in three basic types: read-only, write-once/read, and read/write.

Read-only systems allow only prerecorded disks to be read out. A disk that can only be read from is often referred to as an optical ROM, or OROM. Examples of this type are the 4.7-in. audio compact disks.

Write-once/read systems allow you to write data to a disk, but once the data is written, it cannot be erased or changed. Once data is written, you can read it out as many times as you want. Write-once systems are sometimes referred to by the name DRAW, which stands for *direct read after write*.

Read/write optical-disk systems, as the name implies, allow you to erase recorded data and write new data on a disk. The recording materials and the recording methods are different for these different types of systems.

Disks used for read-only and write-once/read systems are coated with a substance that will be altered when a high-intensity laser beam is focused on it with a lens. The principle here is similar to using a magnifying glass to burn holes in paper, as you may have done at one time or another. In some systems the focused laser light actually produces tiny pits along a track to represent 1s. In other systems a special metal coating is applied to the disk over a plastic polymer layer. When the laser beam is focused on a spot on the metal, heat is transferred to the polymer, causing it to give off a gas. The gas given off produces a microscopic bubble at that spot on the thin metal coating to represent a stored 1. Both of these recording mechanisms are irreversible, so once written, the data can only be read. Data can be read from this type of disk using the same laser diode used for recording, but at reduced power. (A system might, for example, use 25 mW for writing but only 5 mW for reading.) In some systems, such as the one in Figure 13-33, a separate laser is used for reading. The laser beam is focused on the track and a photodiode is used to detect the beam reflected from the data track. A pit or bubble on the track will spread the laser beam light out so that very little of it reaches the photodiode. A spot on the track with no pit or bubble will reflect light to the photodiode. Read-only and write-once systems are less expensive than read/write systems, and for many data-storage applications the inability to erase and rerecord is not a major disadvantage.

For the most common read/write optical-disk system, the disks are coated with an exotic metal alloy that has the required magnetic properties. The read/write head in this type of system has a laser diode and a coil of wire. A current is passed through the coil to produce a magnetic field perpendicular to the disk. At

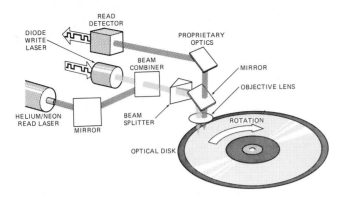

FIGURE 13-33   Read/write mechanism for optical disks.

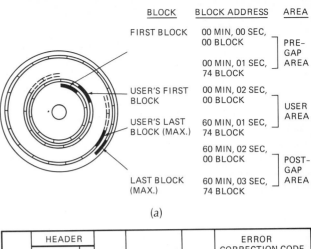

BLOCK	BLOCK ADDRESS	AREA
FIRST BLOCK	00 MIN, 00 SEC, 00 BLOCK	PRE-GAP AREA
	00 MIN, 01 SEC, 74 BLOCK	
USER'S FIRST BLOCK	00 MIN, 02 SEC, 00 BLOCK	USER AREA
USER'S LAST BLOCK (MAX.)	60 MIN, 01 SEC, 74 BLOCK	
	60 MIN, 02 SEC, 00 BLOCK	POST-GAP AREA
LAST BLOCK (MAX.)	60 MIN, 03 SEC, 74 BLOCK	

(a)

SYNC	HEADER				USER DATA	ERROR DETECTION CODE (EDC)	SPACE	ERROR CORRECTION CODE (ECC)	
	BLOCK ADDRESS			MODE				P-PARITY	Q-PARITY
	MINUTE	SECOND	BLOCK						

|←————————————— SCRAMBLED AREA ————————————→|

ONE BLOCK (TOTAL): 2352 BYTES

SYNC:	12 BYTES
HEADER:	4 BYTES
USER DATA:	2 KBYTES (2048 BYTES)
EDC:	4 BYTES
SPACE:	8 BYTES
ECC	
P-PARITY:	172 BYTES (REED SOLOMON CODE)
Q-PARITY:	104 BYTES (REED SOLOMON CODE)

USER DATA

1 BLOCK = 2 KBYTES (2048 BYTES)
1 SECOND = 75 BLOCKS = 150 KBYTES
1 MINUTE = 60 SECONDS = 4500 BLOCKS
1 DISK = 1 HOUR = 60 MINUTES = 270 K BLOCKS

AVERAGE DATA TRANSFER RATE (SEQUENTIAL) = 150 KBYTES/SEC.

(b)

FIGURE 13-34   Industrywide data structure for audio compact disk (CD) optical disks. (a) Disk format. (b) Track format. (*Electronic Engineering Times,* March 25, 1985)

room temperature the applied vertical magnetic field is not strong enough to change the horizontal magnetization present on the disk. To record a 1 at a spot in a data track, a pulse of light from the laser diode is used to heat up that spot. Heating the spot makes it possible for the applied magnetic field to flip the magnetic domains around at that spot and create a tiny vertical magnet. To read data from the disk, polarized laser light is focused on the track. When the polarized light reflects from one of the tiny vertical magnets representing a 1, its plane of polarization is rotated a few degrees. Special optical circuitry can detect this shift and convert the reflections from a data track to a data stream of 1s and 0s. A bit is erased by turning off the vertical magnetic field and heating the spot corresponding to that bit with the laser. When heated with no field present, the magnetism of the spot will flip around in line with the horizontal field on the disk. Other techniques for producing read/write disks are now being researched intensely because of the promise this form of data storage has.

Data is stored on optical disks in several different formats. Figure 13-34 shows the format in which digital data is stored on the 4.7-in. audio compact disks.

As shown in Figure 13-34a, data is stored serially in one long spiral track, starting near the center of the disk. The track is divided into blocks, each containing 2 Kbytes of actual data. Figure 13-34b shows the format for each block. Note that many bytes in each block are used for header, synchronization and error-detecting or error-correcting codes. Extensive error detection and correction is necessary to bring the error rate down to that of magnetic disks. The position of each block on the track is identified with coordinates of minutes, seconds, and block number. As shown in Figure 13-34a, a second represents 75 blocks numbered 0–74. A minute represents 60 seconds, or a total of 4500 blocks. The entire disk represents 1 h, or 270K blocks. Note that although data can be read out from the disk at 150 Kbytes/s (about three times the rate for floppy disks), the disk contains so much data that it takes an hour to read out all the data on the disk. Also note that a large area at the start of the track and a large area at the end of the track are used as gaps. In all, about half of the total area on an optical disk is used for synchronization, identification, and error correction. This is not a big drawback because of the immense amount of data that can be stored on the disk.

Several "jukebox" optical-disk systems, which contain up to 256 disks, are currently available. Typically it takes only a few seconds to access a disk. The potentially low cost of a few cents per megabyte and the hundreds of gigabytes of data storage possible for optical-disk systems may change the way our society transfers and processes information. The contents of a sizable library, for example, could be stored on a few disks. Likewise, the entire financial records of a large company could possibly be kept on a single disk. "Expert" systems for medical diagnosis or legal defense development could use a massive data base stored on disk to do a more thorough analysis. Engineering workstations could use optical disks to store drawings, graphics, or IC-mask layouts. The point here is that optical disks bring directly to your desktop computer a massive data base that previously was available only through a link to large mainframe computers or, in many cases, was not available at all. Perhaps the distribution of data made possible by optical disks will reduce the need for printers, which we discuss in the next section.

PRINTER MECHANISMS

Many different mechanisms and techniques are used to produce printouts, or "hard" copies, of programs and data. This section is intended to give you an overview of the operation and trade-offs of some of the common printer mechanisms. We start with those that mechanically strike the paper in some way.

Formed-Character Impact Printers

Formed-character impact printers function in the same way as typewriters. In fact, the unofficial standard of comparison for print quality is the print produced by the "spinning golf ball" of the IBM Selectric typewriter.

IBM SELECTRIC MECHANISM

To refresh your memory, Figure 13-35 shows how the *IBM Selectric* mechanism works. The entire character set is present as raised type around a sphere. The bottom of the sphere is connected to the drive mechanism. By shifting the ball up or down, rotating it, and tilting it, the character to be printed can be precisely positioned over the desired spot on the paper. When the ball is hit against the ribbon, the letter is printed on the paper. The head is moved across the paper to print a string of characters. Selectric typewriters can be interfaced to computers to do printouts.

The advantages of the Selectric mechanism are the excellent print quality and the fact that the *font* can be changed by simply changing the sphere. (Font is the name used to refer to the character set of a printer.) The disadvantages of this mechanism are that it is mechanically complicated, noisy, and can print only about 14 characters per second (cps).

DAISY-WHEEL PRINTERS

Figure 13-36 shows a drawing of a *daisy-wheel printer* mechanism. Here the raised letters are attached at the ends of spokes of a wheel. To print a letter the wheel is rotated until the desired letter is in position over the paper. A solenoid-driven hammer then hits the "petal" against the ribbon to print the letter.

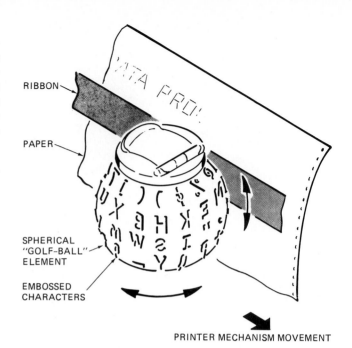

FIGURE 13-35   IBM Selectric printer mechanism. (*Data Products Corporation*)

The advantages of the daisy-wheel mechanism are high print quality, interchangeable fonts, and print speed up to 55 cps. Print quality is not quite as good as that produced by the spinning golf ball.

DRUM, BAND, AND CHAIN PRINTERS

A daisy-wheel produces good-quality print, but for massive data output from large mini- and mainframe computers, 55 cps is not nearly fast enough. For these

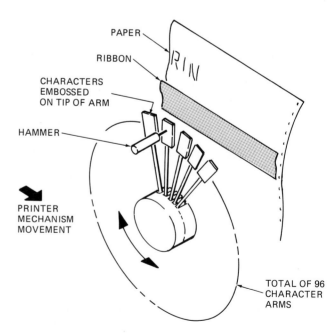

FIGURE 13-36   Daisy-wheel printer mechanism. (*Data Products Corporation*)

systems, *drum, band,* or *chain*-type line printers are used. Figure 13-37 shows a diagram of how a drum type is constructed. A rapidly spinning drum has a complete raised character set constructed around the drum for each character position across the paper. To print characters, magnetically driven hammers in each character position hit the paper and ribbon against the spinning drum. An entire line of characters can be printed during each rotation of the drum. Some drum printers can print 2000 lines/min. If you assume 80-character lines, this corresponds to 2700 cps. However, print lines may be wavy, fonts are not easily changed, and the noise level is high.

In a band printer, several raised character sets are constructed on a metal band, which is rapidly pulled across a line position behind the paper. Each character position has a magnetically driven hammer, such as those shown for the drum printer. When the desired character is under a hammer, the hammer is fired. This hits the ribbon and paper against the letter on the band and prints the character. Some band printers can print up to 2000 lines/min. Print quality is acceptable and fonts are easily changed, but the noise level is high.

Chain printers operate similarly to band printers, except that the character sets are held in a metal or rubber chain and are rotated across the paper along a print line. Another variation of this type of printer is the *train* printer, which rotates metal slugs with characters on them around in a track across the paper. These mechanisms also produce print speeds up to 2000 lines/min and the font is changeable, but they are noisy and the print mechanism tends to wear out.

Dot-Matrix Impact Print Mechanisms

Figure 13-38 shows an *impact-type dot-matrix print head.* Characters are printed as a matrix of dots. Thin print wires driven by solenoids at the rear of the print

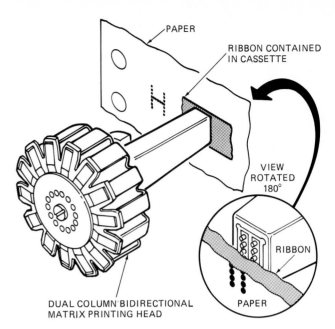

FIGURE 13-38   Impact dot-matrix printer mechanism. (*Data Products Corporation*)

head hit the ribbon against the paper to produce dots. The print wires are arranged in a vertical column so that characters are printed out one dot column at a time as the print head is moved across a line. Early dot-matrix print heads had only 7 print wires, so print quality of these units was not too good. Currently available dot-matrix printers use 9, 14, 18, or even 24 print wires in the print head. Using a large number of print wires and/or printing a line twice, with the dots for the second printing offset slightly from those of the first, produces print that is difficult to tell from that of a Selectric or daisy wheel.

Unlike the formed-character printers, dot-matrix printers can also print graphics. To do this the dot pattern for each column of dots is sent out to the print-head solenoids as the print head is moved across the paper. The principle is similar to the way we produce bit-mapped raster graphics on a CRT screen. By using different color ribbons and making several passes across a line, some dot-matrix impact printers allow you to print color graphics. Most dot-matrix printers now contain one or more microprocessors to control all this.

Print speeds for dot-matrix impact printers range up to 350 cps. Some units allow you to use a low-resolution mode of 200 cps for rough drafts, a medium resolution mode of 100 cps for finished copy, or 50 cps for near-letter-quality printing. A big advantage of dot-matrix impact printers is their ability to change fonts or print graphics under program control.

Dot-Matrix Thermal Print Mechanisms

Most *thermal printers* require paper that has a special heat-sensitive coating. When a spot on this special paper is heated, the spot turns dark. Characters or

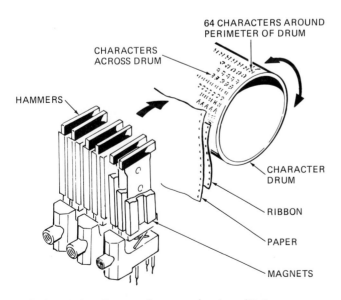

FIGURE 13-37   Drum printer mechanism. (*Data Products Corporation*)

graphics are printed with a matrix of dots. There are two main print-head shapes for producing the dots. For one of these the print head consists of a 5 × 7 or 7 × 9 matrix of tiny heating elements. To print a character the head is moved to a character position and the dot-sized heating elements for the desired character are turned on. After a short time the heating elements are turned off and the head is moved to the next character position. Printing then is done one complete character at a time.

The second print-head configuration for thermal dot-matrix printers has the heating elements along a metal bar that extends across the entire width of the paper. There is a heating element for each dot position on a print line, so this type can print an entire line of dots at a time. The metal bar removes excess heat. Characters and graphics are printed by stepping the paper through the printer one dot line at a time. A few thermal printers can print up to 400 lines/min.

Some of the newer thermal printers have the heat-sensitive material on a ribbon instead of on the paper. When a spot on the ribbon is heated, a dot of ink is transferred to the paper. This approach makes it possible to use standard paper and, by switching ribbons, to print color graphics as well as text.

The main advantage of thermal printers is their low noise. Their main disadvantages are that the special paper or ribbon is expensive, printing carbon copies is not possible, and most thermal printers with good print quality are slow.

Spark Gap Printers

Spark gap printers use a special paper that looks and feels somewhat like aluminum foil. When a spot on the paper is "zapped" with a high voltage, the outer coating at that point is burned off, exposing a dark layer underneath. Characters are printed as a matrix of dots. These printers are often used to print out movie theater tickets because they can print out as many as 2000 cps. Most of the disadvantages relate to the paper, which is expensive, is difficult to handle, is not very durable, and does not produce very good print quality.

Laser and Other Xerographic Printers

Laser printers operate on the same principle as most office copy machines, commonly called "Xerox" machines. The basic approach is first to form an image of the page that is to be printed on a photosensitive drum in the machine. Powdered ink, or "toner," is then applied to the image on the drum. Next the image is electrostatically transferred from the drum to a sheet of paper. Finally, the inked image on the paper is "fused," usually with heat.

In a Xerox machine the image on the photosensitive drum is simply a copy of an original produced with a camera lens. A more computer-compatible method of producing an image on the photosensitive drum is with a laser. Turning a laser on and off as it is swept back and forth across the drum produces an image in about the same way that an image is produced on a raster-scan CRT. Figure 13-39 shows a diagram of how this is done. The rotating mirror sweeps the laser beam across the rotating drum. A modulator controlled by a microcomputer turns the laser beam on or off to produce dots. After the image is inked and transferred to the paper, the drum is cleaned and is ready for the next page.

An alternative to the photosensitive drum is a magnetically sensitive drum used in some units. An image is written on this magnetic drum in the same way that data is recorded on magnetic disks. Magnetized ink particles are then applied to the drum, transferred to the paper, and fused.

Laser and other xerographic printers have the advantages of very high print quality (text and graphics can easily be printed on the same page), very high print speeds (up to 20,000 lines/min), ability to use standard paper, and relatively quiet operation. They have the disadvantages that the copies "look like copies," the machines are very expensive, and the machines require a lot of maintenance.

Ink-Jet Printers

Still another type of printer that uses a dot-matrix approach to produce text and graphics is the *ink-jet printer*. Early ink-jet printers used a pump and a tiny nozzle to send out a continuous stream of tiny ink globules. These ink globules were passed through an electric field, which left them with an electrical charge. The stream of charged ink globules was then electrostatically deflected to produce characters on the paper in the same way that the electron beam is deflected to produce an image on a CRT screen. Excess ink was

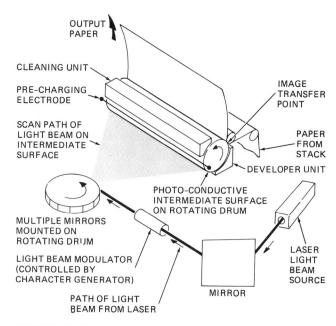

FIGURE 13-39 Laser printer mechanism. (*Data Products Corporation*)

deflected to a gutter and returned to the ink reservoir. These ink-jet printers were relatively quiet, and some of these electrostatically deflected ink-jet printers could print up to 45,000 lines/min. Several disadvantages, however, prevented them from being used more widely. They tended to be messy and difficult to keep working well. Print quality at high speeds was poor and multiple copies were not possible.

Newer ink-jet printers use a variety of approaches to solve these problems. Some, such as the HP Thinkjet, use ink cartridges that contain a column of tiny heaters. When one of these tiny heaters is pulsed on, it caused a drop of ink to explode onto the paper. Others such as the IBM Quietwriter, for example, use an electric current to explode microscopic ink bubbles from a special ribbon directly onto the paper. These last two approaches are really hybrids of thermal and ink-jet technologies. They can produce near-letter-quality print at speeds comparable to those of slower dot-matrix impact printers. A disadvantage of some ink-jet printers is that they require special paper for best results.

SPEECH SYNTHESIS AND RECOGNITION WITH A COMPUTER

In a great many cases it is very convenient for a computer to communicate verbally with a user. Some examples of the use of computer-created speech are talking games, talking cash registers, and text-to-speech machines used by blind people. Other examples are medical monitor systems that give verbal warnings and directions when some emergency condition exists. This use demonstrates some of the major advantages of speech readout. The verbal signal attracts more attention than a simple alarm, and the user does not have to search through a series of readouts to determine the problem.

Adding speech-recognition circuitry to a computer so that it can interpret verbal commands from a user also makes the computer much easier to use. The pilot of a rocket ship or space shuttle, for example, can operate some controls verbally while operating other controls manually. (It probably won't be too long before we eliminate the verbal-manual link and control the whole ship directly from the brain, but that is another story, perhaps in the next book.) Voice-entry systems are also useful for handicapped programmers and other computer users. We first describe for you the different methods used to create speech with a computer and then describe speech-recognition methods.

Speech-Synthesis Methods

There are several common methods of producing speech from a computer. The trade-offs between the different methods are speech quality and the number of bits that must be stored or sent for each word. In other words, the higher the speech quality you want, the more bits you have to store in memory to represent

each word and the faster you have to send bits to the synthesizer circuitry. All the common methods of speech synthesis fall into two general categories: waveform modification and direct digitization. In order to explain how the waveform-modification approaches work, we need to talk briefly about how humans produce sounds.

WAVEFORM-MODIFICATION SPEECH SYNTHESIS

Some sounds, called *voiced sounds*, are produced by vibration of the vocal cords as air passes from the lungs. The frequency of vibration, or *pitch*, the position of the tongue, the shape of the mouth, and the position of the lips determine the actual sound produced. The vowels A and E, when spoken, are examples of voiced sounds. Another type of sound called unvoiced sounds in speech is produced by modifying the position of the tongue and the shape of the mouth as a constant stream of air comes from the lungs. Speaking the letter S is an example of this type of sound. A third type of sound, the nasal sounds called *fricatives*, consists of a mixture of voiced and unvoiced sounds. In electronic terms, then, the human vocal system consists of a variable-frequency signal generator as the source for voiced sounds, a "white" noise signal source for unvoiced sounds, and a series of filters that modify the outputs from the two signal sources to produce the desired sounds. Figure 13-40 shows this in block diagram form.

The three main approaches to implementing this model electronically are *linear predictive coding*, or LPC, *formant*, and *phoneme*. These methods differ mostly in the type of filter used and in how often the filter characteristics are updated.

LPC synthesizers, such as that in the Texas Instruments Speak and Spell, use a digital filter such as we described in Chapter 10 to modify the signals from a pulse and a white noise source. For this type of filter the parameters that must be sent from the microcomputer are the coefficients for the filter and the pitch for the pulse source. Remember from the discussion in Chapter 10 that for a digital filter, the current output value is computed, or "predicted," as the sum of the current input value and portions of previous input values. A high-quality LPC synthesizer may require as many as 16 Kbits/s. One difficulty with most LPC devices has been that complex computer equipment and programs had to be used to analyze a spoken word and determine the series of coefficients required to

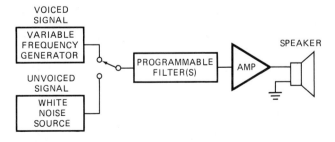

FIGURE 13-40   Electronic model of human vocal track.

produce that word. Usually the IC manufacturer did this for a fee and produced a ROM with the parameters for a particular vocabulary. The General Instruments SP1000, however, has now simplified this process somewhat.

The SP1000 can function as an LPC speech processor, an LPC speech recognizer, and an LPC speech synthesizer under the control of a microcomputer. In learn mode the device generates LPC coefficients for spoken words. The microcomputer reads these coefficients from the SP1000 and stores them in memory. In recognition mode the SP1000 is used to generate the coefficients for the unknown word. These coefficients are then compared with those of known words in memory to identify the unknown word. For use as a speech synthesizer the SP1000 is switched to talk mode, and the coefficients for the desired word are sent to it by the microcomputer. Consult the General Instruments data sheet for more information about this interesting device.

The formant approach uses several resonant, or *formant*, filters to massage the signals from a variable-frequency signal source and a white noise source. Figure 13-41 shows how the frequencies of these formant filters might be arranged for a male and for a female voice. For this type of system the parameters that must be sent from the computer are the pitch of the variable frequency signal, the center frequency for each formant filter, and the bandwidth of each formant filter. The data rate for direct formant synthesis is only about 1 Kbit/s, but the parameters must again be determined with complex equipment. It is then not easy to develop a custom vocabulary for a specific application. A phoneme approach solves this problem and requires a still-lower data rate at the expense of lower speech quality.

Phonemes are fragments of words. An example of a phoneme speech synthesizer is the Votrax SC-01, which we described in Chapter 9. In the case of the SC-01 you get it to sound one of its 64 phonemes by sending it a 6-bit binary code from a computer port. When the SC-01 finishes sending the phoneme, it asserts a REQUEST signal, which indicates that it is ready for the next phoneme. Words are produced by sending a series of phoneme codes. In addition to the 6-bit phoneme code, an additional 2 bits can be sent to specify rising, falling, or flat inflection for each phoneme. Inside the SC-01, the 6-bit phoneme code is

used to control the characteristics of some formant filters, as described in the previous paragraph. Since only one code is sent out for a relatively long period of speech, the required bit rate is only about 70 bits/s. However, the long period between codes gives less control over waveform details and, therefore, sound quality. A phoneme synthesizer has a mechanical sound. One big advantage of phoneme synthesizers is that you can make up any message you want by simply putting together a sequence of phoneme codes. Another example of a phoneme synthesizer is the SSI263 from Silicon Systems, Inc.

DIRECT-DIGITIZATION SPEECH SYNTHESIS

The *direct-digitization* method produces the highest-quality speech because it is essentially just a playback of digitally recorded speech. To start, the word you want the computer to speak is spoken clearly into a microphone. The output voltage from the microphone is amplified and applied to the input of perhaps a 12-bit A/D converter. One approach at this point might be simply to store the A/D samples for the word in a ROM and read the values out to a D/A converter when you want the computer to speak the word. The difficulty with this approach is that if the samples are taken often enough to produce good speech quality, a lot of memory is required to store the samples for a word. To reduce the amount of memory required, several speech-compression algorithms are used. These algorithms are too complex to discuss here, but the basic principles involve storing repeated waveforms only once, taking advantage of symmetry in waveforms, and not storing values for silent periods. To further reduce the memory required for direct digital speech, some systems use differential, or *delta*, modulation. In these systems only a 3-bit or 4-bit code, representing how much a sample has changed from the last sample, is stored in memory instead of the complete 12-bit value. Since audio signals change slowly, this is very acceptable. Even with compression, however, direct digital speech requires considerable memory and a bit rate as high as 64 Kbits/s. The OKI Semiconductor MSM5218RS is an example of a device that functions in this way. In record mode it can be used with an A/D converter to produce the differential codes for a spoken word. In play mode the device produces speech from applied codes using an internal 10-bit D/A converter. Another example of a direct digital system is the National Semiconductor *Digitalker*. For further information, consult the data sheets for these devices.

Speech Recognition

Speech recognition is considerably more difficult than speech synthesis. The process is similar to trying to recognize human faces with a computer vision system. The first step in speech recognition is to train the system, or, in other words, produce templates for each of the words that the system needs to recognize and store these templates in memory. To produce a template for a word, the intended user speaks the word

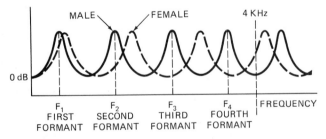

FIGURE 13-41   Filter responses for formant speech synthesizer.

several times into a microphone connected to the system. The system then determines several parameters, or *features*, for each repetition of the word and averages them to produce the actual template.

Different systems extract different parameters to form the template. Figure 13-42 shows a block diagram for one of the most common methods. This method uses a set of formant filters with their center frequencies adjusted to match those of the average speaker. The output amplitudes of these formant filters are averaged to produce a signal proportional to the energy in each of the frequency bands. Also used are one or more zero-crossing detectors to give basic frequency information. The pulse train from the zero-crossing detector is converted to a proportional voltage so it can be digitized along with the outputs from the formant averagers.

Now, when a word is spoken, samples of each of the features are taken and digitized at evenly spaced intervals of 10 to 20 ms during the duration of the word. The features are stored in memory. If this is a training run, this set of samples is averaged with others to form the template for the word. If this is a recognition run, this set of features is compared with the templates stored in memory. The best match is assumed to be the correct word. Currently none of the available voice-recognition systems are 100 percent accurate. The most accurate systems are those that work only with the speaker who trained them and the systems that work only with isolated words. However, considerable progress is being made in this area. The VPC 2000 from VOTAN Inc., for example, is a speech-recognition unit that plugs into IBM PC-compatible computers and can recognize continuous phrases. It also has a built-in voice-activated telephone dialing and answering service. Another PC-compatible unit, the VocaLink from Interstate Voice Products, permits the programming of up to 240 spoken commands to control standard PC software such as word processors and business programs. Perhaps the HAL 9000 is not too far away.

CHECKLIST OF IMPORTANT TERMS AND CONCEPTS IN THIS CHAPTER

If there are terms and concepts in this list you do not remember, use the index to find them in the chapter.

CRT operation
    Raster display
    Field
    Interlaced scanning
    Frame

Video monitor

CRT terminal

Horizontal and vertical sync pulses

Composite video

Character generator

Display refresh RAM
    Dot, undot
    Dot clock
    Overscan

Display page

Attribute code

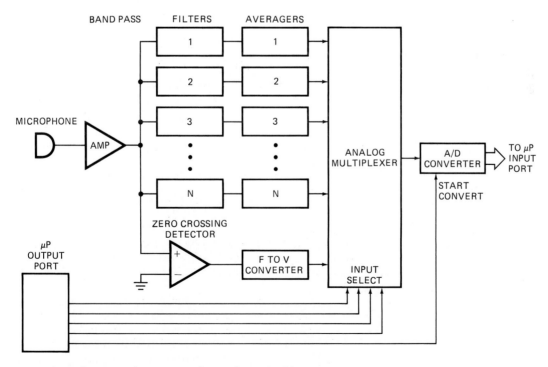

FIGURE 13-42 Block diagram of one type of speech-recognition system.

Bit-mapped raster-scan CRT graphics display
    Picture element (pixel, pel)

Mouse

Composite color monitor

Luminance signal

Chroma signal

Vector-scan CRT displays

Alphanumeric/graphics LCD displays

Computer vision
    Ultrasonic vision
    Video cameras; videcon
    CCD cameras
    OPTICRAM cameras

Floppy disks
    Hard and soft sectoring
    Index holes
    Index, ID, and data fields
    Gaps
    Address marks

Checksums

Cyclic redundancy character

Single and double density

FM and MFM recording

File allocation table

Hierarchical file structure

Root directory and subdirectory

File-control block

File handle

ASCIIZ

RAM disk

Hard-disk systems
    Cylinders
    Partitions

Optical disk systems
    OROM
    DRAW

Printer mechanisms
    IBM Selectric
    Daisy wheel
    Drum, band, and chain
    Dot-matrix impact and thermal
    Spark gap
    Laser and xerographic
    Ink-jet

Speech synthesis
    Pitch, unvoiced sounds, and fricatives
    Linear predictive coding, formant, phoneme
    Direct digitization

Speech recognition

REVIEW QUESTIONS AND PROBLEMS

1. With the help of a simple drawing, explain how a noninterlaced raster is produced on a CRT.

2. Use a simple drawing to help you describe how a display of the letter X is produced on a noninterlaced raster-scan CRT display.

3. Refer to Figure 13-5 to help you answer the following questions.
    a. What is the purpose of the RAM in this circuit?
    b. At what points in displaying a frame do the address inputs of this RAM get changed?
    c. At what points in displaying a frame do the R0–R3 address inputs of the character generator ROM get changed?
    d. What is the purpose of the shift register on the output of the character-generator ROM?
    e. Why is one input of the shift register tied to ground?
    f. At what points in displaying a frame are horizontal sync pulses produced?
    g. At what points in displaying a frame are vertical sync pulses produced?
    h. List the three components of a composite video signal.

4. A CRT display is designed to display 24 character rows with 72 characters in each row. The system uses a 7×9 character generator in a 9×12 dot matrix. Assuming a 60-Hz noninterlaced frame rate, 3 additional character times for horizontal overscan, and 120 additional scan lines for vertical overscan, find the following values.
    a. Total number of character times per row
    b. Total number of scan lines per frame
    c. Horizontal frequency (lines per second)
    d. Dot clock frequency (dots per second)
    e. Minimum bandwidth required for video amplifier
    f. Time between RAM accesses

5. The IBM PC color adapter board uses a 14-MHz dot clock frequency, a 15.750-kHz horizontal scan rate, and a 60-Hz frame rate. Characters are produced in an 8×8 dot matrix. There are 80 characters per row and 25 rows per frame.
    a. What is the total number of dot times per scan line?
    b. How many dot times then are left for horizontal overscan?
    c. What is the total number of scan lines per frame, including overscan?
    d. How many scan lines then are left for vertical overscan?

6. Describe how a DMA controller is used with a CRT controller such as the 8275 to keep a CRT display refreshed.

7. How does the CRT display system in Figure 13-7 arbitrate the dispute that occurs when the 6845 CRT controller and the microprocessor both want to access the display RAM at the same time?

8. Write a program that uses the IBM BIOS procedures to read a string of characters entered from the keyboard, put the key codes in a buffer in memory, and display the characters for the pressed keys on the CRT.

9. How much memory is required to store the pixel data for a bit-mapped display of 640 × 480?

10. What is the difference between a CRT monitor and a CRT terminal?

11. Describe how three electron beams are used to produce all possible colors on a color CRT screen.

12. How much memory is required to store the pixel data for a 512 × 512 display, where each pixel can be any one of 16 colors?

13. Describe how a composite color video signal is produced from the red, blue, green, and sync signals. Include in your answer the function of the 3.579545-MHz signal.

14. Describe how a vector graphics CRT display system produces a display of a triangle on the screen. What is the major problem with the vector approach to CRT graphics?

15. The inputs of an 8-bit D/A converter are connected to port $BF14 of a microcomputer and the output of the D/A converter is connected to the X axis of an oscilloscope. The inputs of another 8-bit D/A converter are connected to port $BF18 of a microcomputer, and the output of this D/A is connected to the Y axis of the oscilloscope. Write a program that uses these D/A converters to display a square on the screen of the oscilloscope. Then modify the program so that the square enlarges after each 100 refreshes.

16. Describe the methods used by CCD and OPTI-CRAM cameras to produce visual images that can be stored in computer memory.

17. How is the read/write head for a disk drive moved into position over a specified track?

18. What additional information besides the actual data is recorded on each track of a soft-sectored floppy disk? Describe the purpose of the CRC bytes included with each block of data recorded on the disk.

19. Why must clock bits be recorded along with data bits on floppy disks? Under what conditions will a clock pulse be inserted in a bit cell when recording data on a disk in MFM format?

20. List the major types of information contained in the directory of a magnetic disk formatted by a DOS. If a data file requires several clusters on a disk, how does a DOS keep track of where the pieces of the file are located?

21. What is meant by the term *hierarchical file structure?* What is a major advantage of this type of file structure?

22. Write a program that uses the Apple Macintosh function calls to read in a string containing your name from the keyboard to a buffer in memory and sends the string to a printer. Remember to use the exit function call to return to the OS at the end of the program.

23. Explain why magnetic hard disks can store much more data than floppy disks and why data can be written or read out much faster from hard disks.

24. Why must hard disks be operated in a dust-free environment?

25. Two terms often encountered in hard-disk system manuals are *cylinder* and *partition*. Define each and tell the difference between these two terms.

26. Describe how stored data is read from optical disks. What advantages does this readout method have over that used for hard magnetic disks?

27. Describe how data bits are recorded in magneto-optic read/write optical-disk systems and in DRAW optical-disk systems.

28. A human brain can store about 10^{10} bits of data and has an access time in the order of about a second. Compare these parameters with those of an optical-disk system such as the Optimem 1000.

29. Describe the operation of the print mechanism for each of the following types of printer. Also give an advantage and a disadvantage for each type.
    a. Spinning golf ball
    b. Daisy-wheel
    c. Drum
    d. Chain or band
    e. Dot-matrix
    f. Thermal
    g. Laser
    h. Ink-jet

30. Draw a block diagram of a waveform-modification type of speech synthesizer. Describe the operation of the LPC, formant, and phoneme types of speech synthesizer that use this model.

31. What are the major differences between an LPC speech synthesizer and a formant speech synthesizer?

32. Describe the operation of a direct-digitization speech synthesizer. What is the major advantage and the major disadvantage of this type?

CHAPTER 14

Data Communication and Networks

In Chapter 2 we discussed "computerizing" an electronics factory. This means that computers are integrated into all the operations of the factory and that each person in the company has access to a computer. The company may have a large centrally located mainframe computer, several minicomputers that serve groups of users, individual computer engineering workstations, and portable computers spread around the world with the salespeople. In order for all these computers to work together, they must be able to communicate with each other in an organized manner. In this chapter we show you some of the devices, signal standards, and systems used for communication with and between computers.

In the first section of the chapter we discuss the hardware and low-level software required to interface microcomputer buses to serial data communication lines. Then we discuss how the serial data signals are transmitted from one place to another. This discussion includes RS-232C-type standards, modems, and fiber-optic cables. The next section of the chapter shows you how to write programs that perform simple serial data communication. As an example, in this section we use a program that allows you to download programs from a Macintosh® computer to an URDA® MDS. In the final sections of the chapter we discuss the operation of several common computer networks.

OBJECTIVES

At the end of this chapter, you should be able to

1. Show and describe the meaning of the bits in the format used for sending asynchronous serial data.

2. Initialize a common UART for transmitting serial data in a specified format.

3. Describe several voltage, current, and light (fiber-optic) signal methods used to transmit serial data.

4. Describe the function of the major signals in the RS-232C standard.

5. Show how to connect RS-232C equipment directly or with a "null-modem" connection.

6. Describe the different types of modulation commonly used by modems.

7. Show the formats for a byte-oriented protocol and for a bit-oriented protocol used in synchronous serial data transmission.

8. Draw diagrams to show the common computer network topologies.

9. Describe the operation of an Ethernet system.

10. Describe the operation of a token-passing ring system.

11. Show the major signal groups for the GPIB (IEEE 488) bus, describe how bus control is managed, and indicate how data is transferred on a handshake basis for the GPIB.

INTRODUCTION TO ASYNCHRONOUS SERIAL DATA COMMUNICATION

Overview

Serial data communication is a somewhat difficult subject to approach because you need pieces of information from several different topics in order for each part of the subject to really make sense. To make this approach easier, we first give an overview of how all the pieces fit together and then describe the details of each piece later in specific sections. A problem with this subject is that it contains a great many terms and acronyms. To help you absorb all these, you may want to make a glossary of terms as you read the chapter.

Within a microcomputer, data is transferred in parallel, because that is the fastest way to do it. For transferring data over long distances, however, parallel data transmission requires too many wires. Therefore, data to be sent long distances is usually converted from parallel form to serial form so that it can be sent on a single wire or pair of wires. Serial data received from a distant source is converted to parallel form so that it can easily be transferred on the microcomputer buses. Three terms often encountered in literature on serial data systems are *simplex, half-duplex,* and *full-duplex.* A simplex data line can transmit data only in one direction. An earthquake sensor sending data back from Mount St. Helens and a commercial radio station are examples of simplex transmission. Half-duplex transmission means that communication can take place in either direction between two systems but can occur in only one direction at a time. An example of half-duplex transmission is a two-way radio system, where one user always listens while the other talks because the receiver circuitry is turned off during transmit. The term full-duplex means that each system can send and receive data at the same time. A normal phone conversation is an example of a full-duplex operation.

Serial data can be sent synchronously or asynchronously. For synchronous transmission, data is sent in blocks at a constant rate. The start and end of a block are identified with specific bytes or bit patterns. In a later section of the chapter we discuss synchronous data transmission in detail. For asynchronous transmission, each data character has a bit that identifies its start and 1 or 2 bits that identify its end. Since each character is individually identified, characters can be sent at any time (asynchronously), in the same way that a person types on a keyboard.

Figure 14-1 shows the bit format often used for transmitting asynchronous serial data. When no data is being sent, the signal line is in a constant high, or marking, state. The beginning of a data character is indicated by the line going low for 1 bit time. This bit is called a start bit. The data bits are then sent out on the line one after the other. Note that the least significant bit is sent out first. Depending on the system, the data word may consist of 5, 6, 7, or 8 bits. Following the data bits is a parity bit, which—as we explained in Chapter 11—is used to check for errors in received data. Some systems do not insert or look for a parity bit. After the data bits and the parity bit, the signal line is returned high for at least 1 bit time to identify the end of the character. This always-high bit is referred to as a stop bit. Some older systems use 2 stop bits. For future reference note that the efficiency of this format is low, because 10 or 11 bit times are required to transmit a 7-bit data word such as an ASCII character.

The term *baud rate* is used to indicate the rate at which serial data is being transferred. Baud rate is defined as 1/(the time between signal transitions). If the signal is changing every 3.33 ms, for example, the baud rate is 1/(3.33 ms) = 1/(0.00333 s), or 300 Bd. There is an almost unavoidable, but incorrect, tendency to refer to this as 300 bits/s. In some cases, the two do correspond, but in other cases 2 or more actual data bits are encoded in one signal transition, so data bits per second and baud do not correspond. Common baud rates are 300, 600, 1200, 2400, 4800, 9600, and 19,200.

To interface a microcomputer with serial data lines, the data must be converted to and from serial form. A parallel in, serial out shift register and a serial in, parallel out shift register can be used to do this. For some cases of serial data transfer, handshaking circuitry is also needed to make sure that a transmitter does not send data faster than it can be read in by the receiving system. Several programmable LSI devices are available that contain most of the circuitry needed for serial communication. A device such as the National INS8250, which can only do asynchronous communication, is often referred to as a *universal asynchronous receiver-transmitter,* or UART. A device such as the Intel 8251A, which can be programmed to do either asynchronous or synchronous communication, is often called a *universal synchronous-asynchronous receiver-transmitter,* or USART.

Once the data is converted to serial form, it must in some way be sent from the transmitting UART to the receiving UART. There are several ways in which serial data is commonly sent. One method is to use a current to represent a 1 in the signal line and no current to represent a 0. We discuss this current-loop approach in a later section. Another approach is to add line drivers on the output of the UART to produce a sturdy voltage signal. The range of each of these methods, however, is limited to a few thousand feet.

For sending serial data over long distances, the standard telephone system is a convenient path, because the wiring and connections are already in place. Standard phone lines, often referred to as switched lines because any two points can be connected together through a series of switches, have a bandwidth of only about 300 to 3000 Hz. Therefore, for several reasons, digital signals of the form shown in Figure 14-1 cannot be sent directly over standard phone lines.

NOTE: Phone lines capable of carrying digital data directly can be leased, but these are somewhat costly and are limited to the specific destination of the line.)

The solution to this problem is to convert the digital

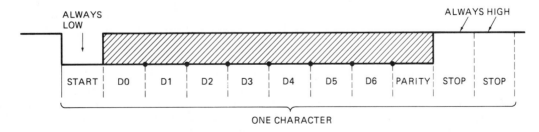

FIGURE 14-1 Bit format used for sending asynchronous serial data.

signals to audio-frequency tones, which are in the frequency range that the phone lines can transmit. The device used to do this conversion and to convert transmitted tones back to digital information is called a *modem.* The term is a contraction of modulator-demodulator. In a later section of this chapter we discuss the operation of some common types of modems. For now, look at Figure 14-2, which shows how two modems can be connected to allow a remote terminal to communicate with a distant mainframe computer over a phone line. Modems and other equipment used to send serial data over long distances are known as *data communication equipment,* or DCE. The terminals and computers that are sending or receiving the serial data are referred to as *data terminal equipment,* or DTE.

The data and handshake signal names shown in Figure 14-2 are part of a serial data communications standard called RS-232C, which we discuss in detail in a later section. For now you just need enough of an overview of these signals so that the initialization of the 8251A UART in the next section makes sense to you. Note the direction arrowheads on each of these signals. Here is a sequence of signals that might occur when a user at a terminal wants to send some data to the computer.

After the terminal power is turned on and the terminal runs any self-checks, it asserts the data-terminal-ready (DTR) signal to tell the modem it is ready. When it is powered up and ready to transmit or receive data, the modem will assert the data-set-ready (DSR) signal to the terminal. Under manual control or terminal control, the modem then dials up the computer.

If the computer is available, it will send back a specified tone. When the terminal has a character actually ready to send, it will assert a request-to-send (RTS) signal to the modem. The modem will then assert its carrier-detect (CD) signal to the terminal to indicate that it has established contact with the computer.

When the modem is fully ready to transmit data, it asserts the clear-to-send (CTS) signal back to the terminal. The terminal then sends serial data characters to the modem. When the terminal has sent all the characters it needs to, it makes its RTS signal high. This causes the modem to unassert its CTS signal and stop transmitting. A similar handshake occurs between the modem and the computer at the other end of the data link. The important point at this time is that a set of handshake signals is defined for transferring serial data to and from a modem.

Now that you have an overview of asynchronous serial data, modems, and handshaking, we describe the operation of a device commonly used to interface a microcomputer to a modem or other device that requires serial data.

An Example USART—The Intel 8251A

SYSTEM CONNECTIONS AND SIGNALS

As we showed you in Chapter 7, an 8251A is used as a serial port. The 8251A is used on the IBM PC synchronous communication board and on many other boards, so we chose to use it as an example here.

Figure 14-3 shows a block diagram and the pin descriptions for the 8251A. Keep a copy of this handy as you work your way through the following discussion.

The eight parallel lines, D7–D0, are used to connect to the host system's data bus so that data words and control/status words can be transferred to and from the device. The chip select (CS) input is connected to an address decoder so the device is enabled when addressed. The 8251A has two internal addresses, a control address, which is selected when the C/D input is high, and a data address, which is selected when the C/D input is low. The RESET, RD, and WR lines are connected to the system signals with the same names. The clock input of the 8251A is usually connected to a signal derived from the system clock to synchronize the internal operations of the USART with the processor timing.

The signal labeled TxD on the upper right corner of the 8251A block diagram is the actual serial data output. The pin labeled RxD is the serial data input. Additional circuitry may be connected to the TxD pin and the RxD to convert the TTL logic levels to and from the 8251A to current-loop or RS-232C signals. We discuss current-loop and RS-232C signal standards a little later.

The shift registers in the USART require clocks to shift the serial data in and out. TxC is the transmit shift-register clock input, and RxC is the receive shift-register clock input. Usually these two inputs are tied together so they are driven by the same signal. The frequency of the signal you choose for TxC and RxC must be 1, 16, or 64 times the transmit and receive baud rate, depending on the mode in which the 8251A is initialized. Using a clock frequency higher than the baud rate allows the receive shift register to be clocked

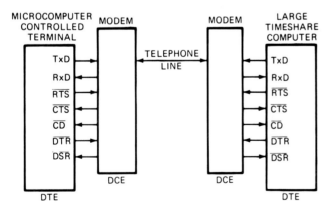

DTE = DATA TERMINAL EQUIPMENT
DCE = DATA COMMUNICATION EQUIPMENT

FIGURE 14-2 Digital data transmission using modems and standard phone lines.

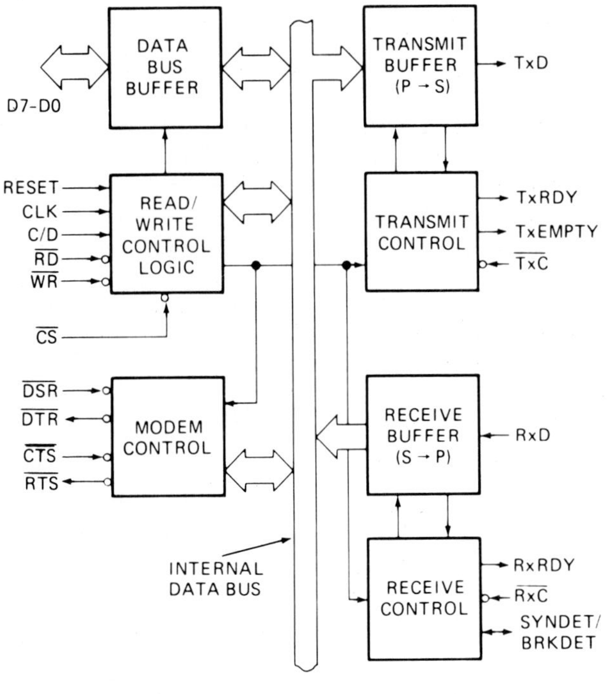

Pin Name	Pin Function
D7–D0	Data bus (8 bits)
C/$\overline{D}$	Control or data is to be written or read
$\overline{RD}$	Read data command
$\overline{WR}$	Write data or control command
$\overline{CS}$	Chip select
CLK	Clock pulse (TTL)
RESET	Reset
$\overline{TxC}$	Transmitter clock
TxD	Transmitter data
$\overline{RxC}$	Receiver clock
RxD	Receiver data
RxRDY	Receiver ready (has character for CPU)
TxRDY	Transmitter ready (ready for char. from CPU)
$\overline{DSR}$	Data set ready
$\overline{DTR}$	Data terminal ready
SYNDET/BD	Sync detect/break detect
$\overline{RTS}$	Request to send data
$\overline{CTS}$	Clear to send data
TxEMPTY	Transmitter empty
V_{cc}	+5-V supply
GND	Ground

(b)

FIGURE 14-3   Block diagram and pin descriptions for the Intel 8251A USART.
(a) Block diagram. (b) Pin descriptions.

at the center of the bit times rather than at leading edges. This reduces the chance of signal noise at the start of the bit time causing a read error.

The 8251A is double-buffered. This means that one character can be loaded into a holding buffer while another character is being shifted out of the actual transmit shift register. The TxRDY output from the 8251A will go high when the holding buffer is empty and another character can be sent from the CPU. The TxEMPTY pin on the 8251A will go high when both the holding buffer and the transmit shift register are empty. The RxRDY pin of the 8251A will go high when a character has been shifted into the receiver buffer and is ready to be read out by the CPU. Incidentally, if a character is not read out before another character is shifted in, the first character will be overwritten and lost.

The sync-detect/break-detect (SYNDET/BD) pin has two uses. When the device is operating in asynchronous mode, in which we are interested here, this pin will go high if the serial data input line, RxD, stays low for more than 2 character times. This signal then indicates an intentional break in data transmission or a break in the signal line. When programmed for synchronous data transmission, this pin will go high when the 8251A finds a specified sync character or characters in the incoming string of data bits.

The four signals connected to the box labeled MODEM CONTROL in the 8251A block diagram are handshake signals, which we described in the previous section.

INITIALIZING AN 8251A

To initialize an 8251A you must first send a mode word and then a command word to the control register address for the device. Figure 14-4 shows the formats for these words and for the 8251A status word, which is read from the same address. Baud rate factor, specified by the two least significant bits of the mode word, is the ratio between the clock signal applied to the TxC-RxC inputs and the desired baud rate. For example, if you want to use a TxC of 19,200 Hz and transmit data at 1200 Bd, the baud rate factor is 19,200/1200,

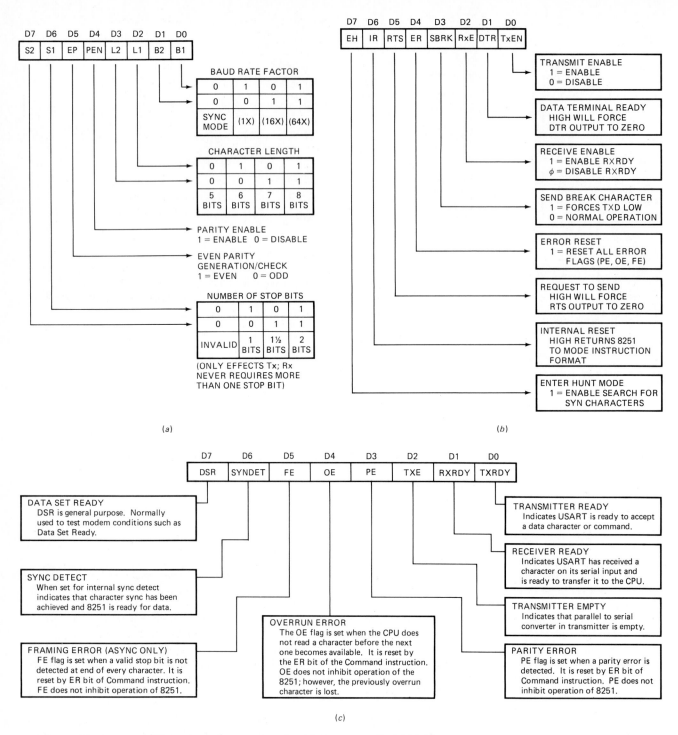

FIGURE 14-4 Formats of 8251A mode, command, and status words. (a) Mode word. (b) Command word. (c) Status word. (Intel Corp.)

or 16. If bits D0 and D1 are both made 0s, the 8251A is programmed for synchronous data transfer. In this case the baud rate will be the same as the applied TxC and RxC. The other three combinations for these 2 bits represent asynchronous transfer. A baud rate factor of 1 can be used for asynchronous transfer only if the transmitting system and the receiving system both use the same TxC and RxC. The character length specified by bits D2 and D3 in the mode word includes only the actual data bits, not the start bit, parity bit, or stop bit(s). If parity is disabled, no parity bit is inserted in the transmitted bit string. If the 8251A is programmed for 5, 6, or 7 data bits, the extra bits in the data character byte read from the device will be 0s.

After you send a mode word to an 8251A, you must then send it a command word. A 1 in the least significant bit of the command word enables the transmitter section of the 8251A and the TxRDY output. When enabled, the 8251A TxRDY output will be asserted high if the CTS input has been asserted low and the transmitter holding buffer is ready for another character from the CPU. The TxRDY signal can be connected to an interrupt input on the CPU or an 8259A, so characters to be transmitted can be sent to the 8251A on an interrupt basis. When a character is written to the 8251A data address, the TxRDY signal will go low and remain low until the holding buffer is again ready for another character. Putting a 1 in bit D1 of the command word will cause the DTR output of the 8251A to be asserted low. As we explained before, this signal is used to tell a modem that a terminal or computer is operational. A 1 in bit D2 of the command word enables the RxRDY output pin of the 8251A. If enabled, the RxRDY pin will go high when the 8251A has a character in its receiver buffer ready to be read. This signal can be connected to an interrupt input so that characters can be read in on an interrupt basis. The RxRDY output is reset when a character is read from the 8251A.

Putting a 1 in bit D3 of the command word causes the 8251A to output a character of all 0s, which is called a *break character*. A break character is sometimes used to indicate the end of a block of transmitted data. Sending a command word with a 1 in bit D4 causes the 8251A to reset the parity, overrun, and framing error flags in the 8251A status register. The meanings of these flags are explained in Figure 14-4c. A 1 in bit D5 of the command word will cause the 8251A to assert its RTS output low. This signal, remember, is sent to a modem to ask whether the modem and the receiving system are ready for a data character to be sent.

Putting a 1 in bit D6 of the command word causes the 8251A to be internally reset when the command word is sent. After a software reset command is sent in this way, a new mode word must be sent. Later we show you how this is used.

The D7 bit in the command word is used only when the device is operating in synchronous mode. A command word with a 1 in this bit position tells the 8251A to look for specified sync character(s) in a stream of bits being shifted in. If the 8251A finds the specified sync character(s), it will assert its SYNDET/BD pin high. We discuss this further in the synchronous data communication section of this chapter.

The initialization sequence for an 8251A is somewhat lengthy for two reasons. First, the 8251A does not always respond correctly to a hardware reset on power-up. Therefore, a series of software commands must be sent to the device to make sure it is reset properly before the desired mode and command words are sent. The device is put into a known state by writing 3 bytes of all 0s to the 8251A control register address, and then it is reset by sending a control word with a 1 in bit D6. After this reset sequence,

the desired mode and control words can be sent to the 8251A. The 8251A distinguishes a command word from a mode word by the order in which they are sent to the device. After reset, a mode word must be sent to the command address. Any words sent to the command address after the mode word are treated as command words until the device is reset.

The second factor that lengthens this initialization is the write-recovery time, TRV, of the 8251A. According to the data sheet the 8251A requires a worst-case recovery time of 16 cycles of the clock signal connected to the CLK input. A simple way to produce the required delay and a margin of safety is to count down in an assembly language loop, as we have seen in previous examples. When writing data characters to an 8251A, you don't have to worry about this recovery time, because a new character will not be written to the 8251A until the previous character has been shifted out. This shifting, of course, requires much more time than TRV.

Once the 8251A is initialized, new control words can be sent at any time to, for example, reset the error flags. Now let's look at how characters are sent to and read from an 8251A.

SENDING AND RECEIVING CHARACTERS WITH AN 8251A

Data characters can be sent to and read from the 8251A on an interrupt basis or on a polled basis. To send characters on an interrupt basis, the TxRDY pin of the 8251A is connected to an interrupt input on the processor or an 8259A priority interrupt controller. The transmitter and the TxRDY output are enabled by putting a 1 in bit D1 of the control word sent to the 8251A during initialization. When the CTS input of the 8251A is asserted low and the 8251A buffer is ready for a character, the TxRDY pin will go high. If the processor and 8259A interrupt path are enabled, the processor will go to an interrupt-service procedure, which writes a data character to the 8251A data address. Writing the data character causes the 8251A to reset its TxRDY output until the buffer is again ready to receive a character. A counter can be used to keep track of how many characters have been sent.

In a similar manner characters can be read from an 8251A on an interrupt basis. In this case the RxRDY output of the 8251A is connected to an interrupt input of the processor or an 8259A, and this output is enabled by putting a 1 in bit D2 of the command word sent during initialization. When a character has been shifted into the 8251A and the character is in the receiver buffer ready to be read, the RxRDY pin will go high. If the interrupt chain through the 8259A and the processor is enabled, the processor will go to an interrupt procedure, which reads in the data character. Reading a data character from the 8251A causes it to reset the RxRDY output signal. This signal will stay low until another character is ready to be read.

To send characters to an 8251A on a polled basis, the 8251A status register is read and checked over and over until the TxRDY bit (D0) is found to be a 1. In most systems you also want to check bit D7 of the status register to make sure the DSR input of the 8251A has been asserted by a signal from a modem, for example. When the required bit(s) of the status register are all high, a data character is then written to the 8251A data address. Writing a data character to the 8251A resets the TxRDY bit in the status register.

Reading a character from the 8251A on a polled basis is a similar process, except that the RxRDY bit (D1) of the status register is polled to determine when a character is ready to be read. When bit D1 is found high, a character is read in from the 8251A data address. Status register bits D3, D4, and D5 can be checked to see if a parity error, overrun error, or framing error has occurred. If an error has occurred, a message to retransmit the data can be sent to the transmitting system.

The next step in our journey into serial data communications is to discuss the signal standards used to connect the serial inputs and outputs of UARTS to modems and other serial devices.

SERIAL DATA TRANSMISSION METHODS AND STANDARDS

In the last section we showed you how a UART or USART is used to interface microcomputer buses with serial data communication lines. The TTL signals output by a USART, however, are not suitable for transmission over long distances, so these signals are converted to some other form to be transmitted. In this section of the chapter we discuss devices and signal types commonly used to send serial data signals over long distances.

Aside from drum beats in the jungle, one of the earliest forms of serial data communication was the telegraph. In a telegraph, pressing a key at one end of a signal line causes a current to flow through the line. When this current reaches the receiving end of the line, it activates a solenoid (sounder), which produces a sound. Letters and numbers are sent using Morse code or some other convenient code. After a hundred years or so, the telegraph key and sounder evolved into the teletypewriter. A teletypewriter terminal has a typewriter-style keyboard so that the user can simply press a key to send a desired letter or number code. A teletype terminal also has a print mechanism, which prints out characters as they are received. Most teletypes use a current to represent a 1 and no current to represent a 0. We start this section by briefly describing the old current-loop standards and then go on to newer methods.

20- and 60-mA Current Loops

In teletypewriters or other current-signal systems, some manufacturers use a nominal current of 20 mA to represent a 1, or mark, and no current to represent a 0, or space. Other manufacturers use a nominal current of 60 mA to represent a 1 and no current to represent a 0. The actual current in a specific system may be considerably different from the nominal value. When connecting these types of current loops to TTL-level electronics, PNP transistors and 74LS14 inverters can be used to "condition" the signals. This conditioning transforms the signals from current-loop to TTL levels and vice versa.

RS-232C Serial Data Standard

OVERVIEW

In the 1960s as the use of timeshare computer terminals became more widespread, modems were developed so that terminals could use phone lines to communicate with distant computers. As we stated earlier, modems and other devices used to send serial data are often referred to as data communication equipment, or DCE. The terminals or computers that are sending or receiving the data are referred to as data terminal equipment, or DTE. In response to the need for signal and handshake standards between DTE and DCE, the Electronic Industries Association (EIA) developed EIA standard RS-232C. This standard describes the functions of 25 signal and handshake pins for serial data transfer. It also describes the voltage levels, impedance levels, rise and fall times, maximum bit rate, and maximum capacitance for these signal lines. Before we work our way through the 25 pin functions, we will take a brief look at some of the other hardware aspects of RS-232C.

RS-232C specifies 25 signal pins, and it specifies that the DTE connector should be a male and the DCE connector should be a female. A specific connector is not given, but the most commonly used connector is the DB-25P male shown in Figure 14-5a. For systems where many of the 25 pins are not needed, a 9-pin DIN connector such as the DE-9P male connector shown in Figure 14-5b is used. When you are wiring up these connectors, it is important to note the order in which the pins are numbered.

The voltage levels for all RS-232C signals are as follows. A logic high, or mark, is a voltage between -3 V and -15 V under load (-25 V under no load). A logic low or space is a voltage between $+3$ V and $+15$ V under load ($+25$ V under no load). Voltages such as ±12 V are commonly used.

RS-232C-TO-TTL INTERFACING

Obviously a USART such as the 8251A is not directly compatible with RS-232C signal levels. One way to interface between RS-232C and TTL levels is with

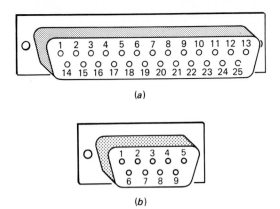

(a)

(b)

FIGURE 14-5   Connectors often used for RS-232C connections. (a) DB-25P 25-pin male connector. (b) DE-9P 9-pin male DIN connector.

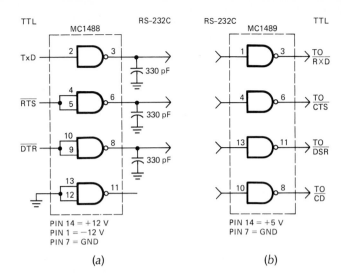

(a)   (b)

FIGURE 14-6   TTL-to-RS-232C-to-TTL signal conversion. (a) MC1488 used to convert TTL to RS-232C. (b) MC1489 used to convert RS-232C to TTL.

MC1488 quad TTL-to-RS-232C drivers and MC1489 quad RS-232C-to-TTL receivers shown in Figure 14-6. The MC1488s require + and − supplies, but the MC1489s require only +5 V. Note the capacitor to ground on the outputs of the MC1488 drivers. To reduce cross talk between adjacent wires, the rise and fall times for RS-232C signals are limited to 30 V/μs. Also note that the RS-232C handshake signals such as RTS are active low. Therefore, if one of these signals is asserted, you will find a positive voltage on the actual RS-232C signal line when you check it during troubleshooting. Now let's look at the RS-232C pin descriptions.

RS-232C SIGNAL DEFINITIONS

Figure 14-7 shows the signal names, signal direction, and a brief description for each of the 25 pins defined for the RS-232C. For most applications only a few of these pins are used, so don't be overwhelmed. Here are a few additional notes about these signals.

First note that the signal direction is specified with respect to the DCE. This convention is part of the standard. We have found it very helpful to put arrowheads on all signal lines, as shown in Figure 14-2, when we are drawing circuits for connecting RS-232C equipment.

Next observe that there is both a chassis ground (pin 1) and a signal ground (pin 7). To prevent large ac-induced ground currents in the signal ground, these two should be connected together only at the power supply in the terminal or the computer.

The TxD, RxD, and handshake signals shown with common names in Figure 14-7 are the ones most often used for simple systems. We gave an overview of their use in the introduction to this section of the chapter and discuss them further in a later section of the chapter on modems. These signals control what is called the *primary*, or *forward*, communications channel of the modem. Some modems allow communication over a *secondary*, or *backward*, channel, which

operates in the reverse direction from the forward channel and at a much lower baud rate. Pins 12, 13, 14, 16, and 19 are the data and handshake lines for this backward channel.

Pins 15, 17, 21, and 24 are used for synchronous data communication. We tell you a little more about these in the section on modems. Next we want to show you some of the tricks in connecting RS-232C-compatible equipment.

CONNECTING RS-232C-COMPATIBLE EQUIPMENT

A major point we need to make is that you can seldom just connect together two pieces of equipment described by their manufacturers as RS-232C compatible and expect them to work the first time. There are several reasons for this. To give you an idea of one of the reasons, suppose that you want to connect the terminal in Figure 14-2 directly to the computer rather than through the modem-modem link. The terminal and the computer probably both have DB-25-type connectors so that, other than a possible male-female mismatch, you might think you could just plug the terminal cable directly into the computer. To see why this doesn't work, hold your fingers over the modems in Figure 14-2 and refer to the pin numbers for the RS-232C signals in Figure 14-7. As you should see, both the terminal and the computer are trying to output data (TxD) from their number 2 pins to the same line. Likewise, they are both trying to input data (RxD) from the same line on their number 3 pins. The same problem exists with the handshake signals. RS-232C drivers are designed so that connecting the lines together in this way will not destroy anything, but connecting outputs together is not a productive relationship. A solution to this problem is to make an

PIN NUMBERS FOR 9 PINS	PIN NUMBERS FOR 25 PINS	COMMON NAME	RS-232C NAME	DESCRIPTION	SIGNAL DIRECTION ON DCE
	1		AA	PROTECTIVE GROUND	—
3	2	TXD	BA	TRANSMITTED DATA	IN
2	3	RXD	BB	RECEIVED DATA	OUT
7	4	$\overline{RTS}$	CA	REQUEST TO SEND	IN
8	5	$\overline{CTS}$	CB	CLEAR TO SEND	OUT
6	6	$\overline{DSR}$	CC	DATA SET READY	OUT
5	7	GND	AB	SIGNAL GROUND (COMMON RETURN)	—
1	8	$\overline{CD}$	CF	RECEIVED LINE SIGNAL DETECTOR	OUT
	9		—	(RESERVED FOR DATA SET TESTING)	—
	10		—	(RESERVED FOR DATA SET TESTING)	—
	11			UNASSIGNED	—
	12		SCF	SECONDARY RECEIVED LINE SIGNAL DETECTOR	OUT
	13		SCB	SECONDARY CLEAR TO SEND	OUT
	14		SBA	SECONDARY TRANSMITTED DATA	IN
	15		DB	TRANSMISSION SIGNAL ELEMENT TIMING (DCE SOURCE)	OUT
	16		SBB	SECONDARY RECEIVED DATA	OUT
	17		DD	RECEIVER SIGNAL ELEMENT TIMING (DCE SOURCE)	OUT
	18			UNASSIGNED	—
	19		SCA	SECONDARY REQUEST TO SEND	IN
4	20	$\overline{DTR}$	CD	DATA TERMINAL READY	IN
	21		CG	SIGNAL QUALITY DETECTOR	OUT
9	22		CE	RING INDICATOR	OUT
	23		CH/CI	DATA SIGNAL RATE SELECTOR (DTE/DCE SOURCE)	IN/OUT
	24		DA	TRANSMIT SIGNAL ELEMENT TIMING (DTE SOURCE)	IN
	25			UNASSIGNED	—

FIGURE 14-7   RS-232C pin names and signal directions.

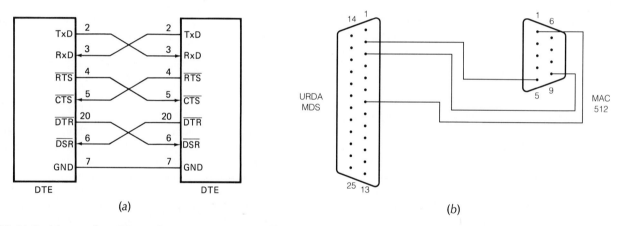

(a)   (b)

FIGURE 14-8   Nonmodem RS-232C connections. (a) Null modem for connecting two RS-232C data terminal–type devices. (b) Macintosh to URDA MDS serial port connection.

FIGURE 14-9   MC3488A driver and MC3486 receiver used for RS-423 signal transmission.

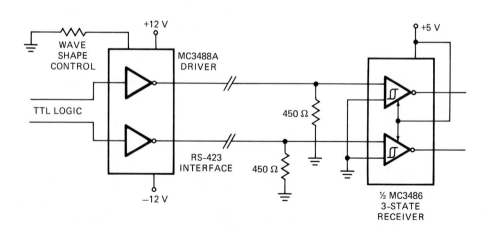

adapter with two connectors so that the signals cross over, as shown in Figure 14-8a. This crossover connection is often called a *null modem.* We have again put arrowheads on the signals in Figure 14-8a to help you keep track of the direction for each. As you can see in the figure, the TxD from the terminal now sends data to the RxD input of the computer. Likewise, the TxD from the computer now sends data to the RxD input of the computer, as desired. The handshake signals also are crossed over, so each handshake output signal is connected to the corresponding input signal.

A second reason that you can't just plug RS-232C-compatible equipment together and expect it to work is that a partial implementation of RS-232C is often used to communicate with printers, plotters, and other computer peripherals besides modems. These other peripherals may be configured as DCE or as DTE. Also, they may use all, some, or none of the handshake signals. As a more complex problem, we can consider connecting two serial ports where one of the ports does not use the RS-232C standard.

The Macintosh uses an RS-422 serial standard, described in the next section. The IBM PC uses an RS-232C standard. However the two can be connected successfully. In order to do so the two systems should be grounded together by connecting the RS-232C pin 7 to the RS-422 pin 1. The transmit data line of the RS-232C (pin 2, TxD) is connected to the RS-422 transmit data positive line (pin 5). The RS-232C receive data line (pin 3, RxD) is connected to the RS-422 receive data negative line (pin 9).

Figure 14-8b shows the connections you make to solve this problem so the Macintosh can talk to the URDA MDS.

The point here is that whenever you have to connect RS-232C-compatible devices such as terminals or serial printers, get the schematic for each and work your way through the connections one pin at a time. Make sure that an output on one device goes to the appropriate input on the other device. Sometimes you have to look at the actual drivers and receivers on the schematic to determine which pins on the connector are outputs and which are inputs. This is necessary because some manufacturers label an output pin connected to pin 3 as RxD, indicating that this signal goes to the RxD input of the receiving system.

If you do not have schematics for the RS-232C equipment you are trying to connect, you can often use a breakout box to determine the correct connections. You insert the breakout box in series with the connecting cable, and LEDs on the box indicate which lines are outputs and which lines are inputs. By throwing switches on the box, you can try different connection combinations until data transfers correctly.

RS-423A and RS-422A

RS-423

A major problem with RS-232C is that it can transmit data reliably only about 50 ft (16.4 m) at its maximum

rate of 20,000 Bd. If longer lines are used, the transmission rate has to be drastically reduced. This limitation is caused by the open signal lines with a single common ground that are used for RS-232C.

Another EIA standard, which is an improvement over RS-232C, is RS-423A. This standard specifies a low-impedance single-ended signal that can be sent over 50-Ω coaxial cable and partially terminated at the receiving end to prevent reflections. Figure 14-9 shows how an MC3488A driver and MC3486 receiver can be connected to produce the required signals. A logic high in this standard is represented by the signal line being between 4 and 6 V negative with respect to ground, and a logic low is represented by the signal line being 4 and 6 V positive with respect to ground.

The RS-423 standard allows a maximum data rate of 100,000 Bd over a 40-ft line or a maximum baud rate of 1000 Bd on a 4000-ft line.

RS-422A

A still-newer standard for serial data transfer, the RS-422A specifies that each signal will be sent differentially over two adjacent wires in a ribbon cable or a twisted pair of wires, as shown in Figure 14-10a.

The term *differential* in this standard means that the signal voltage is developed between the two signal lines rather than between a signal line and ground, as in RS-232C and RS-423. In RS-422A a logic high is transmitted by making the b line more positive than the a line. A logic low is transmitted by making the a line more positive than the b line. The voltage difference between the two lines must be greater than 0.4 V but less than 12 V. Typical drivers such as the MC3487 shown in Figure 14-10a produce a differential voltage of about 2 V. The center, or common-mode, voltage on the lines must be between −7 V and +7 V. RS-422A specifies signal rise and fall times of 20 ns or 0.1 × the time for 1 bit, whichever is greater.

Figure 14-10b shows the relationship between maximum cable length and baud rate for RS-422A line. As you can see in this graph, the maximum data rate for RS-422A lines ranges from 10 million Bd on a line 40 feet long to 100,000 Bd on a 4000-ft line. The reason that the data rates are so much higher than for RS-423 lines is that the differential line functions as a fully terminated transmission line. Common 24-gage twisted-pair wire has a Zo of about 100 Ω, so the line can be terminated with a matching 100-Ω resistor, connected between the signal lines. A more common termination method, however, is to use a 50-Ω resistor from each signal line to ground, as shown in Figure 14-10a. This method helps keep the two signal lines balanced.

A further advantage of differential signal transmission is that any electrical noise induced in one signal line will be induced equally in the other signal line. A differential line receiver such as the MC3486 shown in Figure 14-10a responds only to the voltage difference between its two inputs, so any noise voltage that is

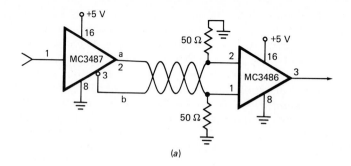

(a)

FIGURE 14-10 (a) MC3487 driver and MC3486 receiver used for RS-422A differential signal.

(b) Maximum line length versus baud rate for RS-422A signal lines.

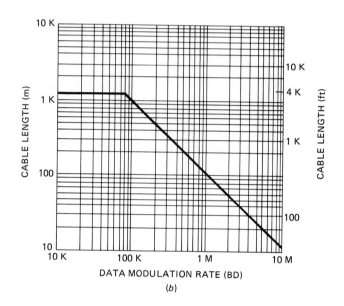

(b)

FIGURE 14-11 Representation of digital 1s and 0s with amplitude-modulated sine waves.

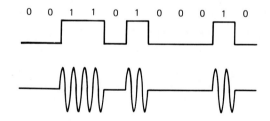

FIGURE 14-12 Representation of digital 1s and 0s with two different frequencies (FSK).

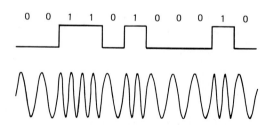

induced equally on the two inputs will not have any effect on the output of the differential receiver.

The RS-422A and RS-423A standards do not specify connector pin numbers or handshake signals the way that RS-232C does. An additional EIA standard, RS-449, does this for the two. RS-449 specifies 37 signal pins on a main connector and 9 additional pins on an optional connector. The signals on these connectors are a superset of the RS-232C signals, so adapters can be used to interface RS-232C equipment with RS-449 equipment.

Now that we have discussed the signals commonly used to interface a computer to a modem, let's take a closer look at how modems transmit signals over standard phone lines.

Modems

INTRODUCTION

As we described in a previous section, a modulator-demodulator, or *modem,* sends digital 1s and 0s over standard phone lines as modulated tones. The frequency of the tones is within the band-pass of the lines. Two organizations are responsible for most of the current standards for modem modulation methods and transmission rates. Older modems in the United States were based on de facto standards from Bell Telephone Company. Examples of these standards are the Bell types 103, 202, 208, and 212A. In the United States modem standards are now handled by the Telecommunications Industry Association, which works very closely with the Comité Consultatif Internationale Téléphonique et Télégraphique (CCITT), which is part of the International Telecommunications Union. CCITT standards relating to modems start with a V. Examples are the V.22 bis, which is a 2400-bit/s modem standard, and the V.29, which is a 9600-bit/s modem standard. As we discuss modem modulation techniques in the following section, we describe these and other standards in greater detail.

INTRODUCTION TO MODEM MODULATION

To represent digital 1s and 0s, a modulator changes some characteristic of an audio signal that has a frequency within the bandwidth of the phone lines. An important point to keep in mind as you read through the following section is that the maximum rate at which the audio tone can be modulated is one-half the bandwidth of the transmission line. If, for example, we assume that the worst-case bandwidth of a two-wire phone line is 2400 Hz, then the maximum modulation rate for a half-duplex signal on the line is 1200 baud. For full-duplex communication, half the bandwidth is used for transmission in each direction, so the maximum modulation rate for each direction on a two-wire phone line is 600 Bd. In a four-wire phone line, which has separate wires for each direction, the maximum modulation rate for each direction is 1200 Bd. One of the goals of this section is to show you the modulation techniques used to overcome these basic limitations.

The major forms of modulation used are amplitude, frequency-shift keying (FSK), phase-shift keying (PSK), and multiple carrier.

As the name implies, amplitude modulation changes the amplitude of the transmitted tone. One common way of doing this is to turn a 387-Hz tone on to represent a 1 and turn the tone off to represent a 0, as shown in Figure 14-11. In other systems that we discuss later, the tone is always present, but its amplitude is changed between two or more values. Amplitude modulation is used only for very low speed reverse-channel transmission or in conjunction with some other type of modulation, such as phase modulation.

FREQUENCY-SHIFT-KEYING MODULATION

Frequency-shift-keying, or FSK, modulation uses one tone to represent a 0 and another tone to represent a 1, as shown in Figure 14-12. In order to allow full-duplex communication, four different frequencies are often used. An old standard, the Bell 103A, 300-Bd FSK modem, for example, uses 2025 Hz for a 0 and 2225 Hz for a 1 in one direction and 1070 Hz for a 0 and 1270 Hz for a 1 in the other direction. Another standard, the Bell 202 modem, permits half-duplex communication at 1200 Bd. The 202 uses 1200 Hz to represent a 0 and 1700 Hz to represent a 1 for the main channel. Different versions of the 202 may also have either a 5-bit/s amplitude-modulated back channel or a 150-bit/s FSK back channel, which uses 387 Hz for a 0 and 487 Hz for a 1.

As we discussed before, simple modulation such as FSK is limited to half-duplex operation at 1200 Bd on two-wire phone lines or 1200 Bd full-duplex on four-wire phone lines. For higher bit rates, some type of phase-shift modulation is used.

PHASE-SHIFT MODULATION VARIATIONS

In the simplest form of phase-shift modulation, called differential phase-shift modulation (DPSK), the phase of a constant-frequency sine-wave carrier of perhaps 1700 Hz is shifted by 180° to represent a change in the data from a 1 to a 0 or a change in the data from a 0 to a 1. Figure 14-13a shows an example of this. As the digital data changes from a 0 to a 1, near the left edge of the figure, the phase of the signal is shifted by 180°. When the data changes from a 1 to a 0, the phase of the carrier is again shifted by 180°. For the next section of the digital data, where the data stays 0 for 3 bit times, the phase of the carrier is not changed. Likewise, in a later section of the waveform, where the data remains at a 1 level for 2 bit times, the phase of the carrier is not changed. Thus the phase of the carrier is shifted by 180° only when the data line changes from a 1 to a 0 or from a 0 to a 1.

The simple phase-shift modulation shown in Figure 14-13a has no real advantage over FSK as far as maximum bit rate is concerned. However, by using phase angles other than 180°, 2 or more data bits can be sent with one phase change. Figure 14-13b shows how the value of 2 bits can be represented by four different phase shifts. If, for example, the value of a dibit, or 2 bits taken together, is 00, the phase of the carrier will be shifted 90° to represent that dibit. The trick here is that the phase of the carrier has to shift only once for each group of 2 transmitted bits.

Remember from a previous discussion that the baud rate limitation we are trying to overcome is the rate at which the carrier is changing. In this case the number of data bits per second is twice the baud rate. Bell 212A and CCITT V.22-type modems use this scheme to transmit 1200 bits/s at an effective baud rate of only 600 Bd. Two carrier frequencies, 1200 Hz and 2400 Hz, are used to permit full-duplex operation at this rate.

A more complex phase-shift-modulation scheme called *quaternary amplitude modulation*, or QAM, enables V.22 bis–type modems to transmit full-duplex data at 2400 bits/s over two-wire phone lines. V.29-type modems also use this type modulation to transmit half-duplex, 9600-bit/s data from facsimile (fax) machines. QAM uses 12 different phase angles and three different amplitudes to encode 4 data bits in each modulation change. Each group of 4 data bits is referred to as a *quadbit*. A phase-amplitude graph such as that shown in Figure 14-14 is often used to represent the phase-amplitude value for each of the 16 possible quadbits. Incidentally, the pattern of phase amplitude points in a graph such as this is commonly referred to as a *constellation*.

Dibit and QAM phase-shift modulations permit higher data rates on phone lines, but correctly demodulating this type of phase-encoded data presents some unique problems. To illustrate the first problem, remember from our previous discussion that in a dibit system the value of a dibit is represented by shifting the phase of a carrier signal some specified number of degrees from a reference phase. In order to detect the amount of phase shift, the receiver and the transmitter must be using the same reference phase. This would be easy if we could just run another wire to carry a synchronizing clock signal. However, since this is not easily done, the synchronizing signal must in some way be included with the data. The carrier signal itself cannot be used directly, because that is the signal whose phase must be detected.

The solution to this problem is to use transitions in the transmitted signal to synchronize a phase-locked-loop oscillator in the receiver. In order for this to work, two factors must be included in the transmitted data. First of all, the system must be operated synchronous-

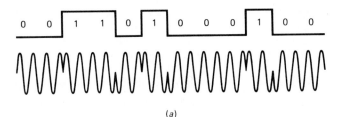

| 0 | 0 | 1 | 1 | 0 | 1 | 0 | 0 | 0 | 1 | 0 | 0 |

(a)

GRAY CODE DIBIT VALUE	DEGREES OF PHASE SHIFT
0 0	0
0 1	90
1 1	180
1 0	270

(b)

GRAY CODE DIBIT VALUE	DEGREES OF PHASE SHIFT
0 0 1	22.5
0 0 0	67.5
0 1 0	112.5
0 1 1	157.5
1 1 1	202.5
1 1 0	247.5
1 0 0	292.5
1 0 1	337.5

(c)

FIGURE 14-13 Phase-shift modulation. (a) Waveforms for simple phase-shift modulation. (b) Set of phase shifts used to represent four possible digit combinations.

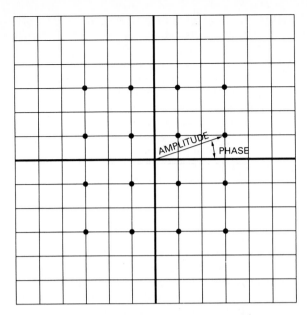

FIGURE 14-14 Phase-amplitude graph showing constellation for quaternary amplitude modulation (QAM).

ly rather than asynchronously, so that data, sync, or null characters are always being received by the receiver. Secondly, the transmitted data must have enough transitions at regular intervals to keep the phase-locked loop locked in the desired phase. The serial-data stream from the USART may not have enough transitions in it to satisfy this second condition, so a special circuit called a scrambler is included in the transmitter part of the modem. The scrambler, which usually consists of a shift register with feedback, puts in extra signal transitions as needed. The output from the scrambler is then used to modulate the phase of the carrier. When the carrier signal reaches the receiver, the signal is demodulated to produce a signal of 1s and 0s. This signal is then passed through a descrambler, which reverses the scrambling process and outputs the original data.

A second problem encountered in high-speed data transmission with modems is error detection/correction. One method used to decrease the error rate is called *trellis coding*. Trellis coding uses a constellation with more points than the minimum required to represent the number of data bit combinations in the group. The information needed to decode each data bit is spread over several transmitted values rather than being encoded in just one, as in straight QAM. This scheme makes it possible for the receiver to detect illegal values caused by errors. V.32-type modems use trellis coding to allow full-duplex, 9600-bit/s transmission on a two-wire phone line with 2400-Bd modulation.

Note that this modulation rate is higher than we told you was possible for a phone-line bandwidth of 2400 Hz. The actual bandwidth of the phone lines is usually 3000 or somewhat more, so it is common practice to

"push" the bandwidth limits to get higher data transmission rates. Most modems are designed to work with several different transmission rates and types of modulation so that they can communicate with a variety of modems. The software controlling the modem usually attempts communication at the highest available data rate, and if the particular phone connection will not support that rate, it "falls back" to a lower data rate, where it can successfully transmit and receive. V.32-type modems also contain echo-cancellation circuitry to reduce errors caused by interference between the signal being sent out and the signal coming in.

Other techniques being used to increase the rate at which modems can transfer data on standard phone lines are error correcting and data compression. CCITT standard V.42 specifies an error detection/correction algorithm that is independent of the data transmission speed and modulation method. CCITT standard V.42 bis specifies data compression algorithms that can be implemented in modems independently of the data transmission rate and the modulation method. The algorithm in this standard allows up to a 4:1 data compression, depending on the amount of redundancy in the data being transmitted. An average increase of about 60 percent in the actual data transmission rate is common with this algorithm.

Still another technique used to increase the data rate on phone lines is Telebit Corporation's Dynamically Adaptive Multicarrier Quadrature Amplitude Modulation (DAMQAM). This scheme uses up to 512 different carrier frequencies within the bandwidth of the phone lines. Data transmission is spread out over a large number of these channels, so the transmission on any one channel can be at a very low rate, even with an overall transmission rate of 19,200 bits/s.

Now that you know about the modulation schemes used in modems, let's take a look at how a high-speed modem can be interfaced with microcomputer buses.

MODEM HARDWARE OVERVIEW

Figure 14-15 shows a block diagram for a combination fax and data modem that interfaces directly to the main buses in a microcomputer. As you can see, the modem contains a dedicated microprocessor to control the operations of the modem. This processor manages handshaking, data formatting, dialing, etc. The ROM or EPROM stores the program for the microprocessor and the RAM stores blocks of data received by the modem and blocks of data waiting to be sent.

As we described before, high-speed data transmission on phone lines requires precisely detecting the amplitude of signals, precisely detecting the phase of signals, noise filtering, and echo cancellation. In current modems these tasks are accomplished with the digital signal processing techniques we described in Chapter 10. As you can see, the modem in Figure 14-15 contains a dedicated digital signal processor to do all this.

The modem in Figure 14-15 contains a fax front end and a data front end. The reason for this is that a fax typically uses V.29-type half-duplex, 9600-bit/s trans-

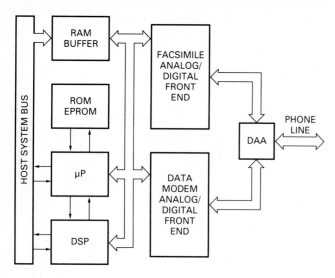

FIGURE 14-15 Block diagram of combination fax and data modem.

mission, and the corresponding data communication uses V.22 bis full-duplex, 2400-bit/s transmission.

The box labeled DAA in Figure 14-15 is the data access arrangement circuitry, which actually interfaces the signals with the phone lines. This circuitry must conform to the provisions of FCC rules, Section 68.

LSI has made it possible to build a modem with very few parts. A device such as the Advanced Micro Devices Am7910, for example, can be used to produce a 1200-Bd FSK modem. The EXAR Corp. XR-2901 and 2902 chip set contains a major part of the circuitry needed to implement a modem that can send or receive facsimile data at 9600 bits/s or send and receive full-duplex modem data at 2400 bits/s.

MODEM HANDSHAKING

Earlier in the chapter we gave an overview of the handshake process between a terminal and a remote computer through modems and the phone lines. Now that you know more about modems, we can take a closer look at the handshake sequence.

Most of the currently available modems contain a dedicated microprocessor. The built-in intelligence allows these units automatically to dial a specified number with either tones or pulses and redial the number if it is busy or doesn't answer. When a smart modem makes contact with another modem, it will automatically try to set its transmit circuitry to match the baud rate of the other modem. Many modems can be set to automatically answer a call after a programmed number of rings so that you can access your computer from a remote location. Some units allow the user to establish voice contact and then switch over to modem operation.

After a modem dials up another modem, a series of handshake signals takes place. The handshake signals may be generated by hardware in the modem or by software in the system connected to the modem. Figure 14-16 shows an example of the data and handshake

waveforms for a modem built with the AM7910 single-chip FSK modem. Other modems may use a slightly different sequence, but the principles are the same.

The modem that makes a call is usually referred to as the *originate modem*, and the modem that receives the call is usually referred to as the *answer modem*. In the following discussion we use the terms *calling modem* and *called modem*, respectively, to agree with the labels on the waveforms in Figure 14-16.

At the left side of the waveforms, a call is being made from one modem to another. Assuming that the DTR of the called modem is asserted, the ringing signal on the line will cause the DAA circuitry to assert the ringing input (RI) of the 7910. In response to this, the 7910 will send out a silent period of about 2 s to accommodate billing signals, and then it will send out an answer tone of 2025 Hz to the calling modem for 2 s. If the DTR and the RTS of the calling modem are asserted, indicating that data is ready to be sent, the calling modem then puts a tone of 2225 Hz (mark) on the line for 8 ms to let the called modem know that contact is complete. In response to this mark, the called modem asserts its carrier-detect (CD) output to enable the receiving UART. The calling modem then sends data until its RTS input is released by the computer or terminal sending the data. While it is receiving data on the main channel, the called modem can send data to the calling modem on the 5-bit/s back channel. Releasing RTS causes the modem to release CTS to the sending computer and remove the carrier from the line. The called modem senses the loss of the carrier and unasserts its CD signal.

If the called system is to send some data back to the calling system on the main channel, it asserts the RTS input to its modem. The called modem sends a marking tone to the calling modem for 8 ms. The calling modem asserts its CD output to its UART. The called modem then sends data to the calling modem on the main channel until its RTS input is unasserted by the called system, indicating no more data to send. While the called modem is transmitting on the main channel, the calling modem can transmit over the back channel if necessary. For a full-duplex system, the handshake is similar, but the data rates are equal in both directions.

Codecs, PCM, TDM, and ISDN

In the previous sections we described how modems produce signals suitable for transmission over standard phone lines. Now we want to discuss briefly how telephone companies actually transmit the signals output by modems and some new developments that we hope will eliminate the need for modems as we know them.

Digital signals have much better noise immunity than analog signals, so as soon as a phone company receives a voice or modem signal in its local branch office, the signal is converted to digital form. A D/A converter at the destination uses the received binary codes to reconstruct a replica of the original analog

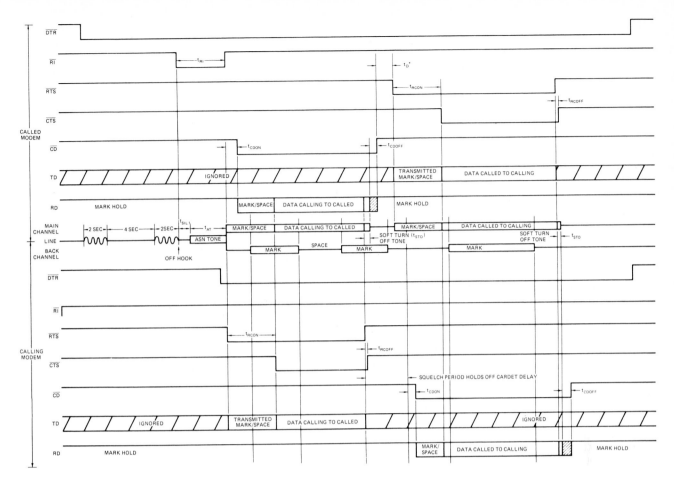

FIGURE 14-16   Handshake sequence for Bell-type 202 FSK modem using
AM7910 modem chip. (*Advanced Micro Devices*)

signal. Sending analog signals, such as phone signals, as a series of binary codes is called pulse-code modulation, or PCM. The A/D converter that produces the binary codes in this application is usually called a *coder,* and the D/A converter that reconstructs the analog signal from the pulse codes is referred to as a *decoder.* Since both a coder and a decoder are needed for two-way communication, they are often packaged in the same IC. This combined coder and decoder is called a *codec.* A common example of a codec is the Intel 2910A. This device contains a sample-and-hold circuit on the analog input, an 8-bit A/D converter, an 8-bit D/A converter, and appropriate control circuitry.

Normal A/D converters are linear, which means that the steps are the same size over the full range of the converters. The A/D converters used in codecs are nonlinear. They have small steps for small signals and large steps for large signals. In other words, for signals near the zero point of the A/D converter, it only takes a small change in the signal to change the code on the output of the A/D. For a signal near the full scale of the converter, a large change in the input signal is required to produce a change in the output binary code. This nonlinearity of the A/D converter is said to *compress* the signal, because it reduces the dynamic range of the signal. Compression in this way greatly improves

the accuracy for small signals where it is needed, without going to a converter with more bits of resolution. The D/A in the codec is nonlinear in the reverse manner, so that when the binary pulse codes are converted to analog, the result is expanded to duplicate the original waveform. A codec that has this intentional nonlinearity is often referred to as a *compander,* or a *companding codec.* Consult the Intel 2910A data sheet for more information about this.

In most systems the output of the codec A/D is not simply sent on a wire by itself; instead, it is multiplexed with the outputs of many other codecs in a manner known as time-division multiplexing, or TDM. There are several different formats used. A simple one will give you the idea of how it's done.

One of the first TDM systems was the T1 or DS-1 system, which multiplexes 24 PCM voice channels onto a single wire. For this system an 8-bit codec on each channel samples and digitizes the input signal at an 8-kHz rate. The 8-bit codes from the codecs are sent to a multiplexer, which sends them out serially, one after the other. One set of bits from each of the 24 codecs plus a framing bit is referred to as a *frame.* Figure 14-17 shows the format of a frame for this system. The framing bit at the start of each frame toggles after each frame is sent. It is used to keep the

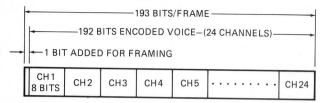

FIGURE 14-17 Frame format for telephone company T1 digital data transmission.

receiver and the transmitter synchronized and to keep track of how many frames have been sent. After it sends the framing bit, the multiplexer sends out the 8-bit code from the first codec, then sends out the 8-bit code from the next codec, and so on, until the codes for all 24 have been sent out. At specified intervals the multiplexer sends out a frame that contains synchronization information and signaling information. This does not seriously affect the quality of the transmitted data.

Since the multiplexer is sending out 193-bit frames at a rate of 8000 per second, the data rate on the wire is 193×8000, or 1.544 Mbits/s. A newer system, known as T4M or DS-4, multiplexes 4032 channels onto a single coaxial cable or optic fiber. The bit rate for this system is 274.176 Mbits/s.

The question that should come to your mind about now is, If the phone company transmits data in high-speed digital form, why do I have to send data as modulated audio tones? The answer to this question is that the circuitry between your phone and the local branch office is a relic from a bygone analog era. This circuitry creates a bottleneck in the communications link.

One attempt to eliminate this bottleneck is a wideband digital connection system known as the *integrated services digital network*, or ISDN. As shown in Figure 14-18a, ISDN replaces the analog connections between your home and the telephone company branch office with relatively high speed digital connections. An ISDN basic-rate service connection gives two 64-Kbit/s voice/data channels and a 16-Kbit/s data/control channel in each direction. The voice/data channels are referred to as B1 and B2. The data/control channel is referred to as the D channel.

Figure 14-18b shows how the B1, B2, D, framing, and other bits are packed in a 48-bit frame for transmission. Note that the B channel has four times as many bits per frame as the D channel, so the bit rate for the B channel is four times the bit rate for the D channel. A 48-bit frame is transmitted every 250 μs, so the basic bit rate on the signal line is 192 Kbits/s. Only 16 of the 48 data bits represent one of the B channels, so the transmission rate for a B channel is 64 Kbits/s.

For voice communication a codec in the telephone converts voice signals to a sequence of 8-bit codes, which are then put in, for example, the B1 channel slots in the 48-bit frames. The codec also converts the

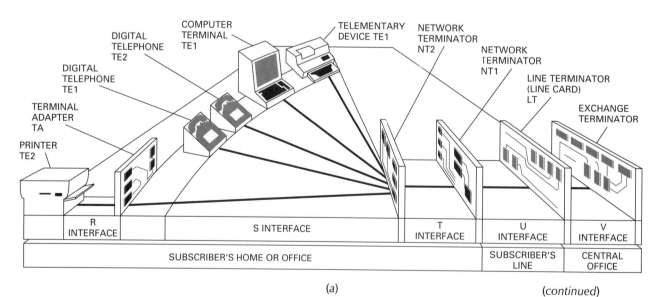

(a)

(continued)

FIGURE 14-18 Integrated services digital network (ISDN). (a) Line connections and interfaces. Reprinted from *EDN*, April 27, 1989, © 1989 Cohners Publishing Company, a division of Reed Publishing USA. (b, p. 478) Example S interface frame format showing how B1, B2, and D channel bits are packaged for transmission. (NOTE: Frames sent from network termination to terminal equipment are offset 2 bits from frames sent from terminal equipment to network termination.)

codes for received voice signals back to analog form to drive a speaker. Some advantages of ISDN for standard telephone communications are that it gives better sound quality and allows identification of the number from which a call is coming.

For data communications an adapter in the computer formats the data to be transmitted in the required frames and adds the framing bits, etc. Since both B channels can be used, the effective data rate is the sum of that for the two channels, or 128 Kbits/s. In some cases the D channel can also be used for data, and the effective rate becomes 144 Kbits/s.

In a large building with main telephones and computers, each phone and computer will communicate with the PBX in the building using a basic ISDN 2B +D service line such as we just described. The PBX will then use a higher-frequency multiplexed line such as the T1 system we described earlier to communicate with the telephone company's central office.

As you can see by the transmission rates for ISDN, it is a big improvement over the old analog connections. As of this writing ISDN is still available only in some major cities and a few different areas. It is slowly spreading to other areas, but if you want to communicate with many different locations, you will probably be stuck with an analog modem for some time. This is unfortunate, because high-speed data communication is a required for interactive graphic user interfaces. In other words, if you want to transmit high-resolution color images rapidly, you need a high-speed communications link. In the next section we discuss fiber-optic systems, which allow the very high speed data transfer needed for this.

Fiber-Optic Data Communication

INTRODUCTION

All the data communication methods we have discussed so far use metallic conductors. Fiber-optic systems use very thin glass or plastic fibers to transfer data as pulses of light. Some of the advantages of fiber-optic links are that they are immune to electrical noise, they can transfer data at very high rates, and they can transfer data over long distances without amplification.

Figure 14-19 shows the connections for a basic fiber-optic data link you can build and experiment with. This type of link might be used to transmit data from a sensor in an electrically noisy environment such as a factory. The light source here is a simple infrared LED. Higher-performance systems use an infrared injection laser diode (ILD) or some other laser driven by a high-speed, high-current driver. Digital data is sent over the fiber by turning the light beam on for a 1 and off for a 0.

> NOTE: If you are working on a fiber-optic system, you should never look directly into the end of the fiber to see if the light source is working, because the light beam from some laser diodes is powerful enough to cause permanent eye damage. Use a light meter or point the cable at a nonreflective surface to see if the light source is working.

To convert the light signal back into an electrical signal at the receiving end, Darlington photodetectors such as the MFOD73 shown in Figure 14-19, p-i-n FET devices, or avalanche photodiodes (APDs) are used. APDs are more sensitive and operate at higher frequencies, but the circuitry for them is more complex. A Schmitt trigger is usually used on the output of the detector to "square up" the output pulses.

The fiber used in a cable is made of special plastic or glass. Fiber diameters used range from 2 to 1000 μm. Larger-diameter plastic fibers are used for short distance, low-speed transmission, and small-diameter glass fibers are used for high-speed applications such as long-distance telephone transmission lines. As shown in Figure 14-20e, the fiber-optic cable consists of three parts. The optical-fiber core is surrounded by a

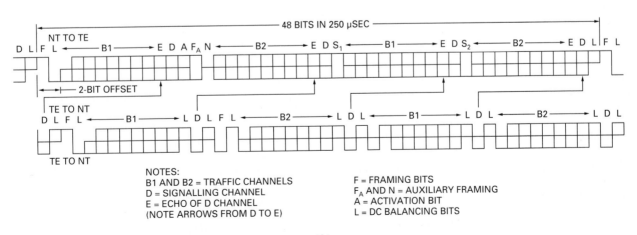

NOTES:
B1 AND B2 = TRAFFIC CHANNELS
D = SIGNALLING CHANNEL
E = ECHO OF D CHANNEL
(NOTE ARROWS FROM D TO E)

F = FRAMING BITS
F$_A$ AND N = AUXILIARY FRAMING
A = ACTIVATION BIT
L = DC BALANCING BITS

(b)

FIGURE 14-18   (continued)

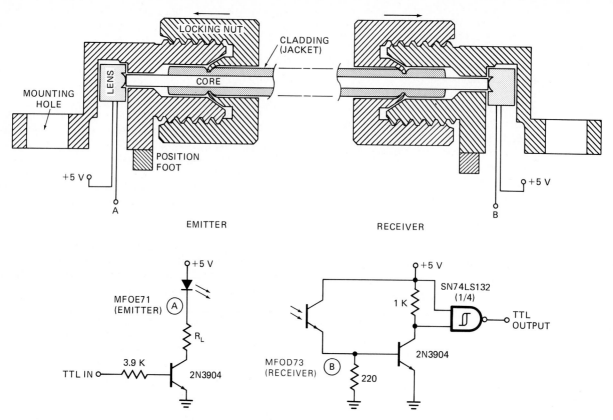

FIGURE 14-19   Components of a simple fiber-optic data link.

cladding material, which is also transparent to light. An outer sheath protects the cladding and prevents external light from entering.

Now that you have an overview of an optical-fiber link, let's take a look at how the light actually propagates through the fiber and the trade-offs with different fibers.

THE OPTICS OF FIBERS

The path of a beam of light going from a material with one optical density to a material of different optical density depends on the angle at which the beam hits the boundary between the two materials. Figure 14-20 shows the path that will be taken by beams of light at various angles going from an optically dense material such as glass to a less dense material such as a vacuum or air. If the beam hits the boundary at a right angle, it will go straight through, as shown in Figure 14-20a. When a beam hits the boundary at a small angle away from the perpendicular, or normal, it will be bent away from the normal when it goes from the more dense to the less dense, as shown in Figure 14-20b. A light beam going in the other direction would follow the same path. A quantity called the index of refraction is used to describe the amount that the light beam will be bent. Using the angle identifications shown in Figure 14-20b, the index of refraction, n, is defined as (sine B)/(sine A). A typical value for the index of refraction of glass is 1.5. The larger the index

of refraction, the more the beam will be bent when it goes from one material to another.

Figure 14-20c shows a unique situation that occurs when a beam going from a dense material to a less dense material hits the boundary at a special angle called the critical angle. The beam will be bent so that it travels parallel to the boundary after it enters the less dense material.

A still more interesting situation is shown in Figure 14-20d. If the beam hits the boundary at an angle greater than the critical angle, it will be totally reflected from the boundary at the same angle on the other side of the normal. This is somewhat like skipping stones across water. In this case the light beam will not leave the more dense material.

To see how all this relates to optical fibers, take a look at the cross-sectional drawing of an optical fiber in Figure 14-20e. If a beam of light enters the fiber parallel to the axis of the fiber, it will simply travel through the fiber. If the beam enters the fiber so that it hits the glass-cladding-layer boundary at the critical angle, it will travel through the fiber-optic cable in the cladding layer, as shown for beam Y in Figure 14-20e. However, if the beam enters the cable so that it hits the glass-cladding-layer boundary at an angle greater than the critical angle, it will bounce back and forth between the walls of the fiber, as shown for beam X in Figure 14-20e. The glass or plastic used for fiber-optic cables has very low absorption, so the beam can bounce back and forth along the fiber for several feet or

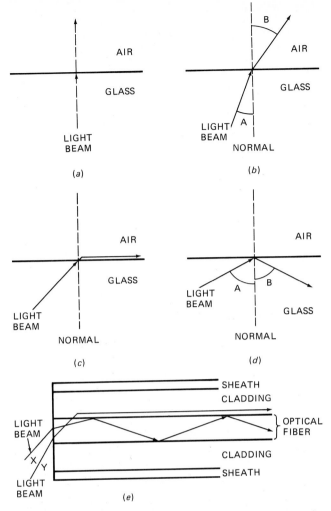

FIGURE 14-20 Light-beam paths for different angles of incidence with the boundary between higher-optical-density and lower-optical-density materials. (a) Right angle. (b) Angle less than critical angle. (c) At critical angle. (d) At angle greater than critical angle. (e) At angle greater than critical angle in optical fiber.

miles without excessive attenuation. Most systems use light with wavelengths of 0.85 μm, 1.3 μm, or 1.500μm, because absorption of light by the optical fibers is minimum at these wavelengths.

If an optical fiber has a diameter many times larger than the wavelength of the light being used, then beams that enter the fiber at different angles will arrive at the other end of the fiber at slightly different times. The different angles of entry for the beams are referred to as *modes*. A fiber with a diameter large enough to allow beams with several different entry angles to propagate through it is called a *multimode fiber*. Since multimode fibers are larger, they are easier to manufacture, are easier to work with manually, and can use inexpensive LED drivers. However, the phase difference between the output beams in multimode fibers causes problems at high data rates. One partial solution to this problem is to dope the glass of the fiber so

that the index of refraction decreases toward the outside of the fiber. Light beams travel faster in the region where the index of refraction is lower, so beams that take a longer path back and forth through the faster outer regions tend to arrive at the end of the fiber at the same time as those that take a shorter path through the slower center region.

A better solution to the phase problems of the multimode fiber is to use a fiber that has a diameter only a few times the wavelength of the light being transmitted. Only beams very nearly parallel to the axis of the fiber can then be transmitted. This is referred to as single-mode operation. Currently available single-mode systems can transmit data a distance of more than 60 km at a rate greater than 1 Gbit/s. An experimental system developed by AT&T multiplexes 10 slightly different wavelength laser beams onto one single-mode fiber. The system can transmit data at an effective rate of 20 Gbits/s over a distance of 68 km without amplification.

One of the main problems with single-mode fibers is the difficulty in making low-loss connections with the tiny fibers. Another difficulty is that in order to get enough light energy into the tiny fiber, relatively expensive laser diodes or other lasers—rather than inexpensive LEDs—must be used.

FIBER-OPTIC CABLE USES

Fiber-optic transmission has the advantages that the signal lines are much smaller than the equivalent electrical signal lines, signals can be sent much longer distances without repeater amplifiers, and very high data rates are possible. One of the first major uses of fiber-optic transmission systems has been for carrying large numbers of phone conversations across oceans and between cities. A single 12-fiber, $\frac{1}{2}$-in.-diameter optical-fiber cable can transmit 1,000,000 simultaneous telephone conversations. These specifications are impressive but relatively primitive as compared to the possibilities shown by laboratory research. In the future it is possible that the high data rate of fiber-optic transmission may make picture phones a household reality, replace TV cables, replace satellite communication for many applications, replace modems, and provide extensive computer networking.

ASYNCHRONOUS COMMUNICATION SOFTWARE ON THE APPLE MACINTOSH

In a previous section of this chapter we discussed how asynchronous serial data can be sent or received with an 8251A on a polled or an interrupt basis. Any serial communication at some point has to get down to that level of hardware interaction. However, as we tried to show you in Chapter 13, you should write programs at the highest language level you have available without excessively sacrificing execution speed, the amount of memory used, or ease of use. In this section we show examples of serial data communication using direct UART interaction.

As an example we show you a program that downloads object code files from the Apple Macintosh to an URDA MDS.

Apple Macintosh–to–URDA MDS Download Program

The main purpose of the program described in this section is to allow the binary codes for programs developed on an Apple Macintosh computer to be downloaded through an RS-232C link to an URDA MDS.

Figure 14-21a and b shows the overall algorithm for the program, first as pseudocode and then as a flowchart.

Figure 14-22 shows the complete program. The main part of the program is several pages long. The code is "real" production code used in the serial interface add-on to the URDA board. One of the key goals of real production code is that it be small. The code is placed in EPROMs shipped with the serial add-on board. If the code is too large, then it won't fit in the EPROMs, or larger, more expensive EPROMs must be used. In the process of getting the code as small as possible, the actual layout of the code is sometimes modified to save some bytes of EPROM memory. For example, the program contains a routine TOMAIN, which is described later and which is called after completing either a program download or a upload. A download moves a file from the Macintosh to the URDA MDS, and an upload moves a file from the URDA MDS to the Macintosh. The routine TOMAIN is found directly after the download routine (MACR). By placing TOMAIN directly after MACR, we can save an instruction word that would be required to branch to TOMAIN at the end of MACR. Notice that at the end of the upload routine (MACW), there is a branch to TOMAIN using the instruction BRA TOMAIN. We will observe several examples like this in the program. This has a tendency to make the code somewhat more difficult to read and follow.

Another aspect of this code that makes it somewhat hard to read is that the actual subroutines are not broken apart from each other with comment statements. That is, labels representing the start of subroutines are not distinguished from labels that are simply internal branch points within a subroutine. The desire to make the code as compact as possible, which causes a blurring of jump points and subroutine entry points, is partially responsible.

OVERVIEW

The first operation that occurs in almost any program is initialization. This occurs in the routine INFO found at the end of the program listing. The place where the program starts executing is actually at the MACW (MACintosh Write) routine for an upload or MACR (MACintosh Read) for a download. These routines are called from the URDA MDS executive loop by following

```
INITIALIZE EVERYTHING
      GET STARTING ADDRESS
      GET END ADDRESS
      INITIALIZE 68681

IF ASCII THEN
      SET UP FOR TWO CHARACTERS PER BYTE

WHILE (COUNT <> 0)
      GET BYTE
      SEND/GET CHARACTER
      IF ASCII THEN
            GET/SEND SECOND CHARACTER
      STORE/SEND BYTE
      DECREMENT COUNT

COMPLETE OPERATION
      DISABLE 68681
      DISPLAY FINAL ADDRESS
```

(a)

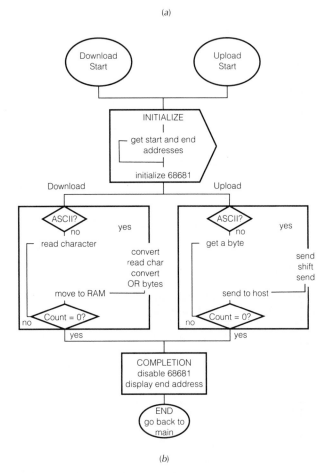

(b)

FIGURE 14-21   Algorithm for Apple Macintosh–to–URDA MDS download program. (a) Pseudocode. (b) Flowchart.

the instructions in the serial download user's manual. Notice that both MACR and MACW have a branch-to-subroutine instruction (BSR INFO) as their first instruction. INFO also performs the input loop shown in Figure 14-21. This input loop reads start and end addresses for the download and upload. Once both

;MEMORY AND I/O ADDRESSES

MRA	EQU	$B000	;ADDRESS OF DUART'S MAR1/MRA2 REGISTERS
SRA	EQU	$B002	;ADDRESS OF DUART'S SRA REGISTER
CRA	EQU	$B004	;ADDRESS OF DUART'S CRA REGISTER
THRA	EQU	$B006	;ADDRESS OF DUART'S THRA REGISTER
ACRA	EQU	$B008	;ADDRESS OF DUART'S ACRA REGISTER
FILE_NAME	EQU	$7FB6	;ADDRESS IN SYSTEM MEMORY CONTAINING LAST FILE ;NAME ENTERED
START	EQU	$7FB8	;ADDRESS IN SYSTEM MEMORY CONTAINING LAST ;STARTING ADDRESS ENTERED

;EXTERNAL REFERENCE TABLE (MONITOR ROUTINES AND THEIR LOCATIONS)

XREF	GET_FILE_NAME	;AT $0A54
XREF	DISPLAY_ERROR	;AT $0978
XREF	GET_START	;AT $0A36
XREF	BOUND_CHECK	;AT $0988
XREF	GET_END	;AT $0A40
XREF	MAIN_RETURN	;AT $04F4
XREF	ADDRESS	;AT $07E8
XREF	FORMAT_CHAR	;AT $076A
XREF	MAIN+	;AT $04DA

ADDR	CODE		INSTRUCTION		COMMENTS
1700	6100 016C	MACW:	BSR	INFO	;GET START,END ADDRESS FROM USER
1704	2C7C 0000 7FB6		MOVEA.L	#FILE_NAME,A6	
170A	3016		MOVE.W	(A6),D0	;GET FILE NAME
170C	0C40 000A		CMPI.W	$000A,D0	;IF ASCII,GO TO AFILE
1710	6708		BEQ	AFILE	
1712	2C7C 0000 0018		MOVEA.L	#(NOCONV-CONV+2),A6	;ELSE SET UP FOR NO COVERSION
1718	6006		BRA	WRITE	
171A	2C7C 0000 0002	AFILE:	MOVEA.L	#(CONV-CONV+2),A6	;SET UP FOR CONVERSION
1720	16BC 0006	WRITE:	MOVE.B	#$06,A3	;ENABLE DUART TO TRANSMIT
1724	4280		CLR.L	D0	;CLEAR D0
1726	4281		CLR.L	D1	;CLEAR D1
1728	1018	SEND:	MOVE.B	(A0)+,D0	;GET NEXT BYTE
172A	4EFB E800		JMP	CONV-2(PC,A6)	
172E	1200	CONV:	MOVE.B	D0,D1	;COPY BYTE TO D1
1730	E818		ROR.B	#4,D0	;GET UPPER NIBBLE
1732	0200 000F		AND.B	#$0F,D0	
1736	103B 0824		MOVE.B	ASCII(PC,D0.L),D0	;GET ASCII VALUE FROM TABLE
173A	6114		BSR	SENDBY	;SEND TO MACINTOSH
173C	0201 000F		AND.B	#$0F,D1	;GET LOWER NIBLE
1740	103B 181A		MOVE.B	ASCII(PC,D1.L),D0	;GET ASCII VALUE FROM TABLE
1744	610A	NOCONV:	BSR	SENDBY	
1746	4A46		TST	D6	;TEST COUNTER
1748	57CE FFDE		DBEQ	D6,SEND	;IF COUNTER <>0,GO TO SEND
174C	6000 007C		BRA	TOMAIN	
1750	1412	SENDBY:	MOVE.B	(A2),D2	;READ DUART STATUS REGISTER
1752	0802 0002		BTST	D2,#2	;IS DUART READ?
1756	67F8		BEQ	SENDBY	;IF NOT, TRY AGAIN
1758	1880		MOVE.B	D0,(A4)	;WITE BYTE TO TX REGISTER
175A	4E75		RTS		
175C	30	ASCII:	DC.B	$30	;ASCII CODE FOR 0
175D	31		DC.B	$31	;ASCII CODE FOR 1
175E	32		DC.B	$32	;ASCII CODE FOR 2
175F	33		DC.B	$33	;ASCII CODE FOR 3
1760	34		DC.B	$34	;ASCII CODE FOR 4
1761	35		DC.B	$35	;ASCII CODE FOR 5
1762	36		DC.B	$36	;ASCII CODE FOR 6
1763	37		DC.B	$37	;ASCII CODE FOR 7
1764	38		DC.B	$38	;ASCII CODE FOR 8
1765	39		DC.B	$39	;ASCII CODE FOR 9
1766	41		DC.B	$41	;ASCII CODE FOR A
1767	42		DC.B	$42	;ASCII CODE FOR B
1768	43		DC.B	$43	;ASCII CODE FOR C

FIGURE 14-22 Subroutines for download program (*continued*).

```
1769   44                          DC.B      $44              ;ASCII CODE FOR D
176A   45                          DC.B      $45              ;ASCII CODE FOR E
176B   46                          DC.B      $46              ;ASCII CODE FOR F

176C   6100 0100        MACR:      BSR       INFO             ;GET START,END ADDR FROM USER
1770   2C7C 0000 7FB6              MOVEA.L   #FILE_NAME,A6
1776   3016                        MOVE.W    (A6),D0          ;GET FILE NAME
1778   0C40 000A                   CMPI.W    $000A,D0         ;IF ASCII,GO TO AAFILE
177C   6708                        BEQ       AAFILE
177E   2C7C 0000 001E              MOVEA.L   #(RNOCOV-RCONV+2),A6   ;ELSE SET UP FOR NO COVERSION
1784   6006                        BRA       READ
1786   2C7C 0000 0002   AAFILE:    MOVEA.L   #(RCONV-RCONC+2),A6    ;SET UP FOR CONVERSION
178C   16BC 0009        READ:      MOVE.B    #$09,(A3)        ;ENABLE DUART TO RECEIVE
1790   4280                        CLR.L     D0               ;CLEAR D0
1792   4281                        CLR.L     D1               ;CLEAR D1
1794   617A                        BSR       NOLIMIT          ;GET FIRST BYTE
1796   4EFB E80C                   JMP       RCONV-2(PC,A6)
179A   223C 0000 0000   RECEIV:    MOVE.L    #$0000,D1        ;CLEAR D1
17A0   617A                        BSR       LIMIT            ;GET NEXT BYTE
17A2   4EFB E800                   JMP       RCONV-2(PC,A6)

17A6   6100 0096        RCONV:     BSR       ASTOBI           ;CONVERT UPPER NIBBLE TO BINARY
17AA   0C00 00FF                   CMPI.B    #$FF,D0          ;WAS AN INVALID CHARACTER SENT?
17AE   67EA                        BEQ       RECEIV           ;IF SO TRY AGAIN
17B0   1200                        MOVE.B    D0,D1            ;PUT UPPER NIBLE IN D1
17B2   E919                        ROL.B     #4,D1            ;ROTATE INTO POSITION
17B4   6166             LOWER:     BSR       LIMIT            ;GET NEXT BYTE
17B6   6100 0086                   BSR       ASTOBI           ;CONVERT LOWER NIBBLE TO BINARY
17BA   0C00 00FF                   CMPI.B    #$FF,D0          ;WAS AN INVALID CHARACTER SENT?
17BE   67F4                        BEQ       LOWER
17C0   8001             OROUT:     OR.B      D1,D0            ;COMBINE UBBER AND LOWER NIBBLE
17C2   10C0             RNOCONV:   MOVE.B    D0,(A0)+         ;WRITE BYTE TO MEMORY
17C4   4A46                        TST       D6               ;TEST D6
17C6   57CE FFD2                   DBEQ      D6,RECEIV        ;LOOP BACK IF COUNT <> ZERO
17CA   16BC 000A        TOMAIN:    MOVE.B    #$0A,(A3)        ;DISABLE DUART
17CE   90FC 0001                   SUB.W     #1,A0            ;FIND LAST ADDRESS
17D2   3408                        MOVE.W    A0,D2            ;PUT ADDRESS IN D2
17D4   163C 0004                   MOVE.B    #4,D3            ;FOUR CHARACTERS TO BE FORMATTED
17D8   4EB8 076A                   JSR       FORMAT_CHAR      ;FORMAR ADDRESS FOR DISPLAY
17DC   227C 0000 7FA0              MOVEA.L   #LAST_KEY,A1
17E2   22C1                        MOVE.L    D1,(A1)+         ;PUT FORMATTED ADDRESS IN BUFFER
17E4   1410                        MOVE.B    (A0),D2          ;PUT DATA IN D2
17E6   163C 0002                   MOVE.B    #2,D3            ;TWO CHARACTERS TO BE FORMATTED
17EA   4EB8 076A                   JSR       FORMAT_CHAR      ;FORMAT DATA FOR DISPLAY
17EE   2281                        MOVE.L    D1,(A1)          ;PUT FORMATTED DATA IN BUFFER
17F0   227C 0000 7F76              MOVEA.L   #USER_ADDRESS,A1
17F6   2288                        MOVE.L    A0,(AI)          ;STORE USER ADDRESS
17F8   227C 0000 7FA0              MOVEA.L   #LAST_KEY,A1
17FE   4EB8 0950                   JSR       LOAD_MESSAGE     ;LOAD DISPLAY
1802   227C 0000 7FA1              MOVEA.L   #$7FA1,A1
1808   12BC 0002                   MOVE.B    #$02,(A1)        ;SET DATA SIZE TO WORD
180C   4EF8 04DA                   JMP       MAIN+            ;BACK TO MAIN PROGRAM


1810   1412             NOLIMIT:   MOVE.B    (A2),D2          ;READ DUART STATUS REGISTER
1812   0802 0000                   BTST      D2,#0            ;IS DUART READY?
1816   67F8                        BEQ       NOLIMIT          ;IF NOT TRY AGAIN
1818   1014                        MOVE.B    (A4),D0          ;GET BYTE FROM DUART
181A   4E75                        RTS

181C   2A3C 0004 FFFF   LIMIT:     MOVE.L    #0004 FFFF,D5    ;SET TIMER
1822   5385             AGAIN:     SUB.L     #1,D5            ;DECREMENT TIMER
1824   670C                        BEQ       TOUT             ;IF TIMER EQ 0, TIME IS UP
1826   1412                        MOVE.B    (A2),D2          ;READ STATUS REGISTER
1828   0802 0000                   BTST      D2,#0            ;IS DUART READY?
182C   67F4                        BEQ       AGAIN            ;IF NOT TRY AGAIN
182E   1014                        MOVE.B    (A4),D0          ;GET BYTE
1830   4E75                        RTS
1832   2C5F             TOUT:      MOVEA.L   (SP)+,A6         ;FIX STACK
1834   103C 0000                   MOVE.B    #$00,D0          ;CLEAR D0
1838   3C38 0000                   MOVE.W    #$0000,D6        ;CLEAR COUNTER
183C   6082                        BRA       OROUT            ;GO TO OROUT

183E   0400 0030        ASTOBI:    SUB.B     #$30,D0
1842   6D0C                        BLT       DATA0
```

```
1844   0C00 0016              CMPI.B      #$16,D0
1848   6E06                   BGT         DATA0
184A   103B 080A              MOVE.B      BINARY(PC,D0.L),D0
184E   4E75                   RTS
1850   103C 00FF     DATA0:   MOVE.B      #$FF,D0
1854   4E75                   RTS

1856   00            BINARY:  DC.B        $00                    ;BINARY FOR ASCII 30
1857   01                     DC.B        $01                    ;BINARY FOR ASCII 31
1858   02                     DC.B        $02                    ;BINARY FOR ASCII 32
1859   03                     DC.B        $03                    ;BINARY FOR ASCII 33
185A   04                     DC.B        $04                    ;BINARY FOR ASCII 34
185B   05                     DC.B        $05                    ;BINARY FOR ASCII 35
185C   06                     DC.B        $06                    ;BINARY FOR ASCII 36
185D   07                     DC.B        $07                    ;BINARY FOR ASCII 37
185E   08                     DC.B        $08                    ;BINARY FOR ASCII 38
185F   09                     DC.B        $09                    ;BINARY FOR ASCII 39
1860   FF                     DC.B        $FF                    ;BINARY FOR ASCII 3A
1861   FF                     DC.B        $FF                    ;BINARY FOR ASCII 3B
1862   FF                     DC.B        $FF                    ;BINARY FOR ASCII 3C
1863   FF                     DC.B        $FF                    ;BINARY FOR ASCII 3D
1864   FF                     DC.B        $FF                    ;BINARY FOR ASCII 3E
1865   FF                     DC.B        $FF                    ;BINARY FOR ASCII 3F
1866   FF                     DC.B        $FF                    ;BINARY FOR ASCII 40
1867   0A                     DC.B        $0A                    ;BINARY FOR ASCII 41
1868   0B                     DC.B        $0B                    ;BINARY FOR ASCII 42
1869   0C                     DC.B        $0C                    ;BINARY FOR ASCII 43
186A   0D                     DC.B        $0D                    ;BINARY FOR ASCII 44
186B   0E                     DC.B        $0E                    ;BINARY FOR ASCII 45
186C   0F                     DC.B        $0F                    ;BINARY FOR ASCII 46
186D   00

186E   2F3C 0000 0978  INFO:  MOVE.L      #DISPLAY_ERROR,-(A7)
1874   4EB8 0A54              JSR         GET_FILE_NAME
1878   0C00 0013              CMPI.B      #$13,D0                ;WAS MINUS PRESSED?
187C   670C                   BEQ         ERROR                  ;IF SO, DISPLAY ERROR
187E   0C42 000A              CMPI.W      #$000A,D2              ;AN ASCII FILE?
1882   670A                   BEQ         CONTIN                 ;IF SO CONTIN
1884   0C42 000B              CMPI.W      #$000B,D2              ;A BINARY FILE?
1888   6704                   BEQ         CONTIN                 ;IF SO CONTIN
188A   4EF8 0978     ERROR:   JMP         DISPLAY_ERROR          ;ELSE DISPLAY ERROR
188E   4EB8 0A36     CONTIN:  JSR         GET_START              ;GET STARTING ADDRESS
1892   0C00 0013              CMPI.B      #$13,D0                ;MINUS KEY PRESSED?
1896   67D6                   BEQ         INFO                   ;IF SO START OVER
1898   4EB8 0988              JSR         BOUND_CHECK            ;CHECK BOUNDS
189C   4EB8 0A40              JSR         GET_END                ;GET END ADSDRESS
18A0   0C00 0013              CMPI.B      #$13,D0                ;MINUS KEY PRESSED?
18A4   67E8                   BEQ         CONTIN                 ;IF SO GET NEW START ADDRESS
18A6   4EB8 0988              JSR         BOUND_CHECK            ;CHECK BOUNDS
18AA   227C 0000 7FB8         MOVEA.L     #START,A1
18B0   3611                   MOVE.W      (A1),D3                ;GET STARTING ADDRESS OUT OF MEMORY
18B2   9443                   SUB.W       D3,D2                  ;END-START=BYTECOUNT
18B4   6BD4                   BMI         ERROR                  ;IF NEGATIVE, GO TO ERROR
18B6   2043                   MOVEA.L     D3,A0                  ;PUT START ADDRESS IN A0
18B8   3C02                   MOVE.W      D2,D6                  ;PUT BYTECOUNT IN D6
18BA   225F                   MOVEA.L     (A7)+,A1

;INITIALIZE DUART

18BC   227C 0000 B000         MOVEA.L     #MRA,A1                ;PUT MRA ADDRESS IN A1
18C2   247C 0000 B002         MOVEA.L     #SRA,A2                ;PUT SRA ADDRESS IN A2
18C8   267C 0000 B004         MOVEA.L     #CRA,A3                ;PUT CRA ADDRESS IN A3
18CE   287C 0000 B006         MOVEA.L     #THRA,A4               ;PUT THRA ADDRESS IN A4
18D4   2A7C 0000 B008         MOVEA.L     #ACRA,A5               ;PUT MRA ADDRESS IN A5

18DA   16BC 002A              MOVE.B      #$2A,(A3)              ;RESET RECEIVER
18DE   16BC 003A              MOVE.B      #$3A,(A3)              ;RESET TRANSMITTER
18E2   1ABC 0080              MOVE.B      #$80,(A5)              ;SELECT SET #1 BUAD RATES
18E6   16BC 001A              MOVE.B      #$1A,(A3)              ;RESET MRA POINTER
18EA   12BC 0013              MOVE.B      #$13,(A1)              ;WRITE 13H TO MRA1
18EE   12BC 0007              MOVE.B      #$07,(A1)              ;WRITE 07H TO MRA2
18F2   14BC 00BB              MOVE.B      #$BB,(A2)              ;SELECT 9600 BUAD

18F6   4E75                   RTS
```

FIGURE 14-22   *continued*

addresses have been read, INFO initializes the USART and returns.

The two routines MACR and MACW are the key routines that actually read or write the file. These routines implement the loop at the bottom of Figure 14-21. This loop actually reads or writes the file.

The last major routine of interest in the program is the TOMAIN routine, which cleans up after the program executes and returns to the URDA executive loop. Normally after this routine returns to the URDA executive, the user would then actually call the program that had just been downloaded, as indicated in the serial add-on user's manual. The clean up that TOMAIN performs consists primarily of disabling the USART.

INITIALIZATION

The UART used on the Apple Macintosh is a custom ACIA manufactured for Apple specifically for use with the Macintosh. The URDA MDS uses a 68681, which is a modern, VLSI dual-port ACIA. The 68681 is initialized very simply with a byte written to the IC's command port and then to the data port, as we have seen previously. The routine starting at the label INFO performs initialization of the 68681. This routine writes to the 68681's memory-mapped registers to perform this initialization in a manner analogous to that which we have seen for an 8251A.

The INFO routine also gets a start and an end address from the user. These addresses are the ones that will be used for the following download or upload. Notice that the addresses are checked as a part of the INFO routine to make sure they are "reasonable." The routine BOUND_CHECK is a routine in the URDA monitor code that makes sure that the address specified is actually a valid RAM address. If it were not, then attempting to write to the address could generate a bus error and cause the program (and the whole URDA executive) to fail with a bus error. The program also checks the start and end addresses by subtracting the start from the end to produce a byte count of the number of bytes to be downloaded. If this count is negative, then that is also an error, and the routine jumps to DISPLAY_ERROR. DISPLAY_ERROR is a routine in the URDA executive code that puts an error message on the LED display and then returns to the URDA executive loop.

The routine INFO uses two other routines provided by the URDA executive, GET_START and GET_END. These routines are the ones that actually gather the user input as keys are pressed. If you would like to see the actual code for these routines, then consult the listing for the URDA executive. This code is available as an option when ordering the URDA MDS. These routines are the same as the ones we have seen previously for reading input from a keyboard and converting it to binary values.

COMPLETION

The routine TOMAIN is called when the download or upload is completed. Notice again that at the end of the routine, MACR is a branch to TOMAIN but that at the end of MACW, the flow of control simply continues on into TOMAIN, so no branch instruction is needed. The routine TOMAIN disables the USART and then it takes the last address that was downloaded into (or uploaded from), formats it, and displays it on the URDA LED display. This allows the user to verify that the proper final address was reached. The routine TOMAIN uses the URDA executive routine FORMAT_CHAR to perform the formatting and the routine LOAD_MESSAGE to display the message. The last thing the routine TOMAIN does is to jump back to the main URDA executive using the instruction JMP MAIN+. MAIN+ is a location in the URDA main executive loop after the initialization. We don't want to reinitialize the URDA executive, since this would clear the LEDs and erase the address that TOMAIN just displayed there.

THE FILE READ SUBROUTINE

The two routines of most interest in this program are the MACR and MACW routines, which actually perform the file download or upload. These routines use a few small "helper" routines also included in the program code. The MACR routine is one of the major entry points of this program (the other is MACW). The first thing MACR does is to call the INFO routine to get the starting and end addresses from the user. The MACR routine then looks at the file name to be downloaded (uploaded) to determine whether it is supposed to perform an ASCII or a binary operation. If an ASCII download is occurring, then each byte comes across the serial line as two ASCII characters that must be read and combined into one byte to be placed in memory. If binary is used, then the bytes come across the serial line as a single byte and are placed in memory directly. MACR contains code to perform both types of operation (reading pairs of ASCII bytes or reading single binary bytes). The address of a location that corresponds to the desired type of operation is placed in A6. This value is a code offset that is used in a PC relative jump instruction: JMP RCONV-2(PC,A6).

Looking at the end of the routine MACR, the label RNOCONV: (Read NO CONVersion) is where the byte that has just been read (or composed from two ASCII bytes) is moved into memory. Then the counter in D6 is decremented, and a branch occurs to get the next byte if the count is not exhausted. If the count is exhausted, then the routine falls into the TOMAIN routine and goes back to the URDA executive main loop. The INFO routine placed bytecount into D6 when it was called at the beginning of MACR.

The RECEIV: label is where 1 byte is read from the serial line. The helper routine LIMIT is used to perform the read. The two helper routines LIMIT and NOLIMIT are where the bytes are actually read from the USART. These routines both loop check the USART status, waiting for it to indicate that a byte is ready. The difference between the two is that the NOLIMIT routine will loop forever waiting for a byte, whereas the LIMIT routine has a counter in the loop, which it counts down. If the counter gets to 0 before a byte is ready, then the LIMIT routine returns without reading a byte. The calling routine MACR or MACW must be absolutely sure a byte is coming before calling NOLIMIT, but it can call LIMIT to check for a byte without fearing that the helper routine may never return.

The JMP RCONV-2(PC,A6) instruction following the RECEIVE: is actually a dual-function instruction. That is, if a binary conversion is occurring, then MACR will have put a value into A6 such that this jump goes directly to RNOCONV. If an ASCII download is occurring, then this jump instruction will simply jump to the CONV: location. At CONV (CONVert from ASCII to binary), a call is made to the ASTOBI (ASCII to BInary) subroutine. ASTOBI is another interesting helper routine that uses an ASCII lookup table to convert the ASCII character just read into its binary equivalent. We have seen several types of ASCII-to-binary conversion routines. This is a slightly different form of one we have seen before. The ASCII character is converted to a binary index, which is used to read the equivalent binary values from the BINARY table.

In the convert routine, the binary value to which the ASCII character was converted is shifted to the upper nibble of the byte. Recall that two hex digits represent the upper 4 and the lower 4 bits of the binary equivalent. The CONV code flow in the MACR routine then reads another character from the USART (using LIMIT again), converts it to binary (using ASTOBI), ORs it with the upper nibble, and finally moves the resulting byte into RAM.

THE FILE WRITE SUBROUTINE

The file write subroutine sends a file from the URDA MDS to the Macintosh. This operation is known as a file *upload.* The routine MACW accomplishes this task. MACW is basically the same as the MACR routine, except that it sends bytes of data to the Macintosh rather than receiving data. The routine is organized similarly to the MACR routine in that it can handle both binary uploads and ASCII uploads. The same type of technique is used, loading an offset into A6 and using that offset to jump to one of two locations. A helper routine, SENDBY, actually sends the bytes to the Macintosh (or IBM PC). SENDBY simply loops, reading the CTS (clear-to-send) line until it is set, indicating that the Macintosh is ready to receive a byte. Then the byte is moved to the USART register, which sends it along the serial line to the Macintosh.

The MACW routine uses two branch targets, CONV and NOCONV to perform either a single-byte (no conversion) upload or an ASCII upload, where each memory byte is sent as two ASCII characters. The MACW routine has an embedded conversion from binary to ASCII using a technique similar to the ASTOBI routine used by MACR. In this case a table of ASCII character values is used, and the upper or lower nibble of the memory byte is used to index into the table.

When MACW starts, it calls INFO just as does MACR, and when it is done, it jumps to TOMAIN.

CONCLUSION

One interesting observation in this program is the use of the JSR instruction to call routines in the URDA executive program and the use of BSR to call local subroutines. The JSR instruction is normally used to call subroutines that are a long way (that is far away in memory) from the current location, whereas BSR is used to call subroutines that are close by.

One item we didn't mention is the TOUT part of the LIMIT routine. The TOUT (TimeOUT) location deals with what happens when the time is counted down to 0 and no character has yet been read from the Macintosh. In such a case, the code simply removes the return address from the stack, clears registers D0 and D6, and jumps back to the end of the RECEIV loop at location OROUT. By clearing the count register, D6, this has the effect of ending the input loop altogether. It is hoped that the user will notice that the end address displayed when the MACW routine ends is not the correct one. Then the user can correct the problem that caused the character not to be received by the URDA MDS (perhaps the serial connector was unplugged somehow) and try again.

This program was written to do a specific job. Space limitations prevented us from making the program as ''friendly'' as we would have liked it to be. Perhaps you can see how the program could easily be modified to, for example, let the user enter the desired communications port number and the desired baud rate.

SYNCHRONOUS SERIAL DATA COMMUNICATION AND PROTOCOLS

Introduction

Most of the discussion of serial data transfer up to this point in the chapter has been about asynchronous transmission. For asynchronous serial transmission, a start bit is used to identify the beginning of each data character, and at least one stop bit is used to identify the end of each data character. The transmitter and the receiver are effectively synchronized on a character-by-character basis. With a start bit, 1 stop bit, and 1 parity bit, a total of 10 bits must be sent for each 7-bit ASCII character. This means that 30 percent of the transmission time is wasted. A more efficient method of transferring serial data is to synchronize the transmitter and the receiver and then send a large block of data characters one after the other, with no time between characters. No start or stop bits are then needed with individual data characters, because the receiver automatically knows that every 8 bits received after synchronization represents a data character. When a block of data is not being sent through a synchronous data link, the line is held in a marking condition. To indicate the start of a transmission, the transmitter sends out one or more unique characters called *sync characters* or a unique bit pattern called a *flag,* depending on the system being used. The receiver uses the sync characters or the flag to synchronize its internal clock with that of the receiver. The receiver then shifts in the data-following characters and converts them to parallel form so they can be read in by a computer. As we said in the discussions of modems and ISDN, high-speed modems and digital communication channels use synchronous transmission.

Recall from a previous section that a hardware-level set of handshake signals is required to transmit asynchronous or synchronous digital data over phone lines with modems. In addition to this handshaking, a higher level of coordination, or protocol, is required between transmitter and receiver to assure the orderly transfer of data. A protocol in this case is an agreed-upon set of rules concerning the form in which the data is to be sent. There are many different serial data protocols. The two most common that we discuss here are the IBM binary synchronous communications protocol, or BISYNC, and the high-level data link control protocol, or HDLC.

Binary Synchronous Communication Protocol (BISYNC)

BISYNC is referred to as a byte-controlled protocol (BCP), because specified ASCII or EBCDIC characters (bytes) are used to indicate the start of a message and to handshake between the transmitter and the receiver. Incidentally, even in a full-duplex system, BISYNC protocol allows data transfer in only one direction at a time.

Figure 14-23 shows the general message format for BISYNC. For our first cycle through this, we will assume that the transmitter has received a message from the receiver that it is ready to receive a transmission. If no message is being sent, the line is in an *idle* condition, with a continuous high on the line. To indicate the start of a message, the transmitting system sends two or more previously agreed-upon sync characters. For example, a sync character might be the ASCII $16. As we said before, the receiver uses these sync characters to synchronize its clock with that of the transmitter. A header may then be sent if desired. The header contents are usually defined for a specific system and may include information about the type, priority, and destination of the message that follows. The start of the header is indicated with a special character called start-of-header (SOH), which in ASCII is represented by $01.

After the header, if present, the beginning of the text portion of the message is indicated by another special character called start-of-text (STX), which is repre-

sented in ASCII by $02. To indicate the end of the text portion of the message, an end-of-text (ETX) character or an end-of-block (ETB) character is sent. The text portion may contain 128 or 256 characters (different systems use different-size blocks of text). Immediately following the ETX character, one or two block check characters (BCC) are sent. For systems using ASCII, the BCC is a single byte representing complex parity information computed for the text of the message. For systems using EBCDIC, a 16-bit cyclic redundancy check is performed on the text part of the message, and the 16-bit result is sent as 2 BCCs. The point of these BCCs is that the receiving system can recompute the value for them from the received data and compare the results with the BCCs sent from the transmitter. If the BCCs are not equal, the receiver can send a message to the transmitter telling it to send the message again. Now let's look at how messages are used for data transfer handshaking between the transmitter and the receiver.

To start, let's assume that we have a remote "smart" terminal connected to a computer with a half-duplex connection. Further, let's assume that the computer is in the receive mode. Now, when the program in the terminal determines that it has a block of data to send to the computer, it first sends a message with the text containing only the single character ENQ (ASCII $05), which stands for enquiry. The terminal then switches to receive mode to await the reply from the computer. The computer reads the ENQ message, and, if it is not ready to receive data, it sends back a text message containing the single character for negative acknowledge, NAK (ASCII $15). If the receiver is ready, it sends a message containing the character for affirmative acknowledge, ACK (ASCII $06). In either case, the computer then switches to receive mode to await the next message from the terminal. If the terminal received a NAK, it may give up, or it may wait a while and try again. If the terminal received an ACK, it will send a message containing a block of text and ending with a BCC character or characters. After sending the message, the terminal switches to receive mode and awaits a reply from the computer as to whether the message was received correctly. The computer, meanwhile, computes the BCC for the received block of data and compares it with the BCC sent with the message. If the two BCCs are not equal, the computer sends an NAK message to the terminal. This tells the terminal to send the message again, because it was not received correctly. If the two BCCs are equal, then the computer sends an ACK message to the terminal, which tells it to send the next message or block of text. In a system where multiple blocks of data are being transferred, an ACK 0 message is usually sent for one block, an ACK 1 message sent for the next, and an ACK 0 again sent for the next. The alternating ACK messages are a further help in error checking. In either case, after the message is sent, the computer switches to receive mode to await a response from the terminal.

A variation of BISYNC commonly used to transfer binary files in the PC environment and between Unix

DIRECTION OF SERIAL DATA FLOW

FIGURE 14-23   General message format for binary synchronous communication (BISYNC).

systems and PCs is called XMODEM. An XMODEM block consists of an SOH character, a block number, 128 bytes of data (padded if necessary to fill the block), and an 8-bit checksum. A transmission starts with the receiver sending a NAK character to the sender. The sender then sends a block of data. If the data is received correctly, the receiver sends back an ACK and the sender sends the next block of data. If the data is not received correctly, the receiver sends a NAK and the sender sends the block again. The transmission is completed when the sender sends an end-of-transmission (EOT) character and the receiver replies with an ACK.

One major problem with a BISYNC-type protocol is that the transmitter must stop after each block of data is transferred and wait for an ACK or NAK signal from the receiver. Due to the wait and line turnaround times, the actual data transfer rate may be only half the theoretical rate predicted by the physical bit rate of the data link. The HDLC protocol discussed in a later section greatly reduces this problem. Next we want to return to the Intel 8251A USART, which is used on the IBM PC Synchronous Communication Adapter, and give you a brief look at how it is used for BISYNC communication.

Using the Intel 8251A USART for BISYNC Communication

We initialize an 8251A by first getting its attention, sending it a mode word, and then sending it a command word. To initialize the 8251A for synchronous communication, 0s are put in the least-significant 2 bits of the mode word. The rest of the bits in the mode word then have the meanings shown in Figure 14-24a. Most of the bit functions should be reasonably clear from the descriptions in the figure, but a couple need a little more explanation.

Bit 6 of the mode word specifies the SYNDET pin on the 8251A to be an input or an output. The pin is programmed to function as an input if external circuitry is used to detect the sync character in the data bit stream. When programmed as an output, this pin will go high when the 8251A has found one or more sync characters in the data bit stream.

Bit 7 of the mode word is used to specify whether one sync character or a sequence of two different sync characters is to be looked for at the start of a message.

To initialize an 8251A for synchronous operation: Send a series of nulls and a software reset command to the control address. Send a mode word based on the format in Figure 14-24a to the control address. Send the desired sync character for that particular system to the control address of the 8251A. If a second sync character is needed, send it to the control address. Send a command word to the control address to enable the transmitter, enable the receiver, and enable the device to look for sync characters in the data bit stream coming in on the RxD input.

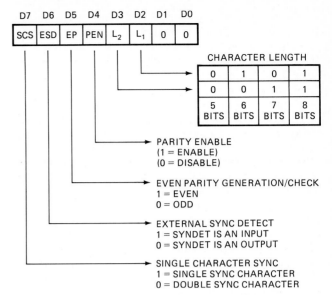

(a)

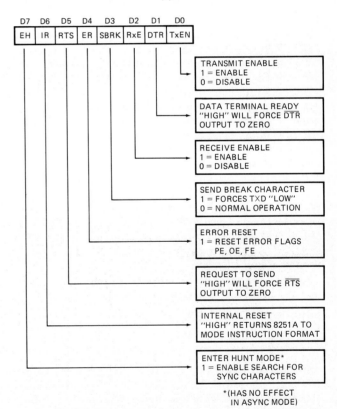

(b)

FIGURE 14-24 8251A synchronous formats. (a) Mode word. (b) Command word.

The command word format is shown in Figure 14-24b. Let's see how the 8251A participates in a synchronous data transfer. Try to keep separate the parts of the process that are done by the 8251A and the parts that are done by software at one end of the link or the other.

To start, let's assume the 8251A is in a terminal that has blocks of data to send to a computer, as we described earlier in this section. Further assume that the computer is in receive mode waiting for a transmission from the terminal and that the 8251A in the terminal has been initialized and is sending out a continuous high on the TxD line.

An I/O driver routine in the terminal will start the transfer process by sending a sync character(s), SOH character, header characters, STX character, ENQ character, ETX character, and BCC byte to the 8251A, one after the other. The 8251A sends the characters out in synchronous serial format (no start and stop bits). If, for some reason such as a high-priority interrupt, the CPU stops sending characters while a message is being sent, the 8251A will automatically insert sync characters until the flow of data characters from the CPU resumes.

After the ENQ message has been sent, the CPU in the terminal awaits a reply from the computer through the RxD input of the 8251A. If the 8251A has been programmed to enter hunt mode by sending it a control word with a 1 in bit 7, it will continuously shift in bits from the RxD line and check after each shift if the character in the receive buffer is a sync character. When it finds a sync character, the 8251A asserts the SYNDET pin high, exits the hunt mode, and starts the normal data read operation. When the 8251A has a valid data character in its receiver buffer, the RxRDY pin will be asserted, and the RxRDY bit in the status register will be set. Characters can then be read in by the CPU on a polled or an interrupt basis.

When the CPU has read in the entire message, it can determine whether the message was a NAK or an ACK. If the message was an ACK, the CPU can then send the actual data message sequence of characters to the 8251A. Handshake and data messages will be sent back and forth until all the desired block of data has been sent to the computer. In the next section we discuss another protocol used for synchronous serial data transfer.

High-level Data Link Control (HDLC) and Synchronous Data Link Control (SDLC) Protocols

The BISYNC-type protocols we discussed in the previous section work only in half-duplex mode; except for XMODEM, have difficulty transmitting pure 8-bit binary data such as object code for programs; and are not easily adapted to serving multiple units sharing a common data link. In an attempt to solve these problems, the International Standards Organization (ISO) proposed the high-level data link control protocol (HDLC) and IBM developed the synchronous data link control protocol (SDLC). The standards are so nearly identical that, for the discussion here, we will treat them together under the name HDLC and indicate any significant differences as needed.

As we said previously, BISYNC is referred to as a byte-controlled protocol because character codes or

bytes such as SOH, STX, and ETX are used to mark off parts of a transmitted message or act as control messages. HDLC is referred to as a bit-oriented protocol (BOP) because messages are treated simply as a string of bits rather than a string of characters. The group of bits that makes up a message is referred to as a frame. The three types of frames used are information, or I, frames, supervisory control sequences, or S frames, and command/response, or U, frames. The three types of frames all have the same basic format.

Figure 14-25a shows the format of an HDLC frame. Each part of the frame is referred to as a field. A frame starts and ends with a specific bit pattern, 0111 1110, called a flag, or flag field. When no data is being sent, the line idles with all 1s, or continuous flags. Immediately after the flag field is an 8-bit address field, which contains the address of the destination unit for a control or information frame and the source of the response for a response frame.

Figure 14-25b shows the meaning of the bits in the 8-bit control field for each of the three types of frames. We don't have the space or the desire to explain the meaning of all these. A little later, however, we explain the use of the Ns and Nr bits in the control byte for an information frame.

The information field, which is present only in information frames, can have any number of bits in HDLC protocol, but in SDLC the number of bits has to be a multiple of 8. In some systems as many as 10,000 or

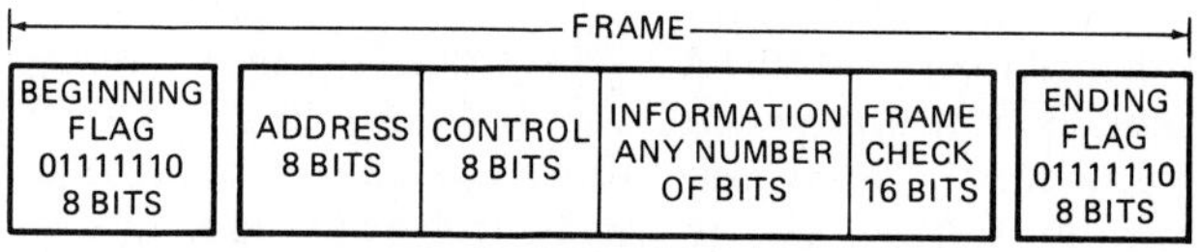

(a)

BITS IN CONTROL FIELD

HDLC FRAME FORMAT	7	6	5	4	3	2	1	0
I-FRAME (INFORMATION TRANSFER COMMANDS/RESPONSES)	Nr	Nr	Nr	P/F	Ns	Ns	Ns	0
S-FRAME (SUPERVISORY COMMANDS/RESPONSES)	Nr	Nr	Nr	P/F	S	S	0	1
U-FRAME (UNNUMBERED COMMANDS/RESPONSES)	M	M	M	P/F	M	M	1	1

SENDING ORDER – BIT 0 FIRST, BIT 7 LAST

NS THE TRANSMITTING STATION SEND SEQUENCE NUMBER, BIT 2 IS THE LOW-ORDER BIT.

P/F THE POLL BIT FOR PRIMARY STATION TRANSMISSIONS, AND THE FINAL BIT FOR SECONDARY STATION TRANSMISSIONS.

Nr THE TRANSMITTING STATION RECEIVE SEQUENCE NUMBER, BIT 6 IS THE LOW-ORDER BIT.

S THE SUPERVISORY FUNCTION BITS

M THE MODIFIER FUNCTION BITS

(b)

FIGURE 14-25 (a) Format of HDLC frame. (b) Meaning of bits in 8-bit control field of frame.

20,000 information bits may be sent per frame. Now, the question may occur to you, What happens if the data contains the flag bit pattern, 0111 1110? The answer to this question is that a special hardware circuit modifies the bit stream between flags so that there are never more than five 1s in sequence. To do this the circuit monitors the data stream and automatically stuffs in a 0 after any series of five 1s. A complementary circuit in the receiver removes the extra 0s. This scheme allows character codes or binary data to be sent without the problems BISYNC has in this area.

The next field in a frame is the 16-bit frame-check sequence (FCS). This is a cyclic redundancy word derived from all the bits between the beginning and end flags, not including 0s inserted to prevent false flag bytes. This CRC value is recomputed by the receiving system to check for errors.

Finally, a frame is terminated by another flag byte. The ending flag for one frame may be the starting flag for another frame.

In order to describe the HDLC data transfer process, we first need to define a couple of terms. HDLC is used for communication between two or more systems on a data link. One of the systems or stations on the link will always be set up as a controller for the link. This station is called the *primary station.* Other stations on the link are referred to as *secondary stations.*

Now, suppose that a primary station—a computer, for example—wants to send several frames of information to a secondary station such as another computer or terminal. Here's how a transfer might take place.

The primary station starts by sending an S frame containing the address of the desired secondary station and a control word that inquires if the receiver is ready. The secondary station then sends an S frame that contains the address of the primary station and a control word that indicates its ready status. If the secondary station receiver is ready, the primary station then sends a sequence of information frames. The information frames contain the address of the secondary station, a control word, a block of information, and the FCS words. For all but the last frame of a sequence of information frames, the P/F bit in the control byte is a 0. The 3 Ns bits in the control byte contain the number of the frame in the sequence.

Now, as the secondary station receives each information frame, it reads the data into memory and computes the frame check sequence for the frame. For each frame in a sequence that the secondary station receives correctly, it increments an internal counter. When the primary station sends the last frame in a sequence of up to seven frames, it makes the P/F bit in the control byte a 1. This is a signal to the secondary station that the primary station wants a response concerning the number of frames that were received correctly. The secondary station responds with an S frame. The Nr bits in the control word of this S frame contain the sequence number of the last frame that was received correctly plus 1. In other words, Ns represents the number of the next expected frame. The primary station compares Ns − 1 with the number of frames sent in the sequence. If the two numbers do not agree, the primary station knows that it must retransmit some frames, because they were not all received correctly. The Nr number tells the primary station at which frame number to start the retransmission. For example, if Nr is 3, the primary station will retransmit the sequence of frames starting with frame 3. If the sequence of frames was received correctly, another series of frames can be sent if desired. Actually, since HDLC operates in full duplex, the receiving station can be queried after each frame is sent to see if the previous frame was received correctly. A similar series of actions takes place when a secondary station transmits to a primary station or to another secondary station.

One advantage of this HDLC scheme is that a large number of bits can be sent in a frame so the framing bit percentage is low. Another advantage is that the transmitter does not have to stop after every short message for an acknowledge, as it does in BISYNC protocol. True, several frames may have to be sent again in case of an error, but in low-error-rate systems, this is the exception. HDLC is often used with high-speed modems, and, as we show in the next section, HDLC is used along with some higher-level protocols for network communication between a wide variety of systems.

A final point to discuss here is how HDLC protocol is implemented with a microcomputer. At the basic hardware level, a standard USART cannot be used because of the need to stuff and strip 0 bits. Instead, specially designed parts such as the Intel 8273 HDLC/SDLC protocol controller are used. Devices such as this automatically stuff and strip the required 0 bits, generate and check frame-check sequence words, and produce the interface signals for RS-232C. The devices interface directly to microcomputer buses.

The actual control of which station uses the data link at a particular time and the formatting of frames is done by the system software. The next section discusses how several systems can be connected together, or *networked,* so they can communicate with each other.

LOCAL AREA NETWORKS

Introduction

The objective of this section is to show you how several computers can be connected together to communicate with each other and to share common peripherals such as printers, large disk drives, fax machines, etc. We will start with simple cases and progress to the type of network that might be used in the computerized electronics factory we described in an earlier chapter.

To communicate between a single terminal and a nearby computer, a simple RS-232C connection is sufficient. If the computer is distant, then a modem and phone line or a leased phone line is used, depending on the required data rate. For a more difficult case, suppose that we have 100 terminals in a university building that need to communicate with a distant computer. We could use 100 phone lines with modems, but this seems quite inefficient. One solution to this problem is to run wires from all the terminals to a central point in the building and then use a multiplexer or data concentrator of some type to send all the communications over one wideband line. Either time-domain multiplexing or frequency-division multiplexing can be used. A demultiplexer at the other end of the line reconstructs the original signals.

As another example of computer communication, suppose that we have several computers in one building or in a complex of buildings and that the computers need to communicate with each other. Our computerized electronics factory is an example of this situation. What is needed in this case is a high-speed network, commonly called a *local area network*, or LAN, connecting the computers together. We start our discussion of LANs by showing you some of the basic ways that the systems on a network are connected together.

LAN Topologies

The different ways of physically connecting devices on a network with each other are commonly referred to as *topologies*. Figure 14-26 shows the five most common topologies and some pertinent data about each, such as examples of commercially available systems that use each type.

In a *star topology* network, a central controller coordinates all communication between devices on the network. The most familiar example of how this works is probably a private automatic branch exchange, or

PABX, phone system. In a PABX all calls from one phone on the system to another or to an outside phone are routed through a central switchboard. The new digital PABX systems allow direct communication between computers within a building at rates up to perhaps 100 Kbits/s.

In the *loop* topology, one device acts as a controller. If a device wants to communicate with one or more other devices on the loop, it sends a request to the controller. If the loop is not in use, the controller enables the one device to output and the other device(s) to receive. The GPIB or IEEE 488 bus described in the last section of this chapter is an example of this topology.

In the *common-bus* topology, control of the bus is spread among all the devices on the bus. The connection in this type of system is simply a wire (usually but not always a coaxial cable), into which any number of devices can be tapped. Any device can take over the bus to transmit data. Data is transmitted in fixed-length blocks called *packets*. One common scheme to prevent two devices from transmitting at the same time is called *carrier sense, multiple access with collision detection*, or CSMA/CD. We discuss the details of CSMA/CD in a later section on Ethernet.

In a *ring* network, the control is also distributed among all the devices on the network. Each device on the ring functions as a repeater, which means that it simply takes in the data stream and passes the data stream on to the next device on the ring if it is not the intended receiver for the data. Data always circulates around the ring in one direction. Any device can transmit on the ring. A token is one common way used to prevent two or more devices from transmitting at the same time. A token is a specific lone byte, such as 0111 1111, which is circulated around the ring when no device is transmitting. A device must possess the token in order to transmit. When a device needs to transmit, it removes the token from the bus, thus preventing any other devices from transmitting. After transmitting one or more packets of data, the transmitting device puts the token back on the ring so another device can grab it and transmit. We discuss this more in a later section.

The final topology we want to discuss here is the *tree-structured network*, which often uses broadband transmission. Before we can really explain this one, we need to introduce you to a couple of terms commonly used with networks. In some networks such as Ethernet, data is transmitted directly as digital signals at rates of up to 10 Mbits/s. With this type of signal, only one device can transmit at a time. This form of data transmission is often referred to as *baseband transmission*, because only one basic frequency is used. The other common form of data transmission on a network is referred to as *broadband transmission*. Broadband transmission is based on a frequency-division multiplexing scheme such as that used for community antenna television (CATV) systems. The radio-frequency spectrum is divided up into 6-MHz-bandwidth channels.

A single device or group of devices can be assigned one channel for transmitting and another for receiv-

TOPOLOGY	TYPICAL PROTOCOLS	TYPICAL NO. OF NODES	TYPICAL SYSTEMS
STAR	RS-232C OR COMPUTER	TENS	PABX, COMPUTER μC CLUSTERS
LOOP	SDLC	TENS	IBM 3600/3700, μC CLUSTERS
COMMON BUS	CSMA/CD OR CSMA WITH ACKNOWLEDGMENT	TENS TO HUNDREDS PER SEGMENT	ETHERNET, NET/ONE, OMNINET, Z-NET μC CLUSTERS
RING	SDLC HDLC (TOKEN PASSING)	TENS TO HUNDREDS PER CHANNEL	PRIMENET, DOMAIN, OMNILINK μC CLUSTERS
OTHER SERVICES BROADBAND BUS	CSMA/CD RS-232C & OTHERS PER CHANNEL	TWO TO HUNDREDS PER CHANNEL	WANGNET, LOCALNET M/A-COM

- • TERMINAL
- ▮ DISTRIBUTED CONTROL
- Ⓒ LOCAL CONTROLLER
- ⓒ MULTINETWORK CONTROLLER
- (FDM) FREQUENCY DIVISION MULTIPLEX

FIGURE 14-26 Summary of common computer network topologies.

ing. Each channel or pair of channels is considered a branch on the tree. Special modems are used to convert digital signals to and from the modulated radio-frequency signals required. The multiple channels and the 6-MHz bandwidth of the channels in a broadband network allow voice, data, and video signals to be transmitted at the same time throughout the network. This is an advantage over baseband systems, which can transmit only one digital data signal at a time, but the broadband system is much more expensive.

Network Protocols

In order for different systems on a network to communicate effectively with each other, a series of rules or protocols must be agreed upon and followed by all the devices on the network. The International Standards Organization, in an attempt to bring some order to the chaos of network communication, has developed a set of standards called the *open systems interconnection* (OSI) model. This model is more of a recommendation than a rigid standard, but to increase compatibility more and more manufacturers are attempting to follow it. The OSI model is a seven-layer hierarchy of protocols, as shown in Figure 14-27. This layered approach structures the design tasks and makes it possible to change, for example, the actual hardware used to transmit the data without changing the other layers. We will use a common network operation, electronic mail, to explain the function of the upper-layers model.

Electronic mail allows a user on one system of a network to send a message to another user on the same system or on another system. The message is actually sent to a "mailbox" in a hard-disk file. Each user on the network periodically checks a personal mailbox to see if it contains any messages. If any messages are present, they can be read out and then deleted from the mailbox.

The application layer of the OSI model specifies the general operation of network services such as elec-

tronic mail, file management, program-to-program communication, and peripheral sharing. For our electronic mail example, this layer of the protocol would specify the format for invoking the electronic mail function.

The presentation layer of the OSI protocol governs the programs which convert messages to the code and format that will be understood by the receiver. For our electronic mail message, this layer might involve translating the message from ASCII codes to EBCDIC codes and formatting the message into packets or frames, such as those we described for HDLC in a previous section on standard file format. Data compression and encryption also fall in this layer of the protocol.

The session layer of the OSI protocol establishes and terminates logical connections on the network. This layer is responsible for opening and closing named files, for translating a user name into a physical network address, and for checking passwords. Electronic mail allows you to specify the intended receiver of a message by name. It is the responsibility of this layer of the protocol to make the connection between the name and the network address of the named receiver.

The transport layer of the protocol is responsible for making sure a message is transmitted and received correctly. An example of the operation of this protocol layer is the ACK or NAK handshake used in BISYNC transmission after the receiver has checked to see if the data was received correctly. For electronic mail, the message can be written to the addressed mailbox and then read back to make sure it was sent correctly.

The network layer of the protocol is used only in multichannel networks. It is responsible for finding a path through the network to the desired receiver by switching between channels. The function of this layer is similar to the function of postal mail routing, which finds a route to get a letter from your house to the addressed destination. Another example of the function performed by this layer is the telephone switching system that finds a route to connect a phone call.

The data link layer of the OSI model is responsible for the transmission of packets or blocks from sender to receiver. At this level the BCC characters or CRC characters are generated and checked, 0s are stuffed in the data, and flags and addresses are added to data frames. The HDLC data transmission protocol described earlier in this chapter is an example of the type of factors involved in this layer.

The physical layer of the OSI model is the lowest level. This layer is used to specify the connectors, cables, voltage levels, bit rates, modulation methods, etc. RS-232C is an example of a standard that falls in this layer of the model.

We don't have space here to discuss all the different networks listed as examples in Figure 14-26, but we do discuss a few of the most common ones. To start, we take a more detailed look at the operation of a very widespread common-bus network, Ethernet. Ethernet is a trademark of Xerox Corporation.

LAYER	LAYER NUMBER	FUNCTION
APPLICATION	7	SELECTS APPROPRIATE SERVICE FOR APPLICATIONS
PRESENTATION	6	PROVIDES CODE CONVERSION, DATA REFORMATTING
SESSION	5	COORDINATES INTERACTION BETWEEN END-APPLICATION PROCESSES
TRANSPORT	4	PROVIDES END-TO-END DATA INTEGRITY AND QUALITY OF SERVICE
NETWORK	3	SWITCHES AND ROUTES INFORMATION
DATA LINK	2	TRANSFERS UNITS OF INFORMATION TO OTHER END OF PHYSICAL LINK
PHYSICAL	1	TRANSMITS BIT STREAM TO MEDIUM

FIGURE 14-27 International Standards Organization open systems interconnection (OSI) model for network communications.

Ethernet

The Ethernet network standard was originally developed by Xerox Corporation. Later Xerox, DEC, and Intel worked on defining the standard sufficiently so that commercial products for implementing the standard were possible. It has now been adopted, with slight changes, as the IEEE 802.3 standard.

Physically, Ethernet is implemented in a common-bus topology with a single 50-Ω coaxial cable. Data is sent over the cable using baseband transmission at 10 Mbits/s. Data bits are encoded using Manchester coding, as shown in Figure 14-28. The advantage of this coding is that each bit cell contains a signal transition. A system that wants to transmit data on the network first checks for these transitions to see if the network is currently busy. If the system detects no transitions, then it can go ahead and transmit on the network.

Figure 14-29 shows how a very simple Ethernet is set up. The backbone of the system is the coaxial cable. Terminations are put on each end of the cable to prevent signal reflections and each unit is connected into the cable with a simple tee-type tap. A transmitter-receiver, or transceiver, sends out data on the coax, receives data from the coax, and detects any attempt to transmit while the coax is already in use. The transceiver is connected to an interface board with a 15-pin connector and four twisted-wire pairs. The transceiver cable can be as long as 15 m. The interface board, as the name implies, performs most of the work of getting data on and off the network in the correct form. The interface board assembles and disassembles data frames, sends out source and destination addresses, detects transmission errors, and prevents transmission while some other unit on the network is transmitting.

The method used by a unit to gain access to the network is CSMA/CD. Before a unit attempts to transmit on the network, it looks at the coax to see if a carrier (Manchester code transitions) is present. If a carrier is present, the unit waits some random length of time and then tries again. When the unit finds no carrier on the line, it starts transmitting. While it is transmitting, it also monitors the line to make sure no other unit is transmitting at the same time. It may occur to you at this point to wonder how another unit can be transmitting at the same time if a unit cannot start transmitting until it finds no carrier on the coax. The answer to this question involves propagation de-lay. Since transceivers can be as much as 2500 m apart, it may take as long as 23 μs for data transmitted from one unit to reach another unit. In other words, one unit may start transmitting before the signal from a transmitter that started earlier reaches it. A situation where two units transmit at the same time is referred to as a *collision*. When a unit detects a collision, it will keep transmitting long enough for all transmitting stations to detect that a collision has occurred and then stop transmitting. Any other transmitting units will also stop transmitting and try again after a random period of time. The term *multiple access* in the CSMA/CD name means that any unit on the network can attempt to transmit. The network has no central controller to control which unit has use of the network at a particular time. Access is gained by any unit using the mechanism we have just described.

The maximum number of units that can be connected on a single Ethernet is 1024. For further information about how an interface board is built, consult the data sheets for the Intel 82586 LAN coprocessor and the data sheets for the Intel 82501 Ethernet serial interface.

One problem with standard Ethernet is the coax cable used to connect units on the network. This cable is expensive and somewhat difficult to get through wiring conduits in existing buildings. To solve these problems, a new Ethernet standard was developed that is called thin Ethernet, or 10BaseT. The 10 in this name indicates 10-Mbit/s transmission and the T in the name stands for twisted-pair telephone wire. By limiting the maximum distance between units to 100 m rather than the 2500-m maximum for standard Ethernet, a 10BaseT network can use standard telephone-type wiring, which is often already installed or can easily be installed. The basic operation of the 10BaseT network is basically the same as that of the standard Ethernet we described previously.

Another problem with Ethernet is that as the amount of traffic on the network increases, the time that a unit on the end of the network has to wait before it can transmit may become very long. As the number of units increases, the number of collisions and the amount of time spent waiting for a "clear shot" increases. This degrades the performance of the network. In the next section we discuss token-passing ring networks, which solve the access problem in a way that degrades less under heavy traffic load.

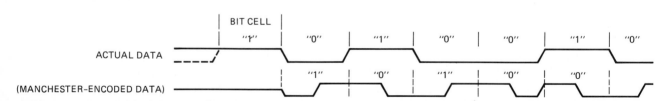

FIGURE 14-28 Manchester coding used for Ethernet data communication.
Note that encoded data has a transition at center of each bit time.

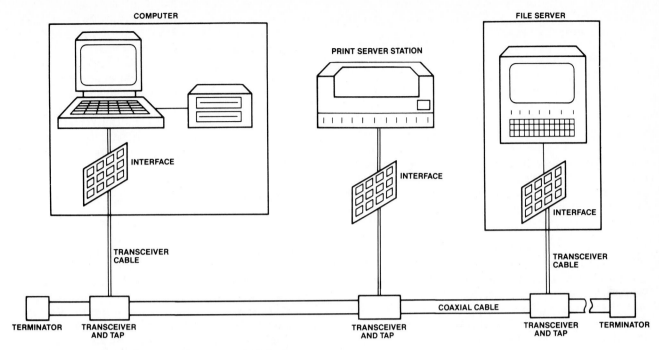

FIGURE 14-29   Block diagram of very simple Ethernet system.

Token-Passing Rings

IEEE standard 802.5 defines the physical layer and the data link layer for a token-passing ring network. As the name implies, systems on a token-passing ring are connected in series around a ring. To simplify wiring, however, token rings are often connected as shown in Figure 14-30. The Multistation access unit, or MAU, is put in a wiring closet or some readily accessible place. Unlike the passive taps used in an Ethernet system, each active station or node on a token ring receives data, examines it to see if the data is addressed to it, and retransmits the data to the next station on the ring. A bypass relay in the MAU will automatically shunt data around defective or inactive nodes. Data always travels in one direction around the ring. Data is transmitted as HDLC or SDLC frames. Early token-passing ring network adapter cards transmitted data at 4 Mbits/s, but 16-Mbit/s network adapter cards are now becoming widely available.

Token-passing ring networks solve the multiple-access problem in an entirely different way than the CSMA/CD approach described for Ethernet. A token is a byte of data with an agreed-upon, unique bit pattern such as 0111 1111. If no station is transmitting, this token is circulated continuously around the ring. When a station needs to transmit, it withdraws the not-busy token, changes it to a busy token of perhaps 0111 1110, and sends the busy token on around the ring. The transmitting unit then sends a frame of data around the ring to the intended receiver(s). When the transmitting station receives the busy token and the data frame back again, it reads them in and removes them from the ring. It then sends out the not-busy token again. As soon as a transmitting station sends

out the not-busy token again, the next station on the loop can grab the token and transmit on the network. The first station that transmitted cannot transmit again until the not-busy token works its way around the ring. This gives all units on the network a chance to transmit in a "round-robin" manner.

NOTE:
Some token-passing ring networks use tokens with priority bits so that high-priority stations

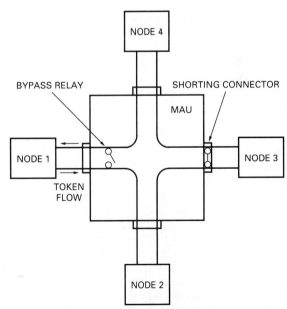

NOTE: MAU = MULTISTATION ACCESS UNIT

FIGURE 14-30   Block diagram of a token ring network system showing multistation access unit (MAU).

can transmit again if necessary before a lower-priority station gets a turn.

Two questions occurred to us the first time we read about token-passing rings; perhaps these same two questions have occurred to you. The first question is, How does a station on the network tell the bit pattern for a token from the same bit pattern in the data frame? The answer to this question is bit-stuffing, the same technique that is used to prevent the flag bit pattern from being present in the data section of an HDLC frame. A hardware circuit in the transmitter alters the data stream so that certain bit patterns are not present. Another hardware circuit in the receiver reconstructs the original data.

The second question is, What happens if the not-busy token somehow gets lost going around the ring? A couple of different approaches are used to solve this problem. One approach uses a timer in each station. When a station has a frame to transmit, it starts a timer. If the station does not detect a token in the data stream before the timer counts down, it assumes that the token was lost and sends out a new token. Another approach used by IBM sets up one station as a network monitor. If this station does not detect a token within a prescribed time, it clears any leftover data from the ring and sends out a new not-busy token.

The Texas Instruments TMS380 chip set can be used to implement a node on a 4-Mbit/s token-passing ring network. Consult the data sheets for these devices to get more information about the operation of a token-passing ring network.

Token-passing ring networks have the disadvantage that more complex hardware is required where each station connects to the network, but as we said earlier, under heavy traffic loads they are more efficient than Ethernets. Also, the receive and transmit circuitry at the connection acts as a repeater, which helps maintain signal quality throughout the network. Since signals travel in only one direction around the ring, this topology is ideally suited for fiber-optic transmission.

A new standard called the fiber distributed data interface (FDDI), or ANSI X3T9.5, describes a fiber-optic token-passing ring network that transmits data at 100 Mbits/s. The FDDI ring actually consists of a fiber that transmits data in one direction around the ring and another fiber that transmits data in the other direction around the ring. This dual-fiber approach allows data transmission to continue if one fiber path is broken or interrupted in some way. Nodes on FDDI can be as far as 2 km from each other, up to 500 nodes can be connected on the ring, and the maximum circumference of the ring can be much as 100 km. The Advanced Micro Devices' Supernet chip set or the National Semiconductor FDDI chip set can be used along with a microcontroller, buffer memory, and an electro-optical interface to build an FDDI node. Consult the data sheets for these devices to get more information about FDDI operation.

Figure 14-31 shows how an FDDI network can serve as a backbone that allows high-speed communication between other networks. Circuits called *bridges*, or *gateways*, interface Ethernets, multiplexed Ethernets, or even T1 type signals with the FDDI. The Pentagon uses a network such as this.

A transmission rate of 100 Mbits/s may at first seem like "overkill," but as we move more and more toward high-resolution interactive video, computer simulations, and massive data storage, this rate is not nearly fast enough. Work is currently underway on fiber-optic networks that transmit data at 250 Mbits/s and 500 Mbits/s and allow nodes to be as much as 50 km apart.

A Network Application Example and LAN Software Overview

As an example of how you put all the pieces of a network together, suppose that you have the job of designing and setting up a general-purpose computer room at a college. The lab is to be used for computer-aided drafting (CAD) with AutoCAD; programming in Pascal, C, and assembly language; mechanical engineering simulations; word processing; and other unspecified applications. All programs that will be run require a 68000-based computer. The computer room is to have 24 workstations, a large plotter, a laser printer, and two letter-quality dot-matrix printers.

The drafting and mechanical engineering instructors indicate that they need the speed of a 68020-based machine and display resolution of 1024×768 pixels. These specifications require that each of the 24 workstations be a 68020-based machine with an 8514/A-type video adapter. Some of the programs that they plan to run are very memory hungry, so the basic workstations need 2 Mbytes or more of RAM.

The systems need to run a very wide variety of programs, so a large amount of hard-disk storage is needed. One alternative is to install a large hard disk in each workstation and install a set of the required programs on each disk. One problem with this approach is the cost of the 24 large hard disks. A second problem with this approach is that it is difficult to maintain the software on all these separate machines. Updating is tedious and time consuming. Still another problem is that on these individual machines it is difficult to protect the application programs from accidental or mischievous corruption by users.

All these problems can be solved by connecting the workstations on a network that includes a fast file server. A single copy of the application programs can be installed on the file server and accessed from each workstation as needed. If the hard disk on the server is large enough, user files can also be stored on it. The plotter and printers can also be connected on the file server so that they are accessible from any workstation.

The file server and its hard disk need to be fast so that they do not create a "bottleneck" in the system. You might choose a 68030-based microcomputer for the file server and equip it with a 250-Mbyte, 16-ms hard disk. If the budget permits, you might also include an optical disk drive in the server so that programming classes could access the very large programmer's li-

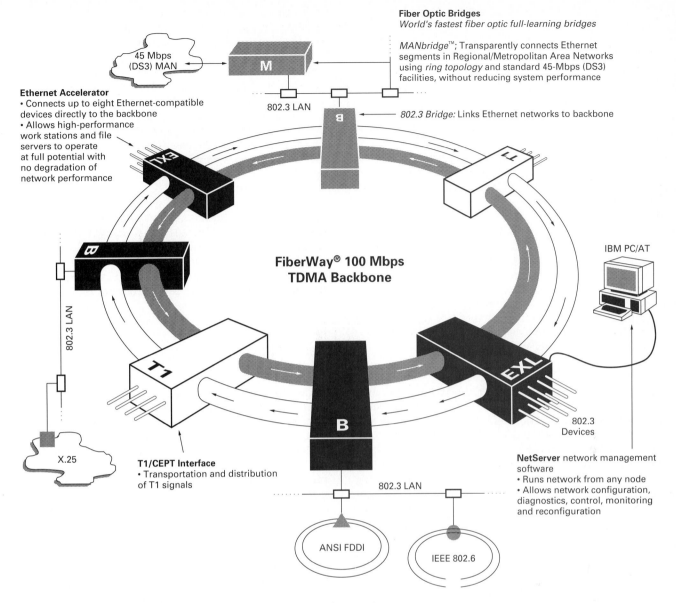

Fiber Optic Bridges
World's fastest fiber optic full-learning bridges

MANbridge™; Transparently connects Ethernet segments in Regional/Metropolitan Area Networks using *ring topology* and standard 45-Mbps (DS3) facilities, without reducing system performance

Ethernet Accelerator
• Connects up to eight Ethernet-compatible devices directly to the backbone
• Allows high-performance work stations and file servers to operate at full potential with no degradation of network performance

45 Mbps (DS3) MAN

802.3 LAN

802.3 Bridge: Links Ethernet networks to backbone

FiberWay® 100 Mbps TDMA Backbone

IBM PC/AT

802.3 LAN

X.25

T1/CEPT Interface
• Transportation and distribution of T1 signals

802.3 Devices

NetServer network management software
• Runs network from any node
• Allows network configuration, diagnostics, control, monitoring and reconfiguration

802.3 LAN

ANSI FDDI

IEEE 802.6

FIGURE 14-31   Fiber distributed data interface (FDDI) network used as "backbone" for different types of networks.

brary that could be made available on CD ROM. The server will also need a 1.2-Mbyte floppy drive and a 1.44-Mbyte floppy drive to transfer software from floppies to the hard disk.

The next step is to decide on the software you want to use to manage the network and to provide the file server and print server functions. The best approach for this is to choose the network software that will do the best job and then choose network hardware compatible with that software.

The typical UNIX® OS works with Ethernet, ARCnet, and IBM's Token Ring boards. Since the workstations in this lab are physically all in the same room, you might consider using the 10BaseT, or Thin Ethernet, network we described earlier, because it is the cheapest of these alternatives. Remember that this type of

network transmits data at 10 Mbits/s over standard twisted-pair phone wire for distances up to 100 m.

UNIX typically requires a minimum 2 Mbytes of memory in the server, and it works better with 8M or 16M, so you should include this in the bid specifications for the server.

While you are waiting for hardware bids to come in, purchase orders to go out, and the hardware to arrive, we will give you an overview of how network software works so you will have some idea how to install and use it.

Part of the network software resides in each workstation and part of it resides in the server. Let's start with the workstation part. To refresh your memory, Figure 14-32*a* shows the software hierarchy for a UNIX-based workstation operating in stand-alone

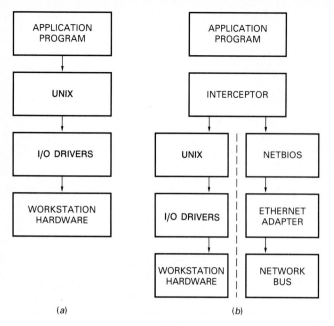

FIGURE 14-32 Software hierarchy on a workstation.
(a) Nonnetworked. (b) Networked.

mode. In this mode an application program such as a word processor uses UNIX OS function calls to access system peripherals. The UNIX OS function calls use OS drivers to interact with the actual hardware.

Figure 14-32b shows the software hierarchy when the workstation is operating in network mode. When the application program attempts to access a disk file, for example, the "interceptor" part of the resident network software determines whether the file is located on the workstation hard disk or on the server hard disk. If the file is on the workstation hard disk, the interceptor simply passes the request on to UNIX, and the access proceeds through UNIX as it would in stand-alone operation. If the file is on the server, the request goes to the request translator to get assembled in the proper packet format for transmission over Ethernet. The output from the request translator then goes to the network communications driver, which sends it to the server over the network.

The server reads the requested file, converts it to packets, and sends it to the workstation. The appropriate driver reads the packets in to the workstation. The reply translator part of the software converts the packets to UNIX file format and loads the file in memory so the application can work with it.

The network software that resides in the server is a complete operating system in itself. Once installed, the network operating system is set up so that only the system administrator can access and change its operation. The system administrator sets up user accounts, assigns passwords, and sets the access rights for files. Application program files are usually specified as read-only so that users cannot accidentally or maliciously modify them. For files that are intended to be accessed and written to by any one of several users, UNIX has a default feature called *file locking,* which prevents one

user from accessing the file until a previous user has finished with it. In this case the "critical region" is the file, and file locking provides a way to protect it.

In addition to allowing users to store and access files, the network operating system has many other useful features. It sets up a queue of files waiting to be printed or plotted so that users can just enter a print command and go on with their work. Most networks have electronic mail, which allows the system administrator to communicate with all users and users to communicate with each other. Most electronic mail systems are set up so you can define a group of users and direct mail messages to just that group.

For the reasons that we have discussed, it is likely that in the near future almost all computers will in some way be networked with other computers through telephone lines or direct connections. In the last section of the chapter we discuss a different type of computer network, which is often used in a factory environment to build a "smart" test system.

THE GPIB, HPIB, OR IEEE488 BUS

The preceding sections of the chapter discussed networks that allow microcomputers to communicate with each other and to share peripherals such as printers. The general-purpose interface bus (GPIB), also known as the Hewlett-Packard interface bus (HPIB) and the IEEE488 bus, that we discuss here is not intended for use as a computer network in the same way that the Ethernet and token rings are used. It was developed by Hewlett-Packard to interface smart test instruments with a computer. Figure 14-33a shows a GPIB connector.

The standard describes three types of devices that can be connected on the GPIB. First is a listener, which can receive data from other instruments or from the controller. Examples of listeners are printers, display devices, programmable power supplies, and programmable signal generators. The second type of device defined is a talker, which can send data to other instruments. Examples of talkers are tape readers, digital voltmeters, frequency counters, and other measuring equipment. A device can be both a talker and a listener. The third type of device on the bus is a controller, which determines who talks and who listens on the bus.

Physically the bus consists of a 24-wire cable with a connector, such as that shown in Figure 14-33a, on each end. Actually, each end of the cable has both a male connector and a female connector, so that cables can daisy-chain from one unit to the next on the bus. Instruments intended for use on a GPIB usually have switches that allow you to select the 4-bit address that the instrument will have on the bus. Standard TTL signal voltage levels are used.

As shown in Figure 14-33b, the GPIB has eight bidirectional data lines. These lines are used to transfer data, addresses, commands, and status bytes among as many as 8 or 10 instruments.

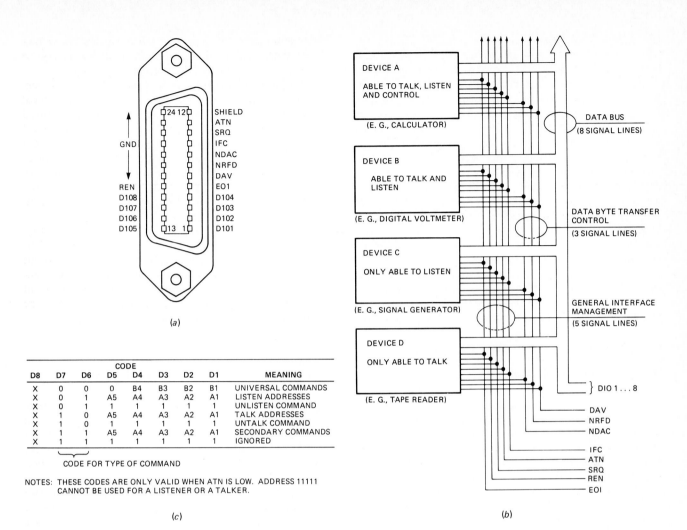

(a)

CODE								MEANING
D8	D7	D6	D5	D4	D3	D2	D1	
X	0	0	0	B4	B3	B2	B1	UNIVERSAL COMMANDS
X	0	1	A5	A4	A3	A2	A1	LISTEN ADDRESSES
X	0	1	1	1	1	1	1	UNLISTEN COMMAND
X	1	0	A5	A4	A3	A2	A1	TALK ADDRESSES
X	1	0	1	1	1	1	1	UNTALK COMMAND
X	1	1	A5	A4	A3	A2	A1	SECONDARY COMMANDS
X	1	1	1	1	1	1	1	IGNORED

CODE FOR TYPE OF COMMAND

NOTES: THESE CODES ARE ONLY VALID WHEN ATN IS LOW. ADDRESS 11111
CANNOT BE USED FOR A LISTENER OR A TALKER.

(c)

(b)

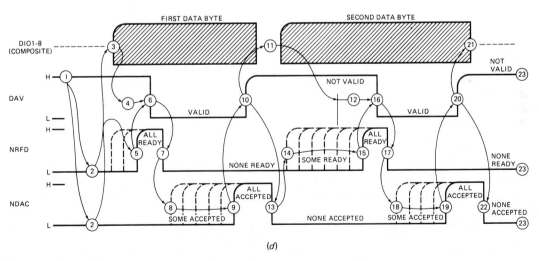

(d)

FIGURE 14-33   GPIB pins, signals, and handshake waveforms. (a) Connector.
(b) Bus structure. (c) Command formats. (d) Data transfer handshake
waveforms.

The GPIB also has five bus-management lines, which function basically as follows. The interface clear line (IFC), when asserted by the controller, resets all devices on the bus to a starting state. It is essentially a system reset. The attention (ATN) line, when asserted (low), indicates that the controller is putting a universal command or an address-command such as "listen" on the data bus. When the ATN line is high, the data lines contain data or a status byte. Service request (SRQ) is similar to an interrupt. Any device that needs to transfer data on the bus asserts the SRQ line low. The controller then polls all the devices to determine which one needs service. When asserted by the system controller, the remote-enable (REN) signal allows an instrument to be controlled directly by the controller rather than by its front panel switches. The end or identify (EOI) signal is usually asserted by a talker to indicate that the transfer of a block of data is complete.

Finally, the bus has three handshake lines that coordinate the transfer of data bytes on the data bus. These are data valid (DAV), not ready for data (NRFD), and not data accepted (NDAC). These handshake signals allow devices with very different data rates to be connected together in a system. A little later we show you how this handshake works. First we give you an overview of general bus operation.

Upon power-up the controller takes control of the bus and sends out an IFC signal to set all instruments on the bus to a known state. The controller then uses the bus to perform the desired series of measurements or tests. To do this the controller sends out a series of commands with the ATN line asserted low. Figure 14-33c shows the formats for the combination command-address codes that a controller can send to talkers and listeners. Bit 8 of these words is a don't care, bits 7 and 6 specify which command is being sent, and bits 5 through 1 give the address of the talker or listener to which the command is being sent. For example, to enable (address) a device at address 04 as a talker, the controller simply asserts the ATN line low and sends out a command-address byte of X1000100 on the data bus. A listener is enabled by sending out a command-address byte of $X01A5A4A3A2A1$, where the lower 5 bits contain the address that the listener has been given in the system. When a data transfer is complete, all listeners are turned off by the controller sending an unlisten command, X0111111. The controller turns off the talker by sending an untalk command, X1011111. Universal commands sent by the controller with bits 7, 6, and 5 all 0s will go to all listeners and talkers. The lower 4 bits of these words specify one of 16 universal commands.

While it is using the bus, the controller periodically checks the SRQ line for a service request. If the SRQ line is low, the controller polls each device on the bus one after another (serial) or all at once (parallel) until it finds the device requesting service. A talker such as a DVM, for example, might be indicating that it has completed a series of conversions and has some data to send to a listener such as a chart recorder. When the controller determines the source of the SRQ, it asserts the ATN line low and sends listener address commands to each listener that is to receive the data and a talk address command to the talker that requested service. The controller then raises the ATN line high, and data is transferred directly from the talker to the listeners using a double-handshake-signal sequence.

Figure 14-33d shows the sequence of signals on the handshake lines for a transfer of data from a talker to several listeners. The DAV, NRFD, and NDAC lines are all open-collector. Therefore, any listener can hold NRFD low to indicate that it is not ready for data or

hold NDAC low to indicate that it has not yet accepted a data byte. The sequence proceeds as follows. When all listeners have released the NRFD line (5 in Figure 14-33d), indicating that they are ready (not not-ready), the talker asserts the DAV line low to indicate that a valid data byte is on the bus. The addressed listeners then all pull NRFD low and start accepting the data. When the slowest listener has accepted the data, the NDAC line will be released high (9 in Figure 14-33d). The talker senses NDAC becoming high and unasserts its DAV signal. The listeners all pull NDAC low again, and the sequence is repeated until the talker has sent all the data bytes it has to send. The rate of data transfer is determined by the rate at which the slowest listener can accept the data.

When the data transfer is complete, the talker pulls the EOI line in the management group low to tell the controller that the transfer is complete. The controller then takes control again and sends an untalk command to the talker. It also sends an unlisten command to turn off the listeners and continues to use the bus according to its internal program.

A standard microprocessor bus can be interfaced to the GPIB with dedicated devices such as the Intel 8291 GPIB talker-listener and 8292 GPIB controller. The importance of the GPIB is that it allows a microcomputer to be connected with several test instruments to form an integrated test system.

CHECKLIST OF IMPORTANT TERMS AND CONCEPTS IN THIS CHAPTER

If there are terms or concepts in this list you do not remember, use the index to find them in the chapter.

Serial data communication
Simplex, half-duplex, full-duplex
Synchronous, asynchronous
Marking state, spacing state
Start bit, stop bit
Baud rate

UART, USART, DTE, DCE

20- and 60-mA current loops

RS-232C, RS-422A, RS-423A, and RS-449 serial data standards

Codecs, TDM, and PCM

ISDN

Modems

Amplitude modulation, FSK, PSK
Quaternary amplitude modulation (QAM)
Scrambler, descrambler

Fiber-optic data communication
Critical angle
Multimode and single-mode fibers

Terminal emulator

Critical region

Binary synchronous communications protocol
   (BISYNC)
   Byte-controlled protocol (BCP)
   Cyclic redundancy check
   XMODEM protocol

HDLC, SDLC protocols
   Bit-oriented protocol (BOP)
   Frame, field, flag
   Frame-check sequence (FCS)

Local area network (LAN)
   Star, loop, ring, common-bus, broadband-bus (tree)
   topologies
   Token
   Baseband and broadband transmission

Electronic mail

Open-system interconnection model (OSI)
   Presentation, session, transport, network, data link
   Physical layers

Ethernet
   Transceiver
   Collision
   CSMA/CD
   10BaseT

Token-passing rings

Fiber distributed data interface (FDDI)

File server, print server

GPIB, HPIB, IEEE 488 bus standard
   Listener, talker, controller

REVIEW QUESTIONS AND PROBLEMS

1. Draw a diagram showing the bit format used for asynchronous serial data. Label the start, stop, and parity bits. Number the data bits to show the order of transmission.

2. A terminal is transmitting simple asynchronous serial data at 1200 Bd.
   a. How much time is required to transmit 1 bit?
   b. Assuming 7 data bits, a parity bit, and 1 stop bit, how long does it take to transmit one character?

3. What is the main difference between a UART and a USART?

4. Define the term modem and explain why a modem is required to send digital data over standard switched phone lines.

5. Describe the functions of the DSR, DTR, RTS, CTS, TxD, and RxD signals exchanged between a terminal and a modem.

6. What frequency transmit clock (TxC) is required by an 8251A in order for it to transmit data at 4800 Bd with a baud rate factor of 16?

7. a. Show the bit pattern for the mode word and the command word that must be sent to an 8251A to initialize the device as follows: baud rate factor of 64, 7 bits/character, even parity, 1 stop bit, transmit interrupt enabled, receive interrupt enabled, DTR and RTS asserted, error flags reset, no hunt mode, no break character.
   b. Show the sequence of instructions required to initialize an 8251A at addresses 80H and 81H with the mode and command words you worked out in part a.
   c. Show the sequence of instructions that can be used to poll this 8251A to determine when the

receiver buffer has a character ready to be read.
   d. How can you determine whether a character received by an 8251A contains a parity error?
   e. What frequency transmit and receive clock will this 8251A require in order to send data at 2400 Bd?
   f. What other way besides polling does the 8251A provide for determining when a character can be sent to the device for transmission? Describe the additional hardware connections required for this method.

8. Give the signal voltage ranges for a logic high and for a logic low in the RS-232C standard.

9. a. Describe the problem that occurs when you attempt to connect together two RS-232C devices that are both configured as DTE.
   b. Draw a diagram that shows how this problem can be solved.

10. a. Why are the two ground pins on an RS-232C connector not just jumpered together?
    b. What symptom will you observe if the wire connected to pin 5 of an RS-232C terminal is broken?

11. Explain why systems that use the RS-422A or RS-423A signal standards can transmit data over longer distances and at higher baud rates than RS-232C systems.

12. a. How does an FSK modem represent digital 1s and 0s in the signal it sends out on a phone line?
    b. How does an FSK modem perform full-duplex communication over standard phone lines?
    c. Approximately what is the maximum bit rate for FSK data transmission on standard switched telephone lines?

13. a. Draw a waveform to show the signal that a simple phase-shift keying (PSK) modem will send out to represent the binary data 0 1101 0100.

b. Describe how phase-shift modulation can be used to transmit 2 data bits with only one carrier change.

c. Describe how quaternary amplitude modulation transmits 4 data bits with only one carrier change.

14. a. Why do telephone companies transmit signals over long distance in digital form rather than in analog form?

b. Describe the operation of a codec.

c. Why are codecs designed with nonlinear response?

d. Explain how telephone companies commonly transmit many phone signals on a single wire or channel.

15. a. Briefly describe the operation of the integrated services digital network.

b. Explain the significance ISDN has for data communication between computers.

16. a. Draw a diagram that shows the construction of a fiber-optic cable, and label each part.

b. Identify two types of devices that are used to produce the light beam for a fiber-optic cable and two devices which are commonly used to detect the light at the receiving end of the fiber.

c. Why should you never look into the end of a fiber-optic cable to see if light is getting through?

d. Describe the difference between a multimode fiber and a single-mode fiber. Give a major advantage and a major disadvantage of each type.

e. What are the major advantages of fiber-optic cables over metallic conductors?

17. The URDA MDS will only accept uppercase letters as commands. The download program in Figure 14-22 would be friendlier if you did not have to remember to press the caps lock key on the Macintosh. Write an assembly language routine that will convert a letter entered in lowercase to uppercase without affecting entered uppercase letters or numbers and describe where you would insert this section of code in the program in Figure 14-22.

18. a. When changing a bit in a control word or interrupt mask word, why should you not alter the other bits in the word?

b. Show the assembly language instructions you would use to unmask IR5 of an 8259A at base address $CF80 without changing the interrupt status of any other bits.

19. Why is synchronous serial data communication much more efficient than asynchronous communication?

20. a. If an 8251A is being used in synchronous mode for a BISYNC data link, what additional initialization word(s) must be sent to the device?

b. How does the 8251A detect the start of a message?

c. How does the 8251A indicate that it has found the start of a message?

d. How does the receiving station in a BISYNC link indicate that it found an error in the received data?

21. a. How is the start of a message frame indicated in a bit-oriented protocol such as HDLC?

b. How does an HDLC system prevent the flag bit pattern from appearing in the data part of the message?

c. How does the receiver in an HDLC system tell the transmitter that an error was found in a transmitted frame?

22. a. Draw simple diagrams that show the five common network topologies.

b. For each topology, identify one commercially available system that uses it.

23. What is the difference between a baseband network and a broadband network?

24. a. List the seven layers of the ISO open systems model.

b. Which of these layers is responsible for assembling messages into frames or packets?

c. Which layer is responsible for making sure the message was transmitted and received correctly?

25. a. Describe the topology, physical connections, and signal type used in Ethernet.

b. Describe the method used by a unit on an Ethernet to gain access to the network for transmitting a message.

c. What response will a transmitting station make if it finds that another station starts transmitting after it starts?

d. What is the term used to refer to this condition?

26. a. Describe the method used by a unit on a token-passing ring to take control of the network for transmitting a message frame.

b. What is the advantage of this scheme over the method used in Ethernet?

c. How can a token-passing ring network recover if the token is lost while being passed around the ring?

27. a. Describe how the software on a network node responds when the user enters a command that accesses the hard disk in the workstation.

b. Describe how the software on a network node responds when the user enters a command that accesses the hard disk on the file server.

c. Describe how the file server software protects application program files from being modified by users.

d. Describe how the file server software protects user files from access by other users.

28. a. For what purpose was the GPIB designed?

b. Give the names for the three types of devices defined by the GPIB.

c. List and briefly describe the function of the three signal groups of the GPIB.

d. Describe the sequence of handshake signals that take place when a talker on a GPIB transfers data to several listeners. How does this handshake scheme make it possible for talkers and listeners with very different data rates to operate correctly on the bus?

Operating Systems, the 68030 Microprocessor, the 68040, and the Future

As we told you in an earlier chapter, a general-purpose operating system in its simplest form is a program that allows a user to create, print, copy, delete, display, and in other ways work with files. It also allows a user to load and execute other programs. The operating system insulates the user from needing to know the intricate hardware details of the system in order to use it. Up to this point in the book we have referred only to single-user operating systems such as the Apple Macintosh® OS. To round out the book we now want to give you an overview of multiuser/multitasking operating systems and an introduction to the 68020 microprocessor. The 68020 (used in the Apple Macintosh II) has advanced features that make it suitable as the CPU in a multitasking system. Finally, in this chapter we discuss a few directions in which microcomputer evolution seems to be heading.

OBJECTIVES

At the conclusion of this chapter, you should be able to

1. Describe the difference between time-slice scheduling and preemptive priority-based scheduling.

2. Define the terms blocked, task queue, deadlock, deadly embrace, critical region, semaphore, kernel, memory-management unit, and virtual memory.

3. Describe two methods that can be used to protect a critical region of code.

4. Show with assembly language instructions how a semaphore can be used to accomplish mutual exclusion.

5. Describe the major features of the UNIX™ operating system and define the terms kernel, pipe, and shell.

6. List and describe the types of "objects" used in the RMX 86 operating system.

7. List and describe the states in which an RMX 86 task can be.

8. Describe the mechanism used to schedule tasks in RMX 86.

9. List some of the differences between UNIX and RMX 86.

10. Draw a block diagram of the internal structure of the 68030.

11. List the major hardware and software features that the 68030 microprocessor has beyond those of the 68000.

12. Show how the 68030 constructs physical addresses in its real address mode and in its protected virtual address mode.

13. Describe how the 68030 uses descriptor tables and call gates to control memory access.

14. Define the term demand-paged virtual memory and describe briefly how the 68040 produces a physical address in paged mode.

OPERATING SYSTEM CONCEPTS AND TERMS

Multiuser/Multitasking Operating System Overview

Newer 16-bit and 32-bit microprocessors are designed to be used as the CPU in multiuser/multitasking microcomputer systems. Therefore, to understand how these processors operate, you need to understand some of the terms and concepts of operating systems.

In Chapter 2 we discussed how several terminals can be connected to a single CPU and operated on a timeshare basis. An operating system that coordinates the actions of a timeshare system such as this is referred to as a *multiuser* operating system. The basic principle of a timeshare system is that the CPU services one terminal for a few milliseconds, then services the next for a few milliseconds, and so on until all the terminals have had a turn. It cycles through all the terminals over and over, fast enough that each user seems to have the complete attention of the CPU. The program or section of a program that services each user is referred to as a *task* or *process.* A multiuser operating system, then, can also be referred to as *multitasking,* but this term is more often used when referring to real-time industrial-control operating systems. With the addition of a user interface, the factory-controller program in Figure 10-35 would be an example of a very simple real-time multitasking operating system.

The multiple tasks that are to be executed by a CPU must in some way be scheduled so that they execute properly. The part of the operating system responsible for this is called the *scheduler, dispatcher,* or *supervisor.* There are several different methods of scheduling tasks, but we are interested primarily in two of them.

The first method is the *time-slice* method, which we discussed previously. In this approach the CPU executes one task for perhaps 20 ms and then switches to the next task. After all tasks have had their turns, execution returns to the first. The UNIX operating system, which we discuss in detail later, uses this scheduling approach for a multiple-user system. The advantage of the time-slice approach in a multiuser system is that all users are serviced at approximately equal time intervals. As more users are added, however, each user gets serviced less often, so each user's program takes longer to execute. This is referred to as *system degradation.* In industrial-control operating systems, this variable time between services is often not acceptable, so a different scheduling method is used.

The second scheduling method in which we are interested is *preemptive priority-based scheduling.* In this approach an executing low-priority task can be interrupted by a higher-priority task. When the high-priority task finishes executing, execution returns to the low-priority task. This approach is well suited to some control applications because it allows the most important tasks to be done first. Priority interrupt controllers such as the 8259A are often used to set up and manage the task service requests. The Motorola PISOS operating system, which we discuss later, uses priority-based scheduling.

In addition to scheduling, several other considerations have to be taken into account with multitasking operating systems. The next section discusses some of these.

Problems Encountered in Building Multitasking Operating Systems

There are a great many operating system variations and many different ways of solving various problems in an operating system. What we have tried to do in this section is use simple enough examples to illustrate the basic problems without getting lost in all the possible variations.

PRESERVING THE ENVIRONMENT

The first problem to be solved in a multitasking system is to preserve the registers, data, and return address (environment) of each task when execution is switched to another task. This is necessary so that the task can be restarted correctly. The usual way to preserve the environment is to keep it on a stack. Often the operating system keeps a separate stack for each task. Current processors such as the 68000 and 68010 have the MOVEM, LINK, and UNLINK instruction to make it easy to save and restore the environment. Any routines used in a multitasking system have to be reentrant.

ACCESSING RESOURCES

The second problem encountered in a multitasking system is assuring that tasks have orderly access to resources such as printers and disk drives. As one example of this, suppose that a user at a terminal needs to read a file from a hard disk and print it on the system printer. Obviously the file cannot be read in from the disk and printed in one of the 20-ms time slices allotted to the terminal service, so several provisions must be made to gain access to the resources and hang on to them long enough to get the job done properly. A flag, or *semaphore,* in memory is used to indicate whether the disk drive is in use by another task or not. Likewise, another semaphore is used to indicate whether the printer is in use. If a task cannot access a resource because it is busy, the task is said to be *blocked.* Rather than making the user type in a print command over and over until the disk drive and the printer are available, most operating systems of this type set up queues of tasks waiting for each resource. When one task finishes with a resource, it resets the semaphore for that resource. The next task in the queue can then set the semaphore to indicate the resource is busy and use the resource.

In order to keep track of the state of a task, a block of data called a *process-control block, process header,* or *process descriptor* is set up by the operating system for each task. Part of the information contained in the process-control block is the progress of the read disk and print job. To simplify the disk and printer queues, all that needs to be put in these queues are pointers to the process-control blocks of tasks that are waiting for access. This is similar to the way a pointer to a string descriptor table is passed to a procedure, rather than passing the string itself, as shown in Figure 13-29. Incidentally, most systems use a separate I/O processor to actually handle disks, printers, and other slow resources so that these do not load down the main processor.

Another problem situation in a multitasking system can occur when two tasks need the same two resources, such as a disk drive and a printer. Suppose that one task gains access to the disk drive and sets its semaphore to indicate that the disk drive is busy at the end of its time slice. The next task finds the disk busy, so its request goes on the queue. However, suppose that the second task finds the printer not busy, so it sets the printer semaphore to indicate it has control of the printer and goes on about its business. When execution returns to the first task, it will try to access the printer so it has both the disk drive and the printer it needs. However, it finds the printer busy, so its request is put on the printer queue. The situation here is that each task controls a resource that the other needs in order to proceed. Therefore, neither can proceed. This condition is called *deadlock*, or *deadly embrace*. The problem can be solved in a number of ways. One way is to link the printer and the disk drive together under one semaphore so that the two resources are accessed with a single action. Another more practical approach is to set up a hierarchy among the tasks, so that if deadlock occurs, the higher-priority task can gain access to all the resources it needs.

Still another interesting problem can occur in a multitasking operating system when two or more users attempt to read and change the contents of some memory locations at the same time. As an example, suppose that an airline ticket-reservation system is operating on a time-slice basis. Now, further suppose that one user examines the memory location that represents a seat on a plane and finds the seat empty, just before the end of its time slice. Another user on the system can then, in its time slice, examine the same memory location, find it empty, mark it full, and print out a reservation confirmed on the CRT. When execution returns to the first user, it has already checked the seat during its previous time slice, so it marks the seat full and prints out a reservation confirmation on the CRT. The two people assigned to the same seat may make nasty remarks about computers unless this problem is solved.

The section of a program where the value of a variable is being examined and changed must be protected from access by other tasks until the operation is complete. The section of code that must be protected is called a *critical region*. A technique called *mutual exclusion* is used to prevent two tasks from accessing a critical region at the same time. In the CHK_N_DISPLAY subroutine in Figure 14-24, we showed one way in which a critical region can be protected from an interrupt-service routine by simply masking the interrupt. In a time-slice system, however, a semaphore is used to provide mutual exclusion.

Figure 15-1 shows how this can be done with 68000 assembly language instructions. The instruction sequence is the same for each task. If task 1 needs to enter a critical section of code, it first loads the semaphore value for critical-region-busy into D0. The single instruction, TSET SEMAPHORE, then tests the semaphore and sets it to a 1. It is important to do this in one instruction so that the time-slice mechanism cannot switch to another task halfway through the test and set and cause our airline problem.

After the semaphore is tested in Figure 15-1, p. 507, the zero flag tells whether the resource is busy. If the critical region is busy, execution will remain in a wait loop for the number of time slices required for the critical region to become free. If the semaphore value is a 0 (i.e., the zero flag is set), indicating not busy, then execution enters the critical region. The TSET instruction has already set the semaphore to indicate the critical region is busy. After execution of the critical region finishes, the MOVE.B #$00,(SEMAPHORE) in-

struction resets the semaphore to indicate that the critical region is no longer busy. Task 2 can then swap the semaphore and access the critical region when needed. The semaphore functions in the same way as the "occupied" sign on a restroom of a plane or train. If you mentally try interrupting each sequence of instructions at different points, you should see that there is no condition under which both tasks can get into the critical region at the same time.

The Need for Protection

Most single-user operating systems do little to prevent user programs from "tromping on" the code or data areas of the operating system. The usual results of this and Murphy's law are that an incorrect address in a user program will cause it to write over critical sections of the operating system. The system then locks up, and the only way to get control again is to reboot the system. In a multitasking system this is intolerable, so several methods are used to protect the operating system.

The major method is to construct the operating system in two or more *layers*. Figure 15-2, p. 508, shows an "onionskin" diagram for a two-layer operating system. The basic principle here is that the inner circle represents the code and data areas used by the operating system. The outer layer represents the code and data areas of user programs or tasks that are being run under control of the operating system. The inner layer is protected because user programs can access operating system resources only through very specific mechanisms rather than a simple, accidental call or jump. The Motorola MC68000 family of microprocessors is designed to accommodate a two-level structure such as this. The MC68000 has two modes of operation, user and supervisory. Certain privileged instructions that affect the operating system can be executed only when the processor is in supervisory mode.

The UNIX operating system, which we discuss in the next major section of the chapter, is an example of a three-layer operating system. Figure 15-3, p. 508, shows the three layers for UNIX. The innermost layer, or *kernel*, contains the major operating system functions such as the scheduler. The middle layer, or *shell*, contains the command line interpreter, which translates user-entered commands to a sequence of kernel operations. The shell level is the user-interface level. The outer layer contains application programs such as data base–management programs. It also contains utilities such as editors and compilers, which programmers can use to write more application programs.

Other systems use even more levels of protection. The Intel 80286 processor has designed into its hardware a mechanism that allows up to four levels of protection to be built into an operating system running on it.

In addition to protecting the operating system from being tromped on by executing tasks, an operating system should provide some way of protecting tasks from each other. Throughout the rest of this chapter

```
;Instructions for accessing critical region of code protected by
; semaphore - User 1

HOLD1:   BSET.B  #2,SEMAPHORE      ; Test and set the semaphore
                                   ;   pretecting the critical region.
                                   ;   The sempahore is bit 2 of memory
                                   ;   location SEMAPHORE.


         BNE     HOLD1             ; Loop and try again if the sempahore
                                   ;   was a 1, that is if the semaphore
                                   ;   had already been set.  A set
                                   ;   semaphore means some other process
                                   ;   is already in the critical region


         ; ...            Instructions for accessing critical region
         ;                of code protected by semaphore are inserted
         ;                here.  This is INSIDE the CRITICAL REGION


         BCLR.B  #2,SEMAPHORE      ; Clear the semaphore indicating that
                                   ;   this proces is done with the
                                   ;   critical region.



;Instructions for accessing critical region of code protected by
; semaphore - User 2

HOLD2:   BSET.B  #2,SEMAPHORE      ; Test and set the semaphore
                                   ;   pretecting the critical region.
                                   ;   The sempahore is bit 2 of memory
                                   ;   location SEMAPHORE.


         BNE     HOLD2             ; Loop and try again if the sempahore
                                   ;   was a 1, that is if the semaphore
                                   ;   had already been set.  A set
                                   ;   semaphore means some other process
                                   ;   is already in the critical region


         ; ...            Instructions for accessing critical region
         ;                of code protected by semaphore are inserted
         ;                here.  This is INSIDE the CRITICAL REGION


         BCLR.B  #2,SEMAPHORE      ; Clear the semaphore indicating that
                                   ;   this proces is done with the
                                   ;   critical region.


;-----------------------------------------------
SEMAPHORE:      DC.B    0          ; The semaphore location


         END
```

FIGURE 15-1 68000 assembly language instruction sequences showing how a
semaphore can be used to provide mutual exclusion for a critical region.

we will be showing you how protection layers are actually implemented, and how tasks can be protected from each other. To start this, we need to introduce you to the concepts of memory management.

Memory Management

There are two major reasons why memory must be specifically managed in a multitasking operating

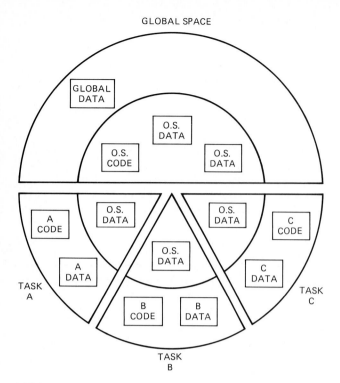

FIGURE 15-2 Onionskin diagram for multitasking operating systems with two levels of protection.

system. The first reason is that the physical RAM is usually not large enough to hold all the operating system and all the application programs that are being executed by the multiple users. The second reason is to make sure that executing tasks do not access protected areas of memory. Memory management can be done totally by the operating system or with the aid of hardware called a *memory-management unit,* or MMU. Before we get into the operation of an MMU, we want to give you a little background on methods used to solve the limited-memory problem.

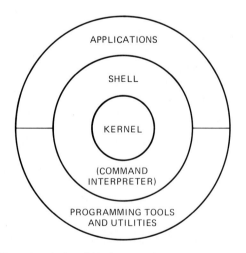

FIGURE 15-3 Onionskin diagram for operating system with three levels, such as UNIX.

A common problem, especially in older, single-user systems, is that the physical RAM is not large enough to hold, for example, an assembler and the program being assembled. The traditional solution to this problem is to write the assembler in modules and use an *overlay scheme.* When the assembler is invoked, the executive module of the assembler is loaded into memory and reserves an additional memory space called the *overlay area.* The assembler then reads through the source program. When it reaches a point where it needs a particular module, it reads that module, referred to as an *overlay,* from the disk into the overlay area reserved in memory. When the assembler reaches a point where it needs another overlay, it reads the overlay from the disk and loads it into the same overlay area in memory. The overlay approach is commonly used and works well for specific cases such as the assembler example we used here, but it is not flexible enough for multitasking systems.

Another approach traditionally used to expand the available memory in a microcomputer is *bank switching.* A system that has only 16 address lines can directly address only 64 Kbytes of memory. As shown in Figure 15-4, however, the addition of some simple selection hardware allows the system to access up to eight memory *banks* of 64 Kbytes each. The hardware is configured so that when the power is turned on, the system is using bank 0. To switch to bank 1, a byte that turns off bank 0 and turns on bank 1 is output to the selection port. Execution then proceeds in bank 1. In practice, some system-dependent tricks are often necessary to get execution smoothly from one bank to another, but the approach does help overcome the memory limits designed into the processor.

To use bank switching in a multiuser system, each user's program might be assigned to a bank. The difficulties with this are that a copy of the operating system kernel must be kept in each bank, the actual memory available for each user is still limited to 64 Kbytes, and users cannot easily share code or data. Thus memory is not very efficiently used. Also, protection is not as easily implemented as it is in the MMU approaches we discuss next.

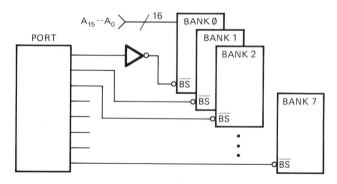

FIGURE 15-4 Block diagram showing how microcomputer memory can be expanded with bank switching.

MMUs

To reduce the burden of memory management on the operating system, most microprocessor manufacturers now have hardware memory-management devices available. The device may be built into the processor, as it is in the 68030, or may be available separately. In either case the MMU is functionally positioned between the processor and the actual memory, as shown in Figure 15-5. The major function of the MMU is to translate logical program addresses to physical memory addresses. We will explain how it does this, but first let's clarify what is meant in this case by logical address and physical address.

When you write an assembly language program, you usually refer to addresses by name. The addresses you work with in a program are called *logical addresses,* because they indicate the logical positions of code and data. An example of this is the 68000 instruction BNZ NEXT. The label NEXT represents a logical address to which execution will go if the zero flag is not set. When a 68000 program is assembled, each logical address is represented with a 32-bit logical address.

When a program is assembled or compiled to run on a system with an MMU, each logical address is represented by two components. In a segment-oriented system the upper component is referred to as a *segment selector,* and the lower component is referred to as the *offset.* In a page-oriented system the upper component is referred to as the *page address,* and the lower component is referred to as the *page offset.* In either case MMU uses the upper component, a segment selector for example, to access a *descriptor* in a table of descriptors in memory rather than just adding it to the

offset in the lower component. A descriptor is a series of memory locations that contain the physical base address for a segment, the privilege level of the segment, and some control bits. As an example, let's assume the selector has 14 address bits and 2 privilege-level bits. The 14 address bits in the selector can select any one of 16,384 descriptors in the descriptor table. If the offset component of the logical address has 16 bits, then each segment can contain 64 Kbytes. Since each descriptor points to a segment, the logical address space for our example system here is 65,536 bytes/segment × 16,384 segments, or about 1 Gbyte. What this means is that the operating system can function as if a gigabyte of memory were available. Now let's see how this relates to the actual semiconductor memory.

Physically the MMU may have perhaps 24 address lines, so it can address only 16 Mbytes of physical memory. The question that may immediately come to mind here is, How can the operating system function as if there were a gigabyte of memory, when the maximum physical memory that the system can have is 16 Mbytes? The answer to this question is that the physical memory, whatever its actual size, is simply a holding place for the segments currently being used by the operating system or user programs.

When the MMU receives a logical address from the CPU, it checks to see if that segment is currently in the physical memory. If the segment is present in physical memory, the MMU adds the offset component of the address to the segment base component of the address from the segment descriptor to form the physical address. It then outputs the physical address to memory on the memory address bus. If the MMU finds that the segment specified by the logical address is not in memory, it sends an interrupt signal to the CPU. In response to the interrupt, the CPU reads the desired code or data segment from a disk or other secondary storage and loads it into the physical memory. The MMU then computes and outputs the physical address as described before. The operation is semiautomatic, so other than a slight delay, the operating system or other program is not aware that the segment had to be loaded. The gigabyte of logical address space that is available to programs is called *virtual memory* and the logical address in this type of system is usually called the *virtual address.* The term virtual means something that appears to be present but actually isn't.

When the CPU or smart MMU wants to load a segment from secondary storage into physical memory, it must first make space for it in the physical memory. Depending on the system, it may do this by compacting the segments already present and changing the descriptors to point to the new physical locations or by swapping the segment being brought in with one currently in physical memory. To help in deciding which segment to swap back to memory, most systems use some bits in the descriptor to keep track of how many times the sector has been used. A low-use segment is the most likely candidate to swap back to memory. Most systems also have a *dirty bit* in each descriptor. This bit will be set if the contents of a

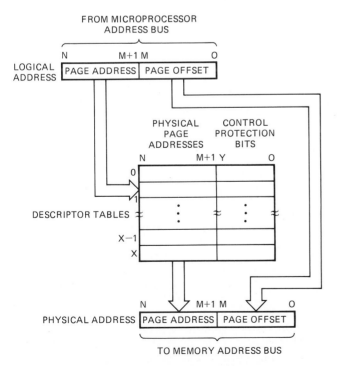

FIGURE 15-5 Block diagram showing operation of a memory-management unit.

segment have been changed. If the dirty bit is set, a segment must be swapped back to secondary storage if its space is needed. If the dirty bit is not set, then the segment has not been altered. The copy of the segment in secondary storage is still correct, so the segment can just be overwritten. This eliminates one write-to-disk operation.

Another term often found in MMU data sheets is the term *hit rate*. Hit rate refers to the percentage of the time that the segment required at a particular time is present in the physical memory. In a well structured system the hit rate may be 85 to 90 percent.

The use of a descriptor table to translate logical addresses to physical addresses has another major advantage besides making virtual memory possible. The selector component of each address contains one or two bits, which represent the privilege level of the program section requesting access to a segment. The descriptor for each segment also contains one or two bits that represent the privilege level of that segment. When an executing program attempts to access a segment, the MMU can compare the privilege level in the selector with the privilege level in the descriptor. If the selector has the same or greater privilege, then the MMU allows the access. If the selector privilege is lower, the MMU can send an interrupt signal to the CPU that indicates a privilege-level violation. The indirect method of producing physical addresses then provides a method of providing privilege levels and protecting program sections such as the operating system kernel.

There are currently two major approaches used by MMUs. One is the segmentation approach we have just described. The logical address in this case consists of a segment selector and an offset within that segment. Segments can be any size from 1 byte to 64 Kbytes in the example we used before. In most segment-oriented systems the segments swapped in and out of physical memory are quite large. The disadvantages of these large segments are the time required to load them and the compaction that often must be done to make space for a segment in physical memory.

The second major approach currently used is called *demand-paged virtual memory*. In this approach the virtual memory is mapped as fixed-length pages of perhaps 4 Kbytes in length. The two components of the virtual address are called the *page address* and the *page offset*. The page offset, as the name implies, contains the offset of a desired byte within a page. The page address is used as a pointer to a descriptor table, just as the selector is in the segmentation approach. The descriptors function in about the same way here that they do in the segmentation scheme. When a demanded page is found to be not present in the physical memory, the MMU or the CPU swaps it in. The typically smaller and fixed lengths of the pages makes the swapping operation much easier.

Before we summarize and go on to the next topic, we need to explain one more term commonly used with MMUs. For some MMUs the descriptor table is stored in a part of the main physical memory. Other MMUs have a built-in, high-speed memory called a *cache* (pronounced "cash"). The descriptors for the currently used segments or pages are kept in the cache memory so that they can be accessed much more quickly than they could if they were in the main memory. The descriptors for pages not currently being used are kept in a table in main memory. If the descriptor for a required page is not present in the cache, then it is read in from the descriptor table in main memory. The descriptor is then used to read in the required page.

To summarize, then, MMUs translate logical program addresses to physical addresses with an indirect method through a descriptor table. This indirect approach makes possible a virtual address space much larger than the physical address space. The indirect approach also makes it possible to protect a memory segment or page from access by a program section with a lower privilege level. You will meet all of these concepts again in a later section, which describes the operation of the 80286 microprocessor. First, however, we want to give you overviews of UNIX, a common multiuser operating system, and RMX 86, a common real-time multitasking operating system.

THE UNIX OPERATING SYSTEM

The purpose of this section is to show you the structure, terminology, and overall operation of the UNIX operating system so you can see how it relates to multiuser microcomputer systems. If you are going to be working with UNIX, there are available several books that use step-by-step examples to illustrate it.

History

In 1969 Ken Thompson, a researcher at Bell Laboratories, decided to write some system programs that would make it easier to develop other programs. Over the next few years, with the help of another researcher, Dennis Richie, these programs evolved into a powerful multiuser operating system. The original versions were written in assembly language for a DEC PDP-7 minicomputer, but when the value of the operating system became obvious, there was a strong desire to write versions for other machines. Adapting an assembly language program to run on another machine with a different CPU means rewriting the whole thing. To help solve this portability problem, Dennis Richie developed a high-level language called C. This language has much of the capability of assembly language to work with hardware and twiddle bits, but it also allows a programmer to write high-level-language structured programs. Adapting a high-level-language program to run on a different machine involves rewriting the I/O sections as needed by the hardware of the new machine and compiling the high-level-language program to the machine code for the new machine. By 1972 a version of UNIX written in C was operating successfully on the DEC PDP-11 computer.

In the following years Western Electric, a parent company of Bell Laboratories, licensed the source code of UNIX to several universities, where it underwent further evolution. A commonly available enhanced version was developed at U.C., Berkeley. The evolution also continued at Bell Labs. In 1979 version 7 was released, and versions III and V were later released by Western Electric.

Unfortunately, the basic structure of UNIX is easy to understand and alter. Therefore, each group using UNIX tended to extend and modify it to fit their specific needs or prejudices. Furthermore, due to licensing difficulties with Western Electric, commercial companies developing UNIX-like operating systems developed their own proprietary versions. The result of all of this is that there are many different versions of UNIX-type operating systems in use. It is hoped that the current efforts to work out a standard will be successful.

UNIX Operating System Structure

As shown in Figure 15-3, the UNIX operating system consists of three layers. The innermost, most privileged layer, or kernel, contains a process scheduler, a hierarchal file structure, and mechanisms for processes to communicate with each other. The middle layer of the operating system, or shell, is the layer with which a user interfaces. This layer contains the command interpreter, which decodes and carries out user-entered commands. The outermost layer contains programming tools such as editors, assemblers, compilers, and debuggers and application programs such as an accounting package. Let's take a closer look at how each of these layers functions and how they operate together.

OPERATIONS OF THE KERNEL

The UNIX operating system was designed to allow several users to share a CPU on a time-slice basis. Each user program is referred to as a *process.* One of the major functions of the kernel is to schedule and service the needs of processes. To do this the kernel keeps two tables in memory.

One of these, the *process table,* contains information about the state of each process. Among other things, the entry in the process table contains the location of the process in memory, the length of the process, the identification number of the process, the identification of the user, and whether the process is active or blocked.

The second type of table maintained by the kernel is called a *user table,* or a *per-process segment.* The user table contains pointers to the data, files, and directories currently being used by the process.

When a user or process is added to a system, the kernel creates a process table entry and a user table for that process. The length of the process table is fixed for each system, so only a set number of processes can be present in the system at one time. A process can create a subprocess, called a *child process.* When a child process is created, an entry is made in the process table for it, and a user table is created for it. When any process is removed from the system, its process table entry and user table are removed to make room for another process.

At any given instant in time, only one process can actually be running, since there is only one CPU on which to run processes. All the other processes are *suspended.* Processes essentially compete with each other for service. The scheduler in the kernel determines which process is to be run at a given time. The scheduling mechanism works as follows.

An external clock signal interrupts the CPU 50 or 60 times a second to produce the basic time slices. The interrupt routine that services this clock interrupt checks the process table entries for each process to determine which process should be run next. The decision as to which process to run is based on several factors. The first factor is whether the process is ready to run or blocked. A process may be blocked, or *put to sleep,* if it has to wait for an input or output operation to complete, a child process to complete, a signal from some other process, an external interrupt signal, or some fixed amount of time before continuing. A sleeping process will not be given a turn until the waited-for event occurs and the process is marked as active (ready to run).

A second factor used to determine which active process should be serviced next is how recently each process has been serviced. An active process that has recently had a turn will have a lower priority than an active process that has not recently had a turn because it just became unblocked or was just *swapped in* from disk. Because there is usually not room enough in memory to store all the suspended processes, some of them are *swapped out* to secondary storage such as a disk. The scheduler decides which processes to swap so that all processes get serviced as needed.

A second major function of the UNIX kernel is to maintain the system file structure. Unix uses a hierarchical file structure, as shown in Figure 15-6. This structure is sometimes called a tree structure because it looks like an inverted tree. The highest level in the hierarchy is the root directory. This directory contains the names of system files and the names of subdirectories. A directory in UNIX is simply a file that contains the name of the directory above it in the hierarchy and names of files or directories below it in the hierarchy. The directory above a file or directory is often referred to as the *parent* directory.

A user logged on to the system is given a directory, labeled usr in Figure 15-6, under the parent directory. The user can then create subdirectories or files under this directory. To refer to other files or directories in the system, a user specifies the directory path to it. For example, a user whose directory is at point 2 in Figure 15-6 can refer to the file at point 8 as /usr/doug/chapt/b. The name of a parent directory is often represented simply by two periods, so ../doug/chap/b can also be used to refer to the file at point 8 in, for example, a copy command. Figure 15-6 shows some other examples of how files, directories, and input/output devices are referred to in this type of file structure.

In addition to names, the directory entry for each file

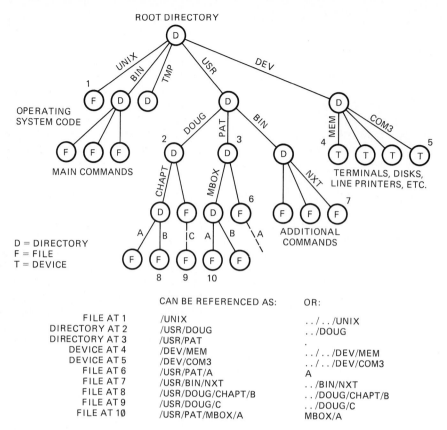

FIGURE 15-6   UNIX hierarchical file structure.

The reference table shown in the figure:

	CAN BE REFERENCED AS:	OR:
FILE AT 1	/UNIX	../../UNIX
DIRECTORY AT 2	/USR/DOUG	../DOUG
DIRECTORY AT 3	/USR/PAT	.
DEVICE AT 4	/DEV/MEM	../../DEV/MEM
DEVICE AT 5	/DEV/COM3	../../DEV/COM3
FILE AT 6	/USR/PAT/A	A
FILE AT 7	/USR/BIN/NXT	../BIN/NXT
FILE AT 8	/USR/DOUG/CHAPT/B	../DOUG/CHAPT/B
FILE AT 9	/USR/DOUG/C	../DOUG/C
FILE AT 10	/USR/PAT/MBOX/A	MBOX/A

and subdirectory contains a 2-byte *inode* number. The inode number identifies the position of the inode for that file or directory in a table of inodes kept by the operating system kernel. An inode is similar to a file-control block, which we discussed in Chapter 12. It contains the type of the file, the length of the file, the location of the file, the identification number of the owner, and the times the file was created, modified, and last accessed. The kernel uses inodes to manipulate files, but normally a user has to be concerned only with the file names.

Still another function of the kernel is to provide a means of communication between processes. The two methods it provides are *signals* and *pipes*. Signals are software interrupts generated by one process to tell another process to stop what it is doing, respond to the signal, and then go on with what it was doing. Signals can also be generated by user commands such as an abort command or by processing errors such as a divide by 0 error.

A pipe is a mechanism for passing the output data from one program directly to another program as input. We discuss how a pipe is used later. Now that you have an overview of some of the kernel functions, let's take a look at some of the shell functions.

THE UNIX SHELL

As we said before, the shell layer of UNIX is the level at which a user usually interacts with the system. The shell executes user commands and programs. It calls

kernel procedures as needed to do this. The UNIX command shell has some interesting features with which we want to acquaint you.

The first feature of the shell to discuss is how it handles I/O. At the user level, UNIX essentially treats I/O devices as files in a directory called dev, as shown in Figure 15-6. A modem connected to the system at point 5 in the system, for example, can be referred to simply as /dev/com3. Devices are opened, read from or written to, and closed, just as other files are. When a process is created, it has three files already open for use. The three are referred to as *standard input*, *standard output*, and *error output*. Standard input usually means the keyboard on the user's terminal. Standard output and error output usually mean the CRT on the user's terminal.

What this means is that when a user enters a command, which requires input, the input will be taken from the keyboard unless otherwise specified. Likewise, a command that produces output data will send it to the user's CRT unless some other destination is indicated. The UNIX command ls, for example, will send a simple list of the user's directory to the CRT on his or her terminal. However, input data or output data can be *redirected* to other devices or files. The < and > symbols are used to indicate redirection. For a user at point 3 in Figure 15-6, the command ls /usr/doug > /dev/com3, for example, reads the directory of /usr/doug and sends it to the device named com3 instead of to the user's CRT. The command sort −d < /usr/pat >

lpr alphabetically sorts the directory /user/pat and sends the result to the line printer. Note that UNIX commands are entered in lowercase letters.

Another feature of the UNIX shell that we mentioned previously is the pipe command. The pipe command allows output data from one program to be passed directly as input data to another program. The unique feature of a pipe is the way that the data is passed between the two. In most other systems data is passed from one program to another through files. One program processes some data and puts the results in a file. When the first program is done, a second program may access the file, further process the data, and put its results in another file, which can be accessed by another program or command. The command ls −1 > myfile, for example, might be used to produce a long listing (including subdirectories, etc.) of a user's directory and put it in a file called myfile. The command sort −d < myfile might then be used to sort the directory listing in the file in alphabetical order and display the result on the user's CRT. The pipe command makes it possible to do both the list and the sort operations without the need for an intermediate file to pass the data between the two commands. The single command ls − 1 | sort −d can be used to do this. The vertical line in the middle of the command indicates that the two commands are to be piped together. When a UNIX user issues a command to pipe two programs together, the kernel makes a connection so that the output from the first program is fed directly to the second program *as it is produced*. The pipe feature is often used with programs called *filters*. A filter is a program that simply performs some operation on a stream of input data and outputs the results. Some common types of filters are programs that format data into columns, sort data in various ways, and translate from one file format to another. As another example of how a filter is used, suppose that a user on the system shown in Figure 15-6 at point 2 wants to sort his or her directory alphabetically and send the result to the line printer. The simple command sort < /usr/doug | lpr will do this. The designated output for the lpr command is the line printer, so no redirection is needed.

Another useful feature of the UNIX command shell allows a user to execute two commands concurrently. As an example of how this capability might be used, suppose that a programmer wants to assemble and print the listing of one program module while editing a second module. The terms *foreground* and *background* are often used to describe the way in which the two processes are executing. For our example here, the compiling and printing are done in the background while editing is done in the foreground. A command followed by & (ampersand) indicates that the command should be carried out in the background mode. The sort and print command from the previous paragraph, for example, can be run as a background process by simply entering the command sort −d < /usr/doug | lpr &.

The kernel actually does the background command by creating a new process for it. The initial user process is referred to as the parent process and the new process is referred to as the child process. The parent process may be put to sleep until the child process finishes, or the parent process and the child process can compete for time slices and execute concurrently, as we described in the previous example.

The UNIX shell also provides a simple way to execute a series of commands over and over again. The commands to be executed are simply written into a named file using the editor. The resulting file is called a *shell file*, or *shell script*. The shell file can be executed with the single command sh followed by the name that was given to the shell file.

One final feature of the UNIX shell and kernel that we want to describe is *spooling*. Spooling is a mechanism that allows users to send files off to get printed without worrying about whether the printer is available at that particular moment. Incidentally, the term spool stands for *simultaneous peripheral operation on line*. Here's how it works. A user sends a file off to the spooler with the lpr command. The file to be printed and another short file containing information about the file are put in a dedicated directory called /usr/lpd. Writing a file in this directory causes a special printer program called the *printer daemon* to start running and print the file. The printer daemon program does this by stealing small amounts of time between other operations. If the printer is busy, then the print request is queued up behind other print requests and eventually gets printed. The main point here is that while all this printing is going on, users can go on editing, compiling, or executing other programs. Now we take a brief look at the programs and utilities included in the outermost UNIX layer.

The UNIX Utilities/Application Layer

Utilities are software tools used to develop, write, compile, debug, and document programs. Because UNIX has been around for so many years, there are a great many utilities available for it. Among these are several powerful editors, programs that format text for typesetting machines, compilers for many high-level languages, and a host of debuggers. For just about any function that a programmer or writer might want, there is probably a UNIX utility that does it. There are also a large number of application programs that will run under UNIX. Application programs, in contrast to utilities, are self-contained, or "canned," programs. Examples of application programs are accounting packages, data base−management packages, and computer-aided engineering design packages.

Some of the advantages of UNIX are its portability to new systems, the shell features we described previously, and the large number of utilities available for it. However, UNIX has various shortcomings, some of which have been remedied in later versions and in newer UNIX-like operating systems. One problem is that a user can load down the system with multiple background programs, fill a disk with files, and even crash the system. Also, a full UNIX system requires 8 to 10 Mbytes of disk space, which makes it more difficult to implement on small systems such as personal computers. Another major problem is that the basic time-slice approach of UNIX, which works well for a time-share system, responds too slowly for many real-time control applications. For these applications, an operating system such as Intel's RMX 86, which we describe in the next section, is used.

THE INTEL RMX 86™ OPERATING SYSTEM

The UNIX operating system, described in the preceding section, is designed to allow several users to develop programs or run application programs on a time-share basis. UNIX and similar operating systems are usually sold to users as complete packages, which can simply be configured to the hardware of a particular system and run. The time-slice approach of UNIX works well for a multiuser timeshare system, but it does not respond fast enough and does not have a suitable priority setup for many real-time control systems. Several companies offer operating systems more suitable to the needs of real-time control systems. One example is the Intel RMX 86 operating system.

RMX 86 is a "building-block" operating system. It is intended primarily to assist OEMs (original equipment manufacturers) in building custom control systems for sale to end users. Therefore, RMX 86 consists of a group of highly structured functional modules and utilities from which a system designer can choose the required functions. The purpose of this section of the chapter is to introduce you to the structure, terminology, and scheduling used in this common operating system.

RMX 86 Structure

Figure 15-7 shows an onionskin diagram of the basic structure of RMX 86. At the center is the *nucleus*, which corresponds to the kernel in UNIX. The nucleus consists mostly of a few dozen routines that system developers can call as needed to implement a desired end-user application program. This is indicated in Figure 15-7 by the fact that the user-application section of the diagram extends all the way to the nucleus.

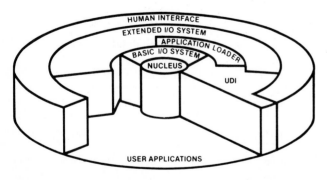

FIGURE 15-7   Onionskin diagram of Motorola RM8 86 operating system.

The nucleus is the only software module required in a system. All the other modules shown in Figure 15-7 are optional.

The *basic input/output system* contains device drivers to interface the system to disk drives, UARTS, keyboards, multiple CRT terminals, parallel printers, and other devices. The *extended input/output system*, or EIOS, contains higher-level I/O routines, which include built-in buffering. The application loader allows user programs to be loaded from disk into memory to be run. The *human interface* part of the system corresponds roughly to the shell in a UNIX system. It decodes and carries out user-entered commands. The basic human interface comes with commands for working with disk files, but other commands can be added as needed for a particular application. The final piece of the puzzle shown in Figure 15-7 is the *universal development interface*, or UDI. This software module, when added to the basic system, allows program-development tools such as editors, assemblers, compilers, and linkers to be loaded and run. Other software modules are also available. The point here is that software modules can be included, added to, or left out to produce a wide variety of custom operating systems. Now let's look a little closer to see how RMX 86 provides for multitasking.

RMX 86 Objects

The basic building blocks for RMX 86 programs are called *objects.* Objects are program structures that are created and manipulated by calls to routines in the nucleus. The major object types are tasks, jobs, segments, mailboxes, regions, and semaphores. We briefly describe each of these types and then show how they are used.

Tasks in RMX 86 are equivalent to processes described previously. Tasks are the only active type of object. As a task executes, it manipulates the other types of objects by calling routines in the nucleus. Tasks compete with each other for CPU time. Tasks are scheduled for execution on a preemptive, priority basis. We talk about this more later, but basically what it means is that if several tasks are ready to run, the task that has been assigned the highest priority will be run first.

A *job* in RMX 86 is a logical environment in which tasks and other objects reside. A job usually corresponds to an application. The system initially has one job called the *root job* and a task that can be used to create other jobs. Tasks use system calls to create jobs. When a job is created, it is given a memory pool. From this memory pool tasks can create child jobs and other objects as needed. Figure 15-8, p. 515, shows a simple diagram to illustrate this hierarchy.

A *segment* in RMX 86 is a contiguous block of memory up to 64 Kbytes in size. When a task requests a segment, the requested memory is taken from the memory pool of the job that contains that task.

A *mailbox* is an object used to pass objects from one task to another. The object being passed through a

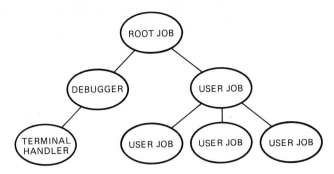

FIGURE 15-8   RMX 86 hierarchy of jobs.

mailbox is usually referred to as a message. What is actually passed through the mailbox is not the object itself, but a 16-bit *token* that represents the object. When each object is created, it is assigned a unique 16-bit number called a token. This approach is similar to the file-handle approach used in some PC DOS function calls. Tasks can create mailboxes, delete mailboxes, send message tokens to mailboxes, and receive message tokens from mailboxes. A mailbox has two queues, one for tasks that are waiting to receive a message (object) and the other for objects that have not yet been received by their destination task. If a task attempts to receive a message and there is no message in the mailbox, the task may be put to sleep for a while to wait for the message. This mechanism can be used to make one task wait at a mailbox until another task is finished before it starts.

A *region* in RMX 86 is one mechanism that can be used to prevent two or more tasks from accessing shared data at the same time. A task can create a region, delete a region, receive control, or send control of a region. If a task has received control of a region (has the token for it), no other task can access the region until the task "sends control" of it (releases the token for it) back to the operating system. A region, then, is usually used to provide mutual exclusion for a collection of data shared by two tasks. To provide mutual exclusion for a single variable or protect a critical region of code, a simpler way is to use a semaphore.

A *semaphore* in its simplest case is simply a 1-bit flag used to indicate that a resource is busy. Figure 15-1 shows an example of how a simple semaphore can be set up to do this. In RMX 86, a semaphore is a *counter*. A task can create a semaphore, delete a semaphore, send units to the semaphore, and receive units from a semaphore. For a simple case such as that shown in Figure 15-1, a semaphore can be created and sent one unit. When a task wants to access the variable protected by the semaphore, it is made to receive one unit from the semaphore. If the variable is not busy, then the semaphore will contain one unit. The task can receive that unit and access the variable. If any other tasks that access that variable are made to receive one unit before accessing the variable, then once one task has received the unit, no other tasks can access it. This is because there is no unit in the

semaphore for the other tasks to receive. When a task has finished with a shared variable or critical region, it sends one unit to the semaphore to release the variable so other tasks can access it. This is the same principle used in the example in Figure 15-1 but described with a different vocabulary. The fact that a semaphore can have values other than 0 or 1 allows it to be used to synchronize two tasks. For example, a task can be written to send one unit to a semaphore each time it executes. A second task can be made to wait at the semaphore until it is able to receive a specified number of units from the semaphore.

In addition to the defined object types, a programmer can create custom objects. Now that we have given you an overview of the types of objects with which RMX 86 works, we will describe how RMX 86 handles task execution.

RMX 86 Task Execution

Real-time control systems usually must respond to asynchronous requests for service in a manner that makes sure the most important request is serviced first. In an RMX 86 system each service for a request is set up as a task. When an RMX 86 task is created, it is assigned a priority number between 0 and 255. The lower the number, the higher the priority. Numbers between 0 and 127 are used for interrupt tasks. RMX 86 supports a single or several cascaded 8259A priority interrupt controllers for multiple-hardware interrupts. Priority numbers between 128 and 255 are used for software tasks. RMX 86 schedules the execution of tasks on a preemptive priority basis. This means that if two or more tasks are ready to run, the task that has been assigned the highest priority will be executed first. This task will execute until it finishes or until it reaches a point where it needs some resource that is not yet available. If a higher-priority task becomes ready while a task is executing, the executing task will be preempted (put to sleep), and the higher priority task will be executed.

Figure 15-9 shows an RMX 86 *task-state diagram*, which is often used to summarize the different states in which a task can be and the conditions necessary to go from one state to another. As we work our way around the numbers in the figure, try to develop some intuitive feel for how it all works.

1. When a task is created, it is placed in the ready state. A task is created, remember, by a call to a routine in the nucleus.

2. A task enters the running state when it has a higher priority than any other ready task or it has been waiting longer than another ready task of the same priority.

3. A task is returned to the ready state when a task with a higher priority becomes ready and preempts it.

4. A task goes from the running state to the asleep state if

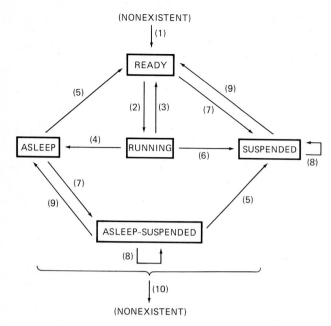

FIGURE 15-9   RMX 86 task state diagram.

a. The task puts itself to sleep with a sleep system call. A task can put itself to sleep for a specified amount of time and then return to the ready state.

b. The task must wait for a semaphore, a message, or a region in order to proceed.

5. Note that there are two 5s on Figure 15-9. A task will go from the asleep state to the ready state or from the asleep-suspended state to the suspended state if
   a. The time specified in the sleep call expires.
   b. The semaphore, message, or region for which the task was waiting becomes available.
   c. The task's waiting-time limit expires without the object for which the task was waiting becoming available.

6. A task goes from the running state to the suspended state when it does a suspend-task system call or a wait-for-interrupt system call.

7. A task in the ready state is suspended when another task suspends it by calling the suspend-task routine from the nucleus.

8. A task remains in a suspended state or an asleep-suspended state until the resume-task nucleus procedure has been called as many times as the suspend-task routine was called for the task.

9. A task in the suspended state will return to the ready state and a task in the asleep-suspended will return to the asleep state when the resume-task system call has been done as many times for the task as the suspend-task system call. Another case where a task may exit from a suspended state is when an interrupt for which the task was waiting occurs.

10. A task can be deleted with the delete-task system call.

A question that might occur to you at this point is, If RMX 86 tasks are executed on a priority basis, how can a multiuser capability be included in a RMX 86–based system? The answer to this question is that a clock tick can be used to produce an interrupt every 20 ms or so. The interrupt-service routine for that interrupt can then cycle around to a different terminal after each interrupt.

The final point we want to make here about RMX 86 is how a designer goes about using it to develop a custom system program. The design steps usually follow a sequence such as the following:

1. Define the system requirements.

2. Break the overall system into logical jobs.

3. Carefully define the functions of each job.

4. Determine the data structures needed for each job.

5. Determine whether jobs need to communicate or share resources.

6. Break down each job into tasks.

7. Write the algorithms for each task, including any needs for shared resources, synchronization, or communication between tasks.

8. Write the system initialization modules that set up the jobs, tasks, segments, regions, and semaphores using nucleus calls.

9. Write and test the program code for each task using system calls to define and manipulate objects as needed.

10. Integrate and test the completed system.

In the next section of this chapter we introduce you to the Motorola 68030 microprocessor, which was designed to be used as the CPU in a multitasking system with virtual memory capability.

THE MOTOROLA 68030 MICROPROCESSOR

We started this chapter with an introduction to some of the needs of multitasking/multiuser operating systems, such as protection, mutual exclusion, and virtual memory capability. Later sections gave brief overviews of UNIX, a common multiuser operating system, and of RMX 86, a common real-time multitasking operating system. The Motorola 68020 and 68030 microprocessors were designed to serve as the CPU in a multitasking microcomputer system such as those we have described. The Apple Macintosh II and several other common systems capable of multitasking operation use the 68020 as their CPU. The 68030 is used in the Apple Macintosh SE30. We have seen the 68020 in previous chapters as a faster, more powerful version of the 68000. The 68020 is used with the 68851 MMU in the Macintosh II. We have selected the 68030 for further discussion in this chapter because it is yet more powerful and because it has a built-in MMU. It is easiest at times to think of the 68030 as a 68020 and a 68851 combined into one IC.

After a brief introduction to the internal architecture, signals, and hardware connections of the 68030, we show you how memory management, task switching, and protection are done with the features built into the device.

68030 Architecture, Signals, and System Connections

Figure 15-10 shows a family summary, including the 68000, 68008, 68010, 68020, and the 68030.

The 68030 is packaged in a 132-pin ceramic flatpack, as shown in Figure 15-11. The 68030 is also available in other packages, such as the pin grid array shown in Figure 15-12, p. 519. Figure 15-13, p. 520, shows an internal block diagram for the 68030. Many of the signals of the 68030 should be familiar to you from our discussion of the 68000 signals in Chapter 7.

Memory for the 68030 is set up as an odd bank and an even bank, just as it is for the 68000.

The machine cycle waveforms for the 68030 are very similar to those of the 68000 that we showed and discussed in earlier chapters. You should be able to work your way through them in the Motorola 68030 data sheets if you need that type of information. In the limited space we have for the remainder of this section, we want to concentrate on the operation of the 68030 in its real address mode and in its protected virtual address mode.

The 68030 Addressing Modes

The instruction set of the 68030 is a *superset* of the 68000 instructions. This means that every instruction

	MC68000	MC68008	MC68010	MC68020	MC68030
Data Bus Size (Bits)	16	8	16	8,16,32	8,16,32
Address Bus Size (Bits)	24	20	24	32	32
Instruction Cache (in words)	—	—	3[1]	128	128
Data Cache (in words)	—	—	—	—	128

Note 1. The MC68010 supports a 3-word cache for the loop mode.

Virtual Memory/Machine MC68010, MC68020, and MC68030	Provide Bus Error Detection, Fault Recovery
MC68030	On-chip MMU
Coprocessor Interface MC68000, MC68008, and MC68010	Emulated in software
MC68020 and MC68030	In Microcode
Word/Long Word Data Alignment MC68000, MC68008, and MC68010	Word/Long Data, Instructions, and Stack Must be Word Aligned
MC68020 and MC68030	Only Instructions Must be Word Aligned (Data Alignment Improves Performance)
Control Registers MC68000 and MC68008	None
MC68010	SFC, DFC, VBR
MC68020	SFC, DFC, VBR, CACR, CAAR
MC68030	SFC, DFC, VBR, CACR, CAAR, CRP, SRP, TC, TT0, TT1, PSR

FIGURE 15-10 M68000 family summary. (*Reprinted with permission of Motorola, Inc.*)

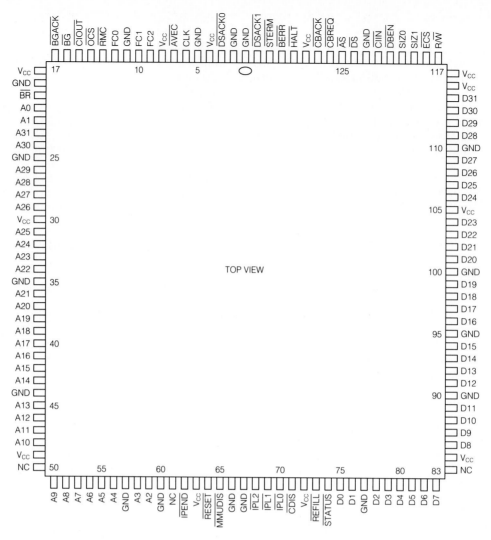

FIGURE 15-11 Pin diagram for 68030 microprocessor ceramic surface-mount package. (*Reprinted with permission of Motorola, Inc.*)

supported by the 68000 is also supported by the 68030; however, the 68030 also supports some additional instructions. The 68030 instruction set is also a superset of the 68020 instruction set.

The 68030 was designed to be upward compatible from the 68000, the 68010, and the 68020 so that the huge amount of software developed for these could easily be transported to the 68030. Previously debugged modules can then be integrated with new program modules written to take advantage of the advanced features of the 68030. Let's take a look at how some of these advanced features work.

68851 Instructions

Motorola offers two memory-management units for use with the 68000 family. The simpler and first-introduced is the 68451. The 68451 provides for a segmented virtual memory environment. That is, the 68451 provides base and bounds registers describing the

various segments of logical memory that are actually in physical RAM. The more recent 68851 provides for demand-paged virtual memory management. That is, the 68851 contains page tables describing the various pages of logical memory that are actually in the physical RAM.

The following brief descriptions are intended to introduce you to the instructions that the 68851 provides. These instructions are built in for the 68030, since the 68030 contains most of the 68851 functions built right into the CPU IC.

PBcc—Branch on MMU condition (68851 only)

PDBcc—Test MMU condition, decrement, and branch (68851 only)

PFLUSH—Flush MMU address translation cache entries

PFLUSHR—Flush MMU ATC entries and root pointer table (68851 only)

The pin diagram content (bottom view):

	1	2	3	4	5	6	7	8	9	10	11	12	13
N	D31	D28	D26	D25	D23	D21	D19	D18	D16	D15	D13	D11	D8
M	DBEN	ECS	D29	D27	D24	D22	D20	D17	D14	D12	D9	D6	D3
L	CIIN	SIZ0	R/W̄	D30	GND	Vcc	GND	GND	GND	D10	D7	D4	D2
K	CBREQ	DS	SIZ1	Vcc	NC*					Vcc	D5	D1	D0
J	CBACK	AS	GND							GND	STATUS	REFILL	
H	BERR	HALT	Vcc							Vcc	CDIS	IPL0	
G	STERM	DSACK1	GND							GND	IPL2	IPL1	
F	DSACK0	Vcc	GND	NC*					NC*	Vcc	RESET	MMUDIS	
E	CLK	AVEC	GND							GND	NC*	IPEND	
D	FC2	FC0	OCS	Vcc	NC*					Vcc	A6	A3	A2
C	FC1	CIOUT	BGACK	A1	GND	Vcc	GND	A18	GND	A11	A9	A5	A4
B	RMC	BG	A31	A29	A27	A25	A22	A20	A16	A14	A12	A8	A7
A	BR	A0	A30	A28	A26	A24	A23	A21	A19	A17	A15	A13	A10

BOTTOM VIEW

*NC — Do not connect to this pin.

Pin Group	Vcc	GND
Address Bus	C6, D10	C5, C7, C9, E11
Data Bus	L6, K10	J11, L9, L7, L5,
ECS, SIZx, DS, AS, DBEN, CBREQ, R/W̄	K4	J3
FC0–FC2, RMC, OCS, CIOUT, BG	D4	E3
Internal Logic, RESET, STATUS, REFILL, Misc.	H3, F2, F11, H11	L8, G3, F3, G11

FIGURE 15-12   Pin diagram for 68030 microprocessor pin grid array package.
(*Reprinted with permission of Motorola, Inc.*)

PLOAD—Load ATC entry

PMOVE—Move MMU register

PRESTORE—Restore MMU state (68851 only)

PSAVE—Save MMU state (68851 only)

PScc—MMU set conditionally (68851 only)

PTEST—Test logical address

PTRAPcc—Trap on MMU condition (68851 only)

PVALID—Validate address (68851 only)

In the remaining sections of this chapter we show you some of the directions beyond the 68020 and 68030 in which microprocessor evolution is heading.

NEW DIRECTIONS

Microprocessor evolution has been proceeding very rapidly in the last few years, and the rate of evolution seems to be increasing. Throughout this book we have tried to point out some of the directions this evolution has been taking. One area of evolution has been from batch processing computer systems to timeshare and multitasking systems. Another direction has been to distributed processing systems linked together in networks such as we described in Chapter 13. Also, the development of optical disk storage makes available at each user's desk more data than was previously available at many large mainframe computers. The overall direction of evolution is toward microcomputers with greater screen resolution, more memory capability,

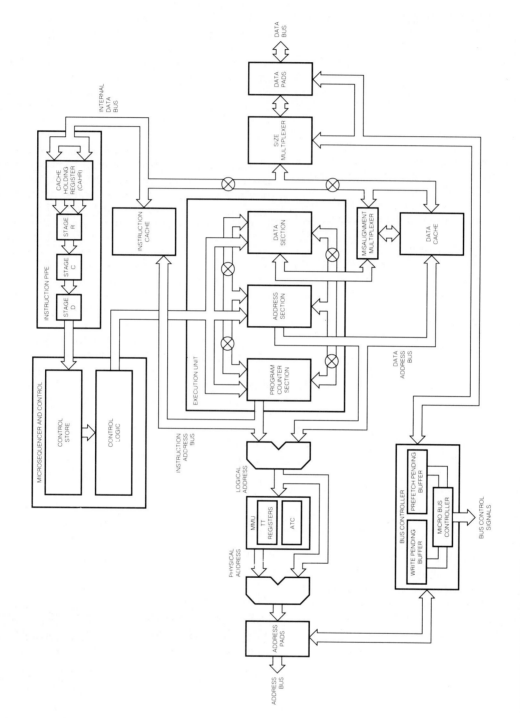

FIGURE 15-13   Internal block diagram of Motorola 68030 microprocessor. *(Reprinted with permission of Motorola, Inc.)*

larger data words, and higher processing speeds. We use the remainder of this chapter to introduce you to some developing areas, the Motorola 68040 32-bit microprocessor, parallel processing, RISC machines, and optical computers.

The Motorola 68040 32-bit Microprocessor

The Motorola 68040 is the most recent, fastest member of the 68000 CPU family. The 68040 is Motorola's third generation of M68000-compatible, high-performance, 32-bit microprocessors. The 68040 can be thought of as a 68030 with most of the 68881 built in and with two 68851s built in. Higher performance is facilitated by a variety of improvements, including, notably, 4K instruction and data caches. By placing the FPU and MMU on a chip, the 68040 can achieve much higher performance than a 68020 or 68030 combined with these ICs off-chip.

The 68040 provides the same programmer's model as does the 68030, 16 general-purpose registers (8 data and 8 address) and eight 80-bit floating-point registers. The addressing modes and MMU/FPU operation are the same as we have studied with the older members of the 68000 family. The 68040 is available in a 179-pin package roughly 1.85 by 1.85 in. in size.

The 68040 is available today in some manufacturers' workstations. 68040s currently can operate with clock speeds of up to 50 MHz.

Parallel Processing

Some computer jobs, such as analyzing weather data, modeling the response of complex drugs, or creating the graphics for high-tech movies such as *The Last Starfighter,* require a type of computer commonly called a *supercomputer.* Supercomputers typically work with 64-bit data words, address large amounts of memory, and execute hundreds of millions of instructions per second. The processing speed of these supercomputers is usually expressed in millions of instructions per second (MIPS) or in millions of floating-point operations per second (megaflops). An example of a floating-point operation is adding together two numbers expressed in floating-point form. One current supercomputer, the X-MP2 from Cray Research, Inc., is capable of about 500 megaflops. Depending on configuration, the X-MP2 costs between $9 million and $12 million. The high price of supercomputers is caused by the fact that in order to achieve their great speed, they have to use large quantities of expensive, state-of-the-art discrete components. Less expensive LSI components are not nearly fast enough for a supercomputer with a traditional one- or two-processor architecture. One solution to this problem is to build a system using many LSI processors that operate in parallel, or *concurrently.* Each processor can then work on a part of the overall problem that the computer is analyzing.

There are several different ways of connecting processors in parallel. The difficulty with a simple bus structure such as this is that processors compete for shared resources such as memory. If one processor is using the bus, others must wait. This slows down the overall processing speed. One of the more efficient multiprocessor architectures is the hypercube topology developed by Seitz and Fox at Caltech. A diagram of this topology is shown in Figure 15-14. Each node in the system consists of a complete processing unit with the ability to communicate with other units. The number of nodes can be expanded to give the power and speed needed to handle the problem the computer is being used to solve. Each processor unit is typically connected to its nearest neighbors, as shown.

Intel has produced the iPSC family of commercial products based on the hypercube topology. The three currently available versions have 32, 64, and 128 nodes. Figure 15-15 shows the components contained on the processor board for each node. Each node is a complete microcomputer with an 80286 processor, 80287 math coprocessor, 500 Kbytes of RAM, 64 Kbytes of ROM, and interface circuitry. The processor board also has an Intel 82586 Ethernet coprocessor to control communications with other nodes. Each processor has seven 10 Mbit/s lines to communicate with other processors and one 10-Mbit/s line to communicate with a central controller. The Intel systems use an Intel 286/310 minicomputer as the central controller for the hypercube. The advantage of this structure is that each processor has enough memory to operate independently, and communication between processors can take any one of several routes, rather than being limited to a single bus. Current systems operate at 2 to 10 megaflops, which puts them in the low end of the supercomputer range. However, because common LSI components are used, the cost is much less than

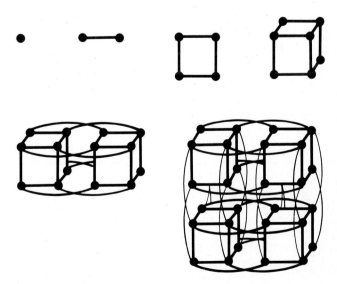

FIGURE 15-14 Hypercube multiprocessor topologies for 1 to 32 nodes.

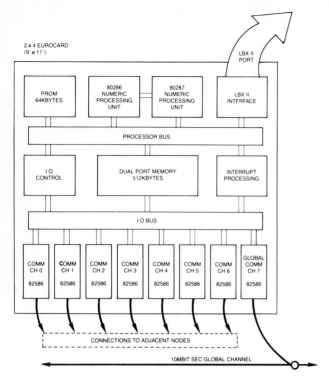

LBX II
PORT

| PROM 64KBYTES | 80286 NUMERIC PROCESSING UNIT | 80287 NUMERIC PROCESSING UNIT | LBX II INTERFACE |

PROCESSOR BUS

| I O CONTROL | DUAL PORT MEMORY 512KBYTES | INTERRUPT PROCESSING |

I O BUS

| COMM CH 0 82586 | COMM CH 1 82586 | COMM CH 2 82586 | COMM CH 3 82586 | COMM CH 4 82586 | COMM CH 5 82586 | COMM CH 6 82586 | GLOBAL COMM CH 7 82586 |

CONNECTIONS TO ADJACENT NODES

10MBIT SEC GLOBAL CHANNEL

FIGURE 15-15   Block diagram of Intel iPSC hypercube node processor board.

that of an equivalent single-processor supercomputer. Adding more nodes should produce faster systems in the future because parallel processors eliminate much of the bottleneck caused by a single serial processor. Another method currently being developed to speed up the operation of processors is to streamline their instruction set.

RISC Machines

The term RISC stands for *reduced instruction set computer.* By designing a microprocessor instruction set with only simple logical and arithmetic instructions, the processor can operate faster. There are several reasons for this. First of all, fewer instructions mean a simpler and faster instruction decoder. Secondly, instruction sequences can be written to do the desired operation most efficiently. The trade-off here, of course, is that writing a program requires more work on the part of the programmer. The RISC designers claim that most programmers do not write in assembly language. Most programmers write in higher-level languages. Thus the RISC programming problems can be addressed by the few programmers who write the high-level language compilers. These compilers are more difficult to write than are compilers for CISC (complex instruction set computers) such as the 68030. However, once the compilers are written properly, the resultant code should execute faster on the faster RISC hardware. This debate still rages in the

computer community. RISC computers are making inroads in certain areas such as the area of computer servers on large networks. CISC-based systems continue to be the dominant machines in terms of numbers of systems sold.

Motorola produces a line of RISC VLSI, the MC88000 family. This family includes the MC88100, a RISC CPU, and the MC88200 cache/memory-management unit (CMMU). The MC88100 has 51 instructions and seven operand types. It includes separate data and instruction memory ports, *pipelined* load and store operations, and support for *big-endian* or *little-endian* byte ordering. Pipelining is an architectural feature used to get higher throughput from existing computer component technology. As an example, let's consider a program that adds a whole sequence of numbers. This happens in several of the programs we have seen as examples in earlier chapters. In a traditional computer each addition is performed sequentially. One addition cannot begin until the one before it is completed. In a pipelined architecture a second and possibly even more additions can begin before the first is completed. The way this works is by breaking the addition circuitry (the ALU) into a series of stages. For example, in order to add two 32-bit integers, the first stage might add the first 8 bits, then the second stage would add the second 8 bits, and so on for four stages. Each stage would possibly pass a carry bit and the result of its 8-bit addition on to the next stage. Thus, we could have up to four additions happening at once, each having a different byte operated on. The four-stage adder is called a pipeline because we move integers into one end and the addition results come out the other end. We could put up to four pairs of integers into the "pipe" at the same time. The MC88100 has a five-stage add pipeline and a six-stage multiply pipeline.

The terms big-endian and little-endian refer to the two ways we can view numbers in memory. That is, if a 4-byte integer is stored in bytes addressed $0000, $0001, $0002, and $0003; which byte is the most significant? With the big-endian view, the "big end" of the number comes first, so the byte at address $0000 is the most significant. The Motorola machines with which we have been working store $0000 as the most significant. So the 68000 family is a family of big-endian machines. The Intel 8086 family is a family of little-endian machines. When the 8086 stores multibyte numbers, the byte at address $0000 is the least significant byte. The MC88100 can be configured when it is reset so that it handles either byte-ordering scheme.

Optical Computers

So far in this book the microcomputer devices we have discussed use electrical currents or voltage levels to represent logic levels. In the final section of this chapter we want to introduce you to experimental computers that use light beams to represent logic levels and switch logic devices on and off. The basic principle is to let a light beam represent a logic 1 and no beam represent a logic 0, just as is done in simple fiber-optic digital signal–transmission systems. Logic gates in an optical computer transmit a beam when switched on and block the light beam when switched off. The logic gates themselves are switched on and off by a light beam shining on them. In other words, logic levels are represented by light or no light, logic gate switches are controlled by the presence or absence of a light beam, and the connecting links between optical logic gates are light beams.

One advantage of optical logic gates and computers is that signals can easily be sent to many elements in parallel. This may lead to their use in parallel processor systems. Another major advantage of optical logic gates is their switching speeds. Even though current optical logic gates are quite primitive, switching speeds are in the picosecond range. Optics researchers believe that switching speeds of a few femtoseconds (10^{-15} s) are possible. Optical computers may be able to run with clocks of several hundred megabytes. A major disadvantage of current optical devices is the relatively large amount of power they require. It is to be hoped that further research will realize the potential of this technology.

EPILOGUE

This book has been able to show you only a small view of where microcomputer electronics is and where it seems to be evolving. It is hoped that it has given you enough of a start for you to proceed on your own and enjoy playing a part in the continuing evolution. As you are faced with learning some new and seemingly difficult material, remember the 5-minute rule and the old saying, "Grapevines and people bear the best fruit on new growth."

CHECKLIST OF IMPORTANT TERMS AND CONCEPTS IN THIS CHAPTER

If there are terms or concepts in this list you do not remember, use the index to find them in this chapter.

Multiuser, multitasking

Scheduler

Time-slice and preemptive priority-based scheduling

Semaphore

Process-control block

Deadlock

Critical region

Application programs

Utilities

Memory management

Overlay

Bank switching

Descriptor table

Virtual memory

Demand-paged virtual memory

Cache

UNIX

Kernel
    Process and user tables
    Child process
    Parent
    Inode number
    Signal
    Pipe

Shell
    Standard input and output, error output
    Redirection
    Spooling

RMX 86
    Nucleus
    Modules
    Basic I/O systems
    Extended I/O systems
    Human interface
    Universal development interface

Objects
    Tasks
    Jobs
    Segments
    Mailboxes
    Regions
    Semaphores

Task state

68030

68040

Parallel processing
    Parallel, or concurrent, operation
    Hypercube topology

RISC machine

Optical computer

5-minute rule

Grapevine

REVIEW QUESTIONS AND PROBLEMS

1. List and briefly describe the two types of scheduling commonly used in multiuser/multitasking operating systems.

2. Suppose that two users in a timeshare computer system each want to print out a file. How can the system be prevented from printing lines from one file between lines of the other file?

3. Define the term deadlock and describe one way it can be prevented.

4. Define the term critical region and show with 68000 assembly language instructions how a semaphore can be used to protect a critical region.

5. The UNIX operating system is set up as a three-layer operating system. What is the major reason it is configured in layers? Identify and describe the function of each of the three layers.

6. Describe how an overlay scheme is used to run programs such as compilers, which are too large to be loaded into physical memory all at once.

7. Define the term virtual memory, and use Figure 15-4 to help you briefly describe how a logical address is converted to a physical address by a memory-management unit using a descriptor table. What action will the MMU take if it finds that a requested segment is not present in physical memory? What is another major advantage of the indirect addressing provided by descriptor tables, besides the ability to address a large amount of virtual memory?

8. How does a UNIX scheduler determine which active process to service next?

9. Define the term hierarchical file structure as used in the UNIX operating system. What is the advantage of this type file structure over a simple list type?

10. In a UNIX system, input or output can be "redirected." Explain briefly what this means.

11. What is meant by the term piping in a UNIX system? What symbol is used to indicate a pipe?

12. A programmer was heard to say that she "sent the file off to the print spooler before going to lunch." What did she mean by this statement?

13. For what types of applications was the RMX 86 operating system designed? Compare the scheduling method of RMX 86 with that of UNIX.

14. List the major processing units in a 68030 microprocessor and briefly describe the function of each.

15. The data sheet for a computer which uses the 68030 as its CPU indicates that the 68030 is operated in its "real address mode." What does this mean?

16. How is a 68030 switched from real address mode to protected virtual address mode operation? How can it be switched back to real address mode operation?

17. Explain the term virtual memory. How much virtual memory can a 68030 address? How much physical memory can a 68030 address?

18. Why is the length of the segment included in the descriptor for the segment? How does the 68030 keep track of where the global descriptor table and the currently used local descriptor table are located in memory?

19. How are tasks in a 68030 system protected from each other?

20. How can operating system kernel procedures and data be protected from access by application programs in an 68030 system?

21. In a 68030 system, a task operating at a level 2 privilege can in a special way call a routine at a higher privilege level. Describe briefly the mechanism that is used to make this access.

22. The 68030 maintains a task state segment for each active task in a system. How are these task state segments accessed?

23. List three major advances that the 68040 microprocessor has over the 68030.

24. What are the major advantages of using parallel processors, such as is done in the Intel hypercube, instead of using a single fast processor?

25. What factor makes optical computers an inviting technology?

BIBLIOGRAPHY

Because of the technical level of this book, the major sources of further information on the topics discussed are manufacturers' data books, application notes, and articles in current engineering periodicals. With the foundation you get from this book you should be able to comfortably read these materials. Listed below, by chapter, are some materials that will give you more details for many of the topics we discuss in the book. Following the chapter listings is a list of periodicals that we have found to be particularly helpful in keeping up with the latest advances in microcomputer evolution and applications.

Chapter 1

Hall, Douglas V., *Digital Circuits and Systems*, McGraw-Hill, Inc., New York, 1989.

Chapters 2–8

Clements, Alan, *68000 Sourcebook*, McGraw-Hill (UK) Limited, Berkshire, 1990.

M68000 8-/16-/32-Bit Microprocessor's Reference Manual, Prentice-Hall, Englewood Cliffs, N.J., fifth edition, 1986.

M6800 Microprocessor Applications Manual, Motorola Inc., 1975.

Macintosh 68000 Development System (MDS) Version 2.0 Update, Consulair Corp., 1986.

Macintosh 68000 Development System User's Manual, Consulair Corp., 1984.

MC68000 16-/32-Bit Microprocessor, Motorola Inc., 1985 (Hardware Databook).

Mick, John, and Jim Brick, *Bit-Slice Microprocessor Design*, McGraw-Hill, Inc., New York, 1980.

P68000 microLab Microprocessor Development System User's Manual, University of Pittsburgh, 1986.

P68681-PC microLab Communications Interface User's Manual, University of Pittsburgh, 1986.

Peripherals, Intel Corporation, Santa Clara, Calif., latest edition (Databook).

Chapters 9–10

Allocca, John A., and Allen Stuart, *Transducers Theory and Applications*, Reston Publishing Company, Inc., Reston, Va., 1984.

AMF Potter & Brumfield Catalog, Potter & Brumfield, Princeton, Ind., latest edition.

Analog Devices Industrial Control Series Data Sheet, Analog Devices, Inc., Norwood, Mass., latest edition.

Apple Numerics Manual, Addison Wesley, Reading, Mass., second edition, 1988.

Auslander, David M., and Paul Sagues, *Microprocessors for Measurement and Control*, Osborne/McGraw-Hill, Berkeley, Calif., 1981.

Chassaing, Rulph, and Darell W. Horning, *Digital Signal Processing with the TMS320C25*, John Wiley & Sons, Somerset, New York, 1990.

Dorf, Richard C., *Robotics and Automated Manufacturing*, Reston Publishing Company, Reston, Va., 1983.

Interfacing Liquid Crystal Displays in Digital Systems, Application Note AN-8, Beckman Instruments, Inc., Scottsdale, Ariz., latest edition.

Johnson, Curtis D., *Process Control Instrumentation Technology*, John Wiley & Sons, New York, latest edition.

M68000 8-/16-/32-Bit Microprocessor's Reference Manual, Prentice-Hall, Englewood Cliffs, N.J., fifth edition, 1986.

Optoelectronics Designer's Catalog, Hewlett-Packard, Palo Alto, Calif., latest edition.

Optoelectronics Device Data Book, DL118R1, Motorola Semiconductor Products Inc., Phoenix, Ariz., latest edition.

Peripherals, Intel Corporation, Santa Clara, Calif., latest edition (Databook).

Sandhu, H. S., *Hands-On-Introduction to ROBOTICS—The Manual for the XR-Series Robots*, Rhino Robots, Champaign, Ill., latest edition.

Seippel, Robert G., *Transducers, Sensors, and Detectors*, Reston Publishing Company, Inc., Reston, Va., 1983.

Sheingold, Daniel H. (ed.), *Transducer Interfacing Handbook—A Guide to Analog Signal Conditioning*, Analog Devices, Inc., Norwood, Mass., latest edition.

Slo-Syn DC Stepping Motors Catalog, DCM1078, Superior Electric Company, Bristol, Conn., latest edition.

Texas Instruments, Inc., *Third Generation TMS320 User's Guide*, Dallas, Tex., latest edition.

Chapter 11

Error Detecting and Correcting Codes, Application Note AP-46, Intel Corporation, Santa Clara, Calif., 1979.

Getting Started With the Numeric Data Processor, Application Note AP-113, Intel Corporation, Santa Clara, Calif., 1981.

Guide to the Macintosh Family Hardware, Addison Wesley, Reading, Mass., 1990.

Hall, Douglas V., *Digital Circuits and Systems*, McGraw-Hill, Inc., New York, 1989. (Chapter 15 on electronic design automation).

Inside Macintosh Volume I, II, and III, Addison Wesley, Reading, Mass., 1985.

M68000 8-/16-/32-Bit Microprocessor's Reference Manual, Prentice-Hall, Englewood Cliffs, N.J., fifth edition, 1986.

Macintosh 68000 Development System User's Manual, Consulair Corp., 1984.

Peripherals, Intel Corporation, Santa Clara, Calif., latest edition (Databook).

Chapter 12

M68000 8-/16-/32-Bit Microprocessor's Reference Manual, Prentice-Hall, Englewood Cliffs, N.J., fifth edition, 1986.

Macintosh 68000 Development System (MDS) Version 2.0 Update, Consulair Corp., 1986.

Programmer's Introduction to the Macintosh Family, Addison Wesley, Reading, Mass., 1988.

THINK C User's Manual, Semantec Corporation, Cupertino, Calif., 1989.

Waite, Michael, and Stephen Prata, *New C Primer Plus,* Howard W. Sams & Company, Carmel, Ind., 1990.

Chapter 13

An Intelligent Data Base System Using the 8272, Application Note AP-116, Intel Corporation, Santa Clara, Calif., 1981. (Old, but good basics.)

Lesea, Austin, and Rodnay Zaks, *Microprocessor Interfacing Techniques,* Sybex Inc., Berkeley, Calif., latest edition.

Peripherals, Intel Corporation, Santa Clara, Calif., latest edition (Databook).

Raster Graphics Handbook, Conrac Corporation, Covina, Calif., latest edition.

Chapter 15

Kaisler, Stephen H., *The Design of Operating Systems for Small Computer Systems,* John Wiley & Sons, New York, 1983.

MC68851 Paged Memory Management Unit User's Manual, Prentice-Hall, Englewood Cliffs, N.J., second edition, 1989.

MC68030 32-Bit Microprocessor User's Manual, Prentice-Hall, Englewood Cliffs, N.J., second edition, 1985.

MC68030 Enhanced 32-Bit Microprocessor User's Manual, Prentice-Hall, Englewood Cliffs, N.J., second edition, 1989.

MC68040 32-Bit Third-Generation Microprocessor User's Manual, Motorola Inc., 1989 (Databook).

Pappas, Chris H., and William H. Murray, *Inside the Model 80,* Osborne/McGraw-Hill, Berkeley, Calif., 1988.

Williams, Steve, *68030 Assembly Language Reference,* Addison Wesley, Reading, Mass., 1989.

Periodicals

BYTE. ISSN 0360-5280. Byte Publications, Inc., 70 Main Street, Peterborough, N.H. 03458.

EDN. ISSN 0012-7515. Cahners Publishing Co., 221 Columbus Avenue, Boston, Mass. 02116.

Electronic Design. USPS-172-080. Hayden Publishing Co., Inc., 50 Essex Street, Rochelle Park, N.J. 07662.

Electronics. ISSN 0013-5070. McGraw-Hill, Inc., 1221 Avenue of the Americas, New York, N.Y. 10020.

Instruments & Control Systems. ISSN 0164-0089. Chilton Company, Chilton Way, Radnor, Penn. 19089.

Electronic Engineering Times. ISSN 0192-1541. Electronic Engineering Times, 600 Community Drive, Manhasset, N.Y. 11030.

APPENDIX A

A.1 INTRODUCTION

This Appendix contains listings of the instruction execution times in terms of external clock (CLK) periods. In this data, it is assumed that both memory read and write cycle times are four clock periods. A longer memory cycle will cause the generation of wait states that must be added to the total instruction time.

The number of bus read and write cycles for each instruction is also included with the timing data. This data is enclosed in parentheses following the number of clock periods and is shown as: (r/w) where r is the number of read cycles and w is the number of write cycles included in the clock period number. Recalling that either a read or write cycle requires four clock periods, a timing number given as 18(3/1) relates to 12 clock periods for the three read cycles, plus 4 clock periods for the one write cycle, plus 2 cycles required for some internal function of the processor.

NOTE
The number of periods includes instruction fetch and all applicable operand fetches and stores.

A.2 OPERAND EFFECTIVE ADDRESS CALCULATION TIMING

Table A-1 lists the number of clock periods required to compute an instruction's effective address. It includes fetching of any extension words, the address computation, and fetching of the memory operand. The number of bus read and write cycles is shown in parenthesis as (r/w). Note there are no write cycles involved in processing the effective address.

Table A-1. Effective Address Calculation Times

Addressing Mode		Byte, Word	Long
Register			
Dn	Data Register Direct	0(0/0)	0(0/0)
An	Address Register Direct	0(0/0)	0(0/0)
Memory			
(An)	Address Register Indirect	4(1/0)	8(2/0)
(An) +	Address Register Indirect with Postincrement	4(1/0)	8(2/0)
− (An)	Address Register Indirect with Predecrement	6(1/0)	10(2/0)
d_{16}(An)	Address Register Indirect with Displacement	8(2/0)	12(3/0)
d_8(An, Xn)*	Address Register Indirect with Index	10(2/0)	14(3/0)
(xxx).W	Absolute Short	8(2/0)	12(3/0)
(xxx).L	Absolute Long	12(3/0)	16(4/0)
d_8(PC)	Program Counter with Displacement	8(2/0)	12(3/0)
d_{16}(PC, Xn)*	Program Counter with Index	10(2/0)	14(3/0)
#<data>	Immediate	4(1/0)	8(2/0)

*The size of the index register (Xn) does not affect execution time.

A.3 MOVE INSTRUCTION EXECUTION TIMES

Tables A-2 and A-3 indicate the number of clock periods for the move instruction. This data includes instruction fetch, operand reads, and operand writes. The number of bus read and write cycles is shown in parenthesis as (r/w).

Table A-2. Move Byte and Word Instruction Execution Times

Source	Destination								
	Dn	An	(An)	(An)+	−(An)	d_{16}(An)	d_8(An,Xn)*	(xxx).W	(xxx).L
Dn	4(1/0)	4(1/0)	8(1/1)	8(1/1)	8(1/1)	12(2/1)	14(2/1)	12(2/1)	16(3/1)
An	4(1/0)	4(1/0)	8(1/1)	8(1/1)	8(1/1)	12(2/1)	14(2/1)	12(2/1)	16(3/1)
(An)	8(2/0)	8(2/0)	12(2/1)	12(2/1)	12(2/1)	16(3/1)	18(3/1)	16(3/1)	20(4/1)
(An)+	8(2/0)	8(2/0)	12(2/1)	12(2/1)	12(2/1)	16(3/1)	18(3/1)	16(3/1)	20(4/1)
−(An)	10(2/0)	10(2/0)	14(2/1)	14(2/1)	14(2/1)	18(3/1)	20(3/1)	18(3/1)	22(4/1)
d_{16}(An)	12(3/0)	12(3/0)	16(3/1)	16(3/1)	16(3/1)	20(4/1)	22(4/1)	20(4/1)	24(5/1)
d_8(An,Xn)*	14(3/0)	14(3/0)	18(3/1)	18(3/1)	18(3/1)	22(4/1)	24(4/1)	22(4/1)	26(5/1)
(xxx).W	12(3/0)	12(3/0)	16(3/1)	16(3/1)	16(3/1)	20(4/1)	22(4/1)	20(4/1)	24(5/1)
(xxx).L	16(4/0)	16(4/0)	20(4/1)	20(4/1)	20(4/1)	24(5/1)	26(5/1)	24(5/1)	28(6/1)
d_{16}(PC)	12(3/0)	12(3/0)	16(3/1)	16(3/1)	16(3/1)	20(4/1)	22(4/1)	20(4/1)	24(5/1)
d_8(PC, Xn)*	14(3/0)	14(3/0)	18(3/1)	18(3/1)	18(3/1)	22(4/1)	24(4/1)	22(4/1)	26(5/1)
#<data>	8(2/0)	8(2/0)	12(2/1)	12(2/1)	12(2/1)	16(3/1)	18(3/1)	16(3/1)	20(4/1)

*The size of the index register (Xn) does not affect execution time.

Table A-3. Move Long Instruction Execution Times

Source	Destination								
	Dn	An	(An)	(An)+	−(An)	d_{16}(An)	d_8(An,Xn)*	(xxx).W	(xxx).L
Dn	4(1/0)	4(1/0)	12(1/2)	12(1/2)	12(1/2)	16(2/2)	18(2/2)	16(2/2)	20(3/2)
An	4(1/0)	4(1/0)	12(1/2)	12(1/2)	12(1/2)	16(2/2)	18(2/2)	16(2/2)	20(3/2)
(An)	12(3/0)	12(3/0)	20(3/2)	20(3/2)	20(3/2)	24(4/2)	26(4/2)	24(4/2)	28(5/2)
(An)+	12(3/0)	12(3/0)	20(3/2)	20(3/2)	20(3/2)	24(4/2)	26(4/2)	24(4/2)	28(5/2)
−(An)	14(3/0)	14(3/0)	22(3/2)	22(3/2)	22(3/2)	26(4/2)	28(4/2)	26(4/2)	30(5/2)
d_{16}(An)	16(4/0)	16(4/0)	24(4/2)	24(4/2)	24(4/2)	28(5/2)	30(5/2)	28(5/2)	32(6/2)
d_8(An,Xn)*	18(4/0)	18(4/0)	26(4/2)	26(4/2)	26(4/2)	30(5/2)	32(5/2)	30(5/2)	34(6/2)
(xxx).W	16(4/0)	16(4/0)	24(4/2)	24(4/2)	24(4/2)	28(5/2)	30(5/2)	28(5/2)	32(6/2)
(xxx).L	20(5/0)	20(5/0)	28(5/2)	28(5/2)	28(5/2)	32(6/2)	34(6/2)	32(6/2)	36(7/2)
d(PC)	16(4/0)	16(4/0)	24(4/2)	24(4/2)	24(4/2)	28(5/2)	30(5/2)	28(5/2)	32(5/2)
d(PC,Xn)*	18(4/0)	18(4/0)	26(4/2)	26(4/2)	26(4/2)	30(5/2)	32(5/2)	30(5/2)	34(6/2)
#<data>	12(3/0)	12(3/0)	20(3/2)	20(3/2)	20(3/2)	24(4/2)	26(4/2)	24(4/2)	28(5/2)

*The size of the index register (Xn) does not affect execution time.

A.4 STANDARD INSTRUCTION EXECUTION TIMES

The number of clock periods shown in Table A-4 indicates the time required to perform the operations, store the results, and read the next instruction. The number of bus read and write cycles is shown in parenthesis as (r/w). The number of clock periods and the number of read and write cycles must be added respectively to those of the effective address calculation where indicated.

In Table A-4 the headings have the following meanings: An = address register operand, DN = data register operand, ea = an operand specified by an effective address, and M = memory effective address operand.

Table A-4. Standard Instruction Execution Times

Instruction	Size	op<ea>, Ant	op<ea>, Dn	op Dn, <M>
ADD/ADDA	Byte, Word	8(1/0) +	4(1/0) +	8(1/1) +
	Long	6(1/0) + **	6(1/0) + **	12(1/2) +
AND	Byte, Word	—	4(1/0) +	8(1/1) +
	Long	—	6(1/0) + **	12(1/2) +
CMP/CMPA	Byte, Word	6(1/0) +	4(1/0) +	—
	Long	6(1/0) +	6(1/0) +	—
DIVS	—	—	158(1/0) + *	—
DIVU	—	—	140(1/0) + *	—
EOR	Byte, Word	—	4(1/0) ***	8(1/1) +
	Long	—	8(1/0) ***	12(1/2) +
MULS	—	—	70(1/0) + *	—
MULU	—	—	70(1/0) + *	—
OR	Byte, Word	—	4(1/0) +	8(1/1) +
	Long	—	6(1/0) + **	12(1/2) +
SUB	Byte, Word	8(1/0) +	4(1/0) +	8(1/1) +
	Long	6(1/0) + **	6(1/0) + **	12(1/2) +

NOTES:

+ add effective address calculation time

† word or long only

* indicates maximum basic value added to word effective address time.

** The base time of six clock periods is increased to eight if the effective address mode is register direct or immediate (effective address time should also be added).

*** Only available effective address mode is data register direct.

DIVS, DIVU — The divide algorithm used by the MC68000 provides less than 10% difference between the best and worst case timings.

MULS, MULU — The multiply algorithm requires $38 + 2n$ clocks where n is defined as:

MULU: n = the number of ones in the <ea>

MULS: n = concatanate the <ea> with a zero as the LSB; n is the resultant number of 10 or 01 patterns in the 17-bit source; i.e., worst case happens when the source is $5555.

A.5 IMMEDIATE INSTRUCTION EXECUTION TIMES

The number of clock periods shown in Table A-5 includes the time to fetch immediate operands, perform the operations, store the results, and read the next operation. The number of bus read and write cycles is shown in parenthesis as (r/w). The number of clock periods and the number of read and write cycles must be added respectively to those of the effective address calculation where indicated.

In Table A-5, the headings have the following meanings: # = immediate operand, Dn = data register operand, An = address register operand, and M = memory operand. SR = status register.

Table A-5. Immediate Instruction Execution Times

Instruction	Size	op #, Dn	op #, An	op #, M
ADDI	Byte, Word	8(2/0)	—	12(2/1) +
	Long	16(3/0)	—	20(3/2) +
ADDQ	Byte, Word	4(1/0)	8(1/0) *	8(1/1) +
	Long	8(1/0)	8(1/0)	12(1/2) +
ANDI	Byte, Word	8(2/0)	—	12(2/1) +
	Long	16(3/0)	—	20(3/1) +
CMPI	Byte, Word	8(2/0)	—	8(2/0) +
	Long	14(3/0)	—	12(3/0) +
EORI	Byte, Word	8(2/0)	—	12(2/1) +
	Long	16(3/0)	—	20(3/2) +
MOVEQ	Long	4(1/0)	—	—
ORI	Byte, Word	8(2/0)	—	12(2/1) +
	Long	16(3/0)	—	20(3/2) +
SUBI	Byte, Word	8(2/0)	—	12(2/1) +
	Long	16(3/0)	—	20(3/2) +
SUBQ	Byte, Word	4(1/0)	8(1/0) *	8(1/1) +
	Long	8(1/0)	8(1/0)	12(1/2) +

+ add effective address calculation time
* word only

A.6 SINGLE OPERAND INSTRUCTION EXECUTION TIMES

Table A-6 indicates the number of clock periods for the single operand instructions. The number of bus read and write cycles is shown in parenthesis as (r/w). The number of clock periods and the number of read and write cycles must be added respectively to those of the effective address calculation where indicated.

Table A-6. Single Operand Instruction Execution Times

Instruction	Size	Register	Memory
CLR	Byte, Word	4(1/0)	8(1/1) +
	Long	6(1/0)	12(1/2) +
NBCD	Byte	6(1/0)	8(1/1) +
NEG	Byte, Word	4(1/0)	8(1/1) +
	Long	6(1/0)	12(1/2) +
NEGX	Byte, Word	4(1/0)	8(1/1) +
	Long	6(1/0)	12(1/2) +
NOT	Byte, Word	4(1/0)	8(1/1) +
	Long	6(1/0)	12(1/2) +
Scc	Byte, False	4(1/0)	8(1/1) +
	Byte, True	6(1/0)	8(1/1) +
TAS	Byte	4(1/0)	10(1/1) +
TST	Byte, Word	4(1/0)	4(1/0) +
	Long	4(1/0)	4(1/0) +

+ add effective address calculation time

A.7 SHIFT/ROTATE INSTRUCTION EXECUTION TIMES

Table A-7 indicates the number of clock periods for the shift and rotate instructions. The number of bus read and write cycles is shown in parenthesis as (r/w). The number of clock periods and the number of read and write cycles must be added respectively to those of the effective address calculation where indicated.

Table A-7. Shift/Rotate Instruction Execution Times

Instruction	Size	Register	Memory
ASR, ASL	Byte, Word	6 + 2n(1/0)	8(1/1) +
	Long	8 + 2n(1/0)	—
LSR, LSL	Byte, Word	6 + 2n(1/0)	8(1/1) +
	Long	8 + 2n(1/0)	—
ROR, ROL	Byte, Word	6 + 2n(1/0)	8(1/1) +
	Long	8 + 2n(1/0)	—
ROXR, ROXL	Byte, Word	6 + 2n(1/0)	8(1/1) +
	Long	8 + 2n(1/0)	—

+ add effective address calculation time for word operands
n is the shift count

A.8 BIT MANIPULATION INSTRUCTION EXECUTION TIMES

Table A-8 indicates the number of clock periods required for the bit manipulation instructions. The number of bus read and write cycles is shown in parenthesis as (r/w). The number of clock periods and the number of read and write cycles must be added respectively to those of the effective address calculation where indicated.

Table A-8. Bit Manipulation Instruction Execution Times

Instruction	Size	Dynamic		Static	
		Register	Memory	Register	Memory
BCHG	Byte	—	8(1/1) +	—	12(2/1) +
	Long	8(1/0) *	—	12(2/0) *	—
BCLR	Byte	—	8(1/1) +	—	12(2/1) +
	Long	10(1/0) *	—	14(2/0) *	—
BSET	Byte	—	8(1/1) +	—	12(2/1) +
	Long	8(1/0) *	—	12(2/0) *	—
BTST	Byte	—	4(1/0) +	—	8(2/0) +
	Long	6(1/0)	—	10(2/0)	—

+ add effective address calculation time
* indicates maximum value; data addressing mode only

A.9 CONDITIONAL INSTRUCTION EXECUTION TIMES

Table A-9 indicates the number of clock periods required for the conditional instructions. The number of bus read and write cycles is indicated in parenthesis as (r/w). The number of clock periods and the number of read and write cycles must be added respectively to those of the effective address calculation where indicated.

Table A-9. Conditional Instruction Execution Times

Instruction	Displacement	Branch Taken	Branch Not Taken
Bcc	Byte	10(2/0)	8(1/0)
	Word	10(2/0)	12(2/0)
BRA	Byte	10(2/0)	—
	Word	10(2/0)	—
BSR	Byte	18(2/2)	—
	Word	18(2/2)	—
DBcc	cc true	—	12(2/0)
	cc false, Count Not Expired	10(2/0)	—
	cc false, Counter Expired	—	14(3/0)

+ add effective address calculation time

*indicates maximum base value

A.10 JMP, JSR, LEA, PEA, AND MOVEM INSTRUCTION EXECUTION TIMES

Table A-10 indicates the number of clock periods required for the jump, jump-to-subroutine, load effective address, push effective address, and move multiple registers instructions. The number of bus read and write cycles is shown in parenthesis as (r/w).

Table A-10. JMP, JSR, LEA, PEA, and MOVEM Instruction Execution Times

Instruction	Size	(An)	(An) +	– (An)	d_{16}(An)	d_8(An,Xn)+	(xxx).W	(xxx).L	d_{16}(PC)	d_8(PC,Xn)*
JMP	—	8(2/0)	—	—	10(2/0)	14(3/0)	10(2/0)	12(3/0)	10(2/0)	14(3/0)
JSR	—	16(2/2)	—	—	18(2/2)	22(2/2)	18(2/2)	20(3/2)	18(2/2)	22(2/2)
LEA	—	4(1/0)	—	—	8(2/0)	12(2/0)	8(2/0)	12(3/0)	8(2/0)	12(2/0)
PEA	—	12(1/2)	—	—	16(2/2)	20(2/2)	16(2/2)	20(3/2)	16(2/2)	20(2/2)
MOVEM M → R	Word	12+4n (3+n/0)	12+4n (3+n/0)	—	16+4n (4+n/0)	18+4n (4+n/0)	16+4n (4+n/0)	20+4n (5+n/0)	16+4n (4+n/0)	18+4n (4+n/0)
	Long	12+8n (3+2n/0)	12+8n (3+2n/0)	—	16+8n (4+2n/0)	18+8n (4+2n/0)	16+8n (4+2n/0)	20+8n (5+2n/0)	16+8n (4+2n/0)	18+8n (4+2n/0)
MOVEM R → M	Word	8+4n (2/n)	—	8+4n (2/n)	12+4n (3/n)	14+4n (3/n)	12+4n (3/n)	16+4n (4/n)	—	—
	Long	8+8n (2/2n)	—	8+8n (2/2n)	12+8n (3/2n)	14+8n (3/2n)	12+8n (3/2n)	16+8n (4/2n)	—	—

n is the number of registers to move

* is the size of the index register (Xn), does not affect the instruction's execution time

A.11 MULTIPRECISION INSTRUCTION EXECUTION TIMES

Table A-11 indicates the number of clock periods for the multiprecision instructions. The number of clock periods includes the time to fetch both operands, perform the operations, store the results, and read the next instructions. The number of read and write cycles is shown in parenthesis as (r/w).

In Table A-11, the headings have the following meanings: Dn = data register operand and M = memory operand.

Table A-11. Multiprecision Instruction Execution Times

Instruction	Size	op Dn, Dn	op M, M
ADDX	Byte, Word	4(1/0)	18(3/1)
	Long	8(1/0)	30(5/2)
CMPM	Byte, Word	—	12(3/0)
	Long	—	20(5/0)
SUBX	Byte, Word	4(1/0)	18(3/1)
	Long	8(1/0)	30(5/2)
ABCD	Byte	6(1/0)	18(3/1)
SBCD	Byte	6(1/0)	18(3/1)

A.12 MISCELLANEOUS INSTRUCTION EXECUTION TIMES

Tables A-12 and A-13 indicate the number of clock periods for the following miscellaneous instructions. The number of bus read and write cycles is shown in parenthesis as (r/w). The number of clock periods plus the number of read and write cycles must be added to those of the effective address calculation where indicated.

Table A-12. Miscellaneous Instruction Execution Times

Instruction	Size	Register	Memory
ANDI to CCR	Byte	20(3/0)	—
ANDI to SR	Word	20(3/0)	—
CHK (No Trap)	—	10(1/0) +	—
EORI to CCR	Byte	20(3/0)	—
EORI to SR	Word	20(3/0)	—
ORI to CCR	Byte	20(3/0)	—
ORI to SR	Word	20(3/0)	—
MOVE from SR	—	6(1/0)	8(1/1) +
MOVE to CCR	—	12(1/0)	12(1/0) +
MOVE to SR	—	12(1/0)	12(1/0) +
EXG	—	6(1/0)	—
EXT	Word	4(1/0)	—
EXT	Long	4(1/0)	—
LINK	—	16(2/2)	—
MOVE from USP	—	4(1/0)	—
MOVE to USP	—	4(1/0)	—
NOP	—	4(1/0)	—
RESET	—	132(1/0)	—
RTE	—	20(5/0)	—
RTR	—	20(5/0)	—
RTS	—	16(4/0)	—
STOP	—	4(0/0)	—
SWAP	—	4(1/0)	—
TRAPV	—	4(1/0)	—
UNLK	—	12(3/0)	—

+ add effective address calculation time

Table A-13. Move Peripheral Instruction Execution Times

Instruction	Size	Register → Memory	Memory → Register
MOVEP	Word	16(2/2)	16(4/0)
MOVEP	Long	24(2/4)	24(6/0)

A.13 EXCEPTION PROCESSING EXECUTION TIMES

Table A-14 indicates the number of clock periods for exception processing. The number of clock periods includes the time for all stacking, the vector fetch, and the fetch of the first two instruction words of the handler routine. The number of bus read and write cycles is shown in parenthesis as (r/w).

Table A-14. Exception Processing Execution Times

Exception	Periods
Address Error	50(4/7)
Bus Error	50(4/7)
CHK Instruction	40(4/3) +
Divide by Zero	38(4/3) +
Illegal Instruction	34(4/3)
Interrupt	44(5/3) *
Privilege Violation	34(4/3)
RESET**	40(6/0)
Trace	34(4/3)
TRAP Instruction	34(4/3)
TRAPV Instruction	34(5/3)

+ add effective address calculation time

* The interrupt acknowledge cycle is assumed to take four clock periods.

** Indicates the time from when RESET and HALT are first sampled as negated to when instruction execution starts.

APPENDIX B

This appendix provides a summary of the primary words in each instruction of the instruction set. The complete instruction definition consists of the primary words followed by the addressing mode operands such as immediate data fields, displacements, and index operands. Table B-1 is an operation code (opcode) map that illustrates how bits 15 through 12 are used to specify the operations.

Table B-1. Operation Code Map

Bits 15 through 12	Operation
0000	Bit Manipulation/MOVEP/Immediate
0001	Move Byte
0010	Move Long
0011	Move Word
0100	Miscellaneous
0101	ADDQ/SUBQ/Scc/DBcc
0110	Bcc/BSR
0111	MOVEQ
1000	OR/DIV/SBCD
1001	SUB/SUBX
1010	(Unassigned, Reserved)
1011	CMP/EOR
1100	AND/MUL/ABCD/EXG
1101	ADD/ADDX
1110	Shift/Rotate
1111	Coprocessor Interface (MC68020)

Table B-2. Effective Addressing Mode Categories

Address Modes	Mode	Register	Data	Memory	Control	Alterable	Assembler Syntax
Data Register Direct	000	reg. no.	X	—	—	X	Dn
Address Register Direct	001	reg. no.	—	—	—	X	An
Address Register Indirect	010	reg. no.	X	X	X	X	(An)
Address Register Indirect with Postincrement	011	reg. no.	X	X	—	X	(An) +
Address Register Indirect with Predecrement	100	reg. no.	X	X	—	X	– (An)
Address Register Indirect with Displacement	101	reg. no	X	X	X	X	(d_{16},An) or $d_{16}(An)$
Address Register Indirect with Index	110	reg. no.	X	X	X	X	(d_8,An,Xn) or $d_8(An,Xn)$
Absolute Short	111	000	X	X	X	X	(xxx).W
Absolute Long	111	001	X	X	X	X	(xxx).L
Program Counter Indirect with Displacement	111	101	X	X	X	—	(d_{16},PC) or $d_{16}(PC)$
Program Counter Indirect with Index	111	011	X	X	X	—	(d_8,PC,Xn) or $d_8(PC,Xn)$
Immediate	111	100	X	X	—	—	# <data>

Table B-3. Conditional Tests

Mnemonic	Condition	Encoding	Test
T*	True	0000	1
F*	False	0001	0
HI	High	0010	$\overline{C} \cdot \overline{Z}$
LS	Low or Same	0011	$C + Z$
CC(HS)	Carry Clear	0100	$\overline{C}$
CS(LO)	Carry Set	0101	C
NE	Not Equal	0110	$\overline{Z}$
EQ	Equal	0111	Z
VC	Overflow Clear	1000	$\overline{V}$
VS	Overflow Set	1001	V
PL	Plus	1010	$\overline{N}$
MI	Minus	1011	N
GE	Greater or Equal	1100	$N \cdot V + \overline{N} \cdot \overline{V}$
LT	Less Than	1101	$N \cdot \overline{V} + \overline{N} \cdot V$
GT	Greater Than	1110	$N \cdot V \cdot \overline{Z} + \overline{N} \cdot \overline{V} \cdot \overline{Z}$
LE	Less or Equal	1111	$Z + N \cdot \overline{V} + \overline{N} \cdot V$

• = Boolean AND
+ = Boolean OR
$\overline{N}$ = Boolean NOT N

*Not available for the Bcc instruction

STANDARD INSTRUCTIONS

OR Immediate

15	14	13	12	11	10	9	8	7	6	5	4	3	2	1	0
										Effective Address					
0	0	0	0	0	0	0	0	Size		Mode			Register		

Size field: 00 = byte   01 = word   10 = long

OR Immediate to CCR

15	14	13	12	11	10	9	8	7	6	5	4	3	2	1	0
0	0	0	0	0	0	0	0	0	0	1	1	1	1	0	0
0	0	0	0	0	0	0	0	Byte Data							

OR Immediate to SR

15	14	13	12	11	10	9	8	7	6	5	4	3	2	1	0
0	0	0	0	0	0	0	0	0	1	1	1	1	1	0	0
Word Data															

Dynamic Bit

15	14	13	12	11	10	9	8	7	6	5	4	3	2	1	0
				Data						Effective Address					
0	0	0	0	Register			1	Type		Mode			Register		

Type field: 00 = TST   10 = CLR
             01 = CHG 11 = SET

MOVEP

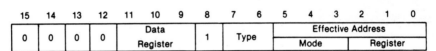

15	14	13	12	11	10	9	8	7	6	5	4	3	2	1	0
				Data									Address		
0	0	0	0	Register			Op-Mode			0	0	1	Register		

Op-Mode field: 100 = transfer word from memory to register
                101 = transfer long from memory to register
                110 = transfer word from register to memory
                111 = transfer long from register to memory

AND Immediate

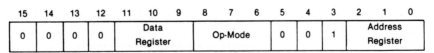

15	14	13	12	11	10	9	8	7	6	5	4	3	2	1	0
										Effective Address					
0	0	0	0	0	0	1	0	Size		Mode			Register		

Size field: 00 = byte   01 = word   10 = long

AND Immediate to CCR

15	14	13	12	11	10	9	8	7	6	5	4	3	2	1	0
0	0	0	0	0	0	1	0	0	0	1	1	1	1	0	0
0	0	0	0	0	0	0	0	Byte Data							

AND Immediate to SR

15	14	13	12	11	10	9	8	7	6	5	4	3	2	1	0
0	0	0	0	0	0	1	0	0	1	1	1	1	1	0	0
Word Data															

SUB Immediate

15	14	13	12	11	10	9	8	7	6	5	4	3	2	1	0
0	0	0	0	0	1	0	0	Size		Effective Address					
										Mode			Register		

Size field: 00 = byte 01 = word 10 = long

ADD Immediate

15	14	13	12	11	10	9	8	7	6	5	4	3	2	1	0
0	0	0	0	0	1	1	0	Size		Effective Address					
										Mode			Register		

Size field: 00 = byte 01 = word 10 = long

Static Bit

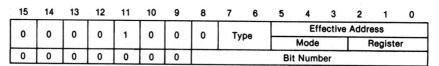

15	14	13	12	11	10	9	8	7	6	5	4	3	2	1	0
0	0	0	0	1	0	0	0	Type		Effective Address					
										Mode			Register		
0	0	0	0	0	0	0	Bit Number								

Type field: 00 = TST   10 = CLR
             01 = CHG 11 = SET

EOR Immediate

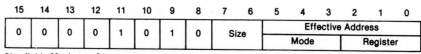

15	14	13	12	11	10	9	8	7	6	5	4	3	2	1	0
0	0	0	0	1	0	1	0	Size		Effective Address					
										Mode			Register		

Size field: 00 = byte 01 = word 10 = long

EOR Immediate to CCR

15	14	13	12	11	10	9	8	7	6	5	4	3	2	1	0
0	0	0	0	1	0	1	0	0	0	1	1	1	1	0	0
0	0	0	0	0	0	0	0	Byte Data							

EOR Immediate to SR

15	14	13	12	11	10	9	8	7	6	5	4	3	2	1	0
0	0	0	0	1	0	1	0	0	1	1	1	1	1	0	0
Word Data															

CMP Immediate

15	14	13	12	11	10	9	8	7	6	5	4	3	2	1	0
										Effective Address					
0	0	0	0	1	1	0	0	Size		Mode			Register		

Size field: 00 = byte 01 = word 10 = long

MOVES (MC68010/MC68012)

15	14	13	12	11	10	9	8	7	6	5	4	3	2	1	0
										Effective Address					
0	0	0	0	1	1	1	0	Size		Mode			Register		
A/D	Register			dr	0	0	0	0	0	0	0	0	0	0	0

dr field: 0 = EA to register
1 = register to EA

MOVE Byte

15	14	13	12	11	10	9	8	7	6	5	4	3	2	1	0
				Destination						Source					
0	0	0	1	Register			Mode			Mode			Register		

Note register and mode locations

MOVEA Long

15	14	13	12	11	10	9	8	7	6	5	4	3	2	1	0
				Destination						Source					
0	0	1	0	Register			0	0	1	Mode			Register		

MOVE Long

15	14	13	12	11	10	9	8	7	6	5	4	3	2	1	0
0	0	1	0	Destination						Source					
				Register			Mode			Mode			Register		

Note register and mode locations

MOVEA Word

15	14	13	12	11	10	9	8	7	6	5	4	3	2	1	0
0	0	1	1	Destination			0	0	1	Source					
				Register						Mode			Register		

MOVE Word

15	14	13	12	11	10	9	8	7	6	5	4	3	2	1	0
0	0	1	1	Destination						Source					
				Register			Mode			Mode			Register		

Note register and mode locations

NEGX

15	14	13	12	11	10	9	8	7	6	5	4	3	2	1	0
0	1	0	0	0	0	0	0	Size		Effective Address					
										Mode			Register		

Size field: 00 = byte 01 = word 10 = long

MOVE from SR

15	14	13	12	11	10	9	8	7	6	5	4	3	2	1	0
0	1	0	0	0	0	0	0	1	1	Effective Address					
										Mode			Register		

CHK

15	14	13	12	11	10	9	8	7	6	5	4	3	2	1	0
0	1	0	0	Data			Size		0	Effective Address					
				Register						Mode			Register		

Size field: 10 = Longword (MC68020)
11 = Word

LEA

15	14	13	12	11	10	9	8	7	6	5	4	3	2	1	0
										Effective Address					
0	1	0	0	Address Register			1	1	1	Mode			Register		

CLR

15	14	13	12	11	10	9	8	7	6	5	4	3	2	1	0
										Effective Address					
0	1	0	0	0	0	1	0	Size		Mode			Register		

Size field: 00 = byte   01 = word   10 = long

MOVE from CCR (MC68010/MC68012)

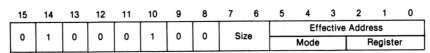

15	14	13	12	11	10	9	8	7	6	5	4	3	2	1	0
										Effective Address					
0	1	0	0	0	0	1	0	1	1	Mode			Register		

NEG

15	14	13	12	11	10	9	8	7	6	5	4	3	2	1	0
										Effective Address					
0	1	0	0	0	1	0	0	Size		Mode			Register		

Size field: 00 = byte   01 = word   10 = long

MOVE to CCR

15	14	13	12	11	10	9	8	7	6	5	4	3	2	1	0
										Effective Address					
0	1	0	0	0	1	0	0	1	1	Mode			Register		

NOT

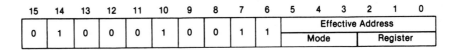

15	14	13	12	11	10	9	8	7	6	5	4	3	2	1	0
										Effective Address					
0	1	0	0	0	1	1	0	Size		Mode			Register		

Size field: 00 = byte   01 = word   10 = long

MOVE to SR

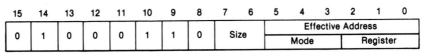

15	14	13	12	11	10	9	8	7	6	5	4	3	2	1	0
										Effective Address					
0	1	0	0	0	1	1	0	1	1	Mode			Register		

NBCD

15	14	13	12	11	10	9	8	7	6	5	4	3	2	1	0
0	1	0	0	1	0	0	0	0	0	\multicolumn{6}{c}{Effective Address}

| | | | | | | | | | | Mode | | | Register | | |

SWAP

15	14	13	12	11	10	9	8	7	6	5	4	3	2	1	0
0	1	0	0	1	0	0	0	0	1	0	0	0	Data Register		

BKPT (MC68010/MC68012)

15	14	13	12	11	10	9	8	7	6	5	4	3	2	1	0
0	1	0	0	1	0	0	0	0	1	0	0	1	BKPT #		

PEA

15	14	13	12	11	10	9	8	7	6	5	4	3	2	1	0
0	1	0	0	1	0	0	0	0	1	\multicolumn{6}{c}{Effective Address}

| | | | | | | | | | | Mode | | | Register | | |

EXT Word

15	14	13	12	11	10	9	8	7	6	5	4	3	2	1	0
0	1	0	0	1	0	0	Type			0	0	0	Data Register		

Type Field: 010 = Extend Word   011 = Extend Long

MOVEM Registers to EA

15	14	13	12	11	10	9	8	7	6	5	4	3	2	1	0
0	1	0	0	1	0	0	0	1	Sz	\multicolumn{6}{c}{Effective Address}

| | | | | | | | | | | Mode | | | Register | | |

Sz field: 0 = word transfer   1 = long transfer

TST

15	14	13	12	11	10	9	8	7	6	5	4	3	2	1	0
										Effective Address					
0	1	0	0	1	0	1	0	Size		Mode			Register		

Size field: 00 = byte   01 = word   10 = long

TAS

15	14	13	12	11	10	9	8	7	6	5	4	3	2	1	0
										Effective Address					
0	1	0	0	1	0	1	0	1	1	Mode			Register		

ILLEGAL

15	14	13	12	11	10	9	8	7	6	5	4	3	2	1	0
0	1	0	0	1	0	1	0	1	1	1	1	1	1	0	0

MOVEM EA to Registers

15	14	13	12	11	10	9	8	7	6	5	4	3	2	1	0
										Effective Address					
0	1	0	0	1	1	0	0	1	Sz	Mode			Register		

Sz field: 0 = word transfer   1 = long transfer

TRAP

15	14	13	12	11	10	9	8	7	6	5	4	3	2	1	0
0	1	0	0	1	1	1	0	0	1	0	0	Vector			

LINK Word

15	14	13	12	11	10	9	8	7	6	5	4	3	2	1	0
0	1	0	0	1	1	1	0	0	1	0	1	0	Address Register		

UNLK

15	14	13	12	11	10	9	8	7	6	5	4	3	2	1	0
0	1	0	0	1	1	1	0	0	1	0	1	1	Address Register		

MOVE to USP

15	14	13	12	11	10	9	8	7	6	5	4	3	2	1	0
0	1	0	0	1	1	1	0	0	1	1	0	0	Address Register		

MOVE from USP

15	14	13	12	11	10	9	8	7	6	5	4	3	2	1	0
0	1	0	0	1	1	1	0	0	1	1	0	1	Address Register		

RESET

15	14	13	12	11	10	9	8	7	6	5	4	3	2	1	0
0	1	0	0	1	1	1	0	0	1	1	1	0	0	0	0

NOP

15	14	13	12	11	10	9	8	7	6	5	4	3	2	1	0
0	1	0	0	1	1	1	0	0	1	1	1	0	0	0	1

STOP

15	14	13	12	11	10	9	8	7	6	5	4	3	2	1	0
0	1	0	0	1	1	1	0	0	1	1	1	0	0	1	0

RTE

15	14	13	12	11	10	9	8	7	6	5	4	3	2	1	0
0	1	0	0	1	1	1	0	0	1	1	1	0	0	1	1

RTD (MC68010/MC68012)

15	14	13	12	11	10	9	8	7	6	5	4	3	2	1	0
0	1	0	0	1	1	1	0	0	1	1	1	0	1	0	0

RTS

15	14	13	12	11	10	9	8	7	6	5	4	3	2	1	0
0	1	0	0	1	1	1	0	0	1	1	1	0	1	0	1

TRAPV

15	14	13	12	11	10	9	8	7	6	5	4	3	2	1	0
0	1	0	0	1	1	1	0	0	1	1	1	0	1	1	0

RTR

15	14	13	12	11	10	9	8	7	6	5	4	3	2	1	0
0	1	0	0	1	1	1	0	0	1	1	1	0	1	1	1

MOVEC (MC68010/MC68012)

15	14	13	12	11	10	9	8	7	6	5	4	3	2	1	0
0	1	0	0	1	1	1	0	0	1	1	1	1	0	1	dr
A/D	Register			Control Register											

dr field: 0 = control register to general register
          1 = general register to control register

Control Register field: $000 = SFC $801 = VBR
                           $001 = DFC $802 = CAAR (MC68020)
                           $002 = CACR (MC68020) $803 = MSP (MC68020)
                           $800 = USP $804 = ISP (MC68020)

JSR

15	14	13	12	11	10	9	8	7	6	5	4	3	2	1	0
0	1	0	0	1	1	1	0	1	0	Effective Address					
										Mode			Register		

JMP

15	14	13	12	11	10	9	8	7	6	5	4	3	2	1	0
0	1	0	0	1	1	1	0	1	1	Effective Address					
										Mode			Register		

ADDQ

15	14	13	12	11	10	9	8	7	6	5	4	3	2	1	0
0	1	0	1	Data			0	Size		Effective Address					
										Mode			Register		

Data field: Three bits of immediate data, 0, 1-7 representing a range of 8,
                     1 to 7 respectively.
Size field: 00 = byte   01 = word   10 = long

Scc

15	14	13	12	11	10	9	8	7	6	5	4	3	2	1	0
0	1	0	1	Condition				1	1	Effective Address					
										Mode			Register		

DBcc

15	14	13	12	11	10	9	8	7	6	5	4	3	2	1	0
0	1	0	1	Condition				1	1	0	0	1	Data Register		

SUBQ

15	14	13	12	11	10	9	8	7	6	5	4	3	2	1	0
0	1	0	1	Data			1	Size		Effective Address					
										Mode			Register		

Data field: Three bits of immediate data, 0, 1-7 representing a range of 8, 1 to 7 respectively.
Size field: 00 = byte   01 = word   10 = long

Bcc

15	14	13	12	11	10	9	8	7	6	5	4	3	2	1	0
0	1	1	0	Condition				8-Bit Displacement							
16-Bit Displacement if 8-Bit Displacement = $00															

BRA

15	14	13	12	11	10	9	8	7	6	5	4	3	2	1	0
0	1	1	0	0	0	0	0	8-Bit Displacement							
16-Bit Displacement if 8-Bit Displacement = $00															

BSR

15	14	13	12	11	10	9	8	7	6	5	4	3	2	1	0
0	1	1	0	0	0	0	1	8-Bit Displacement							
16-Bit Displacement if 8-Bit Displacement = $00															

MOVEQ

15	14	13	12	11	10	9	8	7	6	5	4	3	2	1	0
0	1	1	1	Data Register			0	Data							

Data field: Data is sign extended to a long operand and all 32 bits are transferred to the data register.

OR

15	14	13	12	11	10	9	8	7	6	5	4	3	2	1	0
				Data Register			Op-Mode			Effective Address					
1	0	0	0	Data Register			Op-Mode			Mode			Register		

Op-Mode field:

Byte	Word	Long	Operation
000	001	010	$(<ea>) \lor (<Dn>) \rightarrow <Dn>$
100	101	110	$(<Dn>) \lor (<ea>) \rightarrow <ea>$

DIVU/DIVS Word

15	14	13	12	11	10	9	8	7	6	5	4	3	2	1	0
				Data Register						Effective Address					
1	0	0	0	Data Register			Type	1	1	Mode			Register		

Type field: 0 = DIVU 1 = DIVS

SBCD

15	14	13	12	11	10	9	8	7	6	5	4	3	2	1	0
1	0	0	0	Destination Register*			1	0	0	0	0	R/M	Source Register*		

R/M field: 0 = data register to data register
1 = memory to memory
* If R/M = 0, specifies a data register
If R/M = 1, specifies an address register for the predecrement addressing mode.

SUB

15	14	13	12	11	10	9	8	7	6	5	4	3	2	1	0
				Data Register						Effective Address					
1	0	0	1	Data Register			Op-Mode			Mode			Register		

Op-Mode field:

Byte	Word	Long	Operation
000	001	010	$(<Dn>) - (<ea>) \rightarrow <Dn>$
100	101	110	$(<ea>) - (<Dn>) \rightarrow <ea>$

SUBA

15	14	13	12	11	10	9	8	7	6	5	4	3	2	1	0
				Data Register						Effective Address					
1	0	0	1	Data Register			Op-Mode			Mode			Register		

Op-Mode field:

	Word	Long	Operation
	011	111	$(<An>) - (<ea>) \rightarrow <An>$

SUBX

15	14	13	12	11	10	9	8	7	6	5	4	3	2	1	0
1	0	0	1	Destination Register*			1	Size		0	0	R/M	Source Register*		

Size field: 00 = byte 01 = word 10 = long
R/M field: 0 = data register to data register 1 = memory to memory
* If R/M = 0, specifies a data register
If R/M = 1, specifies an address register for the predecrement addressing mode.

CMP

15	14	13	12	11	10	9	8	7	6	5	4	3	2	1	0
1	0	1	1	Data Register			Op-Mode			Effective Address					
										Mode			Register		

Op-Mode field:

Byte	Word	Long	Operation
000	001	010	(\<Dn\>) − (\<ea\>)

CMPA

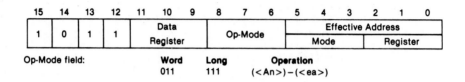

15	14	13	12	11	10	9	8	7	6	5	4	3	2	1	0
1	0	1	1	Data Register			Op-Mode			Effective Address					
										Mode			Register		

Op-Mode field:

	Word	Long	Operation
	011	111	(\<An\>) − (\<ea\>)

EOR

15	14	13	12	11	10	9	8	7	6	5	4	3	2	1	0
1	0	1	1	Data Register			Op-Mode			Effective Address					
										Mode			Register		

Op-Mode field:

Byte	Word	Long	Operation
100	101	110	(\<ea\>) ⊕ (\<Dn\>) → \<ea\>

CMPM

15	14	13	12	11	10	9	8	7	6	5	4	3	2	1	0
1	0	1	1	Destination Register			1	Size		0	0	1	Source Register		

Size field: 00 = byte 01 = word 10 = long

AND

15	14	13	12	11	10	9	8	7	6	5	4	3	2	1	0
1	1	0	0	Data Register			Op-Mode			Effective Address					
										Mode			Register		

Op-Mode field:

Byte	Word	Long	Operation
000	001	010	(\<ea\>)Λ(\<Dn\>) → \<Dn\>
100	101	110	(\<Dn\>)Λ(\<ea\>) → \<ea\>

MULU Word
MULS Word

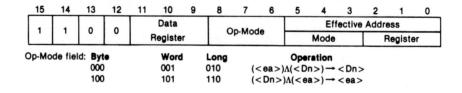

15	14	13	12	11	10	9	8	7	6	5	4	3	2	1	0
1	1	0	0	Data Register			Type	1	1	Effective Address					
										Mode			Register		

Type field: 0 = MULU 1 = MULS

ABCD

15	14	13	12	11	10	9	8	7	6	5	4	3	2	1	0
1	1	0	0	Destination Register*			1	0	0	0	0	R/M	Source Register*		

R/M field: 0 = data register to data register   1 = memory to memory
*If R/M = 0, specifies a data register
If R/M = 1, specifies an address register for the predecrement addressing mode.

EXG Data Registers

15	14	13	12	11	10	9	8	7	6	5	4	3	2	1	0
1	1	0	0	Data Register			1	0	1	0	0	0	Data Register		

EXG Address Registers

15	14	13	12	11	10	9	8	7	6	5	4	3	2	1	0
1	1	0	0	Address Register			1	0	1	0	0	1	Address Register		

EXG Data Register and Address Register

15	14	13	12	11	10	9	8	7	6	5	4	3	2	1	0
1	1	0	0	Data Register			1	1	0	0	0	1	Address Register		

ADD

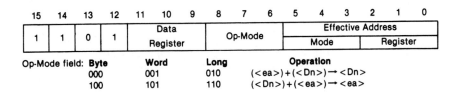

Op-Mode field:

	Byte	Word	Long	Operation
	000	001	010	$(<ea>) + (<Dn>) \rightarrow <Dn>$
	100	101	110	$(<Dn>) + (<ea>) \rightarrow <ea>$

ADDA

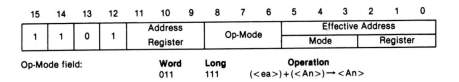

Op-Mode field:

	Word	Long	Operation
	011	111	$(<ea>) + (<An>) \rightarrow <An>$

ADDX

15	14	13	12	11	10	9	8	7	6	5	4	3	2	1	0
1	1	0	1	Destination Register*			1	Size		0	0	R/M	Source Register*		

Size field: 00 = byte 01 = word 10 = long
R/M field: 0 = data register to data register 1 = memory to memory
*If R/M = 0, specifies a data register
 If R/M = 1, specifies an address register for the predecrement addressing mode.

SHIFT/ROTATE — Register

15	14	13	12	11	10	9	8	7	6	5	4	3	2	1	0
1	1	1	0	Count/ Register			dr	Size		i/r	Type		Data Register		

Count/Register field: If i/r field = 0, specifies shift count
                      If i/r field = 1, specifies a data register that con-
                      tains the shift count
dr field: 0 = right 1 = left
Size field: 00 = byte 01 = word 10 = long
i/r field: 0 = immediate shift count 1 = register shift count
Type field: 00 = arithmetic shift 10 = rotate with extend
            01 = logical shift   11 = rotate

SHIFT/ROTATE — Memory

15	14	13	12	11	10	9	8	7	6	5	4	3	2	1	0
1	1	1	0	0	Type		dr	1	1	Effective Address					
										Mode			Register		

Type field: 00 = arithmetic shift 01 = logical shift 10 = rotate with extend 11 = rotate
dr field: 0 = right 1 = left

INDEX

Prototypes for C functions, 409–410

Prototyping, 335–337, 371, 373–376

PSAVE instruction (68851 only), 518

PScc instruction (68851 only), 518

Pseudo-operations. *See* Assembler directives

Pseudocode
CASE structure, 47, 90
comparing strings, 107
data sampling, 119
defined, 46
divide-by-zero program, 203
downloading program, 481
factorials, 132
FOR-DO structure, 102–103
IF-THEN-ELSE structure, 47, 85, 86, 88, 89
IF-THEN structure, 47, 77
moving strings, 105
password checking, 107
REPEAT-UNTIL structure, 47, 96, 97, 99, 105, 107
sequence structure, 47
strobed input, 97
uploading program, 481
WHILE-DO structure, 47, 90, 92

PSK (phase-shift keying) modulation, 473–474

PTEST instruction, 518

PTRAPcc instruction (68851 only), 518

Pulse-code modulation (PCM), 476

Punched cards, 6, 10

Push operations for stacks, 122–124

PVALID instruction (68851 only), 518

Pythagorean theorem, 367, 417–418

QAM (quaternary amplitude modulation), 473, 474

Quadbits, 473

Quaternary amplitude modulation (QAM), 473, 474

Queues, 35–36

R (reset) input, 17

RAM. *See* Random-access memory

Ramp generators (integrators), 294, 297

Random-access memory (RAM)
address decoding for, 180, 182–183
described, 20
display refresh, 427, 428
DRAM. *See* Dynamic random-access memory

Random-access memory (*continued*)
dual-ported, 434
microcomputer use of, 24, 25
OPTICRAM cameras, 439–440
static (SRAM), 20, 348, 355–358
volatile nature of, 20

Random-access memory (RAM) disks, 449–450

Raster-scan graphics, 432–437

Raster scanning, 425–426

RC snubber circuits, 284

Read cycles for 68000 instructions, 527–533

Read-only memory (ROM)
address decoding for, 180–182
character-generator, 427–428
described, 19–20
electrically erasable programmable (EEPROM), 20
erasable programmable (EPROM), 20, 182
mask-programmed, 20
microcomputer use of, 24, 25
nonvolatile nature of, 19
optical (OROM), 451
programmable (PROM), 20

Read-only optical-disk systems, 451

Read/write head for magnetic disks, 441–442

Read/write input, 20

Read/write mechanism for optical disks, 451

Read-write memory. *See* Random-access memory

Read/write optical-disk systems, 451

Real (floating-point) numbers, 62, 361, 362–363

Real-time clocks, 219, 238–240

Recursive subroutines, 132–136

Red-green-blue (RGB) signals, 434, 436–437

Redirected data, 511–512

Reduced instruction set computer (RISC), 521

Reentrant subroutines, 131–133, 504

Refresh controllers, 20, 350

Regions in RMX 86, 514

Register direct addressing mode, 40

Register variables in C, 411–412

Registers
68000 instructions for, 49
accumulators, 27, 35, 36
address (A0–A7, A7′), 35, 36, 115, 117–118, 120–123
bounds, 149

Registers (*continued*)
control, 516
counters using, 99–101
data (D0–D7), 35, 36
data storage, 18
defined, 18
passing parameters in, 124–126
pointers using, 99–101
shift, 18, 439
stack pointer (SP), 35, 36
status, 35, 36–38
supervisor stack pointer (SSP), 35, 36

Relational operators in C, 398–399

Relays, 283–284

Relocatable programs, 65, 79

REPEAT-UNTIL structure, 46–48, 96–109, 403–405

Repetition (iteration) operations for programs, 46–48

Reset (R) input, 17

Reset exception, 202, 208, 212–214

RESET instruction, 51, 157, 533, 544

Reset line, 157

Residual error, 322

Resistor packs, 177, 178

Retriggerable one-shots, 226–228

Return address, 114

Return instructions, 50–51

RGB (red-green-blue) signals, 434, 436–437

Richie, Dennis, 509

Ring networks, 491, 494–496

RISC (reduced instruction set computer), 521

RMX 86 operating system (OS)
objects in, 513–514
overview of, 513
structure of, 513
task execution with, 514–515
task-state diagrams for, 514–515

Robotics, 287–288, 335, 440–441

ROL instruction, 50, 72, 157–158, 531

ROM. *See* Read-only memory

Root directory, 447, 510–511

Root jobs, 513, 514

ROR instruction, 50, 157–158, 531

Rotate instructions, 50, 531, 550

ROXL instruction, 50, 72, 158, 531

ROXR instruction, 50, 158, 531

RS-232C standard, 467–470

RS-422A standard, 470–472

RS-423A standard, 470

RS-449 standard, 472

RTD instruction, 51, 544

URDA MDS (*continued*)
　　initialization list for, 51–52
　　keypad interfacing with,
　　　271–274
　　memory map of, 35, 185
　　monitor program of, 66
　　overview of, 174–178
　　photograph of, 174, 175
　　port address decoding for, 180,
　　　183–186
　　RAM address decoding for, 180,
　　　182–183
　　RAM addresses of, 119, 185
　　ROM address decoding for,
　　　180–182
　　ROM addresses of, 185
　　schematic diagram of, 177, 178
　　start address for RAM on, 119,
　　　185
　　start address for user code, 119
　　troubleshooting, 189–197
　　uploading programs from,
　　　481–486
　　user code start address on, 119
USART (universal
　　synchronous/asynchronous
　　receiver-transmitter), 175,
　　462. *See also* 8251A USART
User bytes (status register), 36–37
User interrupts, 202
User stack, 117
User state, 37, 505
User tables, 510

V (overflow) flag, 37, 77
Variable declarations in C,
　　385–389
Variable types in C, 385–389
Variables
　　automatic, in C, 386, 387,
　　　411–412

Variables (*continued*)
　　char (character) in C, 385–387
　　dummy, 141
　　extern (external), in C, 386,
　　　387, 411–412
　　float (floating-point), in C,
　　　388–389
　　global, in C, 386, 387, 411–412
　　int (integer), in C, 387–388
　　lifetime of, in C, 411–412
　　local, in C, 386, 387, 411–412
　　register, in C, 411–412
　　scope (visibility) of, in C,
　　　411–412
　　static, in C, 411–412
Vector graphics, 437–438
Vector-scan cathode-ray tube
　　(CRT) displays, 437–438
Vectors, exception (interrupt),
　　201, 202, 204–205
Vertical (perpendicular) recording,
　　444
Vertical sync pulse, 426–428
Video cameras, 439
Video information, 425, 427
Video monitors, 426
Video signals, composite, 426,
　　427, 434, 436–437
Vidicons, 439
Virtual addresses, 508, 509
Virtual ground, 296
Virtual memory
　　68010 implementation of, 34
　　demand-paged, 509
　　segmentation approach for, 508
Visibility (scope) of variables in C,
　　411–412
Vocal tract model, 456
Voice coil mechanism, 450
Voiced sounds, 456
Volatile memory, 20

Voltage gain, 293–296
Votrax SC-01A phoneme speech
　　synthesizer, 251–253

.W (word) suffix, 40, 61, 62
Wait states, 527
Waveform-modulation speech
　　synthesis, 456–457
WHILE-DO structure, 46–48, 90,
　　92–96, 403–404
While structure in C, 403–404
Winchester hard disks, 450
Word (16 bits), 1
Word (.W) suffix, 40, 61, 62
Word aligned stacks, 153
Word-type operand, 40
Words
　　binary. *See* Binary words
　　defined, 1
　　extension, 57–58
　　syndrome, 359–360
Write cycles for 68000
　　instructions, 527–533
Write-once/read optical-disk
　　systems, 451

X (extend) flag, 37, 76–77
XDEF (external definition)
　　directive, 136, 137, 164
Xerographic printers, 455
XMODEM protocol, 487–488
XOR (exclusive or) logic gates, 16,
　　17
XREF (external reference)
　　directive, 136, 137, 164

Z80 microprocessor, 33
Zero (Z) flag, 37, 77
Zero divide interrupt, 202–208
Zone bits, 6
Zone coordinates, 177, 178, 369
Zone punches, 6, 10

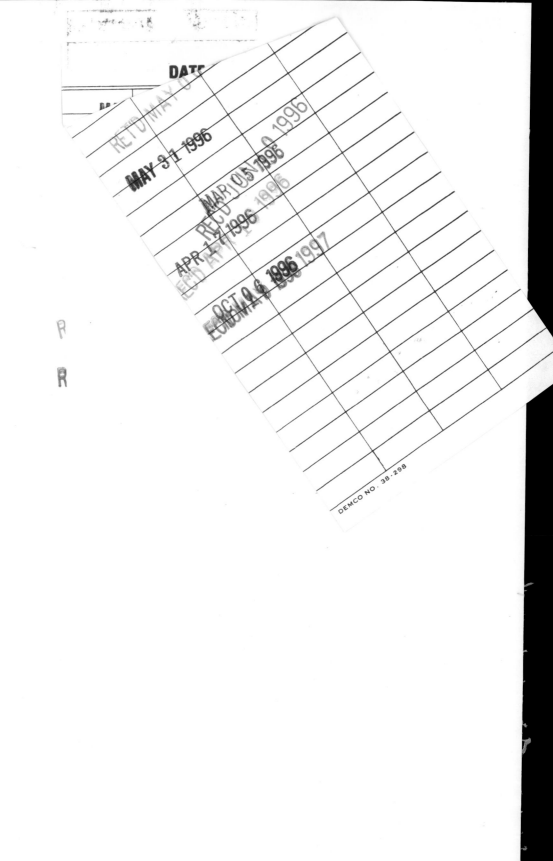